THE EDINBURGH INTERNATIONAL FESTIVAL
1947–1996

To my mother, who did not live to see this book completed, but whose spirit lived on to encourage me. On the many occasions when I was convinced that I could never finish the work on time, a familiar voice would sound in my head, 'Of course you can, if you set your mind to it'.

The Edinburgh International Festival 1947–1996

Eileen Miller

SCOLAR PRESS

Published by

Scolar Press	Ashgate Publishing Company
Gower House	Old Post Road
Croft Road	Brookfield
Aldershot	Vermont 05036-9704
Hants GU11 3HR	USA
England	

British Library Cataloguing-in-Publication data

Miller, Eileen
The Edinburgh International Festival, 1947–1996
1.Edinburgh International Festival – History 2.Festivals – Scotland – Edinburgh – History – 20th century 3.Music festivals – Scotland – Edinburgh – History – 20th century 4.Drama festivals – Scotland – Edinburgh – History – 20th century
I.Title
700.7'94134

Library of Congress Cataloging-in-Publication Data

Miller, Eileen
The Edinburgh International Festival, 1947–1996 / Eileen Miller.
Includes index.
ISBN 1-85928-153-2 (cloth)
1. Edinburgh International Festival. 2. Art festivals—Scotland–Edinburgh. I. Title.
NX430.G72E346 1996
700'.79'4134—dc20 96-258
CIP

ISBN 1 85928 153 2

Typeset in Times by Manton Typesetters, 5–7 Eastfield Road, Louth, Lincolnshire, and printed in Great Britain by Biddles Ltd, Guildford.

Contents

List of plates

Between pages 80 and 81

Foreword to the souvenir programme for the first Edinburgh International Festival 1947

It is with the utmost pleasure that I take this opportunity of prefacing this publication dealing with the International Festival of Music and Drama which we are inaugurating in Edinburgh this summer. The idea is a new one for Edinburgh, but I feel confident we will succeed in establishing our fair city as one of the pre-eminent European Festival Centres.

To succeed, we require the help and co-operation of lovers of art the whole world over, especially as one of our objects is to foster and maintain the international character of the event. We wish to provide the world with a Centre where, year after year, all that is best in music, drama, and the visual arts can be seen and heard amidst ideal surroundings. At the present time all the amenities and ancillaries so essential for the visitors' full enjoyment and appreciation cannot be provided. For example, this year it is not possible for accommodation and catering facilities to be of the very highest standard, but we ask all who are interested to bear with us in these difficult times. In the course of time all these things will be rectified, but we are determined to make a start this year to establish the tradition of Edinburgh as a Festival Centre.

The programmes for the first year are unfolded in the pages which follow and I hope you will believe that in the organisation of the many attractions, we have had ever before us the highest and purest ideals of art in its many and varied forms. May I assure you that this Festival is not a commercial undertaking in any way. It is an endeavour to provide a stimulus to the establishing of a new way of life centred round the arts.

For the three weeks of the Festival, Edinburgh will be wholly given up to Festival affairs – she will surrender herself to the visitors and hopes that they will find in all the performances a sense of peace and inspiration with which to refresh their souls and reaffirm their belief in things other than material.

To all the visitors, whoever they may be and from whatever part of the world they may come, Edinburgh will extend a most warm welcome.

John I. Falconer
Lord Provost

Acknowledgements

I should like to record my grateful thanks to all those who assisted in the compilation of this book. First and foremost to the Festival Directors, Ian Hunter, Robert Ponsonby, Lord Harewood, Peter Diamand, Sir John Drummond, Frank Dunlop and Brian McMaster, who willingly found the time to talk about their experiences and to read and comment on their respective chapters.

Secondly, to the Festival staff, particularly James Waters, Nicholas Dodds, Anne McGee, Ann Monfries, Morag Burnett, Joanna Baker and George Bell; with very special thanks to former staff members, Ellen Valentine and Alastair Dewar, for patiently scrutinising the text for factual errors and omissions.

Thirdly, to the many other people connected with the Festival who have answered questions and provided information: Lord Provosts Eleanor McLaughlin and John McKay, Sheila Colvin, the Hon. Mrs Elizabeth Fairbairn, James Dunbar-Nasmith, Sir Jack Shaw, Ronald Mavor, George Gwilt, William Berry, Tom Fleming, George Bruce, Edward Horton, John Calder, Jenny Brown, Scottish Opera and the Scottish Chamber Orchestra.

To my long-standing friend Sheena McDougall and her staff in the Edinburgh Room, Central Public Library, for good-humouredly fetching large volumes of newspapers, programmes and press cuttings from the bowels of the earth, and for their patience in coaxing readable copies out of a temperamental microfilm copier; to the staff of the Department of Manuscripts, National Library of Scotland for their forbearance in allowing me to rearrange the Festival archives into chronological order, even although it involved transporting hundreds of boxes to and from the stacks; to Lorna Milne, Music Librarian, Edinburgh City Libraries; and to Jayne Fenwick, Archivist, Glyndebourne Festival Opera.

To Rachel Lynch and Ellen Keeling of Scolar Press for guiding a very inexperienced writer through the various stages of publishing.

To the Festival Society for allowing me to reproduce Sir John Falconer's Foreword to the Souvenir Programme of the first Edinburgh International Festival, Lord Harewood and Weidenfeld and Nicolson for permission to quote from *The Tongs and the Bones,* Moira Shearer for permission to quote her article on *The Soldier's Tale,* Hamish Hamilton for permission to quote from *The Life of Kathleen Ferrier* by W. Ferrier and *A Life in the Theatre* by Tyrone Guthrie and Ronald Mavor for permission to quote from the letters of James Bridie. To the editors of the *Sunday Times*, the *Observer*, the *Guardian*, the

Independent, the *Independent on Sunday*, the *Financial Times*, the *Daily Telegraph*, the *Sunday Telegraph*, *Opera*, the *Musical Times*, *Musical Opinion*, the *Scots Magazine* and the *Spectator* for permission to quote reviews from these publications; with particular thanks to James Seaton of the *Scotsman* for kindly allowing me to quote extensively from the *Scotsman* publications, thus filling a number of gaps in the Festival archives.

To the Festival Society, the Scottish Tourist Board, Alex 'Tug' Wilson, Sean Hudson and Scottish Opera for permission to reproduce photographs.

Finally, to my friends Sheena McNeil, Anthony Rudd, Rosemary Dixson and Liz Black for their encouragement and assistance in reading and correcting the text, Marion Ford for her invaluable advice on the complexities of Dos and Windows and for coming to the rescue whenever something went wrong and, above all, to John Hough and Albert Bove for their laborious and painstaking help with proofreading and checking the appendices.

EM

Introduction
Early music festivals 1815–1871

Contrary to general opinion the first Edinburgh musical festival took place, not in 1947, but in 1815. By today's standards the 1815 festival was a much more modest affair, consisting of six concerts and lasting a mere five days. It sprang, as Lord Cockburn succinctly put it, 'more from charity than from love of harmony'.

A small group of Edinburgh music lovers, who had visited some of the festivals in England, were convinced that a similar festival in the Scottish metropolis would help to stimulate public interest in music. Then, on 30 November 1814, Lord Provost Majoribanks chaired a meeting of 'noblemen and gentlemen' to find a way of raising money to meet the demands of various charitable organizations. The success of the English festivals in this direction was discussed and it was resolved that an appeal should be made to the citizens of Edinburgh to support such a venture.

A festival committee was appointed to examine the possibilities and to submit a suitable scheme. Within a month it produced a plan for three morning concerts of sacred music and three evening orchestral concerts. A guarantee fund was to be set up, and they further recommended that the patronage of the nobility be sought. Consequently the Duke of Buccleuch and Queensberry was appointed President, and a further six peers were appointed Vice-Presidents. Thirty gentlemen, including the Lord Provost, the highest law officers in Scotland, and Walter Scott, Esq. were chosen as Extraordinary Directors, and a further 25 representative citizens as Directors. George Hogarth, the editor of the *Evening Chronicle* and later the father-in-law of Charles Dickens, and George Farquhar Graham, a composer who was later to write an account of the festival, were joint secretaries. When the festival ultimately took place these illustrious figures were required to do more than lend their names to the enterprise; they were also expected to take an active role in ensuring that everything ran smoothly.

Charles Ashley of London was contracted to engage a number of prominent singers and instrumentalists, provide the sheet music (a costly item in those days), and to conduct the performances. Another expensive item was the hiring of a grand organ, which was transported to Edinburgh by sea. The principal singers were Madame Marconi, Mrs Salmon and Messrs Braham, Smith, Swift and Rolle, and among the instrumentalists were Mr Lindley (cello), Signor Dragonetti (bass) and Signor Corri (piano). There was an

orchestra of 62 with Felix Yaniewicz (a Polish violinist living in Edinburgh) as leader, and the choir of 58 specially selected voices included local singers as well as choristers from Lancashire, Carlisle and London. The necessity of recruiting choristers from so far afield, who had to travel to Edinburgh by stagecoach, was a considerable drain on the festival resources and drew attention to the desirability of training local singers for future performances.

In the period leading up to the festival public excitement grew to fever pitch. So many people visited Parliament House to witness the arrangements for the first concert that it was decided to charge for admittance. No fewer than 1 235 people duly paid their shilling, increasing the festival receipts by £61. 15*s*.

Visitors from all parts of Scotland and England poured into the city for the festival. There was not a post-horse to be had on any of the roads leading to Edinburgh, and every hotel, inn and hostelry was full to overflowing.

The festival opened on 31 October 1815 with a morning concert in Parliament House. By 8 o'clock the streets were thronged with carriages, chairs and pedestrians, and a patrol of dragoons was required to preserve order in the High Street. On entering the building the patrons were confronted by the spectacle of such eminent personages as the Lord Provost, the Earl of Moray, Sir William Forbes, Lieutenant-General Wynyard and the Lord Advocate acting as stewards, and the Earl of Dalhousie, Sir George Clerk of Penicuik and George Hogarth collecting tickets at the door!

The first part of the concert was devoted to the music of Handel, opening with the Overture to *Esther*, while the second part consisted of an abridged performance of Haydn's oratorio *The Creation*. Handel's *Messiah* was given on 2 November, also in Parliament House, and the final morning concert took place on 4 November with music by Boyce and Handel, concluding with the Coronation Anthem *Zadok the Priest*. The evening concerts on 31 October and 1 and 3 November took place in Corri's Rooms. These were devoted mainly to the 'modern' composers and included symphonies by Haydn, Beethoven and Mozart as well as vocal and instrumental solos.

According to contemporary accounts the festival was an artistic triumph. In his account of the 1923 York Festival, Crosse described the Edinburgh Festival of 1815 as 'one of the great festivals of the country'. Nearly 4 000 people attended the concerts, and what was even more important the festival succeeded in making a profit. Over 9 000 tickets were sold, the receipts amounting to £5 735. 18*s*. 6*d*. After expenses were paid, the princely sum of £1 500 was handed over to the Royal Infirmary and other charitable institutions, 'and we', as Lord Cockburn concluded, 'have become an infinitely more harmonious nation'.

The next Edinburgh music festival took place four years later in 1819 under the presidency of the Duke of Atholl. It began with a concert in the Theatre Royal on the evening of Tuesday 19 October, Corri's Rooms having been sold. This was followed by a morning concert of works by Handel and Mozart on the 20th, a performance of *Messiah* on the 21st, and the festival ended on the Saturday morning with a selection of pieces followed by Beethoven's *The Mount of Olives*, all in Parliament House. Further evening concerts were given in the theatre on the Wednesday and Friday when one of the works performed was a scena *The Last Words of Marmion* by Dr Clarke to words by Walter Scott. Among the performers were Miss Stephens, Miss Goodal, Signora Corri and Mr Braham. The leader of the orchestra was again Mr Yaniewicz and the conductor throughout was Sir George Smart.

From Sir George Smart's own collection of personally annotated programmes, tickets and handbills, all carefully bound and preserved, it would appear that even then the organizers had problems with both performers and traffic. Miss Stephens, in particular, had to be replaced on a number of occasions due to illness. With regard to traffic, one of the handbills reads:

> All carriages going to Parliament House are to line up the High Street and to enter Parliament Square keeping close to the houses on their left and to put down their company at the piazza on the south side of the square to drive off round the statue, keeping close to the wall of the High Church, when they are to turn up Lawn Market and go off by the Mound. They are to take up in the same order. The entry by the Lobby of the Writers' Library will be reserved exclusively for those who come on foot or in chairs, and no carriages will be allowed to enter the area in the Lawn Market before the Public Libraries.

Pasted on the cover of Smart's scrapbook is a cutting from the *Edinburgh Evening Courant* of 1 November stating that 8 526 people attended the concerts. The sums received amounted to £5 256. 17*s*. 1*d*., expenses were £4 024. 7*s*. 1*d*. and the balance of £1 232. 10*s*. was given to the charitable institutions of Edinburgh in the greatest need.

The next festival was held in 1824 when the name of Sir Walter Scott, Bart was again listed among the patrons. In addition to the concerts there was a grand Festival Ball with music by the Military Band of the Royal Dragoons. The tickets cost 10*s*. 6*d*. Sir George's collection for this festival concludes with a 'List of the Order of the Grand Procession of the Royal Society of St. Crispin in honour and memory of King Crispin on Monday 25th October'. This included trumpeters, heralds, the King himself, the Princes, a Highland chieftain and an Indian prince. A glittering occasion indeed!

Queen Victoria and Prince Albert lent their patronage to the festival of 1843 which was presented in the Assembly Rooms in George Street, unfortunately at a loss of £600. This may have dampened the enthusiasm of the organizers as almost 30 years elapsed before the final Edinburgh music festival of this era took place in 1871 when, in celebration of the centenary of the birth of Sir Walter Scott, the prominent Scottish singer, David Kennedy, performed songs to texts by Scott at a concert in the Corn Exchange.

Chapter 1

Rudolf Bing 1947–1949

According to Glyndebourne legend the idea for the current Edinburgh International Festival was born on a clear night in 1942. The English soprano, Audrey Mildmay, and Rudolf Bing, the General Manager of the Glyndebourne Opera, were walking along Princes Street after a performance of Gay's *The Beggar's Opera*. Audrey is said to have looked up at the moonlit castle and given voice to an idea, that had first occurred to her a few years earlier in Salzburg, that the Scottish capital would make a wonderful setting for a festival. The truth was rather more prosaic and was inspired more by the necessity of finding a solution to Glyndebourne's monetary problems than a desire to establish an Edinburgh Festival.

From the opening of the Glyndebourne Festival in 1934 to its sixth season in 1939 Audrey's husband, the rich landowner John Christie, had spent about £100 000 of his own money on his Sussex opera festival. By 1939 it had become apparent that if the festival was to continue an additional source of funding would have to be found. With the declaration of war in September few people, apart from the Glyndebourne authorities, held out much hope for its survival. Plans for the 1940 season had had to be scrapped and replaced by a short tour of *The Beggar's Opera*, which fortunately made a reasonable profit.

During the next few years numerous schemes for ensuring Glyndebourne's future after the war were explored. These included an attempt to present a Glyndebourne season in the USA, a rather far-fetched proposal by John Christie that the opera company at the Royal Opera House, Covent Garden should be run as a joint enterprise with Glyndebourne (the Covent Garden Board were having none of that), and a grandiose plan to stage an annual Wagner festival in London.

While these suggestions were being debated Rudolf Bing came up with a more practical solution to the problem; a music festival, organized in association with Glyndebourne and utilizing the Glyndebourne resources, might be a way of enabling the company to re-establish itself when the war ended. Bing was convinced that no musical festival on anything like a pre-war scale could be held in any of the shattered and impoverished European centres for some time to come. Therefore staging such a festival somewhere in Britain in the summer of 1946 would have little competition and a considerable chance of success. Oxford was his first choice but, although it was discussed in detail and various committees formed, the town was ultimately unable or unwilling to provide the necessary financial support.

In December 1944 Bing met representatives of the British Council over lunch in London to discuss alternative locations for his festival. Henry Harvey Wood, the Scottish representative, put forward the claims of his native Edinburgh. The city had suffered little bomb damage, had great natural beauty, a colourful history and close proximity to the sea and the Scottish Highlands. It was also large enough to accommodate from 50 000 to 150 000 visitors, with hotels, theatres, concert halls and art galleries. Bing was doubtful at first, feeling that Edinburgh was perhaps too large to acquire a proper festival atmosphere, but he was finally persuaded that the city had all the essential qualities required for an international festival. Harvey Wood promised to make preliminary investigations and, if the reactions were favourable, to invite Bing to present his ideas in full to the Town Council.

Harvey Wood then arranged another lunch in Edinburgh when he put Bing's proposals to Lady Rosebery, an influential music lover, Murray Watson, the editor of the *Scotsman*, and Sidney Newman, Professor of Music at Edinburgh University and conductor of the Reid Orchestra. Their response was enthusiastic. It would be a massive undertaking and would involve risking a large sum of money; but if it was organized properly it would be a marvellous prospect, not only for Edinburgh but for the whole of Scotland.

Bing travelled to Edinburgh to meet this small group of supporters. At the same time Harvey Wood arranged a meeting between Bing and the Lord Provost of Edinburgh, Sir John Falconer, at which Bing outlined his proposal for establishing the first post-war European festival of music and drama. In Sir John Falconer, Bing discovered an able and energetic champion of his cause. A lawyer by profession, Sir John had wide experience of civic administration and the vision to realize that such a festival could make an immense contribution to international friendship and understanding, whilst at the same time giving Edinburgh a world-wide reputation as an arts centre, ideals which he later expounded in his foreword to the souvenir programme of the first Edinburgh International Festival. Above all Falconer had the enthusiasm to inspire his colleagues on the council and the determination to steer the scheme safely through the mass of civic obstacles that would inevitably be raised in its path.

Before long the first of these obstructions emerged and flung Bing headlong into Edinburgh city politics. When no progress had been made by May 1945 Bing had written to Harvey Wood asking him if he could find out from the Lord Provost if the city was genuinely interested in the festival idea. As a result of his enquiries Harvey Wood was summoned to the City Chambers to see Bailie Stevenson, who was in charge of the city's parks and halls. Stevenson informed him, somewhat summarily, that the project could not be entertained or supported by the Lord Provost or the magistrates. He argued that it would be unfair to the Reid Orchestra to bring foreign orchestras and conductors to Edinburgh, that there would be insufficient patrons in the city to support additional concerts by visiting orchestras, and concluded by suggesting that Howard and Wyndham, owner of two of the largest theatres, would not easily be persuaded to bring foreign drama companies to Edinburgh! Harvey Wood countered these ridiculously parochial arguments by pointing out that one of the sponsors of the scheme was the conductor of the Reid Orchestra, that tickets for the recent visit by the Hallé Orchestra had been heavily in demand, and that Howard and Wyndham was that month bringing the Comédie Française to perform, in French, in Edinburgh and Glasgow. Bailie Stevenson remained unconvinced and reverted to his fundamental objection that the city could not support a

festival that would compete with his own plans for open-air entertainment and pageantry during the summer months.

Harvey Wood profoundly resented this cavalier treatment, but rather than make an official issue of what might possibly be a mutual misunderstanding, he addressed a personal letter to the Lord Provost (3 July 1945). In it he summarized his meeting with Bailie Stevenson. He requested the Lord Provost to give the matter his personal consideration and let him have in writing his final decision on the Festival, which he could quote in his own reply to Mr Bing.

Sir John promptly invited Harvey Wood to a meeting at which the City Treasurer (Councillor Andrew Murray) and the City Chamberlain (John Imrie) were present. It transpired that the Lord Provost and the Treasurer were still exceedingly enthusiastic about the Festival, while the Chamberlain, although requiring reassurance on a number of points, was open to persuasion. Harvey Wood was asked to invite Bing to return to Edinburgh in September to clarify the points raised.

The burning question was, naturally, how much the Festival would cost. Bing explained that this would obviously depend on the programme and the calibre of the artists engaged. He suggested that a small festival committee be formed to help him programme a three- to four-week festival together with an estimate of expenditure. It would then be possible to ascertain the size of the guarantee fund required. This constituted almost the same procedure as had been adopted for the 1815 festival.

The next stage was to enlist the support of the various interested parties such as the Chamber of Commerce, the Travel Association, the Hotel Associations of Edinburgh and Scotland, the railway companies and the theatrical and musical organizations. Representatives of these bodies were accordingly invited to a meeting on 15 November 1945 at which Bing's proposals were discussed and approved. Those present agreed to form themselves into an interim festival committee. This committee then authorized Bing and the Glyndebourne Society to draw up a festival programme and to ascertain from overseas governments, artists and artistic organizations if they would be willing to participate in a 1947 Edinburgh Festival, and the fees they would expect, but without at this stage making firm commitments. A sum of £1 000 was agreed upon for expenses. The report was to be ready by June 1946 when a final decision would be taken about holding the Festival.

This general committee included prominent citizens such as Herbert Wiseman and Hans Gal representing the musical interests, Stewart Cruikshank, Manager of the Howard and Wyndham theatres, Sir Frank Mears, Director of the Royal Scottish Academy, Sheriff John Cameron (later Lord Cameron) and Dr O.H. Mavor, better known as the playwright James Bridie. These last two men, together with Lady Rosebery, Murray Watson, Sidney Newman and Harvey Wood were to become Bing's greatest allies in the years to come. Immediately after the meeting Bing received the following encouraging letter from Bridie which, at the same time, warned him of the problems he was likely to encounter:

> Your Edinburgh project is a magnificent one and I sincerely hope it may come to fruition. At the same time you have managed to stir up interest in Edinburgh, a city which prides itself on not being interested in anything at all … but I cannot help feeling that a good deal more vital energy than I have hitherto found in contemporary Edinburgh will be required before anything really happens. I hope you will not think this discouraging. It is only fair to say that I am a West of Scotland man myself and that between the West and the East there is a great gulf fixed. It is

> difficult for anyone living outside Scotland to understand the nature of this gulf but it is nevertheless a fact. None of this means that I shall not do all I can to help but it is well to point out one of the primary psychological obstacles to the achievement of your purpose. It can, I think, be overcome, but not by rushing it ...
>
> (Letter from James Bridie to Rudolf Bing, 21 November 1945)

The apathy of the city of Edinburgh and antipathy between the West and the East of Scotland were only two of the minefields in the path of an unsuspecting foreign festival director. During this period Bing succeeded in ruffling a few municipal feathers before he discovered that, understandably, the citizens of Edinburgh did not take kindly to being described as English! But his worst moment, so serious that he later wondered how the Festival idea survived the blunder, was when he proposed to a group of councillors that the Festival should open with a High Mass in the Cathedral. In the strongly Calvinistic city of John Knox and Jenny Geddes (where the latter is said to have thrown a stool at the head of an Anglican priest for having dared to preach a Mass in her ears) such a suggestion was tantamount to heresy! Harvey Wood had to take Bing aside and give him a short lesson on Scottish ecclesiastical history!

In view of the vast amount of work that still had to be done before the Festival project could get off the ground it was necessary to postpone it until the summer of 1947. Bing, however, felt the event should be publicized as soon as possible and accordingly the following communiqué appeared in the *Scotsman*:

> An announcement that should be of the greatest interest to the citizens of Edinburgh is made in our columns today regarding a projected International Festival of Music and Drama to be held in their midst in the summer or early autumn of 1947. Not only the Capital, however, but the whole of Scotland might be expected to benefit from an event which it is hoped would attract visitors from all over the world, and particularly from America ... It is, however, on the outstanding excellence of its presentations that the success of an international festival must be founded. Indeed, it would not be worth undertaking unless everything connected with it were to be of the highest standard. The preliminary announcement indicates clearly that this is what its promoters have in mind. They intend to secure the best that the world has to offer in music, drama and ballet, and it is hoped that in addition to British orchestras, conductors, and dramatic companies foreign organisations and world-famed artists will take part. With the services of the Glyndebourne Festival management at the disposal of the promoters these requirements should be amply met, and if, as may be expected, the Arts Council and the British Council give the project active support its success should be assured. But, of course, that presumes an enthusiastic and adequate response from the citizens themselves to provide the indispensable financial backing for the undertaking. It is encouraging to learn that the Committee who have been concerned in the initial arrangements under the chairmanship of the Lord Provost have already had indications that it is likely to be widely and warmly welcomed, and now that the project has been publicly mooted it will be for the citizens to do their part in bringing it to fruition.
>
> (*Scotsman*, 24 November 1945)

This provoked an avalanche of letters to local newspapers from citizens, both for and against the project. Hoteliers and travel agents contributed articles pointing out the problems that a large influx of visitors would create in a city still subject to food and petrol rationing, and where many hotels had still not reopened after the war. On the whole the comments were favourable, and the hope was expressed that a festival might arouse interest in the arts, and that one day Edinburgh might even have its own symphony orchestra and drama company.

In June 1946 Bing reported that he had had extensive negotiations with British and overseas artistic bodies and individual artists, and he outlined a suggested programme of

orchestral concerts, recitals, chamber music, plays and ballet at a cost of £37 000. After taking organizational expenses and receipts into consideration there would be an estimated deficit of £30 000. Bing also suggested that Glyndebourne would happily provide a season of opera, but since the financial arrangements would be complex it had not been included in the budget submitted. Opera would be the most expensive item and could not be presented without a substantial loss, but he estimated that a three-week season would cost just under £30 000. With takings of £20 000 this would increase the deficit to £40 000. The committee agreed that opera would be an added attraction and that it would be inadvisable to hold a festival without it. A guarantee fund of at least £40 000 would therefore be required before the Festival could take place.

In September 1946 the Town Council unanimously approved the proposals outlined by the Lord Provost for a three-week festival to be held from 24 August to 13 September 1947. The Festival Society was constituted and later incorporated as a company limited by guarantee. The interim committee which had served for the past year became the Council of the Festival Society with the Lord Provost as Chairman, John Reid, the City Social Services Officer was appointed Secretary, the City Chamberlain was invited to become Honorary Treasurer and the Town Clerk, Honorary Legal Adviser. Committees responsible for finance and general purposes, programmes, and reception and membership, with sub-committees to deal with accommodation and catering were set up. An executive committee consisting of the Lord Provost, the Honorary Legal Adviser and the Honorary Treasurer together with the conveners of the various committees was established to deal with matters of urgency and to act in an advisory capacity.

Rudolf Bing was confirmed as Artistic Director with Ian Hunter as his assistant. The Glyndebourne Society would continue in the capacity of Artistic Management, but would not be responsible for any expenses incurred in setting up the Festival or for the Glyndebourne performances at the Festival regardless of ticket sales. Bing emphasized that he and the Glyndebourne Society would only be able to organize the artistic side of the Festival from the Glyndebourne offices in London. It was therefore imperative that a festival office with a responsible manager be set up in Edinburgh to deal with administrative matters such as publicity, press, tickets and accommodation.

Edinburgh City Council voted £20 000 to the guarantee fund and a further £20 000 came from citizens, including the Earl of Rosebery who contributed the proceeds of his recent Derby win! The Arts Council, somewhat reluctant at the outset, eventually gave its support and a grant of £20 000 to be spread over two years. The British Council, although not in a position to contribute to this fund, promised to give the utmost assistance with world publicity.

With new and inexperienced staff, in a city only just returning to normal after six years of war, Bing found himself dealing with numerous mundane matters with which an artistic director should not normally be concerned. Some of the hotels had not yet been de-requisitioned whilst others still had windows blacked-out from wartime, and Bing had to negotiate with the various ministries to de-ration curtain material for the hotels. Additional accommodation had to be organized in hostels and student residences and, in response to an appeal by the Lord Provost, over 6 000 beds were made available in private households. Many were to be taken up during the course of the Festival, frequently by visitors who arrived in the city without making prior arrangements.

With food rationing still in force special arrangements had to be made with the Ministry of Food to ensure sufficient supplies. One of the functions of the Festival Club was to provide meals and during the Festival it served around 2 500 meals a day. The main purpose of the Club, which was situated in the elegant surroundings of the Music Hall and Assembly Rooms in George Street, was to form a focal point where visitors, artists and local residents could meet and exchange ideas. A room was set aside for the reception of distinguished guests; there was also an information bureau and facilities for the press.

Having organized food and accommodation for the visitors, Bing had then to turn his attention to finding venues for Festival events – a problem that was to rack the brains of succeeding directors for nigh on 50 years. Although the city owned the Usher Hall; the Freemasons' Hall and the three main theatres, the King's Theatre, the Lyceum and the Empire were privately owned. These had either to be rented or complicated sharing agreements negotiated between the owners, the guest companies and the Festival Society. None of these theatres was particularly well equipped technically, and the King's Theatre was to become a bone of contention between the city and visiting opera companies for the next 40 years.

As the aim of the Festival was to encourage overseas tourists as well as those from nearer home, tickets had to be available in London, on the Continent and in America. Bing arranged with Thomas Cook, Dean and Dawson and numerous local agents to sell Edinburgh Festival tickets at home and abroad. The Travel Association undertook the task of publicizing the Festival abroad and to supplement the cost, while John Menzies handled the publicity at home. Bing then established a timetable: a date by which the programme would have to be ready, followed by a date for publicity to start and finally a date when tickets would go on sale. At least that was the plan! It was to prove impossible to sustain.

Bing had sold the Festival idea to the City Fathers on the understanding that European governments would be prepared to subsidize the appearance of their artists. The negotiations proved more difficult than he had anticipated. He particularly wanted the Vienna Philharmonic Orchestra, but the Austrian Government could not afford to subsidize its appearance so soon after the war. Eventually a deal was struck which Edinburgh could accept. Bing fared better in Paris and the French Government agreed to send, at its own expense, L'Orchestre des Concerts Colonne and the Louis Jouvet Company.

Not the least of Bing's problems was to persuade artists of the highest calibre to appear at a totally unknown festival, particularly in the early stages when it was still uncertain whether it could take place. He wrote a long letter to his friend Bruno Walter, then resident in America, outlining his plans and inviting him to take part. Walter agreed immediately, and when it became known that he would be present conducting his old orchestra, the Vienna Philharmonic, the requisite standard was assured. No one needed fear that he or she would be appearing in inferior company. The presence of Bruno Walter would also serve to 'de-Nazify' the orchestra and guarantee freedom from the inevitable political demonstrations if it appeared with an Austrian or German conductor. Bing also arranged for his Glyndebourne protégée, Kathleen Ferrier, to audition for Walter who promptly engaged her to sing Mahler's *Das Lied von der Erde*.

Negotiations nearer home resulted in the engagement of the Liverpool Philharmonic Orchestra under Sir Malcolm Sargent, the Hallé Orchestra conducted by John Barbirolli

and the Sadler's Wells Ballet headed by Margot Fonteyn. The chamber music programme was to include a series of concerts by the specially formed partnership of Artur Schnabel, Joseph Szigeti, Pierre Fournier and William Primrose, and two recitals by Lotte Lehmann accompanied by Bruno Walter. Glyndebourne would bring two of its most successful pre-war productions: *Le Nozze di Figaro* with John Brownlee, Italo Tajo, Eleanor Steber and Jarmila Novotná, while Francesco Valentino and Margherita Grandi would repeat their acclaimed performances in Verdi's *Macbeth*.

Drama was the most difficult aspect of the Festival to arrange. The Old Vic was the obvious choice for the British contribution, but the selection of plays was more problematical. James Bridie had been invited to provide a new work for the Festival and had agreed to write a historical play set in the period of Mary, Queen of Scots. Tyrone Guthrie agreed to present it in repertory with Shakespeare's *Richard II* which the Old Vic was putting on in London in March and April. Insurmountable difficulties arose between Bridie and the Old Vic, particularly with regard to casting, and it was June before the Old Vic decided on another of Shakespeare's plays *The Taming of the Shrew* as a substitute for the Bridie play. As tickets had already gone on sale this alteration caused confusion at the box office and many patrons found themselves with tickets for two performances of the same play.

The programme was at last completed but, as with all the best-laid plans, there were inevitable cancellations and last-minute indispositions. Toscanini had originally been asked to conduct *Macbeth* while Bruno Walter had been offered *Figaro*, but both had declined: Toscanini on the grounds that he was 79 years old and had conducted a complete opera in the opera house for the last time at Salzburg in 1937, and Walter because he considered that he would be too busy with his concerts in Edinburgh to undertake an opera as well. In his place he recommended the Hungarian conductor, George Szell, and Tullio Serafin was engaged to conduct *Macbeth*. Serafin was subsequently deterred by the demands of the Inland Revenue so Szell agreed to conduct both operas. Jarmila Novotná, who was to sing Cherubino, withdrew and was replaced by the 37 year-old Giulietta Simionato making a somewhat belated British début. Then the Susanna fell by the wayside. A talented young American soprano, Virginia MacWatters, whom Bing had 'discovered' was offered the part despite some objections from Szell. His doubts proved to have some foundation when she turned up for rehearsal knowing only half the role and, as her facility for learning notes proved inadequate, Szell insisted on her dismissal. Finally, Tatiana Menotti was engaged but could not be present for the early rehearsals which were to take place at Glyndebourne, a factor which did not improve the temper of the irascible Szell.

Matters came to a head at a rehearsal of *Macbeth*. Walter Midgley, who was not a particularly experienced opera singer, tried the patience of Szell a little too far. Turning to him Szell enquired, 'Mr. Midgley, when are you going to sing some of the notes Verdi provided?' Unabashed, Midgley replied in his high-pitched voice with its pronounced Yorkshire accent, 'It's all bloody well for you, you've got the score in front of you'. 'Don't you know Mr Midgley that I never conduct from a score?' came the chilling reply as Szell stomped off. The next morning it was discovered that Szell had packed his bags and departed without a word to anyone. (Many years later, when Szell again walked out on Bing at the Metropolitan Opera in New York, someone remarked to Bing that Szell was his own worst enemy. 'Not while I'm alive', retorted Bing.) With less than a

fortnight to go there was no conductor for either opera! Help was to come from close at hand. Walter Susskind, the conductor of the Scottish Orchestra, which would be playing in the pit, agreed to conduct *Figaro* and the composer, Berthold Goldschmidt, whose own operas had been banned by the Nazi regime in Germany, was engaged for *Macbeth.*

The final catastrophe came three days before the Festival opened when Lotte Lehmann was forced to cancel her recitals because of illness. Schnabel and Szigeti agreed to take over the first recital date and she was replaced at the second by her illustrious compatriot Elisabeth Schumann.

One factor that had worried Bing from the beginning was whether the sombre Scottish capital could acquire the necessary 'festival spirit', as understood in the European festival centres. A feast of music, theatre and dance performed by the world's finest artists does not on its own create a festival. There has to be an air of festivity and gaiety and a camaraderie among the artists, audiences and indeed the whole community which cannot be manufactured. In the period leading up to the Festival there had been no shortage of doubters prophesying doom and financial ruin to the enterprise. Canny Edinburgh citizens had complained about the waste of money and had suggested better ways in which it might be spent. There was real concern on the Festival Council that the citizens would distance themselves from the event as being 'not for them'. According to Harvey Wood there was also criticism (probably from a little further afield) that this was

> not a brave cultural enterprise, but a sordid catch-penny scheme, devised by a city which has no claim to respect in the cultural sphere, a city which cannot maintain a repertory theatre throughout the year, a city which allowed her one and only symphony orchestra to die for want of a paltry grant.
>
> (H. Harvey Wood, *Scotsman*, 7 August 1947)

In the event any fears Bing may have harboured about Edinburgh's suitability as a festival city were proved groundless. Even before the arrival of its visitors the city was alive with anticipation, due in no small measure to the massive press coverage of the Festival. (This was largely the result of a campaign by the editor of the *Scotsman* to interest his fellow editors in the event.) Austerity was banished as Edinburgh adapted to her new role as hostess to the world. Almost overnight an army of workmen converted traffic islands at the West End, Haymarket and the Usher Hall into magnificent floral displays. Baskets of flowers were attached to the tramway stands below attractive thistle lanterns and the tramcars themselves sported bright little pennants. Flags were raised all over the city centre, and the Princes Street shops vied with each other in creating attractive window displays. There was an air of excitement as hotels, restaurants and private households prepared to welcome guests from all parts of the globe. Even the weather joined in the festive spirit as the sun shone gloriously and almost continuously for the entire three weeks. During the day Edinburgh had probably never seen so many brightly coloured summer frocks and at night, long after the theatres and restaurants had closed, Princes Street was still thronged with people, many in full evening dress, enjoying the cool, night air and admiring the magnificent vista of the castle on one side and the elegant New Town on the other. After the grim years of war Edinburgh had suddenly come alive.

The one thing missing was the floodlighting of the castle. A day or two before the Festival the Minister for Fuel and Power had banned the lighting on the grounds that

> at a time when all sections of the community are being continuously urged to effect greater economies in the use of fuel, particularly in electricity, the use of extensive and brilliant outdoor lighting solely for display purposes, although it involves a small consumption of fuel, must necessarily be a cause of criticism and of no encouragement to those members of the public who are trying to meet the Government's call for economies.

Therefore he felt 'unable to agree to the original proposal that Edinburgh Castle should be floodlit throughout the present international Festival'. This ban prompted a flood of letters and telegrams to the City Chambers and newspaper offices from residents offering to give up their ration of coal to enable floodlighting to take place. There were also telegrams from Members of Parliament and other prominent people to the Prime Minister requesting that the decision be reconsidered. So to allow visitors an opportunity of viewing the spectacular sight it was finally agreed that the castle should be floodlit for four nights from dusk until midnight.

When the lights were due to be switched on thousands of people, both tourists and citizens, crowded into Princes Street. Just as nine o'clock struck the first searchlights came on and a hush fell over the vast crowd as the castle, resting solidly on its rock foundation, suddenly seemed to float in the air. At first all that could be heard were gasps of amazement from appreciative spectators, accompanied by clicking cameras. Then came the comments. Even the Festival artists joined in the chorus of approval. Carl Ebert summed up their views when he remarked that now the castle was more impressive than ever, 'So bright in light, so fairylike in the wonderful darkness of the night'. He thought it stood like a 'real symbol of the town' and that 'no one in a life time would ever forget it.'

The honour of opening the first Edinburgh International Festival on 24 August 1947 went to L'Orchestre des Concerts Colonne under the direction of Paul Paray, a fitting tribute to the 'auld alliance' between Scotland and France. Of the opening concert R.H. Westwater wrote in the *Weekly Scotsman* (28 August 1947): 'There has not often been such enthusiasm in the Usher Hall, and it could scarcely be better justified. The "Colonne" and M. Paray gave the Festival a superb send-off.' After the second concert the *Scotsman*'s critic added (28 August 1947): 'Now and again there are concerts which send the critic away walking on air because of the sheer exhilaration of the performance just experienced … Last night's concert was such a concert.'

But there was no doubt that the highlight of the Festival was the eagerly awaited reunion of Bruno Walter with his beloved Vienna Philharmonic Orchestra. They gave six concerts in all, comprising three different and widely differing programmes; the final one being an additional concert to satisfy an exceptional demand for tickets. Queen Elizabeth accompanied by her younger daughter Princess Margaret and the Duchess of Kent attended the second concert of works by Beethoven and Vaughan Williams. Unfortunately there was a hitch at the start. Walter had been briefed to start the 'National Anthem' as soon as the Queen entered the improvised royal box. On seeing a latecomer take a short cut through the box to her seat Dr Walter turned to the orchestra and began the anthem, the Queen and the royal party entering the box as he reached the closing bars! Apart from this the evening was a triumph. At the end the Queen and Princess joined in the enthusiastic applause, while the string players expressed their appreciation by vigorously tapping the music stands with their bows.

To some tastes Walter's rich, expansive reading of Beethoven's sixth and seventh symphonies might have appeared a little over-sentimental, but few could criticize the intensity of his reading of Mahler's moving farewell *Das Lied von der Erde*, or forget the haunting quality of Kathleen Ferrier's magnificent voice dying away into silence in the final 'Ewigkeit'. To many people present this concert remains the most memorable performance of any Edinburgh Festival.

Among the most satisfying and enjoyable performances was the series of morning concerts by the Jacques Orchestra with a distinguished group of soloists including Kathleen Ferrier, Peter Pears and Leon Goossens. The programmes showed considerably more enterprise than those of the larger orchestras. This was followed by a series of quartets and trios by the Menges, Calvet and Masters Quartets and the Carter String Trio, and by two unusual programmes of Czech music by the Czech Nonet. For many visitors these concerts provided an ideal start to a busy festive day.

Chamber music on a grander scale was offered by the intriguing partnership of Schnabel, Szigeti, Primrose and Fournier, quite as much interest being aroused by the players as by the music. There had been qualms as to whether the brilliance of these world-renowned soloists as individuals might detract from the rapport so necessary in great chamber-music playing, but these fears were soon dispelled. The programmes of piano trios and quartets by Brahms, Schubert and Mendelssohn were designed to commemorate their various anniversaries: the one hundred and fiftieth of the birth of Schubert, the one hundredth of the death of Mendelssohn and the fiftieth of the death of Brahms.

Scottish music remained the province of the BBC Scottish Orchestra which, under its permanent conductor Ian Whyte, performed the short *Coronach* by David Stephen and the sole new work to be presented at the Festival, Whyte's own Piano Concerto, with Cyril Smith as soloist. In addition there were two recitals of Scottish song, one of Gaelic airs and the other of Lowland song – the latter given by two local singers, Marie Thomson and her husband John Tainsh. These were well attended, as was the programme by the Glasgow Orpheus Choir under Sir Hugh Roberton, indicating a keenness on the part of visitors to learn something of Scottish culture.

The Glyndebourne performances suffered from the technical shortcomings of the poorly equipped King's Theatre stage and the lacklustre playing of the Scottish Orchestra, but the singing was polished and the productions well integrated. According to the *Scotsman* (26 August 1947), Margherita Grandi was 'excellent as Lady Macbeth. She sang her arias with intensity of feeling and a wonderful variety of tone which seemed never to be studied or exaggerated'. The *Figaro* cast was generally considered excellent, the *Scotsman* singling out the American soprano Eleanor Steber for special praise.

The orchestral playing of an anonymous 'Symphony Orchestra' for the Sadler's Wells Ballet's performances of *The Sleeping Beauty* was criticized and there was some raggedness in the dancing, but these were compensated by the outstanding Aurora of Margot Fonteyn, admirably partnered by Michael Somes.

Pride of place in the drama programme went to the superb Louis Jouvet Company appearing for the first time in this country. Its elaborate productions of Molière's *L'Ecole des Femmes* and Giraudoux's *Ondine* were, according to R.H. Westwater in the *Weekly Scotsman* (11 September 1947), 'in sharply contrasting ways, perfect examples of French taste and artistry'. At the special request of the Queen an additional matinée performance of *L'Ecole des Femmes* was given as the young Princess Margaret had expressed a

particular desire to see it. This resulted in an increased demand for tickets for the remaining performances by the French company. Other members of the royal family in Edinburgh were the Princess Royal and her son, Lord Harewood, who spent a fortnight at the Festival as the guests of Lady Rosebery, thus beginning a close association with the Festival that was to culminate in Lord Harewood becoming Artistic Director in 1961. The Queen also attended the concert by the Glasgow Orpheus Choir (where she joined in the singing of *Auld Lang Syne* at the close), the Glyndebourne opera's *Macbeth* and also visited the Saltire Society's exhibition in Gladstone's Land. This enthusiastic support by the Queen and her family set the final seal of approval on the venture, an example that was followed in subsequent years by royalty and civic dignitaries from all over Europe.

At the suggestion of the Lord Provost various organizations and societies in the city contributed to the Festival in an unofficial way by putting on their own events, many being of a specifically Scottish nature. One of the most important was the *Enterprise Scotland 1947* exhibition in the Royal Scottish Museum, organized by the Scottish Committee of the Council for Industrial Design. Planned and designed by Basil Spence and James Gardner, its aim was to demonstrate the best that Scotland could offer in the realm of industrial design. The official announcement was made in spectacular fashion by means of Scotland's Fiery Cross which had been first raised to summon the clans to repel the Roman invaders and last used in 1745 to call the clansmen to support Bonnie Prince Charlie. This time it bore a more peaceful proclamation inviting Scots communities overseas to the exhibition. The cross, an exact replica of the original one, was ignited with traditional ceremony by the Lord Provost on the battlements of the castle, from whence it was relayed by a team of Scottish athletes to London and then by air to the principal Scottish communities in Europe and the Commonwealth.

The Royal Scottish Academy's summer exhibition was of the works of Vuillard which it agreed to extend until the end of the Festival. The National Gallery of Scotland augmented its important collection of Old Masters for the occasion, whilst in the Synod Hall there was a fascinating exhibition of some 200 early Scottish maps including that of Ptolemy dating from about AD 150 and a selection of German invasion maps and plans for a 'journey that didn't come off'. Other exhibitions were organized by groups such as the Saltire Society, the Dunedin Society, the Church of Scotland and the Artists of the New Gallery.

The Festival also attracted an unofficial or 'fringe' entry from six theatre companies, both amateur and professional, who arrived uninvited, hired their own halls and staged a selection of plays which added to the variety of drama on offer during the period. These included the Glasgow Unity Theatre in Robert McLellan's *The Laird of Tortwatletie* and *The Lower Depths*, a translation into Scots of Gorky's play; the Christine Orr Players in Shakespeare's *Macbeth*; Bridie's *The Anatomist* by members of the Scottish Community Drama Association; Strindberg's *Easter* by the Edinburgh College of Art Theatre Group; while the Pilgrim Players from the Mercury Theatre in London presented two plays by T.S. Eliot, *The Family Reunion* and *Murder in the Cathedral* with Robert Speaight in his original role of Thomas à Becket. There was also a production of the medieval morality play *Everyman* in the abbey in Dunfermline (the old capital of Scotland situated on the other side of the Firth of Forth where Robert the Bruce is buried). From these humble beginnings was born a creative force that in later years was to play as important a part in festival Edinburgh as the official event itself, and which in magnitude was almost to

engulf the International Festival. Certainly what came to be known as the 'Fringe' was to be responsible for staging most of the new and controversial work to be seen at the Festival, and to provide a nursery for many of the great theatrical names of the future.

Another event that was to have a far-reaching effect was the decision by the Edinburgh Film Guild to launch the first International Festival of Documentary Film. This was particularly appropriate as Britain had led the way in making real-life films, and the founder of the movement, John Grierson, was himself a Scot. Some 75 films from 18 countries were shown, most of them receiving their first screening in this country and several of them their world première. This was to develop into the Edinburgh International Film Festival rivalling the Venice and Cannes festivals in size and importance.

However, the most popular of all these extracurricular events, and one which was to contribute handsomely to Festival funds, were the displays of piping and dancing on the castle esplanade organized by the Army's Scottish Command. With the towering battlements of this ancient stronghold forming a magnificent backdrop, illuminated by floodlighting and searchlights, troops from famous Scottish regiments such as the Royal Scots, the Black Watch, the Highland Light Infantry, the King's Own Scottish Borderers, as well as the Seaforth, Gordon, Cameron and the Argyll and Southern Highlanders marched and counter-marched to the accompaniment of their pipes and drums. There were also displays of Highland and Scottish country dancing. On the nights the display was not presented the pipes and drums played 'Retreat' at different points in the city. These became so popular with visitors and citizens alike that in 1950 they developed into the Military Tattoo and thereafter military and naval personnel from all parts of the world would take part.

The first Festival was widely reported in the world's press, 275 journalists representing 153 newspapers and journals being present. This coverage extended to radio, and included some 45 relays to Europe as well as numerous pre-Festival talks. Radio Diffusion de Paris gave no less than 11 broadcasts on the Festival. These were a combination of recordings by the BBC with comments by M. Raymond Barthe, Radio Diffusion's representative in Edinburgh, and included interviews in French with the Lord Provost and Lady Rosebery.

By the end of the three weeks there was no doubt that the Festival had been an unqualified success. Perhaps the most important, though less noticeable, feature had been the highly efficient organization by Rudolf Bing and Ian Hunter which had ensured that everything had gone smoothly, at least as far as the audiences were concerned. The only apparent hitch had been a shortage of programmes for one of the concerts by the Vienna Philharmonic Orchestra. Another significant feature had been the fine Scottish contribution from the voluntary organizations which had greatly enhanced the scope and range of the attractions on offer, and had filled a gap in the official programme. Finally, there was the success of the Festival Club as a meeting place for artists, visitors and local residents. Over 8 000 daily tickets had been sold as well as season tickets and revenue amounted to almost £4 600. There were pleas from local inhabitants that the club should be continued throughout the year as a centre for the encouragement of music and drama, but this was impossible as the premises had only been let to the Festival Society for the duration of the Festival. Artists and visitors were unstinting in their praise of the city, the Festival, the organizers and the friendliness and helpfulness of Edinburgh people. The critics considered the standard of performance exceptionally high, and the City Fathers were satisfied that the original estimate of a deficit of around £20 000 would not be exceeded.

There had, of course, been a few hiccups. The critics had been quick to criticize the arrangements made by the Festival authorities, particularly with regard to the seats allocated to them. These complaints were speedily dealt with, and at a reception for the newspaper representatives given by the Lord Provost as a gesture of appreciation, Sir John referred to the difficulties and inconvenience the journalists had undergone and thanked them for the generous way they had supported the project. Part of the problem had been the exceptionally large number of journalists who had converged on Edinburgh from all corners of the globe.

There was some criticism about the lack of enterprise in programme-planning; a factor which caused one London critic to cancel his visit. No choral music and few contemporary works had been included. Ballet had been inadequately represented, and it was hoped that future festivals would offer a wider selection including perhaps a British ballet. It was also suggested that poetry recitals might be given, with modern poets invited to read their work. The visual arts had been neglected, and there was a strong feeling that they should be considered an essential part of future festivals, and not left to the individual galleries to organize on an *ad hoc* basis. But the most serious criticism came from a number of prominent Scots who felt that there should have been far greater emphasis on Scottish music and drama. The producer and playwright Robert Kemp suggested that a first-rate Scottish company should be assembled for the Festival to present plays by Scottish dramatists.

Harvey Wood, as Chairman of the Programme Committee, admitted that there had been obvious shortcomings and imperfections in this first Festival, but claimed that the programme, which had not been planned as a unit, had not been one of which anybody should be ashamed. He promised that Scottish drama would have a more prominent place in years to come. Not only was his committee anxious to ensure that varied fare was provided from year to year, but that a uniform standard of excellence should be maintained. When they could be sure of that, they would proceed with a Scottish play by a Scottish company.

Now that the Festival had been launched the Council of the Festival Society decided that the time had come to make improvements in administration and consider the appointment of permanent staff. Some members felt that, as the Society was now a bigger organization than Glyndebourne and with Glyndebourne's own future still uncertain, why should it continue to organize the Edinburgh Festival? But Bing made it clear that his first loyalty was to John Christie and that he himself would not be available to Edinburgh apart from Glyndebourne.

This clinched the argument and the Glyndebourne Society was re-engaged as Artistic Management for 1948. However, the Council was adamant that Bing should be responsible directly to it and not to Glyndebourne for the Edinburgh Festival. He was offered a contract as Artistic Director for the period up to and including the 1951 Festival. At the same time he was allowed to continue as General Manager of Glyndebourne, drawing a separate salary for each post.

The programme for 1948 revealed that the Festival Society had taken account of previous press comments particularly with regard to the lack of Scottish music and drama. Robert Kemp's suggestion that a Scottish company be formed to produce a Scottish play was taken up, and Kemp himself was commissioned to produce an acting version of a 400-

year-old morality play by Scotland's first dramatist, Sir David Lyndsay of the Mount, *Ane Satyre of the Thrie Estaites*. The three estates of the title were the three bodies represented in the old Scottish Parliament: the Lords Spiritual, the Lords Temporal and the Merchants. Lyndsay's satire is a protest by the common man against the unprincipled authority of all three but in particular against corruption in the Church. This mammoth seven-hour epic had been first performed at Linlithgow in 1540 for King James V and his Queen, Mary of Guise, and last seen in 1554. The play had so enraged the Scottish clergy that they had ordered the manuscript to be burned by the public executioner in 1558. Since then it had lain almost forgotten, except by scholars, until someone (probably Harvey Wood) proposed that it should be unearthed for the Festival. Kemp reduced the action to about two and a half hours, retaining the general drift of Lyndsay's argument as well as much of his humour. Tyrone Guthrie was invited to direct it, and a cast of 31 actors was drawn from the principal repertory companies in Scotland. The choice of play met with some opposition, not least from the companies from which the cast had been recruited, and with a less brilliant director the result could have been disastrous.

Guthrie's first task was to find a suitable venue. 'Either I have the best theatre in the city or I find somewhere completely out of the ordinary', he declared (*Edinburgh Evening News*, c 25 August 1948). The best theatres had already been earmarked for Glyndebourne, the Sadler's Wells Ballet and the Barrault-Renaud Company, so it had to be 'somewhere out of the ordinary'. The rain poured as he, with Bridie, Kemp and Willy Grahame (all rather inebriated from the tots of whisky they had consumed to keep out the cold) made their way in a Corporation limousine from one unsuitable venue to another across the length and breadth of Edinburgh. They were on the point of giving up when Kemp hesitantly suggested the Assembly Hall of the Church of Scotland! (Inside the Assembly Hall there is a portrait of Guthrie's great-grandfather, a former Moderator of the Church of Scotland, preaching in the open air to a Highland gathering.) In the gloomy, austere setting, with the statue of John Knox in the forecourt seemingly threatening hellfire and destruction to the forces of Mammon, it was almost impossible to envisage anything festive taking place, but with his unerring theatrical acumen Guthrie had no doubts. 'Can we build an apron stage over the moderator's throne?' he asked (*Edinburgh Evening News*, c. 25 August 1948). The twentieth-century clerics, more broad-minded than their sixteenth-century counterparts, agreed to the use of the Assembly Hall and to the alterations, and a makeshift theatre was created that was not only to be the mainstay of drama for almost every future Festival, but was to revolutionize theatre building in Britain and America – the Festival Theatre at Stratford, Ontario, the Guthrie Theatre in Minneapolis, the Chichester Festival Theatre and others were all inspired by the stage Guthrie devised.

This stage was similar in style to that of the sixteenth-century. Built on three levels with surrounding flights of steps it projected into the centre of the auditorium. The audience sat round the stage on three sides, the actors making their entrances and exits down the aisles between the sections of the audience. This staging was ideal for the processions, heraldry and pageantry of Lyndsay's satire, and Molly MacEwen's brilliant costumes more than compensated for the lack of conventional scenery. The long stretches of narrative were punctuated by continual movement as one elaborate grouping merged into another. The large cast led by Duncan Macrae, Bryden Murdoch and Moultrie Kelsall was exemplary, and succeeded in conveying the meaning to a large audience unfamiliar with Lowland Scots. The original and entirely appropriate music by Cedric

Thorpe Davie added the final touch to what the critics unanimously hailed as a thrilling theatrical experience.

Staging a play of which no one outside Scotland, and comparatively few inside, had ever heard as the major dramatic offering at an international festival had been a gamble. The advance bookings had been poor, only 20 per cent of the seats having been sold prior to opening; but after the triumphant first night and the subsequent glowing reviews in the press *The Thrie Estaites* became the smash hit of the Festival. The gamble had paid off, and Scotland had shown that, in one aspect at least, she could hold her own with the best the world had to offer. It was even suggested in many quarters that it should be repeated every year, rather in the manner of *Jedermann* at the Salzburg Festival.

Bing had hoped to bring a production of Shakespeare's *Othello* by Orson Welles and the American Theatre Company, but it had fallen through because of problems with the manufacture of the scenery. It was replaced by an adaptation of *Medea* by Euripides in which the Scottish-Irish actress Eileen Herlie gave an exciting but controversial interpretation of the title role. During the final week Bing followed up the previous year's visit of La Compagnie Jouvet with an appearance by France's other great theatre company, La Compagnie Renaud-Barrault. Barrault himself performed a triple *tour de force*: first as Dorante in a highly praised production of Marivaux's *Les Fausses Confidences*, then by his superb mimicry in the accompanying *Baptiste* and finally, in *Hamlet*, giving what the *Edinburgh Evening News* critic described as 'one of the greatest interpretations of Shakespeare's most controversial character' (8 September 1948).

Another exciting histrionic performance was that of Ljuba Welitsch in Glyndebourne Opera's *Don Giovanni*, although in the wings, unknown to the audience, an equally dramatic incident took place when a piece of heavy stage machinery came loose from the flies. This might have crashed on to the stage, injuring some of the cast, had not the stage manager Jimmy Webb caught the rope to which it was suspended and brought it to a stop only inches above the head of David Franklin as he was about to make his entrance as the Commendatore.

The visit of the St Cecilia Academy Orchestra was marred, first of all, by the absence of Victor de Sabata to whom the financial terms had been unsatisfactory, and then by the illness of Bernardino Molinari which caused a change of programme, but the orchestra was particularly commended for its magnificent string playing. Again it was the morning concerts that proved the most rewarding. Highest praise was reserved for Segovia's three guitar recitals in which his performance of Bach's *Chaconne* was described by Lionel Salter in the *Musical Times* (October 1948) as 'the only reasonable performance of Bach's impossible Chaconne I have ever heard'.

In answer to the previous year's question of 'Where is Scotland's own music?' the Festival Society organized several concerts of Scottish music. These included two programmes by the Glasgow Orpheus Choir, a concert by the Robert Masters Quartet consisting of an unpublished Trio by J.B. McEwen together with works by Alexander Mackenzie and Robin Orr, and a recital by a group of Scottish artists comprising songs by Francis George Scott and a violin sonata by Thorpe Davie. There were also concerts by the Scottish Singers and the Campbeltown Gaelic Choir.

The Scottish contribution extended into the ballet field where the 22 year-old Dunfermline-born ballerina Moira Shearer, in addition to attracting the crowds to her film *The Red Shoes* (being screened as part of the Film Festival), proved herself to be an

equally rewarding dancer on stage. Fonteyn lent her own special blend of radiance, charm and a 'delicious sense of humour' to the role of Swanilda in *Coppélia* and to the central role in *Scènes de Ballet*. But perhaps the greatest impression was made by Helpmann's starkly realistic *Miracle in the Gorbals* depicting life in a Glasgow slum, which at its first performance in 1944 had been hailed as a milestone in the development of ballet.

When the accounts for the year were made up it was discovered that, although expenditure on the Festival had increased from £27 000 in 1947 to £36 000 in 1948, ticket sales had also increased. After taking into consideration the subsidies from Edinburgh Corporation and the Arts Council and £6 000 from private donors, the deficit proved to be £10 500, just over half that of 1947. Edinburgh Corporation agreed to make an annual contribution of £15 000 for the next three years, and with a further grant from the Arts Council of £3 000 in respect of the 1949 Festival, the organizers felt encouraged to plan ahead.

Despite the success of *The Thrie Estaites*, or possibly because of it, the problems of arranging an adequate drama programme continued into 1949. The Old Vic was again approached; as in 1948, it was willing to take part but it was still unable to give details of either repertoire or casting until April. As the tickets had to be on sale by then to enable overseas visitors, particularly from America and the Antipodes, to book passages to Edinburgh, Bing and the Programme Committee had to consider other options. A repeat of *The Thrie Estaites* was a foregone conclusion, but the problem was where to find another Scottish play to present with it. The Programme Committee was keen to reconsider the Bridie play but in a letter to the Festival Society Bridie regretted that he was unwilling to allow *John Knox* to be presented at the Festival unless Guthrie could be persuaded to produce it:

> I feel certain that it would not be in the interests of the Festival or in my own interests to call in another producer. I feel, therefore, bound to withdraw the play from the Committee's consideration and regret that this must be final so far as 1949 is concerned unless Mr. Guthrie changes his mind. If we played Knox, so to speak, on Mr. Guthrie's pitch we would inevitably face awkward comparisons in the press and the fact that Mr. Guthrie had virtually declined to do the play would be a most serious handicap to its success, even if a producer of the first rank could be induced, in the circumstances to tackle the play.
>
> Quite apart from that consideration I do not feel myself disposed to risk Knox in the circumstances and must most gratefully and regretfully ask the Committee to accept my decision.
>
> (Letter from James Bridie to the Festival Society, November 1948)

A copy of an eighteenth-century pastoral comedy *The Gentle Shepherd* by Allan Ramsay was sent to Guthrie for consideration. Although it was a much slighter work than *The Thrie Estaites* Guthrie felt it had possibilities provided it was presented in appropriate surroundings. The ideal setting turned out to be the Upper Hall of the Signet Library where Guthrie envisaged the play's production on an open stage with no scenery and lit entirely by candlelight. The legal society of the Writers to the Signet agreed to let the Hall and even indicated that no rental would be charged, but refused to allow candlelighting. As a result of difficulties with the electrical installations it was thought at first that the play would have to be abandoned. But since the Festival Society had already incurred financial commitments to artists and musicians, Guthrie was asked to find another venue. After examining several halls Guthrie consented to produce the play in the Royal High

School. Feeling that Guthrie was being pressurized into agreement by Kemp and Thorpe Davie, who had been engaged to adapt the play and arrange the music, Bing wrote to the Lord Provost, Sir Andrew Murray, suggesting that the production be discontinued:

> After the world sensation of The Thrie Estaites nothing short of a similar success will do for The Gentle Shepherd. Mr. Guthrie, rightly or wrongly, does not very much believe in the strength of the work, and feels that it requires strong support from a very special atmosphere which in his view only particular surroundings can supply. The Signet Library would have been an ideal frame, and would have supplied all that extra atmosphere and glamour which in Mr. Guthrie's view the work requires. The Royal High School supplies none of the special qualities abundant in the Signet Library … Nothing proves more disastrous in theatrical ventures than trying to force decisions against responsible artists' judgements, and in this case, overwhelming odds.
>
> (Internal Memorandum from Rudolf Bing to Lord Provost, Sir Andrew Murray, 16 May 1949)

In this matter Bing's recommendation was not accepted and the production went ahead.

Possibly to fit in with the neo-classical architecture of the Hall Guthrie updated the play from 1725 to the Regency period, accompanying the action with 14 song arrangements by Thorpe Davie. These were performed by a vocal octet, four wind players and a pianist, all in costume. Although no one could pretend that *The Gentle Shepherd* was another Scottish masterpiece, the production had considerable success. J.C. Trewin wrote:

> I am secretly of the opinion that Tyrone Guthrie enjoys any challenge to do the impossible (which he immediately does) … The play itself is the slightest, simplest affair: what mattered was the art with which Guthrie presented it … The performance began at eleven-thirty p.m. and lasted until one-thirty in the morning. It was a refreshment to sit there in the small hours, listening to Ramsay's rhymes and to the crystal tinkling of the songs while watching again Guthrie's miraculous control of grouping as the phantoms flitted in primrose light.
>
> (J.C. Trewin, *John O'London's Weekly*, n.d.)

Heavier, more intellectual and considerably more controversial fare was provided by the other dramatic presentations. The most animated arguments centred around T.S. Eliot's *The Cocktail Party.* R.H. Westwater in the *Weekly Scotsman* (25 August 1949) found it 'engrossing', adding 'the fact that it is written, with enormous ingenuity and naturalness, in blank verse, increases its distinctiveness'. J.C. Trewin, on the other hand, considered it unmemorable. But if Eliot aroused the most spirited controversy the Festival had yet known, Peter Ustinov excited none. Trewin (*John O'London's Weekly*, n.d.) summed up the general feeling when he added: 'Although I found *The Cocktail Party* mildly tedious, it was certainly a marvel compared with Ustinov's *The Man in the Raincoat* … It is hard to know what possessed him when he wrote this flabby piece.'

To complete the drama programme and to commemorate the two hundredth anniversary of the birth of Goethe, Bing imported the Düsseldorf Theatre Company's production of *Faust.* While the production and the acting were generally praised, dissension of a different kind was raised by the engagement of Gustav Gründgens. This had begun as far back as the previous November when Bing had been approached by the *Sunday Pictorial* and the *Daily Mirror* informing him that Gründgens had been head of the German State Theatre during the Nazi regime. Bing had replied that he was guided on all matters concerning the suitability of artists by the Foreign Office and the Home Office, but a number of individuals were not convinced. On the opening night the proceedings were shattered by a cry from the gallery proclaiming, 'In the name of the people of Edinburgh I protest', followed by a shower of leaflets raining down into the stalls accusing Gründgens

of collaborating with Hitler and Goering. The actors silently left the stage. For a few minutes there was pandemonium whilst the majority of the audience cheered and clapped in an attempt to drown the protest. Eventually, sensing the hostile atmosphere among the audience, the demonstrators rushed out of the theatre and the performance continued. Hurriedly summoned to the Lyceum, Bing went on to the stage at the end and emphatically denied that Gründgens had ever been a Nazi. A demonstration of this nature was in opposition to the tenets on which the Festival had been founded and there was general relief that it had been of short duration.

'On one subject intelligent Festival-goers have been quite unanimous. The Glyndebourne Opera's presentation of "Un Ballo in Maschera" is as near perfection as one may hope to see and hear … What glorious and flawless singing from Ljuba Welitsch, Jean Watson, Alda Noni, Paolo Silveri and Mirto Picchi', wrote R.J.B. Sellar in the *Scots Magazine* (October 1949), adding, of *Così fan tutte*: 'I tasted the rare pleasure of complete enjoyment … A perfect evening.'

The Ballets des Champs-Elysées brought to Edinburgh no less than 24 ballets, many of them unknown in Britain, expertly performed by a talented group of young dancers including Irène Skorik, Nathalie Philippart, Nina Vyroubova, Jean Babilée, Youly Algaroff and the 18-year-old Leslie Caron.

The visit of the Berlin Philharmonic Orchestra showed clearly that inviting an orchestra from abroad to perform music outside its normal repertoire, with guest conductors, was hardly likely to display it at its best. Barbirolli had asked to be released from his contract on the grounds of insufficient rehearsal time, but Bing, believing this to be merely an excuse, had refused. In *Musical Opinion* (October 1949) D.M. commented: 'The Berlin Philharmonic was a sad disappointment in most things … It is interesting enough to see what such an orchestra can *not* do in Elgar, Roussel and Sibelius, but it is comforting to know, that, given music like Symphony no.1 (Mahler), the orchestra is thoroughly good.'

The most effective collaboration between orchestra and conductor was to be found in the three concerts by Sir Thomas Beecham and his hard-working Royal Philharmonic Orchestra which, with its opera performances, played every night of the Festival. Together they demonstrated what can be achieved by an orchestra that is in total rapport with its conductor. The programmes may not have been the most satisfactory from a structural point of view, but there were a number of attractive rarities. At the end of one concert when the orchestra refused to rise and share in the applause, Beecham turned to the delighted audience and complained, 'My orchestra has every conceivable virtue except obedience'. A press conference gave the irrepressible Sir Thomas an even wider platform on which to air his provocative views. After declaring that he was not going to criticize anything or anybody, he proceeded to harangue the critics and grumble in turn about the Arts Council, the proposed Festival of Britain, American money, the Government, the lack of a Scottish national orchestra, even about the Festival itself! Beecham had always been an outspoken critic of the Festival. In 1947 he was reported to have said that 'the people of Scotland are damned fools to throw away £60 000 on a musical festival'. One unsuspecting critic, unaware of Sir Thomas's views, jumped in headlong with the question: 'Do you feel it an honour or a privilege to be playing at the Edinburgh Festival?' Beecham replied:

> Good God, no! It is an honour and a privilege to the Festival for me to come here. This is about the 190th festival in which I have taken part. It seems to be a very nice affair, and if so, it is entirely due to my friend Mr. Bing.

Sir Thomas was obviously in fine fettle, and when another representative asked him whether he felt that, if the loss on the Festival was somewhat less this year, it had been because the Festival had established a record of good music? 'How can anyone establish a record of good music?' he snapped back. 'We have all been making good music for a hundred years and more. What are you talking about? Don't you think there was good music here before the Edinburgh Festival?' He was then asked if he thought the standard was higher? 'I don't know whether it has improved. There are orchestras here which play tolerably well. Some of the ballet companies disport themselves on the stage with fair propriety of movement. This is my first visit.' During his stay in Edinburgh he said he was going to the opera and hoped to see a play or two. 'The other orchestras I am familiar with. I never go to concerts other than my own. I find my own are unpleasant enough without listening to others which I am sure are worse.'

But for once Beecham found himself upstaged by that arch critic of the Festival, Hugh MacDiarmid. Generally considered to be the greatest Scottish poet since Burns, MacDiarmid had been approached by the Festival organizers but had refused to allow his poetry to be read at a Festival which he had publicly denigrated for its 'allegiance to money bags' in a city which he despised as the 'stronghold of bourgeois decadence'.

In a stormy debate with James Bridie initiated in the correspondence columns of the *Scotsman* and reproduced in the *Galliard*, *News Review* and other publications. MacDiarmid had sourly opened his argument by declaring:

> Scotland through the Edinburgh International Festival has gained the whole world with the usual effect on its own soul. I have always been opposed to the notion that cultural advance can be secured by giving any body of people all the culture of the world on tap – and none of their own … This false eclecticism is perhaps the outstanding fault of the Edinburgh Festival.

He went on to say,

> 'It is to my mind absurd that a city which has always treated the arts so meanly should think it can suddenly blossom forth as a great centre of world-culture. It is like giving the content of a University Honours Course all at once to a class of mentally defective children …'

MacDiarmid concluded:

> In consequence I am driven to the conclusion that the Festival is … a huge cultural 'black market' and that here again, as on a famous previous occasion, it is imperative that the money-changers should be driven out of the temple. The worst menace to civilisation lies in the fact that all the arts are being reduced to the level of a mere entertainment – to a Universal Tin Pan Alley.
>
> (H. MacDiarmid, *Galliard*, Autumn 1949)

Bridie countered this outburst by saying, 'Hugh MacDiarmid, the poet, is one of the glories of Scotland … Hugh MacDiarmid, the pamphleteer, is just plain daft.' In Bridie's view 'the Edinburgh Festival is the best thing that has happened in these islands since the Battle of Britain' (*Galliard*, Autumn 1949). In these circumstances, it was hardly surprising that MacDiarmid had declined an invitation from an organization he held in such low esteem.

Early in 1949 Bing had gone to America, at Glyndebourne's expense, to try to arrange a Glyndebourne season there and at the same time to continue negotiations for an American contribution to the Edinburgh Festival. He also seized the opportunity to engage in some canvassing on his own account. Consequently on 27 May the Festival Society received a telegram from Charles Spofford, President of the Metropolitan Opera Association, stating that it wished to offer Bing the position of head of management of the Metropolitan Opera and asking the Festival Society to release him. He added that should the Society be willing the Association would be happy to allow Bing to continue working for the Festival in an advisory capacity. After discussion the Festival Council (31 May 1949) agreed that Bing should be released from his contract on 15 October 1949. The Christies were not quite so conciliatory about Bing's resignation from Glyndebourne and his hasty departure caused bitter feelings.

In Edinburgh a sub-committee was set up to find a suitable successor. Among those suggested were Peter Diamand, Tyrone Guthrie, G.A.M. Wilkinson (the Director of the Cheltenham Arts Festival) and Thomas Bean (the Director of the Hallé Orchestra). Eventually the committee unanimously agreed that the post should remain vacant for the present. Bing was invited to become Honorary Artistic Director and Ian Hunter was designated Artistic Administrator (6 September 1949). This situation continued until 1951 when Hunter was promoted to Artistic Director. Bing was replaced at Glyndebourne by his assistant Moran Caplat. The translation of these two assistants to higher things brought to an end a rather illicit sideline. Since the Festival began Hunter and Caplat had been writing a gossip column for first one and then the other of the Edinburgh evening papers. In his autobiography, *Dinghies to Divas*, Caplat commented that their professional rivals never discovered the identity of the columnist with all the inside information.

Chapter 2

Ian Hunter 1950–1955

Under Rudolf Bing the first three Festivals had been outstandingly successful. He had brought the world's greatest artists to a cold, windy Northern city, not noted for its interest in either music or the performing arts. The Edinburgh Festival had now established itself as one of the major arts festivals in the world, a status that had taken Salzburg more than ten years to attain. The problem facing Ian Hunter was how to consolidate this position and to retain public interest in the Edinburgh Festival in the face of increasing competition, not only from Salzburg and Bayreuth, but also from the many new festivals that were springing up throughout Europe.

The departure of Bing loosened the ties between the Festival Society and Glyndebourne. In his dual role of General Manager of Glyndebourne and Artistic Director of the Edinburgh Festival, Bing had naturally favoured maintaining the closest association between the two organizations. Hunter, on the other hand, was responsible only to Edinburgh, and he had to consider what was best for the Edinburgh Festival; if that involved distancing the Festival from Glyndebourne then it was a risk he had to take. The Glyndebourne Society was still credited with the artistic management, but in effect this meant little more than the two societies sharing the Glyndebourne offices in London, for which Edinburgh paid Glyndebourne an annual rent and a share of the staffing and running expenses. Thanks to a guarantee of £12 500 from John Spedan Lewis of the John Lewis Partnership, which would underwrite the likely deficit of mounting two productions in Sussex in 1950, John Christie was now involved in planning his own festival and therefore, as far as he was concerned, Edinburgh had ceased to be of prime importance.

Although Bing had succeeded in retaining Glyndebourne's services for the opera seasons in Edinburgh it was by no means a *fait accompli* that this state of affairs would continue. Some members of the Festival Council were keen to widen the range of opera at the Festival and, for 1950, tenders were invited from Covent Garden and La Scala as well as from Glyndebourne. David Webster, administrator of the Royal Opera House, suggested presenting the first British performances of Berg's *Wozzeck* together with Verdi's *Otello* and a third opera such as *La Bohème*, with a star cast. He was also in favour of utilizing the Empire Theatre which, with its larger stage, would more easily accommodate the Covent Garden productions. But the Festival Society decided that, in the meantime, opera would have to remain in the King's Theatre. As the pit in this theatre was too small for the orchestra required for *Wozzeck*, Webster (in a letter dated 20 June

1949) proposed a season of 11 performances of *Die Zauberflöte*, in English, with Elisabeth Schwarzkopf, Walter Ludwig, Erich Kunz and Erna Berger, together with seven performances of *Fidelio* with Kirsten Flagstad or Hilde Konetzni in the title role, Franz Lechleitner, Irmgard Seefried, Boris Christoff and Hans Hotter. He also tentatively suggested that there was a possibility that the new Stravinsky opera, *The Rake's Progress*, might be available for 1950. Glyndebourne submitted an estimate for Strauss's *Ariadne auf Naxos* and a new production of either *Figaro* or *Don Giovanni*. These, together with a third opera, Gounod's *Mireille,* to be presented by the Paris Opéra-Comique, would cost £31 000 as opposed to Covent Garden's estimate of £32 000.

In a letter to the Lord Provost, Sir Andrew Murray (7 July 1949), Bing strongly recommended the Glyndebourne/Opéra-Comique option on the grounds that it would be madness for the society to take the unnecessary risk of possibly lowering its operatic standards, particularly when there would be no financial saving. He also pointed out that the high standard of Glyndebourne was well known but there was some uncertainty as to what Covent Garden would provide. Apart from the short international seasons Covent Garden had not yet established its reputation as a major opera house. Another factor to be considered was that the seat prices at Covent Garden were about half those charged for Glyndebourne and if the prices had to be reduced the financial situation would be considerably worsened. As it was by no means certain that *The Rake's Progress* would be ready in time for the 1950 Festival the Programme Committee decided to accept the Glyndebourne tender and to consider *The Rake's Progress* and a new opera by Britten for the following year.

In the meantime Webster, perhaps remembering that Christie had once tried to get a foothold in the Royal Opera House, proposed that the Covent Garden Opera might be prepared to act as organizing centre for the Festival opera. He indicated further that he and his trustees were prepared to meet the committee to consider the proposal in detail. The Programme Committee (22 November 1949) instructed Hunter to continue his negotiations with Webster but without committing the Society. But nothing further was said on this matter and the link with Glyndebourne continued.

By 1950 it had become increasingly difficult to find European orchestras of a sufficiently high calibre that had not already appeared at the Festival. One of Bing's ideas had been to create an Edinburgh Festival Orchestra by bringing together the leading instrumentalists in Britain who would nominate the remaining members of an orchestra of 70 to 80 players. This orchestra would give eight or ten performances during the Festival under three well-known conductors. He discussed the matter with several leading soloists who supported the proposal but, when consulted, Beecham had grave doubts as to whether the project would be successful and the idea was dropped.

As early as 1948 Bing had opened negotiations with the New York Philharmonic Society and with La Scala, Milan, with a view to the appearance of their respective orchestras. The cost of bringing the New York Philharmonic Orchestra would be £25 000 for transport alone, and could not be considered unless £20 000 could be obtained from American sources. When efforts to raise this sum failed Bing formulated an ambitious plan by which the orchestra would give ten concerts in Edinburgh followed by five concerts in London sponsored by the Festival Society. This extension of the Society's activities would help to defray the cost and at the same time enhance the prestige of the Festival. But this scheme also came to nothing and the visit of the orchestra was post-

poned until 1951 when there was a possibility of additional funding from the Festival of Britain authorities.

Hunter continued his negotiations with Ghiringhelli, the Director of La Scala, but by January 1950 these reached stalemate as it was unclear whether the Italian Government would subsidize a second visit to the Festival by one of its orchestras, and the invitation was withdrawn. As Webster was still interested in giving the world première of *The Rake's Progress* in Edinburgh it was decided to channel the money budgeted for the La Scala Orchestra into the opera (Programme Committee 24 January 1950). Two weeks later Covent Garden reported that *The Rake's Progress* would not be ready in time. As the Italian Government had belatedly agreed to subsidize the visit of the La Scala Orchestra, Hunter arranged for Glyndebourne to give three additional performances to cover a gap left by the recent cancellation of *Mireille,* and resumed negotiations with La Scala.

The financial terms for the orchestra had already been agreed. As the Company would be appearing at Covent Garden immediately after the Festival the Society and Covent Garden would share the fares of the orchestra on a pro rata basis. Ghiringhelli's agent suggested that the chorus might also come to Edinburgh to give three concerts with the orchestra. After numerous letters and cables it was agreed that the Society would pay the return fares of the chorus from London to Edinburgh and a contract was sent to La Scala on 23 March. La Scala did not dispute any of the points raised, and in a letter to his agent Ghiringhelli wrote that the deal could be considered settled. But the contract was not returned. Then in a letter dated 18 May, Ghiringhelli raised a number of difficulties, the main one being that the Festival Society should pay the return fares of the orchestra from Milan to Edinburgh regardless of any other performances they might give in this country. At this late stage the Society had no alternative but to agree to the new terms, but Hunter did persuade them to give an additional matinée concert of operatic music on 5 September, when Victoria de los Angeles would be available as soloist, to help defray the increased cost of the fares.

The signing of the contract was not the end of Ian Hunter's problems with La Scala. After a rehearsal of Brahms's *Ein deutsches Requiem* in Milan, de Sabata decided that the standard of performance was not high enough for the Festival and it would be necessary to change the programme. Then, when Victoria de los Angeles and the orchestra came together in Edinburgh to rehearse the matinée concert it was discovered that the arias Victoria de los Angeles had in her repertoire were not acceptable to La Scala. Instead of the operatic programme that had been announced La Scala compiled a programme from the repertoire they had already given that week. With masterly tact Ian Hunter announced to the press,

> throughout all these negotiations there has been the greatest cordiality, and there is no question of temperament on either side. La Scala will not compromise where artistic standards are at stake. Madame de los Angeles, quite rightly, is not prepared to sing arias which she cannot work out to Festival standards.

After her two cancelled performances (she was to have sung the soprano solo in *Ein deutsches Requiem*) Victoria de los Angeles won the hearts of Festival-goers with her Freemasons' Hall recital in which she sang a programme ranging from Monteverdi to modern Spanish songs. Her success was such that Hunter arranged an additional recital a week later.

Under de Sabata the Italian forces gave a full-blooded operatic-style performance of Verdi's *Requiem* with an impressive line-up of soloists; Renata Tebaldi, Fedora Barbieri, Giacinto Prandelli and Cesare Siepi. The young Guido Cantelli proved to be a worthy follower in the great line of Italian conductors, the *Scotsman*'s critic (6 September 1950) describing him as 'a born conductor with the notes and the spirit of the music living in him'. The real orchestral surprise, however, was the standard of the Festival dark horse, alias the Danish State Radio Orchestra which D.M. in *Musical Opinion* (October 1950) considered 'one of the world's great orchestras'.

But the superlatives were reserved for Strauss's *Ariadne auf Naxos* performed in its original version with Molière's *Le Bourgeois Gentilhomme*. It had originally been intended to perform the better known, and vocally easier, later version of the opera but Beecham persuaded the Society to spend another £5 000 on the original version, and his judgement was overwhelmingly vindicated by the critics. Richard Capell's review was short and to the point:

> What a salad is the Straussian 'Ariadne'! It is a salad of such expensive ingredients that only at the grandest of festivals is it possible to serve it up. At Edinburgh we have had it all. First some Molière; then the submergence of Monsieur Jourdain in a rising tide of ballet; and at the end of the evening Strauss's little opera, which is a kind of Wilhelmine triumph – the eclipse of Louis XlV's France by Wilhelm II's Germany.
>
> (R. Capell, *Daily Telegraph*, 26 August 1950)

The choice of drama for the 1950 Festival was subjected to considerable sniping in the press. Perhaps in reply to the Scottish lobby, both within and without the Festival Society, the Glasgow Citizens' Theatre was allocated the Lyceum Theatre for the presentation of three Scottish plays, of which two were world premières. The revival of John Home's eighteenth-century melodrama *Douglas*, which Garrick had once written off as being 'quite unsuitable for the stage', gave Sybil Thorndike an excellent vehicle for displaying her talents. Eric Linklater's *The Atom Doctor* was condemned by many of the critics as too lightweight for an international festival. But Ivor Brown in the *Observer* (27 August 1950) disagreed, considering that it 'offers much better entertainment than Jonson in his own Smithfield, however bravely the "Old Vic" may struggle to state a case for the London comedy'. Although the Old Vic put up the best possible case for the London comedy, Jonson's *Bartholomew Fair,* George Devine was misguidedly given the Assembly Hall for a production that was conceived for subsequent performances on the proscenium stage of the Old Vic, and this naturally presented him with a problem. Furthermore, in the limited rehearsal time available, the actors had insufficient time to adapt their acting to the unfamiliar thrust stage on which the Scottish actors, trained by Guthrie, had proved so adept. This raised the question whether in future years the Assembly Hall should be reserved for Scottish companies, leaving the Lyceum for imported drama.

When the first Festival had been in its planning stage Ian Hunter had suggested to Bing that a Scottish festival would be incomplete without some piping and dancing. Bing replied quickly, 'then you had better do something about it'. Hunter consulted with his brother-in-law in Scottish Command and as a result displays of piping and dancing were organized in the Ross Bandstand in Princes Street Gardens and on the castle esplanade. These were now expanded into a full-scale Military Tattoo, and this was to become the most popular item in this and every succeeding Festival, playing to packed houses every

night. It opened with a historical pageant depicting the installation of the Governor of Edinburgh Castle, the state coach used in the scene having been lent by the King. Then followed the now familiar piping and dancing. Finally came the most moving moment of all when the powerful floodlights were extinguished and a lone piper, spotlighted high on the battlements of the castle, played *The Last Post*.

Ian Hunter's trump card at his first Festival was a totally new departure, when for the first time visual arts were officially included in the programme. In association with the Arts Council of Great Britain he presented the enormously successful Rembrandt Exhibition, organized by Ellis Waterhouse: a representative selection of 36 paintings showing the different stages of his development as an artist culminating in the magnificent *Family Group*.

Hunter was also determined to end the Festival with a bang instead of allowing it to fade away quietly as in previous years, and who better to provide it than the effervescent Beecham? Sir Thomas was in his element when, suitably clad in a steel helmet that had been borrowed from the barracks, he conducted the massed bands and a battery of cannon in a performance of Handel's *Music for the Royal Fireworks*, punctuated by the obligatory fireworks, on the castle esplanade.

Beecham's attitude to festivals, or at least to this one, had mellowed in the intervening year. At another press conference he enthused: 'This is a wonderful festival … Scores of thousands of people troop into the city and put in appearances at concerts with bright, shining countenances, apparently enjoying everything. They attend everything. They applaud and stamp the ground – and it doesn't matter a damn what you play, the enthusiasm is always the same.'

However, the performers were not the only ones to put on an entertainment for the critics. The English press was highly diverted by the political antics of a certain Scottish Provost who, having accepted Lord Provost Sir Andrew Murray's invitation to the Provosts of the other Scottish cities to attend the opening ceremonies, subsequently found it necessary to 'send his apologies'. A prior engagement had come to light: the necessity of welcoming a circus to his own city. In a statement to the deeply interested press he said, 'Had any anxiety been shown about my presence in Edinburgh I might have altered my arrangements'. But a short time later he announced, 'I sincerely hope that when a National Theatre comes to be built it will be built in Glasgow, where the population is and where the theatre- and art-loving communities are'. The denouement came when, on welcoming the circus, he declared: 'I am quite prepared to admit that the pleasure of facing the lions thrills me slightly more than facing the literary lions who are in Edinburgh just now.' Edinburgh, basking in the sunlight of international prestige, had undoubtedly won the latest skirmish in the East–West war, and could afford to maintain a dignified silence.

The main criticism of earlier Festivals had been that they lacked adequate structure. The standard of performance had been extremely high but the programmes had tended to be a hotch-potch of whatever the artists had wanted to perform. This had frequently resulted in unbalanced programmes and, occasionally, the same work being performed by two different orchestras. In 1950 Ian Hunter attempted to change this with his series of chamber concerts of music by Bach and his contemporaries. He continued this practice in 1951 with a survey of Schubert's chamber music and a series of five recitals tracing the development of song, entitled *The Art of Lieder.*

In 1948 the Festival Society had inaugurated a competition for a new orchestral work. It remained open for two years by which time 61 entries from 13 countries had been received. The winner was William Wordsworth for his Symphony No. 2, the second prize going to the Czech-born composer, Karel Jirák. It had not been possible to perform these works in 1950, but in 1951 Hunter gave pride of place to the winning work by including it in the opening concert where it formed part of an all-British programme conducted by Sir Adrian Boult. Jirák's Fifth Symphony was performed at a later concert by the Scottish National Orchestra. The critics were divided about the merits of the compositions, some feeling that the first prize should have gone to Jirák whose symphony was considered to be technically more assured.

The most talked-about musical event of the 1951 Festival was the exclusive visit to this country of the New York Philharmonic Orchestra. Bing and Hunter had achieved a remarkable coup in bringing the orchestra to Edinburgh for no less than 14 concerts. The orchestra and its two conductors, Dimitri Mitropoulos and Bruno Walter, were greeted on their arrival by the City of Edinburgh Police Pipe Band, and received a similar send-off at the end of their visit. Both conductors dispensed with scores; the former also conducted without a baton giving one press wag an excuse for declaring that he also conducted without a beat.

Interposed between the Saturday and Sunday evening concerts by the New York Philharmonic Orchestra, the National Youth Orchestra of Great Britain found itself in the unenviable position of competing with one of the great orchestras of the world. But the 13 to 18 year-olds proved themselves more than equal to the task in an enterprising programme of Wagner, Mozart and Kabalevsky together with a Divertimento written for them by Malcolm Arnold. One of the Edinburgh evening papers reported that Mitropoulos dropped in on the final rehearsal for a few minutes and remained until the end 'astonished and fascinated', while Walter described the performance as 'one of the most inspiring things I have ever heard in my life'.

The enchanting Yugoslav Ballet, with its fascinating amalgamation of folk-dance and classical choreography, received a rapturous reception from the Edinburgh audience, as did the Sadler's Wells Ballet. Moira Shearer danced in both *Swan Lake* and *Ballet Imperial* to great acclaim from the audience, so much so that it caused some controversy in the press and at the morning press conference, where the freedom of audiences to express their appreciation was discussed. It was noticeable that while directors like Carl Ebert and Ninette de Valois were very much against what they called 'indiscriminate applause', the artists, as might be expected, loved it.

When the 1951 programme had been announced to the press, the drama content had again been criticized. The main target had been Shaw's *Pygmalion* which was considered an 'unsuitable' play for the Festival. To make matters worse the leading role was to be played by a popular British film star. When it came to the actual performances many of the play's detractors found themselves forced, albeit reluctantly, to eat their words. Margaret Lockwood was discovered to be a very able stage actress performing her difficult role with great aplomb, and the whole production a delight. Doubts were also expressed about the choice of plays to be given by the Théâtre de l'Atelier. Present Anouilh, by all means, said the critics, but surely one of his more mature plays would have been a more worthwhile choice than the frothy and somewhat inconsequential *Le Bal des Voleurs.* Yet again the performances were witty and enjoyable.

It had been announced that Sadler's Wells Opera would give the world première of Britten's *Billy Budd* during the Festival but because of its financial situation the company had to withdraw leaving only the two Glyndebourne operas. Owing to a traumatic incident when she was attacked and robbed on her way back to her hotel, Genevieve Warner was forced to withdraw from the remaining performances of *Don Giovanni*. Her understudy Roxane Houston ably stepped in for one performance and Léopold Simoneau's wife, Pierrette Alarie, who had accompanied her husband to the Festival, took over the remaining performances. Both operas were conducted by the veteran Fritz Busch, but sadly these were to be his swan-song; his sudden and tragic death from a heart attack was announced less than a week later.

For the closing concert, Ian Hunter came up with the perfect contrast to the 1950 fireworks concert when Mozart's *Eine kleine Nachtmusik* was given by a section of the Hallé Orchestra in the Usher Hall, the platform lit only by candlelight. This was followed by a Farewell Oration written by Robert Kemp and delivered by Lennox Milne and Duncan Macrae with contributions in French and Serbo-Croat from André Barsacq and Mira Sanina. Then Haydn's 'Farewell' Symphony was performed, in traditional style, each player in turn blowing out his candle and tip-toeing from the platform until only the conductor, Sir John Barbirolli, was left apparently asleep in his chair. He was then led off the platform by an attendant in eighteenth-century dress. A distant fanfare was heard and when it finished the lights came on and another Festival ended in rapturous applause.

A sum of £35 000 had been budgeted for opera in 1951 but by the time the final estimates had been submitted the cost had risen to £37 850. The Finance Committee (20 December 1950) accepted this estimate but recommended that in future years the cost of opera should be restricted to £35 000. In an effort to keep within this budget Hunter was considering the possibility of an overseas company, subsidized by its own government, presenting opera in 1952. Both La Scala and the Vienna State Opera had been suggested but because of its commitments in Salzburg there was little likelihood of the latter appearing at the Festival and the King's Theatre stage was far too small to accommodate the La Scala Opera. Hunter felt that a German company might provide a more suitable repertoire. After visiting Berlin, Munich and Hamburg he returned with a package of six operas by the Hamburg State Opera and six by the Bavarian State Opera each at an approximate cost of £30 000. An invitation was then extended to the Bavarian State Opera. Unfortunately the sets for the suggested programme were too heavy to be transported easily and the replacement repertoire, recommended by Munich, included a number of operas already seen in Edinburgh. Another problem was that Georg Solti had left Munich for Frankfurt and the present incumbent was alleged to have Nazi sympathies. Although less prestigious than the Munich ensemble Hunter felt confident in recommending the Hamburg State Opera as an alternative. In his opinion its director, Günther Rennert, was the finest young opera director of the day. There would also be fewer difficulties with scenery as it could be shipped direct from Hamburg to Leith (Programme Committee, 14 August 1951).

John Christie was understandably upset that he had not been consulted about the possible visit of a German company and that he had only been informed when a decision was about to be made. He personally considered that the standard of opera in Germany was low and emphasized that, as the Hamburg State Opera was a national rather than an

international ensemble, it might not offer the same standard as Glyndebourne. At a meeting with the Lord Provost on 29 August 1951 he suggested that if the Festival Society would put off the invitation to Hamburg until 1953 he would be prepared to co-operate, after proper discussions, with an invitation to a German company. But the Festival Council had already made up its mind and, although it was prepared to have Glyndebourne back in 1953, as far as 1952 was concerned it was time for a change.

Later that month Günther Rennert arrived in Edinburgh to inspect the King's Theatre and discuss repertoire. He proposed a new production of Hindemith's *Mathis der Maler* to be mounted specially for the Festival, the Company's recent productions of *Fidelio* and *Die Zauberflöte,* and three other operas from its repertoire, *Der Freischütz, Die Meistersinger* and *Der Rosenkavalier.* The Musicians' Union raised difficulties about the Hamburg Orchestra but Hunter stood firm, pointing out that, apart from the opera, there would only be two foreign orchestras at the Festival giving a total of ten concerts; the remaining concerts would be given by British orchestras.

During the final week of the 1951 Festival rumours began to appear in the press about Glyndebourne being dropped in favour of a German company. At a meeting of the Council the decision to invite the Hamburg State Opera was ratified and an official announcement was made at the final press conference. The statement emphasized that the Society still regarded Glyndebourne as the operatic backbone of the Festival, and had assured Glyndebourne that it would return in 1953.

> The Festival Society are happy to assert that both they and Glyndebourne are most anxious that this collaboration, close and fortunate to both, which has been built up over the past five years shall be fully maintained. The possibilities of inviting other operatic organisations to Edinburgh were explored with the knowledge and concurrence of Glyndebourne in 1947, 1948, 1949 and 1950. Glyndebourne would continue to have artistic management of the Festival.

When he was informed of the Society's statement Caplat commented, 'Glyndebourne having presented its reasons for continuing is disappointed with the decision, but would not seek for one moment to oppose the wishes of the Festival Society. The more distant possibilities can only be evolved by further mutual discussion' (*Scotsman* c. 8 September 1951). This decision caused an outcry amongst music lovers in Edinburgh and angry letters were sent to the local papers pointing out that Glyndebourne was an integral part of the Festival; indeed, that without Glyndebourne there would not have been a Festival. Even the critics voiced their support.

The following April a memo was received from Caplat to the effect that Christie would welcome an opportunity to discuss with the Programme Committee a definite opera policy for the future. Both *La Cenerentola* and *Idomeneo* would be available in 1953 with the possibility of *The Rake's Progress.* Boosey and Hawkes was prepared to allow the first performances in Britain to be given at the Festival. (David Webster of Covent Garden had optimistically hoped to present the world première at a previous Festival, and although Ralph Hawkes had been agreeable, Stravinsky himself had wanted the première to take place at La Fenice in Venice.) The Programme Committee agreed to the proposals (22 April 1952) and, on the surface, cordial relations between the two societies appeared to have been been restored. The decision to invite another opera company had been a particularly difficult one for Hunter. Not only had Christie offered him a job at Glyndebourne at the end of the war but he owed his early training as a conductor to Fritz

Busch. Afterwards Hunter sensed that Christie's attitude towards him had cooled. Perhaps Christie felt that Hunter had been rather disloyal to his former employer.

The visit of the Hamburg State Opera was outstandingly successful and more than justified its inclusion in the programme. The only disappointment was an unimaginative production of *Der Freischütz*, the one opera not directed by Rennert himself. There were many splendid performances by the galaxy of German singers gathered together for the occasion, particularly from Inge Borkh (Leonore), Lisa della Casa (Pamina, Sophie, Marzelline), Anneliese Rothenberger (Regina, Ännchen, Papagena), Elfriede Wasserthal (Ursula), Gottlob Frick (Sarastro, Kaspar, Pogner), and Toni Blankenheim (Beckmesser). In addition to singing Pamina, Eva and Agathe, Elisabeth Grümmer was called back from a short holiday in the Scottish Highlands to take over the role of Octavian when Martha Mödl fell ill. At another performance Lisa Jungkind, who was suffering from a throat infection, acted the role of the First Lady in *Die Zauberflöte* while Clara Ebers sang from the wings. Principals from the company also continued a tradition set by Glyndebourne of giving a concert to patients at the Royal Victoria Hospital. The most important event of the visit, and indeed of the Festival, was the first British stage performances of *Mathis der Maler.* Some of the critics found the music uncompromising and angular with a distinctly unvocal line, but most were impressed by its dramatic and emotional appeal, and Lord Harewood, writing in *Opera* (October 1952), found it 'a moving and exciting experience'.

The only world première was the Cranko ballet *Reflections* to a score by John Gardner which Cyril Beaumont in the *Sunday Times* (24 August 1952) found 'modernist in conception, powerful and impressive'. Fricker's Viola Concerto had been commissioned by the Society, but failed to arrive in time for performance by the Hallé. In its place the 27 year-old Dietrich Fischer-Dieskau sang the *Vier ernste Gesänge* by Brahms, following up his heartfelt performance of Schubert's *Winterreise* of the previous week.

The drama critics had a happier time this year. There were two new plays for them to get their teeth into, although Harold Hobson in the *Sunday Times* (24 August 1952) was somewhat puzzled by the attitude of his fellow critics in Scotland who had showered extravagant praise on *The Highland Fair* which he had found 'an elaborate bore', whilst greeting Charles Morgan's *The River Line* with 'exasperating condescension' – a play which he had considered 'without any shadow of doubt, along with "The Cocktail Party", the most exciting, the most sensitive, the most intellectually and emotionally alive play that any Edinburgh Festival has yet given us'. There was also a splendid production of *Romeo and Juliet* by the Old Vic with Alan Badel and Claire Bloom which, according to the critic of the *Scotsman* (12 September 1952), 'transcended any other play in the Edinburgh Festival. It showed that the open stage is capable of becoming the most compelling feature of the Festival if rightly handled. Only, it must not be used for plays unsuited to it.'

Encouraged by the success of his first exhibition in 1951 Hunter turned to Spain and the result was a fascinating display of El Greco, Goya and Velasquez together with a selection of minor painters. For 1952 he had planned an exhibition of paintings by Renoir but the French Government had been unable to collect sufficient paintings to form a satisfactory exhibition so instead he presented the work of Degas, the first of a splendid series of exhibitions devoted to the work of the French impressionists and their contemporaries.

Four centuries of the violin was chosen as the theme for 1953 enabling Hunter to bring together some of the world's greatest violinists for a celebration of the instrument in all its forms. With the support of Sargent and the BBC Symphony Orchestra, Karajan and the Philharmonia, the Vienna Philharmonic Orchestra with Furtwängler and the Rome Symphony Orchestra under Previtali and Gui, Isaac Stern, Yehudi Menuhin and Gioconda de Vito performed the violin concertos of Brahms, Beethoven and Bartók, and a rarity by Viotti. Then in one of those examples of entreprenerial genius for which Hunter was to become noted he persuaded all three to come together, with the Scottish National Orchestra and Karl Rankl, for Bach's double and Vivaldi's triple violin concertos, the order of the three soloists in the programme being decided by ballot.

Menuhin dedicated his performance of the Beethoven Violin Concerto, with Herbert von Karajan and the Philharmonia, to his friend and mentor, the violinist Jacques Thibaut, who had been killed in an air crash that morning. No applause was requested and at its conclusion the entire audience rose to its feet in a spontaneous act of respect. The Italian group, the Virtuosi di Roma, gave three concerts of concerti by Vivaldi and other eighteenth-century Italian composers. Examples of the violin and piano repertoire were provided by Max Rostal with the Australian pianist, Mewton-Wood. Then a different aspect of the violin was demonstrated in the complete string quartets of Beethoven given in six concerts by the Paganini, Barylli and Loewenguth Quartets, a contest which was won hands down by the Loewenguth. But the Festival's most sustained feat of virtuosity was probably Menuhin's performance of the unaccompanied Violin Sonatas and Partitas of Bach given in two morning recitals.

The concerts by the Vienna Philharmonic Orchestra with Bruno Walter and Wilhelm Furtwängler tended to emphasize the Festival's growing reputation as the Festival of the three Bs: Bach, Beethoven and Brahms, with Bartók replacing Bach in this particular instance. But they did include one rarity, the first British performance of Hindemith's Symphony *(Die Harmonie der Welt)*. Other orchestral concerts included two Festival commissions: the elaborate *Fantasia Concertante on a Theme of Corelli* into which Tippett cleverly interwove a double fugue by Bach; and Fricker's Concerto for Viola, composed for William Primrose, which had been held over from the previous Festival. Other British works included Malcom Arnold's *English Dances* by the National Youth Orchestra of Great Britain, Walton's Symphony No. 1 and the *Sinfonia Antartica* of Vaughan Williams. In the latter work the composer discovered a unique solution to the problem of the wailing of the wind. During a rehearsal of the work one of the horn players jokingly imitated the wind machine. The composer was delighted and the result was a series of banshee howls produced by a row of five horn players simultaneously singing falsetto into their instruments.

The return of 'The Glyndebourne' as it was affectionately known locally was greeted with delight by both critics and patrons. It brought three operas, all in excellent productions by Carl Ebert. The most discussed event was naturally the British première of Stravinsky's *The Rake's Progress*. The critics were divided about the merits of the work but generally in agreement about the excellence of the performance. The other two operas, Rossini's sparkling *La Cenerentola* and Mozart's *Idomeneo* were also highly praised.

A new T.S. Eliot play *The Confidential Clerk*, which had been promised for the previous Festival, was given its world première after a short preview run. A social

comedy, it was much less controversial than *The Cocktail Party* and was generally considered a better play. The demand for more Shakespeare was satisfied by a star-studded production of *Hamlet* by the Old Vic with Richard Burton, Claire Bloom, Michael Hordern and Fay Compton. The bonus of a second Shakespeare play, *Richard II* with Jean Vilar in the title role, was a fortunate result of the unfortunate last-minute cancellation of *La Dame aux Camélias* due to the illness of Edwige Feuillère. This, together with Molière's *L'Avare* by the Théâtre National Populaire and Marcel Marceau's Programme of Pantomimes and Mimodrames won glowing reviews.

But one beloved Festival artist was missing; Kathleen Ferrier had succumbed to the tragic illness that was to bring her short, brilliant career to an end. When Ian Hunter asked Bruno Walter if he could suggest another recitalist, Walter had replied emphatically, 'No. She is one of the few irreplaceable artists'. Instead the Vienna Philharmonic filled the vacant evening in the Usher Hall with an additional orchestral concert. Ferrier had sung at all six Edinburgh Festivals and had won the hearts of Edinburgh people with her radiant singing and warm personality. Of her first appearance she wrote:

> It was unforgettable. The sun shone, the station was decked with flags, the streets were gay. Plays and ballet by the finest artists were being performed, literally morning, noon and night, and hospitality was showered upon guests and visitors by the so-called 'dour' Scots! What a misnomer! It was all so different from previous experiences of concerts ... To be able to unpack for a week and come to a concert fresh and thoroughly rehearsed was novel and delightful.
>
> (W. Ferrier, *The Life of Kathleen Ferrier*, Hamish Hamilton, 1955)

At one of the daily press conferences Hunter reminded Bruno Walter of his prompt agreement to appear at the first Festival explaining that his acceptance had been the catalyst which had encouraged other top-ranking artists to appear. When asked why he had accepted Walter replied without hesitation:

> When the invitation came to me I felt it was enormously important. It was just after the end of the war. Regardless of anything else, I found that from the humane and cultural standpoint it was of the utmost importance and most to be desired that all the ties which had been torn should be re-united. I felt that it was an invitation to be obeyed, as a kind of command. There were a great many puzzles unsolved at that time, but, generally, I believe in a positive standpoint, and the only positive standpoint was to say 'Yes'. What you have seen here in Edinburgh is one of the most magnificent experiences since the war. Here human relations have been renewed. There is really no better way to counter the evil forces which are active in our time and to emphasize the good forces which are always with us, who are only occupied with positive elements of human culture. The war was an interruption of very harmonious personal relationships, and when we met here for the first time after this interruption it was really a meeting of old friends who did not know if they were still friends. But they were.

On 21 September 1953 Ian Hunter wrote to the Executive Committee informing it that, following the death of Harold Holt, he had been offered the post of Director of the well-known firm of artists' agents and requesting permission to accept this post in addition to his Festival one, at the same time reminding it that Rudolf Bing had been General Manager of Glyndebourne as well as Artistic Director of the Festival. The general feeling of the executive committee (19 and 23 October 1953) was that the Society could not contemplate any permanent arrangement whereby the artistic direction of the Festival would be in the hands of a commercial organization. There could be a conflict of interests if the Artistic Director was acting on behalf of artists while simultaneously engaging their services for the Festival. As Hunter's present contract

did not expire until 30 September 1955 it was decided to terminate it and draw up a new contract for the period to September 1955 whereby Hunter would continue as Artistic Director but would still be free to accept the invitation to join Harold Holt Limited on the clear understanding that, during the period of the year when his services were most urgently required, the Festival Society would have full claim on his time. Hunter should also declare his interest whenever an artist registered with Harold Holt was under consideration for the Festival. In the meantime consideration would be given to finding a successor.

In many ways the eighth Festival could lay claim to being the the most successful to date. The standard was as high as ever but there was, in addition, a greater degree of novelty and enterprise in the programme-planning. This was particularly apparent in the orchestral and chamber concerts where more contemporary works than usual were to be found. Two of these, Rawsthorne's *Practical Cats* based on T.S. Eliot, and Ian Whyte's ballet suite *Donald of the Burthens*, were given by the BBC Scottish Orchestra in a concert arranged jointly with the International Music Council, whose conference *Youth and Music* had taken place in Edinburgh during the Festival. A second joint concert was given by the National Youth Orchestra of Great Britain and included Blacher's *Inventions for Orchestra* commissioned for the conference. Another commission, this time by the Festival Society, Hamilton's *Variations on an Original Theme* won approval from the critics; as did a selection of modern works given by the Collegium Musicum of Zürich under Paul Sacher. But for perfection of playing no ensemble came up to the standard of the Philharmonia under Cantelli and Karajan. This was hardly surprising as within its ranks were no less than a dozen well-known soloists whose talents were put to good use in several popular classics.

The outstanding event of 1954 was expected to be the special Festival production of Shakespeare's *A Midsummer Night's Dream* by the Old Vic in association with the Sadler's Wells Ballet and the Scottish National Orchestra which would perform Mendelssohn's incidental music. This attempt to fuse drama, ballet and music which had looked so promising on paper turned out to be, at least according to the drama critics, an elaborate flop. Spectacularly beautiful visually, the production failed as drama. The realistic sets were too bulky for the stage and in order to get from one side to another the cast had to go out into the street behind the theatre! Impeded by his elaborate costume Helpmann had particular difficulty, and was compelled to squeeze himself against the backdrop and creep unobtrusively along it with the assistance of four men to flatten his enormous wings against the wall. Despite the reviews the production was a popular success. For at least one 14 year-old, attending her first adult theatrical performance, it was sheer enchantment from beginning to end. It ignited a love of the performing arts which, fanned by 40 subsequent Festivals, was to culminate in the writing of this book.

A direct result of this ill-fated production of *A Midsummer Night's Dream* was another venture which was to be universally acclaimed by the entire critical corps. The availability of Moira Shearer, Robert Helpmann and Hans Schmidt-Isserstedt inspired Ian Hunter to bring Günther Rennert's production of Stravinsky's *The Soldier's Tale* from Hamburg for four morning performances in the King's Theatre. Sol Hurok, the American impresario who was taking *A Midsummer Night's Dream* to America, was so impressed by the reviews that, without even seeing it, he telephoned Hunter and asked for the entire

production to be sent to New York with *The Dream*. The necessary arrangements were made and *The Soldier's Tale* was given in America with the same cast (all of whom were in *The Dream*) but with a different conductor and instrumental ensemble. Twenty years later, reflecting on the Festival, Moira Shearer gave this graphic description:

> The Festival years I remember most vividly are the early ones … 1954, I remember with a particular, surprised pleasure. I was with the Old Vic, playing Titania in a huge, rambling production of "A Midsummer Night's Dream" destined for a long tour of America and Canada.
>
> We performed at the Empire, under-rehearsed and in rather a mess, with only half of our scenery crammed on to the inadequate stage.
>
> Four of us in the company were asked to give four morning performances at the King's of a Stravinsky curiosity, "The Soldier's Tale" … It was the first time he used rag-time rhythms in a serious work. It's a very strange piece – music, narration, acting and dancing in an oddly angular arrangement.
>
> Anthony Nicholls, Terence Longdon, Robert Helpmann and myself met our director and conductor only three times, in a rehearsal room at the Old Vic. They were great charmers – Günther Rennert of the Hamburg Opera and Hans Schmidt-Isserstedt – but what we were all doing seemed shapeless and quite mad.
>
> We met again on the stage of the King's for a brief dress rehearsal, where it seemed to me even more crazy. My worst moment was discovering that the Princess had to dance on a stage within a stage, completely hollow, making one sound like a cross between a tapping Astaire and a small herd of elephants.
>
> The first performance was at 11 a.m. The musicians, led by puckish Hans Schmidt-Isserstedt, sat on barrels on stage, blowing and sawing quite beautifully. The curtain rose on a packed house with an odd sort of expectancy about it.
>
> Suddenly it was all over, and there was tremendous applause – amazing to us because so unexpected. The other performances had the same reception, and one had the pleasure of realising one had taken part in a most unusual and original production. It is something I look back on with affection and nostalgia.
>
> (M. Shearer, *Scotsman*, 23 August 1976)

Thanks to Michael Benthall, who shared Guthrie's enthusiasm for the open stage (so much so that he advocated that Edinburgh should build a special theatre in the round specially for the Festival) Shakespeare's *Macbeth* was adapted to the Assembly Hall stage. The result was, if not a resounding success, certainly a modified one. But again, the home-grown products were cast into the shade by another French company, the Comédie Française, in a brilliant production of Molière's comedy ballet *Le Bourgeois Gentilhomme*, with incidental music by Lully. They were ably supported by the Saltire Singers, dancers from Margery Middleton's Scottish School of Ballet and by a special Festival Orchestra and Chorus. In parallel with this production Glyndebourne presented the revised version of *Ariadne auf Naxos* in which the play is replaced by an operatic prologue. Beecham may have disapproved of the choice of version, and some in the audience may have missed Beecham's magic touch with the orchestra, but they were amply compensated by a superlative performance of the Composer by Sena Jurinac.

Although Walter Legge had remarked casually to Hunter that it might be a good idea to mount a Diaghilev exhibition he was somewhat annoyed when he discovered that Hunter had taken his advice. Richard Buckle was entrusted with the organization and the result was one of the most outstanding exhibitions of any Festival. Continuing the theme Hunter arranged for the Sadler's Wells Ballet to recreate some of the Diaghilev ballets, notably a brilliant *Firebird* with Margot Fonteyn, who had studied the role with Karsavina, embodying according to the ballet critic of the *Scotsman* (24 August 1954) 'the spirit of

the brilliant-plumaged bird, darting flame-like in red and gold across the stage, her whole body expressing terror at capture by the Tsarevitch, pleading for release'. Another Hunter coup was persuading Ernest Ansermet, who had not conducted a ballet since his days with Diaghilev, to return to the pit, stamping authenticity on every bar of the music.

The major problem facing the Festival Society each year was finance, or more precisely, the lack of it. Rising costs during the past two or three years were now taking their toll and income was not keeping up with expenditure. As far as revenue was concerned the ceiling had almost been reached. Audiences were in the region of 80 per cent of capacity so there was limited scope for increasing the income from the box office except by raising seat prices, which would put Festival performances beyond the reach of the ordinary Edinburgh citizen and exacerbate the growing feeling among the local population that the Festival was a jamboree for wealthy foreigners. The main drain on the resources was opera which, in the view of some members of the Finance Committee, was putting the rest of the Festival in jeopardy. The Diaghilev Exhibition, magnificent as it was, had been expensive to mount, and with the number of visitors lower than expected had resulted in a sizeable loss. The total deficit for 1954 was £30 779 compared with £18 992 in 1953. The only time a deficit on this level had been sustained had been in 1951, Festival of Britain year, the result of the visit of the New York Philharmonic Orchestra and the entire expenses had been borne by the Society. Unless the grants from Edinburgh Corporation and the Scottish Arts Council, and private donations, could be increased the new Festival Director would have a difficult task maintaining the high standard now expected of the Festival and at the same time balancing the books.

At the end of the 1953 Festival it had been announced that Covent Garden might give the world première of *Troilus and Cressida* in 1954, but Walton had been unable to finish revising it in time, so once again Edinburgh had missed out on an important opera première. Caplat had then proposed giving the first performances of Frank Martin's new opera which had been offered to Glyndebourne by the publishers. This would have been an apt choice for the Festival as it was based on Shakespeare's *The Tempest*, but the Programme Committee, whose members tended to be on the conservative side as far as contemporary music was concerned, had turned it down (9 March 1954). Caplat was now making arrangements for both 1955 and 1956 and was anxious to know whether Edinburgh should be included in these plans. Both he and Christie were fully aware that certain members of the Programme Committee were in favour of inviting another overseas opera company in 1955. In a letter dated 26 March 1954 Caplat suggested that this invitation be postponed until 1956 when Glyndebourne was planning to celebrate the bicentenary of Mozart's birth by staging his six major operas and would be unable to prepare anything new for Edinburgh. Hunter thought it would be too early to invite Hamburg back and that it might be difficult to find another overseas company of Festival standard which would be able to present opera in the Kings' Theatre. There had been many complaints from Hamburg about the limitations of the stage, particularly the inadequate space in the wings for a large company, the lack of storage accommodation for scenery and the tiny orchestra pit. All the scenery had had to be stored in a warehouse in Leith and moved back and forth on a daily basis, and several rows of stalls had to be removed to make room for the orchestra to the detriment of the sound. These arguments

prevailed and it was agreed that Glyndebourne would present the 1955 opera season and a company from abroad would be invited in 1956.

Relations with Glyndebourne were strained at this time owing to its having overspent on the opera budget for 1954 (Finance Committee, 10 November). Earlier in the year the Festival Council (13 January) had decided to drop the name of the Glyndebourne Society from official stationery and during the 1954 Festival Christie had formally tendered Glyndebourne's resignation as Artistic Management of the Festival to the Lord Provost. This had become merely a courtesy title as, since Hunter had become Artistic Director, the Festival had been organized entirely independently of Glyndebourne, although the latter had undertaken managerial responsibility for mounting *The Soldier's Tale* for which a separate fee had been negotiated. The only remaining tie between the societies was the sharing of the London office. Then on 24 March 1955 a letter was received from E. Scott Norman, one of the Directors of the new Glyndebourne Trust, to the effect that, with the appointment of a new Artistic Director as well as the possibility of a full-time assistant, Glyndebourne could no longer provide accommodation at Baker Street, and suggesting that the present arrangements be discontinued from 30 September 1955. Whether or not anyone realized it at the time, this was to be the parting of the ways. After 1955 Glyndebourne would make only one further appearance at the Festival.

In the meantime Glyndebourne had another success with a new production of *Falstaff,* a work it had wanted to stage for a number of years but had been unable to find a singer for the title role. Now he had been found in the person of Fernando Corena. Hunter's drama programme suffered a severe blow when Richard Burton, who was to alternate with Paul Scofield as Othello, was forced to cancel because of film commitments. Scofield was unwilling to appear without Burton and at a late stage the Old Vic replaced *Othello* with a good but unremarkable staging of *Julius Caesar.* The new Thornton Wilder play, written specially for the apron stage of the Assembly Hall, gave the critics something to argue about, some finding its classical theme rewarding, others pretentious. But they did agree that it was beautifully acted by Irene Worth and the rest of the company. Montgomery Clift who had been engaged to play King Admetus found himself at odds with the director and refused to continue. Michael Goodliffe had agreed to take over, but by the first performance he too had departed, and the role was eventually played by Robert Hardy. But, yet again, it was the French who took the acting honours with Edwige Feuillère making her belated Festival appearance as Marguerite Gautier in *La Dame aux Camélias* by Alexandre Dumas the younger.

Negotiations for the appearance of the Royal Danish Ballet had begun in 1948 and had continued every year. Finally the financial and technical problems were overcome and the company brought to Edinburgh a selection of Bournonville ballets including the romantic *La Sylphide* (set in Scotland) and the brilliant third act of *Napoli,* which showed off the bravura technique of its male dancers – a revelation to British ballet audiences accustomed to the male dancers taking a more subsidiary role. The main offering was the three-act *Romeo and Juliet* choreographed by Frederick Ashton, with the lyrical Mona Vangsaae, whom Ashton described as a 'divine Juliet', in the title role. (Thirty years later, Vangsaae's son, Peter Schaufuss, re-created this production for the English National Ballet.) The Danes were followed by the colour and splendour of the Azuma Kabuki Dancers and Musicians from Japan, the first time oriental culture had been presented at the Festival. The BBC had planned to televise part of the Kabuki programme but had

been prevented from doing so as the dancers could only perform on their own sacred, consecrated stage, which proved too difficult to dismantle and re-erect elsewhere, and the BBC found it impractical to take the cameras and equipment to the Empire.

Agreement among critics is a wonderful thing and the 1955 Festival won more than its share, when yet again they were united with the *Scotsman*'s critic when he wrote:

> The Festival has for years been experimenting with specially assembled chamber music ensembles. Some have been more successful than others, but there is no doubt that at last the right formula has been found. Within a few bars of the start of last night's concert it was clear that the combination of Francescatti, Fournier, and Solomon was right. Here were three men with world famous reputations as soloists who were in absolute musical and temperamental accord. Their playing was that of true, dedicated chamber musicians. We should not take that for granted. It was a remarkable and very fortunate fusing of superior talents. Ian Hunter has provided numerous artistic experiences over the years, but few more exciting than this, his parting gift to the Edinburgh Festival.
>
> (*Scotsman*, 26 August 1955)

Hunter's greatest achievement was probably the introduction of the visual arts to the official Festival. The Rembrandt and Spanish exhibitions and the series by French artists, Degas, Renoir, Cézanne and Gauguin were of a standard which his successors, with one or two exceptions, were to find difficult to match, let alone surpass.

With the visit of the Hamburg State Opera in 1952 he brought large-scale opera to the Festival and this was the first step in the chain of events that led to the final break with Glyndebourne. Hunter's intention had been to introduce a different company every two or three years to provide an occasional change of repertoire, whilst at the same time retaining Glyndebourne as the mainstay of Festival opera. Whether Glyndebourne could have continued as the official Festival company, or indeed have been willing to do so in the way that the Vienna State Opera is the bedrock of the Salzburg Festival, is a matter for speculation. It is true that in the next 15 years the Festival was enriched by the visits of diverse companies from Germany, Italy and Eastern Europe, with an extensive repertoire which it would not have been possible for Glyndebourne to provide. At the same time many of these operas were too large for the King's Theatre and its primitive technical equipment was unable to cope with the more sophisticated productions. As a result compromises had to be made and many of these were not seen at their best. The Glyndebourne productions were designed for a small house, and fitted the King's Theatre in a way that the Hamburg, Stuttgart, and Prague productions did not. Moreover the standard of Glyndebourne was second to none. Hunter remained convinced that the break was inevitable. The Edinburgh Festival had grown up and had to develop in its own way.

Chapter 3

Robert Ponsonby 1956–1960

In accordance with the Festival Council's decision that immediate steps be taken to find a successor to Ian Hunter, the post was advertised in the world press during the summer of 1954. From 142 applications a short list of four candidates was drawn up. After due consideration the Executive Committee (13 January 1955) recommended to the Festival Council that Robert Ponsonby be appointed. Ponsonby had come to the Festival from Glyndebourne and for the past three years had been employed partly by Glyndebourne and partly by the Festival Society as Ian Hunter's assistant. Lady Rosebery dissented from this decision, suggesting that Peter Diamand (who had been considered for the post on Bing's departure) might be prepared to accept the position if the salary was increased (26 January 1955). In February 1955 several approaches were made to Diamand but he was unwilling to accept a post that encompassed responsibility for only the artistic aspects of the Festival. In addition he felt unable to leave the Holland Festival at a critical time. In a final attempt to persuade him to come to Edinburgh the Secretary and Treasurer visited Amsterdam and suggested that he accept the post on a part-time basis for a year up to August 1956 to allow the Holland Festival time to find a replacement. However, Diamand reluctantly declined the offer and, since only he and Ponsonby had been considered worthy, the Council appointed Robert Ponsonby.

During the summer of 1955 Ponsonby visited Germany, Italy, Czechoslovakia, Switzerland and France. High on his agenda was the necessity of finding a continental opera company for 1956. It had also been suggested that an *ad hoc* opera company, conducted by Beecham, might be formed to present three operas including *A Village Romeo and Juliet* by Delius and Mozart's *Die Entführung aus dem Serail*. Ponsonby's investigations into the financial viability of forming such a company revealed that the cost would be approximately £11 000 more than the the amount paid to Glyndebourne in 1954 and the proposal was dropped. Instead the Hamburg State Opera was invited for 1956 at a cost of £48 270, of which £6 000 would be provided by the West German Government.

Ponsonby had also discussed with Moran Caplat the possibility of Glyndebourne returning in 1957, but in 1956 the Glyndebourne season had been extended until the middle of August, and if this policy was adopted again in 1957 an Edinburgh visit would be out of the question. In this case Ponsonby felt that efforts should be made to bring a distinguished Italian company, preferably the recently formed La Piccola Scala, the visit to be subsidized by the Italian Government. (The previous year La Scala had

opened the 'Little Scala', a small auditorium for the performance of eighteenth-century opera.)

Ponsonby was concerned that if Glyndebourne was not available for future Festivals considerable difficulty would be experienced in maintaining opera presentations of the requisite standard. He suggested that the Society should enter into a long-term agreement with Glyndebourne for the five years from 1958, but Caplat and Christie were unwilling to commit Glyndebourne to appearing at four out of five Festivals and it was agreed that, starting in 1958, the Company would appear every other year. Both parties would have the right to break the agreement at any time, provided two years' notice was given (Programme Committee, 29 October 1956).

During the autumn of 1955 Ponsonby had made a detailed study of every aspect of the Festival and he produced a lengthy report (1 October 1955) in which he pointed out that many aspects of the Festival had fallen far behind the standard of the programme itself. He suggested a number of improvements relating to the opening ceremony, the Festival Club, late licensing, street decorations, artists' receptions, programmes and programme notes, the unsuitability of the Edinburgh office and the desirability of finding a medium-sized concert hall. In particular he emphasized the poorly equipped buildings, many of which were fulfilling a function for which they had never been intended. To strengthen his argument Ponsonby produced a letter from the ballet critic of the *Dancing Times* criticizing the disgraceful conditions under which visiting ballet companies had to perform at the Empire. There was also an article in a Danish publication *Politiken* in which the arts critic questioned whether it had been worth while for the Danish Government to give 200 000 kroner to enable its ballet company to perform in a primitive theatre at the far end of town, and suggesting that the money might have been better spent on a visit to Paris or the USA. Other articles criticizing the Empire, the Usher Hall and the Festival Club had appeared in the *Scotsman, Time and Tide* and *The Times Educational Supplement.*

With regard to finance Ponsonby concluded that although the suggested improvements would absorb much of the Society's bank balance of £60 000 they were essential if the Festival was to be brought up to the same standard as other festivals. Strenuous efforts would have to be made to replenish the fund and to increase revenue for the Festival. The Festival received £15 000 from Edinburgh Corporation and £7 500 from the Scottish Committee of the Arts Council. In return the Festival had created an enormous tourist industry, not just for Edinburgh but for the whole of Scotland – in 1955 the Tourist Board had reported that 84 416 people had been accommodated in hotels and boarding-houses and a further 108 000 had come to the city on coach tours. Ponsonby felt it was now the turn of Scottish industries to help the Festival, so he recommended first the formation of a committee of managing directors of leading Scottish firms, who would act on behalf of the Society in collecting funds either by contribution, through advertising or by covenant; secondly, an appeal to individuals on the mailing list asking for deeds of covenant; and thirdly, the formation of a Festival Guild.

Finally, Ponsonby drew attention to a significant gap in the Festival Society's structure, in that no one was responsible for long-term policy. He accordingly recommended that the Programme Committee be renamed the Policy and Programme Committee, and that the chairmen of the two main committees be appointed vice-chairmen of the Society, supplying an element of continuity which the Lord Provost, by nature of the period of his

office, was unable to do. A special sub-committee was appointed to look into matters concerning capital expenditure and policy-making and to make recommendations.

Ponsonby was aware that the drama content in 1955 had again been the subject of adverse comment in the press and he agreed that the criticism about too few Scottish contributions had been justified. (Hunter had hoped to present McLellan's *Jamie the Saxt* at the Gateway but Duncan Macrae had refused to perform in such a small venue and, as no other theatre had been available, the project had been postponed.) In an attempt to rectify the situation Ponsonby invited the recently formed Gateway Company to present Bridie's *The Anatomist* in 1956. Other projects considered for that year were a production of *Ondine*, in English, with Audrey Hepburn, and a visit by the Berliner Ensemble from East Germany. The former had to be jettisoned because of the unavailability of Hepburn. With regard to the Berliner Ensemble (Programme Committee, 21 February 1956), the Foreign Office had asked the Society to break off negotiations to avoid causing embarrassment to the West German Government which was subsidizing the appearance of the Hamburg State Opera.

In the meantime Guthrie suggested the Stratford Ontario Festival Company. Guthrie had been involved in starting this Festival and had even constructed a larger version of the Assembly Hall stage for the purpose. The Stratford Ontario productions would therefore be ideal for the Assembly Hall. In particular the production of Shakespeare's *Henry V* with Christopher Plummer in the title role was an inspired choice. The dual nationality of the company enabled the English roles to be performed by English-speaking actors while the French Canadian actors in the company undertook the French roles. Another exciting young company, the Piccolo Teatro of Milan, demonstrated *commedia dell'arte* at its best in a brilliant production of *Arlecchino, Servant of Two Masters* by Goldoni. There were doubts about the effectiveness of the attempt to stage Dylan Thomas's radio play, *Under Milk Wood*, but it was an interesting experiment, even if it did not quite come off.

Braving the perils of the Empire Theatre stage were two of the greatest dancers in the world: Margot Fonteyn in perhaps her finest role, Odette/Odile in *Swan Lake*, followed by the colour and splendour of the Indian dancer, Ram Gopal. In his first programme he demonstrated the different schools of the classical Indian tradition and in the second he presented the world première of his own ballet, the spectacular *Legend of the Taj Mahal.*

The music programme was equally strong. In the Usher Hall the Boston Symphony Orchestra under Charles Münch and Pierre Monteux celebrated its seventy-fifth anniversary season with five concerts, each including a work specially commissioned for the season. The final concert of twentieth-century works was a Homage to Sergei Koussevitzky who, in his 25 years as principal conductor, had built the orchestra into one of the finest in the world. There were also five concerts by Beecham and the Royal Philharmonic Orchestra. Included in the opening concert was an overture *Edinburgh* by Sir Arthur Bliss, specially commissioned for the tenth Festival. When Ponsonby asked Beecham if he would mind if the Master of the Queen's Music conducted his new work, Beecham promptly enquired if he would appear in *uniform.* Fortunately, with no royalty present, there was no repeat of a previous Beecham concert when, as Hunter's deputy, Ponsonby had failed to persuade the conductor to wait on the rostrum while members of the Royal Family took their seats in the Grand Tier. 'I don't want to be kept waiting about on that rostrum! I was once kept waiting *twenty minutes* by the Princess Royal. Stuck in a lift she was. Having a baby at the time, I remember.'

Outstanding among the opera presentations was a stunning, if vocally uneven, performance of *Salome* by the young German singer, Helga Pilarczyk, which sent most of the critics into ecstasies. The visual arts were represented by a fine Braque exhibition, which was considered a notable artistic success, but was less popular with the public, raising questions in the minds of some Festival Council members as to the advisability of the Society's presenting these large exhibitions instead of leaving the various galleries to mount their own.

Robert Ponsonby could afford to be satisfied with the outcome of his first Festival which was considered to be one of the best in the series. He also persuaded Edinburgh Corporation to make some badly needed improvements to the Usher Hall, but the owners of the theatres were naturally unwilling to spend vast sums upgrading them for use over a period of only three weeks when they were adequate for the productions presented during the rest of the year. What was needed was a purpose-built opera house capable of staging the productions being brought to the Festival year after year.

Following on Ponsonby's initial report on the theatre situation William Earsman, a member of the Festival Council, took up the cause. He suggested that, as the Festival had become a permanent feature of the city, the time was opportune to consider the acquisition or erection of a suitable Festival Theatre. Accordingly the Executive Committee (28 December 1955) instructed the officials to prepare a report covering the building of a theatre with a seating capacity of about 2 500 to include revenue-producing offices. The topic had been widely discussed during the 1956 Festival, but when it transpired that the cost was likely to be in the region of £1 million any initial enthusiasm shown by either the Society or Edinburgh Corporation quickly waned. In September 1956 Francis Murdoch, the Lord Provost's secretary, uncovered two reports which he sent to Ponsonby explaining that they had been discussed by succeeding committees and then 'conveniently' forgotten. The first was a memorandum on future policy and development, and the second a memorandum prepared in 1948 covering the future development of the city of Edinburgh as an international centre for the teaching of the arts, including the development of a festival centre. This had been based on a project by two young architects, Kenneth Brydon and John Graham, and included plans for a concert hall, an opera house, a theatre, a small concert hall (which could double as a lecture hall), two art exhibition rooms, a restaurant, a library, administrative offices, lounges, reading rooms and practice rooms. The plan went on to suggest the gradual development of schools of music, ballet, drama and opera. Two sites were recommended: the Grassmarket and the area around the Usher Hall. The cost was estimated at £10 million.

On 27 April 1949 this plan had been discussed by the Executive Committee which had decided that the time was inopportune and the idea was, as Murdoch said, forgotten. Ponsonby raised the matter in his report on the 1956 Festival, and it was suggested (Executive Committee 22 January 1957) that a trust fund should be established for the purpose of obtaining capital funds for the provision of a festival centre to include a suitable auditorium and ancillary accommodation for Festival presentations, but in view of the Society's increasing financial problems the matter was later shelved.

Undoubtedly the major event of the 1957 Festival was the visit of La Piccola Scala. However, only one of the four productions, Cimarosa's *Il Matrimonio segreto*, was a Piccola Scala production, the others came from the main theatre, as did the casts. The

opening performance was Bellini's *La Sonnambula* with the celebrated Maria Callas. Though not in her best voice she received a tremendous ovation from the Edinburgh audience and glowing reviews in the press. She was billed to give five performances, but by the third performance she was apparently having vocal problems, and after the fourth she left Edinburgh for Italy. The Festival Society announced that she was ill, but when Callas appeared at one of Elsa Maxwell's parties in Venice on the night she should have been singing in the final performance of *La Sonnambula* the popular press naturally made the most of it, and there were sensational headlines such as 'Callas walks out of the Edinburgh Festival' and 'Walkout Festival star flies to the sun'. Worthy Edinburgh citizens, normally apathetic towards the Festival, were indignant that a singer, even one as famous as Callas, should consider a party more important than an appearance at their Festival. So many conflicting statements were issued that no one knew what to believe, and it was some months before the full story emerged.

La Scala had offered four performances of *La Sonnambula* but when the Festival Director asked for a fifth performance La Scala had been happy to oblige. But for some inexplicable reason Callas had only been contracted to sing four; in typical Italian fashion La Scala had assumed that she would also sing the fifth performance. Callas, however, had been suffering from nervous exhaustion and on 7 August had obtained a medical certificate from her doctors prescribing at least 30 days' rest which she passed on to La Scala. As Callas's name had formed the basis of the contract the administrator of La Scala had prevailed upon her to sing in Edinburgh. But, having fulfilled her contract to sing four performances, Callas had been in no mood to bail La Scala out of a difficulty which it alone had created, and she had steadfastly refused to sing in the final performance. In any case she had already arranged to go to Venice. The resultant barrage of press condemnation was more than even Callas had anticipated. She was furious with La Scala for refusing to make a statement to the press exonerating her, and for two or three months afterwards Callas pleaded, cajoled and threatened Ghiringhelli to release the full story. Finally Ghiringhelli reluctantly made a statement to the Italian press, but by this time the damage to Callas's reputation was irreparable.

Callas was replaced at the final performance of *La Sonnambula* by the 24 year-old Renata Scotto who was in Edinburgh covering the role. A few days earlier Scotto had replaced an indisposed Rosanna Carteri as Adina in *L'Elisir d'Amore*, an occasion which had passed off without comment in the press, but when she took over Callas's role she became famous overnight. Her photograph appeared in the tabloids which hailed her as a new operatic star, and after that one performance her career never looked back.

The premature departure of his prima donna was not Ponsonby's only problem that year. In spite of good intentions 1957 was proving an unlucky year for drama, and the critics (and not only the London ones) were having a field day. Both *Nekrassov* by Sartre and Hasenclever's *Man of Distinction* were considered lightweight, and while one would have been acceptable two were one too many. Anouilh's *La Répétition* (*The Rehearsal*) was beautifully acted by the Renaud-Barrault Company but some of the critics thought that it was not one of his best plays. What should have provided the necessary ballast, a new verse drama *The Hidden King* by Jonathan Griffin, on the open stage of the Assembly Hall, turned out to be the most controversial item in this, or any other Festival. For ten years the critics had been complaining about the lack of new drama at the Festival but when the Society did take the plunge it met with a formidable

phalanx of hostile critics. When asked by a Scottish journalist if he was covering it, Kenneth Tynan's scathing reply in the *Observer* (25 August 1957) was: 'With a sheet, perhaps, on a marble slab. Cover its face. My mind boggles. It died young.' Yet in the same review he remarked that he could see no reason why any non-Scottish play-goer should travel to Edinburgh as, apart from the odd foreign company, drama in Edinburgh was entirely composed of plays that had been induced to use the city as a touring date on their way to London.

In the light of criticism that the play was obscure, over-long and insufficiently theatrical the author, director and cast spent the intervening day working on it and succeeded in clarifying some of the more obscure scenes and shortening it by 20 minutes; at the second performance the play went through without a hitch. At a press conference, where members of the cast were given an opportunity of responding to the critics, the fear was expressed that the drama critics of the popular press, by their present standards of criticism might kill the dramatic side of the Festival and force the Council to keep to non-experimental plays of the kind that are sure to be commercial successes. The actors spoke of the enthusiasm they felt for the play, the magnificent parts it contained and its writing. Michéal MacLiammóir, the distinguished Irish actor and co-founder of the Gate Theatre, hotly defended it saying that all countries were press-ridden. That 'in this country there are six genuine critics and six hundred hooligans. In my country there are seventy hooligans and half a critic'. He went on, 'It is a terrible thing to think that drama is in the grip of apparently potential enemies'.

At the request of the cast Ponsonby arranged a public forum, chaired by Lady Rosebery, at which the cast, critics and public came together to discuss the play. Several hundred members of the public turned up, but few critics took up the challenge. The views of the public were almost unanimously in favour of the play. The only real criticism appeared to be on account of its obscurity, to which Mr MacLiammóir's reply had the audience rocking with laughter. He said he did not think an audience's enjoyment depended on their understanding everything: 'The man who tells me he understands the whole of *Rigoletto* is a liar.'

The problems in connection with *The Hidden King* had begun earlier in the year. A costume drama by an unknown writer and requiring a large cast would inevitably be expensive to produce. The original estimate had been £13 650 but by July this had risen to £17 700. This had irritated members of the Finance Committee (14 August 1957) who had recommended that a sub-committee of three should scrutinize all contracts to ensure that in future the financial arrangements were in accordance with the preliminary budget approved by the Festival Council. Had the play been a success at the box office much of this deficit would have been recovered and the matter forgotten, but there was no doubt that critical condemnation had its effect in keeping the audience away. The continental press were more enthusiastic and after the Festival the rights to present *The Hidden King* were purchased by a German company and in due course it was seen in Freiburg.

With these major crises a fit of temperament on the part of the Scottish National Orchestra's new conductor was all in a day's work for the Director. Hans Swarowsky had been extremely distressed to discover that his photograph had not been included in the souvenir programme and in consequence felt unable to conduct his two concerts. When Lady Rosebery raised the matter at an Executive Committee meeting on 14 August 1957,

Ponsonby replied that, because of the limited number of art pages, it was impossible to include photographs of every artist. Agreeing that the matter was unfortunate but that no artist had an automatic right to have his photograph in the programme, Lord Provost Johnson-Gilbert wrote to Swarowsky expressing regret and explaining the circumstances, after which a mollified Swarowsky consented to conduct.

The 1957 Festival was not without its tragedy. Dennis Brain, probably the best horn player in the world, was killed whilst driving back to London after playing with the Philharmonia Orchestra under Ormandy in a Tchaikovsky programme which closed, almost prophetically, with the 'Pathétique' Symphony. Writing retrospectively about one of the morning concerts in the *Musical Times* (October 1957) Harold Rutland said, 'There he was, as calm and young and happy looking as ever, performing prodigious feats on his chosen instrument.' He had been due to return the following week to play Strauss's Second Horn Concerto with the Concertgebouw Orchestra, but like Kathleen Ferrier, Brain was irreplaceable and Schubert's 'Unfinished' Symphony was substituted.

Feeling that satire should not be solely the preserve of the Fringe, Ponsonby invited the indomitable Anna Russell to present a late-night show at the Lyceum where she gave her classic parody of Wagner's *Ring* and her even more devastating satire on folk-singing. This proved so popular that an extra performance had to be fitted in on the last Friday. With her scheduled Saturday performance Anna Russell had the privilege of closing the eleventh Festival.

Throughout 1957 the Society had been preoccupied with the rapidly deteriorating financial situation. Edinburgh Corporation's grant to the Festival had not increased since 1948 and it had become increasingly apparent that revenue was not keeping up with expenditure. Opera costs over the past ten years had risen by 100 per cent in the case of Glyndebourne and orchestral concerts by up to 200 per cent. In the early days these concerts had made a small profit but that was no longer the case. Negotiations with the Vienna Philharmonic Orchestra, Elisabeth Schwarzkopf and Artur Rubinstein had been broken off over the question of fees. The Festival's great international prestige had been built up and maintained upon the presentation of opera, orchestras and companies of the highest repute. Ponsonby insisted that if the Festival's standards and its position were to be maintained it was vital that the means should be found to enable the Society to continue to afford leading artists and companies.

The temporary offices which the Society had occupied in the Synod Hall since 1947 were quite unsuitable and Ponsonby had finally persuaded the Festival Council of the need for new premises. Accordingly the Society had purchased the disused Highland Church in Cambridge Street next to the Usher Hall, for which the Scottish Arts Council had given an interest-free loan of £5 000. But this had made a sizeable hole in the Festival Fund and a further sum of £15 000 was required for conversion.

If Ponsonby's budget for the 1958 Festival was accepted, the Society would not only have exhausted its working capital but would be in debt to the extent of £19 000. In an attempt to cut costs the Finance Committee (1 October 1957) suggested limiting the opera budget to £48 000, postponing the necessary alterations to the Highland Church and cancelling the proposed Byzantine Exhibition. This exhibition was to have been been held in 1957 but because of the unavailability of some of the exhibits the Victoria and Albert Museum had been reluctant to take the exhibition after the Festival, so it had been decided to

postpone it until 1958 when all the exhibits would be available and the costs could be shared. Because of the advanced state of the negotiations, which had begun in 1954, and the repercussions if it was cancelled, the decision was taken that the exhibition must go ahead, despite the cost of £9 000. It was also felt that it would be inadvisable to delay the conversion of the Highland Church, but the limitation on the opera budget was accepted.

In reply to an appeal from the Festival Council, Edinburgh Corporation agreed to increase its subsidy for the 1958 Festival by £10 000 to £25 000. At the same time it asked for an increase in the number of town councillors on the Festival Council and Executive Committee. The Society agreed and the number of town councillors on the Festival Council was increased from one-third to half the total number, and the Executive Committee to a total of 12 comprising the Lord Provost, six town councillors and five non-town councillors.

During the summer Ponsonby reported to the Programme Committee (5 June 1958) that, in the absence of information about the level of funding, he had been unable to make any arrangements for the 1959 Festival. If artists of international standing were to be engaged it was necessary to act immediately. The Programme Committee instructed him to proceed on the assumption that the budget would be the same as in 1958, and this decision was ratified by the Executive Committee on 6 June 1958. Some members of the Finance Committee (20 June 1958) took exception to this authorization as the special grant of £25 000 from the Corporation applied to 1958 only, and it was by no means certain that a similar grant would be given in 1959. The Finance Committee also recommended, in view of the financial situation, that opera should be omitted from the programme for that year, but as the Executive Committee (23 June) felt that the Festival would be incomplete without it it was agreed that opera should be included but that every effort should be made to keep expenditure down.

It had been announced at the end of the 1957 Festival that Glyndebourne would be returning in 1958. Caplat had again attempted to interest the Society in Frank Martin's *Der Sturm*, but when it was ascertained that neither Fischer-Dieskau nor Ansermet would be available, Ponsonby considered it would be unwise to proceed with the project. Glyndebourne then suggested a new production of *Carmen*, together with *Figaro* and Gluck's *Alceste.* At a meeting with Moran Caplat on 9 October 1957 the Lord Provost referred to the serious financial situation and said that unless drastic action were taken the Festival might cease to exist. Caplat replied that Glyndebourne faced similar circumstances. The best he could offer were nine performances each of *Carmen* and *Figaro* at a cost of £49 175. As the Stuttgart State Opera had proposed 15 performances of four operas for £40 000 the Committee agreed to accept its offer provided there was no breach in the understanding between the Society and Glyndebourne. On the remaining three evenings there would be a Spanish double-bill of Falla's *La Vida Breve* and *El Sombrero de Tres Picos* for which the Spanish Government would pay most of the expenses.

Apart from the usual problems of inadequate lighting facilities and sets that were too large for the King's Theatre stage the visit of the Stuttgart company was received enthusiastically. It brought Wieland Wagner's production of *Tristan und Isolde* with Wolfgang Windgassen and two of the outstanding post-war Wagnerian sopranos, Astrid Varnay and Martha Mödl, to share the role of Isolde. There were also two rarities, Weber's *Euryanthe* and a delightful production of Lortzing's early nineteenth-century

comic opera *Der Wildschütz*. The Spanish Opera-Ballet was notable for the appearance of Victoria de los Angeles as Salud in *La Vida Breve*, but she had to work hard to maintain the audience's interest in the drama in the light of continual interventions by Antonio and his team of dancers, stamping and clicking castanets at every opportunity.

Some of the drama critics accused the Festival Society of 'playing safe' with the drama programme, but with two world premières and one British première 'safe' seems an inappropriate term. The programme was only safe in that it did not arouse the censure of the critics. The two new works were T.S. Eliot's *The Elder Statesman* (another Festival commission) and *The Bonefire* by Gerard McLarnon. The latter was ostensibly having its world première but it had been allowed a week of preview performances in Belfast to 'run it in' before coming to Edinburgh. In his autobiography, Tyrone Guthrie wrote:

> The picture of dear old Belfast which we presented was, in my opinion, true to life. But it was not exactly the version that the Tourist Board might care to exhibit to strangers. There was no end of a hullabaloo. Though there was no demonstration in the theatre, letters poured into the newspapers from those regular correspondents, Disgusted, Pro Bono Publico, and Mother of Nine; questions were asked in Parliament; a deputation of enraged councillors waited upon the Lord Mayor, demanding that he have the offending play withdrawn … Naturally when we got to Edinburgh nobody felt particularly steamed up about the politics, but the energy and skill of the actors was the object of suitable admiration.
>
> (T. Guthrie, *A Life in the Theatre*, Hamish Hamilton, 1960)

Of the Old Vic's contributions, *Twelfth Night* was thought in some quarters to be too popular for the Festival but the critics fully approved of the choice of Schiller's *Mary Stuart.* The New Watergate Theatre Club gave the first British performances of O'Neill's *Long day's journey into night* and the Gateway had a success with *Weir of Hermiston*, based on an unfinished story by Robert Louis Stevenson, in which Tom Fleming gave a fine character study as the 'hanging judge'.

The most joyful occasion of the Festival was when Menuhin, Cassadó and Kentner gave, without fee, a concert for Edinburgh citizens in the Embassy Cinema at Pilton, one of the largest of the city's housing areas. The 1 500 audience, including 600 schoolchildren and a number of Festival visitors, were charged one shilling for admission to cover expenses. Just before the hastily arranged concert began it was discovered that there was insufficient lighting on the music stands and the Lord Provost and Councillor McLaughlin had to borrow a standard lamp from one of the neighbouring houses. Immediately after the concert Menuhin sent a letter to the *Scotsman* saying:

> From the point of view of the performers, the concert was a success beyond our wildest hopes. Knowing audiences as well as I do, having played in public for 36 years and in thousands of circumstances, I can say with complete assurance that the audience this morning was composed overwhelmingly of extremely musical people who had never sat in a concert hall before … Even though the hour was a difficult time for housewives, the fact that 2 000 remained unable to enter the hall proves that there is a vast support, independent of any visitors, for great Festivals and great art in Edinburgh.
>
> (Y. Menuhin, *Scotsman*, c. 13 September 1958)

One of the boldest ventures was the decision to create a special festival ballet company to perform a repertoire of ballets specially commissioned from 12 choreographers. The Company was formed in association with Michael Frostick of Music and Drama Limited who had made the original suggestion. Peggy van Praagh was appointed manager and to her fell the task of scouring the cities of Europe for a corps of dancers to support the

principals suggested by the choreographers. If successful it was hoped it might form a permanent feature of future festivals. Frostick planned a four-month tour of Europe and America after the Festival for which he requested a guarantee of £2 500. In view of the attendant publicity the Council (5 September 1958) agreed. Despite favourable reviews the venture was not a box office success and in October the Company's visit to Sadler's Wells was cancelled because of lack of support, although it did go abroad. Then in December the Company folded and the guarantee was called up.

Three weeks before the 1959 Festival a major political crisis erupted. Ponsonby had successfully arranged for the Czech Philharmonic Orchestra to perform at the Festival, the first visit by an orchestra from behind the Iron Curtain. Karel Ančerl, its resident musical director, would conduct one concert and the other two would be conducted by Hans Schmidt-Isserstedt. The soloists would be Rudolf Firkušný and Johanna Martzy, an expatriate Hungarian violinist then resident in Switzerland. On 15 July the Harold Holt agency, who were acting on behalf of the orchestra, received a message from Prague that the Orchestra refused to accept Johanna Martzy as a soloist, apparently on political grounds. Ponsonby, through the Czech Embassy, informed the Orchestra that it had accepted and signed a contract which stated quite clearly that Miss Martzy would appear. No reply was received from the orchestra and after lengthy discussions between the Festival Society, the agents and the Czech ambassador in London, a representative of Harold Holt flew to Prague for personal talks with the orchestra, which had now been informed that if it persisted in its attitude the contract would be cancelled and the facts made known to the press. Despite these strenuous efforts the orchestra was quite adamant that it would not appear with Miss Martzy. Ponsonby therefore made arrangements with Schmidt-Isserstedt to conduct similar programmes with the Royal Philharmonic Orchestra, and the Czech-born conductor, Walter Susskind (not for the first time) stepped in to conduct the third concert. The simplest solution would have been for the Society to accept the Orchestra's objections and substitute another soloist, but the Festival Director, backed fully by the Lord Provost and the Executive Committee, had no hesitation in adhering to the principles of the Festival that 'art should be above ideologies and political views'.

The new young conductor of the Scottish National Orchestra, Alexander Gibson, the first Scot to hold the position, had a nerve-racking Festival debut when, after conducting Iain Hamilton's Sinfonia for Two Orchestras, there was almost total silence from the bemused audience. No one quite knew what to do! In those appalling soundless moments even clapping out of politeness seemed impossible. Eventually there was some spasmodic applause for the orchestra and conductor, but it was an uncomfortable occasion for all concerned, not least for the enraged Burns Foundation who had been persuaded to collaborate with the Festival Society in commissioning the work, and whose President-elect described it as 'rotten and ghastly'. The next morning Christopher Grier commented:

> For one night, the Festival was jerked, like it or not, into a main stream of current European music making ... To assess the quality of the Sinfonia on so short an acquaintance would be an impertinence ... But of the imagination, seriousness of purpose and skill that went into its making there is no doubt whatever.
>
> (C. Grier, *Scotsman*, 29 August 1959)

The Festival Society had hoped that Jussi Björling might appear with the Stockholm Opera in 1959, but by then ill health and an excess of alcohol had made him increasingly unreliable. Even without its most famous artist the performances revealed a highly musical and professional ensemble in which world-class singers such as Nilsson, Gedda and Söderström collaborated with their accomplished, though less well-known colleagues in extremely well-rehearsed productions, the stars in one performance frequently taking over minor roles in another. The opening opera, *Un Ballo in Maschera*, raised something of a hornet's nest. Based on an actual incident when a former Swedish monarch had been assassinated in his own opera house, the Swedes went all out for authenticity, not merely in the sets and costumes, but in the character of the King himself, who was portrayed as a mincing fop more interested in his page than in Amelia, an interpretation that worked well dramatically, but made nonsense of Verdi's passionate music in the love duet and the Count's jealous rage leading to the final assassination.

The company came into its own with a thrilling *Die Walküre* with Birgit Nilsson, Set Svanholm, Sigurd Björling, Kerstin Meyer and Aase Nordmo-Lövberg. As Harold Rosenthal wrote in *Opera* (October 1959), 'what other company in the world can boast a Walküre cast like this'. But from the point of view of the critics the most interesting event of the Festival was Blomdahl's space travel opera *Aniara* which had been seen for the first time in Stockholm in May. Noël Goodwin in the *Musical Times* (November 1959) described it as 'an arresting if patchwork score'.

As far as the theatre was concerned there had been criticism that the Festival had been handed over to the repertory companies. The Perth, Dundee and Birmingham Repertory Companies together with the Glasgow Citizens' Theatre rose to the challenge and in an enterprising selection of plays, some well off the beaten track, showed that the word 'repertory' need not be synonymous with second-rate.

Les Ballets Babilée, the National Ballet of Finland and Jerome Robbins's Ballets USA presented 23 ballets, all but two either new to the Festival or, like *Giselle*, presented in a new light. The clear winner was the recently formed Jerome Robbins Company. Noël Goodwin wrote:

> In all three weeks of the Festival nothing I came across matched Jerome Robbins's Ballets U.S.A. in brilliance of imagination and breathtaking excitement ... He ranks with Fokine, Balanchine, and Martha Graham as choreographers who have most significantly enriched the vocabulary of dance in this century, and the dancers he brought were a team perfectly tuned to his specifically American style.
>
> (N. Goodwin, *Musical Times*, November 1959)

The company suffered a severe setback when the plane carrying all the props and costumes crashed on its way from Athens to Edinburgh. At the request of the Festival Society W. Mutrie, a local firm of theatrical costumiers, opened early to enable the dancers to select replacement costumes for the show that evening and the performance went on as planned.

Following the previous year's successful Pilton experiment the Swedish mezzo-soprano, Kerstin Meyer, and Gerald Moore announced that they would like to make a similar contribution 'in keeping with the Festival'. This time the Poole's Roxy Cinema was hired and 1 500 excited schoolchildren assembled to hear Gerald Moore give a highly entertaining talk on the art of the accompanist. Then in illustration he and Kerstin Meyer performed songs by Brahms, Schubert and Wolf. At the end the enthusiastic young

audience insisted on an encore, obligingly provided by Meyer and Moore. Afterwards the two artists confessed that performing to an audience of children was more nerve-racking than appearing before adults. 'Children are much more difficult to fool', commented Mr Moore.

Over the years the Festival Fringe had steadily expanded. The original six groups had now grown to more than 25, and many professional actors were beginning to appear. For several years Duncan Macrae, furious at the lack of Scottish drama in the official Festival, had put on his own show at the Palladium. The groups were beginning to work together and in 1958 they had opened their own centralized box office. Now they went even further and formed the Festival Fringe Society offering help and advice to Fringe companies and a special Fringe Club was set up in the YMCA premises in South St Andrew Street. The Scottish Union of Students announced that, beginning in 1960, they would award a trophy for the best student venture on the Fringe. A panel of experts and international celebrities would be appointed to adjudicate.

At a press conference after the première of his new play *Breakspear in Gascony* Eric Linklater set the cat among the pigeons when he agreed with an American journalist that the subsidies from the city to the Festival were inadequate. 'Edinburgh really ought to be prepared to pay for what it has been given in the last thirteen years. The city has been desperately stingy.' He added that it was absolutely miraculous the way the Festival had maintained its high standards and, lamenting the disappearance of Glyndebourne from the Festival programme, suggested that 'If necessary twopence should be put on the rates so that the Festival can afford to bring back Glyndebourne'. After the conference Ponsonby agreed, 'I am very glad he said what he did'. He explained that the Festival Society had been able to bring foreign opera companies to Edinburgh, despite high travelling expenses and other costs, because these companies were subsidized by their own governments. 'But it wouldn't cost us very much more to bring Glyndebourne back, just a few thousand pounds.' The Lord Provost (Johnson-Gilbert), the City Treasurer and the Labour leader, Jack Kane, all disagreed with Mr Linklater, the latter adding that the city had contributed £25 000. Before there was any increase in the rates he would like to see the business communities, the hotel owners and shopkeepers in Princes Street pay more towards the Festival. A recent appeal to them for funds had had very poor results.

Ponsonby found himself in conflict with the Executive Committee (22 July 1959) over his agreement to Tyrone Guthrie's request that James Gibson be paid a fee for his work as associate director on *The Thrie Estaites*, a request which the committee had already turned down as an unnecessary expense. He explained that there had been problems over the division of responsibilities between the Festival Society and Wharton Productions who were acting as management for the production, and he had come to an arrangement by which Wharton would accept responsibility for the cost of the costumes if the Society would meet the cost of Gibson's fee. After a meeting with members of the Council at which the costs of *The Thrie Estaites* had been dissected and analysed in minute detail, Guthrie had departed in a very irate mood. Over lunch with Tom Fleming, who was playing the role of Divine Correction, Guthrie declared emphatically that he would 'have no truck with haberdashers', and in a letter to Ponsonby he complained about the 'overcautious and parsimonious attitude' of the Executive Committee. Because of the Society's attitude over the contract for *The Thrie Estaites* he considered it necessary to terminate his association with the proposed production of Sydney Goodsir Smith's *The*

Wallace, commissioned for the Festival in 1960. After Guthrie's magnificent contribution to the Festival (*The Thrie Estaites* in 1948, 1949, 1951 and 1959, *The Highland Fair* in 1952 and 1953, *The Queen's Comedy, The Atom Doctor, The Matchmaker, A Place in the Sun, Oedipus Rex* and *The Bonefire*) it was regrettable that the Festival's happy association with arguably the greatest theatre director of the day should come to an end over the expenditure of a few pounds.

The Finance Committee's constant scrutiny of the contracts with artists and companies was causing extreme embarrassment to the Artistic Director as it gave him no flexibility in his negotiations. After he had submitted his preliminary estimate in October and a budget had been prepared, he was authorized to commit the Society only to contracts within the narrow limits of this budget. Ponsonby raised this issue with the Executive Committee pointing out that he was not asking for more money, and was prepared to take absolute responsibility within the limits of the budget, but he would like greater freedom and manoeuvrability within the total figure. This matter was discussed at two further meetings of the Executive Committee but a decision was postponed until the preliminary budget for the 1960 Festival was submitted.

Ponsonby was becoming increasingly unhappy at the general policy of the Society, its reluctance to experiment with new works, its concern with the box office appeal of the programme, its tendency to 'play safe', its inclination to cut costs rather than try to increase revenue and its apathy over improving the facilities. These factors were making it almost impossible to maintain standards and, as he did not want to be responsible for running down the Festival, he felt he had no alternative but to resign, which he did in a letter to the Lord Provost dated 12 September, the last day of the 1959 Festival. A press statement was prepared by the Lord Provost, Johnson-Gilbert, and Lord Cameron, but Ponsonby did not agree with the wording, in particular the substitution of the word 'resources' for 'policy'. As no agreement could be reached on this matter (Executive Committee, 21 October 1959), Ponsonby's own version was issued, followed by the views of the Society:

> Mr. Ponsonby has given as the chief reasons for his decision his conviction that neither the standard of performance and presentation which he believes to be essential to an international festival, nor that degree of experiment in new, or unfamiliar, works which he also believes must be a feature of the Festival, can be guaranteed under the policy being pursued by the Society.
>
> The Festival Society does not subscribe to the views implied in the reasons given by Mr. Ponsonby for his resignation. Since its inception the Festival Society has sought to ensure that the annual Festival should be of international standard, and not only has it succeeded in doing this, but it has also experimented in the production of new works on many occasions, and not infrequently at financial loss to the Society. The policy remains the same, and towards this end active steps have been taken to increase the financial resources of the Festival Society. The costs of presenting the Festival have increased substantially within recent years, but despite this, the Society has been able to maintain its position as the leading Festival of its kind in the world.

It was then agreed that neither Ponsonby nor the members of the Council would make any further comment to the media. This secrecy naturally gave rise to speculation in the press that there was something to hide. In the *Scottish Daily Express* (September 1959) Sir Compton Mackenzie challenged the Festival Society to give fuller reasons than those given in the press handout: 'It's no use breaking half a secret. To divulge only a few reasons is to arouse suspicion.' When asked to comment on Sir Compton's remarks,

Ponsonby tactfully declined: 'There is nothing further I can say at this stage.' He remains adamant that his only reason for resigning was his concern over the declining standards of the Festival as a result of the policies of the Council.

Ponsonby was asked to stay and direct the 1960 Festival and, notwithstanding the financial situation, he succeeded in mounting a series of outstanding events for his final Festival. Glyndebourne returned for the last time with a magnificent revival of *Falstaff* with Geraint Evans, ably supported by Ilva Ligabue, Sesto Bruscantini, Oralia Dominguez, Juan Oncina and Hugues Cuenod; an enjoyable triple bill of Busoni's *Arlecchino*, Wolf-Ferrari's *Il Segreto di Susanna* and Poulenc's *La Voix Humaine* with Denise Duval; whilst in *I Puritani* Joan Sutherland followed up her historic Covent Garden triumph as Lucia with another stunning account of an outlandishly difficult coloratura role. The Leningrad Philharmonic Orchestra gave four concerts under Evgeny Mravinsky and Gennadi Rozhdestvensky, at one of which the cellist Mstislav Rostropovich gave a superlative interpretation of the Cello Concerto No. 1 of Shostakovich. Giulini conducted an electrifying performance of Verdi's *Requiem* with Joan Sutherland, Fiorenza Cossotto, Luigi Ottolini and Ivo Vinco. There were chamber concerts by the Beaux Arts Trio, the Amadeus String Trio and the Juilliard Quartet, recitals by Victoria de los Angeles, Hermann Prey, Claudio Arrau, Myra Hess, Witold Malcuzynski, Isaac Stern and Mstislav Rostropovich and the Festival debut of Janet Baker singing the Two Songs for Contralto, Viola and Piano by Brahms. The Royal Ballet returned with two programmes of short ballets including *La Péri* with Margot Fonteyn, and the Old Vic with a production of Chekhov's *The Seagull*. In the Assembly Hall the Festival Society presented the world première of Sydney Goodsir Smith's *The Wallace* and there was a riotous adaptation of *Les Trois Mousquetaires* by La Compagnie Roger Planchon.

Finally, on a less exalted level, there was another event of which Robert Ponsonby was justifiably proud. When his negotiations with Louis Armstrong had broken down at a very late stage Ponsonby, who had always been rather irked by the success of the Fringe's satirical revues, thought 'Why shouldn't the official Festival go one better?' On the recommendation of his assistant, John Bassett, he invited Jonathan Miller, Peter Cook, Alan Bennett and Dudley Moore to present a late-night show at the Lyceum, giving them *carte blanche* to do anything they liked. On attending the dress rehearsal Ponsonby was horrified when the four youngsters fluffed their lines, giggled and frequently broke down. 'What have I done?' he agonized. The first night came, *Beyond the Fringe* became the principal talking point of the Festival, and the rest is history!

Chapter 4

Lord Harewood 1961–1965

Even before Robert Ponsonby had tendered his resignation there had been some speculation about his successor; both Lord Harewood (the Director of the Leeds Festival and a former member of the Board of Directors at the Royal Opera House, Covent Garden) and Peter Diamand (the Director of the Holland Festival) had been named as possibilities. Instead of advertising the post the Executive Committee, probably on the recommendation of Lady Rosebery, decided to approach Lord Harewood to find out whether he would be interested in going to Edinburgh. Following a meeting in London with Lady Rosebery and Councillor Dunbar, Lord Harewood confirmed his interest in the appointment and arrangements were made for him to to meet the Executive Committee on 19 November 1959.

At this meeting Lord Harewood referred to the newspaper reports concerning Ponsonby's reasons for resigning. The Lord Provost replied that the Society was anxious to preserve the Festival as an international event and, while it was willing to experiment, the programme had to be governed by the amount of money available. Whenever there was a shortfall between the programme and finance a decision as to what constituted a justifiable risk had to be taken. Harewood expressed concern at the high level of revenue obtained from the box office, approximately 72 per cent, and remarked that if the box office was to continue to account for such a high proportion there would be a tendency to 'play safe' with the programme and cut down on production costs. Consequently there would be a danger of lowering the standard. The Festival's reputation abroad was still high but he felt that in Britain the critics and other musical highbrows had lost some enthusiasm for the Festival because of the repetitive nature of the programme. In order to recover its prestige it was necessary to devise a programme that would stimulate the interest of the critics. If the press could be persuaded that something festive was going on in Edinburgh they would quickly arouse the enthusiasm of the public. In particular he felt that opera must be given a high profile. He referred to the King's Theatre which was unsuited to opera, other than chamber operas, and therefore made it difficult to maintain the high standard of opera necessary for an international festival. The Committee assured Lord Harewood that the Society was trying to find larger premises.

After the meeting the Committee unanimously recommended to the Council that Harewood should be appointed Artistic Director. Lord Harewood accepted and it was agreed that he should assume duties in March 1960 to enable him to start making plans for the 1961 Festival.

The larger theatre that the Society had in mind was the Playhouse cinema. Originally built as a theatre it had never been used for this purpose. The owners were willing to let it to the Society for the Festival but it required some adaptation before it could be used for opera. Harewood arranged for an architect, Peter Moro, to inspect the theatre and report on what alterations would be necessary. When it transpired that an expenditure of between £25 000 and £50 000 would be required to bring the stage into commission the idea was abandoned.

Harewood was anxious to give the Festival a focal point around which the programme could be built. As 1961 was the one hundred and fiftieth anniversary of his birth Franz Liszt would seem the obvious choice, but in order to attract the attention of the critics Harewood also suggested including a number of works by Schoenberg, who had died ten years before. He hoped to bring the Berlin Philharmonic Orchestra with Karajan, and other conductors would include Stokowski, Klemperer, Giulini and Maazel. He also proposed the inclusion of two or three young artists who were not well known at present, but who showed great promise for the future.

With regard to opera, Harewood suggested inviting the Covent Garden company to present a season of four operas, including a new production, at a cost of around £60 000. The casts would include world class artists such as Joan Sutherland, Teresa Berganza, Boris Christoff, Geraint Evans, Luigi Alva, Carlo Maria Giulini and Georg Solti. It was no longer possible to maintain the Festival standard of opera at the figure of £48 000 set by the Finance Committee. This had only been achieved in the past because the companies from abroad had been heavily subsidized by the governments in question. There was a limit to the willingness of governments to continue sending opera companies as a form of propaganda, and also to the number of companies of sufficient quality to bring to Edinburgh. Several of these were unavailable during August and September because of commitments to festivals at home. Glyndebourne had not been recently because it was unable to mount a new production at the figure offered by the Festival Society. For 1960 it had repeated two productions from the summer season at Glyndebourne and the sole new production, Poulenc's *La voix Humaine*, had only been possible because it had been conceived on the very simplest scale. Furthermore, if opera was provided by a British company with a number of top-ranking guest artists, the Society would have more control over the quality of performance than with an overseas company with only one or two stars on its roster.

To improve the drama content Harewood proposed commissioning a number of playwrights to write works specially for the Festival. In the event of suitable plays being obtained the Society might consider entering into a joint arrangement with a commercial management to present these at the Festival. It was agreed that five plays would be commissioned each year for a period of three years. Ray Lawler and Nigel Dennis accepted but Lawrence Durrell declined to write a play for the Festival until his last play *Sappho* had been produced. In 1950 Margaret Rawlings had purchased an option on *Sappho* but had been unable to persuade a management to produce the play with her in the title role. Her option was due to expire on 1 October 1960 but Harewood felt there might be a moral obligation on the Society to engage her if the play was presented in Edinburgh. The Old Vic was not interested but John Hale of the Bristol Old Vic agreed to present it at the Festival with Rawlings as Sappho.

With regard to the Epstein exhibition which had been under consideration for some time, Lord Harewood suggested it might be possible to obtain a financial sponsor. After

one or two unsuccessful attempts he reported that a Leeds businessman, Jack Lyons, was prepared to present the hangings and to make the pedestals for the portrait bronzes at cost price. Epstein worked on a large scale so Harewood secured the derelict Waverley Market to house the exhibition at no cost to the Society. Richard Buckle, by means of scaffolding and window-dressing material, filled the vast space with corridors, grottoes and huge cathedral-like spaces to display the sculptures and bronzes to the greatest advantage.

The centre-piece was the great alabaster carving of *Adam*. This, together with a number of other Epstein carvings, had formed an almost pornographic sideshow in a flimsy building erected in the owner's garden. Buckle was anxious to borrow this collection for the exhibition but the owner, although unwilling to lend them as it would have meant knocking down a wall to get them out, was quite prepared to sell. On Buckle's assurance that these massive sculptures would be a sound investment, Harewood and Lyons purchased the collection, which they subsequently resold, Harewood retaining *Adam,* which is now the focal point in the main hall at Harewood House.

To advertise the exhibition the plaster cast of the vast statue of St Michael and the Devil, which Epstein had created for Coventry Cathedral, was erected on the corner of Princes Street and the Waverley Bridge. Unfortunately St Michael, having conquered the devil, found himself overcome by the notorious Edinburgh wind and almost lost his spear. A bronze founder was called in to effect repairs and within 24 hours St Michael, his arm suitably strengthened, was once more armed for the fray. During its four-week run the Epstein exhibition achieved a success unrivalled by any other Festival exhibition, attracting over 125 000 visitors, only the Tattoo beating it in attendance figures. It also attracted thousands of ordinary Edinburgh people bringing the Festival to an additional section of the community. Later a small part of the exhibition, some 70 pieces out of a total of 230, was shown at the Tate Gallery in London.

Harewood's efforts to bring Karajan and the Berlin Philharmonic to Edinburgh at a price the Festival could afford proved long and arduous, and at one point he thought it might be necessary to withdraw the invitation. Letters and telephone calls had no result and eventually he had to go to Salzburg to see Karajan in person. On his third evening he managed to obtain a meeting with the conductor during the interval of a performance of *Don Giovanni*. Harewood explained that the theme of the Festival would be Schoenberg and enquired if the orchestra had anything in its repertoire. 'I have never found the necessity', came the reply. A compromise was finally reached and Karajan agreed to include Webern's Six Pieces Op. 6. 'A difficult man, to say the least', was how Harewood summed up his dealings with the conductor.

Michelangeli was equally temperamental. He was engaged to perform Ravel's Piano Concerto in G and the D minor Piano Concerto of Mozart and to give a recital in the Usher Hall. After complaining about his rehearsal schedule which was rearranged to suit him, he then raised difficulties about the transfer of his piano, and finally cancelled his Festival appearances altogether.

Even more problematic was the casting of the leading role in Kenneth MacMillan's version of Kurt Weill's *The Seven Deadly Sins*. Anya Linden was to play the dancing Anna and Weill's widow, Lotte Lenya, the singing Anna. After one rehearsal Lenya decided that the production was not in accordance with her interpretation and declined to take any further part in it. At two weeks' notice the jazz singer, Cleo Laine, agreed to share the part with the Scottish actress Adrienne Corri. Corri also found MacMillan's

concept not to her liking and after several discussions, in which Lord Harewood vainly attempted to arbitrate, she too departed leaving Cleo Laine to sing all the performances.

Kubelik was unable to appear because of a family bereavement, and his programmes were taken over by Jascha Horenstein. Illness forced the cancellation of both Maria Curcio and Teresa Berganza, and the actor Robert Atkins, finding the heat of the Assembly Hall too oppressive and the stage entrances too much for his 75 years, withdrew from the two productions by the Old Vic

But the worst catastrophe of all came in the last week when Joan Sutherland, repeating her sensational performances (which had won her international overnight fame) as Lucia developed an abcess in her ear. By lunchtime it had burst and it became apparent that she would be unable to sing that evening. It being virtually impossible to find another exponent of the difficult role at such short notice a speedy decision was made to replace *Lucia di Lammermoor* with an extra performance of *Il Barbiere di Siviglia.* Frantic telephone calls were made all over Scotland to reassemble the cast, and it was only by a lucky chance that the Covent Garden manager, Patrick Terry, succeeded in contacting Fernando Corena. He was touring the Highlands with his wife when they remembered that they had to take a telephone call from Switzerland at their Edinburgh hotel, and on their return they received a message to contact Terry immediately. Boris Christoff, also on a tour of Scotland, was flagged down by the police, who had been alerted to try to find him, and asked to return to Edinburgh. As Giulini was otherwise engaged at the Usher Hall that evening Edward Downes flew from London to conduct the performance. Despite the pain in her ear Sutherland had hoped to be well enough to sing the final performance of *Lucia* but her doctor refused to allow her to go on. With an extra day at his disposal Terry was able to persuade the French coloratura soprano Mady Mesplé to take over.

In spite of these alarms the 1961 Festival was considered a success even by the critics. Noël Goodwin wrote:

> Lord Harewood, in his first year as artistic director, gave the festival a pattern and design it had hitherto lacked, a purpose to call its own. Edinburgh has sorely needed an identity to set it among, and yet apart from, the major European events of this kind. A musical equivalent of the retrospective exhibition in the visual arts is a solution admirably suited to the festival's character. Except for a series of BBC broadcasts devoted to Schoenberg soon after the composer's death ten years ago, no coherent attempt has been made to acquaint British listeners with one of the chief seminal forces in this century's music … In illustrating his progress at the Edinburgh concerts, however, the performances brought a vitality of interest and a stimulus to thought and imagination such as the festival has never previously had.
>
> (N. Goodwin, *Musical Times*, October 1961)

Having persuaded the Council to commission new plays for the Festival Harewood then raised the question of commissioning musical works. In order to save money Hans Gal recommended that the Society should endeavour to obtain the first performances of new works rather than specially commissioning them, but it was felt that the Society would obtain greater publicity and prestige from commissions. The Programme Committee agreed that the Society should embark on a four-year programme in which one major and one minor work would be commissioned each year and a number of composers including Kodály, Tippett, Henze and Nono were approached with a view to providing a suitable composition.

To widen the appeal of the Festival Harewood suggested inviting the jazz pianist Errol Garner to give a concert. Garner had an enormous gramophone reputation and had never appeared in this country. Dr Firth, Professor Newman and Hans Gal objected seeing no reason why jazz should be included in the Festival. The situation was resolved when it was discovered that Garner was not available, and the question of jazz was postponed for another year.

Ponsonby had succeeded in reducing the deficits on the 1957 and 1958 Festivals to £7 000, but the 1960 Festival had been more expensive, incurring a deficit of just over £24 000. The Scottish Committee of the Arts Council had given a grant of £15 000 for the year ending March 1961 and later they generously agreed to waive the repayment of the loan they had advanced to the Society for the purchase of the Festival Office. As a result of the Lord Provost's annual appeal to business firms in the city £17 000 had been raised. Edinburgh Corporation then decided to make a special contribution of £20 000 to meet the bank overdraft and to increase its contribution for the current year from £25 000 to £50 000. But this additional contribution had not been won easily. Councillor Magnus Williamson, who seconded the Lord Provost's proposal that the increased grant be approved, criticized the Festival Society. 'We intend to provide more money, but we want a bigger control of Festival affairs by the business people of Edinburgh and the Corporation.' He wanted to see the Society run by the Corporation, helped by a number of 'artistically clever' people. 'The present rather arty crafty collection of people on the Society, who have given us a great deal of assistance in the past, should be replaced by new people.' Councillor Pat Rogan, who moved that no additional help be given to the Festival Society unless an investigation was made into the Society's administration, said: 'We are wholeheartedly in favour of the Festival, but we want to know what is happening to our investment. The public are very uneasy about the money being poured into the Society.' The Corporation agreed to make the additional money conditional on the Society's paying more attention to the financial aspects of the Festival and at the same time they asked for even greater representation in the Festival Society and on the Festival Council.

After months of discussion the Festival Council (12 September 1962) agreed that in future it should control both the artistic and financial aspects of the Festival, carrying out the business of the Society with the assistance of a programme advisory panel. The present Council of 45 members would be reduced to 21, 9 non-town council members and 12 town councillors including the Lord Provost, who would continue as Chairman, and the City Treasurer as Vice-Chairman.

Lord Cameron was unhappy with these changes. Initially the Society had been designed as a partnership between Edinburgh Corporation, individuals interested in promoting the Festival and the commercial interests in the city, together with the British Council and the Arts Council of Great Britain. A majority of town councillors both in the Society and on the Festival Council was not in accordance with the original intention. Nor did he consider this change in the best interests of the Festival. The fact that the Corporation had made a contribution of £50 000 to the Society did not justify its claiming controlling rights, particularly in view of the income derived from ticket sales and the donations received from other sources. Both the Lord Provost and the Treasurer had heavy commitments elsewhere and could not devote as much time to the Festival as they might like and therefore Lord Cameron considered that it would be more appropriate for the Society to

appoint a Vice-Chairman from the non-town council members. He raised this again at a Council meeting on 13 January 1964, but it was decided at the Annual General Meeting of the Society on 23 April 1964 that the composition of the Council should remain at the new level. Lord Cameron's motion that a vice-chairman be appointed from the non-council members was also rejected by the Council (on the casting vote of Lord Provost Dunbar).

1962 was the year of the Russian invasion of the Edinburgh Festival. During the visit of the Leningrad Philharmonic Orchestra in Ponsonby's last year Harewood had initiated talks with the Soviet authorities for a visit by a number of Russian artists. The Ministry of Culture expressed an interest in the proposals and Harewood was invited to visit Russia for further discussion. With the assistance of Madame Furtseva, the Minister of Culture, and in spite of the collective hindrances of Soviet politics, Russian bureaucracy and a surfeit of Georgian brandy, Harewood visited musical institutions and attended concerts and opera performances in Moscow, Leningrad and Tbilisi. He had decided to feature the music of Shostakovich in 1962 and the composer had agreed to be present as the Society's guest. Harewood then visited Shostakovich in his apartment to discuss which of his works should be performed, and by whom, and the composer agreed to the Festival's giving the Western première of his Symphony No. 12. Harewood had hoped to persuade Mravinsky to give two concerts with the Philharmonia, one of which would include the Symphony, but he was reluctant to come and Igor Markevich was booked instead. He was also anxious to engage Sviatoslav Richter, whom he considered one of the best pianists in the world, but Richter was a hypersensitive individual with an impressive list of cancellations to his name. Madame Furtseva promised to do everything within her power to persuade him to visit Edinburgh and then stick to the agreement, but admitted that she had little or no control over him. (In the event she failed and, as predicted, Richter cancelled.) However, Harewood succeeded in engaging the Borodin Quartet, Gennadi Rozhdestvensky, Mstislav Rostropovich and Galina Vishnevskaya. He was also keen to arrange visits by the Georgian Ballet Company and the Bolshoi Opera but as these would require a very large stage and good technical facilities they would have to be postponed until a suitable theatre was built.

The opening concert was Beethoven's *Missa Solemnis* conducted by Maazel with Vishnevskaya as the soprano soloist. She arrived in Edinburgh to rehearse with Lorin Maazel having only a very inaccurate idea of the score. As Harewood wrote in his autobiography, *The Tongs and the Bones* (Weidenfeld and Nicolson), Maazel 'restrained his indignation in the interests of international accord, but that could not be said of her fellow-soloists when, having hogged all the rehearsal time in order to get it nearly right, she proceeded on the night to steal the honours of the performance with a nearly flawless display'. Her husband, Rostropovich, accompanied her on the piano in a recital of mainly Russian songs, including a satirical song cycle by Shostakovich which was a great hit with the audience. Then, as a gesture to the Festival, Rostropovich performed, without fee, the Bach Suites for solo cello in St Cuthbert's Church.

Twenty-five compostions by Shostakovich were performed during the three weeks of the Festival. Among these were all the string quartets, the violin and cello concertos (played by Oistrakh and Rostropovich, to whom they were respectively dedicated), six symphonies and miscellaneous other works. The Twelfth Symphony was written off by the critics as a failure, but the others received more favourable comment. At a press conference Shostakovich expressed satisfaction at the performances: 'The Allegri Quartet

performed wonderfully my First, Second and Fifth Quartets. The Ninth Symphony sounded very well. I was not fully satisfied with the performances of my Sixth and Eighth Symphonies. It seemed that the tempo of both these symphonies was a little too slow.' He then had a word of praise for the Scottish forces, 'I attended the rehearsal of my Tenth Symphony conducted by Gibson this morning and was very much impressed'.

The conference began with an amusing incident when it appeared that the composer had acquired a Scots accent, although the pressmen had been assured that he could speak only Russian. In reply to a question about the weather, he replied, 'Absolutely terrible. Edinburgh is awful'. The newsmen were already sharpening their wits for the next day's sensational headlines when the door opened and in walked the real Shostakovich like a German *Doppelgänger*, and they discovered that the man they had mistaken for him was a Glasgow journalist with a close likeness to the composer.

The Russian theme was strengthened by the visit of the Belgrade Opera with a selection of Russian operas: the British premières of Prokofiev's *The Love of Three Oranges* and *The Gambler* and of the Shostakovich version of Mussorgsky's *Khovanshchina,* as well as *Prince Igor* by Borodin, an opera which everyone knew of, but few had actually seen. The fifth opera was another rarity, Massenet's *Don Quichotte*. All were sung in Serbo-Croat, with a pronounced Slavonic wobble. The critics without exception remarked on the poor lighting and the inadequacy of the King's Theatre for opera on this scale but praised the Society for its enterprise in presenting such an interesting and unhackneyed programme.

Festival audiences were introduced to another singer who was to become a great favourite. Teresa Berganza had been forced to cancel her previous year's performances but she more than made up for it with a delightful recital in Leith Town Hall. Another highlight was Béjart's epic ballet *The Four Sons of Aymon* given in Murrayfield Ice Rink. A magnificent extravaganza, it encompassed circus, ballet and theatre, and involved two choreographers and six designers. Unfortunately one performance was interrupted by a gas leak from the the rink's refrigeration plant which was hastily repaired and after an extended interval the performance continued as normal.

The Writers' Conference, which had been suggested and organized by the publisher, John Calder, was very successful. About 150 writers from 11 countries had been invited to take part in a discussion on the modern novel, but about half of them failed to turn up. No explanation was given for the Russian absentees, the French were unable to come for a number of 'domestic' reasons, the South African writer, Alan Paton, had been refused a passport to come to Britain and Sir Compton Mackenzie was ill. Malcolm Muggeridge took over as chairman but left after the second day, partly for personal reasons and partly because he realized he was outclassed. Among those present were Rebecca West, Angus Wilson, Lawrence Durrell and Muriel Spark. The stars of the Conference turned out to be four Americans: Mary McCarthy, Norman Mailer, Henry Miller and William Burroughs, as well as Khushwant Singh from India and the poet Erich Fried. Each day there was a debate with a panel of four commentators, the writers on the platform coming to the microphone one by one to make their points. The Conference also gave Scottish writers an opportunity to meet and debate with their foreign counterparts. On the second day those self-same Scottish writers (rather an argumentative band) put on their own domestic comedy for the visitors, hinging mainly on the old division between the Nationalists and the Internationalists. There were a few flare-ups particularly between the veteran,

Hugh MacDiarmid and the young rebel Alexander Trocchi who, after apologizing to the chairman, departed. As many of the distinguished visitors and the audience were slipping quietly away the platform was taken over by folk-singer, Josh Macrae. One of the subjects discussed later in the week was censorship and after hearing Henry Miller the Conference voted by a majority that censorship should be abolished. As a result Miller's *Tropic of Cancer* was finally published the following year.

Even the Tattoo had its controversial moment. Always anxious to take a chance by introducing innovative material to prevent the event becoming stale, Brigadier MacLean included 'Let's twist again' played by the Band of the Royal Marines. To his horror dozens of paratroopers ran on to the arena, selected girls from the stands, and started twisting on the esplanade, to be joined by hundreds of the audience. Appalled by what he considered 'shockingly poor discipline' the Brigadier was planning what he would say the next morning when a Field Marshal remarked on the 'excellent public relations'. Luckily the Commander-in-Chief agreed. In an interview Brigadier MacLean confessed that he had some difficulty in restraining a three-star general in full mess kit and spurs from dashing down from the Royal Box and joining in the fun. 'I knew there would be repercussions and wondered just what would hit me when I opened the papers the next morning. Our innovation had certainly rocked the English press. *The Times* thought it worth a favourable comment in their leader column.' Afterwards he received 11 letters of protest mainly from young people who, though keen twisters themselves, did not approve of its taking place in the Tattoo, but these were offset by 123 letters of praise.

The critics voted the sixteenth Festival a triumph. Andrew Porter stated:

> Not only was this year's music of exceptional interest; so were the performances. Standard 'celebrity recital' programmes were absent, unless some Bach ones count as that. Edinburgh had a theme, which was Shostakovich; a context for it, Borodin, Mussorgsky, Prokofiev operas; and plenty of subsidiary themes (notably Debussy, Brahms and Bach) ... Lord Harewood has not only given the Festival a shape and purpose, but has also made almost every detail interesting.
>
> (A. Porter, *Musical Times*, October 1962)

1963 could again be described as the Festival of the three Bs, but instead of Bach, Beethoven and Brahms (although all were included), there was Bartók, Berlioz and Britten. None of the Berlioz operas was given but the orchestral concerts included a number of rarely heard works such as *Tristia*, *Lélio* and the *Rob Roy Overture.* Britten was not one of the specially featured composers but there were a number of his compositions in the programme: *The Rape of Lucretia*, his realization of Gay's *The Beggar's Opera*, the *Spring Symphony*, the *Simple Symphony* and the three *Canticles*, performed by Harper, Procter and Pears with Britten himself as accompanist. Bartók was represented by his six string quartets, his three piano concertos (all performed by John Ogdon), his two violin concertos, *Dance Suite, Concerto for Orchestra*, songs and piano works. Of particular interest were his three stage works, the opera *Duke Bluebeard's Castle* and his two ballets, all performed together as he had wanted, but never saw. Though Bartók had not planned them as an entity he is on record as saying that only together could they reveal his full purpose.

There were a great many headaches and displays of temperament when Harewood arranged for the Empire Theatre, by then a bingo palace, to be re-opened for three weeks to house the ballet companies. The bingo session on the Saturday evening, played with

much crude humour directed against the Festival, continued until after 11 p.m. and the Hungarian State Opera and Ballet was kept waiting while the stage was cleared of bingo apparatus. It then came to light that some anti-Festival or anti-communist saboteur had plugged all the wash basins and baths and turned on the taps, flooding the dressing rooms and staircase. By this time the Hungarians had also discovered that the Empire stage was only half the width of their own and their scenery was far too large for the limited space. By 6 a.m. on the Sunday morning the company decided they couldn't appear and the house manager, Edward Horton, had to call in Lord Harewood and in no time at all he persuaded the company not to abandon the Festival. As there was no space backstage for the scenery it had to be stored outside in the yard, but no one had taken the Edinburgh wind into account, and while the sets were being changed on the opening night, it howled across the stage scattering the orchestral parts into the audience.

During the week there were some monumental 'theatrical scenes' when the Martha Graham Company arrived to rehearse and were informed by the Hungarians that 'they' had sole right to the stage that week. This contretemps was somehow resolved only to be replaced by another difficulty when the Graham Company asked for a harpsichord. This had to be transported to and from the Usher Hall each day. The tuner failed to arrive for one rehearsal and the conductor flew into a rage when he discovered the instrument wasn't at concert pitch. Eventually the orchestra had to be tuned to the harpsichord and re-tuned for the evening performance.

By this time Horton, a highly efficient manager but somewhat temperamental himself, was feeling at rather a low ebb from the battering he had received, and apprehensive of what might be in store for him during the last week. However, the Stuttgart Ballet restored his faith in the profession. When he reported this to its director, John Cranko replied that all theatrical artists should have a dash of the gypsy in them, then they wouldn't take themselves as seriously as they took their work.

Within the main Festival was a smaller festival of Indian music, dance and art which captured the imagination of the critics and a large section of the public, most of whom had never heard a note of Indian music. Harewood had also wanted to include an exhibition of Indian bronzes but this had been impossible to arrange. Even without these it was one of the most concentrated, varied and comprehensive promotions of its kind ever attempted in Europe. It opened with a lecture by Dr Narayana Menon and Yehudi Menuhin. Then followed a series of recitals by some of India's most outstanding instrumentalists, some of them demonstrating feats of improvisation that could put even the finest jazz musican into the shade. Larry Adler, Julian Bream, George Malcolm and William Bennett joined the Indian musicians in an experimental concert performing Eastern music and some Bach was performed on the veena, the concert ending with all the participants joining together in a raga. William Mann described these concerts as 'the great converting revelation of the Festival'. They were amusing as well as informative. Mann ended his review:

> What I shall never forget is the comic turn in which Ravi Shankar explained the tabla while Alla Rakha gave examples: 'this sound is called *Ktar*' said Shankar. 'Clunk', responded Rakha's drum. 'And this is *Ktol*'. 'Clunk' answered the drum. 'Tarakatatariko' – 'Tarakatatariklunk', came the reply, pat and prestissimo. On television it would go like a house on fire.
>
> (W. Mann, *Musical Times*, October 1963)

In the lecture hall of the Royal Scottish Museum the greatest exponent of Indian classical dancing, Balasarasvati, enchanted packed houses with her delicate art. A corollary to these performances of music and dancing was an exotic exhibition of *Music and Dance in Indian Art* containing taped illustrations of the ragas, beautiful examples of the instruments, photographs explaining the meaning of the hand gestures in Indian dance, a fantastic collection of devil dancers, masks and costumes from Darjeeling, sculptures of dancing goddesses, miniatures and paintings, and in the background the mesmerizing sound of piped music.

Two of the three new plays became the subject of censorship. The Lawler play, a Festival commission, had originally been called *The Unshaven Cheek of God* but this was considered too blasphemous by one or two of the more Calvinist Council members and so it was billed merely as *The Unshaven Cheek*. More than the title was modified in Ronald Duncan's adaptation of Martin Walser's *The Rabbit Race*. This play had been banned in Germany and had to be revised twice before its first controversial production in Berlin by the Schiller Company. For its British première at the Festival the Lord Chamberlain had insisted on five small cuts which Mr Duncan declared spoilt the rural vitality of the peasant scenes. Walser, in Edinburgh for the première and to take part in the Drama Conference, was surprised and pleased at the reaction of the British audiences, who seemed to grasp what he was trying to say. He confessed that he preferred the Berlin version which had been more stylized, and admitted to a little concern at the English translation, but agreed that the linguistic difficulties had been well overcome.

The withdrawal of Renata Tebaldi gave Festival audiences the opportunity of hearing Magda Olivero in one of her finest roles – Adriana Lecouvreur in the opera by Cilea. It was a performance that drew eloquent, if not totally ecstatic reviews, but allowing for some vocal shortcomings, no one was in any doubt that they had experienced a truly great theatrical performance. However, the visit of the Teatro San Carlo was memorable for more than the singing, as there was a touch of Italian temperament thrown in. During a performance of Verdi's *Luisa Miller* the principal tenor, Renato Cioni deciding, probably rightly, that the applause at the end of the second act was for him, insisted on taking a solo curtain call. When his fellow artist, Paolo Washington, grumbled about this unorthodox procedure, Cioni accused him of jealousy. This was too much for Washington, who promptly lost his temper and let fly with his fist, leaving Cioni to sing the final act of the opera with a bleeding nose!

But this display of Mediterranean volatility was nothing to the *brouhaha* aroused at the Drama Conference where John Calder provided his own brand of excitement, bringing the Festival to an end in a loud explosion of civic indignation. As part of a 'Play of Happenings' organized by Kenneth Dewey, an avant-garde director from Los Angeles, a nude model was wheeled across the organ gallery on a trolley. This episode was seized upon by the reporters from the more popular papers, who gave it more press coverage than almost any other single event in the history of the Festival. The only other incident to equal it had been Callas's abrupt departure from the Festival in 1957. Harewood, who was naturally blamed for the affair, had been aware that two sketches had been planned for the Saturday afternoon session, but had no idea of the details. He regarded the incident as silly and pointless and stated that he believed it had sabotaged the chances of another conference of a similar nature being held. Calder thought it 'very funny'. Not so, Lord Provost Weatherstone, who declared that 'it was a tragedy that three weeks of

glorious Festival should have been ruined by one squalid incident'. Civic anger was excited to such an extent that Calder and the model, Anna Kesseler, were prosecuted for indecency; thereby giving even greater prominence to a trivial incident. A number of well-known figures appeared for the defence which was conducted by Nicholas Fairbairn, and the model was acquitted. Afterwards an uncowed Calder applied to the Festival Society for reimbursement of his legal expenses; a request which the Society chose to ignore.

Harewood's premonition about the possible repercussions of the nude incident proved to be right. A poetry conference had been planned for the following year but the proposal was shelved. Finance was given as the reason but it seems more probable that some members of the Council were unwilling to risk another fiasco. At the Annual General Meeting of the Scottish branch of Equity the members deplored the Festival Society's decision not to proceed with the conference and expressed the fervent hope that, should it be impossible to reverse the decision for 1964, the conference might be included in the following year's Festival, but the Council decided that it would be impracticable at this stage to broaden the base of the Festival by the inclusion of a poetry conference.

Early in 1963 the Festival Society had been faced with its worst financial crisis to date. The 1962 Festival had resulted in a deficit of £18 000 leaving the Society with an overdraft of £22 500. As part of a proposed development for a Festival theatre on Castle Terrace the Corporation was anxious to buy the Festival Office for £37 180 (the purchase price of the building plus renovation expenses) and had offered to provide temporary accommodation in the Evening News building in Market Street at a nominal rent until the Society could move into its new offices within the Festival Theatre. This would wipe out the overdraft and leave about £15 000 as working capital, but after allowing for an estimated deficit on the 1963 Festival, the Society would have no money to pay staff salaries after November and no assets to provide security for an overdraft. The Council therefore decided that the 1964 Festival must be produced within the limits of the estimated revenue of £159 000. Lord Harewood thought it would be possible to arrange a programme within this sum, without reducing standards, but that this measure could only be taken for one year. By filling the programme with celebrity recitals and substituting three concerts by the English Chamber Orchestra for three large orchestral concerts Harewood was able to keep within this budget. At the request of the Society the Corporation undertook the entertainment of Festival artists (but on a smaller scale), cuts were made in advertising and thanks to a concerted effort donations for 1964 were increased by £30 000. The result was a surplus of income over expenditure of £35 637. For the first time in its history the Festival had balanced its books!

For the 1964 Festival Harewood planned a Czech theme with the first visit to this country of the Opera from the Prague National Theatre as its centrepiece. It brought a repertoire of British premières: Smetana's *Dalibor*, Janáček's *From the house of the dead* and *Resurrection* by Jan Cikker, together with Dvořák's *Rusalka* and the first Czech language performances in this country of Janáček's *Káta Kabánova*. Knowing that the Company contained a number of singers now past their best, Harewood went to Prague and personally selected the singers who would appear. The result was a triumph. Harewood was particularly happy about this visit and wrote in the souvenir programme for the 1971 Festival that there was a freshness and co-operative dedication about their performances

which made for true Festival spirit: 'I doubt if any operatic performance for which I was technically responsible gave me more pleasure than theirs of *Katya*; it seemed to me as near a complete realisation of a composer's aim as one is likely to get in an imperfect world.' Harewood's opinion was reiterated by all the critics, without exception. Harold Rosenthal in *Opera* (Autumn 1964) described it as 'One of those rare performances in which all the elements fused together to make it an unforgettable experience'. Rosenthal was almost equally enthusiastic about the other operas. He was unfortunate in not getting the excellent first cast for *Dalibor* (Vilém Přibyl, Alena Miková and Libuše Domanínská) but admitted that 'The chorus singing was outstanding, and the orchestra under Jaroslav Krombholc played magnificently'. In fact the virtuoso playing of the orchestra was a feature of all the operas as were the brilliant productions by Václav Kašlik, Karel Jernek, and Ladislav Štros.

Since Richter's cancellation in 1962 Harewood had been trying to persuade him to come to Edinburgh, but as usual, he was proving elusive and it was July before he confirmed that he would appear with the Orchestre de la RTF on 18 August, and play the Bach Cello Sonatas with Rostropovich on the 20th; but he stated he would be unable to give his planned solo recital on the 23rd. Then just as the Festival was starting he fell ill and cancelled his engagements. The two piano concertos had to be omitted from the programme and replaced with a performance of the *Symphonie Fantastique* of Berlioz. In an endeavour to modify the disappointment of Festival patrons Richter offered to give his solo recital on 2 September and to perform the cello and piano sonatas at a late-night concert on 31 August for half his normal fee.

Richter may have been difficult to deal with but Marlene Dietrich was well nigh impossible. Nervous of new audiences and conscious of her advancing years, her nerves were stretched to the limit and consequently she found an outlet by finding fault with everything, from the loss of some of her luggage by a careless airline to the omission of a credit for her agent in the souvenir programme. With no voice to speak of but with sheer star quality and presence she brought a touch of glamour to her late-night show that delighted and enraptured the audience, if not the Festival Director. In his autobiography Lord Harewood confessed:

> I can safely say that she was the only visitor to the Festival while I was there whom I would happily have consigned to hell. Nothing we did was right for her, and her capacity to express her displeasure was versatile and unrivalled. To cap it all, we were offered her services for the following year. Festival weal overcame prospective private woe, and I re-engaged her. Again the houses were full, and we could but admire the total professionalism of her performance. But she had not changed.
>
> (Harewood, *The Tongs and the Bones*, 1981)

On that occasion Tom Fleming, the Director of the Lyceum Theatre Company, also had problems with her. After complaints from every member of the theatre staff he confronted her in her dressing room and pointed out that he had a theatre to run and he needed staff to help him run it, and would she please stop behaving like a 10 year-old. To his surprise she calmed down and gave no more trouble. Some time later he had a telephone call from the director of another theatre where she was then appearing asking how he had coped with Madame Dietrich as she was creating mayhem and kept saying how well she had been treated at the Lyceum in Edinburgh!

As a result of an appeal by the Lord Provost for additional funding the Corporation offered the Society an additional £25 000 but, as usual, there was a string attached,

namely that a firm of professional management consultants should be brought in to examine the Society's administration procedures. Messrs Urwick, Orr and Partners, recommended by the Corporation's Organization and Methods Officer, found little to criticize in the way the Festival was being organized, but they did come up with one or two rather odd ideas, such as never allowing an artist to know that he or she is the first choice for a particular engagement in order to obtain a more competitive fee! As Harewood commented afterwards, 'Try that on Klemperer or Karajan'. They also recommended some 'improvements' in the management structure, most of which proved to be nothing of the kind, and some were positively disastrous. The most important of these was the transfer of executive power from the Festival Council to the Artistic Director, who would be responsible for all aspects of the Festival administration. For the first time he would have a vote on the Council which from henceforth would become a policy-forming body. The former Secretary, based at the Edinburgh office, would be upgraded to an administrator, responsible to the Festival Director; they also advocated the appointment of a business manager who would undertake sales and marketing. The Festival Council agreed to these recommendations and Lord Harewood was confirmed as the new 'overlord' or Festival Director

The 1964 Festival had been personally a traumatic one for Lord Harewood. Although not yet public knowledge, news of his impending divorce and the birth of a child to the woman he hoped to marry, had reached the ear of the Lord Provost, who was very concerned about the effect this might have on the Festival. Remembering that, at the time of his appointment, one or two members of the Festival Council had expressed some concern about how they could get rid of the Queen's cousin should they ever want to do so, Harewood felt strongly that he must do whatever was necessary to save the Lord Provost and the Council from a potentially embarrassing situation. Although he was reluctant to leave a post which he found challenging and rewarding, he accepted the advice of Lord Cameron and wrote a letter of resignation which the Lord Provost could keep in his safe and use if and when he considered it politic to do so. Lord Provost Weatherstone kept it for several months but by December he was beginning to get cold feet about the Festival being at the centre of yet another scandal and he decided to produce the letter. No reason was given beyond the brief statement: 'During the last few weeks, I have after intensive examination of the position come to the conclusion that the time has come for me to tender my resignation to the Society'. Press speculation as to Harewood's reasons for leaving were rife, and ranged from the Festival's financial problems to Harewood's disappointment at the delay in building the opera house he had been promised; but none came anywhere near the truth. In actual fact the news of the divorce did not become public until January 1967. Thus the Festival lost the services of a Director who might have continued to organize the high-quality, enterprising and stimulating Festivals that had become his trademark, for at least two more years.

Harewood agreed to the Festival Council's request that he continue in office until the end of the 1965 Festival by which time it was hoped a successor would be found. The Council decided not to advertise the post and on the advice of Lady Rosebery approaches were again made to Peter Diamand who, on this occasion, accepted without hesitation.

Arranging a satisfactory opera programme in the King's Theatre at an affordable price was becoming increasingly arduous. In 1965 Harewood hoped to present special productions of *Don Giovanni* and Haydn's *Le Pescatrici* in association with the Holland Festival, the English Opera Group in *Albert Herring* and three performances of Offenbach's *La Belle Hélène* by a French company, but this would have meant exceeding the budget by £10 000. It seemed likely that this programme would have to be curtailed when an anonymous benefactor volunteered the sum of £10 000 to enable the opera season to go ahead as planned. Just before Christmas the French company dropped out. Finding a suitable replacement of an adequate standard at a few months' notice seemed an insurmountable problem when Harewood remembered the tiny court theatre in Munich, known as the Cuvilliés Theatre. Early in January he went to Munich and persuaded the Bavarian State Opera to bring its small-scale productions of *Così fan tutte* and Richard Strauss's autobiographical *Intermezzo* to Edinburgh. The result was a perfect collaboration.

With the joint production of *Don Giovanni* the Festival nearly had its first taste of what we now call producer's opera. When it had been premièred at the Holland Festival the production by Virginio Puecher had been torn to shreds by the critics. The conductor, Carlo Maria Giulini, had been in total disagreement with the producer's concept, and had offered to withdraw from the Edinburgh performances. Harewood, however, refused to accept Giulini's resignation and instead dismissed the producer and designer. In his own words he 'embarked on a lengthy and rather acrimonious correspondence with Puecher and Damiani, offering to pay their fees (but not their fares) for their non-services in Edinburgh, but only on condition they stayed away' (Harewood, *The Tongs and the Bones*, 1981). The sets and costumes were discarded, new costumes commissioned from David Walker, and William Bundy (Covent Garden's lighting expert) was hastily called in to cobble together a production with a minimum of scenery, based mainly on effective lighting. At a press conference Giulini, strongly backed by Lord Harewood and the director designate, Peter Diamand, insisted that 'the musical life of an opera must not be subordinated to a producer's interpretation of the libretto'. Not long afterwards Giulini announced his intention of leaving opera to concentrate on the symphonic repertoire and almost 20 years were to elapse before he ventured back into the opera house.

Harewood's programmes had never lacked enterprise but choosing to feature two such widely different and challenging twentieth-century composers as the avant-garde Boulez and the mystical, searching Tippett, even with a large dose of 'Papa' Haydn thrown in, was an act of unprecedented boldness. On paper this juxtaposition may have looked peculiar but, in fact, it worked out quite well. Tippett's sixtieth birthday made a survey of his work an obvious choice and gave Festival audiences an opportunity of hearing, among other works, his rarely performed Symphony No. 1. Tippett himself conducted his *Little Music*, there was a repeat performance of his *Fantasy Concertante on a Theme of Corelli* originally commissioned for the 1953 Festival and John Ogdon performed the Concerto for Piano and the Piano Sonata No. 1. The Boulez programme, planned in association with the composer, was the largest concentration of his music heard anywhere and included *Le Marteau sans maître* and the first British performance of his massive *Pli selon Pli,* both conducted by the composer who also joined Yvonne Loriod for a performance of the second book of *Structures for 2 Pianos.*

One rather sad incident slightly marred the Festival when Lord Harewood, with deep regret, took the unprecedented step of cancelling a Festival show that was not up to

standard. When the late-night entertainment by Elizabeth Seal and her husband, Zack Matalon, had opened in Cambridge the month before it had been savagely mauled by the critics. The organizer, Gerard Slevin, went to see the show and expressed grave doubts about it to Harewood, but for some inexplicable reason no decision was made until after its first performance in Edinburgh, when the reviews were as bad as expected. The following morning the Festival Council, on the recommendation of the Director, agreed to take it off immediately. To save embarrassment Harewood offered to announce that it was being cancelled due to illness but Matalon, already upset because a number of essential props had not been provided until the last minute, refused and promptly transferred the show to the Fringe. Larry Adler, who was putting on his own show as part of the Fringe, was invited to fill the vacant spot at the Lyceum. Fortunately Adler received 'rave' reviews and the incident was quickly forgotten.

The 1965 Military Tattoo was infiltrated by Goldfinger. In a dastardly attempt to destroy Edinburgh he held James Bond prisoner in a wooden hut high on the northern ramparts of the castle. 'But', commented Brigadier MacLean, 'the City Fathers, always on the ball, are mindful of the situation, and the Royal Marine Commandos have been alerted'. Twenty tough Marines leapt from their assault craft and scaled the castle walls to rescue the agent. According to the Brigadier this was the first time the walls had been scaled since Randolph, Earl of Moray had performed this feat in 1313.

The most notable achievement of 1965, and possibly Harewood's most lasting contribution to the Edinburgh Festival, was the formation of the Scottish Festival Chorus (later renamed the Edinburgh Festival Chorus) for a performance of Mahler's Symphony No. 8. This was not a new idea. Rudolf Bing had discussed just such a proposal in 1948 with Roy Henderson, who had suggested forming a festival chorus of between 150 and 200 voices to be recruited from the Edinburgh and Glasgow areas for the performance of major choral works at the Festival. It had been discussed at a number of committee meetings but was finally abandoned on the advice of Hans Gal, who considered a festival chorus unnecessary in the light of the vast improvement shown by the Edinburgh Choral Union under its new conductor, Herrick Bunney. Fortunately Harewood had more faith in the idea. Arthur Oldham was appointed chorus master and in the pursuit of excellence he held auditions throughout Scotland in a search for the best choral singers. Weekly rehearsals took place in Edinburgh, Aberdeen and Glasgow, the full chorus of 240 voices coming together in Edinburgh only for the final rehearsals. Oldham's dedication and hard work paid off and the chorus made a sensational debut with the Scottish National Orchestra under Gibson in the Mahler Symphony at the opening concert, which was described by Conrad Wilson in the *Scotsman* (23 August 1965) as 'a performance which will surely be remembered as a milestone in the history of the Festival and of music in Scotland'. Two years later its reputation was consolidated when that confirmed perfectionist, Herbert von Karajan, agreed to use it for a performance of Bach's *Magnificat*, after which he declared that it was 'one of the three best choruses in Europe', a fitting climax to an exciting chapter in the history of the Festival.

Chapter 5

Peter Diamand 1966–1972

Diamand had been present in Edinburgh for the 1965 Festival and after the triumphant participation of the Festival Chorus in the opening concert his first question was 'Can they be used in 1966?' At the final press conference he followed the time-honoured custom of giving preliminary details of the following year's programme. After announcing that the Festival Chorus and the Scottish National Orchestra would again open the Festival, he continued: 'The Chorus's debut was one of the events of this year's Festival. It is a particular joy that something has been born that is going to last.' The featured composers would be Schumann and Berg and other plans included the first visit to Edinburgh of the Moscow Radio Orchestra and an exhibition of the works of Georges Rouault. With regard to opera, Diamand stated that in future years he intended to produce opera specially for the Festival. Rejecting criticisms that drama was the weakest part of the Festival he said 'This year's performances were remarkable'. He referred to the old difficulty of engaging actors of international repute who were prepared to commit themselves in advance, and added, 'I have no magic key to solve what has been called "the drama problem of the Edinburgh Festival". I doubt if there is a formula. We will do drama in the best possible way'. He then paid tribute to Lord Harewood, and said, that after attending 12 out of the 19 Festivals, he was tremendously impressed by their development and in the increasing receptiveness of the audiences. 'The standard Lord Harewood has introduced is a very high one, and in my view, one of his many merits is that he has developed the taste of the audience and succeeded in attracting a great many young people.'

Attracting younger audiences to Festival events was one of Diamand's main objectives and in 1966 he presented a series of matinée performances at the Gateway of an enchanting play for children by Nicholas Stuart Gray entitled *The Wrong Side of the Moon*. Based on the tale of Rapunzel by the Brothers Grimm, it featured a man-sized cat called Tomlyn and a lovable raven which, according to Allen Wright in the *Scotsman* (27 August 1966), 'had a better Press that some of the other birds fluttering about the Festival'. These other birds were of the Aristophanic variety in the Lyceum Theatre Company's production of *The Burdies*, a translation into Scots by Douglas Young of Aristophanes' comedy *The Birds*. In spite of an inventive production by Tom Fleming and spectacular and exotic designs by Abd Elkader Farrah the translation attracted the scorn of most of the critics, particularly those from south of the border, who complained that

they couldn't understand it. This wholesale condemnation incited some defensive action on the part of Fleming and Young and the resulting correspondence between Young and Allen Wright in the *Scotsman* provided the touch of dissension without which no Festival was complete. Diamand's Greek theme was continued in the Piraikon Theatre's magnificent productions of *Electra* by Sophocles and Euripides' *Medea* in which the histrionic and highly emotional acting of Elsa Vergi was in sharp contrast to the more subdued English style exhibited in Pop Theatre's production of Euripides' *The Trojan Women*, where Frank Dunlop drew a parallel between the Greeks in Troy and the Americans in Vietnam. Cleo Laine, making her debut as a straight actress in the role of Andromache gave a performance which was, in the words of Allen Wright in the *Scotsman* (30 August 1966), 'one of the glories of this Festival ... she recharged the faltering batteries of Frank Dunlop's production ... even seemed to give fresh inspiration to Flora Robson whose remarkable performance as Hecuba grew in dignity and compassion'.

The Fringe was living up to its reputation as the largest market for young theatrical talent in the world. The Oxford Theatre Group put on the first performance of *Rosencrantz and Guildenstern are Dead* by a promising young dramatist called Tom Stoppard. Most of the reviews were less than appreciative, although in the *Observer* (28 August 1966) Ronald Bryden described it as 'the most brilliant debut by a young playwright since John Arden's'. He later admitted to having prior knowledge that the Royal Shakespeare Company had taken out an option on the play, which was later taken up by the National Theatre.

In order to satisfy the demand for ballet, Diamand compromised (in size but not in quality) by bringing the celebrated Paul Taylor Dance Company whose nine-member troupe played to packed houses in the tiny Church Hill Theatre. But because of technical difficulties one of the ballets, *Junction*, had to be omitted from the first programme.

On the musical side there were auspicious Festival debuts by a number of young artists including Martha Argerich, Claudio Abbado and Carlos Kleiber and tragically, the last appearances of the outstanding lyric tenor, Fritz Wunderlich. He sang Tamino in *Die Zauberflöte* and, as part of his song recital in the Usher Hall, performed Schumann's *Dichterliebe* which Conrad Wilson in the *Scotsman* (5 September 1966) described as 'a deeply felt, carefully graded and original interpretation'. Twelve days later he died of injuries received from a fall down stairs.

In line with his Berg theme Diamand succeeded in arranging performances of all Berg's major works, but he failed to persuade Berg's widow to allow him to present the third act of *Lulu* which had been completed from the composer's notes by Friedrich Cerha. Frau Berg insisted that she must obtain her dead husband's permission before agreeing to a performance of the completed score. Diamand suggested that she let him know as soon as she received Berg's reply. But the spirit world was uncooperative and opera lovers had to wait until Frau Berg's death to hear the third act in its entirety.

The young Carlos Kleiber (whose father, Erich, had conducted the première in 1925) won great critical acclaim for his conducting of *Wozzeck*, in which he used his father's notes, but Edinburgh was destined to see only one performance. A capacity audience was assembled in the King's Theatre eagerly awaiting the rise of the curtain for the second and final performance when it was announced that there would be a short delay as the conductor was unwell. Half an hour later there was another more devastating

intimation that, as there was no other conductor available, there would be no performance. Diamand had been informed at 4.30 p.m. that Kleiber was ill and although a doctor was summoned he felt too ill to conduct. It was too late to fly in another conductor from Stuttgart and the only conductor available in Edinburgh who knew the score was the Director of the company, Ferdinand Leitner. Despite fervent pleas from Diamand he refused to take over with the excuse that he did not have his own score, but there was little doubt that his refusal had more to do with professional jealousy. Later the Company made a payment of £2 250 to the Society in compensation for the lost performance. There was a happier outcome at the Usher Hall when the principal trumpeter of the Moscow Radio Orchestra also fell ill and his opposite number in the Scottish National Orchestra, at less than 24 hours' notice, took his place for a performance of Schedrin's Second Symphony, a work he hadn't even seen until he arrived in Edinburgh for the morning rehearsal.

The following year, 1967, marked the twenty-first anniversary of the Festival and Diamand had planned a programme that would reflect the standing of the Festival as one of the world's major arts events. There were, however, two problems: by June 1966 he had been given no indication of how much money would be allocated for the 1967 Festival, nor did he know which theatres would be available. Diamand raised this as a matter of urgency at a meeting of the Festival Council on 1 June which agreed that he should plan the programme on the assumption that Edinburgh Corporation's contribution would be the same as for 1966, namely £75 000.

The theatre problem was more acute. The Corporation had decided to build two theatres on the derelict Castle Terrace site, a large theatre suitable for opera and a smaller arena theatre, but as yet no progress had been made. The existing theatres were not only unsatisfactory but were rapidly decreasing in number. The Empire, which had originally been used for ballet, was now a bingo hall, and although it had been converted back into a theatre for the 1963 Festival the result had been far from ideal. Since then ballet had been eliminated from the programme as the King's Theatre had been required for opera and the Lyceum had no orchestra pit. The small Gateway Theatre was under threat of closure and arrangements for the King's Theatre had to be suspended as, despite an agreement that the theatre would always be available for the Festival, Howard and Wyndham was considering alternative proposals. In any case it wanted to sell the theatre and was putting pressure on the Corporation to buy it, but with the proposed Castle Terrace development the Corporation was unwilling to assume responsibility for another theatre. Thus Diamand found himself without venues for either opera or ballet, the two most vital elements in his programme which was to feature the works of Stravinsky and Bach. Negotiations were in progress for an exclusive visit by the New York City Ballet and he considered it essential that, in spite of the problems, an attempt should be made to utilize the Empire for this Company. By December 1966 the situation had become critical. After further negotiations Howard and Wyndham consented to let the King's Theatre to the Society at a vastly increased rent and Mecca agreed a rental for the Empire provided the Society paid the conversion costs.

This left the tricky problem of the 1967 budget which, with an estimated loss on the New York City Ballet of £15 000, increased the estimated deficit to £72 000. A number of Council members were in favour of dropping ballet from the programme, but Diamand

stressed its importance in Stravinsky's output and argued that if it was omitted there would be a strong reaction from the press. He stated at a Council meeting on 24 January 1967 that if his budget was not approved he did not know what further action he could take, adding that on his appointment he had been instructed to arrange an appropriate programme for the twenty-first Festival and he had assumed that adequate funds would be made available. The budget was finally accepted on the understanding that every effort would be made to effect savings.

Diamand had arranged for Stravinsky himself to visit the Festival and to conduct several of his own works. Stravinsky expressed delight at the invitation but subsequently was forced to cancel on the advice of his doctors. In recompense he sent the Festival a birthday present in the form of the European première of his *Requiem Canticles* written the previous year for Princeton University.

The twenty-first Festival saw the first appearance of Scottish Opera in two Stravinsky works, *The Rake's Progress* and *The Soldier's Tale.* Since its memorable first season in 1962 the Company, under its founder and musical director Alexander Gibson, had gone from strength to strength and it was generally agreed that the company was fully qualified to represent Scotland at an international festival. Under the title Edinburgh Festival Opera Diamand began to put into action his policy of presenting operas specially tailored for the King's Theatre stage. These were two rarities, Haydn's *Orfeo ed Euridice* with Joan Sutherland and Nicolai Gedda and Bellini's *I Capuleti ed i Montecchi* with Anna Moffo, Giacomo Aragall and Luciano Pavarotti, staged in co-operation with the Holland and Vienna Festivals.

Among the concert highlights were the visits by the Berlin Philharmonic Orchestra with Karajan, the Cleveland Orchestra under Szell and the Netherlands Chamber Orchestra with Giulini. Kertesz and Abbado appeared with the London Symphony Orchestra, the BBC Symphony Orchestra was conducted by Boulez and Colin Davis, and the two Scottish orchestras appeared under the batons of their resident conductors, Alexander Gibson and James Loughran. In addition there was an impressive assembly of soloists. The New York City Ballet brought 12 ballets, 5 by Stravinsky, most of them performed by the original New York casts. Jacques d'Amboise was ill but as a substitute the company was fortunate in obtaining the services of the brilliant Danish dancer, Peter Martins. Other outstanding dancers were Suzanne Farrell, Patricia McBride, Edward Villella and Arthur Mitchell.

Finally there was one of the strongest drama programmes of any Festival so far. Seventeen plays were scheduled including a number of experimental ones such as *Tom Paine*, a new play by Paul Foster, presented by the Traverse Theatre Club and performed by members of the New York La Mama Company. Another New York group, the Haizlip-Stoiber Company, who had brought Baldwin's *The Amen Corner* to the 1965 Festival, had two more winners with O'Neill's *The Emperor Jones* and a stunning musical, *Black New World*. Prospect Productions performed Chekhov's *The Cherry Orchard*, with Lila Kedrova making her British debut in the role of Ranyevskaya, and an adaptation of Forster's novel *A Room with a View,* while in the Assembly Hall Frank Dunlop directed a modern dress version of *A Midsummer Night's Dream* with Cleo Laine as an exotic Titania and Molière's *The Tricks of Scapin* in which pop singer Jim Dale gave an engaging performance in the title role.

In July 1965 Edinburgh Corporation had given the Society an additional £25 000, bringing the total grant for the 1964 Festival to £75 000. Then in July 1967 it dropped a bombshell by cutting the grant for 1968 to £50 000. On being informed of the Corporation's unanimous decision, Diamand is said to have flown to Edinburgh in high dudgeon, threatening to resign. Whether this was true or not, he was extremely outspoken in his criticism of the Corporation's action which he described as 'a vote of censure on the Festival'. He stressed that the 1967 Festival could not be produced on the basis of a £50 000 budget. Diamand stated that he was unwilling to economize by reducing standards, considering that this would be the beginning of the end, but the Council insisted that his estimated deficit of £48 000 would have to be reduced to £25 000 before an appeal could be made to the Corporation to reconsider its subsidy.

On 6 February 1968 Peter Diamand again expressed concern at the uncertainty of the Corporation's contribution to the Festival. Press conferences were to be held in Edinburgh and London to announce the 1968 programme when questions on the financial situation would inevitably be raised and he asked for instructions on how to reply. He added that the Festival had been established as an international festival on a large scale and costs would rise every year. Unless additional money was given the Festival could not continue at its present high artistic level yet no action had been taken to obtain the necessary funds. At every meeting he was made aware that there was a growing resistance within Edinburgh Corporation to the Festival, and particularly to the allocation of funds. He pointed out that even if an additional £25 000 were given this would represent considerably less spending power than in previous years and devaluation had reduced the value even further. When planning recent Festivals he had found it extremely difficult to produce a programme worthy of the Festival with the finance available and now it was becoming almost impossible. It was vital that the Council should urgently consider whether or not the Festival should be continued and, if so, on what conditions. He had made arrangments for the 1968 Festival without knowing for certain whether there would be sufficient funds to meet these commitments.

Two months later (on 8 March 1968) Diamand raised the question of the programme for 1969. He was planning an Italian theme with the Florence Opera as the central feature. While approving the idea, the Council considered that it would be unfair and improper to ask the Festival Director to make arrangements which might result in contracts with artists and companies, knowing that it might not be possible for the Society to honour its obligations. If sufficient income to close the gap between revenue and expenditure was not forthcoming, the Council would have to decide whether or not to proceed with the 1969 Festival. Diamand pointedly asked whether he was to continue preparing a programme for 1969, or if he was to wait until the Council was in a position to issue such instructions. If preparation was discontinued even for a short time, it would be difficult to arrange a programme comparable to that of previous Festivals. In his negotiations with heavily engaged artists it was necessary for him to agree in principle to their appearance at the Festival. Although the contracts were not drawn up until later he had morally committed the Society. It would be impossible, and indeed dangerous, to make any arrangement 'subject to sufficient funds being available for the Festival to be held'. The Lord Provost replied that he could not give clear instructions until the Scottish Arts Council and Edinburgh Corporation had decided on their financial contributions.

It was May before the Corporation granted the additional £25 000 for 1968 but obtaining it had been far from easy and Lord Provost Herbert Brechin, at a Council meeting on 3 May 1968, considered it would be unwise to count on a contribution of £75 000 for the 1969 Festival. A reduction in the Corporation's grant might also mean a reduction in the donation from the Scottish Arts Council. In the circumstances it was not possible for the Festival Director to make provisional engagements for 1969. When Diamand made it clear that, unless an immediate decision was made, he would not wish to be responsible for organizing the 1969 programme, as every day's delay made preparations more difficult and costly, he was authorized to proceed.

The 1968 Festival commemorated both Britten and Schubert. In the opening performances Diamand gave pride of place to the Scottish forces: the Scottish Festival Chorus appearing with the London Symphony Orchestra in a Britten programme on the Sunday, and on the Monday evening Scottish Opera presented Britten's *Peter Grimes* in a production by Colin Graham. The Scots repaid Diamand's faith in them with performances which Diamand described as 'truly outstanding'. Both Benjamin Britten and István Kertesz had been greatly impressed while, in *Opera* (Autumn 1968), Alan Blyth wrote: 'Any adverse criticisms I make hereafter of Scottish Opera's production of *Peter Grimes* must be read in the context of the by-now well-established fact that this company is at present the best *ensemble* in the country.' Nigel Douglas, who was understudying the title role, had to take over the early performances from an indisposed Richard Cassilly. Britten also expressed great satisfaction with the performance of his *War Requiem* by Giulini with the New Philharmonia Orchestra, the Scottish Festival Chorus and the soloists for which it had been written (Vishnevskaya, Pears and Fischer-Dieskau), considering it the 'best performance he had heard'.

The main Schubert event was a concert performance by Gibson and the Scottish National Orchestra of his unknown *Alfonso and Estrella.* This concert overran by almost an hour keeping 2 400 people waiting outside for the late-night Hoffnung concert that was to close the Festival. By the time the Schubert reached its closing pages many of the soldiers who were appearing in the Hoffnung concert were rather drunk and insisted on joining in, causing Gibson to comment on the rich sound of the off-stage band. One town councillor, impatient at the long wait outside, threatened that if the Hoffnung jinks continued into the Sabbath he would call the police and have everyone arrested. Diamand rather drily replied that they would think it was part of the performance.

Since the 'nude' incident at the 1962 Drama Conference there had been little in the official Festival to upset those self-imposed defenders of the city's morals, but that was before the indefatigable Richard Demarco edged his way into official circles with his *Canada 101 Exhibition.* At the opening the eagle eye of Bailie Theurer, a member of the Festival Council, detected one or two four-letter words in an exhibit entitled *Twenty-four Hourly Notes* by Greg Cunroe, and promptly complained to the Lord Provost. The upshot was that the offending parts of the exhibit were removed. This caused an even greater reaction from a group of critics and art lovers, including Nicholas Fairbairn, who promptly sent an open letter of protest to the *Scotsman.* The offending parts of the exhibit were not replaced but Theurer's action ensured a greater degree of publicity for the artist than he had perhaps merited.

Diamand and his assistant, William Thomley, had assembled another strong drama programme. The main attractions were Prospect Theatre's memorable production of the unknown *When We Dead Awaken* by Ibsen and Caspar Wrede's contentious *Hamlet* with Tom Courtenay as the prince. This was condemned by most of the critics but Harold Hobson leapt to its defence:

> Not since 'The Birthday Party' have I found criticism so universally hostile – and so universally wrong. This production of 'Hamlet' is, pre-eminently what has made the official drama of the Festival important and praiseworthy again ... [Mr Wrede] has adopted the view that 'Hamlet' is a reasonable play, and that the actions of Hamlet are logical, and, because they are logical, interesting. This is why, for the first time for many years, I was absolutely absorbed by the action of the play, which no one else has ever made clear to me.
>
> (H. Hobson, *Sunday Times*, 25 August 1968)

The Abbey Theatre from Dublin presented Synge's *The Playboy of the Western World* and there was a brilliant production of *The Resistible Rise of Arturo Ui* from the Traverse Theatre Club. Unfortunately, the opening night of the Laboratory Theatre of Wroclaw's production of *Acropolis* on 21 August had to be cancelled because a pair of specially balanced wheelbarrows had disappeared *en route*. They formed a vital part of the production, the actors having to carry them, act under them and practically perform acrobatics on them, and no suitable substitutes could be found.

The previous day Russian troops had invaded Czechoslovakia and the Festival became embroiled in another political crisis. The USSR State Orchestra was due to give two concerts on 24 and 25 August and the *Scotsman* and *Edinburgh Evening News* offices were inundated with angry letters of protest suggesting either cancelling or boycotting the concerts. Demonstrations were arranged by a number of political groups who urged concert-goers to 'show your disgust' and 'refrain from applause'. The one carried by the Labour MP, Tam Dalyell, proclaimed 'We admire your music, not your tanks'. The demonstrations had little effect on the concerts and the players were greeted with thunderous applause when they walked on to the platform and again at the close. When asked if the demonstrations caused him any embarrassment the Festival Director replied, 'Not at all, so long as the protests do not interfere with the concerts'. He revealed that it was on his authority that the protestors had been allowed close to the players, and added, 'I have the greatest respect for the views of the people here tonight. I think it was absolutely right that the musicians saw the feelings of the people who were demonstrating there.' Afterwards the Russians admitted to both fear and amazement at the silent protest, declaring that they had been taught a lesson in democracy. 'In our country such a demonstration would have been impossible!'

That the Hamburg State Opera's third visit to the Festival did not come up to expectations was hardly the fault of the Company. It had planned to present two newly commissioned operas, *Hamlet* by Humphrey Searle and Goehr's *Arden must Die*, but these had to be cancelled as the large sets would not fit on to the stage. The Company took such a serious view of the situation that it had contemplated cancelling the visit, and it was only after protracted and difficult negotiations that this had been avoided. In order not to let Diamand and the Festival down at a late stage it agreed to reduce the size of three other productions, *Elektra, Ariadne auf Naxos* and *Der Fliegende Holländer*, but as the intendant, Professor Liebermann, informed a press conference: 'The programme is not the choice of Mr. Diamand. It is not the choice of the Hamburg Opera. It is the choice of the stage of

the King's Theatre.' He added that when they started to rehearse they discovered that the orchestra pit was also too small and 16 string players had to be sent home. 'We had a very difficult job balancing the strings and the brass section.'

Professor's Liebermann's criticism of the King's Theatre as the 'worst in the world' was to have repercussions. After the Festival the manager, Peter Donald, informed Diamand that unless Edinburgh Corporation purchased the theatre it would not be available to the Society. This was followed by a letter from Peter Donald to the Festival Society (28 September 1968): 'In view of the adverse criticism directed against the King's Theatre, Edinburgh, on the grounds of its alleged inadequacy to house opera, and the consequent damage done to its reputation as a theatre, my directors have decided that the King's Theatre will no longer be available to the Festival Society.' Donald was informed that the Society could not be held responsible for the opinions expressed by representatives of the Hamburg Opera and reminded that he had given an undertaking the previous year that the theatre would be available for two to three years at a rent of £4 000 per week.

The possibility that the Society might not have the use of the theatre came at a critical time. Diamand was on the point of concluding his negotiations with the Florence Opera when he was informed that no contract must be signed until the theatre's availability was established. This matter concerned not only the Florence Opera, which was subsidizing the visit to the sum of £28 000, but also the Italian Government which had promised to contribute £140 000, making a total of £168 000. The Director reported to the Council on 13 January that he was having great difficulty in not signing the contract for the visit, and it was only after he had reported that the Festival Council would meet on the 27 January that the Company had agreed to delay the signing, but had insisted that it be initialled. By complying he might well have involved the Society in an obligation which would have to be honoured. A large grant from the Scottish Arts Council and a substantial donation from an anonymous Edinburgh citizen enabled the Corporation to purchase the King's Theatre which it subsequently let to the Festival Society at a rent of £1 000 per week.

The Society had made an urgent appeal to the Scottish Arts Council for an increase in subsidy. In his reply, dated 1 November 1968, the Chairman, Colin Mackenzie, proposed that membership of the Festival Council should be broadened to include members representing a wider geographical distribution and wider experience in the arts, commerce and industry, and suggested that the Scottish Arts Council should have the right to nominate members of the Festival Council who would serve as individuals and not as representatives of the Arts Council, so that no one body would dominate the Council's debates. Secondly, he recommended that the Society appoint an outstanding Edinburgh citizen to be its Vice-Chairman. If the Festival Society was prepared to accept these proposals the Scottish Arts Council might match the Corporation's grant to the Festival on a pound for pound basis. In spite of this extremely generous offer the Council felt that a further approach to Edinburgh Corporation at that time would be unproductive. The Scottish Arts Council did however increase its grant by £10 000.

The Florentines were enthusiastic about the Edinburgh visit and went to enormous trouble and expense to provide a carefully balancd repertoire even redesigning the sets of five of the six operas so that they would sit comfortably on a stage half the size of their own. In honour of the Scottish visit they opened with Donizetti's *Maria Stuarda*. Leyla Gencer gave a vocally uneven performance as the ill-fated Scottish queen but showed a

keen dramatic sense in the fictitious confrontational scene, where she spat out the words 'vil bastarda' in a manner that without doubt set the seal on her own death warrant while, in the words of Harold Rosenthal in *Opera* (Autumn 1969), Shirley Verrett as Queen Elizabeth 'sang superbly, and created a very positive figure dramatically'. He was even more adulatory about Renata Scotto's Gilda in *Rigoletto*, describing it as 'possibly the best Gilda of the day, singing like an angel and phrasing and acting in the most natural manner imaginable. A great performance' (ibid.). Tito Gobbi's production of Puccini's *Gianni Schicchi*, built around his own witty and human portrayal, was far from being a one-man show and there were sharply drawn vignettes from an experienced cast as his avaricious relatives. The critics found most of interest in the double bill of *Sette Canzoni* by Malipiero and Dallapiccola's *Il Prigioniero*. Again there were powerful vocal and dramatic interpretations by Magda Olivero, Renato Capecchi and Scipio Colombo.

For the opening performance a reputable Italian public relations firm requested permission to decorate the theatre with flowers, supply special silk programmes and distribute small gifts of perfume to the ladies in the audience. Certain members of the Festival Council had been rather sceptical about this offer and demanded to know what the firm wanted in return. On Diamand's assurance that all they required was a mention in the programme permission was granted. A hitch occurred when the flowers were sent in error to the King's Theatre in Glasgow. The perfume, however, was greatly appreciated by the ladies, although a group of Edinburgh matrons (who had formed a queue at the box office to purchase tickets for the forthcoming pantomime), surprised at being accosted by a bevy of sexily dressed young ladies, with typical Edinburgh suspicion refused the offer of a small gift.

The concerts included a wide range of Italian music from Monteverdi to Nono performed largely by Italian artists such as I Musici, the Trio de Trieste, the Sestetto Luca Marenzio, Giulini, Abbado and Gazzelloni. There was no major Italian symphony orchestra or theatre company and an exhibition of contemporary Italian art had to be postponed on account of the cost. Instead there was a smaller exhibition of *Sixteenth Century Italian Drawings*.

The theatre was dominated by Ian McKellen's remarkable double as Shakespeare's *Richard II* and Marlowe's *Edward II* marking the beginning of a brilliant career. There was also a highly praised production of Shaw's *Widowers' Houses* from the Nottingham Playhouse Company and a satirical debunking of Lord Nelson in *The Hero Rises Up* by John Arden and Margaretta D'Arcy. The hero's first line, 'You are, I take it, Englishmen' elicited the predictable reaction from a largely Scottish audience!

To cater for the tastes of younger people and to arouse their interest Diamand introduced some avant-garde presentations into the 1970 Festival. These took the form of a series of late-night performances of short theatrical works given by the Music Theatre Group, a team of young singers, dancers and instrumentalists brought together by Alexander Goehr. Its purpose was to build up a repertoire of works which had been neglected because they failed to fit into any recognized category, and to bridge the gap between conventional opera and concert music. The four programmes included music by Stravinsky and Berio as well as the first performances of Iain Hamilton's *Pharsalia* and Goehr's *Paraphrase on Il Combattimento di Tancredi e Clorinda* for clarinet, brilliantly performed by Alan Hacker, and *Naboth's Vineyard*, the first part of a proposed *Triptych*. Among the singers was Cathy Berberian.

The visit of the Opera of the Prague National Theatre did not quite match the exceptionally high standard of its previous one, but it enabled British audiences to see the first staged performances in this country of *The Excursions of Mr. Broucek* together with the first Czech language productions of *The Makropoulos Case* and *The Cunning Little Vixen*. The Company had suggested completing its Janáček cycle, begun in 1964, with *Jenůfa* but the Music Advisory Panel had opposed the inclusion of four operas by Janáček and *Jenůfa* was replaced by Smetana's *Dalibor*.

In Frankfurt Diamand had seen a production that he considered brilliant of Prokofiev's *The Fiery Angel*, but the final scene depicted an orgy in which three nuns appeared naked from the waist upwards. The producer regarded this scene as essential to the plot and Diamand himself found it difficult to believe that it could be considered offensive but, knowing the sensitivity of some councillors, he felt it necessary to draw their attention to it (19 January 1970). After looking at photographs and reading reviews of the production in Frankfurt and at the Zürich Festival the Lord Provost, concerned at the possible effect of adverse publicity on private donors and on the reputation of the Festival, expressed misgivings and proposed that he and two other members of the Council, Bailie Theurer and James Dunbar-Nasmith should go to Frankfurt to see the production for themselves. This delay was something of an embarrassment to the Festival Director. As there had been a gap of £8 000 between the cost of bringing the company to Edinburgh and the amount of money available, the company had applied for, and received, financial aid from the German authorities and was now anxious to sign the contract even agreeing that, if requested to do so, it would partially dress the three ladies in question.

After being well entertained by the Frankfurt authorities one or two members of the delegation fell asleep during the performance. Diamand hoped they wouldn't wake up until the end of the scene in question, but he had reckoned without the German media which had expressed a great deal of interest in the visit and were determined that the Scottish visitors should not miss what they had come to see. Making just sufficient noise to ensure they woke up in time the photographers were ready with their cameras. Prudently Diamand had arranged that for that one performance the offending nuns would be kept as far back as possible. The deputation reported favourably and the Council (17 February 1970) agreed by a majority of ten to eight that the production should go ahead with the scene unchanged.

This was not the end of the story. On the first night the 'poltergeists' who had an important role in the action appeared to have attacked the antiquated lighting system of the theatre, and after two false starts the performance ground to a halt. After a delay of an hour the mischievous spirits were successfully exorcised and the performance recommenced. In the meantime Anja Silja had become so nervous that she announced that if the performance didn't start this time she wouldn't be able to go on. She proved to be an almost ideal exponent of the taxing role of Renata but Kašlík's effective production was marred by a number of drastic cuts.

Henze's *Elegy for Young Lovers* was given absolutely complete in a production for Scottish opera by Henze himself superlatively sung by Catherine Gayer, Jill Gomez, John Shirley-Quirk, Sona Cervena and David Hillman. However, Stanley Sadie rather curiously opined in *Opera* (Autumn 1970) that 'Henze's misinterpretation of his own opera is as impertinent as any other producer's would be; he has no right to superimpose on the

work ideas, politically motivated, that have nothing to do with what is actually in it'. Perhaps composers don't always know best!

The Henze theme was continued in the concerts where he conducted the Scottish National Orchestra in the first performance in Great Britain of his Sixth Symphony. In late-night performances at the Gateway, which Diamand again considered would appeal to younger audiences, his latest composition *El Cimarron* was given and, at another concert, his *Essay on Pigs* was coupled with Leo Brouwer's Improvisations for six musical instruments. Here the conductor selected six musicians from the orchestra, produced sheets of music, and invited them to improvise on it. Another example of extemporization was found at one of the morning concerts where, in Stockhausen's *Spiral,* Heinz Holliger was asked to improvise on sounds being broadcast on short wave radio. The noises were uninspiring but the well-mannered Freemasons' Hall audience refrained from following the example of audiences in Paris and Cheltenham by shouting insults at the unfortunate performer!

Again with young people in mind, Diamand hired the Haymarket Ice Rink and put on the first rock musical to be given at the Festival, *Stomp*, presented by a group of American students. Performed on small stages on three sides of the rink the audience was encouraged to take part in the action which was exuberant, frenetic and full of colour and excitement. But the most extraordinary event of the Festival, also in the Ice Rink, was the Teatro Libero's magnificent spectacular, *Orlando Furioso*. Directed by Luca Ronconi, this fantastic production was an entirely new experience in theatre. Many scenes were staged simultaneously in different parts of the rink, the members of the audience moving from one to another as their fancy took them while Orlando and his knights, on high horses mounted on trolleys, charged through them at an alarming rate, scattering people in every direction.

The deaths of Barbirolli and Szell caused changes to the advertised programmes. Colin Davis responded to an appeal by the Festival Society and replaced Barbirolli in the opening concert, an all-Beethoven programme culminating in his Ninth Symphony, in which the Edinburgh Festival Chorus again excelled. Szell's concerts were taken over by Giulini, conducting the London Philharmonic Orchestra for the first time. With the New Philharmonia Orchestra and soloists Heather Harper, Janet Baker, Placido Domingo and Robert El Hage, Giulini conducted what for many music lovers was the highlight of the Festival, a performance of Beethoven's *Missa Solemnis*.

Possibly the happiest and most amusing incident of the Festival took place in a courtyard off the Grassmarket where, at the Traverse Tattoo, Nigel Hawthorne delivered a lecture on slapstick and John Neville and Bryan Pringle joined Fringe performers in a practical demonstration of the delicate art of custard pie throwing.

Peter Diamand planned an appropriate programme to celebrate the twenty-fifth anniversary of the Festival in 1971, but when the preliminary estimate revealed a deficit of £85 000 he was asked to cut the production costs by £40 000. Among the casualties were the première by Scottish Opera of *The Decision* by the Edinburgh composer, Thea Musgrave, for which the society would have had to pay the full costs, and a *Self Portraits* exhibition which at a cost of almost £22 000 proved too expensive. This was replaced by an exhibition based on the Belgian contribution to the Surrealistic Movement which had been offered by the Belgian Government at a cost to the Society of

£5 000, the Belgian Government undertaking responsibility for transport and insurance costs.

Even without these events the 1971 programme still boasted an impressive array of artists and performances. There was no special theme as it was felt that this Festival should have the character of a large birthday party emphasizing the range and diversity that had given the Festival its distinctive reputation. In appreciation of the support given to the Festival by the Edinburgh people over the past 25 years the Society presented a special free concert in the Usher Hall the evening before the Festival opened, the tickets being issued by ballot to Edinburgh citizens. This programme was almost a replica of the opening concert, and included the first performance of a new work commissioned from Thomas Wilson for the Festival Chorus. Yehudi Menuhin, who had been granted the Freedom of the City in 1965, was the soloist in the Beethoven Violin Concerto and generously gave his services free.

The main operatic attraction was a new production of Rossini's *La Cenerentola* mounted specially for Teresa Berganza, supported by Luigi Alva and Renato Capecchi and conducted by Abbado. This was produced in co-operation with the Maggio Musicale, Florence. Abbado had been a little reluctant to conduct an opera which was outside his normal repertoire, but the result was a triumph. The production with an almost identical cast was subsequently presented at La Scala and later taken to Vienna, London and Washington. Diamand also negotiated with Deutsche Grammophon to record the opera, the first of a series of prestigious recordings to be made in association with the Festival.

Scottish Opera revived its acclaimed production of *Die Walküre.* Harold Rosenthal reviewing it for *Opera* (Autumn 1971) claimed: 'The performance was dominated by David Ward's imperious and at the same time, most human Wotan and Helga Dernesch's youthful, girlish and infinitely moving Brünnhilde'. The Deutsche Oper, Berlin brought Reimann's *Melusine* and a mediocre production of *Die Entführung aus dem Serail.* The opening night of the latter was further blighted when Erika Köth in the role of Constanze collapsed during her taxing aria 'Martern aller Arten' and the curtain had to be brought down. A doctor was called in and half an hour later Miss Köth recovered and, somewhat unwisely, continued. She was replaced at the second performance by Bella Jasper. *Melusine* was a replacement for the première of a new opera by Nabokov based on Shakespeare's *Love's Labour's Lost* which the Company had hoped to present but which was not finished.

Notable among the concerts was the first appearance at the Festival of the Israel Philharmonic Orchestra under Mehta with Barenboim and Zukerman as soloists and the Chicago Symphony Orchestra with its contrasting resident conductors, Solti and Giulini. Solti conducted Elliott Carter's Variations for Orchestra, a work rarely if ever heard in Britain, and Mahler's Symphony No. 5 which Conrad Wilson in the *Scotsman* (6 September 1971) considered 'among the impressive events of this year's Festival', while Giulini gave warmly lyrical accounts of Mozart and Haydn and a brilliantly evocative *Firebird Suite* by Stravinsky. But perhaps best of all was a magnificent performance of Mahler's 'Resurrection' Symphony from Abbado and the London Symphony Orchestra with Margaret Price and Janet Baker as the superlative soloists. At St Giles' Cathedral Herrick Bunney repeated his feat of 1967 by performing Bach's complete organ works in 16 recitals, and the Festival's long-standing arrangement with the Leeds Piano Festival was marked with performances by the prize-winners of the first three competitions, Michael

Roll, Rafael Orozco and Radu Lupu, the latter two joining forces with the BBC Scottish Orchestra and James Loughran in a performance of Mozart's Concerto for 2 Pianos.

After *Orlando Furioso* the drama in 1971 lacked an element of adventure. The main Festival production, Prospect Theatre Company's *King Lear*, was not one of their most satisfactory and the critics were divided on its merits. This had been a replacement for *Antony and Cleopatra* which had been cancelled due to casting difficulties. Even more debatable was the Manhattan Project's controversial but fascinating *Alice in Wonderland.* At the Haymarket Ice Rink Frank Dunlop's riotous *Comedy of Errors* transported the action from Ephesus to modern Edinburgh, and the rivalries between Ephesus and Syracuse became a conflict between Edinburgh and London. The twins were smart executives with rolled umbrellas, their servants red-headed clowns in kilts, and Adriana the epitome of a prim middle-class Edinburgh housewife. But despite its many novelties and many jokes, Harold Hobson in the *Sunday Times* (28 August 1971), referred to it as 'a "Comedy of Errors" which has more errors than comedy'. The most talked about company was the Bulandra Theatre from Rumania with an entrancing production of *Leonce and Lena* by Georg Büchner.

The cancellation of *The Decision* left a gap at the King's Theatre which enabled Diamand to bring back classical ballet to the Festival after an absence of many years. The Royal Danish Ballet, not without technical difficulties, gave five performances including two works by the Company's Director, Flemming Flindt, as well as the more traditional Bournonville ballets.

The 1971 Festival made a profit of almost £22 000, only the third time in the Festival's history that a surplus had been achieved. This had been due to careful budgeting and increased revenue from ticket sales which had reached 81 per cent, 5 per cent higher than in 1970. At the Annual General Meeting of the Society on 5 July 1971 Alexander Lowe had suggested that the Council should consider presenting popular concerts and operas, and forget, for a year at least the 'little known and seldom performed works by some great composer or the hitherto unknown grand opera from Outer Mongolia performed in its own native language'. Taking up this point at a Council meeting on 9 November 1971 Treasurer Knox added that the Society could not afford to finance uneconomic productions. Diamand replied that not all Festival events could draw audiences of 73 or 74 per cent. From an artistic point of view it was necessary that events of outstanding cultural importance were included in the programme, even if they attracted limited audiences. It was mainly because of the presentation of such events that the Festival had acquired its reputation. In that context he referred to the Bulandra Theatre which had been praised by audiences and press alike as one of the outstanding events of this year's Festival but attracted an audience of 42 per cent, whereas *Die Entführung* which had played to full houses had been severely criticised. He believed that if the Society tried to play safe in the choice of events the reputation of the Festival would soon be in jeopardy. The Council affirmed that it was essential to maintain the present high standards of the Festival and that the Festival Director should continue to include outstanding cultural events even if they were unable to attract large audiences.

The emphasis of the 1972 Festival was on Polish music and Festival audiences were treated to a representative selection of contemporary works by Penderecki, Lutoslawski, Panufnik and Tadeusz Baird given by the Cracow Philharmonic Orchestra and Chorus

with some well-chosen soloists. Additional contributions came from the Scottish National, BBC Symphony and Royal Philharmonic Orchestras. Szymanowski and Chopin were also represented and Polish music from the fourteenth to the seventeenth centuries was heard in a fascinating concert by the Fistulatores et Tubicinatores Varsovienses. Both Lutoslawski and Penderecki were present in Edinburgh, the latter claiming that his massive *Utrenja* had never received a better performance.

Herbert von Karajan and the Berlin Philharmonic returned for three concerts of mainly German music including an exceptional performance of Mahler's *Das Lied von der Erde* with Christa Ludwig and René Kollo making distinguished Festival debuts. The London Philharmonic Orchestra gave two concerts under Giulini and two performances of Brahms's *Ein deutsches Requiem* under Barenboim with Edith Mathis, Dietrich Fischer-Dieskau and the Edinburgh Festival Chorus. This performance was recorded in Edinburgh a few days later by Deutsche Grammophon.

The Deutsche Oper am Rhein effectively adapted two of its more unusual productions to the King's Theatre and St Mary's Cathedral. In Zimmermann's *Die Soldaten* Catherine Gayer added another striking interpretation of a fiendishly difficult modern role to her growing number of Festival appearances. The same production team was responsible for the simple and beautiful staging of Cavalieri's *Rappresentazione di Anima e di Corpo* in the Cathedral. Part opera and part oratorio this allegorical work was one of the most moving experiences of the Festival.

The visit of the Teatro Massimo from Palermo was less happy and the critics had harsh things to say about its productions of *Attila*, *La Straniera* and, in particular, *Elisabetta, Regina d'Inghilterra*. The BBC even cancelled its projected broadcast of this, although in its defence it did suffer from a late change of conductor and possibly inadequate rehearsal time. Yet the Company gave audiences an opportunity of hearing three non-repertoire works and there were excellent individual performances, notably from Renata Scotto and Ruggero Raimondi. The Italians, however, were put to shame by the home product. Scottish Opera had hoped to mount a new production of Mozart's *La Clemenza di Tito* but because of other commitments Janet Baker had been unable to allocate sufficient rehearsal time and it was decided to revive the 1969 production of *Les Troyens*. In *Opera* (Autumn 1972), Harold Rosenthal considered that this 'would alone have made a journey to Edinburgh worthwhile ... Miss Baker's Dido remains one of the greatest interpretations in present-day opera'.

The Fires of London attracted a predominantly young audience to the Haymarket Ice Rink for a concert of works by Ockeghem, Bruce Cole and Peter Maxwell Davies ending with Davies's *Eight Songs for a Mad King*. Dressed in ermine as George III, and surrounded by members of The Fires enclosed in large wicker cages, William Pearson screamed, moaned and gurgled to splendid effect as he attempted to teach his pet finches to imitate the sounds of a barrel organ.

Frank Dunlop had another popular hit with his *Bible One*, an entertainment based on the book of Genesis. The story of the creation from the Wakefield Mystery plays was followed by Andrew Lloyd Webber's *Joseph and his Amazing Technicolor Dreamcoat*. The Glasgow Citizens' Theatre hung the Assembly Hall with banners and skeletons and spattered the stage with gallons of blood in Keith Hack's arresting and barbaric production of Marlowe's *Tamburlaine*, the only criticism being the arbitrary decision to have three actors play the role of Tamburlaine. Giles Havergal's contentious modern dress

production of *Twelfth Night* went to the opposite extreme by having one actor, Jeremy Blake, play both Viola and her brother Sebastian. Controversy was again rife in the experimental productions by the Gruppo Sperimentazione Teatrale Rome and the Théâtre La Laboratoire Vicinal from Brussels. *Moby Dick* in particular proved too advanced for some members of the audience who left half-way through, and even the critics found it hard going. Anthony Troon in the *Scotsman* (22 August 1972) summed up his review in the opening paragraph, 'The noble story of that mighty white whale is here reduced to a pound of codswallop, and not only that but filleted'. Ian McKellen's Actors' Company, a kind of actors' co-operative, made an auspicious debut with an admirable production of Ford's *'Tis pity she's a Whore* (one councillor raised objections to the title of the piece) and an English adaptation of Feydeau's *Le Dindon* entitled *Ruling the Roost*. The wealth of comic roles gave members of the talented company a chance to exploit their talents to the full, Ian McKellen and Felicity Kendal making the most of their supporting roles as a page and a maid. The exuberance and rhythmic drumming of the Ensemble National du Sénégal contrasted with the stylized serenity and grace of the Hosho Noh Company from Tokyo which presented two programmes of extracts from traditional Noh plays interspersed with comic episodes or Kyogen.

One of the delights of the Edinburgh Festival is that the festive spirit among the audiences communicates itself to the artists, and without fail each Festival produces at least one example. When Julian Bream fell ill only a few hours before his recital, and his hastily found substitute Paco Peña developed qualms, Barenboim and Zukerman and a few members of the English Chamber Orchestra quickly rearranged their morning rehearsal schedule and presented themselves at Leith Town Hall at 11 a.m. Then cool, calm and collected they walked on to the platform and delighted the audience with nearly two hours of polished, exemplary Mozart playing, for which Barenboim charged only a token fee and Zukerman refused any fee at all.

1 *The Thrie Estaites*. EIF production, 1948. (Scottish Tourist Board)

2 Ljuba Welitsch and Paolo Silveri in *Don Giovanni*. Glyndebourne, 1948. (Illustrations Scotland)

3 Helmut Krebs and Sena Jurinac in *Idomeneo*. Glyndebourne, 1953. (Scottish Tourist Board)

4 Christopher Plummer and Ginette Letondal in *Henry V.* Stratford Ontario Festival Company, 1956. (Scottish Tourist Board)

5 Günther Rennert, Moira Shearer, Robert Helpmann and Hans Schmidt-Isserstedt. *The Soldier's Tale*, 1954. (Scottish Tourist Board)

6 Maria Callas in *La Sonnambula.* La Piccola Scala, 1957. (Scottish Tourist Board)

7 Geraint Evans and Judith Blegen in *Le Nozze di Figaro*. EIF production, 1976. (Alex 'Tug' Wilson)

8 Sankai Juku, 1982

9 Janet Baker in *The Trojans*. Scottish Opera, 1972. (Eric Thorburn)

10 Placido Domingo and Teresa Berganza in *Carmen*. EIF production, 1977. (Alex 'Tug' Wilson)

11 Christian Blanc, Marief Guittier and Marie Boitel in *Britannicus*. Théâtre de la Salamandre, 1981. (Alex 'Tug' Wilson)

12 Nuria Espert in *Yerma*. Nuria Espert Company, 1986. (Alex 'Tug' Wilson)

13 Colette Alliot-Lugaz (centre) in *L'Étoile*. Opéra de Lyon, 1985. (Alex 'Tug' Wilson)

14 Désirs Parade. Compagnie Philippe Genty, 1991. (Alex 'Tug' Wilson)

15 Mikijiro Hira and Komaki Kurichara in *Macbeth*. Toho Company, 1985. (Photographer unknown)

16 Galina Gorchakova in *The Legend of the Invisible City of Kitezh*. Kirov Opera, 1995. (Sean Hudson/Keith Brame)

Chapter 6

Peter Diamand 1973–1978

The disappointing press reviews for the Teatro Massimo brought to a head the problems facing the Society in the provision of opera. Diamand expressed his concern at the variable standards of recent years and at the level of the Sicilian company, in particular, which had fallen below expectation. The experience of earlier Festivals had manifested itself yet again; distinguished foreign opera companies accustomed to the loyalty of their home audiences and press often underestimated the effort needed to satisfy Edinburgh Festival audiences. Some opera productions, like wines, did not travel well, and when transported to another theatre in a different country lost much of their flavour. Diamand commented that, 'It is an unsatisfactory situation when we have to import things with which we are unhappy but with companies from abroad we sometimes have to take what we are given which often means accepting artistic – or political – standards which often fall below that of the Edinburgh Festival'. This problem was highlighted by his current difficulties with the Hungarian State Opera which had been invited for 1973. Two performances of Handel's *Rodelinda* with Eva Marton had been arranged but then the company insisted on substituting another singer, whom Diamand felt was not suited to the role, for the second performance. The alternative offered by the Hungarians was to replace the two performances of *Rodelinda* with an extra performance of another programme, the fee for eight performances remaining the same as for nine.

In the early days, because of its high reputation, governments had been ready to grant substantial subsidies to their companies to enable them to 'show the flag' in a centre as important as Edinburgh. Prominent casts were assembled and scenery adapted (often at great expense to the company) to fit the dimensions of the King's Theatre. The performances were on a high level and the reception accorded them by the public and the press was favourable; thus the prestige value of the visit justified the effort and expense. But in the last ten years the situation had changed. With faster air travel leading artists were spreading their activities over a wider geographical area, and with the expansion of the record industry more and more artists were now engaged in recording, for which July to September was the peak period. Furthermore, many more festivals had sprung up and there was increasing competition for the services of the same small group of highly paid singers.

In these circumstances few continental opera companies were able to assemble outstanding casts to bring to Edinburgh. Consequently the artistic level of performances had

dropped, while the expectations of audiences, now accustomed to high-quality recordings, had risen. The recent efforts made by Stuttgart, Hamburg, Florence, Prague, Berlin and Palermo had not resulted in performances as successful or as highly praised as those of former years, and the unfriendly reception by the press had added little to their renown and often had a knock-on effect on their reputations at home. It was small wonder that such companies were less willing to tolerate Edinburgh's outdated theatres, and their governments increasingly reluctant to subsidize them. The exception had been those ensembles which could present either rarely heard or contemporary operas, like *The Fiery Angel* or *Die Soldaten*, but such productions were not available every year, and appealed only to a limited audience. Covent Garden was reluctant to return to Edinburgh until there were more suitable facilities and Glyndebourne's extended season made a visit to Edinburgh difficult.

Scottish Opera had mounted new productions in 1967, 1968 and 1970, and in 1971 and 1972 had presented older productions that had been out of its repertoire for some time. All of these had been exemplary. Artistically Diamand would have liked to see them participating regularly in the Festival, but there was a problem. Scottish Opera did not receive a subsidy for its Festival appearances and had to meet the full cost from its own finances and this was reflected in the fees it demanded from the Society. In 1967 the Society had an agreement with Scottish Opera that the Company would take part as regularly as possible with a new production of a non-repertoire work. But for financial reasons it had now become almost impossible for Scottish Opera to comply with the Society's request that a special Festival production be given each year and not shown elsewhere in Britain for some time after the Festival. Yet there seemed little point in the Company giving repertoire works which had already been seen in Scotland or were to be included in its winter season.

For the future Diamand was convinced that the Festival should fall into line with every other Festival presenting opera, and form its own company to mount special Edinburgh Festival productions. The advantage of such presentations would be that Edinburgh could choose, years ahead, what it wanted to do and engage the most suitable artists. In that way the Society would have full artistic control over every detail of the productions. The initial expense would be high, but he hoped part of this could be recouped by recordings and, perhaps, by selling the productions to other companies. Co-productions with other Festivals were also possible provided they were geared to Edinburgh's standards and physical limitations, together with, whenever possible, new productions (perhaps by Scottish composers) from Scottish Opera and suitable foreign productions when they were available.

But that ugly spectre finance was, as ever, lurking in the background. Diamand's preliminary budget for the 1973 Festival showed an estimated deficit of £91 570. At a Council meeting on 6 November 1972 he insisted that, if the standards of the Festival were to be maintained, expenditure was bound to increase. If the Corporation and the Scottish Arts Council were unable to increase their contributions in line with rising costs then new sources of income would have to be found. He recommended that sponsorship be sought for certain productions. After lengthy discussion the Council decided that the budget would have to be reduced by £50 000. Diamand suggested a number of ways in which these cuts could be achieved. These included either abandoning a new Edinburgh Festival production of *Don Giovanni* or postponing the visit of the Hungarian State

Opera and Ballet. Negotiations for these had reached a stage where, in the event of termination, some indemnification to the artists would be necessary. The other possibility was to cut out performances at the Church Hill Theatre, the Gateway and the Haymarket Ice Rink where negotiations were still at a tentative stage. This would not only upset the balance of the Festival, but the Haymarket Ice Rink, in particular, had attracted a new and younger audience. The Council on 28 November 1972 reluctantly conceded that cutting out these venues would cause the least damage to the Festival's reputation.

Don Giovanni was likely to be the event of the Festival, but at the same time Diamand was taking an enormous risk. The cost was far higher than for any other Festival production and could incur a deficit of £75 000. Barenboim had never conducted an opera before, and though Peter Ustinov's reputation in the theatre was well known, as an operatic director he remained an unknown quantity. The original idea had been to produce *Figaro.* Fischer-Dieskau, who enjoyed working in Edinburgh, was enthusiastic about singing the Count and was prepared to be present throughout the entire rehearsal period. But the 79 year-old Karl Böhm had other ideas. Tearful at the possibility of Fischer-Dieskau not being available for Salzburg he put pressure on him to withdraw from the *Figaro* project, at least as far as 1973 was concerned. Fischer-Dieskau suggested to Diamand that Figaro be postponed until 1974, but as Böhm would then be 80 and his tears were likely to flow even more freely, Diamand was somewhat reluctant to comply. With Fischer-Dieskau out of the cast and news that Scottish Opera was planning a new production of *Figaro* in the spring, Diamand, Barenboim and Ustinov settled on *Don Giovanni.* Roger Soyer was available for the title role and the remainder of the Figaro cast was happy to slot into the corresponding roles in *Don Giovanni* and, equally important, EMI was willing to record it.

The results, if not quite the hoped-for coup, were well worth the risk. The critics had reservations about Ustinov's contribution although there were a number of original touches. In the *Scotsman* (21 August 1973) Conrad Wilson concluded, 'Right or wrong, it is a "Giovanni" with a distinctive point of view. Some people may dislike it very much. I found it compelling, finely sung, the recitatives vividly and appreciatively voiced, the whole conception alive.' Gerald Larner in the *Guardian* (c. 23 August 1973) wrote, 'there has rarely been such a well prepared musical performance at the King's Theatre'.

In the Usher Hall there was another glorious performance of Mahler's 'Resurrection' Symphony by the London Symphony Orchestra and Edinburgh Festival Chorus, this time conducted by Bernstein. Janet Baker was again the mezzo-soprano soloist, partnered on this occasion by Sheila Armstrong. Giulini turned his attention to Schumann's rarely performed *Das Paradies und die Peri* and with the same orchestra and chorus and a strong set of soloists including Edith Mathis, Peter Pears and Thomas Allen gave a moving and eloquent performance. Amidst the main Festival there was a small mini-festival displaying the multifaceted talents of Heinz Holliger as soloist, conductor and composer.

One of the most enjoyable aspects of each Festival is finishing off the evening in a lighter vein at one of the many late-night shows (mostly on the Fringe). But for some peculiar reason, known only to the Almighty and the Festival Director, a recital by Cathy Berberian entitled *A la Recherche de la Musique perdue* or *From the sublime to the ridiculous* took place at 8 p.m. in the austere splendour of the Freemasons' Hall on one of

the wettest Sunday evenings ever experienced at the Festival. However, Miss Berberian quickly dispersed the mood of doom and gloom and enchanted her audience with a recital in the Edwardian style. Treating her accompanist, the cheerful Bruno Canino, with feigned prima donna-like contempt she brought to the songs and her commentary a delightful sense of humorous timing. The programme included some curiosities such as a vocal version of the *Danse Macabre* 'written by Saint-Saens himself' and a song based on Chopin's A major Prelude which the artist averred 'shouldn't be wasted as piano music'.

As well as being concerned about the finances, Diamand deplored the cancellation of what had promised to be a very popular event, the Festival's first promenade concerts. With great difficulty permission had been obtained from the city firemaster for up to 2 500 people to stand in the stalls area of the Usher Hall, but the town council, without consulting either the Festival Society or the Scottish National Orchestra, decided to install new seats which could not be removed.

If the Festival Director had hoped that by giving the press advance warning that the theatre programme had been trimmed because of lack of funds he would silence the drama critics he was quickly proved wrong. Criticism of the drama content reached fever pitch and in some cases almost amounted to hysterical abuse. Diamand was accused of a lack of interest in drama and of devoting too large a proportion of the Festival's resources to music and opera, and not enough to drama and the visual arts; a criticism that was to rumble on throughout his tenure.

Those who complained about the lack of new work at the Festival apparently overlooked the fact that three new plays were presented, and the Actors' Company revived Chekhov's rarely performed *The Wood Demon,* the first version of *Uncle Vanya*, in a sensitive production by David Giles. In the Assembly Hall Bill Bryden bravely mounted a new production of *The Thrie Estaites* of which Michael Billington wrote,

> Outside the Tattoo, I doubt if Edinburgh offers a more impressive physical spectacle; but the great virtue of Bill Bryden's Royal Lyceum Theatre Company Production is that it also focuses attention on language and character ... I grow impatient with an official drama programme that offers no single foreign troupe, or substantial new work; but at least the revival of Lindsay's satire does honour to Scottish theatre.
>
> (M. Billington, *Guardian*, c. 22 August 1973)

The drama critics were not the only people to have doubts about the way the 1973 programme had been trimmed. The Fine Arts Panel (29 November 1972) raised the matter of the curtailment of funds for art exhibitions in 1973 and recommended that, as a matter of policy, the visual arts should continue to be included in the Festival programme and that adequate provision should be made. This was taken up at the Annual General Meeting of the Society when certain members criticized the small part represented by exhibitions in relation to the other arts in the Festival programme. The Scottish Arts Council, at a meeting on 1 March 1973, also expressed concern at the lack of provision and suggested the appointment of an art expert, perhaps on a part-time basis, to enable art exhibitions of an appropriate standard to be featured in each Festival. The Director of the Scottish Arts Council further suggested that £25 000–£30 000 be set aside each year for an exhibition.

In recent years exhibitions had shown deficits of up to £10 000. Insurance and transport costs had increased substantially and exhibition costs were now ten times as high as

in the early 1950s. In May the Treasury had granted indemnity to the Scottish Arts Council for its exhibitions but this did not extend to those arranged by the Festival Society. If the high cost of insurance of major works was to be avoided it would be necessary for such exhibitions to be presented by the Scottish Arts Council although the Society would still be in a position to mount small-scale exhibitions.

Diamand's contract expired after the 1973 Festival and he was offered an extension for a further three years. In spite of the difficulties and frustrations of the job Diamand welcomed this additional term, particularly as it gave him an opportunity of changing the Festival's policy on opera along the lines he had suggested, but at the same time he was reluctant to continue unless he received the financial resources to maintain the international standards of the Festival. In June the Scottish Arts Council increased its grant to £100 000 and introduced a triennial system of estimating which would enable the Festival to plan further ahead. Then in February 1974 Edinburgh Corporation finally agreed to the Society's request that instead of a fixed sum the grant to the Festival would be the product of a halfpenny rate, thus ensuring an automatical rise each year.

In the months following the 1973 Festival attention was given to improving the drama content and various suggestions were put forward including commissioning plays for the Festival and perhaps organizing a special Shakespeare season at the Assembly Hall. With regard to the latter proposal a number of directors had been approached, including David Giles and Richard Cottrell, but none were available for 1974. But in reality it was the same old story. No actor or director of standing was prepared to commit himself more than three or four months in advance for a mere two or three weeks work in case he missed the opportunity of a lucrative film or television contract. Frank Dunlop was not available to direct the Young Vic, and negotiations for presenting the musical *On your Toes* in the Haymarket Ice Rink fell through: as an alternative the Rink was offered to the Young Lyceum to present *Finn MacCool.*

The long-term outlook on the operatic front was much more promising. Teresa Berganza had expressed a wish to sing the role of Carmen for the first time in Edinburgh. To Diamand's great satisfaction Giulini was willing to conduct *Carmen* at the 1976 Festival despite the fact that for more than six years he had adamantly refused to accept any of the countless tempting invitations which opera companies and festivals all over the world had showered on him. Diamand, gratified by the attraction which the Festival exercised on such artists, believed that artistically this would be one of the most exciting projects, even though he did not underrate the considerable financial implications. At least six performances would be given and it would be repeated in 1977. The London Philharmonic Orchestra and the Scottish Opera Chorus would take part and he hoped Nicolai Gedda would be available to sing Don José.

Meanwhile one of the highlights of the 1974 Festival was two performances of the Verdi *Requiem* under Giulini with Arroyo, Cossotto, Pavarotti and Arie. At 3.30 p.m. on the day of the second performance Arroyo reported that she would be unable to sing because of a worsening cold. The Director immediately telephoned Rita Hunter who agreed to catch the 5.25 p.m. plane from Heathrow to Edinburgh. She was met at Turnhouse by a limousine complete with police escort which drove her to her hotel for a ten-minute change into evening dress, and then to the Usher Hall, arriving just in time for the performance.

The opera season was one of the strongest of any Festival. The Barenboim/Ustinov *Don Giovanni* was repeated with almost the same forces, the Stockholm Opera returned with excellent productions of *Elektra, Jenůfa*, Handel's *Il Pastor Fido* and a modern Swedish opera, *The Vision of Thérèse* by Werle, all of which were remarkably well cast, and Scottish Opera had another success with Gluck's *Alceste*, notwithstanding the late withdrawal of Janet Baker. In the *Observer* (25 August 1974) Peter Heyworth considered *Alceste* 'among Scottish Opera's most notable achievements. Certainly, I cannot readily recall a production that has so successfully brought Gluck's neo-classicism to life ... Had it scoured the globe for years it could hardly have alighted on a more impressive protagonist than Julia Varady.'

Not to be outdone the Stockholm Opera also brought a fine crop of outstanding female singers. Of its *Elektra*, Harold Rosenthal wrote:

> The 1968 Hamburg cast, it is true, had one of the most glorious-voiced of present-day Chrysomethises in Leonie Rysanek, and an Orestes who was a tower of strength in Hans Sotin; but Stockholm brought us its own native Birgit Nilsson in the title-role, and a Clytemnestra, Barbro Ericson, whose firmly and excitingly sung performance, and completely integrated character-study of the degraded, neurotic queen, made her encounter with Electra the high spot of the evening. It was interesting to encounter Mme Nilsson in the small confines of the King's Theatre, if only to see how totally immersed she was in the role. Her artistry has certainly deepened over the last few years, and her acting and singing are of a piece.
>
> (H. Rosenthal, *Opera*, Autumn 1974)

But perhaps best of all was the Stockholm Opera's production of *Jenufa* which Rosenthal considered 'one of the most emotionally shattering evenings I have ever experienced in an opera house' (*Opera*, Autumn 1974)

With regard to the drama Robert Cushman was able to write in the *Observer* (8 September 1974): 'This has been a festival full of notable acting: Mr Kay's Tartuffe, Mr McKellen's Faustus, and matching if not overtopping them Sven Vollter's electrically temperamental portrayal of Strindberg's *Gustav III*'. To this list could be added Emrys James's 'chilling imperturbable Mephistophilis'. Also designed by Michael Annals this version of Marlowe's *Dr Faustus* was vastly different to the one given by the Old Vic in 1961, in that John Barton amalgamated two different texts and added 550 lines from Marlowe's source. The critics differed on the merits of the reconstruction, John Barber in the *Daily Telegraph* (c. 28 August 1974) considered that the production was 'flawed' by John Barton's manhandling the text, while the *Guardian*'s Michael Billington (c. 28 August 1974) wrote: 'John Barton's brilliant production and adaptation of "Dr. Faustus" for the first time in my experience transforms Marlowe's broken-backed theological treatise into a thrilling theatrical event.' The Actors' Company's production of *The Bacchae* by Euripides met with general commendation. In the tradition of the Greek theatre the tragedy was followed by a pantomime in which the story of *Jack and the Beanstalk* cleverly echoed the preceding tragedy when Jack triumphantly held up the head of the decapitated giant. This was, in the words of B.A. Young

> a tour de force, hilariously funny from end to end. Who ever expected to see Sharon Duce as a principal boy, Robin Ellis as a dame, Sheila Reid and Paula Dionisotti as the back and front ends of a cow? Here they are, as good as anyone you ever saw at the Palladium. What a remarkable company this is!
>
> (B.A. Young, *Financial Times*, c. 21 August 1974)

Thanks to the generosity of Scottish Television the Haymarket Ice Rink was reinstated as a Festival venue but, after the high standards set by *Orlando Furioso* and Dunlop's *Bible 1* and *The Comedy of Errors,* the Young Lyceum's production of *Finn MacCool* failed to make effective use of the space provided. In addition to criticism of the production there were some complaints about the objectionable language. A member of the Council had vetted the script in advance but at the performances some of the actors had taken it upon themselves to ad lib.

One of the most original shows ever presented at the Festival was given by the Mummenschanz Company at the Church Hill Theatre. The only clue to what could be expected was a cryptic note in the programme, 'It is difficult to describe this essentially non-verbal spectacle in words ...'. The critics had to make the effort but most of them failed. In the *Scotsman* (27 August 1974) Kevin Done reported, 'What is impossible, however, is to avoid the use of superlatives to describe this gloriously imaginative collection of mimes'. But it was mime such as had never been seen before, culminating in an episode with masks in which two members of the company destroy each other's faces. Dance was provided by Israel's Bat-Dor company and by the Kathakali Troupe performing a dance version of the Indian classic the *Mahabharata* which ballet critic Una Flett described as 'a magnificent piece of theatre' (*Scotsman*, 22 August 1974).

With the local government reorganization in May 1975 Edinburgh Corporation ceased to exist and it was agreed that the two new authorities, Edinburgh District Council and Lothian Regional Council, would participate on an equal sharing basis in the financing and the management of the Festival. Each authority would have six representatives on the Festival Council, the Lord Provost of Edinburgh would continue as Chairman and, as the post of City Treasurer no longer existed, the Council finally accepted the Scottish Arts Council's recommendation that the Vice-Chairman could be any member of the Council. Ronald Mavor was appointed, the first non-town councillor to hold the post.

The delays and uncertainty about whether and from where the subsidy was coming did not make Diamand's task easier, and he had to negotiate with companies and artists without being certain that there would be a Festival at all, let alone how much he could spend. He had hoped to bring the English National Opera to the Festival for the first time with Henze's *The Bassarids* and possibly *Beatrice and Benedict* by Berlioz but, although the company was willing to come, the financial terms suggested were beyond the means of the Society. A joint appeal to the Arts Council of Great Britain for a special subsidy was turned down. Instead Diamand negotiated with the Deutsche Oper, Berlin for a return visit. For a time it seemed that these arrangements would also fall through but, thanks to the intervention of the German ambassador and the Governing Mayor of Berlin, additional funds were allocated to the Company by Berlin City Council to enable the visit to take place.

Due to a misunderstanding the Festival Chorus found itself at the centre of a major fiasco involving Bernstein, the Austrian Government and the Festival Society. Shortly before the Festival the chorus was informed that its services would not be required for the performance of Bernstein's *Chichester Psalms* to be conducted by the composer. Bernstein had written the *Psalms* for a boys' choir and, after performing the work in Salzburg with the Vienna Boys' Choir, he had suggested to the Austrian Prime Minister that he would like the Boys to take part in the Edinburgh performance. Assuming that the Festival

Society intended to invite the Choir, the Austrian Government declared itself ready to pay the travelling expenses, Bernstein himself undertaking to pay accommodation and any additional expenditure. Bernstein, however, was advised that there was no accommodation available in Edinburgh. Regardless of its disappointment at being replaced, the Festival Chorus offered to provide hospitality and accommodation for the members of the Vienna Boys' Choir to enable them to take part. When consulted, Diamand refused to accept Bernstein's suggestion and declared in favour of the Festival Chorus. He then announced to the press that

> Bernstein sincerely regrets these misunderstandings. He remembers his happy collaboration with the Edinburgh Festival Chorus and Mr. Arthur Oldham in 1973 and is greatly looking forward to working with them again in the *Chichester Psalms*. I am very satisfied indeed that the original plan will be carried out, grateful for the understanding shown by all who were involved in the matter ... but in particular to Mr. Arthur Oldham and the members of the Edinburgh Festival Chorus whose attitude in the past two weeks has filled me with the greatest admiration.

Having satisfactorily solved the Austrian crisis Diamand found himself with an Italian crisis of more epic proportions on his hands. Ronconi's massive spectacular *Utopia* ran into trouble before it had even left Italy when a spell of torrential rain washed out some open-air previews. Then the plane carrying the props ran out of fuel. At this point the Italian Custom Officials became suspicious of a cargo of theatrical props which contained, in addition to collapsible proscenium arches, a fleet of battered motor cars and an ancient biplane, and insisted on investigating it. When the plane stopped to refuel at Stanstead the British Customs officers were even more intrigued than their Italian comrades and caused another delay. By this time both the Festival Society and Ronconi's company, which had spent £3 000 on this trip, were becoming increasingly irritated. The cargo finally arrived at Turnhouse too late for the first performance which had to be cancelled. When the entertainment actually got on stage the performance lasted for four and a half hours and half the audience left before the end. Diamand and his assistant, William Thomley, had discussions with Ronconi who consented to make cuts in the dialogue. Two shortened versions, each of about two and a half hours duration, were shown on Monday and Wednesday and Tuesday and Friday respectively, and the full version was presented on Friday and Saturday. The final catastrophe came at the Saturday performance when the undercarriage of the plane collapsed and had to be dismantled during the interval.

There were more problems at the King's Theatre with Scottish Opera's *Hermiston.* After being suspended with a rope round his neck for 15 minutes in the hanging scene, Jim Hastie collapsed at the dress rehearsal and again at the first performance, and required medical attention. Afterwards he insisted on continuing. 'This is a very important part of the opera. I think it would ruin it completely if I pulled out.' The director Toby Robertson also complained that he had to make no less than seven alterations which he maintained made geographic nonsense of the set because there was no room at the King's to do what had been possible at the multi-purpose McRobert Centre in Stirling. He commented afterwards, 'I cannot understand why the opera companies of the world still come here. It must be a tribute to Peter Diamand or possibly to Edinburgh'.

Immediately after the Festival Peter Diamand received the greatest blow he had so far experienced at the Festival when, after almost 30 years of discussion, argument, plans,

counter-plans, dithering and procrastination, the new Edinburgh District Council finally decided not to proceed with the building of an opera house. This was a direct result of the Government's withdrawal of its promise to pay half the cost. Thus Edinburgh Corporation's inability to make up its mind and its total lack of initiative had lost the city almost £10 million in Government grant for the theatre, and the Festival was still in the same position with regard to facilities as it had been in 1947.

Diamand was pleased with the financial results of the 1975 Festival which, thanks to an additional £5 000 from the Scottish Arts Council, had resulted in a small surplus of £721 instead of the estimated deficit of £45 000. This was due mainly to increased ticket sales and savings on production costs at the King's Theatre. But inflation and devaluation were still hitting the Society severely. No increase in grant would be forthcoming from the Region and the Labour party members of Edinburgh District Council would not support any application for an increase in its contribution. The Scottish Arts Council expressed a willingness to increase its subvention to the Festival, but would expect similar increases from the local authorities. But later in the year it announced an increase of £75 000 bringing its grant to £225 000. The local authorities again contributed £90 000 each with Edinburgh District Council providing an additional £16 000 to offset a similar increase in rents for the theatres – a perfect example of giving with one hand and taking away with the other.

Diamand's plans for 1976 showed an estimated deficit of £90 000. In presenting this budget to the Finance Committee on 3 December 1975 he emphasized that it was his duty to present a programme which would maintain the existing standards of the Festival both in quality and quantity. He had taken account of both devaluation and inflation and, bearing in mind the need for economy, he felt that his proposed budget was realistic. Councillor Williamson suggested that economies could be made by replacing some of the companies and orchestras proposed with others of comparable quality, but on considerably less onerous terms. Diamand quickly replied that, if this view was shared by the other members of the Committee, he felt that he no longer enjoyed the confidence of the Finance Committee, and therefore his replacement should be recommended to the Council. The Council later authorized the Director to proceed with the 1976 Festival on the understanding that savings of £40 000 were made. Because of the necessity of booking musicians at least a year ahead these economies could only be achieved, yet again, at the expense of drama and the visual arts, and accordingly both the Church Hill Theatre and the Haymarket Ice Rink were excluded. The gymnasium of Moray House College was utilized as a less expensive alternative, but unfortunately there was insufficient space for Andrei Serban's production of *Medea* which had to be replaced by additional performances of *The Trojan Women.*

New ground was broken by Serban, in his productions of *The Trojan Women* and *Electra.* Based loosely on Euripides and Sophocles he employed an incomprehensible mixture of Aztec and American-Indian dialects combined with Greek in an attempt to convey emotion through sound rather than language, with memorable effect. Priscilla Smith had a triple triumph as Andromache, Electra and then as Shen-Te in Brecht's *The Good Woman of Setzuan.* Of the latter Allen Wright wrote in the *Scotsman* (3 August 1976), 'The entire company is impressive but Priscilla Smith's alternation between fragile goodness and surly power is something quite out of the ordinary'.

Arrangements had been made with the English Stage Company to present *Night* by David Storey but the Company reported they were having difficulty casting it and instead

suggested Storey's *Mother's Pay*. This was read by several members of the Drama Advisory Panel who considered the play pornographic and unsuitable for the Festival, an opinion later substantiated by the critics when the play opened in London. In its place the Oxford Playhouse presented the musical *Pal Joey*, an alternative that failed to rouse the enthusiasm of the critics, the *Scotsman*'s Allen Wright (24 August 1976) describing it as 'not just an imitation of the second-rate but the genuine article'. Another unforeseen hitch in the drama programme was the last minute cancellation of the second performance of *Masaniello* when the leading actor, Mariano Rigillo, fell and dislocated his shoulder during the final moments of the opening. On similar lines to *Orlando Furioso*, this was one of the most exciting dramatic productions given at the Festival. The Birmingham Repertory Company's *Measure for Measure* with Anna Calder-Marshall, outstanding in the role of Isabella, was one of the most satisfying Shakespeare productions presented in the Assembly Hall. It was subsequently given at the National Theatre and the company was invited to undertake a continental tour for the British Council.

There was an impressive diary of events in St Cecilia's Hall where the Festival Society paid a somewhat belated tribute to Hugh MacDiarmid with a splendid dramatization by Tom Fleming of his epic poem *A Drunk Man Looks at the Thistle*. Also after years of persuasion the Society finally relented and allowed Fleming to present a programme based on the works of Edwin Muir. The American Bicentennial was commemorated by a dignified, if somewhat staid, poetry recital by Princess Grace of Monaco (the former Grace Kelly) supported more vigorously by Richard Pasco and Richard Kiley, and Ian McKellen demonstrated the richness of the English language in his own compilation ranging from Shakespeare through Keats and Dylan Thomas to the Telephone Directory in *Words, Words, Words*. In *Rogues and Vagabonds* Wendy Hiller, with a disarming frankness and lack of conceit, read a letter written to her 40 years before by George Bernard Shaw, whose devastating comments would have discouraged any but the most dedicated actress from continuing in the profession. All in all the drama programme, albeit curtailed, remained one of the most rewarding of recent years.

Apart from a passing nod in the direction of the centenary of the birth of Falla and the one hundred and fiftieth anniversary of the birth of Weber there was no main musical theme for 1976. Instead Diamand celebrated the thirtieth Festival with a reminder of some of the highlights of those 30 years, and of 1947 in particular. *Macbeth* and *Figaro* were repeated as well as Mahler's *Das Lied von der Erde*. The Vienna Philharmonic Orchestra were invited back and there was the welcome reappearance of a number of artists who had become regular visitors over the years: the New Philharmonia Orchestra, Claudio Abbado, Daniel Barenboim, Carlo Maria Giulini, Clifford Curzon, Heather Harper, Teresa Berganza, Peter Pears, Elisabeth Schwarzkopf and Geoffrey Parsons, who had donned Gerald Moore's mantle as accompanist in residence. There was the chance to compare the newly formed Orchestre de Paris under its dynamic young conductor, Daniel Barenboim, with two old-established European orchestras, also with young conductors: the Leipzig Gewandhaus Orchestra under Kurt Masur and the Vienna Philharmonic with Abbado. But for Desmond Shawe-Taylor in the *Sunday Times* (5 September 1976) the fullest experience of this last great orchestra was the final concert when the octogenarian Karl Böhm conducted the last three symphonies of Mozart: 'Simple choice, simple-seeming performances; to all appearances effortless, yet sublime.' If Scottish Opera's *Macbeth* did not quite match its attainments of earlier years it was still memorable for a

fiery interpretation of Lady Macbeth by Galina Vishnevskaya, and the Deutsche Oper am Rhein triumphantly overcame the perils and hazards of the King's Theatre with distinguished productions of operas rarely, if ever, performed in Edinburgh, Schoenberg's *Moses und Aron,* Wagner's *Parsifal* and Rossini's *L'Italiana in Algeri*, and Edinburgh Festival Opera, in addition to a repeat of *Figaro*, gave a commendable concert performance of another little known work, Weber's *Die drei Pintos*.

Ballet was somewhat sparsely represented with a single programme by the Ballet of the Deutsche Oper of which the most notable item was *Opus 1* by the British trained choreographer, John Cranko, then resident in Germany. The other company was the provocative and very individual Twyla Tharp troupe which David Dougill in the *Sunday Times* described as the 'St. Vitus Dance Ensemble'. Alexander Bland in the *Observer* (12 September 1976) considered her vocabulary trivial, but added at the end, 'It will be interesting to see what she can do when she takes her tongue out of her cheek and puts some heart into her chic'. Owing to an injury Tharp herself only made one appearance.

The Royal Botanic Gardens provided an idyllic setting for an exhibition of late sculptures of Barbara Hepworth. The bronzes were scattered on the lawns amongst the trees and the white marbles displayed in a royal blue setting in the Old Herbareum. There was also a remarkable though unofficial exhibition of 140 watercolours, drawings and paintings by Paul Klee in the nearby National Gallery of Modern Art.

If Diamand had thought Edinburgh District Council's decision to abandon the opera house the nadir of his period of office he had greatly underestimated the situation. The period between the 1976 and 1977 Festivals was to be the most difficult yet. On 15 October 1976 he raised, yet again, the question of financing the 1977 Festival. Arrangements for the production of *Carmen* were nearing completion. While no contracts had been signed he had reached firm understandings with the London Symphony Orchestra, Abbado (replacing Giulini who had decided that he was not yet ready to return to opera), the producer, designer and the principal singers. *Carmen* would almost certainly be broadcast, Deutsche Grammophon was interested in recording it and there was the possibility of a European television company filming the production. Even although the costs involved were high, Diamand had been authorized on a number of occasions to proceed with his negotiations on the understanding that he did not commit the Society to expenditure above the level of the income that had been available for 1976. He now felt personally committed to the artists concerned and should the Council decide not to proceed with the production, considerable claims from the London Symphony Orchestra and individual artists were likely to be made. Worse still, the faith of the artists in the reliability of the Festival and its Director would be severely shaken, and having forfeited the confidence of artists with whom he had been negotiating for three years, he would find it difficult to continue as Director. Apart from two performances of Thea Musgrave's new opera *Mary Queen of Scots* he had made no other commitments for 1977, but it was necessary that negotiations with other artists and orchestras be concluded in the very near future otherwise no artist of standing would be available.

Carmen would be by far the most expensive production ever mounted at the Festival. The estimated deficit on the seven performances would be in the region of £234 000. To make matters worse there was a deficit on the 1976 Festival of more than £36 000. Fortunately the Scottish Arts Council came to the rescue with an additional £30 000

bringing the 1976 deficit down to a more acceptable figure of £6 365 but it still left the problem of where the money for *Carmen* would come from. An approach was made to the Scottish banks but they replied that they were not in a position to donate a substantial sum, and the question of sponsorship, which had been discussed on various earlier occasions but left in abeyance, was again envisaged as the only possible means of raising the necessary finance.

Convinced of the necessity to guarantee the continuation of the Festival, Diamand submitted a revised budget in which he reduced the number of performances from 128 to 110, abandoned proposed performances at the Large Studio Theatre and raised ticket prices. If this revised budget was approved he intended to seek the co-operation of all the artists by pointing out the financial difficulties and asking them to make significant reductions in their fees, but it was vital that a final decision was reached immediately. The Council (1 November 1976) approved the amended budget and Diamand proceeded to exert all his diplomatic skills in an effort to convince a number of top-ranking artists that an appearance at the Festival at a greatly reduced fee would be more prestigious than more lucrative engagements elsewhere. Berganza was prepared to lower her fee as the production had been her idea in the first instance. This set the ball rolling and Claudio Abbado, Placido Domingo and Mirella Freni also agreed to substantial reductions, the latter accepting the lower fee as a 'present to her friend, Teresa', while Domingo even signed his contract with the fee blank, saying he would accept whatever the Society could afford to pay him. Other artists followed suit and Diamand finally managed to put together a programme, but with only nine opera performances and one overseas orchestra the 1977 Festival was far below the standards of quantity and variety necessary to maintain the reputation of the Festival. This programme had been achieved as a result of the generous co-operation of many of the artists taking part, and whilst Diamand was grateful to them, the Festival could not continue on this basis.

Having successfully completed extremely delicate negotiations with stars more accustomed to increasing their fees than reducing them Diamand was highly indignant when one town councillor (based on some misleading information) refuted his claim that reduced fees were being paid, stating that these artists received lower fees at the Royal Festival Hall (21 February 1977). Councillor Williamson refused to substantiate his arguments and a few weeks later resigned from the Finance Committee. Though a staunch supporter of the Festival over many years his local government experience led him to adopt a strictly fiscal attitude towards the budget. He believed that the Festival Director should plan his Festival on the revenue available instead of striving for increased funding to maintain standards.

Although galloping inflation and devaluation had vastly decreased spending power the local authority grants to the Festival had remained pegged at the 1975 level and there seemed little hope of an increased subvention. Edinburgh District Council had also substantially increased the rentals for the venues it owned (although few improvements had been carried out) and now it proposed increasing the rent on the Society's Edinburgh office from £4 250 to £21 000 per annum. The Society's own office had been sold to Edinburgh Corporation to make way for the opera house development on the understanding that the Society would be rehoused within the new building. The proposed theatre complex was now little more than a forlorn dream, and this increase added insult to injury.

In the years leading up to the demise of Edinburgh Corporation the Festival had become a kind of political football kicked about by warring parties within the town council. Since reorganization this situation had deteriorated even further: Edinburgh District Council still had a Conservative majority while Lothian Regional Council was predominantly Labour. Relations between them were strained to say the least, and on any divisions within the Festival Council the two authorities unanimously voted against each other. The Regional councillors had drawn up a list of proposals for 'improvements' in the Society's organization and policies. Before these could be discussed the local press reported that the Conservative members of the Regional Council had recommended that the Region's grant to the Festival be reduced by £50 000. A political row blew up when a 'Festival spokesman' was reported to have said that the Conservatives did not appear to be interested in the Festival. Then on top of this came the devastating announcement that the Region was withdrawing its grant to the Festival completely.

In a bid to take over control of the Festival, Edinburgh District Council offered to increase its grant to £190 000 on condition that all twelve local authority seats on the Festival Council were allocated to members of the District Council. The Lothian Region members on the Council (21 April 1977) proposed that the District Council be requested to reconsider the terms of its offer of financial assistance. The Region had withdrawn its grant towards the 1977 Festival because the Rate Support Grant currently favoured Edinburgh District Council. In 1978, the position could well be reversed. The current financial problems were unlikely to continue indefinitely and they assured the Council that the Region wished to make a substantial contribution as soon as circumstances permitted. But some Festival Council members felt that one of the main causes of the difficulties between the two authorities had been the overlap of responsibilities and that the Festival Council would be strengthened if only one authority was involved in the management of the Festival. The Council therefore accepted the District Council's offer and the change in the constitution of the Council was ratified at an Extraordinary General Meeting of the Society by a vote of 66 to 19.

Close on the heels of the Region's decision to withdraw support for the 1977 Festival a copy of Diamand's draft estimates (including the estimated deficit for *Carmen*) was leaked to three Labour councillors (James Kerr, David Brown and George Monies), who promptly gave the figures to the *Edinburgh Evening News* with the comments:

> We are absolutely incensed by this colossal squandering of public money – squandering which has only come to our notice because we managed to uncover some secret documents of the Festival Society which the public have never been allowed to see. In the interests of the ratepayers of Edinburgh and the people who are subsidising the Festival, we feel it is our duty to tell them the facts which the Festival organisers would prefer to remain unknown.
>
> We also want to draw to the public's attention all the hidden subsidies which are made – the complimentary tickets to VIPs, the receptions in the City Chambers and so on. It is nothing short of scandalous that ratepayers have for years been forking out massive sums of money to a body which then spends it arbitrarily with no public accountability at all. Indeed, the majority of councillors being asked to authorize an extra £100,000 to this year's Festival were not in possession of these figures. Only those councillors on the Festival Society knew of them.
>
> (J. Kerr, D. Brown and G. Monies, *Edinburgh Evening News*, 23 February 1977)

Kerr declared his intention of tabling an emergency resolution for the following day's District Council meeting. After a stormy debate the District Council rejected Labour's demands for a 'full and public examination' of the Festival's finances by 34 votes to 20.

Kerr was harshly condemned by the Tory members who were quick to accuse Labour of making a pre-election attack on the Festival in a bid to 'capture the moron vote'. After the meeting Kerr declared that he would raise the matter again and if they were still denied what he described as 'vital information' he intended to ask the Labour group to make a strong effort to scrap the Festival completely. Two days later the Festival received an enormous vote of confidence when British Petroleum presented a cheque for £35 000 as sponsorship towards *Carmen* – the largest gift thus far received by the Society.

The publication of his draft estimate of expenditure was not the first time the Festival Director had been embarrassed by the leakage of confidential information to the press. In January he had asked the Council's permission to accept an advisory post with La Scala, Milan which, if fruitful, might lead to a more permanent post when his contract with the Festival Society expired in 1978. Immediately afterwards Radio Forth broadcast in its news bulletin distorted details of Diamand's future connection with La Scala, and two days later the *Guardian* erroneously implied that Diamand's impending departure from the Edinburgh Festival was linked with the collapse of the plans for the opera house and with his dissatisfaction at the financial problems of the Festival, at the same time omitting to mention that Diamand's contract expired after the 1978 Festival.

As expected *Carmen* was the highlight of the Festival. Because of commitments at Salzburg, Freni could only sing four performances. Much to everyone's surprise Karajan agreed to change the date of one of her Salzburg performances to enable her to be in Edinburgh for the dress rehearsal and sing in the opening performance of *Carmen*. As one member of the Festival staff remarked, 'this unexpected compliance was almost worrying'. Leona Mitchell was engaged for the remaining performances. Her contract stipulated that although her last scheduled performance was on 7 September she should remain in Edinburgh until the 11th, so that she could 'cover' the final performance, although to save face this was not spelled out in the contract, but her agent was in no doubt as to the reason for this clause (Council, 6 September 1977). As it happened Freni was ill and unable to sing on 10 September but when the Society tried to contact Miss Mitchell they discovered that she had returned to New York. Diamand was so annoyed that he delayed payment of her fee for several months and even considered taking legal proceedings against her for breach of contract, but this was eventually dropped. Albert Lance, who was to sing Don José on the 10th fell out with the conductor and producer, and was replaced by Peyo Garacci.

It was an unlucky year for cancellations. Illness caused Edith Mathis to withdraw from her Usher Hall appearance on 22 August, James Galway was badly injured in a road accident and the second violinist of the Chilingirian Quartet injured his hand. A sudden attack of flu prevented Rupert Frazer from performing in *War Music* on 30 August so it was replaced by a further performance of *All for Love*. After being renovated at a cost of £672 000 the lighting circuit at the Lyceum Theatre failed and the Director of Building Control refused to grant a licence for the opening performance of *Käthchen von Heilbronn* by the Stuttgart Theatre. Hundreds of people had to be given their money back. The company had received substantial support from its government to give three performances at the Festival, but one had to be cancelled because the leading actor had film commitments. The refusal of a performing licence meant that only one performance of the play could be given in Edinburgh. In the light of the high rental charged by the

District Council the Festival Society was justifiably annoyed and the dispute about who should bear the financial loss continued for a number of months before it was finally settled. But the worst casualty of all was the cancellation of the State Theatre of Greece's production of *Medea* caused by the withdrawal of its leading actress, Melina Mercouri, because of a perforated ulcer. At very short notice the Society was able to bring Keith Hack's production of *Hedda Gabler*, currently running at the Duke of York's Theatre in London, to fill the vacant dates.

Particularly memorable among the drama presentations was Julie Harris's portrayal of the poet Emily Dickinson in *The Belle of Amherst.* Hailed on Broadway as the greatest performance by an American actress in the last 25 years, Harris's first appearance on the British stage met with equal praise from the British critics.

At the final press conference Diamand described *Carmen* as the jewel in this year's Festival, and quoted a letter from Lord Harewood who claimed that Miss Berganza's performance as Carmen had been 'as near perfect as any of us is ever likely to see'. A leading Italian newspaper, the *Corriere della Sera*, had said that 'We must only ask ourselves when it will be possible to hear such a *Carmen* in Italy'. The Lord Provost, Kenneth Borthwick, said that 'Mr Diamand has operated under great difficulties on a shoe string budget.' They would look to sponsorship in addition to the contributions from the local authority and the Scottish Arts Council to build up a reserve fund.

But the music and drama performances of the 1977 Festival were put into the shade when, with a cast of hundreds including the Lord Provost, the Festival Society, councillors, politicians, actors, citizens and visitors the final act of the Edinburgh Opera House saga was played out in the full glare of the world's press. Even Cecil de Mille couldn't have staged a more spectacular denouement.

When presenting his preliminary estimate for 1978 (21 February 1977) Diamand stated that it had been prepared on the assumption that the Council wished to present a Festival similar in character and diversity to those of former years and, notwithstanding the financial circumstances, he believed the Council should be aware of the cost of presenting such a Festival. In addition to several performances of *Carmen* which he hoped would be less expensive than in 1977 he proposed to present a new Festival production of *Così fan Tutte* and a new production by Scottish Opera of Monteverdi's *Ulysses.* Although Diamand agreed that savings of £70 000 might be effected by cancelling *Così fan Tutte* and by engaging an overseas company to present opera or ballet the Finance Committee decided that this budget would have to be cut by £100 000. At the same time concern was expressed that the support from the local authorities was no higher than it had been several years ago, and an appeal was made to Edinburgh District Council for an additional grant to offset the increased rents on the Festival Office and the various venues, and to allow for the increase in inflation in 1976 and 1977. The District Council agreed to an additional subsidy of £32 620, and in April they added another £22 680 to offset the loss on the 1977 Festival, and approved a grant of £300 000 for 1978 on condition that the Society did not seek additional support later.

Letters appealing for funds had been sent to large business concerns in Scotland with disappointing results. Out of 151 letters sent to prospective new donors, 9 made donations amounting to £4 875 and 58 refused to contribute at all. Appeals for sponsorship were more successful and in addition to British Petroleum, who had sponsored

Carmen, Elf Acquitaine, IBM, BAA and Scottish Widows agreed to sponsor individual events.

The 1978 Festival was in keeping with the high standard which, with enormous difficulty, Diamand had maintained throughout his 13-year tenure. Opera was high on the agenda, and in addition to a repeat of *Carmen*, the Zürich Opera staged its controversial Monteverdi cycle conducted by Nikolaus Harnoncourt. In place of *Ulysses* Scottish Opera gave *Pelléas et Mélisande* and the Frankfurt Opera paid a return visit with a somewhat unsympathetic production of Janáček's *Káta Kabanová*, redeemed by the lustrous singing of Hildegard Behrens in the title role, and Nono's *Al Gran Sole Carico d'Amore*, but after the trials and tribulations experienced with *The Fiery Angel* the Frankfurt Company decided to play safe with a concert performance only. William Mann, for *Opera* (Autumn 1978), found the Nono 'eventful, excitable, beautiful and ultimately moving, as well as superbly performed'. This opinion was not shared by Felix Aprahamian who wrote in the *Sunday Times* (9 September 1978): 'Ranging from acceptable monody to speculative noise, it was bearable only when merely boring.'

Pina Bausch's Tanztheater Wuppertal made an auspicious first visit to Britain with a trilogy of ballets to music by Stravinsky on the subject of spring entitled *Frühlingsopfer.* The final item, a highly dramatic version of *The Rite of Spring*, caught the imagination of the dance critics. In it Bausch concentrated on the female participants in the rites. Alexander Bland commented,

> The notion of giving the main action to the girls, who start as trembling adolescents and turn into thrashing maenads, is marvellously dramatic ... The final stroke of inspiration is to set the whole action ... on a thick depth of peat ... By the end of the ceremony soil is streaked over the dancers' faces and caked on to their skins.
>
> (*Observer*, 3 September 1978)

For the first time the Festival established its own drama company, Edinburgh Festival Productions, to present Shakespeare's *The Tempest* and *A Midsummer Night's Dream* in the Assembly Hall. The critics were lukewarm in their reactions and the enterprise did not meet with the hoped-for success. A third Shakespeare play was given by the Royal Shakespeare Company in tandem with a magnificent *Three Sisters* by Chekhov. Prospect presented a highly praised production of *Ivanov* with Derek Jacobi, and a further two Russian plays, Gogol's *The Marriage* and Turgenev's *A Month in the Country* were given by the admirable Moscow Drama Theatre. Unfortunately the Groupe TSE from Paris, who had been scheduled to give four performances of *The Heartaches of an English Pussy Cat*, had to cancel its visit and it was impossible to find a replacement in the time available.

When his contract had been renewed in 1975 for a further three years there had been mutual agreement between Diamand and the Festival Council that he would not continue in office for a fourth term, and a sub-committee was set up to find a new Director. John Drummond, the Assistant Head of Music and Arts at the BBC, was chosen from a list of 20 candidates. That year the Festival also said goodbye to the Artistic Assistant, William Thomley, who had been responsible mainly for drama.

At a luncheon given in his honour in the City Chambers Diamand said that he hoped an opera house would be built in Edinburgh in the foreseeable future, adding that 'one of the great disappointments has been that the opera house which so many had hoped for has not been created'. Of his 13 years as director Diamand commented, 'I can say without

any reservation that my association with the Edinburgh Festival has been a tremendous challenge, and summing up all the events and all the experiences it has been a wonderful time. I wish the Festival a very happy and successful future.'

Chapter 7

John Drummond 1979–1983

John Drummond was the exact antithesis of his predecessor. Diamand was a quiet, charming and retiring man who disliked public relations, avoided interviews and was frequently invisible; Drummond was upfront, very visible and very vocal to the press, on radio and on television. Diamand was patient, shrewd, firm but diplomatic in his relations with the local authorities, institutions and the Festival Council; Drummond could be impatient, outspoken and was not always tactful, particularly with people who were being obstructive or who refused to understand his problems, and this could on occasion lead to confrontation. A case in point concerned the Director of the Royal Scottish Museum, who expressed no real interest in the Festival. When Drummond rather pointedly suggested that perhaps he should, he was quickly shown the door.

In 1958 Drummond had been offered a job by Robert Ponsonby but the salary had been so low that he couldn't afford to accept it and instead he had joined the BBC. Up to 1984 he had attended 19 Festivals and for several of these he had been responsible for the BBC's coverage. He therefore knew the Festival and the city well. One or two aspects of the Festival disturbed him. Primarily there was the tension between the citizens of Edinburgh and the Festival itself which led every year to a shower of complaints in the local press about the high cost of the event, and the resulting disruption of the everyday lives of citizens. Although 40 to 60 per cent of the tickets were sold annually to a strong core of loyal supporters in and around Edinburgh, many giving up their holidays to attend performances day after day, Drummond was very much aware there was an even larger number of people to whom the Festival meant nothing. Drummond remembers one such woman accusing him of getting in her way before a concert in the Freemasons' Hall. To which he had replied, 'Yes! That's the whole point of the Festival. To disrupt ordinary life'. Consequently he felt there was a missionary job to be done and he set out by means of talks, lectures and numerous after-dinner speeches to try and make people more receptive to the Festival and what he was trying to do, not only on behalf of those who appreciated the Festival but also for those who had a financial stake in it.

While the Festival was still held in high regard throughout the world, Drummond considered that the programme had become slightly repetitive in that the same roster of top-class artists, occasionally referred to as the 'Diamand Mafia' (Giulini, Abbado, Barenboim, Berganza, Fischer-Dieskau and Stern) appeared year after year, giving rise to a slight feeling of *déjà vu*. The image presented was of an institution that had become a

little settled in its ways. No festival can afford to stand still or become complacent, and to keep its place as the leading arts festival Drummond felt that he must not only retain the high standards of his predecessors but also explore new areas for development and different ways of doing things. As a Scot Drummond also believed that the Festival should involve itself more in Scotland and Scottish life and he resolved to include more Scottish events, provided they were of a sufficiently high quality.

Above all Drummond was concerned about the state of the buildings the Council owned and the fact that each year the District Council clawed back a large part of its subsidy in rents for inadequate buildings. He considered that the Council's attitude to the buildings it owned amounted to an absolute dereliction of public responsibilty. Backstage conditions at the King's Theatre were appalling, and having to take out six rows of the most expensive seats to put in six rows of expensive musicians was ludicrous. The Usher Hall was an excellent concert-hall but it had no supporting facilities for the audience and only one green room that had to be shared by all the principal artists. The Lyceum had been the subject of an expensive refurbishment but this had been entirely confined to the front of the house, whereas the real problem was on the stage. The goodwill on which Edinburgh had depended for so long was running out and foreign governments were no longer prepared to put up vast sums of money just for the glory of coming to Edinburgh. Major opera and ballet companies would take one look at the theatres and say, 'You must be joking. We can't possibly perform here'. So rather than cut down productions that were too large for the accommodation available, Drummond set out to find opera and ballet companies that had stages of similar dimensions to those in Edinburgh.

The governing factor was finance and Drummond was insistent that every effort must be made to increase funding. This was crucial as the 1978 Festival had incurred a deficit of £25 000 and only a supplementary grant from the Scottish Arts Council had prevented its being higher. This shortfall had been largely due to an underestimation of Scottish Opera's production costs. Fluctuation in currency exchange rates had resulted in further losses. Financially the Festival had lived too close to the edge for too long and Drummond believed that the only way of raising sufficient additional income was through sponsorship.

Inexpensive ways of widening the range would be to extend the category of 'associated events' into the field of drama and by seeking closer links with the Film Festival, the Television Festival and the Fringe Society. A number of companies appearing regularly on the Fringe were of a sufficiently high standard to merit inclusion in the Festival programme as 'associated events', and while it might be necessary for the Festival Society to offer these companies some financial guarantee against loss, no responsibility would devolve on the Society apart from ensuring that the content was up to Festival standards. The Fringe attracted a younger and less conservative audience than the official Festival and Drummond thought that, by narrowing the divide between the two events, these younger people could be brought into the main Festival.

Drummond was unhappy with the publicity which he felt needed sharpening, and in order to present a livelier image he changed the Festival motif which had been in use since 1967, and in the interests of efficiency he centralized the design and printing of publicity in Edinburgh. Two years later he also dispensed with the services of the Publicity Officer whose outspoken criticism of the Fringe was having a detrimental effect

on relations between the two organizations. Both Harewood and Diamand had tried to improve relations between the official Festival and the Fringe, but had received little support from either the Festival or the town council. In fact when, on first taking office, Diamand had attended a Fringe reception he had been sternly rebuked by the Lord Provost for accepting the invitation.

Another area Drummond considered in need of improvement was the administrative structure of the Society both in London and Edinburgh; in particular the allocation of responsibilities which, in his view, had been far from ideal. Harewood and Diamand had preferred to concentrate on the musical side of the Festival leaving the drama and visual arts to their assistants. Drummond wanted to be involved in all aspects of the Festival, but in order to do this some delegation was necessary, and he required suitably qualified assistants who could put his plans into operation and deputize for him during his absences abroad. Accordingly Richard Jarman was appointed as Artistic Assistant and Sheila Colvin upgraded to Executive Assistant in London.

The London office had always been considered an extravagance by some members of the Festival Council. Every two or three years it had been suggested that this office be closed and that the Festival Director should work from Edinburgh. Harewood and Diamand had insisted that it was essential that they operate from London which was in effect the musical centre of Europe, and from where it was possible to travel anywhere in the world in the shortest space of time. Drummond approached this contentious issue with caution and asked for a few months to consider the matter and report back. As an experiment he tried not using the London office for a month. But, despite the fact that he was living in his own London flat instead of a hotel, he found it impossible to function without secretarial help, telex or a photocopier. He concluded that, while it was his intention to maintain a greater presence in Edinburgh, only by living in London, with full backup facilities, could he see the number of performances he considered necessary and at the same time liaise personally with artists, agents and other people involved in the arts. While recommending that certain administrative functions be transferred to Edinburgh he considered a London office necessary but suggested that better premises be found. He also questioned the wisdom of the Festival Society paying a high rental to Edinburgh District Council for an Edinburgh office which was far from satisfactory, and suggested that the Society should purchase its own premises in Edinburgh: almost the identical argument that Ponsonby had presented to the Festival Council nearly 30 years before. He was extremely irritated when he discovered that the Trustees of the Capital Fund were unwilling to allocate funds for capital projects.

On the artistic side nothing had been arranged for the 1979 Festival except two concerts by the Boston Symphony Orchestra, which was also appearing at the London Promenade Concerts, so Drummond had to start from scratch. His aim was to expand Harewood's idea of building each Festival around a central theme, but instead of a composer he wanted to find a suitable topic. The 1979 Festival opening on the fiftieth anniversary of the death of Diaghilev gave him an ideal subject, enabling him to link together the different aspects – opera, ballet, drama, concerts and the visual arts – in a way that had never been attempted before. Diaghilev in opera was represented by Scottish Opera's *The Golden Cockerel*, and in drama by *Chinchilla,* a play about Diaghilev written for the Glasgow Citizens' Theatre by Robert David MacDonald, and Goldoni's *The Good-Humoured Ladies,* with designs by Sue Blane based on the original Bakst. The orchestral concerts included music from Stravinsky's ballets.

Particular emphasis was placed on the exhibitions. A Degas Exhibition in the National Gallery made special reference to his ballet paintings and other works completed about 1879, the cost being shared between the Festival Society and the Gallery with additional sponsorship from British Petroleum. A second exhibition of ballet costumes, was organized by Alexander Schouvaloff of the Theatre Museum (part of the Victoria and Albert Museum in London), who was a former Artistic Assistant of the Festival. The Diaghilev theme was completed by a series of lectures on different aspects of his work and influence given by Richard Buckle, Moira Shearer, Anton Dolin, Noël Goodwin, Sir Charles Johnston and the Festival Director himself.

Drummond decided not to use the unsatisfactory Leith Town Hall. Instead he hired the new Queen's Hall which was being adapted from a disused church as a home for the Scottish Chamber Orchestra. It was a calculated risk that paid off. The acoustics proved ideal for the morning concerts and it was more central than Leith Town Hall. For ballet a large tent was erected in the Meadows similar to the one used by the Royal Ballet at Battersea Park in London. Here the Sadler's Wells Royal Ballet presented three different programmes including two premières, David Bintley's *Punch and the Street Party* and MacMillan's *Playground.* The National Ballet of Cuba made its first appearance in Britain with a selection of classical and modern works and its director, the legendary Alicia Alonso, recreated her famous interpretation of *Giselle.* In the third week the Merce Cunningham Dance Company gave a week of workshops and open rehearsals in Moray House Gymnasium. The Tent was an enormous success, but it took 15 months of negotiations with various departments of the District Council before permission was finally granted for its use, the licence arriving only two hours before the first performance was due to start. The cost of £60 000 was also prohibitive and, when the Society became involved in a legal dispute with the owners about who should pay for what, it was unlikely that it could be considered for future Festivals.

Drummond spent six months trying to persuade Paul McCartney and Wings to fill the empty evenings on the castle esplanade, but two weeks before the event they still had not made up their minds whether they wanted to come or not, or what it was going to cost, so Drummond lost patience with them and ceased negotiations.

Another innovation was having an Artist-in-Residence for each week of the Festival. James Galway was in Edinburgh for the first week and in addition to performances in the Usher Hall and Queen's Hall gave three in the Lyceum. In the second week the Netherlands Wind Ensemble agreed to give performances in various parts of the city, travelling between locations by minibus. Richard Rodney Bennett was the resident artist for the third week, giving a recital with Jane Manning and Richard Jackson and several late-night performances with Marian Montgomery. Drummond also arranged for Galway and the Netherlands Wind Ensemble to perform in a variety of spaces at different times of the day, from morning until late evening, as well as giving performances in schools throughout the region.

The concerts featured nine conductors who had never appeared at the Festival, or like Rozhdestvensky, had not appeared for 20 years. Included in the programmes were the world premières of *Sonnets to Orpheus* and the Horn Sonata by Bennett, *Dream Songs* by Gordon Crosse and Iain Hamilton's song cycle *The Spirit of Delight.* After the rich operatic feasts provided by Peter Diamand the 1979 diet, provided by Scottish Opera and the relatively inexperienced Kent Opera, was meagre to say the least. All five operas were

given in English, giving rise to a remark addressed to the Director by Riccardo Muti that in one stroke he had made the Festival provincial. With the exception of David Pountney's exotic *The Golden Cockerel* and Anthony Besch's magnificently atmospheric production of *The Turn of the Screw* the operas could hardly be described as Festival fare. There were some interesting touches in Jonathan Miller's *La Traviata*, but the sets and particularly the costumes were dowdy and the singers not up to their demanding roles.

True international fare was provided by the Rustaveli Company from Georgia in acclaimed performances of Brecht's *The Caucasian Chalk Circle* and Shakespeare's *Richard III*, and one of the most enchanting drama presentations so far seen at the Festival, an adaptation of a story by Balzac entitled *The Heartaches of an English Pussycat* by the Groupe TSE, an Argentinian company based in Paris, while the Traverse Theatre Company presented *Animal*, a new play by Tom McGrath.

To mark the twenty-fifth anniversary of the twinning of Edinburgh and Munich the latter sent an exhibition of the early works of Kandinsky which had never been seen in Britain. With the exception of the hanging, the catalogue and publicity, all charges were borne by the City of Munich.

There was no overall theme for the 1980 Festival. Instead, there was an emphasis on events from Canada and Australia where there was great enthusiasm for the Festival and a willingness to take part. Canadian arts were represented by Canadian Brass, the Toronto Mendelssohn Choir, drama companies from Vancouver and Ottawa, the folk group, Barde, and two exhibitions – a retrospective survey of one of Canada's leading twentieth-century artists, Jack Bush, and *The Legacy*. The latter was a collection of more than a hundred examples of north-west coast Indian art from the British Columbia Provincial Museum, tracing the history of each tribal group from the late eighteenth century to modern times. A live element in this exhibition was provided by the chief carver of the museum, Richard Hunt, who throughout the duration of the exhibition was to be observed in the foyer of the City Art Centre carving a totem pole which was subsequently presented to the City. After several unsuccessful attempts by his predecessors, Drummond at last persuaded a reluctant Festival Council to present the second major jazz event to be given in the official Festival, a concert in the Usher Hall by Oscar Peterson.

From Australia Drummond brought the dynamic young Australian Dance Theatre which had been founded five years before by the ex-Ballet Rambert dancer and choreographer, Jonathan Taylor. It gave the first European performances of Taylor's exciting full-length ballet, *Wildstars*. In the second programme his *Flibbertigibbet* totally captivated the audience as 13 boiler-suited dancers clambered precariously down the outsides of balconies and boxes to the stage where they continued their zany antics to the accompaniment of Bach's Italian Concerto with passing references to *Swan Lake* and *Giselle*.

The National Theatre, making its first appearance at the Festival, had two popular successes in Lillian Hellman's *Watch on the Rhine* with Peggy Ashcroft, and Bill Bryden's modern promenade version of the York and Wakefield mystery plays, *The Passion*, scenes from which were given during the day in Parliament Square. Peter Hall had originally offered a package of two plays: Howard Brenton's *The Romans in Britain*, which would have been very controversial, and an all-star production of *King Lear*. John Gielgud had agreed to give a few performances of Lear in the tiny Cottesloe Theatre, but when he

found he was expected to give a week of performances in the Assembly Hall in Edinburgh he argued that it was impossible. He was too old and his voice was no longer strong enough. After the deal with *King Lear* fell through Drummond lost interest in the Brenton play.

After three successful appearances on the Fringe Tadeusz Kantor's Cricot 2 finally gained official status with its highly dramatic and disturbing production of *Wielepole, Wielepole*. A dream-like evocation of events from the writer's childhood in Poland, it was described by Allen Wright as

> a fearsome dance of death, culminating in a grotesque travesty of the Last Supper, with a forest of bayonets and crucifixes being raised over the final scene of carnage ... These remarkable Poles, whose present base is Florence, never fail to astonish us, but 'Wielepole' must be their greatest achievement, and it is one of the most extraordinary experiences I have had at any Festival.
>
> (*Scotsman*, 27 August 1980)

Another dramatic triumph was the Vancouver East Cultural Centre's production of *Billy Bishop goes to War* with Eric Peterson impersonating not only the First World War air ace, but all the other roles as well. Their French Canadian compatriots from Ottawa presented a haunting puppet version of Strindberg's *Le Songe*, but were rather less successful with Büchner's *Woyzeck* which, in the opinion of James Fenton in the *Sunday Times* (31 August 1980), 'amounted to a sentimental travesty of a great play'.

Fenton found Scottish Opera's version of Berg's *Wozzeck* much more compelling: 'in terms of acting and production, this was a brilliant evocation of the age of expressionism. One saw, vividly, what that age had seen in Buechner ... And the acting was among the best in Edinburgh' (*Sunday Times*, 31 August 1980). Scottish Opera had a second winner with Janáček's *The Cunning Little Vixen* (a joint production with the Welsh National Opera) with Helen Field giving a brilliantly athletic performance as the Vixen. As a replacement for the Opera du Rhin, which had cancelled because of financial and technical difficulties, the Cologne Opera came to the rescue with a charming production of Cimarosa's *Il Matrimonio Segreto*, and a slightly disappointing *Così fan Tutte,* although there were compensations in the singing of Julia Varady and Ann Murray as the sisters and in the conducting of John Pritchard. But the main operatic event was Peter Maxwell Davies's new opera *The Lighthouse*, the first work to be presented by the Festival under the Tennent Caledonian sponsorship scheme for the commissioning of new works. Based on events in the Flannan Islands in 1900 when three lighthouse keepers mysteriously disappeared Maxwell Davies created, in the words of Robert Henderson in *Opera* (Autumn 1980), 'a work of tense, riveting, cumulatively harrowing power ... it is on every level a score of compelling virtuosity'.

The Usher Hall organ, for many years a bone of contention between the Society and the District Council which had steadfastly refused either to replace or repair it, aroused the wrath of Claudio Abbado. After he refused to consider its use for the organ solos in Berlioz's *Te Deum,* arrangements were made for Gillian Weir to perform them on the organ of St Mary's Cathedral a mile away and, by courtesy of the BBC, the sound was relayed to loudspeakers in the Hall and contact maintained by closed circuit television. At the conclusion a police escort brought Miss Weir to the Usher Hall to take her place on the platform for the final calls.

Drummond's extended ballet season in 1981 was not quite the success that he had anticipated. The critics were rather lukewarm in their praise of the San Francisco Ballet and the Dan Wagoner Company, both appearing for the first time in this country. Even London Contemporary Dance Theatre's new work *Dances of Love and Death*, in which Cohan re-created in choreographic terms the conflict of love and death in relation to five mythological and literary couples, was considered over-long.

After a long history of exceptional Festival productions Scottish Opera's *The Beggar's Opera* in an inflated and overelaborate arrangement by Guy Woolfenden, misfired. Far more noteworthy were the contributions by the Scottish Opera Chorus and Scottish Chamber Orchestra to the Cologne Opera's *Il Barbiere di Siviglia* – a new production mounted specially for the Festival. Together with Ponnelle's production of Mozart's *La Clemenza di Tito,* it proved ideal for the King's Theatre stage. The company's third offering was a studio production of Thea Musgrave's *The Voice of Ariadne* but, according to Rodney Milnes in *Opera* (Autumn 1981), it was 'experimental only in so far that it was extremely good ... This engrossing performance ... proved that an opera too many of us had virtually written off seven years ago was a valid and exciting work of art. How nice to be wrong'.

Of the musical premières the most important was John Tavener's deeply moving memorial to Anna Akhmatova which Desmond Shawe-Taylor in the *Sunday Times* (23 August 1981) thought would be 'remembered as the main event of the 1981 Edinburgh Festival'. David Cairns in the same paper (6 September 1981) described Menotti's *Moans,Groans, Cries, Sighs, or a Composer at Work* performed by the King's Singers, as 'a piece of deeply embarrassing naivety', while in the *Scotsman* (4 September 1981) Conrad Wilson thought that the lowest point was Stephen Oliver's *Namings*, 'a nondescript new sub-Brittenish setting of some vivid words, the musical ideas boringly bland, the ideas tantalisingly unseized'. The outstanding Festival discovery was the brilliant young double-bass player, Gary Karr. Of his recital in the Freemasons' Hall, Conrad Wilson commented:

> Mr. Karr is a phenomenon, a virtuoso of the double-bass. With a complete absence of fuss and even a benign smile, he draws Orphean sounds from his 1611 Amati which I would swear were not technically possible. In his hands, an instrument usually considered intractable and gruff, at best corroborative and at worst slightly grotesque, turns into a sweet and versatile singer, capable of sonorous nobility, or noble eloquence and of extraordinary agility.
>
> (C. Wilson, *Scotsman*, 21 August 1981)

The main musical attraction, Abbado's weighty account of Bach's *St Matthew Passion* with the Festival Chorus, London Symphony Orchestra and a star line-up of soloists (Margaret Price, Jessye Norman, Peter Schreier, Hermann Prey, Philip Langridge and Gwynne Howell) drew some scathing comments from the critics but met with the approval of the capacity audience. The performance might have been heavier still had Abbado not pruned the 240-strong chorus to 140, thereby upsetting many choristers who, having thoroughly rehearsed the work, were extremely disgruntled to be informed a few days before that they would not be required. Letters of complaint to the Festival Director were met with the reply that 'it was the conductor's prerogative to decide what forces he required' and a plea that the Chorus should 'behave professionally' – perhaps not the most appropriate comment to make to an amateur body. But much annoyance could have been averted if the conductor had realized earlier that 240 choristers were too many for Bach.

For once the drama programme was greeted with almost complete approval by the critics, particularly Allan Wright who commented in cricketing terms in the *Scotsman* (22 August 1981): 'The pace at which the Festival Director has been bowling bumpers at us this week has been staggering. In six deliveries of drama on successive evenings, John Drummond has taken five wickets.' The one 'miss hit' was the Birmingham Repertory Company's *As You Like It*. When negotiations were in progress Drummond had stressed the neccessity for star casting, and when the company had failed to comply he had considered cancelling the visit. The 'bumpers' included the National Theatre of Rumania in a comedy by Terence, *The Girl from Andros,* and a splendid production of Racine's *Britannicus*, in which the director recreated the Palace of Versailles. In the final week the National Theatre gave the première of Tom Stoppard's *On the Razzle*, with Felicity Kendal, although relations between the Festival Society and the National Theatre were hardly improved when the published text of the play stated that the first performance was at the Lyttleton Theate on 22 September instead of in Edinburgh on 1 September.

An exhibition of Latin American Art had been planned but had had to be cancelled when the Mexican Government refused to lend certain items. Instead the Museum of Modern Art in New York had been extremely helpful in providing alternatives and had offered two exhibitions, one of 40 to 50 paintings and sculptures from its own galleries, and a photography exhibition which had recently been shown in Paris. For these the Museum had obtained a grant of $75 000 from the Heinz Foundation to assist with costs. In the Lyceum Little Gallery there was a curious exhibition of postcards and other exhibits displaying the exploitation of the Scottish image called *Scotch Myths*, organized by Murray and Barbara Grigor.

In association with the Television Festival there was a conference, Television and the Arts, in which Huw Wheldon introduced and chaired six discussions on television's treatment of different aspects of the arts. The contributors included Jeremy Isaacs, Melvyn Bragg, Humphrey Burton, Raymond Leppard, Jonathan Miller and the Festival Director.

Although the 1981 Festival had been a box office success it had nevertheless resulted in a net deficit of over £46 000, the largest in its history. The exhibitions had drawn poor attendances due to the counter attraction of excellent weather. An excessive amount of overtime had to be paid at the King's Theatre in the remaking of sets for the visit of the Cologne Opera, and also at the Lyceum by the National Theatre's production of *On the Razzle*; and there had been the high cost of converting the Assembly Hall and Moray House into theatres

Drummond's contract was due for renewal in September 1983. He had agreed to an extension for a further two years but made it clear that he had no wish to be associated with a Festival of declining standards. He had gathered around him an outstanding team and he felt that such excellence had to be matched by a willingness on the part of the Festival Council to find an answer to the Society's financial problems. The Society was having difficulty attracting new sponsors and Drummond's suggestion that an approach should be made to a firm of professional fund-raisers was accepted. Accordingly Kallaway Associates was appointed to increase sponsorship for the Festival.

In view of the disappointing attendances Drummond had revised his thoughts on the presentation of exhibitions of a similar size and nature. A number of artistic organizations within the city arranged exhibitions during the Festival, and he considered it would be

more appropriate to invite these organizations to continue this practice, leaving the Society to present a major exhibition of outstanding interest every three or four years. For 1982 two official exhibitions had been arranged: *Circles of the World* in the Royal Scottish Museum, which was being financed by American Express, the Society's financial contribution being limited to approximately £2 000 for transport to and from America; and *British Watercolours from 1750 to the present day*, presented in association with the British Council. As there was space in the programme brochure a larger number of 'associated exhibitions' were included.

The current year, 1982, was to be an Italian year but from the beginning everything seemed to go wrong. An exhibition of Italian contemporary art was cancelled for financial reasons (a similar exhibition had been cancelled in 1969) and there were problems finding suitable Italian theatre companies. Drummond and his assistant, Richard Jarman, spent the winter flying to and from the Continent desperately hunting for Italian productions and drawing a blank. In the end they settled for three highly unusual companies: the Akroama Company from Sardinia with *Mariedda*, a folk-musical version of Hans Andersen's *The Little Match Girl*, and the Carlo Colla Marionette Company from Milan with 250 beautifully dressed puppets in re-creations of nineteenth-century theatre productions. The third Italian offering was the Cooperativa Teatromusica from Rome with an almost incomprehensible Metastasian 'opera without music', *L'Olimpiade* which, in spite of a brilliant production by Sandro Sequi, had the usual effect of an opera libretto on an audience, but without the saving grace of the music. Even with music, Peter Ustinov's adaptation of Gogol's *The Marriage* was an expensive failure. La Scala had wanted to stage Mussorgsky's unfinished opera and had commissioned Ustinov to write a play that would contain the opera in its original form. The result was a boring hybrid. To make matters worse the original sets got lost on their way from Milan. As the set consisted of backstage props for an opera, an SOS was sent to Scottish Opera which supplied something similar within a few hours. There were also problems with the British contributions. Drummond's plans had included the National Theatre in a production of *A Midsummer Night's Dream* with Paul Scofield and Susan Fleetwood, but this had come to grief because of timetabling problems. Then the recently formed Scottish Theatre Company, which had been given the Tennent Caledonian Award of £25 000 to produce *Commedia*, a new play by Marcella Evaristi, had to withdraw when Evaristi failed to complete it on time.

When he announced his programme Drummond had predicted that it would plunge the critics into a demarcation dispute with the music, drama and dance critics treading on each other's toes. This, he felt, was all to the good, for the performing arts should be integrated with each other and not placed in separate specialized compartments. Almost every theatrical production turned out to be a blend of drama with some other art form – dance, mime, opera or music.

In line with his stated policy of rotating the balance of different art forms each year, Drummond had decided that the emphasis in 1982 would be on opera with performances by no less than four distinguished companies; an act of atonement for the lean effort of the previous year. Unfortunately a deal with the Florence Maggio Musicale, which was to bring a late seventeenth-century *commedia dell'arte* piece by Leonardo Vinci and Sciarrino's *Macbeth*, collapsed when the director of the Maggio Musicale, Bogianckino, left Florence and Sciarrino did not complete *Macbeth*. At nine months' notice Drummond

managed to get La Piccola Scala. Edinburgh had waited 25 years for a return visit by this company and the witty scintillating production of Rossini's *La Pietra del Paragone* and highly stylized *Ariodante* by Handel, both beautifully sung, were well worth the wait.

Another Handel opera, *Tamburlaine*, was given by the Welsh National Opera in a controversial production by Philip Prowse, though Rodney Milnes in *Opera* (Autumn 1982) failed to see where the 'controversy' came in as, in his view, the production was 'simply ghastly' and an 'act of mindless vandalism'. In particular he, like a number of other critics, objected to the distracting activities of the extras during the arias. On the credit side, though, he found some of the singing 'very fine'. Fine singing, however, was not a feature of the visit by the Dresden State Opera, nor was the conducting beyond criticism, but there was compensation in the beautiful playing of the Dresden Staatskapelle whose 'superb musicality and technical mastery' were, in the words of Peter Heyworth in the *Observer* (29 August 1982), 'an unfailing joy to the ear'. Scottish Opera was represented by its new production of Puccini's *Manon Lescaut* with the Rumanian soprano Nelly Miricioiu in the title role – the first major opera by Puccini to be presented at the Festival

The Italian theme was most apparent in the concerts, where works by 40 Italian composers from Monteverdi to Nono were played. According to David Cairns in the *Sunday Times* (29 August 1982) the opening concert by the London Symphony Orchestra under Abbado 'vindicated Edinburgh's international claims. Any Festival in the world would be pleased to be able to put on two performances of Verdi's *Requiem* with a solo quartet consisting of Margaret Price, Jessye Norman, José Carreras and Ruggero Raimondi'. In the morning concerts there was praise for Dominic Muldowney's Second Quartet (a Festival commission) performed by the Medici Quartet, which David Cairns found 'an attractively whimsical, spiky but fundamentally lyrical work' (ibid.). There was praise, too, for Michael Berkeley's Sonata for Guitar of which Neville Garden wrote in the *Sunday Standard* (29 August 1982), 'Those fearing something "difficult" and highly contemporary, must have been relieved to hear its rich, romantic sonorities. It even had some tunes'. Glamour and excitement were provided by the Labèque sisters in their two-piano recital in the Queen's Hall.

The strangest performance of the Festival was an act called *Sholika*, meaning the hanging of meat in a butcher's shop. It took place in the open air when four nearly naked actors from the Japanese Sankai Juku troupe, braving the Edinburgh elements, were slowly lowered upside down from the top of the 50-foot high Lothian Regional Council Chambers in Parliament Square. (It proved such a sensation that they were persuaded to remain in the city an extra day so that they could give a repeat performance on Fringe Sunday.) This was a foretaste of what was to come in the full-length dance drama *Kinshan Shonen*. The most mesmerizing scene was of a dwarf turning into a man and dancing with a live peacock, which remained on the stage throughout the performance, strutting and preening in a pool of light. The accompanying Western-style music ranged from the the wail of bagpipes, by way of jazz and rock, to the 'New World' Symphony. The other dance company, the Antonio Gades Company, was a late replacement for the Geneva Opera-Ballet which had withdrawn because the director was Argentinian and he felt that the tensions occasioned by the conflict in the Falklands made a visit at this time inappropriate. The Gades Company presented a highly dramatic flamenco version of Lorca's *Blood Wedding*, culminating in a silent slow motion duel with knives in which

both the protagonists were killed. After an agonized pause, punctuated by rhythmic finger clicks, the guests departed to cunningly suggested horse beats. These dance performances were given in a new venue, the Assembly Rooms in George Street, which until 1980 had been used as the Festival Club. In 1981 it had been taken over by Associate Productions Limited, headed by William Burdett-Coutts, as a multiple venue for sub-letting to Fringe groups. Drummond had been impressed with the organization and operation of this venue and believed the Society should become involved, thus creating a half-way house between the Festival and the Fringe. He arranged for the Society to rent certain of the performance areas within the Assembly Rooms complex. Some Council members had expressed concern that if the project was unsuccessful considerable adverse criticism would be directed against the Society, and that there could be problems if events fully financed by the Festival Society were not under its complete control. In the event these fears proved to be groundless.

In his attempts to involve the ordinary citizens in the Festival and increase the festive atmosphere Drummond introduced more street events. In addition to the feats of Sankai Juku there were daily demonstrations of the medieval art of flag-throwing by a group called I Sbandieratori from the Umbrian town of Gubbio, which was similar to the popular Le Contrade di Cori of 1979. But the most popular event of all was a late-night concert, organized by the Scottish Chamber Orchestra in association with Glenlivet, in the Ross Bandstand in Princes Street Gardens. The programme consisted of Haydn's Trumpet Concerto and the coronation anthem *Zadok the Priest* by Handel, culminating in a grand finale as Handel's *Music for the Royal Fireworks* was performed to the accompaniment of a huge barrage of fireworks exploding, cascading and showering down from the battlements of the castle. As on that memorable night in 1947, when permission had been granted for floodlighting the castle, thousands of citizens poured into the centre of the City until the Gardens and the surrounding streets were tightly packed by a solid mass of people, those unable to get near the bandstand listening to the concert on transistor radios. The concert proved so popular that it has been repeated, with variations, every year.

The second Sunday of the Festival was designated 'Fringe Sunday'. In the afternoon the High Street was closed to traffic and about 70 Fringe groups seized the opportunity of gaining free publicity for their shows and performed to an estimated audience of 30 000. The entertainments included a car chase from a Bond film with sound effects from a cast of two, a drama performed by a troupe who emerged from a giant porridge oats packet and a rather more politically conscious group sending up the French Revolution on the back of a lorry! Festival visitors discovered that a Scottish Sunday does not necessarily have to be dull – all that was needed was a lot of people dressing up and doing outrageous things under the very nose of John Knox. Earlier in the day a field of 900 Fringe performers had lined up for the first Fringe Fun Run when Romans, Hawaiian dancers, over-age infants, a group of scouts shackled together, spidermen, a gorilla, and a few eccentrics looking like athletes ran round Holyrood Park, the proceeds going to the Scottish Trust for the Physically Disabled. Then the carnival spilled into Princes Street for the parade to launch the five-day Edinburgh International Jazz Festival where jazz bands 'oompahed' from their floats to the rhythms of New Orleans, cajoling all but the dourest Festival critic away from his Sunday siesta to join in the fun. Another strictly unofficial event took place in Inverleith Park during the following week when teams from La Piccola Scala and Scottish Opera staged a friendly football match.

Although it contained some splendid moments Drummond did not feel that the 1982 Festival would be remembered as among the most outstanding. Attendances at the Usher Hall and King's Theatre were down in comparison with previous years and he attributed this to customer resistance to high ticket prices and unknown works, and too many orchestral concerts. The opera had been well received but had achieved disappointing sales, while drama, which had sold well had attracted much adverse criticism. The public had also been unhappy at the non-use of the Assembly Hall, which had been used every year since 1948. The Festival had been more contentious than previous ones. The Director himself had been disappointed by *Entführung* and the American Repertory Theatre's production of *Lulu*, whilst other productions, especially *The Marriage* had been heavily attacked by the critics. It had been a difficult year brought about by a number of cancellations, and Drummond felt that these problems had not always been acknowledged by the critics.

Drummond and some members of the Council were particularly concerned about the persistent criticism directed at the Festival by Conrad Wilson, the music critic of the *Scotsman*, which might have been instrumental in dissuading people from buying tickets. It was suggested that Wilson should be relieved of his duties as Festival programme editor, but this was a difficult situation which required careful consideration. However, the dilemma was resolved when Wilson, fully aware that the Festival Director was piqued by his comments on the way the musical side of the Festival had been planned since he took over, resigned.

At the Annual General Meeting of the Society on 22 February 1983 the perennial complaint about the lack of Scottish representation at the Festival was raised yet again. Drummond promised that in 1983 there would be a strong Scottish presence and that this representation had been included because of the high quality of the participants. At the same time he defended his invitations to overseas companies on the grounds that audiences in the UK seldom had the chance to see foreign companies and as a large proportion of Festival tickets were taken up by Edinburgh people there seemed little point in promoting purely Scottish events.

Fees already arranged with overseas companies were now being affected by the falling rate of sterling, thus adding to the expenditure on productions. Drummond had been forced to renegotiate a contract with the Hamburg State Opera, and the Opera Theater of St Louis had also asked for an increased payment. This, together with galloping inflation and the rise in rents had encouraged Drummond to hope for an increased grant for 1983. When it was announced at a Council meeting on 7 March 1983 that this would only be 5 per cent higher than the previous year it became apparent that, even though various cuts had already been made in the programme – including a visit by the Ballet of the Komische Opera, Berlin and a contemporary music group – the deficit for 1983 would be around £70 000. Drummond was asked to make further cuts amounting to £30 000. After expressing his extreme disappointment at the level of the grant Drummond proposed that, instead of making further cuts, the Council should help him raise the money. When it refused he abruptly left the meeting. The following Monday, after a weekend of deliberation in which he concluded that he wasn't enjoying the job any more, he announced that he wished to leave when his present contract expired on 30 September 1983.

Anger and disappointment at the curtailing of his carefully laid plans for the 1983 Festival, and the reluctance of the Council to take any responsibility for fund-raising, were not the only reasons for Drummond's decision. During the next few months he was quite outspoken to the press about the reasons for his imminent departure. Near the top of the list was the attitude of the District Council which, while reluctant to spend more money on a Festival which brought an estimated £20 million into the city each year, was prepared to find £13 million for the 1986 Commonwealth Games. He had been forced to spend more time raising money for the Festival than actually organizing it, which was not what he was trained for, or what he had come to Edinburgh to do. Worst of all was the sheer embarrassment of trying to persuade leading opera and dance companies to perform in conditions which made it impossible for them to present their work properly. The alternative was to accept second- or even third-class standards which he was not prepared to do; the Festival had to operate on the highest level or not at all. He found it unacceptable and indefensible that in 1983 the buildings and other facilities were in almost the same condition as they had been 37 years before. It was the Ponsonby story all over again. Without another job in prospect Drummond was prepared to risk unemployment rather than betray 'certain principles'.

In the meantime two other projects were foundering. The Lyceum Company had planned to celebrate the theatre's centenary with an entertainment by Tom Gallagher entitled *Time Present,* tracing the history of the theatre and featuring a number of leading Scottish artists. After reading the script the Drama Advisory Panel on 7 March and 5 July 1983 decided it would have to be revised. There were also doubts about the choice of Leslie Lawton as director as it was felt that some leading actors might not be prepared to appear with him. When Lawton admitted he was experiencing difficulty in casting it Drummond decided not to proceed with *Time Present.* In its place he arranged to bring a production of Chekhov's *The Cherry Orchard* with a very distinguished cast including Joan Plowright and Frank Finlay.

The other problem concerned Scottish Opera. Following a visit to the King's Theatre the designer of the proposed production of *Death in Venice* had concluded that the sets, originally designed for the Playhouse, would be too large for the King's and that the adjustments required would be so extreme that the resulting production would not be worthy of the Festival. This was a joint production with the Opera-Theatre of Geneva and, knowing that the stage in Geneva was twice the size of the King's, Drummond had expressed reservations about its suitability. No contract had yet been signed with Scottish Opera and after discussing various unsatisfactory options the Finance Committee (30 May 1983) took the view that, as the King's had been well known to Scottish Opera for the past 20 years, the blame rested entirely with the company and it was asked to suggest alternative proposals including, if necessary, the preparation of new scenery. Scottish Opera offered to allocate a sum of £3 650 from its own resources towards the estimated cost of £9 500 for redesigning the set to fit the King's. In the end the Society agreed to meet half the costs and Scottish Opera was asked to meet the balance of £4 750 (Council meeting 15 July 1983). Technical difficulties also caused the transfer of the Hungarian State Ballet from the Music Hall to the Playhouse and, as the Musicians' Union would not allow taped music for performances, arrangements were made for a small group of musicians and singers to provide the music

Drummond had for some time been irritated by the infrastructure of advisory committees which were frequently obstructive and time-wasting. His parting gift to the Festival

was a proposal that the structure of the committees be reorganized and his recommendations were submitted to the Finance and General Purposes Committee for consideration.

Had he planned it Drummond could not have chosen a better finale. *Vienna 1900* was the most thoroughly worked-out and integrated of all the Edinburgh Festivals. It was a subject after Drummond's own heart. Schoenberg, Webern, Zemlinsky, Mahler, Rilke, Hoffmansthal. Kokoschka, Werfel and Berg had all been working together in Vienna at that time. Trying to recreate the cultural climate of the period, when new currents of thought were flowing simultaneoulsy in all the arts, gave him an opportunity to bring together the different disciplines to an even greater extent than before; at the same time emphasizing the strengths and the uniqueness of the Edinburgh Festival in a way that no previous director had succeeded in doing. This central theme inspired not only the main *Vienna 1900* exhibition, which brought to Edinburgh designs, furniture and costumes connected with the Viennese Secession, but ran through more than half of the 160 performances, taking in opera, ballet, concerts, drama and lectures. To complement this exhibition the Fine Arts Society reconstructed the Scottish Room designed by Charles Rennie Mackintosh for the Eighth Exhibition of the Vienna Secession. The other main exhibition, a unique exploration of *Man and Music*, took two years to prepare and enabled the Royal Scottish Museum's own magnificent collection of ethnic musical instruments to be displayed for the first time. It was organized by Jean Jenkins, one of the world's foremost authorities on the subject. As part of the exhibition there were concerts by groups of musicians from the countries represented, who also gave performances in various outdoor locations throughout the city. The Royal Scottish Academy exhibited the unique *Rothschild Exhibition* of wine labels designed by Braque, Cocteau, Chagall, Henry Moore, Picasso and others, and in the City Arts Centre there was the Sackler Collection of *Pre-Columbian Art of the Andean Indians.*

The previous year, following the withdrawal of the Scottish Theatre Company, Tennent Caledonian had allowed the award to be transferred to La Piccola Scala. This year it had been awarded to the Ballet Rambert for *Morder, Hoffnung der Frauen*, a ballet by Glen Tetley based on the play by Kokoschka. Drummond had encouraged a group of students to present the original play but Tetley protested and instead the students performed an earlier work by Kokoschka. Drummond thought Tetley's objections unreasonable until he discovered that Tetley had decided not to include the 25 minutes of choreography, for which the company had been awarded the commission, and the dancers performed the play. As most of them were unable to act, the main points of the drama were not made and most of it was inaudible. In the words of Drummond it was a 'total disaster' and one of the few events during his time that he considered a 'terrible failure'. It was unfortunate as, after that, the Tennent Caledonian award lapsed. After three failures in a row to one success it was difficult to present a strong enough argument for its continuation, particularly as the chairman of Bass Charrington had been opposed to the idea from the beginning and it had been the subject of a number of board-room battles, but in spite of these, Hamish Swann of Tennent Caledonian had managed to keep the award going for four years.

Musically the Festival brought to light some of the work of the hitherto unknown Zemlinsky. Indeed it was seeing his two one-act operas in Hamburg that had given Drummond the inspiration for his theme. On his arrival home, one of his staff had inquired, 'Who is Zemlinsky?' Trying to explain this gave him the idea and then it

snowballed. Zemlinsky's operas, and the performance by the Tokyo Quartet of his String Quartet No. 3 were among the highlights of the Festival. The Glasgow Citizens' Theatre Company's contribution to the theme was an imaginative production of *Der Rosenkavalier* (von Hoffmansthal without Strauss) and a four-hour adaptation of Karl Kraus's mammoth *The Last Days of Mankind* in which Kraus as the voice of sanity comments on the enormities of the First World War. Undeniably an apt play for a Festival, it yet proved something of an endurance test for even the most resilient theatre-goer. Kraus's great friend, Otto Weininger, who committed suicide at the age of 23, was the subject of Yehoshua Sobol's extraordinary play *Soul of a Jew* given by the Haifa Municipal Theatre. Both this and *Poppie Nongena*, a heart-breaking picture of the life of a black woman in South Africa movingly portrayed by Thuli Dumakude, were given in Burdett-Coutts's Assembly Rooms complex.

This year also saw the first visit to the Festival by an American opera company. With its productions of *Fennimore and Gerda* by Delius and *The Postman Always Rings Twice* by Paulus, the young Opera Theater of St Louis lived up to Andrew Porter's tribute in *Opera* that it was America's most exciting company: 'It is a combination of adventurous repertory, lustrous young casts, imaginative direction, and the dramatic vividness achieved by singers who sing and act in a language understood which has made it so.' In a concert ambitiously entitled *Stars of St Louis* the young singers showed themselves equally at home in more conventional repertoire . Among the stars were Jerry Hadley, Susanne Mentzer and Frederick Burchinal all making promising UK debuts.

One of Drummond's aims had been to widen the parameters of the Festival and in his second year he organized a Writers' Conference, the first since the ill-fated Drama Conference in 1963, bringing together a large number of prominent writers to discuss the English language. This was followed in 1981 by a conference on *Television and the Arts* and in 1982 by one on *The State and the Arts*. By this time there was a growing feeling in Edinburgh that the Festival embraced all the art forms except literature – a view shared by Drummond himself. With his encouragement a committee was formed under the chairmanship of Lord Balfour of Burleigh (a former chairman of the Scottish Arts Council) to organize a book fair at the 1983 Festival, with funding from the Scottish Arts Council. As a large percentage of the population never entered either a bookshop or a library it was decided to hold it in a large tent in Charlotte Square Gardens. Jenny Brown, formerly Assistant Administrator of the Fringe, was appointed Director with Valerie Bierman as the Children's Fair Organizer. With 120 authors, including John Updike, Anthony Burgess and Anita Desai taking part, and an attendance of about 30 000 people, the Book Festival was an immediate success and it was later established as a biennial event.

John Drummond was perhaps the most multifaceted of all the Festival Directors and his five Festivals were by far the most finely balanced, almost equal emphasis being given to all the art forms. With his championship of Scottish companies, artists and particularly his poetry and prose recitals such as the series on Gaelic culture *Dualchas*, he was the first Director to give Scottish arts and culture a truly prominent place in the Festival. His one regret in this respect was that the upheaval in Scottish Opera's administration on the departure of Peter Hemmings made it difficult for him to maintain the same mutually satisfactory arrangement that had been possible in Diamand's time. Drummond also succeeded in breaking down the barriers between the official Festival and the Fringe,

a factor that had troubled both Harewood and Diamand, but neither had found a solution to the problem. But his greatest contribution was in making the Festival more acceptable to the ordinary people of Edinburgh. He is still unconvinced that his efforts in this direction bore fruit but, as in the case of the theatres, he did the spadework, paving the way for Frank Dunlop who was to follow him.

Chapter 8

Frank Dunlop 1984–1991

The abrupt resignation of John Drummond gave the Council little time to find a successor. Frank Dunlop was one of a list of people whose names had been mentioned as possible candidates for the position of Festival Director. At that time he was earning a great deal of money in America and might not have been interested in the post but, having directed regularly at the Festival over many years, he volunteered to tell the Council what he thought was wrong with the Festival. He then flew overnight to London, caught the shuttle to Edinburgh and arrived at the Caledonian Hotel for a meeting. Exhausted from jet lag he sat down on a sofa and promptly fell asleep. The next thing he knew the secretary of the Council was leaning over him asking if he was Frank Dunlop as they had been searching all over for him. Dunlop insisted that the Festival was not getting through to the ordinary people of Edinburgh who looked on it as too esoteric and 'not for them'. The Festival should be for everybody. He also felt that the Regional Council should come back in to provide additional financial support.

When the word got round that the Festival Council was considering offering Dunlop the post it had been lobbied by some members of the Establishment that he would be a dangerous choice. Instead of deterring them this opposition made some Festival Councillors more eager to appoint Dunlop. They wanted someone who would take a fresh look at the Festival and who would not be afraid to take risks. Dunlop, always willing to take up a challenge, agreed and for the first time in its history the Festival had a theatre man as Director. In announcing the appointment the Lord Provost stated that this should not be regarded as a change in policy in relation to future festivals; not only would the existing high standards of music be maintained, but drama would play a particularly exciting part. The Council also agreed to Dunlop's request that he be allowed to accept occasional outside work in addition to his duties as Director.

Attendances at Festival events had tended to drop during the third week and Dunlop recommended that the Festival should begin a week earlier. The dates had originally been fixed so that Edinburgh would not be competing with other European festivals for the same companies, orchestras and artists, but he felt that this was no longer an important factor. The main event scheduled for the third week of the 1984 Festival was a visit by the Vienna Philharmonic Orchestra but, even with heavy sponsorship, the cost was likely to be far in excess of the normal fee paid by the Society. As Dunlop envisaged no difficulty in finding suitable events for the new first week the Festival

Council, after vociferous discussion, agreed to the change of dates for the 1984 Festival.

Dunlop had been warned by Drummond about the various advisory panels which he had considered unnecessary. Preferring to take advice from individuals rather than wasting time with committees, but not sure how to approach the matter, Dunlop consulted with Lord Cameron. His advice was short and to the point: 'Best thing to do is get rid of them, now! Don't delay and don't be diplomatic about it. Just get rid of them!' Without wasting time, Dunlop wrote and disbanded the panels.

Drummond's legacy to Dunlop was a deficit of just under £175 500, the largest on record. Dunlop was justifiably annoyed at starting off with such a millstone and declared that had he known about it before his appointment he would probably have turned the job down. Approaches were made to Edinburgh District Council and the Scottish Arts Council for assistance to offset this shortfall and to enable the Society to meet its commitments until the District Council's grant towards the 1984 Festival was received in April. The District Council responded with a supplementary grant of £70 000 and the Scottish Arts Council gave an additional £10 000. A further £26 498 came from the Capital Fund. After paying the bills the Society was still left with an overdraft of £22 000.

Dunlop sought the approval of the Finance Committee for the 1984 estimate to be based on a break-even position with no provision being made for paying off the outstanding deficit. Paying it off in one year would involve cutting down drastically on events for 1984. But the Committee felt that, having come through a particularly disappointing financial year, the Society's actions would be under close scrutiny by both funding organizations and therefore Dunlop must try and eliminate as much as possible of the deficit within that year.

Dunlop was also rather unhappy about the performance of the firm of professional fund-raisers appointed to raise sponsorship for the Festival. Kallaway Associates had been concentrating its efforts on finding a 'mega' sponsor but so far had not achieved the results expected. There were fears that such a sponsor would insist on the maximum publicity which could result in the Festival losing its identity. Such massive exposure by one company might also discourage smaller companies from sponsoring individual Festival events. Dunlop believed that the Society should revert to its own sponsorship-seeking arrangements and it was agreed that Kallaway's contract should be terminated when it ran out at the end of 1984, and in 1985 Wendy Stephenson was appointed Sponsorship Manager. But then problems arose with Kallaway which, due to the inadequate wording of the original contract, was claiming commission in perpetuity on the donations from the companies it had secured. An offer of £5 000 was made to Kallaway to terminate the contract but this was rejected and Mr Kallaway threatened that if the full settlement of £15 000 was not made he would place the matter in the hands of his legal advisers, and it was October 1987 before the matter was finally resolved. The decision by the Council to appoint its own fund-raiser was overwhelmingly vindicated when in the intervening two years sponsorship and donations increased from £316 027 in 1985 to £512 873 in 1987, and by the end of Dunlop's period of office in 1991 this had increased to almost £796 681.

In May 1984 another event took place that was to have a far-reaching effect on the Festival when, in the local council elections, the Conservative Group who had been responsible for Dunlop's appointment was ousted and Labour gained control of the

District Council. Almost immediately it announced a change in policy towards the Festival and the arts in general. At a conference on *The Future of the Arts in Edinburgh* the Labour administration announced its intention of 'spreading the Festival atmosphere throughout the rest of the year'. The Festival would no longer be the 'all-consuming aspect of the arts in Edinburgh'. In future the emphasis would be on community events involving people actually doing things rather than on prestigious building projects such as the grandiose opera house plan. It also attacked the ingrained élitism of the Festival and indicated that its grant could be withdrawn if the Festival did not embrace a wider section of the community. The Labour leader Alex Wood was quoted in several national newspapers as stating that unless the Festival got rid off its 'stuffed shirt image' the Council was prepared to 'pull the plug on the Festival' and it 'would do it tomorrow', a statement that he reaffirmed during the Festival on national radio and television. Referring to the resulting carping attacks made on councillors' philistinism Councillor George Kerevan added that these 'proved that there was an arts establishment in Edinburgh', adding, 'we declare war on it; we will abolish it; we will democratize it'.

All these threatening statements were made before any of the Group took the trouble to discover what Dunlop's own plans for the future might be. In an attempt to calm the situation Dunlop requested a meeting with some of the District Councillors in which he declared that he was not their political opponent. He had always loved the Festival and was prepared to fight for it. He pointed out that Edinburgh was a great historical city, a capital without the responsibilities of government, and could become the cultural capital of the world, thus giving the city a true purpose. When it transpired that many of Dunlop's ideas about popularizing the Festival fitted in broadly with those of the District Council a temporary truce was called. In a letter to the Festival Society, August 1983, Councillor Wood welcomed Dunlop's decision to take some Festival events to outlying areas of the capital and hoped that this would be the 'beginning of a truly popular Festival. I consider this to be a major break-through and I trust that it is an indication of the policy of the Festival in the years to come.' In a statement to the press Dunlop said that the Festival had triumphed over the 'hysterical controversy' of recent months. The unusual circumstances had not made his life easy, adding, 'I am hoping and praying that we are going to be left to get on with the job, but I am a little nervous that somebody may say "You are not allowed to spend our money on that"'.

The rift may have been temporarily healed but while it lasted it created a great deal of adverse publicity for the Festival in the national press and even on television. The BBC's *Newsnight* and *The Times* speculated on how long the Festival could survive, the *Guardian* suggested it should be put out to tender like the Olympic Games, but the most unbridled attack came from Rodney Milnes:

> What may happen in Edinburgh has less to do with socialism than with John Knoxery, xenophobia and foam-flecked, purulent hatred of quality and pleasure, all British characteristics from time immemorial but seen at their most virulent in the Scottish capital ... There will be little prospect of largesse in the less immediate future unless the Festival programme is limited to ethnic street theatre (and Scottish ethnic at that) and wholly innocent of militaristic obscenities like the Tattoo and such foreign élitist filth as opera and ballet.
>
> (R. Milnes, *Spectator*, 26 May 1984)

There was no all-embracing theme for the 1984 Festival but ensconced in the drama programme was a mini-festival of the work of Samuel Beckett. There were two pro-

grammes of short plays given by the Harold Clurman Theatre from New York, Max Wall read extracts from *Malone Dies* and John Calder compiled a programme entitled *From its Beginning to its End* which featured extracts from the author's prose, poetry and drama illustrating Beckett's views of life in all its aspects. The Beckett season was completed by an 11-day programme of talks, discussions, films and television programmes – an entirely new innovation for the Festival.

The other important element was an increased emphasis on the visual arts. This was due largely to the efforts of the American multimillionaire Dr Arthur Sackler, who had a vision of Edinburgh as an international centre for the arts and sciences. In 1982 he had lent part of his own collection for the Piranesi Exhibition and the following year his collection of Pre-Columbian Art of the Andean Indians. With his backing, the Smithsonian Institution (the national museum of the USA) lent 250 exhibits for a magnificent exhibition of *Treasures from the Smithsonian Institution*. He also persuaded Princeton University, the Metropolitan Museum and the Smithsonian to lend a series of rare Chinese watercolours, which he had collected and donated to them, for an exhibition in the Old College of Edinburgh Universtiy. Sackler's future plans for the Festival included bringing over an entire opera company and establishing an International Edinburgh Foundation in the USA which would be non-profit-making and which would provide support for the Festival. Dunlop tried to persuade the District Council to make Dr Sackler a Freeman of the City but the Council short-sightedly refused. (A few years earlier a similar proposal to honour the Prince of Wales had also failed to gain the necessary two-thirds majority.) Another boost to the visual arts was the opening of the new Gallery of Modern Art in the former John Watson's School on the edge of Edinburgh's New Town where an exhibition on the theme of modern art and nature entitled *Creation* was shown.

The highlight of the music programme was a concert by the BBC Symphony Orchestra which, under Pierre Boulez, performed Bartók's *The Miraculous Mandarin*, Boulez's own *Notations*, Berg's Three Pieces for Orchestra, Op. 6 and his *Altenberglieder*. The series of concerts by the Smithsonian Chamber Players was also highly praised as was the Scottish première of Lutoslawski's Third Symphony and the contributions by Muti and the young Finnish conductor Esa-Pekka Salonen. These went a little way towards compensating for the poor opera season which many critics considered the worst so far. Dunlop had cancelled the visit of the Welsh National Opera which was scheduled to present Martinů's *The Greek Passion* and a concert performance of *Parsifal* conducted by Reginald Goodall. Goodall, who was not well at the time, pulled out and as he was the main attraction Dunlop refused to consider another conductor. Bookings had been poor and, as the Society's insurance policy would not compensate for a substitute conductor, Dunlop was unwilling at that point to take the risk of a financial disaster: by cancelling, the Society's losses would be covered by the insurance. But it was a calamitous decision for the Welsh National Opera which had succeeded in obtaining sponsorship for the visit. Washington Opera's double bill of Menotti's *The Telephone* and *The Medium* suffered from a poor production but in the opinion of Felix Aprahamian in the *Sunday Times* (19 August 1984) 'the splendid playing of the S.C.O. for Cal Stewart Kellogg and obviously hand-picked casts provided ample scope for Menotti's theatrical genius'. The only new production was an over-blown realization of Cavalli's *Orion* by Raymond Leppard for Scottish Opera. The production by Peter Wood was played for laughs and detracted from the excellent singing and playing of the charming and inventive score. By far the most

satisfactory operatic presentation was a concert performance of Bartók's *Duke Bluebeard's Castle* by the Royal Philharmonic Orchestra under Walter Weller, with Julia Varady and Dietrich Fischer-Dieskau both in splendid form as Judith and Bluebeard.

Complementing the Smithsonian Exhibition was a two-week celebration of American music in all its facets by the Modern Jazz Quartet, Sweet Honey in the Rock, Tommy Flanagan and Barry Harris, Beausoleil and Lawrence Eller. In line with Dunlop's aim of attracting new audiences to the Festival several of these groups also gave concerts in various community centres in the city. Other such events included a performance by the Japanese Temple dancers, Arifuku Kagura, in the Ross Bandstand in Princes Street Gardens and a series of kite-making workshops in Pilton by Da Bei Feng, culminating in a grand Kite Fly-Past in Holyrood Park.

With £200 000 worth of commercial sponsorship and donations of more than $1 million by Americans for the Smithsonian Institution's exhibition the 1984 Festival achieved a surplus of £75 000, a great relief to the Society after the horrendous deficit of the previous year.

One disturbing result of the change in the political climate was the Labour group's insistence that all the local authority places on the Festival Council be held by Labour councillors, who were expected to follow the party line. (At one time all the political parties had been represented on the Council and each member had voted according to his or her own judgement on the matter under discussion but, since the local government reorganization in 1977, the Festival Council had become much more politically motivated.) This, together with Labour's threats to close down the Festival, had an intimidating effect on the non-town council members who were very nervous about disagreeing with the Labour group or even putting forward any view that might run counter to Labour policy; no member wanted to be responsible for the Festival's subsidy being cut. As a result Dunlop frequently found himself without the support or backing of the Council.

Since 1977 James Dunbar-Nasmith, the Vice-Chairman of the Festival Council, had been advocating that in order to take the Festival out of the political arena the number of local authority seats on the Festival Council should be reduced. But with the District Council having overall control, it had been almost impossible to persuade its members to vote for reducing that power. Now with one or two of the middle-of-the-road Labour councillors unhappy about being continually hijacked into supporting policies with which they personally did not agree Dunbar-Nasmith felt that, if he chose his moment carefully, there was a chance that he might be able to push his motion through. He prepared a report on Festival funding which revealed that the District Council's contribution was only 28 per cent of the total. Dunbar-Nasmith then discussed this with Dunlop who considered that, if the worst came to the worst and the District cut off its subsidy, the Festival might still survive financially, albeit with difficulty. To ensure that everyone received copies of this document and would be present to vote, Dunbar-Nasmith delivered copies to each Council member personally. These moves to depoliticize the Festival Council provoked an angry response from the Labour leaders who insisted on their right to a majority, and they threatened not only to stop the grant to the Festival but to withold the use of the District Council's halls and theatres.

A working party was set up to look into the matter for which Dunbar-Nasmith and the new Vice-Chairman, William Berry, prepared a discussion document dealing with the composition of the Council and the Festival Society and the number of committees. In

1986 the motion was passed and the number of local authority seats was cut to one third of the total. At the same time the Labour group succeeded in its own objective of changing the constitution of the Festival Society to open up membership to everyone, instead of being by invitation only.

The 'auld alliance' between Scotland and France provided the inspiration for many features of the 1985 Festival, but some doubts were raised as to whether the alliance would withstand what the Festival did to Molière and Feydeau. *Le Bourgeois Gentilhomme* was given a distinctly Scottish slant in Denise Coffey and Rikki Fulton's heavy-handed adaptation, translated as *A Wee Touch of Class*. Even more eccentric was *Turkey Trot*, an updated version of Feydeau's *Le Dindon* where according to Allen Wright in the *Scotsman* (23 August 1985), 'the women became the lechers, aggressors and leaders, and the men their timid and coy companions who have to suffer the indignity of having their bottoms pinched and their physical appearance absurdly exploited'. On the other hand Molière's *Le Misanthrope* was given an absolutely straight but lifeless production by the Belgian National Theatre. The French contribution to the Festival drama, a revival by the Louis Barrault Company of Victor Hugo's romantic melodrama *Angelo, Tyran de Padoue*, was notable for an exceptionally fine performance of the central role by Geneviève Page. Scotland was represented by a revival of Tom Fleming's 1983 production of *The Thrie Estaites* and a new production of Sydney Goodsir Smith's *The Wallace*. For these Fleming assembled the strongest array of Scottish theatrical talent yet seen at the Festival, proving yet again that the Scottish Theatre can stand comparison with the best in the world. The only new play, a transfer from the Bush Theatre in London of *When I was a Girl I used to Scream and Shout* by the Scottish dramatist Sharman MacDonald, was also the most controversial and gave the professional correspondents to the local papers something to argue about. But the outstanding triumph of the Festival was a Japanese version of *Macbeth* by Yukio Ninagawa for the Toho Theatre of Japan. John Peter for the *Sunday Times* (25 August 1985) wrote, 'Macbeth's final deadly confrontation with Macduff, Samuri swords gleaming amid the falling petals of cherry blossom, is a poignant and haunting theatrical image, and I shall remember it as long as I live'.

Dunlop's musical coup was in securing the brilliant Opéra de Lyon under its English conductor, John Eliot Gardiner. It had the privilege of reopening the King's Theatre after its £1.5 million face-lift, which included a new orchestra pit capable of accommodating 100 musicians. Its delightful production of Chabrier's *L'Étoile* was considered by Max Loppert in the *Financial Times* (c. 14 August 1985) 'one of the most joyous events of 1985'. Its companion piece, an updated conceptual staging of *Pelléas et Mélisande*, presented in its original version carefully restored by Gardiner, was beautifully performed by Diana Montague, José van Dam and François le Roux. Les Arts Florissants, making its first visit to Britain, presented authentically staged versions of baroque operas by Charpentier and Rameau, and in Leith Theatre the Connecticut Opera, by courtesy of Dr Sackler, presented Menotti's *The Consul*, notable for powerful performances by Susan Hinshaw and Beverly Evans.

The French connection was also apparent in the ballet programme with contributions by the Experimental Group from the Paris Opéra. The Scottish-born Michael Clark presented his cacophonous and outrageous *Our caca-phony H*, and Peter Darrell's new ballet *Carmen* was premièred by Scottish Ballet with the young dancer Christine Camillo winning plaudits for her portrayal of the title role. But David Dougill writing in the

Sunday Times (18 August 1985) was most impressed by Elaine McDonald as *La Sylphide* considering that in this role she 'has few peers. She dances it with fleeting ease, poetic grace, and an innocent teasing skittishness – a captivating creature'.

In keeping with the District Council's policy of taking the Festival to the people Dunlop again arranged for some of the official groups to perform in community centres thoughout the city. One of the star attractions was to be a series of workshops for children by Popov the clown from the Moscow State Circus, but somewhere along the line misunderstandings arose. When Popov arrived at St Bride's Centre for the first of these workshops he discovered not only an audience comprised mainly of adults but a poster giving admission prices. Convinced that he had been conned and someone was trying to make money out of him, he refused to perform. Popov's other community shows were cancelled and Dunlop later expressed his disappointment at the apparent unwillingness of the Circus performers to become involved in any happening outside the terms of their contract. Two of the community centres later wrote complaining bitterly about the lack of co-ordination between the Festival authorities and the local community.

During the summer there was another political row when, at a critical stage in the arrangements for the 1986 Festival, Dunlop had to go into hospital. To enable him to organize the Festival from his hospital bed he had to be treated privately and the Festival Council agreed to pay his medical expenses. Edinburgh District Council passed a motion on 19 June deploring this decision and informed the Festival Council that, as custodian of large sums of public funding, there must be no repetition of such abuses. The matter was taken up by the Merchiston and Morningside Labour Party who condemned the payment of the Director's medical expenses on the grounds that it 'perpetrated the view held by many that the Festival Society is an élitist organization, run only to benefit its members and, in this case, principal employee', adding that they 'hoped Edinburgh District Council would take account of this action when considering future grants to the Society'. Dunlop quickly diffused the situation by writing to the Lord Provost, expressing his gratitude to the council for its offer to reimburse his expenses and insisting that this sum be put towards the the 1986 Festival.

In January 1986 Dunlop had been informed that the District's grant to the Festival would be reduced by £47 000 although a further sum of £80 000 would be allocated for activities in community venues, provided the District Council's Recreation Department approved the programme details. A young director, Andy Arnold, was appointed to organize a wide range of popular events in The Dome, a large tent erected in Pilrig Park. Despite favourable publicity the experiment was a failure, attracting very low attendances and incurring a loss of £58 893, and it was not repeated. In the words of Dunlop it 'proved once and for all that the "activists" were wrong'.

Frank Dunlop's third Festival was unashamedly populist. In addition to the community events in Pilrig Park and various centres throughout the city, there were American jugglers at the King's Theatre (formerly the home of Festival opera), jazz at the Usher Hall, Scottish humour at the Lyceum and Leith Theatres, the Chinese Magical Circus at the Playhouse, and Jimmy Logan as Harry Lauder in Portobello Town Hall. But as far as his first World Theatre Season was concerned there was no question of the Festival going down-market. With companies from Poland, France, Germany, Sweden, Spain, South

Africa, the USA and Japan presenting 11 plays it was the most ambitious drama programme the Festival had yet seen, and with it Dunlop more than fulfilled his pledge to restore the balance of the Festival from its former heavy emphasis on music and opera. If one or two of the productions such as the Théâtre de la Salamandre's almost incomprehensible *Le Saperleau*, or 'Superloo' as it was quickly and irreverently named, did not quite come up to expectation they were quickly forgotten. The first week opened with a gripping adaptation of *Crime and Punishment* by the Stary Theatre of Cracow in the small St Bride's Centre where the audience of about 100 was seated on benchs tiered like a large jury box. This was followed by two masterly productions of Scandinavian classics by Ingmar Bergman: Ibsen's *John Gabriel Borkman* for the Bavarian State Theatre and Strindberg's *Miss Julie* for Stockholm's Royal Dramatic Theatre. In the second week there were memorable Spanish productions of Lorca's *Blood Wedding* and *Yerma*, the latter in an imaginative production by Victor Garcia which, when it had first been presented in Spain, had been considered one of the landmarks of European drama.

But, as in 1985, it was Yukio Ninagawa and the Toho Company, this time in Euripides's *Medea,* that had the critics searching for superlatives to describe one of the truly unique experiences of any Festival. More than one person thought Frank Dunlop quite mad to present Greek tragedy late at night in the open air in chilly Edinburgh, but like Guthrie in the Assembly Hall, he confounded his critics. Even in the teeming rain and with a howling east wind the courtyard of Robert Adam's Old College was an ideal setting for Ninagawa's genius. John Peter considered it 'the most magnificent production of a Greek play I've ever seen … a visual and intellectual spectacular which conveyed both the lyricism and the ferocity of Euripides's imagination'. At the end there was a thrilling moment when Medea in her fiery chariot ascended into the Heavens. 'In all my theatregoing life I can remember few moments of such truthful magnificence' was how John Peter summed up his review in the *Sunday Times* (31 August 1986).

With the Scottish Enlightenment (a period in the eighteenth century when the arts and sciences flourished in Edinburgh) as its theme there was also a greater emphasis on Scottish arts. In *A Gallery of Scots* Tom Fleming repeated a series of recitals on the work of eminent Scottish writers given singly at previous Festivals. But the Scottish element really came to the fore in the exhibitions: *A Hotbed of Genius*, *Painting in Scotland – The Golden Age*, *The Enterprising Scot* and, in particular, *Scottish Art Today* when 20 or so young Scottish artists worked in different situations around the city watched by the public. This exhibition revealed an amazing resurgence of Scottish artistic talent which was to form the basis of the following year's exhibition *The Vigorous Imagination.* Dunlop considered this one of the most important happenings of his Festival years.

One of Dunlop's declared intentions on taking office was to slacken the grip of the London orchestras on the Festival. He saw no reason why they should bring tired South Bank programmes to Edinburgh and, at the same time, charge an exorbitant sum for doing so. The previous year he had cut down their contribution to four concerts. In 1986 there was only one, by the BBC Symphony Orchestra under Pritchard, plus two by Neville Marriner's Academy of St Martin-in-the-Fields. Simon Rattle's City of Birmingham Orchestra was invited to give two concerts and there was one by the Hallé under its new conductor Stanislaw Skrowaczevsky. The remainder were given by the Toronto Symphony, the vastly improved Oslo Philharmonic Orchestra under its brilliant young conductor Mariss Jansons, the popular Moscow Virtuosi and the Chamber Orchestra of

Europe conducted by Abbado. Dunlop also accepted an offer from the Pittsburgh Symphony Orchestra which had offered to subsidize itself as Orchestra-in-Residence. The advantage of these arrangements was that Edinburgh could present its own brand of goods rather than repeat a performance planned for the Proms.

One particular brand of Edinburgh goods was the evolution of the Composer's Choice weekend. In conversation with Dunlop Alexander Goehr had bemoaned the passing of the old Freemasons' Hall and Gateway emphasis on modern music. Dunlop took up the challenge and quickly drove the ball back into Goehr's court by inviting him to devise a series of programmes designed to take place during one single weekend to enable those interested to attend all the events. Goehr agreed and the result was an enterprising series of seven concerts of twentieth-century music. One of the highlights was Alan Feinberg's account of the Piano Sonata No. 3 by Roger Sessions which Nicholas Kenyon in the *Observer* (31 August 1986) described as a 'musical event which made the trip to Edinburgh worthwhile'. The series also introduced to Festival audiences some of the works of György Kurtag splendidly sung by Adrienne Csengery.

Dunlop had also expressed a desire to put the Usher Hall to more adventurous use. He felt that previous directors had accepted too readily the obligation to fill it every night with conventional symphony concerts and he wanted to use the space for something more out of the way. His first such divergence in 1985, Nureyev dancing to the music of Bach, had met with hostility from certain music critics but, undeterred, Dunlop invited two of the stars of the National Ballet of Canada, Karen Kain and Peter Ottmann, to perform *The Soldier's Tale* with the Toronto Symphony – a performance which the dance critics greeted with more enthusiasm than they accorded the major ballet events at the Playhouse.

What was even more revolutionary was his idea of turning the Usher Hall into an opera house for his own production of Weber's *Oberon*. In this he almost succeeded in achieving the impossible – an effective staging of what was considered to be an unstageable work. Not all the problems were solved but what emerged was a brilliantly imaginative production, full of witty touches such as an endearingly human horn. As befits a work in which the orchestra plays a major role, the Junge Deutsche Philharmonie was given a prominent position centre stage, surrounded by staircases and platforms on which the action took place. Even the conductor, Seiji Ozawa, was occasionally drawn into the action. This production had evolved almost by accident. After making arrangements with Ozawa to present *Oberon* Dunlop had invited Scottish Opera to participate in the venture but the company had refused as it wanted to mount its own production. Ozawa had then insisted that Dunlop produce it himself. The intention had been to perform it in German but Dunlop persuaded Ozawa to use Planché's original English libretto which was much more humorous than the German version and the result was an unqualified success. In her customary refreshing style the *Scotsman*'s Ruth Wishart (16 August 1986) considered that 'to have devised a production with so much charm, wit and humour that the entire massed ranks of the Amalgamated Union of Critics, Cynics, and Professional Whingers were compelled to applaud without quibble, is in itself a feat of quite major proportions'.

In an attempt to widen the appeal of opera and prove that it need not necessarily be 'élitist' Dunlop brought the Folkopera of Stockholm's celebrated adaptation of *Aida* to Leith Theatre. As the audience entered the foyer it was met by groups of singers wandering around in costume giving a foretaste of what was to come. The auditorium

itself was transformed by a large platform stage thrust deep into the hall bringing the action into the audience and making them a part of it as priests with flaming torches, dancers and singers entered down the aisles. There were no stars, the principal roles being rotated among the company so that one evening's Aida would be singing in the small chorus for the next performance, and most of the critics admitted that the singing was generally first rate. There were some musical compromises in that the small orchestra of two dozen players (positioned on a raised platform behind the stage) was enhanced by the discreet use of a synthesizer, but as David Cairns observed in the *Sunday Times* (31 August 1986): 'For someone who knows the piece well and has groaned under many a routine, top-heavy performance it comes as a rejuvenation: the work, the music, are felt again as new.'

Equally successful were the performances of *The Ragged Child* and Britten's *Let's make an Opera* by the National Youth Music Theatre, the former Children's Music Theatre in a new guise. With one or two exceptions, good singing was not on offer in the Maly Theatre of Leningrad's productions of Tchaikovsky's *Eugene Onegin* and *The Queen of Spades* and a new opera on the subject of Mary, Queen of Scots by Sergei Slonimsky. Nor was imaginative production, although in fairness to the company it did have the usual nightmare of transferring sets made for a stage twice the size to the small proportions of the King's Theatre. Even with £1.5 million of improvements there were still delays caused by scene shifting and at one point in *Onegin* the orchestra even came to a halt as it waited in silence for the stage to be set.

These mishaps gave even more point to Dunlop's well-publicized plea to the civic authorities for a new theatre capable of presenting opera, ballet and large musicals. Much to everyone's surprise one of the leaders of the Labour group, Councillor Kerevan, admitted there was a need for a large theatre and appealed for Government funding. The Arts Minister gave the initiative a cautious welcome, but pointed out that Edinburgh must take the lead in raising the money. This gave Edinburgh some hope that the Labour Council had done a U-turn and now wanted to spend money on an opera house which two years before it had declared was 'selfish, irresponsible and élitist'. The Tory opposition promptly castigated Labour as 'hypocrites of the worst kind' and yet another squabble ensued. Then the Labour leader Mark Lazarowicz dispelled hopes yet again by declaring,

> there is no way that we consider the construction of an opera house in Edinburgh as any type of priority ... It is, of course, sheer hypocrisy for the Conservative Party to argue that they would have built such a building; there was no money set aside for it in the Council Budget as we discovered when we took office in 1984. If the Conservatives really wanted to see an improvement in theatre provision in Edinburgh they should not have sold off, at a knock-down price, the Playhouse which could have been adapted relatively cheaply.'

The losses on The Dome and other venues left the Festival with a reserve of only £26 000. With an estimated deficit of £119 000 on the budget for 1987 the financial situation was serious. As this estimate allowed for a programme of community events at The Dome, Leith Theatre and St Bride's, Dunlop requested a repeat of the previous year's additional grant, but Councillor Vestri insisted that these events should be part of the overall Festival programme and paid from core funding. In April the District Council confirmed that the grant for the forthcoming Festival would be pegged at the 1986 level and as there would be no additional £80 000 Dunlop was forced to cut out the events planned for The Dome. He then successfully negotiated with two London mangements to

take some Festival events after the Edinburgh performances, enabling the costs of these events to be shared. But by June he was becoming increasingly anxious about the financial situation for 1988 and, in view of the planned programme for that year, he considered it imperative that something was done to ensure the Society had sufficient funds to meet commitments. Like Drummond, Dunlop found himself devoting more time to the finances than to the more important artistic aspect of the Festival.

To celebrate the seventieth anniversary of the October Revolution in 1917, Dunlop planned a Russian theme for 1987. What he had hoped for was something on the lines of the Smithsonian Institution's contribution to the 1986 Festival but the compartmentalized system in the Soviet Union presented a problem and it took three years, and no less than five visits by Dunlop and three by his assistant, Sheila Colvin, to organize a representative selection of Soviet culture.

The Soviet authorities had been rather suspicious of Dunlop and on his first visit he had been allocated a filthy room in a seedy hotel. Dunlop promptly phoned the British Embassy and informed the ambassador that he had never slept in such a disgusting room and he was going home. The ambassador pointed out that he was an official guest and he would offend the Soviet authorities. 'I don't care', replied Dunlop. 'They've offended me. And I just want them to know that I'm unhappy, I don't like it here and I want to go home!' Half an hour later a Russian limousine appeared to transport Dunlop to another hotel. The next day he had an extraordinary meeting with a group of about ten people including the minister in charge of culture, who opened the proceedings: 'Mr Dunlop. At last we have you here. Tell us, why did you give up all that money in America to take on the Edinburgh Festival?' In his customary outspoken style Dunlop replied that in the West people occasionally did things for moral rather than financial reasons. There was a sudden silence. Nobody knew what to say as everything was probably being recorded. At that point it occurred to Dunlop that the Soviets probably suspected him of spying for the Americans. Dunlop then informed the Minister that he had done his homework and had a list of the companies he wanted to see. Finally the Minister agreed. 'Very well, you do what you want to do.' After that she became extremely supportive. A KGB agent was assigned to accompany him and eventually he got everything he wanted.

After the support he had obtained from the Ministry of Culture Dunlop was irritated to discover that the head of the National Agency was being very obstructive. Finally Dunlop couldn't take it any longer and, regardless of the listening staff, turned on him and said, 'I've had enough of you. You are a nasty, vicious man.' At that point the man became rather nervous and apologetic but Dunlop interrupted, 'I've now got a headache through talking to you and I'm going to try to find something for my head', and stomped out. A few seconds later an assistant ran after him and offered him some aspirin. 'That was wonderful', he said, and promptly ran back again. Dunlop laughed so much that he decided to keep the aspirin as a souvenir.

The main problem was the perennial one of the lack of adequate facilities making a visit by either the Bolshoi or the Kirov companies out of the question. The Soviet authorities, who considered the Edinburgh Festival the major showcase in the West, would have been more than happy to send either of these companies. Indeed they tried very hard to overcome the problem, working out all kinds of permutations of their stage sets to try to find something suitable, but ultimately they had to admit defeat. Instead of

the Bolshoi and the Kirov opera and ballet companies Dunlop had to settle for the Bolshoi Theatre Orchestra, the Bolshoi Sextet, the Shostakovich Quartet and Siverko, a 100-strong group of folk-dancers and musicians from Archangel. Drama was represented by the Tbilisi State Puppet Theatre and the Gorky Theatre of Leningrad in Chekhov's *Uncle Vanya* and a curiosity by Rozovsky, *The History of a Horse*, based on a story by Tolstoy. The Museum of Oriental Art in Moscow organized an exhibition of the decorative arts from Soviet Central Asia entitled *Tbilisi to Tashkent*. Finally, the Ministry of Culture sent a distinguished delegation of writers, directors, critics and political commentators to take part in a four-day symposium on literature and the arts. Warned by Dunlop that such a conference might be politically explosive, the Minister replied that they were willing to take risks. The result was an entertaining, frank and enlightening series of discussions – the Soviet delegation stressing the new freedom in literature and the theatre, citing the popular magazine *Ogonyok* which was tackling an increasing number of formerly forbidden topics. The star of the show was undoubtedly the poet Evgeny Yevtushenko who, in addition to enlivening the discussions, gave readings of his poetry and, with his colourful personality and dress (on one occasion he appeared in burgundy slacks, a tan leather jacket, pale blue shirt, a red tie with green motifs, green cap and grey blue socks), gave the eager press enough copy for several days.

Michael Ratcliffe wrote:

> Last year's Edinburgh Festival World Theatre season included no fewer than six productions from abroad which will rank historically among the finest of the decade – seven, if you count the ill-received and under-attended Wooster Group from New York, which I do. For the first time in several years the Festival far outclassed, for pleasure and excitement, the Fringe. No more. Even on paper it was clear that the 1987 international season was not going to be half as good ... it would serve Edinburgh ill to pretend that the programme has not been compromised and that all is well with the Festival Director's selection and the public response to it.
>
> (M. Ratcliffe, *Observer*, 23 August 1987)

He went on to describe the 1987 drama programme as a 'homogenising tide of hopefully popular, populist theatre – puppets, acrobats, martial arts – which doubles in drama, folklore, singing and dance'. Fortunately the other critcs were more favourably impressed. If the second World Theatre Season did not have the impact of the first it was a penalty for the first being too good. It is always difficult to follow up on excellence. Nevertheless, in addition to the outstanding contributions from the Gorky Theatre there were successes from the Gate Theatre of Dublin with *Juno and the Paycock*, the Berliner Ensemble's production of *The Caucasian Chalk Circle* by Brecht and the Cameri Theatre of Tel Aviv in *Michael Kohlhaas* by James Saunders based on a work by Heinrich von Kleist. The Kunju *Macbeth* and Raun Raun's trilogy of traditional folk myths in dramatic form were unique in themselves, giving Western audiences a rare opportunity of assessing examples of Oriental culture, surely the purpose of an international festival. This was the first time the Raun Raun company had visited the West and the provision of acceptable meals created a problem for the Festival Society. Fortunately the company discovered Macdonald's and thereafter they refused to eat anything else even to the extent that, when an official reception was arranged for them, hamburgers had to be provided.

There was more justification in the criticism of the music programme, an example of weak and thoughtless planning. Conrad Wilson, the music critic of the *Scotsman* grasped every opportunity to complain about the howlers in the programmes and the unhelpful notes, no doubt in the hope that if he drew attention to them often enough something might be done. Dunlop's ideas on opera were a far cry from the sumptuous star-studded events of Peter Diamand's day, and he grasped every opportunity to make it more popular and accessible. The use of the dingy, out-of-town Leith Theatre for two of the opera productions, leaving the renovated King's Theatre with its new orchestra pit for drama, was a deliberate act of policy, and it paid off. Both Folkopera's *Die Zauberflöte* and the Alte Oper, Frankfurt's production of Henze's *The English Cat*, with its modern sonorities, sold out. But though sparse and bleak on paper, the opera programme turned out to be highly rewarding. The small-scale adaptation of *Die Zauberflöte* was described by Raymond Monelle in *Opera* (Autumn 1987) as 'giddy, gorgeous, infectious and exuberant', while the British premières of *The English Cat* and Merikanto's *Juha* provided stronger meat for the opera buff. In his praise for *Juha, Opera*'s Rodney Milnes (Autumn 1987) castigated his colleagues who failed to attend and at the same time found a small crumb of approbation for the much maligned King's Theatre: 'How nice, for once, to meet a visiting company to whom the King's is luxuriously large … But *Juha* sounded fabulous, fuller and more airy than on home territory.' *Opera* (Autumn 1987) also found space for a comment by Raymond Monnelle on the 'flawless perfection' of the Kunju Theatre's comic opera *The Peony Pavilion*, which he found 'a complete revelation, a perfectly achieved example of an unfamiliar but deeply satisfying operatic style'.

The main exhibition, *The Vigorous Imagination*, again brought Scottish art to the forefront of the Festival: Steven Campbell, Mario Rossi, Ken Currie, Wisniewski and Peter Howson were among the painters selected, with photographs by Calum Colvin and Ron O'Donnell, and there were commissioned works by David Mach, Kate Whiteford and Sam Ainsley. Stephen Conroy, a 23-year-old graduate from the Glasgow College of Art, had an overnight success, selling three of his five paintings on show, his mysterious half-lit groups attracting clusters of intent viewers every day. The grotesque and violent imagery of the American David Salle was on show at the Fruitmarket Gallery, the Scottish Arts Council's main showcase, where the controversy surrounding this exhibition and the avant-garde policies of its director, Mark Francis, led to his resignation in the middle of the Festival.

During the Festival Glasgow announced that it was doubling its grant to the arts. Not to be outdone, Edinburgh's Councillor Kerevan informed a press conference that Edinburgh would be adopting Britain's first 'Percentage for Art' policy by earmarking 1 per cent of the budget for each of its new buildings for the commissioning of associated works of art. He was unable to specify just how much would be spent beyond 'hundreds of thousands' over the first three or four years. Referring to the Glasgow initiative he said that Glasgow was now 'catching up' by spending £1 million a year on the arts, compared with Edinburgh's £1.3 million. Kerevan concluded by maintaining that the £533 000 grant for the Festival, in spite of a 15 per cent budget cut, was 'quite heroic'. Opinions were equally divided as to which city had won that particular battle.

Plans were in motion for an Italian Festival in 1988 with a visit by the San Carlo, which was celebrating its two hundred and fiftieth anniversary, as the main feature. When the

company increased its fee and asked for two or three times the amount agreed, Dunlop went to Italy and suggested various ways in which the expenses could be reduced but, despite the intervention of the Italian Government who were subsidizing the company, it refused and without an increase in grant Dunlop was forced to cancel the visit. He had already cut out a major orchestra and was having to decide whether to use the Assembly Hall or Leith Theatre. The editor of the *Scotsman* was approached and the newspaper agreed to launch a festival fund and to underwrite it to the tune of £60 000 if the response proved poor. As a result of this appeal 2 000 readers sent in cheques and many businesses who had never before given to the Festival added their support. A total of £90 000 was raised enabling the Festival to bring over the Houston Grand Opera's production of John Adams's *Nixon in China.* This response from the Edinburgh citizens not only saved the Festival opera but also gave a new lease of life to a thoroughly disheartened Dunlop. Criticism from the establishment who wanted more stars, sniping from the left who wanted more 'commitment', on top of dwindling funds had taken their toll and Dunlop was on the point of handing in his resignation. But in the face of that fantastic support from the ordinary citizens of Edinburgh he decided he could not go.

Apart from Ninagawa's spectacular and visually thrilling *Tempest*, the 1988 programme seemed more like an example of populist entertainment than a serious World Theatre Season. From France there was a production of Marivaux's *Le Jeu de L'amour et du Hasard* by the Groupe TSE performed in monkey masks, and a geriatric vaudeville *Les Petits Pas* from the Compagnie Jérôme Deschamps. From Canada came two productions, *B-Movie* and *The Rez Sisters*, the latter written and presented by an amateur Eskimo group, which would have fitted more comfortably into the Fringe. Italy's contribution was a company of Sicilian puppets and *Miseria e Nobilta*, a stultified reproduction of a hundred-year-old Neapolitan comedy. Cape Town's Baxter Theatre brought a musical based on the contentious bulldozing by the South African Government of a multiracial district of Cape Town which, had it been given a less glossy Hollywood treatment and more authentic African music, would have been more moving. But perhaps bottom of the league was the Schiller Company's heavily Germanic, almost Brechtian, treatment of Offenbach's *La Périchole* and a German-language version of a vampirish play by Fassbinder, of which an English version was concurrently running on the Fringe. Needless to say the London critics were not impressed and there were more articles questioning the future of the Festival in the light of the parsimony and the anti-élitist bias of Edinburgh District Council.

The music programme met with equal hostility. There were complaints about an absence of top-class international stars, a lack of contemporary music and unimaginative programme-planning. Grand opera was conspicuous by its absence. Instead of the promised San Carlo Company there was a musical entertainment based on Neapolitan folklore, *La Gatta Cenerentola*, by the former director of the San Carlo, Roberto de Simone. Admirable though it might be as music theatre, it could hardly be described as an opera. The Stockholm Folkopera returned with its scaled-down version of Puccini's *Turandot* which, though it played to packed houses, was ruined for some by the amplified sound. Dunlop, however, did secure a coup with the British première of Turnage's opera *Greek*, based on a play running in London by Steve Berkoff. Berkoff had been unhappy with the political implications in the adaptation of his play and had even threatened to stop the Edinburgh performances, but after hearing a tape of the

opera he had been reconciled to it. But it was the British première of *Nixon in China*, in a spectacular production by Peter Sellars, which gave the opera programme viability. The most memorable features of the concert programme were the visit by the USSR State Orchestra and the Shostakovich Quartet's performances of all Shostakovich's string quartets.

Balletomanes were also enchanted by the Matsayuma Ballet and in particular by its ethereal prima ballerina, Yoko Morishita, who gave a touching and persuasive portrayal of Giselle, admirably supported by a superbly synchronised corps de ballet.

For Dunlop's Spanish Festival in 1989 the Spanish Government sent over 400 musicians, dancers and actors, one of the largest contingents ever sent to the Festival. The National Opera of Spain from the Teatro La Zarzuela in Madrid presented what was purported to be the first complete performance of a zarzuela to be given in Britain, Moreno Torroba's three-act *La Chulapona*, the National Orchestra of Spain under Rafael Frühbeck de Burgos gave concert performances of Falla's *Atlántida* and *La Vida Breve*, classical Spanish ballet was provided by the Spanish National Ballet and flamenco dancing by the Cristina Hoyos Company. The most entertaining of the Spanish companies was a brilliant group of street entertainers, Els Comediants, with *Dimonis* given in the grounds of George Heriot's School and *La Nit* at the Lyceum. John Clifford wrote:

> It would be an understatement to describe what they achieved as amazing. It surpassed that wildest collection of extravagant superlatives you could ever imagine. They filled the air with screaming banshees. They had the battlements bathed in flares. They made the whole night vibrate with drums ... And the night after that they did the same to the Lyceum. They covered the audience with a net of silver bells; they hoisted it to the ceiling and transformed it into a starry sky. And at the end, with a characteristic playful tenderness they tucked the moon to bed before the coming of the dawn.
>
> (J. Clifford, *Scotland on Sunday*, 20 August 1989)

Finally there were performances of *La Celestina* by Fernando de Rojas and Calderón's *The Mayor of Zalamea* by the Compania Nacional Teatro Clasico. (Two other plays by Calderón, *Life is a Dream* and *Schism in England* were presented by Cracow's Stary Theatre and the Royal National Theatre Studio.) The Spanish Government had been unwilling to lend any paintings but an imaginative exhibition *El Greco: Mystery and Illumination*, built around its recent acquisition *Fábulo*, was mounted in the National Gallery of Scotland. Two other versions of this painting were also on view as was the magnificent *View of Toledo* from the Metropolitan Museum in New York. One of the dance highlights was Martha Clarke's *The Garden of Earthly Delights*, based on the Híeronymus Bosch triptych in the Prado Museum, and comprising scenes from the Garden of Eden and the seven deadly sins and ending with a descent into hell. Although there were complaints that the Spanish theme had been insufficiently representative, particularly the musical side, it was popular with the public.

The principal complaint on the dramatic front was the absence of a major production in the Assembly Hall. However unsatisfactory this venue might be for the actors the audience loved it. Dunlop had hoped to present R.S. Silver's play *The Bruce*, but negotiations for this had broken down. The World Theatre Season was varied and full of novelties: the colourful, sensuous splendour of the Yokohama Boat Theatre was in stark contrast to

Wajda's compelling staging of Ansky's *The Dybuk* for the Stary Theatre of Cracow. But perhaps Dunlop's greatest success was in securing the first performances in Britain by Moscow's Taganka Theatre (now reunited with its former director, Yuri Lyubimov, after his expulsion for criticizing the Party six years before) in a modern dress staging of *Boris Godunov.*

Equally dramatic and theatrical was Kresnik's original, but horrifying and sadistic balletic version of *Macbeth*, while Richard Jones's Opera North production of Prokofiev's *The Love of Three Oranges*, with its smells and spells was, in the opinion of Paul Driver in the *Sunday Times* (27 August 1989), 'one of the most brilliant I have ever seen of any opera anywhere. It is relentlessly inventive, transparently simple, and completely magical. By itself, it made the week worthwhile'.

Dunlop's most interesting idea was the coupling of Strauss's *Salome* with the Oscar Wilde original, as presented by Dublin's Gate Theatre, in a mesmerizing, slow-motion, mimed production by Steven Berkoff. An intriguing double that might well have been a triple had Dunlop's original plan for including Maxwell Davies's ballet on the same subject come off. Dunlop would have liked to produce the opera himself in the Usher Hall, with a large orchestra centre stage encircled by the action, as he had done so spectacularly in *Oberon*, but this was another plan that did not materialize. Instead he had to settle for a scaled-down, cheaper version, using Strauss's own reduced orchestration. Building on the success of the Stockholm Folkopera at the previous three fesivals, he invited the Stockholm team of conductor Kerstin Nerbe and producer Claes Fellbom to devise a special Festival Folkopera production with British singers supported by the Scottish Chamber Orchestra. The result was the main talking point of the Festival, receiving lavish praise and total condemnation in roughly equal proportions. The main bones of contention were the explicitly sexual scene of desire and violence between the child prinçess and the prophet, which runs counter to both text and music, and the placing of the orchestra behind the singers, inevitably obscuring much of Strauss's lush orchestral sound, a vital feature of the opera. On the credit side it was, on its own terms, a dramatically thrilling experience sporting two admirable casts of young singers. Dunlop had hoped that Festival Folkopera might become a permanent feature of the Festival, operating from Leith Theatre. Edinburgh District Council were favourably disposed to the idea. Indeed they would have been more than happy for the Festival Society to rent Leith Theatre on an all-year basis, but the Scottish Arts Council was unwilling to fund Folkopera, feeling that it might conflict with the activities of Scottish Opera.

But the concert and recital programmes were severely castigated for being tame, conservative and lacking in imagination. The Oslo Philharmonic Orchestra's programme of *Don Juan* by Strauss (tenth Festival performance), Grieg's Piano Concerto (being performed for the first time at the Festival) and the Second Symphony of Brahms (receiving its seventeenth Festival performance) was the prime target, though there were compensations in the luminous playing of the orchestra under Mariss Jansons. In the early years there had been suggestions that the Festival should forget about drama and concentrate on music, now the music critics were putting forward a case for the music being dropped altogether and the Festival becoming purely a dramatic event!

In addition to the El Greco exhibition the Festival Society also mounted the popular Tartan exhibition. This had started life at the Fashion Institute of Technology in New York, where it had been seen by Dunlop. By the time he had secured enough money to

bring the exhibition to the Festival the exhibits had been returned to their owners. The Society approached the National Museum of Scotland, who had provided some of the material but, knowing how difficult it would be to restage the exhibition, it politely declined. The National Gallery was also reluctant to help. After considerable horse-trading behind the scenes the exhibition was eventually mounted in the Talbot Rice Gallery at Edinburgh University. In the time available it was not possible to reassemble all the original exhibits but, with the assistance of the El Fayed's, Dunlop was able to obtain the most important part, the collection of the Duke of Windsor.

Taking *The Vigorous Imagination* exhibition of 1987 a step further the National Galleries mounted a series of exhibitions which provided a remarkable survey of Scottish artists over 300 years. One of the most outstanding was the tercentenary display devoted to the life and times of William Adam, the father of the Adam brothers and an outstanding architect in his own right, numbering among his achievements Haddo House, Hopetoun House and Floors Castle. There was *Patrons and Painters: Art in Scotland 1650–1760* at the National Portrait Gallery, *Scottish Art since 1900* at the National Gallery of Modern Art, while the Royal Scottish Academy mounted an exhibition of the work of one of its former presidents, William McTaggart, in which his massive seascapes took pride of place. Another exhibition displaying the work of his descendants together with other Scottish artist families was to be seen at the Fine Art Society and there was a *Robin Philipson Restrospective* in the Sculpture Court of Edinburgh College of Art.

But the Festival had not been without its alarms. The first row concerned the Glenlivet Fireworks concert, normally a happy event, but the choice of Elgar's *Pomp and Circumstance March No. 1* had upset a large number of the watching crowd who responded to the tune Land of Hope and Glory with boos and jeers. The Scottish National Party took up the cause, describing the playing of the tune as 'offensive to the vast majority of Scots', and in a letter to Dunlop the Secretary complained that the tune had been hijacked by the Tory party as their semi-official anthem, and had been written to celebrate the worst sort of English imperialism. As the Glenlivet event was organized entirely by the Scottish Chamber Orchestra the Society left the orchestra to answer the criticisms. But, when challenged, the Orchestra's manager was unrepentant: 'I think there has been an over sensitive reaction to this. The pieces are chosen because they are good music and because they are a perfect companion to fireworks. No one has objected to Handel written for English royal occasions.'

There were three major cancellations. Arleen Augér was unable, through illness, to give her recital in the Queen's Hall and as a replacement could not be found at short notice the ticket money had to be refunded. Tango Argentina had also withdrawn and the Society was considering legal action in the American courts to try to recoup the costs, though this was later dropped. The third casualty was La Zattera di Babele which was to have performed Shakespeare's *Macbeth* on the island of Inchcolm in the Firth of Forth, and which had pulled out ten days before because the director, Carlo Quartucci, and his leading lady wife, Carla Tato, had suffered nervous breakdowns. Richard Demarco, who was presenting the play in association with the Italian Institute, replaced the Sicilian group with a 'promenade production' by notable Scottish actors. Ticket holders were offered refunds or the opportunity to exchange their tickets for the new show. Unfortunately the Society had been unable to contact all the ticket holders by letter. This chaotic situation was exacerbated by Mr Demarco who started selling tickets from his own art

gallery without ensuring that there would be sufficient available for those turning up with the original tickets, so about 30 people were left on the quayside at South Queensferry as there was no room for them on the boat.

But the ticket fiasco was only the beginning of the problems besetting this production of Shakespeare's 'unlucky Scottish play'. Rain, a decrepit boat and temperamental loudspeakers also played their part and just as Macbeth, alias John Cairney, was congratulating himself on having escaped disaster he discovered his car had been caught by the incoming tide and was almost submerged in sea water. For the audience braving the pouring rain and the buffeting wind it was an amazing and unforgettable experience as Shakespeare's poetry rang out in the ruined abbey to the accompaniment of screeching gulls and the lapping of the waves. Even the actors who had laboured for seven days with little sleep, were not immune to the spell, but whether they would care to repeat the experience was another matter!

Dunlop found himself in hot water when, at a press conference, he nonchalantly aired a suggestion that Edinburgh might benefit from a closer liaison with Glasgow, the 1990 European City of Culture. On being closely questioned about the possibility of the Festival alternating between Edinburgh and Glasgow, he replied that the notion might be worthy of discussion. These remarks so angered a Tory District Councillor that he tabled an emergency motion at a council meeting strongly condemning Dunlop's remarks as 'dangerously irresponsible'. Stopping short of demanding Dunlop's resignation he ended by inviting Mr. Dunlop to 'consider his postion'. According to a statement by the Festival's press officer the shared Festival idea had been put forward by a 'bone-headed London critic!'

But the Press had prepared an even hotter bath for the Festival Director. Throughout the Festival the London music critics (never particularly well disposed towards the Festival) had been positively vitriolic in their comments. Hugh Canning, summed up the gist of these remarks in what could only be described as a hatchet job on the Festival:

> Edinburgh's claim to be a music festival – among other things – of international standing no longer bears too much scrutiny. It has become self-satisfied, complacent and parochial, scarcely worth the five-hour train journey from London ... Who is to blame? It would be unjust, I think, to heap it all on to the head of the beleaguered festival director, who has never made any secret of his inexperience in matters musical. The warning shots of Edinburgh's decline were fired by his predecessor, John Drummond ... When he left, the legendary miserliness of the City Fathers conspired with the insatiable greed of 'international' musicians to seal Edinburgh's lapse into provincialism. Indeed, many Edinburgh-watchers have always assumed this was Dunlop's brief: to downgrade the costly musical content of the festival in favour of the cheaper, more flexible dramatic arts. By that yardstick, then, Dunlop's sixth Festival has been a triumphant success, since the music programme has reached a nadir below which it surely could not sink ... If Frank Dunlop cannot come up with some new ideas to meet the challenge of Glasgow's Cultural Capital of Europe jamboree next year, then it might be worth thinking of hiving off the musical events of the Festival in perpetuity to the city where most of Scotland's musical resources concentrate – no doubt thanks to the meaness of the Edinburgh City Fathers.
>
> (H. Canning, *Sunday Times*, 3 September 1989)

Fortunately Michael Billington (admittedly a theatre rather than a music critic) had a few kind words to say.

> Edinburgh District Council, reputedly mean, has in fact more than quintupled its grant to the Festival in the last 12 years while the Scottish Arts Council has barely doubled its subvention

> … last year's Festival ended up with a tiny deficit of £1 529 which on a turnover of close to £3 million is not bad. Frank Dunlop clearly must be doing something right. And, even in an age when festivals have bred like rabbits, Edinburgh still retains its omnivorous primacy.
>
> (M. Billington, *Guardian*, Festival Supplement, 1989)

By the final press conference the temperature of the water had risen yet again and some of Dunlop's critics could barely restrain their hostility. Above all he was blamed for what had been called 'The fall of the House of Usher', a drastic decline in the standard of concerts at the Usher Hall. Dunlop had been warned that the *Sunday Times* was planning a four-page scandalous exposé of his policies with its climax at the final conference where Hugh Canning was to stand up and destroy Dunlop and it would all be reported in the paper. He therefore prepared a speech in which he answered all the press complaints before they even had a chance to make them. Dunlop began by stating that he thought there was an error in people's perceptions of the Festival:

> This is no longer a Festival of blockbusters – I know people are looking for blockbusters because that makes big news. It's more a Festival about discovery and when you are making discoveries you take risks; and when you take risks you sometimes fall on your face and sometimes you have a glorious success … A legend has grown up in the past few years that because the present incumbent of the hot seat did have a sort of long career in the theatre he must have come in and moved all the money from the music to theatre events. It's untrue. This year at least two-thirds of the available subsidy was used for music and opera. The other third went to drama, dance and all other events including art exhibitions.

This speech had the effect of provoking Canning and when he became obstreperous Dunlop interrupted, 'You just sit down, Fred'. 'My name is not Fred. Don't you know who I am,' spluttered Canning. 'Who are you?' replied Dunlop. Joyce MacMillan of the *Guardian* jumped in and, amidst applause from the world's pressmen, called out to Canning: 'Why don't you just sit down. Who do you think you are?' Instead of attacking Dunlop the press representatives turned on Canning. Dunlop was delighted, thinking of the marvellous publicity he would get for the Festival in the press and on television, only to find himself upstaged by a lion that had escaped from its cage somewhere in the wilds of Scotland, and all the television reporters were diverted to look out for it.

In his summary of the Festival Allen Wright suggested that perhaps it should be left to the Fringe to take risks and that the Festival might

> concentrate on mounting a few block-busters, or at least major productions on a scale which Fringe groups can not afford. That would seem to be more sensible than competing with such an enormous enterprise as the Fringe which, in itself, is the biggest arts festival in the world – though I don't believe it could flourish for long without the main Festival as its backbone.
>
> (A. Wright, *Scotsman*, 4 September 1989)

Earlier in the year a public forum on the future of the Festival had been held. This had been initiated by the District Council, and the *Scotsman* had agreed to organize it; the funding coming from the District Council, the Chamber of Commerce, the Bank of Scotland, the Royal Bank of Scotland, Scottish Financial Enterprise, IBM and BP. Delegates were invited from the Festival staff and other arts organizations, the financial and business community and local politicians. There were two open sessions for all the delegates and six workshops devoted to specific areas; the speakers included Dunlop, Martin Segal, the Director of the New York Festival, and Sheila Colvin, now Director of the Aldeburgh Festival. This forum raised a number of important issues including spon-

sorship, marketing and, above all, the structure of the Festival Society itself. A direct result of the Forum was the decision by the Festival Council to set up a working party to review the role, size, membership and structure of both the Society and the Council, the role of the Director and the management of the Festival.

About the same time Dunlop, in association with Mike Hathorn, the Associate Director for Finance and Administration, drew up a three-year business plan. The aims, as set out in the document, were to increase income from advertising, merchandising, sponsorship (particularly from overseas) and the exploitation of the Society's own productions by means of recordings and video; to strengthen the management team by the appointment of a marketing director and to explore new initiatives to increase ticket sales; the setting up of a permanent unit to produce the Society's own theatrical events which could then be toured throughout the UK and abroad; the formation of a Festival theatre company utilizing the best of Scottish and international dramatic talent, and an intimate opera company on the lines of Folkopera with Leith Theatre as its base. Dunlop felt very strongly that the Festival should become a producing festival rather than just a receiving one. Above all he considered it essential that one of the city's theatres should be converted into a Festival theatre capable of taking opera, ballet and large-scale musicals, and which would incorporate the Festival Office and Management, thus providing a permanent home for the Festival.

In 1986 Dunlop had suggested that an effort should be made to nominate Edinburgh as European City of Culture in 1990, and had even recommendeded that if Edinburgh and Glasgow put in a joint bid the result would be a foregone conclusion. The Labour Party was not prepared to consider a joint application and approaches were made to the EEC Council of Ministers for Edinburgh to be considered on its own. Unfortunately it did not make a proper presentation and the leaders of the main cultural organizations were not invited to present their case to the European representatives, and Glasgow became the 1990 European City of Culture. Hiding its bitter disappointment Edinburgh put on a show of nonchalance and even allowed Glasgow to advertise in the Festival programmes and elsewhere, no doubt at a cost. Festival visitors were subsequently surprised to see slogans such as 'Glasgow's miles better' and 'You are now only 44 miles from the cultural capital of Europe' prominently displayed on buses and hoardings throughout the city. But there was no doubt that Glasgow's success was a severe blow to Edinburgh's pride and caused the District Council to reconsider its attitude to the arts and, in particular, to the funding of the Festival.

After 40 years and countless appeals from the Festival Society, Edinburgh District Council and the Scottish Arts Council at last agreed to a definite commitment to the Festival by guaranteeing funding over a three-year period. Lothian Region was showing an increasing interest in renewing its support for the Festival and, in addition, an endowment fund had been set up with Sir Thomas Risk and Professor Jack Shaw as the main trustees. The aim was to raise £10 million and, thanks to the efforts of Sir Thomas, the Fund quickly reached £700 000. With sponsorship having now reached a figure of £550 000 the Festival found itself in a reasonably stable financial situation, and for the first time the Festival Director could plan ahead without worrying whether there would be money available to honour contracts. It also enabled him to spend more money on the music programme, particularly opera, and to bring back a few of the 'stars' who had been absent from the last few Festivals.

Dunlop was concerned to learn that, as part of its 1990 City of Culture celebrations, Glasgow had signed the Bolshoi to present three operas in Glasgow the week before the Festival. This could seriously affect the Festival's own presentations by the Slovak National Opera. So when he discovered that Glasgow was having difficulty raising the money required for the visit he offered to take the smallest production, Prokofiev's *Betrothal in a Monastery*, which would fit comfortably on to the stage of the Playhouse, and to share the costs. At the same time he arranged for the Bolshoi Orchestra to give two concerts in the Usher Hall as a replacement for the USSR State Orchestra which had cancelled its visit.

This year, 1990, was the centenary of the birth of Martinů and, in celebration, Dunlop organized the most comprehensive survey of his works ever heard in Britain, including two of his operas, *The Greek Passion* in a concert performance by the Prague Symphony Orchestra, and his surrealistic opera *Julietta*. His other theme that year focused on the arts and culture of the countries of the Pacific Rim with companies from Korea, Japan and California including the celebrated Saito Kinen Orchestra conducted by Seiji Ozawa and the San Francisco Symphony Orchestra, together with the Cleveland San José Ballet, which is based for half the year in California. To commemorate the hundredth anniversary of Robert Louis Stevenson's arrival in Samoa, Dunlop produced an adaptation of *Treasure Island* in the Assembly Hall.

Dunlop was extremely upset to discover that, having initiated the negotiations and campaigned strenuously for almost two years for the conversion of the Empire into a Festival Theatre, he and the Festival Society were not being consulted on the final plans for the theatre. He was appalled when it was revealed that the original scheme had been amended and no longer included space for the Festival offices within the theatre. Dunlop's cherished plan that the Festival should manage the theatre on a 52-week basis had also been scrapped. This was a severe blow to the Festival Society which had fully expected that it would have rent-free accommodation throughout the year and a free venue for Festival events as well as a theatre in which to mount its own productions. In an attempt to salvage something of the original scheme a service contract was drawn up which suggested sharing the Festival's computerized box office system and the sharing of box office and technical staff, which would have considerable savings for both the Society and the Festival Theatre, but this also fell by the wayside.

Initially Dunlop had succeeded in raising a certain amount of support from the Festival Council for his three-year plan, but when he appeared to show more interest in running the Festival Theatre than the Festival some of that support began to fall away. Although the concept was sound there were doubts as to whether Dunlop had the necessary administrative qualities to carry it through. Dunlop also failed to gain the full backing of one or two members of his staff, which was essential if a plan of such magnitude was to be successful. There was also criticism that the music programme was never organized in time making it difficult for him to engage top artists and companies. Used to last-minute arrangements in the theatre, Dunlop had difficulty gearing himself up to engaging opera companies and musicians several years ahead, although it has to be emphasized that erratic funding made this difficult. These factors together with the strong press criticism that the standard of music had deteriorated during the past eight years convinced some members of the Festival Council that it was time for a change.

Dunlop was convinced that there was a cabal on the Festival Council determined to get rid of him, one of whose members was deliberately leaking to the press tales of dissension at Council meetings. These suspicions were confirmed when, after a caucus meeting of the Council on 11 November 1989, the *Scotsman* reported that the Festival Director was to be 'dumped'. Though notice had been given that the meeting would take place it was estimated that only about a dozen of the 21 members were present. Some members felt that it was unconstitutional for such an important decision to be taken by so few Council members, and there was widespread criticism that, as the meeting was declared 'informal', no minutes were taken. Dunlop justifiably complained to the Executive Committee (6 December 1990) that such a situation placed him in an impossible position and suggested that whoever leaked the information should resign. The Lord Provost, Eleanor McLaughlin, explained that, whilst the matter of his contract had been discussed, it was only to suggest that he be asked to find someone to 'shadow' him in the post until such time, not yet determined, when he would retire. At another Council meeting on the 17th December 1990 it was agreed unanimously that Dunlop should be asked to extend his contract for a further year to take in the 1992 Festival – an offer which Dunlop declined. In a letter to the Lord Provost dated 12 January 1991 he stated, 'I love the Festival and Edinburgh and I would have been happy to lead my staff toward a successful completion of the three years plan that both council and officers had agreed. Now, a large number of the council do not appear to accept the full implementation of that plan'. If his plans could not be put into action Dunlop had no desire to continue.

The District Council had finally authorized the much needed improvements to the Lyceum Theatre but doubts had arisen as to whether the work would be completed in time for the 1991 Festival. According to the terms of the lease with the District Council, the Lyceum's management was obliged to make the theatre available to the Society during the Festival period, and in January Dunlop wrote to the Manager giving notice that they would be liable for costs in the event of the Festival being unable to use the theatre, but to no effect. At a cost of around £155 000, approximately £100 000 more than the rent of the Lyceum, Dunlop made arrangements for the Empire to be opened up to take the shows scheduled for the Lyceum. It was suggested that, in order to recover the costs, legal action be taken against the Lyceum, particularly as the Lyceum Company planned to reopen immediately after the Festival with its own production and Dunlop was convinced that, with a little extra effort, the work could have been finished in time for the Festival. (The Lyceum Company had always resented having to give up the theatre during the Festival.) Eventually the Society was persuaded to drop this action as a successful outcome would bankrupt the Lyceum.

Another expensive headache for Dunlop was the cancellation of *Peter Pan* which was to be given by the Ship's Company and directed by Bill Bryden. When the Tramway Theatre in Glasgow, who along with the BBC were assisting with the costs, dropped out of the arrangements the Ship's Company asked for an additional £100 000. As the Festival Society was in no position to find this extra money Dunlop refused and Bill Bryden backed out. With four weeks to go Dunlop had no major production for the Assembly Hall. Tom Fleming came to the rescue and managed to assemble sufficient Scottish actors to revive his production of *The Thrie Estaites*. Two other major shows also came to grief at the last moment. *Lady Chatterley on Trial* had to be cancelled for financial (not censorship) reasons, and as a result of a personal quarrel between the

writers Barrie Keefe and Alan Plater the rock musical *I Only Want To Be With You* to be given by the Theatre Royal, Stratford East was replaced by *Shooting Ducks*. These alterations entailed reprinting the programme brochure, but with copies of the original still in circulation, there was considerable confusion and, with little advance publicity, it was difficult to find an audience to fill the Assembly Hall for a three-week run of *The Thrie Estaites,* and it was not a success at the box office.

With increases of around £40 000 from both Edinburgh District Council and the Scottish Arts Council, and a large increase in sponsorship, Dunlop was able to present one of the strongest music programmes for many years. Scottish Opera (after a long period of changes within its management which had made it difficult to enter into any satisfactory joint planning arrangements) returned with a new production of Mozart's *La Clemenza di Tito*. The orchestras included the Czech Philharmonic, the Philharmonia and the Royal Scottish Orchestra (the former Scottish National Orchestra having now received Royal status) and there was a splendid series of recitals by Margaret Price, Felicity Lott, Jessye Norman, Thomas Allen, Tatyana Nikolaeva, Peter Donohoe, Josef Suk, Igor Oistrakh and Steven Isserlis. Continuing his links with the Soviet Union Dunlop invited the Bolshoi Opera to return with productions of Rimsky-Korsakov's *Christmas Eve* and Tchaikovsky's *Eugene Onegin*. The Kirov Opera under its dynamic music director, Valery Gergiev, performed all Mussorgsky's operas, with staged performances of *Khovanshchina* and *The Marriage* and concert performances of *Boris Godunov*, *Sorotchinsky Fair* and *Salammbó*. These performances by Russia's two leading opera companies introduced to British audiences a host of exciting young Russian singers such as Olga Borodina, Elena Prokina, Nina Rautio, Ludmilla Nam, Ekaterina Kudriavchenko, Larissa Diadkova, Yuri Marusin and Vladimir Redkin, many of whom were to reappear in leading roles with the major British companies. Three further concerts were given by the Leningrad Philharmonic Orchestra under Temirkanov with a group of Soviet soloists and the Lenkom Theatre of Moscow presented its brilliantly satirical production of Ostrovsky's *Too Clever by Half*. Unable to be present Hugh Canning later commented to Dunlop, 'I hear the music at the Festival was very good this year'. To which Dunlop replied, 'Yes, Hugh. For the first time we had the money to do what we wanted to do! Why don't you print that?' But Canning never did!

On the morning the Bolshoi were due to leave Moscow Dunlop woke up and turned on the television in time to see tanks rumbling down the main street in Moscow. As soon as he reached the office he rang the Bolshoi to find out what was happening, to be told that everything was all right. Thanks to the warm relationship that had been built up between the Soviet authorities and the Festival Society the only aircraft being allowed out were the chartered planes transporting the Bolshoi company to Edinburgh. Following the successful coup by the Kremlin hardliners to overthrow Gorbachov, the stage doorman's office at the Playhouse, with its television set, became the focal point each evening as terrified singers rushed from the stage and crowded the staircase, desperately trying to find out what was happening at home. In the Usher Hall Yuri Temirkanov conducted the Leningrad Philharmonic Orchestra with the Festival Chorus and a quartet of Russian soloists in an overweight but, in the circumstances, infinitely moving performance of Mozart's *Requiem*. The hearts of the entire audience went out to the artists who were in an agony of suspense wondering who would be in power, and what kind of situation they would face on their return.

Attention was briefly drawn from the Russian crisis by the enfant terrible, Nigel Kennedy when, after an operation on his shoulder, he had to cancel his advertised recital of classical music. Without consulting the Festival Society he arranged with the sponsor to give a programme of pop music playing from the hip, country style. Had Dunlop known about this in time Kennedy could have done an alternative concert for the Festival.

Frank Dunlop's genius for arousing controversy continued until the end. At a lunch with arts journalists he stirred things up by agreeing with one of the critics that the standard of the Fringe had gone down enormously. That it had become 'smug and self-satisfied' and was 'reminiscent of a modern Tower of Babel of the arts'. While no one could deny that there was a great deal of truth in his remarks it was perhaps hardly politic for the Festival Director to state his views so publicly. These outspoken remarks irritated the Lord Provost, Eleanor McLaughlin, to such an extent that she issued a statement declaring:

> I have remained silent for some time now while Frank Dunlop has made critical and divisive comments which have done little to enhance the reputation of Edinburgh both as a city and as a venue for the arts. However, enough is enough and his recent statements on the Fringe are nothing short of outrageous.

Adding, 'Mr Dunlop has no right to interfere with the Fringe. There are more constructive ways for him to spend his time'. Then, referring to the cancellation of Nigel Kennedy's concert, she commented, 'Perhaps Frank Dunlop should stop throwing tantrums and put his energy into filling the large hole this has left in the Festival programme and leave the running of the Fringe to the people who have made it the success it is today'. The Lord Provost's statement created an even greater furore, not only in the press but among members of the Society (some of whom supported Dunlop's views and felt that the matter should have been dealt with privately).

Dunlop's frustration and anger at his long-running feud with the District Council surfaced when, on the eve of his departure, he gave an interview to the *Scotsman* in which he accused some of the Labour leaders of major interference and an anti-Festival attitude during his eight years in charge. It was not a case of his not being able to get on with the city fathers, but their 'not being able to get on with me'.

In spite of the ever-widening gulf between the volatile Frank Dunlop and the District Council, Dunlop was undoubtedly the right Director at the time. In a 50-year history, not unnoted for its political problems, Dunlop's period of office coincided with by far the most difficult political situation that any Director had to endure. Although some earlier Directors would certainly have dealt more diplomatically with the city fathers it is impossible to imagine their views and policies being politically acceptable to the extremists in power at the time. Dunlop and the Labour District Council were in broad agreement on principles but not necessarily on how these should be carried out. With a considerably reduced Labour majority on the District Council and with the District Council no longer having its former controlling interest on the Festival Council the time was ripe for a change of direction. But as the impish Dunlop chuckled gleefully in an interview with Owen Dudley Edwards, the press will 'have to make the most of me. They'll never get any off-the-cuff clangers from Brian' [McMaster].

Chapter 9

Brian McMaster 1992–

After the outspoken, erudite, multifaceted Drummond and the flamboyant, puckish and equally forthright Dunlop the appointment of the small, bearded, self-effacing Brian McMaster with the general air and appearance of a senior civil servant startled many people. Brian McMaster? Everybody tried to recall what they knew about the new occupant of one of the most prestigious international appointments in the arts. They remembered that he had run the Welsh National Opera for what seemed like an eternity, putting what had formerly been a provincial opera company on the world map. There was also his sponsorship of East German directors such as Joachim Herz, Harry Kupfer and Ruth Berghaus, some of whose work had been controversial to say the least. Was the Edinburgh Festival to become a bastion of modern, conceptual opera production? Such a possibility might intrigue the critics but could equally alienate Edinburgh's relatively conservative audience. How would he cope with non-vocal music, drama, dance and the visual arts? It then came to light that he had at one time worked for EMI. Perhaps his general musical experience was wider than anyone had realized? His emphasis on opera production might also conceal an interest in the theatre! But the world would have to wait and see: apart from the occasional hint, the reticent Brian McMaster was unlikely to reveal his hand to the media. But he had a reputation as an efficient administrator and, after the chaotic and turbulent Dunlop years, a period of tranquillity might not be a bad thing for the Festival.

McMaster brought to an end the long-standing and frequently acrimonious dispute about the London office by moving to Edinburgh, a very popular decision with the staff and the local community. The insistence of the previous directors on running the Festival from London had frequently been interpreted as arrogance. Now the Festival could be wholly identified with the city. This also improved relations within the Festival office itself. In the massive operation of putting on almost 200 performances by some 60 companies and orchestras with a small permanent staff, strengthened by dozens of part-time operatives, there had always been a certain amount of tension when the London staff appeared for four weeks in the year and took over.

Due to losses caused by the closure of the Lyceum, the cancellation of *Peter Pan*, and the collapse of a joint deal with Dublin to share the costs of the Bolshoi Opera's visit, together with a reduction in ticket sales caused by the economic downturn, the 1991 Festival had resulted in a deficit of £198 000. Therefore any hopes or fears that the opera

programme would be dominated by the East German school of direction were not to be realized. There was no money to spare for an expensive opera season and any large-scale projects would have to be postponed until the new Festival Theatre had been completed. McMaster wanted to give the Festival a more distinctive character by reducing the number of fringe-type events, particularly in the drama programme. He felt the role of the official Festival should be to present high-quality, large-scale performances of the kind that the Fringe groups could not afford. In order to maintain a tighter control on quality he wanted to exclude from the Festival programme all events that were not organized and promoted by the Society. Another stated aim was to reflect the best of Scottish culture and enable Scottish arts organizations to present their work to a worldwide audience.

One problem that has troubled all the directors, except possibly Lord Harewood, has been the curiously belligerent attitude towards the Festival of the London critics. As far back as 1947 one critic refused to cover the Festival because of its 'unenterprising' programme. Though after six years of sparse culture, even in London, how anyone could consider Bruno Walter and the Vienna Philharmonic, L'Orchestre des Concerts Colonnne, Glyndebourne Opera, the Old Vic, Jouvet, Fonteyn, Schnabel, Schumann, Ferrier et al., not worthy of a visit is beyond comprehension. As soon as the programme was announced each year the complaints would begin. Some critics found it possible to criticize the Festival without attending a single event. Sheridan Morley wrote in the *Spectator* (12 September 1992): 'I have managed to miss most of the last ten Edinburgh Festivals, ever since making the discovery that anything good there came immediately to London and anything bad got desperately overpraised by those with vested interests in keeping what is clearly still a thin drama programme alive.' Who the people with vested interests were was a mystery; certainly not the Edinburgh critics as one or two of them could on occasion be equally censorious. Furthermore, the period from 1982 to 1991 covered Frank Dunlop's World Theatre Seasons which were unique to Edinburgh.

Why these critics have been so persistently hostile to the Festival is a question to which even they might not have an answer. Was it because they objected to Edinburgh's pretensions to high cultural status? Did they resent the fact that for three weeks in the year Edinburgh challenged London's supremacy as the cultural capital of Britain, even of the world? Did they really believe that nothing worthwhile occurred north of Watford? There was of course the inconvenience of travelling 400 miles to Edinburgh when they might prefer to remain comfortably at home covering London openings and ignoring the rest of the country! An even more probable answer was that, unlike the paying audiences who tended to sample a cross-selection of what was on offer, the critics only attended performances in their own speciality subject and cheerfully ignored everything else. Consequently, after reviewing two or three drama openings a theatre critic might give extensive coverage to a mediocre stand-up comic on the Fringe rather than attend a major opera or dance programme, even though it might provide an equally enthralling theatrical experience. As a result, if a critic was unfortunate enough to experience a couple of less inspiring performances that reviewer would promptly write off the Festival as a disaster, oblivious to the fact that there may have been wonderful performances in a different sphere. John Drummond had his own views on this subject. He succeeded during a couple of Festivals in forcing the critics to widen their horizons but the effect was short-lived. This negative attitude was galling to the organizers who had to suffer the slings and arrows of disgruntled critics, allied to the continual worry that a few uncomplimentary

reviews for performances which had been cheered to the rafters by the audience could have a disastrous effect on ticket sales, not only for the current Festival but for future Festivals, and might even discourage visitors. As the Festival had always depended on the box office to provide a large percentage of its funding this was quite a serious threat.

McMaster's first Festival, in 1992, was no exception. There were four themes: the music of Tchaikovsky, a series of concerts devoted to Scottish classical music through the centuries, and retrospectives of two almost forgotten playwrights, Harley Granville Barker and C.P. Taylor (a new departure for the Festival), supported by lectures, symposia and the publication of study guides and the texts of the plays. Shortly before the Festival one detractor, Waldemar Januszczak, an arts editor for Channel 4, wrote that he wasn't going to Edinburgh this year because of what he described as 'misplaced nationalism'. Continuing,

> Edinburgh first gained its reputation as the greatest arts festival in the world not by rescuing obscure Scotsmen from well-deserved obscurity but by bringing the best international art and theatre to Britian … I shall miss Edinburgh but I am simply not interested in witnessing one more stage of its horrible and relentless and, yes, tragic transformation into a minor, local event.
>
> (W. Januszczak, *Guardian*, Festival Supplement, 1992)

Michael White, in the *Independent* (16 August 1992), was hardly more complimentary: 'With Tchaikovsky as its music focus this year Edinburgh seems to be making a recessionary appeal to the box office, and not much appeal to anyone who expects a major arts festival to offer something more than you'd find in an average family pops night.' This view was shared by one of the *Daily Telegraph*'s reviewing team who questioned whether a once great international festival should go so completely overboard for music that can be heard all the year round. The fact that the programme included a number of the composer's rarely heard works was almost ignored.

In an editorial Magnus Linklater was provoked into retaliation:

> Broadsides from various Fleet Street papers, notably the *Guardian*, have pronounced the Festival as 'boring, wretched, dated, and artless' … It is, of course, a trifle inconvenient for these arbiters of modern taste to discover that their own newspapers disagree with them, to the point of devoting more space than ever to the Festival, spending large sums of money on advertising their wares, and boasting about their coverage. It is even more inconvenient to discover that Edinburgh audiences not only seem to be ignoring their advice but, despite the recession, have been filling houses, crowding theatres, and generally enjoying themselves no end. More than this, there has been a cultural richness that is simply not available to the lamentable provincialism that is the metropolitan tendency these days. No one (including, by the way, several London critics who seem not to have been properly briefed) could mistake the performance of Els Joglars for anything other than superb theatre, of an energy and depth which is simply not to be found in the West End. No one (except those for whom journeying north of the Wash instils paralysis of the brain) could claim that staging *Moses and Aaron* in the Usher Hall was safe and traditional. Anyone who fails to understand that Allan Ramsay is central to the one of the greatest periods of European art, is probably visually impaired. Untroubled by these crippling deficiencies, we can safely say that the Festival has been a success, and in some respects a triumph. Musically it has produced at least four perfomances of the kind Kenneth Tynan used to call 'high definition' – the Schoenberg, the first St. Petersburg concert, Olga Borodina and Janice Watson. Dance was particularly strong, with the Mark Morris Group, but it was the theatre which finally came good. The nominees for the new *Scotsman* awards would stand scrutiny with any drama in the world. Indeed, the point is that it was *world* drama, and that includes the two Scottish theatre groups who made it to the finals.

> But to see Scottish actors and directors in a global context is a concept too taxing for those who can only judge it from the fastnesses of the Farringdon Road.
>
> (M. Linklater, *Scotsman*, September 1992)

The opening concert, *Moses and Aaron*, was a triumph for all concerned, particularly the Festival Chorus, the first amateur body to tackle the work. The singers found the music thankless and frustratingly difficult to learn, and few in the audience could have appreciated the time and effort that had gone into it, but the resulting performance enhanced the chorus's already formidable reputation. Later in the Festival it performed Tchaikovsky's unknown *Cantata Moscow* and his unaccompanied *Liturgy of St John Chrysostom*. His operatic output was represented by a concert performance of his early opera *The Oprichnik* with largely Russian soloists and by Opera North's production of *Yolanta*, mistakenly presented in tandem with a quirky though amusing modern version of *The Nutcracker* by Adventures in Motion Pictures. In three morning concerts the Borodin Quartet performed all three of Tchaikovsky's string quartets together with the more or less contemporaneous quartets of Brahms. Peter Donohoe, the foremost Tchaikovsky interpreter of the day, presented a substantial selection of his piano works in three recitals and some of his songs were performed by Olga Borodina and Dmitri Hvorostovsky. Of the non-Tchaikovsky works the St Petersburg Philharmonic under Mariss Jansons, in the words of Mary Miller in the *Scotsman* (22 August 1992), played Shostakovich's fifth Symphony 'as though laying out a carpet of all human emotion. Some people were able to shout at the end. Others, though, stumbled home humbled, unable to speak'. The Bartók Quartet gave authentic performances of the six Bartók quartets and there were notable recital debuts by Janice Watson, Barbara Bonney, Andreas Schmidt and Benjamin Frith. One of McMaster's innovations was the successful introduction of a number of late-night concerts in the Usher Hall which included Mahler's arrangement of his *Das Lied von der Erde* for contralto, tenor and piano and Schoenberg's arrangement of the same work for voices and chamber ensemble.

But at least one English critic, Paul Driver, reacted favourably and commented:

> Edinburgh music is in safe hands again, to judge from Brian McMaster's first set of programmes. Although his choice of Tchaikovsky for the main theme might seem unadventurous, it has so far proved highly rewarding. The composer's very popularity has masked his achievement, and we have been enjoyably able to reassess the latter both in terms of its variety and its quality.
>
> (P. Driver, *Sunday Times*, 23 August 1992)

He went on to praise McMaster's scholarly approach to the programme planning and his 'collector's instinct' which inspired him to offer almost complete sets of Taylor and Barker plays and Tchaikovsky quartets and piano music. 'McMaster has initiated a good deal of scholarly documentation of his themes – that kind of challenging, intellectually curious approach is precisely, it seems to me, what a good festival of the arts should now be risking.'

With regard to McMaster's Scottish themes Januszczak's prognosis had some justification. While one concert of Scottish music might have been greeted with enthusiam, five underlined how meagre and lightweight Scotland's contribution in this genre is. By far the most interesting items were the contemporary works by Thea Musgrave and James MacMillan. Of the other Scottish theme Michael Coveney reported in the *Observer* (30 August 1992): 'The C.P. Taylor retrospective has assumed the proportions of a genuine

débâcle'. *The Ballachulish Beat* should perhaps have remained in oblivion, *And a nightingale sang* and *Operation Elvis* were hardly worthy of revival, *The Black and White Minstrels* was handicapped by a bad production and *Walter* suffered from insufficient rehearsal; only *Schippel* and *Good* appeared to justify Taylor's reputation as a dramatist.

The Granville Barker season was a more rewarding experience. In addition to rehearsed readings of four plays, McMaster negotiated with three companies to stage his major works including the hitherto unperformed *His Majesty* by the Orange Tree Company and a weighty production of *The Voysey Inheritance* by William Gaskill for the Lyceum Theatre Company. But the highlight of the drama programme was Peter James's brilliantly imaginative staging of *The Madras House* for the Lyric Theatre, Hammersmith, of which Alastair Macaulay wrote in the *Financial Times* (27 August 1992): 'No brief newspaper review can convey the way this play's detail becomes so enthralling. I had not seen it before; hours after I am still electrified. No British play of this century has so excited me.' Cleverly surmounting the problem of the large cast, and at the same time underlining the play's theme of the exploitation of women, James double-cast each of his actresses as the six wealthy, unmarried Huxtable girls and as the sales assistants in the family drapery business and, between the scenes, deployed them as a mute, resentful chorus shifting scenery in their underwear.

When the accounts were made up, it was discovered that in one stroke McMaster had achieved a surplus of almost £190 000 and written off the deficit from the previous year. With increases in subsidy from the various funding bodies McMaster was able to plan a more ambitious Festival for 1993.

McMaster's second Festival started off with a major disaster when four days prior to the opening the backstage area of the Playhouse Theatre went up in flames. As with the King's and the Lyceum there had been a niggling fear that the complicated electrical and technical facilities required might not be ready on time after the theatre's £2 million refurbishment, but no one had envisaged an ill-timed accident turning doubt into certainty. With the help of Edinburgh District Council arrangements were made to transfer the Mark Morris Dance Group, which had been due to open the theatre, to Meadowbank Stadium but the Playhouse stage was the only one in Edinburgh that could take *Falstaff* and the Canadian Opera Company's double bill of Bartók's *Bluebeard's Castle* and Schoenberg's *Erwartung,* and without it these operas would have to be cancelled. A close inspection revealed that the damage was less widespread than had been feared and there was a possibility that the theatre could be made ready for the opera. Apollo Leisure, however, wanted to close down completely in order to carry out the repairs and the redecoration of the smoke-damaged building for a 17-week run of the Cameron Mackintosh show, *Les Misérables,* beginning in September. After two days of tense negotiations a deal was struck with Apollo Leisure to postpone the redecoration until the following year. In return the Festival and Edinburgh District Council agreed to help meet any additional costs.

The transfer of his performances to a sports stadium was insufficient to deter the ebullient Mark Morris, who declared that the members of his company were so keen to come to Edinburgh that they would perform in a swamp if they had to. Morris had stunned the Edinburgh audiences the previous year when he had danced both Dido and the Sorceress in his version of Purcell's *Dido and Aeneas*. Later he had remarked to the *Scotsman*'s ballet critic Christopher Bowen (29 August 1992): 'Well it's *my* ballet and they're the best parts'. To which one dancer had added: 'That's Mark, he just wants to be

Krystle *and* Alexis!' In 1993 he brought two programmes, one made up entirely of new works, but it was his *New Love Song Waltzes* to music by Brahms that entranced his many Edinburgh devotees.

Since the previous year the London press appeared to have undergone a sea-change and McMaster's 1993 programme, in which he juxtaposed works by Schubert and Janáček as well as featuring Verdi and the Scottish composer James McMillan, was for once greeted with enthusiasm. Hugh Canning (the scourge of Frank Dunlop) commented

> In less than two years as festival director, Brian McMaster has reversed what had seemed the inexorable decline of classical music at Edinburgh ... McMaster's wide-ranging musical contacts are already producing dividends in the 1993 programme ... his operatic fare, however, has still to recover from the lean Dunlop years ... McMaster has cleverly combined the thorny problems of new and Scottish music in one glamorous, user-friendly package: the talented attention-seeking, Catholic-socialist-Scottish Nationalist composer, James MacMillan, who is treated to a high-profile mini-festival within the context of the wider event.
>
> (H. Canning, *Sunday Times*, 15 August 1993)

The drama critics were no less enthusiastic. The opportunity of seeing the work of no fewer than four internationally renowned directors comes rarely to Britain and therefore the promise of Peter Sellars, Peter Stein, Robert Wilson and Robert Lepage created an excited buzz of anticipation within their ranks.

When it came to the point the illustrious four unleashed a minor war, with the critics and everybody else joyfully taking sides. Peter Sellars fired the first deafening salvo with his updated production of *The Persians* attributed to Aeschylus who, no doubt to his amazement, found himself transported in time to the Gulf War trying to put up a case for Saddam Hussein. This wholesale slaughter of a notable anti-war play enraged most of the critics – and inspired them to even greater heights of eloquence: only *The Times* and the *Guardian,* with its sister publication the *Observer*, finding anything praiseworthy to say. Irving Wardle in the *Independent on Sunday* (5 September 1993) accused Sellars of 'having broken all records for crimes against the classics in the name of topical relevance'.

Then the skies were lit up by an explosion of bombshells in Robert Wilson's fascinating production of Gertrude Stein's opera libretto that never was, *Dr Faustus lights the lights,* which was variously described as 'a thrilling piece of impersonal abstraction' (John Peter, *Sunday Times*), 'a hallucination' (Martin Hoyle, *Mail on Sunday*) and an 'entertaining absurdist façade' (Alastair Macaulay, *Financial Times*). Its verbal exercises inciting comments such as 'I enjoyed because I enjoyed. It I enjoyed.' from Kirsty Milne in the *Sunday Telegraph* (29 August 1993) and 'A waste, is a waste is a waste' from John Peter in the *Sunday Times* (29 August 1993).

In the last week Peter Stein sent in the storm troopers, all 200 of them, in Shakespeare's *Julius Caesar.* Despite some excellent performances by the leading actors, in particular Gert Voss as Mark Antony and Thomas Holtzmann as Brutus, the general feeling was that by the scale of the production, transferred from the Felsenreitschule in Salzburg to the Royal Exhibition Hall, Ingliston, Stein diminished the play and made nonsense of the conspiratorial scenes, forcing the characters to shout their secrets across a 180 foot-wide acting area. John Peter in the *Sunday Times* (5 September 1993) considered it 'relentlessly and thuddingly grand, hugely and self-consciously theatrical, but without the energy of drama'. On the other hand the *Guardian*'s Michael Billington (3 September 1993) argued

that 'Never before in Julius Caesar have I also been so aware of the sense of characters in the grip of some invisible destiny ... Stein uses drama to reclaim history which is why I judge his production a down-right, unforgettable masterpiece.' There were also wide-ranging opinions of the Citizens' Theatre Company's production of *The Soldiers* by Jacob Lenz, formerly seen in Edinburgh in operatic guise as *Die Soldaten*.

Peace was negotiated with the Tag Theatre Company's simple but moving production of Alastair Cording's adaptation of Lewis Grassic Gibbon's classic trilogy *A Scot's Quair*, which almost united the critics. Here 12 almost unknown actors skilfully undertook more than 50 roles. Charles Spencer in the *Daily Telegraph* (23 August 1993) considered that 'The Edinburgh Festival certainly has showier productions than this, but none I suspect, that will speak with such truth and tenderness of the promptings of the human heart'.

The last of the big four, Robert Lepage, turned his attention to opera, and with the support of the outstanding Canadian Opera Company led the victory celebrations with his brilliantly integrated double bill of *Bluebeard's Castle* by Bartók and a Freudian interpretation of Schoenberg's *Erwartung*, which was generally considered the major sensation of the Festival, and for which the Company received the Scotsman/Hamada award. (These awards, begun in 1992, were funded by the Hamada Foundation and organized by the *Scotsman*.) The other major opera presentations featured Verdi 'from first to last' with a revival of Welsh National Opera's classic production by Peter Stein of his final opera *Falstaff* and a revelatory concert performance of his first opera *Oberto,* thrillingly performed by the Festival Chorus and the Royal Scottish National Orchestra with a magnificent team of soloists. Scottish Opera had a slight problem with *I Due Foscari* when Frederick Burchinal as the elder Foscari lost his voice and was reduced to miming the role while his understudy, Phillip Joll, sang from the wings. As he became increasingly involved in the drama Joll emerged further and further on to the stage giving rise to a remark by Scottish Opera's Managing Director that the opera should be renamed *I Tre Foscari*!

McMaster's brave enterprise in presenting 17 of the works of James MacMillan revealed that Scotland was beginning to take an honoured place in the contemporary musical scene. Apart from a disappointing one-act opera *Tourist Variations* which Richard Morrison in *The Times* considered 'the first serious *faux pas* of MacMillan's career', the season was a great success with both public and critics. Gerald Larner commenting on his *Visitatio Sepulchro* in the *Scotsman* (28 August 1993) wrote: 'Macmillan's musical imagery continues to develop in eloquence and his textures to accumulate in interest.'

Illness played havoc with McMaster's concert schedule, particularly the conductors' roster. Klaus Tennstedt and Erich Leinsdorf both cancelled and Sir Edward Downes underwent a serious eye operation which left him almost blind. David Robertson bravely stepped in to conduct *Oberto*, a rarely performed opera that he had almost certainly never conducted before and Welser-Möst took over Tennstedt's Mahler programme. The Leinsdorf concerts with the Philharmonia were reassigned to Edo de Waart, but he too cried off, and at the very last moment Marek Janowski and Mark Elder came to the rescue. There were also problems in the soprano wing when Karen Huffstodt, Alessandra Marc and Joan Rodgers all had to be replaced. But McMaster's Associate Director, James Waters, still goes white at the gills when he remembers his boss's terse announcement on his return from a trip to Paris in March that he was cancelling a major opera production

which he had found unsatisfactory. The show had been booked, the sets built and the brochure had already gone to the printers. With one thing and another the 1993 Festival is one that will linger in their memories for some time to come.

McMaster may have won the critics round but with his policy on art exhibitions he was sailing into treacherous waters. The question of exhibitions had always been a very grey area. In the fifties the main Festival exhibitions had been presented by the Society in association with the Royal Scottish Academy and the Arts Council of Great Britain, who had undertaken the organization. In the sixties Harewood had invited Richard Buckle to mount the Epstein Exhibition on behalf of the Festival Society and this was followed by a number of additional exhibitions which were accommodated in either the National Gallery of Scotland or the Royal Scottish Museum. Then in 1974 Peter Diamand began the practice of including in the programme some 'Associate Exhibitions' which were not organized by the Society. The number of these increased during Frank Dunlop's time until in 1991 over 40 exhibitions were included in the *Official Souvenir Guide.* At this point Brian McMaster put his foot down and in 1992 only the exhibitions in the National Galleries were advertised in the brochure.

In the following year, unwilling to make arbitrary decisions as to which exhibitions were of a high enough standard to be considered, McMaster took the perfectly logical view that since all the music, theatre and dance in the Festival programme had been organized by him, the same should apply to the visual arts. Consequently only the Society's own exhibition *The Waking Dream: Photography's First Century* (an enormously popular exhibition of photography from the Gilman collection in New York) was included in the Festival brochure. This decision naturally upset all the galleries which had relied on the free publicity . The directors of the National galleries also objected to their exhibitions being demoted to the level of 'Fringe' events. Duncan MacMillan, Director of the Talbot Rice Gallery, raised the matter at a Festival Council meeting pointing out that the exhibitions were an important part of the overall attraction of the Festival and that the Society could benefit from the exploitation of the resource provided by the main galleries. While acknowledging the importance of the visual arts in the Festival and the contribution made by the galleries McMaster was adamant that the Festival could not be expected to promote exhibitions which were the responsibility of other autonomous bodies.

The press quickly took up the matter, particularly as that year there had been at least three exhibitions at the National Galleries and several others which were undoubtedly of Festival standard. After seeing the extent and standard of the visual arts programme presented in 1993 McMaster relented, and in 1994 the major exhibitions were once again listed in the brochure and a separate guide to all the exhibitions was produced which the Festival helped to distribute. This compromise satisfied most of the galleries, although one or two directors are still slightly disgruntled at their exhibitions not being accorded official status. More debatable is McMaster's current view that the 'route forward is to find ways such as this in which the Festival can back up the excellent work of the whole visual arts community, rather than attempt to replicate it in our own programme' and, as a result, the visual arts have now been dropped from the official programme.

At last, after 47 years of argument, Edinburgh had its own opera house. It was not to be called an opera house but as far as the Festival was concerned the new multi-purpose theatre, with its vast stage and state-of-the art technology, was the opera house the city

had been waiting for. The Festival Director could now go shopping for productions anywhere in the world confident that they could be fitted on to the stage and that the technical installations could cope with even the most complicated technology. The Empire Theatre with its rebuilt stage, refurbished auditorium and new glass and steel frontage had reopened in June as the Festival Theatre and in celebration Brian McMaster had planned an exciting programme of Festival events to fill it.

In keeping with his Beethoven theme for 1994 he organized a marathon, 12-hour *Fidelio* day. It began with a talk by H.C. Robbins Landon followed by a concert given by the Scottish Chamber Orchestra consisting of two early overtures to the opera and the *Cantata on the Death of Emperor Joseph II*, which contained some of the music later recycled for *Fidelio.* In the afternoon there was a concert performance of the early version of the opera, *Leonore*, and in the evening the final reworking given by Scottish Opera in the new theatre. 'The whole day was an unforgettable example of what a festival should do', wrote Michael Kennedy in the *Sunday Telegraph* (21 August 1994).

Fidelio was followed by Mark Morris's full length ballet *L'Allegro, Il Penseroso ed Il Moderato*, a joyful fusion of dance with Handel's music and Milton's poetry and probably his finest work. Then in the second week the stage was filled by Australian Opera's sumptuous production of Britten's *A Midsummer Night's Dream,* which transplanted the action to India under the British Raj, with the mechanicals as a group of soldiers engaged in amateur theatricals and a host of fairies called gopies. The single set, reminiscent of Dunlop's *Oberon*, consisted of a large bandstand on which the Scottish Chamber Orchestra and conductor Roderick Brydon, decked in scarlet uniforms, performed as if for a vice-regal entertainment. The roof of the stand was the realm of Oberon and Puck and underneath was a river with rafts which conveyed the characters to and fro. It was described by Mary Miller as

> brilliant, blazing entertainment. It is wildly funny, elevates bad taste at least to the level of designer advertising, and it has all the dreamy, glistening beauty of an Eastern night and the hot and hazy days of the Empire. Its fairies, so pink and twinkly that they are almost edible, roll glittery eyes and behave with enchanting horridness, the set is green and rippled with light, purple and erotic, mottled and misty. One couldn't dream of anything more magical.
>
> (M. Miller, *Scotsman*, 26 August 1994)

Purists such as Andrew Porter in the *Observer* (4 September 1994) complained that 'amid the riot of cartwheels, fairy lights, and scampering about between and during phrases, the romance and the more poignant emotions of Britten's opera were lost … It was all a bit coarse and unerotic, undisturbing. But it was a spirited show.' He was right but few in the audience cared. It was the spectacle they had waited for and they revelled in it.

The season in the Festival Theatre was completed by one of the most unusual drama productions ever seen at the Festival; a play without dialogue by Peter Handke entitled *The Hour We Knew Nothing of Each Other.* Directed by Luc Bondy, the stage was filled with over 400 characters, real and mythological, brought to life by a cast of 33 actors. Some found it boring, others enthralling; but it certainly provided food for debate. More heated argument was provoked by the world première of the first part of Robert Lepage's epic drama *The Seven Streams of the River Ota* presented in Meadowbank Sports Centre. There were also controversial productions of two of Shakespeare's plays: a satirical *Antony and Cleopatra* by Peter Zadek for the Berliner Ensemble with Gert Voss and Eva

Mattes in the title roles, and a visually beautiful but slow-moving *Winter's Tale* by the brilliant young French director Stéphane Braunschweig. The highlight of the drama programme was Peter Stein's magnificent seven-hour long production of the *Oresteia* by Aeschylus, in Russian, in Murrayfield Ice Rink. The topicality of this 2 500 year-old drama which, in its final section, depicts the birth of civil law and a new democratic order was fully brought home to its Russian cast who only five years before had taken part in their country's first free elections.

In addition to *Fidelio* the Beethoven season included all the piano concertos performed by Andras Schiff with Bernard Haitink and the London Philharmonic, ten of the string quartets by the Borodin Quartet, recitals by Richard Goode, Alfred Brendel and Piotr Anderszewski of the piano sonatas, and all the symphonies, some performed on original or pseudo-original instruments, giving rise to a welter of stimulating discussion as to how Beethoven should or should not be performed. The Festival Chorus performed two versions to Goethe's texts of the Faust legend: Mahler's Symphony No. 8 and Schumann's *Scenes from Goethe's Faust* and, linking the Chabrier and Goethe themes, McMaster resurrected Chabrier's uncompleted last opera *Briséïs*, based on a play by Goethe. The turgid score, owing much to Wagner, had the critics reeling. Michael White commented:

> Not many at the Usher Hall can have been prepared for the impact of Act 1 of *Briséis* ... the music is astonishing: a feast of colour, richly textured, brilliantly imagined and – surprisingly – with backbone. The playing by the BBC Scottish Orchestra under Jean Yves Ossonce, was magnificent with superb singing from Joan Rodgers, Kathryn Harries and the Scottish Opera Chorus. If ever a discovery at Edinburgh cried out for repetition down south, here it is.
>
> (M. White, *Independent on Sunday*, 21 August 1994)

The Goethe celebrations were completed by Robert David MacDonald's production of his *Torquato Tasso* for the Citizens' Theatre which, in spite of an elegantly beautiful set and inspired direction, failed to instil any sense of drama into the work. Continuing the Chabrier theme Gerald Larner devised an entertaining late-night cabaret in which Denis Quilley revealed the composer's not so respectable side and Opera North brought its productions of *L'Étoile* and *Le Roi Malgré-lui*, Jeremy Sams's rewriting of the latter giving rise to another critical explosion.

But 1994 will be remembered primarily as the year dance finally came into its own: five diverse companies from America and Canada gave 19 performances of 14 works by some of the most influential dance creators of the twentieth century – a superb programme by any standard. In addition to Mark Morris there were the pure, exquisite forms of the 75 year-old guru of modern dance, Merce Cunningham, the stark minimalism allied to modern film techniques of Lucinda Childs and the theatricality of Jean-Pierre Perreault. But the real surprise was the brilliance and exuberance of Edward Villella's young Miami City Ballet in two programmes of works by George Balanchine including the British première of his full-length ballet *Jewels*.

Mark Morris, now a regular visitor to the Festival, and the Miami City Ballet returned in 1995 with contrasting productions of Tchaikovsky's *The Nutcracker*. Edward Villella revived Balanchine's production which was seen for the first time outside America but the critics were more intrigued by Morris's *The Hard Nut*; an updated, hilariously funny and undoubtedly more adult version conforming more closely to the original Hoffmann story with its darker resonances. The snowflake scene where the men, dressed in silver tutus and *on point*, joined the women in a travesty of a classical ensemble, crossing and

recrossing the stage in a series of arabesques while scattering armfuls of snowflakes until the stage was white, practically had the audience rolling in the aisles. Carpeting the stage with thousands of plastic carnations Pina Bausch proceeded to put her company through a series of grotesque scenes, dressing the men in badly fitting silk gowns, confronting them with howling alsatians, rubbing their faces in raw onions, and finally sending them out to hug members of the audience. Some found it too bizarre and left, a few requested their money back, while others remained mesmerized to the end.

Even more harrowing was *Still/Here* by the Bill T. Jones/Arnie Zane Company where Jones incorporated videotaped testimonies of people suffering from aids and other terminal illnesses in which they discussed how they coped with dying. This piece had invoked a howl of protest when it had first been performed in America. The dance critic of the *New Yorker*, Arlene Croce, refused to see it and instead wrote a 4 000-word article in which she declared the work to be 'undiscussable' and 'a step too far', whereupon dozens of celebrities joined in the controversy. The British critics were less passionate in their reactions but lukewarm in their judgements of its merits. Sophie Constanti in the *Independent* (28 August 1995) considered the work all controversy and no choreography: 'like most of Jones's work it trivialises rather than matches an important issue to dance.'

The music programme, which featured Dvořák, was of an exceptionally high standard. The concert by the St Petersburg Philharmonic Orchestra conducted by Mariss Jansons was probably the highlight of the whole Festival. Geoffrey Norris wrote in the *Daily Telegraph* (23 August 1995) that 'even in this pre-eminent league of music-making their concert of Dvořák and Prokofiev achieved astonishing new heights'. Opera lovers were excited by the visit of the Kirov Opera with two of Rimsky-Korsakov's rarely performed works, *The Invisible City of Kitezh* and *Sadko,* and a concert performance of *Ruslan and Ludmilla* by Glinka. The critics praised the performances but found the productions, particularly *Sadko*, old-fashioned and Gerald Larner's review in the *Scotsman* inspired a number of the audience to put pen to paper in protest. However, most people agreed that Scottish Opera's production of Dvořák's *The Jacobin* by Christine Mielitz with designs by Reinhart Zimmermann was ugly and misconceived. *I was Looking at the Ceiling and then I Saw the Sky*, a piece of musical theatre about the Los Angeles earthquake, written by John Adams and directed by Peter Sellars in his least self-indulgent manner, had a mixed reception from the critics. Finally, in the Usher Hall, Charles Mackerras almost proved that directors are unnecessary in a semi-staged performance of *Don Giovanni*, the third of the series of Mozart operas presented by the Edinburgh Festival in association with a record company, in this case Telarc. With an excellent cast, including Felicity Lott, Christine Brewer, Nuccia Focile, Boje Skovhus, Alessandro Corbelli and Jerry Hadley, and a minimum of props it was as effective dramatically as musically. But McMaster's musical coup was undoubtedly Zimmermann's rarely performed *Requiem for a Young Poet.* Organized in association with the Salzburg Festival, the Festival d'Automne Paris, the Berlin Festwochen and the SWF Symphony Orchestra, Baden-Baden, it was magnificently performed by massed choirs from Cologne, Stuttgart, Bratislava and Edinburgh and an impressive team of soloists conducted by Michael Gielen, who had directed the 1969 world première. The composer dedicated the work to three poets who had committed suicide and eight months after its first performance he too followed their example. Andrew Porter in the *Observer* (3 September 1995) considered it a 'mid-century period piece but also a masterpiece' while Philip Henscher in the *Daily Telegraph* (*c.* 30 August

1995) summed it up as 'an anguished experience we cannot fully understand, and from which we have eventually to turn aside'.

The previous year the Scottish National Party, ever on the alert for perceived slights to the home country, complained that no major Scottish event had been included in the Festival. Needless to say the other political parties leapt to the defence. McMaster responded with a series of 21 late-night concerts of *Folk Songs of North-East Scotland* by some of Scotland's best-known folk singers. The other Scottish event *Lanark*, an attempt by the Tag Theatre to follow up its success with *A Scot's Quair*, flopped. The novel, dependent on its poetic imagery and description did not translate well to the stage and most people found the plot obscure. It was the parent company, the Citizens' Theatre, that took the Festival honours with a brilliant production by Philip Prowse of Schiller's *Don Carlos* in a translation by Robert David MacDonald. Dublin's Abbey Theatre brought its powerful award-winning anti-war play *Observe the Sons of Ulster Marching towards the Somme*. The surprising factor was that this play about a group of Ulstermen who volunteer to fight as a mark of their loyalty to Britain, linked with their fears of a united Ireland, should have been written by a Republican Catholic, Frank McGuinness. The final week was again dominated by three prominent directors. Peter Zadek and the Berliner Ensemble returned with Shakespeare's *The Merchant of Venice* in which a blond, blue-eyed Gert Voss gave a somewhat unusual portrayal of Shylock. More food for argument was provided by *Dans la Solitude des Champs de Coton*, a duologue by Bernard-Marie Koltès about a mysterious seller who refused to reveal what he has to sell and a potential buyer who is reticent about what he wants to buy, in which Patrice Chéreau both performed and directed. After all the heavyweights, the Festival was brought to an end with two French farces by Sacha Guitry, *The Illusionist* and *Let's Dream*, directed by Luc Bondy for the Schaubühne am Lehniner Platz, Berlin. Gert Voss, following his performances as Shylock, developed a throat infection and was admitted to hospital for intravenous antibiotics but he insisted on rising from his sickbed to perform in *The Illusionist*, returning to hospital at the end of the performance.

In addition to being an artistic success the forty-ninth Festival broke all records at the box office. While much of the Edinburgh Festival's current success is due to the reigning Festival Director, he has also received considerable support from Edinburgh District Council which, over the past six years has steadily increased its grant from £600 000 in 1989 to £950 000 in 1994. After cutting off its subsidy in 1977 Lothian Regional Council (who in the intervening years had assisted in sponsoring individual events) finally came back into the fold and in 1990 donated £150 000, rising to £350 000 in 1994. The grant from the Scottish Arts Council had similarly increased by some £230 000 to its current level of £735 000. There was also a massive increase in sponsorship which in 1989 stood at £783 687 and in 1994 reached £1 078 555. These increases have not been won easily but so far the Director has succeeded in obtaining the additional money he requires. Now a cloud has appeared on the horizon. Under local government reorganization in May 1995 Lothian Regional Council ceased to exist and the Festival lost one of its main sources of funding. With the expenses of the reorganization it is probably unreasonable to hope that the new Edinburgh City Council will be able to make up the difference, which doesn't augur well for the future. Sponsorship at home is reaching saturation point and unless overseas companies can be

persuaded to support the Festival there seems little hope of substantial increases in that direction.

As a result of this period of financial and political stability, the first ever enjoyed by the Festival, McMaster has succeeded in reviving musical standards and giving dance a worthier place in the programme while at the same time keeping the drama programme on an international level. With the Film, Jazz, Book and Television Festivals, the Military Tattoo, and an estimated 14 000 performances on the Fringe, the Edinburgh Festival still retains its position as the largest, most comprehensive arts festival in the world. By presenting within one Festival artists of the calibre of Claudio Abbado, Pierre Boulez, Sir Charles Mackerras, John Eliot Gardiner, Mariss Jansons, Andras Schiff, Peter Schreier, Felicity Lott, Galina Gorchakova, Anne Sofie von Otter, Yo-Yo Ma, Alicia de Larrocha, Gert Voss, Peter Sellars, Peter Zadek, Patrice Chéreau and Luc Bondy, and companies such as the Kirov Opera, Pina Bausch, Mark Morris and the Berliner Ensemble, as well as the St Petersburg Orchestra, the NDR Symphony Orchestra and the Ensemble Intercontemporain, there is no doubt that artistically the official event has regained its pre-eminent position.

In the meantime there are exciting plans for the future. A £7 million project for a Festival Centre in the Highland Tolbooth Kirk, adjacent to the castle, is on the drawing board, but this can only be achieved if £3.9 million is forthcoming from the Scottish Arts Council's lottery funds. This would incorporate the Festival Offices and provide a permanent base for the development of all the festivals, as well as a Festival club and home for the Festival visitor. There are also plans to celebrate the fiftieth Festival in 1996 in association with the Festival Fringe and the Film Festival, both of which also have their fiftieth event that year.

Brian McMaster's current contract expires after the 1996 Festival but after the undoubted success of the four Festivals under his direction, it is no surprise that he has been offered an extension, and that he will lead the Edinburgh Festival into the next millennium. After 50 years Sir John Falconer's vision remains firm and strong and the Edinburgh International Festival still stands as a symbol for world peace and unity through the Arts.

Chapter 10

The hole in the ground

Plans for an opera house on the Castle Terrace site had begun in 1960 when, following his appointment, Lord Harewood began to campaign for a suitable theatre for staging large-scale opera. When it became apparent that the cost of extending and upgrading the Playhouse stage would be prohibitive he turned his attention to the possibility of building a purpose-built theatre which would seat 2 000. He won a certain amount of cautious support from Lord Provost Dunbar, although Dunbar insisted that the theatre must also have some use during the remaining 49 weeks of the year.

That year an Edinburgh property dealer, Meyer Oppenheim, purchased the Lyceum Theatre and suggested to Edinburgh Corporation that it associate with him in building a theatre together with a conference hall, hotel, restaurant and an office block on the site. The Corporation was enthusiastic and set about acquiring nearby buildings which would be demolished to enlarge the site. But in 1964 Oppenheim pulled out of the scheme and sold the Lyceum to the Corporation. By this time the much more enthusiastic Duncan Weatherstone had become Lord Provost and under his leadership the Corporation decided that the site should be developed as a large 1 600-seat theatre with a smaller 800-seat arena theatre underneath, together with a multi-storey hotel. These theatres would link up with the Usher Hall to form a complete Festival Centre.

William Kininmonth, who had originally been engaged for the Oppenheim plan, was sent by the city to study opera houses and theatres abroad and in July 1965 he produced an outline plan in association with Scottish and Newcastle Brewers. The Company had agreed to lease a portion of the site, at a substantial ground rent for a period of 122 years and to erect a 120-room hotel and a conference hall, the whole scheme to be completed in time for the 1971 Festival.

Weatherstone was succeeded as Lord Provost by Herbert Brechin, who was more interested in building an olympic-sized swimming pool and other facilities for the Commonwealth Games than an opera house, and a series of delays and procrastinations followed while the Corporation sought financial support from the Government. Both the Minister for the Arts, Jennie Lee, and Lord Goodman, Chairman of the Arts Council, supported the project and throughout the coming-of-age Festival in 1967 hopes were high that the Government would pay half the cost. At the final press conference Lord Provost Brechin announced that they were negotiating for a Government grant of nearly £2 million, emphasizing that they had no intention of starting the scheme before the Govern-

ment agreed the grant: 'We would make a false step if we were to move before a decision was given. It is well worth waiting a few months.' In January 1968 Scottish and Newcastle, worried at the delays and sharply rising costs which had now reached £4 million, withdrew from the project.

During the next few months experts examining the proposed development announced that the site would be overcrowded. It was then decided that the Lyceum would be retained, and only one large theatre built on the site, so Kininmonth was instructed to draw up new plans. On 4 December 1969 the Corporation approved the new design and finally made a definite commitment to building the opera house, but there was still no firm promise from the Government regarding its share of the funding. Kininmonth warned the Corporation that the cost of building was rising by approximately £250 000 a year. Then, with a fine sense of timing, Edward Heath arrived for the twenty-fifth Festival in 1971 and announced that the Government would contribute £2.5 million towards the cost of the opera house.

At that point when it might have been expected that the Corporation would have seized the proferred pot of gold and started building without further delay, Edinburgh Corporation began to have misgivings about the design. A new city architect, Brian Annable, had recently been appointed and he, with the aid of consultants whom he appointed to advise him, drew up a new and more ambitious brief which included the Lyceum Theatre, a studio theatre and other facilities at an estimated cost of £9 million. This found favour with the small sub-committee set up by the Corporation to deal with the opera house project which, without the knowledge of the majority of the Town Council, sacked Kininmonth. Sir Robert Matthew, a member of the Royal Fine Art Commission and adviser on architectural matters to the Secretary of State for Scotland, was appointed to draw up a new and more elaborate design, regardless of the fact that the site had already been described as grossly overloaded.

As Sir Robert worked inflation soared and the cost reached £18 million. Further financial discussions with the Government resulted in a renewed grant of £9 million on condition that there would be stricter financial control, no further delays and that the plan was approved by the Royal Fine Art Commission. In August 1974 the final plan failed to gain its approval because of the volume of building being forced on to a limited site. While descibing the design as 'bold, ingenious and of high architectural quality', they considered the scheme would have a 'damaging visual impact and an adverse effect on environmental quality and character'. As a result the Government insisted that no grant would be made towards the cost of the opera house until the plans had been modified. After the height of the fly-tower had been reduced by about 4 metres approval was finally granted.

By the following year Edinburgh District Council had taken over from Edinburgh Corporation and the Government had begun to curtail public expenditure. Tacit agreement had been reached between the Scottish Office and officials of Edinburgh District Council to abandon the project, but neither wished to lose face by being the first to renege on the agreement. With the Government's clampdown on spending, the Secretary of State for Scotland was clearly unable to spend £10 million on an opera house, while the Labour group on the District Council had declared their opposition to the scheme. Backed by the smaller political groups they were almost certain to carry the day.

A special meeting of Edinburgh District Council was called in September 1975 to enable the officials involved to explain the plans and the building programme, after

which a vote would be taken. This proved to be no more than window-dressing. Peter Diamand and Tom Fleming arrived, complete with detailed plans, to present their arguments. They were not even given a hearing but were simply informed that the project was 'off'. As they left the City Chambers Diamand remarked, 'That is the shortest funeral I have ever attended.'

During the debate Lord Provost Millar maintained that by scrapping the scheme they would be allowing the £1 million spent so far to 'go down the drain' adding, 'Let us show the people we have got guts, boldness and initiative. I am trying to keep this thing alive. It is terribly important for the future of the city and of the Festival. If it dies, it will never be revived'. In favour of abandoning the scheme, Councillor James Kerr (Labour) asked the Council to decide 'perhaps reluctantly' to bury what he was certain was nothing more than 'a huge, colossal white elephant'. When the vote was taken the District Council decided by a majority of 32 votes to 27 to abandon the scheme (two councillors, Waugh and Crombie, acting in defiance of the party whip, voted with the Labour group while two others abstained thus ensuring a Labour victory).

This was not to be the end of the story. The penultimate chapter was written in the following August when the Conservative group on the District Council proposed selling off the entire Castle Terrace site to a developer despite a bid by the Lyceum Theatre for approximately 9 per cent of the site for extensions to the theatre. As the voting was likely to be close a demonstration by actors and companies appearing at the Festival was arranged in support of the bid. Toby Robertson made a fervent plea from the Assembly Hall stage asking the audience to join in. Even the Scottish Arts Council condemned the Conservatives, urging the councillors to 'think again before committing the ratepayers of Edinburgh to a course of action which we believe is likely to prove short-sighted, expensive and wrong'. The Scottish Trades Union Congress (STUC) also joined the campaign and in a statement supporting the Scottish Arts Council stand, James Milne, General Secretary of the STUC said it was essential that part of the Castle Terrace site should be made available to the Lyceum, so that necessary additions could be provided and the Little Lyceum Theatre continue to operate next door. He repeated the campaign's arguments that the Lyceum was the nucleus for a National Theatre for Scotland.

Councillor Waugh, the Tory group leader, hit back at the Scottish Arts Council by pointing out that they had already informed the Arts Council that they had a full commitment of expenditure on the King's Theatre and there was no finance available for the Lyceum, adding 'If this is, as they say, a national theatre then why should Edinburgh ratepayers pay for it?' A counter-motion by a Tory rebel, Brian Meek, that the site should be advertised but that preference be given to developers willing to present a joint plan for a hotel and theatre extension, together with plans to rehouse the Little Lyceum within the site, was defeated. When voting took place on the main issue it proved to be exactly even, whereupon the Lord Provost, Kenneth Borthwick, used his casting vote to sell the entire site.

As a result, the Lord Provost found himself at the centre of a furious row. The next morning the following editorial appeared in the *Scotsman*:

> MISCAST VOTE The conduct of local government stands low enough in the public estimation without the Lord Provost of Edinburgh descending to the level he did yesterday. As Chairman of the District Council he should have acted impartially on such a controversial issue. It was unwise of him to move and vote for anything so contentious. It was an abuse of his casting vote

to use it for altering the status quo. It is equally reprehensible that he should defy so much expert opinion, and the carefully considered advice of the Scottish Arts Council. The Festival and Lyceum Theatre Company are national assets and not simply local amenities, and the Secretary of State should intervene on behalf of the Government. While he may have no power to alter the decision it would be permissible for him to express his views. If developers knew the Government were unlikely to look favourably on the project, they might not be so ready to grasp the District Council's offer of the site. The independent stance taken by a few members of that group is to be applauded. It should never have been a party political issue. It has been done so insensitively that lasting damage has probably been inflicted on the relationship between Edinburgh District Council and artistic organisations. For Councillor Waugh, leader of the ruling group to quote grossly misleading statistics to promote his cause is inexcusable, and the conflict between region and district surely reached its nadir when the Lord Provost summoned the Police to remove the convener of Lothian Region from the Public Gallery. It is lamentable that this sorry affair should come to its conclusion in the first week of the great international festival, which one of Edinburgh's most enlightened Lord Provosts helped to establish, and which his successors have upheld till now.

Numerous letters were written to the *Scotsman* and two former Lord Provosts, Jack Kane and John Millar joined an attempt to call a special meeting of the Festival Society to discuss the implications of the District Council's decision which was, according to Millar, a complete reversal of the policies operating when he was Lord Provost. 'We cannot go on in this way and still claim we have the best Festival in Europe,' he said. Other Festival Council members wanted to go further and call an extraordinary general meeting of the Society to change the Articles of Association removing the automatic right of the Lord Provost to be the Chairman of the Society. A few days later a deal was struck among all the political parties on the District Council and in *A Statement of Clarification* the Lord Provost said that 'Any sceme for the development of the Castle Terrace site must not be prejudicial to the necessary upgrading of the back stage facilities of the Royal Lyceum Theatre and the Director of Architecture would be instructed by the Lord Provost to define the necessary upgrading required.' There was no financial commitment for the provision of a new auditorium for the Little Lyceum Theatre. It was agreed by all concerned that

if extra theatrical needs were required especially with regard to a new auditorium on the Castle Terrace site, then the funding of this must come from outwith the Council and those requesting those facilities would have to negotiate with the developers concerned themselves.

The Extraordinary General Meeting of the Festival Society accepted the Lord Provost's statement that the need for the special meeting had been removed by the clarification statement, and that any scheme for the Castle Terrace site would not prejudice the upgrading of the Lyceum Theatre. Agreement was then reached that Edinburgh District Council should consult with the Festival Society over the future development of the site.

The issue of a new theatre on the Castle Terrace site was briefly revived. John Richards of Robert Matthew Johnson-Marshall and Partners was commissioned to draw up yet another theatre plan for the notorious 'hole in the ground' as it had become known. This slightly reduced £14 million scheme was put to a meeting of the full District Council on 30 March 1984, and despite Labour criticism that the theatre proposal was élitist the motion to go ahead with the project was passed by a vote of 30 to 7. But this project never got off the ground. In the May local government elections Labour gained control and one of its first actions was to cancel the theatre plan, and finally in 1988 the site was

leased to Scottish Metropolitan Property for the building of a financial centre together with a 250-seat studio theatre to replace the old Traverse Theatre.

As there no longer seemed any likelihood of a multi-purpose theatre being built Frank Dunlop opened discussions with Apollo Leisure regarding the possible conversion of the Playhouse. In 1986 plans for a Festival theatre and Administrative Centre were drawn up but foundered on a number of rocks, in particular Apollo Leisure's insistence that the theatre be leased back to them and run by them, and the Government's reluctance to help fund the project. The campaign for an International Opera House on a site at the Victoria Docks in Leith also fell through. Then, by chance, Dunlop found himself sitting opposite the head of Mecca, the owner of the Empire Theatre, at a reception in London and in his customary forthright manner exclaimed, 'Oh, you're the one that is putting bingo in the best theatre in Edinburgh'. After further discussions with Mecca it transpired that it might be willing to sell the theatre if the right situation arose. Dunlop and Sandy Orr, formerly of the Scottish Arts Council, negotiated with the architects, Law and Dunbar-Nasmith, to produce a plan for converting the Empire into a suitable Festival theatre for staging large-scale productions together with accommodation for the Festival offices, management and box office.

In November 1989 Edinburgh District Council representatives asked to take over the negotiations with Mecca and the following August the theatre was offered to the District Council at a knock-down price of £2 million. As Mecca had just been acquired by the Rank Organisation a final decision was required by 27 August. The Conservatives on the District Council agreed on condition that, when the theatre became operational, the King's Theatre was either sold or leased and that the plans for the new Traverse Theatre on the old Castle Terrace site were reconsidered. But despite the pleas of their leader, Mark Lazarowicz, the Labour councillors were unable to make up their minds in time and the offer to sell the theatre was rescinded. On receipt of a letter of appeal from Malcolm Rifkind, the Secretary of State for Scotland, the chairman of Rank replied that the theatre would be valued along with other Mecca properties and the District Council would be offered first refusal to purchase the theatre at the valuation figure. Seven months later, in March 1991, the District Council unanimously agreed to buy the Empire for £2.6 million. A further £11 million was required to convert and refurbish the theatre of which the District Council agreed to provide half, the remainder coming from Lothian Regional Council, Lothian and Edinburgh Enterprise Limited, the Scottish Arts Council, the Scottish Tourist Board, the Historic Buildings Council and the private sector. A trust was established to undertake the development and refurbishment works and on completion to operate the theatre.

The new Festival Theatre was opened in June 1994 with a Scottish Variety performance followed by Scottish Opera's production of Wagner's *Tristan und Isolde* conducted by Richard Armstrong, with Anne Evans and Jeffrey Lawton.

Bibliography

Bing, Rudolf, *5000 Nights at the Opera*

Bruce, George, *Festival in the North*, Robert Hale, 1975

Caplat, Moran, *Dinghies to Divas*, Collins

Edinburgh International Festival. A Review of the First Ten Years, 1956

Ferrier, Winifred, *The Life of Kathleen Ferrier*, Hamish Hamilton, 1955

Guthrie, Tyrone, *A Life in the Theatre*, Hamish Hamilton, 1960

Harewood, Lord, *The Tongs and the Bones*, Weidenfeld and Nicolson, 1981

Hughes, Spike, *Glyndebourne*, Methuen, 1965

Jellinek, George, *Callas: Portrait of a Prima Donna*, Gibbs & Phillips, 1961

Meneghini, Giovanni Battista, *My Wife Maria Callas*, Farrar, Straus & Giroux, 1982

Scotto, Renata and Roca, Octavio, *Scotto: More than a Diva*, Robson Books, 1986

Notes To Appendices

Performances are listed under seven main headings: Opera, Orchestral Concerts, Chamber Concerts, Drama, Poetry and Prose Recitals, Dance, and Exhibitions, with additional headings when necessary.

Late changes in programmes and casting are included when known, and are indicated in the Programmes section by an asterisk. Some errors in the original programmes have been corrected.

In some cases Slavonic names have been standardised so that only one form of name is used for each artist, e.g. Jovanka Bjegojevic was listed in the original programmes variously as Jovanka Bjegojevic, Yovanka Byegoyevitch and Iovanka Biegovitch.

Knighthoods have been assigned from the date they were received.

The names of orchestras and companies are given in the form in use at the time and brought together in the Index under the latest form, e.g. performances by the Scottish National Orchestra, Royal Scottish Orchestra and Royal Scottish National Orchestra are indexed under the current form of Royal Scottish National Orchestra.

Artists in the Indexes are listed under the last part of their names, e.g. Stefano, Giuseppe di

Musical works are listed in accordance with normal library practice:

1. Capitals are used for the first word in a title, for proper names and German nouns.

2. French, German, Spanish and Italian titles are listed in the original language, titles in other languages are translated into English unless the title is better known in the original language, e.g. *Haugtussa*. For works performed in a language other than the original, the language is given in brackets after the title.

3. Excerpts are listed after the main work, e.g. Fidelio: Overture.

4. Works in a particular form are listed by form rather than instrument, e.g. Concerto for violin and cello, Quartet for oboe and strings. This avoids the inconsistency of having some works listed under form and some under instrument.

Quartets and *Trios* are for strings unless stated otherwise.

The English term *Songs* is used for Lieder, mélodies, romances, chansons etc.

The numbering throughout is taken from *The Gramophone Classical Catalogue*.

Abbreviations

act	actor
anon	anonymous
arr	arranged, arranger
attrib	attributed
b-bar	bass-baritone
bar	baritone
bas hn	basset horn
bn	bassoon
boy sop	boy soprano
bp	bagpipe
bs	bass
c ten	counter tenor
cl	clarinet
comp	composer
conc perf	Concert performance
cont	contralto
cor ang	Cor anglais
dan	dancer
db	double bass
des	designer
dir	director
ed	edited
Eng	English
EF Chorus	Edinburgh Festival Chorus
EIF	Edinburgh International Festival
ent	entertainer
exc.Sund	except Sundays
exh dir	exhibition director
f-pf	fortepiano
flugel hn	flugel horn
fl	flute
Fr	French
Ger	German
gtr	guitar
hn	horn
hp	harp
hpd	harpsichord
Ind fl	Indian flute
interp	interpreter
It	Italian
Jap	Japanese
jun	junior
kbds	keyboards
lect	lecturer
light	lighting designer
mez	mezzo soprano
Mod Greek	Modern Greek
mus	musician
mus dir	music director
narr	narrator
ob	oboe
ob d'amore	oboe d'amore
orch	orchestra
org	organ
perc	percussion
Pol	Polish
prod	producer
rdr	reader
read	rehearsed reading
rev	revised
RSNO	Royal Scottish National Orchestra
RSO	Royal Scottish Orchestra
Rum	Rumanian
Rus	Russian
S.Croat	Serbo-Croat
sax	saxophone
sngr	singer
SNO	Scottish National Orchestra
Soc.	Society
sop	soprano
sop sax	soprano saxophone
Sp	Spanish
spk	speaker
Swed	Swedish
synth	synthesizer
tbn	trombone
ten	tenor
ten sax	tenor saxophone
timp	timpani
tpt	trumpet
transcr	transcribed
va	viola
va da gamba	viola da gamba
vc	cello
vn	violin
ww	woodwind

Programmes 1947-1996

1947

OPERA

GLYNDEBOURNE OPERA
25, 27, 29 Aug. 2, 4, 6, 8, 10, 12 Sep.
19.00 *King's Theatre*
MACBETH Verdi
Macbeth Francesco Valentino
Lady Macbeth Margherita Grandi
Banquo Italo Tajo
Owen Brannigan
Macduff Walter Midgley
Malcolm Andrew McKinley
Gentlewoman Vera Terry
Doctor André Orkin
Servant Robert Vivian
Murderer Edward Thomas
Scottish Orchestra
Conductor Berthold Goldschmidt
Director Carl Ebert
Designer Caspar Neher

26, 28, 30 Aug. 1, 3, 5, 9, 11, 13 Sep.
19.00 *King's Theatre*
LE NOZZE DI FIGARO Mozart
Figaro Italo Tajo
Susanna Tatiana Menotti
Ayhan Alnar
Count John Brownlee
Countess Eleanor Steber
Cherubino Giulietta Simionato
Dr Bartolo Owen Brannigan
Marcellina Catherine Lawson
Don Basilio Bruce Flegg
Barbarina Barbara Trent
Don Curzio Gwent Lewis
Antonio Ernest Frank
Scottish Orchestra
Conductors Walter Susskind
Renato Cellini
Director Carl Ebert
Scenery Hamish Wilson
Costumes Ann Litherland

ORCHESTRAL CONCERTS

L'ORCHESTRE DES CONCERTS COLONNE
Conductor Paul Paray
24 Aug. 19.30 *Usher Hall*
Haydn Symphony no.94 in G (Surprise)
Schumann Symphony no.4 in D minor, op.120
Franck Symphony in D minor

27 Aug. 19.30 *Usher Hall*
Bax Overture to a picaresque comedy
Mendelssohn A midsummer night's dream: Nocturne *and* Scherzo
Saint-Saëns Concerto for piano no.4 in C minor, op.44
Beethoven Symphony no.3 in E flat (Eroica), op.55
Soloist Robert Casadesus (pf)

29 Aug. 14.30 *Usher Hall*
Berlioz Le carnaval romain - Overture
Lalo Concerto for cello in D minor
Fauré Pelléas et Mélisande - Suite
Ravel Daphnis et Chloë - Suite no.2
Debussy Prélude à l'après-midi d'un faune
Dukas L'apprenti sorcier
Soloist Bernard Michelin (vc)

HALLÉ ORCHESTRA
Conductor John Barbirolli
31 Aug. 19.30 *Usher Hall*
Weber Euryanthe: Overture
Delius A song of summer
Mozart Concerto for violin no.4 in D, K218
Elgar Symphony no.2 in E flat, op.63
Soloist Joseph Szigeti (vn)

2 Sep. 19.30 *Usher Hall*
Rossini La gazza ladra: Overture
Elgar Introduction and allegro, op.47
Haydn Concerto for cello no.2 in D
Berlioz Symphonie fantastique
Soloist Pierre Fournier (vc)

LIVERPOOL PHILHARMONIC ORCHESTRA
Conductor Sir Malcolm Sargent
3 Sep. 19.30 *Usher Hall*
Bach Passacaglia in C minor; arr. Respighi
Beethoven Concerto for piano no.4 in G, op.58
Brahms Symphony no.2 in D, op.73
Soloist Artur Schnabel (pf)

5 Sep. 14.30 *Usher Hall*
Britten The young person's guide to the orchestra
Walton Concerto for viola in A minor
Holst The planets
Soloist William Primrose (va)

SCOTTISH ORCHESTRA
7 Sep. 19.30 *Usher Hall*
Smetana The bartered bride: Overture
Ravel Concerto for piano in G
Britten Peter Grimes: Four sea interludes
Dvorák Symphony no.8 in G, op.88
Conductor Walter Susskind
Soloist
Arturo Benedetti Michelangeli (pf)

VIENNA PHILHARMONIC ORCHESTRA
Conductor Bruno Walter
8, 9 Sep. 19.30 *Usher Hall*
V. Williams Fantasia on a theme by Tallis
Beethoven Symphony no.6 in F (Pastoral), op.68
Beethoven Symphony no.7 in A, op.92
Conductor Bruno Walter

11 Sep. 19.30 12 Sep. 14.30 *Usher Hall*
Schubert Symphony no.8 in B minor (Unfinished), D759
Mahler Das Lied von der Erde
Soloists Kathleen Ferrier (cont), Peter Pears (ten)

13 Sep. 14.30 and 19.30 *Usher Hall*
Haydn Symphony no.102 in B flat
Mozart Eine kleine Nachtmusik
Schubert Rosamunde: Overture *and* Ballet music
Suppé Die schöne Galathée: Overture
J. Strauss Der Zigeunerbaron: Overture
J. Strauss Die Fledermaus: Overture
J. Strauss Kaiser Walzer

BBC SCOTTISH ORCHESTRA
10 Sep. 19.30 *Usher Hall*
Purcell Chaconne in G minor; arr. Whittaker
Whyte Concerto for piano
D. Stephen Coronach
Sibelius Symphony no.2 in D, op.43
Conductor Ian Whyte
Soloist Cyril Smith (pf)

JACQUES ORCHESTRA
Conductor Reginald Jacques
26 Aug. 11.00 *Freemasons' Hall*
Mozart Eine kleine Nachtmusik
V. Williams Five variants on 'Dives and Lazarus'
Barber Adagio for strings, op.11
Debussy Danse sacrée et danse profane
Bliss Music for strings
Soloist Marie Korchinska (hp)

27 Aug. 11.00 *Freemasons' Hall*
Handel Concerto grosso in B flat, op.6/11
Bach Cantata no.51
Byrd Fantasia no.2 in C minor
Schubert Salve regina in A, D676
Tchaikovsky Serenade for strings, op.48
Soloist Ena Mitchell (sop)

28 Aug. 11.00 *Freemasons' Hall*
Corelli Concerto grosso in G minor (Christmas), op.6/8
Bach Brandenburg concerto no.6 in B flat
Finzi Let us garlands bring
Britten Variations on a theme of Frank Bridge
Soloist Robert Irwin (bar)

29 Aug. 11.00 *Freemasons' Hall*
Handel Concerto grosso in G, op.6/l
Bach Concerto for 2 violins in D minor
Galuppi Adagio and giga
Bach Cantata no.170
Mozart Divertimento (Salzburg Symphony) no.1 in D, K.136
Soloists Nancy Evans (cont), Ruth Pearl, Mary Carter (vn)

30 Aug. 11.00 *Freemasons' Hall*
Handel Ottone: Overture
Bach Brandenburg concerto no.1 in F
Finzi Dies natalis
Mozart Divertimento no.17 in D, K.334
Handel Solomon: Arrival of the Queen of Sheba
Soloist Eric Greene (ten)

1 Sep. 11.00 *Freemasons' Hall*
Handel Samson: Overture
Mozart Exsultate, jubilate
Sibelius Rakastava
Rubbra Soliloquy
Arensky Variations on a theme of Tchaikovsky
Soloists Margaret Field Hyde (sop), Harvey Phillips (vc)

2 Sep. 11.00 *Freemasons' Hall*
Handel Concerto grosso in B flat, op.6/7
Bach Concerto for oboe d'amore in A; arr.. Tovey
Corelli Concerto grosso; arr. Barbirolli
Marcello Concerto for oboe in C minor
Moszkowski Prelude and fugue
Soloist Leon Goossens (ob)

3 Sep. 11.00 *Freemasons' Hall*
Handel Alcina: Overture
Bach Concerto for harpsichord in D minor
Purcell Chaconne in G minor
Bach Cantata no. 82
Bach Brandenburg concerto no.2 in F
Soloists William Parsons (bs), Thornton Lofthouse (hpd)

4 Sep. 11.00 *Freemasons' Hall*
Bach Brandenburg concerto no.5 in D
Britten Les illuminations
Bartók Divertimento for strings
Soloist Peter Pears (ten)

5 Sep. 11.00 *Freemasons' Hall*
Bach Brandenburg concerto no.4 in G
Bach Christmas oratorio: Bereite dich, Zion (Eng)
Bach Cantata no.53
Bach Suite no.2 in B minor
Bach Brandenburg concerto no.3 in G
Soloists Kathleen Ferrier (cont), John Francis (fl)

CHAMBER CONCERTS

FESTIVAL PIANO QUARTET
Schnabel, Szigeti, Primrose, Fournier
28 Aug. 19.30 *Usher Hall*
Brahms Trio for piano and strings no.3 in C minor, op.101
Schubert Trio for piano and strings no.2 in E flat, D929
Brahms Quartet for piano and strings no.2 in A, op.26

30 Aug. 14.30 *Usher Hall*
Brahms Quartet for piano and strings no.3 in C minor, op.60
Mendelssohn Trio for piano and strings no.1 in D minor, op.49
Brahms Trio for piano and strings no.1 in B, op.8

1 Sep. 14.30 *Usher Hall*
Brahms Trio for piano and strings no.2 in C, op.87
Schubert Trio for piano and strings no.1 in B flat, D898
Brahms Quartet for piano and strings no.1 in G minor, op.25

CZECH NONET
6 Sep. 11.00 *Freemasons' Hall*
Borkovec Nonet
Ha'ba Fantasia for nonet, op.40
Beethoven Septet, op.20

8 Sep. 11.00 *Freemasons' Hall*
Jirák Variations, scherzo and finale, op.45a
Krejci Divertimento for nonet
Ridky Nonet no.2, op.39

MENGES QUARTET
9 Sep. 11.00 *Freemasons' Hall*
Beethoven Quartet no.13 in B flat, op.130
Beethoven Quartet no.7 in F (Rasumovsky), op.59/1

CALVET QUARTET
11 Sep. 11.00 *Freemasons' Hall*
Mozart Quartet no.21 in D, K575
Beethoven Quartet no.8 in E minor (Rasumovsky), op.59/2
Ravel Quartet in F

ROBERT MASTERS PIANO QUARTET
12 Sep. 11.00 *Freemasons' Hall*
Mozart Quartet for piano and strings in G minor, K.478
Françaix Trio for strings in C
Dvořák Quartet for piano and strings no.2 in E flat, op.87

CARTER TRIO
13 Sep. 11.00 *Freemasons' Hall*
Beethoven Trio no.4 in C minor, op.9/3
Moeran Fantasy quartet for oboe and strings
Purcell Three 3-part fantasias
Mozart Quartet for oboe and strings in F, K.370
with Leon Goossens (ob)

SCOTTISH CONCERTS

CONCERT OF GAELIC SONGS
29 Aug. 19.30 *Freemasons' Hall*
Evelyn Campbell, James Campbell, Kitty MacLeod, Allan Macritchie (sngr), Duncan Morrison (pf). Introduced by Hector Maclver

CONCERT OF SCOTTISH LOWLAND SONGS
5 Sep. 19.30 *Freemasons' Hall*
Marie Thomson (sop), John Tainsh (ten), Ian Whyte (pf). Introduced by John Oliver

GLASGOW ORPHEUS CHOIR
6 Sep. 19.30 *Usher Hall*
Conductor Sir Hugh Roberton
Soloists Betty Watson, Annie Tait, Alexander McKay (sngr), Ailie Cullen (pf)

RECITALS

ELISABETH SCHUMANN (sop)
BRUNO WALTER (pf)
6 Sep. 14.30 *Usher Hall*
Songs by Schubert

TODD DUNCAN (bar)
WILLIAM ALLEN (pf)
8 Sep. 14.30 *Usher Hall*
Songs by Handel, Scarlatti, Brahms, R. Strauss, Massenet, Rachmaninov, Mussorgsky, Tchaikovsky *and* Spirituals

ROY HENDERSON (bar)
GERALD MOORE (pf)
10 Sep. 11.00 *Freemasons' Hall*
Songs by Hume, Pilkington, Bartlet, Purcell, Arne, Boyce, Warlock, Stanford, V. Williams, Ferguson, Moeran

JOSEPH SZIGETI (vn)
ARTUR SCHNABEL (pf)
4 Sep. 19.30 *Usher Hall*
Brahms Sonatas nos.1-3

DRAMA

OLD VIC
26, 27, 28 Aug. 1, 5, 6 Sep. 19.15
27 Aug. 6 Sep. 14.30 *Lyceum Theatre*
THE TAMING OF THE SHREW
Shakespeare
Petruchio Trevor Howard
Katharina Patricia Burke
Hortensio Harry Andrews
Bianca Renée Asherson
Lucentio George Rose
Tranio Peter Copley
Baptista Mark Dignam
Gremio Cecil Winter
Biondello Frank Duncan
Grumio George Relph
Vincentio Kenneth Edwards
Curtis Aubrey Richards
Christopher Sly Bernard Miles
Other parts played by Norma Shebbeare, David Kentish, Denis McCarthy, Robert Perceval, Christopher Beedell, Kenneth Connor, Peter Varley, Michael Raghan, Penelope Munday, Rosalind Atkinson, Pietro Nolte, Reginald Hearne, John Garley, James Lytton, John Biggerstaff, Patrick Jordan
Director John Burrell
Scenery Kathleen Ankers
Costumes Alix Stone, Audrey Cruddas

29, 30 Aug. 2, 3, 4 Sep. 19.15 *30 Aug.*
3 Sep. 14.30 *Lyceum Theatre*
RICHARD II Shakespeare
King Richard II Alec Guinness
John of Gaunt Mark Dignam
Edmund, Duke of York George Relph
Bolingbroke Harry Andrews
Earl of Northumberland Nicholas Hannen
Thomas Mowbray, Duke of Norfolk Peter Copley
Duke of Aumerle John Garley
Bishop of Carlisle Cecil Winter
Henry Percy Frank Duncan
Duke of Surrey George Rose
Bushy David Kentish
Bagot Peter Varley
Green Pietro Nolte
Earl of Salisbury/Sir Pierce of Exton Denis McCarthy
Lord Berkeley/Lord Fitzwater James Lytton
Lord Ross/Abbot of Westminster John Biggerstaff
Lord Willoughby Christopher Beedell
Sir Stephen Scroope Michael Raghan
Queen Renée Asherson
Duchess of Gloucester Rosalind Atkinson
Captain Aubrey Richards
Groom Kenneth Connor
Servant to York Patrick Jordan
Director Ralph Richardson
Designer Michael Warre

LA COMPAGNIE JOUVET DE THÉÂTRE DE L'ATHENÉE, Paris
8, 9, 10 Sep.19.15 *10 Sep. 14.30*
Lyceum Theatre
L'ÉCOLE DES FEMMES Molière
Horace Jean Richard
Arnolphe Louis Jouvet
Chrysalde Leo Lapara
Alain René Busson
Georgette Monique Melinand
Agnes Dominique Blanchar
Notary Michel Etcheverry
Notary's clerk Jacques Mauclair
Servant Paul Rieger
Enrique Georges Riquier
Oronte Pierre Renoir
Director Louis Jouvet
Designer Christian Bérard

11, 12, 13 Sep. 17.15 *13 Sep. 14.30*
Lyceum Theatre
ONDINE Giraudoux
Ondine Dominique Blanchar
Hans Louis Jouvet
Auguste Jean Dalmain
Eugenie Monique Melinand
King of the water sprites Maurice Lagrenée
Chamberlain Michel Etcheverry
Superintendant of the theatre George Riquier
Seal-keeper Jacques Monod
Poet Jean Richard
Venus/Grete Jacqueline Hebel
Bertha Wanda
Violante/Daughter of Vaiselle Camille Rodrigue
Bertram Leo Lapara
King Hubert Buthion
Queen Yseult Yolande Laffon
Swineherd René Busson
Ulrich Jacques Mauclair
Director Louis Jouvet
Designer Pavel Tchelitchev

DANCE

SADLER'S WELLS BALLET
25, 26, 27, 28, 29, 30 Aug. 1, 2, 3, 4, 5, 6 Sep. 19.15 27, 30 Aug. 3, 6 Sep. 14.30
Empire Theatre
THE SLEEPING BEAUTY
Choreographers
Marius Petipa, Nicholas Sergeyev
Music Tchaikovsky
Designer Oliver Messel
Dancers Margot Fonteyn, Pamela May, Beryl Grey, Violetta Prokhorova, Margaret Dale, Pauline Clayden, Julia Farron, Anne Negus, Gerd Larsen, Gillian Lynne, Avril Navarre, Palma Nye, Lorna Mossford, Alexis Rassine, Michael Somes, Harold Turner, John Hart, Richard Ellis, Leslie Edwards, Franklin White, Alexander Grant
Symphony Orchestra
Conductors Geoffrey Corbett, Hugo Rignold

1948

OPERA

GLYNDEBOURNE OPERA
23, 25, 27, 31 Aug. 2, 4, 6, 8, 10 Sep. 19.00 *King's Theatre*
DON GIOVANNI Mozart
Don Giovanni Paolo Silveri
Donna Anna Ljuba Welitsch
Donna Elvira Christina Carroll
Don Ottavio Richard Lewis
Leporello Vito de Taranto
Zerlina Hilde Güden
Ann Ayars
Masetto Ian Wallace
The Commendatore David Franklin
Royal Philharmonic Orchestra
Conductor Rafael Kubelik
Director Carl Ebert
Scenery Hamish Wilson
Costumes Hein Heckroth

24, 26, 28, 30 Aug. 1, 3, 7, 9, 11 Sep. 19.00 *King's Theatre*
COSÌ FAN TUTTE Mozart
Fiordiligi Suzanne Danco
Dorabella Eugenia Zareska
Ferrando Petre Munteanu
Guglielmo Erich Kunz
Despina Hilde Güden
Don Alfonso Mariano Stabile
Royal Philharmonic Orchestra
Conductor Vittorio Gui
Director Carl Ebert
Designer Rolf Gérard

ORCHESTRAL CONCERTS

CONCERTGEBOUW ORCHESTRA, Amsterdam
22 Aug. 19.30 *Usher Hall*
Mendelssohn Symphony no.4 in A (Italian), op.90
Bruckner Symphony no.7 in E
Conductor Eduard van Beinum

23 Aug. 19.30 *Usher Hall*
Beethoven Symphony no.4 in B flat, op.60
Debussy Images: Ibéria
Honegger Symphony no.3 (Liturgique)
Conductor Charles Münch

24 Aug. 19.30 *Usher Hall*
Schubert Symphony no.9 in C (Great), D944
Martinů Concerto grosso
Roussel Symphony no.3 in G minor, op.42
Conductor Charles Münch

25 Aug. 19.30 *Usher Hall*
Handel Water music; arr. Harty
Mozart Symphony no.38 in D (Prague), K504
Berlioz Symphonie fantastique
Conductor Charles Münch

26 Aug. 19.30 *Usher Hall*
Diepenbrock The birds - Overture
Haydn Symphony no.96 in D (Miracle)
Debussy La mer
Bartók Concerto for orchestra
Conductor Eduard van Beinum

LIVERPOOL PHILHARMONIC ORCHESTRA
Conductor Sir Malcolm Sargent
27 Aug. 19.30 *Usher Hall*
Beethoven Coriolan - Overture
Clementi Symphony in C
Mozart Concerto for piano no.24 in C minor, K491
Mozart Concerto for piano no.15 in B flat, K450
Soloist Artur Schnabel (pf)

28 Aug. 19.30 *Usher Hall*
Gluck Alceste: Overture
Fauré Requiem
Walton Belshazzar's feast
Soloists Isobel Baillie (sop), Harold Williams (bar), Huddersfield Choral Soc.

29 Aug. 14.30 *Usher Hall*
Bach Mass in B minor
Soloists Isobel Baillie (sop), Kathleen Ferrier (cont), Eric Greene (ten), Owen Brannigan (bs), Huddersfield Choral Soc.

BBC SCOTTISH ORCHESTRA
Conductor Ian Whyte
29 Aug. 19.30 *Usher Hall*
Mendelssohn A midsummer night's dream: Overture
Beethoven Concerto for violin in D, op.61
V. Williams The wasps: Overture
Sibelius Symphony no.1 in E minor, op.39
Soloist Yehudi Menuhin (vn)

6 Sep. 19.30 *Usher Hall*
Gluck Iphigénie en Tauride: Overture
Prokofiev Symphony no.1 in D (Classical), op.25
Mozart Concerto for piano no.20 in D minor, K466
Mozart Concerto for piano no.17 in G, K453
Beethoven Symphony no.8 in F, op.93
Soloist Artur Schnabel (pf)

HALLÉ ORCHESTRA
Conductor John Barbirolli
30 Aug. 19.30 *Usher Hall*
Barbirolli An Elizabethan suite
Mozart Symphony no.35 in D (Haffner), K385
Villa-Lobos Descrobimento do Brasil - Suite no.1
Stravinsky Concerto in D
Sibelius Symphony no.5 in E flat, op.82

1 Sep. 19.30 *Usher Hall*
Haydn Symphony no.83 in G minor (The hen)
Dvořák Concerto for cello in B minor, op.104
Brahms Symphony no.1 in C minor, op.68
Soloist Gregor Piatigorsky (vc)

BBC SYMPHONY ORCHESTRA
Conductor Sir Adrian Boult
3 Sep. 19.30 *Usher Hall*
Beethoven Leonore: Overture no 3
Mozart Concerto for piano no.27 in B flat, K595
Elgar Falstaff
Stravinsky The firebird - Suite
Soloist Artur Schnabel (pf)

4 Sep. 19.30 *Usher Hall*
Mozart Die Zauberflöte: Overture
Brahms Concerto for violin and cello in A minor, op.102
Ravel Daphnis et Chloë - Suite no.2
V. Williams Symphony no.6 in E minor
Soloists Yehudi Menuhin (vn), Gregor Piatigorsky (vc)

SANTA CECILIA ACADEMY ORCHESTRA, Rome
7 Sep. 19.30 *Usher Hall*
Geminiani Concerto grosso no.2
Schubert Symphony no.5 in B flat, D485
Weber Oberon: Overture
Pizzetti La pisanella - Suite
Ravel Le tombeau de Couperin
Verdi Les vêpres Siciliennes: Overture
Conductor Carlo Zecchi

8 Sep. 19.30 *Usher Hall*
Cherubini Anacréon: Overture
Brahms Symphony no.2 in D, op.73
Beethoven Concerto for violin, cello and piano in C, op.56
Beethoven Leonore: Overture no.3
Conductor Wilhelm Furtwängler
Soloists Gioconda de Vito (vn), Enrico Mainardi (vc), Arturo Benedetti Michelangeli (pf)

9 Sep. 19.30 *Usher Hall*
Ghedini Partita
R. Strauss Tod und Verklärung
Beethoven Symphony no.5 in C minor, op.67
Conductor Wilhelm Furtwängler

10 Sep. 19.30 *Usher Hall*
Rossini La cenerentola: Overture
Schumann Concerto for piano in A minor, op.54
Brahms Symphony no.3 in F, op.90
Dukas L'apprenti sorcier
Conductor Vittorio Gui
Soloist
Arturo Benedetti Michelangeli (pf)

11 Sep. 19.30 *Usher Hall*
Haydn Symphony no.88 in G
Boccherini Concerto for cello no.9 in B flat
Mortari Music for strings
Schumann Symphony no.4 in D minor, op.120
Conductor Carlo Zecchi
Soloist Enrico Mainardi (vc)

12 Sep. 14.30 *Usher Hall*
Beethoven Egmont: Overture
Brahms Concerto for violin in D, op.77
Mozart Sinfonia concertante for wind, K.297b
Respighi Belfagor: Overture
Franck Psyché: Sommeil de Psyché *and* Psyché et Eros
Conductor Vittorio Gui
Soloist Gioconda de Vito (vn)

BOYD NEEL ORCHESTRA
Conductor Boyd Neel

23 Aug. 11.00 *Freemasons' Hall*
Avison Concerto in E minor
J.C. Bach Symphony in B flat, op.21/3
Britten Variations on a theme of Frank Bridge
Honegger Symphony for strings

24 Aug. 11.00 *Freemasons' Hall*
Ariosti Overture in Vespasian
Boccherini Concerto for cello no.9 in B flat
Bartók Music for strings, percussion and celesta
Soloist James Whitehead (vc)

25 Aug. 11.00 *Freemasons' Hall*
Mozart Divertimento (Salzburg symphony) no.2 in B flat, K137
Bach Concerto for piano in D minor
Schoenberg Verklärte Nacht
Soloist Kathleen Long (pf)

26 Aug. 11.00 *Freemasons' Hall*
Bach (ascrib.) Overture in G minor
D. Scarlatti Concerto for viola; arr. Bayan
Mozart Fantasia in F minor, K.608
Elgar Introduction and allegro, op.47
Soloist Max Gilbert (va)

27 Aug. 11.00 *Freemasons' Hall*
Howard The amorous goddess: Overture
V. Williams Concerto for oboe in A minor
Ireland Concertino pastorale
Tippett Concerto for double string orchestra
Soloist Leon Goossens (ob)

28 Aug. 11.00 *Freemasons' Hall*
Handel Concerto grosso in F, op.6/9
Pergolesi Concertino in F minor
Milhaud Concertino de printemps for violin
Wolf Italian serenade
Shostakovich Prelude and scherzo, op.11
Soloist Maurice Clare (vn)

30 Aug. 11.00 *Freemasons' Hall*
Stanley Concerto grosso in B flat, op.6/2
Méhul L'avoir qu'une pensée
Dourlen Je sais attacher les rubans
Monsigny Il regardait mon bouquet
Garat Dans le printemps de mes années
Pergolesi La serva padrona: Serpina's aria (Fr.)
Suk Serenade in E flat, op.6
Chausson Poème de l'amour et de la mer
Soloist Maggie Teyte (sop)

31 Aug. 11.00 *Freemasons' Hall*
Vivaldi Concerto grosso in D minor
Jacob Concerto for bassoon
R. Strauss Metamorphosen for 23 solo strings
Soloist Archie Camden (bn)

1 Sep. 11.00 *Freemasons' Hall*
Boyce Symphony no.1 in B flat, op.2/1
Bach Musikalisches Opfer: Ricercar
Rawsthorne Concerto for piano, strings and percussion
Stravinsky Apollon musagète
Soloist Kendal Taylor (pf)

2 Sep. 11.00 *Freemasons' Hall*
Handel Concerto grosso in D, op.6/5
Abel Symphony in E flat, op.10/3
Britten Serenade for tenor, horn and strings
Dvorák Serenade for strings in E, op.22
Soloists John Tainsh (ten), Dennis Brain (hn)

CHAMBER CONCERTS

HUNGARIAN QUARTET

3 Sep. 11.00 *Freemasons' Hall*
Mozart Quartet no.14 in G, K387
Bartók Quartet no.5
Schubert Quartet no.14 in D minor (Death and the maiden), D810

4 Sep. 11.00 *Freemasons' Hall*
Beethoven Quartet no.10 in E flat (Harp), op.74
Beethoven Quartet no.15 in A minor, op.132
Beethoven Quartet no.6 in B flat, op.18/6

TRIO DI TRIESTE

7 Sep. 11.00 *Freemasons' Hall*
Brahms Trio for piano and strings no.3 in C minor, op.101
Beethoven Variations in E flat, op.44
Ravel Trio for piano and strings in A minor

8 Sep. 11.00 *Freemasons' Hall*
Mozart Trio for piano and strings no.3 in B flat, K502
Dvorák Trio for piano and strings no.4 in E minor (Dumky), op.90
Schubert Trio for piano and strings no.1 in B flat, D898

ROBERT MASTERS PIANO QUARTET

9 Sep. 20.00 *Freemasons' Hall*
A.C. Mackenzie Quartet for piano and strings in E flat, op.11
Orr Sonatine in 1 movement for cello and piano (World première)
J.B. McEwen Trio for strings no.5 (Attica) (World première)
Fauré Quartet for piano and strings no.1 in C minor, op.15

CARTER TRIO

11 Sep. 11.00 *Freemasons' Hall*
Boyce Trio sonata no.8 in E flat
Gal Trio for oboe, violin and viola
Wordsworth Trio for strings in G minor
Mozart Quartet for oboe and strings in F, K370
with Leon Goossens (ob)

SCOTTISH CONCERTS

JANETTE SCLANDERS, ALEXANDER CARMICHAEL (sngr), SYBIL TAIT (pf)

25 Aug. 20.00 *Freemasons' Hall*
Scottish folk songs arr. by Moffat, Diack, Stephen, Whyte

CAMPBELTOWN GAELIC CHOIR

27 Aug. 20.00 *Central Hall*
Conductor Malcolm G. MacCallum
Soloists Helen Macmillan, Jean Baines, Morag Macdonald, Neil Maclean, Alasdair Matheson, Angus Whyte (sngr), Margaret Hill Boyle (pf)

SCOTTISH SINGERS

6 Sep. 20.00 *Freemasons' Hall*
Finzi Lo, the full, final sacrifice
Anon. Dunkeld music book: 2 Pieces
Britten A ceremony of carols
Kennedy-Fraser *arr.* Songs of the Hebrides
Folk songs arr. by Holst, Stanford, Bantock, V. Williams, Hughes, Shaw, Roberton, Stephen
Conductor Joyce Fleming
Soloists Evelyn Campbell (sngr), Andrew Bryson, Ruth D'Arcy Thompson (pf), Margery Davidson (hp), R.C. Howells (org)

GLASGOW ORPHEUS CHOIR
Conductor Sir Hugh Roberton

11 Sep. 14.30 *Usher Hall*
Soloists Betty Watson, Mina Bell, Maxwell Kennedy (sngr), David Anderson (pf)

12 Sep. 19.30 *Usher Hall*
Soloists Jean Houston, Annie Tait, Alexander McKay (sngr), David Anderson (pf)

RECITALS

KATHLEEN FERRIER (cont)
GERALD MOORE (pf)

26 Aug. 20.00 *Freemasons' Hall*
Songs by Schubert, Brahms, Parry, Stanford, Moeran, Warlock

MAGGIE TEYTE (sop)
GERALD MOORE (pf)

1 Sep. 20.00 *Freemasons' Hall*
Songs by Webber, Ravel, Debussy, Fauré. Stravinsky, Hahn

ROY HENDERSON (bar)
GERALD MOORE (pf)

9 Sep. 11.00 *Freemasons' Hall*
Butterworth A Shropshire lad
Songs by Schubert, Parry, Stanford, Wood, Delius, Warlock, Ireland, Bairstow, Davidson

ALFRED CORTOT (pf)

4 Sep. 14.30 *Usher Hall*
A recreation of a recital by Chopin in 1848

LOUIS KENTNER (pf)

6 Sep. 11.00 *Freemasons' Hall*
Schubert Fantasia in C (Wanderer), D.760
Schubert Moments musicaux, D.780
Schubert Sonata no.21 in B flat, D.960

YEHUDI MENUHIN (vn)
LOUIS KENTNER (pf)

31 Aug. 19.30 *Usher Hall*
Beethoven Sonatas nos.1-4

2 Sep. 19.30 *Usher Hall*
Beethoven Sonatas nos.5-7

5 Sep. 19.30 *Usher Hall*
Beethoven Sonatas nos.8-10

GREGOR PIATIGORSKY (vc)
IVOR NEWTON (pf)

5 Sep. 14.30 *Usher Hall*
Works by Boccherini, Bach, Beethoven, Schubert, Debussy, Fauré, Saint-Saëns, Stravinsky, Paganini

SEGOVIA (gtr)

7 Sep. 20.00 *Freemasons' Hall*
Guitar works by A. Scarlatti, D. Scarlatti, Rameau, Haydn, Bach, Crespo, Tansman, Turina, Granados, Albeniz

8 Sep. 20.00 *Freemasons' Hall*
Guitar works by Milan, Weiss, Couperin, Sor, Bach, Torroba, Ponce, Granados, Castelnuovo-Tedesco, Albeniz

10 Sep. 11.00 *Freemasons' Hall*
Guitar works by Dowland, Purcell, Haydn, Handel, Castelnuovo-Tedesco, Ponce, Villa-Lobos, Espla, Granados, Albeniz

JOAN ALEXANDER (sop), ELIZABETH LOCKHART (vn), HUBERT GREENSLADE, AILIE CULLEN (pf)

24 Aug. 20.00 *Freemasons' Hall*
Thorpe Davie Sonata for violin and piano
Suk 4 Pieces for violin and piano, op.17: Quasi ballata *and* Appassionata
Franck Sonata for violin and piano in A
F.G. Scott Songs

DRAMA

THE SCOTTISH THEATRE
24 Aug.-11 Sep. 19.30 (exc. Sun) 24, 28, 31 Aug. 4, 7, 11 Sep 14.30 Assembly Hall
THE THRIE ESTAITES Lyndsay
(Adapted by Robert Kemp)
Diligence C.R.M. Brookes
King Bryden Murdoch
Wantonness Douglas Campbell
Placebo Peter MacDonell
Solace James Stuart
Sensualitie Molly Urquhart
Hameliness Jean Carrol
Danger Audrey Moncrieff
Fund-Jennet Dudley Stuart White
Gude Counsel Moultrie Kelsall
Flatterie/Pardoner Duncan Macrae
Falsehood James Gibson
Deceit James Sutherland
Veritie Lennox Milne
Chastitie Jean Taylor Smith
Spiritualitie Andrew P. Wilson
Prioress Edith Ruddick
Abbot/Tailor's wife Graham Squire
Parson Bruce Morgan
Acolyte Fred Law
Temporalitie Robert McLauchlan
Merchant John Main
Soutar Jack Maguire
Soutar's wife Monty Landstein
Tailor William Young
Correction's varlet Stanley Baxter
Divine Correction Ian Stewart
Poor man Jack Lynn
John the Common-Weal Archie Duncan
Sergeant Andrew Gray
Director Tyrone Guthrie
Designer Molly MacEwen
Music Cedric Thorpe Davie

TENNENT PRODUCTIONS LTD
23 Aug.- 4 Sep. 19.15 (exc.Sun) 25, 28 Aug. 1, 4 Sep. 14.30 *Lyceum Theatre*
MEDEA Euripides
(Eng. Adapted by Robinson Jeffers)
Medea Eileen Herlie
Jason Ralph Michael
Creon Hector MacGregor
Aegeus Robert Marsden
Nurse Cathleen Nesbitt
Tutor Lee Fox
Children Anthony Linke, Stanley Foreman
Chorus Elspeth March, Helen Horsey, Sandra Jennings
Other parts played by Terence Longdon, David Oxley, Alan Brown, Josephine Dent, Violet Coleman
Director John Gielgud
Designer Leslie Hurry

LA COMPAGNIE RENAUD-BARRAULT, Paris
7, 9, 11 Sep. 19.15 11 Sep. 14.30
Lyceum Theatre
HAMLET Shakespeare
(Fr. Translated by André Gide)
Hamlet Jean-Louis Barrault
Ophelie Eleonore Hirt
Gertrude Marie-Hélène Dasté
Claudius Jacques Dacqmine
Polonius André Brunot
Horatio Jean Desailly
Laertes Gabriel Cattand
Fortinbras Bernard Noel
Osric Jean-Pierre Granval
Ghost Georges Le Roy
Rosencrantz Jacques Blondeau
Guildenstern Bernard Dhéran
Player king Beauchamp
Player queen Simone Valère
Other parts played by Régis Outin, Jean Juillard, Albert Medina
Director Jean-Louis Barrault
Designer André Masson
Music Honegger
Music director Pierre Boulez

6, 8, 10 Sep. 19.15 10 Sep. 14.30
Lyceum Theatre
LES FAUSSES CONFIDENCES
Marivaux
Araminte Madeleine Renaud
Dorante Jean Desailly
M. Rémi André Brunot
Madame Argante Catherine Fonteney
Arlequin Jean-Pierre Granval
Dubois Jean-Louis Barrault
Marton Simone Valère
Le comte Régis Outin
L'orfevre Gabriel Cattand
Le valet Jacques Blondeau
Director Jean-Louis Barrault
Designer Maurice Brianchon
BAPTISTE Prevert
(Pantomime from *Enfants du paradis*)
La statue/La duchesse Madeleine Renaud
La chanteur Jean Desailly
Baptiste Jean-Louis Barrault
Le gardien de square Jean Juillard
Arlequin Marcel Marceau
La petite fille Mireille Labaye
La lavandière Simone Valère
Le bijoutier Jean-Pierre Granval
Le laquais Albert Medina
Le marchand d'Habits Beauchamp
Director Jean-Louis Barrault
Designer Mayo

POETRY AND PROSE RECITALS

APOLLO SOCIETY
29 Aug. 20.00 *Freemasons' Hall*
Peggy Ashcroft, John Laurie, Cecil Day Lewis (rdr), Natasha Litvin (pf)

5 Sep. 20.00 *Freemasons' Hall*
Dame Edith Evans, Dylan Thomas, Michel St Denis (rdr), Franz Osborn (pf)

DANCE

SADLER'S WELLS BALLET
30, 31 Aug. 1 Sep. 19.15 1 Sep. 14.30
Empire Theatre
LA BOUTIQUE FANTASQUE
Choreographer Léonide Massine
Music Rossini; arr. Respighi
Designer André Derain
MIRACLE IN THE GORBALS
Choreographer Robert Helpmann
Music Bliss
Designer Edward Burra
SYMPHONIC VARIATIONS
Choreographer Frederick Ashton
Music Franck
Designer Sophie Fedorovitch

2, 3, 4 Sep. 19.15 4 Sep.14.30
Empire Theatre
COPPÉLIA
Choreographers Petipa, Cecchetti, Sergeyev
Music Delibes
Designer William Chappell
CHECKMATE
Choreographer Ninette de Valois
Music Bliss
Designer E. McKnight Kauffer

6, 7, 8 Sep 19.15 8 Sep. 14.30
Empire Theatre
CLOCK SYMPHONY
Choreographer Léonide Massine
Music Haydn
Designer Christian Bérard
SCÈNES DE BALLET
Choreographer Frederick Ashton
Music Stravinsky
Designer André Beaurepaire
MAM'ZELLE ANGOT
Choreographer Léonide Massine
Music Lecocq; arr. Jacob
Designer André Derain

9, 10, 11 Sep. 19.15 11 Sep. 14.30
Empire Theatre
LES SYLPHIDES
Choreographer Mikhail Fokine
Music Chopin
Designer Alexander Benois
JOB
Choreographer Ninette de Valois
Music V. Williams
Designer John Piper
THE THREE-CORNERED HAT
Choreographer Léonide Massine
Music Falla
Designer Pablo Picasso
Dancers Margot Fonteyn, Robert Helpmann, Pamela May, Moira Shearer, Beryl Grey, Violetta Elvin, Alexis Rassine, Michael Somes, Harold Turner, John Hart, Margaret Dale, Pauline Clayden, Julia Farron, Gerd Larsen, June Brae, Anne Negus, Gillian Lynne, Avril Navarre, Rosemary Lindsay, Lorna Mossford, Palma Nye, Alexander Grant, John Field, Leslie Edwards, Richard Ellis, Ray Powell, Franklin White
Covent Garden Orchestra
Conductor Warwick Braithwaite

1949

OPERA

GLYNDEBOURNE OPERA
22, 24, 26, 29, 31 Aug. 1, 3, 5, 6, 8, 10 Sep. 19.00 *King's Theatre*
UN BALLO IN MASCHERA Verdi
Riccardo Mirto Picchi, William Horne
Renato Paolo Silveri
Amelia Ljuba Welitsch, Margherita Grandi
Ulrica Jean Watson, Amalia Pini
Oscar Alda Noni
Samuel Ian Wallace
Tom Hervey Alan
Silvano Francis Loring
Judge George Israel
Servant Leslie Fyson
Royal Philharmonic Orchestra
Conductors Vittorio Gui, Hans Oppenheim
Director Carl Ebert
Designer Caspar Neher

23, 25, 27, 30 Aug. 2, 7, 9 Sep. 19.00
King's Theatre
COSÌ FAN TUTTE Mozart

Fiordiligi Suzanne Danco
Dorabella Sena Jurinac
Ferrando Petre Munteanu
Guglielmo Marko Rothmüller
Despina Irene Eisinger
Don Alfonso John Brownlee
Royal Philharmonic Orchestra
Conductors Vittorio Gui
Hans Oppenheim
Director Carl Ebert
Designer Rolf Gérard

ORCHESTRAL CONCERTS

ROYAL PHILHARMONIC ORCHESTRA
Conductor Sir Thomas Beecham
21 Aug. 19.30 *Usher Hall*
Berlioz King Lear - Overture
Brahms Variations on a theme by Haydn (St Antoni, op.56a)
Franck Le chasseur maudit
Sibelius Tapiola
Dvořák Symphonic variations, op.78

28 Aug. 19.30 *Usher Hall*
Handel Il pastor fido - Suite; arr. Beecham
Haydn Symphony no.97 in C
Paisiello Nina: Overture
Schubert Symphony no.6 in C, D589

4 Sep. 19.30 *Usher Hall*
Schumann Symphony no.1 in B flat (Spring), op.38
Bantock Hebridean symphony
Delius Folkeraadet
Debussy L'enfant prodigue: Cortège and air de danse
Chabrier España

BERLIN PHILHARMONIC ORCHESTRA
22 Aug. 19.30 *Usher Hall*
Wagner Die Meistersinger: Overture
Elgar Introduction and allegro, op.47
Roussel Bacchus et Ariane - Suite no.2
Sibelius Symphony no.2 in D, op.43
Conductor Sir John Barbirolli

23 Aug. 19.30 *Usher Hall*
Rossini Semiramide: Overture
Mozart Symphony no.39 in E flat, K543
Barber Adagio for strings, op.11
Elgar Variations on an original theme (Enigma)
Conductor Sir John Barbirolli

24 Aug. 19.30 *Usher Hall*
Rossini Semiramide: Overture
Barber Adagio for strings, op.11
Roussel Bacchus et Ariane - Suite no.2
Sibelius Symphony no.2 in D, op.43
Conductor Sir John Barbirolli

25 Aug. 19.30 *Usher Hall*
Elgar Cockaigne - Overture
Dukas La Péri
Hindemith Symphonic metamorphosis on themes of Weber
Mahler Symphony no.1 in D
Conductor Eugene Goossens

26 Aug. 14.30 *Usher Hall*
Beethoven Coriolan - Overture
Mozart Symphony no.41 in C (Jupiter), K551
Harris Symphony no.3
E. Goossens Concerto for oboe
Antill Corroboree - Suite
Conductor Eugene Goossens
Soloist Leon Goossens (ob)

26 Aug. 19.30 *Usher Hall*
Beethoven Coriolan - Overture
Mozart Symphony no.41 in C (Jupiter), K551
Mahler Symphony no.1 in D
Conductor Eugene Goossens

BBC SCOTTISH ORCHESTRA
27 Aug. 19.30 *Usher Hall*
Ireland A London overture
D'Albert Concerto for cello in C, op.20
Haydn Symphony no.88 in G
Whyte Symphony no.1
Conductor Ian Whyte
Soloist Guilhermina Suggia (vc)

3 Sep. 19.30 *Usher Hall*
Thorpe Davie The beggar's benison
Bloch Concerto symphonique (World première)
Gal Lilliburlero
Bax Symphony no.1 in E flat
Conductors Ian Whyte
Ernest Bloch
Soloist Corinne Lacomblé (pf)

ORCHESTRE DE LA SUISSE ROMANDE
Conductor Ernest Ansermet
30 Aug. 19.30 *Usher Hall*
Haydn Symphony no.101 in D (Clock)
Martin Symphonie concertante
Honegger Prelude, fugue and postlude 'Amphion'
Ravel Concerto for piano (Left hand)
Ravel Rapsodie espagnole
Soloist Jacqueline Blancard (pf)

31 Aug. 19.30 *Usher Hall*
Mozart Symphony no.38 in D (Prague), K504
Debussy Nocturnes
Martinů Sonata da camera for cello and orchestra
Stravinsky Petrushka: Scenes 1 *and* 4
Soloist Henri Honegger (vc)
Scottish Singers members

PHILHARMONIA ORCHESTRA
Conductor Rafael Kubelik
1 Sep. 19.30 *Usher Hall*
Martinů Concerto for double string orchestra
Beethoven Concerto for piano no.5 (Emperor), op.73
Dvořák Symphony no.8 in G, op.88
Soloist Rudolf Serkin (pf)

2 Sep. 19.30 *Usher Hall*
Mendelssohn Meeresstille und glückliche Fahrt - Overture
Dvořák Concerto for violin in A minor, op.53
Beethoven Symphony no.7 in A, op.92
Soloist Adolf Busch (vn)

PARIS CONSERVATOIRE ORCHESTRA
5, 9 Sep. 19.30 *Usher Hall*
Beethoven Egmont: Overture
Beethoven Symphony no.1 in C, op.21
Beethoven Symphony no.3 In E flat (Eroica), op.55
Conductor Bruno Walter

6 Sep. 19.30 *Usher Hall*
Berlioz Le carnaval romain - Overture
Sibelius Concerto for violin in D minor, op.47
Honegger Symphony for strings
Stravinsky The firebird - Suite
Conductor André Cluytens
Soloist Ginette Neveu (vn)

8, 10 Sep. 19.30 *Usher Hall*
Berlioz Benvenuto Cellini: Overture
Debussy Prélude à l'après-midi d'un faune
Mahler Kindertotenlieder
Brahms Symphony no.4 in E minor, op.98
Conductor Bruno Walter
Soloist Kathleen Ferrier (cont)

11 Sep. 14.30 *Usher Hall*
Lalo Le roi d'Ys: Overture
Ravel Ma mère l'oye
Rivier Concerto for piano in C
Duruflé Scherzo
Mussorgsky Pictures at an exhibition; orch. Ravel
Conductor André Cluytens
Soloist Monique de la Bruchollerie (pf)

JACQUES ORCHESTRA
Conductor Reginald Jacques
24 Aug. 11.00 *Freemasons' Hall*
Handel Concerto grosso in A minor, op.6/4
Mozart Eine kleine Nachtmusik
V. Williams Fantasia on a theme by Tallis
Bliss Music for strings

25 Aug. 11.00 *Freemasons' Hall*
Bach Concerto for flute, violin and harpsichord
Gibbons Pavane and Galliard
D. Scarlatti Suite for flute and strings in A; arr. Benjamin
Corelli Concerto grosso; arr. Barbirolli
Soloists Gareth Morris (fl), Irene Richards (vn), Thornton Lofthouse (hpd)

27 Aug. 11.00 *Freemasons' Hall*
Corelli Concerto grosso in G minor (Christmas), op.6/8
Bach Brandenburg Concerto no.6 in B flat
Bach Concerto for 2 violins in D minor
Bach Brandenburg Concerto no.3 in G
Soloists Irene Richards, Mary Carter (vn), Thornton Lofthouse (hpd)

29 Aug. 11.00 *Freemasons' Hall*
Handel Suite from the overtures; arr. Jacques
Stamitz Concerto for clarinet
Tippett Little music for strings
Arnold Concerto for clarinet, op20
Barber Adagio for strings, op11
Soloist Frederick Thurston (cl)

30 Aug. 11.00 *Freemasons' Hall*
Pergolesi Concertino no.3 in A
Gurney Songs; arr. Finzi
Mozart Divertimento no.17 in D, K334
Soloist Joan Alexander (sop)

1 Sep. 11.00 *Freemasons' Hall*
Handel Concerto grosso in B minor, op.6/12
Albinoni Concerto for oboe in D, op.7/6
Purcell Chaconne in G minor
Jacob Concerto for oboe
Goossens Concertino for string orchestra
Soloist Leon Goossens (ob)

2 Sep. 11.00 *Freemasons' Hall*
Handel Concerto grosso in E minor, op.6/3
Bach Cantata no.85: Seht was die Liebe tut! (Eng)
Byrd Fantasia no.2 in C minor
V. Williams Four hymns for tenor, viola and strings
W. Schuman Symphony for strings
Soloists Richard Lewis (ten), Margot Stebbing (va)

5 Sep. 11.00 *Freemasons' Hall*
Handel Concerto grosso in D minor, op.6/10
Bach Mass in B minor: Laudamus te

Mozart Serenade no.6 in D (Serenata notturna), K239
L. Berkeley Four poems by St Teresa of Avila
Gal Concertino for organ and strings
Soloists Kathleen Ferrier (cont), Irene Richards, Mary Carter (vn), Margot Stebbing (va), John Walton (db), Herrick Bunney (org)

7 Sep. 11.00 *Freemasons' Hall*
Handel Faramondo: Overture
Bach Brandenburg concerto no.5 in D
Corelli Concerto grosso in B flat, op.6/11
Bach Brandenburg concerto no.4 in G
Soloists Irene Richards (vn), Geoffrey Gilbert, Harold Clarke (fl), Ernest Lush (pf)

8 Sep. 11.00 *Freemasons' Hall*
Vivaldi Concerto grosso in E minor
Handel Concerto for harp and 2 flutes in B flat, op.4/6
L. Berkeley Serenade for strings, op.12
Debussy Danse sacrée et danse profane
Gluck Orfeo ed Euridice: Dance of the blessed spirits
Elgar Introduction and allegro, op.47
Soloists Marie Korchinska (hp), Geoffrey Gilbert, Harold Clarke (fl)

CHAMBER CONCERTS

GRILLER QUARTET
22 Aug. 11.00 *Freemasons' Hall*
Mozart Quartet no.14 in G, K387
Beethoven Quartet no.11 in F minor (Serioso), op.95
Purcell Chaconne in G minor

23 Aug. 11.00 *Freemasons' Hall*
Bartók Quartet no.2
Brahms Quartet no.1 in C minor, op.51/1

BUSCH QUARTET
27 Aug. 14.30 *Usher Hall*
Beethoven Septet, op.20
Schubert Octet, D803
with Frederick Thurston (cl), Paul Draper (bn), Dennis Brain (hn), James Merrett (db)

29 Aug. 19.30 *Usher Hall*
Brahms Quintet for piano and strings in F minor, op.34
Dvořák Quintet for piano and strings in A, op.81
with Rudolf Serkin (pf)

31 Aug. 11.00 *Freemasons' Hall*
Haydn Quartet in D (Lark), op.64/5
Tovey Air with variations, op.11
Beethoven Quartet no.12 in E flat, op.127

3 Sep. 11.00 *Freemasons' Hall*
Brahms Quartet no.2 in A minor, op.51/2
Mendelssohn Capriccio in E minor
Beethoven Quartet no.7 in F (Rasumovsky), op.59/1

PRAGUE TRIO
9 Sep. 11.00 *Freemasons' Hall*
Ravel Trio for piano and strings in A minor
Smetana Trio for piano and strings in G minor

10 Sep. 11.00 *Freemasons' Hall*
Shostakovich Trio for piano and strings no.2 in E minor, op.67
Dvořák Trio for piano and strings no.3 in F minor, op.65

CLOISTER SINGERS OF ST ANDREW'S
24 Aug. 20.00 *Freemasons' Hall*
Madrigals, lute songs, Scottish folk songs
Conductor Charles Guild
with Isla Hunter (pf)

PRO MUSICA ANTIQUA ENSEMBLE, Brussels
9 Sep. 20.00 *Freemasons' Hall*
Medieval and Renaissance music

10 Sep. 20.00 *Freemasons' Hall*
Medieval and Renaissance music

GLASGOW ORPHEUS CHOIR
11 Sep. 19.30 *Usher Hall*
Conductor Sir Hugh Roberton
Soloists Annie Tait, Mina Bell, Betty Watson, Alexander McKay (sngr), David Anderson (pf)

RECITALS

AULIKKI RAUTAWAARA (sop)
JUSSI JALAS (pf)
26 Aug. 11.00 *Freemasons' Hall*
Songs by Sibelius

AKSEL SCHIOTZ (ten)
GERALD MOORE (pf)
6 Sep. 11.00 *Freemasons' Hall*
Schubert Die schöne Müllerin

KATHLEEN FERRIER (cont)
BRUNO WALTER (pf)
7 Sep. 19.30 *Usher Hall*
Schumann Frauenliebe und -leben
Songs by Schubert and Brahms

JOHN TAINSH (ten), WALDO CHANNON (vn), ALAN RICHARDSON, AILIE CULLEN (pf)
1 Sep. 20.00 *Freemasons' Hall*
Dunlop Four settings of William Soutar
Richardson Sonata for violin and piano no.1
Thorpe Davie Six poems by Violet Jacob
Richardson Sonatina for piano
F.G. Scott Songs

RUDOLF SERKIN (pf)
3 Sep. 14.30 *Usher Hall*
Bach Concerto in the Italian style
Beethoven Sonata no.29 in B flat (Hammerklavier), op.106
Schubert Fantasia in C (Wanderer), D760

ADOLF BUSCH (vn)
RUDOLF SERKIN (pf)
28 Aug. 15.00 *Freemasons' Hall*
Schumann Sonata no.1 in A minor, op.105
Beethoven Sonata no.10 in G, op.96
Brahms Sonata no.3 in D minor, op.108

4 Sep. 15.00 *Freemasons' Hall*
Mozart Sonata no.32 in B flat, K454
Reger Sonata in C minor, op.139
Schubert Fantasia in C, D934

GINETTE NEVEU (vn)
JEAN NEVEU (pf)
10 Sep. 14.30 *Usher Hall*
Fauré Sonata no.1 in A, op.13
Debussy Sonata
Franck Sonata in A

GUILHERMINA SUGGIA (vc)
IVOR NEWTON (pf)
25 Aug. 20.00 *Freemasons' Hall*
Works by Bach, Senaillé, Arne, Sammartini, Brahms, Bridge, Glazunov, Schmitt, Ravel, Falla

DRAMA

THE SCOTTISH THEATRE
22 Aug.-10 Sep. 19.30 (exc.Sun) 23, 27, 30 Aug. 3, 6, 10 Sep.14.30 Assembly Hall
THE THRIE ESTAITES Lyndsay
(Adapted by Robert Kemp)
Diligence C.R.M. Brookes
King Bryden Murdoch
Wantonness Robert Urquhart
Placebo Peter MacDonell
Solace James Stuart
Sensualitie Catherine Lawson
Hameliness Jean Carrol
Danger Audrey Moncrieff
Fund-Jennet Dudley Stuart White
Gude Counsel Moultrie Kelsall
Flatterie/Pardoner Duncan Macrae
Falsehood James Gibson
Deceit James Sutherland
Veritie Lennox Milne
Chastitie Jean Taylor Smith
Spiritualitie Andrew P. Wilson
Prioress Edith Ruddick
Abbot Stanley Baxter
Parson Bruce Morgan
Acolyte Ian Scott
Temporalitie James Cairncross
Merchant Mayne Lynton
Soutar Abe Barker
Soutar's wife Monty Landstein
Tailor William Young
Tailor's wife Stanley Baxter
Correction's varlet Andrew Keir
Divine Correction Ian Stewart
Poor man Jack Lynn
John the Common-Weal Douglas Campbell
Sergeant David Orr
Director Tyrone Guthrie
Designer Molly MacEwen
Music Cedric Thorpe Davie

21, 25, 26, 29, 31 Aug. 2, 5, 7, 9 Sep. 23.30 *Royal High School*
THE GENTLE SHEPHERD Ramsay
(Adapted by Robert Kemp)
Sir William Worthy James Cairncross
Patie Robert Urquhart
Roger Douglas Campbell
Symon James Gibson
Glaud C.R.M. Brookes
Bauldy Duncan Macrae
Peggy Moira Robertson
Jenny Gudrun Ure
Mause Jean Cadell
Madge Lennox Milne
Singers Joan Alexander, Catherine Lawson, Jean Carroll, Audrey Moncrieff, William Herbert, Alexander Carmichael, Andrew Downie, Robert Nicholl Easton
Royal Philharmonic Orchestra members
Director Tyrone Guthrie
Designer Ruth Keating
Music Cedric Thorpe Davie

HENRY SHEREK
22-27 Aug. 19.15 24, 27 Aug. 14.30
Lyceum Theatre
THE COCKTAIL PARTY Eliot
(EIF commission)
The unidentified guest Alec Guinness
Edward Chamberlayne Robert Flemyng
Julia Shuttlethwaite Cathleen Nesbitt
Celia Coplestone Irene Worth
Alexander MacGolgie Gibbs Ernest Clark
Peter Quilpe Donald Houston
Lavinia Chamberlayne Ursula Jeans
A nurse secretary Christina Horniman

2 Caterer's men
Donald Bain, Martin Beckwith
Director E. Martin Browne
Designer Anthony Holland

29 Aug.-3 Sep. 19.15 31 Aug. 3 Sep. 14.30 *Lyceum Theatre*
THE MAN IN THE RAINCOAT Ustinov
(World première)
Helen Mary Ellis
Standing Percy Cartwright
Philip Jessup George Coulouris
Mr Justice Moy Alan Wheatley
The man in the raincoat Julian Somers
Director Peter Ustinov
Designer Anthony Holland

DÜSSELDORF THEATRE COMPANY
5-10 Sep. 19.15 7, 10 Sep. 14.30
Lyceum Theatre
FAUST Goethe
The Lord's voice, Michael, Raphael, Gabriel, Mephistopheles
Gustaf Gründgens
Faust Horst Caspar
Wagner Rudolf Therkatz
Scholar Max Eckard
Frosch Siegmund Giesecke
Brander Hans Müller-Westernhagen
Siebel/Valentin Gerhard Geisler
Altmeyer Bert Ledwoch
Witch Emmy Graetz
Margarete Antje Weisgerber
Marthe Elisabeth Flickenschildt
Lieschen Erna Möller
Director Gustaf Gründgens
Designer Herta Böhm
Conductor Heinz Rockstroh

DANCE

LES BALLETS DES CHAMPS-ELYSÉES
22-24 Aug. 19.30 *Empire Theatre*
13 DANCES
Choreographer Roland Petit
Music Grétry
Designer Christian Dior
THE NUTCRACKER: Pas de deux
Choreographer
Gordon Hamilton *after* Saint-Léon
Music Tchaikovsky
JEU DE CARTES
Choreographer Janine Charrat
Music Stravinsky
Designer Pierre Roy
LES FORAINS
Choreographer Roland Petit
Music Sauguet
Costumes Christian Bérard
SWAN LAKE: Black swan pas de deux (22 Aug)
Choreographer Petipa *and* Ivanov
Music Tchaikovsky
Designer Jean-Denis Malclès

25-27 Aug. 19.30 *Empire Theatre*
LA SYLPHIDE
Choreographer
Victor Gsovsky *after* Taglioni
Music Schneitzhoffer
Designer Serebriakov
Costumes Christian Bérard
SWAN LAKE: Black swan pas de deux (exc.25 Aug.)
THE SLEEPING BEAUTY: Pas de deux (25 Aug.)
Choreographer Victor Gsovsky, Petipa
Music Tchaikovsky
LE JEUNE HOMME ET LA MORT
Choreographer Roland Petit
Music Bach
Designer Georges Wakhevitch

29, 31 Aug. 19.30 *Empire Theatre*
MASCARADE
Choreographer Victor Gsovsky
Music Bizet
Designer Vertès
LE RENDEZVOUS
Choreographer Roland Petit
Music Kosma
Scenery Brassai
Costumes Mayo
SWAN LAKE: Pas de deux
LA RENCONTRE
Choreographer David Lichine
Music Sauguet
Designer Christian Bérard

30 Aug. 19.30 *Empire Theatre*
13 DANCES
THE NUTCRACKER: Grand pas classique
LA RENCONTRE
SWAN LAKE: Pas de deux
LES FORAINS

1-3 Sep. 19.30 *Empire Theatre*
LA FIANCÉE DU DIABLE
Choreographer Roland Petit
Music Paganini; arr. Hubeau
Designer Jean-Denis Malclès
LA NUIT
Choreographer Janine Charrat
Music Sauguet
Designer Christian Bérard
THE SLEEPING BEAUTY: Bluebird pas de deux
Choreographer Petipa
Music Tchaikovsky
Costumes Christian Bérard
LE BAL DES BLANCHISSEUSES
Choreographer Roland Petit
Music Vernon Duke
Designer Stanislav Lepri

5-7 Sep. 19.30 *Empire Theatre*
FÊTE GALANTE
Choreographer Victor Gsovsky
Music Claude Arrieu
Designer André Beaurepaire
LA CREATION
Choreographer David Lichine
SWAN LAKE: Pas de deux
LE PORTRAIT DE DON QUICHOTTE
Choreographer Aurel M. Milloss
Music Petrassi
Designer T. Keogh
VALSE CAPRICE
Choreographer David Lichine
Music Fauré; arr. Vaubourgoin
Costumes Christian Bérard

8-10 Sep. 19.30 *Empire Theatre*
COPPÉLIA: Act 2
Choreographer Saint-Léon
Music Delibes
Designer D. Bouchene
L'AMOUR ET SON AMOUR
Choreographer Jean Babilée
Music Franck
Designer Jean Cocteau
SWAN LAKE: Pas de deux
LES AMOURS DE JUPITER
Choreographer Roland Petit
Music Ibert
Designer Jean Hugo
Dancers Irène Skorik, Jean Babilée, Youly Algaroff, Nathalie Philippart, Leslie Caron, Tutti Enderlé, Danielle Darmance, Christian Foye, Hélène Constantine, Hélène Varenova, Youra Loboff, Nicholas Polajenko, Hélène Sadovska, Deryk Mendel, Teddy Rodolphe, Nina Vyroubova
Festival Ballet Orchestra
Conductor André Girard

1950

OPERA

GLYNDEBOURNE OPERA
21, 23, 25, 29, 31 Aug. 2, 4, 6, 8 Sep. 19.00 *King's Theatre*
ARIADNE AUF NAXOS R. Strauss
(1st version)
Ariadne Hilde Zadek
Zerbinetta Ilse Hollweg
Bacchus Peter Anders
Najade Maureen Springer
Dryade Marjorie Thomas
Echo April Cantelo
Harlekin Douglas Craig
Brighella Murray Dickie
Scaramuccio Alexander Young
Truffaldin Bruce Dargavel
Royal Philharmonic Orchestra
Conductor Sir Thomas Beecham
LE BOURGEOIS GENTILHOMME
Molière
(Eng. Translated by Miles Malleson)
Monsieur Jourdain Miles Malleson
Madame Jourdain Dandy Nichols
Nicoline Ilona Ference
Dorimène Tatiana Lieven
Music master Wensley Pithy
Composer John Ebdon
Dancing master Graham Stark
Philosopher Harold Scott
Fencing master Peter Copley
Dorante David King-Wood
Flunkies Norman Welsh, Alan Gordon
Singer April Cantelo
Director Carl Ebert
Designer Oliver Messel
Choreographer Michael Holmes

22, 24, 26, 28, 30 Aug. 1, 5, 7, 9 Sep. 19.00 *King's Theatre*
LE NOZZE DI FIGARO Mozart
Figaro George London
Susanna Elfriede Trötschel
Count Marko Rothmüller
Countess Clara Ebers
Cherubino Sena Jurinac
Dr Bartolo Ian Wallace
Marcellina Jean Watson
Don Basilio Murray Dickie
Barbarina April Cantelo
Don Curzio Leslie Fyson
Antonio Dennis Wicks
Royal Philharmonic Orchestra
Conductor Ferenç Fricsay
Director Carl Ebert
Designer Rolf Gérard

ORCHESTRAL CONCERTS

ORCHESTRE NATIONAL DE LA RADIODIFFUSION FRANÇAISE
20 Aug. 19.30 *Usher Hall*
Bizet L'Arlésienne - Suite
Fauré Ballade for piano and orchestra, op.19
Roussel Suite in F, op.33
Ravel Concerto for piano in G
Ravel La valse
Conductor Roger Désormière
Soloist Marguerite Long (pf)

21 Aug. 19.30 *Usher Hall*
Bach Brandenburg concerto no.5 in D
Liszt Fantasia 'Ad nos, ad salutarem undam'; arr. Dupré
Shostakovich Symphony no.5 in D minor, op.47

Conductor Leonard Bernstein
Soloist Marcel Dupré (org)

22 Aug. 19.30 *Usher Hall*
Méhul Les deux aveugles de Tolède: Overture
Grétry Zémire et Azor - Suite
Lalo Symphony in G minor
Poulenc Sinfonietta
Delibes Le roi s'amuse - Suite
Conductor Sir Thomas Beecham

23 Aug. 19.30 *Usher Hall*
W. Schuman American festival overture
Beethoven Concerto for piano no.1 in C, op.15
Schumann Symphony no.2 in C, op.61
Conductor and soloist Leonard Bernstein (pf)

24 Aug. 19.30 *Usher Hall*
Beethoven Symphony no.8 in F, op.93
Fauré Pavane, op.50
Bloch Schelomo
Boccherini Concerto for cello no.9 in B flat
Balakirev Tamara
Chabrier Joyeuse marche
Conductor Sir Thomas Beecham
Soloist Pierre Fournier (vc)
Edinburgh Royal Choral Union

25 Aug. 19.30 *Usher Hall*
Bach Suite no.3 in D
Mozart Concerto for piano no.24 in C minor, K491
Debussy Marche écossaise
d'Indy Symphony on a theme montagnard
Conductor Roger Désormière
Soloist Robert Casadesus (pf)

ROYAL PHILHARMONIC ORCHESTRA
Conductor Sir Thomas Beecham
27 Aug. 19.30 *Usher Hall*
Mozart Symphony no.31 in D (Paris), K297
Handel Concerto for piano; arr. Beecham
Haydn Symphony no.40 in F
V. Thomson Concerto for cello in D
Mozart March in D, K249
Soloists Betty Humbie (pf), Anthony Pini (vc)

3 Sep. 19.30 *Usher Hall*
Haydn Die Jahreszeiten (Eng)
Soloists Isobel Baillie (sop), Richard Lewis (ten), Trevor Anthony (bs), Edinburgh Royal Choral Union

DANISH STATE RADIO ORCHESTRA
26 Aug. 19.30 *Usher Hall*
Dvořák Carnival overture
Reger Variations and fugue on a theme of Mozart, op.132
Mozart Symphony no.40 in G minor, K550
R. Strauss Till Eulenspiegels lustige Streiche
Conductor Fritz Busch

28 Aug. 19.30 *Usher Hall*
Horneman Aladdin - Overture
Hindemith Symphonic metamorphosis on themes of Weber
Brahms Rhapsody for contralto, op.53
Brahms Symphony no.1 in C minor, op.68
Conductor Fritz Busch
Soloist Kathleen Ferrier (cont)
Edinburgh Royal Choral Union

29 Aug. 19.30 *Usher Hall*
Weber Oberon: Overture
Beethoven Concerto for piano no.3 in C minor, op.37
Nielsen Symphony no.5, op.50
Conductor Erik Tuxen
Soloist Claudio Arrau (pf)

BBC SCOTTISH ORCHESTRA
30 Aug. 19.30 *Usher Hall*
Busoni Tanzwalzer, op.53
Tchaikovsky Concerto for violin in D, op.35
Brahms Serenade no.1 in D, op.11
Conductor Ian Whyte
Soloist Nathan Milstein (vn)

HALLÉ ORCHESTRA
Conductor Sir John Barbirolli
31 Aug. 19.30 *Usher Hall*
Verdi La forza del destino: Overture
Debussy Sarabande; arr. Ravel
V. Williams Symphony no.5 in D
Brahms Symphony no.2 in D, op.73

1 Sep. 19.30 *Usher Hall*
Ireland Satyricon - Overture
Fauré Pelléas et Mélisande - Suite
Sibelius Symphony no.7 in C, op.105
Brahms Concerto for piano no.2 in B flat, op.83
Soloist Clifford Curzon (pf)

2 Sep. 19.30 *Usher Hall*
Beethoven Die Geschöpfe des Prometheus: Overture
Bartók Concerto for viola
Mozart Symphony no.29 in A, K201
Schubert Symphony no.9 in C (Great), D944
Soloist William Primrose (va)

ORCHESTRA OF LA SCALA, MILAN
4, 9 Sep. 19.30 *Usher Hall*
Verdi Requiem
Conductor Victor de Sabata
Soloists Renata Tebaldi (sop), Fedora Barbieri (mez), Giacinto Prandelli (ten), Cesare Siepi (bs), Chorus of La Scala, Milan

5 Sep. 19.30 *Usher Hall*
Schubert Symphony no.2 in B flat, D125
Ghedini Concerto dell'albatro
Tchaikovsky Symphony no.5 in E minor, op.64
Conductor Guido Cantelli
Soloists Ornella Puliti Santoliquido (pf), Enrico Minetti (vn), Massimo Amfitheatroff (vc), Leslie French (narr)

6 Sep. 19.30 *Usher Hall*
Haydn Symphony no.93 in D
Stravinsky The song of the nightingale
Rossini Semiramide: Overture
Beethoven Symphony no.7 in A, op.92
Conductor Guido Cantelli

7 Sep. 19.30 *Usher Hall*
Brahms Symphony no.4 in E minor, op.98
Pizzetti Fedra: Overture
Wagner Tannhäuser: Venusburg music
Ravel Daphnis et Chloë - Suite no.2
Conductor Victor de Sabata
Chorus of La Scala, Milan

8 Sep. 19.30 *Usher Hall*
Monteverdi Magnificat
Mozart Requiem, K626
Conductor Guido Cantelli
Soloists Renata Tebaldi (sop), Fedora Barbieri (mez), Giacinto Prandelli (ten), Cesare Siepi (bs), Chorus of La Scala, Milan

9 Sep. 11.00 *Usher Hall*
Monteverdi Magnificat
Tchaikovsky Symphony no.5 in E minor, op.64
Conductor Guido Cantelli
Chorus of La Scala, Milan

LONDON HARPSICHORD ENSEMBLE
'Bach and his Contemporaries'
Commemorating the bicentenary of the death of J.S. Bach
Instrumental soloists John Francis, Albert Honey (fl), Manoug Parikian, Hans Geiger (vn), Bernard Davis (va), George Roth (vc), Millicent Silver (hpd)
Bach cantatas conducted by Hans Oppenheim

20 Aug. 20.00 *Freemasons' Hall*
Bach Suite no.2 in B minor
Bach Cantata no.104
Bach Concerto for violin in E
Bach Cantata no.140
Soloists Ena Mitchell (sop), Richard Lewis (ten), William Parsons (bs), Edinburgh University Singers

22 Aug. 11.00 *Freemasons' Hall*
Bach Art of fugue; arr. Isaacs

24 Aug. 11.00 *Freemasons' Hall*
Bach Suite no.1 in C
Bach Cantata no.56
Bach Concerto for flute, violin and harpsichord
Soloist William Parsons (bs)
Edinburgh University Singers

26 Aug. 11.00 *Freemasons' Hall*
Bach Sonata for flute and harpsichord no.1 in B minor
Handel Deutsche Arien: In den angenehmen Büschen *and* Meine Seele hört im Sehen
Bach Concerto in the Italian style
Bach Bist du bei mir
Bach Cantata no.68: Mein glaübiges Herze
Bach Trio sonata no.3 in G
Soloist Ena Mitchell (sop)

29 Aug. 11.00 *Freemasons' Hall*
Rameau Concerto no.4 for harpsichord, flute and cello
Pergolesi Se tu m'ami
Marcello Quella fiamma che m'accende
Bach Sonata for violin no.1 in G minor
Bach Cantata no.142: Jesu, Dir sei Preis
Bach Cantata no.85: Jesus ist ein guter Hirt
Bach Trio sonata no.4 in G
Soloist Flora Nielsen (sop)

31 Aug 11.00 *Freemasons' Hall*
Telemann Suite in A minor for flute
Rameau Le berger fidèle
Bach Sonata for violin and harpsichord no.6 in G
Bach Cantata no.208: Schafe können sicher weiden
Bach Cantata no.206: Hört doch der sanften Flöten Chor
Soloist Elisabeth Schwarzkopf (sop)

2 Sep. 11.00 *Freemasons' Hall*
A. Scarlatti Sonata for flute, harpsichord and strings in D; arr. Tebaldini
J.C. Bach Concerto for harpsichord in E flat, op.7/5
Bach Cantata no.189
Bach *(attrib)* Trio sonata no.2 in C (Goldberg)
Soloist Peter Pears (ten)

4 Sep. 11.00 *Freemasons' Hall*
Bach Concerto for harpsichord in D minor
Bach Suite for flute in A minor
Bach Cantata no.211 (Coffee cantata)
Soloists Elisabeth Schwarzkopf (sop), John Tainsh (ten), George James (bs)

6 Sep. 11.00 *Freemasons' Hall*
Frederick II of Prussia Concerto for flute in G
Bach Musikalisches Opfer

8 Sep. 11.00 *Freemasons' Hall*
Bach Cantata no.54
Bach Brandenburg concerto no.4 in G
Bach Cantata no.106
Soloists April Cantelo (sop), Alfred Deller (c ten), Richard Lewis (ten), William Parsons (bs), Edinburgh University Singers

CHAMBER CONCERTS

LOEWENGUTH QUARTET
21 Aug. 11.00 *Freemasons' Hall*
Haydn Quartet in G minor (Rider), op.74/3
Beethoven Quartet no.11 in F minor (Serioso), op.95
Rainier Quartet

23 Aug. 11.00 *Freemasons' Hall*
Schumann Quartet no.1 in A minor, op.41/1
Rueff Quartet (World première)
Beethoven Quartet no.8 in E minor (Rasumovsky), op.59/2

ORCHESTRE NATIONAL WIND QUINTET
28 Aug. 11.00 *Freemasons' Hall*
Mozart Quintet for piano and wind in E flat, K452
Milhaud Le cheminée du Roi René
Françaix Quintet for wind
Poulenc Sextet for piano and wind
with Jean Françaix (pf)

GRILLER QUARTET
30 Aug. 11.00 *Freemasons' Hall*
Haydn Quartet in F minor, op.20/5
Kodály Quartet no.2, op.10
Beethoven Quartet no.15 in A minor, op.132

1 Sep. 11.00 *Freemasons' Hall*
Mozart Quartet no.15 in D minor, K421
Bliss Quartet no.2 (World première)
Brahms Quintet for clarinet and strings in B minor, op.115
with Frederick Thurston (cl)

BUDAPEST QUARTET
5 Sep. 11.00 *Freemasons' Hall*
Haydn Quartet in D, op.76/5
Bartók Quartet no.2
Beethoven Quartet no.8 in E minor (Rasumovsky), op.59/2

7 Sep. 11.00 *Freemasons' Hall*
Beethoven Quartet no.1 in F, op.18/1
Hindemith Quartet no.5 in E flat
Brahms Quartet no.3 in B flat, op.67

9 Sep. 11.00 *Freemasons' Hall*
Mozart Quartet no.14 in G, K387
Milhaud Quartet no.15
Beethoven Quartet no.12 in E flat, op.127

GLASGOW ORPHEUS CHOIR
26 Aug. 14.30 *Usher Hall*
Scottish and choral songs

9 Sep. 14.30 *Usher Hall*
Scottish and choral songs
Conductor Sir Hugh Roberton
Soloists Mina Bell, Alexander McKay, Mina Forrest, Elizabeth Scott, Agnes MacGregor (sngr), David Anderson (pf)

EDINBURGH UNIVERSITY SINGERS
7 Sep. 20.00 *Freemasons' Hall*
Whyte Biblical songs (World première)
Britten Hymn to St Cecilia
Madrigals by Morley, Bateson, Wilbye, Byrd. Choral part songs arr. by Holst, V. Williams, Thorpe Davie
Conductor Ian Pitt-Watson
Soloists John Tainsh (ten), Ian Whyte (pf)

RECITALS

VICTORIA DE LOS ANGELES (sop)
GERALD MOORE (pf)
27 Aug. 20.00 *Freemasons' Hall*
Arias and songs by Monteverdi, Handel, A. Scarlatti, Weber, Schubert, Schumann, R. Strauss, Nin, Granados, Falla, Turina

4 Sep. 20.00 *Freemasons' Hall*
Arias and songs by Monteverdi, Campra, Handel, Schubert, Schumann, Brahms, R. Strauss, Respighi, Ravel, Granados, Guridi, Falla, Turina

JENNIE TOUREL (mez)
GEORGE REEVES (pf)
29 Aug. 20.00 *Freemasons' Hall*
Arias and songs by Cherubini, Handel, Purcell, Mozart, Offenbach, Debussy, Mussorgsky, Bizet, Liszt

31 Aug. 20.00 *Freemasons' Hall*
Hindemith Das Marienleben (rev. version)

PETER PEARS (ten)
BENJAMIN BRITTEN (pf)
3 Sep. 20.00 *Freemasons' Hall*
Purcell Morning hymn
Purcell Evening hymn
Britten The holy sonnets of John Donne
Oldham Five Chinese lyrics
Tippett Boyhood's end
Copland Old American songs: Set 1

ELISABETH SCHWARZKOPF (sop)
GERALD MOORE ((pf)
5 Sep. 20.00 *Freemasons' Hall*
Songs by Wolf

CLAUDIO ARRAU (pf)
27 Aug. 14.30 *Usher Hall*
Mozart Rondo in A minor, K511
Beethoven Sonata no.26 in E flat (Farewell), op.81a
Schumann Fantasia in C, op.17
Ravel Miroirs
Debussy Preludes: La puerta del vino *and* Feux d'artifice

EMIL TELMÁNYI (vn)
MILLICENT SILVER (hpd)
22 Aug. 20.00 *Freemasons' Hall*
Bach Sonata for solo violin no.3 in C
Bach Sonata for violin and harpsichord no.2 in A
Bach Partita for solo violin no.2 in D minor

NATHAN MILSTEIN (vn)
ARTUR BALSAM (pf)
3 Sep. 14.30 *Usher Hall*
Tartini Sonata in G minor (Devil's trill)
Bach Partita for solo violin no.1 in B minor
Beethoven Sonata no.8 in G, op.30/3
Brahms Sonata no.3 in D minor, op.108

WILLIAM PRIMROSE (va)
CLIFFORD CURZON (pf)
3 Sep. 15.00 *Freemasons' Hall*
Beethoven Notturno in D, op.42
Hindemith Sonata, op.11/4
A. Paul Sonata
Brahms Sonata no.2 in E flat, op.120/2

PIERRE FOURNIER (vc)
ERNEST LUSH (pf)
27 Aug. 15.00 *Freemasons' Hall*
Beethoven Sonata no.4 in C, op.102/1
Schubert Sonata in A minor (Arpeggione), D821
Brahms Sonata no.2 in F, op.99
Debussy Sonata
Stravinsky Pulcinella: Suite Italienne

MONA BENSON (sop), JOAN DICKSON (vc), HESTER DICKSON, BETTY BROWN (pf)
24 Aug. 20.00 *Freemasons' Hall*
Beethoven Sonata for cello and piano no.1 in F, op.5/1
Tovey Elegiac variations, op.25
Barber Sonata for cello and piano, op.6
Songs by Schubert, Respighi

MAX ROSTAL (vn), DENNIS BRAIN (hn), FRANZ OSBORN (pf)
25 Aug. 11.00 *Freemasons' Hall*
Beethoven Sonata for horn and piano in F, op.17
Walton Sonata for violin and piano
Brahms Trio for horn, violin and piano in E flat, op.40

DRAMA

OLD VIC
21 Aug.-9 Sep. 19.30 (exc.Sun) 22, 26, 29 Aug. 2, 6, 9 Sep. 14.30 Assembly Hall
BARTHOLOMEW FAIR Jonson
(1st public performance for 220 years)

John Littlewit	Anthony van Bridge
Win-the-fight Littlewit	Dorothy Tutin
Winwife	John van Eyssen
Tom Quarlous	Esmond Knight
Humphrey Waspe	Alec Clunes
Bartholomew Cokes	Robert Eddison
Dame Overdo	Ursula Jeans
Grace Wellborn	Heather Stannard
Dame Purecraft	Dorothy Green
Zeal-of-the-land Busy	Mark Dignam
Adam Overdo	Roger Livesay
Lanthorn Leatherhead	Pierre Lefevre
Joan Trash	Sheila Ballantine
Nightingale	Leo McKern
Ursula	Nuna Davey
Mooncalf	Brian Smith
Dan Jordan Knockem	William Devlin
Ezekial Edgeworth	Paul Hansard
Costardmonger	Lee Montague
Corn cutter	Leonard Maley
Captain Whit	Douglas Wilmer
Bristle	Rupert Davies
Bookholder	Richard Pasco
Scrivener/Haggis	Peter Duguid
Trouble-all/Stagekeeper	Paul Rogers
Val Cutting/Mousetrap man	James Grout
Northern/Filcher	James Wellman
Puppy/Sharkwell	Richard Walter
Puppeteers	George Speaight, Leonard Maley
Director	George Devine
Designer	Motley

CITIZENS' THEATRE, Glasgow
21, 22, 23, 31 Aug. 1, 9 Sep. 19.15
23 Aug. 9 Sep. 14.30 *Lyceum Theatre*
THE QUEEN'S COMEDY Bridie
(World première)
Jupiter Walter Fitzgerald
Juno Sonia Dresdel
Neptune John Young
Minerva Lennox Milne
Venus Rona Anderson
Apollo James Gilbert
Mars Lea Ashton
Vulcan Duncan Macrae
Mercury Stanley Baxter
Hebe Moira Robertson
Thetis Wendy Noel
Sleep James Cairncross
Agamemnon Nigel Fitzgerald
Ulysses Douglas Campbell
Diomede Ian Macnaughton
Nestor Laurence Hardy
Machaon Kenneth Mackintosh
Hecamede Dorothy Primrose
Medical orderly Roddy McMillan
Infantryman Eric Woodburn
Directors
Tyrone Guthrie, John Casson
Designer Molly MacEwen

24, 25, 26, 30 Aug. 4, 5 Sep. 19.15
26, 30 Aug. 14.30 *Lyceum Theatre*
THE ATOM DOCTOR Linklater
(World première)
Shurie James Gibson
Connie May Patricia Burke
Professor Mortimer Duncan Macrae
Mrs Bonamy Betty Henderson
Miss Sobieski-Smith Madeleine Christie
Miss Julia Sobieski-Smith Lennox Milne
Alfred Shinney Stanley Baxter
Tom Thistleton John Young
Mrs Thistleton Dorothy Primrose
Duke of Applecross Laurence Hardy
Mrs Shinney Marjorie Thomson
Major Kernay Kenneth Mackintosh
Soldier Fulton Mackay
Policeman Douglas Campbell
Director Tyrone Guthrie
Designer John Russell

28, 29 Aug. 2, 6, 7, 8 Sep. 19.15
2, 6 Sep. 14.30 *Lyceum Theatre*
DOUGLAS Home
Lady Randolph Sybil Thorndike
Lord Randolph Lewis Casson
Douglas Douglas Campbell
Glenalvon Laurence Hardy
Anna Lennox Milne
Old Norval James Gibson
Director John Casson
Designer Molly MacEwen
Music Cedric Thorpe Davie

DANCE

AMERICAN BALLET THEATRE
21-26 Aug. 19.30 23, 26 Aug. 14.30
Empire Theatre
THEME AND VARIATIONS
Choreographer George Balanchine
Music Tchaikovsky
Designer Woodman Thompson
FALL RIVER LEGEND
Choreographer Agnes de Mille
Music Gould
Scenery Oliver Smith
Costumes Miles White
FANCY FREE
Choreographer Jerome Robbins
Music Bernstein
Scenery Oliver Smith
Costumes Kermit Love
Dancers Nora Kaye, Alicia Alonso, Igor Youskevitch, John Kriza, Mary Ellen Moylan, Norma Vance, Paul Godkin, Allyn McLerie, James Mitchell, Lucia Chase
Festival Ballet Orchestra
Conductor Alexander Smallens

GRAND BALLET DU MARQUIS DE CUEVAS
28, 29, 30 Aug. 19.30 30.Aug. 14.30
Empire Theatre
SWAN LAKE: Act 2
Choreographers Petipa *and* Ivanov
Music Tchaikovsky
Designer Jean Robier
A TRAGEDY IN VERONA
Choreographer George Skibine
Music Tchaikovsky
Designer Delfoe
SWAN LAKE: Black swan pas de deux
Choreographer Marius Petipa
Music Tchaikovsky
Costumes Jean Robier
LE BEAU DANUBE
Choreographer Léonide Massine
Music J. Strauss; arr. Désormière
Designer Constantin Guys

31 Aug. 1, 2 Sep. 19.30 2 Sep. 14.30
Empire Theatre
GISELLE
Choreographers Coralli *and* Perrot *after* Petipa
Music Adam
Scenery *after* Alexander Benois
Costumes Jean Robier
PETRUSHKA
Choreographer Mikhail Fokine
Music Stravinsky
Designer Alexander Benois
Dancers Rosella Hightower, André Eglevsky, George Skibine, Marjorie Tallchief, Ethéry Pagava, Ana Ricarda, Nicholas Orloff, Léonide Massine, Tania Karina, Helga Monson, René Bon, Raoul Celada, Harriet Toby, Serge Golovine, Evaryste Madejsky, Michel Reznikoff, Vladimir Oukhtomsky, Oleg Sabline
Festival Ballet Orchestra
Conductor Gustave Cloez

ROSARIO AND ANTONIO
4-6 Sep. 19.30 *Empire Theatre*
Programme 1 Spanish dances

7-9 Sep. 19.30 9 Sep. 14.30
Empire Theatre
Programme 2 Spanish dances
with Alfredo Rodriguez Mendoza, Pablo Miquel (pf), Juan Garcia de la Mata (gtr)

EXHIBITIONS

National Gallery of Scotland
REMBRANDT VAN RHYN
Director Ellis Waterhouse
(In association with the Arts Council of Great Britain)

CLOSING CEREMONY

9 Sep. 23.00 *Castle Esplanade*
MASSED MILITARY BANDS
Handel Music for the royal fireworks
Conductor Sir Thomas Beecham

1951

OPERA

GLYNDEBOURNE OPERA
20, 22, 24, 28, 30 Aug. 1, 3, 5, 7 Sep.
19.00 *King's Theatre*
LA FORZA DEL DESTINO Verdi
Leonora Walburga Wegner
Don Alvaro David Poleri
Don Carlo Marko Rothmüller
Preziosilla Mildred Miller
Padre Guardiano Bruce Dargavel
Fra Melitone Owen Brannigan
Marchese di Calatrava Stanley Mason
Curra Bruna MacLean
Alcade Dennis Wicks
Trabuco Robert Thomas
Surgeon Philip Lewtas
Royal Philharmonic Orchestra
Conductor Fritz Busch
Director Carl Ebert
Designer Leslie Hurry

21, 23, 25, 27, 29, 31 Aug. 4, 6, 8 Sep.
19.00 *King's Theatre*
DON GIOVANNI Mozart
Don Giovanni Mario Petri
Donna Anna Hilde Zadek
Donna Elvira Dorothy MacNeil
Suzanne Danco*
Don Ottavio Léopold Simoneau
Leporello Alois Pernerstorfer
Owen Brannigan
Zerlina Genevieve Warner
Roxane Houston*
Pierrette Alarie*
Masetto Geraint Evans
The Commendatore Bruce Dargavel
Royal Philharmonic Orchestra
Conductors Fritz Busch
John Pritchard
Director Carl Ebert
Designer John Piper

ORCHESTRAL CONCERTS

LONDON PHILHARMONIC ORCHESTRA
Conductor Sir Adrian Boult
19 Aug. 19.30 *Usher Hall*
Walton Scapino - Overture
Wordsworth Symphony no.2 in D, op.34 (EIF commission)
Elgar Concerto for violin in B minor, op.61
Soloist Ida Haendel (vn)

20 Aug. 19.30 *Usher Hall*
Schubert Symphony no.5 in B flat, D485
Bach Concerto for oboe d'amore in A; arr. Tovey
Kodály Dances from Galánta
Dvořák Symphony no.6 in D, op.60
Soloist Leon Goossens (ob d'amore)

NEW YORK PHILHARMONIC ORCHESTRA
22 Aug. 19.30 *Usher Hall*
Weber Euryanthe: Overture
Mozart Symphony no.39 in E flat, K543
Mahler Symphony no.4 in G
Conductor Bruno Walter
Soloist Irmgard Seefried (sop)

23 Aug. 19.30 *Usher Hall*
Beethoven Coriolan - Overture
Beethoven Symphony no.4 in B flat, op.60
Prokofiev Symphony no.5 in B flat, op.100
Conductor Dimitri Mitropoulos

24, 30 Aug. 19.30 *Usher Hall*
Brahms Tragic Overture
Brahms Variations on a theme by Haydn (St Antoni), op.56a
Brahms Schicksalslied (Eng)
Brahms Symphony no.2 in D, op.73
Conductor Bruno Walter
Edinburgh Royal Choral Union

25 Aug. 19.30 *Usher Hall*
Schumann Overture, scherzo and finale, op.52
Haydn Sinfonia concertante in B flat, op.84
Křenek Symphonic elegy for strings
Beethoven Concerto for piano no.4 in G, op.58
Conductor Dimitri Mitropoulos
Soloist Myra Hess (pf)*

26 Aug. 19.30 *Usher Hall*
Beethoven Leonore: Overture no.2
Haydn Symphony no.88 in G
Bruckner Symphony no.4 in E flat (Romantic)
Conductor Bruno Walter

27 Aug. 19.30 *Usher Hall*
Weber Der Beherrscher der Geister: Overture
V. Williams Symphony no.4 in F minor
Beethoven Concerto for violin in D, op.61
Conductor Dimitri Mitropoulos
Soloist Zino Francescatti (vn)

28 Aug. 19.30 *Usher Hall*
Handel Concerto grosso in G minor, op.6/6
Wagner Siegfried idyll
Schubert Symphony no.9 in C (Great), D944
Conductor Bruno Walter

29 Aug. 19.30 *Usher Hall*
Weber Der Freischütz: Overture
Beethoven Concerto for piano no.5 in E flat (Emperor), op.73
Mendelssohn Symphony no.3 in A minor (Scottish), op.56
Gould Philharmonic waltzes
Conductor Dimitri Mitropoulos
Soloist Robert Casadesus (pf)

31 Aug. 19.30 *Usher Hall*
Bax Overture to a picaresque comedy
Swanson Short symphony
Berlioz La damnation de Faust: Minuet; Dance of the sylphs; Rákóczy march
Brahms Concerto for piano no.1 in D minor, op.15
Conductor Dimitri Mitropoulos
Soloist Solomon (pf)

1 Sep. 19.30 *Usher Hall*
Cherubini Le deux journées: Overture
Beethoven Symphony no.2 in D, op.36
Schumann Concerto for piano in A minor, op.54
Falla El sombrero de tres picos: Neighbour's dance; Miller's dance; Final dance
Conductor Dimitri Mitropoulos
Soloist Myra Hess (pf)

2, 4 Sep. 19.30 *Usher Hall*
V. Williams Fantasia on a theme by Tallis
Beethoven Symphony no.9 in D minor (Choral), op.125
Conductor Bruno Walter
Soloists Frances Yeend (sop), Martha Lipton (cont), David Lloyd (ten), Mack Harrell (bar), Edinburgh Royal Choral Union

3 Sep. 19.30 *Usher Hall*
Berlioz Le carnaval romain - Overture
Saint-Saëns Concerto for cello in A minor, op.33
Malipiero Concerto for piano no.4
Rachmaninov Symphony no.2 in E minor, op.27
Conductor Dimitri Mitropoulos
Soloists Leonard Rose (vc), Dimitri Mitropoulos (pf)

SCOTTISH NATIONAL ORCHESTRA
26 Aug. 14.30 *Usher Hall*
Berlioz Waverley - Overture
Delius A song of summer
Mendelssohn Concerto for violin in E minor, op.64
Jirák Symphony no.5 (EIF commission)
Conductor Walter Susskind
Soloist Gioconda de Vito (vn)

NATIONAL YOUTH ORCHESTRA OF GREAT BRITAIN
2 Sep. 14.30 *Usher Hall*
Wagner Rienzi: Overture
Mozart Concerto for clarinet in A, K622
Arnold Divertimento
Kabalevsky Symphony no.2 in C minor, op.19
Conductor Walter Susskind
Soloist Colin Bradbury (cl)

BBC SCOTTISH ORCHESTRA
5 Sep. 19.30 *Usher Hall*
Suk Fantastic scherzo
Mozart Exsultate, jubilate
Elgar Introduction and allegro, op.47
Turina Canto a Sevilla
Shostakovich Symphony no.1 in F, op.10
Conductor Ian Whyte
Soloist Victoria de los Angeles (sop)

HALLÉ ORCHESTRA
Conductor Sir John Barbirolli
7 Sep. 19.30 *Usher Hall*
Rossini L'Italiana in Algeri: Overture
Mozart Symphony no.25 in G minor, K183
Chausson Poème de l'amour et de la mer
Berlioz Harold in Italy
Soloists Kathleen Ferrier (cont), George Alexander (va)

8 Sep. 19.30 *Usher Hall*
Haydn Symphony no.83 in G minor (The hen)
Moeran Serenade in G
Elgar Symphony no.1 in A flat, op.55

8 Sep. 23.00 *Usher Hall*
Closing Ceremony
Mozart Eine kleine Nachtmusik
Farewell oration by Robert Kemp
Haydn Symphony no.45 in F sharp minor (Farewell)
Thorpe Davie Fanfares
Soloists Lennox Milne, Duncan Macrae, André Barsacq, Mira Sanina (rdr)

BOYD NEEL ORCHESTRA
Conductor Boyd Neel
21 Aug. 11.00 *Freemasons' Hall*
J.C. Bach Symphony in B flat, op.21/3
Hamerik Symphony no.6 in G (Spirituelle), op.38
Handel Concerto grosso in G, op.6/1

22 Aug. 11.00 *Freemasons' Hall*
Handel Concerto grosso in A, op.6/11
Vivaldi Concerti, op.8: Nos.1-4 (The four seasons)
Shostakovich Prelude and scherzo, op.11
Soloist Maurice Clare (vn)

23 Aug. 11.00 *Freemasons' Hall*
Handel Concerto for oboe no.3 in G minor
Stravinsky Concerto in D
Vivaldi Concerto for oboe in D minor
Handel Concerto grosso in B flat, op.6/7
Soloist Leon Goossens (ob)

24 Aug. 11.00 *Freemasons' Hall*
Handel Concerto grosso in A minor, op.6/4
Stravinsky Apollon musagète
Françaix Symphony for strings

25 Aug. 11.00 *Freemasons' Hall*
Corelli Concerto grosso in D, op.6/7
Britten Les illuminations
Handel Concerto grosso in F, op.6/9
Soloist Richard Lewis (ten)

27 Aug. 11.00 *Freemasons' Hall*
Handel Concerto grosso in C minor, op.6/8
Stravinsky Concerto in E flat (Dumbarton Oaks)
Schubert Totus in corde in C, D136
Schubert Salve regina in F, D223
Vivaldi Concerto grosso in D minor, F11/10
Soloists Suzanne Danco (sop), Jack Brymer (cl)

LONDON MOZART PLAYERS
Conductor Harry Blech
31 Aug. 11.00 *Freemasons' Hall*
Mozart March in D, K445
Haydn Symphony no.49 in F minor (La passione)
Mozart Concerto for piano no.14 in E flat, K449
Mozart Symphony no.29 in A, K201
Soloist Nina Milkina (pf)

1 Sep. 11.00 *Freemasons' Hall*
Mozart March in F, K248
Haydn Symphony no.44 in E minor (Trauersinfonie)
Haydn Concerto for horn in D
Mozart Symphony no.33 in B flat, K319
Soloist Dennis Brain (hn)

3 Sep. 11.00 *Freemasons' Hall*
Mozart March in C, K408/1
Haydn Armida: Overture
Haydn Symphony no.85 in B flat (La reine)
Mozart Symphony no.34 in C, K338

4 Sep. 11.00 *Freemasons' Hall*
Geminiani Concerto grosso in C minor, op.2/2
Mozart Divertimento no.11 in D, K251
Mozart Sinfonia concertante for violin and viola, K364
Soloists Norbert Brainin (vn), Peter Schidlof (va)

CHAMBER CONCERTS

GRILLER QUARTET
20 Aug. 11.00 *Freemasons' Hall*
Haydn Quartet in C (Bird), op.33/3
Schubert Quartet no.13 in A minor, D804

21 Aug. 19.30 *Usher Hall*
Schubert Quintet for strings in C, D956
Brahms Quintet for piano and strings in F minor, op.34
with Myra Hess (pf), Harvey Phillips (vc)

NEW ITALIAN QUARTET
28 Aug. 11.00 *Freemasons' Hall*
Haydn Quartet in G, op.77/1
Verdi Quartet in E minor

Debussy Quartet in G minor, op.10/1

29 Aug. 11.00 *Freemasons' Hall*
Mozart Adagio and fugue in C minor, K546
Schubert Quartet no.8 in B flat, D112
Schumann Quartet no.2 in F, op.41/2

AMADEUS QUARTET
6 Sep. 20.00 *Freemasons' Hall*
Haydn Quartet in C, op.54/2
Tippett Quartet no.2
Schubert Quartet no.15 in G, D887

8 Sep. 11.00 *Freemasons' Hall*
Haydn Quartet in F, op.77/2
Brahms Quartet no.1 in C minor, op.51/1

EDINBURGH UNIVERSITY SINGERS
3 Sep. 20.00 *Freemasons' Hall*
Britten Rejoice in the lamb
Britten Five flower songs
Madrigals by Bennet, Gibbons, Wilbye, Tomkins, Bateson. Tudor church music by Redford, Morley, Gibbons, Byrd.
Tudor music for organ by Gibbons, Blow
Conductor Ian Pitt-Watson
with Herrick Bunney (org)

VIENNA ACADEMY CHAMBER CHOIR
Conductor Ferdinand Grossmann
4 Sep. 20.00 *Freemasons' Hall*
Austrian sacred music by Gallus, Fux, Lotti, David, Heiller, Schiske, Angerer, Haydn, M. Haydn, Mozart, Bruckner

5 Sep. 20.00 *Freemasons' Hall*
Bach Motet no.3. Jesu meine Freude
Sacred music by Ockeghem, Byrd, Victoria, Schütz, Hindemith, Kodály, Poulenc, Heiller, Vecchi, Josquin Desprez, Lassus

7 Sep. 11.00 *Freemasons' Hall*
Brahms Liebeslieder Walzer
Austrian secular music by Peuerl, Isaac, Von Bruck, Schoenberg, Gal, Hauer, David, Haydn, Schubert *and* Anon.
with Elfriede Hofstätter, Franz Bauer (pf)

NETHERLANDS CHAMBER CHOIR
Conductor Felix de Nobel
5 Sep. 11.00 *Freemasons' Hall*
Stravinsky Mass
Choral works by Josquin Desprez, Clemens non Papa, Monteverdi, Poulenc, Ravel
with Instrumental ensemble

6 Sep. 11.00 *Freemasons' Hall*
Hopkins Five studies (World première)
Choral works by Clemens non Papa, Obrecht, Brumel, Josquin Desprez, Lassus, Sweelinck, Martin, Badings

SCOTTISH CONCERTS

Folk Music of Scotland
23 Aug. 20.00 *Freemasons' Hall*
Soloists Joan Alexander, Alexander Carmichael, James Macphee, John Mearns (sngr), Andrew Bryson, Norman Whitelaw (pf), Jimmy Shand (accordion), Jimmy Taylor (va), Angus White (mouth music). Introduced by Dr Herbert Wiseman

Composed Music of Scotland
29 Aug. 20.00 *Freemasons' Hall*
Conductor John Hopkins
Soloists John Tainsh (ten), Edna Arthur (vn), Gervase Markham (fl), Andrew Bryson (pf), Scottish Singers

RECITALS

FANÉLY REVOIL (sop)
WILLY CLÉMENT (bar)
22 Aug. 20.00 *Freemasons' Hall*
Excerpts from French operettas
Introduced and accompanied by Stanford Robinson

THE ART OF SONG

IRMGARD SEEFRIED (sop)
GERALD MOORE (pf)
24 Aug. 20.00 *Freemasons' Hall*
Songs by Schubert

MACK HARRELL (bar)
GERALD MOORE (pf)
28 Aug. 20.00 *Freemasons' Hall*
Beethoven An die ferne Geliebte
Schubert Schwanengesang: 6 Heine Lieder
V. Babin Beloved stranger
Brahms Vier ernste Gesänge

SUZANNE DANCO (sop)
GERALD MOORE (pf)
31 Aug. 20.00 *Freemasons' Hall*
Arias and songs by Monteverdi, Bononcini, Grandi, Ariosti, Milhaud, Ravel *and* Anon

PIERRE BERNAC (bar)
FRANCIS POULENC (pf)
2 Sep. 20.00 *Freemasons' Hall*
Songs by Duparc, Debussy, Ravel, Poulenc

KATHLEEN FERRIER (cont)
BRUNO WALTER (pf)
6 Sep. 19.30 *Usher Hall*
Songs by Schubert, Mahler, Brahms

SOLOMON (pf)
1 Sep. 14.30 *Usher Hall*
Beethoven Sonatina no.2 in F
Beethoven Sonata no.3 in C, op.2/3
Beethoven Sonata no.23 in F minor (Appassionata), op.57
Beethoven Sonata no.32 in C minor, op.111

ETHEL BARTLETT, RAE ROBERTSON (2 pf)
30 Aug. 11.00 *Freemasons' Hall*
Mozart Sonata in D, K448
Brahms Variations on a theme by Haydn (St Antoni), op.56b
Martinů 3 Czech dances
Rachmaninov Suite no.2, op.17: Waltz
Rachmaninov Suite no.1, op.5: Tears
Milhaud Scaramouche: Brazileira

ZINO FRANCESCATTI (vn)
ROBERT CASADESUS (pf)
26 Aug. 15.00 *Freemasons' Hall*
Beethoven Sonata no.3 in E flat, op.12/3
Beethoven Sonata no.7 in C minor, op.30/2
Beethoven Sonata no.9 in A (Kreutzer), op.47

2 Sep. 15.00 *Freemasons' Hall*
Mozart Sonata no.17 in C, K296
Brahms Sonata no.3 in D minor, op.108
Franck Sonata in A

DRAMA

CITIZENS' THEATRE, Glasgow
20 Aug.-8 Sep. 19.30 (exc.Sun) 21, 25, 28, 1, 4, 8 Sep. 14.30 *Assembly Hall*
THE THRIE ESTAITES Lyndsay
(Adapted by Robert Kemp)
Diligence C.R.M. Brookes
King Fulton Mackay
Wantonness Andrew Downie
Placebo Ignatius McFadyen
Solace James Stuart
Sensualitie Madeleine Christie
Hameliness Jean Carrol
Danger Audrey Moncrieff
Fund-Jennet Paul Curran
Gude Counsel David Steuart
Flatterie Duncan Macrae
Falsehood James Gibson
Deceit James Sutherland
Veritie Lennox Milne
Chastitie Jean Taylor Smith
Spiritualitie Eric Woodburn
Prioress Josephine Crombie
Abbot/Tailor Leonard Maguire
Parson Bruce Morgan
An acolyte Graham Buchanan
Temporalitie Graham Squire
Merchant James Gilbert
Soutar James Copeland
Soutar's wife Nell Ballantyne
Tailor's wife Helena Gloag
Correction's varlet Ian Macnaughton
Divine Correction James Cairncross
Poor man Roddy McMillan
John the Common-Weal Andrew Keir
Sergeant Robert Erskine
Minstral Henry Bardon
Directors
Tyrone Guthrie, Moultrie Kelsall
Designer Molly MacEwen
Music Cedric Thorpe Davie

HENRY SHEREK
20-25 Aug. 19.15 22, 25 Aug. 14.15
Lyceum Theatre
PYGMALION Shaw
Eliza Doolittle Margaret Lockwood
Henry Higgins Alan Webb
Colonel Pickering R. Stuart Lindsell
Alfred Doolittle Charles Victor
Mrs Eynsford Hill Dorothy Reynolds
Miss Eynsford Hill Gillian Howell
Freddy Eynsford Hill John Warner
Mrs Higgins Gladys Boot
Mrs Pearce Beatrice Varley
Parlourmaid Mary Walklett
Bystanders Frank Royde, John Allen
Director Peter Potter
Designer Hutchinson Scott

TENNENT PRODUCTIONS LTD
28 Aug.-1 Sep. 19.15 29, 31 Aug. 1 Sep. 14.15 *Lyceum Theatre*
THE WINTER'S TALE Shakespeare
Leontes John Gielgud
Hermione Diana Wynyard
Paulina Flora Robson
Antigonus Lewis Casson
Perdita Frances Hyland*
Florizel Richard Gale
Old shepherd George Howe
Autolycus George Rose
Camillo Michael Goodliffe
Young shepherd Philip Guard
Mamillius Robert Anderson
Polixenes Brewster Mason
Emilia Hazel Terry
Gaoler John Whiting
Dorcas Joy Rodgers
Mopsa Charlotte Mitchell
Bear Churton Fairman
Time Norman Bird

Other parts played by John Moffatt, Paul Hardwick, Margaret Wolfit, Hugh Stewart, Kenneth Edwards, Michael Nightingale
Director Peter Brook
Designer Sophie Fedorovitch
Music Christopher Fry
(In association with the Arts Council of Great Britain)

LE THÉÂTRE DE L'ATELIER, Paris
3, 4, 5 Sep. 19.15 5 Sep. 14.15
Lyceum Theatre
L'ENTERREMENT Monnier
M. Belhamy Pierre Goutas
M. Préparé/M. Avére Jean Francel
Adèle/Mme Philidor Simone Chambord
Le garcon livreur/M. Beaufrère/
M. Versepuy Cécilia Paroldi
M. Tétrot/M. Tardiveau/M. Poireau
Charles Nugue
M. Mouin/M. Beaufumé/M. Lanoy
Pierre Jacques Moncorbier
M. Meslin/M. Moutardier José Quaglio
M. Dupré/M. Vidal/L'ecclésiastique
Maurice Jacquemont
M. Philibert/M. Poissy/M. Lorrain
M. Prêcheur/M. Tétard René Clermont
Le commissaire des morts
Michel Herbault
M. Duplan/Le cocher/Le croquemort
Jean Bertho
Director André Barsacq
LE BAL DES VOLEURS Anouilh
Le musicien Jacques Ramade
Hector Jean Francel
Eva Simone Chambord
Le crieur public Charles Nugue
Peterbono Paul Ville
Gustave Jean Bertho
Juliette Cécilia Paroldi
Lady Hurf Madeleine Geoffroy
Lord Edgard Pierre Jacques Moncorbier
Dupont-Dufort Pére Maurice Jacquemont
Dupont-Dufort Fils René Clermont
La petite fille Nadine Nattier
Agents Pierre Goutas, Charles Nugue
Director André Barsacq
Music Milhaud

6-8 Sep. 19.15 8 Sep. 14.15
Lyceum Theatre
LE RENDEZ-VOUS DE SENLIS Anouilh
Georges Michel Herbault
La propriétaire Lise Berthier
Le maître d'hôtel
Pierre-Jacques Moncorbier
Philémon Paul Ville
Mme de Montalembreuse
Madeleine Geoffroy
Barbara Simone Chambord
Robert José Quaglio
M. Delachaume Maurice Jacquemont
Edmée Jacqueline Moresco
Mme Delachaume Gabrielle Roanne
Isabelle Loleh Bellon
Le docteur Charles Nugue
Director André Barsacq

DANCE

SADLER'S WELLS BALLET
20, 21, 22, 27, 28, 29 Aug. 19.30
22, 29 Aug. 14.30 Empire Theatre
SWAN LAKE
Choreographers Petipa *and* Ivanov
Music Tchaikovsky
Designer Leslie Hurry

23, 24 Aug. 19.30 Empire Theatre
LES PATINEURS
Choreographer Frederick Ashton
Music Meyerbeer; arr. Lambert
Designer William Chappell
A WEDDING BOUQUET
Choreographer Frederick Ashton
Music and design Lord Berners
TIRESIAS
Choreographer Frederick Ashton
Music Constant Lambert
Designer Isabel Lambert

25 Aug. 14.30 and 19.30 Empire Theatre
CHECKMATE
Choreographer Ninette de Valois
Music Bliss
Designer E. McKnight Kauffer
SYMPHONIC VARIATIONS
Choreographer Frederick Ashton
Music Franck
Designer Sophie Fedorovitch
DON QUIXOTE
Choreographer Ninette de Valois
Music Gerhard
Designer Edward Burra

30, 31 Aug. 1 Sep. 19.30 Empire Theatre
THE RAKE'S PROGRESS
Choreographer Ninette de Valois
Music Gavin Gordon
Designer Rex Whistler *after* Hogarth
BALLET IMPERIAL
Choreographer George Balanchine
Music Tchaikovsky
Designer Eugene Berman
JOB
Choreographer Ninette de Valois
Music V. Williams
Designer John Piper

1 Sep. 14.30 Empire Theatre
LES PATINEURS
BALLET IMPERIAL
JOB

1 Sep. 19.30 Empire Theatre
THE RAKE'S PROGRESS
BALLET IMPERIAL
JOB
Dancers Margot Fonteyn, Moira Shearer, Violetta Elvin, Pamela May, Nadia Nerina, Michael Somes, John Field, Alexander Grant, John Hart, Alexis Rassine, Brian Shaw, Pauline Clayden, Margaret Dale, Julia Farron, Anne Heaton, Rowena Jackson, Gerd Larsen, Rosemary Lindsay, Gillian Lynne, Lorna Mossford, Avril Navarre, Philip Chatfield, Leslie Edwards, Richard Ellis, Henry Legerton, Kenneth MacMillan, Kenneth Melville, Ray Powell, Alfred Rodrigues, Gilbert Vernon, Franklin White
Covent Garden Orchestra
Conductors John Hollingsworth, Robert Irving

BELGRADE OPERA BALLET
3, 4, 5 Sep. 19.30 5 Sep. 14.30
Empire Theatre
THE LEGEND OF OHRID
Choreographer Margarita Froman
Music Stevan Hristić
Scenery Stasha Belozanski
Costumes Milica Babić

6, 7, 8 Sep. 19.30 8 Sep. 14.30
Empire Theatre
THE BALLAD OF A MEDIEVAL LOVE: Scenes
Choreographer Pia *and* Pino Mlakar
Music Fran Lhotka
Scenery Miomir Denić
Costumes Milica Babić
THE GINGERBREAD HEART
Choreographer Dimitri Parlić
Music Krešimir Baranović
Scenery Miomir Denić
Costumes Milica Babić
Dancers Mira Sanina, Dimitri Parlić, Ruth Parnel, Boyana Perić, Vera Kostić, Nenad Lhotka, Dušan Trninić, Jovanka Bjegojević, Branko Marković, Katarina Obradović, Nevenka Bigin, Milan Momcilović, Sonia Kastl, Neda Tchonić, Liubitza Stefanović, Veronika Mlakar
Scottish National Orchestra
Conductors Oskar Danon, Stevan Hristić, Bogdan Babić

LECTURES

15.00 Pollock Memorial Hall
23 Aug. Bruno Walter
24 Aug. Ninette de Valois The development of British ballet
27 Aug. Boyd Neel The future of the chamber orchestra
28 Aug. Dimitri Mitropoulos Future trends in music
30 Aug. John Gielgud Shakespeare production, old and new
31 Aug. Gerald Moore The art of accompaniment
3 Sep. Mrs De Witt Peltz Opera in America
6 Sep. Robert Kemp The revival of The thrie estaites
7 Sep. André Barsacq Jean Anouilh (Fr)

EXHIBITIONS

National Gallery of Scotland
SPANISH PAINTINGS: El Greco to Goya
Director Ellis Waterhouse
(In association with the Arts Council of Great Britain)

1952

OPERA

HAMBURG STATE OPERA
18, 20 Aug. 1, 4 Sep. 19.00 King's Theatre
FIDELIO Beethoven
Leonore Inge Borkh
Martha Mödl
Florestan Peter Anders
Rocco Theo Herrmann
Don Pizarro Josef Metternich
Marzelline Lisa della Casa
Jacquino Kurt Marschner
Don Fernando Caspar Bröcheler
Prisoners Fritz Göllnitz, Toni Blankenheim
Conductor Leopold Ludwig
Director Günther Rennert
Designer Alfred Siercke

22, 25, 27 Aug. 19.00 King's Theatre
DER FREISCHÜTZ Weber
Max Peter Anders
Agathe Elisabeth Grümmer
Clara Ebers
Ännchen Anneliese Rothenberger
Kaspar Gottlob Frick
Caspar Bröcheler
Kuno Toni Blankenheim
Kilian Kurt Marschner
Ottokar Georg Mund
Hermit Theo Herrmann
Gottlob Frick
Bridesmaids Christine Görner, Ilse Wallenstein, Ursula Nettling

Samiel — Wolfgang Rottsieper
Conductor — Joseph Keilberth
Director — Oscar Fritz Schuh
Designer — Caspar Neher

19, 21, 23, 26 Aug. 19.00 *King's Theatre*
DIE ZAUBERFLÖTE Mozart
Tamino — Rudolf Schock
Pamina — Elisabeth Grümmer, Lisa della Casa
Papageno — Horst Günter
Sarastro — Gottlob Frick
Queen of the Night — Valerie Bak
Speaker — Josef Metternich
1st Lady — Lisa Jungkind, Clara Ebers*
2nd Lady — Ilse Koegel
3rd Lady — Maria von Ilosvay
Papagena — Anneliese Rothenberger
Monostatos — Kurt Marschner
3 Boys — Christine Görner, Ilse Wallenstein, Gisela Litz
2 Armed men — Helmut Melchert, Jean Pfendt
2 Priests — Robert Helma, Karl Otto
Conductor — Georg Solti
Director — Günther Rennert
Designer — Alfred Siercke

28, 30 Aug. 5 Sep. 18.00 *King's Theatre*
DER ROSENKAVALIER R. Strauss
Marschallin — Clara Ebers
Octavian — Martha Mödl, Elisabeth Grümmer*
Sophie — Lisa della Casa
Ochs — Theo Herrmann
Faninal — Caspar Bröcheler
Marianne Leitmetzerin — Lisa Bischof
Valzacchi — Fritz Göllnitz
Annina — Hedy Gura
Italian singer — Rudolf Schock, Fritz Lehnert
Police commissioner — Jean Pfendt
Major domo (Marschallin) — Horst Wegner
Major domo (Faninal)/Landlord — Kurt Marschner
Notary — Karl Otto
Hairdresser — Frank Hoopmann
Conductors — Joseph Keilberth, Leopold Ludwig
Director — Günther Rennert
Designer — Alfred Siercke

29 Aug. 2 Sep. 19.00 *King's Theatre*
MATHIS DER MALER Hindemith
Mathis — Mathieu Ahlersmeyer
Regina — Anneliese Rothenberger
Ursula — Elfriede Wasserthal
Albrecht von Brandenburg — Helmut Melchert
Lorenz von Pommersfelden — Toni Blankenheim
Wolfgang Capito — Fritz Lehnert
Riedinger — Theo Herrmann
Hans Schwalb — Heinrich Bensing
Prefect of Waldburg — Jean Pfendt
Sylvester von Schaumburg — Kurt Marschner
Countess Helfenstein — Lisa Jungkind
Count Helfenstein — Guido Diemer
Conductor — Leopold Ludwig
Director — Günther Rennert
Scenery — Helmut Jürgens
Costumes — Alfred Siercke

3, 6 Sep. 17.00 *King's Theatre*
DIE MEISTERSINGER Wagner
Hans Sachs — Otto Edelmann
Walther — Peter Anders
Eva — Elisabeth Grümmer
David — Kurt Marschner
Beckmesser — Toni Blankenheim
Magdalena — Gisela Litz
Pogner — Gottlob Frick
Vogelgesang — Fritz Lehnert
Nachtigall — Martin Schramm
Kothner — Caspar Bröcheler
Zorn — Erich Zimmermann
Eisslinger — Peter König
Moser — Robert Bodewig
Ortel — Karl Otto
Schwarz — Jean Pfendt
Foltz — Josef Vetter
Nightwatchman — Horst Günter
Conductor — Leopold Ludwig
Director — Günther Rennert
Scenery — Helmut Jürgens
Costumes — Rosemarie Jakameit

ORCHESTRAL CONCERTS

ROYAL PHILHARMONIC ORCHESTRA

17 Aug. 20.00 *Usher Hall*
Sibelius — Symphony no.7 in C, op.105
Sibelius — The tempest - Incidental music
Sibelius — Symphony no.1 in E minor, op.39
Conductor — Sir Thomas Beecham

18 Aug. 20.00 *Usher Hall*
Schumann — Manfred: Overture
Rawsthorne — Concerto for piano no.2
Mozart — Concerto for piano no.23 in A, K488
Debussy — La mer
Conductor — John Pritchard
Soloist — Clifford Curzon (pf)

19 Aug. 20.00 *Usher Hall*
Mozart — Symphony no.34 in C, K338
Mozart — Symphony no.38 in D (Prague), K504
R. Strauss — Ein Heldenleben
Conductor — Sir Thomas Beecham

20 Aug. 20.00 *Usher Hall*
Beethoven — Symphony no.3 In E flat (Eroica), op.55
Britten — Sinfonia da requiem
Ravel — Rapsodie espagnole
Conductor — Vittorio Gui

22 Aug. 20.00 *Usher Hall*
Haydn — Symphony no.94 in G (Surprise)
Haydn — Symphony no.99 in E flat
Delius — Appalachia
Conductor — Sir Thomas Beecham
Soloist — Robert Nicoll Easton (bar)
Edinburgh Royal Choral Union

23 Aug. 20.00 *Usher Hall*
Porpora — Sonata in D; arr. for orchestra
Haydn — Symphony no.88 in G
Martin — Concerto for violin
Mendelssohn — A midsummer night's dream: Nocturne *and* Scherzo
Rossini — L'Italiana in Algeri: Overture
Conductor — Vittorio Gui
Soloist — Joseph Szigeti (vn)

24 Aug. 14.30 *Usher Hall*
Berlioz — L'enfance du Christ
Conductor Sir Thomas Beecham
Soloists Arda Mandikian (cont), Léopold Simoneau (ten), Bruce Boyce, Robert Nicoll Easton, Julian Smith (bar), André Vessières (bs), Edinburgh Royal Choral Union

SCOTTISH NATIONAL ORCHESTRA

21 Aug. 20.00 *Usher Hall*
Walton — Portsmouth Point - Overture
Brahms — Concerto for violin and cello in A minor, op.102
V. Williams — Symphony no.2 (A London symphony)
Conductor — Walter Susskind
Soloists Joseph Szigeti (vn), Pierre Fournier (vc)

CONCERTGEBOUW ORCHESTRA, Amsterdam

25 Aug. 20.00 *Usher Hall*
Mendelssohn — The Hebrides (Fingal's cave) - Overture
Beethoven Symphony no.6 in F (Pastoral), op.68
Stravinsky — The rite of spring
Conductor — Eduard van Beinum

26 Aug. 20.00 *Usher Hall*
Smetana — The bartered bride: Overture
Suk — Meditation on an old Czech hymn (St Wenceslas)
Janáček — Taras Bulba
Mahler — Symphony no.1 in D
Conductor — Rafael Kubelik

28 Aug. 20.00 *Usher Hall*
Mozart — Symphony no.33 in B flat, K319
Mahler — Das Lied von der Erde
Conductor — Eduard van Beinum
Soloists Kathleen Ferrier (cont), Julius Patzak (ten)

29 Aug. 20.00 *Usher Hall*
Gluck — Iphigénie en Aulide: Overture
Mengelberg — Magnificat
Bartók — Music for strings, percussion and celesta
Beethoven — Symphony no.7 in A, op.92
Conductor — Rafael Kubelik
Soloist — Annie Woud (cont)

31 Aug. 14.30 *Usher Hall*
Berlioz — Benvenuto Cellini: Overture
Debussy — Prélude à l'après-midi d'un faune
Pijper — Symphony no.3
Brahms Symphony no.1 in C minor, op.68
Conductor — Eduard van Beinum

1 Sep. 20.00 *Usher Hall*
Haydn — Symphony no.82 in C (The bear)
Elgar — Concerto for cello in E minor, op.85
Dvořák — Symphony no.9 in E minor (New World), op.95
Conductor — Rafael Kubelik
Soloist — Pierre Fournier (vc)

NATIONAL YOUTH ORCHESTRA OF GREAT BRITAIN

30 Aug. 20.00 *Usher Hall*
Glinka — Ruslan and Ludmilla: Overture
Haydn — Concerto for oboe in C
Britten — The young person's guide to the orchestra
Dvořák — Symphony no.8 in G, op.88
Conductor — Walter Susskind
Soloist — Adèle Karp (ob)

BBC SCOTTISH ORCHESTRA

3 Sep. 20.00 *Usher Hall*
Mozart — Concerto for violin no.5 in A, K219
Whyte — Theme and variations (Marmion)
Chisholm — Concerto for violin (World première)
Dohnányi — The veil of Pierrette: Walzer Reigen *and* Hochzeits Walzer
Conductor — Ian Whyte
Soloist — Max Rostal (vn)

HALLÉ ORCHESTRA

Conductor Sir John Barbirolli
4 Sep. 20.00 *Usher Hall*
Donizetti — Don Pasquale: Overture
Haydn — Symphony no.6 in D (La matin)
Brahms — Vier ernste Gesänge; orch. Sargent
Sibelius — Symphony no.5 in E flat, op.82

Soloist Dietrich Fischer-Dieskau (bar)

5 Sep. 20.00 *Usher Hall*
Elgar The dream of Gerontius
Soloists Kathleen Ferrier (cont), Richard Lewis (ten), Marian Nowakowski (bs), Hallé Choir

6 Sep. 19.30 *Usher Hall*
Handel Messiah
Soloists Irmgard Seefried (sop), Kathleen Ferrier (cont), William Herbert (ten), Marian Nowakowski (bs), Hallé Choir

ROYAL PHILHARMONIC CHAMBER ORCHESTRA
25 Aug. 11.00 *Freemasons' Hall*
J.C. Bach Sinfonia in G minor, op.6/6
R. Strauss Duet concertino for clarinet and bassoon
Sibelius Rakastava
Mozart Symphony no.28 in C, K200
Conductor John Pritchard
Soloists Jack Brymer (cl), Gwydion Brooke (bn)

26 Aug. 11.00 *Freemasons' Hall*
Abel Symphony in E flat, op.10/3
Mozart Concerto for horn no.4 in E flat, K495
Copland Quiet city
Mozart Symphony no.28 in C, K200
Conductor John Pritchard
Soloist Dennis Brain (hn)

27, 28 Aug. 11.00 *Freemasons' Hall*
Purcell My heart is inditing
Purcell Ode for St Cecilia's day
Conductor Hans Oppenheim
Soloists Ena Mitchell (sop), Ella McConnell (mez), Evelyn Saren (cont), Alfred Deller (c ten), Richard Lewis (ten), Julian Smith (bar), William Parsons, Bruce Clark (bs), Kirkcaldy Choral Union

29, 30 Aug. *Freemasons' Hall*
Handel Acis and Galatea
Conductor Hans Oppenheim
Soloists Joan Alexander, April Cantelo (sop), Richard Lewis (ten), William Parsons (bs), Kirkcaldy Choral Union

STUTTGART CHAMBER ORCHESTRA
Conductor Karl Münchinger
2 Sep. 11.00 *Freemasons' Hall*
Bach Brandenburg concerto no.1 in F
Pergolesi (attrib) Concertino no.4 in F minor
Bach Brandenburg concerto no.2 in F

3 Sep. 11.00 *Freemasons' Hall*
Bach Brandenburg concerto no.6 in B flat
Hindemith Five pieces for strings, op.44
Respighi Ancient airs and dances: Set 3

5 Sep. 11.00 *Freemasons' Hall*
Bach Brandenburg concerto no.5 in D
Mozart Divertimento (Salzburg symphony) no.1 in D, K136
Beethoven Grosse Fuge in B flat, op.133

6 Sep. 11.00 *Freemasons' Hall*
Bach Brandenburg concerto no.3 in G
Bach Concerto for oboe and violin in D minor
Bach Brandenburg concerto no.4 in G

CHAMBER CONCERTS

QUINTETTE DE L'ATELIER
18 Aug. 11.00 *Freemasons' Hall*
Schumann Quintet for piano and strings in E flat, op.44
Fauré Quintet for piano and strings no.2 in C minor, op.115

20 Aug. 11.00 *Freemasons' Hall*
Dvořák Quintet for piano and strings in A, op.81
Franck Quintet for piano and strings in F minor

AMADEUS QUARTET
19 Aug. 11.00 *Freemasons' Hall*
Beethoven Quartet no.11 in F minor (Serioso), op.95
Beethoven Quartet no.9 in C (Rasumovsky), op.59/3

21 Aug. 11.00 *Freemasons' Hall*
Mozart Quartet no.18 in A, K464
Haydn Quartet in C, op.74/1

VEGH QUARTET
22 Aug. 11.00 *Freemasons' Hall*
Haydn Quartet in F, op.77/2
Beethoven Quartet no.12 in E flat, op.127

23 Aug. 11.00 *Freemasons' Hall*
Mozart Quartet no.21 in D, K575
Bartók Quartet no.1

FESTIVAL PIANO QUARTET
Curzon, Szigeti, Primrose, Fournier
24 Aug. 20.00 *Usher Hall*
Mozart Quartet for piano and strings in G minor, K.478
Fauré Quartet for piano and strings no.1 in C minor, op.15
Brahms Quartet for piano and strings no.2 in A, op.26

27 Aug. 20.00 *Usher Hall*
Brahms Trio for horn, violin and piano in E flat, op.40
Schubert Quintet for piano and strings in A (The trout), D667
Brahms Quartet for piano and strings no.3 in C minor, op.60
with Dennis Brain (hn), James Merrett (db)

31 Aug. 20.00 *Usher Hall*
Mozart Quartet for piano and strings in E flat, K493
Bridge Phantasy quartet
Brahms Quartet for piano and strings no.1 in G minor, op.25

ROBERT MASTERS PIANO QUARTET
29 Aug. 20.00 *Freemasons' Hall*
Fauré Quartet for piano and strings no.2 in G minor, op.45
Wordsworth Trio for piano and strings
Dvořák Quartet for piano and strings no.2 in E flat, op.87

LONDON CZECH TRIO
1 Sep. 11.00 *Freemasons' Hall*
Beethoven Trio for piano and strings no.5 in D (Ghost), op.70/1
Dvořák Trio for piano and strings no.3 in F minor, op.65

4 Sep. 11.00 *Freemasons' Hall*
Dvořák Trio for piano and strings no.4 in E minor (Dumky), op.90
Beethoven Trio for piano and strings no.7 in B flat (Archduke), op.97

SCOTTISH JUNIOR SINGERS
22 Aug. 20.00 *Freemasons' Hall*
Folk songs, English songs, Scottish songs, lute works, Italian canzonets, madrigals
Conductor Agnes Duncan
Soloists Diana Poulton (lute), Sybil Tait (pf)

IRMGARD SEEFRIED (sop), KATHLEEN FERRIER (cont), JULIUS PATZAK (ten), HORST GÜNTER (bar), CLIFFORD CURZON, HANS GAL (pf)
2 Sep. 20.00 *Usher Hall*
Schubert Fantasia for piano duet in F minor, D940
Brahms An die Heimat
Brahms Der Abend
Brahms Fragen
Brahms Liebeslieder Walzer
Brahms Neue Liebeslieder Walzer: Zum Schluss
Schubert Piano works

RECITALS

FLORA NIELSEN (sop)
GERALD MOORE (pf)
19 Aug. 20.00 *Freemasons' Hall*
Songs by Schumann, Fauré, Brahms

JULIUS PATZAK (ten)
GERALD MOORE (pf)
26 Aug. 20.00 *Freemasons' Hall*
Schubert Die schöne Müllerin

SOPHIE WYSS (sop)
GERALD MOORE (pf)
30 Aug. 20.00 *Freemasons' Hall*
French songs through the ages

DIETRICH FISCHER-DIESKAU (bar)
GERALD MOORE (pf)
31 Aug. 15.00 *Freemasons' Hall*
Schubert Winterreise

IRMGARD SEEFRIED (sop)
GERALD MOORE (pf)
4 Sep. 20.00 *Freemasons' Hall*
Schumann Frauenliebe und -leben
Songs by Mozart, Hindemith, Wolf

JOAN ALEXANDER (sop), MARY GRIERSON, AILIE CULLEN (pf)
1 Sep. 20.00 *Freemasons' Hall*
Schubert Sonata for piano no.18 in G, D894
H. Ferguson Five Bagatelles, op.9
Albeniz Ibéria for piano: Evocación
Granados Goyescas: El fandango de Cadil
Songs by Kilpinen, F.G. Scott

DRAMA

OLD VIC and CITIZENS' THEATRE, Glasgow
18-30 Aug. 19.30 (exc.Sun) 19, 23, 26, 30 Aug. 14.30 *Assembly Hall*
THE HIGHLAND FAIR Mitchell
(A ballad opera adapted by Robert Kemp)
Bracken John Thorburn
MacFadyean James Gibson
Alaster Andrew Downie
Nanny Iris Russell
Kenneth Andrew Keir
Maggy Elizabeth French
Gregor A. Maxwell Curr
Ian Kenneth McKellar
Anna Nancy Scott
Margaret Easson*
Ellen Grace Morrison
Catriona Madeleine Christie

Grelloch Robert Buchanan
Miss Watt Lennox Milne
Hector James Cairncross
Jeany Marion Studholme
Nancy Scott*
Hamish Niven Miller
Alan Terence Conoley
Elspeth Anne Edwards
Fiona Audrey Moncrieff
Devorguilla Denne Parker
Capt. Morgan Evans Roderick Jones
Sgt Swilly Ian Wallace
Nicol Roddy McMillan
Attendant Lloyd Reckord
Dancers Alasdair Drummond, Patrick Donnelly, John McDonald, Jack Johnstone
Director Tyrone Guthrie
Designer Molly MacEwen
Music Cedric Thorpe Davie

OLD VIC
1-6 Sep. 19.30 2, 6 Sep. 14.30
Assembly Hall
ROMEO AND JULIET Shakespeare
Romeo Alan Badel
Juliet Claire Bloom
Mercutio Peter Finch
Benvolio William Squire
Capulet John Phillips
Lady Capulet Yvonne Coulette
Montague Rupert Harvey
Lady Montague Daphne Heard
Nurse Athene Seyler
Tybalt Laurence Payne
Paris John Warner
Friar Laurence Lewis Casson
Friar John/Old Capulet Robert Welles
Chorus/Escalus William Devlin
Sampson/Apothecary Wolfe Morris
Gregory George Murcell
Abraham Hugh David
Balthasar John Breslin
Peter Newton Blick
Page to Paris Alan Dobie
Director Hugh Hunt
Designer Roger Furse

TENNENT PRODUCTIONS LTD
18, 19, 20, 22, 23 Aug. 19.15 20, 22, 23 Aug. 14.15 Lyceum Theatre
THE RIVER LINE Morgan
(World première)
Marie Chassaigne Pamela Brown
Philip Sturgess Paul Scofield
Commander Wyburton Michael Goodliffe
Mrs Muriven Marjorie Fielding
Valerie Barton Virginia McKenna
Major John Lang (Heron) John Westbrook
Dick Frewer Robert Hardy
Pierre Chassaigne Marcel Poncin
Director Michael MacOwan
Scenery Alan Tagg
Costumes Motley

EDINBURGH INTERNATIONAL FESTIVAL
21, 25, 31 Aug. 19.15 28 Aug. 2 Sep. 14.15 Lyceum Theatre
BLEAK HOUSE Dickens
Emlyn Williams as Charles Dickens

HENRY SHEREK
26 Aug.-6 Sep. 19.15 27-30 Aug. 3, 6 Sep. 14.15 Lyceum Theatre
THE PLAYER KING Hassall
(World première)
Margaret, Duchess of Burgundy Cathleen Nesbitt
Lady Katherine Gordon Heather Stannard
Richard of York Tony Britton
Sir William Stanley/Abbot of Beaulieu Milton Rosmer
Henry of Bergen Kenneth Edwards
Henry VII Noel Howlett
James IV Andrew Faulds
Roderigo de Puebla Kenneth Hyde
Sir Robert Clifford/Pedro de Ayala Ernest Clark
Cicely Lampson Josephine Griffin
Sir George Neville/Peasant Geoffrey Bayldon
Robert Erskine/Officer Dan Cunningham
Peasant's wife Beatrice Rowe
John Kinch/Porter Peter Bryant
Officer of the bodyguard Edwin Apps
Director Norman Marshall
Designer Anthony Holland

DANCE

SADLER'S WELLS THEATRE BALLET
18-20 Aug. 19.30 20 Aug. 14.30
Empire Theatre
COPPÉLIA
Choreographers Ivanov, Cecchetti, Sergeyev
Music Delibes
Designer Loudon Sainthill

21-23 Aug. 19.30 23 Aug. 14.30
Empire Theatre
LES RENDEZVOUS
Choreographer Frederick Ashton
Music Auber
Designer William Chappell
REFLECTION (World première)
Choreographer John Cranko
Music John Gardner
Designer Keith New
PINEAPPLE POLL
Choreographer John Cranko
Music Sullivan; arr. Mackerras
Designer Osbert Lancaster
Dancers Elaine Fifield, Svetlana Beriosova, Patricia Miller, Maryon Lane, Sheilah O'Reilly, David Blair, Donald Britton, Pirmin Trecu, David Poole, Stanley Holden, Maureen Bruce, Stella Claire, Pauline Harrop
Conductors Charles Mackerras, John Lanchbery

NEW YORK CITY BALLET
25-27 Aug. 19.30 27 Aug. 14.30
Empire Theatre
SWAN LAKE: Act 2
Choreographer George Balanchine
Music Tchaikovsky
Designer Cecil Beaton
THE CAGE
Choreographer Jerome Robbins
Music Stravinsky
Costumes Ruth Sabotka
PICNIC AT TINTAGEL
Choreographer Frederick Ashton
Music Bax
Designer Cecil Beaton
BOURRÉE FANTASQUE
Choreographer George Balanchine
Music Chabrier
Costumes Barbara Karinska

28-30 Aug. 19.30 30 Aug. 14.30
Empire Theatre
CARACOLE
Choreographer George Balanchine
Music Mozart
Designer Christian Bérard
TYL ULENSPIEGEL
Choreographer George Balanchine
Music R. Strauss
Designer Esteban Frances
THE FIREBIRD
Choreographer George Balanchine
Music Stravinsky
THE PIED PIPER
Choreographer Jerome Robbins
Music Copland
Dancers Maria Tallchief, Tanaquil Leclercq, Melissa Hayden, Nora Kaye, Diana Adams, Beatrice Tompkins, Patricia Wilde, Yvonne Mounsey, Nicholas Magallanes, Francisco Moncion, Herbert Bliss, Hugh Laing, Todd Bolender, Frank Hobi, Michael Maule, Roy Tobias
Scottish National Orchestra
Conductor Leon Barzin

GRAND BALLET DU MARQUIS DE CUEVAS
1-3 Sep.19.30 3 Sep.14.30
Empire Theatre
CONCERTO BAROCCO
Choreographer George Balanchine
Music Bach
Costumes Barbara Karinska
SCARAMOUCHE
Choreographer Rosella Hightower
Music Sibelius
Scenery Georges Wakhevitch
Costumes Raoul Pen du Bois
PAQUITA: Pas de trois
Choreographer George Balanchine
Music Minkus
Costumes Pierre Balmain
PRISONER IN THE CAUCASUS
Choreographer George Skibine
Music Khachaturian; arr. Stein
Designer Mstislav *and* Rostislav Dobujinsky

4-6 Sep. 19.30 6 Sep. 14.30
Empire Theatre
NIGHT SHADOW
Choreographer George Balanchine
Music Rieti *after* Bellini
Designer André Delfau
INES DE CASTRO
Choreographer Ana Ricarda
Music Serra
Designer Celia Hubbard
TARASIANA
Choreographer John Taras
Music Gluck, Mozart, Tchaikovsky
Designer Jean Robier
DEL AMOR Y DE LA MUERTE
Choreographer Ana Ricarda
Music Granados
Designer Celia Hubbard
Dancers Rosella Hightower, George Skibine, Serge Golovine, George Zoritch, Vladimir Skouratoff, Ana Ricarda, Jacqueline Moreau, Andrea Karlsen, Jocelyne Vollmar, Dolores Starr, Tania Karina, Helga Monson, Oleg Sabline, Michel Reznikoff
Festival Ballet Orchestra
Conductor Mac Dermott

EXHIBITIONS

Royal Scottish Academy
DEGAS
Director Derek Hill
(In association with the Royal Scottish Academy and the Arts Council of Great Britain)

LECTURES

15.00 Central Hall
20 Aug. Sir Thomas Beecham
21 Aug. Tyrone Guthrie Music in the theatre
22 Aug. Mary Garden Grand opera - Paris 1900
25 Aug. Philip Hope-Wallace

26 Aug. George Balanchine Tradition in ballet
27 Aug. Rafael Kubelik
28 Aug. Prof. J. Stewart Deas
29 Aug. Christopher Hassall
1 Sep. Gerald Moore
2 Sep. Norman Marshall
4 Sep. Dr Günther Rennert

1953

OPERA

GLYNDEBOURNE OPERA
24, 26, 28, 31 Aug. 8, 10, 12 Sep. 19.00
King's Theatre
LA CENERENTOLA Rossini
Cenerentola Marina de Gabarain
Don Ramiro Juan Oncina
Dandini Sesto Bruscantini
Don Magnifico Ian Wallace
Clorinda Alda Noni
Tisbe Fernanda Cadoni
Alidoro Hervey Alan
Royal Philharmonic Orchestra
Conductors Vittorio Gui
John Pritchard
Director Carl Ebert
Designer Oliver Messel

25, 27, 29 Aug. 2, 4 Sep. 19.00
King's Theatre
THE RAKE'S PROGRESS Stravinsky
Anne Elsie Morison
Tom Rakewell Richard Lewis
Trulove Hervey Alan
Nick Shadow Jerome Hines
Mother Goose Mary Jarred
Baba the Turk Nan Merriman
Sellem Murray Dickie
Keeper Dennis Wicks
Royal Philharmonic Orchestra
Conductor Alfred Wallenstein
Director Carl Ebert
Designer Osbert Lancaster

1, 3, 5, 7, 9, 11 Sep. 19.00 King's Theatre
IDOMENEO Mozart
Idomeneo Richard Lewis
Ilia Sena Jurinac
Idamante Helmut Krebs
Electra Jennifer Vyvyan
Arbace John Cameron
High Priest John Carolan
Voice of Neptune Hervey Alan
Royal Philharmonic Orchestra
Conductor John Pritchard
Director Carl Ebert
Designer Oliver Messel

ORCHESTRAL CONCERTS

RAI SYMPHONY ORCHESTRA, Rome
23 Aug. 20.00 Usher Hall
Corelli Concerto grosso in F, op.6/2
Schubert Symphony no.4 in C minor (Tragic), D417
Viotti Concerto for violin no.22 in A minor
Rossini Guillaume Tell: Overture
Conductor Fernando Previtali
Soloist Gioconda de Vito (vn)

25 Aug. 20.00 Usher Hall
Gluck Iphigénie en Aulide: Overture
Brahms Symphony no.3 in F, op.90
Ghedini Pezzo concertante for 2 violins and viola
Respighi The pines of Rome
Conductor Vittorio Gui

26 Aug. 20.00 Usher Hall
Verdi La forza del destino: Overture
Beethoven Grosse Fuge in B flat, op.133
Mozart Symphony no.40 in G minor, K550
Petrassi La follia di Orlando: Excerpts
Stravinsky The firebird - Suite
Conductor Fernando Previtali

27 Aug. 20.00 Usher Hall
Frescobaldi Four pieces; arr. Ghedini
Brahms Concerto for violin in D, op.77
Mendelssohn Symphony no.4 in A (Italian), op.90
Conductor Vittorio Gui
Soloist Isaac Stern (vn)

BBC SYMPHONY ORCHESTRA
Conductor Sir Malcolm Sargent
28 Aug. 20.00 Usher Hall
Delius Paris (The song of a great city)
Beethoven Concerto for piano no.3 in C minor, op.37
Walton Symphony no.1 in B flat minor
Soloist Solomon (pf)

29 Aug. 20.00 Usher Hall
Tippett Fantasia concertante on a theme of Corelli (EIF commission)+
V. Williams Symphony no.7 (Sinfonia Antartica)
Brahms Symphony no.4 in E minor, op.98
Conductor Michael Tippett+
Soloist Joan Alexander (sop)
Edinburgh Royal Choral Union members

30 Aug. 20.00 Usher Hall
Haydn Die Schöpfung
Soloists Eleanor Steber (sop), William Herbert (ten), Jerome Hines (bs), Edinburgh Royal Choral Union

NATIONAL YOUTH ORCHESTRA OF GREAT BRITAIN
31 Aug. 20.00 Usher Hall
Brahms Academic festival overture
Saint-Saëns Concerto for cello in A minor, op.33
Arnold English dances nos.1, 3, 5, 8
Sibelius Symphony no.1 in E minor, op.39
Conductor Sir Adrian Boult
Soloist Carol Sansom (vc)

PHILHARMONIA ORCHESTRA
1 Sep. 20.00 Usher Hall
Britten Variations on a theme of Frank Bridge
Debussy La mer
Beethoven Symphony no.7 in A, op.92
Conductor Herbert von Karajan

2 Sep. 20.00 Usher Hall
Handel Water music; arr. Harty
Beethoven Concerto for violin in D, op.61
Bartók Concerto for orchestra
Conductor Herbert von Karajan
Soloist Yehudi Menuhin (vn)

3 Sep. 20.00 Usher Hall
Walton Orb and sceptre - Coronation march
Mozart Sinfonia concertante for violin and viola, K364
Fricker Concerto for viola, op.18 (EIF commission)
Elgar Variations on an original theme (Enigma)
Conductor Sir Adrian Boult
Soloists Isaac Stern (vn), William Primrose (va)

4 Sep. 20.00 Usher Hall
Mozart Divertimento no.15 in B flat, K287
Ravel Rapsodie espagnole
Tchaikovsky Symphony no.5 in E minor, op.64
Conductor Herbert von Karajan

SCOTTISH NATIONAL ORCHESTRA
6 Sep. 20.00 Usher Hall
Weber Euryanthe: Overture
Bach Concerto for 2 violins in D minor
Schoenberg Chamber symphony no.1, op.9
Vivaldi Concerto for 3 violins in F
R. Strauss Till Eulenspiegels lustige Streiche
Conductor Karl Rankl
Soloists Gioconda de Vito, Yehudi Menuhin, Isaac Stern (vn)

VIENNA PHILHARMONIC ORCHESTRA
6 Sep. 14.30 7 Sep. 20.00 Usher Hall
Beethoven Egmont: Overture
Beethoven Symphony no.4 in B flat, op.60
Beethoven Symphony no.3 In E flat (Eroica), op.55
Conductor Wilhelm Furtwängler

8, 10 Sep. 20.00 Usher Hall
Brahms Tragic overture
Brahms Variations on a theme by Haydn (St Antoni), op.56a
Brahms Ein deutsches Requiem
Conductor Bruno Walter
Soloists Irmgard Seefried (sop), Dietrich Fischer-Dieskau (bar), Edinburgh Royal Choral Union

9 Sep. 20.00 Usher Hall
Wagner Die Meistersinger: Prelude
Hindemith Symphony (Die Harmonie der Welt)
Schubert Symphony no.9 in C (Great), D944
Conductor Wilhelm Furtwängler

11 Sep. 20.00 Usher Hall
R. Strauss Don Juan
Bartók Concerto for violin
Brahms Symphony no.1 in C minor, op.68
Conductor Wilhelm Furtwängler
Soloist Yehudi Menuhin (vn)

12 Sep. 19.30 Usher Hall
Weber Der Freischütz: Overture
Mozart Symphony no.41 in C (Jupiter), K551
Beethoven Symphony no.6 in F (Pastoral), op.68
Conductor Bruno Walter

12 Sep. 23.00 Usher Hall
Schubert Rosamunde: Overture
J. Strauss Der Zigeunerbaron: Overture
J. Strauss Kaiser Walzer
J. Strauss G'schichten aus dem Wiener Wald
J. Strauss Die Fledermaus: Overture
Thorpe Davie *arr.* Auld lang syne
Epilogue by Robert Kemp
Conductor Bruno Walter
Soloists Lennox Milne, Iris Russell, James Cairncross (rdr)

LONDON MOZART PLAYERS
Conductor Harry Blech
24 Aug. 11.00 Freemasons' Hall
Mozart Lucio Silla: Overture
Mozart Symphony no.28 in C, K200
Mozart Thamos, König in Ägypten: Intermezzi nos.2 *and* 3
Haydn Symphony no.86 in D

25 Aug. 11.00 *Freemasons' Hall*
Mozart Symphony no.36 in C (Linz), K425
Mozart Concerto for bassoon in B flat, K191
Mozart Symphony no.35 in D (Haffner), K385
Soloist Gwydion Brooke (bn)

26 Aug. 11.00 *Freemasons' Hall*
Haydn Symphony no.52 in C minor
Mozart Concerto for violin no.3 in G, K216
Mozart Symphony no.29 in A, K201
Soloist Isaac Stern (vn)

27 Aug. 11.00 *Freemasons' Hall*
Mozart Adagio and fugue in C minor, K546
Mozart Concerto for piano no.9 in E flat, K271
Haydn Symphony no.49 in F minor (La passione)
Soloist Nina Milkina (pf)

VIRTUOSI DI ROMA
Conductor Renato Fasano
1 Sep. 11.00 *Freemasons' Hall*
Albinoni Sonata for strings in A, op.2/3
Anon. Concerto for oboe in C minor
Vivaldi Concerto for violin and cello in B flat
Cambini Concerto for piano in G
Rossini Sonata for strings no.3 in C

2 Sep. 11.00 *Freemasons' Hall*
Vivaldi Concerto for violin in G minor
Vivaldi Concerto for viola d'amore in D minor
Vivaldi Concerto for oboe in D minor
Vivaldi Concerto for cello in G
Vivaldi Concerto for strings in A

3 Sep. 11.00 *Freemasons' Hall*
Marcello Introduction, aria and presto
Paisiello Concerto for piano in C
Corelli Concerto grosso in F, op.6/6
Bonporti Concerto for violin in F: Recitative
Vivaldi Concerto for 2 violins in A minor

CHAMBER CONCERTS

CARTER TRIO
24 Aug. 20.00 *Freemasons' Hall*
Pergolesi Quartet for oboe and strings in D; arr. Sampson
Beethoven Trio for strings no.2 in G, op.9/1
Wordsworth Quartet for oboe and strings in D, op.44
A. Cooke Trio for strings
Mozart Quartet for oboe and strings in F, K370
with Leon Goossens (ob)

BEETHOVEN STRING QUARTETS

PAGANINI QUARTET
28 Aug. 11.00 *Freemasons' Hall*
Nos. 3 in D; 5 in A; 10 in E flat

29 Aug. 11.00 *Freemasons' Hall*
Nos. 6 in B flat; 11 in F minor; 14 in C sharp minor

BARYLLI QUARTET
4 Sep. 11.00 *Freemasons' Hall*
Nos. 2 in G; 9 in C; 12 in E flat

5 Sep. 11.00 *Freemasons' Hall*
Nos. 4 in C minor; 13 in B flat; Grosse Fuge in B flat, op.133

LOEWENGUTH QUARTET
11 Sep. 11.00 *Freemasons' Hall*
Nos. 7 in F; 15 in A minor

12 Sep. 11.00 *Freemasons' Hall*
Nos. 1 in F; 8 in E minor; 16 in F

VIENNA OCTET
5 Sep. 20.00 *Usher Hall*
Mozart Divertimento no.17 in D, K334
Schubert Octet, D803

ALBAN TRIO
7 Sep. 20.00 *Freemasons' Hall*
Mozart Trio for piano and strings no.3 in B flat, K502
N. Fulton Trio for piano and strings no.1
Smetana Trio for piano and strings in G minor, op.15

SALTIRE SINGERS
30 Aug. 20.00 *Freemasons' Hall*
17th century music for voices and instruments by Schütz, Janequin, Monteverdi, Purcell
Conductor Hans Oppenheim
Soloists Paul Collins, Angela Richey (vn), Joan Dickson (vc)

ITALIAN OPERA QUARTET
6 Sep. 20.00 *Freemasons' Hall*
Italian operatic and vocal music of the 17th, 18th and 19th centuries by Monteverdi, Cesti, A. Scarlatti, Paisiello, Cavalli, Durante, Pergolesi, Piccinni, Cimarosa, Rossini, Bellini, Donizetti
Alda Noni (sop), Fernanda Cadoni (mez), Juan Oncina (ten), Sesto Bruscantini (bar), John Pritchard (pf). Introduced by Moran Caplat

CAMBRIDGE UNIVERSITY MADRIGAL SINGERS
Conductor Boris Ord
8 Sep. 11.00 *Freemasons' Hall*
Madrigals and songs

9 Sep. 11.00 *Freemasons' Hall*
Taverner Mass 'Western wynde'
Bach Motet no.2. Geist hilft unsrer Schwachheit
Kodály Missa brevis
with William Minay (org)

RECITALS

VLADIMIR RUZDJAK (bar)
26 Aug. 20.00 *Freemasons' Hall*
Schumann Dichterliebe
Songs by Schubert, Gotovac, Ravel

BRUCE BOYCE (bar)
28 Aug. 20.00 *Freemasons' Hall*
Songs by Schubert, Schumann, Loewe, Wolf

ELEANOR STEBER (sop)
1 Sep. 20.00 *Freemasons' Hall*
Songs by Schubert, Mahler, R. Strauss, Wolf, Debussy, Stanford, Wilda, Barber, Duke, Dougherty

DIETRICH FISCHER-DIESKAU (bar)
3 Sep. 20.00 *Freemasons' Hall*
Songs by Beethoven

IRMGARD SEEFRIED (sop)
5 Sep. 15.00 *Freemasons' Hall*
Songs by Mozart, Schubert, Bartók, Brahms

IRMGARD SEEFRIED (sop)
DIETRICH FISCHER-DIESKAU (bar)
9 Sep. 20.00 *Freemasons' Hall*
Wolf Italienisches Liederbuch
All with **GERALD MOORE (pf)**

SOLOMON (pf)
30 Aug. 14.30 *Usher Hall*
Mozart Sonata no.11 in A, K331
Schubert Sonata no.14 in A minor, D784
Beethoven Sonata no.26 in E flat (Farewell), op.81a
Chopin Ballade no.3 in A flat, op.47
Chopin Andante spianato and grande polonaise, op.22

YEHUDI MENUHIN (vn)
31 Aug. 11.00 *Freemasons' Hall*
Bach Sonata no.1 in G minor
Bach Partita no.1 in B minor
Bach Sonata no.3 in C

7 Sep. 11.00 *Freemasons' Hall*
Bach Sonata no.2 in A minor
Bach Partita no.3 in E
Bach Partita no.2 in D minor

MAX ROSTAL (vn)
MEWTON-WOOD ((pf)
10 Sep. 11.00 *Freemasons' Hall*
Mozart Sonata no.32 in B flat, K454
Stravinsky Duo concertant
Beethoven Sonata no.9 in A (Kreutzer), op.47

DRAMA

OLD VIC
24 Aug.-5 Sep. 19.15 (exc.Sun) 25, 29 Aug. 1, 5 Sep. 14.15 *Assembly Hall*
HAMLET Shakespeare
Hamlet Richard Burton
Ophelia Claire Bloom
Gertrude Fay Compton
Claudius Laurence Hardy
Polonius Michael Hordern
Horatio William Squire
Laertes Robert Hardy
Fortinbras John Neville
Osric Timothy Bateson
Bernardo Jeremy Geidt
Francisco John Lamin
Marcellus Ronald Hines
Ghost Bernard Horsfall
Rosencrantz David William
Guildenstern John Dearth
Player (King)/1st Gravedigger Edgar Wreford
Player (Queen) Clifford Williams
Player (Lucianus) Maxwell Gardiner
2nd Gravedigger/Player Bruce Sharman
Priest Job Stewart
Director Michael Benthall
Designer Kenneth Rowell
Music John Gardner

CITIZENS' THEATRE, Glasgow
7-12 Sep. 19.15 8, 9, 11, 12 Sep 14.15
Assembly Hall
THE HIGHLAND FAIR Mitchell
(A ballad opera adapted by Robert Kemp)
Bracken Tom Fordyce
MacFadyean James Gibson
Alaster John Cairney
Nanny Iris Russell
Kenneth Ian Macnaughton
Maggy Elizabeth French
Gregor Robert Taylor
Ian Denis Hall
Anna Ruth Clark
Ellen Mary Dean
Catriona Madeleine Christie

Grelloch Scott Logan
Miss Watt Lennox Milne
Hector James Cairncross
Jeany Nancy Scott
Hamish Niven Miller
Alan Terence Conoley
Elspeth Anne Edwards
Fiona Audrey Moncrieff
Devorguilla Elise Gunn
Capt. Morgan Evans Roderick Jones
Sgt Swilly George James
Nicol Roddy McMillan
Attendant Lyn Braham
Dancers L. Wood, Patrick Donnelly, John McDonald, Jack Johnstone
Director Tyrone Guthrie
Designer Molly MacEwen
Music Cedric Thorpe Davie

HENRY SHEREK
25 Aug.-5 Sep. 19.15 (exc.Sun) 26, 28, 29 Aug. 2, 5 Sep. 14.15 Lyceum Theatre
THE CONFIDENTIAL CLERK Eliot
(EIF commission)
Sir Claude Mulhammer Paul Rogers
Eggerson Alan Webb
Colby Simpkins Denholm Elliott
Lucasta Angel Margaret Leighton
B. Kaghan Peter Jones
Lady Elizabeth Mulhammer Isabel Jeans
Mrs Guzzard Alison Leggatt
Director E. Martin Browne
Designer Hutchinson Scott

LE THÉÂTRE NATIONAL POPULAIRE, Paris
7, 9 Sep. 19.15 Lyceum Theatre
L'AVARE Molière
Herpagon Jean Vilar
Cléante Jean-Pierre Darras
Elise Monique Chaumette
Valère Jean Deschamps
Mariane Christiane Minazzoli
Anselme Georges Wilson
Frosine Lucienne Le Marchand
Maître Simon/Brindavoine Coussonneau
Maître Jacques Jean-Paul Moulinot
La Flèche Daniel Sorano
Dame Claude Zanie Campan
La Merluche André Schlesser
Le commissaire Georges Riquier
Le clerc Philippe Noiret
Director Jean Vilar
Designer Léon Gischia
Music Maurice Jarre

8 Sep.19.15 9 Sep.14.15 Lyceum Theatre
RICHARD II Shakespeare (Fr)
Richard II Jean Vilar
Jean de Gand Jean-Paul Moulinot
Bolingbroke Jean Deschamps
Comte de Northumberland Georges Wilson
Thomas Mowbray Georges Lycan
Le Marechal d'Angleterre Guy Provost
Green Pierre Hatet
Bushy Jean-Pierre Darras
Bagot Jacques Dasque
Duchesse de Gloucester Lucienne le Marchand
Duc d'Aumerle Jean-Pierre Jorris
1 ere Hérault André Schlesser
2 eme Hérault/Le palefrenier Coussonneau
La Reine Monique Chaumette
1 ere Suivante Zanie Campan
2 eme Suivante Christiane Minazzoli
Lord Ross Jacques le Marquet
Lord Willoughby Guy Provost
Duc d'York Daniel Sorano
Henry Percy Roger Mollien
Sir Etienne Scroop Philippe Noiret
Evêque de Carlisle Georges Riquier
La jardiniere du Duc d'York Jean Paul Moulinot
L'aide jardiniere Laurence Badie
Lord Fitzwater Jean-Pierre Darras
L'Abbe de Westminster Guy Provost
Sir Pierce d'Exton Philippe Noiret
Un serviteur d'Exton Pierre Hatet
Le geôlier Georges Lycan
Director Jean Vilar
Scenery Camille Demangeat
Costumes Léon Gischia
Music Maurice Jarre

LA COMPAGNIE DE MIME MARCEL MARCEAU, Paris
10-12 Sep. 19.15 12 Sep. 14.15
Lyceum Theatre
A programme of pantomimes and mimodrames including:
LES PANTOMIMES DE BIP
Bip Marcel Marceau
THE COAT (from a story by Gogol)
Ist Clerk Marcel Marceau
2nd Clerk Roger Desmare
3rd Clerk Gilles Segal
4th Clerk Pierre Verry
The chief clerk Michel Trevières
The tailor Gilles Léger
His daughter Sabine Lods
The chief clerk's wife Edith Perret
The wife of the 2nd official Regine Maupre
A servant Pierre Verry
Director Marcel Marceau
Designer Jacques Noël

DANCE

AMERICAN BALLET THEATRE
24-26 Aug. 19.30 26 Aug 14.30
Empire Theatre
CONSTANTIA
Choreographer William Dollar
Music Chopin
Designer Robert Davison
CIRCO DE ESPANA
Choreographer Carmelita Maracci
Music Albanese, Turina, Granados, Falla
Designer Rico Lebrun
SWAN LAKE: Black swan pas de deux
Choreographer Marius Petipa
Music Tchaikovsky
RODEO
Choreographer Agnes de Mille
Music Copland
Scenery Oliver Smith
Costumes Saul Bolasni

27-29 Aug. 19.30 29 Aug. 14.30
Empire Theatre
BILLY THE KID
Choreographer Eugene Loring
Music Copland
Designer Jared French
SCHUMANN CONCERTO
Choreographer Bronislava Nijinska
Music Schumann
Designer Stewart Chaney
GRADUATION BALL
Choreographer David Lichine
Music J. Strauss; arr. Dorati
Dancers Alicia Alonso, Igor Youskevitch, John Kriza, Mary Ellen Moylan, Melissa Hayden, Ruth Ann Koesun, Eric Braun, Lillian Lanese, Michael Lland, Jenny Workman, Kelly Brown, Dorothy Scott, Liane Plane, Barbara Lloyd, Scott Douglas
Scottish National Orchestra
Conductors Joseph Levine, Paul Strauss

SPANISH BALLET OF PILAR LÓPEZ
31 Aug.-2 Sep. 19.30 2 Sep. 14.30
Empire Theatre
Spanish dances and music including
CONCIERTO DE ARANJUEZ (López)
Music Rodrigo

3-5 Sep. 19.30 5 Sep. 14.30
Empire Theatre
Spanish dances and music including
FANTASIA GOYESCA
Music Granados
SUITE ARGENTINA
Music Guastavino
Choreographer Pilar López
Dancers Pilar López, Elvira Real, Dorita Ruiz, Encarnacion Mendoza, Alberto Lorca, Paco de Ronda, Roberto Ximénez, Manolo Vargas, Pilar Calvo
with Ramon de Loja (sngr), Luis Maravilla (gtr), Abraham Thevenet Echániz (pf)
Festival Ballet Orchestra
Conductor José María Franco

SADLER'S WELLS THEATRE BALLET
7-9 Sep.19.30 9 Sep.14.30
Empire Theatre
THE RAKE'S PROGRESS
Choreographer Ninette de Valois
Music Gavin Gordon
Designer Rex Whistler *after* Hogarth
PASTORALE
Choreographer John Cranko
Music Mozart
Designer Hugh Stevenson
BLOOD WEDDING
Choreographer Alfred Rodrigues
Music Denis Apivor
Designer Isabel Lambert

10-12 Sep.19.30 12 Sep.14.30
Empire Theatre
LA FÊTE ÉTRANGE
Choreographer Andrée Howard
Music Fauré; arr. Warrack
Designer Sophie Fedorovitch
HARLEQUIN IN APRIL
Choreographer John Cranko
Music Richard Arnell
Designer John Piper
CARTE BLANCHE (World première)
Choreographer Walter Gore
Music John Addison
Designer Kenneth Rowell
Dancers Elaine Fifield, Maryon Lane, Gerd Larsen, Patricia Miller, Sheilah O'Reilly, Donald Britton, David Poole, Pirmin Trecu, Margaret Hill, Sara Neil, Annette Page, Stanley Holden, Kenneth MacMillan, Gilbert Vernon
with Marion Studholme (sop)
Conductors John Lanchbery, Richard Arnell

EXHIBITIONS

Royal Scottish Academy
RENOIR
(In association with the Royal Scottish Academy and the Arts Council of Great Britain)

Royal Scottish Museum
MEDIEVAL FRESCOES FROM YUGOSLAVIA
(In association with the Scottish Committee of the Arts Council of Great Britain)

1954

OPERA

GLYNDEBOURNE OPERA
23, 25, 27, 30 Aug. 1, 4, 7 Sep. 19.00
King's Theatre
LE COMTE ORY Rossini
Count Ory — Juan Oncina
Countess Adèle — Sari Barabas
Raimbaud — Sesto Bruscantini
Isolier — Fernanda Cadoni
Alice — Halinka de Tarczynska
Ragonde — Monica Sinclair
Tutor — Ian Wallace
Cavalier — Dermot Troy
Royal Philharmonic Orchestra
Conductor — Vittorio Gui
Director — Carl Ebert
Designer — Oliver Messel

24, 26, 28 Aug. 3, 8, 10 Sep. 19.00
King's Theatre
ARIADNE AUF NAXOS R. Strauss
(Revised version)
Ariadne — Lucine Amara
Bacchus — Richard Lewis
Zerbinetta — Mattiwilda Dobbs
Composer — Sena Jurinac
Harlekin — Kurt Gester
Scaramuccio — Juan Oncina
Truffaldin — Fritz Ollendorf
Brighella/Dancing master — Murray Dickie
Music master — Geraint Evans
Major domo — Peter Ebert*
James Atkins
Naiade — Maureen Springer
Dryade — Noreen Berry
Echo — Elaine Malbin
Officer — John Carolan
Wig maker — Gwyn Griffiths
Lackey — James Atkins
Royal Philharmonic Orchestra
Conductor — John Pritchard
Director — Carl Ebert
Designer — Oliver Messel

31 Aug. 2, 6, 9, 11 Sep. 19.00
King's Theatre
COSÌ FAN TUTTE Mozart
Fiordiligi — Sena Jurinac
Dorabella — Magda Laszlo
Ferrando — Richard Lewis
Juan Oncina
Guglielmo — Geraint Evans
Despina — Alda Noni
Don Alfonso — Sesto Bruscantini
Royal Philharmonic Orchestra
Conductors — Vittorio Gui
John Pritchard
Director — Carl Ebert
Scenery — Rolf Gérard
Costumes — Rosemary Vercoe

ORCHESTRAL CONCERTS

DANISH STATE RADIO ORCHESTRA
22 Aug. 20.00 — Usher Hall
Nielsen — Maskarade: Overture
Mozart — Sinfonia concertante for wind, K297b
Prokofiev — Symphony no.5 in B flat, op.100
Conductor — Erik Tuxen

23 Aug. 20.00 — Usher Hall
Dvořák — Carnival - Overture
Sibelius — Concerto for violin in D minor, op.47
Nielsen — Symphony no.4 (Inextinguishable), op.29
Conductor — Thomas Jensen
Soloist — Isaac Stern (vn)

24 Aug. 20.00 — Usher Hall
Beethoven — Leonore: Overture no.3
Beethoven — Symphony no.2 in D, op.36
Tchaikovsky — Symphony no.6 in B minor (Pathétique), op.74
Conductor — Eugene Ormandy

SCOTTISH NATIONAL ORCHESTRA
Conductor — Karl Rankl
25 Aug. 20.00 — Usher Hall
Schoenberg — Gurrelieder
Soloists Sylvia Fisher (sop), Constance Shacklock (cont), William Herbert, Murray Dickie (ten), Owen Brannigan (bs), Alvar Liddell (narr), Edinburgh Royal Choral Union, West Calder and District Male Choir

5 Sep. 20.00 — Usher Hall
Wagner — Lohengrin: Prelude
Rachmaninov — Rhapsody on a theme of Paganini
Mahler — Symphony no.5 in C sharp minor
Soloist — Artur Rubinstein (pf)

BBC SCOTTISH ORCHESTRA
26 Aug. 14.30 — Usher Hall
Britten — The young person's guide to the orchestra
Mendelssohn — Concerto for violin in E minor, op.64
Rawsthorne — Practical cats (EIF commission)
Whyte — Donald of the Burthens - Suite
Conductor — Ian Whyte
Soloists Isaac Stern (vn), Alvar Lidell (narr), Pipe Major Robert Reid (bp)

ORCHESTRE NATIONAL DE LA RADIODIFFUSION FRANÇAISE
Conductor — Charles Münch
26 Aug. 20.00 — Usher Hall
Handel — Concerto grosso in A minor, op.6/4
Mozart — Symphony no.31 in D (Paris), K297
Roussel — Bacchus et Ariane - Suite no.2
Saint-Saëns — Symphony no.3 in C minor (Organ), op.78
Soloist — Herrick Bunney (hpd, org)

27 Aug. 20.00 — Usher Hall
Mozart — Divertimento (Salzburg Symphony) no.1 in D, K136
Bach — Concerto for violin in A minor
Prokofiev — Concerto for violin no.1 in D, op.19
Brahms — Symphony no.4 in E minor, op.98
Soloist — Isaac Stern (vn)

29 Aug. 20.00 — Usher Hall
Gluck — Alceste: Overture
Haydn — Symphony no.100 in G (Military)
Ravel — Concerto for piano in G
Ravel — Le tombeau de Couperin
Ravel — Daphnis et Chloë - Suite no.2
Soloist — Nicole Henriot (pf)

NATIONAL YOUTH ORCHESTRA OF GREAT BRITAIN
28 Aug. 20.00 — Usher Hall
Weber — Euryanthe: Overture
Mozart — Concerto for piano no.17 in G, K453
Blacher — Inventions for orchestra (World première)
Tchaikovsky — Symphony no.5 in E minor, op.64
Conductor — Jean Martinon
Soloist — Allan Schiller (pf)

NDR SYMPHONY ORCHESTRA, Hamburg
Conductor — Hans Schmidt-Isserstedt
30 Aug. 20.00 — Usher Hall
Mozart — Symphony no.29 in A, K201
Mozart — Concerto for violin no.5 in A, K219
Blacher — Variations on a theme of Paganini
Beethoven — Symphony no.5 in C minor, op.67
Soloist — Wolfgang Schneiderhan (vn)

31 Aug. 20.00 — Usher Hall
Stravinsky — Symphony in 3 movements
Chopin — Concerto for piano no.2 in F minor, op.21
Brahms — Symphony no.2 in D, op.73
Soloist — Claudio Arrau (pf)

1 Sep. 20.00 — Usher Hall
Pachelbel — Canon and gigue in D
Haydn — Symphony no.96 in D (Miracle)
Hindemith — Concerto for horn
R. Strauss — Don Quixote
Soloists Dennis Brain (hn), Arthur Tröster (vc)

HALLÉ ORCHESTRA
Conductor — Sir John Barbirolli
2 Sep. 20.00 — Usher Hall
Mozart — La clemenza di Tito: Overture
Mozart — Symphony no.36 in C (Linz), K425
Mahler — Symphony no.9 in D

3 Sep. 20.00 — Usher Hall
Verdi — Les vêpres Siciliennes: Overture
Debussy — Prélude à l'après-midi d'un faune
Wordsworth — Symphony no.4 in E flat, op.54 (World première)
Brahms — Concerto for piano no.2 in B flat, op.83
Soloist — Artur Rubinstein (pf)

4 Sep. 20.00 — Usher Hall
Verdi — Requiem
Soloists Elisabeth Schwarzkopf (sop), Constance Shacklock (cont), Richard Lewis (ten), Hans Hotter (b-bar), Sheffield Philharmonic Chorus

PHILHARMONIA ORCHESTRA
6 Sep. 20.00 — Usher Hall
Berlioz — Symphonie fantastique
Schumann — Concerto for piano in A minor, op.54
Wagner — Tristan und Isolde: Prelude and Liebestod
Conductor — Herbert von Karajan
Soloist — Claudio Arrau (pf)

7 Sep. 20.00 — Usher Hall
Beethoven — Egmont: Overture
Beethoven — Symphony no.4 in B flat, op.60
Beethoven — Symphony no.3 In E flat (Eroica), op.55
Conductor — Herbert von Karajan

8 Sep. 20.00 — Usher Hall
Mozart — Symphony no.35 in D (Haffner), K385
R. Strauss — Till Eulenspiegels lustige Streiche
Brahms — Symphony no.1 in C minor, op.68
Conductor — Herbert von Karajan

9 Sep. 20.00 — Usher Hall
Schumann — Manfred: Overture
Schumann — Symphony no.4 in D minor, op.120

Debussy Le martyre de St Sébastien - Suite
Debussy La mer
Conductor Guido Cantelli

10 Sep. 20.00 *Usher Hall*
Beethoven Symphony no.6 in F (Pastoral), op.68
Wagner Siegfried idyll
Hindemith Mathis der Maler - Symphony
Conductor Guido Cantelli

11 Sep. 19.30 *Usher Hall*
Mussorgsky Pictures at an exhibition; orch. Ravel
Tchaikovsky Symphony no.4 in F minor, op.36
Conductor Guido Cantelli

JACQUES ORCHESTRA
Conductor Reginald Jacques
23 Aug. 11.00 *Freemasons' Hall*
Bach Brandenburg concerto no.3 in G
Jacob Concerto for flute
Purcell Chaconne in G minor
Bartók Divertimento for strings
Soloist Geoffrey Gilbert (fl)

24 Aug. 11.00 *Freemasons' Hall*
Arensky Variations on a theme of Tchaikovsky
Byrd Fantasia no.2 in C minor
Arnold Concerto for oboe, op.39
Dvořák Serenade for strings in E, op.22
Soloist Leon Goossens (ob)

26 Aug. 11.00 *Freemasons' Hall*
Hamilton Variations on an original theme, op.1
Bach Concerto for piano in D minor
Bliss Music for strings
Soloist James Ching (pf)

27 Aug. 11.00 *Freemasons' Hall*
Tippett Concerto for double string orchestra
Bach Concerto for violin in E
V. Williams Fantasia on a theme by Tallis
Soloists Emanuel Hurwitz (vn), Herrick Bunney (hpd)

DANISH STATE RADIO CHAMBER ORCHESTRA
25 Aug. 11.00 *Freemasons' Hall*
Handel Concerto grosso in B flat, op.3/2
Bach Brandenburg concerto no.5 in D
Nielsen Concerto for clarinet, op.57
Haydn Symphony no.91 in E flat
Conductor Mogens Wöldike
Soloist Ib Eriksson (cl)

COLLEGIUM MUSICUM, Zürich
Conductor Paul Sacher
2 Sep. 11.00 *Freemasons' Hall*
Handel Concerto grosso in A minor, op.6/4
Purcell Sonata in 4 parts no.6 in G minor
W. Burkhard Concertino for 2 flutes and harpsichord (World première)
Mozart Divertimento (Salzburg symphony) no.1 in D, K136
Soloists André Jaunet, Ursula Burkhard (fl), Hans Andreae (hpd)

3 Sep. 11.00 *Freemasons' Hall*
Pergolesi Concertino no.5 in E flat
Schoeck Concerto for horn
Bach Suite no.2 in B minor
Soloists Dennis Brain (hn), André Jaunet (fl)

4 Sep. 11.00 *Freemasons' Hall*
W.F. Bach Sinfonia in D minor for 2 flutes
C.P.E. Bach Sinfonia in B flat
Martin Ballade for flute, piano and strings
Honegger Symphony no.2
Soloists André Jaunet (fl), Hans Andreae (fl)

CHAMBER CONCERTS

AMADEUS QUARTET
28 Aug. 11.00 *Freemasons' Hall*
Mozart Quartet no.19 in C (Dissonance), K465
Brahms Quintet no.2 in G, op.111
with Cecil Aronowitz (va)

29 Aug. 20.00 *Freemasons' Hall*
Mozart Quintet no.3 in G minor, K516
Schubert Quintet in C, D956
with Cecil Aronowitz (va), William Pleeth (vc)

31 Aug. 11.00 *Freemasons' Hall*
Mozart Quartet no.21 in D, K.575
Brahms Sextet no.1 in B flat, op.18
with Cecil Aronowitz (va), William Pleeth (vc)

1 Sep. 20.00 *Freemasons' Hall*
Haydn Quartet in C, op.54/2
Beethoven Quartet no.16 in F, op.135
Mozart Quintet no.2 in C, K515
with Cecil Aronowitz (va)

KEHR TRIO
7 Sep. 11.00 *Freemasons' Hall*
Reger Trio in A minor, op.77b
Mozart Divertimento in E flat, K563

8 Sep. 11.00 *Freemasons' Hall*
Mozart Adagio and fugue in F minor, K.404a
Beethoven Serenade in D, op.8
Dohnányi Serenade for 2 violins and viola, op.10

PASCAL QUARTET
9 Sep. 11.00 *Freemasons' Hall*
Mozart Quartet no.14 in G, K387
Milhaud Quartet no.4
Beethoven Quartet no.8 in E minor (Rasumovsky), op. 59/2

10 Sep. 11.00 *Freemasons' Hall*
Mozart Quartet no.19 in C (Dissonance), K465
Schumann Quartet no.1 in A minor, op.41/1
Bartók Quartet no.1

11 Sep. 11.00 *Freemasons' Hall*
Debussy Quartet in G minor, op.10/1
Fauré Quartet in E minor, op.121
Ravel Quartet in F

GOLDEN AGE SINGERS
Director Margaret Field Hyde
30 Aug. 11.00 *Freemasons' Hall*
Madrigals and chansons by Weelkes, Farmer, Monteverdi, Morley, Bertrand, Costeley, Lassus, Janequin, Wilbye, Greaves, Tomkins

1 Sep. 11.00 *Freemasons' Hall*
Byrd Mass in 4 parts
Madrigals, canzonets, chansons by Bennet, Weelkes, Farnaby, Wilbye, Bateson, Lassus, Janequin

SOIRÉE OFFENBACH
5 Sep. 20.00 *Freemasons' Hall*
Arias, duets and trios from the operettas
Liliane Berton (sop), Raymond Amade (ten), Bernard Lefort (bar), Germaine Tailleferre (pf). Introduced by Jean-Jacques Oberlin

RECITALS

MATTIWILDA DOBBS (sop)
25 Aug. 20.00 *Freemasons' Hall*
Songs by Rodrigo, Schubert, R. Strauss, Pizzetti, Milhaud, Respighi, Castelnuovo-Tedesco, Egk

HANS HOTTER (b-bar)
30 Aug. 20.00 *Freemasons' Hall*
Goethe settings by Loewe, Schubert, Schumann, Wolf

ELISABETH SCHWARZKOPF (sop)
31 Aug. 20.00 *Freemasons' Hall*
Goethe settings by Mozart, Beethoven, Schumann, Schubert

ELISABETH SCHWARZKOPF (sop)
HANS HOTTER (b-bar)
2 Sep. 20.00 *Freemasons' Hall*
Goethe settings by Wolf

IRMGARD SEEFRIED (sop)
7 Sep. 20.00 *Freemasons' Hall*
Songs by Mahler, Mussorgsky, Pfitzner, R. Strauss

IRMGARD SEEFRIED (sop), WOLFGANG SCHNEIDERHAN (vn), CARL SEEMANN (pf)
9 Sep. 20.00 *Freemasons' Hall*
Arias for soprano, violin and piano by Mozart, Bach. Songs by Beethoven. Violin works by Mozart, Bach
All with **GERALD MOORE (pf)**

JAMES CHING (pf)
27 Aug. 20.00 *Freemasons' Hall*
Bach Fantasia in C minor
Bach French suite no.5 in G
Bach Chromatic fantasia and fugue in D minor
Bach Das wohltemperirte Klavier: Preludes and fugues nos.1-4
Bach Partita no.1 in B flat

CLAUDIO ARRAU (pf)
4 Sep. 14.30 *Usher Hall*
Liszt Sonata in B minor
Chopin Ballade no.4 in F minor, op.52
Chopin Nocturne no.17 in B, op.62/1
Chopin Scherzo no.4 in E, op.54
Liszt Légendes
Chopin Sonata no.3 in B minor, op.58

ARTUR RUBINSTEIN (pf)
8 Sep. 14.30 *Usher Hall*
Beethoven Sonata no.21 in C (Waldstein), op.53
Chopin Ballade no.1 in G minor, op.23
Chopin Étude no.17 in E minor, op.25/5
Chopin Étude no.4 in C sharp minor, op.10/4
Chopin Nocturne no.8 in D flat, op.27/2
Chopin Polonaise no.6 in A flat, op.53
Schumann Carnaval
Stravinsky Petrushka: 3 movements; arr. for piano

ISAAC STERN (vn)
ALEXANDER ZAKIN (pf)
29 Aug. 14.30 *Usher Hall*
Beethoven Sonata no.2 in A, op.12/2
Bartók Sonata no.1
Brahms Sonata no.3 in D minor, op.108

DRAMA

TENNENT PRODUCTIONS LTD
23 Aug.- 4 Sep. 19.30 (exc.Sun) 25, 28 Aug. 1, 4 Sep. 14.30 Lyceum Theatre
THE MATCHMAKER Wilder
(World première)
Mrs Levi — Ruth Gordon
Mrs Irene Molloy — Eileen Herlie
Horace Vandergelder — Sam Levene
Miss Van Huysen — Esmé Church
Cornelius Hackl — Arthur Hill
Malachi Stack — Patrick McAlinney
Ermengarde — Prunella Scales
Barnaby Tucker — Alec McCowen
Rudolph — Timothy Findley
Joe Scanlon/Musician — Peter Sallis
Minnie Fay — Rosamund Greenwood
Gertrude — Henzie Raeburn
Miss Van Huysen's cook — Daphne Newton
August — John Milligan
Ambrose Kemper — Lee Montague
Cabman — Peter Bayliss
Director — Tyrone Guthrie
Designer — Tanya Moiseiwitsch

LA COMÉDIE FRANÇAISE
6-11 Sep. 19.30 8, 11 Sep. 14.30 Lyceum Theatre
LE BOURGEOIS GENTILHOMME
Molière
Monsieur Jourdain — Louis Seigner
Madame Jourdain — Andrée de Chauveron
Nicole — Béatrice Bretty
Dorimène — Marie Sabouret
Music master — Jacques Rameau* Robert Hirsch ?
Covielle — Jean Meyer
Dancing master — Jacques Charon
Philosopher — Georges Chamarat
Fencing master — Michel Galabru
Dorante — Maurice Escande
Cléonte — Jean Piat
Tailor — Robert Manuel
Tailor's assistant — Teddy Bilis
Lackies — Arsène Drancourt, Charles Millot
Lucile — Micheline Boudet
Saltire Singers, Students from the Scottish Ballet School, Festival Chorus & Orchestra
Director — Jean Meyer
Designer — Suzanne Lalique
Music — Lully
Conductor — André Jolivet

GATEWAY COMPANY
23 Aug.-11 Sep. 19.30 (exc.Sun) 26, 28 Aug. 2, 4, 9, 11 Sep. 14.30 Gateway Theatre
THE OTHER DEAR CHARMER Kemp
Robert Burns — Tom Fleming
Nancie Maclehose (Clarinda) — Iris Russell
Mirren — Meg Buchanan
Lord Craig — George Davies
Miss Nimmo — Lennox Milne
Miss Peacock — Sheila Prentice
Robert Ainslie — Michael Elder
Jenny Clow — Marillyn Gray
Rev. John Kemp — Bill Crichton
Director — Peter Potter
Designer — Molly MacEwen

OLD VIC
23 Aug.- 4 Sep. 19.15 (exc.Sun) 24, 28, 31 Aug. 4 Sep. 14.15 Assembly Hall
MACBETH Shakespeare
Macbeth — Paul Rogers
Lady Macbeth — Ann Todd
Banquo — Eric Porter
Macduff — John Neville
Duncan — Robert Hardy
Malcolm — Paul Daneman
Donalbain — Nicholas Amer
Fleance — Robert Gillespie
Lennox — John Wood
Ross — Meredith Edwards
Seyton — Alan Dobie
Doctor — Geoffrey Chater
Porter — Laurence Hardy
Lady Macduff — Gwen Cherrell
Gentlewoman — Mary Hignett
Witches — Rachel Roberts, Clifford Williams, Job Stewart
Son to Macduff — Bunny May
Murderers — Donald Moffatt, Aubrey Morris
Sergeant — Brian Rawlinson
Director — Michael Benthall
Designer — Audrey Cruddas
Music — Brian Easdale

EDINBURGH INTERNATIONAL FESTIVAL
31 Aug.-11 Sep. 19.30 (exc.Sun) 1, 3, 4, 8, 11 Sep. 14.30 Empire Theatre
A MIDSUMMER NIGHT'S DREAM
Shakespeare
Titania — Moira Shearer
Oberon — Robert Helpmann
Lysander — Terence Longdon
Helena — Joan Benham
Demetrius — Patrick Macnee
Hermia — Ann Walford
Theseus — Anthony Nicholls
Hippolyta — Margaret Courtenay
Bottom — Stanley Holloway
Starveling — Daniel Thorndike
Snug — Michael Redington
Flute — Philip Locke
Quince — Eliot Makeham
Snout — Norman Rossington
Puck — Philip Guard
Philostrate — Peter Johnson
Peaseblossom — Jocelyn Britton
Cobweb — Tania D'Avray
Moth — Sheila Wright
Mustardseed — Joan King
Egeus — John Dearth
Indian boy — Anne Brown
Scottish National Orchestra
Conductor — Hugo Rignold
Director — Michael Benthall
Designers — Robin *and* Christopher Ironside
Choreographers
Robert Helpmann, Frederick Ashton
Music — Mendelssohn
(In association with the Old Vic, Sadler's Wells Ballet and the Scottish National Orchestra)

6, 7, 9, 10 Sep. 11.00 King's Theatre
THE SOLDIER'S TALE Stravinsky
(Eng. Translated by Michael Flanders *and* Kitty Black)
Princess — Moira Shearer
Devil — Robert Helpmann
Soldier — Terence Longdon
Narrator — Anthony Nicholls
Instrumental Ensemble
Conductor — Hans Schmidt-Isserstedt
Director — Günther Rennert
Scenery — Alfred Mahlau
Costumes — Ita Maximowna
Choreographer — Robert Helpmann
(In association with Glyndebourne Opera)

6-11 Sep. 19.15 7, 11 Sep. 14.15 Assembly Hall
HAIL CALEDONIA!
An entertainment of Scottish singing, dancing and piping devised by Robert Kemp
John Mearns (sngr), Jack Johnstone (dan), Norman Quinney (gtr), John Burgess (bp), Campbeltown Gaelic Choir, Falkirk Choral Society, Newhaven Fisher Lassies' Choir, Royal Scottish Country Dance Society, Tim Wright's Country Dance Band.
Introduced by Roddy McMillan
Director — Norman Marshall
Designer — Audrey Cruddas
Music — Cedric Thorpe Davie

DANCE

SADLER'S WELLS BALLET
23-28 Aug. 19.30 25, 28 Aug. 14.30 Empire Theatre
Homage To Diaghilev
LA BOUTIQUE FANTASQUE
Choreographer — Léonide Massine
Music — Rossini; arr. Respighi
Designer — André Derain
THE FIREBIRD
Choreographer — Mikhail Fokine (reproduced by Grigoriev and Tchernicheva)
Music — Stravinsky
Designer — Nathalia Goncharova
THE THREE-CORNERED HAT
Choreographer — Léonide Massine
Music — Falla
Designer — Pablo Picasso
Dancers Margot Fonteyn, Violetta Elvin, Rowena Jackson, Nadia Nerina, Michael Somes, John Field, Alexander Grant, John Hart, Alexis Rassine, Svetlana Beriosova, Brian Shaw, Pauline Clayden, Margaret Dale, Mary Drage, Julia Farron, Anne Heaton, Gerd Larsen, Anya Linden, Rosemary Lindsay, Avril Navarre, Valerie Taylor, Meriel Evans, Bryan Ashbridge, David Blair, Michael Boulton, Philip Chatfield, Ronald Hynd, Peter Clegg, Desmond Doyle, Leslie Edwards, Henry Legerton, Ray Powell, Douglas Steuart, Franklin White, Harold Turner
Conductor — Ernest Ansermet

EXHIBITIONS

Royal Scottish Academy
CÉZANNE
Director — Lawrence Gowing
(In association with the Royal Scottish Academy and the Arts Council of Great Britain)

National Gallery of Scotland
TREASURES FROM THE BARBER INSTITUTE

Edinburgh College of Art
HOMAGE TO DIAGHILEV
Director — Richard Buckle

1955

OPERA

GLYNDEBOURNE OPERA
22, 24, 26, 31 Aug. 6, 9 Sep. 19.00
King's Theatre
IL BARBIERE DI SIVIGLIA Rossini
Figaro Sesto Bruscantini
Rosina Gianna D'Angelo
Count Almaviva Juan Oncina
Dr Bartolo Ian Wallace
Don Basilio Cristiano Dalamangas
Berta Monica Sinclair
Fiorello Gwyn Griffiths
Ambrogio Harold Williams
Officer David Kelly
Notary Daniel McCoshan
Royal Philharmonic Orchestra
Conductor Alberto Erede
Director Carl Ebert
Designer Oliver Messel

23, 25, 27, 29 Aug. 2, 7 Sep. 19.00
King's Theatre
FALSTAFF Verdi
Falstaff Fernando Corena
Alice Anna Maria Rovere
Meg Fernanda Cadoni
Mistress Quickly Oralia Dominguez
Nanetta Eugenia Ratti
Ford Walter Monachesi
Fenton Juan Oncina
Kevin Miller
Dr Caius Dermot Troy
Bardolph Daniel McCoshan
Pistol Marco Stefanoni
Innkeeper Harold Williams
Royal Philharmonic Orchestra
Conductor Carlo Maria Giulini
Director Carl Ebert
Designer Osbert Lancaster

30 Aug. 1, 3, 5, 8, 10 Sep. 19.00
King's Theatre
LA FORZA DEL DESTINO Verdi
Leonora Sena Jurinac
Don Alvaro David Poleri
Don Carlo Marko Rothmüller
Preziosilla Marina de Gabarain
Padre Guardiano Hervey Alan
Fra Melitone Ian Wallace
Marchese di Calatrava David Kelly
Curra Monica Sinclair
Trabuco John Carolan
Alcade James Atkins
Surgeon Niven Miller
Royal Philharmonic Orchestra
Conductor John Pritchard
Director Peter Ebert
Designer Leslie Hurry

ORCHESTRAL CONCERTS

BERLIN PHILHARMONIC ORCHESTRA
21 Aug. 20.15 *Usher Hall*
Brahms Academic festival overture
Beethoven Concerto for piano no.4 in G, op.58
Franck Symphony in D minor
Conductor Eugene Ormandy
Soloist Solomon (pf)

22 Aug. 20.00 *Usher Hall*
Egk French suite
Mozart Concerto for clarinet in A, K622
Tchaikovsky Symphony no.4 in F minor, op.36
Conductor Wolfgang Sawallisch
Soloist Reginald Kell (cl)

23 Aug. 20.00 *Usher Hall*
Prokofiev Symphony no.1 in D (Classical), op.25
Brahms Concerto for violin in D, op.77
Stravinsky Petrushka: Scenes 1, 2 *and* 4
Ravel La valse
Conductor Eugene Ormandy
Soloist Zino Francescatti (vn)

24 Aug. 20.00 *Usher Hall*
Bach Suite no.4 in D
Hindemith Concerto for cello
Brahms Variations on a theme by Haydn (St.Antoni), op.56a
Hindemith Concert music, op.50
Conductor Paul Hindemith
Soloist Enrico Mainardi (vc)

26 Aug. 20.00 *Usher Hall*
Haydn Symphony no.94 in G (Surprise)
Bartók Concerto for piano no.2
Schumann Symphony no.4 in D minor, op.120
Conductor Joseph Keilberth
Soloist Géza Anda (pf)

27 Aug. 20.00 *Usher Hall*
Weber Euryanthe: Overture
Mahler Lieder eines fahrenden Gesellen
Martin Six monologues from 'Jedermann'
Beethoven Symphony no.3 in E flat (Eroica), op.55
Conductor Joseph Keilberth
Soloist Dietrich Fischer-Dieskau (bar)

I MUSICI
22 Aug. 11.00 *Freemasons' Hall*
Pergolesi Concertino no.1 in G
Vivaldi Concerto for strings in A
Vivaldi Concerto for 3 violins in F
Leo Concerto for cello in D
Rossini Sonata for strings no.3 in C

23 Aug. 11.00 *Freemasons' Hall*
Corelli Concerto grosso in D, op.6/4
Giordani Concerto for piano in C
Vivaldi Concerti, op.8: nos.1-4 (The four seasons)

24 Aug. 11.00 *Freemasons' Hall*
Torelli Concerto for 2 violins
Vivaldi Concerto for violin in B flat
Marcello Introduction, aria and presto
Marcello Concerto grosso*
[Change of programme]

SCOTTISH NATIONAL ORCHESTRA
Conductor Karl Rankl
28 Aug. 20.00 *Usher Hall*
Beethoven The consecration of the house - Overture
Beethoven Concerto for violin, cello and piano in C, op.56
Dvořák Symphony no.7 in D minor, op.70
Soloists Solomon (pf), Zino Francescatti (vn), Pierre Fournier (vc)

4 Sep. 20.00 *Usher Hall*
Smetana The bartered bride: Overture
Dvořák Concerto for cello in B minor, op.104
Brahms Symphony no.3 in F, op.90
Soloist Pierre Fournier (vc)

BBC SYMPHONY ORCHESTRA
Conductor Sir Malcolm Sargent
29 Aug. 20.00 *Usher Hall*
Elgar Symphony no.2 in E flat, op.63
Walton Belshazzar's feast
Soloist Dietrich Fischer-Dieskau (bar)
Edinburgh Royal Choral Union

30 Aug. 20.00 *Usher Hall*
Bach Suite no.3 in D
Brahms Concerto for violin and cello in A minor, op.102
Shostakovich Symphony no.10 in E minor, op.93
Soloists Zino Francescatti (vn), Pierre Fournier (vc)

31 Aug. 20.00 *Usher Hall*
Sibelius Symphony no.3 in C, op.52
Castelnuovo-Tedesco Concerto for guitar no.1, op.99
Beethoven Symphony no.5 in C minor, op.67
Soloist Segovia (gtr)

NETHERLANDS CHAMBER ORCHESTRA
Conductor and soloist Szymon Goldberg
2 Sep. 20.00 *Usher Hall*
Bach Concerto for violin in E
Bach Brandenburg concerto no.5 in D
Bach Brandenburg concerto no.6 in B flat
Bach Brandenburg concerto no.1 in F

4 Sep. 14.30 *Usher Hall*
Bach Brandenburg concerto no.3 in G
Bach Brandenburg concerto no.4 in G
Bach Concerto for piano in D minor
Bach Brandenburg concerto no.2 in F
Soloist Rosalyn Tureck (pf)

NATIONAL YOUTH ORCHESTRA OF WALES
3 Sep. 14.30 *Usher Hall*
Humperdinck Hänsel und Gretel: Overture
Beethoven Ah! perfido
Dvořák Symphony no.9 in E minor (New World), op.95
G. Williams Penillion (Composed for visit to EIF)
Massenet Le Cid: Ballet music
Conductor Clarence Raybould
Soloist Joan Davies (sop)

NEW YORK PHILHARMONIC ORCHESTRA
5 Sep. 20.00 *Usher Hall*
Gould Show piece
Beethoven Concerto for piano no.3 in C minor, op.37
V. Williams Symphony no.4 in F minor
Conductor Dimitri Mitropoulos
Soloist Myra Hess (pf)

6 Sep. 20.00 *Usher Hall*
Rossini L'assedio di Corinto: Overture
Brahms Symphony no.1 in C minor, op.68
Debussy Nocturnes: Nuages *and* Fêtes
Ravel Daphnis et Chloë - Suite no.2
Conductor Guido Cantelli

7 Sep. 20.00 *Usher Hall*
Barber Adagio for strings, op.11
Beethoven Symphony no.7 in A, op.92
Copland El salón México
Mussorgsky Pictures at an exhibition; orch. Ravel
Conductor Guido Cantelli

8 Sep. 20.00 *Usher Hall*
Brahms Symphony no.4 in E minor, op.98
Brahms Concerto for piano no.1 in D minor, op.15
Conductor George Szell
Soloist Clifford Curzon (pf)

9 Sep. 20.00 *Usher Hall*
Wagner Die Meistersinger: Prelude
Wagner Siegfried idyll
Wagner Lohengrin: Prelude

Wagner Rienzi: Overture
Sibelius Symphony no.2 in D, op.43
Conductor George Szell

10 Sep. 19.30 *Usher Hall*
Weber Der Freischütz: Overture
Mendelssohn Symphony no.5 in D (Reformation), op.107
Skalkottas Five Greek dances
Brahms Symphony no.2 in D, op.73
Conductor Dimitri Mitropoulos

LONDON BAROQUE ENSEMBLE
Conductor Karl Haas
8 Sep. 11.00 *Freemasons' Hall*
R. Strauss Serenade for 13 wind instruments
C.P.E. Bach Sonata for wind no.2 in G
C.P.E. Bach Sonata for wind no.4 in F
C.P.E. Bach Sonata for wind no.6 in A
R. Strauss Symphony for 16 wind instruments

9 Sep. 11.00 *Freemasons' Hall*
R. Strauss Suite no.1 for 13 wind instruments
C.P.E. Bach Sonata for wind no.1 in E flat
C.P.E. Bach Sonata for wind no.3 in C
C.P.E. Bach Sonata for wind no.5 in D
R. Strauss Suite no.2 for 16 wind instruments

10 Sep. 11.00 *Freemasons' Hall*
Mozart Serenade no.12 in C minor, K388
Mozart 6 Notturni for 2 sopranos and baritone, K346, K436, K437, K438, K439, K549
Mozart Serenade no.11 in E flat, K375
Soloists Anne Balfour, Emerentia Scheepers (sop), Thomas Hemsley (bar)

CHAMBER CONCERTS

FESTIVAL PIANO TRIO
Solomon, Francescatti, Fournier
25 Aug. 20.00 *Usher Hall*
Beethoven Trio for piano and strings no.1 in E flat, op.1/1
Beethoven Trio for piano and strings no.5 in D (Ghost), op.70/1
Beethoven Trio for piano and strings no.7 in B flat (Archduke), op.97

1 Sep. 20.00 *Usher Hall*
Mozart Trio for piano and strings no.3 in B flat, K502
Brahms Trio for piano and strings no.3 in C minor, op.101
Schubert Trio for piano and strings no.1 in B flat, D898

GRILLER QUARTET
with Reginald Kell (cl)
25 Aug. 11.00 *Freemasons' Hall*
Haydn Quartet in G, op.76/1
Milhaud Quartet no.1
Mozart Quintet for clarinet and strings in A, K581

26 Aug. 11.00 *Freemasons' Hall*
Haydn Quartet in D minor (Fifths), op.76/2
Brahms Quintet for clarinet and strings in B minor, op.115

27 Aug. 11.00 *Freemasons' Hall*
Haydn Quartet in C (Emperor), op.76/3
Wordsworth Quintet for clarinet and strings (World première)
Mozart Quartet no.20 in D (Hoffmeister), K499

WIGMORE ENSEMBLE
Director Geoffrey Gilbert
29 Aug. 11.00 *Freemasons' Hall*
Françaix Quintet for flute, harp and strings
Ibert Cinq pièces en trio for oboe, clarinet and bassoon
Roussel Trio for flute, viola and cello, op.40
Poulenc Sextet for piano and wind
Ravel Introduction and allegro for flute, clarinet, harp and strings

30 Aug. 11.00 *Freemasons' Hall*
Beethoven Septet, op.20
Ferguson Octet, op.4

31 Aug. 11.00 *Freemasons' Hall*
Malipiero Sonata à cinque for flute, harp and strings
Mozart Quintet for piano and wind in E flat, K452
Debussy Sonata for flute, viola and harp
Damase Theme and 17 variations

NEW EDINBURGH QUARTET
2 Sep. 11.00 *Freemasons' Hall*
Haydn Quartet in G, op.54/1
R. Crawford Quartet, op.4
Dvořák Quartet no.10 in E flat, op.51

HUNGARIAN QUARTET
5 Sep. 11.00 *Freemasons' Hall*
Beethoven Quartet no.7 in F (Rasumovsky), op.59/1
Bartók Quartet no.4

6 Sep. 11.00 *Freemasons' Hall*
Beethoven Quartet no.8 in E minor (Rasumovsky), op.59/2
Bartók Quartet no.5

7 Sep. 11.00 *Freemasons' Hall*
Bartók Quartet no.6
Beethoven Quartet no.9 in C (Rasumovsky), op.59/3

SALTIRE SINGERS
4 Sep. 15.00 *Freemasons' Hall*
Anon. Musica Scotica: 6 songs
Buxtehude Jesu, meine Freude
Handel Look down, harmonious saint
Schütz Der zwölfjährige Jesus im Tempel
Musgrave Cantata for a summer's day
Conductor Hans Oppenheim
Soloists Sebastian Forbes (boy sop), Bryden Murdoch (rdr), Thea Musgrave (martinette organ), New Edinburgh Quartet, Royal Philharmonic Orchestra members

RECITALS

GÉRARD SOUZAY (bar)
DALTON BALDWIN (pf)
25 Aug. 20.00 *Freemasons' Hall*
Songs by Lully, Fauré, Duparc, Debussy, Roussel, Ravel

DIETRICH FISCHER-DIESKAU (bar)
GERALD MOORE (pf)
31 Aug. 20.00 *Freemasons' Hall*
Songs by Brahms

2 Sep. 20.00 *Freemasons' Hall*
Schubert Schwanengesang: 6 Heine Lieder
Schumann Dichterliebe

JENNIE TOUREL (mez)
GEORGE REEVES (pf)
4 Sep. 20.00 *Freemasons' Hall*
Songs by Torelli, A. Scarlatti, Rossini, Debussy, Schubert, Brahms, Offenbach, Tchaikovsky, Gretchaninov, Dargomizhsky

7 Sep. 20.00 *Freemasons' Hall*
Songs and arias by Monteverdi, Chelleri, Duparc, Ravel, Debussy, Mahler, R. Strauss, Tchaikovsky, Mussorgsky, Villa-Lobos, Guarnieri, Offenbach

GÉZA ANDA (pf)
23 Aug. 20.00 *Freemasons' Hall*
Beethoven Sonata no.7 in D, op.10/3
Schumann Études symphoniques, op.13
Bartók Suite for piano
Brahms Variations on a theme by Paganini

ROSALYN TURECK (pf)
1 Sep. 11.00 *Freemasons' Hall*
Bach Goldberg variations

SOLOMON (pf)
3 Sep. 20.00 *Usher Hall*
Bach Concerto in the Italian style
Brahms Intermezzo in E flat minor, op.118/6
Brahms Intermezzo in E, op.116/4
Brahms Intermezzo in C, op.119/3
Beethoven Sonata no.28 in A, op.101
Chopin Ballade no.4 in F minor, op.52
Chopin Nocturne no.1 in B flat minor, op.9/1
Debussy Preludes: Général Lavine - eccentric; La cathédrale engloutie
Debussy L'isle joyeuse

RALPH KIRKPATRICK (hpd)
3 Sep. 11.00 *Freemasons' Hall*
Sonatas by D. Scarlatti

SEGOVIA (gtr)
28 Aug. 15.00 *Freemasons' Hall*
Guitar works by Galilei, Visée, Bach, Schubert, Tansman, Villa-Lobos, Castelnuovo-Tedesco, Granados, Albeniz

DRAMA

TENNENT PRODUCTIONS LTD
22 Aug.-10 Sep. 19.15 (exc.Sun) 23, 27, 30 Aug. 3, 6, 10 Sep.14.15 Assembly Hall
A LIFE IN THE SUN Wilder
(EIF commission)
Alcestis Irene Worth
Admetus Robert Hardy
Aglaia Madeleine Christie
Teiresias Geoffrey Dunn
Hercules Rupert Davies
Cheriander Michael Bates
Epimenes Alexander Davion
King Agis Robert Speaight
1st Watchman Laurence Hardy
2nd Watchman Peter Bayliss
Death John Kidd
Apollo Michael David
Boy David Gloag
Herdsmen Philip Guard, John Scholan, Peter Fox, Peter Duguid
Director Tyrone Guthrie
Designer Tanya Moiseiwitsch

OLD VIC
22 Aug.-3 Sep. 19.30 (exc.Sun) 24, 27, 31 Aug. 3 Sep. 14.30 Lyceum Theatre
JULIUS CAESAR Shakespeare
Julius Caesar Gerald Cross
Brutus Paul Rogers
Portia Wendy Hiller
Mark Antony John Neville
Cassius Richard Wordsworth

Casca Jack Gwillim
Calpurnia Rosemary Harris
Cinna the conspirator/Lepidus Dudley Jones
Cimber Harold Kasket
Cicero/Titinius Denis Holmes
Octavius Caesar John Fraser
Artemidorus/Lucilius Derek Francis
Cinna the poet/Dardanius Aubrey Morris
Decius Brutus John Wood
Marullus Charles Gray
Flavius John Woodvine
Citizen/Pindarus Clifford Williams
Soothsayer/ Clitus Job Stewart
Other parts played by David Saire, Anthony White, James Villiers, Edward Harvey, Ronald Allen, Tom Kneebone, Bryan Pringle, Keith Taylor, John Greenwood, Derry Nesbitt
Director Michael Benthall
Designer Audrey Cruddas
Music Frederick Marshall

LA COMPAGNIE EDWIGE FEUILLÈRE
5-10 Sep. 19.30 7, 10 Sep. 14.30
Lyceum Theatre
LA DAME AUX CAMÉLIAS Dumas
Marguerite Gautier Edwige Feuillère
Armand Duval Jacques Dacqmine
M. Duval Jacques Berlioz
Nanine Madeleine Clervanne
Varville Marcel Journet
Nichette Simone Matile
Valentin Jean Breck
Olympe Jacqueline Marbaux
Saint-Gaudens Maurice Varny
Prudence Charlotte Clasis
Gaston Maurice Bray
Giray Pierre Le Coq
Gustave Michel Maurette
Un commissionaire Yves Martin
Le docteur André Laurent
Anais Pierrette Tison
Arthur Yves Sergent
Esther Catherine Brieux
Un valet de pied François Ducar
Director Edwige Feuillère
Designer Bernard Evein

DANCE

ROYAL DANISH BALLET
23-25 Aug. 19.30 24 Aug. 14.30
Empire Theatre
LA SYLPHIDE
Choreographer August Bournonville
Music Løvenskjold
CAPRICIOUS LUCINDA
Choreographer Niels Bjørn Larsen
Music Jørgen Jersild
Designer Helge Refn

26-29 Aug. 19.30 27 Aug. 14.30
Empire Theatre
ROMEO AND JULIET
Choreographer Frederick Ashton
Music Prokofiev
Designer Peter Rice

30 Aug.-1 Sep. 19.30 31 Aug. 14.30
Empire Theatre
NAPOLI: Act 3
Choreographer August Bournonville
Music Paulli, Helsted, Gade, Lumbye
GRADUATION BALL
Choreographer David Lichine
Music J. Strauss; arr. Dorati
Designer Ove Christian Pedersen

2, 3 Sep. 14.30 and 19.30 Empire Theatre
THE WHIMS OF CUPID AND THE BALLET MASTER
Choreographer Vincenzo Galeotti
Music Jens Lolle
Designer Ove Christian Pedersen
LA SYLPHIDE
NAPOLI: Act 3
Dancers Gerda Karstens, Mona Vangsaae, Borge Ralov, Kirsten Ralov, Margrethe Schanne, Inge Sand, Svend Erik Jensen, Hans Brenaa, Frank Schaufuss, Stanley Williams, Fredbjørn Bjørnsson, Erik Bruhn, Henning Kronstam, Niels Bjørn Larsen
Scottish National Orchestra
Conductors Johan Hye-Knudsen, Henrik Sachsenskjold

AZUMA KABUKI DANCERS AND MUSICIANS
5-7 Sep. 19.30 7 Sep. 14.30
Empire Theatre
Programme 1

8-10 Sep. 19.30 10 Sep. 14.30
Empire Theatre
Programme 2
Choreographer Masaya Fujima
Scenery Motohiro Nagasaka
Costumes Seison Maeda, Kiyokata Kaburagi
Dancers Tsurunosuke Bando, Tokuho Azuma, Masaya Fujima, Shusai Fujima, Mitsuemon Bando, Umesuke Onoe, Haruyo Azuma, Tomiko Azuma, Yukiko Azuma, Keiko Bando, Setsuko Bando, Kanchie Fujima, Wakana Hanayagi and Musicians
Musical director Katsusaburo Kineya

EXHIBITIONS

Royal Scottish Academy
GAUGUIN
Director Douglas Cooper
(In association with the Royal Scottish Academy and the Arts Council of Great Britain)

1956

OPERA

HAMBURG STATE OPERA
20, 22, 24, 27, 29, 31 Aug. 3 Sep. 19.00
King's Theatre
DIE ZAUBERFLÖTE Mozart
Tamino Rudolf Schock, Heinz Hoppe
Pamina Elisabeth Grümmer, Anny Schlemm
Papageno Horst Günter
Sarastro Arnold van Mill
Queen of the Night Colette Lorand
Speaker James Pease
1st Lady Oda Balsborg
2nd Lady Margarete Ast
3rd Lady Gisela Litz
Papagena Anneliese Rothenberger, Erna Maria Duske
Monostatos Kurt Marschner
3 Boys Christian Fischer, Gerd Mathieu, Harry Reichenberg
2 Armed men Jürgen Förster, Jean Pfendt
2 Priests Peter Markwort, Georg Mund
Conductor Rudolf Kempe
Director Günther Rennert
Designer Ita Maximowna

21, 28 Aug. 5 Sep. 19.00 King's Theatre
OEDIPUS REX Stravinsky
Oedipus Helmut Melchert
Jocasta Maria von Ilosvay
Creon James Pease
Tiresias Arnold van Mill
Shepherd Fritz Lehnert
Messenger Caspar Bröcheler
Narrator Gerard Slevin
MAVRA Stravinsky
Paracha Melitta Muszely
Neighbour Margarete Ast
Mother Gisela Litz
Hussar Jürgen Förster
Conductor Leopold Ludwig
Director Günther Rennert
Designer Teo Otto

23, 25 Aug. 7 Sep. 19.00 King's Theatre
DER BARBIER VON BAGDAD Cornelius
Caliph Georg Mund
Baba Mustapha Kurt Marschner
Margiana Melitta Muszely
Bostana Gisela Litz
Nureddin Sándor Kónya, Heinz Hoppe
Abul Hassan Ali Ebn Bekar Arnold van Mill
Slave Jürgen Förster
Conductor Albert Bittner
Director Günther Rennert
Designer Alfred Siercke

30 Aug. 1, 4, 6, 8 Sep. 19.00
King's Theatre
SALOME R. Strauss
Salome Helga Pilarczyk, Inge Borkh*
Jokanaan Caspar Bröcheler, Josef Metternich
Herod Peter Markwort, Helmut Melchert
Herodias Siw Ericsdotter
Narraboth Fritz Lehnert
Page Margarete Ast
5 Jews Kurt Marschner, Jürgen Förster, Hans Böhm, Victor Gawlitzek, Karl Ott
2 Nazarenes Arnold van Mill, Erich Zimmermann
2 Soldiers Horst Günter, Jean Pfendt
Cappadocian Georg Mund
Slave Werner Hecker
Conductor Leopold Ludwig
Director Wolf Völker
Designer Alfred Siercke

ORCHESTRAL CONCERTS

ROYAL PHILHARMONIC ORCHESTRA
Conductor Sir Thomas Beecham
19 Aug. 20.00 Usher Hall
Elgar *arr.* National anthem
Beethoven Symphony no.9 in D minor (Choral), op.125
Soloists Sylvia Fisher (sop), Nan Merriman (mez), Richard Lewis (ten), Kim Borg (bs), Edinburgh Royal Choral Union

20 Aug. 20.00 Usher Hall
Bliss Edinburgh: Overture (Presented by the composer on the 10th anniversary of the EIF)+
Bliss Concerto for violin+
Brahms Symphony no.2 in D, op.73
Conductor Sir Arthur Bliss+
Soloist Alfredo Campoli (vn)

22 Aug. 20.00 Usher Hall
R. Strauss Don Quixote
Berlioz Harold in Italy
Soloists Frederick Riddle (va), John Kennedy (vc)

23 Aug. 20.00 *Usher Hall*
Boccherini Overture in D
Grétry Zémire et Azor - Suite; arr. Beecham
Beethoven Concerto for piano no.4 in G, op.58
Balakirev Symphony no.1 in C
Soloist Robert Casadesus (pf)

24 Aug. 20.00 *Usher Hall*
Schubert Symphony no.6 in C, D589
Delius In a summer garden
Arnell Landscapes and figures (World première)
Sibelius Symphony no.6 in D minor, op.104
Berlioz Waverley - Overture

BBC SCOTTISH ORCHESTRA
21 Aug. 14.30 *Usher Hall*
Fauré Masques et bergamasques
Dohnányi Variations on a nursery theme
Smetana Ma vlast: Vltava
Bizet Symphony in C
Conductor Ian Whyte
Soloist Ernst von Dohnányi (pf)

SCOTTISH NATIONAL ORCHESTRA
Conductor Karl Rankl
25 Aug. 20.00 *Usher Hall*
Schumann Genoveva: Overture
Bartók Concerto for violin no.2
Dvořák Symphony no.9 in E minor (New World), op.95
Soloist Isaac Stern (vn)

1 Sep. 20.00 *Usher Hall*
Rossini La gazza ladra: Overture
Mozart Concerto for piano no.21 in C, K467
Bruckner Symphony no.4 in E flat (Romantic)
Soloist Myra Hess (pf)

BOSTON SYMPHONY ORCHESTRA
26 Aug. 20.00 *Usher Hall*
Haydn Symphony no.102 in B flat
Piston Symphony no.6
R. Strauss Don Juan
Dukas L'apprenti sorcier
Conductor Charles Münch

27 Aug. 20.00 *Usher Hall*
Creston Symphony no.2, op.35
Bartók Concerto for orchestra
Schubert Symphony no.9 in C (Great), D944
Conductor Pierre Monteux

28 Aug. 20.00 *Usher Hall*
Copland Symphonic ode (rev. version)
Beethoven Concerto for violin in D, op.61
Schumann Symphony no.2 in C, op.61
Conductor Charles Münch
Soloist Isaac Stern (vn)

29 Aug. 20.00 *Usher Hall*
Freed Festival overture
Brahms Symphony no.3 in F, op.90
Franck Symphonic variations, op.56
Ravel Concerto for piano (Left hand)
R. Strauss Der Rosenkavalier - Suite
Conductor Pierre Monteux
Soloist Robert Casadesus (pf)

30 Aug. 20.00 *Usher Hall*
Homage to Koussevitzky
Hanson Elegy in memory of Koussevitzky
Schumann Concerto for piano in A minor, op.54
Honegger Symphony no.5 (Di tre re)
Debussy La mer
Conductor Charles Münch
Soloist Clifford Curzon (pf)

NATIONAL YOUTH ORCHESTRA OF GREAT BRITAIN
31 Aug. 20.00 *Usher Hall*
Berlioz Le corsaire - Overture
Haydn Sinfonia concertante in B flat, op.84
Frankel A Shakespeare overture (World première)
Beethoven Symphony no.5 in C minor, op.67
Conductor Walter Susskind

LONDON MOZART PLAYERS
Conductor Harry Blech
2 Sep. 20.00 *Usher Hall*
Haydn Symphony no.48 in C (Maria Theresia)
Mozart Concerto for piano no.27 in B flat, K595
Bartók Divertimento for strings
Schubert Symphony no.3 in D, D200
Soloist Robert Casadesus (pf)

3 Sep. 20.00 *Usher Hall*
Haydn Symphony no.103 in E flat (Drumroll)
Mozart Concerto for violin no.4 in D, K218
Mozart Il rè pastore: L'amerò sarò costante
Mozart Mass no.18 in C minor (Great), K427: Et incarnatus est
Beethoven Symphony no.2 in D, op.36
Soloists Irmgard Seefried (sop), Wolfgang Schneiderhan (vn)

4 Sep. 20.00 *Usher Hall*
Haydn Symphony no.85 in B flat (La reine)
Mozart Sinfonia concertante for violin and viola, K364
Mozart Concerto for oboe in C, K314
Arriaga Symphony in D minor
Soloists Leon Goossens (ob), Norbert Brainin (vn), Peter Schidlof (va)

VIENNA HOFMUSIKKAPELLE
Conductor Rudolf Moralt
6 Sep. 20.00 *Usher Hall*
Mozart Mass no.16 in C (Coronation), K317
Mozart Ave verum corpus
Mozart Requiem, K626
Soloists Richard Lewis (ten), Oscar Czerwenka (bs)

7 Sep. 20.00 *Usher Hall*
Schubert Offertorium 'Tres sunt'
Schubert Auguste jam coelestium
Schubert Magnificat in C, D486
Schubert Mass no.6 in E flat, D950
Soloists Richard Lewis (ten), Oscar Czerwenka (bs)

8 Sep. 19.30 *Usher Hall*
Beethoven Fantasia for piano, chorus and orchestra, op.80
Beethoven Mass in C, op.86
Soloists Richard Lewis (ten), Oscar Czerwenka (bs), Carl Seemann (pf)

CHAMBER CONCERTS

MELOS ENSEMBLE
20 Aug. 11.00 *Freemasons' Hall*
Schoenberg Pierrot lunaire
Walton Facade
Conductor and soloist Peter Stadlen (pf)
Soloists Hedli Anderson (sop), Dame Edith Sitwell (narr)

21 Aug. 11.00 *Freemasons' Hall*
Beethoven Trio no.2 in G, op.9/1
Bliss Quintet for clarinet and strings
Mozart Quartet for flute and strings no.1 in D, K285

NEW EDINBURGH QUARTET
23 Aug. 11.00 *Freemasons' Hall*
Beethoven Quartet no.1 in F, op.18/1
Dohnányi Quintet for piano and strings no.2 in E flat minor, op.26
with Ernst von Dohnányi (pf)

BOSTON BRASS ENSEMBLE
28 Aug. 11.00 *Freemasons' Hall*
Gabrieli Canzona septimi toni no.1
Bonelli Toccata
Poulenc Sonata for horn, trumpet and trombone
Sanders Quintet in B flat
Berezowsky Brass suite for 7 instruments
Director Roger Voisin

AMADEUS QUARTET
30 Aug. 11.00 *Freemasons' Hall*
Mozart Quintet no. 5 in D, K593
Mozart Quintet no.3 in G minor, K516
with Cecil Aronowitz (va)

31 Aug. 11.00 *Freemasons' Hall*
Haydn Quartet in G, op.77/1
Beethoven Quintet in C, op.29
with Cecil Aronowitz (va)

1 Sep. 11.00 *Freemasons' Hall*
Mozart Quartet for oboe and strings in F, K370
Mozart Divertimento in E flat, K563
with Leon Goossens (ob)

2 Sep. 20.00 *Freemasons' Hall*
Haydn Quartet in C, op.74/1
Schubert Quartet no.13 in A minor, D804
Beethoven Quartet no.12 in E flat, op.127

VEGH QUARTET
6 Sep. 11.00 *Freemasons' Hall*
Bartók Quartet no.5
Ravel Quartet in F

8 Sep. 11.00 *Freemasons' Hall*
Seiber Quartet no.3 (Quartetto lirico)
Beethoven Quartet no.7 in F (Rasumovsky), op.59/1

RENAISSANCE SINGERS
Director Michael Howard
24 Aug. 20.00 *Freemasons' Hall*
Palestrina Missa Papae Marcelli
Palestrina Exaltabo te
Palestrina Sicut cervus
Palestrina O salutaris hostia
Palestrina Tantum ergo sacramentum
Palestrina Stabat Mater

25 Aug. 11.00 *Freemasons' Hall*
Taverner Mass 'Small devotion'
Anon. (?Carver) Mass 'Rex virginum':Kyrie
R. Johnson Deus misereatur
D. Peebles Quam multi, domine
A. Blackhall Of mercy and of judgement both
Anon. Psalms 18 and 113 (in Reports)
Anon. Mass 'Felix namque': Kyrie *and* Gloria

EDINBURGH UNIVERSITY SINGERS
4 Sep. 11.00 *Freemasons' Hall*
Choral music by Byrd, Josquin d'Ascanio, Josquin Desprez, Passereau, Bach, Kodály, V. Williams, Walton, Britten
Director Herrick Bunney

RECITALS

GERHARD HÜSCH (bar)
GERALD MOORE (pf)
27 Aug. 15.00 *Freemasons' Hall*
Songs by Schubert, Brahms, Wolf, Kilpinen

JOAN ALEXANDER (sop)
ERNEST LUSH (pf)
31 Aug. 15.00 *Freemasons' Hall*
Songs by Cornelius, Brahms, Schubert

IRMGARD SEEFRIED (sop)
ERIK WERBA (pf)
2 Sep.15.00 7 Sep. 20.00
Freemasons' Hall
Songs by Mozart, Schumann, Wolf, Egk

IRMGARD SEEFRIED (sop),
WOLFGANG SCHNEIDERHAN (vn),
ERIK WERBA, CARL SEEMANN (pf)
5 Sep. 20.00 *Usher Hall*
Schumann Sonata no.1 in A minor, op.105
Schumann Frauenliebe und -leben
Brahms Sonata no.3 in D minor, op.108
Brahms Songs

ROSALYN TURECK (pf)
22 Aug. 11.00 *Freemasons' Hall*
Bach Partitas nos.1, 2, 6

23 Aug. 15.00 *Freemasons' Hall*
Bach Partitas nos.3-5

NINA MILKINA (f-pf, pf)
24 Aug. 11.00 *Freemasons' Hall*
Mozart Variations in F on an allegretto, K547a
Mozart Sonata no.1 in C, K279
Mozart Sonata no.8 in A minor, K310
Mozart Adagio in B minor, K540
Mozart Sonata no.18 in D, K576

MYRA HESS (pf)
26 Aug. 14.30 *Usher Hall*
Beethoven Sonata no.30 in E, op.109
Beethoven Sonata no.31 in A flat, op.110
Beethoven Sonata no.32 in C minor, op.111

29 Aug. 11.00 *Freemasons' Hall*
Beethoven Variations on an original theme in F, op.34
Beethoven Sonata no.7 in D, op.10/3
Beethoven Sonata no.23 in F minor (Appassionata), op.57

ROBERT CASADESUS (pf)
27 Aug. 11.00 *Freemasons' Hall*
Schumann Fantasia in C, op.17
Schumann Waldszenen
Schumann Études symphoniques, op.13

CLIFFORD CURZON (pf)
3 Sep. 11.00 *Freemasons' Hall*
Schubert Fantasia in C (Wanderer), D760
Schubert Impromptus, D935
Schubert Sonata no.17 in D, D850

LOUIS KENTNER (pf)
5 Sep. 11.00 *Freemasons' Hall*
Piano works by Liszt

ALFREDO CAMPOLI (vn)
ERNST VON DOHNÁNYI (pf)
26 Aug. 20.00 *Freemasons' Hall*
Mozart Sonata no.35 in A, K526
Dohnányi Sonata in C sharp minor, op.21
Dohnányi Six pieces for piano, op.41
Dohnányi Ruralia Hungarica

ISAAC STERN (vn)
ALEXANDER ZAKIN (pf)
1 Sep. 14.30 *Usher Hall*
Brahms Sonata no.1 in G, op.78
Prokofiev Sonata no.1 in F minor, op.80
Franck Sonata in A

WOLFGANG SCHNEIDERHAN (vn)
CARL SEEMANN (pf)
7 Sep. 11.00 *Freemasons' Hall*
Mozart Sonata no.32 in B flat, K454
Mozart Sonata no.28 in E flat, K380
Mozart Sonata no.24 in F, K376
Mozart Sonata no.23 in D, K306

SEBASTIAN SHAW (rdr)
NINA MILKINA (pf)
21 Aug. 20.00 *Freemasons' Hall*
R. Strauss Enoch Arden (Tennyson)

DRAMA

STRATFORD ONTARIO FESTIVAL COMPANY
28, 29, 30, 31 Aug. 1, 4, 6, 8 Sep. 19.30
30 Aug. 1, 4, 8 Sep. 14.30 Assembly Hall
HENRY V Shakespeare
Henry V Christopher Plummer
Chorus William Needles
Duke of Gloucester William Shatner
Duke of Bedford Grant Reddick
Duke of Exeter Robert Goodier
Earl of Salisbury/Bardolph Anthony van Bridge
Earl of Westmorland Donald Davis
Archbishop of Canterbury William Hutt
Bishop of Ely Robert Christie
Earl of Cambridge/Bates Bruce Swerdfager
Lord Scroop/Court Richard Easton
Sir Thomas Grey Max Helpmann
Sir Thomas Erpingham Robert Christie
Gower David Gardner
Fluellen Eric House
MacMorris Ted Follows
Jamy Roland Hewgill
Williams Douglas Rain
Pistol Douglas Campbell
Nym Bruno Gerussi
Charles VI Gratien Gelinas
Dauphin Roger Garceau
Duke of Burgundy Lloyd Bochner
Duke of Orleans Jean Louis Roux
Duke of Bourbon Gabriel Gascon
Constable of France Jean Gascon
Montjoy Jean Coutu
Governor of Harfleur Guy Hoffman
Queen Isabel Eleanor Stuart
Katharine Ginette Letondal
Alice Germaine Giroux
Mistress Quickly Helene Winston
Boy Robin Gammell
Bretagne Aime Major
Director Michael Langham
Designer Tania Moiseiwitsch
Music Louis Applebaum

3, 5, 7 Sep. 19.30 6 Sep. 14.30
Assembly Hall
OEDIPUS REX Sophocles
(Eng. Translated by W.B. Yeats)
Oedipus Douglas Campbell
Jocasta Eleanor Stuart
Creon Robert Goodier
Tiresias Donald Davis
Shepherd/Priest Eric House
Messenger Douglas Rain
Man from Corinth Anthony van Bridge
Ismene Amelia Hall
Antigone Lois Shaw
Nurse Sharon Acker
Leader of the chorus William Hutt
Chorus Members of the Company
Director Tyrone Guthrie
Designer Tania Moiseiwitsch
Music Cedric Thorpe Davie

TENNENT PRODUCTIONS LTD
21-25 Aug. 19.30 22, 23, 25 Aug. 14.30
Lyceum Theatre
UNDER MILK WOOD Thomas
(1st professional stage production)
Actors Donald Houston, Diana Maddox, Jessie Evans, Joan Newell, Betty Lloyd Davies, Peter Halliday, John Gill, Gareth Jones, Cliff Gordon, Patricia Mort, Gwyneth Owen, William Squire, Raymond Llewellyn, Catherine Dolan, Richard Curnock, David Rees, Aubrey Richards, Peter Murphy, Buddug-Mair Powell, Claudine Morgan, Daphne Shaven, T.H. Evans, Dorothea Phillips, Denys Graham, Barbara Alleyn, Angela Crow, Margot Jenkins, Judy Manning, Virginia Graham
Directors Douglas Cleverdon, Edward Burnham
Designer Michael Trangmar

PICCOLO TEATRO, Milan
27-29 Aug. 19.30 29 Aug. 14.30
Lyceum Theatre
ARLECCHINO Goldoni
Arlecchino Marcello Moretti
Pantalone Antonio Battistella
Clarice Relda Ridoni
Dr Lombardi Checco Rissone
Silvio Giulio Chazalettes
Beatrice Valentina Fortunato
Florindo Aretusi Tino Carraro
Brighella Gianfranco Mauri
Smeraldina Marina Bonfigli
Waiters Franco Graziosi, Raoul Consonni, Ezio Marano
Porter Ottavio Fanfani
Director Giorgio Strehler
Designer Ezio Frigerio
Music Fiorenzo Carpi

30 Aug.-1 Sep. 19.30 1 Sep. 14.30
Lyceum Theatre
QUESTA SERA SI RECITA A SOGGETTO (Tonight we improvise)
Pirandello
Dr Hinkfuss Marcello Moretti
Heavy woman (Ignazia) Giuso Dandolo
Low comedian (Palmiro) Antonio Battistella
Mommina Valentina Fortunato
Totina Relda Ridoni
Dorina Gabriella Giacobbe
Nenè Ornella Vanoni
Leading man (Rico Verri) Tino Carraro
Sarelli Ottavio Fanfani
Pomarici Enzo Tarascio
Nardi Franco Graziosi
Mangini Giulio Chazalettes
Pometti Ezio Marano
Chanteuse Marina Bonfigli
Customers Checco Rissone, Andrea Matteuzzi, Gianfranco Mauri, Raoul Consonni
Director Giorgio Strehler
Scenery Luciano Damiani
Costumes Ezio Frigerio
Music Gino Neri

HENRY SHEREK
3-8 Sep. 19.30 5, 8 Sep. 14.30
Lyceum Theatre
VILLAGE WOOING Shaw
Z Brenda Bruce
A Michael Denison
Director Roy Rich
Designer Finlay James

FANNY'S FIRST PLAY Shaw
Fanny/Margaret Knox Jacqueline Mackenzie
Mr Gilbey George Benson
Mrs Gilbey Lally Bowers
Juggins Robin Bailey
Dora Delaney Brenda Bruce
Mrs Knox Jean Taylor Smith
Mr Knox Michael O'Halloran
M. Duvallet Michael Denison
Bobby Gilbey David Evans
Director Douglas Seale
Designer Finlay James

GATEWAY COMPANY
20 Aug.-8 Sep. 19.30 (exc.Sun) 23, 25, 30 Aug. 1, 6, 8 Sep. 14.30
Gateway Theatre
THE ANATOMIST Bridie
Dr Knox Tom Fleming
Mary Dishart Mary Helen Donald
Amelia Dishart Lennox Milne
Walter Anderson Michael Elder
Jessie Ann Sheila Donald
Raby Norman Fraser
Landlord John Young
Mary Paterson Marillyn Gray
Janet Marion Wishart
Davie Paterson George Davies
Burke Brian Carey
Hare Roddy McMillan
Director James Gibson
Designer Peter Norris

EDINBURGH INTERNATIONAL FESTIVAL
20-25 Aug. 19.30 21, 25 Aug. 14.30
Assembly Hall
PLEASURE OF SCOTLAND
An entertainment of traditional Scottish dancing, singing and piping devised by George Scott Moncrieff
Jameson Clark, Mary O'Hara, Joan Mackenzie, John Burgess, Jeannie Robertson, James Campbell, Jack Johnstone, Festival Chorus
Director Anthony Besch
Designer Molly MacEwen
Music arrangements Francis Collinson

DANCE

SADLER'S WELLS BALLET
20-22 Aug. 19.30 22 Aug. 14.30
Empire Theatre
THE LADY AND THE FOOL
Choreographer John Cranko
Music Verdi; arr. Mackerras
Designer Richard Beer
NOCTAMBULES
Choreographer Kenneth MacMillan
Music Searle
Designer Nicholas Georgiadis
BIRTHDAY OFFERING
Choreographer Frederick Ashton
Music Glazunov; arr. Irving
Designer André Levasseur

23-25 Aug. 19.30 25 Aug. 14.30
Empire Theatre
COPPÉLIA
Choreographer Ivanov *and* Cecchetti
Music Delibes
Designer Osbert Lancaster

27, 28 Aug. 19.30 *Empire Theatre*
THE MIRACULOUS MANDARIN (World première)
Choreographer Alfred Rodrigues
Music Bartók
Designer Georges Wakhevitch

LES SYLPHIDES
Choreographer Mikhail Fokine
Music Chopin; arr. Douglas
Designer *after* Benois
HOMAGE TO THE QUEEN
Choreographer Frederick Ashton
Music Arnold
Designer Oliver Messel

29 Aug. 14.30 *Empire Theatre*
LES SYLPHIDES
HOMAGE TO THE QUEEN
COPPÉLIA: Act 3

29 Aug. 19.30 *Empire Theatre*
LES SYLPHIDES
THE MIRACULOUS MANDARIN
HOMAGE TO THE QUEEN

30 Aug.-1 Sep. 19.30 1 Sep. 14.30
Empire Theatre
SWAN LAKE
Choreographer Petipa *and* Ivanov
Music Tchaikovsky
Designer Leslie Hurry
Dancers Dame Margot Fonteyn, Beryl Grey, Nadia Nerina, Rowena Jackson, Svetlana Beriosova, Michael Somes, Brian Shaw, Alexander Grant, Philip Chatfield, David Blair, Mary Drage, Julia Farron, Elaine Fifield, Anya Linden, Rosemary Lindsay, Meriel Evans, Maryon Lane, Gerd Larsen, Annette Page, Brenda Taylor, Valerie Taylor, Bryan Ashbridge, Gary Burne, Peter Clegg, Desmond Doyle, Leslie Edwards, Ronald Hynd, Ronald Plaisted, Ray Powell, Douglas Steuart, Pirmin Trecu, Franklin White, John Hart, Alexis Rassine
Conductors Robert Irving, John Hollingsworth

RAM GOPAL INDIAN BALLET
3-5 Sep. 19.30 5 Sep. 14.30
Empire Theatre
A programme of Indian dance of the four classical schools - Bharata Natya, Kathakali, Manipuri, Kathak *and* Folk dance

6-8 Sep. 19.30 8 Sep. 14.30
Empire Theatre
THE LEGEND OF THE TAJ MAHAL (World première)
Choreographers Ram Gopal, Yogen Desai
Music Comolata Dutt
Designer Frieda Harris
Dancers Ram Gopal, Kumudini Devi, Yogen Desai, Shevanti Devi, Anura Satyavati, Yaron Yalton, Namboodri, Surendra Sinha, Satyavan, Ramanlal, Amala, with Musicians

EXHIBITIONS

Royal Scottish Academy
BRAQUE
Director Douglas Cooper
(In association with the Royal Scottish Academy and the Arts Council of Great Britain)

1957

OPERA

LA PICCOLA SCALA, Milan
19, 21, 26, 29 Aug. 3 Sep. 19.00
King's Theatre
LA SONNAMBULA Bellini
Amina Maria Callas
Renata Scotto*
Elvino Nicola Monti
Count Rodolfo Nicola Zaccaria
Teresa Fiorenza Cossotto
Lisa Greta Rapisardi
Alessio Dino Mantovani
Notary Franco Ricciardi
Conductor Antonino Votto
Director Luchino Visconti
Designer Piero Tosi

20, 22, 24, 28 Aug. 19.00
King's Theatre
IL MATRIMONIO SEGRETO Cimarosa
Carolina Graziella Sciutti
Paolino Luigi Alva
Geronimo Carlo Badioli
Elisetta Eugenia Ratti
Fidalma Gabriella Carturan
Count Robinson Franco Calabrese
Conductor Nino Sanzogno
Director Giorgio Strehler
Scenery Luciano Damiani
Costumes Ezio Frigerio

23, 27, 31 Aug. 5, 7 Sep. 19.00
King's Theatre
L'ELISIR D'AMORE Donizetti
Adina Rosanna Carteri
Renata Scotto*
Nemorino Giuseppe di Stefano
Nicola Monti*
Belcore Giulio Fioravanti
Dr Dulcamara Fernando Corena
Giannetta Greta Rapisardi
Conductor Nino Sanzogno
Director Franco Enriquez
Designer Mario Vellani Marchi

30 Aug. 2, 4, 6 Sep. 19.00
King's Theatre
IL TURCO IN ITALIA Rossini
Selim Sesto Bruscantini
Fiorilla Eugenia Ratti
Narciso Luigi Alva
Geronio Franco Calabrese
Prosdocimo Fernando Corena
Zaida Fiorenza Cossotto
Albazar Angelo Mercuriali
Conductor Gianandrea Gavazzeni
Director and designer Franco Zeffirelli

ORCHESTRAL CONCERTS

HALLÉ ORCHESTRA
Conductor Sir John Barbirolli
18 Aug. 20.00 *Usher Hall*
Elgar Centenary Programme
Cockaigne - Overture
Concerto for cello in E minor, op.85
Symphony no.1 in A flat, op.55
Soloist Janos Starker (vc)

20 Aug. 20.00 *Usher Hall*
Stravinsky Symphony of psalms
Brahms Ein deutsches Requiem
Soloists Lois Marshall (sop), Heinz Rehfuss (bar), Hallé Choir

21 Aug. 20.00 *Usher Hall*
Mozart Die Entführung aus dem Serail: Overture
Mozart Concerto for piano no.27 in B flat, K595
Mahler Symphony no.1 in D
Soloist Clara Haskil (pf)

BAVARIAN RADIO SYMPHONY ORCHESTRA
23 Aug. 20.00 *Usher Hall*
Beethoven Egmont: Overture
Beethoven Symphony no.4 in B flat, op.60
Beethoven Symphony no.3 In E flat (Eroica), op.55
Conductor Otto Klemperer

24 Aug. 20.00 *Usher Hall*
Hindemith Symphonic dances
R. Strauss Vier letzte Lieder
Brahms Symphony no.1 in C minor, op.68
Conductor Eugen Jochum
Soloist Lois Marshall (sop)

25 Aug. 20.00 *Usher Hall*
Bach Suite no.3 in D
Stravinsky Pulcinella - Suite
Brahms Symphony no.4 in E minor, op.98
Conductor Otto Klemperer

26 Aug. 20.00 *Usher Hall*
Mozart Le nozze di Figaro: Overture
Mozart Concerto for piano no.19 in F, K459
Bruckner Symphony no.7 in E
Conductor Eugen Jochum
Soloist Clara Haskil (pf)

CONVIVIUM MUSICUM
27 Aug. 20.00 *Usher Hall*
Bach Suite no.1 in C
Bach Brandenburg concerto no.5 in D
Mozart Concerto for flute and harp in C, K299
Mozart Divertimento no.11 in D, K251

SCOTTISH NATIONAL ORCHESTRA
Conductor Hans Swarowsky
28 Aug. 20.00 *Usher Hall*
Hindemith Mathis der Maler - Symphony
Berlioz Les nuits d'été
Beethoven Symphony no.7 in A, op.92
Soloist Victoria de los Angeles (sop)

1 Sep. 20.00 *Usher Hall*
Mozart Die Zauberflöte: Overture
Brahms Concerto for piano no.1 in D minor, op.15
Blacher Variations on a theme of Paganini
R. Strauss Till Eulenspiegels lustige Streiche
Soloist Rudolf Firkušný (pf)

PHILHARMONIA ORCHESTRA
29 Aug. 20.00 *Usher Hall*
Mozart Symphony no.29 in A, K201
Mahler Das Lied von der Erde
Conductor Otto Klemperer
Soloists Anton Dermota (ten), Dietrich Fischer-Dieskau (bar)

30 Aug. 20.00 *Usher Hall*
Dvořák Symphonic variations, op.78
Martinů Concerto for piano no.4 (Incantation)
Beethoven Symphony no.5 in C minor, op.67
Conductor Rafael Kubelik
Soloist Rudolf Firkušný (pf)

31 Aug. 20.00 *Usher Hall*
Tchaikovsky Serenade for strings, op.48
Tchaikovsky Romeo and Juliet - Fantasy overture
Tchaikovsky Symphony no.6 in B minor (Pathétique), op.74
Conductor Eugene Ormandy

CONCERTGEBOUW ORCHESTRA, Amsterdam
3 Sep. 20.00 *Usher Hall*
Weber Der Freischütz: Overture
Beethoven Concerto for piano no.3 in C minor, op.37
Berlioz Symphonie fantastique
Conductor Eduard van Beinum
Soloist Rudolf Firkušný (pf)

4 Sep. 20.00 *Usher Hall*
Cornelius Der Barbier von Bagdad: Overture
Kox Sinfonia concertante
Mendelssohn Concerto for violin in E minor, op.64
Debussy Prélude à l'après-midi d'un faune
Debussy La mer
Conductor Eduard van Beinum
Soloist Szymon Goldberg (vn)

6 Sep. 20.00 *Usher Hall*
Schubert Symphony no.8 in B minor (Unfinished), D759
R. Strauss Don Juan
R. Strauss Ein Heldenleben
Conductor Eugene Ormandy

7 Sep. 19.30 *Usher Hall*
Schubert Symphony no.6 in C, D589
Debussy Nocturnes
Stravinsky The firebird - Suite
Ravel Daphnis et Chloë - Suite no.2
Conductor Eduard van Beinum
Edinburgh Royal Choral Union members

BBC SCOTTISH ORCHESTRA
5 Sep. 20.00 *Usher Hall*
Sullivan Iolanthe: Overture
Mozart Symphony no.35 in D (Haffner), K385
Elgar The wand of youth - Suite no.2
Beethoven Concerto for piano no.1 in C, op.15
Whyte Scottish dance - Eightsome reel
Conductor Ian Whyte
Soloist Nina Milkina (pf)

CHAMBER CONCERTS

DENNIS BRAIN WIND ENSEMBLE
22 Aug. 20.00 *Usher Hall*
Mozart Divertimento no.14 in B flat, K270
Mozart Quintet for piano and wind in E flat, K452
Hindemith Kammermusik, op.24/2
Poulenc Sextet for piano and wind

24 Aug. 11.00 *Freemasons' Hall*
Beethoven Quintet for piano and wind in E flat, op.16
Malipiero Dialogue no.4 for wind quintet
Dukas Villanelle for horn and piano
Fricker Quintet for wind, op.5

ROBERT MASTERS PIANO QUARTET
26 Aug. 11.00 *Freemasons' Hall*
Brahms Quartet for piano and strrings no.1 in G minor, op.25
Martinů Quartet for piano and strings

28 Aug. 11.00 *Freemasons' Hall*
Brahms Quartet for piano and strings no.3 in C minor, op.60
Walton Quartet for piano and strings

HOLLYWOOD QUARTET
27 Aug. 11.00 *Freemasons' Hall*
Beethoven Quartet no.12 in E flat, op.127
Beethoven Quartet no.14 in C sharp minor, op.131

29 Aug. 11.00 *Freemasons' Hall*
Beethoven Quartet no.13 in B flat, op.130
Beethoven Grosse Fuge in B flat, op.133

31 Aug. 11.00 *Freemasons' Hall*
Beethoven Quartet no.15 in A minor, op.132
Beethoven Quartet no.16 in F, op.135

NEW EDINBURGH QUARTET
3 Sep. 11.00 *Freemasons' Hall*
Haydn Quartet in C, op.54/2
Schumann Quintet for piano and strings in E flat, op.44
with Nina Milkina (pf)

PARRENIN QUARTET
5 Sep. 11.00 *Freemasons' Hall*
Debussy Quartet in G minor, op.10/1
Bartók Quartet no.3
Arriaga Quartet no.1 in D minor

6 Sep. 11.00 *Freemasons' Hall*
Ravel Quartet in F
Milhaud Quartet no.13, op.268
Mendelssohn Quartet no.2 in A minor, op.13

MUSICA SCOTICA
Directed by Thurston Dart (hpd)
SALTIRE SINGERS
19 Aug. 11.00 *Freemasons' Hall*
Early Scottish chamber music for voices and instruments including works by Johnson, Kinloch, Burnett
with Desmond Dupré (lute, cittern)

21 Aug. 11.00 *Freemasons' Hall*
Early Scottish chamber music for voices and instruments including works by Lauder, Black, Johnson
with Jacobean Ensemble

EARLY ENGLISH MUSIC
DELLER CONSORT
2 Sep. 11.00 *Freemasons' Hall*
Anthems, madrigals and songs by Tallis, Morley, Byrd, Campion, Dowland, Cornyshe, Weelkes, Eccles, Bennet, Ward, Vautor, Wilbye, Dering

4 Sep. 11.00 *Freemasons' Hall*
Madrigals, part songs and folk songs by Weelkes, Wilbye, Dowland, Purcell, Morley, Parsons, Travers, Vautor, Johnson

RECITALS

HEINZ REHFUSS (bar)
GERALD MOORE (pf)
22 Aug. 20.00 *Freemasons' Hall*
Mussorgsky Songs and dances of death
Songs by Schubert, Wolf, Debussy

VICTORIA DE LOS ANGELES (sop)
GERALD MOORE (pf)
25 Aug. 14.30 *Usher Hall*
Songs and arias by Sacrati, A. Scarlatti, Handel, Schubert, Schumann, Brahms, Stravinsky, Ravel, Duparc, Halffter, Vives, Nin, Obradors

1 Sep. 14.30 *Usher Hall*
Mozart Ch'io mi scordi di te
Songs by Schubert, Brahms, Fauré, Granados, Nin, Rodrigo, Falla, Turina

LOIS MARSHALL (sop)
WELDON KILBURN (pf)
27 Aug. 20.00 *Freemasons' Hall*
Schumann Frauenliebe und -leben
Britten The holy sonnets of John Donne
Songs by Mahler, Debussy, Purcell

ANTON DERMOTA (ten)
HILDE DERMOTA (pf)
31 Aug. 20.00 *Freemasons' Hall*
Songs by Schubert, Schumann, Wolf, Strauss

DIETRICH FISCHER-DIESKAU (bar)
GERALD MOORE (pf)
2 Sep. 20.00 *Usher Hall*
Songs by Schubert

PIERRE BERNAC (bar)
FRANCIS POULENC (pf)
5 Sep. 20.00 *Freemasons' Hall*
Poulenc Le travail du peintre (World première)
Ravel Don Quichotte à Dulcinée
Songs by Fauré, Schumann, Poulenc

CLARA HASKIL (pf)
23 Aug. 11.00 *Freemasons' Hall*
Mozart Sonata no.10 in C, K330
Beethoven Sonata no.18 in E flat, op.31/3
Schubert Sonata no.21 in B flat, D960

SZYMON GOLDBERG (vn)
GERARD HENGEVELD (pf)
30 Aug. 11.00 *Freemasons' Hall*
Mozart Sonata no.25 in F, K377
Bartók Sonata for solo violin
Beethoven Sonata no.10 in G, op.96

1 Sep. 15.00 *Freemasons' Hall*
Beethoven Sonata no.3 in E flat, op.12/3
Bach Partita for solo violin no.2 in D minor
Stravinsky Duo concertant
Debussy Sonata

JANOS STARKER (vc)
20 Aug. 11.00 *Freemasons' Hall*
Bach Suite no.2 in D minor
Bach Suite no.6 in D

22 Aug. 11.00 *Freemasons' Hall*
Bach Suite no.4 in E flat
Bach Suite no.1 in G

25 Aug. 15.00 *Freemasons' Hall*
Bach Suite no.5 in C minor
Bach Suite no.3 in C

DRAMA

EDINBURGH INTERNATIONAL FESTIVAL
20 Aug.-7 Sep. 19.00 (exc.Sun) 22, 24, 27, 29, 31 Aug. 3, 7 Sep. 14.00
Assembly Hall
THE HIDDEN KING Griffin (World première)
Dom Sebastian, King of Portugal/The Stranger Robert Eddison
Dom Diego de Brito Robert Speaight
Dom Cristóvão de Moura Micheál MacLiammóir
Borazzo Sebastian Shaw
Cardinal of Pisa Ernest Thesiger
Veronica Pauline Jameson
Lena Rosalind Atkinson
Fausta Clare Austin
Beth Boyd*
Dom João Mascarenhas Robert Bernal
Cardinal Henry/Grand Duke of Tuscany Leo Ciceri
Duke of Alba/Doge Iain Cuthbertson
Pietro Paladino Edward Palmer
Father Sampayo Richard Dare
Spanish ambassador/Nuno da Costa Bernard Horsfall
Don Francisco/Dom Luis/Cneio Belegno John Bennett
Pantaleão Pesóa/Herald Hugh Cross
Marco Quirini/Venetian Pretor Ronald Harwood
Sebastião Figueiras/Courtier Morris Perry
Antonio Pimentel/Courtier Derek Nimmo
Dom João de Castro/Courtier Frank Thornton
De Negron John Bryans
Da Silva/Dom Cristóvão de Távora David Fleming
Bawd/Gypsy Beth Boyd
Other parts played by David Kelly, John Dunbar, William Lyon Brown, Gordon Gilmour
Director Christopher West
Designer Leslie Hurry
(In association with Stephen Mitchell)

ENGLISH STAGE COMPANY
19-24 Aug. 19.30 21, 24 Aug. 14.30
Lyceum Theatre
NEKRASSOV Sartre (Eng. Translated by Sylvia *and* George Leeson)
Georges de Valéra Robert Helpmann
Jules Palotin Harry H. Corbett
Sibilot George Benson
Mouton Felix Felton
Demidoff Martin Miller
Irma Margo Cunningham
Robert/Lerminier George Merritt
Inspector Goblet Roddy McMillan
Perigord Ronald Barker
Mayor de Travaja/Charivet Percy Cartwright
Interpreter/Bergerat Kerry Jordan
Veronique Jane Downs
Nerciat Bernard Kay
Inspector Baudoin Milo Sperber
Inspector Chapuis John Wood
Madame Bounoumi Margery Caldicott
Other parts played by Nicholas Brady, James Villiers, Anna Steele, Kendrick Owen, Anthony Creighton, Robert Aldous, Ann Davies
Director George Devine
Designer Richard Negri
Music Thomas Eastwood

HENREY SHEREK
26-31 Aug. 19.30 28, 31 Aug. 14.30
Lyceum Theatre
MAN OF DISTINCTION Hasenclever
Hugo Möbius Anton Walbrook
Lia Compass Moira Shearer
Herr Compass Eric Porter
Captain von Schmettau Peter Bull
Harry Compass John Warner
Rasper Aubrey Richards
Aline Prunella Scales
Frau Compass Yvonne Coulette
Secretary Roger Ostime
Frau Schnütchen Olga Lindo
Policeman Neil Wilson
Director Denis Carey
Designer Peter Rice

LA COMPAGNIE RENAUD-BARRAULT, France
2-7 Sep. 19.30 *Lyceum Theatre*
LA RÉPÉTITION (The rehearsal) Anouilh
Countess Madeleine Renaud
Hortensia Anne Carrere
Lucile Simone Valère
Count Jean-Louis Barrault
M. Damiens Pierre Bertin
Villebosse Gabriel Cattand
Hero Jacques Dacqmine
Director Jean-Louis Barrault
Designer Jean-Denis Malclès

4, 7 Sep. 14.30 *Lyceum Theatre*
CONNAISSANCE DE CLAUDEL
A dramatic anthology arranged and introduced by Jean-Louis Barrault
Madeleine Renaud, Anne Carrere. Simone Valère, Pierre Bertin, Jacques Dacqmine, Gabriel Cattand

GATEWAY COMPANY
19 Aug.-7 Sep. 19.30 (Exc. Sun) 22, 24, 29, 31 Aug. 5, 7 Sep. 14.30
Gateway Theatre
THE FLOUERS O' EDINBURGH McLellan
Jock Carmichael Walter Carr
Kate Mair Pamela Bain
Lady Athlestane Lennox Milne
Lord Stanebyres Tom Fleming
Charles Gilchrist Bryden Murdoch
Rev. Daniel Dowie John Young
John Douglas of Baldernock Michael Elder
Rev. Alexander Lindsay Norman Fraser
Captain Sidney Simkin John Gayford
Mistress Bell Baxter Nell Ballantyne
Susie Sheena Pow
Bailie Gleg George Davies
Thomas Auchterleckie Duncan Macrae
Siva Richard Whytock
General Brian Carey
Jeanie Anne Scotland
Caddies William Simpson, Stuart Henry
Director James Gibson
Designer Peter Norris

26 Aug. 15.00 *Freemasons' Hall*
SIR JOHN GIELGUD (rdr)
The ages of man
From the anthology by George Rylands

LATE NIGHT ENTERTAINMENT

26, 28, 30 Aug. 2, 4, 6, 7 Sep. 23.00
Freemasons' Hall
ANNA RUSSELL
Satire and song
with Joseph Cooper (pf)

DANCE

ROYAL SWEDISH BALLET
19-21 Aug. 19.30 *Empire Theatre*
GISELLE
Choreographers Jean Coralli, Mary Skeaping
Music Adam
THE PRODIGAL SON
Choreographer Ivo Cramer
Music Alfvén
Designer Rune Lindström

21 Aug. 14.30 *Empire Theatre*
GISELLE
GAIETÉ PARISIENNE
Choreographer Léonide Massine
Music Offenbach; arr. Rosenthal
Designer Etienne de Beaumont *after* Winterhalter

22, 23 Aug. 19.30 24 Aug. 14.30
Empire Theatre
CUPID OUT OF HIS HUMOUR
Choreographer Mary Skeaping
Music Purcell
RAYMONDA: Grand pas classique
Choreographer Albert Kozlovsky
Music Glazunov
SISYPHUS
Choreographer Birgit Akesson
Music Blomdahl
Designer Tor Hörlin
MISS JULIE
Choreographer Birgit Cullberg
Music Rangstrom; arr. Grossman
Designer *after* Sven Erixson

24 Aug. 19.30 *Empire Theatre*
THE PRODIGAL SON
RAYMONDA: Grand pas classique
MISS JULIE
GAIETÉ PARISIENNE
Dancers Mariane Orlando, Elsa Marianne von Rosen, Gerd Andersson, Anne-Mari Lagerborg, Birgit Grefveberg, Wiweka Ljung, Yvonne Brosset, Kerstin Lust, Vera Kihlgren, Monica Tropp, Anne-Marie Wallin, Björn Holmgren, Teddy Rhodin, Willy Sandberg, Mario Mengarelli, Caj Selling, Bengt Andersson, Verner Klavsen, Elis Gustavsson, Gunnar Randin, Jacques Delisle
Scottish National Orchestra
Conductors Sixten Ehrling, Herbert Sandberg

BALLETS AFRICAINS DE KEITA FODÉBA
26-31 Aug. 19.30 28, 31 Aug. 14.30
Empire Theatre
Director Keita Fodéba
Designers Bernard Daydé
Keita Fodéba

GRAND BALLET DU MARQUIS DE CUEVAS
2-4 Sep. 19.30 4 Sep. 14.30
Empire Theatre
LES SYLPHIDES
Choreographer Mikhail Fokine
Music Chopin; arr. Baron
Scenery Eugene Dunkeel *after* Corot
Costumes Monique Cheseaud
LA FEMME MUETTE
Choreographer Antonia Cobos
Music Paganini; arr. Rieti
Designer Rico Lebrun
SWAN LAKE: Black swan pas de deux
Choreographer *after* Marius Petipa
PETRUSHKA
Choreographer Mikhail Fokine
Music Stravinsky
Costumes Barbara Karinska

5-7 Sep. 19.30 7 Sep. 14.30
Empire Theatre
CONCERTO BAROCCO
Choreographer George Balanchine
Music Bach
Costumes Jean Robier
SOIRÉE MUSICALE: Pas de deux
Choreographer John Taras
Music Rossini; arr. Britten
Costumes André Levasseur
SONG OF UNENDING SORROW (World première)
Choreographer Ana Ricarda
Music Christopher Headington
Designer N.H. Stubbing
LE SPECTRE DE LA ROSE
Choreographers
Mikhail Fokine, Bronislava Nijinska
Music Weber

LA TERTULIA
Choreographers
Ana Ricarda, Irène Lidova
Music Manuel Infante
Scenery Capuletti
Dancers Rosella Hightower, Nina Vyroubova, Serge Golovine, Jacqueline Moreau, Vladimir Skouratoff, Ana Ricarda, Genia Melikova, George Zoritch, Nicholas Polajenko, Wasil Tupin, Georges Goviloff, Beatriz Consuelo, Daphne Dale, Solange Golovina
Scottish National Orchestra
Conductors Gustave Cloez, Foster Clark

EXHIBITIONS

Royal Scottish Academy
MONET
Director Douglas Cooper
(In association with the Arts Council of Great Britain)

1958

OPERA

WÜRTTEMBERG STATE OPERA, Stuttgart
25, 27, 29 Aug. 4, 10, 12 Sep. 19.00
King's Theatre
DIE ENTFÜHRUNG AUS DEM SERAIL Mozart
Belmonte Josef Traxel
Fritz Wunderlich
Constanze Wilma Lipp
Ruth-Margret Pütz
Blonde Lotte Schädle
Pedrillo Alfred Pfeifle
Gerhard Unger
Osmin Fritz Linke
Otto von Rohr
Bassa Selim Heinz Cramer
Conductors Ferdinand Leitner
Lovro von Matacic
Director Kurt Puhlmann
Designer Leni Bauer-Ecsy

26 Aug. 3, 8 Sep. 19.00 *King's Theatre*
EURYANTHE Weber
Euryanthe Lore Wissmann
Adolar Josef Traxel
Eglantine Inge Borkh
Lysiart Gustav Neidlinger
King Louis VI Alexander Welitsch
Messenger Hubert Buchta
Conductor Lovro von Matacic
Director Kurt Puhlmann
Designer Gerd Richter

28, 30 Aug. 2, 5 Sep.17.00 King's Theatre
TRISTAN UND ISOLDE Wagner
Tristan Wolfgang Windgassen
Isolde Martha Mödl
Astrid Varnay
Brangäne Grace Hoffman
Kurvenal Gustav Neidlinger
King Mark Otto von Rohr
Melot Hans Günter Nöcker
Young sailor Josef Traxel
Fritz Wunderlich
Shepherd Alfred Pfeifle
Steersman Kurt Egon Opp
Conductor Ferdinand Leitner
Director and designer
Wieland Wagner

1, 6 Sep. 19.00 *King's Theatre*
DER WILDSCHÜTZ Lortzing
Count of Eberbach Karl Schmitt-Walter
Countess Hetty Plümacher
Baron Kronthal Fritz Wunderlich
Baroness Freimann Lore Wissmann
Nanette Sieglinde Kahmann
Baculus Fritz Linke
Gretchen Friederike Sailer
Pancratius Hubert Buchta
Conductor Ferdinand Leitner
Director Günther Rennert
Designer Alfred Siercke

SPANISH OPERA-BALLET
9, 11, 13 Sep. 19.00 *King's Theatre*
LA VIDA BREVE Falla
Salud Victoria de los Angeles
Paco Bernabé Martínez
Grandmother Rosario Gómez
Uncle Salvador Joaquín Deus
Pepe Manuel Ausensi
Carmela Julita Bermejo
Manuel Manuel Albalat
Voice in the smithy Jesús Aguirre
Voice of a hawker Rafael Maldonado
Street vendors Anita Fernández del Pozo, Emilia García Manzanares, Elia López
Antonio and his Spanish Ballet Company
Cantores de Madrid,
Orquesta de Madrid
Conductor Eduardo Toldrá
Scenery José Caballero
Costumes Leo Anchóriz
EL SOMBRERO DE TRES PICOS Falla
Miller Antonio
Miller's wife Rosita Segovia
Governor Rodolfo Otero
Governor's wife Carmen Rollán
Dandy Enrique Gutiérrez
Antonio and his Spanish Ballet Company
Orquesta de Madrid
Choreographer Antonio
Conductor Benito Lauret
Designer Manuel Muntañola

ORCHESTRAL CONCERTS

PHILHARMONIA ORCHESTRA
24 Aug. 20.00 *Usher Hall*
Beethoven The consecration of the house - Overture
Beethoven Symphony no.6 in F (Pastoral), op.68
Beethoven Symphony no.5 in C minor, op.67
Conductor Otto Klemperer

25 Aug. 20.00 *Usher Hall*
Glinka Ruslan and Ludmilla: Overture
Shostakovich Concerto for violin no.1 in A minor, op.99
Tchaikovsky Symphony no.6 in B minor (Pathétique), op.74
Conductor Ernest Ansermet
Soloist Yehudi Menuhin (vn)

26 Aug. 20.00 *Usher Hall*
Haydn Symphony no.101 in D (Clock)
Bruckner Symphony no.4 in E flat (Romantic)
Conductor Otto Klemperer

27 Aug. 20.00 *Usher Hall*
Berlioz Le carnaval romain - Overture
Berlioz Roméo et Juliette: Queen Mab scherzo
Beethoven Concerto for piano no.4 in G, op.58

Schumann Symphony no.4 in D minor, op.120
Conductor Wolfgang Sawallisch
Soloist Hans Richter-Haaser (pf)

28 Aug. 20.00 *Usher Hall*
Beethoven Symphony no.4 in B flat, op.60
Debussy Images: Ibéria
Bartók Concerto for orchestra
Conductor Ernest Ansermet

SCOTTISH NATIONAL ORCHESTRA
Conductor Hans Swarowsky
29 Aug. 20.00 *Usher Hall*
Mozart Symphony no.36 in C (Linz), K425
Brahms Concerto for violin and cello in A minor, op.102
Hindemith Symphonic metamorphosis on themes of Weber
Stravinsky The firebird - Suite
Soloists Yehudi Menuhin (vn), Gaspar Cassadó (vc)

3 Sep. 20.00 *Usher Hall*
Hamilton Bartholomew Fair - Overture
Brahms Symphony no.3 in F, op.90
Schumann Concerto for piano in A minor, op.54
Respighi The pines of Rome
Soloist Hans Richter-Haaser (pf)

7 Sep. 20.00 *Usher Hall*
Bach Magnificat in D
Haydn Mass no.11 in D minor (Nelson)
Soloists Maria Stader, Jennifer Vyvyan (sop), Maureen Forrester (cont), Nicolai Gedda (ten), Kim Borg (bs), Edinburgh Royal Choral Union

ROYAL DANISH ORCHESTRA
30 Aug. 20.00 *Usher Hall*
Nielsen Maskarade: Overture
R. Strauss Till Eulenspiegels lustige Streiche
Beethoven Concerto for piano no.3 in C minor, op.37
Brahms Symphony no.1 in C minor, op.68
Conductor Georg Solti
Soloist Louis Kentner (pf)

31 Aug. 20.00 *Usher Hall*
Haydn Die Schöpfung
Conductor Mogens Wöldike
Soloists Jennifer Vyvyan (sop), Nicolai Gedda (ten), Kim Borg (bs), Royal Danish Chapel Choir

1 Sep. 20.00 *Usher Hall*
Weber Der Freischütz: Overture
Nielsen Symphony no.2 (The four temperaments), op.16
Mozart Concerto for violin no.3 in G, K216
Ravel Daphnis et Chloë - Suite no.2
Conductor John Frandsen
Soloist Yehudi Menuhin (vn)

ORCHESTRA OF THE ROYAL OPERA HOUSE, COVENT GARDEN
4 Sep. 20.00 *Usher Hall*
Stravinsky Apollon musagète - Suite
Stravinsky La baiser de la fée - Divertimento
Stravinsky Petrushka - Suite (1911 version)
Conductor Ernest Ansermet

5 Sep. 20.00 *Usher Hall*
Britten Peter Grimes: Four sea interludes *and* Passacaglia
Britten Les illuminations
Britten Spring symphony
Conductors Ernest Ansermet
Benjamin Britten
Soloists Jennifer Vyvyan (sop), Norma Procter (cont), Peter Pears (ten), Royal Opera House Chorus, Boys of the Royal Danish Chapel Choir

6 Sep. 20.00 *Usher Hall*
Ravel Rapsodie espagnole
Turina Canto a Sevilla
Falla El amor brujo: Gypsy scene
Albeniz Ibéria; orch. Arbós
Conductor Enrique Jorda
Soloist Victoria de los Angeles (sop)

VIENNA SYMPHONY ORCHESTRA
Conductor Josef Krips
9 Sep. 20.00 *Usher Hall*
Weber Oberon: Overture
Brahms Concerto for piano no.2 in B flat, op.83
Schubert Symphony no.9 in C (Great), D944
Soloist Claudio Arrau (pf)

10 Sep. 20.00 *Usher Hall*
Haydn Symphony no.94 in G (Surprise)
Mozart Exsultate, jubilate
Bruckner Symphony no.7 in E
Soloist Maria Stader (sop)

12 Sep. 20.00 *Usher Hall*
Mozart Symphony no.39 in E flat, K543
Mozart Concerto for piano no.24 in C minor, K491
Mozart Symphony no.41 in C (Jupiter), K551
Soloist Claudio Arrau (pf)

13 Sep. 19.30 *Usher Hall*
Beethoven Leonore: Overture no.3
Schmidt Concertante variations on a theme by Beethoven
Beethoven Symphony no.3 In E flat (Eroica), op.55
Soloist Alexander Jenner (pf)

13 Sep. 22.45 *Usher Hall*
J. Strauss Die Fledermaus: Overture
J. Strauss Der Zigeunerbaron: Overture
J. Strauss G'schichten aus dem Wienerwald
J. Strauss Pizzicato polka
J. Strauss Perpetuum mobile
J. Strauss Kaiser Walzer
J. Strauss, *the elder* Radetzky march

ZAGREB SOLOISTS' ENSEMBLE
Conductor and soloist Antonio Janigro
11 Sep. 11.00 *Freemasons' Hall*
Corelli Sarabande, gigue and badinerie; arr. Arbós
Vivaldi Concerto for cello in D
Telemann Concerto for violin in A minor
Rossini Sonata for strings no.3 in C
Mozart Divertimento (Salzburg symphony) no.3 in F, K138
Britten Simple symphony
Soloist Jelka Stanic Krek (vn)

13 Sep. 11.00 *Freemasons' Hall*
Albinoni Concerto a cinque in B flat
Boccherini Concerto for cello no.9 in B flat
Rossini Sonata for strings no.1 in G
Hindemith Trauermusik
Kelemen Concertante improvisations
Mozart Divertimento (Salzburg symphony) no.1 in D, K136
Soloist Stefano Passaggio (va)

CHAMBER CONCERTS

BERLIN PHILHARMONIC OCTET
25 Aug. 11.00 *Freemasons' Hall*
Ferguson Octet, op.4
Beethoven Septet, op.20

27 Aug. 11.00 *Freemasons' Hall*
Copland Sextet
Schubert Octet, D803

VEGH QUARTET
26 Aug. 11.00 *Freemasons' Hall*
Haydn Quartet in D, op.76/5
Brahms Quartet no.2 in A minor, op.51/2

28 Aug. 11.00 *Freemasons' Hall*
Beethoven Quartet no.11 in F minor (Serioso), op.95
Schubert Quartet no.13 in A minor, D804

NEW EDINBURGH QUARTET
LYRA QUARTET
29 Aug. 11.00 *Freemasons' Hall*
Hamilton Octet, op.24
Mendelssohn Octet, op.20

JUILLIARD QUARTET
Bartók String Quartets
30 Aug. 11.00 *Freemasons' Hall*
Nos. 1 *and* 4
1 Sep. 11.00 *Freemasons' Hall*
Nos. 2 *and* 5
3 Sep. 11.00 *Freemasons' Hall*
Nos. 3 *and* 6

PASQUIER TRIO
6 Sep. 11.00 *Freemasons' Hall*
Mozart Divertimento in E flat, K563
Fauré Quartet for piano and strings no.1 in C minor, op.15
with Kathleen Long (pf)

8 Sep. 11.00 *Freemasons' Hall*
Beethoven Trio no.2 in G, op.9/1
Beethoven Trio no.4 in C minor, op.9/3
Fauré Quartet for piano and strings no.2 in G minor, op.45
with Kathleen Long (pf)

MENUHIN - CASSADÓ - KENTNER TRIO
8 Sep. 20.00 *Usher Hall*
Mozart Trio for piano and strings no.4 in E, K542
Schubert Trio for piano and strings no.1 in B flat, D898
Brahms Trio for piano and strings no.1 in B, op.8

11 Sep. 20.00 *Usher Hall*
Mendelssohn Trio for piano and strings no.1 in D minor, op.49
Ravel Trio for piano and strings in A minor
Beethoven Trio for piano and strings no.7 in B flat (Archduke), op.97

12 Sep. 11.00 *Embassy Cinema*
Mendelssohn Trio for piano and strings no.1 in D minor, op.49
Beethoven Trio for piano and strings no.7 in B flat (Archduke), op.97

QUINTETTO CHIGIANO
10 Sep. 11.00 *Freemasons' Hall*
Boccherini Quintet for piano and strings in C
Milhaud La création du monde - Suite
Brahms Quintet for piano and strings in F minor, op.34

12 Sep. 11.00 *Freemasons' Hall*
Shostakovich Quintet for piano and strings in G minor, op.57
Dvořák Quintet for piano and strings in A, op.81

EDINBURGH UNIVERSITY SINGERS
31 Aug. 15.00 *Freemasons' Hall*
Palestrina Stabat Mater
V. Williams Mass in G minor
Choral works by Lassus, Janequin, Costeley, Passereau, Ravel
Director Herrick Bunney

MONTREAL BACH CHOIR
7 Sep. 15.00 *Freemasons' Hall*
Choral works by Sweelinck, Lassus, Bach, Mouton, Mauduit, Brumel, Charpentier, Britten, Janequin, K. Jones, V. Archer, J. Coulthard
Conductor George Little

RECITALS

PETER PEARS (ten)
JULIAN BREAM (lute, gtr)
27 Aug. 20.00 *Freemasons' Hall*
Works for voice, lute and guitar by Dowland, Morley, Campion, Ford, Cutting, Britten, L. Berkeley, Seiber

PETER PEARS (ten)
BENJAMIN BRITTEN (pf)
3 Sep. 20.00 *Freemasons' Hall*
Schumann Liederkreis, op.39
Britten Winter words
Songs by Schubert, Britten

NICOLAI GEDDA (ten)
GERALD MOORE (pf)
4 Sep. 20.00 *Freemasons' Hall*
Songs by Stradella, A. Scarlatti, Schubert, R. Strauss, Hahn, Debussy, Rachmaninov

KIM BORG (bs)
GERALD MOORE (pf)
10 Sep. 20.00 *Freemasons' Hall*
Mozart Cosi dunque tradisci...Aspri rimorsi atroci
Ravel Don Quichotte à Dulcinée
Songs by Haydn, Schubert, Sibelius, Mussorgsky

MAUREEN FORRESTER (cont)
JOHN NEWMARK (pf)
12 Sep. 20.00 *Freemasons' Hall*
Poulenc La fraîcheur et le feu
Brahms Zigeunerlieder
Britten A charm of lullabies
Songs by C.P.E. Bach, Franck, Schubert, Loewe

LOUIS KENTNER (pf)
2 Sep. 20.00 *Usher Hall*
Beethoven Sonata no.7 in D, op.10/3
Beethoven Sonata no.21 in C (Waldstein), op.53
Beethoven Sonata no.32 in C minor, op.111
Beethoven Sonata no.23 in F minor (Appassionata), op.57

5 Sep. 11.00 *Freemasons' Hall*
Mozart Fantasia in C minor, K475
Mozart Sonata no.14 in C minor, K457
Schubert Sonata no.20 in A, D959
Liszt Années de pèlerinage 2: Sonetti del Petrarca
Liszt Venezia e Napoli: Tarantella

CLAUDIO ARRAU (pf)
7 Sep. 14.30 *Usher Hall*
Piano works by Chopin

YEHUDI MENUHIN (vn)
LOUIS KENTNER (pf)
31 Aug. 14.30 *Usher Hall*
Beethoven Sonata no.10 in G, op.96
Mozart Sonata no.35 in A, K526
Franck Sonata in A

THOMAS MATTHEWS (vn)
EILEEN RALF (pf)
9 Sep. 11.00 *Freemasons' Hall*
Brahms Sonata no.1 in G, op.78
Brahms Sonata no.2 in A, op.100
Brahms Sonata no.3 in D minor, op.108

GASPAR CASSADÓ (vc)
WIGHT HENDERSON (pf)
2 Sep. 11.00 *Freemasons' Hall*
Brahms Sonata for cello and piano no.1 in E minor, op.38
Brahms Piano pieces, op.119
Brahms Sonata for cello and piano no.2 in F, op.99

JULIAN BREAM (lute, gtr)
4 Sep. 11.00 *Freemasons' Hall*
Works for lute and guitar by Dowland, Bacheler, Johnson, Cutting, Bach, Sor, Granados, Villa-Lobos, Turina, Albéniz

DRAMA

OLD VIC
25-30 Aug. 19.15 26, 30 Aug. 14.15
Assembly Hall
TWELFTH NIGHT Shakespeare
Viola Barbara Jefford
Orsino John Humphry
Olivia Jane Downs
Sir Toby Belch Joss Ackland
Sir Andrew Aguecheek John Neville
Malvolio Richard Wordsworth
Maria Judi Dench
Feste Dudley Jones
Curio Thomas Johnston
Valentine Peter Cellier
Sea captain David Gardner
Sebastian Gerald Harper
Antonio Oliver Neville
Fabian James Culliford
Page Simon Fraser
Officers Harold Innocent, James Mellor
Priest John Gay
Director Michael Benthall
Designer Desmond Heeley
Music arrangement Gordon Jacob

2-13 Sep. 19.15 (exc.Sun) 3, 5, 6, 9, 13 Sep. 14.15 *Assembly Hall*
MARY STUART Schiller
(Eng. Translated by Stephen Spender)
Mary Stuart Irene Worth
Queen Elizabeth Catherine Lacey
Hanna Kennedy Rosalind Atkinson
Leicester John Phillips
Mortimer Ronald Lewis
Paulet Derek Francis
Talbot Ernest Thesiger
Kent Dennis Chinnery
Melvil Jack May
Bellievre Edward Hardwicke
O'Kelly Barrie Ingham
Lord Burleigh Kenneth Mackintosh
Sir William Davison Gerald James
Count Aubespine Norman Scace
Sir Drue Drury Jeremy Kemp
Officer Charles West
Sheriff of Northampton Brian Jackson
Director Peter Wood
Designer Leslie Hurry
Music John Hotchkis

HENRY SHEREK
25-30 Aug. 19.30 27, 30 Aug. 14.30
Lyceum Theatre
THE ELDER STATESMAN Eliot
(EIF commission)
Lord Claverton Paul Rogers
Monica Claverton-Ferry Anna Massey
Frederico Gomez William Squire
Mrs Carghill Eileen Peel
Charles Hemington Richard Gale
Michael Claverton-Ferry Alec McCowen
Mrs Piggott Dorothea Phillips
Lambert Geoffrey Kerr
Director E. Martin Browne
Designer Hutchinson Scott

ULSTER GROUP THEATRE
1-6 Sep. 19.30 3, 6 Sep. 14.30
Lyceum Theatre
THE BONEFIRE McLarnon
(World première)
James Mitchell J.G. Devlin
Davy Marr James Ellis
Mrs McComb Irene Bingham
Mrs Jefferson Elizabeth Begley
Mr Lindsay James Boyce
Sam Kyle John McBride
Mr McNulty Harold Goldblatt
Willy McNulty Denys Hawthorne
Vanessa Lindsay Margaret D'Arcy
Jim Hanna Maurice O'Callaghan
Kevin McAlinden Colin Blakely
Mrs Hanna Catherine Gibson
Director Tyrone Guthrie
Designer Frederick Crooke

NEW WATERGATE THEATRE CLUB
8-13 Sep. 19.00 *Lyceum Theatre*
LONG DAY'S JOURNEY INTO NIGHT O'Neill
James Tyrone Anthony Quayle
Mary Tyrone Gwen Ffrangcon Davies
James Tyrone, jun Ian Bannen
Edmund Tyrone Alan Bates
Cathleen Etain O'Dell
Director José Quintero
Designer David Hays

GATEWAY COMPANY
25 Aug.-13 Sep. 19.30 (exc.Sun)
28, 30 Aug. 4, 6, 11, 13 Sep. 14.30
Gateway Theatre
WEIR OF HERMISTON Sellar
(Adapted from Robert Louis Stevenson)
Weir of Hermiston Tom Fleming
Archie Weir Frank Wylie
Frank Innes William Simpson
Kirsty Elliott Lennox Milne
Christina Elliott Pamela Bain
Hob Elliott John Young
Clem Elliott Walter Carr
Gib Elliott Gino Coia
McKillop James Gibson
Prison governor Callum Mill
Haxton Leonard Maguire
Jean Haxton Christine Turnbull
Ecky Paul Young
Director Brian Carey
Designer David Sidey

POETRY AND PROSE RECITALS

APOLLO SOCIETY
9 Sep. 14.30 *Lyceum Theatre*
PORTRAITS OF WOMEN: FROM CHAUCER TO DYLAN THOMAS
Dame Peggy Ashcroft (rdr), Osian Ellis (hp)

11 Sep. 14.30 *Lyceum Theatre*
A RECITAL OF VERSE AND MUSIC
Selections from Shakespeare, Byron, Wilde, Fry
Dame Edith Evans, Christopher Hassall (rdr), Natasha Litvin (pf)

DANCE

EDINBURGH INTERNATIONAL BALLET
BALLET PREMIÈRES
25-27 Aug. 19.30 27 Aug. 14.30
Empire Theatre
CIRCLE OF LOVE
Choreographer Birgit Cullberg
Music Hilding Hallnås
Designer Sonja Carlsson
THE NIGHT AND SILENCE
Choreographer Walter Gore
Music Bach; arr. Mackerras
Designer Ronald Wilson
SECRETS
Choreographer John Cranko
Music Poulenc
Designer John Piper
CONCERTO FOR DANCERS
Choreographer Wendy Toye
Music Joseph Horovitz
Designer Alix Stone

28-30 Aug. 19.30 30 Aug. 14.30
Empire Theatre
SECRETS
THE NIGHT AND SILENCE
LES FACHEUSES RENCONTRES
Choreographer George Skibine
Music Maurice Jarre
Designer Alwyne Camble
OCTET
Choreographer John Taras
Music David Wooldridge
Scenery John Diebel
Costumes Elaine Bromwich

1-3 Sep. 19.30 3 Sep. 14.30
Empire Theatre
OCTET
DREAMS
Choreographer Dimitri Parlić
Music Dušan Radić
Designer Dušan Ristić
LES FACHEUSES RENCONTRES
MIDSUMMER'S VIGIL
Choreographer Björn Holmgren
Music Alfvén; arr. Mackerras
Designer Allan Fridericia

4-6 Sep. 19.30 6 Sep. 14.30
Empire Theatre
DREAMS
LA BELLE DAME SANS MERCI
Choreographer and designer
Andrée Howard
Music Goehr
THE SEVENTH SACRAMENT
Choreographer Deryk Mendel
Music Guy Morançon
Designer Monica Koenig
MIDSUMMER'S VIGIL

8-10 Sep. 19.30 10 Sep. 14.30
Empire Theatre
THE SEVENTH SACRAMENT
CHANGEMENT DE PIEDS
Choreographer and designer
Alan Carter
Music Martin
LA BELLE DAME SANS MERCI
THE GREAT PEACOCK
Choreographer Peter Wright
Music Searle
Designer Yolande Sonnabend

11-13 Sep. 19.30 13 Sep. 14.30
Empire Theatre
CONCERTO FOR DANCERS
THE NIGHT AND SILENCE
CHANGEMENT DE PIEDS
THE GREAT PEACOCK

Dancers Carla Fracci, Françoise, Paula Hinton, Beryl Kaye, Gillian Lynne, Yvonne Meyer, Elsa Marianne von Rosen, Kirsten Simone, Marjorie Tallchief, Wendy Toye, Margot Werner, Max Bozzoni, Irving Davies, Dominique, Heino Hallhuber, Björn Holmgren, Henning Kronstam, Milorad Miskovitch, George Skibine, Paddy Stone, Claudie Algeranova, Yvonne Cartier, Wish Mary Hunt, Gayrie MacSween, Yemaiel Oved, Prudence Rodney, Irene Siegfried, Jenny Trevelyan, Peter Cazalet, Dennis Griffiths, Christopher Lyall, David Poole, Ronald Reay, Peter Wright
with Jan Cervenka, Maurits Sillem, Hazel Vivienne (pf)
Edinburgh International Ballet Orch.
Conductors Charles Mackerras, Maurits Sillem
(In association with Michael Frostick)

EXHIBITIONS

Royal Scottish Museum
BYZANTINE ART
Director David Talbot Rice
(In association with the Royal Scottish Museum and the Victoria and Albert Museum)

Royal Scottish Academy
MOLTZAU COLLECTION: Cézanne to Picasso
(Sponsored and arranged by the Royal Scottish Academy)

1959

OPERA

ROYAL OPERA, STOCKHOLM
24, 29 Aug. 4, 12 Sep. 19.00
King's Theatre
UN BALLO IN MASCHERA Verdi (Swed)
Gustav III of Sweden Ragnar Ulfung
Count Holberg Erik Saedén
Hugo Hasslo
Amelia Birgit Nilsson
Aase Nordmo-Lövberg
Ulrica Kerstin Meyer
Barbro Ericson
Otto Birgit Nordin
Count Horn Bo Lundborg
Count Anckarström Arne Tyrén
Matts Ingvar Wixell
Bishop Arne Ohlson
Servant Sven Erik Vikström
Conductor Sixten Ehrling
Director Göran Gentele
Designer Sven-Erik Skawonius

25, 27 Aug.1, 9, 11 Sep. 19.00
King's Theatre
RIGOLETTO Verdi
Rigoletto Hugo Hasslo
Duke Nicolai Gedda
Uno Stjernqvist
Gilda Margareta Hallin
Maddalena Kerstin Meyer
Barbro Ericson
Sparafucile Arne Tyrén
Giovanna Barbro Ericson
Margit Sehlmark
Count Monterone Sigurd Björling
Anders Näslund
Marullo Anders Näslund
Erik Saedén
Borsa Olle Sivall
Count Ceprano Ingvar Wixell
Countess Ceprano Ingeborg Kjellgren
Page Birgit Nordin
Officer Bo Lundborg
Conductor Fausto Cleva
Director Bengt Peterson
Designer Birger Bergling

26, 28, 31 Aug. 2, 7 Sep. 18.00
King's Theatre
DIE WALKÜRE Wagner
Brünnhilde Birgit Nilsson
Siegmund Set Svanholm
Sieglinde Aase Nordmo-Lövberg
Wotan Sigurd Björling
Fricka Kerstin Meyer
Margareta Bergström
Hunding Leon Björker
Gerhilde Anna-Greta Söderholm
Ortlinde Elisabeth Söderström
Waltraute Ingeborg Kjellgren
Schwertleite Margit Sehlmark
Helmwige Kjerstin Dellert
Siegrune Barbro Ericson
Grimgerde Margareta Bergström
Rossweise Kerstin Meyer
Conductor Sixten Ehrling
Director Bengt Peterson
Designer Tor Hörlin

3, 5 Sep. 19.00 *King's Theatre*
ANIARA Blomdahl
Blind poetess Margareta Hallin
Daisi Doody/La garçonne Kjerstin Dellert
The Mimarobe Anders Näslund
Erik Saedén
Chefone 1 and 2 Arne Tyrén
Chief engineer 1 Sven Erik Vikström
Chief engineer 2 Arne Ohlson
Chief engineer 3 Bo Lundborg
Sandon Olle Sivall
Isagel Mariane Orlando
Stone-mute deaf Ragnar Ulfung
Blind one Sven Erik Vikström
Conductor Sixten Ehrling
Director Göran Gentele
Designer Sven Erixson

8, 10 Sep. 19.00 *King's Theatre*
WOZZECK Berg
Wozzeck Anders Näslund
Erik Saedén
Marie Elisabeth Söderström
Drum-major Conny Söderström
Andres Arne Ohlson
Captain Sven Erik Vikström
Doctor Arne Tyrén
Margret Margareta Bergström
Apprentices Bo Lundborg, Ingvar Wixell
Idiot Olle Sivall
Marie's child Michel Rhodin
Soldier Tore Persson
Conductor Sixten Ehrling
Director Göran Gentele
Designer Sven Erixson

ORCHESTRAL CONCERTS

ROYAL PHILHARMONIC ORCHESTRA
23 Aug. 20.00 *Usher Hall*
Walton Partita for orchestra
Walton Concerto for cello
Walton Symphony no.1 in B flat minor
Conductor Sir William Walton
Soloist Pierre Fournier (vc)

25 Aug. 20.00 *Usher Hall*
R. Strauss Don Juan
Bartók Concerto for piano no.2

Beethoven Symphony no.5 in C minor, op.67
Conductor Rudolf Kempe
Soloist Hans Richter-Haaser (pf)

26 Aug. 20.00 *Usher Hall*
Beethoven Leonore: Overture no.2
Mozart Sinfonia concertante for wind, K297b
Berlioz Symphonie fantastique
Conductor Rudolf Kempe
Soloists Terence MacDonagh (ob), Jack Brymer (cl), Gwydion Brooke (bn), Andrew Woodburn (hn)

10 Sep. 20.00 *Usher Hall*
Haydn Symphony no.96 in D (Miracle)
Dvořák Concerto for violin in A minor, op.53
Beethoven Symphony no.7 in A, op.92
Conductor Hans Schmidt-Isserstedt
Soloist Johanna Martzy (vn)

11 Sep. 20.00 *Usher Hall*
Suk Fairy tale - Suite
Dvořák Concerto for piano in G minor, op.33
Brahms Symphony no.1 in C minor, op.68
Conductor Walter Susskind
Soloist Rudolf Firkušný (pf)

12 Sep. 19.30 *Usher Hall*
Mozart Symphony no.39 in E flat, K543
Tchaikovsky Concerto for violin in D, op.35
Brahms Symphony no.2 in D, op.73
Conductor Hans Schmidt-Isserstedt
Soloist Johanna Martzy (vn)

SCOTTISH NATIONAL ORCHESTRA
28 Aug. 20.00 *Usher Hall*
Berlioz Le corsaire - Overture
Beethoven Concerto for piano no.5 in E flat (Emperor), op.73
Hamilton Sinfonia for 2 orchestras (Commissioned by the EIF and the Burns Foundation)
Elgar Variations on an original theme (Enigma)
Conductor Alexander Gibson
Soloist Wilhelm Kempff (pf)

30 Aug. 20.00 *Usher Hall*
Beethoven Egmont: Overture
Dvořák Concerto for cello in B minor, op.104
Sibelius Symphony no.2 in D, op.43
Conductor Alexander Gibson
Soloist Pierre Fournier (vc)

6 Sep. 20.00 *Usher Hall*
Vaughan Williams Memorial Programme
Concerto for 2 pianos
Symphony no.1 (A sea symphony)
Conductor Sir Adrian Boult
Soloists Heather Harper (sop), John Cameron (bar), Vronsky *and* Babin (pf), Edinburgh Royal Choral Union

LONDON MOZART PLAYERS
31 Aug. 20.00 *Usher Hall*
Haydn Symphony no.98 in B flat
Mozart Concerto for 2 pianos in F, K242
Mozart Three German dances, K605
Mozart Mauerische Trauermusik
Schubert Symphony no.5 in B flat, D485
Conductor Harry Blech
Soloists Vronsky *and* Babin (pf)

1 Sep. 20.00 *Usher Hall*
Prokofiev Symphony no.1 in D (Classical), op.25
Mozart Concerto for flute and harp in C, K299
R. Strauss Metamorphosen for 23 solo strings
Haydn Symphony no.93 in D
Conductor Rudolf Kempe
Soloists Jean-Pierre Rampal (fl), Nicanor Zabaleta hp)

2 Sep. 20.00 *Usher Hall*
Mozart Symphony no.32 in G, K318
Mozart Concerto for piano no.22 in E flat, K482
Stravinsky Danses concertantes
Mozart Symphony no.41 in C (Jupiter), K551
Conductor Colin Davis
Soloist Hans Richter-Haaser (pf)

LUCERNE FESTIVAL STRINGS
Leader Rudolf Baumgartner
4 Sep. 20.00 *Usher Hall*
Vivaldi Concerto for strings in A
Purcell Pavane and chaconne
Bach Concerto for violin in E
Bach Cantata no.202 (Wedding cantata)
Hindemith Five pieces for strings, op.44
Soloists Irmgard Seefried (sop), Wolfgang Schneiderhan (vn)

6 Sep. 20.00 *Usher Hall*
Handel Concerto grosso in D, op.6/5
Tartini Concerto for violin in D minor
Bach Cantata no.56
Purcell The married beau - Suite
Bach Concerto for 2 violins in D minor
Soloists Dietrich Fischer-Dieskau (bar), Wolfgang Schneiderhan, Rudolf Baumgartner (vn)

CHAMBER CONCERTS

LOEWENGUTH QUARTET
STROSS QUARTET
24 Aug. 11.00 *Freemasons' Hall*
Brahms Sextet no.2 in G, op.36
Milhaud Octet (From Quartets nos.14 and 15)

26 Aug. 11.00 *Freemasons' Hall*
Beethoven Quintet in C, op.29
Mendelssohn Octet, op.20

STROSS QUARTET
28 Aug. 11.00 *Freemasons' Hall*
Beethoven Quartet no.14 in C sharp minor, op.131
Beethoven Quartet no.7 in F (Rasumovsky), op.59/1

LOEWENGUTH QUARTET
29 Aug. 11.00 *Freemasons' Hall*
Mozart Quartet no.16 in E flat, K428
Wolf Italian serenade
Debussy Quartet in G minor, op.10/1

AMICI QUARTET
29 Aug. 20.00 *Freemasons' Hall*
Janáček Quartet no.2 (Intimate letters)
Janáček Diary of one who disappeared with Josephine Veasey (mez), Richard Lewis (ten), Gerald Moore (pf), University Singers members

7 Sep. 11.00 *Freemasons' Hall*
Saygun Quartet, op.27
Brahms Quintet for clarinet and strings in B minor, op.115
With Gervase de Peyer (cl)

PROMETHEUS ENSEMBLE
1 Sep. 11.00 *Freemasons' Hall*
Mozart Quintet for horn and strings in E flat, K407
Hindemith Octet
Spohr Nonet, op.31

2 Sep. 11.00 *Freemasons' Hall*
Frankel Five bagatelles for 11 instruments (World première)
Ravel Introduction and allegro for flute, clarinet, harp and strings
Beethoven Septet, op.20

LEPPARD ENSEMBLE
Director Raymond Leppard
8 Sep. 11.00 *Freemasons' Hall*
Purcell Sonata in 4 parts no.2 in E flat
Handel Tra le fiamme (Il consiglio)
Handel Trio sonata in D for flute, oboe and continuo
Haydn Trio for harpsichord and strings in E flat
Soloist Jennifer Vyvyan (sop)

10 Sep. 11.00 *Freemasons' Hall*
Handel Trio sonata for 2 violins and continuo in G minor
Haydn Arianna a Naxos
Haydn Trio for harpsichord and strings in C
Purcell Theatre music: Act tunes and airs
Soloist Jennifer Vyvyan (sop)

AMADEUS QUARTET
9 Sep. 11.00 *Freemasons' Hall*
Walton Quartet in A minor
Brahms Quartet no.3 in B flat, op.67

11 Sep. 11.00 *Freemasons' Hall*
Mozart Quartet no.20 in D (Hoffmeister), K499
Mozart Quintet for clarinet and strings in A, K581
with Gervase de Peyer (cl)

12 Sep. 11.00 *Freemasons' Hall*
Haydn Quartet in G, op.54/1
Beethoven Quartet no.15 in A minor, op.132

EDINBURGH UNIVERSITY SINGERS
30 Aug. 15.00 *Freemasons' Hall*
Choral music by Victoria, Sermisy, Bonnet, Le Jeune, Josquin d'Ascanio, Lassus, V. Williams, Debussy, Hopkins
Director Herrick Bunney
with Wight Henderson (pf)

SESTETTO ITALIANO LUCA MARENZIO
6 Sep. 15.00 *Freemasons' Hall*
Gastoldi Tutti, venite armati
Banchieri Il festino della sena del giovedi grasso avanti cena
Gesualdo Luci serene e chiare
Monteverdi Invettiva di Armida
Monteverdi O Mirtillo, Mirtillo
Croce Canzone del cucco e del rossignolo con sentenza del pappagallo
Marenzio Inno a Roma

RECITALS

RICHARD LEWIS (ten)
GERALD MOORE (pf)
27 Aug. 20.00 *Freemasons' Hall*
Tippett The heart's assurance
Songs by Purcell, V. Williams, Bax, Butterworth, Howells, Fauré

IRMGARD SEEFRIED (sop)
ERIK WERBA (pf)
5 Sep. 20.00 *Usher Hall*
Songs by Haydn, Schumann, Hindemith, Mendelssohn, Pfitzner, R. Strauss

IRMGARD SEEFRIED (sop), DIETRICH FISCHER-DIESKAU (bar), ERIK WERBA, GERALD MOORE (pf)
7 Sep. 20.00 *Usher Hall*
Wolf Spanisches Liederbuch

DIETRICH FISCHER-DIESKAU (bar) GERALD MOORE (pf)
9 Sep. 20.00 *Usher Hall*
Schubert Die schöne Müllerin

KERSTIN MEYER (mez) GERALD MOORE (pf)
10 Sep. 11.00? *Roxy Cinema*
Concert for children

WILHELM KEMPFF (pf)
29 Aug. 20.00 *Usher Hall*
Bach French suite no.5 in G
Kempff Praeambulum-Scherzo-Introduzione-Toccata
Beethoven Sonata no.28 in A, op.101
Brahms Variations and fugue on a theme by Handel

RUDOLF FIRKUŠNÝ (pf)
8 Sep. 20.00 *Freemasons' Hall*
Beethoven Variations on a theme by Salieri
Brahms Piano pieces, op.119
Chopin Sonata no.3 in B minor, op.58
Schumann Davidsbündlertänze
Janáček Sonata 1 X 1905
Smetana Czech dances: Excerpts

VRONSKY *and* BABIN (pf)
4 Sep. 11.00 *Freemasons' Hall*
Mozart Sonata for piano duet in F, K497
Stravinsky Concerto for 2 solo pianos
Schubert Fantasia for piano duet in F minor, D940

WOLFGANG SCHNEIDERHAN (vn) CARL SEEMANN (pf)
3 Sep. 20.00 *Freemasons' Hall*
Schubert Sonata in A (Duo), D574
Brahms Sonata no.1 in G, op.78
Mozart Sonata no.26 in B flat, K378
Beethoven Sonata no.7 in C minor, op.30/2

PIERRE FOURNIER (vc) WILHELM KEMPFF (pf)
25 Aug. 11.00 *Freemasons' Hall*
Beethoven Sonata no.1 in F, op.5/1
Beethoven Sonata no.4 in C, op.102/1
Beethoven Sonata no.5 in D, op.102/2

27 Aug. 11.00 *Freemasons' Hall*
Beethoven Sonata no.2 in G minor, op.5/2
Beethoven Sonata no.3 in A, op.69

JEAN-PIERRE RAMPAL (fl) ROBERT VEYRON-LACROIX (pf)
3 Sep. 11.00 *Freemasons' Hall*
Bach Sonata no.4 in C
Bach Sonata in G minor
Bach Sonata no.3 in A
Bach Sonata no.2 in E flat

5 Sep. 11.00 *Freemasons' Hall*
Bach Sonata no.6 in E
Bach Sonata no.1 in B minor
Bach Sonata for solo flute in A minor
Bach Sonata no.5 in E minor

NICANOR ZABALETA (hp)
31 Aug. 11.00 *Freemasons' Hall*
Music by Rosetti, Corelli, Beethoven, C.P.E. Bach, Hindemith, Křenek, Fauré, Prokofiev

DRAMA

EDINBURGH INTERNATIONAL FESTIVAL
24 Aug.-12 Sep. 19.15 (exc. Sun) 25, 29 Aug. 1, 5, 8, 12 Sep. 14.15 Assembly Hall
THE THRIE ESTAITES Lyndsay
Diligence Eric Woodburn
King John Cairney
Wantonness Andrew Downie
Placebo William Simpson
Solace Norman Fraser
Sensualitie Constance Mullay
Hameliness Joan Summers
Danger Margery Harris
Fund-Jennet Brian Carey
Gude Counsel Bryden Murdoch
Flatterie Duncan Macrae
Falsehood James Gibson
Deceit Walter Carr
Veritie Grace McClery
Chastitie Marjorie Thomson
Spiritualitie Roddy McMillan
Prioress Pamela Bain
Abbot Alexander Allan
Parson Edmund Sulley
Vicar John Rae
Temporalitie Michael Elder
Merchant Norman McLeod
Divine Correction Tom Fleming
Poor man George Davies
Pardoner Duncan Macrae
John the Common-Weal Andrew Keir
Red sergeant Michael Deacon
Black sergeant William Nicol
Director Tyrone Guthrie
Designer Molly MacEwen
Music Cedric Thorpe Davie
(In association with Wharton Productions)

OLD VIC
24-29 Aug. 19.00 29 Aug. 14.15
Lyceum Theatre
THE DOUBLE-DEALER Congreve
Maskwell Donald Houston
Lord Touchwood Charles West
Mellefont John Justin
Careless John Woodvine
Lord Froth Joss Ackland
Brisk Alec McCowen
Sir Paul Plyant Miles Malleson
Saygrace Norman Scace
Lady Touchwood Ursula Jeans
Cynthia Judi Dench
Lady Froth Moyra Fraser
Lady Plyant Maggie Smith
Boy Gordon Gardner
Footmen Douglas Harris, Stephen Moore
Director Michael Benthall
Designer Desmond Heeley
Music John Lambert

BIRMINGHAM REPERTORY THEATRE
31 Aug.-5 Sep. 19.00 5 Sep. 14.15
Lyceum Theatre
GAMMER GURTON'S NEEDLE Master S. Master of Arts (Identity uncertain)
Diccon Terence Lodge
Hodge Paul Williamson
Tib Thelma Barlow
Gammer Gurton Marigold Sharman
Cock Mark Kingston
Dame Chat Elizabeth Spriggs
Doctor Rat Ian Richardson
Master Bailey Arthur Pentelow
Doll Nancie Jackson
Scapethrist John Carlin
FRATRICIDE PUNISHED
Night Marigold Sharman
1st Fury/Ophelia Thelma Barlow
2nd Fury Elizabeth Spriggs
3rd Fury/Queen of Denmark Nancie Jackson
1st Sentinel/Carl/2nd Pirate Terence Lodge
Ghost of Hamlet's father William McAllister
2nd Sentinel/1st Pirate Paul Williamson
Horatio Arthur Gross
Francisco/Jens/Leonhardus Ian Richardson
Hamlet Mark Kingston
Phantasmo Derek Hunt
Corambus Arthur Pentelow
King of Denmark John Carlin
Player queen Christine Jones
Actor David Trevena
Director Bernard Hepton
Designer Paul Shelving

ENGLISH STAGE COMPANY
7-12 Sep. 19.00 12 Sep. 14.15
Lyceum Theatre
COCK-A-DOODLE DANDY O'Casey
The Cock Berto Pasuka
Michael Marthraun J.G. Devlin
Sailor Mahan Wilfred Lawson
Lorna Pauline Flanagan
Loreleen Joan O'Hara
Marion Etain O'Dell
Shanaar Eamon Keane
1st Rough fellow Alex Farrell
2nd Rough fellow Colin Blakely
Father Domineer Patrick Magee
Sergeant/Mayor John Kelly
Julia Jeanne Hepple
Jack/Julia's father Robert Arnold
Porter Charles Wade
One-eyed Larry Bil Keating
Mace-bearer/Bellman Stephen Dartnell
Messenger Norman Rodway
Director George Devine
Designer Sean Kenny
Music Geoffrey Wright

PERTH REPERTORY THEATRE
24-29 Aug. 19.30 27, 29 Aug. 14.30
Gateway Theatre
BREAKSPEAR IN GASCONY Linklater (World première)
Alys Claire Isbister
Walter Breakspear Christopher Burgess
Sir William David Steuart
Martin Ian Cowan
Geoffrey Neville Barber
Simkin Leader Hawkins
Lady Saill Valerie Lush
Lady Héloise Diana Beaumont
Brother Melchior Wilfred Bentley
Sir Thomas Turton Johnson Bayly
Bertram Geoffrey Rose
English sentry Anthony Negus
Hobden Peter Penry-Jones
Tobias of Lincoln Graham Roberts
Director Julian Herington
Scenery Mary Purvis
Costumes Wendy Doncaster

DUNDEE REPERTORY THEATRE
31 Aug.-5 Sep. 19.30 3, 5 Sep. 14.30
Gateway Theatre
CANDIDA Shaw
Prosperine Garnett Rowena Cooper
Rev. James Mavor Morell Raymond Westwell
Rev. Alexander Mill James Ward
Burgess John Walters
Candida Joan MacArthur
Eugene Marchbanks Neil Curnow
Director Raymond Westwell
Scenery Edward Furby
Costumes Wendy North

CITIZENS' THEATRE, Glasgow
7-12 Sep. 19.30 10, 12 Sep. 14.30
Gateway Theatre
THE BAIKIE CHARIVARI Bridie
Sir James Pounce-Pellott Iain Cuthbertson
Lady Pounce-Pellott Elaine Wells
Miss Pounce-Pellott Amanda Grinling
Rev. Dr Marcus Beadle Donald Douglas
Councillor John Ketch John Grieve
Joe Mascara Clarke Tait
Toby Messan Bruce McKenzie
Dr Jean Pothecary Ann Gudrun
Mrs Jemima Lee Crowe Pat Heywood
Robert Copper David MacMillan
Lady Maggie Revenant Helena Gloag
The De'il Leonard Maguire
Director Peter Duguid
Scenery David Jones
Costumes Elisabeth Friendship

POETRY AND PROSE RECITALS

ROBERT BURNS (1759-1796)
Produced by Gerard Slevin
22.45 *Lyceum Theatre*
24, 28 Aug. Joan Alexander, Meta Forrest, Ian Gilmour
26 Aug. 8 Sep Roberta McEwan, Roddy McMillan
10, 12 Sep. James Kelman, Iain Cuthbertson
with Alexander Kelly (pf)
At each performance
THE JOLLY BEGGARS Thorpe Davie
(Words by Robert Burns)
with Saltire Singers, Amici Quartet
Conductor Hans Oppenheim
Based on the original production by Peter Potter

2 Sep. 14.15 *Lyceum Theatre*
Burns: Readings from his verse and prose
Sir Compton Mackenzie, Meta Forrest, Ian Gilmour, James Gibson (rdr)
Director Gerard Slevin

26 Aug. 14.15 *Lyceum Theatre*
JOHN BETJEMAN (rdr)
Works by Hardy, Barham, Betjeman *and others*
(In association with the Apollo Society)

9 Sep. 14.15 *Lyceum Theatre*
DAME EDITH SITWELL (rdr)
Works by Shakespeare, Herrick, Milton, Tennyson, Swinburne, Yeats, Edith, Osbert and Sacheverell Sitwell *and others*
(In association with the Apollo Society)

LATE NIGHT ENTERTAINMENT

25, 27, 29, 31 Aug. 2, 4 Sep. 22.45
Lyceum Theatre
MICHAEL FLANDERS *and* DONALD SWANN
AT THE DROP OF A HAT

1, 3, 5, 7, 9, 11 Sep. 22.45
Lyceum Theatre
ANNA RUSSELL makes fun of the Festival
with Eugene Rankin (pf)

DANCE

LES BALLETS BABILÉE, France
24-26 Aug. 19.30 26 Aug. 14.30
Empire Theatre
SUITE EN BLANC
Choreographer Serge Lifar
Music Lalo
VARIATION
Choreographer Léonide Massine
Music Manino
ORPHÉE
Choreographer Adolfo Andrade
Music Liszt
BALANCE À TROIS
Choreographer Jean Babilée
Music Jean-Michel Damase
Designer Tom Keogh
BALLETINO
Choreographer Dick Sanders
Music Ibert
LE JEUNE HOMME ET LA MORT
Choreographer Roland Petit
Music Bach
Scenery Georges Wakhevitch
Costumes Barbara Karinska

27-29 Aug. 19.30 29 Aug. 14.30
Empire Theatre
SABLE
Choreographer Jean Babilée
Music Le Roux
Costumes Lila de Nobili
FUGUE
Choreographer Janine Charrat
Music Bach
DIVERTIMENTO
Choreographer Jean Babilée
Music Jean-Michel Damase
LA BOUCLE
Choreographer Jean Babilée
Music Jean-Michel Damase
Scenery Michel Drach
Costumes Sylvia Braverman
ADAGIO
Choreographer Gérard Ohn
Music Albinoni
LA CRÉATION
Choreographer David Lichine
L'EMPRISE
Choreographer Dick Sanders
Music Delerue
Designer François Ganeau
Dancers Claire Sombert, Jean Babilée, Jovanka Bjegojević, Gérard Ohn, Adolfo Andrade, Josette Clavier, Catherine Verneuil
Festival Ballet Orchestra
Conductor Daniel Stirn

NATIONAL BALLET OF FINLAND
31 Aug. 1, 2, 5, Sep. 19.30
Empire Theatre
L'ÉPREUVE D'AMOUR
Choreographer George Gé *after* Fokine
Music Mozart
Scenery Janos Horvath
Costumes Martha Platonoff
SCARAMOUCHE
Choreographer Irja Koskinen
Music Sibelius
Designer Paul Suominen
DON QUICHOTTE
Choreographer George Gé
Music Minkus
Scenery Seppo Nurmimaa
Costumes Martha Platonoff

2, 5 Sep. 14.30 *Empire Theatre*
CIRCLE OF ROSES
Choreographer Elsa Sylvestersson
Music Sonninen
Designer Seppo Nurmimaa
VALSE TRISTE
Choreographer Elsa Sylvestersson
Music Sibelius
DANCE OF THE SPIDER
Choreographer Irja Koskinen
Music Sonninen
THREE HARLEQUINS
Choreographer George Gé
Music Rinkama
SWAN LAKE: Black swan pas de deux
Choreographer Petipa *and* Ivanov
Music Tchaikovsky
DON QUICHOTTE

3, 4 Sep. 19.30 *Empire Theatre*
GISELLE
Choreographer Coralli, Perrot, Petipa rev. Léonid Lavrovsky
Music Adam
Designer Paul Suominen
Dancers Margaretha von Bahr, Doris Lainë, Maj-Lis Rajala, Lisa Taxell, Uno Onkinen, Jaakko Lätti, Klaus Salin, Heikki Värtsi
Festival Ballet Orchestra
Conductors Jussi Jalas, Nisse Rinkama

JEROME ROBBINS - BALLETS: USA
7-12 Sep. 19.30 9,12 Sep. 14.30
Empire Theatre
MOVES
Choreographer Jerome Robbins
Lighting Nananne Porcher
AFTERNOON OF A FAUN
Choreographer Jerome Robbins
Music Debussy
Scenery Jean Rosenthal
Costumes Irene Sharaff
NY EXPORT, Op. JAZZ
Choreographer Jerome Robbins
Music Robert Prince
Scenery Ben Shahn
Costumes Ben Shahn, Florence Klotz
THE CONCERT
Choreographer Jerome Robbins
Music Chopin
Scenery Saul Steinberg
Costumes Irene Sharaff
Dancers Jamie Bauer, Muriel Bentley, Wilma Curley, Patricia Dunn, Gwen Lewis, Erin Martin, Christine Mayer, Jane Mason, Barbara Milberg, Beryl Towbin, Tommy Abbott, Bob Bakanic, Lawrence Gradus, John Jones, Michael Maule, James Moore, Jay Norman, Bill Reilly, Doug Spingler, James White
with Betty Walberg (pf)
Scottish National Orchestra
Conductor Werner Torkanowsky

EXHIBITIONS

Royal Scottish Academy
MASTERPIECES OF CZECH ART
(In association with the Royal Scottish Academy and the Arts Council of Great Britain)

1960

OPERA

GLYNDEBOURNE OPERA
23, 25, 27, 29 Aug. 2, 6, 9 Sep. 19.00
King's Theatre
FALSTAFF Verdi
Falstaff Geraint Evans
Alice Ilva Ligabue
Meg Anna Maria Rota
Mistress Quickly Oralia Dominguez
Nanetta Mariella Adani
Ford Sesto Bruscantini
Fenton Juan Oncina
Dr Caius Hugues Cuenod
Bardolph Mario Carlin
Pistol Marco Stefanoni
Innkeeper Harold Williams
Royal Philharmonic Orchestra
Conductor Vittorio Gui
Director Peter Ebert (orig. Carl Ebert)
Designer Osbert Lancaster

24, 26, 31 Aug. 3, 8, 10 Sep. 19.00
King's Theatre
I PURITANI Bellini
Elvira Joan Sutherland
Arturo Nicola Filacuridi
Giorgio Giuseppe Modesti
Queen Henrietta Monica Sinclair
Riccardo Ernest Blanc
Sir Bruno John Kentish
Lord Walton David Ward
Royal Philharmonic Orchestra
Conductors Vittorio Gui
Bryan Balkwill
Director Franco Enriquez
Designer Desmond Heeley

30 Aug. 1, 5, 7 Sep. 19.00 King's Theatre
IL SEGRETO DI SUSANNA Wolf-Ferrari
Gil Sesto Bruscantini
Countess Mariella Adani
Sante Heinz Blankenburg
Director Peter Ebert
Designer Carl Toms
LA VOIX HUMAINE Poulenc
Elle Denise Duval
Director and designer Jean Cocteau
ARLECCHINO Busoni
Arlecchino Heinz Blankenburg
Colombina Helga Pilarczyk
Ser Matteo Ian Wallace
Abbate Cospicuo Gwyn Griffiths
Doctor Bombasto Carlos Feller
Leandro Dermot Troy
Annunziata Silvia Ashmole
Royal Philharmonic Orchestra
Director Peter Ebert
Designer Peter Rice
Conductor (all operas) John Pritchard

ORCHESTRAL CONCERTS

PHILHARMONIA ORCHESTRA
21 Aug. 20.00 *Usher Hall*
Verdi Requiem
Conductor Carlo Maria Giulini
Soloists Joan Sutherland (sop), Fiorenza Cossotto (mez), Luigi Ottolini (ten), Ivo Vinco (bs), Philharmonia Chorus

22 Aug. 20.00 *Usher Hall*
Rezniček Donna Diana: Overture
Brahms Concerto for violin in D, op.77
Dvořák Symphony no.4 in G, op.88
Conductor Wolfgang Sawallisch
Soloist Gioconda de Vito (vn)

24 Aug. 20.00 *Usher Hall*
Mozart Symphony no.39 in E flat, K543
Beethoven Concerto for piano no.1 in C, op.15
Brahms Symphony no.1 in C minor, op.68
Conductor Carlo Maria Giulini
Soloist Claudio Arrau (pf)

25 Aug. 20.00 *Usher Hall*
Mendelssohn A midsummer night's dream: Overture
Brahms Variations on a theme by Haydn (St Antoni), op.56a
Mahler Des Knaben Wunderhorn: Das irdische Leben; Wo die schönen Trompeten blasen; Rheinlegendchen
Beethoven Symphony no.7 in A, op.92
Conductor Wolfgang Sawallisch
Soloist Ursula Boese (mez)

SCOTTISH NATIONAL ORCHESTRA
28 Aug. 20.00 *Usher Hall*
Schumann Manfred: Overture
Chopin Concerto for piano no.1 in E minor, op.11
Mahler Symphony no.1 in D
Conductor Alexander Gibson
Soloist Claudio Arrau (pf)

31 Aug. 20.00 *Usher Hall*
Mozart Symphony no.34 in C, K338
Beethoven Concerto for piano no.2 in B flat, op.19
Bartók Concerto for orchestra
Conductor Alexander Gibson
Soloist Myra Hess (pf)

4 Sep. 20.00 *Usher Hall*
Carissimi Jephte
Rossini Stabat Mater
Conductor Vittorio Gui
Soloists Victoria de los Angeles (sop), Oralia Dominguez (mez), Richard Lewis (ten), Giuseppe Modesti (bs), Edinburgh Royal Choral Union

10 Sep. 22.45 *Usher Hall*
A Scottish Serenade
Arnold Tam o' Shanter - Overture
Whyte Scottish dance - Eightsome reel
Hamilton Scottish dances
Gibilaro Scottish fantasia
Trad. Scottish songs
Conductor Alexander Gibson
Soloist Ian Wallace (bs)

SACHER CHAMBER ORCHESTRA, Zürich
Conductor Paul Sacher
29 Aug. 20.00 *Usher Hall*
Haydn Symphony no.87 in A
Mozart Concerto for piano no.19 in F, K459
Mozart Rondo for piano and orchestra in A, K386
Martin Études for string orchestra
Soloist Paul Badura-Skoda (pf)

30 Aug. 20.00 *Usher Hall*
Mozart Divertimento no.11 in D, K251: 4 movements
Haydn Concerto for violin in C
Mozart Concerto for violin no.3 in G, K216
Honegger Symphony no.2
Soloist Isaac Stern (vn)

ROYAL LIVERPOOL PHILHARMONIC ORCHESTRA
Conductor John Pritchard
2 Sep. 20.00 *Usher Hall*
Haydn Symphony no.95 in C minor
Ravel Alborada del gracioso
Berg Concerto for violin
Walton Symphony no.2 (World première)
Soloist Isaac Stern (vn)

3 Sep. 20.00 *Usher Hall*
Searle Symphony no.3, op.36 (World première)
Berg Lulu - Suite
Soloist Helga Pilarczyk (sop)
Introduced by John Carewe

LENINGRAD SYMPHONY ORCHESTRA
6 Sep. 20.00 *Usher Hall*
Shostakovich Symphony no.5 in D minor, op.47
Tchaikovsky Symphony no.5 in E minor, op.64
Conductor Evgeny Mravinsky

7 Sep. 20.00 *Usher Hall*
Mozart Le nozze di Figaro: Overture
Beethoven Symphony no.7 in A, op.92
Tchaikovsky Symphony no.6 in B minor (Pathétique), op.74
Conductor Evgeny Mravinsky

9 Sep. 20.00 *Usher Hall*
Britten Variations and fugue on a theme of Purcell, op.34
Shostakovich Concerto for cello no.1 in E flat, op.107
Miaskovsky Symphony no.21 in F sharp minor, op.51
Tchaikovsky Francesca da Rimini
Conductor Gennadi Rozhdestvensky
Soloist Mstislav Rostropovich (vc)

10 Sep. 19.30 *Usher Hall*
Glinka Ruslan and Ludmilla: Overture
Prokofiev Symphony no.6 in E flat minor, op.111
Tchaikovsky Symphony no.4 in F minor, op.36
Conductor Evgeny Mravinsky

10 Sep. 11.00 *Freemasons' Hall*
Haydn Toy symphony
A public rehearsal and performance by Festival artists and personalities

CHAMBER CONCERTS

JUILLIARD QUARTET
22 Aug. 11.00 *Freemasons' Hall*
Piston Quartet no.1
Schubert Quartet no.14 in D minor (Death and the maiden), D810

24 Aug. 11.00 *Freemasons' Hall*
Schubert Quartet no.13 in A minor, D804
Berg Lyric suite

26 Aug. 11.00 *Freemasons' Hall*
Musgrave Quartet no.1
Schubert Quartet no.15 in G, D887

AMADEUS TRIO
29 Aug. 11.00 *Freemasons' Hall*
Mozart Quartet for piano and strings in G minor, K478
Mozart Quartet for piano and strings in E flat, K493
with Denis Matthews (pf)

31 Aug. 11.00 *Freemasons' Hall*
Beethoven Serenade in D, op.8
Mozart Divertimento in E flat, K563

BEAUX ARTS TRIO
3 Sep. 11.00 *Freemasons' Hall*
Beethoven Variations on 'Ich bin der Schneider Kakadu'
Ravel Trio for piano and strings in A minor

Mendelssohn Trio for piano and strings no.2 in C minor, op.66

6 Sep. 11.00 *Freemasons' Hall*
Beethoven Trio for piano and strings no.3 in C minor, op.1/3
Copland Vitebsk; Study on a Jewish theme
Brahms Trio for piano and strings no.1 in B, op.8

KOECKERT QUARTET
5 Sep. 11.00 *Freemasons' Hall*
Mozart Quartet no.17 in B flat (Hunt), K458
Beethoven Quartet no.12 in E flat, op.127

Schumann
7 Sep. 11.00 *Freemasons' Hall*
Trio for piano and strings no.1 in D minor, op.63
Quartet no.1 in A minor, op.41/1
Quintet for piano and strings in E flat, op.44
with Geoffrey Parsons (pf)

9 Sep. 11.00 *Freemasons' Hall*
Quartet no.2 in F, op.41/2
Trio for piano and strings no.2 in F, op.80
Quartet no.3 in A, op.41/3
with Geoffrey Parsons (pf)

RECITALS

VICTORIA DE LOS ANGELES (sop)
27 Aug. 20.00 *Usher Hall*
Songs of the Spanish Renaissance
with Ars Musicae Ensemble

1 Sep. 20.00 *Usher Hall*
Songs by A. Scarlatti, Handel, R. Strauss, Ravel, Hemsi, Granados
with Gerald Moore (pf)

URSULA BOESE (mez)
GERALD MOORE (pf)
28 Aug. 15.00 *Freemasons' Hall*
Songs by Purcell, Schubert, Dvořák, Brahms, Mahler

HERMANN PREY (bar)
GERALD MOORE (pf)
4 Sep. 15.00 *Freemasons' Hall*
Schubert settings of Schiller and Goethe

ADAM HARASIEWICZ (pf)
23 Aug. 11.00 *Freemasons' Hall*
Piano works by Chopin

GEORGE MALCOLM (hpd)
25 Aug. 11.00 *Freemasons' Hall*
Bach Goldberg variations

CLAUDIO ARRAU (pf)
26 Aug. 20.00 *Usher Hall*
Beethoven Sonata no.13 in E flat, op.27/1
Schumann Fantasia in C, op.17
Ravel Gaspard de la Nuit
Smetana Macbeth and the witches
Liszt Concert study no.2 (Gnomenreigen)
Liszt Étude d'execution transcendante no.10 in F minor

HALINA CZERNY-STEFANSKA (pf)
30 Aug. 11.00 *Freemasons' Hall*
Piano works by Chopin

MYRA HESS (pf)
4 Sep. 14.30 *Usher Hall*
Schumann Bunte Blätter: Albumblätter
Schumann Papillons
Schubert Sonata no.21 in B flat, D960
Beethoven Sonata no.32 in C minor, op.111

WITOLD MALCUZYNSKI (pf)
8 Sep. 20.00 *Usher Hall*
Piano works by Chopin

ISAAC STERN (vn), MYRA HESS (pf)
28 Aug. 14.30 *Usher Hall*
Brahms Sonata no.2 in A, op.100
Schubert Sonatina no.1 in D, D384
Ferguson Sonata no.2, op.10
Beethoven Sonata no.10 in G, op.96

JOAN DICKSON (vc)
HESTER DICKSON (pf)
27 Aug. 11.00 *Freemasons' Hall*
Bach Sonata no.2 in D
Gal Sonata
Chopin Sonata in G minor, op.65

ENRICO MAINARDI (vc)
GERALD MOORE (pf)
2 Sep. 11.00 *Freemasons' Hall*
Bach Suite no.4 in E flat
Mainardi Sonata for solo cello (World première)
Schubert Sonata in A minor (Arpeggione), D821

MSTISLAV ROSTROPOVICH (vc)
ALEXANDER DEDUKHIN (pf)
8 Sep. 11.00 *Freemasons' Hall*
Brahms Sonata no.2 in F, op.99
Bach Suite for solo cello no.3 in C
Prokofiev Sonata in C, op.119

ERNST WALLFISCH (va), LORY WALLFISCH (pf), JANET BAKER (mez)
1 Sep. 11.00 *Freemasons' Hall*
Brahms Sonata no.1 in F minor, op.120/1
Brahms Two songs for contralto, viola and piano
Brahms Sonata no.2 in E flat, op.120/2

DRAMA

EDINBURGH INTERNATIONAL FESTIVAL
22 Aug.-10 Sep. 19.15 (exc.Sun) 23, 27, 30 Aug. 3, 6, 10 Sep.14.15 Assembly Hall
THE WALLACE Goodsir Smith
(World première)
William Wallace Iain Cuthbertson
Robert Bruce John McGregor
Mirren Braidfute Rona Anderson
Jean Mairhi Russell
Queen Margaret Ruth Lodge
Sir Thomas Braidfute Alexander Allan
Ailish Rae Amanda Walker
Sandy Fraser/Edward, Prince of Wales Walter Carr
Sir John Menteith Robert James
Sir John Lovell/Herald Patrick Godfrey
Scottish chronicler James Gibson
Sir John Comyn John Grieve
Macduff/Sir Geoffrey de Hartlepool Bryden Murdoch
English chronicler Stanley Ratcliffe
Donald Frank Wylie
Sir John Graham/Sir Ralph John Mackenzie
Andrew Murray/Majordomo Michael Elder
Sir William Heselrig/Sir Peter Mallory Hugh Cross
Sir John Stewart of Bonkill David Orr
Sir John Segrave Lauriston Shaw
King Edward 1 Clive Morton
Lady Isabella Morag Forsyth
Earl of March/John de Backwell William Lyon Brown
Earl of Angus Iain Dunnett
Sir Ralph Haliburton Alistair Colledge
Archbishop of Canterbury Edmund Sulley
Director Peter Potter
Designer Audrey Cruddas
Music Iain Hamilton
(In association with Stephen Mitchell)

5-10 Sep. 19.00 7, 10 Sep. 14.15
Lyceum Theatre
THE DREAM OF PETER MANN Kops
(World première)
Sonia Mann Hermione Baddeley
Peter Mann Robert Hardy
Jason Martin Miller
Alex Michael Warre
Penny Valerie Gearon
Tom Groom Oscar Quitak
Mrs Butcher Eileen Way
Mr Green Will Stampe
Mrs Green Peggy Rowan
Mr Fish George Innes
Mrs Fish Doria Noar
Mr Butcher Norman Scace
Sylvia Paddy Edwards
John John Maynard
Jack Thomas Lennon
Director Frank Dunlop
Designer Richard Negri
Lighting Richard Pilbrow
(In association with Lynoq Productions)

OLD VIC
22-27 Aug. 19.00 24, 27 Aug. 14.15
Lyceum Theatre
THE SEAGULL Chekhov (Eng)
Medvedyenko Derek Smith
Masha Georgine Anderson
Peter Sorin Cyril Luckham
Konstantin Treplyev Tom Courteney
Nina Zarechnaya Ann Bell
Polina Sylvia Coleridge
Dr Dorn Ralph Michael
Irina Arkadina Judith Anderson
Boris Trigorin Tony Britton
Shamrayev Gerald James
Cook David Lloyd Meredith
Yakov Charles West
Housemaid Rosemarie Dunham
Director John Fernald
Scenery Paul Mayo
Costumes Beatrice Dawson

LA COMPAGNIE ROGER PLANCHON, France
29 Aug.-3 Sep. 19.00 31 Aug. 3 Sep. 14.15 *Lyceum Theatre*
LES TROIS MOUSQUETAIRES
Planchon (Adapted from the story by Alexandre Dumas)
Louis XIII Claude Lochy
La Reine Isabelle Sadoyan
Duc de Richelieu Henri Galiardin
Duc de Buckingham Jean-Pierre Barnard
Milady de Winter Julia Dancourt
Lord de Winter Jean Bouise
La père d'Artagnan Michel Robin
La mère d'Artagnan Ferna Claude
La frère/Planchet/Patrick Julien Mallier
Athos Jean Jacques Lagarde
Porthos Armand Meffre
Aramis Jean-Baptiste Thiérée
D'Artagnan Roger Planchon
M. de Tréville Pierre Meyrand
Boistracy/Felton Pierre Vassas
Ferenzac Daniel Laloux
Rochefort Jean Leuvrais
Jussac Gilbert Vilhon
Biscarat Bernard Jousset
Boisrenard Paul Planchon
Cahusac Philippe Morel
Le Chancelier Seiguier/L'Aubergiste Roger Saget

M. Bonacieux Marc Dudicourt
Madame Bonacieux Colette Dompietrini
Estafena Madeleine Berthelot
Director Roger Planchon
Scenery René Allio
Costumes Isabelle Sadoyan

CITIZENS' THEATRE, Glasgow
22-27 Aug. 19.30 25, 27 Aug. 14.30
Gateway Theatre
ROMULUS THE GREAT Dürrenmatt
(Eng. Translated by Nell Moody)
Romulus Augustus Joseph Greig
Julia Geraldine Newman
Rea Joanna Morris
Zeno the Isaurian Charles Baptiste
Emilian Hugh Sullivan
Mares John Ruck Keene
Tullius Rotundus Martin Heller
Spurius Titus Mamma Clarke Tait
Achilles Ian Trigger
Pyramus Roy Boutcher
Apollyon Ken Jones
Caesar Skinnem Dallas Cavell
Phylax/Odoaker Glyn Jones
Theodoric James Grant
Phosphoridos Gino Coia
Sulphurides Roy Hanlon
Cook Kalman Glass
Director Callum Mill
Designer Sally Hulke
Costumes Elisabeth Friendship

GATEWAY COMPANY
29 Aug.-10 Sep. (exc.Sun) 19.30 1, 3, 8, 10 Sep. 14.30 Gateway Theatre
MARY STUART IN SCOTLAND Bjørnson
(Eng. Translated by Elizabeth Sprigge)
Mary Stuart Patricia Kneale
Darnley Tom Criddle
James, Earl of Moray Bill Cartwright
Duchess of Argyle Margaret Robertson
Lethington Trevor Baxter
Rizzio Christopher Guinee
Bothwell Tom Fleming
Morton John Young
Ruthven Paul Kermack
Lindsay Brown Derby
Kerr Brian Carey
Taylor Alan Thompson
Erskine Anthony Moore
Knox Leonard Maguire
Lord James Hamilton Gary Hope
Director Richard Mathews
Designer David Lovett

30 Aug. 1, 3 Sep. 20.30 Freemasons' Hall
MARK TWAIN TONIGHT!
Hal Holbrook as Mark Twain
Director Joseph Keating

LATE NIGHT ENTERTAINMENT

22-27 Aug. 22.45 Lyceum Theatre
BEYOND THE FRINGE
Alan Bennett, Peter Cook, Jonathan Miller, Dudley Moore
Director John Hammond

29 Aug.-3 Sep. 22.45 Lyceum Theatre
LES FRÈRES JACQUES
with Pierre Philippe (pf)
Designer Jean-Denis Malclès

5-10 Sep. 22.45 Lyceum Theatre
A LATE EVENING WITH BEATRICE LILLIE
with Howard Godwin (pf)
Director John Philip

DANCE

THE ROYAL BALLET
22-24 Aug. 19.30 24 Aug. 14.30
Empire Theatre
DANSES CONCERTANTES
Choreographer Kenneth MacMillan
Music Stravinsky
Designer Nicholas Georgiadis
LA BAISER DE LA FÉE
Choreographer Kenneth MacMillan
Music Stravinsky
Designer Kenneth Rowell
PETRUSHKA
Choreographer Mikhail Fokine
Music Stravinsky
Designer Alexander Benois

25-27 Aug. 19.30 27 Aug. 14.30
Empire Theatre
BALLABILE
Choreographer Roland Petit
Music Chabrier; arr. Lambert
Designer Antoni Clavé
LA PÉRI
Choreographer Frederick Ashton
Music Dukas
Designer André Levasseur
THE PRINCE OF THE PAGODAS: Act 3
Choreographer John Cranko
Music Britten
Scenery John Piper
Costumes Desmond Heeley
Dancers Margot Fonteyn, Nadia Nerina, Svetlana Beriosova, Anya Linden, Annette Page, Michael Somes, Brian Shaw, Alexander Grant, David Blair, Donald Macleary, Maryon Lane, Julia Farron, Merle Park, Antoinette Sibley, Gary Burne, Leslie Edwards, Stanley Holden, Ronald Hynd, Ray Powell, Graham Usher, Franklin White, Christine Beckley, Georgina Parkinson, Petrus Bosman, Richard Farley, Bryan Lawrence, Christopher Newton, Ronald Plaisted, Derek Rencher, Keith Rosson, John Sale, Douglas Steuart, William Wilson
City of Birmingham Symphony Orch.
Conductor John Lanchbery

SUSANA Y JOSÉ, Spain
29, 31 Aug. 19.30 Empire Theatre
THE BALLAD OF CARMEN AND DON JOSÉ and other dances
Music Robledo
Designer Max Röthlisberger

30 Aug. 19.30 31 Aug. 14.30
Empire Theatre
Spanish folk dances
Dancers Susana Audeoud, José Udaeta, Manuel Mairene, Paco Hernandez
with Armin Janssen (pf), René Gerber (perc)

LITTLE BALLET TROUPE, Bombay
2 Sep. 14.30 3 Sep. 19.30
Empire Theatre
PANCHATANTRA

2 Sep. 19.30 3 Sep. 14.30
Empire Theatre
RAMAYANA
Choreographer Shanti Bardhan
Music Bahadur Hussain Khan
Dancers Gyan Sharma, Appuni Karta, Th. Babu Singh, Gul Bardhan, Sarmishtha Bardhan, Reva Chaudhari, Vatsala Rao, Rekha Rao, Prabhat Ganguli, Hasmukh Chavda, Narayan Swami, Sana Tomba, Suryamukhi Devi

BALLETS EUROPÉENS de Nervi
5-7 Sep. 19.30 7 Sep. 14.30
Empire Theatre
SCHÉHÉRAZADE
Choreographer Mikhail Fokine
Music Rimsky-Korsakov
Designer Léon Bakst
CHOREARTIUM
Choreographer Léonide Massine
Music Brahms
Scenery Eugene Lourie, André Beaurepaire
Costumes Constantine Terechkovich
LE BEAU DANUBE
Choreographer Léonide Massine
Music J. Strauss
Designer Constantin Guys

8-10 Sep. 19.00 10 Sep. 14.30
Empire Theatre
LA COMMEDIA UMANA
Choreographer Léonide Massine
Music Arrieu
Designer Alfred Manessier
Dancers Carla Fracci, Vjera Markovic, Tatiana Massine, jun, Yvonne Meyer, Nicole Nogaret, Duška Sifnios, Adolfo Andrade, Paolo Bortoluzzi, Ivan Dragadze, Harry Haythorne, Alfredo Kollner, Léonide Massine, jun, Nicolas Petrov, Enrico Sportiello, Wassili Sulich, Léon Woizikowsky, Milorad Miskovitch
Scottish National Orchestra
Conductor Marcel Couraud

EXHIBITIONS

Royal Scottish Academy
BLUE RIDER GROUP
(Arranged in association with the Arts Council of Great Britain and the Royal Scottish Academy)

1961

OPERA

COVENT GARDEN OPERA
21, 23, 26, 30 Aug. 4 Sep. 19.00
King's Theatre
IPHIGÉNIE EN TAURIDE Gluck
Iphigénie Rita Gorr
Oreste Robert Massard
Pylade André Turp
Thoas Louis Quilico
Diana Margreta Elkins
Greek woman Jeannette Sinclair
Priestesses Jenifer Eddy, Janet Coster
Scythian Victor Godfrey
Servant David Kelly
Conductors Georg Solti
Bryan Balkwill
Director Göran Gentele
Designer Carl Toms

25, 28 Aug. 1, 9 Sep. 19.00
King's Theatre
LUCIA DI LAMMERMOOR Donizetti
Lucia Joan Sutherland
Mady Mesplé*
Edgardo André Turp
Enrico John Shaw
Raimondo Joseph Rouleau
Arturo Kenneth Macdonald
Alisa Margreta Elkins
Normanno Edgar Evans
Conductor John Pritchard
Director and designer Franco Zeffirelli
*Performance on 7 Sep.cancelled and replaced with *Il barbiere di Sivigliia*

31 Aug. 2, 5, 7, 8 Sep. 19.00
King's Theatre
IL BARBIERE DI SIVIGLIA Rossini
Figaro Rolando Panerai
Rosina Bianca-Maria Casoni
Count Almaviva Luigi Alva
Dr Bartolo Fernando Corena
Don Basilio Boris Christoff
Berta Josephine Veasey
Fiorello Ronald Lewis
Ambrogio Leonard Fenton
Officer Robert Bowman
Conductors Carlo Maria Giulini
Edward Downes*
Director Maurice Sarrazin
Designer Jean-Denis Malclès

22, 24, 29 Aug. 6 Sep. 19.00 2 Sep. 14.00 *King's Theatre*
A MIDSUMMER NIGHT'S DREAM
Britten
Tytania Joan Carlyle
Oberon Russell Oberlin
Lysander John Dobson
Helena Irene Salemka
Demetrius Peter Glossop
Hermia Janet Coster
Theseus Forbes Robinson
Hippolyta Margreta Elkins
Noreen Berry
Bottom Geraint Evans
Starveling Joseph Ward
Snug David Kelly
Flute John Lanigan
Quince Michael Langdon
Snout Kenneth Macdonald
Puck Nicholas Chagrin
Philostrate Leonard Fenton
Conductors Georg Solti
Meredith Davies
Director John Gielgud
Designer John Piper

ORCHESTRAL CONCERTS

LONDON SYMPHONY ORCHESTRA
20 Aug. 20.00 *Usher Hall*
Schoenberg Gurrelieder
Conductor Leopold Stokowski
Soloists Gré Brouwenstijn (sop), Nell Rankin (mez), James McCracken, John Lanigan (ten), Forbes Robinson (bs), Alvar Lidell (narr), Edinburgh Royal Choral Union

21 Aug. 20.00 *Usher Hall*
Britten Sinfonia da requiem
Ravel Concerto for piano in G
Berlioz Symphonie fantastique
Conductor Colin Davis
Soloist Monique Haas (pf)

22 Aug. 20.00 *Usher Hall*
Gabrieli Sonata pian e forte a 8
Tippett Concerto for double string orchestra
Liszt Mephisto waltz no.1
Shostakovich Symphony no.5 in D minor, op.47
Conductor Leopold Stokowski

23 Aug. 20.00 *Usher Hall*
Schoenberg Five orchestral pieces, op.16
Liszt Concerto for piano no.1 in E flat
Haydn Sinfonia concertante in B flat, op.84
Stravinsky Symphony in 3 movements
Conductor Colin Davis
Soloists Annie Fischer (pf), Hugh Maguire (vn), Kenneth Heath (vc), Roger Lord (ob), William Waterhouse (bn)

SCOTTISH NATIONAL ORCHESTRA
Conductor Alexander Gibson
24 Aug. 20.00 *Usher Hall*
Britten Peter Grimes: Four sea interludes *and* Passacaglia
Mozart Concerto for piano no.20 in D minor, K466
Schoenberg Variations, op.31
Liszt Prometheus
Soloist Paul Badura-Skoda (pf)

2 Sep. 20.00 *Usher Hall*
Berlioz Benvenuto Cellini: Overture
Schoenberg Concerto for violin, op.36
Liszt A Faust symphony
Soloists Wolfgang Marschner (vn), Murray Dickie (ten), Edinburgh Royal Choral Union

BERLIN PHILHARMONIC ORCHESTRA
25 Aug. 20.00 *Usher Hall*
Webern Six pieces, op.6
Mozart Symphony no.39 in E flat, K543
Brahms Symphony no.1 in C minor, op.68
Conductor Herbert von Karajan

26 Aug. 20.00 *Usher Hall*
Bach Suite no.2 in B minor
Stravinsky Symphony in C
R. Strauss Ein Heldenleben
Conductor Herbert von Karajan

27 Aug. 20.00 *Usher Hall*
Blacher Fantasia, op.51
Britten Concerto for piano in D, op.13
Dvořák Symphony no.9 in E minor (New World), op. 95
Conductor Rudolf Kempe
Soloist Maureen Jones (pf)

28 Aug. 20.00 *Usher Hall*
Brahms Variations on a theme by Haydn (St Antoni), op.56a
Mendelssohn Concerto for violin in E minor, op.64
Hindemith Symphonic metamorphosis on themes of Weber
Stravinsky The firebird - Suite
Conductor Rudolf Kempe
Soloist Henryk Szeryng (vn)

30 Aug. 20.00 *Usher Hall*
Gluck Iphigénie en Aulide: Overture
Janáček Taras Bulba
Beethoven Symphony no.3 in E flat (Eroica), op.55
Conductor Jascha Horenstein

31 Aug. 20.00 *Usher Hall*
Mozart Concerto for piano no.27 in B flat, K595
Mahler Symphony no.5 in C sharp minor
Conductor Jascha Horenstein
Soloist Clifford Curzon (pf)

BBC SYMPHONY ORCHESTRA
3 Sep. 20.00 *Usher Hall*
Schubert Symphony no.4 in C minor (Tragic), D417
Schoenberg Six songs, op.8
Schoenberg Film music, op.34
Mozart Ch'io mi scordi di te
Liszt Hunnenschlacht
Conductor Norman del Mar
Soloists Elisabeth Söderström (sop), David Wilde (pf)

ENGLISH CHAMBER ORCHESTRA
4 Sep. 20.00 *Usher Hall*
Arriaga Symphony (1825)
Handel Alcina: Tornami a vagheggiar *and* Ombre pallide
Stravinsky Concerto in E flat (Dumbarton Oaks)
Rossini Sonata for strings no.3 in C
Bellini Beatrice di Tenda: Oh! miei fedeli
Haydn Symphony no.80 in D minor
Conductor John Pritchard
Soloist Joan Sutherland (sop)

6 Sep. 20.00 *Leith Town Hall*
Arriaga Los esclavos felices: Overture
Berg Lyric suite: 3 movements
Mozart Concerto for piano no.23 in A, K488
Bizet Symphony in C
Conductor John Pritchard
Soloist Annie Fischer (pf)

7 Sep. 11.00 *Leith Town Hall*
Bach Brandenburg concerto no.3 in G
Stravinsky Movements for piano and orchestra
Telemann Concerto for viola in G
Schubert Symphony no.3 in D, D200
Conductor Meredith Davies
Soloists Bruno Giuranna (va), John Ogdon (pf)

9 Sep. 11.00 *Leith Town Hall*
Cimarosa Il maestro di cappella
Music in miniature by Haydn, Casella, Handel, Stravinsky, Rameau, Purcell, Gluck, Arnold
Conductor Raymond Leppard
Soloist Geraint Evans (bar)

PHILHARMONIA ORCHESTRA
5 Sep. 20.00 *Usher Hall*
Mendelssohn A midsummer night's dream: Overture *and* Incidental music
Bartók Divertimento for strings
Schumann Symphony no.4 in D minor, op.120
Conductor Otto Klemperer

7 Sep. 20.00 *Usher Hall*
Tchaikovsky Symphony no.6 in B minor (Pathétique), op.74
Mussorgsky Khovanshchina: Overture
Mussorgsky Pictures at an exhibition; orch. Ravel
Conductor Carlo Maria Giulini

8 Sep. 20.00 *Usher Hall*
Mahler Symphony no.2 in C minor (Resurrection)
Conductor Otto Klemperer
Soloists Heather Harper (sop), Janet Baker (mez), Edinburgh Royal Choral Union

9 Sep. 19.30 *Usher Hall*
Mozart Symphony no.35 in D (Haffner), K385
Mozart Sinfonia concertante for violin and viola, K.364
Britten Serenade for tenor, horn and strings
Britten The young person's guide to the orchestra
Conductor Carlo Maria Giulini
Soloists Peter Pears (ten), Alan Civil (hn), Szymon Goldberg (vn), Bruno Giuranna (va)

9 Sep. 22.45 *Usher Hall*
Offenbach La belle Hélène: Overture
J. Strauss Kaiser Walzer
R. Strauss Der Rosenkavalier: Waltzes
Berlioz La damnation de Faust: Rákóczy march
Klemperer Merry waltz and one-step
Conductor Otto Klemperer

CHAMBER CONCERTS

DROLC QUARTET
21 Aug. 11.00 *Freemasons' Hall*
Schoenberg Quartet no.1 in D minor, op.7
Haydn Quartet in D, op.76/5

23 Aug. 11.00 *Freemasons' Hall*
Schoenberg Quartet no.3, op.30
Haydn Quartet in B flat, op.1/1
Beethoven Quartet no.7 in F (Rasumovsky), op.59/1

25 Aug. 11.00 *Freemasons' Hall*
Schoenberg Quartet no.4, op.37
Schoenberg Quartet no.2 in F sharp minor, op.10
with Heather Harper (sop)

CONCERTGEBOUW WIND QUINTET, Amsterdam
with Lamar Crowson (pf)
22 Aug. 11.00 *Freemasons' Hall*
Schoenberg Quintet for wind, op.26
Beethoven Quintet for piano and wind in E flat, op.16

24 Aug. 11.00 *Freemasons' Hall*
Seiber Permutazioni a cinque
Badings Quintet for wind no.2
Rossini Quartet for wind no.5 in D
Mozart Quintet for piano and wind in E flat, K452

TRIO DI TRIESTE
26 Aug. 11.00 *Freemasons' Hall*
Shostakovich Trio for piano and strings no.2 in E minor, op.67
Schubert Trio for piano and strings in E flat, D929

28 Aug. 11.00 *Freemasons' Hall*
Ravel Trio for piano and strings in A minor
Beethoven Trio for piano and strings no.7 in B flat (Archduke), op.97

ANNIE FISCHER (pf)
ALLEGRI QUARTET
29 Aug. 20.00 *Usher Hall*
Mozart Quartet for piano and strings in G minor, K478
Beethoven Sonata no.21 in C (Waldstein), op.53
Schumann Quintet for piano and strings in E flat, op.44

JOHN OGDON (pf), ALLEGRI QUARTET
31 Aug. 11.00 *Freemasons' Hall*
Schubert Quartet no.12 in C minor (Quartetsatz), D703
Liszt Lugubre gondola
Liszt Valse oubliée no.2
Liszt Années de pèlerinage 3: Le jeux d'eau à la Villa d'Este
Liszt Don Giovanni fantasia
Brahms Quintet for piano and strings in F minor, op. 34

CLIFFORD CURZON (pf)
AMADEUS QUARTET
3 Sep. 14.30 *Usher Hall*
Schubert Quartet no.8 in B flat, D112
Schubert Impromptus for piano, D899
Schubert Quintet for piano and strings in A (The trout), D667
with James Merrett (db)

AMADEUS QUARTET
4 Sep. 11.00 *Freemasons' Hall*
Seiber Quartet no.3 (Quartetto lirico)
Haydn Quartet in D minor (Unfinished), op.103
Beethoven Quartet no.8 in E minor (Rasumovsky), op.59/2

NEW MUSIC ENSEMBLE
6 Sep. 11.00 *Freemasons' Hall*
P.M. Davies Ricercar and doubles on 'To many a well'
Schoenberg Serenade, op.24
Conductor John Carewe
Soloist John Shirley-Quirk (bar)
(In association with the Music Section of the Institute of Contemporary Arts)

EDINBURGH UNIVERSITY SINGERS
27 Aug. 15.00 *Freemasons' Hall*
Bach Motet no.3. Jesu meine Freude
Britten Hymn to St Cecilia
Mozart Canons, K555, K348, K232
Leighton Hymn of the Nativity
Seiber Three nonsense songs
Songs of the French Renaissance by Lassus, Costeley, Jacotin, Certon, Passereau
Conductor Herrick Bunney

GREGG SMITH SINGERS
8 Sep. 11.00 *Freemasons' Hall*
Works by Bach, Schoenberg, Britten, Victoria, Byrd, Mendelssohn, Ives, Salisbury, Billings, Biggs, G. Smith
Conductor Gregg Smith

JOAN CARLYLE (sop), JOSEPHINE VEASEY (mez), JOHN LANIGAN (ten), MICHAEL LANGDON (bs), EDWARD DOWNES, ROBERT KEYS (pf)
1 Sep. 11.00 *Leith Town Hall*
Rossini Serate musicale
Brahms Liebeslieder Walzer

ELECTRONIC CONCERT
5 Sep. 20.00 *Freemasons' Hall*
Stockhausen Study 2
Berio Momenti
Nono Omaggio a Emilio Vedova
Electronic compositions by Eimert, Castiglioni, Kotonski, Arel, Walter, Schaeffer, Olnick
Presented by Daphne Oram

RECITALS

LUIGI ALVA (ten), GERALD MOORE (pf)
27 Aug. 20.00 *Freemasons' Hall*
Arias by Paisiello, Gluck, Handel, Mozart
Songs by Nin, Obradors, Morales, Arias

PETER PEARS (ten)
BENJAMIN BRITTEN (pf)
2 Sep. 11.00 *Leith Town Hall*
Purcell Morning hymn
Purcell Alleluia
Schumann Dichterliebe
Debussy Trois ballades de François Villon
Britten 6 Hölderlin fragments
Britten Folk song arrangements: Sally in our alley; Tom Bowling; The Lincolnshire poacher

ELISABETH SÖDERSTRÖM (sop)
CLIFFORD CURZON
GERALD MOORE (pf)
5 Sep. 11.00 *Leith Town Hall*
Songs and piano works by Liszt

ANNIE FISCHER (pf)
27 Aug. 14.30 *Usher Hall*
Beethoven Sonata no.30 in E, op.109
Brahms Sonata no.3 in F minor, op.5
Bartók Fifteen Hungarian peasant songs
Liszt Concert study no.1 (Waldesrauschen)
Dohnányi Rhapsody no.3 in C, op.11/3
Liszt Études d'exécution transcendante d'apres Paganini: A minor (Theme and variations)

BRENTON LANGBEIN (vn)
MAUREEN JONES (pf)
30 Aug. 11.00 *Freemasons' Hall*
Schumann Sonata no.1 in A minor, op.105
Debussy Sonata
Prokofiev Sonata no.2 in D, op.94a

JOAN DICKSON (vc)
GEORGE MALCOLM (hpd)
29 Aug. 11.00 *Freemasons' Hall*
Bach Overture (Partita) for harpsichord in the French style
Bach Suite for solo cello no.5 in C minor
Bach Sonata for cello and harpsichord no.3 in G

JULIAN BREAM (lute, gtr)
3 Sep. 15.00 *Freemasons' Hall*
Eastwood Capriccio (World première)
Lute works by Dowland, Johnson, Bacheler, Rossiter. Guitar works by Frescobaldi, Bach, Handel, Villa-Lobos, Albeniz

GAELIC CONCERTS

(In association with An Comunn Gaidhealach)
1 Sep. 20.00 *Usher Hall*
Soloists Rhona MacLeod, Donald MacVicar, Iain R. Douglas, Joan M. MacKenzie, James C. Smith, Evelyn Campbell, Kenna Campbell, Archie MacLean (sngr), Florence V. Wilson (clarsach), Jean Campbell (pf), Pipe Major John MacLellan, Royal Scottish Pipers' Society, Edinburgh Gaelic Choir, Glasgow Gaelic Musical Association,

Greenock Gaelic Choir and Choral Society, Lothian Celtic Choir, Royal Scottish Country Dance Society, Scottish Official Board of Highland Dancing

8 Sep. 20.00 *Leith Town Hall*
CEILIDH
Soloists Archie MacLean, Alasdair B. Gillies, Carol Galbraith, Nan D. Hunter, Sheila A. McDougall, Hugh MacInnes, Aunice M. Gillies, Nina MacCallum, Catherine A. MacNiven, Neiliann MacLennan, John A. MacRae (sngr), Chris Turner (pf), Edinburgh Gaelic Choir, Lothian Celtic Choir, Edinburgh Highland Reel and Strathspey Society, Royal Scottish Pipers' Society, John M. Bannermann (Fear-an-tighe)

DRAMA

OLD VIC
21-26 Aug. 4, 5 Sep. 19.15 22, 26 Aug. 5 Sep. 14.15 *Assembly Hall*
DOCTOR FAUSTUS Marlowe
Faustus Paul Daneman
Mephistophilis Michael Goodliffe
Chorus Walter Hudd
Wagner Stephen Moore
Good angel Charles West
Evil angel Peter Ellis
Lucifer Robert Eddison
1st Scholar Brian Hawksley
2nd Scholar Roger Grainger
3rd Scholar Leon Shepperdson
Valdes Leader Hawkins
Cornelius Brian Spink
The Pope/Wrath David Bird
Charles, the German Emperor Maurice Good
Cardinal of Lorraine/Pride William McAllister
Old man/Gluttony Robert Atkins
Alexander Anthony Moore
Friar Michael Turner
Sloth Vernon Dobtcheff
Lechery/Empress Rosemarie Dunham
Covetousness Sylvia Coleridge
Alexander's paramour Dona Martyn
Helen of Troy Meredith Kinmont
Envy Emrys James
Knight Victor Winding
Director Michael Benthall
Designer Michael Annals
Music John Lambert

28-31 Aug. 1, 2, 6, 7, 8, 9 Sep. 19.15 29 Aug. 2, 9 Sep. 14.15 *Assembly Hall*
KING JOHN Shakespeare
King John Maurice Denham
Philip Faulconbridge Paul Daneman
Prince Henry Gilbert Wynne
Arthur Hugh Janes, Jonathan Collins
Pembroke David Bird
Essex Stephen Moore
Salisbury Michael Turner
Bigot Brian Hawksley
Hubert Michael Goodliffe
Robert Faulconbridge Leader Hawkins
James Gurney Roger Grainger
Peter of Pomfret Victor Winding
King of France Robert Eddison
Lewis, the Dauphin Jerome Willis
Lymoges, Duke of Austria Robert Atkins, Roger Frith
Pandulph Walter Hudd
Melun William McAllister
Chatillon Emrys James
Citizens Charles West, Maurice Good, David Tudor-Jones
French herald Brian Spink
English herald Peter Ellis
Executioner Maurice Good
Queen Elinor Rosalind Atkinson
Constance Maxine Audley
Lady Faulconbridge Sylvia Coleridge
Blanch of Spain Jane Downs
Director Peter Potter
Designer Audrey Cruddas
Music Peter Racine Fricker

ENGLISH STAGE COMPANY
21 Aug.-2 Sep. 19.30 (exc.Sun) 23, 26, 30 Aug. 2 Sep. 14.30 *Empire Theatre*
LUTHER Osborne
Martin Luther Albert Finney
Knight Julian Glover
Prior/Eck James Cairncross
Hans Bill Owen
Lucas Peter Duguid
Weinand Dan Meaden
Tetzel Peter Bull
Staupitz Carleton Hobbs
Cajetan John Moffatt
Miltitz Robert Robinson
Leo Charles Kay
Katherine Meryl Gourley
Director Tony Richardson
Designer Jocelyn Herbert
Music John Addison

4-9 Sep. 19.00 6, 9 Sep. 14.15
Lyceum Theatre
AUGUST FOR THE PEOPLE Dennis (EIF commission)
Sir Augustus Thwaites Rex Harrison
Toastmaster/Press attaché John Junkin
Mr Bolt George Benson
Angela Pauline Munro
Mrs Fulton Rachel Roberts
Lord Woodham William Kendall
Mr Glumly Cyril Raymond
Dr Swinburne Hugh Latimer
Thompson Gordon Rollings
Mrs Thompson Kate Lansbury
Beamer Arthur Mullard
Miss Willoughby Laura Graham
The Lichee of Tambucca Edric Connor
Reporters Prior Pitt, Terence Brook, Kenneth McClellan
French lady reporter Paulette Preney
Lady reporter Constance Lorne
American reporter Don Sutherland
1st Man visitor Douglas Ditta
Women visitors Caroline John, Gwen Nelson
Maid Elizabeth Bell
Aide to the Lichee Yemi Ajibade
Director George Devine
Designer Stephen Doncaster

BRISTOL OLD VIC
21-26 Aug. 19.00 23, 26 Aug. 14.15
Lyceum Theatre
SAPPHO Durrell
Sappho Margaret Rawlings
Chloe Diane Aubrey
Thais Anna Palk
Phoebe Bridget Wood
Diomedes Willoughby Goddard
Minos Norman Tyrrell
Phaon Richard Gale
Pittakos Nigel Davenport
Adamanthis Peter Birrel
Pythocritos Henry Woolf
Kleis Jane Barlow
Kreon Frederick Farley
Messenger Robin Phillips
Slave Michael Lynch
Soldier Michael Goldie
Director John Hale
Designer Jane Graham

28-30 Aug. 19.00 30 Aug. 14.15
Lyceum Theatre
LE MISANTHROPE Molière
Alceste Jacques François
Philinte Bernard Dhéran
Oronte Raymond Gérôme
Célimène Madeleine Dalavaivre
Eliante Josette Harmina
Arsinoë Maria Tamar
Acaste Jacques Toja
Clitandre Guy Jacquet
Basque Jean-Marie Lormont
Dubois Clément Michu
Un garde Charles Trombetta
Director Bernard Dhéran
Scenery Roger Dornés
Costumes Pierre Cardin, Pierre Larsen
Tapestries Jean Lurçat
(In association with Jan de Blieck and the Association Française d'Action Artistique)

31 Aug.-2 Sep. 19.00 2 Sep. 14.15
Lyceum Theatre
JEAN DE LA LUNE Achard
Jef Jacques François
Louis Jean-Marie Lormont
Clotaire Clément Michu
Marceline Madeleine Delavaivre
Richard Bernard Dhéran
Etienne Josette Harmina
Director Bernard Dhéran
Scenery Bernard Evein
Costumes Pierre Cardin

GATEWAY COMPANY
21 Aug.-9 Sep. 19.30 (exc.Sun) 24, 26, 31 Aug. 2, 7, 9 Sep. 14.30
Gateway Theatre
LET WIVES TAK' TENT Kemp
(Based on Molière's L'ecole des femmes)
Mr Oliphant Duncan Macrae, Walter Carr
Mr Gilchrist James Gibson
Agnes Margo Croan
Walter Laidlaw Dalling
Alan Walter Carr, William Lyon Brown
Alison Effie Morrison
Law agent Bryden Murdoch
Mr Montgomerie Alexander Allan
Mr Reekie Alexander McCrindle
Street musician John Duncanson
Director Tom Fleming
Designer Molly MacEwen
Music Cedric Thorpe Davie

POETRY AND PROSE RECITALS

23, 30 Aug. 6 Sep. 15.00
Freemasons' Hall
META FORREST, IAN GILMOUR (rdr)
3 recitals of Scottish verse from William Dunbar to the present day
with William McPherson (vn)

LATE NIGHT ENTERTAINMENT

21-26 Aug. 22.45 *Lyceum Theatre*
SONGS OF BATTLE, BED AND BOTTLE
Michael Barne, Rory and Alex McEwen, Jimmy MacGregor, Robin Hall

28 Aug.-2 Sep. 22.45 *Lyceum Theatre*
'5 + 1' ... A REVUE
by Steven Vinaver and Carl Davis
Fenella Fielding, Dilys Laye, Anton Rodgers, Robin Ray, Riggs O'Hara, Annette Robertson

Designer Sally Jacobs
Musical direction Anthony Bowles

4-9 Sep. 22.45 *Lyceum Theatre*
AN EVENING WITH JULIETTE GRECO
with Henri Patterson and his Ensemble, Freddy Balta (accordion)

DANCE

EDINBURGH INTERNATIONAL FESTIVAL
4-9 Sep. 19.30 6, 9 Sep. 14.30
Empire Theatre
TRIPLE BILL
A fusion of dance and song in a dramatic presentation
SALADE Milhaud
(Eng. Translated by Rollo Myers)
Choreographer Peter Darrell
Designer Barry Kay
RENARD Stravinsky (Eng)
Choreographer Alfred Rodrigues
Designer Arthur Boyd
THE SEVEN DEADLY SINS Weill
(Eng. Translated by W.H. Auden)
Choreographer Kenneth MacMillan
Designer Ian Spurling
Anna Cleo Laine, Anya Linden
Dancers Brenda Last, Hazel Merry, Gail Donaldson, Suzanne Musitz, Yvonne Joseph, Clover Roope, Sylvia Wellman, Erling Sunde, Peter Cazalet, Dennis Griffiths, Laverne Meyer, Gilda Proudley, Oliver Symons, Max Natiez, Victor Maynard
Singers Dorothy Dorow, Murray Dickie, John Lawrenson, Trevor Anthony, Alfred Mallett
Western Theatre Ballet
Scottish National Orchestra
Conductor Alexander Gibson

EXHIBITIONS

Waverley Market
EPSTEIN MEMORIAL EXHIBITION
Arranged by Richard Buckle

Royal Scottish Academy
MASTERPIECES OF FRENCH PAINTING FROM THE BÜHRLE COLLECTION
Selected by Douglas Cooper
(In association with the Royal Scottish Academy and the Arts Council of Great Britain)

1962

OPERA

BELGRADE OPERA
20, 22, 25 Aug. 19.00 *King's Theatre*
PRINCE IGOR Borodin (S.Croat)
Igor Dušan Popović
Yaroslavna Milka Stojanović
Vladimir Zvonimir Krnetić
Galitzky Miroslav Čangalović
Žarko Cvejić
Kontchak Miroslav Čangalović
Djordje Djurdjević
Kontchakovna Biserka Cvejić
Skoula Ladko Korošec
Eroshka Franjo Paulik
Ovlour Živojin Milosavljević
Yaroslavna's nurse Ljubica Vrsajkov
Polovtsian girl Djurdjevka Čakarević
Dancers Katarina Obradović, Jovanka Bjegojević, Žarko Prebil
Conductor Oskar Danon
Dušan Miladinović
Director Branko Gavela
Designer Miomir Denić
Costumes Milica Babic

21, 23 Aug. 19.00 *King's Theatre*
THE LOVE OF THREE ORANGES
Prokofiev (S.Croat)
King of Clubs Žarko Cvejić
Prince Stjepan Andrašević
Princess Clarissa Milica Miladinović
Leander Jovan Gligorijević
Truffaldino Franjo Paulik
Pantaloon Stanoje Janković
Chelio Djordje Djurdjević
Fata Morgana Valerija Hejbalova
Linetta Ljubica Vrsajkov
Nicoletta Anica Jelinek
Ninetta Dobrila Bogošević
Cook Aleksandar Djokić
Farfarello Živojin Milosavljević
Smeraldina Djurdjevka Čakarević
Herald Ilija Gligorijević
Master of ceremonies Nikola Jančić
Dancers Ljiljana Dulovic, Milan Momčilović
Conductor Oskar Danon
Director Mladen Sabljić
Designer Miomir Denić
Costumes Mira Glišić

24, 31 Aug. 19.00 *King's Theatre*
DON QUICHOTTE Massenet (S.Croat)
Don Quichotte Miroslav Čangalović
Dulcinea Biserka Cvejić
Sancho Panza Ladko Korošec
Pedro Dobrila Bogošević
Garcias Ljubica Vrsajkov
Rodriguez Nikola Jančić
Juan Drago Starc
Fool Zivojin Mitrović
Dancer Nevena Mirić
Conductor Oskar Danon
Director Mladen Sabljić
Designer Miomir Denić
Costumes Mira Glišić

27, 29 Aug. 1 Sep. 19.00 *King's Theatre*
KHOVANSHCHINA Mussorgsky
(S.Croat. Orchestrated by Shostakovich)
Prince Ivan Khovansky Žarko Cvejić
Prince Andrei Khovansky Zvonimir Krnetić
Prince Vassily Galitsin Franjo Paulik
Shaklovity Dušan Popović
Stanoje Janković
Dosifey Miroslav Čangalović
Djordje Djurdjević
Marfa Melanija Bugarinović
Milica Miladinović
Scribe Vladan Cvejić
Emma Milka Stojanović
Varsonofiev Velizar Maksimović
Kouzka Zivojin Milosavljević
1st Streltsy Aleksandar Djokić
2nd Streltsy Ilija Gligorijević
Streshniev Ivan Murgaški
Herald Nikola Jančić
Conductor Krešimir Baranović
Dušan Miladinović
Director Mladen Sabljić
Designer Miomir Denić
Costumes Milica Babić

28, 30 Aug. 19.00 *King's Theatre*
THE GAMBLER Prokofiev (S.Croat)
General Žarko Cvejić
Pauline Valerija Hejbalova
Alexei Drago Starc
Babushka Djurdjevka Čakarević
Marquis Stjepan Andrašević
Mr Astley Stanoje Janković
Blanche Milica Miladinović
Prince Nilsky Nikola Jančić
Baron Wirmerhelm Gradimir Hadži-Slavcović
Potapitch Zivojin Mitrović
Director Ilija Gligorijević
Croupiers Zvonimir Krnetić, Živojin Iovanović
Fat Englishman Aleksandar Djokić
Thin Englishman Djordje Djurdjević
Merry lady Dobrila Bogošević
Pale lady Anica Jelinek
Coquettish lady Ljubica Vrsajkov
Respectable lady Milka Stojanović
Doubtful lady Mira Djordjević
Eager gambler Dragomir Perić
Sick gambler Nikola Stefanović
Hunchbacked gambler Dragi Dimitrijević
Unsuccessful gambler Živojin Milosavljević
Old gambler Velizar Maksimović
Conductor Oskar Danon
Director Mladen Sabljić
Designer Miomir Denić
Costumes Milica Babić

ENGLISH OPERA GROUP
3, 5, 7 Sep. 19.00 *King's Theatre*
THE TURN OF THE SCREW Britten
Prologue Peter Pears
Gerald English
Governess Jennifer Vyvyan
Miles Kevin Platts
Flora Ellen Dales
Mrs Grose Sylvia Fisher
Quint Peter Pears
Gerald English
Miss Jessel Elisabeth Fretwell
Conductor Meredith Davies
Director Basil Coleman
Designer John Piper

ORCHESTRAL CONCERTS

LONDON SYMPHONY ORCHESTRA
19 Aug. 20.00 *Usher Hall*
Beethoven Mass in D (Missa solemnis), op.123
Conductor Lorin Maazel
Soloists Galina Vishnevskaya (sop), Marga Höffgen (cont), Richard Lewis (ten), Frederick Guthrie (bs), Leeds Festival Chorus

21 Aug. 20.00 *Usher Hall*
Sibelius Symphony no.7 in C, op.105
Shostakovich Concerto for cello no.1 in E flat, op.107
Brahms Symphony no.2 in D, op.73

Conductor Lorin Maazel
Soloist Mstislav Rostropovich (vc)

22 Aug. 20.00 *Usher Hall*
Mozart Symphony no.31 in D (Paris), K297
Nono Sul Ponte di Hiroshima (EIF commission)
Tchaikovsky Romeo and Juliet: Love duet (completed by Taneyev)
Debussy Nocturnes
Conductor John Pritchard
Soloists Dorothy Dorow, Marie Collier (sop), June Holden (mez), Richard Lewis (ten), Edinburgh Royal Choral Union

24 Aug. 20.00 *Usher Hall*
Falla Atlántida (completed by Halffter)
Conductor Igor Markevich
Soloists Teresa Berganza (mez), Raimundo Torres (bar), Orfeon Donostiarra

26 Aug. 20.00 *Usher Hall*
Tchaikovsky Francesca da Rimini
Shostakovich Lady Macbeth of Mtsensk: Once I saw from my window *and* Far off in a forest
Mussorgsky Six songs; orch. Markevich
Stravinsky The rite of spring
Conductor Igor Markevich
Soloist Galina Vishnevskaya (sop)

POLISH RADIO SYMPHONY ORCHESTRA
25 Aug. 20.00 *Usher Hall*
Britten Variations on a theme of Frank Bridge
Szymanowski Concerto for violin no.1, op.35
Brahms Symphony no.4 in E minor, op.98
Conductor Jan Krenz
Soloist Tadeusz Wronski (vn)

27 Aug. 20.00 *Usher Hall*
Shostakovich Symphony no.9 in E flat, op.70
Scriabin Concerto for piano in F sharp minor, op.20
Mozart Symphony no.25 in G minor, K183
Dvořák Symphonic variations, op.78
Conductor Charles Mackerras
Soloist Paul Badura-Skoda (pf)

28 Aug. 20.00 *Usher Hall*
Shostakovich Two pieces for strings, op.11
Beethoven Concerto for piano no.3 in C minor, op.37
Debussy Jeux
Lutoslawski Concerto for orchestra
Conductor Jan Krenz
Soloist Maureen Jones (pf)

29 Aug. 20.00 *Usher Hall*
Beethoven Symphony no.8 in F, op.93
Shostakovich Symphony no.8 in C minor, op.65
Conductor Jan Krenz

BBC SCOTTISH ORCHESTRA
Conductor Norman del Mar
26 Aug. 15.00 *Leith Town Hall*
Mozart Adagio and Fugue in C minor, K546
Berg Chamber concerto
Stravinsky Four études
Wagner Siegfried idyll
Britten Canadian carnival overture
Soloists Brenton Langbein (vn), Maureen Jones (pf)

1 Sep. 20.00 *Usher Hall*
Tippett Suite in D; A birthday suite for Prince Charles
Mahler Des Knaben Wunderhorn
Shostakovich Symphony no.6 in B minor, op.54
Soloists Elisabeth Söderström (sop), Thomas Hemsley (bar)

SCHOLA CANTORUM BASILIENSIS
Director August Wenzinger
1 Sep. 11.00 *Leith Town Hall*
Bach Brandenburg concerto no.5 in D
Telemann Suite in E minor for 2 flutes, strings and continuo
Telemann Quartet for flute, oboe, violin and continuo in G
Bach Brandenburg concerto no.4 in G

2 Sep. 15.00 *Leith Town Hall*
Bach Brandenburg concerto no.1 in F
A. Scarlatti Sinfonia no.4 in E minor
Vivaldi Concerto in G minor (Dresden), R577
Handel Water music: Suite in F
Bach Brandenburg concerto no.2 in F

3 Sep. 11.00 *Leith Town Hall*
Bach Suite no.2 in B minor
Bach Brandenburg concerto no.6 in B flat
Bach Concerto for harpsichord in F minor
Bach Brandenburg concerto no.3 in G

SCOTTISH NATIONAL ORCHESTRA
Conductor Alexander Gibson
2 Sep. 20.00 *Usher Hall*
Delius Paris (The song of a great city)
Mozart Bella mia fiamma
Walton Concerto for cello
Mozart Mass no.16 in C (Coronation), K317 (*with* Sonata for organ, K329)
Soloists Stefania Woytowicz (sop), Janet Baker (mez), Alexander Young (ten), Thomas Hemsley (bar), Joan Dickson (vc), Herrick Bunney (org), Edinburgh Royal Choral Union

3 Sep. 20.00 *Usher Hall*
Shostakovich Festival overture
Shostakovich Symphony no.10 in E minor, op.93
Brahms Concerto for violin in D, op.77
Soloist David Oistrakh (vn)

PHILHARMONIA ORCHESTRA
4 Sep. 20.00 *Usher Hall*
Shostakovich Lady Macbeth of Mtsensk - Suite (World première)
Shostakovich Symphony no.12 in D minor (The year 1917), op.112
Prokofiev Symphony no.3 in C minor, op.44
Conductor Gennadi Rozhdestvensky

6 Sep. 20.00 *Usher Hall*
Rossini Guillaume Tell: Overture
Dvořák Concerto for cello in B minor, op.104
Brahms Symphony no.1 in C minor, op.68
Conductor Carlo Maria Giulini
Soloist Mstislav Rostropovich (vc)

7 Sep. 20.00 *Usher Hall*
Shostakovich Concerto for violin no.1 in A minor, op.99
Shostakovich Symphony no.4 in C minor, op.43
Conductor Gennadi Rozhdestvensky
Soloist David Oistrakh (vn)

8 Sep. 19.30 *Usher Hall*
Beethoven Symphony no.6 in F (Pastoral), op.68
Britten Peter Grimes: Four sea interludes
Debussy La mer
Conductor Carlo Maria Giulini

CHAMBER CONCERTS

ALLEGRI QUARTET
20 Aug. 11.00 *Freemasons' Hall*
Shostakovich Quartet no.1 in C, op.49
Shostakovich Quartet no.2 in A, op.68
Mozart Quintet no.6 in E flat, K.614
with Cecil Aronowitz (va)

21 Aug. 11.00 *Freemasons' Hall*
Shostakovich Quartet no.5 in B flat, op.92
Brahms Sextet no.2 in G, op.36
with Cecil Aronowitz (va), Terence Weil (vc)

MELOS ENSEMBLE
24 Aug. 11.00 *Freemasons' Hall*
Ravel Introduction and allegro for flute, clarinet, harp and strings
Debussy Sonata for flute, viola and harp
Bliss Quintet for clarinet and strings

25 Aug. 11.00 *Freemasons' Hall*
Mozart Quartet for flute and strings no.1 in D, K285
Debussy Quartet in G minor, op.10/1
Brahms Quintet for clarinet and strings in B minor, op.115

BORODIN QUARTET
26 Aug. 20.30 *Leith Town Hall*
Shostakovich Quartet no.3 in F, op.73
Shostakovich Quartet no.7 in F sharp minor, op.108
Beethoven Quartet no.14 in C sharp minor, op.131

29 Aug. 11.00 *Leith Town Hall*
Borodin Quartet no.2 in D
Shostakovich Quartet no.4 in D, op.83
Shostakovich Quartet no.7 in F sharp minor, op.108

31 Aug. 20.00 *Leith Town Hall*
Brahms Quartet no.2 in A minor, op.51/2
Shostakovich Quartet no.8 in C minor, op.110
Ravel Quartet in F

2 Sep. 14.30 *Usher Hall*
Tchaikovsky Quartet no.3 in E flat minor, op.30
Britten Quartet no.2 in C, op.36
Shostakovich Quintet for piano and strings in G minor, op.57
with Lev Oborin (pf)

BRENTON LANGBEIN (vn), MAUREEN JONES (pf), BARRY TUCKWELL (hn)
31 Aug. 11.00 *Freemasons' Hall*
Banks Trio for horn, violin and piano (EIF commission)
Beethoven Sonata for violin and piano no.7 in C minor, op.30/2
Brahms Trio for horn, violin and piano in E flat, op.40

WIND ENSEMBLE
7 Sep. 11.00 *Freemasons' Hall*
Dittersdorf Partita for brass in D
Locke Music for His Majesty's cornets and sackbuts
Mozart Divertimento no.9 in B flat, K240
Beethoven Three equali for brass
Mozart Divertimento no.14 in B flat, K270
Director Meredith Davies

ACCADEMIA MONTEVERDIANA
Conductor Denis Stevens
27 Aug. 11.00 *Freemasons' Hall*
Monteverdi Ballo: Movete al mio bel suon
Monteverdi Hor ch'el ciel e la terra
Monteverdi Il combattimento di Tancredi e Clorinda
Monteverdi Dolcissimo uscignuolo
Monteverdi Lamento della ninfa
Monteverdi Altri canti di Marte

28 Aug. 11.00 *Freemasons' Hall*
Music at the court of Ferrara by Wert, Monteverdi, Frescobaldi, Rore, Marenzio, Luzzaschi, Gesualdo, Striggio

JACQUELINE DU PRÉ (vc), MARGARET KITCHIN, ERNEST LUSH (pf), ENGLISH STRING QUARTET
3 Sep. 20.00 *Freemasons' Hall*
BBC Invitation Concert
P.M. Davies Quartet no.2
Tippett Sonata for piano no.2 (World première)
Shostakovich Quartet no.6 in G, op.101
Brahms Sonata for cello and piano no.2 in F, op.99

RECITALS

TERESA BERGANZA (mez)
FELIX LAVILLA (pf)
20 Aug. 20.00 *Leith Town Hall*
Songs and arias by Handel, A. Scarlatti, Purcell, Pergolesi, Mahler, Wolf, Debussy, Villa-Lobos, Granados

PETER PEARS (ten)
YVONNE LEFEBURE (pf)
22 Aug. 11.00 *Freemasons' Hall*
Debussy Preludes: Book 1
Debussy Ariettes oubliées
Debussy Masques
Debussy L'isle joyeuse
Debussy Fêtes galantes: Sets 1 and 2
Debussy Images: Poissons d'or

GALINA VISHNEVSKAYA (sop)
MSTISLAV ROSTROPOVICH (pf, vc)
23 Aug. 20.00 *Usher Hall*
Mussorgsky Songs and dances of death
Villa-Lobos Bachianas brasileiras nos.1, 5
Shostakovich Five satires (Scenes from the past)
Tchaikovsky Songs
with 7 celli from the London Symphony Orchestra

PETER PEARS (ten)
JULIAN BREAM (lute, gtr)
1 Sep. 18.00 *Freemasons' Hall*
Britten Songs from the Chinese
Songs and lute solos by Rosseter, Frescobaldi, Dowland, Monteverdi, Bach, Caccini, Stradella

STEFANIA WOYTOWICZ (sop)
GEOFFREY PARSONS (pf)
5 Sep. 11.00 *Freemasons' Hall*
Arias and songs by Caldara, Sarti, Pergolesi, A. Scarlatti, Cesti, Bach, Schumann, Fauré, Rachmaninov, Wiechowicz

ELISABETH SÖDERSTRÖM (sop), JANET BAKER (mez), PETER PEARS (ten), THOMAS HEMSLEY (bar), GEOFFREY PARSONS (pf)
8 Sep. 11.00 *Leith Town Hall*
Schumann Spanisches Liederspiel
Shostakovich From Jewish folk poetry

JOHN OGDON (pf)
30 Aug. 11.00 *Freemasons' Hall*
Beethoven Sonata no. 32 in C minor, op.111
Debussy En blanc et noir
Bartók Sonata for 2 pianos and percussion
with Brenda Lucas (pf), James Blades, Stephen Whittaker (perc)

6 Sep. 11.00 *Leith Town Hall*
Bach Art of fugue: Contrapuncti nos. 1, 3, 4
Brahms Variations on a theme by Schumann
Debussy Études nos.1, 2, 5
Shostakovich Preludes and fugues, op.87: C major
Scriabin Sonata no.5, op.53
Balakirev Islamey

ROSALYN TURECK (pf)
2 Sep. 20.30 *Leith Town Hall*
Bach Das wohltemperirte Klavier: Preludes and fugues nos.1, 2, 5, 8
Bach Partita no.2 in C minor
Bach Chromatic fantasia and fugue in D minor
Bach Concerto in the Italian style
Bach Two-part inventions: C minor, D minor, E, A minor

ROSALYN TURECK (hpd)
4 Sep. 11.00 *Freemasons' Hall*
Rameau Tambourin
Rameau Aria and variations in A minor
Bach Das wohltemperirte Klavier: Preludes and fugues nos. 3, 5, 14
Bach Chromatic fantasia and fugue in D minor
Bach Partita no.2 in C minor

WOLFGANG MARSCHNER (vn)
GEOFFREY PARSONS (pf)
23 Aug. 11.00 *Freemasons' Hall*
Mozart Sonata no.24 in F, K376
Bach Partita for solo violin no.3 in E
Webern Four pieces, op.7
Bartók Rhapsody no.2

DAVID OISTRAKH (vn)
LEV OBORIN (pf)
30 Aug. 20.00 *Usher Hall*
Beethoven Sonata no.5 in F (Spring), op.24
Beethoven Sonata no.7 in C minor, op.30/2
Beethoven Sonata no.8 in G, op.30/3

DAVID OISTRAKH (vn)
FRIDA BAUER (pf)
5 Sep. 20.00 *Usher Hall*
Leclair Sonata in D
Beethoven Sonata no.9 in A (Kreutzer), op.47
Debussy Sonata
Shostakovich Three fantastic dances, op.5
Schubert Fantasia in C, D934

MSTISLAV ROSTROPOVICH (vc)
27 Aug. 18.00 *St Cuthbert's Church*
Bach Suites nos.1-3

28 Aug. 18.00 *St Cuthbert's Church*
Bach Suites nos. 4-6

JULIAN BREAM (lute, gtr)
2 Sep. 20.00 *Freemasons' Hall*
Lute and guitar works by Dowland, Molinaro, Besard, Byrd, Weiss, Bach, Berkeley, Turina

GAELIC CONCERTS

(Arranged in association with An Commun Gaidhealach)
CEILIDH
24 Aug. 20.00 *Leith Town Hall*
Soloists Calum Cameron, Kenna Campbell, Alasdair B. Gillies, Sheila A. McDougall, Joan Mackenzie, Archie MacLean, Johan Macleod, Flora MacNeil (sngr), Royal Scottish Pipers' Society, Fergie MacDonald and his Hebridean Ceilidh Band, John M. Bannerman (Fear-an-tighe)

31 Aug. 20.00 *Usher Hall*
Soloists Hugh Macinnes, Donald Macleod, Evelyn Campbell, Carol Galbraith, Catherine A. MacNiven, Helen T. Macmillan, George J. Clavey (sngr), Florence V. Wilson (clarsach), Royal Scottish Pipers' Society, Ayr Junior Gaelic Choir, Edinburgh Gaelic Choir, Lothian Celtic Choir, Glasgow Gaelic Musical Association, Greenock Gaelic Choir and Choral Society, Royal Scottish Country Dance Society, Scottish Official Board of Highland Dancing

DRAMA

EDINBURGH INTERNATIONAL FESTIVAL
20 Aug.-8 Sep. 19.15 (exc.Sun) 21, 25, 28 Aug. 1, 4, 8 Sep. 14.15 Assembly Hall
THE DOCTOR AND THE DEVILS
Thomas

Dr Robert Knox	Leonard Maguire
Narrator	Bryden Murdoch
Elizabeth	Ellen MacIntosh
Hare	Walter Carr
Nelly	Mairhi Russell
Burke	James Mellor
Annabella	Hilary Mason
John Murray	Frank Wylie
Mary Paterson	Morag Forsyth
Meg	Nan Kerr
Davie Forsythe	Alexander McCrindle
Chairman	Christopher Page
Mrs Flynn	Katy Gardiner
Dr Green	Iain Dunnett
Dr Monro	Alastair Audsley
Fiddler/Grocer	George Harvey-Webb
Merrylees/Lord Justice Clerk	Roy Hanlon
Mrs Grey/Rosie/Abigail	Julia McCarthy
Janet	Dorothy Bibby
Mole	Ian Trigger
Harding	Stuart Henry
Daft Jamie	Tom Conti
Potman	Campbell Godley
Maggie Bell	Brenda Turnbull

Other parts played by George Cormack, Joseph Dunlop, John Young, Ian Fraser
Director Callum Mill
Designer Sally Hulke
(In association with Gervase Farjeon and Richard O'Donoghue)

ROYAL SHAKESPEARE COMPANY
20-25 Aug. 19.00 22, 25 Aug. 14.15
Lyceum Theatre
TROILUS AND CRESSIDA Shakespeare

Prologue	Trevor Martin
Priam	Donald Layne-Smith
Hector	Derek Godfrey
Troilus	Ian Holm
Paris	John Ronane
Deiphobus	Shaun Curry
Helenus/Alexander	Roger Croucher
Margarelon	Mark Moss
Aeneus	Brian Smith
Antenor	Edward Argent
Calchas	John Hussey

Cressida Dorothy Tutin
Pandarus Max Adrian
Cassandra Sonia Fraser
Andromache Cherry Morris
Servant Paul Dawkins
Page Ian Ricketts
Agamemnon John Nettleton
Menelaus Trevor Martin
Ulysses Michael Hordern
Ajax Roy Dotrice
Achilles Patrick Allen
Nestor Ken Wynne
Patroclus Peter McEnery
Diomedes David Buck
Thersites Gordon Gostelow
Helen Maxine Audley
Director Peter Hall
Designer Leslie Hurry
Music Humphrey Searle

27 Aug.-1 Sep. 19.00 29 Aug. 1 Sep. 14.15 Lyceum Theatre
THE DEVILS Whiting
Mannoury John Nettleton
Adam Gordon Gostelow
Louis Trincant John Hussey
Phillipe Trincant Marian Diamond
Jean d'Armagnac Paul Dawkins
de Cerisay David Buck
Sewerman Ken Wynne
Urbain Grandier Richard Johnson
Ninon Susan Engel
de la Rochepozay/Father Ambrose Roy Dotrice
Father Rangier Roger Croucher
Father Barre Max Adrian
Sister Jeanne Dorothy Tutin
Sister Claire Cherry Morris
Sister Louise Sonia Fraser
de Laubardemont Peter McEnery
Father Mignon Donald Layne-Smith
Sister Gabrielle Madoline Thomas
Prince Henri de Conde Alan Dobie
Richelieu/Clerk Trevor Martin
Bontemps Edward Argent
Louis XIII Darryl Kavann
Director Peter Wood
Scenery Sean Kenny
Costumes Desmond Heeley

4-8 Sep. 19.00 5, 6, 8 Sep. 14.15 Lyceum Theatre
CURTMANTLE Fry (World première in Eng)
Barber/Monk John Hussey
Constance Susan Engel
Huckster/Monk Ken Wynne
Blae Patsy Byrne
Anesty/Captain Trevor Martin
Eleanor Maxine Audley
William Marshall Roy Dotrice
Henry Derek Godfrey
Becket Alan Dobie
Cleric Donald Layne-Smith
Gilbert Foliot John Nettleton
Earl of Leicester Paul Dawkins
Young Henry Roger Croucher
Richard David Buck
Geoffrey Ian McCulloch
John Martin Norton
Roger Brian Smith
Margaret Marian Diamond
Philip of France Peter McEnery
Juggler Robert Jennings
Messenger Shaun Curry
Old woman Madoline Thomas
Director Stuart Burge
Designer Abd'Elkader Farrah
Music Richard Rodney Bennett

GATEWAY COMPANY
20 Aug.- 8 Sep. 19.30 (exc.Sun) 23, 25, 30 Aug. 1, 6, 8 Sep 14.30. Gateway Theatre
YOUNG AUCHINLECK McLellan
Mrs Dodds Magda Miller
James Boswell John Cairney
Lord Auchinleck Brown Derby
John Bruce James Gibson
Thomas Glenn Williams
John Johnston of Grange Victor Carin
Mrs Montgomerie-Cunningham Lennox Milne
Peggie Montgomerie Anne Kristen
Mrs Blair Jean Taylor Smith
Kate Blair Janet Michael
Susie Margery Mitchinson
Aunt Boyd Doreen Peck
Councillor Boyd Colin Miller
Mrs Boyd Isobel Paton
Mary Anne Boyd Maureen Morris
Miss Betty Boswell Jean Faulds
Seamas/Joseph Sean Cotter
Mrs MacBride Marsail McCuish
Director Kenneth Parrott
Asst. Director James Gibson
Designer Neil Parkinson

LATE NIGHT ENTERTAINMENT

20-25 Aug. 22.45 Lyceum Theatre
WHAT NEXT
A unique entertainment from Prague of mostly invisible men and movable objects

27 Aug.-1 Sep. 22.45 Lyceum Theatre
AMALIA RODRIGUES
Portuguese fados and songs
with Guilermino Antonio de Castro Mota, Domingos Augusto Camarinha (gtr)

3-8 Sep. 22.45 Lyceum Theatre
PLAIN SONG AND ALL THAT JAZZ
Rory and Alex McEwen
with Al Fairweather-Sandy Brown All-Stars and George Melly, Carolyn Hester and Dick Farina, and guest stars

DANCE

BALLET DU XXe SIÈCLE, Brussels
27 Aug.-8 Sep. 19.30 (exc.Sun) 29 Aug. 1, 5, 8 Sep. 14.30 Murrayfield Ice Rink
THE FOUR SONS OF AYMON
Choreographers Janine Charrat, Maurice Béjart
Music Fernand Schirren
Designers Francis André, Thierry Bosquet, Germinal Casado, Georgette Lanc, Didi Mahillon, Joëlle Roustan
Speakers Paul Anrieu, Iain Cuthbertson
Dancers Tania Bari, Dolorès Laga, Andrée Marliere, Duška Sifnios, Marie-Claire Carrié, Jaleh Kérendi, Lydie Brackeleer, Louba Dobrievich, Nicole Karys, Lise Pinet, Mathé Souverbie, Nicole Raes, Jeanine Renguet, Madeleine Bart, Francine Cramer, Blanche Aubrée, Nicole Floris, Nicole Delvaux, Françoise Dubois, Colette Ludo, Michèle Rimbold, Jeanine Wisniewski, Arlette van Boven, Germinal Casado, André Leclair, Paolo Bortoluzzi, Antonio Cano, Pierre Dobrievich, Vittorio Biagi, Flavio Bennati, Jorg Lanner, Daniel Lambo, Grégor Thorndike, Arnold Poels, Guy Brasseur, Anthony Hulbert, Serge Marakoff, Christian Hudec, Jean-Pierre Bras, Franco Romano, Mayan Bayer, Donald Mahler

BELGRADE OPERA BALLET
4, 6, 8 Sep. 19.00 King's Theatre
THE INFANTA'S BIRTHDAY
Choreographer Dimitri Parlić
Music Fortner
Designer Dušan Ristić
THE MIRACULOUS MANDARIN
Choreographer Dimitri Parlić
Music Bartók
Designer Dušan Ristić
KOŠTANA
Choreographer Dimitri Parlić
Music Petar Konjović
Designer Milo Milunović
Dancers Jovanka Bjegojević, Katarina Obradović, Žarko Prebil, Branko Marković, Duška Sifnios, Dušan Trninić, Milan Momčilović, Višnja Djordjević, Ruth Parnel, Gradimir Hadži-Slavković, Stevan Žunac, Borivoje Mladenović, Milica Jovanović, Miodrag Mirković, Dragan Seferović, Miodrag Panić, Marica Ristić, Magdalena Janeva, Lidia Pilipenko, Temira Pokorni, Sima Laketić
with Melanija Bugarinović (mez)
Conductor Oskar Danon

INTERNATIONAL WRITERS' CONFERENCE

20-24 Aug. 14.30 McEwan Hall
Malcolm Muggeridge, Stephen Spender, David Daiches, Mary McCarthy, Rebecca West, Hugh MacDiarmid, Alexander Reid, Robin Jenkins, Walter Keir, Douglas Young, Alexander Trocchi, Fionn MacColla, William Burroughs, Edwin Morgan, Neil Paterson, James Baldwin, Robert Jungk, Angus Wilson, Michel Butor, William Golding, Roberto Fernandez-Retamar, Rayner Heppenstall, Aldous Huxley, Colin MacInnes, Henry Miller, Rosamund Lehmann, Lawrence Durrell, Norman Mailer, Khushwant Singh, Erich Fried, Muriel Spark, L.P.H. Hartley
Organized by John Calder

EXHIBITIONS

National Gallery of Scotland
YUGOSLAV MODERN PRIMITIVES

Royal Scottish Academy
SONJA HENIE-NIELS ONSTAD COLLECTION
(In association with the Arts Council of Great Britain and the Royal Scottish Academy)

1963

OPERA

ENGLISH OPERA GROUP
19, 21, 23 Aug. 19.00 *King's Theatre*
THE RAPE OF LUCRETIA Britten
Lucretia Kerstin Meyer
Tarquinius Peter Glossop
Collatinus Forbes Robinson
Lucia Elizabeth Vaughan
Bianca Helen Watts
Junius John Shirley-Quirk
Male chorus Ronald Dowd
Female chorus Sylvia Fisher
English Chamber Orchestra
Conductor Meredith Davies
Director Colin Graham
Designer Tony Walton

20, 22, 24 Aug. 19.00 *King's Theatre*
THE BEGGAR'S OPERA Gay
(Edited by Benjamin Britten)
Captain Macheath Peter Pears
Polly Janet Baker
Lucy Heather Harper
Mr Peachum David Kelly
Mrs Peachum Anna Pollak
Lockit Bryan Drake
Jenny Diver Joan Edwards
Filch Bernard Dickerson
Mrs Trapes Edith Coates
Beggar Roger Jerome
English Chamber Orchestra
Conductor Benjamin Britten
Director and Scenery Colin Graham
Costumes Alix Stone

TEATRO SAN CARLO, Naples
26, 28, 31 Aug. 4 Sep. 19.00
King's Theatre
LUISA MILLER Verdi
Luisa Margherita Roberti
Rodolfo Renato Cioni
Miller Piero Cappuccilli
Count Walter Paolo Washington
Federica Anna Maria Rota
Laura Anna di Stasio
Wurm Franco Ventriglia
Un Contadino Vittorio Pandano
Conductor Alberto Erede
Director Franco Enriquez
Designer Attilio Colonnello

27, 30 Aug. 2, 6 Sep. 19.00
King's Theatre
ADRIANA LECOUVREUR Cilea
Adriana Magda Olivero
Maurice Juan Oncina
Michonnet Sesto Bruscantini
Princess de Bouillon Adriana Lazzarini
Prince de Bouillon Enrico Campi
Abbot de Chazeuil Piero de Palma
Quinnault Augusto Frati
Poisson Vittorio Pandano
Mlle Jouvenot Elena Barcis
Mlle Dangeville Anna di Stasio
Dancers Tony Ferrante, Lino Vacca, A. Maria Siniscalco, Aurora Vuoto, Rita Romanelli
Conductor Oliviero de Fabritiis
Director Aldo Mirabella Vassallo
Designer Camillo Parravicini
Choreographer Bianca Gallizia

29 Aug. 3, 5, 7 Sep. 19.00 King's Theatre
DON PASQUALE Donizetti
Don Pasquale Fernando Corena
Norina Gianna d'Angelo
Ernesto Alfredo Kraus
Dr Malatesta Renato Capecchi
Notary Augusto Frati
Conductor Alberto Erede
Director Eduardo de Filippo
Designer Ezio Frigerio

HUNGARIAN STATE OPERA AND BALLET
19, 20, 21, 23 Aug. 19.00 Empire Theatre
DUKE BLUEBEARD'S CASTLE Bartók
Judith Klára Palánkay
Olga Szönyi
Duke András Faragó
Conductor János Ferencsik
Director Kálmán Nádasdy
Scenery Zoltán Fülöp
Costumes Tivadar Márk
with The miraculous mandarin *and* The wooden prince *See* Dance

ORCHESTRAL CONCERTS

ORCHESTRA OF THE ROYAL OPERA HOUSE, COVENT GARDEN
18 Aug. 20.00 *Usher Hall*
Berlioz La damnation de Faust
Conductor Georg Solti
Soloists Josephine Veasey (mez), Nicolai Gedda (ten), George London, Robert Savoie (bar), Royal Opera House Chorus, Boys of St Mary's R.C. Cathedral

19 Aug. 20.00 *Usher Hall*
Schubert Symphony no.5 in B flat, D485
Bartók Concerto for violin no.2
Stravinsky The rite of spring
Conductor Georg Solti
Soloist Yehudi Menuhin (vn)

20 Aug. 20.00 *Usher Hall*
Berlioz Rob Roy - Overture
Berlioz Tristia
Berlioz Les Troyens: Royal hunt and storm
Britten Spring symphony
Conductor John Pritchard
Soloists Ella Lee (sop), Norma Procter (cont), William McAlpine (ten), Royal Opera House Chorus, Boys of St Mary's R.C. Cathedral

21 Aug. 20.00 *Usher Hall*
Mozart Symphony no.40 in G minor, K550
R. Strauss Three hymns, op.71
Berlioz Harold in Italy
Conductor John Pritchard
Soloists Ella Lee (sop), Paul Doktor (va)

BBC SCOTTISH ORCHESTRA
22 Aug. 20.00 *Usher Hall*
Berlioz King Lear - Overture
Tippett The midsummer marriage: Ritual dances
Elgar Concerto for violin in B minor, op.61
Conductor Norman del Mar
Soloist Yehudi Menuhin (vn)

LONDON SYMPHONY ORCHESTRA
23 Aug. 20.00 *Usher Hall*
Brahms Variations on a theme by Haydn (St Antoni), op.56a
Henze Symphony no.5
Schubert Symphony no.9 in C (Great), D944
Conductor Hans Werner Henze

24 Aug. 20.00 *Usher Hall*
Berlioz Symphonie fantastique
Berlioz Lélio
Conductor Colin Davis
Soloists Alexander Young (ten), Peter Glossop (bar), Paul Daneman (narr)

25 Aug. 20.00 *Usher Hall*
Beethoven Symphony no.4 in B flat, op.60
Bartók Concerto for piano no.1
Dvořák Symphony no.8 in G, op.88
Conductor István Kertész
Soloist John Ogdon (pf)

27 Aug. 20.00 *Usher Hall*
Berlioz Le corsaire - Overture
Mozart Symphony no.29 in A, K201
Beethoven Concerto for piano no.2 in B flat, op.19
Bartók Concerto for orchestra
Conductor István Kertész
Soloist Hephzibah Menuhin (pf)

28 Aug. 20.00 *Usher Hall*
Mozart Symphony no.32 in G, K318
Tippett Concerto for orchestra (EIF commission)
Mozart Concerto for violin no.5 in A, K219
Stravinsky Eight instrumental miniatures
Mozart Symphony no.39 in E flat, K543
Conductor Colin Davis
Soloist Isaac Stern (vn)

HURWITZ CHAMBER ENSEMBLE
25 Aug. 15.00 *Leith Town Hall*
Handel Concerto grosso in A, op.6/11
Mozart Divertimento (Salzburg symphony) no.1 in D, K136
Bartók Rumanian folk dances
Rossini Sonata for strings no.1 in G
V. Williams Romance for harmonica
Britten Simple symphony
Director and leader Emanuel Hurwitz
Soloist Larry Adler (harmonica)

SCOTTISH NATIONAL ORCHESTRA
30 Aug. 20.00 *Usher Hall*
Prokofiev Symphony no.5 in B flat, op.100
Bloch Schelomo
Beethoven Concerto for violin, cello and piano in C, op.56
Berlioz Le carnaval romain - Overture
Conductor Alexander Gibson
Soloists Isaac Stern (vn), Leonard Rose (vc), Eugene Istomin (pf)

BOURNEMOUTH SYMPHONY ORCHESTRA
31 Aug. 20.00 *Usher Hall*
Tchaikovsky Manfred symphony
Stravinsky The song of the nightingale
Enesco Rumanian rhapsody no.1 in A, op.11/1
Conductor Constantin Silvestri

BBC SYMPHONY ORCHESTRA
1 Sep. 20.00 *Usher Hall*
Mahler Symphony no.10: Adagio
Bartók Concerto for piano no.2
Beethoven Symphony no.7 in A, op.92
Conductor Lorin Maazel
Soloist John Ogdon (pf)

2 Sep. 20.00 *Usher Hall*
Berlioz Benvenuto Cellini: Overture
Mozart Mentre ti lascio
Wolf Prometheus
Mahler Symphony no.6 in A minor
Conductor Norman del Mar
Soloist David Ward (bs)

PHILOMUSICA OF LONDON
Director and soloist George Malcolm (hpd)
1 Sep. 15.00 *Leith Town Hall*
Pergolesi Concertino no.4 in F minor
Arne Concerto for harpsichord no.5 in G minor
Bartók Divertimento for strings
Bach Concerto for oboe in F

Rossini Sonata for strings no.3 in C
Soloist Heinz Holliger (ob)

3 Sep. 11.00 *Leith Town Hall*
Mozart Nine country dances and quadrilles, K510
Mozart Concerto for piano no.12 in A, K414
Handel Solomon: Arrival of the Queen of Sheba
Haydn Symphony no.43 in E flat (Mercury)

CONCERTGEBOUW ORCHESTRA, Amsterdam
3 Sep. 20.00 *Usher Hall*
Leeuw Mouvements rétrogrades
Schumann Concerto for piano in A minor, op.54
Mahler Symphony no.1 in D
Conductor Bernard Haitink
Soloist Eugene Istomin (pf)

4 Sep. 20.00 *Usher Hall*
Bartók Dance suite
Stravinsky Concerto for violin in D
Brahms Symphony no.2 in D, op.73
Conductor Bernard Haitink
Soloist Isaac Stern (vn)

6 Sep. 20.00 *Usher Hall*
Mozart Symphony no.41 in C (Jupiter), K551
Bartók Concerto for piano no.3
Debussy La mer
Conductor George Szell
Soloist John Ogdon (pf)

7 Sep. 19.30 *Usher Hall*
Beethoven Egmont: Overture
Beethoven Concerto for piano no.4 in G, op.58
Beethoven Symphony no.5 in C minor, op.67
Conductor George Szell
Soloist Clifford Curzon (pf)

CHAMBER CONCERTS

JULIAN BREAM CONSORT
19 Aug. 11.00 *Leith Town Hall*
Dowland Lachrymae
Dowland Lute songs, solos and music for voice and viols
with Peter Pears (ten)

6 Sep. 11.00 *Leith Town Hall*
Music by Robinson, Dowland, Morley, Gibbons, Allison, Britten, Byrd, Phillips, Campion, Hollowe, Bacheler

TATRAI QUARTET
22 Aug. 11.00 *Freemasons' Hall*
Purcell Chaconne in G minor
Bartók Quartet no.5
Schubert Quartet no.13 in A minor, D804

25 Aug. 20.30 *Leith Town Hall*
Bartók Quartet no.1
Haydn Quartet in E flat (Joke), op.33/2
Fricker Quartet in one movement, op.8
Brahms Quintet for piano and strings in F minor, op.34
with David Wilde (pf)

28 Aug. 11.00 *Freemasons' Hall*
Bartók Quartet no.2
Bartók Quartet no.3
Mozart Quartet no.14 in G, K387

YEHUDI MENUHIN (vn), GERVASE DE PEYER (cl), HEPHZIBAH MENUHIN (pf)
25 Aug. 14.30 *Usher Hall*
Bartók Sonata for violin and piano no.1
Bartók Contrasts for violin, clarinet and piano
Beethoven Sonata for violin and piano no.10 in G, op.96

ISAAC STERN (vn), LEONARD ROSE (vc), EUGENE ISTOMIN (pf)
26 Aug. 20.00 *Usher Hall*
Beethoven Trio for piano and strings no.2 in G, op.1/2
Ravel Trio for piano and strings in G
Schubert Trio for piano and strings no.1 in B flat, D898

1 Sep. 14.30 *Usher Hall*
Beethoven Trio for piano and strings no.3 in C minor, op.1/3
Beethoven Trio for piano and strings no.5 in D (Ghost), op.70/1
Beethoven Trio for piano and strings no.7 in B flat (Archduke), op.97

5 Sep. 20.00 *Usher Hall*
Beethoven Variations on 'Ich bin der Schneider Kakadu'
Mendelssohn Trio for piano and strings no.1 in D minor, op.49
Schubert Trio for piano and strings no.2 in E flat, D929

LARRY ADLER (harmonica)
GEOFFREY PARSONS (pf)
EDINBURGH QUARTET
29 Aug. 11.00 *Leith Town Hall*
Adler Theme and variations
Gershwin Lullaby for harmonica and string quartet (World première)
Gershwin Porgy and Bess: Suite; arr. Adler
Jacob Divertimento for harmonica and strings
Works by Bach, Milhaud, Bloch, Gershwin

INSTRUMENTAL ENSEMBLE
29 Aug. 20.00 *Usher Hall*
Brahms Sextet no.1 in B flat, op.18
Schubert Octet, D803
Yehudi Menuhin, Robert Masters (vn), Cecil Aronowitz, Ernst Wallfisch (va), Maurice Gendron, Derek Simpson (vc), Eugene Cruft (db), Gervase de Peyer (cl), Archie Camden (bn), Barry Tuckwell (hn)

AMADEUS QUARTET
31 Aug. 11.00 *Leith Town Hall*
Mozart Quartet for oboe and strings in F, K370
Bartók Quartet no.4
Britten Six metamorphoses after Ovid for oboe
Mozart Quartet no.19 in C (Dissonance), K465
with Heinz Holliger (ob)

1 Sep. 20.30 *Leith Town Hall*
Haydn Quartet in G, op.76/1
Bartók Quartet no.6
Beethoven Quartet no.10 in E flat (Harp), op.74

HEATHER HARPER (sop), NORMA PROCTER (cont), PETER PEARS (ten), FORBES ROBINSON (bs), BARRY TUCKWELL (hn), BENJAMIN BRITTEN (pf)
26 Aug. 11.00 *Leith Town Hall*
Schumann Minnespiel
Schumann Adagio and allegro for horn and piano, op.70
Britten Canticles nos.1, 2,

RECITALS

ELLA LEE (sop), GERALD MOORE (pf)
23 Aug. 11.00 *Freemasons' Hall*
Haydn Arianna a Naxos
Schubert Der Hirt auf dem Felsen
Songs by Schumann, Wolf, R. Strauss
with Thea King (cl)

OLGA SZÖNYI (mez), ANDRÁS FARAGÓ (b-bar), DAVID WILDE (pf)
27 Aug. 11.00 *Freemasons' Hall*
Bartók Sonata for piano
Bartók Suite for piano, op.14
Bartók Songs, folksongs and piano music

JOHN OGDON (pf)
5 Sep. 11.00 *Leith Town Hall*
Clementi Sonata for piano no.64 (Didone abbandonata), op.50/3
Busoni Sonatina for piano no.2
Liszt Mephisto waltz no.1
Bartók Sonata for 2 pianos and percussion
with Brenda Lucas (pf), James Blades, Stephen Whittaker (perc)

INDIAN MUSIC

(Introduced by Narayana Menon)
20 Aug. 11.00 *Freemasons' Hall*
INDIAN MUSIC AND THE EDINBURGH FESTIVAL
An illustrated talk and discussion
Yehudi Menuhin, Narayana Menon

21 Aug. 11.00 *Freemasons' Hall*
ALI AKBAR KHAN (sarode), ALLA RAKHA (tabla)

24 Aug. 11.00 *Leith Town Hall*
LARRY ADLER (harmonica), JULIAN BREAM (gtr), GEORGE MALCOLM (hpd), WILLIAM BENNETT (fl), ALI AKBAR KHAN (sarode), ALLA RAKHA (tabla), T. VISWANATHAN (Ind fl)
East-West miscellany

27 Aug. 18.00 *St Cuthbert's Church*
YEHUDI MENUHIN (vn), RAVI SHANKAR (sitâr), ALI AKBAR KHAN (sarode), GEORGE MALCOLM (hpd)
Bartók Sonata for solo violin
Bach English suite no.6 in D minor
Bach Partita for violin no.2: Chaconne
Improvisations on Râga Sudh Kalyan
Improvisations on Râga Malkaus

30 Aug. 11.00 *Freemasons' Hall*
RAVI SHANKAR (sitâr)

30 Aug. 2 Sep. 20.00 *Freemasons' Hall*
SUBBULAKSHMI (sop)
with accompaniment of violin, mrdangam, ghatan, tambura

2 Sep. 11.00 *Freemasons' Hall*
RAVI SHANKAR (sitâr), ALI AKBAR KHAN (sarode), ALLA RAKHA (tabla)

4 Sep. 11.00 *Freemasons' Hall*
PALGHAT RAGHU (Mrdangam)
ALLA RAKHA (tabla)
T.VISWANATHAN (Ind fl)

22, 23, 24, 26, 27, 28, 29, 31 Aug. 20.00
Royal Scottish Museum
BALASARASVATI (dan)
Bharata Natyam - The classical dance of South India
with K. Ganesan (cymbal),

S. Narasimhulu, S. Kumaraswami (sngr), T. Ranganathan (mrdangam), T. Viswanathan (Ind fl), S. Dhanalakshmi (tambura)

SCOTTISH CONCERTS

SCOTTISH CONCERT
4 Sep. 20.00 *Leith Town Hall*
Songs of Robert Burns
Music from Musica Scotica
Scottish dance music
Elizabeth Robson (sop), Kenneth McKellar (ten), Andrew Bryson (pf), Jimmy Shand (accordion), Ronald Gonella (fiddle), Pipe-Major John MacLellan, Pipe-Major George Stoddart (bp), Kinghorn Choir, Edinburgh Players
Conductor James Sloggie

SCOTTISH POETRY AND MUSIC
7 Sep. 11.00 *Leith Town Hall*
Poetry by Robert Burns and Hugh MacDiarmid, read and sung to the traditional tunes selected by Burns and settings of Francis George Scott
Marion Studholme (sop), Kenneth McKellar (ten), David Ward (bs), Andrew Bryson (pf), Bryden Murdoch, Hugh MacDiarmid (rdr)

GAELIC CONCERT
23 Aug. 20.00 *Leith Town Hall*
Soloists Anne Gillies, Archie MacLean, Ewen MacLachlan, Rhona MacLeod, George J. Clavey, Evelyn Campbell, George T. MacCallum (sngr), Janet McGilp (pf), Scottish Pipers' Association, Govan Gaelic Choir, Oban Gaelic Choir, Ayr Junior Gaelic Choir, Team from Scottish Official Board of Highland Dancing
(In association with An Comunn Gaidhealach)

CEILIDH
6 Sep. 20.00 *Leith Town Hall*
Soloists Donald MacRae, Carol Galbraith, Angus C. MacLeod, Nan D. Hunter, John A. Macrae, Ann MacLean, Joan M. Mackenzie, Kenneth MacRae (sngr), Chris Turner (pf), Jean Reynolds School of Dancing, Glasgow Angus Dance Band, Scottish Pipers' Association, Donald Thomson (Fear-an-tighe)
(In association with An Comunn Gaidhealach)

DRAMA

CHICHESTER FESTIVAL THEATRE
2-7 Sep. 19.15 3, 7 Sep. 14.15
Assembly Hall
SAINT JOAN Shaw
Joan Joan Plowright
Captain Robert de Baudricourt Martin Boddey
Steward Keith Marsh
Bertrand de Poulengey Richard Hampton
Archbishop of Rheims Dudley Foster
Monseigneur de la Tremouille Peter O' Shaughnessy
Gilles de Rais Terence Knapp
The Dauphin Robert Stephens
Captain la Hire Michael Turner
Duchess de la Tremouille Marion Mathie
Dunois Peter Cellier
Pages John Rogers, Trevor Hadley
Earl of Warwick Anthony Nicholls
John de Stogumber Frank Finlay
Bishop of Beauvais Robert Lang
Warwick's page Raymond Clarke
Inquisitor Max Adrian
Canon John d'Estivet Peter Russell
Canon de Courcelles Reginald Greene
Brother Martin Roger Heathcott
Executioner Dan Meaden
English soldier Norman Rossington
Gentleman Michael Rothwell
Director John Dexter
Designer Michael Annals

EDINBURGH INTERNATIONAL FESTIVAL
19-31 Aug. 19.15 (exc.Sun) 20, 24, 27, 31 Aug. 14.15 *Assembly Hall*
THE RABBIT RACE Walser
(Eng. Adapted by Ronald Duncan)
Alois Grubel Paul Massie
Anna Sheila Brennan
Kreisleiter Gorbach John Chandos
Professor Potz Frank Gatliff
Dr Zerlebeck John Crocker
Zenker David Lyell
Joseph Schmidt Denis McCarthy
Maschnik Duncan Lewis
Herr Woizele Denis Thorne
Jerzy Keith Goodman
Semper Derek Tansley
Blad Billy John
Maria Maria Lennard
Director Chloe Gibson
Designer Peter Rice
(In association with Marlan Productions)

19-24 Aug. 19.00 21, 24 Aug. 14.15
Lyceum Theatre
THE UNSHAVEN CHEEK Lawler
(World première)
Charlie Lewis Alfred Marks
Roy Lewis Walter Brown
Graham Corry
Lonnie Lewis Paul Dawkins
Eva Lewis June Jago
Blowfly Skuse Reg Lye
Lily Skuse Bettina Dickson
Nick Hannon Alister Williamson
Bernie Ward Bernard Hopkins
Fay Brewer Amanda Reiss
Director Frith Banbury
Scenery Loudon Sainthill
(In association with Frith Banbury)

59 THEATRE COMPANY
26-31 Aug. 19.00 28, 31 Aug. 14.15
Lyceum Theatre
LITTLE EYOLF Ibsen
(Eng. Translated by Michael Meyer)
Alfred Allmers James Maxwell
Rita Dilys Hamlett
Asta Allmers Avril Elgar
Borghejm Eric Thompson
Rat wife Catherine Lacey
Eyolf Stevie Walters
Director Michael Elliott
Designer Riette Sturge Moore
(In association with Gleneagles Productions Ltd)

ENGLISH STAGE COMPANY
2-7 Sep. 19.00 4, 7 Sep. 14.15
Lyceum Theatre
EXIT THE KING (Le Roi se meurt) Ionesco
(Eng. Translated by Donald Watson)
Berenger the First Alec Guinness
Queen Marguerite Googie Withers
Queen Marie Natasha Parry
Doctor Graham Crowden
Juliette Eileen Atkins
Guard Peter Bayliss
Director George Devine
Designer Jocelyn Herbert

GATEWAY COMPANY
19 Aug.-7 Sep. 19.30 (exc.Sun) 22, 24, 29, 31 Aug. 5, 7 Sep. 14.30
Gateway Theatre
ALL IN GOOD FAITH McMillan
Robert Bryson John Grieve
Agnes Bryson Marjorie Thomson
Jadie Bryson Walter Carr
Nicoll Bryson James Maguire
Rena Bryson Morag Forsyth
Colin Harry Walker
Peter James Grant
Lawyer Bryden Murdoch
Tina Gibb Irene Sunters
The gancher Lea Ashton
The craitur John Morton
Allan Bryson Leo Maguire
Director Victor Carin
Designer David Lovett

LATE NIGHT ENTERTAINMENT

19-31 Aug. 22.45 *Lyceum Theatre*
SET THEM REELING
Robin Hall and Jimmy MacGregor, Jimmy Shand and his Band, Doris Gilfeather, Gay Gordon Dance Team

2-7 Sep. 22.45 *Lyceum Theatre*
EX-AFRICA
A "Black odyssey" in jazz, rhyme, and calypso from the Negro's past
Shake Keane, Isabelle Lucas, Carmen Munroe, Joe Harriott Band, Emile Roumer, Derek Walcott, Richard Wright, Bobby Orr, Pat Smythe, Coleridge Goode
Directed by Bari Jonson

DANCE

HUNGARIAN STATE OPERA AND BALLET
19, 20, 21, 23 Aug. 19.00 *Empire Theatre*
THE WOODEN PRINCE
THE MIRACULOUS MANDARIN
Choreographer Gyula Harangozó
Music Bartók
Scenery Zoltán Fülöp
Costumes Tivadar Márk
with Duke Bluebeard's castle *See* Opera

22, 24 Aug. 19.00 *Empire Theatre*
THE SLY STUDENTS
Choreographer Gyula Harangozó
Music Farkas
Scenery Zoltán Fülöp
Costumes Tivadar Márk
SWAN LAKE: Act 2
Choreographers Lev Ivanov, Asaf Messerer
Music Tchaikovsky
GAYANEH
Choreographer Nina Anissimova
Music Khachaturian
Costumes Gizella Szeitz

22 Aug. 14.15 *Empire Theatre*
THE SLY STUDENTS
THE NUTCRACKER: Pas de deux
Choreographer Voinonen
Music Tchaikovsky
WALTZ
Choreographer Voinonen
Music Moskowski
GISELLE: Pas de deux (Act 2)
Choreographer Lavrovsky
Music Adam
THE BRIDE'S KERCHIEF: Pas de deux
Choreographer Gyula Harangozó
Music Kenessey

SWAN LAKE: Black swan pas de deux
GAYANEH: Act 3

24 Aug. 14.15 *Empire Theatre*
THE SLY STUDENTS
GISELLE: Pas de deux (Act 1)
SPRING WATERS
Choreographer Asaf Messerer
Music Rachmaninov
GISELLE: Pas de deux (Act 2)
SWAN LAKE: Black swan pas de deux
THE BRIDE'S KERCHIEF: Pas de deux
GAYANEH: Act 3
Dancers Zsuzsa Kún, Gabriella Lakatos, Adél Orosz, Klotild Ugray, Ágoston Balogh, Viktor Fülöp, Andar Gál, Gyula Harangozó, Ferenc Havas, Viktor Róna, Zoltán Sallay, Levente Sipeki
Conductors János Ferencsik, Pétar Tóth, Gedeon Fráter

MARTHA GRAHAM DANCE COMPANY, USA
26 Aug. 19.30 *Empire Theatre*
SERAPHIC DIALOGUE
Music Norman Dello-Joio
SECULAR GAMES
Music Robert Starer
PHAEDRA
Music Robert Starer

27 Aug. 19.30 *Empire Theatre*
DIVERSION OF ANGELS
Music Norman Dello-Joio
LEGEND OF JUDITH
Music Mordecai Seter
ACROBATS OF GOD
Music Carlos Surinach

28 Aug. 14.30 *Empire Theatre*
SECULAR GAMES
EMBATTLED GARDEN
Music Carlos Surinach
PHAEDRA

28, 30 Aug. 19.30 *Empire Theatre*
CLYTEMNESTRA
Music Halim El-Dabh

29 Aug. 19.30 *Empire Theatre*
SERAPHIC DIALOGUE
EMBATTLED GARDEN
NIGHT JOURNEY
Music W. Schuman

31 Aug. 14.30 *Empire Theatre*
DIVERSION OF ANGELS
NIGHT JOURNEY
ACROBATS OF GOD

31 Aug. 19.30 *Empire Theatre*
SERAPHIC DIALOGUE
SECULAR GAMES
LEGEND OF JUDITH
Choreographer (all ballets) Martha Graham
Designer (all ballets) Isamu Noguchi
Lighting (all ballets) Jean Rosenthal
Dancers Martha Graham, Bertram Ross, Helen McGehee, Linda Hodes, Robert Cohan, Yuriko, David Wood, Ethel Winter, Mary Hinkson, Robert Powell, Richard Gain, Gene McDonald, Peter Randazzo, Takako Asakawa, Carol Fried, Clive Thompson, Dudley Williams, Juliet Fisher, Phyllis Gutelius, Noemi Lapzeson with Rosalia Maresca (sop), Mario Laurenti (bar)
Conductor Robert Irving

STUTTGART BALLET
2-4 Sep. 19.30 4 Sep. 14.30
Empire Theatre
DAPHNIS AND CHLOË
Choreographer John Cranko
Music Ravel
Designer Nicholas Georgiadis
TREDE VARIATIONS
Choreographer John Cranko
Music Yngve Trede
QUINTET
Choreographer Peter Wright
Music Ibert
Costumes Walter Gayer
THE MIRROR WALKERS
Choreographer Peter Wright
Music Tchaikovsky

5-7 Sep. 19.30 *Empire Theatre*
THE CATALYST
Choreographer John Cranko
Music Shostakovich
Designer Werner Schachteli
LAS HERMANAS
Choreographer Kenneth MacMillan
Music Martin
Designer Nicholas Georgiadis
L'ESTRO ARMONICO
Choreographer John Cranko
Music Vivaldi

7 Sep. 14.30 *Empire Theatre*
MUSICAL CHAIRS
Choreographer John Cranko
Music Stolze
Designer Wilfried Gronwald
LAS HERMANAS
L'ESTRO ARMONICO
Dancers Marcia Haydée, Birgit Keil, Anita Cardus, Ilse Wiedmann, Henning Kronstam, Ray Barra, Hugo Delavalle, Graeme Anderson, Egon Madsen, Chesterina Sim Zecha, Richard Cragun
Bournemouth Symphony Orchestra
Conductors Josef Dünnwald, Kurt-Heinz Stolze

INTERNATIONAL DRAMA CONFERENCE

2-7 Sep. 14.30 *McEwan Hall*
Kenneth Tynan, J.B.Priestley, Martin Esslin, Peter Brook, Harold Clurman, Joan Greenwood, Wolf Mankowitz, Arnold Wesker, David Frost, Arthur Kopit, Erich Fried, Alexander Reid, Dorothy Tutin, Sir Laurence Olivier, Robert McLellan, Judith Anderson, Friedrich Luft, Lillian Helmann, Peter Shaffer, Bernard Levin, Jan Kott, Arnold Wesker, John Arden, Harold Pinter, Marguerite Duras, Arthur Adamov, Barry Reckford, Alain Robbe-Grillet, Jack Gelber, Jack Garfein, Charles Marowitz, Henry McNicol, George Devine, Martin Walser, Alan Schneider, Edward Albee, Bamber Gascoigne, Joan Plowright, Wole Soyinka, Habib Tanvir, Duncan Macrae, Cees Nootebloom, Jack Gerson, Kenneth Dewey, Jovan Hristic, Joan Littlewood, Carol Baker, Alan Kaprow, Jack Fitzgerald, Ronald Duncan, Peter Hall, Agnes Moorehead, Hilton Edwards,
Organized by John Calder

EXHIBITIONS

Royal Scottish Academy
MODIGLIANI
Director John Russell
SOUTINE
Director David Sylvester

Royal Scottish Museum
MUSIC AND DANCE IN INDIAN ART
Director Philip Rawson

1964

OPERA

PRAGUE NATIONAL THEATRE
17, 20, 22, 27 Aug. 3 Sep. 19.00
King's Theatre
DALIBOR Smetana
Dalibor Vilém Přibyl, Beno Blachut
Milada Alena Miková, Libuše Prylová, Milada Šubrtová
Jitka Libuše Domanínská, Helena Tattermuschová
Vitek Viktor Kočí, Zdeněk Švehlá
Budivoy Antonín Švorc
Benes Eduard Haken, Dalibor Jedlička
Vladislav Václav Bednář, Jindřich Jindrák
Judge Dalibor Jedlička, Jaroslav Horáček
Conductor Jaroslav Krombholc
Director Václav Kašlík
Scenery Josef Svoboda
Costumes Jarmila Konečná

18, 26 Aug. 19.00 *King's Theatre*
RESURRECTION Cikker
Prince Dmitri Teodor Šrubař
Sophia Ivanovna Milada Čadikovičová
Maria Ivanovna Naděžda Kniplová
Katharina Maslov (Káta) Alena Miková
Smelkov Milan Karpíšek
Euphemia Bochkov Helena Tattermuschová
Kartinkin Jiří Joran
Mme Kitayev Jaroslava Procházková
President of the court Karel Berman
Prosecutor Jindřich Jindrák
Defending counsel Antonín Votava
Prison inspector Dalibor Jedlička
Simonson Beno Blachut
Piotr Jaroslav Horáček
Marfa Jaroslava Dobrá
Singer/Young prisoner Zdeněk Švehla
Head juryman Miroslav Šindelář
Tichon Otakar Havránek
Prostitue Sona Rudišová
1st Woman Edita Denková
2nd Woman/2nd Prisoner Anna Rousková
1st Prisoner Božena Novotná
Prisoner in chains Jan Hadraba
Lieutenant Václav Pokorný
Serge/Court room recorder Emanuel Hruška
Wardresses Alena Šlaisová, Jana Kostelecká
Governor of the prison Ferdinand Kotas
Officer Bohumír Lalák
Usher Zdeněk Duda
Conductor Jaroslav Krombholc
Director Karel Jernek
Designer Zbyněk Kolář
Costumes Olga Filipi

19, 21, 25, 29, 31 Aug. 19.00
King's Theatre
RUSALKA Dvořák
Rusalka Milada Šubrtová, Libuše Domanínská
Prince Ivo Žídek, Beno Blachut
Foreign princess Libuše Prylová, Naděžda Kniplová
Water sprite Eduard Haken, Karel Berman

Witch — Marta Krásová / Jaroslava Dobrá / Jaroslava Procházková
Game keeper — Jiří Joran / Antonín Votava
Cook — Helena Tattermuschová
1st Wood nymph — Sylvia Kodetová
2nd Wood nymph — Miloslava Fidlfrová
3rd Wood nymph — Ivana Mixová
Hunter — Václav Bednář / Teodor Šrubař / Přemysl Kočí
Conductor — Jan Hus Tichý
Director — Václav Kašlík
Scenery — Josef Svoboda
Costumes — Jarmila Konečná

24 Aug. 1, 4 Sep. 19.00 — *King's Theatre*
KÁTA KABANOVÁ Janáček
Káta — Libuše Domanínská / Eva Zikmundová / Alena Miková
Boris — Viktor Kočí / Beno Blachut
Marfa Kabanová — Jaroslava Procházková / Jaroslava Dobrá
Dikoy — Karel Berman
Tichon Kabanov — Jaroslav Stříška
Vanya — Zdeněk Švehla
Varvara — Ivana Mixová
Kuligin — Jindřich Jindrák
Glasha — Sylvia Kodetová
Feklusha — Milada Čadikovičová
Conductor — Jaroslav Krombholc
Director — Hanuš Thein
Scenery — Josef Svoboda
Costumes — Marcel Pokorný

28 Aug. 2, 5 Sep. 19.00 — *King's Theatre*
FROM THE HOUSE OF THE DEAD
Janáček
Alexander — Dalibor Jedlička
Alyeya — Helena Tattermuschová
Filka Morozov — Beno Blachut
Big prisoner — Jaroslav Stříška
Little prisoner — Karel Berman
Prison commander — Jaroslav Horáček / Antonín Švorc
Old prisoner — Antonín Votava
Skuratov — Ivo Žídek
Chekunov — Jindřich Jindrák
Drunk prisoner — Miroslav Mach
Cook — Miroslav Šindelář
Blacksmith — Jiří Joran
Priest — Jaromír Bělor
Young prisoner — Jindřich Jindrák
Young harlot — Eva Zikmundová
Shapkin/Kedril — Milan Karpíšek
Shishkov — Přemysl Kočí
Cherevin — Viktor Kočí
Don Juan/Brahmin — Jiří Joran
Conductor — Bohumil Gregor
Director — Ladislav Štros
Designer — Vladimír Nývlt
Costumes — Marcel Pokorný

ORCHESTRAL CONCERTS

ORCHESTRE NATIONAL DE LA RADIODIFFUSION FRANÇAISE

16 Aug. 20.00 — *Usher Hall*
Berlioz — Grande messe des morts (Requiem)
Conductor — Charles Münch
Soloist William McAlpine (ten), Choeurs de la Radiodiffusion Française, Tullis Russell Mills Band

17 Aug. 20.00 — *Usher Hall*
Berlioz — Roméo et Juliette
Conductor — Lorin Maazel
Soloists Anna Reynolds (mez), Camille Maurane (bar), Joseph Rouleau (bs), Choeurs de la Radiodiffusion Française

18 Aug. 20.00 — *Usher Hall*
Bach — Suite no.4 in D
Stravinsky — Symphony in three movements
Berlioz — Symphonie fantastique
Conductor — Lorin Maazel

19 Aug. 20.00 — *Usher Hall*
Fauré — Pelléas et Mélisande - Suite
Roussel — Symphony no.3 in G minor, op.42
Berlioz — Les nuits d'été
Ravel — Boléro
Conductor — Charles Münch
Soloist — Marilyn Horne (mez)

SCOTTISH NATIONAL CHAMBER ORCHESTRA
Conductor Alexander Gibson

17 Aug. 11.00 — *Leith Town Hall*
Mozart — Symphony no.34 in C, K338
Lampugnani — Meraspe: Superbo di me stesso
Beethoven — Ah! perfido
Haydn — Symphony no.98 in B flat
Soloist — Marilyn Horne (mez)

29 Aug. 11.00 — *Leith Town Hall*
Britten — Sinfonietta, op.1
Mozart — Symphony no.32 in G, K318
Rodrigo — Concierto de Aranjuez for guitar
Haydn — Symphony no.84 in E flat
Soloist — Julian Bream (gtr)

LONDON SYMPHONY ORCHESTRA

22 Aug. 20.00 — *Usher Hall*
Tchaikovsky — Hamlet - Fantasy overture
Britten — Symphony for cello and orchestra, op.68
Janáček — Sinfonietta
Prokofiev — Overture on Jewish themes
Conductor — Gennadi Rozhdestvensky
Soloist — Mstislav Rostropovich (vc)

23 Aug. 20.00 — *Usher Hall*
Berlioz — King Lear - Overture
Henze — Ariosi (EIF commission)
Elgar — Symphony no.1 in A flat, op.55
Conductor — Colin Davis
Soloists Irmgard Seefried (sop), Wolfgang Schneiderhan (vn)

24 Aug. 20.00 — *Usher Hall*
Berlioz — L'enfance du Christ
Conductor — Colin Davis
Soloists April Cantelo (sop), Alexander Young, Edgar Fleet (ten), Thomas Hemsley (bar), Joseph Rouleau, John Frost (bs), London Symphony Orchestra Chorus

ENGLISH CHAMBER ORCHESTRA
Conductor Alexander Schneider

25 Aug. 20.00 — *Usher Hall*
Mozart — Symphony no.20 in D, K133
Mozart — Concerto for piano no.12 in A, K414
Mozart — Concerto for piano no. 21 in C, K467
Soloist — Rudolf Serkin (pf)

26 Aug. 20.00 — *Usher Hall*
Mozart — Concerto for piano no.16 in D, K451
Mozart — Concerto for piano no.11 in F, K413
Mozart — Concerto for 2 pianos in E flat, K365
Soloists — Rudolf *and* Peter Serkin (pf)

28 Aug. 20.00 — *Usher Hall*
Mozart — March in D, K335
Mozart — Concerto for piano no.14 in E flat, K449
Mozart — Six German dances, K571
Mozart — Concerto for piano no.20 in D minor, K466
Soloist — Rudolf Serkin (pf)

SCOTTISH NATIONAL ORCHESTRA
Conductor Alexander Gibson

27 Aug. 20.00 — *Usher Hall*
Berlioz — Les francs-juges - Overture
Webern — Six pieces, op.6
Schumann — Concerto for cello in A minor, op.129; ed. Shostakovich
Berlioz — Te deum
Soloists Charles Craig (ten), Mstislav Rostropovich (vc), Alexander Anderson (org), Scottish Junior Singers, Scottish Opera Chorus

1 Sep. 20.00 — *Usher Hall*
Berlioz — Waverley - Overture
Janáček — The cunning little vixen - Suite
Beethoven — Concerto for piano no.5 in E flat (Emperor), op.73
Elgar — Falstaff
Soloist — Rudolf Serkin (pf)

BBC SCOTTISH ORCHESTRA

29 Aug. 20.00 — *Usher Hall*
R. Strauss — Macbeth
Beethoven — Concerto for piano no.3 in C minor, op.37
Janáček — Jealousy
Britten — The prince of the pagodas: Prelude and dances
Conductor — Norman del Mar
Soloist — Rudolf Firkušný (pf)

PRAGUE NATIONAL THEATRE CHORUS and ORCHESTRA

30 Aug. 20.00 — *Usher Hall*
Smetana — Má vlast: Vltava, Tábor, Blanik
Janáček — Glagolitic mass
Conductor — Jaroslav Krombholc
Soloists Libuše Domanínská (sop), Marta Krásová (cont), Beno Blachut (ten), Eduard Haken (bs), Alexander Anderson (org).

PITTSBURGH SYMPHONY ORCHESTRA
Conductor William Steinberg

3 Sep. 20.00 — *Usher Hall*
Schuller — Seven studies on themes of Paul Klee
Mendelssohn — Concerto for violin in E minor, op.64
Elgar — Symphony no.2 in E flat, op.63
Soloist — Charles Treger (vn)

4 Sep. 20.00 — *Usher Hall*
P. Mennin — Canto for orchestra
Mahler — Kindertotenlieder
Mahler — Symphony no.7 in E minor
Soloist — Dietrich Fischer-Dieskau (bar)

5 Sep. 20.00 — *Usher Hall*
Schubert — Symphony no.2 in B flat, D125
W. Mellers — 'Alba' in nine metamorphoses
Berlioz — Béatrice et Bénédict: Overture
Tchaikovsky — Concerto for violin in D, op.35
Copland — El salón México
Soloists Manoug Parikian (vn), Bernard Goldberg (fl)

CHAMBER CONCERTS

OROMONTE STRING TRIO

18 Aug. 11.00 — *Freemasons' Hall*

Mozart Adagio and fugue in G minor, K404a/2
Schoenberg Trio, op.45
Mozart Divertimento in E flat, K563

21 Aug. 11.00 Freemasons' Hall
Mozart Adagio and fugue in D minor, K404a/1
Rainier Quanta for oboe and strings
Mozart Quartet for oboe and strings in F, K370
Beethoven Trio no.2 in G, op.9/1
with Janet Craxton (ob)

JULIAN BREAM (lute, gtr), ALEXANDER YOUNG (ten), JULIAN BREAM CONSORT
20 Aug. 11.00 Leith Town Hall
Vivaldi Concerto for lute in D
Haydn Cassation in C, op.1/6
Eastwood Solitudes (World première)
Britten Nocturnal after John Dowland for guitar
Schubert Quartet for guitar and strings in G, D96

MSTISLAV ROSTROPOVICH (vc)
PARK LANE ENSEMBLE
23 Aug. 14.30 Usher Hall
Vivaldi Concerto for cello in C, P31
Vivaldi Concerto for cello in G minor, P369
Vivaldi Concerto for cello in G, P120
Tartini Concerto for cello in A
Boccherini Concerto for cello in D

JANÁČEK QUARTET
24 Aug. 11.00 Freemasons' Hall
Beethoven Quartet no.1 in F, op.18/1
Janáček Quartet no.1 (The Kreutzer sonata)
Dvořák Quartet no.14 in A flat, op.105

26 Aug. 11.00 Freemasons' Hall
Haydn Quartet in D minor (Fifths), op.76/2
Janáček Quartet no.2 (Intimate letters)
Smetana Quartet no.1 in E minor (From my life)

RUDOLF FIRKUŠNÝ (pf)
ENGLISH CHAMBER ORCHESTRA members
27 Aug. 11.00 Leith Town Hall
Janáček Concertino for piano and chamber ensemble
Janáček In the mist
Janáček Capriccio for piano (Left hand) and chamber ensemble
Mozart Quintet for piano and wind in E flat, K452

RUDOLF FIRKUŠNÝ (pf)
ALLEGRI QUARTET
31 Aug. 20.00 Usher Hall
Mozart Quartet no.14 in G, K387
Haydn Quartet in D (Lark), op.64/5
Janáček Sonata 1 X 1905
Dvořák Quintet for piano and strings in A, op.81

SCOTTISH PIANO TRIO
4 Sep. 11.00 Freemasons' Hall
Beethoven Trio for piano and strings no.1 in E flat, op.1/1
Rawsthorne Trio for piano and strings
Schubert Notturno in E flat, D897
Brahms Trio for piano and strings no.3 in C minor, op.101

PRAGUE NATIONAL THEATRE WIND BAND
5 Sep. 11.00 Leith Town Hall
Kramář Harmonie in E flat, op.71
Janáček Mládi
Mozart Serenade no.12 in C minor, K388

EDINBURGH UNIVERSITY SINGERS
28 Aug. 11.00 Freemasons' Hall
Bonnet Francion vint l'autre jour
Sermisy Au joly boys
Janequin Ce moys de may
Monte Derriere un beau prunier
Arcadelt Margot labourez les vignes
Monteverdi Missa in illo tempore
Bach Motet no.1. Singet dem Herrn
Conductor Herrick Bunney

HEATHER HARPER (sop), CATHERINE WILSON (sop), KENNETH McKELLAR (ten), NEIL HOWLETT (bar), ROBERT KEYS (pf)
22 Aug. 11.00 Leith Town Hall
Berlioz Chansons d'Irlande
Donizetti Nuits d'été a Pausilippe

MARIA TAUBEROVÁ (sop), IVANA MIXOVÁ (mez), BENO BLACHUT, IVO ŽIDEK (ten), PŘEMYSL KOČÍ, JINDŘICH JINDRÁK (bar), JAN HUS TICHÝ, JIRÍ POKORNÝ (pf)
1 Sep. 11.00 Freemasons' Hall
Janáček Diary of one who disappeared
Songs by Smetana, Dvořák

RECITALS

CAMILLE MAURANE (bar)
ROBERT KEYS (pf)
19 Aug. 11.00 Freemasons' Hall
Fauré L'horizon chimérique
Fauré Mirages
Debussy Trois ballades de François Villon
Debussy Le promenoir des deux amants
Duparc Songs

IRMGARD SEEFRIED (sop)
ERIK WERBA (pf)
21 Aug. 20.00 Leith Town Hall
Mussorgsky The nursery
Songs by Mozart, Schumann, Schubert, Hindemith, R. Strauss

KENNETH McKELLAR (ten)
DENIS WOOLFORD (pf)
28 Aug. 20.00 Leith Town Hall
Schumann Dichterliebe (Transl. into Scots)
Britten *arr.* Scots songs from 'The beggar's opera'
Trad. Folk songs

DIETRICH FISCHER-DIESKAU (bar)
GERALD MOORE (pf)
2 Sep. 20.00 Usher Hall
Songs by Busoni, Mahler, R. Strauss

RUDOLF SERKIN (pf)
30 Aug. 14.30 Usher Hall
Schubert Sonata no.20 in A, D959
Beethoven Bagatelles nos.8-18, op.119
Beethoven Sonata no.21 in C (Waldstein), op.53

SVIATOSLAV RICHTER (pf)
2 Sep. 14.30 Usher Hall
Schubert Sonata no.21 in B flat, D960
Mendelssohn Variations sérieuses, op.54
Brahms Ballade no.2 in D, op.10/2
Brahms Piano pieces, op.76: Capriccio in C
Brahms Piano pieces, op.116: Excerpts

MICHAEL ROLL (pf)
3 Sep. 11.00 Freemasons' Hall
D. Scarlatti Sonata no.12 in D minor, L413
D. Scarlatti Sonata no.13 in D minor, L422
Beethoven Sonata no.23 in F minor (Appassionata), op.57
Britten Notturno
Chopin Scherzo no.2 in B flat minor, op.31
Mussorgsky Pictures at an exhibition

MANOUG PARIKIAN (vn)
DAVID WILDE (pf)
2 Sep. 11.00 Freemasons' Hall
Bach Sonata no.2 in A minor for solo violin
Janáček Sonata for violin and piano
Henze Sonata for piano
Beethoven Sonata for violin and piano no.6 in A, op.30/1

JOAN DICKSON (vc)
HESTER DICKSON (pf)
31 Aug. 11.00 Freemasons' Hall
Beethoven Variations on' Ein Mädchen oder Weibchen' (Mozart)
Henze Serenade for solo cello
Janáček Fairy tale (Pohádka)
Franck Sonata for cello and piano in A

MSTISLAV ROSTROPOVICH (vc)
SVIATOSLAV RICHTER (pf)
31 Aug. 22.30 Usher Hall
Beethoven Sonatas nos.1-5

SCOTTISH CONCERTS

GAELIC CONCERT
21 Aug. 20.00 Usher Hall
Soloists Ann Gillies, Joan Mackenzie, Ian A. Carmichael, George J. Clavey (sngr), Janet McGilp (pf), Anne Macdearmid (clarsach), Ronald Gonella (fiddle), Pipe-Major Donald MacLeod (bp), Iain C. Macdonald (Highland dancer), Edinburgh City Police Pipe Band, Edinburgh Gaelic Choir, Lothian Celtic Choir, Glasgow Islay Gaelic Choir, Glasgow Gaelic Musical Association, Greenock Gaelic Choir, Govan Gaelic Choir
(In association with An Comunn Gaidhealach)

ELIZABETH ROBSON (sop), KENNETH McKELLAR (ten), WILLIAM McCUE (bs), ANDREW BRYSON (pf), BRYDEN MURDOCH (rdr)
25 Aug. 11.00 Leith Town Hall
Songs of Scotland
Poems on Edinburgh by William Dunbar and the makars of the 14th century to the present day

MUSIC OF SCOTLAND
4 Sep. 20.00 Leith Town Hall
Soloists Elizabeth Robson (sop), Duncan Robertson (ten), Ronald Gonella (fiddle), Julian Dawson (hpd, pf), Pipe-Major George Stoddart, Pipe-Major John MacLellan (bp), Rowallan Singers, Edinburgh Players
Conductor James Sloggie
Introduced by Robin Richardson

DRAMA

THEATRE WORKSHOP
17 Aug.-5 Sep 19.15 (exc.Sun) 18, 22, 25, 29 Aug. 1, 5 Sep. 14.15 Assembly Hall
HENRY IV Parts 1 *and* 2 Shakespeare
King Henry IV Richard Goorney
Henry, Prince of Wales Frank Coda

Earl of Westmoreland/Ostler
Richard Curnock
Sir Walter Blunt/Vintner George Sewell
Earl of Northumberland/Sheriff
Peter Dalton
Henry Percy (Hotspur) Julian Glover
Earl of Worcester/Bardolph Brian Murphy
Owen Glendower/Poins Victor Spinetti
Sir John Falstaff George Cooper
Gadshill/Earl of March/Sir Richard Vernon
Murray Melvin
Lady Percy/Doll Tearsheet Myfanwy Jenn
Lady Mortimer Fanny Carby
Mistress Quickly Avis Bunnage
Chamberlain/Pistol Howard Goorney
Ralph Larry Dann
Earl of Douglas/Bishop Ian Paterson
Servant to Hotspur Colin Kemball
Francis/Scrivener Jeremy Spenser
Director Joan Littlewood
Designer John Bury

EDINBURGH INTERNATIONAL FESTIVAL
17-22 Aug. 19.00 19, 22 Aug. 14.15
Lyceum Theatre
HAMP Wilson
Private Arthur Hamp John Hurt
Corporal Malcolm Tierney
Guard John Croft
Lieutenant Hargreaves Richard Briers
Lieutenant Webb Leonard Rossiter
President of the court/Guards major
Noel Coleman
'Buffs' major Christopher Greatorex
'Loyals' captain/Orderly officer
Jeremy Conway
Lieutenant Prestcott Michael Deacon
Captain Midgeley Charles Hodgson
Padre Tom Watson
Captain O'Sullivan Kevin Flood
Director John Gibson
Designer Christopher Morley
(In association with Michael White)

BRISTOL OLD VIC
24, 28, 29 Aug. 19.00 29 Aug. 14.15
Lyceum Theatre
HENRY V Shakespeare
King Henry V Richard Pasco
Chorus David Dodimead
Duke of Gloucester Michael Fleming
Duke of Bedford Noel Thorpe-Tracey
Duke of Exeter Richard Mayes
Earl of Salisbury/Sir Thomas Grey
Charles Pemberton
Earl of Westmoreland Leader Hawkins
Archbishop of Canterbury James Cossins
Bishop of Ely/Duke of Orleans
Julian Battersby
Earl of Cambridge/Jamy Michael Quinto
Lord Scroop/Williams Michael Jayston
Sir Thomas Erpingham/Bardolph
Julian Curry
Gower Peter Baldwin
Fluellen Russell Hunter
MacMorris/Duke of Burgundy
James Cossins
Bates/Charles VI Frank Middlemass
Pistol Christopher Benjamin
Nym/French soldier Alan Collins
Louis, the Dauphin Terrence Hardiman
Duke of Bourbon Antony Vogel
Constable of France Geoffrey Toone
Montjoy Sebastian Breaks
Queen Isabel/Mistress Quickly
Eithne Dunne
Katharine Rowena Cooper
Alice Barbara Leigh-Hunt
Ladies Bonnie Hurren, Joy Ring
Director Stuart Burge
Designer Graham Barlow

25-27 Aug. 19.00 26 Aug. 14.15
Lyceum Theatre
LOVE'S LABOUR'S LOST Shakespeare
Ferdinand David Dodimead
Berowne Richard Pasco
Longaville Michael Jayston
Dumaine Peter Baldwin
Dull Julian Curry
Costard Russell Hunter
Don Adriano de Armado
Christopher Benjamin
Moth Stanley Bates
Jaquenetta Jennie Woodford
Boyet Terrence Hardiman
Princess of France Eithne Dunne
Rosaline Barbara Leigh-Hunt
Katharine Rowena Cooper
Maria Bonnie Hurren
Lord Michael Fleming
Foresters Julian Battersby, Michael Quinto
Sir Nathaniel Frank Middlemass
Holofernes James Cossins
Chamberlain Leader Hawkins
Clerk Alan Collins
Mercade Sebastian Breaks
Lords Alan Knight, Antony Vogel
Director Val May
Designer Michael Annals

GATEWAY COMPANY
17 Aug.-5 Sep. 19.30 (exc.Sun) 20, 22, 27, 29 Aug. 3, 5 Sep. 14.30
Gateway Theatre
THE GOLDEN LEGEND OF SHULTS
Bridie
Davie Cooper Alex McAvoy
Annie Morag Forsyth
Lord Auchtertyre Brown Derby
Nurse Clare Richards
Prison chaplain James Gibson
Doctor Stanley Stewart
Adolf Phil McCall
Provost McGlashan John Dunbar
Women Jean Faulds, Pekoe Ainley
Ida Schuster
Harry Brown Laidlaw Dalling
Joe Robinson Hugh Evans
Tom Jones Christopher Page
Dick Smith Alec Monteith
Musician Pat Cresswell
Other parts played by William McCabe, Brian Marjoribanks, Richard Finlay, Joe Dunlop, Alan Tennock, Malcolm Terris, Kenneth Bryers, Lars Macfarlane, Ogilvie Crombie, John Kirkwood, Margaret Leslie, Alistair Kerr, Rosemary Curr, John Morton
Director Victor Carin
Designer Juanita Waterson

18, 21, 25, 28 Aug. 1, 4 Sep. 14.30
Gateway Theatre
THE HEART IS HIGHLAND Kemp
Lennox Milne

LATE NIGHT ENTERTAINMENT

17-22 Aug. 22.45 *Lyceum Theatre*
ONE HAND CLAPPING
A review directed by Charles Marowitz with material by Paul Ableman
Leon Eagles, Graham Lines, Marigold Sharman, Bill Wallis, Nicholas Smith
Music Richard Peaslee
Designer Suzanne Glanister
(In association with Camden Playhouse Productions Ltd)

24-29 Aug. 22.45 *Lyceum Theatre*
CHAGANOG
Julian Chagrin, George Ogilvie, Patsy Rowlands, Sheila O'Neill, David Toguri
Director Braham Murray
Designer Claude Chagrin
(In association with Peter Bridge)

31 Aug-5 Sep. 22.45 *Lyceum Theatre*
MARLENE DIETRICH
with Orchestra conducted by Burt Bacharach
(In association with John Coast and Donald Langdon)

DANCE

LES BALLETS AFRICAINS
The National Company of Guinea
31 Aug.-5 Sep. 19.00 2, 5 Sep. 14.15
Lyceum Theatre
BAGATAI
THE FOREST
TOUTOU DIARRA
MIDNIGHT
INITIATION
SOUNDIATA
DOUNDOUMBA (Dance of retired warriors)
TIRANKE who could not make up her mind
Director Amadou Sissoko
Scenery Jacques Noël
Costumes Apsita Sissoko

EXHIBITIONS

Royal Scottish Academy
DELACROIX EXHIBITION

Waverley Market
THE SHAKESPEARE EXHIBITION
Director Richard Buckle

1965

OPERA

EDINBURGH INTERNATIONAL FESTIVAL
23, 25, 28 Aug. 1, 3 Sep. 19.00
King's Theatre
DON GIOVANNI Mozart
Don Giovanni — Renato Capecchi
Donna Anna — Luisa Bosabalian
Donna Elvira — Ilva Ligabue
Don Ottavio — Richard Lewis
Leporello — Paolo Montarsolo
Zerlina — Mariella Adani
Masetto — Leonardo Monreale
Commendatore — Giorgio Tadeo
Netherlands Chamber Choir
New Philharmonia Orchestra
Conductor — Carlo Maria Giulini
Lighting — William Bundy
Costumes — David Walker
(In association with the Holland Festival)

24, 26, 27 Aug. 19.00 *Kings' Theatre*
LE PESCATRICI Haydn
Eurilda — Ruza Pospis
Lindoro — Ugo Trama
Lesbina — Maddalena Bonifaccio
Burlotto — Umberto Grilli
Nerina — Adriana Martino
Frisellino — Giacomo Aragall
Mastricco — Carlos Feller
Netherlands Chamber Choir
New Philharmonia Orchestra
Conductor — Alberto Erede
Director — Werner Düggelin
Designer — Jörn Zimmermann
(In association with the Holland Festival)

ENGLISH OPERA GROUP
31 Aug. 2, 4 Sep. 19.00 *King's Theatre*
ALBERT HERRING Britten
Albert Herring — Kenneth Macdonald
Florence Pike — Johanna Peters
Miss Wordsworth — April Cantelo
Mr Gedge — Bryan Drake
Mr Upfold — Edgar Evans
Superintendant Budd — Harold Blackburn
Lady Billows — Sylvia Fisher
Emmie — Sheila Amit
Cis — Jennifer Lilleystone
Harry — Robert Mulcahy
Sid — Benjamin Luxon
Nancy — Anne Pashley
Mrs Herring — Sheila Rex
English Chamber Orchestra
Conductor — Vilem Tausky
Director — Colin Graham
Designer — John Piper

BAVARIAN STATE OPERA, Munich
6, 7, 8, 10 Sep. 19.00 *King's Theatre*
COSÌ FAN TUTTE Mozart (Ger)
Fiordiligi — Claire Watson
Leonore Kirschstein
Dorabella — Hertha Töpper
Lilian Benningsen
Ferrando — Fritz Wunderlich
Donald Grobe
Guglielmo — Raimund Grumbach
Despina — Hanny Steffek
Gertrud Freedman
Don Alfonso — Keith Engen
Karl Christian Kohn
Conductor — Hans Gierster
Director — Rudolf Hartmann
Scenery — Helmut Jürgens
Costumes — Charlotte Flemming

9, 11 Sep. 19.00 *King's Theatre*
INTERMEZZO R. Strauss
Christine — Hanny Steffek
Robert Storch — Hermann Prey
Franz — Hamid Nasseri
Anna — Gertrud Freedman
Baron Lummer — Ferry Gruber
Notary — Josep Knapp
His wife — Annelie Waas
Kapellmeister — Friedrich Lenz
Commercial councellor — Karl Christian Kohn
Barrister — Hans Hermann Nissen
Kammersänger — Max Proebstl
Fanny — Paula Meyer
Housemaid — Monika Kienzl
Resi — Rose Marie Freni
Conductor — Meinhard von Zallinger
Director — Rudolf Hartmann
Designer — Jean-Pierre Ponnelle

ORCHESTRAL CONCERTS

SCOTTISH NATIONAL ORCHESTRA
Conductor Alexander Gibson
22 Aug. 20.00 *Usher Hall*
Mahler — Symphony no.8 in E flat
Soloists Heather Harper, Gwyneth Jones, Gwenyth Annear (sop), Janet Baker (mez), Norma Procter (cont), Vilém Přibyl (ten), Vladimir Ruzdjac (bar), Donald McIntyre (b-bar), Scottish Festival Chorus

24 Aug. 20.00 *Usher Hall*
Sibelius Symphony no.4 in A minor, op.63
Sibelius — Concerto for violin in D minor, op.47
Sibelius — Symphony no.5 in E flat, op.82
Soloist — Henryk Szeryng (vn)

3 Sep. 20.00 *Usher Hall*
Haydn — Symphony no.61 in D
Tippett — Concerto for piano
Orr — Symphony in one movement
Dvořák — Symphonic variations, op.78
Soloist — John Ogdon (pf)

NDR SYMPHONY ORCHESTRA, Hamburg
26 Aug. 20.00 *Usher Hall*
Wagner Der fliegende Holländer: Overture
Beethoven Concerto for violin in D, op.61
Brahms Symphony no.1 in C minor, op.68
Conductor — Hans Schmidt-Isserstedt
Soloist — Henryk Szeryng (vn)

27 Aug. 20.00 *Usher Hall*
Haydn — Symphony no.86 in D
Tippett Fantasia concertante on a theme of Corelli
Mozart — Exsultate, jubilate
Stravinsky — The firebird - Suite
Conductor — Hans Schmidt-Isserstedt
Soloist — Friederike Sailer (sop)

28 Aug. 20.00 *Usher Hall*
Beethoven — Symphony no.2 in D, op.36
Messiaen — Oiseaux exotiques
Webern — Symphony, op.21
Debussy — La mer
Conductor — Pierre Boulez
Soloist — Yvonne Loriod (pf)

29 Aug. 20.00 *Usher Hall*
Boulez — Pli selon pli
Conductor — Pierre Boulez
Soloist — Halina Lukomska (sop)

NEW PHILHARMONIA CHAMBER ORCHESTRA
28 Aug. 11.00 *Leith Town Hall*
Haydn — Symphony no.6 in D (Le matin)
Haydn — Symphony no.7 in C (Le midi)
Haydn — Symphony no.8 in G (Le soir)
Conductor — Alberto Erede

NEW PHILHARMONIA ORCHESTRA
31 Aug. 20.00 *Usher Hall*
Mozart Divertimento no.15 in B flat, K287
Mozart — Serenade no.10 in B flat (Gran partita), K361
Conductor — Carlo Maria Giulini

4 Sep. 20.00 *Usher Hall*
Haydn — Symphony no.94 (Surprise)
Beethoven — Concerto for piano no.1 in C, op.15
Schumann — Symphony no.3 in E flat (Rhenish), op.97
Conductor — Carlo Maria Giulini
Soloist — Claudio Arrau (pf)

6 Sep. 20.00 *Usher Hall*
Elgar — Introduction and allegro, op.47
Beethoven — Concerto for piano no.5 in E flat (Emperor), op.73
Nielsen — Symphony no.5
Conductor — Sir John Barbirolli
Soloist — Claudio Arrau (pf)

7 Sep. 20.00 *Usher Hall*
Haydn — Symphony no.98 in B flat
Britten — Concerto for violin in D minor, op.15
Tchaikovsky — Symphony no.5 in E minor, op.64
Conductor — Sir John Barbirolli
Soloist — Wanda Wilkomirska (vn)

NETHERLANDS CHAMBER ORCHESTRA
30 Aug. 20.00 *Usher Hall*
Conductor Szymon Goldberg
Bach — Concerto for violin in A minor
Bach — Suite no.2 in B minor
Bach — Suite no.1 in C
Bach — Brandenburg concerto no.4 in G
Soloists Szymon Goldberg (vn), Severino Gazzelloni, Gareth Morris (fl)

31 Aug. 18.00 *St Cuthbert's Church*
Haydn — The seven last words of our Saviour from the cross, for orchestra

1 Sep. 20.00 *Usher Hall*
Haydn — Symphony no.57 in D
Boccherini (attrib.) Concerto for flute in D, op.27
Bach — Brandenburg concerto no.3 in G
Schoenberg — Quartet no.2 in F sharp minor, op.10
Erna Spoorenberg (sop), Severino Gazzelloni (fl)

2 Sep. 20.00 *Usher Hall*
Bach — Concerto for 2 violins in D minor
Mozart Concerto for violin no.4 in D, K218
Badings — Largo and allegro
Webern — Five pieces, op.5
Dvořák — Serenade for strings in E, op.22
Soloist — Thomas Magyar (vn)

LONDON MOZART PLAYERS
5 Sep. 20.00 *Usher Hall*
Conductor Harry Blech
Mozart — Adagio and fugue in C minor, K546
Haydn — Berenice che fai
Mozart — Un bacio di mano
Mozart — Symphony no.41 in C (Jupiter), K551
Haydn — Mass no.11 in D minor (Nelson)
Soloists Erna Spoorenberg (sop),

Helen Watts (cont), Gerald English (ten), Forbes Robinson (bs), Netherlands Chamber Choir

6 Sep. 11.00 *Leith Town Hall*
Haydn Armida: Overture
Tippett Divertimento 'Sellinger's round'
Mozart Concerto for oboe in C, K314
Haydn Symphony no.44 in E minor (Trauersinfonie)
Soloist Heinz Holliger (ob)

BBC SCOTTISH ORCHESTRA
8 Sep. 20.00 *Usher Hall*
Busoni Comedy overture
Tippett Symphony no.1
Brahms Concerto for piano no.1 in D minor, op.15
Conductor Norman del Mar
Soloist Claudio Arrau (pf)

11 Sep. 22.45 *Usher Hall*
Berlioz Le corsaire - Overture
Prokofiev Romeo and Juliet - Suite
Chabrier España
Dankworth Zodiac variations: Excerpts
Seiber-Dankworth Improvisations for jazz band and orchestra
John Dankworth Band
Conductor James Loughran

BBC CONCERT ORCHESTRA
Conductor Vilem Tausky
9 Sep. 20.00 *Usher Hall*
Haydn Symphony no.48 in C (Maria Theresia)
Williamson Symphonic variations (World première)
Prokofiev Concerto for violin no.1 in D, op.19
Tchaikovsky Capriccio Italien
Soloist Wanda Wilkomirska (vn)

11 Sep. 19.30 *Usher Hall*
Smetana The bartered bride: Overture
Haydn Concerto for trumpet in E flat
Haydn Arie des Schutzgeistes
Haydn Aria di Cardellina
Svendsen Carnival in Paris
Hamilton Concerto for jazz trumpet
Gershwin Porgy and Bess: Excerpts
Soloists Mattiwilda Dobbs (sop), Inia Te Wiata (bs), David Mason, George Swift (tpt)

CHAMBER CONCERTS

NEW PHILHARMONIA ENSEMBLE
23 Aug. 11.00 *Leith Town Hall*
Haydn Trio for horn, violin and cello
Mozart Quintet for clarinet and strings in A, K581
Tippett Little music for strings+
Beethoven Sextet in E flat, op.81b
Conductor Michael Tippett+

5 Sep. 14.30 *Usher Hall*
Haydn Nocturne in G (Military)
Nielsen Quintet for wind, op.43
Beethoven Septet, op.20

PARRENIN QUARTET
30 Aug. 11.00 *Leith Town Hall*
Haydn Quartet in G minor (Rider), op.74/3
Stravinsky Concertino
Debussy Quartet in G minor, op10/1

1 Sep. 11.00 *Leith Town Hall*
Mozart Quartet no.14 in G, K387
Boulez Livre pour quatuor: 2 movements
Beethoven Quartet no.6 in B flat, op.18/6

PIERRE BOULEZ, YVONNE LORIOD (2 pf), SEVERINO GAZZELLONI (fl), MARGARET KITCHIN (pf)
2 Sep. 11.00 *Freemasons' Hall*
Boulez Sonatine for flute and piano
Boulez Structures pour 2 pianos: Livre 2
Debussy Syrinx for flute
Debussy En blanc et noir

HAMBURG TRIO
3 Sep. 11.00 *Freemasons' Hall*
Schubert Trio in B flat (one movement), D471
Webern Trio, op.20
Beethoven Trio no.2 in G, op.9/1
Britten 6 Metamorphoses after Ovid for oboe
Britten Phantasy quartet for oboe and strings
with Heinz Holliger (ob)

NEW MUSIC ENSEMBLE
4 Sep. 11.00 *Leith Town Hall*
Boulez Le marteau sans maître
Schoenberg Pierrot lunaire
Conductor Pierre Boulez
Soloist Jeanne Deroubaix (vocalist)

HUNGARIAN QUARTET
9 Sep. 11.00 *Leith Town Hall*
Tippett Quartet no.2
Beethoven Quartet no.12 in E flat, op.127

11 Sep. 11.00 *Leith Town Hall*
Haydn Quartet in C (Bird), op.33/3
Haydn Quartet in F, op.77/2
Haydn Quartet in D, op.76/5

NETHERLANDS CHAMBER CHOIR
25 Aug. 11.00 *Freemasons' Hall*
Schütz Das deutsche Magnificat
Choral music by Lassus, Sweelinck, Andriessen, Badings, Ketting, Dresden, Debussy, Dallapiccola

RECITALS

HANS HOTTER (b-bar)
ERNEST LUSH (pf)
25 Aug. 20.00 *Usher Hall*
Songs by Schubert, Wolf, Loewe

JOHN OGDON (pf)
23 Aug. 20.00 *Usher Hall*
Beethoven Sonata no.3 in C, op.2/3
Beethoven Sonata no.31 in A flat, op.110
Ravel Gaspard de la nuit
Tippett Sonata no.1

YVONNE LORIOD (pf)
31 Aug. 11.00 *Freemasons' Hall*
Mozart Sonata no.11 in A, K331
Messiaen Catalogue d'oiseaux: La rousserolle effarvatte
Debussy Études: Pour les arpèges composés
Debussy Études: Pour les huits doigts
Boulez Sonata no.2

DANIEL BARENBOIM (pf)
10 Sep. 20.00 *Usher Hall*
Beethoven Sonata no.26 in E flat (Farewell), op.81a
Beethoven Sonata no.23 in F minor (Appassionata), op.57
Beethoven Sonata no.29 (Hammerklavier), op.106

HENRYK SZERYNG (vn)
MARINUS FLIPSE (pf)
29 Aug. 14.30 *Usher Hall*
Brahms Sonata no.1 in G, op.78
Brahms Sonatensatz
Bach Partita for solo violin no.2 in D minor
Ponce Sonata breve
Prokofiev Sonata no.2 in D, op.94a

ROBERT TEAR (ten), JOAN DICKSON (vc), MARGARET KITCHIN (pf)
27 Aug. 11.00 *Freemasons' Hall*
Bach Suite for solo cello no.4 in E flat
Tippett The heart's assurance
Hamilton Sonata for cello and piano
Beethoven An die ferne Geliebte

GAELIC CONCERT

THE MUSIC OF THE GAEL
3 Sep. 20.00 *Leith Town Hall*
Soloists Evelyn Campbell, Anne Gillies, Kirsteen Grant, Joan Mackenzie, Rhona MacLeod, George J. Clavey, Angus M. Ruthven (sngr), Kathleen MacLeod Stage (pf), Florence V. Wilson (clarsach), Pipe-Major George Stoddart, Hector MacFadyen (bp), Peter Carmichael (fiddle), Lothian Celtic Choir, Stirling Gaelic Choir, Dancers from 1st Battalion Royal Scots, Eagle Pipers' Society, (In association with An Comunn Gaidhealach)

INDIAN MUSIC

7 Sep. 11.00 *Freemasons' Hall*
BISMILLAH KHAN (shanai)
North Indian music

8 Sep. 11.00 *Freemasons' Hall*
K.V. NARAYANASWAMY (sngr)
PALGHAT MANI IYER (Mrdangam)
M. RAJAMANI (kanjira)
LALGUDI JAYARAMAN (vn)
KAMALA KRISHNAN (tambura)
South Indian music

10 Sep. 11.00 *Freemasons' Hall*
VILAYAT KHAN (sitâr), IMRAT KHAN (surbahar), SHANTA PRASAD (tabla)
North Indian Music
Concerts Introduced by K. Kothari

DRAMA

TRAVERSE FESTIVAL PRODUCTIONS
23 Aug.-11 Sep. 19.15 (exc.Sun) 24, 28, 31 Aug. 4, 7, 11 Sep.14.15 Assembly Hall
MACBETH Shakespeare
Macbeth Leonard Maguire
Lady Macbeth Meg Wynn Owen
Banquo Robert James
Macduff Jeremy Young
Duncan/Doctor Donald Bisset
Malcolm Ian Paterson
Donalbain/Young Siward Robin John
Fleance Lee Menzies
Lennox Alexander Allan
Ross Alex McAvoy
Seyton/Captain Henry Stamper
Porter Duncan Macrae, Matt McGinn
Lady Macduff Annabel Barton
Gentlewoman Katy Gardiner
Witches Rosemary Davey, Brigit Forsyth, Anne Raitt
Son of Macduff Jennifer Angus
Angus James Fairley
Old man/Caithness George Cormack
Murderers David Kincaid, Matt McGinn
Menteith David Strong
Siward John Lancaster
Director Michael Geliot
Designer Annena Stubbs

HAIZLIP- STOIBER PRODUCTIONS, New York
23-28 Aug. 19.00 25, 28 Aug. 14.15
Lyceum Theatre
THE AMEN CORNER Baldwin
Sister Margaret Claudia McNeil
Odessa Theresa Merritt
David Antonio Fargas
Luke Julius W. Harris
Ida Jackson Leu Camacho
Sister Boxer Helen Martin
Sister Moore Georgia Burke
Brother Boxer Richard Ward
Sister Douglas Lillian Hayman
Sister Rice Minnie Gentry
Sister Sally/2nd Woman Urylee Leonardos
Sister Williams/1st Woman Tina Sattin
Brother Davis Bernard Mavritte
Brother Washington/Man Kevin Lovette
Director Lloyd Richards
Scenery Ed Wittstein
Costumes Ronald L. Williams
Music director Howard A. Roberts

TEATRO STABILE, Genoa
30 Aug.- 4 Sep. 19.00 1, 4 Sep. 14.15
Lyceum Theatre
I DUE GEMELLI VENEZIANI Goldoni
Dr Balanzoni Mario Bardella
Rosaura Paola Mannoni
Pancrazio Camillo Milli
Zanetto/Tonino Alberto Lionello
Lelio Eros Pagni
Beatrice Marzia Ubaldi
Florindo Emilio Cappuccio
Brighella Omero Antonutti
Colombina Margherita Guzzinati
Arlecchino Giancarlo Maestri
Tiburzio Luigi Carubbi
Sheriff Enrico Ardizzone
Bobbies Gianni Fenzi, Giuliano Disperati
Porter Sandro Rossi
Groom Giuliano Disperati
Director Luigi Squarzina
Designer Gianfranco Padovani

BRIDGE PRODUCTIONS LTD
6-11 Sep. 19.00 8, 11 Sep. 14.15
Lyceum Theatre
TOO TRUE TO BE GOOD Shaw
Nurse Sweetie Dora Bryan
Sergeant Fielding George Cole
Burglar Kenneth Haigh
Miss Mopply June Ritchie
Mrs Mopply Athene Seyler
Colonel Tallboys Alastair Sim
Microbe Terry Scully
Doctor Anthony Oliver
Private Meek James Bolam
Mr Bagot Laurence Hardy
Director Frank Dunlop
Designer Tom Lingwood

GATEWAY COMPANY
23 Aug.-11 Sep. 19.30 (exc.Sun) 26, 28 Aug. 2, 4, 9, 11 Sep. 14.30
Gateway Theatre
THE MAN FROM THERMOPYLAE Kay
Geron Bernard Lloyd
Girl Rosemary Curr
Old woman Jean Taylor Smith
Pantites Victor Carin
Philander Bryden Murdoch
Polixenes Tony Kinnie
Melissa Clare Richards
Penthessilea Judith Carey
Iolaus William Moore
Scorpias Brian Carey
Helena Jennifer Claire
Hippias James Locker
Cleon Brown Derby
Cleisthenes James Gibson
Priest Ted Richards
Director Richard Mathews
Designer Hamish Henderson

POETS IN PUBLIC

24 Aug. 11.00 Freemasons' Hall
John Betjeman, R.S. Thomas, David Wevill, Martin Bell (rdr)

25 Aug. 14.30 Freemasons' Hall
Ted Hughes, Peter Porter, Jon Silkin, Charles Causley, W.D. Snodgrass, Harvey Hall (rdr)

26 Aug. 11.00 Freemasons' Hall
Hugh MacDiarmid, Thomas Kinsella, Norman MacCaig, Richard Murphy, Harvey Hall (rdr)

27 Aug. 20.00 Freemasons' Hall
W.H. Auden, Stevie Smith, George Barker, Charles Causley, Harvey Hall (rdr) with Frankie Armstrong (folk sngr), Michael Jessett (gtr), Larry Adler (harmonica)
Chairman John Wain

LATE NIGHT ENTERTAINMENT

23-28 Aug. 22.45 Lyceum Theatre
MARLENE DIETRICH
with Orchestra conducted by Burt Bacharach
(In association with John Coast and David Langdon)

30 Aug. 22.45 Lyceum Theatre
ELIZABETH SEAL, ZACK MATALON
Have bird, will travel
*Subsequent performances cancelled and replaced by Larry Adler

4-11 Sep. 22.45 Lyceum Theatre
LARRY ADLER (Harmonica)
One man's show
Directed by George Mully

EXHIBITIONS

Royal Scottish Academy
COROT EXHIBITION
(In association with the Arts Council of Great Britain and the Royal Scottish Academy)

Royal Scottish Museum
RUMANIAN ART TREASURES
(In association with the Rumanian State Committee for Culture and the British Council)

1966

OPERA

WÜRTTEMBERG STATE OPERA, Stuttgart
26, 29, 31 Aug. 2, 5 Sep. 19.00
King's Theatre
DIE ZAUBERFLÖTE Mozart
Tamino Waldemar Kmentt, Fritz Wunderlich
Pamina Gundula Janowitz, Liselotte Rebmann
Papageno Karlheinz Peters
Sarastro Otto von Rohr, Fritz Linke
Queen of the Night Sylvia Geszty
Speaker Raymond Wolansky, Stefan Kosso
1st Lady Elizabeth Löw-Szöky
2nd Lady Hetty Plümacher
3rd Lady Claudia Hellmann
Papagena Lily Sauter
Monostatos Herold Kraus
3 Boys Liselotte Becker-Egner, Franziska Wachmann, Hannelore Schulz-Pickard
2 Armed men James Harper, Klaus Bertram/Stefan Kosso
2 Priests Stefan Schwer, Frithjof Sentpaul
Conductor Ferdinand Leitner
Director Leopold Lindtberg
Designer Leni Bauer-Ecsy

27 Aug. 19.00 King's Theatre
WOZZECK Berg
Wozzeck Gerhard Stolze
Marie Irmgard Seefried
Drum-Major Günther Treptow
Andres Sigurd Björnsson
Captain Kurt Marschner
Doctor Fritz Linke
Margret Hetty Plümacher
Apprentices Klaus Bertram, Karlheinz Peters
Idiot Hubert Buchta
Marie's child Tilman Ruess
Soldier Siegfried Fischer-Sandt
Conductor Carlos Kleiber
Director Günther Rennert
Designer Leni Bauer-Ecsy
*Performance on 3 Sep. cancelled

30 Aug. 1, 7, 9 Sep. 19.00 King's Theatre
LOHENGRIN Wagner
Lohengrin Wolfgang Windgassen
Elsa Hildegard Hillebrecht, Elizabeth Löw-Szöky
Telramund Gustav Neidlinger
Ortrud Grace Hoffman
Henry the Fowler Otto von Rohr
Herald Raymond Wolansky, Karlheinz Peters
Gottfried Bernhard Stierle
Conductor Ferdinand Leitner, Heinrich Hollreiser
Director and designer Wieland Wagner

6, 8, 10 Sep. 19.00 King's Theatre
LULU Berg
Lulu Anja Silja
Countess Geschwitz Sona Cervena
Dr Schön Carlos Alexander
Alwa Richard Holm
Painter James Harper
Schigolch Willy Ferenz
Rodrigo Caspar Bröcheler
Dr Goll Engelbert Czubok
Schoolboy Hannelore Schulz-Pickard
Prince Stefan Schwer

Theatre director Heinz Cramer
Wardrobe-mistress Paula Brivkalne
Valet Kurt-Egon Opp
Negro Klaus Hirte
Animal tamer/Jack the Ripper Rudolf Knoll
Conductor Ferdinand Leitner
Director and designer Wieland Wagner

ORCHESTRAL CONCERTS

SCOTTISH NATIONAL ORCHESTRA
Conductor Alexander Gibson
21 Aug. 20.00 *Usher Hall*
Britten Cantata academica
Tippett A child of our time
Soloists Elizabeth Vaughan (sop), Janet Baker (mez), Richard Lewis (ten), Forbes Robinson (bs), Scottish Festival Chorus

28 Aug. 20.00 *Usher Hall*
Mahler Symphony no.8 in E flat
Soloists Heather Harper, Gwyneth Jones, Gwenyth Annear (sop), Yvonne Minton (mez), Norma Procter (cont), Vilém Přibyl (ten), Vladimir Ruzdjak (bar), Donald McIntyre (b-bar), Scottish Festival Chorus

MOSCOW RADIO ORCHESTRA
Conductor Gennadi Rozhdestvensky
22 Aug. 20.00 *Usher Hall*
Tchaikovsky Hamlet - Fantasy overture
Tchaikovsky Variations on a Rococo theme
Tchaikovsky Symphony no.5 in E minor, op.64
Soloist Natalia Shakhovskaya (vc)

23 Aug. 20.00 *Usher Hall*
Schumann Manfred: Overture
Prokofiev Concerto for piano no.3 in C, op.26
Shostakovich Symphony no.5 in D minor, op.47
Soloist Nikolai Petrov (pf)

24 Aug. 20.00 *Usher Hall*
Prokofiev They are seven
Shostakovich Concerto for violin no.1 in A minor, op.99
Berlioz Symphonie fantastique
Soloists Mikhail Waiman (vn), Vilém Přibyl (ten), Scottish Festival Chorus

25 Aug. 20.00 *Usher Hall*
Shchedrin Symphony no.2
Mozart Concerto for piano no.24 in C minor, K491
Stravinsky The firebird - Suite
Soloist Annie Fischer (pf)

VIRTUOSI DI ROMA
Conductor Renato Fasano
28 Aug. 14.30 *Usher Hall*
Albinoni Sonata for strings in A, op.2/3
Anon. Concerto in C minor
Corelli Concerto grosso in D, op.6/4
Vivaldi Concerti, op.3: No.1 in D
Vivaldi Concerti, op.3: No.4 in E minor
Vivaldi Concerti, op.3: No.7 in F
Vivaldi Concerti, op.3: No.10 in B minor

30 Aug. 11.00 *Leith Town Hall*
Vivaldi Concerti, op.3: No.2 in G minor
Vivaldi Concerti, op.8: No.12 in C
Vivaldi Concerti, op.8: No.5?*
Vivaldi Concerti, op.3: No.8 in A minor
Vivaldi Concerti, op.9: No.9 in B flat
Vivaldi Concerti, op.4: No.5 in A*
Vivaldi Concerti, op.3: No.11 in D minor

NEW PHILHARMONIA ORCHESTRA
29 Aug. 20.00 *Usher Hall*
Mozart Symphony no.38 in D (Prague), K504
Mahler Symphony no.4 in G
Conductor Rafael Kubelik
Soloist Elsie Morison (sop)

30 Aug. 20.00 *Usher Hall*
Schumann Overture, scherzo and finale, op.52
Schumann Concerto for piano in A minor, op.54
Schumann Symphony no.2 in C, op.61
Conductor Rafael Kubelik
Soloist Annie Fischer (pf)

1 Sep. 20.00 *Usher Hall*
Schubert Symphony no.3 in D, D200
Schumann Concerto for cello in A minor, op.129
Berg Three orchestral pieces, op.6
Ravel Daphnis et Chloë - Suite no.2
Conductor Claudio Abbado
Soloist Pierre Fournier (vc)

2 Sep. 20.00 *Usher Hall*
Schumann Genoveva: Overture
Beethoven Concerto for piano no.1 in C, op.15
Schumann Introduction and allegro appassionato, op.92
Beethoven Symphony no.7 in A, op.92
Conductor Claudio Abbado
Soloist Daniel Barenboim (pf)

SCOTTISH NATIONAL CHAMBER ORCHESTRA
3 Sep. 11.00 *Leith Town Hall*
Schubert Symphony no.5 in B flat, D485
Berg Chamber concerto
Conductor Alexander Gibson
Soloists Brenton Langbein (vn), Maureen Jones (pf)

NATIONAL YOUTH ORCHESTRA OF CANADA
3 Sep. 20.00 *Usher Hall*
Smetana The bartered bride: Overture
Schumann Manfred: Excerpts
Mozart Ch'io mi scordi di te
Berg Der Wein
R. Strauss Till Eulenspiegels lustige Streiche
Conductor and soloist Walter Susskind (pf)
Soloist Evelyn Lear (sop)

4 Sep. 20.00 *Usher Hall*
Berlioz Benvenuto Cellini: Overture
Ravel Concerto for piano in G
Mercure Triptyque
Mussorgsky Pictures at an exhibition; orch. Ravel
Conductor Walter Susskind
Soloist Martha Argerich (pf)

BBC SCOTTISH ORCHESTRA
Conductor James Loughran
6 Sep. 20.00 *Usher Hall*
R. Strauss Don Juan
Berg Five orchestral Lieder on texts by Altenberg
Wilson Symphony no.2
Mahler Rückert Lieder: Ich bin der Welt
Wolf Mignon 'Kennst du das Land'
R. Strauss Wiegenlied
Mahler Des Knaben Wunderhorn: Rheinlegendchen
Wagner Tannhäuser: Overture
Soloist Irmgard Seefried (sop)

7 Sep. 20.00 *Usher Hall*
Brahms Variations on a theme by Haydn (St Antoni), op.56a
Chavez Concerto for violin
Schumann Symphony no.1 in B flat (Spring), op.38
Soloist Henryk Szeryng (vn)

HALLÉ ORCHESTRA
Conductor Sir John Barbirolli
8 Sep. 20.00 *Usher Hall*
Rawsthorne Street corner - Overture
Satie Gymnopédies nos.1 *and* 3; arr. Debussy
Beethoven Concerto for piano no.4 in G, op.58
Dvořák Symphony no.7 in D minor, op.70
Soloist Emil Gilels (pf)

9 Sep. 20.00 *Usher Hall*
Haydn Symphony no.104 in D (London)
Berg Concerto for violin
Schumann Symphony no.4 in D minor, op.120
Soloist Henryk Szeryng (vn)

10 Sep. 19.30 *Usher Hall*
V. Williams Symphony no.8 in D minor
Elgar Sea pictures
Brahms Symphony no.4 in E minor, op.98
Soloist Janet Baker (mez)

10 Sep. 22.45 *Usher Hall*
Farewell Symphony
Mozart La clemenza di Tito: Overture
Weill Alabama song
Weill As you make your bed you must lie there
Dessau Friedenslied
Wagner Tannhäuser: Dich teure Halle
Beethoven Sonata no.26 in E flat (Farewell), op.81a
Haydn Symphony no.45 in F sharp minor (Farewell)
Soloists Bettina Jonič, Anja Silja (sop), Janet Baker (mez), Daniel Barenboim, Paul Hamburger (pf)
Introduced by Tom Fleming

CHAMBER CONCERTS

OROMONTE PIANO TRIO
22 Aug. 11.00 *Freemasons' Hall*
Mozart Trio for piano and strings no.3 in B flat, K502
Schumann Trio for piano and strings no.2 in F, op.80
Beethoven Trio for piano and strings no.5 in D (Ghost), op.70/1

OROMONTE STRING TRIO
25 Aug. 11.00 *Freemasons' Hall*
Mozart Quartet for piano and strings in E flat, K493
Skalkottas Trio
Schumann Quartet for piano and strings in E flat, op.47
with Nina Milkina (pf)

DELME QUARTET
24 Aug. 11.00 *Freemasons' Hall*
Haydn Quartet in E flat, op.76/6
Schumann Quartet no.2 in F, op.41/2
Berg Quartet, op.3

26 Aug. 11.00 *Freemasons' Hall*
Beethoven Quartet no.6 in B flat, op.18/6
Berg Lyric suite
Verdi Quartet in E minor

AMADEUS QUARTET
27 Aug. 11.00 *Leith Town Hall*

Haydn Quartet in G, op.77/1
Schubert Quartet no.12 in C minor (Quartetsatz), D703
Schumann Quartet no.3 in A, op.41/3

29 Aug. 11.00 *Leith Town Hall*
Haydn Quartet in C (Emperor), op.76/3
Beethoven Quartet no.11 in F minor (Serioso), op.95
Schumann Quintet for piano and strings in E flat, op.44
with Annie Fischer (pf)

DANZI QUINTET
1 Sep. 11.00 *Freemasons' Hall*
Gebauer Quintet for wind no.2 in E flat
Reicha Quintet for wind in C, op.91/1
Hindemith Kammermusic no.2, op.24/2
Françaix Quintet for wind

2 Sep. 11.00 *Freemasons' Hall*
Seiber Permutazioni a cinque
Birtwistle Refrains and choruses
Schat Improvisations and symphonies
Schoenberg Quintet for wind, op.26

EDINBURGH UNIVERSITY SINGERS
31 Aug. 11.00 *Freemasons' Hall*
Victoria Missa 'Ascendens Christus in altum'
Leighton Mass, op.44
Choral works by Le Jeune, Janequin, Jacotin, Certon, Sermisy, Bonnet, Lassus
Conductor Herrick Bunney

RECITALS

ELISABETH SCHWARZKOPF (sop)
JÖRG DEMUS (pf)
31 Aug. 20.00 *Usher Hall*
Songs by Schumann, Wolf

FRITZ WUNDERLICH (ten)
HUBERT GIESEN (pf)
4 Sep. 14.30 *Usher Hall*
Schumann Dichterliebe
Songs by Beethoven, Schubert

EVELYN LEAR (sop), IRWIN GAGE (pf)
7 Sep. 11.00 *Freemasons' Hall*
Songs by Schumann, Berg, Wolf, R. Strauss

JANET BAKER (mez)
PAUL HAMBURGER (pf)
9 Sep. 11.00 *Leith Town Hall*
Schumann Frauenliebe und -leben
Songs by Purcell, Schubert, Berlioz, Fauré

JÖRG DEMUS (pf)
23 Aug. 11.00 *Freemasons' Hall*
Schumann Papillons
Schumann Sonata no.2 in G minor, op.22
Schumann Kinderszenen
Schumann Études symphoniques, op.13

ANNIE FISCHER (pf)
27 Aug. 20.00 *Usher Hall*
Beethoven Variations and fugue on an original theme 'Eroica'
Schumann Sonata no.1 in F sharp minor, op.11
Beethoven Sonata no.8 in C minor (Pathétique), op.13
Schumann Fantasiestücke, op.12

EMIL GILELS (pf)
5 Sep. 20.00 *Usher Hall*
Beethoven Sonata no.28 in A, op.101
Schumann Presto passionato in G minor
Schumann Nachtstücke, op.23
Prokofiev Sonata no.8 in B flat, op.84

MARTHA ARGERICH (pf)
6 Sep. 11.00 *Freemasons' Hall*
Schumann Toccata in C, op.7
Schumann Fantasia in C, op.17
Chopin Barcarolle, op.60
Chopin Scherzo no.3 in C sharp minor, op.39
Prokofiev Sonata no.7 in B flat, op.83

DANIEL BARENBOIM (pf)
10 Sep. 11.00 *Leith Town Hall*
Berg Sonata, op.1
Beethoven Sonata no.32 in C minor, op.111
Schumann Carnaval

BRENTON LANGBEIN (vn)
MAUREEN JONES (pf)
8 Sep. 11.00 *Freemasons' Hall*
Schumann Sonata no.1 in A minor, op.105
Banks Sonata
Beethoven Sonata no.9 in A (Kreutzer), op.47

PIERRE FOURNIER (vc)
JEAN FONDA (pf)
5 Sep. 11.00 *Leith Town Hall*
Beethoven Variations on 'See the conquering hero comes' (Handel)
Beethoven Sonata no.3 in A, op.69
Schumann Adagio and allegro, op.70
Schumann Fantasiestücke, op.73
Chopin Introduction and polonaise brillante, op.3

CHILDREN'S CONCERT
WÜRTTENBERG STATE OPERA Members
7 Sep. 11.00 *Leith Town Hall*

CEILIDH

26 Aug. 20.00 *Leith Town Hall*
Soloists Evelyn Campbell, Kenna Campbell, Carol Galbraith, Alasdair B. Gillies, Kirsteen Grant, Cameron MacKichan, Angus C. MacLeod, Archie McTaggart, Mary Sandeman (sngr), Kathleen MacLeod Stage (pf), Hugh MacGilp (fiddle), Glasgow Gaelic Musical Association, Greenock High School Gaelic Choir, Edinburgh City Police Pipe Band, Jean Carnie School of Dancing (In association with An Comunn Gaidhealach)

DRAMA

POP THEATRE
22-27, 31 Aug. 1, 2, 6, 7, 10 Sep. 19.15
23, 27 Aug. 6 Sep. 14.15 *Assembly Hall*
THE WINTER'S TALE Shakespeare
Leontes Laurence Harvey
Hermione Moira Redmond
Paulina Diana Churchill
Antigonus Alan Foss
Perdita Jane Asher
Florizel David Weston
Old shepherd/Gaoler Edward Jewesbury
Autolycus Jim Dale
Camillo Esmond Knight
Mamillius Simon Orr
Polixenes David Sumner
Clown John Gray
Emilia Cherry Morris
Dorcas Joanna Wake
Mopsa Joy Ring
Lord David Orr
Lady Janet Moffatt
Gentleman to the King Michael Irving
Cleomenes Terry Palmer
Mariner/1st Gentleman Gavin Reed
2nd Gentleman Tom Baker
Servant Charmian Eyre
Steward Michael Murray
Director Frank Dunlop
Designer Carl Toms
Lighting Francis Reid
Music Jim Dale

29, 30 Aug. 3, 5, 8, 9 Sep. 19.15 30 Aug. 3, 10 Sep. 14.15 *Assembly Hall*
THE TROJAN WOMEN Euripides
(Eng. Translated by Ronald Duncan)
Hecuba Flora Robson
Cassandra Jane Asher
Helen Moira Redmond
Andromache Cleo Laine
Menelaus Esmond Knight
Poseidon Edward Jewesbury
Pallas Athene Cherry Morris
Talthybios Michael Murray
Astyanax Gavin Orr
Chorus leader Diana Churchill
Director Frank Dunlop
Designer Carl Toms
Lighting Francis Reid

ROYAL LYCEUM THEATRE COMPANY
22-27 Aug. 19.00 24, 27 Aug. 14.15
Lyceum Theatre
THE BURDIES (The birds) Aristophanes
(Eng. Adapted and translated by Douglas Young)
Mr Wylie Callum Mill
Jock Hope Harry Walker
Servant bird Jean Taylor Smith
Hoopoo/Poet Duncan Macrae
Coryphaeus Fulton Mackay
Priest/Blackmailer Malcolm Hayes
Beadle Dudley Stuart White
Horace Scope/Prometheus George Cormack
Meton/Triballian God Martin Heller
Inspector-General/Poseidon Leon Sinden
Regulation-Monger Lennox Milne
Iris Eliza Ward
Herald bird David Kincaid
Daddie-Dadder Brian Cox
Cinesias Paul Chapman
Hercules Brian Coburn
Nightingale Joyce Bell
Basileia Sandra Duncan
Chorus leaders David MacMillan, Morag Forsyth
Director Tom Fleming
Designer Abd' Elkader Farrah
Lighting André Tammes

PIRAIKON THEATRE, Greece
29 Aug. 1, 3 Sep. 19.00 31 Aug. 14.15
Lyceum Theatre
ELECTRA Sophocles
(Mod Greek. Translated by I. Gryparis)
Electra Elsa Vergi
Orestes K. Galanakis, N. Lykomitros
Chrysothemis H. Karolou, N. Vorrea
Clytemnestra Rika Sifaki, E. Konstantinou
Aegisthus N. Lykomitros
Pylades D. Gennimatas
Tutor A. Xenakis, D. Stefanopoulos
Director D. Rondiris
Choreographer Loukia

30, 31 Aug. 2 Sep. 19.00 3 Sep. 14.15
Lyceum Theatre
MEDEA Euripides
(Mod Greek. Translated by D. Sarros)
Medea Elsa Vergi

Jason — A. Xenakis, N. Lykomitros
Creon — D. Stefanopoulos
Aegeus — K. Galanakis
Nurse — K. Sifaki, E. Konstantinou
Tutor — D. Stefanopoulos, D. Gennimatas
Messenger — N. Lykomitros, K. Galanakis
Director — D. Rondiris
Choreographer — Loukia

EDINBURGH INTERNATIONAL FESTIVAL
5-10 Sep. 19.00 7, 10 Sep. 14.15
Lyceum Theatre
A PRESENT FOR THE PAST Hailstone
(World première)
Elspeth — Renée Asherson
Trudie — Hazel Hughes
Martha — Wendy Hiller
Baroness — Gwen Ffrangcon-Davies
Alexander — Mark Dignam
Charles — David Knight
Mr James — James Ottaway
Director — Robert Chetwyn
Designer — Hutchinson Scott
Lighting — Francis Reid
(In association with Michael Codron)

22 Aug.-3 Sep. 14.30 (exc.Sun)
GatewayTheatre
THE WRONG SIDE OF THE MOON Gray
Tomlyn — Nicholas Stuart Gray
Marshall — Michael Atkinson
Mother Gothel — Jenny Laird
Jarvis — Malcolm Young
Cornella — Josephine Stuart
Rapunzel — Gemma Jones
Batty pan — Stanley Beard
Robert — Richard Kay
Director — Joan Knight
Designer — Joan Jefferson Farjeon
(In association with John Ridley Ltd)

22-27 Aug. 19.30 *Gateway Theatre*
AN EVENING WITH GBS
Max Adrian as George Bernard Shaw
Devised by Michael Voysey
Director — Ronald Hayman
(In association with Bradbury Plays Ltd)

29 Aug.-3 Sep. 19.30 1, 3 Sep. 14.30
Church Hill Theatre
THE LITTLE MEN Aleichem
(Eng. Translated by Joseph Leftwich)
George Murcell, Eliahu Goldenberg, Jonathan Lynn
Director — Eliahu Goldenberg
(In association with Bernard Delfont)

POLISH MIME THEATRE, Wroclaw
5-10 Sep. 19.30 10 Sep. 14.30
Church Hill Theatre
Liliana Bobrowska, Elzbieta Bojanowicz, Ewa Czekalska, Krystyna Marynowska, Ewa Warwas, Stanislaw Brzozowski, Leszek Czarnota, Leon Górecki, Anatol Krupa, Rajmund Klechot, Wlodzimierz Kowalewski, Jerzy Kozlowski, Stefan Niedzialkowski, Janusz Pieczuro, Pawel Rouba, Andrzej Szczuzewski, Ryszard Staw, Jan Uryga, Zbigniew Zukowski
Director — Henryk Tomaszewski
Costumes — Jerzy Lawacz, Krzysztof Pankiewicz, Kazimierz Wišniak

MOSCOW PUPPETS
29 Aug.-3 Sep. 19.30 *Gateway Theatre*
with Sergei Obraztsov (dir, puppeteer), Olga Obraztsova (pf), Anna Barr (interp)

TRAVERSE THEATRE CLUB
6-10 Sep. 19.30 8, 10 Sep. 14.30
Gateway Theatre
LORCA Jonič
Tony Beckley, Bettina Jonič, Nicholas Chagrin, Pamela Miles, John English, Christian Hughes, David Strong, Michael Henderson, Shane Younger, Margaret Leslie, Joseph Morris
Director — Ande Anderson
Designer — Tom Lingwood
Music — Harrison Birtwistle

LATE NIGHT ENTERTAINMENT

ROYAL LYCEUM THEATRE COMPANY
22-27 Aug. 22.45 *Lyceum Theatre*
10.45 AND A' THAT
Devised by George Bruce
Fulton Mackay, Duncan Macrae, Eileen McCallum, Diana Olsson, Paul Chapman, Martin Heller (act), Margaret Fraser, Harry Stevenson (sngr), Philip Green (cl), Andrew Shivas (perc), Bernard Sumner (pf, hpd)
Director — Iain Cuthbertson
Designer — Hamish Henderson
Lighting — André Tammes

29 Aug.-3 Sep. 22.45 *Lyceum Theatre*
CATHERINE SAUVAGE
with Claude Artur (pf)

5-10 Sep. 22.45 *Lyceum Theatre*
CLEO LAINE
with John Dankworth, Laurie Holloway (pf)

DANCE

PAUL TAYLOR DANCE COMPANY, New York
22-27 Aug. 19.30 27 Aug. 14.30
Church Hill Theatre
3 EPITAPHS
Music — American folk music
Costumes — Robert Rauschenberg
DUET
Music — Haydn
Costumes — George Tacit
ORBS
Music — Beethoven
Designer — Alex Katz
**Junction* cancelled

Programme 2
AUREOLE
Music — Handel
FROM SEA TO SHINING SEA
Music — McDowell
Designer — John Rawlings
SCUDORAMA
Music — Clarence Jackson
Designer — Alex Katz
Choreographer (all ballets) Paul Taylor
Lighting — Jennifer Tipton, Thomas Skelton
Dancers Paul Taylor, Dan Wagoner, Bettie de Jong, Molly Reinhart, Carolyn Adams, Daniel Williams, Janet Aaron, Jane Kosminsky, Eileen Cropley
Conductor — John Perras

EXHIBITIONS

Royal Scottish Academy
GEORGES ROUAULT
(In association with the Arts Council of Great Britain and the Royal Scottish Academy)

1967

OPERA

SCOTTISH OPERA
21, 26, 31 Aug. 8 Sep. 19.00
King's Theatre
THE RAKE'S PROGRESS Stravinsky
Anne — Elizabeth Robson
Tom Rakewell — Alexander Young
Trulove — David Kelly
Nick Shadow — Peter van der Bilt
Mother Goose — Johanna Peters
Baba the Turk — Sona Cervena
Sellem — Francis Egerton
Keeper — Ronald Morrison
Scottish National Orchestra
Conductor — Alexander Gibson
Director — Peter Ebert
Designer — Ralph Koltai
Lighting — Charles Bristow

4-9 Sep. 11.00 *Assembly Hall*
THE SOLDIER'S TALE Stravinsky
(Eng. Translated by Michael Flanders and Kitty Black)
Princess — Una Stubbs
Devil — Patrick Wymark
Soldier — Nicky Henson
Narrator — Gordon Jackson
Scottish Opera Chamber Ensemble
Conductor — Alexander Gibson
Director — Wendy Toye
Designer — Carl Toms
Lighting — Charles Bristow

EDINBURGH INTERNATIONAL FESTIVAL
25, 29 Aug. 1, 4, 6, 9 Sep. 19.00
King's Theatre
ORFEO ED EURIDICE Haydn
Orfeo — Nicolai Gedda
Euridice — Joan Sutherland
Creonte — Spiro Malas
Pluto — Simon Gilbert
Genio — Mary O'Brien
Chorista — Malcolm King, John Graham
Scottish National Orchestra
Scottish Opera Chorus
Conductor — Richard Bonynge
Director — Rudolf Hartmann
Designer — Heinz Ludwig
(Co-production with the Wiener Festwochen)

30 Aug. 2, 5, 7 Sep. 19.00 *King's Theatre*
I CAPULETI ED I MONTECCHI Bellini
Giulietta — Anna Moffo
Romeo — Giacomo Aragall
Lorenzo — Walter Monachesi
Tebaldo — Luciano Pavarotti
Capellio — Giovanni Foiani
London Symphony Orchestra
Scottish Opera Chorus
Conductor — Claudio Abbado
Director — Antonello Madau-Diaz
(In association with the Holland Festival)

ORCHESTRAL CONCERTS

CLEVELAND ORCHESTRA
Conductor George Szell
20 Aug. 20.00 *Usher Hall*
Bach — Suite no.3 in G
Mozart — Symphony no.40 in G minor, K550
Walton — Variations on a theme by Hindemith
Stravinsky — The firebird - Suite (1919 version)

21 Aug. 20.00 *Usher Hall*
Weber Oberon: Overture
Mozart Concerto for piano no.24 in C minor, K491
Beethoven Symphony no.3 In E flat (Eroica), op.55
Soloist Clifford Curzon (pf)

22 Aug. 20.00 *Usher Hall*
R. Strauss Don Juan
Beethoven Romance for violin and orchestra no.2 in F, op.50
Mozart Concerto for violin no.5 in A, K219
Sibelius Symphony no.2 in D, op.43
Soloist Leonid Kogan (vn)

23 Aug. 20.00 *Usher Hall*
Stravinsky Pulcinella - Suite
Beethoven Concerto for piano no.5 in E flat Emperor), op.73
Brahms Symphony no.2 in D, op.73
Soloist Clifford Curzon (pf)

BBC SCOTTISH SYMPHONY ORCHESTRA
24 Aug. 20.00 *Usher Hall*
Wilson Concerto for orchestra (World première)
Elgar Concerto for cello in E minor, op.85
C.P.E. Bach Concerto for cello in A
Beethoven Symphony no.4 in B flat, op.60
Conductor James Loughran
Soloist Pierre Fournier (vc)

NETHERLANDS CHAMBER ORCHESTRA
26, 27 Aug. 20.00 *Usher Hall*
Bach Mass in B minor
Conductor Carlo Maria Giulini
Soloists Irmgard Stadler (sop), Janet Baker (mez), Richard Lewis (ten), Robert El Hage (bs), New Philharmonia Chorus

28 Aug. 20.00 *Usher Hall*
Bach Brandenburg Concerti nos. 6, 1, 4
Bach Concerto for harpsichord in A
Conductor Szymon Goldberg
Soloists Janny van Wering (hpd), Adriaan Bonsel, Koos Verheul (fl)

29 Aug. 20.00 *Usher Hall*
Bach Brandenburg concerti nos. 3, 5, 2
Bach Cantata no.192
Conductor Szymon Goldberg
Soloists Janny van Wering (hpd), Adriaan Bonsel (fl), Harvard Glee Club, Radcliffe Choral Society

SCOTTISH NATIONAL ORCHESTRA
Conductor Alexander Gibson
30 Aug. 20.00 *Usher Hall*
Stravinsky Ode
Stravinsky Petrushka
Brahms Concerto for piano no.1 in D minor, op.15
Soloist Rafael Orozco (pf)

7 Sep. 20.00 *Usher Hall*
Stravinsky Fireworks
Stravinsky Capriccio for piano and orchestra
Mahler Symphony no.10; ed. Cooke
Soloist André Tchaikovsky (pf)

LONDON SYMPHONY ORCHESTRA
31 Aug. 20.00 *Usher Hall*
Mozart Symphony no.25 in G minor, K183
Stravinsky Concerto for piano and wind
Bartók Duke Bluebeard's castle
Conductor István Kertész
Soloists Olga Szönyi (mez), András Faragó (b-bar), Martha Argerich (pf)

6 Sep. 20.00 *Usher Hall*
Kodály Psalmus Hungaricus
Stravinsky Concerto for violin in D
Brahms Symphony no.4 in E minor, op.98
Conductor István Kertész
Soloists Lajos Kozma (ten), Szymon Goldberg (vn), Scottish Festival Chorus

8 Sep. 20.00 *Usher Hall*
Stravinsky Oedipus Rex
Bach Musikalisches Opfer; arr. Abbado
Conductor Claudio Abbado
Soloists Shirley Verrett (mez), Lajos Kozma, Loren Driscoll (ten), Spiro Malas, Giovanni Foiani (bs), Keith Michell (narr), Scottish Festival Chorus

9 Sep. 19.30 *Usher Hall*
Tchaikovsky Romeo and Juliet - Fantasy overture
Stravinsky Symphony of psalms
Vivaldi Gloria in D, RV589
Verdi Four sacred pieces:Te deum
Conductor Claudio Abbado
Soloists Edda Moser (sop), Shirley Verrett (mez), Scottish Festival Chorus

9 Sep. 22.30 *Usher Hall*
Farewell Symphony
Verdi Don Carlos: O don fatale
Schubert Rondo for piano duet in A, D951
Ravel Ma mère l'oye
Mozart Die Zauberflöte: O zittre nicht
Verdi Ernani: Infelice
Conductor Claudio Abbado
Soloists Edda Moser (sop), Shirley Verrett (mez), Spiro Malas (bs), Cleo Laine (sngr), Walter Baracchi, Laurie Holloway (pf), John Dankworth
Introduced by Tom Fleming

BBC SYMPHONY ORCHESTRA
1 Sep. 20.00 *Usher Hall*
Bartók Music for strings, percussion and celesta
Bartók Concerto for piano no.2
Stravinsky Abraham and Isaac
Stravinsky Symphony in three movements
Conductor Colin Davis
Soloists Stephen Bishop-Kovacevich (pf), Günter Reich (bar)

2 Sep. 20.00 *Usher Hall*
Stravinsky The song of the nightingale
Stravinsky Requiem canticles
Stravinsky Symphonies of wind instruments
Stravinsky The rite of spring
Conductor Pierre Boulez
Soloists Yvonne Minton (mez), Günter Reich (bar), John Alldis Choir

BERLIN PHILHARMONIC ORCHESTRA
Conductor Herbert von Karajan
3 Sep. 20.00 *Usher Hall*
Mozart Divertimento no.15 in B flat, K287
Tchaikovsky Symphony no.4 in F minor, op.36

4 Sep. 20.00 *Usher Hall*
Handel Concerto grosso in B minor, op.6/12
Stravinsky Symphony in C
Beethoven Symphony no.5 in C minor, op.67

5 Sep. 20.00 *Usher Hall*
Bach Magnificat in D
Brahms Symphony no.1 in C minor, op.68
Soloists Helen Donath (sop), Josephine Veasey (mez), Robert Tear (ten), Gérard Souzay (bar), Scottish Festival Chorus

CHAMBER CONCERTS

SMETANA QUARTET
23 Aug. 11.00 *Freemasons' Hall*
Mozart Quartet no.17 in B flat (Hunt), K458
Janáček Quartet no.1 (The Kreutzer sonata)
Beethoven Quartet no.15 in A minor, op.132

25 Aug. 11.00 *Freemasons' Hall*
Haydn Quartet in D (Lark), op.64/5
Martinů Quartet no.4
Smetana Quartet no.1 in E minor (From my life)

BERLIN PHILHARMONIC OCTET
6 Sep. 11.00 *Leith Town Hall*
Mozart Divertimento (Salzburg symphony) no.2 in B flat, K137
Mozart Quintet for clarinet and strings in A, K581
Beethoven Septet, op.20

HARVARD GLEE CLUB
RADCLIFFE CHORAL SOCIETY
Conductor Elliot Forbes
28 Aug. 11.00 *Leith Town Hall*
Choral works by Bach, Josquin Desprez, Stravinsky, Britten, Rossi, Milhaud, Fine, Haydn, Brahms, Gabrieli, Villa-Lobos *and* Spirituals

30 Aug. 11.00 *Leith Town Hall*
Choral works by Morley, Haydn, Stravinsky, Lassus, Bartók, Schubert, Caplet, Sermisy, Consilium, Regnard, J. Strauss

INSTRUMENTAL ENSEMBLE
Director Raymond Leppard (hpd)
7 Sep. 11.00 *Leith Town Hall*
Vocal works by Monteverdi, Cavalli
Soloists Heather Harper (sop), Robert Tear (ten)

9 Sep. 11.00 *Leith Town Hall*
Vocal works by Monteverdi, Cavalli
Soloists Heather Harper (sop), Robert Tear, Gerald English (ten), Christopher Keyte (bs)

RECITALS

GÉRARD SOUZAY (bar)
DALTON BALDWIN (pf)
3 Sep. 15.00 *Freemasons' Hall*
Poulenc Chansons villageoises
Martin Six monologues from 'Jedermann'
Songs by Louis XIII, Bataille, Guedron, Boësset, Boismortier, Debussy, Fauré

SHIRLEY VERRETT (mez)
ROBERT SUTHERLAND (pf)
5 Sep. 11.00 *Freemasons' Hall*
Brahms Vier ernste Gesänge
Milhaud Chansons de négresse
Songs by Granados, Nin, Obradors, Debussy *and* Spirituals

GEORGE MALCOLM (hpd)
21 Aug. 11.00 *Freemasons' Hall*
Bach Overture (Partita) in the French style
Rameau Suite in A minor
Bach English suite no.6 in D minor
D. Scarlatti Sonatas

29 Aug. 11.00 *Freemasons' Hall*
Farnaby Works for virginals

Bach	Partita no.4 in D
F. Couperin	Suite no.8 in B minor
Bach	Chromatic fantasia and fugue in D minor

CLAUDIO ARRAU (pf)
25 Aug. 20.00 *Usher Hall*

Beethoven	Variations and fugue on an original theme (Eroica)
Mozart	Fantasia in C minor, K475
Mozart	Sonata no.14 in C minor, K457
Debussy	Estampes
Chopin	Scherzo no.1 in B minor, op.20
Chopin	Ballade no.3 in A flat, op.47
Chopin	Ballade no.4 in F minor, op.52

RAFAEL OROZCO (pf)
1 Sep. 11.00 *Freemasons' Hall*

Chopin	Preludes nos.1-24, op.28
Bach	English suite no.3 in G minor
Prokofiev	Sonata no.2 in D minor, op.14

ANDRÉ TCHAIKOVSKY (pf)
4 Sep. 11.00 *Freemasons' Hall*

Bach	Goldberg variations
Beethoven	Sonata no.30 in E, op.109

MARTHA ARGERICH (pf)
8 Sep. 11.00 *Freemasons' Hall*

Bach	English suite no.2 in A minor
Schumann	Sonata no.2 in G minor, op.22
Ravel	Jeux d'eau
Liszt	Funérailles
Chopin	Ballade no.3 in A flat, op.47
Chopin	Mazurkas nos. 23, 26, 40
Chopin	Scherzo no.2 in B flat minor, op.31

LEONID KOGAN (vn)
NAUM WALTER (pf)
24 Aug. 11.00 *Leith Town Hall*

Bach	Sonata no.1 in B minor
Bach	Suite no.3 in D: Air
Bach	Sonata for solo violin no.3 in C
Prokofiev	Sonata no.2 in D, op.94a
Paganini	Cantabile, op.17
Ravel	Tzigane

SZYMON GOLDBERG (vn)
JANNY VAN WERING (hpd)
2 Sep. 11.00 *Leith Town Hall*

Bach	Sonata no.3 in E
Bach	Partita for solo violin no.2 in D minor
Bach	Partita for solo violin no.3 in E
Bach	Sonata no.6 in G

PIERRE FOURNIER (vc)
GEORGE MALCOLM (hpd)
26 Aug. 11.00 *Leith Town Hall*

Bach	Sonata no.1 in G
Bach	Sonata no.2 in D
Bach	Suite for solo cello no.1 in G
Bach	Sonata no.3 in G minor

ELAINE SHAFFER (fl)
GEORGE MALCOLM (hpd)
31 Aug. 11.00 *Freemasons' Hall*

Bach	Sonata no.6 in E
Bach	Sonata no.1 in B minor
Bach	Sonata no.2 in E flat
Bach	Sonata no.5 in E minor

FRANS BRÜGGEN (rec)
22 Aug. 11.00 *Freemasons' Hall*
Works by Eyck, Telemann, Bach, Andriessen, Berio

HERRICK BUNNEY (org)
21, 22, 23, 24, 25, 26, 29, 30, 31 Aug. 1, 2, 5, 6, 7, 8, 9 Sep. 17.00
St Giles' Cathedral
Bach — Complete organ works

CEILIDH

1 Sep. 20.00 *Leith Town Hall*
Soloists MacDonald Sisters (sngr), Innis Gaels, The Albanachs, Nancy Dickson MacLeod Dancers and Pipers, Pat McNulty, Grace and Eric Hughes, Aedin Ni Choileain
(In association with An Comunn Gaidhealach)

DRAMA

POP THEATRE
21-26, 28, 29 Aug. 1, 6-9 Sep. 19.15
22, 26, 29 Aug. 14.15 *Assembly Hall*
A MIDSUMMER NIGHT'S DREAM Shakespeare

Titania/Hippolyta	Cleo Laine
Oberon/Theseus	Robin Bailey
Lysander	Peter Gilmore
Helena	Anna Gilcrist
Demetrius	Job Stewart
Hermia	Denise Coffey
Bottom	Jim Dale
Starveling	Gavin Reed
Snug	Albert Rofrano
Flute	Graham James
Quince	Bernard Bresslaw
Snout	Alan Foss
Puck	Hywel Bennett
Philostrate	Andrew Robertson
Peaseblossom	Edward Arthur
Cobweb	Bill Jarvis
Moth	Suzanne Mokler
Mustardseed	Richard Smith
Egeus	Edward Jewesbury
Director	Frank Dunlop
Designer	Carl Toms
Lighting	Charles Bristow
Music	John Dankworth

30, 31 Aug. 2, 4, 5 Sep. 19.15 2, 5, 9 Sep. 14.15 *Assembly Hall*
THE LESSON Ionesco
(Eng. Translated by Donald Watson)

Maid	Cleo Laine
Pupil	Denise Coffey
Professor	Bernard Bresslaw
Director	Johan Fillinger
Designer	Carl Toms
Lighting	Charles Bristow

THE TRICKS OF SCAPIN (Les fourberies de Scapin) Molière (Eng)

Octavio	Peter Gilmore
Sylvester	Bernard Bresslaw
Scapin	Jim Dale
Hycintha	Suzanne Mokler
Argante	Edward Jewesbury
Geronte	Job Stewart
Leander	Graham James
Carlo	Albert Rofrano
Zerbinetta	Anna Gilcrist
Director	Frank Dunlop
Designer	Carl Toms
Lighting	Charles Bristow

HAIZLIP-STOIBER PRODUCTIONS, New York
21, 23, 25, 26 Aug. 19.00 23 Aug. 14.15
THE EMPEROR JONES O'Neill
Lyceum Theatre

Brutus Jones	James Earl Jones
Henry Smithers	Edward Zang
Old woman	Miriam Burton
Congo witch-doctor	William Louther
Lem	Charles Berry

Other parts played by Mary Barnett, John Parks, Trina Parks, Rodney Griffin, Jerry Grimes, Geraldine Seignious, Richild Springer, Clay Taliaferro, George Tipton, Clyde Turner, Sylvia Walters

Director	Gene Frankel
Scenery	Robin Wagner
Costumes	Jeanne Button
Lighting	Nikola Cernovitch
Choreographer	Louis Johnson

22, 24 Aug. 19.00 26 Aug. 14.15
Lyceum Theatre
BLACK NEW WORLD McKayle
Company William Louther, Mary Barnett, Charles Berry, Miriam Burton, Rodney Griffin, Jerry Grimes, Sally Neal, Richild Springer, Clay Taliaferro, Sylvia Waters, Clyde Turner (act), Trina Parks, John Parks, Geraldine Seignious (sngr), Antonio Callender (drums), Charles Sullivan (tpt), Larry Dismond (gtr)

Narrator	George Tipton
Music	Dorothea Freitag, Howard A. Roberts
Costumes	Normand Maxon, Bernard Johnson
Lighting	Nikola Cernovitch
Choreographer	Donald McKayle
Conductor-pianist	Margaret Harris

PROSPECT PRODUCTIONS
28, 30 Aug. 1 Sep. 19.00 30 Aug. 14.15
Lyceum Theatre
THE CHERRY ORCHARD Chekhov
(Eng. Translated by Richard Cottrell)

Madame Ranyevskaya	Lila Kedrova
Anya	Marty Cruickshank
Varya	Stephanie Bidmead
Gayev	James Cairncross
Lopakhin	Patrick Wymark
Trofimov	Terry Scully
Simeonov-Pishchik	John Byron
Charlotta Ivanovna	Hazel Hughes
Yepihodov	Laurence Carter
Dunyasha	Bridget Turner
Firs	Edward Atienza
Yasha	Barry Warren
Passer by	Michael Elphick
Station master	Christopher Cabot
Post office clerk	Roger Gartland
Director	Richard Cottrell
Designer	Hutchinson Scott
Lighting	John B. Read

29, 31 Aug. 2 Sep. 19.00 2 Sep. 14.15
Lyceum Theatre
A ROOM WITH A VIEW Sieveking *and* Cottrell (Adapted from the novel by Forster) (World première)

Mrs Honeychurch	Hazel Hughes
Lucy Honeychurch	Fiona Walker
Freddy Honeychurch	Barry Warren
Charlotte Bartlett	Jean Anderson
Mr Emerson	Timothy West
George Emerson	Laurence Carter
Rev. Mr Beebe	James Cairncross
Cecil Vyse	Neil Stacy
Eleanor Lavish	Hazel Coppen
Marie	Delia Lindsay
Angelo	Michael Elphick
Clergyman	Christopher Cabot
Travellers	Christine Reid, Roger Gartland, Richard Morant
Director	Toby Robertson
Designer	Robin Archer
Lighting	John B. Read

EDINBURGH INTERNATIONAL FESTIVAL
4-9 Sep. 19.00 6, 8 14.15 Lyceum Theatre
COUNTRY DANCE Kennaway

Sir Charles Ferguson	Edward Fox
Hilary Ferguson	Joanna van Gyseghem
Douglas Dow	Stuart Mungall
Rosie	Janet Michael
Director	James Roose-Evans
Designer	Julia Trevelyan Oman

(In association with Michael Codron)

21-26 Aug. 19.30 24, 26 Aug. 14.30
Gateway Theatre
MARCEL MARCEAU, France
with Pierre Verry

CLOSE THEATRE CLUB
28 Aug.-2 Sep. 19.30 31 Aug. 2 Sep. 14.30 Gateway Theatre
TRIPLE IMAGE Wymark
Lunchtime concert; The inhabitants; Coda
Woman Zoë Hicks
Man Arthur Cox
Boy Bernard Hopkins
Voice Noel Davies
Director Michael Meacham
Costumes Jennifer Noone
Lighting George Rhodie
(In association with Citizens' Theatre, Glasgow)

MARIONETTEATERN, Stockholm
4-9 Sep. 14.30 Gateway Theatre
THE WIZARD OF OZ Meschke (Eng. Adapted from the story by L. Frank Baum)
with the voices of Doreen Denning, Ann Bibby, Johnny Young, Sidney Coulson, Michael Meschke, Allan Blair, Benita Booth, Lorrie Holmin
Director Michael Meschke
Scenery Arnaud Laval

5-9 Sep. 19.30 Gateway Theatre
UBU ROI Jarry
(Swed. Translated by Sture Pyk)
with the voices of Allan Adwall, Ingvar Kjellson, Margareta Krook, Hakan Serner, Nils Eklund, Michael Meschke, Birgitta Vahlberg, Ulla Sjöblom, Björn Gustafson
Director Michael Meschke
Scenery Franciszka Themerson
Music Penderecki

HAMPSTEAD THEATRE CLUB
21-26 Aug. 19.30 24, 26 Aug. 14.30
Church Hill Theatre
NATHAN AND TABILETH Bermange
Nathan Robert Bernal
Tabileth June Jago
Bernie James Culliford
OLDENBERG Bermange
Man Roger Booth
Woman June Jago
Oldenberg James Culliford
Director James Roose-Evans
Designer Harry Waistnage

VOYAGE THEATRE
28 Aug.-2 Sep. 19.30 31 Aug. 2 Sep. 14.30 Church Hill Theatre
MACBETH IN CAMERA Lang
Director Harold Lang
Actors Nicholas Amer, Greville Hallam
Geoffrey Keir David Kelsey
MAN SPEAKING Lang
Nicholas Amer, Greville Hallam, Harold Lang
Director Harold Lang
Designers Peter Key, Daphne Eales

TRAVERSE THEATRE CLUB
4-9 Sep. 19.30 7, 9 Sep. 14.30
Church Hill Theatre
TOM PAINE Foster
John Bakos, Mari-Claire Charba, Peter Craig, Jerry Cunliffe, Claris Erickson, Victor Lipari, Kevin O'Connor, Beth Porter, Michael Warren Powell, Marilyn Roberts, Robert Thirkield
Director Tom O'Horgan
Designer Hamish Henderson
Lighting André Tammes
(Actors from La Mama Company, NY)

LATE NIGHT ENTERTAINMENT

4-9 Sep. 22.45 Lyceum Theatre
CHARLES AZNAVOUR
with Instrumental ensemble
Director Dany Brunet

2 Sep. 22.45 Usher Hall
JACQUES LOUSSIER TRIO/PLAY BACH

DANCE

NEW YORK CITY BALLET
28 Aug. 1 Sep. 19.30 Empire Theatre
BUGAKU
Choreographer George Balanchine
Music Toshiro Mayuzumi
Scenery and lighting David Hays
Costumes Barbara Karinska
VARIATIONS
Choreographer George Balanchine
Music Stravinsky
TARANTELLA
Choreographer George Balanchine
Music Gottschalk; arr. Hershy Kay
Lighting David Hays
Costumes Barbara Karinska
RAGTIME
Choreographer George Balanchine
Music Stravinsky
Lighting Ronald Bates
APOLLO
Choreographer George Balanchine
Music Stravinsky
Lighting David Hays

29, 31 Aug. 19.30 Empire Theatre
DONIZETTI VARIATIONS
Choreographer George Balanchine
Music Donizetti
Costumes Barbara Karinska
Lighting David Hays
CONCERTO BAROCCO
Choreographer George Balanchine
Music Bach
Lighting David Hays
PAS DE DEUX
Choreographer George Balanchine
Music Tchaikovsky
Costumes Barbara Karinska
Lighting David Hays
MEDITATION
Choreographer George Balanchine
Music Tchaikovsky
Costumes Barbara Karinska
Lighting David Hays
AGON
Choreographer George Balanchine
Music Stravinsky
Lighting Nananne Porcher

30 Aug. 14.30 Empire Theatre
APOLLO
TARANTELLA
EBONY CONCERTO
Choreographer John Taras
Music Stravinsky
Scenery and lighting David Hays
PAS DE DEUX
DONIZETTI VARIATIONS

30 Aug. 19.30 2 Sep. 14.30
Empire Theatre
BUGAKU
INTERMEZZO
Choreographer George Balanchine
Music Brahms
Scenery Peter Harvey
Costumes Barbara Karinska
Lighting Ronald Bates
EBONY CONCERTO
TARANTELLA
APOLLO
Dancers Suzanne Farrell, Conrad Ludlow, Patricia McBride, Arthur Mitchell, Edward Villella, Peter Martins*, Karin von Aroldingen, Elaine Comsudi, Penelope Gates, Deni Lamont, Robert Maiorano, Paul Mejia, Marnee Morris, Patricia Neary, Susan Pilarre, John Prinz, Richard Rapp, Earle Sieveling, Bettijane Sills, Carol Sumner, Gloria Govrin, Sara Leland, Rosemary Dunleavy, Gail Crisa
with Gordon Boelzner (pf)
BBC Scottish Symphony Orchestra
Conductor Robert Irving

EXHIBITIONS

Royal Scottish Academy
DERAIN
(Arranged by the Arts Council of Great Britain in association with the Royal Scottish Academy)

Waverley Market
TWO HUNDRED SUMMERS IN A CITY

Royal Scottish Museum
TREASURES FROM SCOTTISH HOUSES

David Hume Tower
EDINBURGH OPEN 100

1968

OPERA

SCOTTISH OPERA
19, 21, 23, 26 Aug. 19.00 King's Theatre
PETER GRIMES Britten
Peter Grimes — Nigel Douglas*, Richard Cassilly
Ellen Orford — Phyllis Curtin
Nieces — Ann Baird, Patricia Hay
Mrs Sedley — Johanna Peters
Auntie — Elizabeth Bainbridge
Bob Boles — William McAlpine
Rev. Horace Adams — John Robertson
Captain Balstrode — John Shaw
Ned Keene — Michael Maurel
Swallow — Harold Blackburn
Hobson — John Graham
John — Dennis Sheridan
Dr Crabbe — Robert Harvey
Scottish National Orchestra
Conductor — Alexander Gibson
Producer — Colin Graham
Designer — Alix Stone

ENGLISH OPERA GROUP
22, 24 Aug. 19.30 King's Theatre
PUNCH AND JUDY Birtwistle
Choregos — Geoffrey Chard
Punch — John Cameron
Judy — Maureen Morelle
Lawyer — John Winfield
Doctor — Wyndham Parfitt
Pretty Polly — Jenny Hill
Conductor — David Atherton
Director — Anthony Besch
Designer — Peter Rice
Choreographer — Alfred Rodrigues

26, 28, 31 Aug. 20.00 29 Aug. 18.30
St Mary's Cathedral
THE PRODIGAL SON Britten
Tempter (Abbot) — Peter Pears, Robert Tear
Father — Bryan Drake, John Shirley-Quirk
Elder son — Bryan Drake, Benjamin Luxon, Malcolm Rivers
Younger son — Bernard Dickerson, Robert Tear
Musical direction — Benjamin Britten
Director and Scenery — Colin Graham
Costumes — Annena Stubbs

27 Aug. 20.00 30 Aug. 21.15
St Mary's Cathedral
CURLEW RIVER Britten
Abbott — Harold Blackburn
Ferryman — Benjamin Luxon, John Shirley-Quirk
Traveller — Malcolm Rivers, Bryan Drake
Madwoman — Robert Tear
Musical direction — Viola Tunnard, Steuart Bedford
Director and Scenery — Colin Graham
Costumes — Annena Stubbs

29 Aug. 21.15 30 Aug. 18.30
St Mary's Cathedral
THE BURNING FIERY FURNACE Britten
Astrologer (Abbot) — Bryan Drake, Malcolm Rivers
Nebuchadnezzar — Kenneth Macdonald
Ananias — Benjamin Luxon
Misael — Robert Tear, Bernard Dickerson
Azarias — Paschal Allen
Angel — Robert Alder
Herald — Peter Leeming
Musical direction — Viola Tunnard, Steuart Bedford
Director and designer — Colin Graham
Costumes — Annena Stubbs

HAMBURG STATE OPERA
29 Aug. 3, 6 Sep. 19.00 King's Theatre
ELEKTRA R. Strauss
Elektra — Gladys Kuchta
Orestes — Hans Sotin
Chrysothemis — Leonie Rysanek*, Ingrid Bjoner
Clytemnestra — Regina Resnik
Aegisthus — Helmut Melchert
Tutor — Carl Schultz
Confidant — Ursula Nettling
Trainbearer — Rosemarie Hartung
Young servant — Wilfried Plate
Old servant — Franz Grundheber
Overseer — Edith Lang
Maidservants Cvetka Ahlin, Ursula Boese, Regina Marheineke, Ingeborg Krüger, Inger Paustian
Conductor — Leopold Ludwig
Director — Wolf Völker
Designer — Alfred Siercke

30 Aug. 4, 7 Sep. 19.00 King's Theatre
ARIADNE AUF NAXOS R. Strauss
(Revised version)
Ariadne — Arlene Saunders
Bacchus — Ernst Kozub
Zerbinetta — Sylvia Geszty
Composer — Tatiana Troyanos
Harlekin — Heinz Blankenburg
Scaramuccio — Wilhelm Brokmeier
Truffaldin — Noel Mangin
Brighella/Dancing master — Gerhard Unger
Music master — Herbert Fliether
Major domo — Toni Blankenheim
Naiade — Regina Marheineke
Dryade — Cvetka Ahlin
Echo — Helga Thieme
Officer — Rudolf Mandak
Wig maker — Hans Sotin
Lackey — Franz Grundheber
Conductor — Leopold Ludwig
Director — Ulrich Wenk
Designer — Alfred Siercke

31 Aug. 2, 5 Sep. 19.00 King's Theatre
DER FLIEGENDE HOLLÄNDER Wagner
Dutchman — David Ward*, Theo Adam
Senta — Anja Silja
Daland — Ernst Wiemann
Erik — Richard Cassilly
Mary — Ursula Boese
Steersman — Gerhard Unger
Conductor — Bernhard Klee
Director and designer — Wieland Wagner

ORCHESTRAL CONCERTS

LONDON SYMPHONY ORCHESTRA
18 Aug. 20.00 Usher Hall
Britten *arr.* — National anthem
Britten — Voices for today
Britten — Concerto for violin in D minor, op.15
Britten — Spring symphony
Conductor — István Kertész
Soloists Sir Yehudi Menuhin (vn), Elly Ameling (sop), Helen Watts (cont), Peter Pears (ten), Scottish Festival Chorus, Boys of St Mary's R.C. Cathedral

19 Aug. 20.00 Usher Hall
Schubert — Symphony no.5 in B flat, D485
Dvořák — Concerto for cello in B minor, op.104
Bartók — Concerto for orchestra
Conductor — István Kertész
Soloist — Jacqueline du Pré

21 Aug. 20.00 Usher Hall
Schoenberg — Erwartung
Debussy — Rhapsody for clarinet and orchestra
Schubert — Symphony no.6 in C, D589
Conductor — Pierre Boulez
Soloists Helga Pilarczyk (sop), Gervase de Peyer (cl)

SCOTTISH NATIONAL ORCHESTRA
Conductor — Alexander Gibson
22 Aug. 20.00 Usher Hall
Schubert Overture in the Italian style in C, D591
Beethoven Concerto for violin in D, op.61
Dvořák Symphony no.7 in D minor, op.70
Soloist — Sir Yehudi Menuhin (vn)

7 Sep. 19.30 Usher Hall
Schubert — Alfonso und Estrella
Soloists Phyllis Curtin, Patricia Hay (sop), Richard Lewis, Duncan Robertson (ten), Thomas Hemsley, John Shaw (bar), Josef Greindl (bs), Scottish Opera Chorus

ENGLISH CHAMBER ORCHESTRA
23 Aug. 11.00 Leith Town Hall
Bach — Brandenburg concerto no.3 in G
Bach — Cantata no.73
Britten — Cantata misericordium
Conductor — Benjamin Britten
Soloists Peter Pears (ten), Dietrich Fischer- Dieskau (bar), John Alldis Choir

23 Aug. 20.00 Usher Hall
Schubert — Symphony no.3 in D, D200
Mozart — Concerto for piano no.20 in D minor, K466
Schubert — Rosamunde: Entracte in B flat *and* Ballet music in G
Mozart — Symphony no.39 in E flat, K543
Conductor and soloist — Daniel Barenboim (pf)

USSR STATE ORCHESTRA
24 Aug. 20.00 Usher Hall
Pärt — Perpetuum mobile, op.10
Britten Symphony for cello and orchestra, op.68
Rachmaninov Symphony no.2 in E minor, op.27
Conductor — Evgeny Svetlanov
Soloist — Mstislav Rostropovich (vc)

25 Aug. 20.00 Usher Hall
Brahms Symphony no.4 in E minor, op.98
Mozart Concerto for violin no.5 in A, K219
R. Strauss — Till Eulenspiegels lustige Streiche
Conductor and soloist — David Oistrakh (vn)

NEW PHILHARMONIA ORCHESTRA
28 Aug. 20.00 Usher Hall
Rossini — La gazza ladra: Overture
Bartók — Concerto for piano no.1
Schubert — Symphony no.2 in B flat, D125
Wagner — Tristan und Isolde: Prelude and Liebestod
Conductor — Claudio Abbado
Soloist — Daniel Barenboim (pf)

30 Aug. 20.00 Usher Hall
Mahler — Symphony no.9 in D
Conductor — Otto Klemperer

31 Aug. 20.00 Usher Hall
Schubert — Symphony no.4 in C minor (Tragic), D417

Schubert Mass no.6 in E flat, D950
Conductor Carlo Maria Giulini
Soloists Anne Pashley (sop), Sybil Michelow (cont), David Hughes, Duncan Robertson (ten), William McCue (bs), Scottish Festival Chorus

1 Sep. 20.00 *Usher Hall*
Britten War Requiem
Conductors
Carlo Maria Giulini, Benjamin Britten
Soloists Galina Vishnevskaya (sop), Peter Pears (ten), Dietrich Fischer-Dieskau (bar), Scottish Festival Chorus, Boys of St Mary's R.C. Cathedral, Melos Ensemble

BAVARIAN RADIO SYMPHONY ORCHESTRA
Conductor Rafael Kubelik
2 Sep. 20.00 *Usher Hall*
Britten Sinfonia da requiem
Mahler Symphony no.1 in D

3 Sep. 20.00 *Usher Hall*
Schubert Symphony no.8 in B minor (Unfinished), D759
Hartmann Gesangsszene
Beethoven Symphony no.7 in A, op.92
Soloist Dietrich Fischer-Dieskau (bar)

4 Sep. 20.00 *Usher Hall*
Mendelssohn A midsummer night's dream: Overture, Nocturne *and* Scherzo
Mozart Concerto for piano no.17 in G, K453
Schubert Symphony no.9 in C (Great), D944
Soloist Ingrid Haebler (pf)

BBC SCOTTISH SYMPHONY ORCHESTRA
5 Sep. 20.00 *Usher Hall*
Beethoven Symphony no.8 in F, op.93
Britten Concerto for piano in D, op.13
Musgrave Concerto for orchestra
Mozart Concerto for piano no.15 in B flat, K450
Conductors James Loughran
Benjamin Britten
Soloist Peter Frankl (pf)

7 Sep. 22.30 *Usher Hall*
Hoffnung Concert
Beethoven/Strasser Leonore no.4 overture
Jaja/Searle Punkt Kontrapunkt
Arnold The United Nations
Chagrin French patrol
Arnold Fanfare to end all fanfares
Arnold A grand, grand overture
Horovitz Metamorphosis on a bedtime theme
Reizenstein Concerto populare
Jacob Variations on Annie Laurie
Conductors James Loughran, Lawrence Leonard, Joseph Horovitz
Director Colin Graham
Soloists April Cantelo (sop), Eric Shilling (bar), Amadeus Quartet, Massed bands

CHAMBER CONCERTS

ISAAC STERN (vn), LEONARD ROSE (vc), EUGENE ISTOMIN (pf)
27 Aug. 20.00 *Usher Hall*
Haydn Trio for piano and strings no.20 in E flat
Beethoven Trio for piano and strings no.3 in C minor, op.1/3
Schubert Trio for piano and strings in E flat, D929

29 Aug. 20.00 *Usher Hall*
Beethoven Variations on 'Ich bin der Schneider Kakadu'
Schubert Trio for piano and strings no.1 in B flat, D898
Brahms Trio for piano and strings no.2 in C, op.87

AMADEUS QUARTET
28 Aug. 11.00 *Leith Town Hall*
Schubert Quartet no.14 in D minor (Death and the maiden), D810
Schubert Quartet no.13 in A minor, D804

29 Aug. 11.00 *Leith Town Hall*
Purcell When night her purple veil
Britten Quartet no.2 in C, op.36
Britten Songs and proverbs of William Blake
with Dietrich Fischer-Dieskau (bar), Benjamin Britten (pf)

31 Aug. 11.00 *Leith Town Hall*
Schubert Quartet no.8 in B flat, D112
Schubert Quintet in C, D956
with Mstislav Rostropovich (vc)

4 Sep. 11.00 *Leith Town Hall*
Schubert Quartet no.9 in G minor, D173
Schubert Quintet for piano and strings in A (The trout), D667
with Jörg Demus (pf), James Merrett (db)

6 Sep. 11.00 *Leith Town Hall*
Schubert Quartet no.10 in E flat, D87
Schubert Quartet no.12 in C minor (Quartetsatz), D703
Schubert Quartet no.15 in G, D887

MELOS ENSEMBLE
30 Aug. 11.00 *Freemasons' Hall*
Musgrave Chamber concerto no.3
Schubert Octet, D803

2 Sep. 11.00 *Freemasons' Hall*
Berwald Septet
Britten Sinfonietta, op.1
Mozart Quintet for clarinet and strings in A, K581

JOHN ALLDIS CHOIR
24 Aug. 11.00 *Freemasons' Hall*
Britten Five flower songs
Britten A hymn to the Virgen
Messiaen Cinq rechants
Choral works by Schubert, Le Jeune
Conductor John Alldis
Soloists Jessica Cash (sop), Sarah Walker (mez), Ian Partridge, Philip Langridge (ten), John Huw Davies (bs)

RECITALS

PETER PEARS (ten)
BENJAMIN BRITTEN (pf)
20 Aug. 11.00 *Freemasons' Hall*
Schubert Winterreise

DIETRICH FISCHER-DIESKAU (bar)
JÖRG DEMUS (pf)
26 Aug. 20.00 *Usher Hall*
Songs by Schubert

GALINA VISHNEVSKAYA (sop)
MSTISLAV ROSTROPOVICH (pf)
27 Aug. 11.00 *Leith Town Hall*
Britten The poet's echo
Songs by Rachmaninov, Rimsky-Korsakov, Tchaikovsky, Stravinsky

RICHARD LEWIS (ten)
GEOFFREY PARSONS (pf)
5 Sep. 11.00 *Freemasons' Hall*
Songs by Schubert and Beethoven

PETER FRANKL (pf)
19 Aug. 11.00 *Freemasons' Hall*
Bartók Fifteen Hungarian peasant songs
Schubert Fantasia in C (Wanderer), D760
Schubert Sonata no.9 in B, D575
Bartók Dance suite

SEMYON KRUCHIN (pf)
21 Aug. 11.00 *Freemasons' Hall*
Beethoven Sonata no.28 in A, op.101
Prokofiev Sonata no.7 in B flat, op.83
Liszt Sonata in B minor

DANIEL BARENBOIM (pf)
25 Aug. 14.30 *Usher Hall*
Schubert Moments musicaux, D780
Schubert Sonata no.15 in C (Unfinished), D840
Schubert Impromptus, D935

PETER WILLIAMS (hpd)
26 Aug. 15.00 *St Cecilia's Hall*
L. Couperin Suite in C
F. Couperin Ordre no.3 in C minor: Suite
Froberger Lament on the death of Ferdinand IV
Bach Partita no.2 in C minor

INGRID HAEBLER (pf)
7 Sep. 11.00 *Freemasons' Hall*
Schubert Sonata no.18 in G, D894
Schubert Sonata no.21 in B flat, D960

SIR YEHUDI MENUHIN (vn)
24 Aug. 18.00 *St Cuthbert's Church*
Bach Sonata no.3 in C
Bartók Sonata

SIR YEHUDI MENUHIN (vn)
HEPHZIBAH MENUHIN (pf)
20 Aug. 20.00 *Usher Hall*
Schubert Fantasia in C, D934
Bartók Sonata no.1
Beethoven Sonata no.9 in A (Kreutzer), op.47

ISAAC STERN (vn)
EUGENE ISTOMIN (pf)
1 Sep. 14.30 *Usher Hall*
Schubert Sonata in A minor, D385
Brahms Sonata no.1 in G, op.78
Beethoven Sonata no.5 in F (Spring), op.24

MSTISLAV ROSTROPOVICH (vc)
28 Aug. 18.00 *St Cuthbert's Church*
Bach Suite no.1 in G
Bach Suite no.2 in D minor
Britten Suite no.1, op.72

30 Sep. 18.00 *St Cuthbert's Church*
Bach Suite no.3 in C
Bach Suite no.4 in E flat
Britten Suite no.2, op.80

2 Sep. 18.00 *St Cuthbert's Church*
Bach Suite no.5 in C minor
Bach Suite no.6 in D

JACQUELINE DU PRÉ (vc)
DANIEL BARENBOIM (pf)
26 Aug. 11.00 *Leith Town Hall*
Beethoven Variations on 'Bei Männern' (Mozart)
Beethoven Sonata no.5 in D, op.102/2
Brahms Sonata no.2 in F, op.99

ELLY AMELING (sop), JÖRG DEMUS (pf), GERVASE DE PEYER (cl)
22 Aug. 11.00 Freemasons' Hall
Schubert Der Hirt auf dem Felsen
Schubert Sonata for piano no.13 in A, D664
Schubert Fantasia in C minor on themes by Mozart, D993
Schubert Sonata for piano no.14 in A minor, D784
Schubert Songs

PETER PEARS (ten)
BENJAMIN BRITTEN (pf)
MSTISLAV ROSTROPOVICH (vc)
3 Sep. 11.00 Leith Town Hall
Schubert Sonata for cello and piano in A minor (Arpeggione), D821
Britten Winter words
Britten Sonata for cello and piano in C, op.65

DRAMA

69 THEATRE COMPANY
19-24, 28, 30 Aug. 2, 5, 7 Sep. 19.15
20, 24, 27, 29, 31 Aug. 3 Sep. 14.15
Assembly Hall
HAMLET Shakespeare
Hamlet Tom Courtenay
Ophelia Anna Calder-Marshall
Gertrude Dilys Hamlett
Claudius Glyn Owen
Polonius Jeffry Wickham
Horatio Trevor Peacock
Laertes John Nettles
Fortinbras Kiffer Weisselberg
Osric Ian Marter
Bernardo/Captain John Donovan
Francisco/Player (Lucianus) Russell Hunter
Marcellus Malcolm Rennie
Ghost/Player (King) Edgar Wreford
Rosencrantz David Horovitch
Guildenstern David Carson
Player (Queen)/Priest Christopher Cabot
Gravediggers Russell Hunter, John Donovan
Others parts played by Paul Sanders, Geoffrey Case
Director Caspar Wrede
Designer Malcolm Pride
Lighting John B. Read

WHEN WE DEAD AWAKEN Ibsen
(Eng. Translated by Michael Meyer)
26, 27, 29, 31 Aug. 3, 4, 6 Sep. 19.15
7 Sep. 14.15 Assembly Hall
Arnold Rubek Alexander Knox
Maja Irene Hamilton
Irene Wendy Hiller
Ulfhejm Brian Cox
Inspector Roger Swaine
Nun Brenda McGuinne
Director Michael Elliott
Scenery Johanna Bryant
Costumes Malcolm Pride
Lighting Richard Pilbrow

PROSPECT PRODUCTIONS
19-24 Aug. 19.00 21, 24 Aug. 14.15
Lyceum Theatre
THE BEGGAR'S OPERA Gay
Captain Macheath Peter Gilmore
Polly Jan Waters
Lucy Frances Cuka
Mr Peachum James Cossins
Mrs Peachum/Mrs Trapes Hy Hazell
Lockit John Cater
Jenny Diver Angela Richards
Filch Peter Kenton
Beggar Richard Durden
Matt of the Mint David Calder
Nimming Ned Tony Robinson
Ben Budge Gordon Reid
Jemmy Twitcher Adam Deane
Crook-fingered Jack Peter Forest
Wat Dreary Kenneth Shanley
Mrs Coaxer Carol Gillies
Dolly Trull Patricia Fuller
Mrs Vixen Jessie Barclay
Betty Doxy Margaret Blay
Mrs Slammekin Pamela Miles
Suky Tawdry Suzanne Heath
Molly Brazen Vivian Brooks
Brewers/Constables Colin Prockter, Alan Tennock
Director Toby Robertson
Scenery Voytek
Costumes Nadine Baylis
Lighting Tony Corbett
Music *arr.* Benjamin Pearce Higgins

CITIZENS' THEATRE, Glasgow
27-31 Aug. 19.00 28, 31 Aug. 14.15
Lyceum Theatre
THE RESISTIBLE RISE OF ARTURO UI
Brecht (Eng. Adapted by George Tabori)
The barker Bernard Martin
Old Dogsborough/4th grocer James Gibson
Givola Steven Berkoff
Giri Harold Innocent
Arturo Ui Leonard Rossiter
Clark Donald Douglas
Sheet/Goldman/Dullfeet Bruce Myles
Bowl/Preacher Douglas Malcolm
Roma Del Henney
Young Dogsborough Michael Harrigan
Dockdaisy Mairhi Russell
Ragg/Fish/1st Chicago grocer James Kennedy
Butcher Bernard Martin
O'Casey Blain Fairman
Actor John Lancaster
Bodyguards Max Latimer, John Sinclair
Woman Ida Schuster
Betty Dullfeet Louise Breslin
Young Inna/3rd Chicago grocer Peter Lincoln
Shorty Walter Jackson
2nd Chicago grocer Ian Dempsey
Director Michael Blakemore
Designer Annena Stubbs
Lighting Tony Jones

ABBEY THEATRE, Dublin
2-7 Sep. 19.00 4, 7 Sep. 14.15
Lyceum Theatre
THE PLAYBOY OF THE WESTERN WORLD Synge
Michael James Flaherty Geoffrey Golden
Margaret Flaherty (Pegeen) Aideen O'Kelly
Shawn Keogh Patrick Laffan
Philly Cullen Michéal O'Briain
Jimmy Farrell Harry Brogan
Christopher Mahon Vincent Dowling
Old Mahon Eamon Kelly
Widow Quin Máire Ní Dhomhnaill
Sara Tansey Fidelma Murphy
Susan Brady Bernadette McKenna
Honor Blake Máire Ní Ghráinne
Nelly Reilly Leslie Lawlor
A bellman Patrick O'Callaghan
Director Tomás MacAnna
Scenery Brian Collins
Costumes Anne McCabe
Lighting Leslie Scott

TRINITY SQUARE REPERTORY COMPANY, USA
19-24 Aug. 19.30 22, 24 Aug. 14.30
Church Hill Theatre
YEARS OF THE LOCUST Holland
Oscar Wilde Richard Kneeland
Martin William Damkoehler
Matthews James Gallery
Chief Anthony Palmer
1st class prisoner Ed Hall
Prisoners Bree Cavazos, James Eichelberger
Isaacson Clinton Anderson
Nelson William Cain
Lord Queensberry/Fingers Robert Colonna
Lord Alfred Douglas/Davey Cross Peter Gerety
Lady Wilde Marguerite Lenert
Lady Mandrake Barbara Orson
Frank Harris Ronald Frazier
Constance Wilde Katherine Helmond
Chaplain Robert Patterson
Director Adrian Hall
Scenery Eugene Lee
Costumes John Lehmeyer
Lighting Roger Morgan

TRAVERSE THEATRE CLUB
2-7 Sep. 19.30 Church Hill Theatre
MOURNING BECOMES ELECTRA
O'Neill
Seth Beckwith/A chantyman Thick Wilson
Amos Ames/Josiah Borden William Simons
Louisa/Mrs Borden Sheila Grant
Minnie/Mrs Hills Gwynyth Marshall-Jones
Lavinia Mannon Valerie Sarruff
Hazel Niles Corinna Marlowe
Captain Peter Niles Peter Harlowe
Christine Mannon Judy Campbell
Captain Adam Brant William Russell
Brigadier-General Mannon Robert Harris
Dr Joseph Blake/Abner Small Richard Wilson
Orin Mannon John Fraser
Ira Mackel Michael Murray
Director Gordon McDougall
Lighting André Tammes

LABORATORY THEATRE, Wroclaw
22-24, 26-30 Aug. 20.00
11 Cambridge Street
ACROPOLIS Wyspianski
Jacob/Harpist Zygmunt Molik
Rebecca/Cassandra Rena Mirecka
Isaac/Trojan guard Antoni Jaholkowski
Ezau/Hector Ryszard Cieślak
Angel/Paris Zbigniew Cynkutis
Stanislaw Scierski
Andrzej Paluchiewicz
Director Jerzy Grotowski
Scenery Jerzy Gurawski
Costumes Józef Szajna
*Performance on 21 Aug. cancelled

DAME EDITH EVANS (rdr)
5 Sep. 15.00 St Cecilia's Hall
Reading for pleasure

DANCE

ALVIN AILEY AMERICAN DANCE THEATER
26, 29 Aug. 19.30 31 Aug. 14.30
Church Hill Theatre
TOCCATA
Choreographer Talley Beatty
Music Dizzy Gillespie
Lighting Thomas Skelton
REFLECTIONS IN D
Choreographer Alvin Ailey
Music Duke Ellington
Lighting Nikola Cernovitch
ICARUS
Choreographer Lucas Hoving
Music Shin-Ichi Matsushita
Costumes Beni Montresor
Lighting Thomas Skelton

BLACK DISTRICT
Choreographer Talley Beatty
Music Duke Ellington
Costumes Edward Burbridge
Lighting Thomas Skelton
REVELATIONS
Choreographer Alvin Ailey
Music Trad.
Designer Ves Harper
Lighting Nikola Cernovitch

27, 30 Aug. 19.30 Church Hill Theatre
CONGO TANGO PALACE
Choreographer Talley Beatty
Music Miles Davis
Costumes Matthew Cameron
Lighting Nikola Cernovitch
CREDO
Choreographer John Fealy
Music Stravinsky
Lighting Thomas Skelton
METALLICS
Choreographer and designer Paul Sanasardo
Music Henk Badings, Henry Cowell
Lighting Nikola Cernovitch
PRODIGAL PRINCE
Choreog., music, design Geoffrey Holder
BLACK DISTRICT

29 Aug. 14.30 Church Hill Theatre
CONGO TANGO PALACE
CREDO
METALLICS
PRODIGAL PRINCE
REVELATIONS

28, 31 Aug. 19.30 Church Hill Theatre
CONGO TANGO PALACE
ICARUS
QUINTET
Choreographer Alvin Ailey
Music Laura Nyro
Costumes M. Cameron, George Faison
JOURNEY
Choreographer and designer Joyce Trisler
Music Ives
KNOXVILLE: SUMMER 1915 (World Première)
Choreographer Alvin Ailey
Music Barber
Costumes Joop Stokvis
REVELATIONS
Dancers Consuela Atlas, Judith Jamison, Michele Murray, Linda Kent, Alma Robinson, Eleanor McCoy, Miguel Godreau, Michael Peters, George Faison, Dudley Williams, Kelvin Rotardier, Ernest Pagnano, Freddy Romero

EXHIBITIONS

Royal Scottish Museum
CHARLES RENNIE MACKINTOSH
(Sponsored by the EIF and arranged by the Scottish Arts Council)

Royal Scottish Museum
FRITZ WOTRUBA

Royal Scottish Academy
BOUDIN TO PICASSO

College of Art
CANADA 101

English Speaking Union
HOFFNUNG

1969

OPERA

TEATRO COMUNALE, Florence
25, 28 Aug. 1, 8 Sep. 19.30
King's Theatre
MARIA STUARDA Donizetti
Maria Stuarda Leyla Gencer
Elisabetta Shirley Verrett
Leicester Franco Tagliavini
Talbot Agostino Ferrin
Cecil Giulio Fioravanti
Anna Anna di Stasio
Herald Mario Frosini
Conductor Nino Sanzogno
Director Giorgio de Lullo
Designer Pier Luigi Pizzi

26, 30 Aug. 3, 9, 13 Sep. 19.30
King's Theatre
RIGOLETTO Verdi
Rigoletto Mario Zanasi
Duke Renato Cioni
Gilda Renata Scotto
Maddalena Biancarosa Zanibelli
Sparafucile Franco Ventriglia
Giovanna Anna Falcone
Count Monterone Plinio Clabassi
Marullo Giorgio Giorgetti
Borsa Dino Formichini
Count Ceprano Mario Frosini
Countess Ceprano Giuliana Matteini
Usher Guerrando Rigiri
Conductor Alberto Erede
Director Sandro Sequi
Designer Pier Luigi Pizzi

29 Aug. 5, 11 Sep. 19.30 King's Theatre
SETTE CANZONI Malipiero
Ballad singer/Drunk Renato Capecchi
Mother Magda Olivero
Inner voice Guerrando Rigiri
Lover Giuseppe Baratti
Bell ringer Scipio Colombo
Lamplighter Giorgio Giorgetti
IL PRIGIONIERO Dallapiccola
Mother Claudia Parada
Prisoner Scipio Colombo
Gaoler/Grand inquisitor Mirto Picchi
Priests Dino Formichini, Giorgio Giorgetti
Conductor Nino Sanzogno
Director Alessandro Fersen
Designer Emanuele Luzzati

4, 6, 10, 12 Sep. 19.30 King's Theatre
IL SIGNOR BRUSCHINO Rossini
Bruschino, son Valiano Natali
Bruschino, father Renato Capecchi
Sofia Jolanda Meneguzzer
Gaudenzio Claudio Desderi
Florville Giuseppe Baratti
Commissioner of police Paolo Pedani
Filiberto Graziano del Vivo
Marianna Anna di Stasio
Conductor Aldo Ceccato
Director Filippo Crivelli
Designer Gianni Vagnetti
GIANNI SCHICCHI Puccini
Gianni Schicchi Tito Gobbi
Lauretta Maddalena Bonifaccio
Rinuccio Ugo Benelli
Zita Flora Rafanelli
Gherardo Dino Formichini
Nella Giuliana Matteini
Gherardino Carlo Formichini
Betto di Signa Graziano del Vivo
Simone Plinio Clabassi
Marco Giorgio Giorgetti
La Cesca Anna di Stasio
Maestro Spinelloccio Augusto Frati
Ser Amantio Paolo Pedani
Pinellino Mario Frosini
Guccio Valiano Natali
Conductor Aldo Ceccato
Director Tito Gobbi
Designer Ferdinando Ghelli

MUSIC THEATRE ENSEMBLE
27 Aug. 22.30 Freemasons' Hall
Goehr Triptych: Naboth's vineyard
Conductor Alexander Goehr
Director John Cox
Soloists Gloria Jennings (cont), Philip Langridge (ten), Michael Rippon (bs), Mark Furneaux, Richard Dennis (mimes)
Goehr Paraphrase on 'Il combattimento di Tancredi e Clorinda' (Monteverdi) (World première)
Soloist Alan Hacker (cl)
Hamilton Pharsalia (World première)
Conductor David Atherton
Director John Cox
Designer Bernard Culshaw
Soloists Philip Langridge (narr), Teresa Cahill, Yvonne Fuller (sop), Gloria Jennings (cont), Alexander Oliver (ten), Michael Rippon, Joseph Rouleau (bs)

28 Aug. 22.30 Freemasons' Hall
Hamilton Pharsalia
Berio Visage
Berio Sequenza III for voice
Soloist Cathy Berberian (sop)
Stravinsky Renard
Conductor David Atherton
Designers Ian Mackintosh, Vincent Yorke
Choreographer David Drew
Soloists Jane Landon, Wayne Sleep, Alexander Grant, Donald Britton (dancers) Philip Langridge, Alexander Oliver (ten), Michael Rippon, Joseph Rouleau (bs)

29 Aug. 22.30 Freemasons' Hall
Monteverdi Il Combattimento di Tancredi e Clorinda
Tancredi Alexander Oliver
Clorinda Yvonne Fuller
Testo Philip Langridge
Mimes Mark Furneaux, Richard Dennis
Conductor Alexander Goehr
Director John Cox
Designer Bernard Culshaw
Berio Visage
Berio Sequenza III for voice
Stravinsky Renard

30 Aug. 22.30 Freemasons' Hall
Monteverdi Il combattimento di Tancredi e Clorinda
Goehr Paraphrase on 'Il combattimento di Tancredi e Clorinda' (Monteverdi)
Goehr Triptych: Naboth's vineyard

ORCHESTRAL CONCERTS

SCOTTISH NATIONAL ORCHESTRA
24 Aug. 20.00 Usher Hall
Britten The building of the house - Overture
Bennett Concerto for piano
Berlioz Te deum
Conductor Alexander Gibson
Soloists Stephen Bishop-Kovacevich (pf), John Mitchinson (ten), EF Chorus, Boys of St Mary's R.C. Cathedral

6 Sep. 20.00 Usher Hall
Malipiero Sinfonia delle campane
Chopin Concerto for piano no.1 in E minor, op.11

Sibelius Symphony no.5 in E flat, op.82
Conductor Sir John Barbirolli
Soloist Claudio Arrau (pf)

BBC SCOTTISH RADIO ORCHESTRA
25 Aug. 20.00 *Usher Hall*
A programme of Scottish light music
Conductor Iain Sutherland
Soloists Patricia MacMahon (sop), Ronald Morrison (bar), Angus Cameron (fiddle), George McIlwham (bp)

LONDON SYMPHONY ORCHESTRA
26 Aug. 20.00 *Usher Hall*
Mozart Symphony no.31 in D (Paris), K297
Mahler Lieder eines fahrenden Gesellen
Beethoven Symphony no.3 In E Flat (Eroica), op.55
Conductor Hans Schmidt-Isserstedt
Soloist Barry McDaniel (bar)

27 Aug. 20.00 *Usher Hall*
Mendelssohn Symphony no.4 in A (Italian), op.90
Prokofiev Concerto for violin no.2 in G minor, op.63
Petrassi Concerto for orchestra no.1
R. Strauss Till Eulenspiegels lustige Streiche
Conductor Hans Schmidt-Isserstedt
Soloist Itzhac Perlman (vn)

29 Aug. 20.00 *Usher Hall*
Beethoven Die Geschöpfe des Prometheus: Overture
Mozart Vorrei spiegarvi o Dio
Nono Intolleranza - Suite (World première)
Brahms Symphony no.2 in D, op.73
Conductor Claudio Abbado
Soloist Catherine Gayer (sop)

30 Aug. 20.00 *Usher Hall*
Donatoni Puppenspiel no.2
Prokofiev Concerto for piano no.3 in C, op.26
Debussy Nocturnes
Ravel Daphnis et Chloë - Suite no.2
Conductor Claudio Abbado
Soloists Martha Argerich (pf), Severino Gazzelloni (fl), EF Chorus

BBC SCOTTISH SYMPHONY ORCHESTRA
28 Aug. 20.00 *Usher Hall*
Verdi La forza del destino: Overture
Dallapiccola Piccola musica notturna
Liszt Concerto for piano no.2 in A
Berlioz Harold in Italy
Conductor James Loughran
Soloists Nikita Magaloff (pf), Peter Schidlof (va)

CZECH PHILHARMONIC ORCHESTRA
1 Sep. 20.00 *Usher Hall*
Dvořák Carnival - Overture
Martinů Concerto for piano no.2
Dvořák Symphony no.7 in D minor, op.70
Conductor Vaclàv Neumann
Soloist Rudolf Firkušný (pf)

2 Sep. 20.00 *Usher Hall*
Fišer Fifteen pages after Dürer's Apocalypse
Tchaikovsky Concerto for violin in D, op.35
Smetana Má vlast: From Bohemia's woods and groves; Tábor; Blanik
Conductor Vaclàv Neumann
Soloist Nathan Milstein (vn)

4 Sep. 20.00 *Usher Hall*
Schumann Manfred: Overture
Beethoven Concerto for piano no.5 in E flat (Emperor), op.73
Bartók Concerto for orchestra
Conductor Lorin Maazel
Soloist Annie Fischer (pf)

I MUSICI
3 Sep. 20.00 *Usher Hall*
Corelli Concerto grosso in C minor, op.6/13
Bucchi Concerto grottesco for double bass and vibraphone
Paisiello Concerto for harpsichord in C
Vivaldi Concerti, op.8: Nos.1-4 (The four seasons)
Soloists Roberto Michelucci (vn), Lucio Buccarella (db), Maria Teresa Garatti (hpd)

5 Sep. 20.00 *Usher Hall*
Vivaldi Concerto for 2 violins and 2 cellos in G
Vivaldi Concerti, op.11: No.2 in E minor (Il favorito)
Vivaldi O qui coeli terraeque
Vivaldi Concerto for 2 violins in A minor
Rolla Concertino for viola in E flat
Locatelli Concerto for 4 violins in F minor
Soloist Catherine Gayer (sop)

NEW PHILHARMONIA ORCHESTRA
7 Sep. 20.00 *Usher Hall*
Berlioz Béatrice et Bénédict: Overture
Berlioz Les nuits d'été
Bruckner Symphony no.7 in E
Conductor Daniel Barenboim
Soloist Janet Baker (mez)

9 Sep. 20.00 *Usher Hall*
Bonporti Concerto a quattro in D, op.11/8
Petrassi Magnificat
Rossini Stabat Mater
Conductor Carlo Maria Giulini
Soloists Angeles Gulin Dominguez, Catherine Gayer (sop), Janet Baker (mez), Nicolai Gedda (ten), Raffaele Arie (bs), EF Chorus

11 Sep. 20.00 *Usher Hall*
Busoni Rondo Arlecchinesco
Rachmaninov Rhapsody on a theme of Paganini
Schumann Symphony no.4 in D minor, op.120
Conductor Alberto Erede
Soloist Misha Dichter (pf)

12 Sep. 20.00 13 Sep. 19.30 *Usher Hall*
Verdi Requiem
Conductor Carlo Maria Giulini
Soloists Angeles Gulin Dominguez (sop), Shirley Verrett (mez), Nicolai Gedda (ten), Raffaele Arie (bs), New Philharmonia Chorus

SCOTTISH NATIONAL CHAMBER ORCHESTRA
12 Sep. 11.00 *Leith Town Hall*
Mozart Symphony no.32 in G, K318
Carissimi Domine deus meus
Castiglioni A solemn music II (1965 version)
Petrassi Estri for 15 instruments
Dallapiccola Sex carmina alcaei
Haydn Symphony no.61 in D
Conductor Alexander Gibson
Soloist April Cantelo (sop)

CHAMBER CONCERTS

BARTÓK QUARTET
25 Aug. 11.00 *Freemasons' Hall*
Mozart Quartet no.15 in D minor, K421
Bartók Quartet no.3
Verdi Quartet in E minor

27 Aug. 11.00 *Freemasons' Hall*
Haydn Quartet in G minor (Rider), op.74/3
Bartók Quartet no.4
Debussy Quartet in G minor, op.10/1

TRIO DI TRIESTE
28 Aug. 11.00 *Freemasons' Hall*
Haydn Trio for piano and strings in E
Casella Sonata a tre, op.62
Schumann Trio for piano and strings no.1 in D minor, op.63

31 Aug. 15.00 *Freemasons' Hall*
Vivaldi Sonata for violin, cello and piano in C minor
Brahms Trio for piano and strings no.2 in C, op.87
Ravel Trio for piano and strings in A minor

SESTETTO ITALIANO LUCA MARENZIO
8 Sep. 11.00 *Freemasons' Hall*
Vecchi L'amfiparnaso
Verretti Dulcissime Jesu
Verretti Ecce crucem Domini
Petrassi Nonsense

10 Sep. 11.00 *Freemasons' Hall*
Works by Lassus, Monteverdi, Bussotti

AEOLIAN QUARTET
9 Sep. 11.00 *Freemasons' Hall*
Haydn Quartet in G, op.54/1
Petrassi Quartet
Beethoven Quartet no.9 in C (Rasumovsky), op.59/3

11 Sep. 11.00 *Freemasons' Hall*
Mozart Quartet no.14 in G, K387
Walton Quartet in A minor
Beethoven Quartet no.14 in C sharp minor, op.131

RECITALS

RENATO CAPECCHI (bar), EDOARDO MÜLLER (pf)
26 Aug. 11.00 *Freemasons' Hall*
Italian songs from the 15th to the 20th centuries

BARRY McDANIEL (bar)
GEOFFREY PARSONS (pf)
31 Aug. 20.00 *Usher Hall*
Schubert Die schöne Müllerin

CATHERINE GAYER (sop)
HANS HILSDORF (pf)
1 Sep. 11.00 *Freemasons' Hall*
Songs by Monteverdi, Caldara, A. Scarlatti, Busca, Bellini, Rossini, Donizetti, Verdi, Malipiero, Dallapiccola, Pizzetti

JANET BAKER (mez)
RAYMOND LEPPARD (hpd)
4 Sep. 11.00 *Leith Town Hall*
A. Scarlatti Sarei troppo felice
D. Scarlatii Salve regina
Handel Lucrezia
Purcell Songs

NICOLAI GEDDA (ten)
GEOFFREY PARSONS (pf)
7 Sep. 15.00 *Usher Hall*
Songs by Schubert, Glinka, Mussorgsky, Tchaikovsky

SHIRLEY VERRETT (mez)
WARREN WILSON (pf)
10 Sep. 20.00 — *Usher Hall*
Handel — Alcina: Mi lusinga *and* È gelosia
Schumann — Frauenliebe und -leben
Donizetti — Anna Bolena: Sposa a Percy...Per questa fiamma indomita
Spirituals — Give me Jesus; Hold on; Oh glory
Dvořák — Gypsy melodies

NIKITA MAGALOFF (pf)
30 Aug. 11.00 — *Leith Town Hall*
D. Scarlatti — Sonata in D, L14
D. Scarlatti — Sonata in B minor, L33
D. Scarlatti — Sonata in D, L361
Chopin — Sonata in B minor, op.58
Dallapiccola — Sonatina canonica
Liszt — Études d'exécution transcendante d'après Paganini

RUDOLF FIRKUŠNÝ (pf)
3 Sep. 11.00 — *Leith Town Hall*
Haydn — Sonata in E flat
Schubert — Sonata no.16 in A minor, D845
Dvořák — Theme and variations in A flat, op.36
Smetana — Czech dances: Medved; Polka; Furiant

ANNIE FISCHER (pf)
6 Sep. 11.00 — *Leith Town Hall*
Mozart — Sonata no.8 in A minor, K310
Beethoven — Sonata no.19 in G minor, op.49/1
Beethoven — Sonata no.31 in A flat, op.110
Schumann — Kreisleriana

CLAUDIO ARRAU (pf)
8 Sep. 20.00 — *Usher Hall*
Mozart — Sonata no.18 in D, K576
Schumann — Fantasia in C, op.17
Debussy — Pour le piano
Liszt — Ballade no.2 in B minor
Liszt — Études d'ecécution transcendante: Harmonies du soir *and* No.10 in F minor

MISHA DICHTER (pf)
13 Sep. 11.00 — *Freemasons' Hall*
Beethoven — Andante favori in F
Schubert — Sonata no.13 in A, D664
Rachmaninov — Prelude no.12 in C, op.32/1
Rachmaninov — Prelude no.13 in B flat minor, op.32/2
Rachmaninov — Étude tableau in E flat minor, op.39/5
Rachmaninov — Prelude no.3 in B flat, op.23/2
Prokofiev — Sonata no.7 in B flat, op.83

NATHAN MILSTEIN (vn)
6 Sep. 17.30 — *St Cuthbert's Church*
Bach — Sonata no.1 in G minor
Bach — Partita no.2 in D minor
Paganini — Caprice no.11 in C
Paganini — Caprice no.13 in B flat minor
Paganini — Caprice no.16 in G minor
Bach — Sonata no.3 in C

ITZHAC PERLMAN (vn)
BRUNO CANINO (pf)
29 Aug. 11.00 — *Freemasons' Hall*
Vivaldi — Sonata in A
Brahms — Sonata no.3 in D minor, op.108
Debussy — Sonata
Paganini — Caprices nos.19, 9, 5
Sarasate — Carmen fantasia

SZYMON GOLDBERG (vn), RUDOLF FIRKUŠNÝ (pf), COLIN BRADBURY (cl)
5 Sep. 11.00 — *Leith Town Hall*
Mozart — Sonata for violin and piano no.28 in E flat, K380
Beethoven — Sonata for violin and piano no.10 in G, op.96
Berg — Adagio for violin, clarinet and piano
Beethoven — Sonata for violin and piano no.3 in E flat, op.12/3

SEVERINO GAZZELLONI (fl)
BRUNO CANINO (hpd, pf)
2 Sep. 11.00 — *Freemasons' Hall*
Rimini — Sonata in F
Vinci — Sonata in D
Veracini — Sonata in G
Petrassi — Souffle for flute in G, flute in C and piccolo
Castiglioni — Gymel
Berio — Sequenza I for flute
Maderna — Honeyreves

CEILIDH

12 Sep. 20.00 — *Leith Town Hall*
Soloists Evelyn Campbell, James Smith, John MacFadyen, Joan Mackenzie, Norman Maclean, Duncan Morison (sngr), Govan Gaelic Choir
Introduced by Norman Maclean
(In association with An Comunn Gaidhealach)

DRAMA

PROSPECT THEATRE COMPANY
27, 28, 29 Aug. 2, 3, 5, 10, 13 Sep. 19.00
2, 13 Sep. 14.15 — *Assembly Hall*
EDWARD II Marlowe
King Edward II — Ian McKellen
Prince Edward — Myles Reithermann
Edmund, Earl of Kent — Peter Bourne
Pierce Gaveston — James Laurenson
Guy, Earl of Warwick — Paul Hardwick
Thomas, Earl of Lancaster — Trevor Martin
Aymer de Valence — Stephen Greif
Edmund Fitzalan — Colin Fisher
Henry, Earl of Leicester — Richard Morant
Roger Mortimer of Chirk — Michael Spice
Roger Mortimer of Wigmore — Timothy West
Hugh le Despenser (elder) — Andrew Crawford
Hugh le Despenser (younger) — David Calder
John Stratford — Michael Godfrey
Robert Baldock — Luke Hardy
Sir John Maltravers — Paul Hardwick
Lightborn — Robert Eddison
Queen Isabella — Diane Fletcher
Lady Margaret de Clare — Lucy Fleming
Lady in waiting — Charmian Eyre
Sir Thomas Berkeley — Colin Fisher
Thomas Gurney — Terence Wilton
Director — Toby Robertson
Designer — Kenneth Rowell
Lighting — John B. Read
Music — Carl Davis

25, 26, 30 Aug. 1, 4, 6, 8, 9, 11, 12 Sep. 19.00 30 Aug. 4, 6, 11 Sep. 14.15
Assembly Hall
RICHARD II Shakespeare
Richard II — Ian McKellen
John of Gaunt — Paul Hardwick
Edmund, Duke of York — Robert Eddison
Bolingbroke — Timothy West
Earl of Northumberland — Trevor Martin
Thomas Mowbray, Duke of Norfolk — Stephen Greif
Duke of Aumerle — Terence Wilton
Bishop of Carlisle — Andrew Crawford
Henry Percy — Myles Reithermann
Bushy — Colin Fisher
Bagot — Luke Hardy
Green/Abbot of Westminster — Peter Bourne
Earl of Salisbury — Richard Morant
Lord Ross — David Calder
Lord Willoughby — Michael Spice
Sir Pierce of Exton — James Laurenson
Queen — Lucy Fleming
Duchess of Gloucester — Charmian Eyre
Duchess of York — Peggy Thorpe-Bates, Charmian Eyre*
Other parts played by Jeremy Nicholas, Michael Godfrey, David Nicholas, Nicolas Olivier, John Cording, Nigel Crewe, Nigel Havers, Michael Howarth, William Smith
Director — Richard Cottrell
Designer — Tim Goodchild
Lighting — John B. Read

SCOTTISH ACTORS' COMPANY
25-30 Aug. 19.15 27, 30 Aug. 14.15
Lyceum Theatre
THE WILD DUCK Ibsen
(Eng. Translated by Michael Meyer)
Haakon Werle — Robin Bailey
Gregers Werle — Brian Cox
Old Ekdal — Callum Mill
Hjalmar Ekdal — Leonard Maguire
Gina Ekdal — Una McLean
Hedvig — Anna Calder-Marshall
Mrs Soerby — Helen Dorward
Relling — David Burke
Molvik/Petterson — Roy Hanlon
Graaberg — Hamish Roughhead
Jensen — Phil McCall
Pale gentleman — Brown Derby
Balding gentleman — Alastair Hunter
Short-sighted gentleman — Bryden Murdoch
Others — Derek Anders, Edmund Sulley, Jimmy Gavigan
Waiters — Michael Bruce, Ian McDiarmid
Director — Fulton Mackay
Designer — Sally Hulke
Lighting — André Tammes
Music — David Dorward

BRIDGE PRODUCTIONS LTD
1-6 Sep. 19.15 3, 6 Sep. 14.15
Lyceum Theatre
ZOO, ZOO, WIDDERSHINS ZOO Laffan
Mave — Lynn Redgrave
Chris — Gordon Waller
Minnie — Sandra Caron
Bill — Nicky Henson
Ray — Richard Warwick
Milton — Larry Aubrey
Janet — Yvonne Antrobus
Director — Frank Dunlop
Designer — Tom Lingwood
Lighting — John de Lannoy

NOTTINGHAM PLAYHOUSE
8-10 Sep. 19.15 10 Sep. 14.15
Lyceum Theatre
THE HERO RISES UP Arden *and* D'Arcy
Nelson — Robin Parkinson
Sir William Hamilton — David Dodimead
Admiral Lord Keith/Prince/Parker — Peter Whitbread
St Vincent Caracciolo — Bruce Myles
Hardy/Allen — Donald Gee
King of Naples/Clergyman — Bruce Purchase
Nisbett — Trevor Smith
Cardinal/Old relative — Francis Thomas
Bosun — Nicholas Clay
Host/Blackwood — John Manford
Lady Emma Hamilton — Thelma Ruby
Lady Nelson — Kathleen Michael
Mrs Cadogan — Anna Wing
Queen of Naples — Penelope Wilton
Director — Bill Hays
Scenery — Patrick Robertson
Costumes — Rosemary Vercoe
Lighting — Michael Outhwaite

11-13 Sep. 19.15 13 Sep. 14.15
Lyceum Theatre
WIDOWERS' HOUSES Shaw

Cokane	Frank Middlemass
Trench	Robin Ellis
Sartorius	Anthony Newlands
Blanche	Nicola Pagett
Porter	Francis Thomas
Waiter	Nicholas Clay
Lickcheese	Larry Noble
Maid	Penelope Wilton
Director	Michael Blakemore
Designer	John Elvery
Lighting	Michael Outhwaite

THEATRE ON THE BALUSTRADE, Prague
25, 26, 30 Aug. 20.00 30 Aug. 14.30
Church Hill Theatre
THE FOOLS Fialka

27, 28, 29 Aug. 20.00 28 Aug. 14.30
Church Hill Theatre
THE BUTTON Fialka
Actors Ludmila Kovářová, Zdenka Kratochvílová, Jana Pešková, Olga Przygrodská, Božena Věchetová, Josef Fajta. Jiří Kaftan, Ivan Lukeš, Richard Weber, Ladislav Fialka

Director	Ladislav Fialka
Scenery	Boris Soukup
Costumes	Mirka Kovářová
Masks	Rudolf Hammer

STABLES THEATRE COMPANY, Manchester
1-6 Sep. 20.00 4, 6 Sep. 14.30
Church Hill Theatre
WOULD YOU LOOK AT THEM SMASHING ALL THOSE LOVELY WINDOWS! Wright
Company Katherine Barker, Carla Challenor, Sam Dastor, John Fraser, Zoë Hicks, Richard Howard, Maureen Pryor, John Shrapnel, William Simons, Brian Smith, André van Gyseghem, Paul Williamson, Richard Wilson

Director	Barry Davis
Designer	Jo Provan
Lighting	Ivor Dykes

CENTRAL PUPPET THEATRE, Sofia
8, 9,12,13 Sep. 20.00 Church Hill Theatre
PRINCE MARCO Theofilov

Narrator	Bryan Stanyon
Directors	Ivan Theofilov, Ivan Tsonev
Designer	Ivan Tsonev

10-12 Sep. 17.15 Church Hill Theatre
PINOCCHIO Collodi

Director	Liliana Docheva
Designer	Ivan Tsonev

10, 11 Sep. 20.00 13 Sep. 14.30
Church Hill Theatre
THE MISANTHROPE after Molière

Director	Liuben Grois
Designer	Ivan Tsonev

with the voices of John Rye, David Spenser, Jonathan Scott, Shirley Dixon, Sheila Grant, Elizabeth Morgan, Fraser Kerr, Leslie Heritage

POETRY AND PROSE RECITALS

27-29 Aug. 15.00 St Cecilia's Hall
DAME SYBIL THORNDIKE (rdr)
A personal anthology and reminiscences of Ellen Terry
Arranged by John Carroll

1-6 Sep. 15.00 St Cecilia's Hall
WENDY HILLER, ROBERT HARDY (rdr)
The letters and poety of Elizabeth Barrett and Robert Browning

LATE NIGHT ENTERTAINMENT

2-6 Sep. 22.45 Lyceum Theatre
CABARET RIVE GAUCHE, Paris
Béatrice Arnac, Bernard Haller, Jacques Marchaix, Michel Villard, Paul Villaz

EXHIBITIONS

Merchant's Hall
ITALIAN SIXTEENTH CENTURY DRAWINGS FROM BRITISH PRIVATE COLLECTIONS

Scottish National Gallery of Modern Art
CONTEMPORARY POLISH ART

Royal Incorporation of Architects
JACK COIA

Royal Scottish Museum
POMP

1970

OPERA

FRANKFURT OPERA
24, 26 Aug. 19.30 King's Theatre
THE FIERY ANGEL Prokofiev

Renata	Anja Silja
Ruprecht	Rudolf Constantin
Innkeeper	Rosl Zapf
Potboy	Vladimir de Kanel
Fortune teller	Sona Cervena
Jakob Glock	Alfred Vökt
Agrippa von Nettesheim	Willy Müller
Count Heinrich von Otterheim	Stephan Mettin
Servant	Armin Maeder
Doctor	Kurt Wolinski
Mathias	Edwin Feldmann
Abbess	Agnes Baltsa
Inquisitor	Dieter Weller
Nuns	Marlise Wendels, Ena Lewgowd
Conductor	Christoph von Dohnányi
Director	Václav Kašlík
Scenery	Josef Svoboda
Costumes	Jan Skalicky

SCOTTISH OPERA
25, 27, 29 Aug. 19.30 King's Theatre
ELEGY FOR YOUNG LOVERS Henze

Hilda Mack	Catherine Gayer
Elisabeth Zimmer	Jill Gomez
Carolina	Sona Cervena
Toni Reischmann	David Hillman
Dr Reischmann	Lawrence Richard
Gregor Mittenhofer	John Shirley-Quirk
Josef Mauer	John Graham
Conductor	Alexander Gibson
Director	Hans Werner Henze
Scenery	Ralph Koltai
Costumes	Fausto Moroni

PRAGUE NATIONAL THEATRE
31 Aug. 4, 11 Sep. 19.30 King's Theatre
THE BARTERED BRIDE Smetana

Marenka	Daniela Šounová
	Marcela Machotková
Jeník	Ivo Žídek
Vašek	Milan Karpíšek
	Oldřich Lindauer
Kecal	Eduard Haken
Krušina	Jindrich Jindřák
Ludmila	Štěpánka Jelínková
Micha	Zdeněk Otava
Háta	Jaroslava Procházková
Circus master	Rudolf Vonásek
Esmeralda	Nada Šormová
Red Indian	Otakar Havránek
	Jan Hadraba
Conductor	Jaroslav Krombholc
Director	Luděk Mandaus
Designer	Karel Svolinský

1, 7, 12 Sep. 19.30 King's Theatre
DALIBOR Smetana

Dalibor	Ivo Žídek
	Vilém Přibyl
Milada	Naděžda Kniplová
	Alena Miková
Jitka	Eva Zikmundová
	Helena Tattermuschová
Vítek	Viktor Kočí
Budivoy	Rudolf Jedlička
Benes	Jaroslav Horáček
	Eduard Haken
Vladislav	Jindřich Jindrák
Judge	Dalibor Jedlička
	Jaroslav Horáček
Conductor	Jaroslav Krombholc
Director	Václav Kašlík
Scenery	Josef Svoboda
Costumes	Jarmila Konečná

2, 10 Sep. 19.30 King's Theatre
THE CUNNING LITTLE VIXEN Janáček

Vixen	Helena Tattermuschová
Fox	Eva Zikmundová
Forester	Jindrich Jindrák
His wife/Owl	Jaroslava Procházková
Schoolmaster/Gnat	Jan Hlavsa
Vicar/Badger	Dalibor Jedlička
Harasta	Josef Heriban
Pásek	Rudolf Vonásek
Pásková/Woodpecker	Jaroslava Dobrá
Lapák	Eva Hlobilová
Cock/Jay	Marcela Machotková
Hen	Štěpánka Jelínková
Frantík	Věra Starková
Pepík	Ludmila Erbenová
Conductor	Bohumil Gregor
Director	Ladislav Štros
Scenery	Vladimír Nývlt
Costumes	Marcel Pokorný

3, 8 Sep. 19.30 King's Theatre
THE MAKROPOULOS AFFAIR Janáček

Emilia Marty	Naděžda Kniplová
Albert Gregor	Ivo Žídek
	Jan Hlavsa
Jaroslav Prus	Rudolf Jedlička
Janek	Viktor Kočí
Kolenatý	Karel Berman
Vítek	Rudolf Vonásek
Kristina	Helena Tattermuschová
Hauk/Sendorf	Milan Karpíšek
Charwoman	Jaroslava Procházková
Stagehand	Jiří Joran
Chamber maid	Eva Hlobilová
Conductor	Bohumil Gregor
Director	Václav Kašlík
Scenery	Josef Svoboda
Costumes	Jindřiška Hirschová

5, 9 Sep. 19.30 King's Theatre
THE EXCURSIONS OF MR BROUCEK Janáček

Broucek	Beno Blachut

Málinka/Etherea/Kunka
Helena Tattermuschová
Mazal/Azurean/Petrík Ivo Žídek
Sacristan/Lunobor/Domsík
Dalibor Jedlička
Würfl/Wonderglitter Karel Berman
Waiter/Child prodigy/Pupil
Marcela Lemariová
Housekeeper/Kedruta
Jaroslava Procházková
Cloudy/Vasek/Rainbowglory/Miroslav
Milan Karpíšek
Harper/Vojta Rudolf Vonásek
Svatopluk Cech Zdeněk Otava
1st Taborite Jaroslav Horáček, Jiří Schiller
2nd Taborite
Rudolf Vonásek, Lubomir Havlák
Conductor Jaroslav Krombholc
Designer Oldřich Šimáček
Director Hanuš Thein
Costumes Jan Skalický

ORCHESTRAL CONCERTS

NEW PHILHARMONIA ORCHESTRA
23 Aug. 19.30 *Usher Hall*
Beethoven Symphony no.1 in C, op.21
Beethoven Symphony no.9 in D minor (Choral), op.125
Conductor Colin Davis
Soloists Heather Harper (sop), Janet Baker (mez), Ronald Dowd (ten), Raimund Herincx (bar), EF Chorus

24 Aug. 20.00 *Usher Hall*
Goehr Symphony in one movement, op.29
Wagner Wesendonck Lieder
Dvořák Symphony no.8 in G, op.88
Conductor Edward Downes
Soloist Helga Dernesch (sop)

27 Aug. 20.00 *Usher Hall*
Beethoven Mass in D (Missa solemnis), op.123
Conductor Carlo Maria Giulini
Soloists Heather Harper (sop), Janet Baker (mez), Placido Domingo (ten), Robert El Hage (bs), EF Chorus

28 Aug. 20.00 *Usher Hall*
Mozart Symphony no.35 in D (Haffner), K385
Goehr Concerto for violin, op.13
Schumann Symphony no.4 in D minor, op.120
Conductor Daniel Barenboim
Soloist Ruggiero Ricci (vn)

BBC SYMPHONY ORCHESTRA
30 Aug. 20.00 *Usher Hall*
Stravinsky Agon
Beethoven Concerto for piano no.3 in C minor, op.37
Elgar Falstaff
Conductor Colin Davis
Soloist Radu Lupu (pf)

ACADEMY OF ST MARTIN-IN-THE-FIELDS
Conductor Neville Marriner
31 Aug. 20.00 *Usher Hall*
Mendelssohn Symphony for strings no.10 in B minor (Spring)
J.C. Bach Concerto for oboe in F
Rossini Sonata for strings no.3 in C
Webern Five pieces, op.5
Mozart Concerto for piano no.14 in E flat, K449
Mozart Divertimento (Salzburg symphony) no.1 in D, K136
Soloists Heinz Holliger (ob), Peter Frankl (pf)

2 Sep. 20.00 *Usher Hall*
Bach Suite no.2 in B minor
Bach Musikalisches Opfer: Ricercar à 6
Bach Cantata no.158
Bach Concerto for oboe in F
Bach Cantata no.56
Soloists Dietrich Fischer-Dieskau (bar), Heinz Holliger (ob), Karlheinz Zöller (fl), Members of the BBC Scottish Choral Society

SCOTTISH NATIONAL ORCHESTRA
1 Sep. 20.00 *Usher Hall*
Mozart Sonata for organ and orchestra no.14 in C, K278
Mozart Sonata for organ and orchestra no.16 in C, K329
Mozart Sonata for organ and orchestra no.17 in C, K336
Mozart Sinfonia concertante for violin and viola, K364
Henze Symphony no.6
Conductor Hans Werner Henze
Soloists Norbert Brainin (vn), Peter Schidlof (va), Peter Williams (org)

8 Sep. 22.30 *Gateway Theatre*
Henze Essay on pigs
Brouwer Exaedros for 6 instruments and their multiples
Conductors Hans Werner Henze, Leo Brouwer
Soloists William Pearson (bar), Stomu Yamash'ta (perc)

12 Sep. 19.30 *Usher Hall*
Beethoven Concerto for piano no.5 in E flat (Emperor), op.73
Beethoven Symphony no.2 in D, op.36
Beethoven Fantasia for piano, chorus and orchestra, op.80
Conductor Alexander Gibson
Soloist Clifford Curzon (pf)
EF Chorus

STOCKHOLM PHILHARMONIC ORCHESTRA
Conductor Antal Dorati
3 Sep. 20.00 *Usher Hall*
Blomdahl Sisyphus
Beethoven Concerto for piano no.2 in B flat, op.19
Sibelius Symphony no.2 in D, op.43
Soloist
Stephen Bishop-Kovacevich (pf)

5 Sep. 20.00 *Usher Hall*
Dvořák Requiem mass
Soloists Elisabeth Söderström (sop), Birgit Finnilä (mez), Sven Olof Eliasson (ten), Arne Tyrén (bs), Stockholm Philharmonic Choir

LONDON PHILHARMONIC ORCHESTRA
Conductor Carlo Maria Giulini
4 Sep. 20.00 *Usher Hall*
Haydn Symphony no.99 in E flat
Mahler Kindertotenlieder
Schumann Symphony no.3 (Rhenish), op.97
Soloist Dietrich Fischer-Dieskau (bar)

6 Sep. 20.00 *Usher Hall*
Beethoven Egmont: Overture
Beethoven Concerto for piano no.4 in G, op.58
Beethoven Symphony no.7 in A, op.92
Soloist Clifford Curzon (pf)

CONCERTGEBOUW ORCHESTRA, Amsterdam
7 Sep. 20.00 *Usher Hall*
Berlioz Benvenuto Cellini: Overture
Van Delden Musica sinfonica, op.93
Mahler Das Lied von der Erde
Conductor Bernard Haitink
Soloists Janet Baker (mez), Vilém Přibyl (ten)

9 Sep. 20.00 *Usher Hall*
Beethoven Leonore: Overture no.3
Beethoven Concerto for piano no.1 in C, op.15
Beethoven Symphony no.5 in C minor, op.67
Conductor Eugen Jochum
Soloist Alfred Brendel (pf)

10 Sep. 20.00 *Usher Hall*
Mozart Concerto for piano no.18 in B flat, K456
Bruckner Symphony no.8 in C minor
Conductor Bernard Haitink
Soloist Geza Anda (pf)

BBC SCOTTISH SYMPHONY ORCHESTRA
8 Sep. 20.00 *Usher Hall*
Musgrave Memento vitae
Dvořák Concerto for violin in A minor, op.53
Shostakovich Symphony no.5 in D minor, op.47
Conductor James Loughran
Soloist Josef Suk (vn)

CHAMBER CONCERTS

AMADEUS QUARTET
Beethoven String Quartets
24 Aug. 11.00 *Leith Town Hall*
Nos. 1 in F; 2 in G; 15 in A minor

26 Aug. 11.00 *Leith Town Hall*
Nos. 3 in D; 10 in E flat; 13 in B flat

28 Aug. 11.00 *Leith Town Hall*
Nos. 7 in F; 12 in E flat

1 Sep. 11.00 *Leith Town Hall*
Nos. 4 in C minor; 11 in F minor
14 in C sharp minor

3 Sep. 11.00 *Leith Town Hall*
Nos. 5 in A; 8 in E minor
Grosse Fuge in B flat, op.133

7 Sep. 11.00 *Leith Town Hall*
Nos. 6 in B flat; 9 in C; 16 in F

MADELEINE RENAUD, JEAN-LOUIS BARRAULT, NEW YORK CHAMBER SOLOISTS
4 Sep. 11.00 *Assembly Hall*
Words and music from the court of the Sun-King, Louis XIV

5 Sep. 11.00 *Assembly Hall*
Poesie amoureuse

EDINBURGH QUARTET
9 Sep. 11.00 *Freemasons' Hall*
Haydn Quartet in G, op.76/1
Gal Quartet no.3 (World première)
Dvořák Quartet no.10 in E flat, op.51

NETHERLANDS WIND ENSEMBLE
11 Sep. 11.00 *Freemasons' Hall*
Gounod Petite symphonie
Janáček Mládi
Beethoven Rondino in E flat
Mozart Serenade no.12 in C minor, K388

PURCELL CONSORT OF VOICES
8 Sep. 11.00 *Freemasons' Hall*

English madrigals by Monteverdi, Vecchi, Gesualdo, East, Weelkes, Tomkins. French chansons by Poulenc, D'Indy, Auric. English part songs by Crosse, Burgon, Hames

WILLIAM PEARSON (bar), LEO BROUWER (gtr), STOMU YAMASH'TA (perc), KARLHEINZ ZÖLLER (fl)
8 Sep. 22.30 *Gateway Theatre*
Henze El Cimarrón

RECITALS

DIETRICH FISCHER-DIESKAU (bar)
DANIEL BARENBOIM (pf)
29 Aug. 20.00 *Usher Hall*
Songs by Beethoven including
Six Gellert Lieder
An die ferne Geliebte

EVA BERNÁTHOVÁ (pf)
27 Aug. 11.00 *Freemasons' Hall*
Beethoven Sonata no.30 in E, op.109
Janáček Sonata 1 X 1905
Kabeláč Eight preludes, op.30
Liszt Sonata in B minor

RADU LUPU
2 Sep. 11.00 *Freemasons' Hall*
Beethoven Sonata no.19 in G minor, op.49/1
Beethoven Sonata no.21 in C (Waldstein), op.53
Schubert Sonata no.18 in G, D894

CLIFFORD CURZON (pf)
11 Sep. 20.00 *Usher Hall*
Schumann Fantasia in C, op.17
Beethoven Variations and fugue on an original theme (Eroica)
Schubert Sonata no.21 in B flat, D960

ALFRED BRENDEL (pf)
12 Sep. 11.00 *Leith Town Hall*
Beethoven Bagatelles nos.19-24, op.126
Beethoven Sonata no.5 in C minor, op.10/1
Beethoven Sonata no.29 in B flat (Hammerklavier), op.106

RUGGIERO RICCI (vn)
31 Aug. 11.00 *Freemasons' Hall*
Bach Partita no.3 in E
Bartók Sonata
Hindemith Sonata, op.31/2
Ysaÿe Sonata no.3 in D minor, op.27/3
Paganini Introduction and variations on 'Nel cor piu non mi sento' (Paisiello)

GYÖRGY PAUK (vn)
PETER FRANKL (pf)
25 Aug. 11.00 *Freemasons' Hall*
Beethoven Sonata no.6 in A, op.30 /1
Bartók Sonata no.2
Beethoven Sonata no.7 in C minor, op.30/2

JOSEF SUK (vn)
STEPHEN BISHOP-KOVACEVICH (pf)
10 Sep. 11.00 *Freemasons' Hall*
Beethoven Sonata no.1 in D, op.12/1
Janáček Sonata
Beethoven Sonata no.10 in G, op.96

JACQUELINE DU PRÉ (vc)
DANIEL BARENBOIM (pf)
25 Aug. 20.00 *Usher Hall*
Beethoven Sonata no.1 in F, op.5/1
Beethoven Sonata no.4 in C, op.102/1
Beethoven Variations on 'See the conquering hero comes' (Handel)
Beethoven Sonata no.3 in A, op.69

26 Aug. 20.00 *Usher Hall*
Beethoven Sonata no.2 in G minor, op.5/2
Beethoven Variations on 'Ein Mädchen oder Weibchen' (Mozart)
Beethoven Variations on 'Bei Männern' (Mozart)
Beethoven Sonata no.5 in D, op.102/2

HEINZ HOLLIGER (ob)
CHRISTIANE JACCOTTET (hpd)
NORMAN JONES (vc)
29 Aug. 11.00 *Freemasons' Hall*
F. Couperin Concerto no.5 from Les goûts réünis
Rameau Harpsichord works
Babell Sonata for oboe and continuo in C minor, op.1/2
Handel Sonata for oboe and continuo in G minor, op.1/6
Berio Sequenza VII for oboe
Stockhausen Spiral fo oboe

DRAMA

PROSPECT THEATRE COMPANY
24-26 Aug. 1, 4, 5, 8, 9, 12 Sep. 19.30
1, 5, 8, 12 Sep. 14.30 *Assembly Hall*
MUCH ADO ABOUT NOTHING
Shakespeare
Beatrice Sylvia Syms
Benedick John Neville
Hero Barbara Ewing
Claudio John Castle
Don Pedro Timothy West
Leonato John Byron
Young officer James Faulkner
Friar Francis Henry Moxon
Don John Julian Glover
Borachio Peter Clay
Conrade Paul Stender
Antonio John Rogan
Balthazar Tim Piggott-Smith
Margaret Pamela Miles
Ursula Carol Gillies
Dogberry Bryan Pringle
Verges Clifford Rose
Director Toby Robertson
Designer Robin Archer
Lighting John B. Read
Music Alexander Faris

27, 28, 29, 31 Aug. 2, 3, 7, 10, 11 Sep. 14.30 29 Aug. 14.30 *Assembly Hall*
BOSWELL'S LIFE OF JOHNSON Dufton *and* Thorne (World première)
Dr Johnson Timothy West
James Boswell Julian Glover
David Garrick John Neville
Dr Oliver Goldsmith Clifford Rose
Sir John Hawkins Bryan Pringle
Hassan/Richard Savage Peter Clay
King George III/Lord Chesterfield John Byron
Frank Barber George Baizley
Hester Thrale Sylvia Syms
Fanny Burney Barbara Ewing
Mrs Pritchard/Miss Anna Seward Wynne Clark
Tom Davies/Lord Auchinleck Henry Moxon
Joseph Joseph Charles
Henry Thrale John Byron
Lady of the town/Confidante Carol Gillies
Mr Paton John Rogan
Sir Thomas Robinson Paul Stender
Louisa Lewis Pamela Miles
Director Toby Robertson
Designer Robin Archer
Lighting John B. Read

DEUTSCHES THEATER, Berlin
24, 26, 28, 29 Aug. 19.15 Lyceum Theatre
PEACE Aristophanes
(Ger. Adapted by Peter Hacks)
Trygaios Fred Düren
His daughters
Mathilde Danegger, Trude Bechmann
Slaves Johannes Maus, Peter Dommisch
Hermes Klaus Piontek
War Rudolph Christoph
Tumult Kaspar Eichel
Helmet maker Lothar Förster
Arms dealers
Adolf-Peter Hoffman, Hans Lucke
Hierokles Dietrich Körner
Harvest Home Elsa Grube-Deister
Spring's Delight Brigitte Soubeyran
Peace Johanna Clas
Chorus leader Reimar Joh. Baur
Papa Binnes Jazzband
Director Benno Besson
Designer Heinrich Kilger
Music André Asriel

ROYAL SHAKESPEARE COMPANY
25, 27 Aug. 19.15 *Lyceum Theatre*
PLEASURE AND REPENTANCE
Devised and directed by Terry Hands
Janet Suzman, Barrie Ingham, Brewster Mason, Richard Pasco

ROYAL LYCEUM THEATRE COMPANY
7, 8, 11 Sep. 19.15 12 Sep. 14.15
Lyceum Theatre
RANDOM HAPPENINGS IN THE HEBRIDES McGrath
Jimmy John Thaw
Aeny Joseph Greig
John James John Cairney
Catriona Elizabeth MacLennan
Irishwoman Zoë Hicks
Andy Brown Derby
Calum John Shedden
Mary Maggie Jordan
Pauline Moreen Scott
Macalaster Bill McCabe
Tom Bryden Murdoch
Peter Fraser Michael Harrigan
Macdonald Jimmy Gavigan
Donaldson Matt McGinn
Macbeth Arthur Cox
Fishermen Iain Agnew, Dennis Lawson, Ian Ireland
Doctor Martin Heller
Mrs Macdonald Sheila Latimer
Teresa Sandra Buchan
Rachel Kate Binchy
Mr Macdonald Kevin Collins
Andy's wife May Henry
Director Richard Eyre
Scenery John Gunter
Costumes Lorraine McKee
Lighting Andy Phillips

9, 10, 12 Sep. 19.15 10 Sep. 14.15
Lyceum Theatre
THE CHANGELING Middleton *and* Rowley
Beatrice-Joanna Anna Calder-Marshall
Vermandero Brown Derby
Tomazo de Piracquo Frank Moorey
Alonzo de Piracquo Bryan Stanyon
Alsemero Arthur Cox
Jasperino Tom Watson
Alibius Martin Heller
Lollio Joseph Greig
Pedro Michael Harrigan
Antonio Roland Curram
Franciscus John Shedden
De Flores David Burke
Diaphanta Cleo Sylvestre
Isabella Kate Binchy
Director Richard Eyre

Designer John Gunter
Lighting Andy Phillips
Music Adrian Secchi

TEATRO LIBERO, Rome
1-5 Sep. 20.15 *Haymarket Ice Rink*
ORLANDO FURIOSO Ariosto
(Adapted by Eduardo Sanguineti)
Dorotea Aslanidis, Piero Baldini, Rodolfo Baldini, Gianfranco Barra, Marco Berneck, Giovanni Bignamini, Elettra Bisetti, Liú Bosisio, Gaetano Campisi, Francesco Censi, Vittorio di Bisogno, Luigi Diberti, Antonio Fattorini, Giorgio Favretto, Massimo Foschi, Marco Galletti, Paola Gassman, Cesare Gelli, Graziano Giusti, Maria Grazia Grassini, Giorgio Maich, Paolo Malco, Marzio Margine, Loredana Martinez, Mariangela Melato, Aldo Miranda, Carlo Montagna, Sergio Nicolai, Anna Nogara, Giancarlo Prati, Armando Pugliese, Aldo Puglisi, Anna Rossini, Rosabianca Scerrino, Paola Tanziani, Gabriele Tozzi, Barbara Valmorin, Renata Zamengo
Director Luca Ronconi
Scenery Uberto Bertacca
Costumes Elena Mannini

THE COMBINE, USA
24-29 Aug. 7-12 Sep. 22.30
Haymarket Ice Rink
STOMP
George Barnes, Joey Ely, Bruce Gambill, Milton Gambill, Linda Gamble, Steven Garfinkel, Elisabeth Herring, Deborah Kramer, Rena Porter, Nicholas Rawson, Dave Ringland, Jo Ann Schatz, Patrick Shanley (act), Robert Bachman, Ronnie MacKey, Rickey Lansford, Joe Mulherin (mus)

LEEDS PLAYHOUSE
7-12 Sep. 19.45 9, 12 Sep. 14.30
Church Hill Theatre
HENRY IV Pirandello
(Eng. Translated by John Wardle)
Henry IV Alfred Burke
Donna Matilde Kathleen Michael
Frida Susan Macready
Marquess Carlo di Nolli Nigel Terry
Baron Tito Belcredi Timothy Bateson
Doctor Dionisio Genoni Jerome Willis
Landolf (Lolo) Harry Meacher
Harold (Franco) Andrew Dallmeyer
Ordulf (Momo) John Nightingale
Bertold (Fino) Tony Robinson
Giovanni James Garbutt
Menservants
Gareth Armstrong, Kenneth Shaw
Director Bill Hays
Scenery Brian Currah
Costumes Andrew Gagg

PRODUCTIONS D'AUJOURD'HUI, Paris
25-27 Aug. 22.30 *Gateway Theatre*
INÉDITS Ionesco
Anne Alexandre, Suzy Hannier, Michel Paulin, Jean Rougerie, André Chaumeau
Director Jean Rougerie

POETRY AND PROSE RECITALS

27-29 Aug. 15.00 *St Cecilia's Hall*
MARY STUART, QUEEN OF SCOTS
Letters, prose, poetry and music
Vivien Merchant, John Westbrook (rdr), Robert Spencer (ten and lute)
Devised by John Carroll

31 Aug.-3 Sep. 15.00 *St Cecilia's Hall*
ELIZABETH TUDOR, QUEEN OF ENGLAND
Letters, prose, poetry and music
Dame Flora Robson, John Westbrook (rdr),
Robert Spencer (ten and lute)
Devised by John Carroll

DANCE

NETHERLANDS DANCE THEATRE
31 Aug.-3 Sep. 19.15 2 Sep. 14.15
Lyceum Theatre
SQUARES
Choreographer Hans van Manen
Music Zoltan Szilassy
Designer Bonies
FIVE SKETCHES
Choreographer Hans van Manen
Music Hindemith
Designer Jan van der Wal
NOUVELLES AVENTURES
Choreographer Jaap Flier
Music Ligeti
Designer Jan van der Wal
IMAGINARY FILM
Choreographer Glen Tetley
Music Schoenberg
Designer Nadine Baylis

4, 5 Sep. 19.15 5 Sep. 14.15
Lyceum Theatre
SITUATION
Choreographer Hans van Manen
Designer Jean-Paul Vroom
Lighting Oliver Wood
SOLO FOR VOICE 1
Choreographer Hans van Manen
Music Cage
Costumes Jan van der Wal
BRANDENBURG
Choreographer Charles Czarny
Music Bach
Costumes Joop Stokvis
MYTHICAL HUNTERS
Choreographer Glen Tetley
Music Oedoen Partos
Costumes Anthony Binstead
Dancers Arlette van Boven, Kathy Gosschalk, Kerstin Lidstrom, Marian Sarstadt, Mea Venema, Jaap Flier, Hans Knill, Gerard Lemaitre, Jan Nuyts, Moira Bosman, Anja Licher, Conny Lodewijk, Rita Poelvoorde, Anne van Tol, Carina Verzijl, Yteke Waterbolk, Lenny Westerdijk, Jon Benoit, Nils Christe, David Gordon, Leon Koning, Johan Meyer, Hormen Tromp, Frans Vervenne, Rob van Woerkom
Conductor Jan Stulen

EXHIBITIONS

Royal Scottish Academy
EARLY CELTIC ART
Director Prof. Stuart Piggott
(In association with the Arts Council of Great Britain)

College of Art
CONTEMPORARY GERMAN ART FROM DÜSSELDORF
Director Karl Ruhrberg
(In association with the City of Düsseldorf, Goethe Institute and the Scottish Arts Council)

1971

OPERA

EDINBURGH FESTIVAL OPERA
23, 25, 27 Aug. 7, 9 Sep. 19.30
King's Theatre
LA CENERENTOLA Rossini
Angelina Teresa Berganza
Don Ramiro Luigi Alva
Dandini Renato Capecchi
Don Magnifico Paolo Montarsolo
Clorinda Eugenia Ratti
Margherita Guglielmi
Tisbe Laura Zannini
Alidoro Ugo Trama
London Symphony Orchestra
Scottish Opera Chorus
Conductor Claudio Abbado
Director and designer
Jean-Pierre Ponnelle
(In association with Maggio Musicale, Florence)

SCOTTISH OPERA
26, 28, 31 Aug. 18.00 *King's Theatre*
DIE WALKÜRE Wagner
Brünnhilde Helga Dernesch
Wotan David Ward
Siegmund Charles Craig
Sieglinde Leonore Kirschstein
Hunding William McCue
Fricka Anna Reynolds
Gerhilde Heather Howson
Ortlinde Nancy Gottschalk
Waltraute Patricia Purcell
Schwertleite Johanna Peters
Helmwige Patricia Hay
Siegrune Phyllis Cannan
Grimgerde Joan Clarkson
Rossweise Claire Livingstone
Scottish National Orchestra
Conductor Alexander Gibson
Director Peter Ebert
Designer Michael Knight
Lighting Charles Bristow

DEUTSCHE OPER, Berlin
30 Aug. 1, 3 Sep. 19.30 *King's Theatre*
DIE ENTFÜHRUNG AUS DEM SERAIL
Mozart
Belmonte Werner Hollweg
Constanze Erika Köth
Bella Jasper*
Blonde Carole Malone
Pedrillo Martin Vantin
Osmin Bengt Rundgren
Josef Greindl
Bassa Selim Walter Dicks
Conductor Heinrich Hollreiser
Director Gustav Rudolf Sellner
Designer Wilhelm Reinking

2, 4 Sep. 19.30 *King's Theatre*
MELUSINE Reimann
Melusine Catherine Gayer
Pythia Martha Mödl
Madame Lapérouse Gitta Mikes
Oleander Donald Grobe
Count von Lusignan Barry McDaniel
Surveyor Ivan Sardi
Mason Klaus Lang
Architect Loren Driscoll
Oger Josef Greindl
Foreman Thomas Brennicke
Worker Lothar Wehrle
Secretary Walter Dicks
Conductor Reinhard Peters
Director Gustav Rudolf Sellner
Designer Gottfried Pilz

MUSIC THEATRE ENSEMBLE
1 Sep. 22.45 *Gateway Theatre*
Goehr Triptych (Naboth's vineyard, Shadowplay-2, Sonata about Jerusalem)
Purcell Fantasy for strings; arr. Goehr, in memory of Annon Lee Silver

2 Sep. 22.45 *Gateway Theatre*
Babbitt Philomel
Ligeti Aventures et nouvelles aventures+
Daiken Mayakovsky and the sun (EIF commission)

3 Sep. 22.45 *Gateway Theatre*
Ligeti Aventures et nouvelles aventures+
Goehr Triptych: Shadowplay-2
Daiken Mayakovsky and the sun
Jane Manning, Hazel Holt (sop), Margaret Lensky (mez), Philip Langridge (ten), Michael Rippon (bs), Richard Dennis, Mark Furneaux, John Trigger (act)
Conductors
Alexander Goehr, Elgar Howarth+
Director John Cox
Designer Bernard Culshaw

ORCHESTRAL CONCERTS

SCOTTISH NATIONAL ORCHESTRA
21 Aug. 19.30 *Usher Hall*
Britten *arr.* National anthem
Wilson Te deum (EIF commission)
Beethoven Concerto for violin in D, op.61
Walton Belshazzar's feast
Conductor Alexander Gibson
Soloists Sir Yehudi Menuhin (vn), John Shirley-Quirk (bar), EF Chorus

22 Aug. 19.30 *Usher Hall*
Stravinsky Ave Maria
Stravinsky Pater noster
Wilson Te deum (EIF commission)
Elgar Concerto for violin in B minor, op.61
Walton Belshazzar's feast
Conductor Alexander Gibson
Soloists Sir Yehudi Menuhin (vn), John Shirley-Quirk (bar), EF Chorus

11 Sep. 19.30 *Usher Hall*
Berio Bewegung (Definitive version - World première)
Berio Sinfonia
Stravinsky Ode
Janáček Sinfonietta
Conductors
Alexander Gibson, Luciano Berio
Swingle Singers

LONDON PHILHARMONIC ORCHESTRA
23 Aug. 20.00 *Usher Hall*
Mussorgsky A night on the Bare Mountain
Tchaikovsky Concerto for piano no.1 in B flat minor, op.23
Shostakovich Symphony no.10 in E minor, op.93
Conductor Bernard Haitink
Soloist Andre Watts (pf)

24 Aug. 20.00 *Usher Hall*
Mozart Symphony no.32 in G, K318
Verdi Otello: Piangea cantando *and* Ave Maria
Bruckner Symphony no.3 in D minor; arr. Oeser
Conductor Bernard Haitink
Soloists Victoria de los Angeles (sop), Margreta Elkins (mez)

26 Aug. 20.00 *Usher Hall*
R. Strauss Le bourgeois gentilhomme - Suite
Schumann Concerto for cello in A minor, op.129
Mozart Symphony no.41 in C (Jupiter), K551
Conductor Josef Krips
Soloist Pierre Fournier (vc)

27 Aug. 20.00 *Usher Hall*
Berg Chamber concerto
Schubert Symphony no.9 in C (Great), D944
Conductor Josef Krips
Soloists Wolfgang Schneiderhan (vn), Walter Klien (pf)

NATIONAL YOUTH ORCHESTRA OF GREAT BRITAIN
25 Aug. 20.00 *Usher Hall*
Bartók Music for strings, percussion and celesta
Berg Concerto for violin
Webern Six pieces, op.6
Debussy La mer
Conductor Pierre Boulez
Soloist Sir Yehudi Menuhin (vn)

ISRAEL PHILHARMONIC ORCHESTRA
Conductor Zubin Mehta
28 Aug. 20.00 *Usher Hall*
Maayani Qumran - symphonic metaphor
Brahms Concerto for piano no.1 in D minor, op.15
Berlioz Symphonie fantastique
Soloist Daniel Barenboim (pf)

30 Aug. 20.00 *Usher Hall*
Brahms Symphony no.3 in F, op.90
Schumann Concerto for piano in A minor, op.54
Bartók The miraculous mandarin
Soloist Daniel Barenboim (pf)

31 Aug. 20.00 *Usher Hall*
Webern Im Sommerwind
Mendelssohn Concerto for violin in E minor, op.64
Mahler Symphony no.1 in D
Soloist Pinchas Zukerman (vn)

LONDON SYMPHONY ORCHESTRA
1 Sep. 20.00 *Usher Hall*
Berlioz Rob Roy - Overture
Musgrave Concerto for clarinet
Rachmaninov Symphony no.2 in E minor, op.27
Conductor André Previn
Soloist Gervase de Peyer (cl)

2 Sep. 20.00 *Usher Hall*
Mozart Vesperae solennes de confessore: Laudate dominum
Mozart Non temer amato bene
Mahler Symphony no.2 in C minor (Resurrection)
Conductor Claudio Abbado
Soloists Margaret Price (sop), Janet Baker (mez), EF Chorus

3 Sep. 20.00 *Usher Hall*
Mendelssohn Die schöne Melusine - Overture
Brahms Concerto for violin in D, op.77
Brahms Variations on a theme by Haydn (St Antoni), op.56a
Prokofiev Romeo and Juliet - Suite
Conductor Claudio Abbado
Soloist Henryk Szeryng (vn)

8 Sep. 20.00 *Usher Hall*
Stravinsky The song of the nightingale
Beethoven Concerto for piano no.3 in C minor, op.37
R. Strauss Also sprach Zarathustra
Conductor André Previn
Soloist Michael Roll (pf)

CHICAGO SYMPHONY ORCHESTRA
4 Sep. 20.00 *Usher Hall*
Mendelssohn A midsummer night's dream: Overture
Carter Variations for orchestra
Brahms Symphony no.1 in C minor, op.68
Conductor Sir Georg Solti

5 Sep. 20.00 *Usher Hall*
Mozart Concerto for piano no.20 in D minor, K466
Mahler Symphony no.5 in C sharp minor
Conductor Sir Georg Solti
Soloist Vladimir Ashkenazy (pf)

6 Sep. 20.00 *Usher Hall*
Berlioz Roméo et Juliette: Excerpts
Mozart Symphony no.39 in E flat, K543
Stravinsky The firebird - Suite
Conductor Carlo Maria Giulini

7 Sep. 20.00 *Usher Hall*
Brahms Tragic Overture
Prokofiev Concerto for piano no.2 in G minor, op.16
Haydn Symphony no.94 in G (Surprise)
Ravel Rapsodie espagnole
Conductor Carlo Maria Giulini
Soloist Rafael Orozco (pf)

BBC SCOTTISH SYMPHONY ORCHESTRA
9 Sep. 20.00 *Usher Hall*
Bliss Meditations on a theme of John Blow
Mozart Concerto for 2 pianos in E flat, K365
Elgar Variations on an original theme (Enigma)
Conductor James Loughran
Soloists
Radu Lupu, Rafael Orozco (pf)

BBC SCOTTISH RADIO ORCHESTRA
11 Sep. 22.45 *Usher Hall*
Farewell to the 25th Festival
Conductor Iain Sutherland
Soloists Helga Dernesch (sop), Martha Schlamme (folk sngr), Ronald Morrison (bar), William McCue (bs), Alasdair Graham (pf)

CHAMBER CONCERTS

ENGLISH CONSORT OF VIOLS
24 Aug. 11.00 *Freemasons' Hall*
Works by Ferrabosco, Byrd, Bull, Campion, Johnson, Jones, Coprario, Banchieri, Segni, Trabaci, Dlugoraj, Vasquez, Purcell, Jenkins
with Martyn Hill (ten), Anthony Rooley (lute)

FINE ARTS QUARTET
26 Aug. 11.00 *Freemasons' Hall*
Haydn Quartet in C (Bird), op.33/3
Husa Quartet no.3
Ravel Quartet in F

27 Aug. 11.00 *Freemasons' Hall*
Mozart Quartet no.21 in D, K575
Bartók Quartet no.6
Mendelssohn Quartet no.2 in A minor, op.13

THE MATRIX
4 Sep. 11.00 *Freemasons' Hall*
Gabrieli Canzona
Mozart Adagio for 3 basset horns and bassoon, K410

Webern — Five canons, op.16
Webern — Three songs, op.23
Schumann — Papillons
Dalby — The keeper of the pass (EIF commission)
Coe — Improvisation on tenor sax
Birtwistle — Ring a dumb carillon
Stravinsky — Elegy for JFK
Jane Manning (sop), Alan Hacker, Tony Coe, Francis Christou (cl), Paul Crossley (pf, org), Tristan Fry (perc)

TRIO ITALIANO
8 Sep. 11.00 — *Freemasons' Hall*
Beethoven — Trio no.2 in G, op.9/1
Petrassi — Trio
Mozart — Divertimento in E flat, K563

10 Sep. 11.00 — *Freemasons' Hall*
Mozart — Duo for violin and viola in B flat, K424
Schoenberg — Trio, op.45
Beethoven — Trio no.4 in C minor, op.9/3

EARLY MUSIC CONSORT OF LONDON
9 Sep. 11.00 — *Freemasons' Hall*
Five centuries of popular music
Director — David Munrow
Soloist — James Bowman (c ten)

RECITALS

BENJAMIN LUXON (bar)
DAVID WILLISON (pf)
23 Aug. 11.00 — *Freemasons' Hall*
Schumann — Dichterliebe
Stravinsky — Pribaoutki
Dalby — Eight songs from the Chinese
Poulenc — Banalités

VICTORIA DE LOS ANGELES (sop)
MIGUEL ZANETTI (pf)
29 Aug. 15.00 — *Usher Hall*
Lorca *arr.* Canciones populares españolas
Songs by Monteverdi, Pergolesi, Marcello, Galuppi, Schumann, Debussy

MARGARET PRICE (sop)
JAMES LOCKHART (pf)
31 Aug. 11.00 — *Freemasons' Hall*
Britten — The poet's echo
Songs by Bellini, Donizetti, Verdi, Rossini, Schubert, Rachmaninov, Britten *and* Folksongs

MATTIWILDA DOBBS (sop), PETER KATIN, PETER GELLHORN (pf)
1 Sep. 11.00 — *Freemasons' Hall*
Sir Walter Scott in music and song
Works by Schubert, Liszt, F.G. Scott, Rossini, Ricci, Donizetti

TERESA BERGANZA (mez)
FELIX LAVILLA (pf)
2 Sep. 11.00 — *Leith Town Hall*
Haydn — Arianna a Naxos
Mussorgsky — The nursery
Falla — Siete canciones populares españolas
Songs by Anchieta, De la Torre, Granados, Esteve

RENATO CAPECCHI (bar)
ENZA FERRARI (pf)
10 Sep. 20.00 — *Freemasons' Hall*
'For ever' ... Italian cabaret songs

CLAUDE FRANK (pf)
25 Aug. 11.00 — *Freemasons' Hall*
Mozart — Sonata no.12 in F, K332
Martin — Eight preludes
Beethoven — Sonata no.32 in C minor, op.111

PETER WILLIAMS (hpd)
30 Aug. 15.00 — *St Cecilia's Hall*
Bach — Goldberg variations

MICHEL BLOCK (pf)
3 Sep. 11.00 — *Freemasons' Hall*
Debussy — Suite bergamasque
Barber — Sonata, op.26
Chopin — Sonata no.3 in B minor, op.58

RADU LUPU (pf)
7 Sep. 11.00 — *Leith Town Hall*
Beethoven Sonata no.14 in C sharp minor (Moonlight), op.27/2
Brahms — Rhapsodies, op.79
Schubert — Sonata no.16 in A minor, D845

MICHAEL ROLL (pf)
11 Sep. 11.00 — *Freemasons' Hall*
Bach — Concerto in the Italian style
Schumann — Kreisleriana
Liszt — Sonata in B minor

SIR YEHUDI MENUHIN (vn)
26 Aug. 17.30 — *St Cuthbert's Church*
Bach — Partita no.3 in E
Bartók — Sonata
Bach — Partita no.2 in D minor

PINCHAS ZUKERMAN (vn)
DANIEL BARENBOIM (pf)
29 Aug. 20.00 — *Usher Hall*
Mozart — Sonata no.32 in B flat, K454
Beethoven — Sonata no.10 in G, op.96
Schoenberg — Fantasia, op.47
Schumann — Sonata no.1 in A minor, op.105

WOLFGANG SCHNEIDERHAN (vn)
WALTER KLIEN (pf)
30 Aug. 11.00 — *Leith Town Hall*
Schubert — Sonata in A (Duo), D574
Prokofiev — Sonata no.2 in D, op.94a
Brahms — Sonata no.3 in D minor, op.108

PIERRE FOURNIER (vc)
JEAN FONDA (pf)
28 Aug. 11.00 — *Leith Town Hall*
Debussy — Sonata
Mendelssohn — Variations concertantes, op.17
Martinů — Sonata no.1
Brahms — Sonata no.2 in F, op.99

PETER LUKAS GRAF (fl)
JÖRG-EWALD DÄHLER (pf)
1 Sep. 15.00 — *St Cecilia's Hall*
Handel — Sonata no.1 in E minor, op.1/1
Varèse — Density 21.5 for solo flute
Bach — Sonata no.1 in B minor
Handel — Sonata no.2 in G, op1/5
Fukushima — Mei for solo flute
Bach — Sonata no.5 in E minor

HERRICK BUNNEY (org)
23, 24, 25, 26, 27, 28, 31 Aug. 1, 2, 3, 4, 7, 8, 9, 10, 11 Sep. 17.00
St Giles' Cathedral
Bach — Complete organ works

GERALD ENGLISH (ten)
BARRY TUCKWELL (hn)
MARGARET KITCHIN (pf)
6 Sep. 11.00 — *Freemasons' Hall*
Schubert — Schwanengesang: Excerpts
Beethoven — Sonata for horn and piano in F, op.17
Debussy — Proses lyriques
Schubert — Auf dem Strom, D943
Boulez — Sonata for piano no.1
Britten — Canticle no.3

RAVI SHANKAR (sitâr)
ALLA RAKHA (tabla)
KAMALA CHAKRAVARTY (tambura)
29 Aug. 19.30 — *Assembly Hall*
A recital of indian music

DRAMA

PROSPECT THEATRE COMPANY
23 Aug.-11 Sep. 19.30 (exc. Sun)
Assembly Hall
KING LEAR Shakespeare
King Lear — Timothy West
Goneril — Caroline Blakiston
Regan — Diane Fletcher
Cordelia — Fiona Walker
Edgar — John Shrapnel
Edmund — Matthew Long
Duke of Burgundy/Captain — James Snell
Duke of Cornwall — Terence Bayler
Duke of Albany — Michael Griffiths
Earl of Kent — Trevor Martin
Earl of Gloucester — John Bailey
Fool — Ronnie Stevens
King of France — Walter McMonagle
Oswald — Michael Graham Cox
Knight/Old man/Doctor — Henry Moxon
Messenger — Peter Clough
Director — Toby Robertson
Designer — Robin Archer
Lighting — Michael Outhwaite
Music — Carl Davis

YOUNG VIC
23 Aug.-1 Sep. 20.15 (exc. Sun) 27 Aug. 19.15 and 22.15 28 Aug. 2, 4, 9, 11 Sep. 14.30 — *Haymarket Ice Rink*
THE COMEDY OF ERRORS
Shakespeare
Antipholus of Edinburgh — Sam Kelly
Antipholus of London — Edward Fox
Dromio of Edinburgh — Andrew Robertson
Dromio of London — Gavin Reed
Adriana — Denise Coffey
Luciana — Alison Groves
Duke — Alex McAvoy
Aegeon — Edward Jewesbury
Balthazar/Pinch — Ian Trigger
Angelo — Paul Brooke
Aemilia — Joan Heal
Merchants
Seymour Matthews, Robert Gillespie
Gaoler — David Wynn
Luce — Julia McCarthy
Lady of the town — Joanna Wake
Nun — Barbara Courtney
Police officer — Ray Davis
Business woman — Charmian Eyre
Singer — Iain Dunn
Directors — Frank Dunlop, Peter James
Designer — Nadine Baylis
Lighting — Derek J. Brown

ROYAL LYCEUM THEATRE COMPANY
23-28 Aug. 19.15 25, 28 Aug. 14.15
Lyceum Theatre
CONFESSIONS OF A JUSTIFIED SINNER Hogg (Adapted by Ronder)
James Hogg — Russell Hunter
Colwan — Andrew Crawford
Rev. Wringham — Robert James
Mrs Colwan — June Watson
Robert Wringham — Richard Kane
Gil-Martin — Jack Shepherd
George — Jack Galloway
Miss Logan — Mairhi Russell
Bell — Clare Richards
Drummond — Colin McCormack

Woman Jean Taylor Smith
Bessy Jennifer Lee
Blanchard Brown Derby
Editor Tom Buchan
Printer/Lawyer James Kennedy
Friends/Officers
Michael Harrigan, Will Knightly
Girl Christie McKenna
Fiddlers Robin Park, Alan Ross
Director Richard Eyre
Designer David Collis
Costumes Lorraine McKee
Lighting André Tammes

BULANDRA THEATRE, Bucharest
30 Aug. 2, 3, 4 Sep. 19.15 1 Sep. 14.15
Lyceum Theatre
CARNIVAL SCENES Caragiale (Rum)
Nae Girimea Octavian Cotescu
Iancou Pompon Toma Caragiu
Machae Razachescu Marin Moraru
Supernumerary Aurel Cioranu
Iordache Stefan Banica
Florian Pittis
Didine Mazu Rodica Tapalaga
Mitza Baston Gina Patrichi
Police officer Mihai Mereuta
Director Lucian Pintilie
Scenery Liviu Ciulei, Giulio Tincu
Costumes Ovidiu Bubulac
Translation read by Brian Wallworth

31 Aug. 1 Sep. 19.15 4 Sep. 14.15
Lyceum Theatre
LEONCE AND LENA Büchner (Rum)
King Peter Marin Moraru
Prince Leonce Ion Caramitru
Princess Lena Irina Petrescu
Valerio Virgil Ogasanu
Rosetta Ileana Predescu
Governess Vally Voiculescu
Major-domo Nicky Welcz
President Gheorghe Oprina
Policemen Mihai Mereuta, Marius Pepino
Director and scenery Liviu Ciulei
Costumes Ioana Gardescu
Translation read by Brian Wallworth

LONG WHARF THEATRE COMPANY, USA
6, 8, 10 Sep. 19.15 11 Sep. 14.15
Lyceum Theatre
SOLITAIRE Anderson
Sam Bradley Richard Venture
Madame Ruth Nelson
Daughter Patricia Pearcy
Brother Will Fenno
Wife Joyce Ebert
Father John Cromwell
Captain William Swetland
DOUBLE SOLITAIRE Anderson
Charley Richard Venture
Barbara Joyce Ebert
Mrs Potter Ruth Nelson
Mr Potter John Cromwell
Sylvia Martha Schlamme
George William Swetland
Peter Will Fenno
Director Arvin Brown
Scenery Kert Lundell
Costumes Lewis Rampino
Lighting Ronald Wallace

7, 9, 11 Sep. 19.15 8 Sep. 14.15
Lyceum Theatre
YOU CAN'T TAKE IT WITH YOU Hart *and* Kaufman
Penelope Sycamore Teresa Wright
Essie Laurie Kennedy
Paul Sycamore William Swetland
Mr De Pinna David Spielberg
Ed Tom Atkins
Donald Chuck Turner
Martin Vanderhof Emery Battis
Alice Patricia Pearcy
Henderson Will Fenno
Tony Kirby James Naughton
Gay Wellington Joyce Ebert
Mr Kirby John Cromwell
Mrs Kirby Ruth Nelson
Olga Martha Schlamme
Director Arvin Brown
Scenery Kert Lundell
Costumes James Edmund Brady
Lighting Ronald Wallace

THE MANHATTAN PROJECT
31 Aug.-11 Sep. 22.45 (exc.Sun)
11 Cambridge Street
ALICE IN WONDERLAND
(Based on Lewis Carroll)
Gerry Bamman, Tom Costello, Saskia Noordhoek Hegt, Jerry Mayer, Angela Pietropinto, Larry Pine
Director André Gregory
Designers
Eugene Lee, Franne Newman

POETRY AND PROSE RECITALS

31 Aug. 15.00 St Cecilia's Hall
A SINGULAR GRACE
A programme for the bicentenary of the birth of Sir Walter Scott
Lennox Milne, Tom Fleming, Richard Todd (rdr)
Devised by John Carroll and Royce Ryton

4 Sep. 20.00 Freemasons' Hall
POETRY SESSION
Charles Causley, Norman McCaig, Stephen Spender (rdr)

5 Sep. 20.00 Freemasons' Hall
POETRY SESSION
George Bruce, Alan Jackson, Pete Morgan, Robert Tait (rdr)

LATE NIGHT ENTERTAINMENT

30 Aug.-6 Sep. 22.45 (exc.Sun)
Lyceum Theatre
THE CORRIES
Two programmes of Scottish folksongs

10 Sep. 22.45 Usher Hall
SWINGLE SINGERS
with Jacky Cavellero (db), Roger Fugen (perc)

DANCE

ROYAL DANISH BALLET
6 Sep. 19.30 King's Theatre
THE LESSON
Choreographer Flemming Flindt
Music George Delerue
Designer Bernard Daydé
CARMEN
Choreographer Roland Petit
Music Bizet
Designer Antoni Clavé
THE LIFE GUARDS ON AMAGER
Choreographers
August Bournonville, Hans Brenaa
Music V.C. Holm
Designer Bjørn Wiinblad

8 Sep. 19.30 King's Theatre
LE CONSERVATOIRE
Choreographer August Bournonville
Music Paulli
Designer Ove Chr. Pedersen
THE YOUNG MAN MUST MARRY
Choreographer Flemming Flindt
Music Per Nørgaard
Designer Jacques Noël
JEU DE CARTES
Choreographer John Cranko
Music Stravinsky
Designer Dorothee Zippel

10 Sep. 19.30 King's Theatre
THE YOUNG MAN MUST MARRY
NIGHT SHADOW
Choreographer George Balanchine
Music Bellini; arr. Rietti
Designer André Delfau
JEU DE CARTES

11 Sep. 14.30 King's Theatre
LE CONSERVATOIRE
NIGHT SHADOW
THE LIFE GUARDS ON AMAGER

11 Sep. 19.30 King's Theatre
THE LESSON
CARMEN
THE LIFE GUARDS ON AMAGER
Dancers Kirsten Simone, Anna Laerkesen, Henning Kronstam, Flemming Flindt, Inge Sand, Solveig Østergaard, Vivi Flindt, Mette Hønningen, Inge Olafsen, Sorella Englund, Niels Bjørn Larsen, Fredbjørn Bjørnsson, Niels Kehlet, Palle Jacobsen, Flemming Halby, Flemming Ryberg, Aage Poulsen, Anne Marie Vessel, Johnny Eliasen
Bournemouth Sinfonietta
Conductors Arne Hammelboe, Tamás Vetö

EXHIBITIONS

Royal Scottish Academy
THE BELGIAN CONTRIBUTION TO SURREALISM

Parliament House
THE PARLIAMENT HOUSE EXHIBITION

Waverley Market
WRITER TO THE NATION
Director John L. Paterson

Demarco Gallery
CONTEMPORARY RUMANIAN ART

French Institute
COIA CARICATURES

1972

OPERA

DEUTSCHE OPERA AM RHEIN, Düsseldorf-Duisburg
21, 22 Aug. 19.30 King's Theatre
DIE SOLDATEN Zimmermann
Wesener Marius Rintzler
Marie Catherine Gayer
Charlotte Trudeliese Schmidt
Mother Henny Ekström
Stolzius Peter-Christoph Runge
His mother Gwynn Cornell
Colonel von Spannheim Georg Paucker
Desportes Anton de Ridder
Hunter Franz Radinger
Pirzel Albert Weikenmeier
Eisenhardt Richard Allen
Haudy Wilhelm Ernest
Mary Wicus Slabbert
Countess de la Roche Faith Puleston
Young Count Nicola Tagger
Servant Kurt Wagner
Mme Bischof Renate Dreis
Mdlle Bischof Josephine Engelskamp
Lady from Andalusia Tilly Söffing
Mme Roux Margarete Rübsam
Officers
Matti Juhan, Wolf Appel, Norbert Orth
Ensigns
Max Tichauer, Jan Hain, Lothar Spiller
Young ensign Werner Leuwer
Drunken officer Karl Vüllings
Conductor Günther Wich
Director Georg Reinhardt
Scenery Heinrich Wendel
Costumes Günter Kappel

24, 25 Aug. 20.00 St Mary's Cathedral
RAPPRESENTAZIONE DI ANIMA E DI CORPO Cavalieri
Body Peter-Christoph Runge
Soul Rachel Yakar
Intellect Alva Tripp
Good Counsel Malcolm Smith
Time Toshimitsu Kimura
Pleasure Faith Puleston
Pleasure's companions
Alfred Beckles, Zenon Kosnowski
Guardian angel William Holley
World Marius Rintzler
Worldy life Trudeliese Schmidt
Blessed soul Josephine Engelskamp
Damned soul Zenon Kosnowski
Bochum Symphony Orchestra
Conductor Alberto Erede
Scenery Georg Reinhardt, Heinrich Wendel, Erich Walter, Liselotte Erler

SCOTTISH OPERA
24, 26 Aug. 6 Sep. 17.30 King's Theatre
LES TROYENS Berlioz (Eng)
Cassandra Helga Dernesch
Ascanius Patricia Hay
Hecuba Patricia Purcell
Aeneus Gregory Dempsey
Choroebus Delme Bryn-Jones
Pantheus John Graham
Ghost of Hector/Narbal Joseph Rouleau
Priam Norman White
Mercury/Trojan soldier Gordon Sandison
Helenus/Hylas John Robertson
Andromache Elaine McDonald
Dido Janet Baker
Anna Bernadette Greevy
Iopas Derek Blackwell
Soldiers Gordon Sandison, Norman White
Scottish Theatre Ballet
Scottish National Orchestra
Conductor Alexander Gibson
Director Peter Ebert
Scenery Hans Ulrich Schmückle
Costumes Sylta Busse-Schmückle
Choreographer Laverne Mayer

TEATRO MASSIMO, Palermo
28, 30 Aug. 1 Sep. 19.30 King's Theatre
ATTILA Verdi
Attila Ruggero Raimondi
Odabella Luisa Maragliano
Maria Parazzini*
Ezio Renato Bruson
Foresto Bruno Prevedi
Uldino Umberto Scala
Pope Leone I Franco Pugliese
Conductor Giuseppe Patanè
Director Aldo Mirabella Vassallo
Designer Giulio Coltellacci

31 Aug. 2, 5, 8 Sep. 19.30 King's Theatre
LA STRANIERA Bellini
Alaide Renata Scotto
Signore di Montolino Guido Mazzini
Isoletta Elena Zilio
Arturo Ottavio Garaventa
Baron of Valdeburgo Domenico Trimarchi
Prior of Spendalieri Enrico Campi
Osburgo Gian Paolo Corradi
Conductor Nino Sanzogno
Director Mauro Bolognini
Designer Marcel Escoffier

4, 7, 9 Sep. 19.30 King's Theatre
ELISABETTA, REGINA D'INGHILTERRA Rossini
Elizabeth Leyla Gencer
Leicester Umberto Grilli
Matilde Margherita Guglielmi
Enrico Giovanna Vighi
Norfolk Pietro Bottazzo
Guglielmo Gian Paolo Corradi
Conductors Nino Sanzogno
Giacomo Zani
Director Mauro Bolognini
Designer Gaetano Pompa

ORCHESTRAL CONCERTS

ROYAL PHILHARMONIC ORCHESTRA
20 Aug. 19.30 Usher Hall
V. Williams Dona nobis pacem
V. Williams Job
Conductor Sir Adrian Boult
Soloists Felicity Palmer (sop), John Carol Case (bar), EF Chorus

21 Aug. 20.00 Usher Hall
Debussy Images for orchestra: Ibéria
Chopin Concerto for piano no.2 in F minor, op.21
Tchaikovsky Symphony no.4 in F minor, op.36
Conductor Rudolf Kempe
Soloist Shura Cherkassky (pf)

22 Aug. 20.00 Usher Hall
Schubert Overture in the Italian style in C, D591
Tippett Symphony no.1
Beethoven Concerto for piano no.5 in E flat (Emperor), op.73
Conductor Lawrence Foster
Soloist Alfred Brendel (pf)

23 Aug. 20.00 Usher Hall
Ives Three places in New England
Szymanowski Concerto for violin no.1, op.35
Penderecki Capriccio for violin and orchestra
Beethoven Symphony no.2 in D, op.36
Conductor Lawrence Foster
Soloist Wanda Wilkomirska (vn)

24 Aug. 20.00 Usher Hall
Schumann Symphony no.4 in D minor, op.120
Mahler Des Knaben Wunderhorn: Wo die schönen Trompeten blasen; Das irdische Leben
Mahler Rückert Lieder: Liebst du um Schönheit; Ich atmet einen Lindenduft; Ich bin der Welt
Janáček Taras Bulba
Conductor Rudolf Kempe
Soloist Jessye Norman (sop)

ENGLISH CHAMBER ORCHESTRA
25 Aug. 20.00 Usher Hall
Haydn Symphony no.99 in E flat
Mozart Concerto for piano no.24 in C minor, K491
Mozart Concerto for piano no.22 in E flat, K482
Conductor and soloist
Daniel Barenboim (pf)

26 Aug. 20.00 Usher Hall
Handel Concerto for oboe no.3 in G minor
Bach Concerto for violin in A minor
Mozart Serenade no.7 in D (Haffner), K250
Conductor and soloist
Pinchas Zukerman (vn)
Soloist Neil Black (ob)

28 Aug. 20.00 Usher Hall
Stravinsky Octet
Mendelssohn Concerto for piano no.1 in G minor, op.25
Wagner Siegfried idyll
Mozart Symphony no.38 in D (Prague), K504
Conductor Uri Segal
Soloist Joseph Kalichstein (pf)

LONDON PHILHARMONIC ORCHESTRA
27 Aug. 20.00 Usher Hall
Shostakovich Symphony no.14, op.135
Tchaikovsky Symphony no.2 in C minor (Little Russian), op.17
Conductor Carlo Maria Giulini
Soloists Stefania Woytowicz (sop), Raffaele Arie (bs)

29, 30 Aug. 20.00 Usher Hall
Bruckner Locus iste
Bruckner Ave Maria
Brahms Ein deutsches Requiem
Conductor Daniel Barenboim
Soloists Edith Mathis (sop), Dietrich Fischer-Dieskau (bar), EF Chorus

31 Aug. 20.00 Usher Hall
Mahler Symphony no.9 in D
Conductor Carlo Maria Giulini

SCOTTISH NATIONAL ORCHESTRA
2 Sep. 20.00 Usher Hall
Forbes Symphony in two movements (EIF commission)
Chopin Concerto for piano no.1 in E minor, op.11
Penderecki Concerto for cello no.1 (World première)
Sibelius Symphony no.5 in E flat, op.82
Conductor Alexander Gibson
Soloists Tamás Vásáry (pf), Siegfried Palm (vc)

9 Sep. 19.30 Usher Hall
Lutoslawski Trois poèmes d'Henri Michaux
Walton Concerto for violin in B minor
Stravinsky Symphony of psalms

Conductors Alexander Gibson
Witold Lutoslawski
Soloist Christian Ferras (vn), EF Chorus

BERLIN PHILHARMONIC ORCHESTRA
Conductor Herbert von Karajan
3 Sep. 20.00 *Usher Hall*
Bach Brandenburg concerto no.3 in G
Berg Three orchestral pieces, op.6
Beethoven Symphony no.3 In E flat (Eroica), op.55

4 Sep. 20.00 *Usher Hall*
Mahler Das Lied von der Erde
Soloists Christa Ludwig (mez), René Kollo (ten)

5 Sep. 20.00 *Usher Hall*
Stravinsky Apollon musagète
Brahms Symphony no.2 in D, op.73

CRACOW PHILHARMONIC ORCHESTRA
Conductor Jerzy Katlewicz
6 Sep. 20.00 *St Giles' Cathedral*
Penderecki Utrenja
Soloists Stefania Woytowicz sop), Krystyna Szczepanska (mez), Kazimierz Pustelak (ten), Bernard Ladysz (bar), Peter Lagger (bs), Cracow Philharmonic Chorus

7 Sep. 20.00 *Usher Hall*
Szymanowski Stabat Mater
Lutoslawski Livre pour orchestra
T. Baird Four Shakespeare sonnets
Penderecki Dies irae
Soloists Stefania Woytowicz (sop), Krystyna Szczepanska (mez), Andrzej Hiolski (bar), Cracow Philharmonic Chorus

BBC SCOTTISH SYMPHONY ORCHESTRA
8 Sep. 20.00 *Usher Hall*
Walton Partita for orchestra
Hamilton Concerto for violin no.2 (Amphion) (World première)
Lutoslawski Funeral music
Panufnik Sinfonia sacra
Conductor Christopher Seaman
Soloist Paul Zukofsky (vn)

CHAMBER CONCERTS

SCOTTISH BAROQUE ENSEMBLE
23 Aug. 11.00 *Freemasons' Hall*
McGibbon Sonata in B minor for strings, violin and harpsichord
Foulis Sonata in A
Anon. Airs and dances of Renaissance Scotland
Wilson Ritornelli per archi (World première)
Earl of Kelly Trio sonata in C
Lauder Pavan and galliard
McGibbon Sonata in G for strings
Director Leonard Friedman
Soloist Kenneth Elliott (hpd)

DANIEL BARENBOIM (pf), PINCHAS ZUKERMAN, KENNETH SILLITOE (vn), CECIL ARONOWITZ (va), DOUGLAS CUMMINGS (vc)
26 Aug. 11.00 *Leith Town Hall*
Mozart Quartet for piano and strings in G minor, K478
Mozart Quartet for piano and strings in E flat, K493
Mozart Sonata for violin and piano no.32 in B flat, K454

MELOS ENSEMBLE
1 Sep. 11.00 *Leith Town Hall*
Haydn Quartet for guitar and strings in D, op.2/2
L. Berkeley Trio for strings, op.19
Walton Five bagatelles for guitar
Bennett Concerto for guitar
Conductor David Atherton
Soloist Julian Bream (gtr)

FIRES OF LONDON
2 Sep. 11.00 *Haymarket Ice Rink*
Ockeghem Ut heremita solus; arr. Birtwistle
P.M. Davies Hymnos for clarinet and piano
B. Cole Caesura
P.M. Davies Eight songs for a mad king
Conductor Peter Maxwell Davies
Soloists William Pearson (bar), Stephen Pruslin (pf), Alan Hacker (cl)

AEOLIAN QUARTET
4 Sep. 11.00 *Freemasons' Hall*
Haydn Quartet in G minor (Rider), op.74/3
Webern Quartet, op.28
Brahms Sextet no.2 in G, op.36
with Kenneth Essex (va), Terence Weil (vc)

5 Sep. 11.00 *Freemasons' Hall*
Mozart Quintet no.5 in D, K593
Mozart Quintet no.3 in G minor, K516
with Kenneth Essex (va)

8 Sep. 11.00 *Freemasons' Hall*
Haydn Quartet in G, op.76/1
Stravinsky Concertino for string quartet
Brahms Sextet no.1 in B flat, op.18
with Kenneth Essex (va), Terence Weil (vc)

DIETRICH FISCHER-DIESKAU (bar) BERLIN PHILHARMONIC SOLOISTS
6 Sep. 11.00 *Usher Hall*
Bach Musikalisches Opfer: Trio sonata in C minor
Bach Cantata no.13: Ächzen und erbärmlich Weinen
Bach Cantata no.152: Tritt auf die Glaubensbahn
Bach Cantata no.157: Ja, ja, ich halte Jesum feste
Telemann Ihr Völker hört
Telemann Trio sonata in D minor
Telemann Trauermusik eines kunsterfahrnen Canarienvogels

BERLIN PHILHARMONIC SOLOISTS
7 Sep. 11.00 *Freemasons' Hall*
Britten Phantasy quartet for oboe and strings, op2
Zimmermann Tempus loquendi for flute
Mozart Quartet for oboe and strings in F, K370
Ravel Sonata for violin and cello
Mozart Quartet for flute and strings no.1 in D, K285

KING'S SINGERS
21 Aug. 11.00 *Freemasons' Hall*
Works by Forbes, Carver, Penderecki, Banchieri, Lassus, Passereau, Janequin, Poulenc, Ridout *and* Anon.

FISTULATORES ET TUBICINATORES VARSOVIENSES
25 Aug. 11.00 *Freemasons' Hall*
Works by Nicholas of Cracow, Gomólka, Jarzebski *and* Anon.

SALTIRE SINGERS
28 Aug. 15.00 *St Cecilia's Hall*
Scottish Renaissance music
Works by Janequin, Costeley, Lassus, Certon, Musgrave, Hamilton, Maw, Anon.

RECITALS

JESSYE NORMAN (sop)
IRWIN GAGE (pf)
29 Aug. 11.00 *Freemasons' Hall*
Songs by Schubert, Brahms, Ravel, R. Strauss

CATHERINE GAYER (sop)
ARIBERT REIMANN (pf)
31 Aug. 11.00 *Freemasons' Hall*
Songs by Schubert, Chopin, Debussy, Webern, Reimann, R. Strauss

DIETRICH FISCHER-DIESKAU (bar)
DANIEL BARENBOIM (pf)
1 Sep. 20.00 *Usher Hall*
Songs by Wolf

ANNE HOWELLS (mez)
GEOFFREY PARSONS (pf)
9 Sep. 11.00 *Freemasons' Hall*
Songs by Pergolesi, Cavalli, Debussy, Poulenc, Fauré, Mompou, Rodrigo, Obradors, Granados

JOSEPH KALICHSTEIN (pf)
24 Aug. 11.00 *Freemasons' Hall*
Schumann Davidsbündlertänze
Mendelssohn Fantasia in F sharp minor (Sonata écossaise), op.28
Bartók Sonata

ALFRED BRENDEL (pf)
28 Aug. 11.00 *Leith Town Hall*
Beethoven Sonata no.7 in D, op.10/3
Beethoven Sonata no.27 in E minor, op.90
Schubert Sonata no.16 in A minor, D845

HELEN SCHNABEL
KARL ULRICH SCHNABEL (pf duet)
22 Aug. 11.00 *Freemasons' Hall*
Mozart Andante and variations in G, K501
Schubert Sonata in B flat, D617
Schnabel Seven pieces
Weber Eight pieces, op.60: Tema variato, Marcia, Rondo
Mendelssohn Theme and variations, op.83a

CHRISTIAN FERRAS (vn)
JEAN-CLAUDE AMBROSINI (pf)
6 Sep. 20.00 *Freemasons' Hall*
Beethoven Sonata no.5 in F (Spring), op.24
Bach Sonata for solo violin no.1 in G minor
Schumann Sonata no.2 in D minor, op.121

SIEGFRIED PALM (vc)
MARGARET KITCHIN (pf)
30 Aug. 11.00 *Freemasons' Hall*
Chopin Sonata in G minor, op.65
Webern Three little pieces, op.11
Zimmermann Sonata for solo cello
Penderecki Capriccio for Siegfried Palm
Mendelssohn Sonata no.1 in B flat, op.45

DRAMA

CITIZENS' THEATRE, Glasgow
21-26 Aug. 6-9 Sep. 19.30 24, 26 Aug. 9 Sep. 14.30 *Assembly Hall*
TAMBURLAINE THE GREAT Marlowe

Tamburlaine — Rupert Frazer, Jeffery Kissoon, Mike Gwilym
Bajazeth — Ian McDiarmid
Mycetes — Murray Salem
Cosroe — Lewis Collins
Theridamas — James Aubrey
Techelles — Dave Yelland
Usumcasane — Christopher Brown
Agydas — Douglas Heard
Soldan of Egypt — Jonathan Levy
Amyras — Colin Haigh
Calyphas — Jeremy Blake
Celebinus — Laurance Rudic
Callapine — Jonathan Kent
Zenocrate — Paola Dionisotti
Zabina — Jill Spurrier
Olympia — Angela Chadfield
Anippe — Celia Foxe
Director — Keith Hack
Designer — Philip Prowse
Lighting — Gerry Jenkinson

28 Aug.-5 Sep. 19.30 (exc.Sun) 29 Aug. 2, 5 Sep. 14.30 *Assembly Hall*
TWELFTH NIGHT Shakespeare
Viola/Sebastian — Jeremy Blake
Orsino — Jonathan Kent
Olivia — Celia Foxe
Sir Toby Belch — Ian McDiarmid
Sir Andrew Aguecheek — James Aubrey
Malvolio — Mike Gwilym
Maria — Angela Chadfield
Feste — Christopher Brown
Antonio — Douglas Heard
Director — Giles Havergal
Designer — Philip Prowse
Lighting — Gerry Jenkinson

YOUNG VIC
21, 22, 23, 28, 29 Aug. 1, 2, 5, 6, 7 Sep. 20.00 23, 29 Aug. 2, 7 Sep. 14.30
Haymarket Ice Rink
BIBLE ONE
Part 1 Medieval Mystery Plays
Adam — Gary Bond
God — Paul Brooke
Rachel — Barbara Courtney
Rebecca — Alison Groves
Esau/Cain — Richard Kane
Old Isaac — Alex McAvoy
Noah's wife — Julia McCarthy
Abel — Riggs O'Hara
Abraham — Gavin Reed
Jacob — Peter Reeves
Lucifer — Andrew Robertson
Noah — Ian Trigger
Noah's sons — Alex McAvoy, David Wynn, Ian Charleson
Noah's daughters-in-law — Alison Groves, Barbara Courtney, Joanna Wake
Eve — Joanna Wake
Young Isaac — Jeremy James Taylor
Angel — Ian Charleson
Part 2 Joseph and the amazing technicolor dreamcoat Webber
Jacob — Alex McAvoy
Jacob's wife/Potiphar's wife — Joan Heal
Joseph — Gary Bond
Reuben/Pharaoh — Gordon Waller
Simeon/Potiphar — Gavin Reed
Levi — Simon Taylor
Napthali — Richard Kane
Isaachar — Andrew Robertson
Asher — Paul Brooke
Dan — Ian Trigger
Zebulum — David Wynn
Gad — Ian Charleson
Benjamin — Jeremy James Taylor
Judah — Riggs O'Hara
Director — Frank Dunlop
Designer — Nadine Baylis
Musical director — Alan Doggett
Choreographer — Christopher Bruce

25, 26, 30, 31 Aug. 4, 8, 9 Sep. 20.00 26, 31 Aug. 9 Sep.14.30 *Haymarket Ice Rink*
THE COMEDY OF ERRORS
Shakespeare
Antipholus of Edinburgh — Richard Kane
Antipholus of London — Gary Bond
Dromio of Edinburgh — Andrew Robertson
Dromio of London — Gavin Reed
Adriana — Denise Coffey
Luciana — Alison Groves
Aegeon — Peter Reeves
Balthazar/Pinch — Ian Trigger
Duke — Alex McAvoy
Angelo — Paul Brooke
Aemilia — Joan Heal
Merchants — David Wynn, Riggs O'Hara
Gaoler — Jeremy James Taylor
Luce — Julia McCarthy
Lady of the town — Joanna Wake
Nun — Barbara Courtney
Police officer — Ian Charleson
Singer — Iain Dunn
Directors — Frank Dunlop, Peter James
Designer — Nadine Baylis

HOSHO NOH THEATRE, Japan
21 Aug. 19.15 23 Aug. 14.15
Lyceum Theatre
SUMIDAGAWA (The Sumida River)
KAKI YAMABUSHI (Kyogen)
HAGOROMO (A robe of feathers)

22, 23 Aug. 19.15 *Lyceum Theatre*
KIYOTSUNE (Tied to the cudgel)
BOSHIBARI (Kyogen)
AYANOTSUZUMI (The damask drum)
Fusao Hosho, Fusatero Hosho, Tokio Otsubo, Yoshihisa Noguchi, Takashi Tatsumi,Yasuo Imai, Yoshinaga Takeda, Toshio Tamaki, Fusataka Honma, Yoshio Terai, Yasuo Kamei, Yoshiro Kobayashi, Ryuzo Tazaki, Haruhiro Maeda (Shite group), Yaichi Hosho, Kan Hosho (Waki group), Daigoro Fujita, Hisashi Uzawa, Haruo Yasufuku, Shinichi Uno, Jun Kunikawa (Musicians), Yasuyuki Izumi, Ukon Miyake, Hiroshi Wada (Kyogen group)
Interpreter — Eiho Shizuru
Lecturer — Yoshitaka Takahashi

ACTORS' COMPANY
28 Aug.-2 Sep.19.15 30 Aug. 2 Sep. 14.15 *Lyceum Theatre*
RULING THE ROOST (Le dindon)
Feydeau
(Eng. Translated by Richard Cottrell)
Vatelin — Tenniel Evans
Lucienne — Moira Redmond
Pontagnac — Ronnie Stevens
Clotilde — Marian Diamond
Redillon — Robin Ellis
Armandine — Caroline Blakiston
Pinchard — Robert Eddison
Madame Pinchard — Margery Mason
Soldignac — Frank Middlemass
Maggy — Sheila Reid
Hotel manager — Edward Petherbridge
Maid — Felicity Kendal
Page boy — Ian McKellen
Policemen — Jack Shepherd, Juan Moreno
Jean — Matthew Long
Gerome — John Tordoff
Director — Richard Cottrell
Designer — Robin Archer
Lighting — Michael Outhwaite

4-9 Sep.19.15 6, 9 Sep.14.15
Lyceum Theatre
'TIS PITY SHE'S A WHORE Ford
Bonaventura — Robert Eddison
Cardinal — Juan Moreno
Soranzo — Edward Petherbridge
Florio — Frank Middlemass
Donado — Tenniel Evans
Grimaldi — Robin Ellis
Giovanni — Ian McKellen
Bergetto — John Tordoff
Richardetto — Ronnie Stevens
Vasques — Jack Shepherd
Poggio — Matthew Long
Annabella — Felicity Kendal
Hippolita — Moira Redmond
Philotis — Sheila Reid
Putana — Margery Mason
Director — David Giles
Designer — Kenneth Mellor
Lighting — Michael Outhwaite

GRUPPO SPERIMENTAZIONE TEATRALE, Rome
21-26 Aug. 20.30 24, 26 Aug. 14.30
Church Hill Theatre
MOBY DICK Ricci (after Melville)
Angela Diana, Deborah Hayes, Lillo Monachesi, Carlo Montesi, Luigi Perrone, Claudio Previtera
Voice — Dario Mazzoli
Director — Mario Ricci
Scenery — Carlo Montesi, Claudio Previtera, Mario Romano
Costumes — Angela Diana
Film — Guido Cosulich. Mario Ricci, Angela Reddini

THÉÂTRE LABORATOIRE VICINAL, Brussels
28, 29 Aug. 1, 2 Sep. 21.00
Gateway Theatre
TRAMP Spilliaert

31 Aug. 21.00 2 Sep. 15.00
Gateway Theatre
LUNA PARK
Baba, Frédéric Flamand, Rafael Godinho, Jean de la Fontaine, France Joset, Anne West
Director — Frédéric Flamand

POETRY AND PROSE RECITALS

DAME PEGGY ASHCROFT (rdr)
JULIAN BREAM (lute, gtr)
3 Sep. 20.00 *Assembly Hall*
A dialogue of poetry and music
Donne, C.Day Lewis, Dowland, Britten

THE BARROW POETS
24, 25, 26 Aug. 22.45 *Freemasons' Hall*
An entertainment with words and music

25 Aug. 15.00 26 Aug. 11.00
Assembly Hall
A summer Howyahooha for children

DANCE

24-26 Aug. 19.15 26 Aug. 14.15
Lyceum Theatre
ENSEMBLE NATIONAL DU SÉNÉGAL
Ballet director — Jean-Pierre Leurs
Artistic director — Mamadou M'Baye

EXHIBITIONS

Merchants' Hall
17th CENTURY ITALIAN DRAWINGS

Demarco Gallery
POLISH CONTEMPORARY ART

Royal Scottish Academy
ALAN DAVIE Paintings 1952-1972

1973

OPERA

EDINBURGH FESTIVAL OPERA
20, 23, 25 Aug. 6, 8 Sep. 19.30
King's Theatre
DON GIOVANNI Mozart
Don Giovanni — Roger Soyer
Donna Anna — Antigone Sgourda
Donna Elvira — Heather Harper
Don Ottavio — Luigi Alva
Leporello — Geraint Evans
Zerlina — Helen Donath
Masetto — Alberto Rinaldi
The Commendatore — Peter Lagger
English Chamber Orchestra
Scottish Opera Chorus
Conductor — Daniel Barenboim
Director and designer — Peter Ustinov
Lighting — John B. Read

HUNGARIAN STATE OPERA
24, 28, 30 Aug. 19.30 King's Theatre
DUKE BLUEBEARD'S CASTLE Bartók
Judith — Katalin Kasza
Olga Szönyi
Duke — György Melis
András Faragó
Conductor — János Ferencsik
Director — András Miko
Scenery — Gábor Forray
Costumes — Tivadar Márk
with The miraculous mandarin *See* Ballet

27, 29 Aug. 19.30 King's Theatre
BLOOD WEDDING Szokolay
Mother — Erzsébet Komlóssy
Bridegroom — Ferenc Szönyi
Bride — Erzsébet Házy
Neighbour — Katalin Kasza
Leonardo — András Faragó
Leonardo's wife — Stefánia Moldován
Mother-in-law — Anita Szabó
Father — Endre Várhelyi
Servant — Irén Szecsódy
Bridesmaids — Eva Andor, Marta Szabó
Best man — András Rajna
Wood cutters — Csaba Otvös, István Gáti, László Polgár
Moon — Sándor Palcsó
Death — Zsuzsa Barlay
Conductor — András Kórodi
Director — András Mikó
Scenery — Zoltán Fülöp
Costumes — Tivadar Márk

ENGLISH OPERA GROUP
4, 7 Sep. 19.30 King's Theatre
DEATH IN VENICE Britten
Gustav von Aschenbach — Peter Pears
Traveller/Fop/Gondolier/Hotel manager/Barber/Leader of the players/Voice of Dionysus — John Shirley-Quirk
Voice of Apollo — James Bowman
Polish mother — Deanne Bergsma
Tadzio — Robert Huguenin
Daughters — Elizabeth Griffiths, Melanie Phillips
Governess/Street dancer — Sheila Humphreys
Jaschiu — Nicholas Kirby
Waiter/Steward — Stuart Harling
Strawberry-seller — Iris Saunders
Guide/German father — Robert Carpenter Turner
Glass-maker — Stephen James Adams
Lace-seller/English lady — Sheila Brand
Beggar-woman/French mother — Anne Wilkens
Newspaper-seller — Alexandra Browning
Flower seller — Anne Conoley
Strolling players — Neville Williams, Penelope MacKay
English clerk/Jaschiu's father — Peter Leeming
Russian mother — Alexandra Browning
Russian father — Michael Follis
Russian nanny — Angela Vernon Bates
German mother — Helen Attfield
Other parts played by Thomas Edmonds, James Graham, Michael Bauer, Norman Lloyd-Miller, Arnost Kopecky, Wendy Pashley, Keith Jones, Victor Kravchenko, Janice Hooper-Roe, Ronald Murdoch, Robin Bell, Kathleen Smales, Anna Vincent, Wyndham Parfitt
English Chamber Orchestra
Conductor — Steuart Bedford
Director — Colin Graham
Scenery — John Piper
Costumes — Charles Knode
Choreographer — Sir Frederick Ashton

ORCHESTRAL CONCERTS

SCOTTISH NATIONAL ORCHESTRA
Conductor Alexander Gibson
19 Aug. 19.30 Usher Hall
Messiaen — Hymne au St Sacrement
Sibelius — Concerto for violin in D minor
Verdi — Four sacred pieces
Soloists Sheila Armstrong (sop), Henryk Szeryng (vn), EF Chorus

20 Aug. 20.00 Usher Hall
R. Strauss — Don Juan
Bartók — Concerto for piano no.3
Brahms — Symphony no.2 in D, op.73
Soloist — Annie Fischer (pf)

LONDON SYMPHONY ORCHESTRA
21 Aug. 20.00 Usher Hall
Ravel — Ma mère l'oye
Ravel — Concerto for piano (Left hand)
Walton — Symphony no.2
Conductor — André Previn
Soloist — Leon Fleischer (pf)

23 Aug. 20.00 Usher Hall
Schumann — Das Paradies und die Peri
Conductor — Carlo Maria Giulini
Soloists Edith Mathis, Sheila Armstrong (sop), Delia Wallis, Valerie Johnston (mez), Peter Pears, Anthony Rolfe Johnson (ten), Wolfgang Brendel, Thomas Allen (bar), EF Chorus

24 Aug. 20.00 Usher Hall
Webern — Passacaglia, op.1
Mozart — Concerto for piano no.20 in D minor, K466
Schubert — Symphony no.9 in C (Great), D944
Conductor — Carlo Maria Giulini
Soloist — Annie Fischer (pf)

29 Aug. 20.00 Usher Hall
Schumann Concerto for piano in A minor, op.54
Shostakovich Symphony no.8 in C minor, op.65
Conductor — André Previn
Soloist — Radu Lupu (pf)

27, 28 Aug. 20.00 Usher Hall
Mahler — Symphony no.2 in C minor (Resurrection)
Conductor — Leonard Bernstein
Soloists Sheila Armstrong (sop), Janet Baker (mez), EF Chorus

ENGLISH CHAMBER ORCHESTRA
22 Aug. 20.00 Usher Hall
Mozart — Divertimento no.17 in D, K334
Stravinsky — The soldier's tale
Conductor — Daniel Barenboim
Soloist — Peter Ustinov (narr)

1 Sep. 20.00 Usher Hall
Weber — Symphony no.2 in C
Beethoven — Concerto for piano no.2 in B flat, op.19
Beethoven — Concerto for piano no.1 in C, op.15
Conductor and soloist — Daniel Barenboim (pf)

BBC SYMPHONY ORCHESTRA
Conductor Pierre Boulez
25 Aug. 20.00 Usher Hall
Ravel — Valses nobles et sentimentales; arr. for orchestra
Berlioz — Les nuits d'été
Bartók — Concerto for orchestra
Soloist — Jane Berbié (mez)

26 Aug. 20.00 Usher Hall
Stravinsky — The song of the nightingale
Boulez — ee cummings ist der dichter
Holliger — Siebengesang
Berg — Three orchestral pieces, op.6
Soloist — Heinz Holliger (ob)
Schola Cantorum of Stuttgart

BBC SCOTTISH SYMPHONY ORCHESTRA
31 Aug. 20.00 Usher Hall
Ravel — Rapsodie espagnole
Tchaikovsky Concerto for violin in D, op.35
Elgar — Symphony no.1 in A flat, op.55
Conductor — Christopher Seaman
Soloist — Ida Haendel (vn)

NEW PHILHARMONIA ORCHESTRA
2 Sep. 20.00 Usher Hall
Nordheim — Epitaffio for orchestra and tape
Chopin — Concerto for piano no.1 in E minor, op.11
Schumann — Symphony no.1 in B flat (Spring), op.38
Conductor — Zubin Mehta
Soloist — Martha Argerich (pf)

3 Sep. 20.00 Usher Hall
Chihara — Forest music
Debussy — La mer
Brahms — Concerto for violin in D, op.77
Conductor — Zubin Mehta
Soloist — Isaac Stern (vn)

5 Sep. 20.00 Usher Hall
Vivaldi — Concerto for harpsichord in A, R158
Cherubini Requiem mass no.2 in D minor
Franck — Symphony in D minor
Conductor — Riccardo Muti
EF Chorus

6 Sep. 20.00 Usher Hall
Berlioz — Waverley - Overture
Mozart — Concerto for piano no.21 in C, K467
Prokofiev — Symphony no.3 in C minor, op.44
Conductor — Riccardo Muti
Soloist — Murray Perahia (pf)

ORCHESTRE DE PARIS
7 Sep. 20.00 Usher Hall
Amy — d'un espace déployé
Berlioz — Symphonie fantastique
Conductors — Sir Georg Solti, Gilbert Amy
Soloist — Christiane Eda-Pierre (sop)

8 Sep. 19.30 *Usher Hall*
Roussel Symphony no.3 in G minor, op.42
Ravel Shéhérazade
Stravinsky The rite of spring
Conductor Sir Georg Solti
Soloist Régine Crespin (sop)

CHAMBER CONCERTS

GYÖRGY PAUK (vn), RALPH KIRSHBAUM (vc), PETER FRANKL (pf)
21 Aug. 11.00 *Freemasons' Hall*
Mozart Divertimento for piano and strings in B flat, K254
Schumann Trio for piano and strings no.2 in F, op.80
Mendelssohn Trio for piano and strings no.2 in C minor, op.66

GYÖRGY PAUK (vn), ALAN HACKER (cl, bas hn), PETER FRANKL (pf)
23 Aug. 11.00 *Freemasons' Hall*
Brahms Sonata for violin and piano no.3 in D minor, op.108
Bartók Contrasts for violin, clarinet and piano
Birtwistle Chanson de geste for basset horn and pre-recorded tape (World première)
Ravel Sonata for violin and piano

GABRIELI QUARTET
24 Aug. 11.00 *Freemasons' Hall*
Beethoven Quartet no.2 in G, op.18/2
Ravel Quartet in F
Janáček Quartet no.2 (Intimate letters)

HEINZ HOLLIGER (ob)
URSULA HOLLIGER (hp)
JÖRG WYTTENBACH (pf, hpd)
29 Aug. 11.00 *Freemasons' Hall*
Rossini Andante con variazioni for oboe and harp
Schumann Three romances; transcr. for oboe and harp, op.94
Holliger Elis; 3 nocturnes for piano
Schumann Fantasiestücke, op.73 (version for oboe d'amore and piano)
Spohr Sonata for oboe and harp in A flat, op.115
Bach Sonata for violin and continuo in G minor; transc. for oboe and harpsichord

LES PERCUSSIONS DE STRASBOURG
30 Aug. 11.00 *Leith Town Hall*
Kabeláč Eight inventions
Aperghis Kryptogramma
Varèse Ionisation
Serocki Continuum

1 Sep. 11.00 *Leith Town Hall*
Cage First construction (in metal)
Scherchen Shen
Xenakis Persephassa

HOLLIGER ENSEMBLE
31 Aug. 11.00 *Freemasons' Hall*
Boulez Sonata for piano no.3: Trope
Debussy Syrinx for flute
Debussy Sonata for flute, viola and harp
Huber Noctes for oboe and harpsichord
Holliger Erde und Himmel
Holliger Trio for oboe doubling cor anglais, viola and harp
with Philip Langridge (ten)

1 Sep. 22.45 *Assembly Hall*
Wyttenbach Exécution ajournée for string quartet
Globokar Note for piano
Globokar Échange for trombone
Holliger Cardiophonie
Holliger Kreis for 4 to 7 players
Wyttenbach Kunststücke, die Zeit totzuschlagen
Open improvisations

AMADEUS QUARTET
With Cecil Aronowitz (va)
5 Sep. 11.00 *Leith Town Hall*
Haydn Quartet in B flat, op.64/3
Mozart Quintet no.5 in C, K515
Haydn Quartet in G, op.64/4

7 Sep. 11.00 *Leith Town Hall*
Haydn Quartet in C, op.54/2
Mozart Quintet no.6 in E flat, K614
Haydn Quartet in B flat, op.55/3

8 Sep. 11.00 *Leith Town Hall*
Mozart Quartet no.19 in C (Dissonance), K465
Mozart Quintet no.3 in G minor, K516

ENGLISH CHAMBER ORCHESTRA WIND ENSEMBLE
6 Sep. 11.00 *Freemasons' Hall*
Donizetti Sinfonia in G minor
Gounod Petite symphonie
Mozart Serenade no.12 in C minor, K388
Mozart La ci darem; arr for wind

SCHOLA CANTORUM OF STUTTGART
Director Clytus Gottwald
25 Aug. 11.00 *Freemasons' Hall*
Josquin Desprez Pater noster
Kagel Hallelujah
Finck Sanctus
Holliger Dona nobis pacem
Messiaen O sacrum convivium

27 Aug. 11.00 *Freemasons' Hall*
Josquin Desprez Baisez-moy
Josquin Desprez Petite camusette
Bussotti Ancora odono i colli
Schnebel AMN
Holliger Psalm
Cage Song books

KING'S SINGERS
3 Sep. 11.00 *Freemasons' Hall*
Medieval English music
16th century Scottish music
Wert Three Italian madrigals
Berio 'Cries' of London (EIF commission)
Bennett The house of sleepe
Poulenc Trois chansons

RECITALS

EDITH MATHIS (sop)
THOMAS STUMPF (pf)
20 Aug. 11.00 *Freemasons' Hall*
Songs by Mozart, Debussy, Brahms

CATHY BERBERIAN (sop)
BRUNO CANINO (pf)
30 Aug. 2 Sep. 20.00 *Freemasons' Hall*
A la recherche de la musique perdue

PETER WILLIAMS (hpd)
Les Clavecinistes Français
21 Aug. 15.00 *St Cecilia's Hall*
F. Couperin Suite no.5 in A
F. Couperin Suite no.26
F. Couperin Suite no.8 in B minor

27 Aug. 15.00 *St Cecilia's Hall*
L. Couperin Suite in D minor
F. Couperin Les folies françoises
Forqueray Suite in G
Rameau Gavotte 'La triomphante' with 6 doubles
Lebegue Trois noels

JEAN-RODOLPHE KARS (pf)
22 Aug. 11.00 *Freemasons' Hall*
Debussy Children's corner suite
Prokofiev Sonata no.2 in D minor, op.14
Messiaen Vingt regards sur l'enfant Jesus: Nos. 5, 6, 13, 20

ANNIE FISCHER (pf)
26 Aug. 15.00 *Usher Hall*
Mozart Sonata no.14 in C minor, K457
Schumann Sonata no.1 in F sharp minor, op.11
Beethoven Sonata no.19 in G minor, op.49/1
Beethoven Sonata no.23 in F minor (Appassionata), op.57

ANTHONY GOLDSTONE (pf)
28 Aug. 11.00 *Freemasons' Hall*
Janáček Sonata 1 X 1905
Beethoven Variations and fugue on an original theme (Eroica)
Schumann Carnaval

MARTHA ARGERICH (pf)
4 Sep. 11.00 *Leith Town Hall*
Bach Toccata and fugue in C minor
Mozart Sonata no.13 in B flat, K333
Debussy Estampes
Chopin Preludes nos.1-24, op.28

ISAAC STERN (vn)
DANIEL BARENBOIM (pf)
4 Sep. 20.00 *Usher Hall*
Mozart Sonata no.33 in E flat, K481
Brahms Sonata no.1 in G, op.78
Franck Sonata in A

DRAMA

ROYAL LYCEUM THEATRE COMPANY
20 Aug.-8 Sep.19.30 (exc.Sun) 21, 25, 28 Aug. 1, 4, 8 Sep. 14.30 *Assembly Hall*
THE THRIE ESTAITES Lyndsay
(Adapted by Tom Wright)
Diligence James Cairncross
King James Grant
Wantonness William Armour
Placebo John Shedden
Solace Paul Young
Sensualitie Eileen McCallum
Hameliness Vivien Heilbron
Danger Janet Michael
Gude Counsel Bryden Murdoch
Flatterie Rikki Fulton
Falset John Cairney
Dissait John Grieve
Veritie Lennox Milne
Chastitie Edith Macarthur
Spiritualitie Roddy McMillan
Prioress Clare Richards
Abbot Phil McCall
Parson James Kennedy
Merchant Brown Derby
Soutar Jackie Farrell
Soutar's wife Jan Wilson
Tailor Alec Heggie
Tailor's wife Mary McCusker
Jennie Ann Maley
Correction's varlet/Scribe Andrew Byatt
Divine Correction Tom Fleming
Poor man Joseph Brady
John the Common-Weal Fulton Mackay
Lord John Young
Sergeants Ian Ireland, Ron Bain
Covetice Patrick Malahide
Public Oppression Tony Roper
Doctor Ian Stewart
Folly Walter Carr
Director Bill Bryden
Scenery Geoffrey Scott
Costumes Deirdre Clancy

Lighting André Tammes
Music Cedric Thorpe Davie

27 Aug.-31 Sep. 12.30 *Lyceum Studio*
THE KNIFE Brown
Mr Grant John Cairney
Mr Pringle Roland Oliver
Mrs Allan Clare Richards
Mr Masterson Brown Derby
Director John David
Designer Poppy Mitchell
Lighting André Tammes

YOUNG LYCEUM COMPANY
27, 29, 30, 31 Aug. 14.30 *Assembly Hall*
WOYZECK Büchner (Eng)
Woyzeck Ron Bain
Marie Jane Fox
Drum major Barry Woolgar
Andres Alan Hunter
Captain Sean McCarthy
Doctor Patrick Malahide
Margaret Mary McCusker
Apprentices Martin Black, Tony Roper
Grandmother Susan Brown
Jew Simon Callow
Karl Peter Davison
Girl/Barker's wife Jeni Giffen
Landlord Alec Heggie
Kathe Leslie Mackie
Girl Ann Maley
Sergeant David Rintoul
Barker Julian Tew
Showman Peter Whitman
Old man Benny Young
Director Radu Penciulescu
Designer Bruce Macadie
Lighting André Tammes

PROSPECT THEATRE COMPANY
20-25 Aug. 19.15 22, 25 Aug. 14.15
Lyceum Theatre
PERICLES Shakespeare
Pericles Derek Jacobi
Thaisa/Marina Marilyn Taylerson
Gower Ronnie Stevens
Antiochus/Bawd Harold Innocent
Thaliard/Leonine John Cording
Daughter of Antiochus
Jamie MacDonald Reid
Helicanus Henry Moxon
Cleon Trevor Martin
Dionyza/Boult Jan Waters
Philoten Barry Warren
Pilch James Hunter
Patchbreech Tim Barker
Simonides Michael David
Lychorida Patricia Gerrard
Cerimon Timothy Davies
Diana Penelope Potter
Pandar Willoughby Goddard
Lysimachus Rupert Frazer
Fisherman Henry Szeps
Sailor Frank Mughan
Gentleman Jonathan Hyde
Whores Robert Swales, Robin Sachs
Waiter David Mayberry
Director Toby Robertson
Designer Robin Archer
Lighting Michael Outhwaite
Music Carl Davis

ACTORS' COMPANY
27 Aug.-1 Sep. 19.15 29 Aug. 1 Sep.
14.15 *Lyceum Theatre*
THE WOOD DEMON Chekhov
(Eng. Translated by Ronald Hingley)
Khruschov Ian McKellen
Serebryakov Robert Eddison
Helen Marian Diamond
Sonya Sheila Reid
Madame Voynitsky Margery Mason
Voynitsky Tenniel Evans
Zheltukin Juan Moreno
Julia Sharon Duce
Orlovsky John Woodvine
Theodore Robin Ellis
Dyadin John Tordoff
Simon Edward Petherbridge
Vassili Robert Davey
Servant girl Elaine Strickland
Director David Giles
Scenery Kenneth Mellor
Costumes
Stephen and Wendy Doncaster
Lighting Howard Eldridge

3-8 Sep. 19.15 5, 8 Sep. 14.15
Lyceum Theatre
THE WAY OF THE WORLD Congreve
Mirabell Edward Petherbridge
Fainall Robin Ellis
Witwoud John Tordoff
Petulant Matthew Long
Sir Wilfull Witwoud John Woodvine
Waitwell Tenniel Evans
Messenger Robert Davey
Chauffeur Juan Moreno
Billy Robert Eddison
Servant Ian McKellen
Lady Wishfort Margery Mason
Mrs Millamant Caroline Blakiston
Mrs Marwood Paola Dionisotti
Mrs Fainall Marian Diamond
Foible Sharon Duce
Mincing Sheila Reid
Peg Elaine Strickland
Director David William
Designer Karen Mills
Lighting Howard Eldridge

3, 4, 6, 7 Sep. 12.30 *Lyceum Studio*
FLOW Josipovici
A Tenniel Evans
B Caroline Blakiston
C Robert Eddison
D Sheila Reid
E Robin Ellis
KNOTS (From the book by R.D. Laing)
Sharon Duce, Paola Dionisotti, Caroline Blakiston, Sheila Reid, Robert Eddison, Robin Ellis, Matthew Long, Juan Moreno, Edward Petherbridge, Tenniel Evans, Ian McKellen
Director Edward Petherbridge

POETRY AND PROSE RECITALS

22-24 Aug. 15.00 *St Cecilia's Hall*
BORDER AND BALLAD: Early Scottish poetry and ballads
Tom Fleming, Edith Macarthur (rdr)
Devised by Tom Fleming

29-31 Aug. 15.00 2 Sep. 15.00 and 20.00
St Cecilia's Hall
THE PRINCE AND THE '45: Prince Charles Edward Stuart in Scotland
Prince Charles Edward Ian Charleson
Scottish narrator Bryden Murdoch
English narrator John Westbrook
with Clifford Hughes (ten *exc.*2 *Sep. 20.00*)
Devised by John Carroll and Royce Ryton

LATE NIGHT ENTERTAINMENT

PROSPECT THEATRE COMPANY
21-23 Aug. 22.45 *Lyceum Theatre*
DON JUAN IN LOVE
Barbara Leigh-Hunt, Harold Innocent, Derek Jacobi
Devised and directed by Kenny McBain
Music arr. and played by Anthony Saunders

6-8 Sep. 22.45 *Lyceum Theatre*
MILVA SINGS BRECHT
with Walter Baracchi (pf)
Devised by Giorgio Strehler

23 Aug.-1 Sep. 22.45
Lodge Canongate Kilwinning
RABELAIS
Readings from J.M. Cohen's English translation.
Russell Hunter, Rose McBain

DANCE

HUNGARIAN STATE BALLET
24, 28, 30 Aug. 19.30 *King's Theatre*
THE MIRACULOUS MANDARIN
Choreographer László Seregi
Music Bartók
Scenery Gábor Forray
Costumes Tivadar Márk
with Duke Bluebeard's castle *See* Opera

31 Aug. 1,3 Sep. 19.30 *King's Theatre*
SPARTACUS
Choreographer László Seregi
Music Khachaturian
Scenery Gábor Forray
Costumes Tivadar Márk
Dancers Viktor Róna, Ferenc Havas, Adél Orosz, Lilla Pártay, Imre Dózsa, Levente Sipeki, Zoltán Nagy, Jenó Gál, László Sterbinszky, Vera Szumrák, Mária Kékesi, Katalin Csarnóy, Zoltán Fülöp, Sándor Erdélyi, Katalin Sebestény, László Pethó, Arpád Bozsó, Gyózó Ziahi, Mária Béreczes, Agoston Balogh, Viktor Fülöp
Conductor Tamás Pál

EXHIBITIONS

Royal Scottish Academy
PERMANENCES DE L'ART FRANÇAIS

City of Edinburgh Art Gallery
OBJECTS USA

Assembly Hall Forecourt
TYRONE GUTHRIE EXHIBITION

1974

OPERA

SCOTTISH OPERA
19. 22, 24, 27 Aug. 19.30 King's Theatre
ALCESTE Gluck
Alceste Julia Varady
Admète Robert Tear
Apollo/High priest Peter van der Bilt
Hercules Delme Bryn-Jones
Evander David Fieldsend
Thanatos Norman White
Herald/Oracle Arthur Jackson
Scottish National Orchestra
Scottish Ballet
Conductor Alexander Gibson
Director Anthony Besch
Designer John Stoddart
Lighting Charles Bristow
Choreographer Peter Darrell

EDINBURGH FESTIVAL OPERA
21, 23, 26 Aug. 19.30 King's Theatre
DON GIOVANNI Mozart
Don Giovanni Roger Soyer
Donna Anna Antigone Sgourda
Donna Elvira Heather Harper
Don Ottavio Luigi Alva
Leporello Geraint Evans
Zerlina Danièle Perriers
Masetto Alberto Rinaldi
The Commendatore Peter Lagger
Scottish Opera Chorus
English Chamber Orchestra
Conductor Daniel Barenboim
Director and designer Peter Ustinov
Lighting John B. Read

ROYAL OPERA, STOCKHOLM
29 Aug. 1, 6 Sep. 20.00 King's Theatre
ELEKTRA R. Strauss
Elektra Birgit Nilsson
Danica Mastilovic
Orestes Erik Saedén
Chrysothemis Berit Lindholm
Clytemnestra Barbro Ericson
Aegisthus Kolbjörn Höiseth
Ragnar Ulfung
Tutor Björn Asker
Confidant Kjerstin Dellert
Trainbearer Sylvia Lindenstrand
Young servant John-Erik Jacobsson
Old servant Paul Höglund
Overseer Margareta Bergström
Maidservants Ileana Peterson, Margot Rödin, Dorrit Kleimert, Hillevi Blylods, Laila Andersson
Conductor Berislav Klobucar
Director Ann-Margret Pettersson
Designer Jan Brazda
(Original production Rudolf Hartmann)

31 Aug. 4, 7 Sep. 19.30 King's Theatre
JENŮFA Janáček (Swed)
Jenufa Elisabeth Söderström
Laila Andersson
Kostelnicka Kerstin Meyer
Laca Kolbjörn Höiseth
Matti Kastu
Števa Jonny Blanc
Grandmother Buryja Margareta Bergström
Foreman Bo Lundborg
Mayor Sten Wahlund
His wife Kjerstin Dellert
Karolka Hillevi Blylods
Barena Solweig Lindström
Jano Gunilla Slättegård
Maid Margareta Sundman
Conductor Berislav Klobucar
Director Götz Friedrich
Scenery Reinhart Zimmermann
Costumes Jan Skalicky

3, 5 Sep. 19.30 King's Theatre
IL PASTOR FIDO Handel
Terpsichore Berit Sköld
Bass solo Ragne Wahlroth
Mirtillo/Apollo Margot Rödin
Amarilli/Erato Laila Andersson
Dorinda Sylvia Lindenstrand
Silvio Tord Slättegård
Eurilla Ileana Peterson
Tirenio Sten Wahlund
Dancers
Tommy Widerberg, Lillemor Arvidsson
Conductor Charles Farncombe
Director Bengt Peterson
Costumes David Walker
Choreographer Mary Skeaping

2, 3 Sep. 20.00 Gateway Theatre
THE VISION OF THÉRÈSE Werle
Thérèse Edith Thallaug
The stranger Fredrik Söderling
Julien Erik Saedén
Françoise Busk Margit Jonsson
Street-sweeper Margareta Bergström
Blind violin-player Lucian Savin
Factory girls
Gunilla Slättegård, Hillevi Bylods
Colombel Kåge Jehrlander
Drunken officers Kolbjörn Höiseth, Bo Lundborg, Paul Höglund
Maid Elizabeth Russell
Conductor Thomas Schuback
Director Lars Runsten
Costumes Kerstin Hedeby

ORCHESTRAL CONCERTS

SCOTTISH NATIONAL ORCHESTRA
18 Aug. 19.30 Usher Hall
Beethoven Leonore: Overture no.3
Mozart Concerto for piano no.23 in A, K488
Tippett Symphony no.3
Conductors Alexander Gibson, Sir Michael Tippett
Soloists Margaret Kingsley (sop), Sir Clifford Curzon (pf)

5 Sep. 20.00 Usher Hall
Nielsen Helios - Overture
Musgrave Concerto for horn
Liszt Concerto for piano no.2 in A
Sibelius Symphony no.2 in D, op.43
Conductors Alexander Gibson, Thea Musgrave
Soloists John Ogdon (pf), Barry Tuckwell (hn)

LONDON PHILHARMONIC ORCHESTRA
20, 21 Aug. 20.00 Usher Hall
Verdi Requiem
Conductor Carlo Maria Giulini
Soloists Martina Arroyo/Rita Hunter (sop), Fiorenza Cossotto (mez), Luciano Pavarotti (ten), Raffaele Arie (bs), EF Chorus

23 Aug. 20.00 Usher Hall
Mozart Symphony no.25 in G minor, K183
Schoenberg Erwartung
Mendelssohn Symphony no.3 in A minor (Scottish), op.56
Conductor Bernard Haitink
Soloist Anja Silja (sop)

25 Aug. 20.00 Usher Hall
Beethoven Symphony no.4 in B flat, op.60
Wolf Der Feuerreiter
Bruckner Te deum in C
Conductor Daniel Barenboim
Soloists Heather Harper (sop), Helen Watts (cont), Luigi Alva (ten), Peter Lagger (bs), EF Chorus

26 Aug. 20.00 Usher Hall
Mozart Le nozze di Figaro: Overture
Bartók Concerto for piano no.1
Bruckner Symphony no.4 in E flat (Romantic); ed. Haas
Conductor Bernard Haitink
Soloist Jean-Bernard Pommier (pf)

28 Aug. 20.00 Usher Hall
Elgar Falstaff
Mahler Lieder eines fahrenden Gesellen
Elgar Variations on an original theme (Enigma)
Conductor Daniel Barenboim
Soloist Dietrich Fischer-Dieskau (bar)

ENGLISH CHAMBER ORCHESTRA
Conductor Andrew Davis
22 Aug. 20.00 Usher Hall
Haydn Symphony no.44 in E minor (Trauersinfonie)
Mozart Concerto for piano no.17 in G, K453
Elgar Serenade for strings in E minor, op.20
Stravinsky Pulcinella - Suite
Soloist Richard Goode (pf)

24 Aug. 20.00 Usher Hall
Stravinsky Danses concertantes
Mozart Concerto for violin no.5 in A, K219
Musgrave Night music
Beethoven Symphony no.1 in C, op.21
Soloist Szymon Goldberg (vn)

BBC SCOTTISH SYMPHONY ORCHESTRA
30 Aug. 20.00 Usher Hall
Holst The perfect fool: Ballet music
Petrassi Concerto no.5
Weber Konzertstück for piano in F minor, op.79
Franck Symphony in D minor
Conductors Christopher Seaman, Goffredo Petrassi
Soloist Moura Lympany (pf)

VIENNA SYMPHONY ORCHESTRA
Conductor Carlo Maria Giulini
1 Sep. 20.00 Usher Hall
J.C. Bach Sinfonia concertante for violin and cello in A
Hindemith Mathis der Maler - Symphony
Mahler Symphony no.1 in D

2 Sep. 20.00 Usher Hall
Beethoven Concerto for piano no.4 in G, op.58
Bruckner Symphony no.2 in C minor
Soloist Alexis Weissenberg (pf)

LONDON SINFONIETTA
3 Sep. 20.00 Usher Hall
Dvořák Serenade for wind in D minor, op.44
Ligeti Chamber concerto for 13 instruments
Walton Facade
Conductor David Atherton
Soloists Mary Thomas, Derek Hammond-Stroud (spk)

4 Sep. 20.00 Usher Hall
Tchaikovsky Souvenir de Florence - string sextet, op.70
Křenek Exercises of a late hour

Mozart Serenade no.10 in B flat (Gran partita), K361
Conductors David Atherton, Ernst Krenek

SYDNEY SYMPHONY ORCHESTRA
6 Sep. 20.00 *Usher Hall*
Britten Sinfonia da requiem
Sculthorpe Sun music IV
Rodrigo Concierto de Aranjuez for guitar
Dvorák Symphony no.8 in G, op.88
Conductor Charles Mackerras
Soloist John Williams (gtr)

7 Sep. 20.00 *Usher Hall*
Beethoven Egmont: Overture
Mozart Concerto for piano no.25 in C, K503
Ravel Daphnis et Chloë
Conductor Willem van Otterloo
Soloist Roger Woodward (pf)
EF Chorus

CHAMBER CONCERTS

TRIO DI MILANO
20 Aug. 11.00 *Freemasons' Hall*
Mozart Trio for piano and strings no.3 in B flat, K502
Canino Labirinto no.5
Beethoven Trio for piano and strings no.7 in B flat (Archduke), op.97

22 Aug. 11.00 *Freemasons' Hall*
Haydn Trio for piano and strings no.25 in G
Ives Trio for piano and strings
Ravel Trio for piano and strings in A minor

MATRIX
24 Aug. 11.00 *Freemasons' Hall*
Music from the 14th-16th centuries arr. Hacker, Birtwistle, Schoenberg
Mozart Eine kleine deutsche Kantate
Searle Cat variations
C. Davis Countdown (1st public performance)
with Jane Manning (sop)

TUCKWELL WIND QUINTET
26 Aug. 11.00 *Freemasons' Hall*
Danzi Quintet for wind in F, op.68
Rossini Quartet for wind no.6
Schoenberg Quintet for wind, op.26

NEW MUSIC GROUP OF SCOTLAND
27 Aug. 11.00 *Freemasons' Hall*
Musgrave Chamber concerto no.2
Wilson Sonata for cello and piano
McGuire Rebirth
Dalby Whisper music
Director Edward Harper

NASH ENSEMBLE
27 Aug. 20.00 *Freemasons' Hall*
Bennett Commedia 1
Ives Songs
Forbes Partita for clarinet, cello and piano
Schoenberg Pierrot lunaire
Conductor Elgar Howarth
Soloist Cleo Laine (sop)

TEL AVIV QUARTET
28 Aug. 11.00 *Freemasons' Hall*
Haydn Quartet in D, op.20/4
Schoenberg Quartet no.2 in F sharp minor, op.10
Mendelssohn Quartet no.4 in E minor, op.44/2
with Heather Harper (sop)

30 Aug. 11.00 *Freemasons' Hall*
Tal Quartet no.1
Beethoven Quartet no.11 in F minor (Serioso), op.95
Schubert Quartet no.15 in G, D887

KING'S SINGERS
6 Sep. 11.00 *Freemasons' Hall*
Tallis The lamentations of Jeremiah
Dickinson Winter afternoons
Poulenc Laudes de Saint Antoine de Padoue
English madrigals by Farmer and Weelkes.
Songs with double bass
with Daryl Runswick (db)

7 Sep. 11.00 *Freemasons' Hall*
Patterson Time piece
Dvorák Five settings of Lithuanian folk song texts
Songs and madrigals of the 16th century
Arrangements in close harmony

RECITALS

CATHERINE GAYER (sop)
RICHARD RODNEY BENNETT (pf)
19 Aug. 11.00 *Freemasons' Hall*
Schoenberg Cabaret songs
Schoenberg Herzgewächse
Schoenberg Song arrangements

JESSYE NORMAN (sop)
IRWIN GAGE (pf)
23 Aug. 11.00 *Leith Town Hall*
Songs by Wolf, Mahler, Poulenc

ELISABETH SÖDERSTRÖM (sop)
KERSTIN MEYER (mez)
GEOFFREY PARSONS (pf)
29 Aug. 11.00 *Freemasons' Hall*
Songs and duets by Fauré, Rachmaninov. Sjögren, Rangström, J.C. Bach, Kodály, Morley, Lindblad, Geijer, Wennerberg, Rossini

DIETRICH FISCHER-DIESKAU (bar)
31 Aug. 20.00 *Usher Hall*
Schubert Winterreise
with Daniel Barenboim (pf)

3 Sep. 11.00 *Leith Town Hall*
Webern Four songs by Stefan George
Krenek Spätlese
Schoenberg Songs
with Aribert Reimann, Ernst Krenek (pf)

JOHN OGDON (pf)
19 Aug. 20.00 *Freemasons' Hall*
Beethoven Sonata no.30 in E, op.109
Ravel Gaspard de la Nuit
Ives Sonata no.2 (Concord)

RICHARD GOODE (pf)
21 Aug. 11.00 *Freemasons' Hall*
Mozart Sonata no.15 in F, K533/494
Brahms Piano pieces, op.116
Beethoven Sonata no.31 in A flat, op.110

ROGER WOODWARD (pf)
5 Sep. 11.00 *Freemasons' Hall*
Takemitsu Undisturbed rest
Takemitsu Piano distance
Takemitsu For away
A. Boyd Angklung
R. Meale Coruscations
Takahashi Cromamorphe II
Beethoven Sonata no.32 in C minor, op.111

SZYMON GOLDBERG (vn)
RADU LUPU (pf)
31 Aug. 11.00 *Leith Town Hall*
Mozart Sonata no.25 in F, K377
Mozart Sonata no.26 in B flat, K378
Mozart Sonata no.20 in C, K303
Mozart Sonata no.33 in E flat, K481

2 Sep. 11.00 *Leith Town Hall*
Mozart Sonata no.24 in F, K376
Mozart Sonata no.28 in E flat, K380
Mozart Sonata no.27 in G, K379
Mozart Sonata no.23 in D, K306

JOHN WILLIAMS (gtr)
4 Sep. 11.00 *Leith Town Hall*
Praetorius Terpsichore: 3 dances
Visée Suite in G
Bach Suite in E minor
Petrassi Nunc
Villa Lobos Five preludes
Bennett Five impromptus

DRAMA

ACTORS' COMPANY
19-24, 30, 31 Aug. 2, 3 Sep. 19.30 20, 24, 31 Aug. 14.30 *Assembly Hall*
TARTUFFE Molière
(Eng. Translated by Richard Wilbur)
Madame Pernell Sheila Burrell
Elmire Sheila Reid
Mariane Sharon Duce
Dorine Paola Dionisotti
Damis Juan Moreno
Cléante Robert Eddison
Orgon Windsor Davies
Valère Edward Petherbridge
Tartuffe Charles Kay
M. Loyal Robin Ellis
Officer Mark McManus
Filipote Judith Orbach
Director Peter James
Designer Geoffrey Scott
Lighting Mick Hughes

26-29 Aug. 4-7 Sep. 19.30 27 Aug. 7 Sep. 14.30 *Assembly Hall*
THE BACCHAE Euripides
(Eng. Translated by William Arrowsmith)
Dionysus Mark McManus
Chorus Paola Dionisotti, Sharon Duce, Sheila Reid
Teiresias Edward Petherbridge
Cadmus Robert Eddison
Pentheus Robin Ellis
Attendant Juan Moreno
Messengers Windsor Davies, Charles Kay
Agave Sheila Burrell
JACK AND THE BEANSTALK
(Revised by Edward Petherbridge)
Jack Sharon Duce
His mother Robin Ellis
Cow Paola Dionisotti, Sheila Reid
Bailiff's men Windsor Davies, Charles Kay
Cattle dealer Juan Moreno
Fairy godmother Sheila Burrell
Giant Mark McManus
Others
Robert Eddison, Edward Petherbridge
Director Edward Petherbridge
Scenery Geoffrey Scott
Costumes Chris Kinman
Lighting Mick Hughes

GOTHENBURG CITY THEATRE
23, 24 Aug. 19.15 24 Aug. 14.15
Lyceum Theatre
GUSTAV III Strindberg
Thorild/Kexell Dan Sjögren
Papillon/Lady Schröderheim Ebon Sorin
Halldin/Ribbing Ola Lindegren

Holmberg/Elis Schröderheim
Martin Berggren
Horn Lars Green
Anckarström/Chamberlain Sten Ljunggren
Munck/De Geer Christian Fiedler
General Pechlin Rune Turesson
Hallman/Armfelt Måns Westfelt
Fersen/Liljensparre Sven Berle
Olof Olsson Ingemar Carlehed
Taube Tomas von Brömssen
Gustav III/Captain Nordström Sven Wollter
Badin Leo Cullborg
Queen Sofia Magdalena Birgitta Palme
Bellman Sven-Eric Johanson
Director Lennart Hjulström
Designer Olle Montelius
Lighting Jan Holmgren, Ray Jönsson

ROYAL SHAKESPEARE COMPANY
26-31 Aug. 19.15 28, 31 Aug. 14.15
Lyceum Theatre
DOCTOR FAUSTUS Marlowe
Faustus Ian McKellen
Mephistophilis Emrys James
Beelzebub Richard Mayes
Lucifer Clement McCallin
Wagner Terence Wilton
1st Scholar/Frederick/Duke of Vanholt
Malcolm Armstrong
2nd Scholar/Charles V Leon Tanner
3rd Scholar/Benvolio Julian Barnes
Old man/Duke of Saxony John Boswall
Duchess of Vanholt Jean Gilpin
Countess Meriel Brook
Horse dealer Denis Holmes
Director John Barton
Designer Michael Annals
Lighting Michael Murray

ABBEY THEATRE, Dublin
3-7 Sep. 19.15 4, 7 Sep. 14.15
Lyceum Theatre
KING OEDIPUS Sophocles
(Eng. Adapted by W.B Yeats)
Oedipus Desmond Cave
Jocasta Angela Newman
Creon Patrick Laffan
Tiresias Eamon Kelly
Herdsman Michéal O Briain
1st Messenger Micheal O Aonghusa
2nd Messenger Bosco Hogan
Ismene Mandy Ratcliffe
Antigone Gabrielle Reidy
Priest Geoffrey Golden
Director Michael Cacoyannis
Designer Alan Barlow
Lighting Howard Eldridge

YOUNG LYCEUM COMPANY
*19 Aug.-7 Sep. 20.00 (exc.Sun) 22, 24, *28, 29, 31 Aug. 5, 7 Sep. 14.30*
Haymarket Ice Rink
THE FANTASTICAL FEATS OF FINN MacCOOL McCarthy
Finn Tony Haygarth
Grainne Jeni Giffen
King Ron Bain
Sava Jeananne Crowley
Dougal Patrick Malahide
Diarmuid Alex Norton
Cam Bill Paterson
Oisin Tony Rohr
Niaf Muriel Romanes
Queen Jan Wilson
Enemy/Dougie Kevin Costello
Druid Dermot Crowley
Nevin/Surly/Singer Hamish Imlach
Singer Dolina MacLennan
Patrick/Goll Michael Harrigan
Sgeolan/Oscar Julian Tew
Miscellaneous roles John Bett
Director Ian Ireland
Scenery John Byrne
Costumes Priscilla Truett
Lighting André Tammes
Music comp. and perf'd by Planxty
*Extra performance

MUMMENSCHANZ COMPANY
26-31 Aug. 19.45 29, 31 Aug. 14.45
Church Hill Theatre
Andres Bossard, Bernie Schurch, Floriana Frassetto

PERFORMANCE GROUP
30 Aug.-7 Sep. 22.45 (exc.Sun)
Cambridge Street Studio
THE TOOTH OF CRIME Shepard
Becky Lou Joan MacIntosh
Star/Ref Elizabeth Le Compte
Doc/Galactic Max
Stephen Borst/Leeny Sack
Cheyenne James Griffiths
Hoss Spalding Gray
Crow Timothy Shelton
Director Richard Schechner
Costumes
Franne Lee, Patricia Barnes

POETRY AND PROSE RECITALS

21-23 Aug. 15.00 *St Cecilia's Hall*
CARLYLE AND JANE
Arr. from the letters and papers of Thomas Carlyle and Jane Welsh by Henry Donald
Tom Fleming, Edith Macarthur (rdr)

28-30 Aug. 15.00 *St Cecilia's Hall*
ROBERT FERGUSSON
Tom Fleming, James Cairncross (rdr), Clifford Hughes (ten)
Devised by Tom Fleming

25 Aug. 20.00 *St Cecilia's Hall*
LOVE AND MARRIAGE
Moira Shearer, Ludovic Kennedy (rdr), Martin Best (lute, gtr)
Devised by Patrick Garland

1 Sep. 20.00 2-4 Sep. 15.00
St Cecilia's Hall
QUEEN VICTORIA IN THE HIGHLANDS
Barbara Leigh-Hunt, Margaretta Scott, James Cairncross (rdr), Marie Korchinska (hp)
Devised by John Carroll

LATE NIGHT ENTERTAINMENT

22-24 Aug. 22.45 *Lyceum Theatre*
ALAN STIVELL and his Folk Ensemble

29-31 Aug. 22.45 *Lyceum Theatre*
CLEO LAINE and JOHN DANKWORTH

31 Aug. 6, 7 Sep. *Haymarket Ice Rink*
PLANXTY

DANCE

KATHAKALI DANCE TROUPE
19 Aug. 19.15 *Lyceum Theatre*
THE MAN-LION
THE RISE OF RAVANA

20 Aug. 19.15 *Lyceum Theatre*
THE RAMAYANA

21 Aug. 14.15 *Lyceum Theatre*
THE SONS OF PANDU

21 Aug. 14.15 *Lyceum Theatre*
THE MAHABHARATA
Padmasri Kalamandalam Krishnan Nayar, Mankompu Sivasankara Pillai, Pandalam Kerala Varma, Kalamandalam Vasudevan Pisharoty, Kalamandalam Hyderali, Kesavadev, Kalamandalam Karunakaran, Kunju Panicker, Nambisan, Kalamandalam Kesavan, Peethambaran Ramakrishnan, Kalamandalam Unnikrishnan Kurup, Kalamandalam Gopi, Udyogamandal Padmanabhan, Kangazha Madhavan, Nelliyode Vasudevan Nambudin, Parameswaran

BAT-DOR DANCE COMPANY
19, 20, 22 Aug. 19.45 23 Aug. 14.45
Church Hill Theatre
FROM HOPE TO HOPE
Choreographer Michael Descombey
Music Bernard Parmegiane
Designer Moshe Ben-Shaul
REQUIEM FOR SOUNDS
Choreographer Gene Hill Sagan
Music Zvi Avni, Barber
Costumes Gene Hill Sagan
MOVEMENTS IN A ROCKY LANDSCAPE
Choreographer Rudi van Dantzig
Music Ligeti
Designer Toer van Schayk
AND AFTER
Choreographer Gene Hill Sagan
Music Bach
Scenery Dani Karavan
Costumes Lea Ladman

21 Aug. 19.45 22 Aug. 14.45 24 Aug. 20.30 *Church Hill Theatre*
COUPLES
Choreographer Rudi van Dantzig
Music Zvi Avni
Designer Toer van Schayk
METALLICS
Choreographer Paul Sanasardo
Music Cowell, Badings
Costumes Avigail Ewert
PALOMAS
Choreographer and designer
Manuel Alum
Music Pauline Oliveros
THE WAIT
Choreographer Michael Descombey
Music Sergio Natra
Designer Eric Smith
Dancers Jeanette Ordman, Yehuda Maor, Igal Berdichevsky, Nira Paaz, Bert Terborgh, Miriam Zamir, Igal Perry, Anna Marie Tannenbaum, Meira Banai, David Rapoport, Lea Lichtenstein, Dahlia Dvir, David Dvir, Ora Dror, Elinor Ambash, Eddi Vinocur, Karen Paskow, Abigail Ben Ari, Margalit Rubin
Musica Viva of London
Conductor Michael Reeves

EXHIBITIONS

Royal Scottish Academy
AACHEN INTERNATIONAL 70/74
Contemporary art from the Ludwig Collection

ASSOCIATED EXHIBITIONS
(Not organized by the Festival Society)

City of Edinburgh Art Centre
18th CENTURY MUSICAL INSTRUMENTS

Fruit Market Gallery
ELEVEN DUTCH ARTISTS

1975

OPERA

EDINBURGH FESTIVAL OPERA
25, 28, 30 Aug. 7 Sep.19.00 10 Sep. 20.00 *King's Theatre*
LE NOZZE DI FIGARO Mozart
Figaro Geraint Evans
Susanna Ileana Cotrubas
Count Dietrich Fischer-Dieskau
Countess Heather Harper
Cherubino Teresa Berganza
Dr Bartolo William McCue
Marcellina Birgit Finnilä
Don Basilio John Fryatt
Barbarina Danièle Perriers
Don Curzio John Robertson
Antonio Malcolm Donnelly
Peasant girls Elizabeth Ritchie, Patricia O'Neill
Scottish Opera Chorus
English Chamber Orchestra
Conductor Daniel Barenboim
Director Sir Geraint Evans
Designer John Fraser
Lighting Charles Bristow

SCOTTISH OPERA
27, 29 Aug. 19.30 *King's Theatre*
HERMISTON Orr (World première)
Lord Hermiston Michael Langdon
Archie Weir Lenus Carlson
Frank Innes Nigel Douglas
Kirstie Elliott Patricia Kern
Christina Catherine Gayer
Dand Gordon Sandison
Parson Arthur Jackson
Groom Peter Bodenham
Shepherd Norman White
Milkmaid Linda Finnie
Grieve Bruce Budd
Duncan Jopp Jim Hastie
Scottish Chamber Orchestra
Conductor Alexander Gibson
Director Toby Robertson
Designer Robin Archer
Lighting Robert Ornbo

DEUTSCHE OPER, BERLIN
9, 12 Sep. 19.30 *King's Theatre*
LULU Berg
Lulu Catherine Gayer
Countess Geschwitz Patricia Johnson
Dr Schön Hans Günter Nöcker
Alwa Donald Grobe
Painter Loren Driscoll
Schigolch Josef Greindl
Rodrigo/Animal-tamer Gerd Feldhoff
Dr Goll/Jack the Ripper Walter Dicks
Schoolboy Barbara Scherler
Prince Martin Vantin
Theatre-director Ernst Krukowski
Wardrobe-mistress Maria José Brill
Valet Leopold Clam
Negro Manfred Haake
Clown Martin Rosenthal
Conductor Reinhard Peters
Director Gustav Rudolf Sellner
Designer Filippo Sanjust

11, 13 Sep. 20.00 *King's Theatre*
SALOME R. Strauss
Salome Ursula Schröder-Feinen
Jokanaan William Dooley
Herod Hans Beirer
Herodias Astrid Varnay
Narraboth Peter Gougaloff
Page Maria José Brill
5 Jews Martin Vantin, Cornelis van Dijk, Helmut Krebs, William Wu, Josef Becker
2 Nazarenes Josef Greindl, Walter Dicks
Soldiers Ernst Krukowski, Victor von Halem, Klaus Lang
Slave Barbara Scherler
Conductor Gerd Albrecht
Director and designer Wieland Wagner

ORCHESTRAL CONCERTS

SCOTTISH NATIONAL ORCHESTRA
Conductor Alexander Gibson
24 Aug. 19.30 *Usher Hall*
Orr Symphony no.2
Beethoven Concerto for piano no.5 in E flat (Emperor), op.73
Prokofiev Romeo and Juliet - Suite
Soloist Daniel Barenboim (pf)

31 Aug. 20.00 *Usher Hall*
C.P.E. Bach Sinfonia in B flat
Monteverdi L'incoronazione di Poppea: Addio Roma
Vivaldi Giuditta triumphans: Aria del Vagante
Haydn Symphony no.61 in D
Haydn Giannina's aria (Giannina e Bernadone)
Mozart La clemenza di Tito: Deh, per questo instante solo *and* Parto, parto
Mozart Symphony no.29 in A, K201
Soloist Teresa Berganza (mez)

11 Sep. 20.00 *Usher Hall*
Mozart March in D, K249
Mozart Divertimento no.17 in D, K334: Minuet
Mozart Die Zauberflöte: O Isis und Osiris *and* Das klinget so herrlich
Mozart A questo seno
Mozart Serenade no.6 in D (Serenata notturna), K239
Mozart Alma grande e nobil core
Mozart Three German dances, K605
J. Strauss Egyptischer Marsch
J. Strauss Tik-Tak polka
J. Strauss Die Fledermaus: Czardas
J. Strauss Tritsch Tratsch polka
J. Strauss Sängerslust polka
J. Strauss Covent Garden waltz
J. Strauss Pizzicato polka
J. Strauss Perpetuum mobile
J. Strauss An der schönon blauen Donau
Soloist Gundula Janowitz (sop)
SNO Chorus

LONDON PHILHARMONIC ORCHESTRA
26 Aug. 20.00 *Usher Hall*
Mozart Sinfonia concertante for wind, K297b
Beethoven Symphony no.9 in D minor (Choral), op.125

27 Aug. 20.00 *Usher Hall*
Haydn Sinfonia concertante in B flat, op.84
Beethoven Symphony no.9 in D minor (Choral), op.125
Conductor Carlo Maria Giulini
Soloists Helen Donath (sop), Alfreda Hodgson (cont), Anthony Rolfe Johnson (ten), Marius Rintzler (bs), EF Chorus

30 Aug. 20.00 *Usher Hall*
Mussorgsky A night on the Bare Mountain
Mussorgsky Songs and dances of death; orch. Shostakovich
Tchaikovsky Symphony no.4 in F minor, op.36
Conductor Mstislav Rostropovich
Soloist Galina Vishnevskaya (sop)

ENGLISH CHAMBER ORCHESTRA
27 Aug. 11.00 *Leith Theatre*
Handel Concerto grosso in A, op.6/11
Haydn Symphony no.7 in C (Le midi)
Torelli Concerto for trumpet in D
Stravinsky Concerto in E flat (Dumbarton Oaks)
Haydn Concerto for trumpet in E flat
Conductor Carl Pini
Soloist Maurice André (tpt)

NEW YORK PHILHARMONIC ORCHESTRA
Conductor Pierre Boulez
28 Aug. 20.00 *Usher Hall*
Berlioz Roméo et Juliette: Excerpts
Carter Concerto for orchestra
Stravinsky Petrushka (1911 version)

29 Aug. 20.00 *Usher Hall*
Beethoven Symphony no.7 in A, op.97
Ligeti Lontano
Mahler Symphony no.10: 1st movement
Bartók The miraculous mandarin - Suite

ISRAEL PHILHARMONIC ORCHESTRA
Conductor Zubin Mehta
1 Sep. 20.00 *Usher Hall*
Schubert Symphony no.3 in D, D200
Berg Concerto for violin
Dvořák Symphony no.7 in D minor, op.70
Soloist Itzhac Perlman (vn)

3 Sep. 20.00 *Usher Hall*
Schoenberg Variations, op.31
Mozart Concerto for piano no.9 in E flat, K271
Berlioz Harold in Italy
Soloists Alfred Brendel (pf), Daniel Benyamini (va)

4 Sep. 20.00 *Usher Hall*
Mozart Symphony no.34 in C, K338
Mahler Kindertotenlieder
Stravinsky The rite of spring
Soloist Janet Baker (mez)

LONDON SYMPHONY ORCHESTRA
2 Sep. 20.00 *Usher Hall*
Prokofiev Sinfonia concertante for cello in E minor, op.125
Prokofiev Alexander Nevsky
Conductor Claudio Abbado
Soloists Galina Vishnevskaya (sop), Mstislav Rostropovich (vc), EF Chorus

5 Sep. 20.00 *Usher Hall*
Brahms Concerto for piano no.2 in B flat, op.83
Brahms Symphony no.4 in E minor, op.98
Conductor Claudio Abbado
Soloist Rafael Orozco (pf)

6 Sep. 20.00 *Usher Hall*
Haydn Symphony no.88 in G
Prokofiev Concerto for violin no.1 in D, op.19
Prokofiev Symphony no.5 in B flat, op.100
Conductor André Previn
Soloist Kyung-Wha Chung (vn)

8 Sep. 20.00 *Usher Hall*
V. Williams Symphony no.5 in D
Rachmaninov The bells
Conductor André Previn
Soloists Sheila Armstrong (sop), Robert Tear (ten), John Shirley-Quirk (bar), EF Chorus

10 Sep. 20.00 *Usher Hall*
Bernstein Chichester psalms
Mozart Concerto for piano no.17 in G, K453
Sibelius Symphony no.5 in E flat, op.82
Conductor and soloist Leonard Bernstein (pf)

ORCHESTRE NATIONAL DE FRANCE
12, 13 Sep. 20.00 *Usher Hall*
Ravel Alborada del gracioso
Ravel Shéhérazade
Ravel Concerto for piano in G
Ravel Tzigane for violin and orchestra
Ravel La valse
Conductor Leonard Bernstein
Soloists Marilyn Horne (mez), Boris Belkin (pf)

CHAMBER CONCERTS

THE CONSORT OF MUSICKE
25 Aug. 11.00 *Freemasons' Hall*
A handefull of pleasant delites: domestic music of Britain c.1600
Works by Ravenscroft, Holborne, Corkine, Bacheler, R. Johnson, Ford, Danyel, Cavendish, Allison, J. Johnson *and* Anon.

CANTILENA
25 Aug. 23.00 *Signet Library*
Director Adrian Shepherd
Gabrieli Canzona à 8
Ferrabosco II Pavane no.2
Bartolini Canzona à 8
Bach Concerto for violin and oboe in D minor
Farina Pavane
Corelli Concerto grosso in G minor (Christmas), op.6/8

2 Sep. 23.00 *Signet Library*
Widmann Canzona, Intrada, Canzona
Vivaldi Concerto for flute in F (La tempesta di mare), op.10/1
Ferrabosco II Pavane no.3
Telemann Concerto for viola in G
Gabrieli Canzona à 7
Albinoni Concerto for oboe in D minor, Op.9/2
Vivaldi Concerti, op.3 (L'estro armonico): No.11 in D minor

12 Sep. 23.00 *Signet Library*
Widmann Canzona, Galliard, Intrada
Ferrabosco II Pavane no.4
Gussago Canzona à 8
Bach Concerto for 2 violins in D minor
Purcell Chaconne in G minor
Locatelli Concerto grosso in F minor

TOKYO QUARTET
26 Aug. 11.00 *Freemasons' Hall*
Haydn Quartet in B flat, op.50/1
Bartók Quartet no.2
Beethoven Quartet no.9 in C (Rasumovsky), op.59/3

28 Aug. 11.00 *Freemasons' Hall*
Mozart Quartet no.21 in D, K575
Bartók Quartet no.3
Brahms Quartet no.3 in B flat, op.67

NEW MUSIC GROUP OF SCOTLAND
30 Aug. 11.00 *Freemasons' Hall*
M. Wilkins Circus (World première)
Dorward Capriccio for viola
Maderna Serenata no.2
Dallapiccola Quaderno musicale di Annalibera
Harper Ricercare in memoriam Luigi Dallapiccola (World première)
Director Edward Harper

AMADEUS QUARTET
6 Sep. 11.00 *Leith Theatre*
Haydn Quartet in E flat, op.64/6
Mozart Quartet no.14 in G, K387
Schubert Quartet no.13 in A minor, D804

8 Sep. 11.00 *Leith Theatre*
Beethoven Quartet no.1 in F, op.18/1
Beethoven Quartet no.14 in C sharp minor, op.131

VESUVIUS ENSEMBLE
9 Sep. 11.00 *Freemasons' Hall*
Mozart Adagio and rondo for glass harmonica, K617
Prokofiev Overture on Jewish themes
Mozart Quartet for oboe and strings in F, K370
Boulez Sonatine for flute and piano
Lutyens Concertante for 5 players, op.22
Ravel Introduction and allegro for flute, clarinet, harp and strings

11 Sep. 11.00 *Freemasons' Hall*
Prokofiev Quintet for oboe, clarinet and strings in G minor, op.39
Mozart Quartet for flute and strings no.1 in D, K285
Rossini Quartet no.4 in B flat
Janáček Concertino for piano and chamber ensemble

PLEETH, WALLFISCH, DE PEYER TRIO
10 Sep. 11.00 *Freemasons' Hall*
Beethoven Trio for clarinet cello and piano, op.11
Leighton Fantasy for clarinet, cello and piano, op.70
Brahms Trio for clarinet, cello and piano in A minor, op.114

ALLEGRI QUARTET
12 Sep. 11.00 *Freemasons' Hall*
Shostakovich Quartet no.8 in C minor, op.110
Gal Quartet no.4, op.99
Beethoven Quartet no.8 in E minor (Rasumovsky), op.59/2

RECITALS

CATHERINE GAYER (sop)
ARIBERT REIMANN (pf)
1 Sep. 11.00 *Freemasons' Hall*
Reimann Six poems by Sylvia Plath
Dallapiccola Quattro liriche de Antonio Machado
Songs by Ravel, R. Strauss

GALINA VISHNEVSKAYA (sop)
MSTISLAV ROSTROPOVICH (pf)
4 Sep. 11.00 *Leith Theatre*
Songs by Tchaikovsky, Rachmaninov, Mussorgsky, Prokofiev, Stravinsky

ANTHONY ROLFE JOHNSON (ten)
DAVID WILLISON (pf)
13 Sep. 11.00 *Freemasons' Hall*
Schumann Liederkreis, op.39
V. Williams Songs of travel
Poulenc Songs

EMANUEL AX (pf)
25 Aug. 20.00 *Usher Hall*
Bach Partita no.1 in B flat
Schoenberg Klavierstücke, op.19
Beethoven Sonata no.21 in C (Waldstein), op.53
Chopin Sonata no.3 in B minor, op.58

ALFRED BRENDEL (pf)
31 Aug. 15.00 *Usher Hall*
Schubert Klavierstücke, D946
Schubert Fantasia in C (Wanderer), D760
Schubert Sonata no.17 in D, D850

RAFAEL OROZCO (pf)
2 Sep. 11.00 *Leith Theatre*
Beethoven Sonata no.27 in E minor, op.90
Schumann Fantasia in C, op.17
Chopin Nocturne no.18 in E, op.62/2
Chopin Scherzo no.4 in E, op.54
Prokofiev Sonata no.7 in B flat, op.83

BRUNO CANINO
ANTONIO BALLISTA (pf)
5 Sep. 11.00 *Freemasons' Hall*
Mozart Sonata for 2 pianos in D, K448
Brahms Hungarian dances for piano duet: Excerpts
Bussotti Tableaux vivants for 2 pianos
Stravinsky Concerto for 2 pianos

ITZHAC PERLMAN (vn)
BRUNO CANINO (pf)
3 Sep. 11.00 *Freemasons' Hall*
Schubert Sonatina no.1 in D, D384
Bach Sonata for solo violin no.2 in A minor
Prokofiev Sonata no.2 in D, op.94a
Kreisler Liebesfreud
Kreisler Liebeslied
Kreisler Tambourin chinois, op.3

MSTISLAV ROSTROPOVICH (vc)
6 Sep. 18.00 *St Cuthbert's Church*
Bach Suites nos. 2, 3, 6

DRAMA

PROSPECT THEATRE COMPANY
26 Aug.-13 Sep. 19.30 (exc.Sun) 30 Aug. 6, 13 Sep. 14.30 *Assembly Hall*
PILGRIM (A musical based on Bunyan's *A pilgrim's progress*)
Christian Paul Jones
Christian's wife Joanna Carlin
Evangelist John Bowe
Worldly Wiseman/Diffidence/Talkative Paul Nicholas
Appolyon/Vanity Fair/Giant Despair Peter Straker
Faithful Ben Cross
Hopeful Geoffrey Burridge
Knowledge/Voice of the Shining One Ena Cabayo
Malice/Sincere Christopher Asante
Narrator/ Faint Heart/ Lord Hategood/ Watchful Ken Bones
Superstition David Freedman
Leading Tongue Kim Goody
Atheist Stafford Gordon
Ignorance Julian Littman
Charity Verity Anne Meldrum
Mistrust/Experience Terence Molloy
Guilt/Envy Joshua Smith
Other parts played by Stephen Earle, George Farmer, Robert Farrant, Peter Leech, Ben Overhead, Tim Rice, Josephine Welcome
Adapted by Jane McCulloch
Music Carl Davis
Director Toby Robertson
Designer Robin Archer
Choreographer Robert North
Lighting John B. Read

ROYAL LYCEUM THEATRE COMPANY
25-30 Aug. 19.15 27, 30 Aug. 14.15
Lyceum Theatre

HOW MAD TULLOCH WAS TAKEN AWAY Morris

Tulloch — James Grant
Macadam — Paul Young
Archie — Ian Ireland
Grey — Alec Heggie
Duffy — Benny Young
Major Hait — Timothy Carlton
Sergeant Prickle — Rikki Fulton
Lydia — Vivien Heilbron
Padre — John Grieve
Hewitt — Roddy McMillan
Fraser — James Cairncross, John Young
Corporal Rock — Martin Black
Corporal Grunt — William Armour
Sergeant — John Young, Jay Smith
Fusilier — Dermot Crowley
2nd Soldier — Jay Smith
Barman — Harry Fox
Girl — Doreen Cameron
Piper — Ronnie Ackroyd
Director — Bill Bryden
Scenery — Hayden Griffin
Costumes — Deirdre Clancy
Lighting — Andy Phillips

NOTTINGHAM PLAYHOUSE
1-6 Sep. 19.15 3, 6 Sep.14.15
Lyceum Theatre
AS YOU LIKE IT Shakespeare

Rosalind — Jane Lapotaire
Orlando — John Price
Oliver — David Bailie
Jaques de Boys/Dennis — Malcolm Ingram
Celia — Susan Tracy
Touchstone — Alun Armstrong
Duke Frederick — Paul Dawkins, Anthony Douse
Duke Senior — Patrick Holt
Amiens — Archie Tew
Jaques — John Normington
Sir Oliver Martext/Adam — Leslie Sarony
Le Beau — Peter Myers
Charles — Garry McDermott
Corin/Hymen — Anthony Douse
Silvius — James Hazeldine
Audrey — Susan Porrett
Phebe — Caroline Hutchison
William — Matthew Scurfield
Director — Peter Gill
Scenery — William Dudley
Costumes — Deirdre Clancy
Lighting — Rory Dempster

THE COMPANY/THE SPACE, South Africa
27 Aug.-6 Sep. 19.45 (exc.Sun) 30 Aug. 4, 6 Sep. 14.45 — *Church Hill Theatre*
DIMETOS Fugard

Dimetos — Carel Trichardt
Lydia — Vanessa Cooke
Sophia — Yvonne Bryceland
Danilo — Wilson Dunster
Director — Athol Fugard
Designer — Douglas Heap

COOPERATIVA TUSCOLANO
5, 6, 8-13 Sep. 20.00 — *Haymarket Ice Rink*
UTOPIA Aristophanes
(It. Adapted by Luca Ronconi)
Maria Acevedo, Maria Teresa Albani, Mauro Avogardo, Francesco Capitano, Gianfilippo Carcano, Alberto Cracco, Maria Cumani-Quasimodo, Ruggero de Daninos, Massimo de Rossi, Sarah di Nepi, Antonello Fassari, Nestor Garay, Cesare Gelli, Claudia Giannotti, Paulo Granata, Nicoileta Languasco, Anita Laurenzi, Roberto Longo, Giuliano Manetti, Gabriele Martini, Lorenzo Minniti, Carlo Monni, Alessandro Quasimodo, Franco Patano, Elisabetta Pedrazzi, Giancarlo Prati, Marilù Prati, Aldo Puglisi, Rosabianca Scerrino, Tullio Valli, Nico Vassallo, Gabriella Zamparini

Director — Luca Ronconi
Designer — Luciano Damiani

POETRY AND PROSE RECITALS

27-29 Aug. 15.00 — *St Cecilia's Hall*
KING JAMES VI and I
Lennox Milne, James Cairncross, John Westbrook (rdr)
Devised by Caroline Bingham
Directed by John Carroll

31 Aug. 20.00 1, 2 Sep. 15.00
St Cecilia's Hall
LOVE AMONG THE SCOTS
Moira Shearer, Ludovic Kennedy (rdr), Clifford Hughes (ten)
Directed by Patrick Garland

4, 5 Sep. 15.00 — *St Cecilia's Hall*
MR TOPHAM'S DIARY
Mr Topham — Timothy West
with Helen McArthur (sop), Edna Arthur (vn), Moray Welsh (vc), Sandra Brown (hpd)
Devised by David Johnson

10-12 Sep. 15.00 — *St Cecilia's Hall*
IS THERE ANYBODY THERE?
A programme on the supernatural and the macabre
Judi Dench, Gabriel Woolf (rdr)
Devised by John Carroll

LATE NIGHT ENTERTAINMENT

4-6 Sep. 22.45 — *Lyceum Theatre*
NUOVA COMPAGNIA DI CANTO POPOLARE, Italy
Fausta Vetere, Nunzio Areni, Giuseppe Barra, Eugenio Bennato, Giovanni Mauriello, Patrizio Trampetti
Co-ordinated by Roberto de Simone

DANCE

ROYAL BALLET
1, 2 Sep. 19.30 — *King's Theatre*
RAYMONDA: Act 3
Choreographer — Rudolf Nureyev *after* Petipa
Music — Glazunov
Designer — Barry Kay
GROSSE FUGE
Choreographer — Hans van Manen
Music — Beethoven
Scenery — Jean-Paul Vroom
Costumes — Hans van Manen
ROMEO AND JULIET: Balcony scene
Choreographer — Kenneth MacMillan
Music — Prokofiev
Designer — Nicholas Georgiadis
PRODIGAL SON
Choreographer — George Balanchine
Music — Prokofiev
Designer — Georges Rouault

3, 4 Sep. 19.30 — *King's Theatre*
CONCERTO
Choreographer — Kenneth MacMillan
Music — Shostakovich
Designer — Jürgen Rose
GISELLE
Choreographers — Nicholas Sergeyev *after* Coralli *and* Perrot
Music — Adam
Designer — Peter Farmer

5, 6 Sep. 19.30 — *King's Theatre*
THE DREAM
Choreographer — Sir Frederick Ashton
Music — Mendelssohn; arr.Lanchbery
Designer — Peter Farmer
APOLLO
Choreographer — George Balanchine
Music — Stravinsky
EL AMOR BRUJO (World première)
Choreographer — Peter Wright
Music — Falla
Designer — Stefanos Lazaridis
Dancers Lynn Seymour, Rudolf Nureyev, Margaret Barbieri, Alain Dubreuil, Stephen Jefferies, Nicholas Johnson, Brenda Last, Vyvyan Lorrayne, Lois Strike, Marion Tait
Conductor — Barry Wordsworth

NIKOLAIS DANCE THEATER, USA
8-10 Sep. 19.15 10 Sep. 14.15
Lyceum Theatre
SANCTUM: Group dance
VAUDEVILLE OF THE ELEPHANTS: Trio
MASKS, PROPS AND MOBILES: Noumenon
FOREPLAY
CROSS-FADE

11-13 Sep. 19.15 13 Sep. 14.15
Lyceum Theatre
TEMPLE
SCENARIO
SOMNILOQUY: Duet
MASKS, PROPS AND MOBILES: Tensile involvement
THE TRIBE
Choreography, design and sound — Alwin Nikolais
Dancers Lisbeth Bagnold, Suzanne McDermaid, Bill Groves, Jessica Sayre, Chris Reisner, Gerald Otte, Karen Sing, Carlo Pellegrini, James Teeters, Joe Zina

EXHIBITIONS

Royal Scottish Museum
JAMES VI and I

Royal Scottish Academy
CERI RICHARDS

Scottish National Gallery of Modern Art
KANDINSKY

ASSOCIATED EXHIBITIONS
(Not organized by the Festival Society)

Scottish Arts Council Gallery
A KIND OF GENTLE PAINTING

Fruit Market Gallery
EIGHT FROM BERLIN

Canongate Tolbooth Museum
HERITAGE

1976

OPERA

SCOTTISH OPERA
23, 26, 28, 30 Aug. 19.30 King's Theatre
MACBETH Verdi
Macbeth Norman Bailey
Lady Macbeth Galina Vishnevskaya
Banquo David Ward
Macduff David Hillman
Malcolm Graham Clark
Gentlewoman Lola Biagioni
Doctor/Lieutenant Arthur Jackson
Duncan Alexander Rose
Scottish Philharmonia
Conductor Alexander Gibson
Director David Pountney
Designer Ralph Koltai
Lighting Nick Chelton

DEUTSCHE OPER AM RHEIN
2, 4 Sep. 18.00 King's Theatre
PARSIFAL Wagner
Parsifal Sven Olof Eliasson, Werner Götz
Kundry Eva Randova
Amfortas Leif Roar
Gurnemanz Peter Meven, Malcolm Smith
Titurel Constantin Dumitru, Marius Rintzler
Klingsor Zenon Kosnowski
Esquires Miya Majima, Patricia Parker, Heinz Leyer, Helmut Pampuch
Knights Wilhelm Richter, E. Lee Davis
Voice from above Keiko Yano
Flowermaidens Nassrin Azarmi, Reingard Didusch, Patricia Parker, Rachel Yakar, Brigitte Dürrler, Keiko Yano
Dancers Helena Pejskova, Niloufer Pieris, Roswitha Rossack
Conductor Günther Wich
Director Georg Reinhardt
Scenery Heinrich Wendel
Costumes Günter Kappel

5, 8, 10 Sep. 19.30 King's Theatre
L'ITALIANA IN ALGERI Rossini
Isabella Julia Hamari
Lindoro Ugo Benelli
Mustafà Constantin Dumitru
Taddeo Zenon Kosnowski
Elvira Nassrin Azarmi
Zulma Patricia Parker
Haly Toshimitsu Kimura
Conductor Peter Schneider
Director and designer Jean-Pierre Ponnelle

7, 11 Sep. 19.30 King's Theatre
MOSES UND ARON Schoenberg
Moses Peter Meven
Aron Sven Olof Eliasson
Young girl Nassrin Azarmi
Young man Alva Tripp
Another man Jaroslav Stajnc
Priest Helmut Fehn
Sick woman Keiko Yano
Ephraimit Kurt Gester
Naked girls Miya Majima, Brigitte Dürrler, Patricia Parker, Ingrid Karrasch
Tribe leaders Andrzej Saciuk, Wilhelm Schaefer, E. Lee Davis
Dancers Inge Koch, Mirja Tervamaa, Tilly Söffing, Linda Thorp, Lazo Turozi, Petr Vondruska
Conductor Günther Wich
Director Georg Reinhardt
Scenery Heinrich Wendel
Costumes Günter Kappel, Pet Halmen

EDINBURGH FESTIVAL OPERA
25, 27, 29, 31 Aug. 19.00 King's Theatre
LE NOZZE DI FIGARO Mozart
Figaro Geraint Evans
Susanna Judith Blegen
Count Dietrich Fischer-Dieskau
Countess Heather Harper
Cherubino Teresa Berganza
Dr Bartolo William McCue
Marcellina Birgit Finnilä
Don Basilio John Fryatt
Barbarina Elizabeth Gale
Don Curzio John Robertson
Antonio Malcolm Donnelly
Peasant girls Elizabeth Ritchie, Patricia O'Neill
Scottish Opera Chorus
English Chamber Orchestra
Conductor Daniel Barenboim
Director Sir Geraint Evans
Designer John Fraser
Lighting Charles Bristow

BBC SCOTTISH SYMPHONY ORCHESTRA
25 Aug. 20.00 Usher Hall
DIE DREI PINTOS Weber (arr. Mahler)
Don Pantaleone Richard Gill
Don Gomez Hermann Winkler
Clarissa Sona Ghazarian
Laura Bernadette Greevy
Don Gaston Michael Cousins
Don Pinto Dieter Weller
Ines Sarah Walker
Ambrosio Peter-Christoph Runge
Host/Narrator Ian Wallace
John Alldis Choir
Conductor Alberto Erede

ORCHESTRAL CONCERTS

SCOTTISH NATIONAL ORCHESTRA
22 Aug. 20.00 Usher Hall
Weber Oberon: Overture
Britten Cantata academica
Dvorák Symphony no.9 in E minor (New World), op.95
Conductor Mstislav Rostropovich
Soloists Sheila Armstrong (sop), Helen Watts (cont), Anthony Rolfe Johnson (ten), Thomas Allen (bar), EF Chorus

4 Sep. 20.00 Usher Hall
Nielsen Helios - Overture
Sibelius Concerto for violin in D minor, op.47
Elgar Symphony no.1 in A flat, op.55
Conductor Alexander Gibson
Soloist Miriam Fried (vn)

LONDON SINFONIETTA
24 Aug. 20.00 Usher Hall
Stravinsky Concerto in E flat (Dumbarton Oaks)
Telemann Concerto for oboe d'amore no.1 in G
Henze Katarina Blum - Concert suite
Donizetti Concertino in G for cor anglais
Weber Concerto for oboe and 10 instruments
Copland Appalachian spring - Suite
Conductor Mark Elder
Soloist Heinz Holliger (ob)

LONDON PHILHARMONIC ORCHESTRA
Conductor Carlo Maria Giulini
26 Aug. 20.00 Usher Hall
Haydn Symphony no.94 in G (Surprise)
Mahler Das Lied von der Erde
Soloists Julia Hamari (mez), John Mitchinson (ten)

28, 29 Aug. 20.00 Usher Hall
Beethoven Mass in D (Missa solemnis), op.123
Soloists Edda Moser (sop), Anna Reynolds (mez), Robert Tear (ten), Gwynne Howell (bs), EF Chorus

LEIPZIG GEWANDHAUS ORCHESTRA
Conductor Kurt Masur
30 Aug. 20.00 Usher Hall
Beethoven Symphony no.1 in C, op.21
Schumann Concerto for piano in A minor, op.54
Shostakovich Symphony no.1 in F minor, op.10
Soloist Stephen Bishop-Kovacevich (pf)

31 Aug. 20.00 Usher Hall
Szymanowski Concerto for violin no.2, op.61
Bruckner Symphony no.7 in E; arr.Hass
Soloist Wanda Wilkomirska (vn)

VIENNA PHILHARMONIC ORCHESTRA
1 Sep. 20.00 Usher Hall
Schubert Symphony no.2 in B flat, D125
Mahler Symphony no.4 in G
Conductor Claudio Abbado
Soloist Frederica von Stade (mez)

2 Sep. 20.00 Usher Hall
Webern Passacaglia, op.1
Schoenberg A survivor from Warsaw
Brahms Concerto for piano no.1 in D minor, op.15
Conductor Claudio Abbado
Soloists Maurizio Pollini (pf), Günter Reich (bar), Cappella Singers

3 Sep. 20.00 Usher Hall
Mozart Symphony no.39 in E flat, K543
Mozart Symphony no.40 in G minor, K550
Mozart Symphony no.41 in C (Jupiter), K551
Conductor Karl Böhm

MONTEVERDI ORCHESTRA AND CHOIR
5 Sep. 20.00 Usher Hall
Handel Jephtha
Conductor John Eliot Gardiner
Soloists Jennifer Smith, Daryl Greene (sop), Sarah Walker (mez), John Angelo Messana (c ten), Peter Pears (ten), David Wilson-Johnson (bar)

NEW PHILHARMONIA ORCHESTRA
6 Sep. 20.00 Usher Hall
Weber Der Beherrscher der Geister: Overture
Beethoven Concerto for piano no.1 in C, op.15
Bartók Two pictures, op.10
Stravinsky The firebird - Suite (1919 version)
Conductor Riccardo Muti
Soloist Radu Lupu (pf)

7 Sep. 20.00 Usher Hall
Schumann Symphony no.4 in D minor, op.120
Beethoven Christus am Ölberge
Conductor Riccardo Muti
Soloists Elizabeth Harwood (sop), Lajos Kozma (ten), Gwynne Howell (bs), EF Chorus

8 Sep. 20.00 Usher Hall
Dvorák Symphony no.8 in G, op.88

Falla Noches en los jardines de España
Falla El sombrero de tres picos - 2 suites
Conductor Rafael Frühbeck de Burgos
Soloist Alicia de Larrocha (pf)

ORCHESTRE DE PARIS
Conductor Daniel Barenboim
9 Sep. 20.00 *Usher Hall*
Ravel Le tombeau de Couperin
Mozart Concerto for piano no.27 in B flat, K595
Brahms Symphony no.1 in C minor, op.68
Soloist Sir Clifford Curzon (pf)

11 Sep. 20.00 *Usher Hall*
Boulez Pli selon pli: Tombeau
Berlioz Te deum
Soloists Jean Dupouy (ten), Jean Guillou (org), EF Chorus, Southend Boys' Choir,

CHAMBER CONCERTS

VERMEER QUARTET
24 Aug. 11.00 *Freemasons' Hall*
Beethoven Quartet no.3 in D, op.18/3
Ginastera Quartet no.2, op.26
Mendelssohn Quartet no.2 in A minor, op.13

26 Aug. 11.00 *Freemasons' Hall*
Haydn Quartet in G, op.77/1
Stravinsky Concertino
Beethoven Quartet no.15 in A minor, op.132

MUSIC PARTY
25 Aug. 11.00 *Freemasons' Hall*
Beethoven Trio for clarinet, cello and piano, op.11
Weber Trio for flute, cello and piano, op.63
Weber Quintet for clarinet and strings, op.34

AMERICAN BRASS QUINTET
30 Aug. 11.00 *Freemasons' Hall*
Coprario Two fancies
Holborne Elizabethan dance suite
Carter Quintet for brass
Poulenc Sonata for horn, trumpet and trombone
Bach Art of fugue: Contrapuncti 3, 9
Dahl Music for brass instruments

1 Sep. 11.00 *Freemasons' Hall*
Druckman Other voices (World première)
Works by Gabrieli, Lawes, Simon, Purcell (arr. Carter), Coprario, Lovelock, Anon.

FIRES OF LONDON
3 Sep. 11.00 *Freemasons' Hall*
Kinloch Kinloche his fantassie; arr. P.M. Davies
P.M. Davies From stone to thorn
McQueen *arr.* 18th century Scottish dances
P.M. Davies Ave maris stella
Director Peter Maxwell Davies
with Timothy Walker (gtr)

ALBAN BERG QUARTET
8 Sep. 11.00 *Freemasons' Hall*
Schubert Quartet no.8 in B flat, D112
Berg Quartet, op.3
Mozart Quartet no.23 in F, K590

10 Sep. 11.00 *Freemasons' Hall*
Schubert Quartet no.12 in C minor (Quartetsatz), D703
Berg Lyric suite
Brahms Quartet no.1 in C minor, op.51/1

SCOTTISH BAROQUE ENSEMBLE
10 Sep. 20.00 *Hopetoun House*
Corelli Concerto grosso in C, op.6/10
Elgar Sospiri for strings, harp and organ, op.70
Elgar Elegy for string orchestra, op.58
Janáček Idyll
Dvořák Bagatelles, op.47
Goehr Little music for strings
Goehr Fugue on the theme of the psalm
Handel Concerto grosso in A, op.6/11
Conductors
Leonard Friedman, Alexander Goehr

KING'S SINGERS
11 Sep. 11.00 *Leith Theatre*
French chansons of the 16th century
Elgar Five part songs from the Greek Anthology
Berio 'Cries' of London (rev. version)
Cordell Seeds of envy
Five arrangements in close harmony

RECITALS

ELISABETH SCHWARZKOPF (sop)
GEOFFREY PARSONS (pf)
23 Aug. 20.00 *Usher Hall*
Songs by Wolf, Schubert, Wolf-Ferrari, Liszt, Schumann, R. Strauss, Brahms

FREDERICA VON STADE (mez)
MARTIN ISEPP (pf)
31 Aug. 11.00 *Freemasons' Hall*
Mahler Lieder eines fahrenden Gesellen
Songs by Dørumsgaard, Ives, Poulenc
Folk song arrangements by Britten

PETER PEARS (ten), OSIAN ELLIS (hp)
7 Sep. 11.00 *Freemasons' Hall*
Purcell Morning hymn
Britten Canticle no.5
Maconchy Three songs
Caplet Deux sonnets
Poulenc A sa guitare
Ravel Rêves
Ravel Sainte
Ravel Cinq mélodies populaires grecques
Britten Suite for harp in C, op.83
Britten A birthday hansel

JENNIFER SMITH (sop)
JOHN FRASER (pf)
9 Sep. 11.00 *Freemasons' Hall*
Songs by Weber, Schumann, Brahms, Debussy, Poulenc

ANDRAS SCHIFF (pf)
23 Aug. 11.00 *Freemasons' Hall*
Bach Clavierübung: Part 2
Bach Concerto in the Italian style
Bach Overture (Partita) in the French style
Weber Sonata no.4 in E minor
Bartók Dance suite

ALICIA DE LARROCHA (pf)
28 Aug. 11.00 *Freemasons' Hall*
Soler Sonata in F sharp
Soler Sonata in D
Schubert Sonata no.21 in B flat, D960
Falla El sombrero de tres picos: Danza de la molinera
Falla Cuatro piezas españolas
Falla Fantasía bética

RADU LUPU (pf)
4 Sep. 11.00 *Leith Theatre*
Haydn Variations in F minor
Schubert Sonata no.9 in B, D575
Schumann Bunte Blätter, op.99
Weber Aufforderung zum Tanze

WANDA WILKOMIRSKA (vn)
TADEUSZ CHMIELEWSKI (pf)
2 Sep. 11.00 *Freemasons' Hall*
Beethoven Sonata no.5 in F (Spring), op.24
Grieg Sonata no.3 in C minor, op.45
Delius Sonata no.2 in C
Wieniawski Polonaise brillante in A
Szymanowski Nocturne and tarantella, op.28

MARIUS MAY (vc)
PAUL HAMBURGER (pf)
6 Sep. 11.00 *Freemasons' Hall*
Bach Suite for solo cello no.1 in G
Brahms Sonata no.1 in E minor, op.38
Janáček Fairy tale (Pohádka)
Fauré Elégie, op.24
Dvořák Rondo in G minor, op.94
Chopin Introduction and polonaise brillante, op.3

JAMES GALWAY (fl)
ANTHONY GOLDSTONE (pf)
27 Aug. 11.00 *Freemasons' Hall*
L. Berkeley Sonatina, op.13
Chopin Andante spianato and grande polonaise, op.22
Hindemith Sonata
Musgrave Orfeo 1 for flute and tape
Martinů Sonata

DRAMA

BIRMINGHAM REPERTORY THEATRE
23-28 Aug. 2, 3, 8, 9, 10 Sep. 19.30
28 Aug. 4 Sep. 14.30 *Assembly Hall*
MEASURE FOR MEASURE
Shakespeare
Vincentio Bernard Lloyd
Escalus Peter Vaughan
Angelo David Burke
Lucio David Suchet
Isabella Anna Calder-Marshall
Juliet Janet Maw
Mistress Overdone Ursula Smith
Pompey Russell Hunter
Provost Richard Butler
Claudio William Lindsay
Friar Peter Alan Rickman
Francisca/Citizen Elizabeth Revill
Nun Susan Parriss
Justice James Irwin
Elbow Roger Kemp
Froth Allan Corduner
Mariana Elizabeth Power
Abhorson Chris Ryan
Barnadine David Foxxe
Duke's servant Derek Ware
Angelo's servant John Rainer
Boy Michael Criswell
Gentlemen Roy Finn, Michael Jackson
Director Stuart Burge
Designer Robin Archer
Lighting Robert Ornbo
Music John Leach

30, 31 Aug. 1, 4, 6, 7, 11 Sep. 19.30 31 Aug. 7, 11 Sep. 14.30 *Assembly Hall*
THE DEVIL IS AN ASS Jonson
(Adapted by Peter Barnes)
Satan Bernard Lloyd
Pug Chris Ryan
Fabian Fitzdotterel Peter Vaughan
Meercraft Russell Hunter
Everill Roger Kemp
Wittipol Alan Rickman
Eustace Manly William Lindsay
Engine David Burke
Trains David Foxxe
Thomas Gilthead David Suchet
Plutarchus Allan Corduner

Sir Paul Eitherside — Richard Butler
Mrs Frances Fitzdotterel — Anna-Calder Marshall
Lady Eitherside — Ursula Smith
Lady Tailbush — Elizabeth Power
Pitfall — Janet Maw
Ambler — Frederick Marks
Whore — Elizabeth Revill
Constable/Sledge — Martin Milman
Shackles — Derek Ware
Vices — Roy Finn, Michael Jackson, John Rainer, James Irwin
Director — Stuart Burge
Designer — Robin Archer
Lighting — Robert Ornbo
Music — John Leach

LA MAMA COMPANY, New York
23-27 Aug. 20.30 — Moray House
THE TROJAN WOMEN Inspired by Euripides
Hecuba — Natalie Gray
Cassandra — Valois Mickens
Andromache — Priscilla Smith
Helen — Onni Johnson
Menelaus — Jorge Takla
Astyanax — Diane Lane
Rapist/Bear — Peter Jon de Vries
Voice of the flute — Mimi Locadio
Weaver/Suicide — Neal Harris
Achilles/Soldier — Charles Hayward
Polixena/Dancer — Rosemary Jeanes
Captain/Brutal master — William Duff-Griffin
Helen's last choice — Patrick Burke
New soldier — Justin Rashid
Woman — Rhida El Khouri
One of 'them' — Jerry Cunliffe
Another one of 'them' — James Siering
Director — Andrei Serban
Scenery — Jun Maeda
Costumes — Sandra Muir
Lighting — Larry Steckman
Music — Elizabeth Swados

28, 30, 31 Aug. 20.30 — Moray House
ELECTRA Inspired by Sophocles
Electra — Priscilla Smith
Orestes — Patrick Burke
Chrysothemis — Valois Mickens, Onni Johnson
Clytemnestra — Natalie Gray, Valois Mickens
Aegisthus — William Duff-Griffin
Pylades — Charles Hayward
Tutor — Peter Jon de Vries
Agamemnon — Justin Rashid
Image of Antigone — Diane Lane
Image of Oedipus — Jorge Takla
Orestes as a child — Ted Lambert
Musicians — William Ruyle, Paul Harris
Director — Andrei Serban
Designer — Jun Maeda
Lighting — Larry Steckman
Music — Elizabeth Swados

2-4 Sep. 20.30 — Moray House
THE GOOD WOMAN OF SETZUAN Brecht (English version by Eric Bentley)
Wong — Valois Mickens
Shen-Te — Priscilla Smith
Mrs Shin — Natalie Gray
Husband — Richard Jakiel
Wife — Rhida El Khouri
Brother — Jorge Takla
Sister-in-law — Mimi Locadio
Grandfather/Unemployed man/Policeman — Charles Hayward
Nephew — John Ahlburg
Niece/Old woman/Mrs Yang — Neal Harris
Child — Diane Lane
Mrs Mi Tzu — Onni Johnson
Yang Sun — Peter Jon de Vries
Mr Shu Fu — William Duff-Griffin
Carpenter — James Siering
Gods — Patrick Burke, Jerry Cunliffe, Justin Rashid
Director — Andrei Serban
Scenery — Jun Maeda
Costumes — Sandra Muir
Lighting — Larry Steckman
Music — Elizabeth Swados

TEATRO LIBERO, Rome
6, 8-11 Sep. 20.00 — Moray House
MASANIELLO Porta and Pugliese
Masaniello — Mariano Rigillo
Marco Vitale — Lucio Allocca
Giulio Genoino — Corrado Annicelli
Maso Carrese — Tommaso Bianco
Cacace/Basile — Vittorio de Bisogno
Andrea Naclerio — Nando di Lena
Viceroy — Lombardo Fornara
Lazzaro/Peasant — Carlo Frataccio
Fishmonger — Bruno Gaudieri
Bernadina — Angela Pagano
Vicereine — Anna Rossini
Lazzaro/Bisagnano — Luca Sallustio
Beggar/Carafa/Palumbo — Armando Cavaliere
Other parts played by Antonio Ferrante, Marisa Laurito, Nicola di Pinto, Girolamo Marzano, Gigio Morra, Giovanni Poggiali, Giancarlo Santelli, Lina Sastri, Enzo Scudellaro
Director — Armando Pugliese
Designer — Bruno Garofalo
Music — Roberto de Simone
*Performance on 7 Sep. cancelled

OXFORD PLAYHOUSE
23-28 Aug. 19.15 25, 28 Aug. 14.15
Lyceum Theatre
PAL JOEY
Joey — Bob Sherman
Vera — Pat Kirkwood
Linda — Patricia Hodge
Gladys — Joyce Blair
Mike — Colin Bennett
Valerie — Clovissa Newcombe
Pearl — Maria Heidler
Dolores — Anna Macleod
Sandy — Vivienne McKee
Victor — Peter Durken
Louis — Garry Ginivan
Other parts played by Anna Quayle, Arthur Nightingale, Peter Pacey, Tony Scannell, Thick Wilson
Music — Richard Rodgers
Lyrics — Lorenz Hart
Book — John O'Hara
Director — Philip Hedley
Designer — David Fisher
Lighting — Mick Hughes

BUNRAKU National Puppet Theatre of Japan
30, 31 Aug. 3 Sep. 19.15 Lyceum Theatre
HEIKE NYOGONOSHIMA (The priest in exile)
SONEZAKI SHINJU (The double suicide at Sonezak)

1, 2 Sep. 19.15 1 Sep. 14.15
Lyceum Theatre
EHON TAIKOKI (The exploits of the tycoon)
SHIMPAN UTAZAIMON (The triangular love)

I COLOMBAIONI (The clowns)
9-11 Sep. 19.15 8, 11 Sep. 14.15
Lyceum Theatre
Carlo and Alberto Colombaioni

POETRY AND PROSE RECITALS

ROYAL EXCHANGE THEATRE, Manchester
25-27 Aug. 15.00 — St Cecilia's Hall
ROGUES AND VAGABONDS
Dame Wendy Hiller, Edward Fox, Graham Crowden (rdr)
Devised by Michael Meyer
Directed by Michael Elliott

1-3 Sep. 15.00 — St Cecilia's Hall
THE VIEW FROM EDEN
From the writings of Edwin and Willa Muir
Tom Fleming, Edith Macarthur (rdr)
Compiled by Henry Donald

4 Sep. 20.00 — St Cecilia's Hall
A DRUNK MAN LOOKS AT THE THISTLE MacDiarmid
Tom Fleming

5 Sep. 20.00 — St Cecilia's Hall
WORDS, WORDS, WORDS: A personal choice
Ian McKellen (rdr)

6-9 Sep. 20.00 — St Cecilia's Hall
AN AMERICAN HERITAGE
Princess Grace of Monaco, Richard Kiley, Richard Pasco (rdr)
Devised by John Carroll

LATE NIGHT ENTERTAINMENT

24-28 Aug. 22.45 — Lyceum Theatre
FENELLA FIELDING
Fielding convertible
with Tudor Davies and a Musical Quartet
Directed by Bill Hays

DANCE

BALLET OF THE DEUTSCHE OPER AM RHEIN
3, 9 Sep. 19.30 — King's Theatre
OPUS 1
Choreographer — John Cranko
Music — Webern
DER TOD UND DAS MÄDCHEN
Choreographer — Erich Walter
Music — Schubert
Costumes — Pet Halmen
SYMPHONY NO.3
Choreographer — Erich Walter
Music — Scriabin
Scenery — Heinrich Wendel
Costumes — Jan Skalicky
Dancers Geneviève Chaussat, István Herczog, Paolo Bortoluzzi, Joan Cadzow, Monique Janotta, Peter Breuer, Falco Kapuste, Petr Vondruska, Eva Grobstas, Inge Koch, Yolande Straudo, Wolfgang Enck, Attila Szilveszter, Lazo Turozi
Kruschek Quartet, Düsseldorf Symphony Orchestra
Conductors Robert Schaub, Boguslav Madey

TWYLA THARP DANCE FOUNDATION, USA
4 Sep. 19.15 6 Sep. 14.15
Lyceum Theatre
COUNTRY DANCES+
THE FUGUE
EIGHT JELLY ROLLS#

6, 8 Sep. 19.15 *Lyceum Theatre*
COUNTRY DANCES+
FROM HITHER AND YON+
SUE'S LEG

7 Sep. 19.15 *Lyceum Theatre*
COUNTRY DANCES+
FROM HITHER AND YON+
THE FUGUE
Choreographer Twyla Tharp
Costumes Santo Loquasto, Kermit Love#
Lighting Marty Kapell+, Jennifer Tipton
Dancers Twyla Tharp, Rose Marie Wright, Kenneth Rinker, Tom Rawe, Christine Uchida, Jennifer Way, Shelley Washington

EXHIBITIONS

Royal Scottish Academy
1826-1976

Royal Botanic Gardens
HEPWORTH

1977

OPERA

EDINBURGH FESTIVAL OPERA
22, 25, 28, 31 Aug. 3, 7, 10 Sep. 19.30
King's Theatre
CARMEN Bizet
Carmen Teresa Berganza
Don José Placido Domingo
Peyo Garacci
Micaela Mirella Freni
Leona Mitchell
Yvonne Kenny*
Escamillo Tom Krause
Frasquita Nan Christie
Yvonne Kenny
Mercédès Alicia Nafé
Moralès Stuart Harling
Zuniga Jean Lainé
El Dancairo Gordon Sandison
El Remendado Geoffrey Pogson
Dancers Mariemma, Tomas de Madrid
Scottish Opera Chorus
George Watson's Boys' Chorus
London Symphony Orchestra
Conductor Claudio Abbado
Director Piero Faggioni
Designer Ezio Frigerio
Lighting Victor Lockwood
Choreographer Mariemma

SCOTTISH OPERA
6, 8 Sep. 19.30` *King's Theatre*
MARY, QUEEN OF SCOTS Musgrave (World première)
Mary Catherine Wilson
Bothwell Gregory Dempsey
Earl of Moray Jake Gardner
Cardinal Beaton/David Rizzio Stafford Dean
Ruthven John Robertson
Morton Ian Comboy
Gordon William McCue
Lord Darnley David Hillman
Mary Seton Linda Ormiston
Mary Beaton Eryl Royle
Mary Livingstone Una Buchanan
Mary Fleming Barbara Barnes
Scottish Chamber Orchestra
Conductor Thea Musgrave
Director Colin Graham
Scenery Robin Don, Colin Graham
Costumes Alex Reid
Lighting Charles Bristow

ORCHESTRAL CONCERTS

SCOTTISH NATIONAL ORCHESTRA
21 Aug. 20.00 *Usher Hall*
Britten Sinfonia da requiem
Britten Phaedra
Walton Improvisations on an impromptu of Benjamin Britten
Oldham Psalms in times of war (World première)
Conductor Sir Alexander Gibson
Soloists Dame Janet Baker (mez), Thomas Allen (bar), EF Chorus

NEW PHILHARMONIA ORCHESTRA
Conductor Carlo Maria Giulini
22, 23 Aug. 20.00 *Usher Hall*
Mozart Symphony no.36 in C (Linz), K425
Mozart Requiem, K626
Soloists Margaret Marshall*/Edith Mathis (sop), Helen Watts (mez), Robert Tear (ten), John Shirley-Quirk (bar), EF Chorus

25 Aug. 20.00 *Usher Hall*
Bruckner Symphony no.8 in C minor (1889-90)

CONCERTGEBOUW ORCHESTRA, Amsterdam
27 Aug. 20.00 *Usher Hall*
Ravel Valses nobles et sentimentales; arr. for orch.
Ravel Concerto for piano (Left hand)
Berlioz Symphonie fantastique
Conductor Kyril Kondrashin
Soloist Michel Béroff (pf)

28 Aug. 20.00 *Usher Hall*
Shostakovich The bolt - Suite
Prokofiev Concerto for violin no.2 in G minor, op.63
Tchaikovsky Suite no.3 in G, op.55
Conductor Kyril Kondrashin
Soloist Mayumi Fujikawa (vn)

30 Aug. 20.00 *Usher Hall*
R. Strauss Don Quixote
Beethoven Symphony no.6 in F (Pastoral), op.68
Conductor Bernard Haitink
Soloist Paul Tortelier (vc)

31 Aug. 20.00 *Usher Hall*
Debussy Prélude à l'après-midi d'un faune
Lutoslawski Mi-parti
Debussy La mer
Beethoven Concerto for piano no.5 in E flat (Emperor), op.73
Conductor Bernard Haitink
Soloist Maurizio Pollini (pf)

LONDON SYMPHONY ORCHESTRA
1 Sep. 20.00 *Usher Hall*
Beethoven Symphony no.8 in F, op.93
Wagner Wesendonck Lieder
Wagner Tristan und Isolde: Prelude and Liebestod
Schumann Symphony no.2 in C, op.61
Conductor Erich Leinsdorf
Soloist Jessye Norman (sop)

2 Sep. 20.00 *Usher Hall*
Mozart Serenade no.9 in D (Posthorn), K320
R. Strauss Also sprach Zarathustra
Conductor Erich Leinsdorf

4 Sep. 20.00 *Usher Hall*
Ligeti Atmosphères
Schumann Concerto for cello in A minor, op.129
Tchaikovsky Symphony no.6 in B minor (Pathétique), op.74
Conductor Claudio Abbado
Soloist Heinrich Schiff (vc)

6 Sep. 20.00 *Usher Hall*
Beethoven Die Geschöpfe des Prometheus: Overture
Beethoven Ah! perfido
Mahler Rückert Lieder
Beethoven Symphony no.7 in A, op.92
Conductor Claudio Abbado
Soloist Dame Janet Baker (mez)

9 Sep. 20.00 *Usher Hall*
Mozart Kyrie in D minor, K341
Mozart Concerto for piano no.24 in C minor, K491
Stravinsky Le roi des étoiles
Debussy Nocturnes
Ravel Daphnis et Chloë - Suite no.2
Conductor Claudio Abbado
Soloist Annie Fischer (pf)
EF Chorus

ROYAL PHILHARMONIC ORCHESTRA
8 Sep. 20.00 *Usher Hall*
Walton Variations on a theme by Hindemith
Rainier Concerto for violin - Due canti e finale (World première)
Bach Concerto for violin in A minor
Roussel Symphony no.3 in G minor, op.42
Conductor Sir Charles Groves
Soloist Sir Yehudi Menuhin (vn)

10 Sep. 20.00 *Usher Hall*
Haydn Symphony no.3 in G
Beethoven Concerto for violin in D, op.61
Bartók Concerto for orchestra
Conductor Antal Dorati
Soloist Sir Yehudi Menuhin (vn)

CHAMBER CONCERTS

CHILINGIRIAN QUARTET
22 Aug. 11.00 *Freemasons' Hall*
Mozart Quartet for flute and strings no.3 in C, K285b
Beethoven Serenade for flute, violin and viola in D, op.25
Schubert Trio in B flat (one movement), D471
Mozart Quartet for flute and strings no.1 in D, K285
with Susan Milan (fl)

26 Aug. 11.00 *Freemasons' Hall*
Beethoven Quintet in C minor, op.104
Beethoven Fugue in D, op.137
Beethoven Duo for viola and cello in E flat
Beethoven Quintet in C, op.29
With Roger Best (va)

CLEVELAND QUARTET
25 Aug. 11.00 *Freemasons' Hall*
Mendelssohn Quartet no.1 in E flat, op.12
Ives Quartet no.2
Beethoven Quartet no.13 in B flat, op.130

27 Aug. 11.00 *Freemasons' Hall*
Barber Quartet in B minor, op.11
Prokofiev Quartet no.2 in F, op.92
Beethoven Quartet no.7 in F (Rasumovsky), op.59/1

BARRY TUCKWELL (hn), JOHN GEORGIADIS (vn), MARTIN JONES (pf)

31 Aug. 11.00 *Leith Theatre*
Beethoven Sonata for horn and piano in F, op.17
Musgrave Music for horn and piano
Schumann Adagio and allegro, op.70
Brahms Trio for horn, violin and piano in E flat, op.40

MELOS QUARTET
1 Sep. 11.00 *Freemasons' Hall*
Mozart Five fugues (from Bach), K405
Janáček Quartet no.2 (Intimate letters)
Schubert Quartet no.14 in D minor (Death and the maiden), D810

2 Sep. 11.00 *Freemasons' Hall*
Mozart Quartet no.15 in D minor, K421
Ravel Quartet in F
Beethoven Quartet no.12 in E flat, op.127

BEAUX ARTS TRIO
5 Sep. 11.00 *Freemasons' Hall*
Haydn Trio for piano and strings no.18 in A
Ravel Trio for piano and strings in A minor
Brahms Trio for piano and strings no.2 in C, op.87

7 Sep. 11.00 *Freemasons' Hall*
Mozart Trio for piano and strings no.5 in C, K548
Shostakovich Trio for piano and strings no.2 in E minor, op.67
Beethoven Trio for piano and strings no.5 in D (Ghost), op.70/1

AMADEUS QUARTET
9 Sep. 11.00 *Leith Theatre*
Schubert Quartet no.10 in E flat, D87
Schubert Quartet no.12 in C minor (Quartetsatz), D703
Schubert Quintet for piano and strings in A (The trout), D667
with Sir Clifford Curzon (pf), Georg Hörtnagel (db)

10 Sep. 11.00 *Leith Theatre*
Mozart Quartet no.3 in G, K156
Britten Quartet no.3, op.94
Mozart Quartet for piano and strings in G minor, K478
with Sir Clifford Curzon (pf)

BBC SINGERS
23 Aug. 11.00 *Freemasons' Hall*
Britten Five flower songs
Schubert Psalm 23, D706
Schubert Rosamunde: Shepherd's chorus
Schubert Gott in der Natur
Schubert Des Tages Weine
Britten Hymn to St Cecilia
Schurmann The double heart
Brahms O schöne Nacht
Director John Poole

RECITALS

TOM KRAUSE (bar), IRWIN GAGE (pf)
24 Aug. 11.00 *Freemasons' Hall*
Ravel Don Quichotte à Dulcinée
Schumann Dichterliebe
Songs by Schubert, Brahms

JESSYE NORMAN (sop)
DALTON BALDWIN (pf)
30 Aug. 11.00 *Leith Theatre*
Songs by Handel, Schubert, R. Strauss, Poulenc, Gounod, Debussy

HERMANN PREY (bar)
GEOFFREY PARSONS (pf)
3 Sep. 11.00 *Leith Theatre*
Songs by Beethoven

SARAH WALKER (mez), THOMAS ALLEN (bar), ROGER VIGNOLES (pf)
8 Sep. 11.00 *Freemasons' Hall*
Sea songs and duets by Ireland, Haydn, Dibdin, Walton, Wolf, Fauré, Schubert, Borodin, Debussy, Britten, Schumann, Ives, Bizet, Berlioz, Mendelssohn

DANIEL BARENBOIM (pf)
26 Aug. 20.00 *Usher Hall*
Beethoven Variations on a waltz by Diabelli
Beethoven Sonata no.23 in F minor (Appassionata), op.57

29 Aug. 20.00 *Usher Hall*
Beethoven Sonata no.30 in E, op.109
Beethoven Sonata no.31 in A flat, op.110
Beethoven Sonata no.32 in C minor, op.111

MAURIZIO POLLINI (pf)
3 Sep. 20.00 *Usher Hall*
Schubert Sonata no.20 in A, D959
Beethoven Sonata no.29 in B flat (Hammerklavier), op.106

ANNIE FISCHER (pf)
5 Sep. 20.00 *Usher Hall*
Beethoven Sonata no.15 in D (Pastoral), op.28
Beethoven Sonata no.8 in C minor (Pathétique), op.13
Beethoven Sonata no.12 in A flat, op.26
Beethoven Sonata no.28 in A, op.101

SIR YEHUDI MENUHIN (vn)
LOUIS KENTNER (pf)
7 Sep. 20.00 *Usher Hall*
Beethoven Sonata no.7 in C minor, op.30/2
Beethoven Sonata no.10 in G, op.96
Beethoven Sonata no.9 in A (Kreutzer), op.47

PAUL TORTELIER (vc)
MARIA DE LA PAU (pf)
29 Aug. 11.00 *Leith Theatre*
Boccherini Sonata no.6 in A
Bach Suite for solo cello no.6 in D
Brahms Sonata no.2 in F, op.99
Paganini Introduction and variations on 'Dal tuo stellatto soglio' (Rossini)

HEINRICH SCHIFF (vc)
MICHAEL ISADOR (pf)
6 Sep. 11.00 *Freemasons' Hall*
Beethoven Variations on 'Ein Mädchen oder Weibchen' (Mozart)
Beethoven Sonata no.4 in C, op.102/1
Lutoslawski Sacher variations
Webern Sonata
Webern Two pieces
Franck Sonata in A

DRAMA

PROSPECT THEATRE COMPANY
21, 22, 24, 26, 31 Aug. 2, 6, 10 Sep. 19.30 25, 27, 30 Aug. 1, 3 Sep. 14.30
Assembly Hall
ANTONY AND CLEOPATRA Shakespeare
Cleopatra Dorothy Tutin
Antony Alec McCowen
Enobarbus Timothy West
Octavius Caesar Derek Jacobi
Jeffrey Daunton
Soothsayer/Schoolmaster/Clown Robert Eddison
Lepidus John Nettleton
Pompey/Dolabella Rupert Frazer
Scarus/Demetrius Kenneth Gilbert
Menas/Seleucus Michael Howarth
Agrippa Philip York
Alexas/Proculeius Neil McCaul
Philo/Ventidius/Canidius John Rowe
Maecenas/Thidias Jeffrey Daunton
Decretas David Shaughnessy
Mardian Andrew Seear
Eros Paul Vaughan Teague
Diomedes Terence Wilton
Iras Suzanne Bertish
Charmian Zöe Hicks
Octavia Bernice Stegers
Varrius Philip Bloomfield
Director Toby Robertson
Designer Nicholas Georgiadis
Lighting Mick Hughes

*23, 25, 27, *30 Aug, 1, 8 Sep. 19.30*
Assembly Hall
ALL FOR LOVE Dryden
Cleopatra Barbara Jefford
Antony John Turner
Alexas Robert Eddison
Serapion John Nettleton
Ventidius Kenneth Gilbert
Dolabella Michael Howarth
Priest/Myris Neil McCaul
Gentlemen David Shaughnessy, Philip Bloomfield
Octavia Suzanne Bertish
Iras Zöe Hicks
Charmian Bernice Stegers
Children
Sasha Robertson, Joshua Robertson
Director Frank Hauser
Designer Nicholas Georgiadis
Lighting Mick Hughes
*Additional performance replacing *War music*

29 Aug. 1 Sep. 19.30 10 Sep. 14.30
Assembly Hall
WAR MUSIC Logue
(An adaptation of Homer's Iliad)
Achilles Rupert Frazer
Briseis Alice Stopczynski
Rosamond Freeman-Attwood
Karen Bowen
Agamemnon John Turner
Storyteller Timothy West
Patroclus Michael Howarth
Hector Philip York
Thestor William Louther
Zeus and Hera Neil McCaul
Sarpedon Terence Wilton
Glaucus Andrew Seear
Antiokhos Jeffrey Daunton
Thetis Barbara Jefford
Odysseus Kenneth Gilbert
Talthybuis Philip Bloomfield
Director Toby Robertson
Designer Pamela Howard
Lighting Mick Hughes
Choreographer William Louther
*Performance on 30 Aug. cancelled and replaced with *All for love*

5, 7, 9 Sep. 19.30 6 Sep. 14.30
Assembly Hall
HAMLET Shakespeare
Hamlet Derek Jacobi
Ophelia Suzanne Bertish
Gertrude Barbara Jefford
Claudius Timothy West
Polonius John Nettleton
Horatio John Rowe
Laertes Terence Wilton
Fortinbras/Lucianus Rupert Frazer
Osric/Barnardo Neil McCaul
Francisco/Cornelius/Reynaldo
Jeffrey Daunton

Marcellus/Priest/Captain Kenneth Gilbert
Voltimand David Shaughnessy
Ghost/Lucianus John Turner
Rosencrantz Michael Howarth
Guildenstern Philip York
Player king
Paul Vaughan Teague, Graeme Edler
Player queen
Andrew Seear, Alice Stopczynski
Gravediggers
John Nettleton, Paul Vaughan Teague
Director Toby Robertson
Designer Robin Archer
Lighting Mick Hughes

4 Sep. 19.00 *Assembly Hall*
MILTON PARADISE LOST
(Adapted by Gordon Honeycombe)
Milton (Narrator) Timothy West
Satan Alec McCowen
Beelzebub/Michael John Turner
Melech/Gabriel Kenneth Gilbert
Belial/Raphael John Rowe
God Robert Eddison
Christ Terence Wilton
Eve Barbara Jefford
Adam Neil McCaul
Director Martin Jenkins

WÜRTTEMBERG STATE THEATRE
23 Aug. 19.15 *Lyceum Theatre*
DAS KÄTHCHEN VON HEILBRONN
Von Kleist
Emperor Traugott Burke
Friedrich Wetter Martin Lüttge
Countess Helena Maria Wiecke
Sir Flammberg/Jakob Pech
Hansjürgen Gerth
Gottschalk Branko Samarovski
Brigitte Karin Schlemmer
Kunigunde von Thurneck Kirsten Dene
Rosalie Charlotte Joss
Sybille/Count von Stein Martin Schwab
Theobald Friedeborn Wolfgang Höper
Käthchen Lore Brunner
Gottfried Friedeborn Marcus Fritsche
Maximilian Gert Voss
Georg von Waldstätten Ignaz Kirchner
Friedrich von Herrnstadt Bert Oberdorfer
Eginhardt von der Wart Peter Saltman
Simultaneous translation
Michael Mellinger
Director Claus Peymann
Designer Achim Freyer
*Performance on 22 Aug. cancelled

NOTTINGHAM PLAYHOUSE
26, 27 Aug. 2, 3 Sep. 19.15 27 Aug.
3 Sep. 14.15 *Lyceum Theatre*
TOUCHED Lowe
Pauline Donna Owen/Seanna Watkinson
Betty Kay Adshead
Johnny Mick Ford
Bridie Annie Hayes
Keith Malcolm Storry
Sandra Marjorie Yates
Joan Susan Tracy
Mary Lorraine Peters
Mother Kristine Howarth
Harry Brian Glover
Director Richard Eyre
Scenery William Dudley
Costumes Pippy Bradshaw
Lighting Rory Dempster

29 Aug.-1 Sep. 19.15 31 Aug. 14.15
Lyceum Theatre
WHITE SUIT BLUES Mitchell
Mark Twain Trevor Peacock
Other parts played by Kay Adshead, Helen Brammer, Duncan Faber, Mick Ford, Annie Hayes, Robert Hickson, Jim Hooper, Sylvester McCoy, Judy Riley, Antony Sher, Malcolm Storry, Larry Walker, Polly Warren, Lola Young
Director Richard Eyre
Designer Pamela Howard
Lighting Geoffrey Mersereau
Music Mike Westbrook

FORUM THEATRE, BILLINGHAM
8-10 Sep. 19.15 10 Sep. 14.15
Lyceum Theatre
HEDDA GABLER Ibsen
(Eng. Adapted by David Essinger)
Hedda Janet Suzman
Jörgen Tesman John Shrapnel
Judge Brack Ian Bannen
Thea Elvsted Rosemary McHale
Eilert Lövberg Jonathan Kent
Juliana Tesman Gwen Nelson
Bertha Renee Goddard
Director Keith Hack
Designer Maria Bjørnson
Lighting Victor Lockwood

DOME PRODUCTIONS
5, 6 Sep. 19.15 *Lyceum Theatre*
THE BELLE OF AMHERST Luce
Emily Dickinson Julie Harris
Director Charles Nelson Reilly
Scenery H.R. Poindexter
Costumes Theoni V. Aldredge

POETRY AND PROSE RECITALS

24, 26 Aug. 5 Sep. 15.00 *St Cecilia's Hall*
THE SMITH OF SMITHS
Sydney Smith Timothy West
with Prunella Scales, John Rowe (rdr), Donald Fraser (hpd)
Devised by Jane McCulloch
Director Toby Robertson

IAN McKELLEN
28 Aug. 15.00 and 20.00 *St Cecilia's Hall*
Acting Shakespeare

29 Aug. 15.00 *St Cecilia's Hall*
Words, words, words: a personal choice

REX HARRISON
30 Aug.-3 Sep. 15.00 *St Cecilia's Hall*
Our theatre in the nineties - Theatre criticisms of Bernard Shaw
Devised by Patrick Garland

HE AND SHE
6-8 Sep. 15.00 *St Cecilia's Hall*
Dorothy Tutin, Alec McCowen, Frank Muir (rdr)
Compiled by Michael Meyer

LATE NIGHT ENTERTAINMENT

30 Aug.-3 Sep. 22.45 *Lyceum Theatre*
PACO PEÑA'S FLAMENCO PURO
Cristina Hoyos, Margarita, Faiquillo de Cordoba (dancers), Barrilito, Miguel Maya (sngr), Fernando Carranza, Paco Peña (gtr)

6, 8-10 Sep. 22.45 *Lyceum Theatre*
BUSTER
Buster Keaton Max Wall
with Jan Waters, Trevor Ingman
Music Donald Fraser
Book/Lyrics Jane McCulloch
Director Toby Robertson
Designer Hugh Durrant
Lighting Keith Edmundson

DANCE

SCOTTISH BALLET
24, 26, 27 Aug. 19.30 *King's Theatre*
LA SYLPHIDE
Choreographer August Bournonville
Music Løvenskjold
Designer Peter Cazalet
Lighting Charles Bristow
THREE DANCES TO JAPANESE MUSIC
Choreographer Jack Carter
Music Trad. arr. Katada
Designer Norman McDowell
Lighting Charles Bristow

29, 30 Aug. 19.30 *King's Theatre*
LES SYLPHIDES
Choreographer Mikhail Fokine
Music Chopin
Scenery Peter Cazalet
Costumes Janet Etta Roberts
Lighting Dee Ashworth
OTHELLO
Choreographer Peter Darrell
Music Liszt
Designer Peter Farmer
Lighting Peter Searle
DON QUIXOTE: Pas de deux
Choreographer *after* Marius Petipa
Music Minkus
THE SCARLET PASTORALE
Choreographer Peter Darrell
Music Martin
Designer Philip Prowse
Lighting Charles Bristow
Dancers Natalia Makarova, Fernando Bujones (guest artists), Linda Anning, Jane Ball, Graham Bart, William Bowen, Pauline Laverty, Anna McCartney, Kenneth Burke, Veronica Butcher, Roy Campbell-Moore, Sally Collard-Gentle, Linden Currey, Andrea Durant, Vincent Hantam, Michael Harper, Louise Hellewell, Kit Lethby, Christopher Long, Elaine McDonald, Linda Martin, Patricia Merrin, Judy Mohekey, Eleanor Moore, Jeanette Newell, Noriko Ohara, Elizabeth Peden, Ruth Prior, Wendy Roe, Peter Royston, Robert Ryan, Kenneth Saunders, Ann Sholem, Nigel Spencer, Dianne Storer, Paul Tyers, Anastasio Vitoros
Conductor Allan Morgan

EXHIBITIONS

Royal Scottish Academy
THE MODERN SPIRIT: American painting 1908-35

ASSOCIATED EXHIBITIONS
(Not organized by the Festival Society)

Scottish National Gallery of Modern Art
AMERICA AMERICA

Scottish Arts Council Gallery
IMPERIAL IMAGES IN PERSIAN MINIATURE PAINTING

1978

OPERA

EDINBURGH FESTIVAL OPERA
21, 24, 27, 30 Aug. 2 Sep. 19.30
King's Theatre
CARMEN Bizet
Carmen Teresa Berganza
Don José Pedro Lavirgen
Micaela Ileana Cotrubas
Yvonne Kenny
Escamillo Tom Krause
Frasquita Nan Christie
Patricia Greig
Yvonne Kenny
Mercédès Alicia Nafé?
Susan Daniel
Moralès Stuart Harling
Zuniga Jean Lainé
Dancairo Gordon Sandison
Remendado Geoffrey Pogson
Dancers Mariemma, Tomas de Madrid
Scottish Opera Chorus
George Watson's Boys' Chorus
London Symphony Orchestra
Conductor Claudio Abbado
Director Piero Faggioni
Designer Ezio Frigerio
Lighting Victor Lockwood
Choreographer Mariemma

SCOTTISH OPERA
23, 25, 26 Aug. 19.30 *King's Theatre*
PELLÉAS ET MÉLISANDE Debussy
Pelléas Thomas Allen
Mélisande Anne Howells
Golaud Lenus Carlson
Arkel Joseph Rouleau
Geneviève Anna Reynolds
Gillian Knight
Yniold Gillian Ramsden
Shepherd/Doctor Norman White
Conductor Sir Alexander Gibson
Director Colin Graham
Designer John Fraser
Lighting Charles Bristow

ZÜRICH OPERA
29, 31 Aug. 19.30 *King's Theatre*
L'ORFEO Monteverdi
Orfeo Philippe Huttenlocher
Euridice Reingard Didusch
La Musica/Speranza Trudeliese Schmidt
Messenger/Prosperina Glenys Linos
Caronte Hans Franzen
Plutone Werner Gröschel
Apollo Roland Hermann
Ninfa Suzanne Calabro
1st Shepherd Peter Keller
2nd Shepherd/1st Spirit Francisco Araiza
3rd Shepherd/2nd Spirit
Rudolf A. Hartmann
4th Shepherd/3rd Spirit József Dene
Conductor Nikolaus Harnoncourt
Director and Scenery
Jean-Pierre Ponnelle
Costumes Pet Halmen

1, 4 Sep. 19.30 *King's Theatre*
IL RITORNO D'ULISSE IN PATRIA
Monteverdi
Penelope Ortrun Wenkel
Ulisse/L' Humana Fragilità
Werner Hollweg
Telemaco Francisco Araiza
Tempo Werner Gröschel
Fortuna/Giunone Renate Lenhart
Giove József Dene
Nettuno Hans Franzen
Minerva Helrun Gardow
Antinöo Simon Estes
Pisandro Peter Straka
Anfinomo Paul Esswood
Eurimaco Peter Keller
Iro Arley Reece
Melanto Sylvia Greenberg
Ericlea Maria Minetto
Amore Klaus Brettschneider
Conductor Nikolaus Harnoncourt
Director and Scenery
Jean-Pierre Ponnelle
Costumes Pet Halmen

3, 5 Sep. 19.30 *King's Theatre*
L'INCORONAZIONE DI POPPEA
Monteverdi
Poppea Rachel Yakar
Nerone Eric Tappy
Ottavia Trudeliese Schmidt
Ottone Paul Esswood
Seneca Matti Salminen
Drusilla Elizabeth Gale
Nutrice Maria Minetto
Arnalta Alexander Oliver
Lucano Philippe Huttenlocher
Servants
Martin Schomberg, Werner Gröschel
Liberto Rudolf A. Hartmann
Valetto Peter Keller
Damigella Suzanne Calabro
Soldiers Peter Straka, Fritz Peter
Amore Andreas Riedman
Fortuna Renate Lenhart
Virtù Helrun Gardow
Conductor Nikolaus Harnoncourt
Director and Scenery
Jean-Pierre Ponnelle
Costumes Pet Halmen

FRANKFURT OPERA
7, 9 Sep. 19.30 *King's Theatre*
KÁTA KABANOVÁ Janáček (Ger)
Káta Hildegard Behrens
Boris Werner Götz
Marfa Kabanová Sona Cervena
Dikoy Heinz Hagenau
Tichon Kabanov William Cochran
Vanya Heinz Meyen
Varvara Pari Samar
Kulighin Francesch Chico-Bonet
Glasha Elsie Maurer
Feklusha Maria Kouba
Woman Margarete Nedelko
Conductor Michael Gielen
Director Volker Schlöndorff
Designer Ekkehard Grübler

8 Sep. 19.30 *King's Theatre*
AL GRAN SOLE CARICO D'AMORE
Nono (Concert performance)
Soloists June Card, Deborah Cook, Franca Fabbri, Tamar Rachum, Margit Neubauer, Sona Cervena (Mother), Willy Müller, Heinz Meyen, Francesch Chico-Bonet, Tadao Yoshie, Franz Mayer, Carlos Krause
Conductor Michael Gielen

ORCHESTRAL CONCERTS

INTERNATIONAL YOUTH ORCHESTRA
20 Aug. 20.00 *Usher Hall*
Mozart Concerto for violin no.3 in G, K216
Beethoven Symphony no.9 in D minor (Choral), op.125
Conductor Carlo Maria Giulini
Soloists Isaac Stern (vn), Sheila Armstrong (sop), Helen Watts (cont), Robert Tear (ten), Marius Rintzler (bs), International Youth Chorus

LONDON PHILHARMONIC ORCHESTRA
22 Aug. 20.00 *Usher Hall*
Berlioz La damnation de Faust
Conductor Daniel Barenboim
Soloists Jessye Norman (sop), Stuart Burrows (ten), Jules Bastin, Don Garrard (bs), EF Chorus, SNO Junior Chorus

25, 26 Aug. 20.00 *Usher Hall*
Brahms Tragic overture
Brahms Ein deutsches Requiem
Conductor Carlo Maria Giulini
Soloists Ileana Cotrubas (sop), Dietrich Fischer-Dieskau (bar), EF Chorus

25 Aug. 22.45 *Usher Hall*
A Festival Garland
In honour of Peter Diamand
Teresa Berganza, Ileana Cotrubas, Catherine Gayer, Jessye Norman, Claudio Abbado, Daniel Barenboim, Dietrich Fischer-Dieskau, Isaac Stern, Sir Alexander Gibson, Carlo Maria Giulini, Ian Robertson, EF Chorus

LONDON SYMPHONY ORCHESTRA
23 Aug. 20.00 *Usher Hall*
Berlioz Le carnaval romain - Overture
Sibelius Concerto for violin in D minor, op.47
Janáček Sinfonietta
Conductor Claudio Abbado
Soloist Isaac Stern (vn)

28 Aug. 20.00 *Usher Hall*
Bernstein Candide: Overture
Chopin Concerto for piano no.1 in E minor, op.11
Shostakovich Symphony no.5 in D minor, op.47
Conductor Evgeny Svetlanov
Soloist Krystian Zimerman (pf)

29 Aug. 20.00 *Usher Hall*
Rimsky-Korsakov The Maid of Pskov: Overture
Beethoven Concerto for piano no.3 in C minor, op.37
Rimsky-Korsakov Shéhérazade
Conductor Evgeny Svetlanov
Soloist Alfred Brendel (pf)

1 Sep. 20.00 *Usher Hall*
Schubert Symphony no.8 in B minor (Unfinished), D759
Mozart Cosi dunque tradisci
Mozart Un bacio di mano
Mozart Mentre ti lascio
Stravinsky Pulcinella
Stravinsky The firebird - Suite
Conductor Claudio Abbado
Soloists Teresa Berganza (mez), Ryland Davies (ten), Dietrich Fischer-Dieskau (bar)

ENGLISH CHAMBER ORCHESTRA
31 Aug. 20.00 *Usher Hall*
Vivaldi Concerti, op.8: Nos. 1-4 (The four seasons)
Schubert Polonaise for violin in B flat, D580
Schubert Symphony no.2 in B flat, D125
Conductor and soloist
Pinchas Zukerman (vn)

BBC SYMPHONY ORCHESTRA
Conductor Pierre Boulez
2 Sep. 20.00 *Usher Hall*
Schoenberg Verklärte Nacht
Mahler Das Lied von der Erde
Soloists Yvonne Minton (mez), Werner Götz (ten)*

3 Sep. 20.00 *Usher Hall*
Boulez Rituel
Stravinsky The nightingale
Soloists Phyllis Bryn-Julson (sop), Anne Howells (mez), Ortrun Wenkel (cont), Ian Partridge (ten), Peter Knapp (bar), Don Garrard, Jules Bastin (bs), BBC Singers

DRESDEN STAATSKAPELLE
Conductor Herbert Blomstedt
5 Sep. 20.00 *Usher Hall*
Beethoven Concerto for piano no.4 in G, op.58
Bruckner Symphony no.4 in E flat (Romantic)
Soloist Zoltán Kocsis (pf)

6 Sep. 20.00 *Usher Hall*
Beethoven Symphony no.4 in B flat, op.60
Mozart Concerto for violin no.2 in D, K211
Reger Variations and fugue on a theme by Mozart, op.132
Soloist Vladimir Spivakov (vn)

CHICAGO SYMPHONY ORCHESTRA
Conductor Sir Georg Solti
7 Sep. 20.00 *Usher Hall*
Beethoven Symphony no.1 in C, op.21
Mahler Symphony no.1 in D

8 Sep. 20.00 *Usher Hall*
Brahms Symphony no.3 in F, op.90
Brahms Symphony no.4 in E minor, op.98

SCOTTISH NATIONAL ORCHESTRA
9 Sep. 20.00 *Usher Hall*
Dvořák Te deum
Mozart Concerto for piano no.21 in C, K467
Janáček Glagolitic mass
Conductor Sir Alexander Gibson
Soloists Sir Clifford Curzon (pf), Wendy Fine (sop), Anne Collins (cont), Vilém Přibyl (ten), John Shirley-Quirk (bar), John Birch (org), EF Chorus

CHAMBER CONCERTS

LaSALLE QUARTET
21 Aug. 11.00 *Freemasons' Hall*
Purcell Three 4-part fantasias (E minor, F, G)
Webern Quartet (1905)
Beethoven Grosse Fuge in B flat, op.133
Mozart Quartet no.16 in E flat, K428

23 Aug. 11.00 *Freemasons' Hall*
Beethoven Quartet in F (Arrangement of Sonata for piano, op.14/1)
Lutoslawski Quartet (1964)
Brahms Quartet no.3 in B flat, op.67

NASH ENSEMBLE
22 Aug. 11.00 *Freemasons' Hall*
Baermann Adagio for clarinet and string quintet in E flat, op.23
L. Berkeley Trio for strings, op.19
Schubert Octet, D803

24 Aug. 11.00 *Freemasons' Hall*
Schubert Adagio and rondo concertante for piano and strings, D487
Schubert Der Hirt auf dem Felsen
Messiaen Quatuor pour la fin du temps
with Sheila Armstrong (sop)

COMPOSER'S PROGRAMME: GOEHR
26 Aug. 11.00 *Freemasons' Hall*
Mozart Divertimento for 3 basset horns, K439b
Goehr Trio for piano and strings, op.20
Goehr Introduction and fugue for 3 clarinets (World première)
Webern Six songs on texts of Georg Traekl
Webern Three little pieces for cello and piano, op.11
Webern Three traditional rhymes, op.17
Webern Variations for piano, op.27
Webern Quartet for violin, clarinet, tenor sax and piano, op.22
Conductor Alexander Goehr
Soloists Catherine Gayer (sop), Alan Hacker, Francis Christou, Edward Pillinger (cl, bas hn), Orion Piano Trio

RUDOLF FIRKUŠNÝ (pf)
SONA CERVENA (mez)
PHILIP LANGRIDGE (ten)
31 Aug. 11.00 *Freemasons' Hall*
Mozart Variations on a minuet by Duport, K573
Schubert Klavierstücke, D946
Janáček Diary of one who disappeared

LONDON SYMPHONY ORCHESTRA WIND ENSEMBLE
2 Sep. 11.00 *Freemasons' Hall*
Janáček Mládi
L. Berkeley Quintet for piano and wind, op.90
Mozart Serenade no.11 in E flat, K375
with Howard Shelley (pf)

FIRES OF LONDON
6 Sep. 20.00 *St Mary's Cathedral*
P.M. Davies Runes from a Holy Island (1st public performance)
Dalby The dancer Eduardova
P.M. Davies Renaissance Scottish dances
P.M. Davies Le jongleur de Notre Dame (staged)
Director Peter Maxwell Davies
with Michael Rippon (bs), Rhubarb the Clown (mime, juggler)

PETER FRANKL (pf), GYÖRGY PAUK (vn), RALPH KIRSHBAUM (vc)
6 Sep. 11.00 *Freemasons' Hall*
Brahms Sonata for violin and piano no.1 in G, op.78
Debussy Sonata for cello and piano
Schubert Trio for piano and strings no.1 in B flat, D898

8 Sep. 11.00 *Freemasons' Hall*
Brahms Sonata for cello and piano no.2 in F, op.99
Debussy Sonata for violin and piano
Schubert Trio for piano and strings in E flat, D929

AMADEUS QUARTET
9 Sep. 11.00 *Leith Theatre*
Schubert Quartet no.10 in E flat, D87
Schubert Quartet no.12 in C minor (Quartetsatz), D703
Schubert Quintet in C, D956
with William Pleeth (vc)

JOHN ALLDIS CHOIR
28 Aug. 11.00 *Freemasons' Hall*
Schubert Lebenslust
Schubert Ständchen, D921
Ligeti Lux aeterna
Holloway Hymn for voices
Schubert Psalm 23, D706
Janáček Two Moravian choruses (O lasko; Vilůzka)
Debussy Trois chansons de Charles d'Orléans
Conductor John Alldis

RECITALS

JESSYE NORMAN (sop)
DALTON BALDWIN (pf)
25 Aug. 11.00 *Freemasons' Hall*
Schubert Songs
Messiaen Poèmes pour Mi
Ravel Chansons madécasses
with Richard Chester (fl), Adrian Shepherd (vc)

DIETRICH FISCHER-DIESKAU (bar)
DANIEL BARENBOIM (pf)
30 Aug. 20.00 *Usher Hall*
Songs by Schubert

TERESA BERGANZA (mez)
ERNESTO BITETTI (gtr)
5 Sep. 15.00 *Leith Theatre*
Spanish music from the 14th to 20th centuries including:
Falla Siete canciones populares españolas

PETER WILLIAMS (hpd)
21 Aug. 15.00 *St Cecilia's Hall*
Bach Partitas nos.1, 3, 6

26 Aug. 15.00 *St Cecilia's Hall*
Bach Partitas nos. 5, 2, 4

DANIEL BARENBOIM (pf)
24 Aug. 20.00 *Usher Hall*
Schubert Impromptus, D935
Schubert Sonata no.21 in B flat, D960

4 Sep. 20.00 *Usher Hall*
Schubert Impromptus, D899
Schubert Moments musicaux, D780
Schubert Sonata no.19 in C minor, D958

ALFRED BRENDEL (pf)
27 Aug. 15.00 *Usher Hall*
Haydn Sonata no.59 in E flat
Beethoven Sonata no.21 in C (Waldstein), op.53
Schubert Sonata no.18 in G, D894

RUDOLF FIRKUŠNÝ (pf)
29 Aug. 11.00 *Freemasons' Hall*
Beethoven Bagatelles nos.19-24, op.126
Beethoven Sonata no.7 in D, op.10/3
Janáček Sonata 1 X 1905
Janáček In the mist
Janáček On an overgrown path: Book 2

ZOLTÁN KOCSIS (pf)
7 Sep. 11.00 *Freemasons' Hall*
Kocsis Tristan und Isolde: Prelude (Wagner)
Liszt Tristan und Isolde: Liebestod (Wagner)
Bartók Allegro barbaro
Bartók Fifteen Hungarian peasant songs
Bartók Six Rumanian folk dances
Bartók Eight improvisations on Hungarian peasant songs
Chopin Piano works

LILIAN KALLIR
CLAUDE FRANK (2 pf)
1 Sep. 11.00 *Freemasons' Hall*
Mozart Fantasia in F minor, K608
Schubert Andantino varié in B minor, D823
Schubert 2 Marches militaires, D733
Schubert Fantasia in F minor, D940
Mozart Sonata in D, K448

ISAAC STERN (vn)
DANIEL BARENBOIM (pf)

27 Aug. 20.00 *Usher Hall*
Schubert Sonata in G minor, D408
Schubert Sonata in A (Duo), D574
Schubert Fantasia in C, D934

VLADIMIR SPIVAKOV (vn)
BORIS BECHTEREV (pf)
4 Sep. 11.00 *Freemasons' Hall*
Schubert Sonata in A minor, D385
Brahms Sonata no.2 in A, op.100
Bartók Sonata no.2
Paganini Le streghe

JAMES GALWAY (fl), PHILLIP MOLL (pf)
30 Aug. 11.00 *Leith Theatre*
L. Berkeley Sonatina, op.13
Schubert Sonata in A minor (Arpeggione), D821
L. Berkeley Sonata (World première)
Schubert Introduction and variations on Trock'ne Blumen

DRAMA

EDINBURGH FESTIVAL PRODUCTIONS
20-23, 28, 31 Aug. 1, 4, 7, 8 Sep. 19.30
29 Aug. 14.30 *Assembly Hall*
THE TEMPEST Shakespeare
Prospero Alan Dobie
Miranda Janet Maw
Alonso William Whymper
Sebastian Desmond Adams
Antonio Rod Beacham
Ferdinand Jack Galloway
Gonzalo Paddy Ward
Adrian Colin Spaull
Caliban Richard Easton
Trinculo Colin Farrell
Stephano Jeffrey Holland
Ariel Adam Bareham
Iris Marilyn Taylerson
Ceres Janice Halsey
Juno Holly Wilson
Master Martin Sadler
Boatswain Alec Bregonzi
Director David Giles
Scenery Kenneth Mellor
Costumes Pauline Whitehouse
Lighting Keith Edmundson

24-26, 29, 30 Aug. 2, 5, 6, 9 Sep. 19.30
26 Aug. 2, 5, 9 Sep. 14.30 *Assembly Hall*
A MIDSUMMER NIGHT'S DREAM Shakespeare
Titania/Hippolyta Marilyn Taylerson
Oberon/Theseus Richard Easton
Lysander Adam Bareham
Helena Holly Wilson
Demetrius Desmond Adams
Hermia Janet Maw
Bottom Alan Dobie
Starveling William Whymper
Snug Jeffrey Holland
Flute Colin Farrell
Quince Paddy Ward
Snout Rod Beacham
Puck Jack Galloway
Philostrate/Cobweb Colin Spaull
Peaseblossom Martin Sadler
Moth Janice Halsey
Mustardseed/Egeus Alec Bregonzi
Director David Giles
Scenery Kenneth Mellor
Costumes Pauline Whitehouse
Lighting Keith Edmundson

ROYAL SHAKESPEARE COMPANY
21-24 Aug. 1-2 Sep. 19.30 24 Aug. 2 Sep. 14.30
Daniel Stewart's and Melville College
TWELFTH NIGHT Shakespeare
Viola Emily Richard
Orsino Edward Petherbridge
Olivia Suzanne Bertish
Sir Toby Belch Ian McKellen
Sir Andrew Aguecheek Roger Rees
Malvolio Bob Peck
Maria Bridget Turner
Feste Christopher Hancock
Curio/Officer Alec Wallis
Valentine/Fabian Clyde Pollitt
Sea captain/Priest Griffith Jones
Sebastian Jeremy Blake
Antonio Patrick Godfrey
Director Jon Amiel
Designer John Napier
Lighting Brian Harris

25, 26, 28-31 Aug. 19.30 26 Aug. 14.30
Daniel Stewart's and Melville College
THREE SISTERS Chekhov
(Eng. Translated by Richard Cottrell)
Andrei Sergyeich Prozorov Ian McKellen
Natalya Ivanova Susan Tracy
Olga Bridget Turner
Masha Suzanne Bertish
Irina Emily Richard
Fiodor Ilyich Kulighin Patrick Godfrey
Alexander Ignatyevich Vershinin Edward Petherbridge
Nikolai Lvovich Tusenbach Roger Rees
Vassily Vassilich Soliony Bob Peck
Ivan Romanych Chebutikin Griffith Jones
Alexei Petrovich Fedotik Jeremy Blake
Vladimir Karlovich Rode Christopher Hancock
Ferapont Clyde Pollitt
Anfisa Rose Hill
Orderly/Musician Alec Wallis
Director Trevor Nunn
Designer John Napier
Lighting Brian Harris

MOSCOW DRAMA THEATRE, Malaya Bronnaya Street
21, 23, 26 Aug. 19.15 26 Aug. 14.15
Lyceum Theatre
THE MARRIAGE Gogol
Podkolyosin Nikolai Volkov, Andrei Martynov
Stepan Alexei Ushakov
Fyokla Ivanovna Antonina Dmitreyeva, Irena Kirichenko
Kochkaryov Mikhail Kozakov
Agafya Tikhonovna Olga Yakovleva, Anna Kamenkova
Arena Panteleymonovna Maria Andrianova
Yaichnitsa (Omelette) Leonid Bronevoy
Zhevakin Lev Durov
Anuchkin Dmitry Dorliak
Panteleyev Victor Kamayev
Dunyashka Vera Mayorova
Merchant Kyrill Glazunov
Clerks Anatoly Grachyov, Grigory Lyampe, Arcady Peselev
Nun Elena Koreneva
Merchant's wife Albina Matveyeva
Clerk's wife Irena Kirichenko
Director Anatoli Efros
Designer Valery Leventhal

22, 24, 25 Aug. 19.15 *Lyceum Theatre*
A MONTH IN THE COUNTRY Turgenev
Natalia Petrovna Islayeva Olga Yakovleva
Mikhail Alexandrovich Rakitin Mikhail Kozakov
Anna Semyonovna Islayeva Maria Andrianova
Alexei Nikolayevich Belyaev Oleg Dal, Anatoly Grachyov
Ignaty Ilyich Shpigelsky Leonid Bronevoy
Verochka Elena Koreneva
Arcady Sergeyevich Islayev Isaac Kastrel
Elizaveta Bogdanovna Albina Matveyeva
Afanasy Ivanovich Bolshintsov Leo Durov, Kyrill Glazunov
Director Anatoli Efros
Scenery Dmitry Krymov
Costumes Ekaterina Sokolskaya, Dmitry Krymov

PROSPECT THEATRE COMPANY
4-9 Sep. 19.15 6, 9 Sep. 14.15
Lyceum Theatre
IVANOV Chekhov (Eng)
Nikolai Ivanov Derek Jacobi
Anna Petrovna Louise Purnell
Matvei Shabelsky John Savident
Pavel Lebedev Michael Denison
Zinaida Sheila Mitchell
Sasha Jane Wymark
Dr Lvov Clive Arrindell
Marfa Babinka Brenda Bruce
Nikolai Kosykh Oz Clarke
Mikhail Borkin John Cording
Avdotya Nazarovna Janet Henfrey
Yegorushka Neil Gibson
Peter Malcolm Hughes
Gavrila Jeffrey Daunton
Director Toby Robertson
Designer Robin Archer
Lighting Mick Hughes

POETRY AND PROSE RECITALS

23-25 Aug. 15.00 *St Cecilia's Hall*
FUN AND GAMES
Diana Rigg, Frank Muir, Robert Powell (rdr)
Devised by Michael Meyer

27 Aug. 15.00 and 20.00 *St Cecilia's Hall*
THE SMITH OF SMITHS
Sydney Smith Timothy West
with Prunella Scales, John Rowe (rdr), Donald Fraser (hpd)
Compiled by Jane McCullogh
Directed by Toby Robertson

29 Aug.-1 Sep. 15.00 *St Cecilia's Hall*
ROBERT BURNS
Tom Fleming (rdr), Jean Redpath (sngr)
Devised by Tom Fleming

31 Aug. 15.00 *St Cecilia's Hall*
WILLIAM SOUTAR
Tom Fleming (rdr), Clifford Hughes (ten), Ronald Stevenson (pf)
Devised by Tom Fleming and George Bruce

3, 4 Sep. 15.00 *St Cecilia's Hall*
FENELLA FIELDING
A personal choice
with Nigel Stock (rdr), Bunny Thompson (pf)

6, 7 Sep. 15.00 *St Cecilia's Hall*
THE LANGUAGE OF THE HEART
Love letters from Antonia Fraser's anthology
Judi Dench, John Stride (rdr)
Devised by John Carroll

DANCE

TANZTHEATER WUPPERTAL
28-30 Aug. 19.30 *Lyceum Theatre*
FRÜHLINGSOPFER
Three ballets by Pina Bausch
WIND VON WEST
DER ZWEITE FRÜHLING
LE SACRE DU PRINTEMPS

Music Stravinsky
Designer Rolf Borzik
Dancers Malou Airaudo, Annemarie Benati, Elisabeth Clarke, Mari DiLena, Silvia Kesselheim, Anne Martin, Jo-Anne Endicott, Beatrice Libonati, Yolanda Meier, Vivienne Newport, Barbara Passow, Monika Sagon, Dana Robin Sapiro, Meryl Tankard, Monica Wacker, Arnaldo Alvarez, Fernando Cortizo, Gary Austin Crocker, Lutz Förster, John Giffin, Ed Kortlandt, Luis P. Layag, Dominique Mercy, Jean Mindo, Jacques Antoine Petarozzi, Heinz Samm

LECTURES

Earl of Harewood Maria Callas

EXHIBITIONS

Royal Scottish Museum
GIAM BOLOGNA

ASSOCIATED EXHIBITIONS
(Not organized by the Festival Society)

Scottish Arts Council Gallery
BULGARIAN ICONS

Royal Scottish Academy
ARMAND HAMMER COLLECTION

Scottish National Gallery of Modern Art
RUSSIAN NON-OBJECTIVE ART

1979

OPERA

KENT OPERA
21, 23, 25, 27 Aug. 19.30 King's Theatre
LA TRAVIATA Verdi (Eng)
Violetta Jill Gomez
Elaine Woods*
Alfredo Keith Lewis
Giorgio Thomas Hemsley
Flora Elaine Woods
Annina Eirian James
Gaston Paul Whitmarsh
Baron Douphol William Shimell
Marquis d'Obigny Paul Wilson
Dr Grenvil Colin Iveson
Giuseppe Christopher Adams
Messenger Martin Nelson
Servant Michael Hartley
Conductor Roger Norrington
Director Jonathan Miller
Designer Bernard Culshaw
Lighting Nick Chelton

22, 24, 26 Aug. 19.30 King's Theatre
IPHIGÉNIE EN TAURIDE Gluck (Eng)
Iphigénie Eiddwen Harrhy
Oreste Jonathan Summers
Pylade Anthony Roden
Thoas Robert Bateman
Diana Elaine Woods
Greek woman Daryl Greene
Priestesses Una Barry, Alison Mary Sutton
Scythian Philip Curtis
Servant Andrew Shore
Conductor Roger Norrington
Director Norman Platt
Designer Roger Butlin
Lighting Nick Chelton

SCOTTISH OPERA
29, 31 Aug. 7 Sep. 19.30 King's Theatre
THE GOLDEN COCKEREL
Rimsky-Korsakov (Eng)
Astrologer John Winfield
King Dodon William McCue
Prince Afron Donald Maxwell
Prince Guidon John Robertson
Queen of Shemakhan Elizabeth Gale
Voice of the Cockerel Marie Slorach
Amelfa Claire Livingstone
General Polkan Norman White
Cockerel Inga-Lise
Parrot Jim Hastie
BBC Scottish Symphony Orchestra
Conductor Henry Lewis
Director David Pountney
Scenery Sue Blane
Costumes Maria Bjørnson
Lighting Charles Bristow

1, 4, 6, 8 Sep. 19.30 King's Theatre
EUGENE ONEGIN Tchaikovsky (Eng)
Onegin John Shirley-Quirk
Tatiana Lilian Sukis
Olga Cynthia Buchan
Lensky Anthony Rolfe Johnson
Madame Larina Claire Livingstone
Filipievna Noreen Berry
Gremin Stafford Dean
M. Triquet Francis Egerton
Zaretski Norman White
Captain Halcro Johnston
Scottish National Orchestra
Conductor Sir Alexander Gibson
Director David Pountney
Scenery Roger Butlin
Costumes Deirdre Clancy
Lighting Nick Chelton

3, 5 Sep. 19.30 King's Theatre
THE TURN OF THE SCREW Britten
Prologue Peter Pears
Governess Catherine Wilson
Miles Kenneth Love
Flora Rosanne Brackenridge
Mrs Grose Patricia Kern
Quint George Shirley
Miss Jessel Milla Andrew
Scottish Chamber Orchestra
Conductor Roderick Brydon
Director Anthony Besch
Designer John Stoddart
Lighting Charles Bristow

ORCHESTRAL CONCERTS

BBC SYMPHONY ORCHESTRA
Conductor Gennadi Rozhdestvensky
19 Aug. 20.00 Usher Hall
Prokofiev Chout
Stravinsky The rite of spring
Soloist Andrew Cruickshank (narr)

20 Aug. 20.00 Usher Hall
Shostakovich Symphony no.14, op.135
Britten Spring symphony
Soloists Felicity Palmer, Margaret Marshall (sop), Helen Watts (cont), Sir Peter Pears (ten), Nicola Ghiuselev (bs), EF Chorus, SNO Junior Chorus

SCOTTISH CHAMBER ORCHESTRA
20 Aug. 11.00 Queen's Hall
Boyce Symphony no.4 in F, op.2/4
Nielsen Concerto for flute
Crosse Dream songs (World première)
Bach Suite no.2 in B minor
Conductor Roderick Brydon
Soloist James Galway (fl)

26 Aug. 20.00 Usher Hall
Bartók Divertimento for strings
Mozart Concerto for 2 pianos in E flat, K365
Mozart Ch'io mi scordi di te
Mozart Voi avete un cor fedele
Mendelssohn Symphony no.4 in A (Italian), op.90
Conductor and soloist
Tamás Vásáry (pf)
Soloists Elly Ameling (sop), Peter Frankl (pf)

SCOTTISH NATIONAL ORCHESTRA
Conductor Sir Alexander Gibson
21 Aug. 20.00 Usher Hall
Weber Aufforderung zum Tanze; orch. Berlioz
Berlioz Les nuits d'été
Rachmaninov Symphony no.2 in E minor, op.27
Soloist Jessye Norman (sop)

5 Sep. 20.00 Usher Hall
Debussy Jeux
Lutoslawski Concerto for cello+
Brahms Symphony no.1 in C minor, op.68
Conductor Witold Lutoslawski+
Soloist Roman Jablonski (vc)

LONDON SYMPHONY ORCHESTRA
22 Aug. 20.00 Usher Hall
Mahler Symphony no.3 in D minor
Conductor Claudio Abbado
Soloist Lucia Valentini-Terrani (mez)
EF Chorus, SNO Junior Chorus

24 Aug. 20.00 Usher Hall
Debussy Prélude à l'après-midi d'un faune
Chopin Concerto for piano no.2 in F minor, op.21

Tchaikovsky Symphony no.4 in F minor, op.36
Conductor Claudio Abbado
Soloist Maurizio Pollini (pf)

25 Aug. 20.00 *Usher Hall*
Schumann Symphony no.1 in B flat (Spring), op.38
Reinecke Concerto for flute in D, op.283
Tchaikovsky Romeo and Juliet - Fantasy overture
Conductor Riccardo Chailly
Soloist James Galway (fl)

ACADEMY OF ANCIENT MUSIC
26 Aug. 15.00 *Queen's Hall*
Music and words by Purcell, Humphrey, Blow, Clarke, D. Purcell
Conductor Christopher Hogwood
Soloists James Bowman (c ten), James Cairncross (rdr)

28 Aug. 11.00 *Queen's Hall*
Mozart Symphony in D, K141a
Mozart Andante for flute in C, K315
Mozart Symphony no.29 in A, K201
Mozart Concerto for violin no.3 in G, K216
Mozart Symphony no.20 in D, K133
Conductor Christopher Hogwood
Soloists Jaap Schröder (vn), Stephen Preston (fl)

PHILHARMONIA ORCHESTRA
28 Aug. 20.00 *Usher Hall*
Mussorgsky A night on the Bare Mountain
Tchaikovsky Concerto for violin in D, op.35
Ravel Rapsodie espagnole
Falla El sombrero de tres picos: Neighbour's dance; Miller's dance; Final dance
Conductor Riccardo Muti
Soloist Salvatore Accardo (vn)

29 Aug. 20.00 *Usher Hall*
Mozart Symphony no.24 in B flat, K182
Penderecki Symphony no.1
Liszt Die Loreley
Liszt Die Vätergruft
Liszt Die drei Zigeuner
Liszt Mignons Lied
Liszt Les préludes
Conductor Riccardo Muti
Soloist Dame Janet Baker (mez)

31 Aug. 20.00 *Usher Hall*
Haydn Symphony no.60 in C (Il distratto)
Mozart Concerto for piano no.26 in D (Coronation), K537
Franck Symphonic variations, op.46
Poulenc Les biches
Conductor Simon Rattle
Soloist Sir Clifford Curzon (pf)

2 Sep. 20.00 *Usher Hall*
Schumann Manfred: Overture
Brahms Concerto for piano no.1 in D minor, op.15
Mussorgsky Pictures at an exhibition; orch. Ravel
Conductor Jesus Lopez-Cobos
Soloist Krystian Zimerman (pf)

POLISH CHAMBER ORCHESTRA
1 Sep. 20.00 *Usher Hall*
Conductor Jerzy Maksymiuk
Tchaikovsky Serenade for strings, op.48
Mozart Concerto for violin no.5 in A, K219
Bach Concerto for violin in A minor
Mozart Divertimento (Salzburg symphony) no.1 in D, K136
Soloist Henryk Szeryng (vn)

3 Sep. 11.00 *Queen's Hall*
Bacewicz Concerto for string orchestra
Bujarski Musica domestica
Górecki Three pieces in an old style
Rossini Sonata for strings no.3 in C
Haydn Symphony no.47 in G

HALLÉ ORCHESTRA
Conductor James Loughran
3 Sep. 20.00 *Usher Hall*
Berlioz Benvenuto Cellini: Overture
Bennett Sonnets to Orpheus (EIF commission)
Elgar Symphony no.2 in E flat, op.63
Soloist Heinrich Schiff (vc)

4 Sep. 20.00 *Usher Hall*
Beethoven Symphony no.7 in A, op.92
Walton Belshazzar's feast
Soloist Benjamin Luxon (bar), EF Chorus

BOSTON SYMPHONY ORCHESTRA
Conductor Seiji Ozawa
7 Sep. 20.00 *Usher Hall*
Beethoven Symphony no.4 in B flat, op.60
R. Strauss Ein Heldenleben

8 Sep. 20.00 *Usher Hall*
Bartók Music for strings, percussion and celesta
Ravel Daphnis et Chloë
EF Chorus

CHAMBER CONCERTS

LINDSAY QUARTET
22 Aug. 11.00 *Freemasons' Hall*
Beethoven Quartet no.11 in F minor (Serioso), op.95
Tippett Quartet no.4
Mozart Quintet for clarinet and strings in A, K581
with Janet Hilton (cl)

PHILIP JONES BRASS ENSEMBLE
23 Aug. 11.00 *Queen's Hall*
French Renaissance dance music
Early English music
Dodgson Fantasia for six brass
Britten Fanfare for St Edmundsbury
Ewald Theme and variations, op.6

NETHERLANDS WIND ENSEMBLE
27 Aug. 11.00 *Queen's Hall*
Rossini Il barbiere di Siviglia: Overture; arr. for wind
Seiber Serenade for wind
Kramář Partita in E flat, op.79
Beethoven Rondino in E flat
Mozart Serenade no.11 in E flat, K375

30 Aug. 22.45 *Usher Hall*
Serenade concert

STUTTGART PIANO TRIO
1 Sep. 11.00 *Freemasons' Hall*
Haydn Trio for piano and strings no.27 in C
Ravel Trio for piano and strings in A minor
Schubert Trio for piano and strings in E flat, D929

MEDICI QUARTET
2 Sep. 15.00 *Usher Hall*
Shostakovich Quartet no.8 in C minor, op.110
Dvořák Quintet for piano and strings in A, op.81
Ravel Quartet in F
with Sir Clifford Curzon (pf)

SCOTTISH BAROQUE ENSEMBLE
6 Sep. 11.00 *Queen's Hall*
Anon. Airs and dances of Renaissance Scotland
Lully Le bourgeois gentilhomme - Suite
Handel Concerto grosso in A minor, op.6/4
Milhaud Octet (From Quartets nos.14 and 15)
Skalkottas Five Greek dances
Director Leonard Friedman

BEAUX ARTS TRIO
7 Sep. 11.00 *Queen's Hall*
Mozart Trio for piano and strings no.4 in E, K542
Beethoven Variations on 'Ich bin der Schneider Kakadu'
Tchaikovsky Trio for piano and strings in A minor, op.50

SCHÜTZ CHOIR
LONDON BAROQUE PLAYERS
30 Aug. 20.00 *Queen's Hall*
Monteverdi Vespro della beata vergine (1610)
Conductor Roger Norrington

MUSIC FROM CHINA
21 Aug. 11.00 *Queen's Hall*
Classical and modern Chinese music
Ensemble of Chinese instrumentalists

RECITALS

JESSYE NORMAN (sop)
DALTON BALDWIN (pf)
23 Aug. 20.00 *Usher Hall*
Haydn Arianna a Naxos
Brahms Two songs for contralto, viola and piano, op.91
Ravel Shéhérazade
Songs by Brahms, R. Strauss
with James Galway (fl), John Harrington (va)

ELLY AMELING (sop)
DALTON BALDWIN (pf)
25 Aug. 11.00 *Queen's Hall*
Poulenc Fiançailles pour rire
Songs by Mozart, Fauré, Schubert

HÅKAN HAGEGÅRD (bar)
THOMAS SCHUBACK (pf)
31 Aug. 11.00 *Freemasons' Hall*
Ravel Don Quichotte à Dulcinée
Songs by Schubert, Brahms, R. Strauss, Stenhammar *and* Swedish folk songs

ELISABETH SÖDERSTRÖM (sop)
MARTIN ISEPP (pf)
4 Sep. 11.00 *Queen's Hall*
Mussorgsky The nursery
Songs by Sjögren, Grieg, Tchaikovsky

CHRISTA LUDWIG (sop)
GEOFFREY PARSONS (pf)
6 Sep. 20.00 *Usher Hall*
Songs by Schubert, Schumann, Brahms, R. Strauss, Mahler, Wolf

MICHEL DALBERTO (pf)
24 Aug. 11.00 *Freemasons' Hall*
Debussy Children's corner suite
Scriabin Sonata no.3 in F sharp minor, op.23
Schumann Theme and variations on the name 'Abegg'
Schumann Humoresque in B flat, op.20

MAURIZIO POLLINI (pf)
27 Aug. 20.00 *Usher Hall*
Schubert Klavierstücke, D946
Schubert Sonata no.14 in A minor, D784
Schumann Gesänge der Frühe
Schumann Fantasia in C, op.17

KRYSTIAN ZIMERMAN (pf)
30 Aug. 20.00 *Usher Hall*
Brahms Sonata no.2 in F sharp minor, op.2
Mozart Sonata no.10 in C, K330
Chopin Sonata no.3 in B minor, op.58

JEAN-PHILIPPE COLLARD (pf)
5 Sep. 11.00 *Freemasons' Hall*
Debussy Estampes
Ravel Gaspard de la Nuit
Rachmaninov Études tableaux, op.39: Nos. 5, 9
Rachmaninov Sonata no.2 in B flat minor, op.36 (1st version)

PETER FRANKL, TAMÁS VÁSÁRY (pf)
29 Aug. 11.00 *Freemasons' Hall*
Bizet Jeux d'enfants
Ravel Ma mére l'oye
Stravinsky The rite of spring; arr. for 2 pianos

SALVATORE ACCARDO (vn)
BRUNO CANINO (pf)
30 Aug. 11.00 *Freemasons' Hall*
Schumann Sonata no.1 in A minor, op.105
Brahms Sonata no.1 in G, op.78
Prokofiev Sonata no.1 in F minor, op.80
Ravel Tzigane

JANE MANNING (sop), RICHARD JACKSON (bar), BARRY TUCKWELL (hn), RICHARD RODNEY BENNETT (pf)
8 Sep. 11.00 *Freemasons' Hall*
R. Strauss Introduction, theme and variations for horn and piano
Saint-Saens Romance for horn and piano in F, op.36
Bennett Sonata for horn (World première)
Hamilton The spirit of delight (World première)

JAZZ

MIKE WESTBROOK ORCHESTRA
26 Aug. 18.00 and 21.00 *Moray House*
Westbrook The cortège

DRAMA

BRISTOL OLD VIC
20, 21, 25, 29-31 Aug. 7, 8 Sep. 19.30 25, 29 Aug. 8 Sep. 14.30 *Assembly Hall*
TROILUS AND CRESSIDA Shakespeare
Prologue/Achilles Robert O'Mahoney
Priam/Nestor James Cairncross
Hector William Hoyland
Troilus Jonathan Kent
Paris Clive Wood
Deiphobus Daniel Day Lewis
Helenus Gregory Martyn
Aeneus Miles Anderson
Antenor Albie Woodington
Calchas/Servant David Foxxe
Cressida Meg Davies
Pandarus John Warner
Cassandra Sarah Collier
Andromache Caroline Holdaway
Page to Paris Christopher Hurst
Page to Troilus Leo Wringer
Agamemnon Andrew Hilton
Menelaus Patrick Connor
Ulysses Peter Postlethwaite
Ajax Sean Scanlan
Patroclus Michael Derrington
Diomedes Jack Klaff
Thersites Ian MacKenzie
Helen Elizabeth Richardson
Director Richard Cottrell
Designer John McMurray
Lighting Francis Reid

22-24, 27, 28 Aug. 1, 3-6 Sep. 19.30 1, 5 Sep. 14.30 *Assembly Hall*
THE RECRUITING OFFICER Farquhar
Prologue Robert O'Mahoney
Mr Balance James Cairncross
Mr Scale Andrew Hilton
Mr Scruple Albie Woodington
Mr Worthy William Hoyland
Captain Plume Miles Anderson
Captain Brazen Neil Stacy
Kite Peter Postlethwaite
Bullock David Foxxe
Costar Pearmain Clive Wood
Thomas Appletree Ian MacKenzie
Thomas, a smith Michael Derrington
Bridewell Patrick Connor
Collier Mark Lambert
Drummer Leo Wringer
Worthy's servant Christopher Hurst
Balance's steward Gregory Martyn
Melinda Meg Davies
Silvia Lindsay Duncan
Lucy Elizabeth Richardson
Rose Caroline Holdaway
Poacher's wife Sarah Collier
Director Adrian Noble
Designer Bob Crowley
Lighting John A. Williams

RUSTAVELI THEATRE COMPANY, USSR
20, 21, 25 Aug. 19.30 25 Aug. 14.30
Lyceum Theatre
THE CAUCASIAN CHALK CIRCLE
Brecht (Rus. Translated by Djordjanely)
Narrator J. Lolashvili
Musician L. Sikmashvili
Governor/Prince Kazbeki/Monk/Corporal G. Sagaradze
Natella M. Tbileli
Mikhail N. Chinchaladze
Messenger F. Guledani
1st Doctor/Shalva/Policeman D. Papuashvili
2nd Doctor/Nephew/1st Lawyer R. Chkhaidze
Simon Chachava K. Kavsadze
Grusha Vachnadze T. Dolidze
Nurse L. Burbutashvili
Cook E. Chavchavadze
Servants G. Bakradze, N. Saradjishvili
Grand Duke/Peasant/Husband K. Sakandelidze
Wife L. Chkheidze
Noble ladies T. Tarkhnishvili, T. Dolidze
Peasant woman L. Gambashidze
Brother/Father-in-law Dj. Gaganidze
Aniko/Jujuna M. Gamtsemlidze
Mother-in-law L. Dzigrashvili
Dubina/ Josef/2nd Lawyer V. Gogitidze
Azdak R. Chkhikvadze
Doctor D. Uplisashvili
Invalid O. Zautachvili
Musician/Cripple O. Lomidze
Ostler S. Abramishvili
Director R. Sturua
Designer G. Meskhishvili
Music G. Kancheli

22-24 Aug. 19.30 *Lyceum Theatre*
RICHARD III Shakespeare
(Rus. Translated by Z. Kiknadze)
Edward IV/Archbishop of Canterbury/Fool A. Makharadze
Prince Edward M. Ninidze
Richard, Duke of York M. Tsiklauri
George, Duke of Clarence G. Kharabadze
Richard III R. Chkhikvadze
Henry, Earl of Richmond A. Khidasheli
Duke of Buckingham G. Gegechkori
Earl Rivers V. Ninidze
Marquess of Dorset D. Chkhikvadze
Lord Grey S. Lagidze
Lord Hastings K. Kavsadze
Lord Stanley B. Kobakhidze
Sir William Catesby K. Sakandelidze
Sir Robert Brackenbury R. Mikaberidze
Sir James Tyrell Dzh. Gaganidze
Murderer E. Sakhlukhutsishvili
Queen Elizabeth S. Kanchelli
Queen Margaret M. Chakhava
Duchess of York M. Tbileli
Lady Anne N. Pachuashvili
Director R. Sturua
Designer M. Shvelidze
Music G. Kancheli

CITIZENS' THEATRE, Glasgow
28, 30, 31 Aug. 19.30 30 Aug. 14.30
Lyceum Theatre
CHINCHILLA MacDonald
Socrate David Beckford
Tancredi Rupert Farley
Clorindo Robert Burbage
Konstantin John Breck
Maxim Nofel Nawras
Chinchilla Gerard Murphy
Mimi Jill Spurrier
Liovka Jonathan Hyde
Ilya Giles Havergal
Gabriel Robert David MacDonald
Fedya Paul Bentall
Vatza David Hayman
Tamara Sian Thomas
Nina Johanna Kirby
Director and designer Philip Prowse
Lighting Gerry Jenkinson

29 Aug. 1 Sep. 19.30 1 Sep. 14.30
Lyceum Theatre
THE GOOD-HUMOURED LADIES
Goldoni (Eng. Adapted by Robert David MacDonald)
Silvestra Jonathan Hyde
Mariuccia Johanna Kirby
Costanza Celia Foxe
Felicita Sian Thomas
Dorotea Jill Spurrier
Pasquina Celia Imrie
Count Rinaldo David Hayman
Nicolo Nofel Nawras
Cavaliere Odoardo Gerard Murphy
Leonardo Paul Bentall
Battistino John Breck
Luca David Beckford
Tancredi Rupert Farley
Clorindo Robert Burbage
Director Robert David MacDonald
Designer (after Bakst) Sue Blane

GROUPE TSE, Paris
3-8 Sep. 19.30 *Lyceum Theatre*
PEINES DE COEUR D'UN CHATTE ANGLAISE Serreau (From a story by Balzac)
Christy/Tomcat/Doctor/Altolaguirre Jacques Jolivet
Pussycat/Amandine/Cactus Amélie Berg
Old girl/Brisquet/Puss-in-boots Facundo Bo
Minister/Tomcat/Beggar Larry Hager
Mother of Beauty/Ernestine/Rose Raquel Iruzubieta
Beauty Marilù Marini
Mother of Amandine/Puff Horacio Pedrazzini
Peer/Thistle Zobeida Juau

Puck/Tomcat Alain Salomon
Arabelle/Butterfly Jérôme Nicolin
Rabbit guitarist Raymond Couste
Dog viola player Jean-Jacques Guéroult
Director Alfredo Rodrigues Arias
Scenery Emilio Carcano
Costumes Claudie Gastine
Masks Rostislav Doboujinsky
Lighting Jacques Duhamel

TRAVERSE THEATRE COMPANY
20-25, 28-30 Aug. 19.30 27, 31 Aug. 1 Sep. 15.00 *Moray House*
ANIMAL McGrath (World première)
Bampot Richard Albrecht
Beard Martin Black
Barbie Elaine Collins
Boo Paul Dalton
Bebop Peter Dawson
Lynn Jill Fenner
Chancer Stuart Hopps
Nunko David Blake Kelly
Spike Peter Kelly
Chick Frances Low
Lorne Karen Mann
Giant Robert Oates
Ma Ann Scott-Jones
Nerves Josephine Welcome
Blue Benny Young
Dieter Christian Burgess
Director Chris Parr
Designer Grant Hicks
Lighting Gerry Jenkinson

27, 31 Aug. 1 Sep. 19.30 20-25, 28-30 Aug. 15.00 *Moray House*
THE RED RUNNER Connolly (World première)
Isa Sara Ballintyne
Psychiatrist/Prison warden Peter Lincoln
Saffron Doreen Cameron
George Alexander Morton
Peter Jim Kennedy
Alfie Tony Roper
Director Campbell Morrison
Designer Grant Hicks
Lighting Gerry Jenkinson

POETRY AND PROSE RECITALS

22 Aug. 15.00 *St Cecilia's Hall*
POET'S CHOICE
Norman MacCaig, Iain Crichton-Smith (rdr)

23 Aug. 15.00 *St Cecilia's Hall*
POET'S CHOICE
Norman MacCaig, Sorley MacLean (rdr)

24 Aug. 15.00 *St Cecilia's Hall*
A STRONG DOSE OF MYSELF
Dannie Abse (rdr)

25 Aug. 11.00 *St Cecilia's Hall*
BEDSIDE MANNERS
Dannie Abse, Nigel Stock (rdr)

26, 27 Aug. 20.00 *St Cecilia's Hall*
AN ALPHABET: A personal anthology
Judi Dench, Michael Williams (rdr)

28, 29 Aug. 15.00 *St Cecilia's Hall*
MacDIARMID: A celebration
Dolina MacLennan, Sandy Neilson (rdr)
Written by Owen Dudley Edwards

31 Aug. 3 Sep. 15.00 *St Cecilia's Hall*
WORDS BY ELGAR, MUSIC BY SHAW
Hubert Gregg (rdr)

2 Sep. 15.00 and 20.00 *St Cecilia's Hall*
VOICES FROM ARMAGEDDON
John Westbrook, Richard Denning (rdr)
Devised by John Carroll

6, 8 Sep. 15.00 *Lyceum Theatre*
BRONTËS: THE PRIVATE FACES
Joan Bakewell, Judith Paris, Tony Church (rdr)
Designed and directed by Jack Emery

LATE NIGHT ENTERTAINMENT

22-24 Aug. 22.45 *Lyceum Theatre*
JAMES GALWAY AND FRIENDS
Robert White (ten), Moray Welsh (vc), Phillip Moll (pf)

4, 5, 7 Sep. 22.45 *Lyceum Theatre*
MARIAN MONTGOMERY
RICHARD RODNEY BENNETT
Portrait of ladies

6 Sep. 22.45 *Lyceum Theatre*
BENJAMIN LUXON, BILL CROFUT
In concert: an evening of American and English folk music

DANCE

SADLER'S WELLS ROYAL BALLET
20, 21 Aug. 19.30 *The Tent*
LES SYLPHIDES
Choreographer Mikhail Fokine
Music Chopin; arr. Douglas
Designer Alexander Benois
THE PRODIGAL SON
Choreographer George Balanchine
Music Prokofiev
Designer Rouault
PUNCH AND THE STREET PARTY (World première)
Choreographer David Bintley
Music Lane, Lord Berners
Designer Mike Becket
Lighting John Hall

22, 23 Aug. 19.30 *The Tent*
LES RENDEZVOUS
Choreographer Sir Frederick Ashton
Music Auber; arr. Lambert
Designer William Chappell
THE TWO PIGEONS
Choreographer Sir Frederick Ashton
Music Messager
Designer Jacques Dupont

24, 25 Aug. 19.30 *The Tent*
CONCERTO
Choreographer Kenneth MacMillan
Music Shostakovich
Designer Jürgen Rose
PLAYGROUND (World première)
Choreographer Kenneth MacMillan
Music Crosse
Designer Yolande Sonnabend
ELITE SYNCOPATIONS
Choreographer Kenneth MacMillan
Music Scott Joplin *and others*
Costumes Ian Spurling
Dancers David Ashmole, Margaret Barbieri, Alain Dubreuil, June Highwood, Desmond Kelly, Vyvyan Lorrayne, Carl Myers, Lois Strike, Marion Tait, Christine Aitken, Brian Bertscher, Anya Evans, Sherilyn Kennedy, Murray Kilgour, Petal Miller, David Morse, Derek Purnell, Kim Reeder, Judith Rowann
Conductors Barry Wordsworth, Colin Metters

NATIONAL BALLET OF CUBA
27 Aug. 1 Sep. 19.30 1 Sep. 14.30
The Tent
GISELLE
Choreographers Coralli, Alicia Alonso
Music Adam
Designer Salvador Fernández

28 Aug. 19.30 *The Tent*
APOLLO
Choreographer George Balanchine
Music Stravinsky
TARDE EN LA SIESTA
Choreographer Alberto Méndez
Music Ernesto Lecuona
Designer Salvador Fernández
BLOOD WEDDING
Choreographer and lighting Antonio Gades
Music Castaño de Diego
Designer Francisco Nieva
CANTO VITAL
Choreographer André Plissetsky
Music Mahler
Designer Salvador Fernández
RARA AVIS
Choreographer Alberto Méndez
Music Handel, Marcello

29, 31 Aug. 19.30 *The Tent*
GRAND PAS DE QUATRE
Choreographer Alicia Alonso *after* Perrot
Music Pugni
Designer Salvador Fernández
MUÑECOS
Choreographer Alberto Méndez
Music Egües
Designer Salvador Fernández
PAS DE TROIS
Choreographer Alberto Méndez
Music Mauri
Designer Salvador Fernández
OEDIPUS REX
Choreographer *after* Jorge Lefèbre
Music Leo Brouwer
Designer J. Ch. Aimée, Salvador Fernández

30 Aug. 19.30 *The Tent*
APOLLO
BLOOD WEDDING
TARDE EN LA SIESTA
RARA AVIS
SWAN LAKE: Act 2: Pas de deux
Choreographer Lev Ivanov
Music Tchaikovsky
Dancers Alicia Alonso, Loipa Araújo, Aurora Bosch, Marta García, María Elena Llorente, Josefina Méndez, Mirta Plá, Lázaro Carreño, Jorge Esquivel, Orlando Salgado, Cristina Álvarez, Mirta García, Pablo Moré, Andrés Williams, José Zamorano, Amparo Brito, Clara Carranco, Ofelia González, Caridad Martínez, Rosario Suárez, Raúl Bustabad, Hugo Guffanti, Fernando Jhones
Sadler's Wells Royal Ballet Orchestra
Conductors José Ramon Urbay, Rembert Egües

MERCE CUNNINGHAM DANCE COMPANY, USA
4, 5, 7, 8 Sep. 19.30 8 Sep. 13.30
Moray House
Events: Informal performances of complete dances, and excerpts of dances from the repertory

5, 7 Sep. 14.00 *Moray House*
Open rehearsal

6 Sep. 10.00 *Moray House*
Workshop day
Dancers Karole Armitage, Louise Burns, Ellen Cornfield, Merce Cunningham, Meg Eginton, Susan Emery, Lisa Fox, Lise Friedman, Alan Good, Catherine Kerr, Chris Komar, Robert Kovich, Joseph Lennon, Robert Remley, Jim Self, Takehisa Kosugi

ARTISTS-IN-RESIDENCE

Week 1 **JAMES GALWAY**
Week 2 **NETHERLANDS WIND ENSEMBLE**
Week 3 **RICHARD RODNEY BENNETT**

LECTURES

15.00 *St Cecilia's Hall*
20 Aug. The legacy of Diaghilev — Richard Buckle
21 Aug. Portrait of Diaghilev — Moira Shearer
27 Aug. Memories of Diaghilev — Anton Dolin
30 Aug. Diaghilev and music — Noël Goodwin
4 Sep. Translating Pushkin's Onegin — Charles Hepburn Johnston
7 Sep. One world for the arts — John Drummond

EXHIBITIONS

National Gallery of Scotland
DEGAS 1879
Organized by the Festival Society and the National Galleries of Scotland in collaboration with the Glasgow Museums and Art Galleries

Edinburgh College of Art
PARADE: Dance costumes of three centuries
Designer John L. Paterson
In association with the Theatre Museum (Victoria and Albert Museum), London

Scottish Arts Council Gallery
KANDINSKY: The Munich years 1900-14
Organized by the Festival Society and the Scottish Arts Council in association with the Lenbachhaus, Munich

ASSOCIATED EXHIBITIONS
(Not organized by the Festival Society)

Scottish National Gallery of Modern Art
WILHELM LEHMBRUCK

Royal Scottish Museum
ART NOUVEAU IN FINLAND

Fruit Market Gallery
STANISLAW IGNACY WITKIEWICZ 1885-1939

HENRYK STAZEWSKI Recent paintings

STREET EVENTS

21-27 Aug. **LE CONTRADE DI CORI**
28, 30 Aug. **NETHERLANDS WIND ENSEMBLE**

1980

OPERA

COLOGNE OPERA
17, 19, 21 Aug. 19.30 *King's Theatre*
COSÌ FAN TUTTE Mozart
Fiordiligi — Julia Varady
Dorabella — Ann Murray
Ferrando — Rüdiger Wohlers
Guglielmo — Claudio Nicolai
Despina — Georgine Resick
Don Alfonso — Carlos Feller
Gürzenich Orchestra of Cologne
Conductor — John Pritchard
Director and designer — Jean-Pierre Ponnelle

23, 25 Aug. 19.30 *King's Theatre*
IL MATRIMONIO SEGRETO Cimarosa
Geronimo — Erik Saedén
Elisetta — Barbara Daniels
Carolina — Krisztina Laki
Fidalma — Marta Szirmay
Count Robinson — Peter Christoph Runge
Paolino — David Kuebler
Servant — Werner Sindemann
Scottish Chamber Orchestra
Conductor — John Pritchard
Director — Michael Hampe
Scenery — Jan Schlubach
Costumes — Martin Rupprecht

SCOTTISH OPERA
27, 29 Aug. 19.30 *King's Theatre*
THE CUNNING LITTLE VIXEN Janáček (Eng)
Vixen — Helen Field
Fox — Arthur Davies
Forester — Phillip Joll
Parson — Curt Appelgren
School master — Nigel Douglas
Poacher — Malcolm Donnelly
Forester's wife — Moyra Patterson
Inn keeper — Nigel Hamilton Shaw
Inn keeper's wife — Jane Guy
Dog — Halcro Johnston
Badger — Keith Brookes
Rooster — John Robertson
Owl — Linda Ormiston
Hen — Elaine MacKillop
Mosquito — John Brackenridge
Woodpecker — Peter Bodenham
Jay — Una Buchanan
Dragonfly — Graham Andrew Hamilton
Spirit of the Vixen/Dragonfly — Elaine Bryce
Frantic — Lyndall Trottman
Pepik — Rosanne Brackenridge
Young vixen — Denise Ashwood
Frog — Andrew Watt
Cricket — Douglas Cowie
Conductor — Richard Armstrong
Director — David Pountney
Designer — Maria Bjørnson
Lighting — Nick Chelton

28, 30 Aug. 19.30 *King's Theatre*
WOZZECK Berg
Wozzeck — Benjamin Luxon
Marie — Elise Ross
Drum major — Arley Reece
Andres — Gordon Christie
Captain — Francis Egerton
Doctor — Roderick Kennedy
Margret — Linda Ormiston
Idiot — Alexander Oliver
Marie's child — David Simandi
Soldiers — Norman White, Donald Maxwell
Scottish National Orchestra
Conductor — Sir Alexander Gibson
Director — David Alden
Designer — David Fielding
Lighting — Charles Bristow

FIRES OF LONDON
2, 3, 5, 6 Sep. 20.00 *Moray House*
THE LIGHTHOUSE P.M. Davies (World première)
Sandy/Officer 1 — Neil Mackie
Blazes/Officer 2 — Michael Rippon
Arthur/Officer 3 — David Wilson-Johnson
Voice of the cards — Fires of London
Conductor — Richard Dufallo
Director — David William
Designer — Finlay James
Lighting — Mick Hughes

ORCHESTRAL CONCERTS

PHILHARMONIA ORCHESTRA
17 Aug. 20.00 *Usher Hall*
Beethoven — Fantasia for piano, chorus and orchestra in C minor, op.80
Beethoven — Concerto for piano no.3 in C minor, op.37
Schubert — Symphony no.9 in C (Great), D944
Conductor — Riccardo Muti
Soloist — Peter Frankl (pf)
EF Chorus

18 Aug. 20.00 *Usher Hall*
Mozart — Symphony no.41 in C (Jupiter), K551
Brahms — Concerto for piano no.2 in B flat, op.83
Conductor — Riccardo Muti
Soloist — Emil Gilels (pf)

21 Aug. 20.00 *Usher Hall*
Mendelssohn — Meeresstille und glückliche Fahrt - Overture
R. Strauss — Vier letzte Lieder
Elgar — Symphony no.1 in A flat, op.55
Conductor — Andrew Davis
Soloist — Kiri Te Kanawa (sop)

22 Aug. 20.00 *Usher Hall*
Tippett — The midsummer marriage: Ritual dances
Delius — Sea drift
Dvořák — Symphony no.8 in G, op.88
Conductor — Andrew Davis
Soloist — Thomas Allen (bar)
Toronto Mendelssohn Choir

SCOTTISH NATIONAL ORCHESTRA
19 Aug. 20.00 *Usher Hall*
Mozart — Mauerische Trauermusik
Mozart — Symphony no.25 in G minor, K183
Tippett — A child of our time
Conductor — Sir Alexander Gibson
Soloists Jessye Norman (sop), Alfreda Hodgson (cont), Robert Tear (ten), Norman Bailey (bar), EF Chorus

EUROPEAN COMMUNITY YOUTH ORCHESTRA
23 Aug. 20.00 *Usher Hall*
Mozart — Die Zauberflöte: Overture+
Bach — Concerto for 2 violins in D minor
Bartók — The miraculous mandarin - Suite
Brahms — Symphony no.2 in D, op.73
Conductors — Claudio Abbado, Edward Heath+
Soloists Salvatore Accardo, Shlomo Mintz (vn)

NEW YORK PHILHARMONIC ORCHESTRA
Conductor Zubin Mehta
24 Aug. 20.00 *Usher Hall*

Penderecki Symphony no.2 (Christmas)
Beethoven Symphony no.3 In E flat (Eroica), op.55

25 Aug. 20.00 *Usher Hall*
Webern Six pieces, op.6
Mahler Rückert Lieder
Mahler Symphony no.1 in D
Soloist Jessye Norman (sop)

SCOTTISH CHAMBER ORCHESTRA
26 Aug. 20.00 *Usher Hall*
Cimarosa I traci amanti: Overture
Mozart Ah, lo previdi
Mozart Symphony no.34 in C, K338
Mendelssohn Infelice
R. Strauss Le bourgeois gentilhomme - Suite
Conductor Raymond Leppard
Soloist Margaret Marshall (sop)

LONDON PHILHARMONIC ORCHESTRA
27 Aug. 20.00 *Usher Hall*
Haydn Die Schöpfung
Conductor Jesus Lopez-Cobos
Soloists Helen Donath (sop), David Rendall (ten), Gwynne Howell (bs), EF Chorus

29 Aug. 20.00 *Usher Hall*
Mahler Symphony no.7 in E minor
Conductor Klaus Tennstedt

LEIPZIG GEWANDHAUS ORCHESTRA
Conductor Kurt Masur
30 Aug. 20.00 *Usher Hall*
Mozart Symphony no.35 in D (Haffner), K385
Beethoven Concerto for piano no.4 in G, op.58
Tchaikovsky Symphony no.5 in E minor, op.64
Soloist Claudio Arrau (pf)

31 Aug. 20.00 *Usher Hall*
Mendelssohn Ruy Blas - Overture
Prokofiev Sinfonia concertante for cello in E minor, op.125
Brahms Symphony no.4 in E minor, op.98
Soloist Natalia Gutman (vc)

LONDON SYMPHONY ORCHESTRA
2 Sep. 20.00 *Usher Hall*
Barber Adagio for strings, op.11
Copland Concerto for clarinet
Orff Carmina burana
Conductor John Pritchard
Soloists Sheila Armstrong (sop), John van Kesteren (ten), Håkan Hagegård (bar), Richard Stoltzman (cl), EF Chorus, SNO Junior Chorus

3 Sep. 20.00 *Usher Hall*
Berlioz Les francs-juges - Overture
Mendelssohn Concerto for violin in E minor, op.64
Walton Symphony no.1 in B flat minor
Conductor John Pritchard
Soloist Mayumi Fujikawa (vn)

5 Sep. 20.00 *Usher Hall*
Mozart Concerto for piano no.27 in B flat, K595
Mahler Symphony no.5 in C sharp minor
Conductor Claudio Abbado
Soloist Alfred Brendel (pf)

6 Sep. 20.00 *Usher Hall*
Debussy Nocturnes
Ravel La valse
Berlioz Te deum
Conductor Claudio Abbado
Soloists Philip Langridge (ten), Gillian Weir (org), EF Chorus, SNO Junior Chorus

CHAMBER CONCERTS

KALICHSTEIN-LAREDO-ROBINSON TRIO
20 Aug. 11.00 *Queen's Hall*
Haydn Trio for piano and strings no.25 in G
Mendelssohn Trio for piano and strings no.1 in D minor, op.49
Schubert Trio for piano and strings in E flat, D929

CANADIAN BRASS
22 Aug. 11.00 *Queen's Hall*
Works by Scheidt, Handel, Purcell, Gabrieli, Bach, Debussy, J. Beckwith

EDINBURGH QUARTET
23 Aug. 11.00 *Freemasons' Hall*
Mendelssohn Capriccio in E minor
Gal Quartet no.2 in A minor, op.35
Shostakovich Quintet for piano and strings in G minor, op.57
with Roger Woodward (pf)

ALBAN BERG QUARTET
26 Aug. 11.00 *Queen's Hall*
Mendelssohn Quartet, op.81: Andante
Wimberger Quartet
Beethoven Quartet no.15 in A minor, op.132

28 Aug. 11.00 *Queen's Hall*
Mozart Quartet no.23 in F, K590
Bartók Quartet no.3
Debussy Quartet in G minor, op.10

SCOTTISH BAROQUE ENSEMBLE
25 Aug. 20.00 *Hopetoun House*
Williamson Birthday ode to Queen Elizabeth, the Queen Mother (1st public performance)
Works by Henry VIII, Quantz, Frederick II of Prussia, Mendelssohn, Albert, Duke of Edinburgh, Walton, Francis I of France, Henry IV of France, Mary, Queen of Scots, Louis XIII of France, Anne Boleyn, Charles, Duke of Orléans
Conductor Leonard Friedman
Soloists Dennis O'Neill (ten), Eugenia Zukerman (fl)

MUSICA ANTIQUA COLOGNE
1 Sep. 11.00 *Queen's Hall*
Reincken Suite in A minor
Pachelbel Suite in E minor
Schenk Scherzi musicali: Suite no.9
Pachelbel Aria variata in A
Buxtehude Sonata in B flat
Handel Sonata for violin in F, op.1/12
F. Couperin Sonata (La sultane)

FIRES OF LONDON
5 Sep. 11.00 *Moray House*
Kinloch Kinloche his fantassie; arr. P.M. Davies
P.M. Davies The kestrel paced round the sun
Weir King Harald sails to Byzantium
P.M. Davies Stedman doubles
Carter Sonata for cello and piano
McGuire Euphoria - a sense of well-being (World première)
P.M. Davies The two fiddlers: Dances
Conductor Peter Maxwell Davies

AMADEUS QUARTET
6 Sep. 11.00 *Queen's Hall*
Haydn Quartet in C, op.74/1
Mozart Quartet no.15 in D minor, K421
Beethoven Quartet no.8 in E minor (Rasumovsky), op.59/2

TORONTO MENDELSSOHN CHOIR
CANADIAN BRASS
20 Aug. 20.00 *St Mary's Cathedral*
Works by Somers, Paynter, H. Willan, Gabrieli, Pachelbel, R.M. Schafer, Bach, Rachmaninov, Handel, Reeves, Kokkonen
Conductor Elmer Iseler

BBC NORTHERN SINGERS
27 Aug. 11.00 *Queen's Hall*
Gesualdo Gioite voi col canto
Gesualdo Tall'or sano desio
Gesualdo Alme d'amor rubelle
Gesualdo Tu piangi, o filli mia
Williamson Symphony for voices
Schumann Vier Doppelchörige Gesänge, op.141
Maw The ruin (World première)
Brahms Fest und Gedenksprüche
Conductor Stephen Wilkinson
with Jonathan Goodall (hn)

SCHÜTZ CONSORT OF LONDON
LONDON BAROQUE PLAYERS
4 Sep. 20.00 *Queen's Hall*
Monteverdi Il ballo delle ingrate
Monteverdi Il combattimento di Tancredi e Clorinda (Eng)
Monteverdi Sestina
Conductor Roger Norrington
Soloists Rosemary Hardy (sop), Neil Jenkins (ten)

RECITALS

LUCIA POPP (sop)
GEOFFREY PARSONS (pf)
18 Aug. 11.00 *Queen's Hall*
Songs by Prokofiev, Kodály, Dvořák, Mahler, Brahms

JESSYE NORMAN (sop)
PHILLIP MOLL (pf)
22 Aug. 15.00 *Queen's Hall*
Schubert Auf dem Ström, D943
Schubert Ständchen, D921
Schubert Miriams Siegesgesang
Songs by Schubert, Brahms
with Michael Thompson (hn), EF Chorus members

SARAH WALKER (mez)
ROGER VIGNOLES (pf)
29 Aug. 11.00 *Freemasons' Hall*
Schumann Gedichte der Königin Maria Stuart
Debussy Trois chansons de Bilitis
Songs by Wolf, Debussy, Ives

DAME JANET BAKER (mez)
GEOFFREY PARSONS (pf)
1 Sep. 20.00 *Usher Hall*
Songs by Schubert, Fauré

CÉCILE OUSSET (pf)
19 Aug. 11.00 *Freemasons' Hall*
Piano works by Chopin, Liszt, Debussy, Pagodes, Saint-Saëns

EMIL GILELS (pf)
20 Aug. 20.00 *Usher Hall*
Mozart Sonata no.15 in F, K533
Beethoven Variations and fugue on a theme from 'Prometheus'
Scriabin Études, op.8: Nos. 2, 12
Scriabin Five preludes, op.74
Ravel Pavane pour une infante défunte
Ravel Jeux d'eau

Ravel Miroirs: Alborada del gracioso

GUSTAV LEONHARDT (hpd)
21 Aug. 11.00 Queen's Hall
Works by Balbastre, D. Scarlatti, Bach

JORGE BOLET (pf)
25 Aug. 11.00 Freemasons' Hall
Bach Partita for violin no.2 in D minor: Chaconne; arr. Busoni
Brahms Variations and fugue on a theme by Handel
Weber Aufforderung zum Tanze; arr. Godowsky
Liszt Années de pèlerinage 2: Sonetti del Petrarca nos. 104, 123
Liszt Années de pèlerinage 2: Après une lecture du Dante (Sonata)

CLAUDIO ARRAU (pf)
28 Aug. 20.00 Usher Hall
Beethoven Sonata no.7 in D, op.10/3
Beethoven Sonata no.23 in F minor (Appassionata), op.57
Debussy Images: Book 1
Liszt Ballade no.2 in B minor
Liszt Années de pèlerinage 3: Les jeux d'eau à la Villa d'Este
Chopin Scherzo no.1 in B minor, op.20

DMITRI ALEXEEV (pf)
30 Aug. 11.00 Freemasons' Hall
Shostakovich Preludes and fugues, op.87: Nos. 3, 5
Brahms Piano pieces, op.76
Chopin Mazurkas nos. 46-49, op.68
Chopin Sonata no.3 in B minor, op.58

EMANUEL AX (pf)
2 Sep. 11.00 Queen's Hall
Schoenberg Klavierstücke, op.11
Schoenberg Klavierstücke, op.19
Beethoven Sonata no.26 in E flat (Farewell), op.81a
Chopin Scherzi nos.1-4

NATALIA GUTMAN (vc)
ANATOLY VEDERNIKOV (pf)
3 Sep. 11.00 Queen's Hall
Bach Sonata no.2 in D
Beethoven Sonata no.2 in G minor, op.5/2
Shostakovich Sonata in D minor, op.40
Debussy Sonata in D minor

RICHARD STOLTZMAN (cl)
EMANUEL AX (pf)
4 Sep. 11.00 Queen's Hall
Weber Grand duo concertant
Brahms Sonata no.1 in F minor, op.120/1
Stravinsky Three pieces for clarinet
Schubert Sonata in A minor (Arpeggione), D821; arr. for clarinet and piano
Schumann Fantasiestücke, op.73

JOS VAN DER KOOY (org)
19 Aug. 17.00 Reid Concert Hall
Organ works by Sweelinck, J.S. Bach, C.P.E. Bach, Buxtehude *and* Anon.
Improvisation on a given theme

GILLIAN WEIR (org)
5 Sep. 12.00 St Mary's Cathedral
Bach Prelude and fugue in E flat (St Anne)
Alain Trois danses
Buxtehude Ciacona in E minor
Reger Fantasia and fugue in D minor, op.135b
Eben Sunday music: Moto ostinato

RAVI SHANKAR (sitâr)
ALLA RAKHA (tabla)
31 Aug. 15.00 and 20.00 Queen's Hall
Indian classical music

MASTER CLASSES

ELISABETH SCHWARZKOPF
2-5 Sep. 14.30 Freemasons' Hall
Jane MacKenzie, Christine Taylor (sop), Marilyn de Blieck, Christine Cairns (mez), Richard Lloyd-Morgan (bar), Brian Scott (b.bar) with Roger Vignoles (pf)

DRAMA

NATIONAL THEATRE
THE PASSION
(A selection of the York and Wakefield Mystery plays by the company and Tony Harrison) *Assembly Hall*
19, 22, 26 Aug. 19.30 18, 21, 24, 28 Aug.15.00
Part 1 - Creation to Nativity (World première)
God Brian Glover
Lucifer Jack Shepherd
Gabriel Don Warrington
Adam Dai Bradley
Eve Valerie Whittington
Cain John Salthouse
Abel/Herod's son Philip Donaghy
Noah J.G. Devlin
Mrs Noah/Mak's wife Edna Doré
Joseph Dave Hill
Mary Brenda Blethyn
Shepherds Kenny Ireland, John Salthouse, John Tams
Mak Barrie Rutter
Wise men Jeffrey Chiswick, Tony Haygarth, Olu Jacobs
Herod Bryan Pringle
18, 20, 21, 23, 24, 27-30 Aug. 19.30
Part 2 - Nativity to Judgement
Jesus Philip Donaghy
John the Baptist Dave Hill
Angel Dai Bradley
Peter Don Warrington
Philip John Tams
Blind man J.G. Devlin
Cayphas Bryan Pringle
Annas Dave Hill
Pontius Pilate Tony Haygarth
Mary Mother Edna Doré
Mary Magdalene Brenda Blethyn
Mary Salome Valerie Whittington
Barrabas Jeffrey Chiswick
Simon of Cyrene Olu Jacobs
Judas Jack Shepherd
Soldiers Brian Glover, Kenny Ireland, Barrie Rutter, John Salthouse
Albion Band
Director Bill Bryden
Designer William Dudley
Lighting William Dudley, Andy Phillips

1-6 Sep. 19.30 3 Sep. 14.30
Lyceum Theatre
WATCH ON THE RHINE Hellman
Anise Pauline Jameson
Joseph Frank Singuineau
Fanny Farrelly Peggy Ashcroft
David Farrelly John Quayle
Marthe de Brancovis Deborah Grant
Teck de Brancovis Sandor Elès
Sara Müller Susan Engel
Bodo Müller Timothy Breeze/James Downer
Joshua Müller Adam Godley
Babette Müller Donna Angell/Tanya Ronder
Kurt Müller David Burke
Director Mike Ockrent
Scenery Eileen Diss
Costumes Jessica Gwynne
Lighting Leonard Tucker

COMPAGNIE DE THÉÂTRE DU CENTRE NATIONAL DES ARTS, Ottawa
25-27 Aug. 19.30 27 Aug. 14.30
Lyceum Theatre
WOYZECK Büchner
(Eng. Adapted by Jean Herbiet)

28-30 Aug. 19.30 30 Aug. 14.30
Lyceum Theatre
LE SONGE Strindberg
(Fr. Adapted by Jean Herbiet)
Voices Claire Faubert, Claude Marquis, Guy Mignault, Gilles Provost
Puppets created by Felix Mirbt
Directors Jean Herbiet, Felix Mirbt
Scenery Michael Eagan
Costumes Michael Eagan, Janet Logan
Lighting Pierre-René Goupil

ROYAL SHAKESPEARE COMPANY
Daniel Stewart's and Melville College
25, 28 Aug. 1, 4 Sep. 19.30 27, 30 Aug. 3, 6 Sep. 14.30
HENRY IV Part 1 Shakespeare
26, 27, 29, 30 Aug. 2, 3, 5, 6 Sep. 19.30
HENRY IV Part 2 Shakespeare
King Henry IV/Warwick Bernard Lloyd
Henry, Prince of Wales David Rintoul
Earl of Westmoreland John Hartley
Sir Walter Blunt/Sherriff Peter Holmes
Earl of Northumberland/Pistol John Burgess
Henry Percy (Hotspur)/Gower Stuart Wilson
Earl of Worcester/Shallow Willoughby Gray
Owen Glendower/Lord Chief Justice/Sir Richard Vernon James Garbutt
Sir John Falstaff Alfred Marks
Bardolph Tim Stern
Poins/Clarence/Hastings Simon Haywood
Lady Percy Juliet Stevenson
Lady Mortimer/Doll Tearsheet Patti Love
Mistress Quickly Barbara Jefford
Douglas/Davy Ken Drury
Peto/Lancaster/Coleville Martin Howells
Mowbray/Mortimer/Lancaster (pt.2)/ Warwick Andrew Jarvis
Archbishop of York/Harcourt Rhys McConnochie
Sir Michael/Francis/Gloucester David Shaw-Parker
Director Bill Alexander
Designer Douglas Heap
Lighting Brian Wigney

VANCOUVER EAST CULTURAL CENTRE
18-23 Aug. 20.00 Moray House
BILLY BISHOP GOES TO WAR Gray
Characters all portrayed by Eric Peterson
Directors John Gray, Eric Peterson
Scenery David Gropman
Lighting Jennifer Tipton

MOVING PICTURE MIME SHOW
20, 21, 23 Aug. 17.30 Moray House
CITY LIMITS
THE EXAMINATION
Paul Filipiak, David Gaines, Toby Sedgwick

CRICOT 2, Florence
26-29 Aug. 20.00 30 Aug. 17.00 and 21.00 Moray House
WIELEPOLE WIELEPOLE Kantor

Uncle Jozef/Priest Stanislaw Rychlicki
Grandmother Katarzyna Jan Ksiazek
Helka Ludmila Ryba
Father Martin/1st Conscript Andrzej Welminski
Aunt Manka Maria Kantor
Aunt Józka Ewa Janicka
Uncle Karol Waclaw Janicki
Uncle Olek Leslaw Janicki
Uncle Stasio/Convict Maria Krasicka
Adas/2nd Conscript Lech Stangret
Widow of the photographer Miroslawa Rychlicka
Conscripts Marzia Loriga, Jean-Marie Barotte, Luigi Arpini. Giovan Battista Storti, Loriano della Rocca
Director Tadeusz Kantor

PROSE AND POETRY RECITALS

18, 20 Aug. 15.00 *Queen's Hall*
AN HOUR OF AMERICAN HUMOUR
Alistair Cooke (rdr)

19, 21, 23, 25 Aug. 15.00
St Cecilia's Hall
DUALCHAS - HERITAGE
4 programmes celebrating the Gaelic language in words and music
Iain Crichton-Smith, Sorley MacLean, Derick Thomson, Aonghas MacNeacail, Maire Mhac an-t-Saoi (rdr). Flora MacNeil, Carol Galbraith, Kathleen MacDonald, Mary Sandeman, Donnie MacLeod, Ian Mackay (sngr), Isobel Mieras (hp), Alison Kinnaird (clarsach), Bob Christie (fiddle), Pipe-Major George Stoddart (bp), Catherine Murray's Waulking Team, John MacInnes, Finlay J. MacDonald (lect)
Devised and presented by Dolina MacLennan

20, 22, 24 Aug. 15.00 24 Aug. 20.00
St Cecilia's Hall
D.H. LAWRENCE - THE TARNISHED PHOENIX
Ian McKellen, Sheila Allen (rdr)
Compiled by Roger Pringle
Directed by John Tydeman

LATE NIGHT ENTERTAINMENT

19, 22 Aug. 22.45 *Music Hall*
CANADIAN BRASS
Musical fun and games

23 Aug. 22.00 *Usher Hall*
OSCAR PETERSON IN CONCERT

27, 30 Aug. 22.45 *Music Hall*
ALBION BAND

28, 29 Aug. 22.45 *Music Hall*
BARDE

2, 4 Sep. 22.45 *Lyceum Theatre*
RICHARD STOLTZMAN (cl)
BILL DOUGLAS
Versatility, improvisation and jazz

DANCE

AUSTRALIAN DANCE THEATRE
18 Aug. 19.30 *Lyceum Theatre*
LABYRINTH
Choreographer Christopher Bruce
Music Subotnik
IMPROMPTU
Choreographer Julia Blaikie
Music Schubert
FLIBBERTIGIBBET+
Choreographer Jonathan Taylor
Music Bach
TRANSFIGURED NIGHT
Choreographer Jonathan Taylor
Music Schoenberg

19 Aug. 19.30 *Lyceum Theatre*
SEVEN SONGS
Choreographer Norman Morrice
Music Canteloube
INCIDENT AT BULL CREEK
Choreographer Jonathan Taylor
Music Carl Vine
FLIBBERTIGIBBET+
LABYRINTH

20-23 Aug. 19.30 23 Aug. 14.30
Lyceum Theatre
WILDSTARS#
Choreographer Jonathan Taylor
Design and soundtrack Nigel Triffitt
Costumes Elizabeth Raupach, Ann Sinclair, Lawrence Blake
Lighting William Akers, Martin Smith#, Kenneth Rayner+
Dancers Alain Israel, Julia Blaikie, Joseph Scoglio, Margaret Wilson, Pamela Buckman, Linda Gay, Shelley Linden, Vanessa McIntosh, Madonna Petersen, Claire Stonier, Roslyn Watson, Robert Canning, Glen Murray, John Nobbs, John Salisbury, Don Secomb, Ronald Van den Bergh
Conductor Bramwell Tovey

SCOTTISH BALLET
2-4 19.30 4 Sep. 14.30 *King's Theatre*
VESPRI
Choreographer André Prokovsky
Music Verdi
Designer Norman McDowell
Lighting Peter Searle
CHÉRI (World première)
Choreographer Peter Darrell
Music David Earl
Designer Philip Prowse
Lighting Ian Irving
NAPOLI: Act 3
Choreographer August Bournonville
Music Gade, Helsted, Paulli, Lumbye
Designer Peter Cazalet
Lighting John B. Read

5, 6 Sep. 19.30 6 Sep. 14.30
King's Theatre
TALES OF HOFFMANN
Choreographer Peter Darrell
Music Offenbach; arr. Lanchbery
Designer Alistair Livingstone
Lighting John B. Read
Dancers Patrick Bissell, Galina Samsova (guest artists), Christopher Blagdon, William Bowen, Veronica Butcher, Roy Campbell-Moore, Sally Collard-Gentle, Linden Currey, Fiona Dear, Gwendoline Edmonds, Catherine Evers, Timothy Flynn, Christopher Gillard, Robert Hampton, Vincent Hantam, Louise Hellewell, Pauline Laverty, Kit Lethby, Christopher Long, Anna McCartney, Elaine McDonald, Seonaid Macleod, Patricia Merrin, Judy Mohekey, Eleanor Moore, Leslie Morrison, Jeanette Newell, Noriko Ohara, Alison O'Neal, Linda Packer, Wendy Roe, Peter Royston, Robert Ryan, Elspeth Shaw, Ann Sholem, June Skinner, Nigel Spencer, Tara Stewart, Garry Trinder, Paul Tyers, Jonathan Williams, Patrick Wood
Conductor Bramwell Tovey

RITHA DEVI
27 Aug. 20.00 *Queen's Hall*
MAHARI NRITYA (Temple-Odissi)
KUCHIPUDI
PRAK-PRATEECHI (East-West)
Choreographer Ritha Devi
Singers Garth Taylor, Ann Estill
Narrator Ritha Devi

WRITERS' CONFERENCE

WHOSE LANGUAGE IS IT ANYWAY...?
26-30 Aug. 10.30 *Assembly Rooms*
26 Aug Use and abuse of the English language
Dr. Robert Burchfield, Prof. Randolph Quirk, Frank Muir, John Mortimer, Sir Victor Pritchett, Dr Anne Smith, John Wells, John Whale, Ion Trewin, Betty Fitzpatrick

27 Aug. The inhuman condition
Penelope Lively, Beryl Bainbridge, Melvyn Bragg, Gore Vidal, Joan Bakewell, Elizabeth Smart, George Barker, Anthony Burgess, Frank Delaney

28 Aug. But is it English...?
Scott Berg, George Steiner, Christopher Logue, Roland McHugh, Anthony Burgess, Richard Ellmann, Dougald McMillan

29 Aug. Language and dialogue
John McGrath, John Byrne, Bill Bryden, Peter Shaffer, Michael Frayn, Sir Peter Hall, Edward Thomas, Donald Campbell

30 Aug. A poet's morning
Edwin Morgan, Sorley MacLean, Iain Crichton-Smith, Ron Butlin, Valerie Gillies, Seamus Heaney, Barbara Jefford, Kingsley Amis, Jonathan Miller, John Drummond

EXHIBITIONS

City Art Centre
THE LEGACY
(From the British Columbia Provincial Museum)

Royal Scottish Academy
DOVECOT TAPESTRY

Demarco Gallery
JOSEPH BEUYS
(Public debates *1-6 Sep. 10.00, 14.00. 17.00*)

ASSOCIATED EXHIBITIONS
(Not organized by the Festival Society)

City Art Centre
PRESCOTE IN EDINBURGH

Royal Scottish Museum
LION RUGS OF FARS

Talbot Rice Art Centre
JACK BUSH

Fruit Market Gallery
NEW NEW MEXICO
(A Scottish Arts Council exhibition in association with the Linda Durham Gallery, Santa Fe, New Mexico

1981

OPERA

COLOGNE OPERA
17, 19, 21, 23 Aug. 19.30 *King's Theatre*
IL BARBIERE DI SIVIGLIA Rossini
Figaro Leo Nucci
Rosina Alicia Nafé
Count Almaviva Luigi Alva
Dr Bartolo Carlos Feller
Don Basilio Justino Diaz
Berta Edith Kertész-Gabry
Fiorello Klaus Bruch
Ambrogio Peter Nikolaus Kante
Officer Eberhard Katz
Scottish Opera Chorus
Scottish Chamber Orchestra
Conductor John Pritchard
Director Michael Hampe
Designers
Ezio Frigerio, Mauro Pagano

27, 29 Aug. 19.30 *King's Theatre*
LA CLEMENZA DI TITO Mozart
Tito Werner Hollweg
Vitellia Kathryn Montgomery
Sesto Brigitte Fassbaender
Servilia Georgine Resick
Annio Daphne Evangelatos
Publio Thomas Thomaschke
Gürzenich Orchestra
Conductor John Pritchard
Director and designer
Jean-Pierre Ponnelle

COLOGNE OPERA STUDIO
24, 26 Aug. 19.30 *Lyceum Theatre*
THE VOICE OF ARIADNE Musgrave
Count Marco Valerio Norman Phillips
Countess Stella Kleindienst
Mr Lamb Neal Schwantes
Marchesa Bianca Bianchi
Marijke Hendriks
Mrs Tracy Marita Knobel
Baldovino Gary Bennett
Gualtiero Eberz Peter Nikolaus Kante
Giovanni Alfons Eberz
Voice of Ariadne Joan Davies
Scottish Chamber Orchestra
Conductor Hilary Griffiths
Director Willy Decker
Scenery Ulrich Erich Milatz
Designer Uschi Köhl

SCOTTISH OPERA
1, 3, 5 Sep. 19.30 *King's Theatre*
THE BEGGAR'S OPERA Gay
(Edited by Guy Woolfenden)
Captain Macheath Thomas Allen
Polly Kate Flowers
Lucy Patricia Hay
Mr Peachum William McCue
Mrs Peachum Linda Ormiston
Lockit Norman White
Jenny Diver Kathleen McCarney
Filch John Brackenridge
Mrs Trapes Una McLean
Beggar John Warner
Matt of the Mint Alan Oke
Nimming Ned Ian McKinven
Ben Budge Grant Richards
Jemmy Twitcher James Paterson
Crook-fingered Jack Thom Irvine
Wat Dreary Philip Cox
Harry Paddington Anthony Davis
Robin of Bagshot David Aldred
Slippery Sam Nigel Hamilton Shaw
Lightning Luke Malcolm Aitken
Johnny Grab/Jailer Paul Strathearn
Tom Tipple/Chaplain Robert Alderson
Mrs Coaxer Alison Doig
Dolly Trull Marjorie Williamson
Mrs Vixen Ann Dempsey
Betty Doxy Ellen Jackson
Mrs Slammekin Una Buchanan
Suky Tawdry Jane Guy
Molly Brazen/Eazie Lee Julia Birch
Madge Fadge Janet Henderson
Amazing Grace Lesley Boyd
Trixie Trade Elaine MacKillop
Greasy Joan Jane Oakland
Drawer Declan McCusker
Executioner Robert Crowe
The Management Geoffrey Edwards
Conductor Guy Woolfenden
Director David William
Scenery Michael Annals
Costumes Alex Reid
Lighting Spike Gaden

ORCHESTRAL CONCERTS

LONDON SYMPHONY ORCHESTRA
Conductor Claudio Abbado
16 Aug. 17.45 18 Aug. 18.00 *Usher Hall*
Bach Passion according to St Matthew
Soloists Margaret Price, Jessye Norman (sop), Peter Schreier, Philip Langridge (ten), Hermann Prey (bar), Gwynne Howell (bs), EF Chorus, SNO Junior Chorus

19 Aug. 20.00 *Usher Hall*
Wagner Lohengrin: Preludes to Acts I *and* 3
Bartók Concerto for violin no.2
Mussorgsky Pictures at an exhibition; orch. Ravel
Soloist Salvatore Accardo (vn)

BBC SYMPHONY ORCHESTRA
20 Aug. 20.00 *Usher Hall*
Conductor Gennadi Rozhdestvensky
Schreker Prelude to a drama
Haydn Sinfonia concertante in B flat, op.84
Tavener Akhmatova requiem (World première)
Soloists Phyllis Bryn-Julson (sop), John Shirley-Quirk (bar), Rodney Friend (vn), Ross Pople (vc), John Anderson (ob), Geoffrey Gambold (bn)

21 Aug. 20.00 *Usher Hall*
Dvořák Symphony no.5 in F, op.76
Elgar Concerto for cello in E minor, op.85
Ives Three places in New England
Soloist Yo-Yo Ma (vc)

NATIONAL YOUTH ORCHESTRA OF GREAT BRITAIN
22 Aug. 20.00 *Usher Hall*
Dvořák Carnival - Overture
Tchaikovsky Concerto for violin in D, op.35
Stravinsky Petrushka
Conductor Charles Dutoit
Soloist Kyung-Wha Chung (vn)

LONDON SINFONIETTA
22 Aug. 11.00 *Queen's Hall*
Henze L'autunno
Henze Quartet no.4
Henze Kammermusik (1958)
Conductor Hans Werner Henze
Soloists Philip Langridge (ten), Timothy Walker (gtr)

24 Aug. 11.00 *Queen's Hall*
Stravinsky Octet
Stravinsky Ragtime
Weill Das Berliner Requiem
Weill Kleine Dreigroschenmusik
Conductor Riccardo Chailly
Soloists Neil Mackie (ten), David Wilson-Johnson (bar), Michael Rippon (bs)

POLISH CHAMBER ORCHESTRA
Conductor Jerzy Maksymiuk
23 Aug. 20.00 *Usher Hall*
Vivaldi Concerti, op.8: Nos. 1-4 (The four seasons)
Mozart Concerto for oboe in C, K314
Britten Variations on a theme of Frank Bridge
Soloists Krzysztof Jakowicz (vn), Maurice Bourgue (ob)

25 Aug. 11.00 *Queen's Hall*
Mozart Divertimento (Salzburg symphony) no.3 in F, K138
Dragonetti Concerto for double bass in A
Elgar Serenade for strings in E minor, op.20
Vivaldi Concerti, op.3 (L'estro armonico): No.5 in A
Bartók Divertimento for strings
Soloist Gary Karr (db)

LONDON PHILHARMONIC ORCHESTRA
25 Aug. 20.00 *Usher Hall*
Beethoven Die Geschöpfe des Prometheus: Overture
Beethoven Concerto for piano no.1 in C, op.15
Sibelius Night-ride and sunrise
Sibelius Symphony no.7 in C, op.105
Conductor Raymond Leppard
Soloist Murray Perahia (pf)

26 Aug. 20.00 *Usher Hall*
Schumann Concerto for piano in A minor, op.54
Verdi Quartet in E minor; arr. for string orchestra
Verdi Four sacred pieces: Stabat Mater *and* Te deum
Conductor Riccardo Chailly
Soloist Maurizio Pollini (pf)
EF Chorus

28 Aug. 20.00 *Usher Hall*
Glinka Ruslan and Ludmilla: Overture
Bartók Concerto for piano no.3
Brahms Symphony no.1 in C minor, op.68
Conductor Klaus Tennstedt
Soloist Michel Béroff (pf)

SCOTTISH CHAMBER ORCHESTRA
28 Aug. 11.00 *Queen's Hall*
Rameau Dardanus - Suite
F. Couperin L'apothéose de Lulli
Bach Cantata no.202
Haydn Symphony no.98 in B flat
Conductor Raymond Leppard
Soloist Isobel Buchanan (sop)

PHILHARMONIA ORCHESTRA
29 Aug. 20.00 *Usher Hall*
Berlioz Roméo et Juliette
Conductor Riccardo Muti
Soloists Julia Hamari (mez), Lajos Kozma (ten), John Paul Bogart (bs), EF Chorus

30 Aug. 20.00 *Usher Hall*
Schumann Die Braut von Messina - Overture
Schumann Concerto for violin in D minor
Tchaikovsky Symphony no.6 in B minor (Pathétique), op.74
Conductor Riccardo Muti
Soloist Gidon Kremer (vn)

1 Sep. 20.00 *Usher Hall*
Ravel Alborada del gracioso
Stravinsky Le roi des étoiles
Mahler Symphony no.2 in C minor (Resurrection)
Conductor Simon Rattle
Soloists Jill Gomez (sop), Alfreda Hodgson (cont), EF Chorus

CAMERATA LYSY, Gstaad
4 Sep. 20.00 *Usher Hall*
Bartók Rumanian folk dances
Vivaldi Concerto for 2 violins in C minor
Bach Concerto for violin in E
Atterberg Suite no.3 for violin and viola, op.19/1
Puccini Crisantemi
Mozart Divertimento (Salzburg symphony) no.1 in D, K136
Soloists Sir Yehudi Menuhin, Alberto Lysy (vn), Paul Coletti (va)

SCOTTISH NATIONAL ORCHESTRA
5 Sep. 20.00 *Usher Hall*
V. Williams Serenade to music
Brahms Concerto for violin and cello in A minor, op.102
Bartók Concerto for violin no.1
Bruckner Te deum in C
Conductor Sir Alexander Gibson
Soloists Felicity Lott (sop), Penelope Walker (mez), John Mitchinson (ten), Marius Rintzler (bs), Sir Yehudi Menuhin (vn), Felix Schmidt (vc), EF Chorus

CHAMBER CONCERTS

CAPRICORN
18 Aug. 11.00 *Queen's Hall*
Janáček Concertino for piano and chamber ensemble
Bartók Contrasts for violin, clarinet and piano
Bainbridge Landscapes and magic words (World première)
Beethoven Septet, op.20
Conductor Simon Bainbridge
Soloist Lynda Richardson (sop)

CONSORT OF MUSICKE
SCATTER'D MUSICK'S ORNAMENT
Music of the Stuart Court 1600-1650
24 Aug. 17.45 and 22.45 *Canongate Kirk*
Brittania triumphans: James VI and I
Works by Weelkes, Dowland, Greaves

25 Aug. 17.45 and 22.45 *Canongate Kirk*
Heaven's Hostage:
Henry, Prince of Wales
Works by Jones, Ford, Handford, Ferrabosco, Campion, Coprario, Ward

27 Aug. 17.45 and 22.45 *Canongate Kirk*
The King's Arcadia: Charles I
Works by Vautor, Porter, W. Lawes

28 Aug. 17.45 and 22.45 *Canongate Kirk*
The Untuning of the Skies: Civil War
Works by H. Lawes, W. Lawes, Tomkins, Hilton, Coleman
Director Anthony Rooley
Soloists Emma Kirkby (sop), David Thomas (bs)

PETER FRANKL, TAMÁS VÁSÁRY (pf), JAMES HOLLAND, TRISTAN FRY (perc)
26 Aug. 11.00 *Queen's Hall*
Debussy Nocturnes: Nuages *and* Fêtes; arr. for 2 pianos by Ravel
Bartók Sonata for 2 pianos and percussion
Brahms Quintet for piano and strings in F minor, op.34; arr. for 2 pianos

BARTÓK QUARTET
27 Aug. 11.00 *Freemasons' Hall*
Bartók Quartet no.2
Mozart Quartet no.14 in G, K387
Bartók Quartet no.1

29 Aug. 11.00 *Freemasons' Hall*
Bartók Quartet no.3
Mozart Quartet no.16 in E flat, K428
Bartók Quartet no.4

31 Aug. 11.00 *Freemasons' Hall*
Bartók Quartet no.6
Mozart Quartet no.19 in C (Dissonance), K465
Bartók Quartet no.5

BEAUX ARTS TRIO
27 Aug. 20.00 *Usher Hall*
Haydn Trio for piano and strings no.18 in A
Mendelssohn Trio for piano and strings no.1 in D minor, op.49
Beethoven Trio for piano and strings no.7 in B flat (Archduke), op.97

JULIAN BREAM LUTE CONSORT
2 Sep. 20.00 *Queen's Hall*
Works by Allison, Phillips, Coprario, Bacheler, Dowland *and* Anon.
With Robert Tear (ten)

4 Sep. 11.00 *Queen's Hall*
Music of the English Renaissance
Works by Byrd, Danyel, Phillips, Dowland, Gibbons, Morley *and* Anon.
with Robert Tear (ten)

KREUZBERGER QUARTET
5 Sep. 11.00 *Freemasons' Hall*
Haydn Quartet in E flat (Joke), op.33/2
Reimann Unrevealed (Lord Byron to Augusta Leigh)
Mendelssohn Quartet no.3 in D, op.44/1
with Barry McDaniel (bar)

KING'S SINGERS
31 Aug. 20.00 *Usher Hall*
Menotti Moans, groans, cries, sighs, or a composer at work (World première)
The old music master: a tribute to Hoagy Carmichael; arr. Runswick
Madrigals, Victorian songs, Arrangements in close harmony

2 Sep. 11.00 *Queen's Hall*
Forbes Latin motets
Hassler Secular and sacred pieces
Canteloube Songs of the Auvergne; arr. Richards
Madrigals and French chansons

EDINBURGH FESTIVAL CHORUS
3 Sep. 20.00 *Usher Hall*
Oliver Namings (EIF commission)
Tallis Spem in alium
Works by Bartók, Bruckner, Rameau, Poulenc, Verdi
Conductor John Currie
Equale Brass

RECITALS

HERMANN PREY (bar)
GEOFFREY PARSONS (pf)
17 Aug. 11.00 *Queen's Hall*
Schumann Liederkreis, op.24
Schumann Dichterliebe
and other songs to poems by Heine

MARGARET PRICE (sop)
JAMES LOCKHART (pf)
21 Aug. 11.00 *Queen's Hall*
Songs by Schubert, Duparc, Granados, Rodrigo, Obradors
with Roy Jowitt (cl)

BRIGITTE FASSBAENDER (mez)
IRWIN GAGE (pf)
1 Sep. 11.00 *Queen's Hall*
Schoenberg Das Buch der hängenden Gärten
Milhaud Chansons de négresse
Mahler Lieder eines fahrenden Gesellen

ZOLTÁN KOCSIS (pf)
17 Aug. 20.00 *Usher Hall*
Piano works by Liszt, Chopin, Bartók, Wagner, Kocsis

YOURI EGOROV (pf)
19 Aug. 11.00 *Freemasons' Hall*
Haydn Sonata no.33 in C minor
Schumann Carnaval
Prokofiev Sonata no.8 in B flat, op.84

MAURIZIO POLLINI (pf)
24 Aug. 20.00 *Usher Hall*
Chopin Sonata no.3 in B minor, op.58
Bartók Out of doors
Piano works by Chopin, Liszt

VLADIMIR ASHKENAZY (pf)
2 Sep. 20.00 *Usher Hall*
Beethoven Sonata no.31 in A flat, op.110
Beethoven Sonata no.32 in C minor, op.111
Chopin Nocturnes nos. 7 *and* 8, op.27
Chopin Sonata no.2 (Funeral march), op.35

SIR YEHUDI MENUHIN, ALBERTO LYSY (vn), PAUL COKER (pf)
3 Sep. 11.00 *Queen's Hall*
Bartók Duos for 2 violins: Nos. 33, 35, 36, 37, 40, 42
Bartók Sonata for violin
Enescu Sonata for violin and piano no.3 in A minor

GARY KARR (db)
HARMON LEWIS (kbds)
20 Aug. 11.00 *Freemasons' Hall*
Eccles Sonata in A minor
Schubert Sonata in A minor (Arpeggione), D821
Copland Sonata for violin and piano; transcr. for double bass
Hindemith Sonata
Koussevitzky Andante cantabile and Valse miniature
Paganini Fantasy on themes from 'Mosé' (Rossini)

VIOLINS, FIDDLES AND FOLLIES
1, 2 Sep. 15.00 *St Cecilia's Hall*
Presented by Susan Baker with Anthony Saunders (pf, spinet)

JAZZ

OSCAR PETERSON
18, 20, 22 Aug. 20.00 *King's Theatre*

DRAMA

BIRMINGHAM REPERTORY THEATRE
16, 17, 21, 24, 26, 29, 30 Aug. 1, 3 Sep. 19.30 22, 27 Aug. 5 Sep. 14.30
Assembly Hall
AS YOU LIKE IT Shakespeare
Rosalind Lynn Dearth
Orlando David Rintoul
Oliver Christopher Brown

Jacques de Boys/Sir Oliver Martext — Mason Taylor
Celia — Alice Krige
Touchstone — Nickolas Grace
Duke Frederick — Denis Holmes
Duke Senior — Denys Hawthorne
Amiens — William Relton
Jaques — John Quentin
Le Beau — Floyd Bevan
Charles — Kevin Quarmby
Corin — Paul Imbusch
Silvius — Reece Dinsdale
Phebe — Yvonne Edgell
Audrey — Nichola McAuliffe
Dennis — Tano Rea
Adam — Robin Wentworth
William — Pat Doyle
Lords — Mark Wynter, Steve O'Hara
Hymen — Mark Wynter
Juno — Carole Brooke
Ceres — Christine Taylor
Director — Clive Perry
Scenery — Poppy Mitchell
Costumes — Hugh Durrant
Lighting — Brian Harris

19, 20, 22, 25, 27, 28, 31 Aug. 2, 4, 5 Sep. 19.30 29 Aug. 14.30 Assembly Hall
CANDIDE Bernstein
Candide — William Relton
Cunegonde — Rosemary Ashe
Voltaire/Dr Pangloss/Governor/Host/Sage — Nickolas Grace
Paquette — Yvonne Edgell
Old Lady — Nichola McAuliffe
Maximilian — Mark Wynter
Other parts played by Christopher Brown, Jenny Michelmore, Pat Doyle, Carole Brooke, Kevin Quarmby, Mason Taylor, Tano Rea, Caroline Ashbourne, Jan Hartley, Christine Taylor, Steve O'Hara, Tricia Deighton, Annie Wensak, Floyd Bevan
Lyrics — Richard Wilbur, Stephen Sondheim, John Latouche
Conductor — Grant Hossack
Director — Peter Farago
Designer — Poppy Mitchell
Lighting — Brian Harris

AMPHI-THEATRE, Athens
18-22 Aug. 19.30 Lyceum Theatre
IPHIGENIA IN LIXOURION Katsaitis
(Adapted by Spyros A. Evangelatos)
Poet — Stephanos Kyriakidis
Agamemnon — Kostas Tsianos
Sganarellos — Panos Skouroliakos
Halkias — Giorgos Tsidimis
Odysseus — Tassos Yfantis
Menelaus — Stathis Kakkavas
Tiburgios — Elias Asproudis
Clytemnestra — Rika Sifaki
Iphigenia — Leda Tassopoulou
Achilles/Angiolis — Michalis Mitroussis
High priest/Barlacchias — Dimitris Katalifos
Fenissos/Vincentzo — Vassilis Goustis
Captain Cuviellos — Kostas Kapodistrias
Scapinos — Giannis Stamatakis
Simona — Melina Botelli
Giacumina — Zoe Rigopoulou
Director — Spyros A. Evangelatos
Designer — Giorgos Patsas

NATIONAL THEATRE
1-5 Sep. 19.30 2, 5 Sep. 14.30
Lyceum Theatre
ON THE RAZZLE Stoppard (Adapted from Nestroy) (World première)
Weinberl — Ray Brooks
Christopher — Felicity Kendal
Melchior — Michael Kitchen
Zangler — Dinsdale Landen
August Sonders — Barry McGinn
Coachman — Harold Innocent
Marie — Mary Chilton
Gertrud — Hilda Braid
Foreigner — Paul Gregory
Hupfer/Italian waiter — John Challis
Philippine — Allyson Rees
Madame Knorr — Rosemary McHale
Frau Fischer — Deborah Norton
German couple — Teresa Codling, Clyde Gatell
Scottish couple — Greta Watson, Andrew Cuthbert
2nd Waiter — Philip Talbot
Constable — Alan Haywood
Fraulein Blumenblatt — Joan Hickson
Lisette — Marianne Morley
Ragamuffin — Courtney Roper-Knight, Adam Woodyatt
Other parts played by Catherine Harding, Thomas Henty, Timothy Hick
Director — Peter Wood
Designer — Carl Toms
Lighting — Robert Bryan

THÉÂTRE DE LA SALAMANDRE
16-19 Aug. 20.00 19 Aug. 14.30
Moray House
BRITANNICUS Racine
Burrhus — Christian Blanc
Albine — Marie Boitel
Néron — Jacques Bonnaffé
Britannicus — Bruno Choël
Narcisse — Guy Perrot
Agrippine — Marief Guittier
Junie — Agnès Mallet
with Armand Didier
Director — Gildas Bourdet, Alain Milianti
Scenery — Gildas Bourdet
Costumes — Françoise Chevalier

NATIONAL THEATRE OF RUMANIA
21, 22, 24, 25 Aug. 20.00 23 Aug. 15.00
Moray House
THE GIRL FROM ANDROS Terence
Simo — Mihai Malaimare
Chremes — Raducu Ictus
Pamphilus — Bogdan Stanoevici
Charinus — Mihai Nicolescu
Crito — Bogdan Musatescu
Byrria/Sosia — Radu George
Dromo/Davos — Alexander Georgescu
Mysis/Lesbia — Olga Delia Mateescu
Glyceria — Tamara Cretulescu
Maidservant — Eugenia Maci
Director — Grigore Gonta
Designer — Dan Erceanu

BRIGHTON THEATRE
19-29 Aug. 20.00 (exc.Sun)
Freemasons' Hall Theatre
BROTHERS KARAMAZOV Dostoyevsky
(Eng. New version by Richard Crane)
(World première)
Dmitry — Bruce Alexander
Ivan — Alan Rickman
Alyosha — Stephen Boxer
Smerdyakov — Peter Kelly
Director and scenery — Faynia Williams
Costumes — Anne Menzies
Lighting — Richard Johnson

POETRY AND PROSE RECITALS

23, 26 Aug. 20.00 25 Aug.14.30
Moray House
ST MARK'S GOSPEL
Alec McCowen (rdr)

17, 18 Aug. 15.00 St Cecilia's Hall
PIOBAIREACHD
Pibroch: the ancient music of the Highland bagpipe
David Murray (lect), Pipe-Major Iain Morrison (bp)

21 Aug. 15.00 St Cecilia's Hall
AN GAIDHEAL ANN AN COGADH
(The Gael at war)
Presented by John MacInnes
Compiled by Dolina MacLennan

22 Aug. 15.00 St Cecilia's Hall
AIR LORG NAN EILEAN
(The road to the Isles)
Presented by Finlay J. MacDonald
Compiled by Dolina MacLennan

19, 20 Aug. 15.00 St Cecilia's Hall
ANNA AKHMATOVA
Faith Brook, Miki Iveria (rdr)
Compiled and introduced by John Drummond

23 Aug. 14.30 and 19.30 St Cecilia's Hall
POETRY FOR TWO
Joy Parker, Paul Scofield (rdr)

30 Aug. 20.00 31 Aug. 15.00
St Cecilia's Hall
A PERSONAL ANTHOLOGY
Tom Fleming (rdr)

3, 4, 5 Sep. 15.00 St Cecilia's Hall
HE AND SHE
Frank Muir, Judi Dench, Michael Williams
Compiled by Michael Meyer

DANCE

SAN FRANCISCO BALLET
18-19 Aug. 19.30 22 Aug. 14.30 and 20.00 Playhouse
ROMEO AND JULIET
Choreographer — Michael Smuin
Music — Prokofiev
Designer — William Pitkin

20, 21 Aug. 19.30 Playhouse
STRAVINSKY CAPRICCIO FOR PIANO AND ORCHESTRA
Choreographer — Robert Gladstein
Music — Stravinsky
Costumes — Willa Kim
A SONG FOR DEAD WARRIORS
Choreographer — Michael Smuin
Music — Charles Fox
Designer — Willa Kim
VARIATIONS DE BALLET
Choreographer — Lew Christensen
Music — Glazunov
Costumes — Sandra Woodall

24 Aug. 19.30 Playhouse
INTRODUCTION AND ALLEGRO
Choreographer — Tomm Ruud
Music — Elgar
Costumes — Sandra Woodall
TEALIA
Choreographer — John McFall
Music — Holst
Costumes — Victoria Gyorfi
SONGS OF MAHLER
Choreographer — Michael Smuin
Music — Mahler
Costumes — Michael Smuin
CON AMORE
Choreographer — Lew Christensen
Music — Rossini
Designer — Seppo Nurmimaa

25 Aug. 19.30 Playhouse
DIVERTIMENTO NO.15
Choreographer — George Balanchine

Music Mozart
Costumes Sandra Woodall
VIVALDI CONCERTO GROSSO
Choreographer Lew Christensen
Music Vivaldi
Costumes Sandra Woodall
Q.a V. (Quattro a Verdi)
Choreographer Michael Smuin
Music Verdi
Costumes Sandra Woodall
PROSPERO'S MASQUE FROM 'THE TEMPEST'
Choreographer Michael Smuin
Music Chihara
Lighting (all ballets)
Sara Linnie Slocum
Dancers Carmen Barth, Damara Bennett, Lori Bodine, Madeleine Bouchard, Val Caniparoli, Horacio Cifuentes, Evelyn Cisneros, Nigel Courtney, Allyson Deane, Nancy Dickson, Betsy Erickson, Attila Ficzere, Alexander Filipov, Ann Foley, Michael Hazinski, Eda Holmes, Antonio Lopez, Tracy-Kai Maier, John McFall, David McNaughton, Lynda Meyer, Jonathan Miller, Linda Montaner, Victoria Morgan, John Mourelatos, Russell Murphy, Gina Ness, Anita Paciotti, Victor Pesina, Zoltan Peter, Kirk Peterson, Andre Reyes, Paul Russell, Tomm Ruud, Don Schwennesen, Jim Sohm, Robert Sund, Alexander Topciy, Paula Tracy, Wendy van Dyck, Vane West, Diana Weber, Carmela Zegarelli, Jamie Zimmerman
with Sara Walker (mez), Bryn Turley (pf)
BBC Scottish Symphony Orchestra
Conductors Denis de Coteau, Jean-Louis LeRoux

LONDON CONTEMPORARY DANCE THEATRE
31 Aug.-5 Sep. 20.00 5 Sep. 14.30
Moray House
DANCES OF LOVE AND DEATH (World première)
Choreographer Robert Cohan
Music Carl Davis, Conlon Nancarrow
Designer Norberto Chiesa
Lighting John B. Read

OPEN SESSIONS
28 Aug. 16.00 Lighting session
29 Aug. 11.00 Company class
2 Sep. 14.30 Introduction
4 Sep. 16.00 Rehearsal
1, 3, Sep. 11.00 Masterclasses
Dancers Christopher Bannerman, Darshan Bhuller, Siobhan Davies, Paul Douglas, Sallie Estep, Anca Frankenhaeuser, Philippe Giraudeau, Anita Griffin, Patrick Harding Irmer, Kate Harrison, Celia Hulton, Tom Jobe, Charlotte Kirkpatrick, Jayne Lee, Jonathan Lunn, Namron, Lauren Potter, Lizie Saunderson, Michael Small, Philip Taylor, Anne Went

DAN WAGONER AND DANCERS, USA
27 Aug. 19.30 29 Aug. 14.30
Lyceum Theatre
A PLAY WITH IMAGES AND WALLS
Music Natalie Gilbert
Costumes Pat Varney
LILA'S GARDEN OX+
Music Bach
Costumes Pat Varney
YONKER DINGLE VARIATIONS
Music Michael Sahl
Costumes Remy Charup

28, 29 Aug. 19.30 *Lyceum Theatre*
SUMMER RAMBO
Music Bach
Costumes Kae Yoshida
STOP STARS (World première)
Music Recorded natural sounds
Costumes James Welty
SPIKED SONATA
Music
Radio theme music of the 1930's
Costumes James Welty
Choreographer (all ballets)
Dan Wagoner
Lighting
Jennifer Tipton, Thomas Rowe+
Dancers Heidi Bunting, Dennis Flemming, Edward Henry, JoAnn Fregalette-Jansen, Diann Sichel, Lisa Taylor, Dan Wagoner
with Natalie Gilbert, Alexandra Colmant (sngr), Daphne Godson (vn), Michael Chibbett (hpd), George Montgomery (narr.)

CONFERENCE

TELEVISION AND THE ARTS
24-29 Aug. 15.00 *St Cecilia's Hall*
Chairman Huw Wheldon
24 Aug. Television and the arts
Brian Wenham, Jeremy Isaacs, Chris Dunkley

25 Aug. The visual arts on television
Marina Vaizey, Robert Hughes, Edwin Mulling

26 Aug. Music on television
Humphrey Burton, Raymond Leppard, John Drummond

27 Aug. Literature on television
Melvyn Bragg, Michael Helroyd, Owen Dudley-Edwards

28 Aug. Television and the past
John Julius Norwich, Magnus Magnusson, Patrick Nuttgens

29 Aug. Television and the theatre
Jonathan Miller, John Mortimer

EXHIBITIONS

City Art Centre and Fruit Market Gallery
AMERICAN ABSTRACT EXPRESSIONISTS
(From The Museum of Modern Art, New York)

City Art Centre
MIRRORS AND WINDOWS
American photography since 1960
(Organized under the auspices of the International Council of the Museum of Modern Art, New York)

Lyceum Little Gallery
SCOTCH MYTHS
Devised by Murray and Barbara Grigor

ASSOCIATED EXHIBITIONS
(Not organized by the Festival Society)

Royal Scottish Museum
TREASURES IN TRUST

National Gallery of Scotland
SEEING IS NOT BELIEVING

Royal Scottish Academy
HONORÉ DAUMIER, 1808-1879

1982

OPERA

DRESDEN STATE OPERA
23, 25, 28 Aug. 19.30 *King's Theatre*
ARIADNE AUF NAXOS R. Strauss
(Revised version)
Ariadne Ana Pusar
Bacchus Klaus König
Reiner Goldberg
Zerbinetta Jana Jonasova
Ulrike Joannou
Composer Elisabeth Hornung
Ute Walther
Harlekin Jürgen Freier
Jürgen Hartfiel
Scaramuccio Karl-Heinz Koch
Günter Neef
Truffaldin Günter Dressler
Rolf Wollrad
Brighella Milos Jezil
Dancing master Karl Friedrich Hölzke
Music master Werner Haseleu
Majordomo Gunter Emmerlich
Naiade Helga Termer
Andrea Ihle
Dryade Elisabeth Wilke
Ilse Ludwig
Echo Gabriele Auenmüller
Barbara Hoene
Officer Rainer Zakowsky
Wigmaker Jürgen Hartfiel
Jürgen Commichau
Lackey Jürgen Commichau
Günter Dressler
Conductor Siegfried Kurz
Director Joachim Herz
Designer Bernhard Schröter

24, 26, 29 Aug. 19.30 *King's Theatre*
DIE ENTFÜHRUNG AUS DEM SERAIL
Mozart
Belmonte Armin Ude
Günther Neumann
Constanze Carolyn Smith-Meyer
Blonde Barbara Sternberger
Pedrillo Uwe Peper
Osmin Rolf Tomaszewski
Bassa Selim Werner Haseleu
Conductor Hiroshi Wakasugi
Director Harry Kupfer
Designer Peter Sykora

LA PICCOLA SCALA, Milan
4, 6, 7 Sep. 19.30 *King's Theatre*
LA PIETRA DEL PARAGONE Rossini
La Marchesa Clarice Julia Hamari
Donna Fulvia Marta Taddei
Baronessa Aspasia Gloria Banditelli
Giocondo Paulo Barbacini
Il Conte Asdrubale Justino Diaz
Pacuvio Alessandro Corbelli
Macrobio Claudio Desderi
Fabrizio Armando Ariostini
Conductor Roberto Abbado
Director Eduardo de Filippo
Scenery Mario Chiari
Costumes Maria de Matteis

10, 11 Sep. 19.30 *King's Theatre*
ARIODANTE Handel
Ariodante Carolyn Watkinson
Ginevra Lella Cuberli
Polinesso Jeffrey Gall
Dalinda Lucia Aliberti
Lurcanio Ernesto Palacio
King of Scotland Alfredo Zanazzo
Odoardo Ernesto Gavazzi

Solo dancers Raffaella Bagetto, Gloria Brandani, Vittorio Biagi
Conductor Roger Norrington
Director and designer Pier Luigi Pizzi
Choreographer Vittorio Biagi

WELSH NATIONAL OPERA
1, 5 Sep. 19.30 *King's Theatre*
TAMERLANO Handel (Eng.)
Asteria Eiddwen Harrhy
Irene Caroline Baker
Tamburlaine Robin Martin-Oliver
Bajazet Anthony Rolfe Johnson
Andronicus Brian Gordon
Leone Peter Savidge
Scottish Chamber Orchestra
Conductor Julian Smith
Director and designer Philip Prowse
Lighting Gerry Jenkinson

SCOTTISH OPERA
22, 27, 31 Aug. 19.30 *King's Theatre*
MANON LESCAUT Puccini
Manon Lescaut Nelly Miricioiu
Chevalier des Grieux Peter Lindroos
Lescaut Gino Quilico
Geronte Raimund Herincx
Edmondo Gordon Christie
Innkeeper Norman White
Dancing master Jim Croom
Musician Clare Moll
Lamplighter Paul Strathearn
Naval captain Alan Oke
Wigmaker John Brackenridge
Sergeant Brian Bannatyne-Scott
Conductor Sir Alexander Gibson
Director John Cox
Scenery Allen Charles Klein
Costumes Alix Stone

6-11 Sep. 17.30 *St Mary's Cathedral*
NOYE'S FLUDDE Britten
Voice of God Sandy Neilson
Noye William McCue
Mrs Noye Linda Ormiston
Orchestra and Chorus of 200 from Edinburgh schools
Conductor Dennis Townhill
Director Pat Tulloch

ORCHESTRAL CONCERTS

LONDON SYMPHONY ORCHESTRA
Conductor Claudio Abbado
22, 24 Aug. 20.00 *Usher Hall*
Verdi Requiem
Soloists Margaret Price, Jessye Norman (sop), José Carreras (ten), Ruggero Raimondi (bs), EF Chorus

23 Aug. 20.00 *Usher Hall*
Beethoven Concerto for piano no.2 in B flat, op.19
Berlioz Symphonie fantastique
Soloist Maurizio Pollini (pf)

MONTEVERDI CHOIR
ENGLISH BAROQUE SOLOISTS
Conductor John Eliot Gardiner
26 Aug. 20.00 *Usher Hall*
Vivaldi La sena festeggiante: Concerto in G minor
Vivaldi Gloria in D
Vivaldi Sinfonia (Al Santo sepulchro)
Vivaldi Beatus vir in C
Soloists Jennifer Smith, Patrizia Kwella (sop), Catherine Denley (mez), William Kendall (ten)

27 Aug. 22.30 *St Cuthbert's Church*
Gesualdo Ave, dulcissima Maria
Monteverdi Exultent caeli
Cavalli Salve regina
D. Scarlatti Stabat Mater

DRESDEN STAATSKAPELLE
27 Aug. 20.00 *Usher Hall*
Mozart Symphony no.29 in A, K201
Mozart Concerto for piano no.24 in C minor, K491
Mozart Symphony no.38 in D (Prague), K504
Conductor Hiroshi Wakasugi
Soloist Radu Lupu (pf)

SCOTTISH NATIONAL ORCHESTRA
28 Aug. 20.00 *Usher Hall*
Mendelssohn Symphony no.4 in A (Italian), op.90
Liszt Concerto for piano no.2 in A
Elgar Falstaff
Verdi La forza del destino: Overture
Conductor Sir Alexander Gibson
Soloist Jorge Bolet (pf)

I MUSICI
29 Aug. 20.00 *Usher Hall*
Corelli Concerto grosso in B flat, op.6/5
Vivaldi Concerti, op.11: No.2 in E minor (Il favorito)
Bach Concerto for harpsichord in A
Donizetti Concerto in D minor
Rossini Sonata for strings no.1 in G
Mozart Serenade no.6 (Serenata notturna), K239

SCOTTISH CHAMBER ORCHESTRA
31 Aug. 20.00 *Usher Hall*
Schubert Overture in the Italian syle in C, D591
Schubert Salve regina in F, D223
Schubert Symphony no.3 in D, D200
Pergolesi Orfeo
Stravinsky Pulcinella - Suite
Conductor Raymond Leppard
Soloist Ileana Cotrubas (sop)

2 Sep. 22.30 *Ross Bandstand*
Fireworks Concert
Handel Zadok the Priest - Coronation anthem
Haydn Concerto for trumpet in E flat
Handel Music for the royal fireworks
Conductor Trevor Pinnock
Soloist Crispian Steele-Perkins (tpt)
Scottish Philharmonic Singers

BBC SYMPHONY ORCHESTRA
1 Sep. 20.00 *Usher Hall*
Conductor Maxim Shostakovich
Stravinsky Fireworks
Stravinsky Concerto for violin in D
Tchaikovsky Manfred symphony
Soloist Ida Haendel (vn)

2 Sep. 20.00 *Usher Hall*
R. Strauss Don Juan
Shostakovich Concerto for piano no.2, op.102
Berlioz Harold in Italy
Soloists Peter Donohoe (pf), Bruno Giuranna (va)

PHILHARMONIA ORCHESTRA
3 Sep. 20.00 *Usher Hall*
Conductor Simon Rattle
Stravinsky Apollon musagète
Ravel Concerto for piano (Left hand)
Fauré Requiem
Soloists Jennifer Smith (sop), Dale Duesing (bar), Pascal Rogé (pf), EF Chorus

4 Sep. 20.00 *Usher Hall*
Haydn Symphony no.95 in C minor
Sibelius Concerto for violin in D minor, op.47
Bartók Concerto for orchestra
Soloist Kyung Wha Chung (vn)

LONDON PHILHARMONIC ORCHESTRA
5 Sep. 20.00 *Usher Hall*
Mahler Symphony no.3 in D minor
Conductor Sir Georg Solti
Soloist Faith Wilson (mez), EF Chorus members, SNO Junior Chorus

6 Sep. 20.00 *Usher Hall*
Dvořák Carnival - Overture
Bruch Concerto for violin no.1 in G minor, op.26
Brahms Symphony no.2 in D, op.73
Conductor James Conlon
Soloist Salvatore Accardo (vn)

8 Sep. 20.00 *Usher Hall*
Beethoven Mass in D (Missa solemnis), op.123
Conductor Sir Georg Solti
Soloists Helen Donath (sop), Doris Soffel (mez), Siegfried Jerusalem (ten), Hans Sotin (bs), EF Chorus

PHILADELPHIA ORCHESTRA
Conductor Riccardo Muti
10 Sep. 20.00 *Usher Hall*
Schumann Symphony no.4 in D minor, op.120
Prokofiev Romeo and Juliet - Suite

11 Sep. 20.00 *Usher Hall*
Barber Essay for orchestra no.2, op.17
Ravel Daphnis et Chloë - Suite no. 2
Mahler Symphony no.1 in D

CHAMBER CONCERTS

MEDICI QUARTET
25 Aug. 11.00 *Freemasons' Hall*
Mozart Quintet no.2 in C, K515
Muldowney Quartet no.2 (World première)
Tchaikovsky Souvenir de Florence - string sextet, op.70
with Michael Cookson (va), David Smith (vc)

LONDON EARLY MUSIC GROUP
27 Aug. 11.00 *Queen's Hall*
Italian Music from the Age of Monteverdi
Works by Vecchi, Marini, Frescobaldi, Monteverdi, Corbetta, Bassano, Zannetti, Rossi, Negri, Stefani, Riccio, Cima, Anon.
Director James Tyler
Soloists Glenda Simpson (mez), Philip Doghan (ten)

SCOTTISH BAROQUE ENSEMBLE
29 Aug. 15.00 *Queen's Hall*
Percy Grainger Centenary Concert
Delius Two aquarelles
Leighton Octet (Homage to Percy Grainger), op.87 (World première)
Delius Air and dance
Songs and piano works by Percy Grainger
Conductor Eric Fenby
Soloists David Wilson-Johnson (bar), Peter Evans (pf)

CLEVELAND QUARTET
30 Aug. 11.00 *Queen's Hall*
Haydn Quartet in D (Lark), op.64/5
Tippett Quartet no.1
Brahms Quartet no.3 in B flat, op.67

1 Sep. 11.00 *Queen's Hall*
Beethoven Quartet no.11 in F minor (Serioso), op.95
Beethoven Quartet no.2 in G, op.18/2
Brahms Quartet no.2 in A minor, op.51/2

INSTRUMENTAL ENSEMBLE
31 Aug. 11.00 *Queen's Hall*
Berio Sequenzas (complete)
Cathy Berberian (sop), Carlo Chiarappa (vn), Aldo Bennici (va), Roberto Fabbriciani (fl), Melinda Maxwell (ob), Antony Pay (cl), Stuart Dempster (tbn), Francis Pierre (hp), Katia Labèque (pf)

NASH ENSEMBLE
3 Sep. 11.00 *Queen's Hall*
Mozart Quintet for piano and wind in E flat, K452
Respighi Il tramonto
Rossini Quartet for wind no.1 in F
Dallapiccola Piccola musica notturna
Berio Folksongs
Conductor Lionel Friend
Soloist Sarah Walker (mez)

5 Sep. 15.00 *Queen's Hall*
Mozart Trio for piano, clarinet and viola, K498
Casella Serenata
Malipiero Sonata à cinque for flute, violin, viola, cello and harp
Stravinsky Pulcinella: Suite Italienne
Ponchielli Quartet for piano, flute, oboe and clarinet

BRANDIS QUARTET
7 Sep. 11.00 *Freemasons' Hall*
Mozart Quartet no.14 in G, K387
Wolf Italian serenade
Schubert Quartet no.14 in D minor (Death and the maiden), D810

9 Sep. 11.00 *Freemasons' Hall*
Mozart Quartet no.23 in F, K590
Kurtág Twelve mikroludes
Schubert Quartet no.15 in G, D887

NEW MUSIC GROUP OF SCOTLAND
10 Sep. 11.00 *Queen's Hall*
Harper Intrada after Monteverdi (World première)
Donatoni Etwas ruhiger im Ausdruck
Castiglioni Tropi
Harper Ricercari in memoriam Luigi Dallapiccola
Cresswell Soliloquy on a lambent tailpiece
Dalby O bella e vaga aurora (EIF commission)
Director Edward Harper

RECITALS

ELISABETH SÖDERSTRÖM (sop)
HÅKAN HAGEGÅRD (bar)
LENNART RÖNNLUND (pf)
28 Aug. 11.00 *Queen's Hall*
Wolf Italienisches Liederbuch

LUIGI ALVA (ten), RICHARD AMNER (pf)
4 Sep. 11.00 *Queen's Hall*
Songs by A. Scarlatti, Beethoven, Mozart, Schubert, Bellini, Rossini, Verdi, Silva, Morales

JESSYE NORMAN (sop)
GEOFFREY PARSONS (pf)
9 Sep. 20.00 *Usher Hall*
Brahms Zigeunerlieder
Songs by Wolf, Gounod, R. Strauss

YVONNE KENNY (sop)*
DAVID HARPER (pf)*
11 Sep. 11.00 *Queen's Hall*
Songs by Schubert, R. Strauss, Mahler, Liszt, Hahn, Walton

ELISABETH LEONSKAJA (pf)
24 Aug. 11.00 *Freemasons' Hall*
Brahms Sonata no.3 in F minor, op.5
Liszt Années de pèlerinage 1: Vallée d'Obermann
Liszt Années de pèlerinage 3: Aux cyprès de la Villa d'Este *and* Le jeux d'eaux à la Villa d'Este
Liszt Années de pèlerinage 2: Après une lecture du Dante (Sonata)

MAURIZIO POLLINI (pf)
25 Aug. 20.00 *Usher Hall*
Beethoven Sonata no.27 in E minor, op.90
Beethoven Sonata no.28 in A, op.101
Schoenberg Klavierstücke, op.23
Webern Variations, op.27
Nono ...sofferte onde serene...

RADU LUPU (pf)
30 Aug. 20.00 *Usher Hall*
Mozart Sonata no.8 in A minor, K310
Schubert Impromptus, D935
Schumann Kreisleriana

JORGE BOLET (pf)
6 Sep. 11.00 *Freemasons' Hall*
Beethoven Sonata no.26 in E flat (Farewell), op.81a
Rachmaninov Variations on a theme of Chopin, op.22
Liszt Années de pèlerinage 2: Sposalizio; Il penseroso; Canzonetta del Salvatore Rosa
Liszt Grandes études de Paganini: La campanella

KATIA and MARIELLE LABÈQUE (pf)
2 Sep. 11.00 *Queen's Hall*
Debussy En blanc et noir
Stravinsky Petrushka: 3 movements; arr. for piano
Ravel Ma mère l'oye
Gershwin Rhapsody in blue

SALVATORE ACCARDO (vn)
8 Sep. 11.00 *Queen's Hall*
Paganini Caprices, op.1: Nos. 1-24

SYLVIA ROSENBERG (vn)
CLIFFORD BENSON (pf)
26 Aug. 11.00 *Freemasons' Hall*
Stravinsky Pulcinella: Suite Italienne
Walton Sonata
Mozart Sonata no.28 in E flat, K380
Brahms Sonata no.1 in G, op.78

JULIAN BREAM (gtr)
23 Aug. 11.00 *Queen's Hall*
M. Berkeley Sonata for guitar (World première)
Works by Visée, Weiss, Sor, Granados, Falla

DRAMA

COOPERATIVA TEATROMUSICA, Rome
23, 26 Aug. 20.30 25 Aug. 14.30
Lyceum Theatre
L'OLIMPIADE Metastasio
Clistene Rodolfo Traversa
Aristea Elisabetta Piccolomini
Argene Marisol Gabbrieli
Licida Stefano Onafri
Megacle Franco Castellano
Arminta Maurizio Gueli
Alcandro Antonella Fattori
Lady Anita Marini
Director and scenery Sandro Sequi
Costumes Giuseppe Crisolini Malatesta
English commentary Irene Worth

AMERICAN REPERTORY THEATRE
24, 25, 27, 28 Aug. 19.30 28 Aug. 14.30
Lyceum Theatre
SGANARELLE Molière (Eng)
(An evening of four Molière farces, translated by Albert Bermel)
Thomas Derrah, John Bottoms, Jeremy Geidt, Richard Grusin, Cherry Jones, Tony Shalhoub, Karen MacDonald, Marianne Owen, Harry S. Murphy, Stephen Rowe,
Director Andrei Serban
Scenery Michael H. Yeargan
Costumes Dunya Ramicova
Lighting James F. Ingalls

29-31 Aug. 19.30 *Lyceum Theatre*
LULU Wedekind
(Eng. Adapted by Michael Feingold)
Lulu Catherine Slade
Lady Swetting (Countess Geschwitz) Karen MacDonald
Louis B. Lebow (Dr Schön) Frederick Neumann
Alan B. Lebow (Alwa) Thomas Derrah
Pittsburgh (Schigolch) Jeremy Geidt
Juan Dos Tres (Rodrigo) Stephen Rowe
Gall (Dr Goll)/Toshu Richard Grusin
Prince (Escerny)/Casti-Piani Tony Shalhoub
Jack Harry S. Murphy
Carbone (Schwarz) John Bottoms
Carmen (Magelone) Marianne Owen
Claudia Cherry Jones
Director Lee Breuer
Scenery Adrianne Lobel
Costumes Rita Ryack
Lighting Paul Gallo

EDINBURGH INTERNATIONAL FESTIVAL
2, 3, 4, 6, 7 Sep. 20.30 5 Sep. 19.30
4 Sep. 14.30 *Lyceum Theatre*
THE MARRIAGE
(Adapted by Peter Ustinov from Mussorgsky and Gogol.
Opera translated by Stephen Oliver)
Stage manager Peter Ustinov
Young girl Pavla Ustinov
Drozdov/Podkolyosin Marius Rintzler
Erofeyev/Stepan David Wilson-Johnson
Rimsky-Korsakov Charles Kay
Mokrovsky/Kochkarov Francis Egerton
Rudina/Fyokla Patricia Johnson
Prof. Shpanko Roger Vignoles
Mme Shpanko Faith Brook
Man John Bett
Prompter Barry Thomas
Director Peter Ustinov
Designer Nana Cecchi
Lighting André Tammes
Pianist Roger Vignoles

AKROAMA, Teatro Laboratorio Sardinia
8-11 Sep. 20.30 *Lyceum Theatre*
MARIEDDA Lecis (Based on *The little matchgirl* by Andersen)
Mariedda Elisabetta Podda
Peppantionia Rosalba Piras
Ballioccu Maurizio Masia
Pistilloni Marcello Enardu
Director and scenery Lelio Lecis
Costumes Anna Lughia Carrucciu

COMPAGNIA MARIONETTISTICI CARLO COLLA, Milan
24-28 Aug. 20.00 26, 28 Aug. 15.00

Church Hill Theatre
PROMETHEUS Colla

30 Aug.-3 Sep. 20.00 1, 3, 4 Sep. 15.00
Church Hill Theatre
CINDERELLA Colla
Designers Maurizio Dotti, Riccardo Isotta
Costumes Pierluigi Bottazzi
Orchestra Ambrosiana
Conductor Michael Summers

POETRY AND PROSE RECITALS

29 Aug. 15.00 St Cecilia's Hall
WALTER SCOTT AND EUROPEAN OPERA
John Warrack (lect)

30 Aug. 15.00 St Cecilia's Hall
AMERICAN THEATRE TODAY
A discussion of current trends
Robert Brustein, Lee Breuer, Frank Dunlop
Chairman Michael Billington

31 Aug.-2 Sep. 15.00 St Cecilia's Hall
BEOWULF
Julian Glover (rdr)

DANCE

ANTONIO GADES BALLET, Spain
1-5 Sep. 19.30 5 Sep. 14.30 Music Hall
BLOOD WEDDING
Choreographer Antonio Gades
Music Emilio de Diego, Perelló Monreal
Designer Francisco Nieva
FLAMENCO SUITE
Choreographers Cristina Hoyos, Antonio Gades
Dancers Cristina Hoyos, Antonio Gades, Juan Antonio, Tauro, Enrique Esteve, Antonio Quintana, Antonio Benitez, Rocio Navarrete, Carmen Villa, Maria Fernanda, Stella Arauzo, Ana Gaviño, Maria José Gaviño
With Gomez de Jerez, Manolo Sevilla (sngr), Antonio Solera, Manuel Rodriquez (gtr)

SANKAI JUKU, Japan
23, 25-28 Aug. 19.30 Music Hall
KINKAN SHONEN
Created and directed by Ushio Amagatsu
Designer Tamotsu Sasagawa
Lighting Hiromichi Takeyama
Dancers Ushio Amagatsu, Goro Namerikawa, Keiji Morita, Yoshiyuki Takada, Atsushi Ogata

CONFERENCE

THE STATE AND THE ARTS
3-4 Sep. St Cecilia's Hall
3 Sep. 11.00 The responsibility
Rt Hon. Paul Channon, Hans Werner Henze, Jean Gattegno, Sergio Romano

3 Sep. 15.00 The audience
Rt Hon. Roy Hattersley, Frans de Ruiter, Peter Ustinov

4 Sep. 11.00 The money
Massimo Bogianckino, Jean-Albert Cartier, George Christie, John Cox

4 Sep. 15.00 The investment
Lord Goodman, Rt Hon. David Steel, Melvyn Bragg, John Drummond
Chairman John Mortimer

EXHIBITIONS

Royal Scottish Academy
BRITISH WATERCOLOURS AND DRAWINGS
(Organized by the British Council)

Royal Scottish Museum
CIRCLES OF THE WORLD: Traditional art of the Plains Indians
(Organized by the Denver Art Museum)
Illustrated Lectures
19 Aug.15.00 Dream clothing and magic lodges
25 Aug.15.00 People of the Buffalo
3 Sep.15.00 Art of the Native American Church - Peyote Religion
13 Sep.15.00 Plains Indians in pictures

Usher Hall
WILLIAM WALTON EXHIBITION
Compiled by Gillian Widdicombe

ASSOCIATED EXHIBITIONS
(Not organized by the Festival Society)

Royal Scottish Academy
CODEX HAMMER
(Armand Hammer Foundation)

City Art Centre
I MACCHIAIOLI: Italian Impressionists

City Art Centre
PIRANESI DRAWINGS AND ETCHINGS
(From the Arthur M. Sackler Collections)

Royal Scottish Academy
MAN RAY
(In association with the Musée National d'Art Moderne, Centre Georges Pompidou)

National Gallery of Scotland
LOOKALIKE: Themes and variations in art

Scottish National Gallery of Modern Art
MIRÓ'S PEOPLE

Scottish National Portrait Gallery
JOHN MICHAEL WRIGHT: The King's painter

National Museum of Antiquities
ANGELS, NOBLES AND UNICORNS: Art and patronage in medieval Scotland

Fruitmarket Gallery
SCOTTISH ARTS NOW

Richard Demarco Gallery
HEBRIDEAN LIGHT: Photographs by Gus Wylie

ASSOCIATED EVENTS

1st EDINBURGH INTERNATIONAL HARPSICHORD COMPETITION
21-28 Aug. St Cecilia's Hall

STREET EVENTS

I SBANDIERATORI: Flag wavers from Gubbio
SANKAI JUKU

1983

OPERA

HAMBURG STATE OPERA
22, 24 Aug. 19.30 King's Theatre
EINE FLORENTINISCHE TRAGÖDIE Zemlinsky
Guido Bardi Kenneth Riegel
Simone Guillermo Saràbia
Bianca Elisabeth Steiner
DER GEBURTSTAG DER INFANTIN (Der Zwerg) Zemlinsky
Donna Clara Inga Nielsen
Ghita Béatrice Haldas
Don Estoban Dieter Weller
Dwarf Kenneth Riegel
Maids Yoko Kawahara, Marianne Hirsti, Olive Fredricks
Conductor Gerd Albrecht
Director Adolf Dresen
Designer Margit Bárdy

23, 25, 27 Aug. 19.30 Playhouse
DIE ZAUBERFLÖTE Mozart
Tamino Rüdiger Wohlers
Pamina Helen Donath
Papageno Mikael Melbye
Sarastro Robert Lloyd* Harald Stamm
Queen of the Night Carla del Re
Speaker Franz Ferdinand Nentwig
1st Lady Heide Christians
2nd Lady Hildegard Hartwig
3rd Lady Marjana Lipovsek
Papagena Marianne Hirsti
Monostatos Norbert Orth
3 Boys Soloists of the Tölzer Boys' Choir
2 Armed men Werner Götz, Carl Schultz
Priest Frieder Stricker
Conductor Christoph von Dohnányi
Director and designer Achim Freyer

SCOTTISH OPERA
26 Aug. 19.30 King's Theatre
DEATH IN VENICE Britten
Gustav von Aschenbach Anthony Rolfe Johnson
Traveller/Fop/Gondolier/Hotel manager/Barber/ Leader of the players/Voice of Dionysus Barry Mora
Voice of Apollo Andrew Dalton
Polish mother Catherine Wilson
Tadzio Craig Fraser
Steward/Boatman/Waiter/Guide/Priest/ English clerk Alan Oke
Strawberry-seller/Lace-seller/Newspaper-seller/Strolling player Una Buchanan
Hotel porter John Robertson
Glass-maker/Strolling player Grant Richards
Beggar-woman Carol Rowlands
Russian mother Elaine MacKillop
Russian father Ian McKinven
Russian nanny Jane Guy
German mother Ann Scott
German father Anthony Davis
Danish lady Jane Oakland
English lady Ann Dempsey
French mother Ellen Jackson
French girl Yvonne Barclay
Other parts played by John Brackenridge, Malcolm Aitken, Alexander Morrison, Thom Irvine, Declan McCusker, Richard Perrett, James Paterson
Conductor Roderick Bryden
Director François Rochaix
Designer Jean-Claude Maret
Lighting Jean-Philippe Roy

OPERA THEATER OF ST LOUIS
6, 9 Sep. 19.30 *King's Theatre*
THE POSTMAN ALWAYS RINGS TWICE Paulus
Nick Papadakis Michael Myers
Cora Karen Hunt
Frank Chambers David Parsons
Sackett Daniel Sullivan
1st Cop (Motorcycle)/Kennedy David Evitts
2nd Cop (Jail) Gordon Holleman
Katz Carroll Freeman
Scottish Chamber Orchestra
Conductor C. William Harwood
Director Colin Graham
Scenery John Conklin
Costumes John Carver Sullivan
Lighting Peter Kaczorowski

8, 10 Sep. 19.30 *King's Theatre*
FENNIMORE AND GERDA Delius
Niels Stephen Dickson
Fennimore Kathryn Bouleyn
Gerda Kathryn Gamberoni
Erik David Bankston
Consul Claudi/Distiller Daniel Sullivan
Frau Claudi Gayle Greene
Offstage voice John La Pierre
Lady Kerry McCarthy
Sportsman Gordon Holleman
Skinnerup/Town councillor Paul Kilmer
Tutor James Daniel Frost
Maid/Marit Brenda Everett
Lila Dayne Renz
Ingrid Dorothy Rhodes
Scottish Chamber Orchestra
Conductor Christopher Keene
Director Frank Corsaro
Designer Ronald Chase
Lighting Peter Kaczorowski

ORCHESTRAL CONCERTS

PHILHARMONIA ORCHESTRA
21 Aug. 20.00 *Usher Hall*
Berg Three orchestral pieces, op.6
Beethoven Symphony no.9 in D minor (Choral), op.125
Conductor Andrew Davis
Soloists Linda Esther Gray (sop), Carolyn Watkinson (mez), John Mitchinson (ten), Robert Lloyd (bs), EF Chorus

ACADEMY OF ST MARTIN-IN-THE-FIELDS
22 Aug. 20.00 *Usher Hall*
Schubert Symphony no.3 in D, D200
Mozart Concerto for clarinet in A, K622
R. Strauss Metamorphosen for 23 solo strings
Conductor Neville Marriner
Soloist Antony Pay (cl)

LONDON SYMPHONY ORCHESTRA
Conductor Claudio Abbado
24 Aug. 20.00 *Usher Hall*
Wagner A Faust overture
Webern Six pieces, op.6
Wagner Lohengrin: Act 2
Soloists Rosalind Plowright (sop), Eva Randová (mez), Siegfried Jerusalem (ten), Hartmut Welker, Siegfried Lorenz (bar), Robert Lloyd (bs), EF Chorus

25 Aug. 20.00 *Usher Hall*
Schoenberg Erwartung
Beethoven Symphony no.3 In E flat (Eroica), op.55
Soloist Phyllis Bryn-Julson (sop)

NATIONAL YOUTH ORCHESTRA OF SCOTLAND
27 Aug. 20.00 *Usher Hall*
Mendelssohn The Hebrides (Fingal's cave) - Overture
Webern Six pieces, op.6
Ravel Shéhérazade
Nielsen Symphony no.4 (Inextinguishable), op.29
Conductor Sir Alexander Gibson
Soloist Isobel Buchanan (sop)

STARS OF ST LOUIS
SCOTTISH CHAMBER ORCHESTRA
28 Aug. 20.00 *Usher Hall*
Works by Mozart, Verdi, Rossini, Puccini, Flotow, R. Strauss, Barber, Loesser, Bernstein, Cardillo, Gershwin
Conductor Bruce Ferden
Soloists Luvenia Garner, Erie Mills (sop), Susanne Mentzer (mez), Jerry Hadley (ten), Frederick Burchinal (bar)
Introduced by Alistair Cooke

SCOTTISH CHAMBER ORCHESTRA
1 Sep. 22.00 *Ross Bandstand*
Fireworks Concert
Sharpe Fanfare for a festival
Handel Music for the royal fireworks
Fletcher Spirit of pageantry
Tchaikovsky 1812 overture
Regimental Band of the Royal Scots
Conductor Gustav Kuhn

LONDON PHILHARMONIC ORCHESTRA
Conductor Klaus Tennstedt
29 Aug. 20.00 *Usher Hall*
Mozart Concerto for violin no.4 in D, K218
Mahler Das Lied von der Erde
Soloists Brigitte Fassbaender (mez), Hermann Winkler (ten), Miriam Fried (vn)

30 Aug. 20.00 *Usher Hall*
R. Strauss Don Juan
R. Strauss Burleske for piano in D
Wagner Götterdämmerung: Siegfried's journey to the Rhine
Weber Konzertstück for piano and orchestra in F minor, op.79
J. Strauss Kaiser Walzer
Soloist Philip Fowke (pf)*

CONCERTGEBOUW ORCHESTRA, Amsterdam
Conductor Bernard Haitink
31 Aug. 20.00 *Usher Hall*
Beethoven Concerto for piano no.1 in C, op.15
Bruckner Symphony no.9 in D minor
Soloist Alfred Brendel (pf)

1 Sep. 20.00 *Usher Hall*
Schoenberg Verklärte Nacht
Mahler Symphony no.4 in G
Soloist Roberta Alexander (sop)*

CITY OF BIRMINGHAM SYMPHONY ORCHESTRA
Conductor Simon Rattle
2 Sep. 20.00 *Usher Hall*
Britten Sinfonia da requiem
Mahler Symphony no.10 in F sharp; arr. Cooke

3 Sep. 20.00 *Usher Hall*
Webern Passacaglia, op.1
Saint-Säens Concerto for piano no.2 in G minor, op.22
Liszt Tannhauser: Overture (Wagner) for piano
Sibelius Symphony no.5 in E flat, op.82
Soloist Shura Cherkassky (pf)

FRANZ LISZT CHAMBER ORCHESTRA, Hungary
Leader Janos Rolla
3 Sep. 11.00 *Queen's Hall*
Handel Concerto grosso in G, op.6/1
Handel Concerto grosso in E minor, op.6/3
Bach Concerto for piano in D minor
Dvořák Serenade for strings in E, op.22
Soloist Zoltán Kocsis (pf)

5 Sep. 11.00 *Queen's Hall*
Corelli Concerto grosso in D, op.6/4
Bach Brandenburg concerto no.3 in G
Mozart Concerto for piano no.12 in A, K414
Szöllösy Concerto no.3 for 16 strings
Mendelssohn Symphony for strings no.9 in C
Soloist Zoltán Kocsis (pf)

SCOTTISH NATIONAL ORCHESTRA
4 Sep. 20.00 *Usher Hall*
Schoenberg Gurrelieder
Conductor Sir Alexander Gibson
Soloists Marilyn Zschau (sop), Ann Murray (mez), Jon Frederic West, Philip Langridge (ten), Nikolaus Hillebrand (bar), Hans Hotter (narr), EF Chorus

8 Sep. 20.00 *Usher Hall*
Wagner Wesendonck Lieder
Bruckner Mass in F minor
Conductor Jesus Lopez-Cobos
Soloists Margaret Marshall (sop), Florence Quivar (mez), Graham Clark (ten), Gwynne Howell (bs), EF Chorus

10 Sep. 20.00 *Usher Hall*
R. Strauss Le bourgeois gentilhomme - Suite
R. Strauss Capriccio: Intermezzo *and* Closing scene
Josef Strauss Dynamiden
Lehár Der Graf von Luxemburg: Lieber Freund, man greift nicht
Lehár Zigeunerliebe: Ich bin ein Zigeuner
J. Strauss Unter Donner und Blitz
J. Strauss Pizzicato polka
Lehár Giuditta: Meine Lippen, sie küssen so heiss
Lehár Die lustige Witwe: Vilja
R. Strauss Der Rosenkavalier: Walzes
Conductor Neeme Järvi
Soloists Elisabeth Söderström (sop), John Hancorn (bar)

CZECH PHILHARMONIC ORCHESTRA
5 Sep. 20.00 *Usher Hall*
Zemlinsky Sinfonietta, op.23
Dussek Concerto for 2 pianos, op.63
Dvořák Symphony no.7 in D minor, op.70
Conductor Jiří Bělohlávek
Soloists Katia and Marielle Labèque (pf)

6 Sep. 20.00 *Usher Hall*
Smetana Má vlast
Conductor Vaclàv Neumann

ORCHESTRA OF THE EIGHTEENTH CENTURY
7 Sep. 20.00 *Usher Hall*
Rameau Le temple de la gloire - Suite
Mozart Sinfonia concertante for violin and viola, K364
Mozart Symphony no.39 in E flat, K543
Conductor Frans Brüggen
Soloists Daniel Stepner (vn), Lucy van Dael (va)

CHAMBER ORCHESTRA OF EUROPE
9 Sep. 20.00 *Usher Hall*
Haydn Symphony no.49 in F minor (La passione)
Mozart Sinfonia concertante for wind, K297b
Beethoven Concerto for violin, cello and piano in C, op.56
Conductor Alexander Schneider
with Beaux Arts Trio

CHAMBER CONCERTS

DELME QUARTET
23 Aug. 11.00 *Queen's Hall*
Debussy Quartet in G minor, op.10
Caplet Conte fantastique (Le masque de la mort rouge)
Ravel Quartet in F
with John Marson (hp)

MELOS QUARTET OF STUTTGART
25 Aug. 11.00 *Queen's Hall*
Mozart Quartet no.14 in G, K387
Zemlinsky Quartet no.3, op.19
Schumann Quartet no.3 in A, op.41/3

BOSTON MUSICA VIVA
26 Aug. 11.00 *Queen's Hall*
Thow All Hallows
Zwilich Passages
Cage Credo in US
Schoenberg Chamber symphony no.1, op.9; arr. Webern
Conductor Richard Pittman

YOUNG UCK KIM (vn), YO-YO MA (vc), EMANUEL AX (pf)
29 Aug. 11.00 *Queen's Hall*
Mozart Trio for piano and strings no.6 in G, K564
Dvořák Trio for piano and strings no.3 in F minor, op.65
Brahms Trio for piano and strings no.1 in B, op.8

TOKYO QUARTET
6 Sep. 11.00 *Queen's Hall*
Haydn Quartet in G, op.77/1
Berg Quartet, op.3
Beethoven Quartet no.9 in C (Rasumovsky), op.59/3

SCHOENBERG ENSEMBLE
8 Sep. 11.00 *Queen's Hall*
Debussy Prélude à l'après-midi d'un faune arr. Sachs
Busoni Berceuse élégiaque; arr. Schoenberg
Reger Eine romantische Suite, op.125 arr. Schoenberg and Kolisch
Songs by Zemlinsky, Schoenberg; arr. Stein
Conductor Reinbert de Leeuw

8 Sep. 22.30 *Queen's Hall*
Schoenberg Pierrot lunaire
Eisler Palmström
Schoenberg Cabaret songs
J. Strauss Rosen aus dem Süden; arr.Schoenberg
Schoenberg Die eiserne Brigade
Conductor Reinbert de Leeuw

10 Sep. 11.00 *Queen's Hall*
Zemlinsky Trio for clarinet, cello and piano in D minor, op.3
Zemlinsky Six Maeterlinck songs, op.13
Schoenberg Eight songs, op.6
Webern Slow movement for string quartet
Webern Six bagatelles for string quartet, op.9

RECITALS

BARBARA HENDRICKS (sop)
RALF GOTHONI (pf)
24 Aug. 11.00 *Queen's Hall*
Poulenc La courte paille
Songs by Schubert, Wolf, Debussy

LUCIA POPP (sop), IRWIN GAGE (pf)
30 Aug. 11.00 *Queen's Hall*
Songs by Schubert, Schoenberg, R. Strauss

ILEANA COTRUBAS (sop)
GEOFFREY PARSONS (pf)
7 Sep. 11.00 *Queen's Hall*
Songs by Liszt, Berg, Wolf

SONGMAKERS' ALMANAC
31 Aug. 11.00 *Queen's Hall*
Alma Mahler
Felicity Palmer (sop), Anthony Rolfe Johnson (ten), Richard Jackson (bar), Graham Johnson (pf)
with Janet Suzman as Alma Mahler

CÉCILE OUSSET (pf)
22 Aug. 11.00 *Queen's Hall*
Debussy Études nos. 5, 7, 11
Fauré Theme and variations in C sharp minor, op.73
Fauré Nocturne no.5 in B flat, op.37
Fauré Impromptu no.3 in A flat, op.34
Fauré Barcarolle no.6 in E flat, op.70
Brahms Variations on a theme by Paganini: Book 1
Prokofiev Ten pieces, op.12

SHURA CHERKASSKY (pf)
1 Sep. 11.00 *Queen's Hall*
Bach Partita for violin no.2 in D minor: Chaconne; arr. Busoni
Beethoven Sonata no.13 in E flat, op.27/1
Brahms Variations on a theme by Paganini: Book 2
Scriabin Sonata no.4 in F sharp, op.30
Berg Sonata, op.1
Chopin Nocturne no.8 in D flat, op.27/2
Chopin Nocturne no.19 in E minor, op.72/1
Chopin Polonaise no.6 in A flat, op.53

CHARLES ROSEN (pf)
9 Sep. 11.00 *Queen's Hall*
Beethoven Sonata no.21 in C (Waldstein), op.53
Webern Variations, op.27
Schoenberg Klavierstücke, op.19
Schumann Fantasia in C, op.17

KATIA AND MARIELLE LABÈQUE (pf)
7 Sep. 22.30 *Queen's Hall*
Works for 2 pianos by Gershwin, Joplin, Mayerl, Johnson

9 Sep. 22.30 *Queen's Hall*
Brahms Hungarian dances for piano duet nos. 1-5, 12, 18-21
Brahms Waltzes for piano duet, op.39

PINCHAS ZUKERMAN (vn, va)
MARC NEIKRUG (pf)
26 Aug. 20.00 *Usher Hall*
Brahms Sonatensatz for violin and piano
Brahms Sonata for violin and piano no.1 in G, op.78
Brahms Sonata for viola and piano no.1 in F minor, op.120/1

28 Aug. 15.00 *Usher Hall*
Brahms Sonata for violin and piano no.2 in A, op.100
Brahms Sonata for viola and piano no.2 in E flat, op.120/2
Brahms Sonata for violin and piano no.3 in D minor, op.108

YO-YO MA (vc), EMANUEL AX (pf)
27 Aug. 11.00 *Queen's Hall*
Beethoven Sonata no.2 in G minor, op.5/2
Chopin Sonata in G minor, op.65
Brahms Sonata no.2 in F, op.99

JENNIFER BATE (org)
2 Sep. 11.00 *St Mary's Cathedral*
Reger Introduction and passacaglia in D minor
Mozart Fantasia in F minor and major, K594
Karg-Elert Chorale improvisations: Herr, wie du willst *and* Jerusalem du hochgebaute Stadt
Bach Prelude and fugue in E flat (St Anne)
Messiaen Apparition de l'église éternelle
Messiaen Livre d'orgue: Les mains de l'abîme
Vierne Pièces en stile libre: Scherzetto
Bate Introduction and variations on an old French carol

MASTER CLASSES

HANS HOTTER
6-9 Sep. 14.30 *Reid School of Music*
Patricia Rozario, Jane Streeton (sop), Elizabeth-Anne Price (mez), Mark Tinkler, John Hancorn (bar), Stephen Richardson (b-bar) with David Willison (pf)

DRAMA

CITIZENS' THEATRE, Glasgow
21-27 Aug. 5, 6, 9 Sep. 19.00
Assembly Hall
KRAUS THE LAST DAYS OF MANKIND
(Eng. Translated by Robert David MacDonald)
Kraus Giles Havergal
Restaurateur Derwent Watson
Waitress Katherine Kitovitz
Officers Robert Gwilym, Ian Puleston-Davies, Garry Roost
A patriot and optimist Patrick Hannaway
Reader of newspapers Rupert Farley
Man of science Lorcan Cranitch
Lady of means Yolanda Vasquez
Journalist Shaun Behan
Photographer Jonathan Scott-Taylor
Man of iron Laurance Rudic
Man of steel Robin Hooper
Man of government Ciaran Hinds
Waiter John Breck
Tart Charon Bourke
Man of God Gary Oldman
Lady of ends Johanna Kirby
Actress Jill Spurrier
War correspondent Jane Bertish
Director Robert David MacDonald
Designer Terry Bartlett
Lighting Gerry Jenkinson

30 Aug.-3 Sep. 7, 8, 10 Sep. 19.30 1, 3, 10 Sep. 14.30 *Assembly Hall*
HOFMANNSTHAL ROSENKAVALIER
(Eng. Translated by Robert David MacDonald)
Marschallin Katherine Kitovitz
Octavian Gary Oldman
Sophie Yolanda Vasquez
Ochs Robert David MacDonald
Faninal Laurance Rudic
Marianne Leitmetzerin Jane Bertish
Valzacchi Ciaran Hinds

Annina — Johanna Kirby
Italian singer — Stephen Hill
Police commissioner — Patrick Hannaway
Major domo (Marschallin) — Derwent Watson
Major domo (Faninal) — Robin Hooper
Landlord — Lorcan Cranitch
Dressmaker — Jonathan Scott-Taylor
Animal seller — Shaun Behan
Noble widow — Jill Spurrier
Noble orphans — Charon Bourke, Rupert Farley
Notary — Robert Gwilym
Leopold — Stewart Porter
Mahomed — Carl Bridgeman
Director and designer — Philip Prowse
Lighting — Gerry Jenkinson

COMPAÑIA DE NURIA ESPERT, Spain
30 Aug.-3 Sep. 19.30 2 Sep. 14.30
Lyceum Theatre
DOÑA ROSITA, THE SPINSTER Lorca
Doña Rosita — Nuria Espert
Child's nurse — Julia Martinez
Aunt — Carmen Bernardos
Uncle — Carlos Lucena
Nephew — Juan Miralles
Three Manolas — Cristina Higueras, Veronica Lujan, Mercedes Gimenez
Professor of economy — Joaquin Molina
Mother of the spinsters — Esperanza Grases
Spinsters — Oliva Cuesta, Ana Frau, Carmen Liaño
Servant — Patricia Escudero
Misses Ayola — Mireia Ros, Covadonga Cadenas
Don Martin — Rafael Anglada
Worker — José Roberto Añibarro
Young man — Manuel de Benito
Director — Jorge Lavelli
Designer — Max Bignens
Lighting — Vincente Mayoral
Music — Anton Garcia Abril

TRIUMPH APOLLO PRODUCTIONS LTD
5-10 Sep. 19.30 8, 10 Sep. 14.30
Lyceum Theatre
THE CHERRY ORCHARD Chekhov (Eng)
Madame Ranyevskaya — Joan Plowright
Anya — Cora Kinnaird
Varya — Joanna David
Gayev — Leslie Phillips
Lopakhin — Frank Finlay
Trofimov — Frank Grimes
Simeonov-Pishchik — Bill Fraser
Charlotta Ivanovna — Catherine Willmer
Yepihodov — David Battley
Dunyasha — Bernadette Shortt
Firs — Bernard Miles
Yasha — Michael Siberry
Station master — John Jefferson-Hayes
Tramp — David Kincaid
Director — Lindsay Anderson
Scenery — Kenneth Mellor
Costumes — Mark Negin
Lighting — James Baird

HAIFA MUNICIPAL THEATRE, Israel
22-27 Aug. 19.30 *Music Hall*
THE SOUL OF A JEW Sobol
Otto Weininger — Doron Tavory
Leopold — Anatol Constantin
Adelaide/Adela — Leora Rivlin
Berger/Prostitute — Guri Segal
Clara — Dalia Shimko
Tietz/Strindberg/Mobius — Yusof Abu-Warda
Freud — Michael Kfir
Otto's double/Prostitute — Tehiya Danon
Director — Gedalia Besser
Scenery — Adrian Vaux
Costumes — Edna Sobol
Lighting — Yehiel Orgal

7:84/GENERAL GATHERING
29 Aug.-3 Sep. 19.30 *Music Hall*
WOMEN IN POWER Aristophanes (Eng. Adapted by John McGrath)
Praxagora — Carol Kidd
Kleonike — Elizabeth MacLennan
Agatha — Anne Myatt
Beatrice — Judith Sweeney
Clarinda — Mary-Anne Coburn
Euphrosyne — Andrea Miller
Doris — Linda Muchan
Blepyros/Tripe seller — Kenneth Bryans
Countrywoman — Peggy Mackenzie
Pheidolos/Nikias — Bill Pheely Johnstone
Chremes/Demosthenes/Paphlagonian — Jimmy Chisholm
Director — John McGrath
Designer — Jenny Tiramani
Lighting — Kris Misselbrook
Music — Thanos Mikroutsikos
Musical director — Robert Pettigrew

POPPIE NONGENA COMPANY, New York
5-10 Sep. 19.30 *Assembly Rooms*
POPPIE NONGENA Kotze *and* Joubert
Poppie — Thuli Dumakude
Ouma Hannie/Ma Lena — Sophie Mgcina
Mosie — Seth Sibanda
Plank — Tsepo Mokone
Jakkie/Preacher — Fana Kekana
Pengi/Suitor/Stone — Lowell Williams
Other parts played by Maggie Soboil, Alex Wipf
Director — Hilary Blecher
Scenery — Jon Ringbom
Costumes — Shura Cohen
Lighting — William Armstrong

ACCLAIM PRODUCTIONS
22-25 Aug. 19.30 *Church Hill Theatre*
221B Read
Dr. Watson — Nigel Stock
Director — Jack Emery
Designer — Pamela Howard
Lighting — John B. Williams

SHAKESPEARE LADY: The life and times of Fanny Kemble
27-30 Aug. 19.30 *Church Hill Theatre*
Estelle Kohler, Bill Homewood

POETRY AND PROSE RECITALS

26, 29 Aug. 17.30 *Queen's Hall*
ALISTAIR COOKE (rdr)

31 Aug.-3 Sep. 19.30 *Church Hill Theatre*
THESE ARE WOMEN: A portrait of Shakespeare's heroines
Claire Bloom (rdr)

COFFEE AND DREAMS: Life and letters in Austria 1895-1925
30, 31 Aug. 14.45 *St Cecilia's Hall*
LOOKING GLASS GLORY

1, 2 Sep. 14.45 *St Cecilia's Hall*
THE DECADENT MUSE
Hetty Baines, David Rintoul, Stephen MacDonald, Tom Watson, Paul Young (rdr), Belvedere Trio
Compiled by Anthony Vivis

LATE NIGHT ENTERTAINMENT

22 Aug. 22.30 *Music Hall*
RAJASTHANI FOLK MUSICIANS

23-26 Aug. 22.30 *Music Hall*
I COLOMBAIONI
Carlo and Alberto Colombaioni

27 Aug.-3 Sep. 22.30 *Music Hall*
GAMELAN ORCHESTRA AND DANCERS

DANCE

BALLET RAMBERT
29-31 Aug. 19.30 30 Aug. 14.30
King's Theatre
PRIBAOUTKI
Choreographer — Robert North
Music — Stravinsky
Designer — Andrew Storer *after* Picasso
Lighting — John B. Read
CONCERTINO
Choreographer — Christopher Bruce
Music — Janácek
Designer — Walter Nobbe
Lighting — Nick Chelton
MURDERER HOPE OF WOMEN
Kokoschka (Performed as a play. Eng)
Choreographer — Glen Tetley
Music — Schoenberg
Designer — Nadine Baylis
Lighting — John B. Read

1-3 Sep. 19.30 3 Sep. 14.30
King's Theatre
FIELDING SIXES
Choreographer — Merce Cunningham
Music — Cage
Designer and lighting — Mark Lancaster
CHICAGO BRASS
Choreographer and designer — Richard Alston
Music — Hindemith
Lighting — Peter Mumford
COLOUR MOVES (World première)
Choreographer — Robert North
Music — Christopher Benstead
Scenery — Bridget Riley
Costumes — Andrew Storer
Lighting — John B. Read
Dancers Catherine Becque, Lucy Bethune, Lucy Burge, Frances Carty, Hugh Craig, Mary Evelyn, Rebecca Ham, Michael Ho, Ikky Maas, Paul Melis, Bruce Michelson, Cathrine Price, Robert North, Albert van Nierop, Michael Popper, Diane Walker, Quinny Sacks, Elizabeth Wright
Mercury Ensemble
Conductor — Nicholas Carr

HUNGARIAN STATE BALLET
5-10 Sep. 19.30 *Playhouse*
PRÓBA (A rock ballet)
Choreographer — Antal Fodor
Music — Bach, Gábor Presser
Scenery — Róbert Wegenast
Costumes — Judit Schäffer
Dancers Imre Dózsa, Jeno Locsey, Ildikó Pongor, Márta Metzger, Nora Szony, Gábor Kevehází, György Szakály, Imre Eck, Zoltán Nagy, István Balikó, István Urbán, János Krasznai

LECTURES

VIENNA 1900 AND ITS INFLUENCE
23 Aug. 14.45
Art and society in Vienna — Peter Vergo
The Vienna circle — Sir Alfred Ayer
24 Aug. 14.45 *Church Hill Theatre*
Schoenberg the painter — Georg Eisler
Schoenberg the musician — Leonard Stein
25 Aug. 14.45 *Church Hill Theatre*
Literature and theatre in Vienna — Martin Esslin

Hanging garden falling down - Music in Vienna before 1918 Alexander Goehr
26 Aug. 14.45 *Church Hill Theatre*
A discussion on the legacy of Vienna

EXHIBITIONS

National Museum of Antiquities
VIENNA 1900
Devised by Peter Vergo

Fine Art Society
VIENNA 1900 - THE SCOTTISH ROOM

Royal Scottish Museum
MAN AND MUSIC

ASSOCIATED EXHIBITIONS
(Not organized by the Festival Society)

Royal Scottish Academy
MOUTON ROTHSCHILD: Paintings for the labels 1945-1981
(Baroness Philippine de Rothschild)

National Gallery of Scotland
ROBERT SCOTT LAUDER'S MASTER CLASS
McTaggart, Orchardson, Pettie and their Edinburgh contemporaries

Fruitmarket Gallery
SANDRO CHIA
(Organized by the Scottish Arts Council in association with the Stedelijk Museum, Amsterdan)

369 Gallery
SCOTTISH EXPRESSIONISM

City Art Centre
ART OF THE ANDES
(From the Arthur M. Sackler Collections)
HUNDERTWASSER
(Subsidised by the Scottish Arts Council)
SCOTTISH CRAFTS NOW

Richard Demarco Gallery
THE VARESE ENGAGEMENT WITH MODERN ART 1955-75
International Conference
Towards the housing of art in the 21st century

Festival Club
CENTRE STAGE: An exhibition of 20th century materials from the Scottish Theatre Archive

Talbot Rice Art Centre
PAUL-EMILE BORDUAS 1905-1960

Canongate Tolbooth Museum
THE ART OF THE DOLL-MAKER
THE PROUD BASSOON

Royal Botanic Gardens
FROM SUNRISE TO SUNSET: A presentation of Wagner's Ring Cycle
Devised by John L. Paterson

STREET EVENTS

STREET MUSICIANS, MEXICO
RAGASTHANI FOLK MUSICIANS,
STEEL BAND, WEST INDIES
FOLK MUSICIANS, MOROCCO
PRAISE SINGERS, IVORY COAST
PIPERS AND FIDDLERS from 4 countries

1984

OPERA

WASHINGTON OPERA
12, 13, 14, 16 Aug. 19.30 *King's Theatre*
THE TELEPHONE Menotti
Lucy — Sheryl Woods
Ben — Wayne Turnage
THE MEDIUM Menotti
Monica — Nadia Pelle
Madame Flora — Beverly Evans
Mrs Gobineau — Elisabeth Carron
Mr Gobineau — John Fiorito
Mrs Nolan — Judith Weyman
Toby — Francis Menotti
Scottish Chamber Orchestra
Conductor — Cal Stewart-Kellogg
Director — Gian Carlo Menotti
Designer — Zack Brown
Lighting — John McLain

SCOTTISH OPERA
21, 23, 25 Aug. 19.30 *King's Theatre*
ORION Cavalli (Eng)
Diana — Anne Howells
Nymphs — Faith Elliot, Clare Moll
Filotero — Barry Mora
Vulcan — Willard White
Steropes — Alexander Morrison
Bronte — Norman White
Amor — Lillian Watson
Orion — Michael Myers
Venus — Ann Howard
Aurora — Linda Ormiston
Titon — Keith Latham
Apollo — Peter Jeffes
Neptune — Brian Bannatyne-Scott
Eolo — Anne Rodger-Bowen
Jove — Donald Stephenson
Amorettino — Stephen McAuslan
Conductor — Raymond Leppard
Director — Peter Wood
Designer — John Bury
Lighting — Robert Bryan

CHILDRENS' MUSIC THEATRE
25, 27 Aug.-1 Sep. 17.30
St Mary's Cathedral
THE TOWER OF BABEL Nield
Nimrod — Richard Morton
His wife — Gillian Fisher
Nahor — Nicholas Rae
Morden — Robin Blaze
God — Michael George
Soloists from Magdalen College Choir, Oxford, 100 children from Daniel Stewart's and Melville College and the Mary Erskine School
Written and directed by Jeremy James Taylor
Scenery — Christopher Richardson
Costumes — Alix Stone

ORCHESTRAL CONCERTS

PHILHARMONIA ORCHESTRA
12 Aug. 20.00 *Usher Hall*
Beethoven — Symphony no.2 in D, op.36
Rossini — Stabat Mater
Conductor — Riccardo Muti
Soloists Cecilia Gasdia (sop), Ann Murray (mez), Francisco Araiza (ten), James Morris (bs), EF Chorus

14 Aug. 20.00 *Usher Hall*
Ravel — Le tombeau de Couperin
Mussorgsky — Songs and dances of death; orch. Shostakovich
Sibelius Symphony no.1 in E minor, op.39
Conductor — Esa-Pekka Salonen
Soloist — Tom Krause (bar)

15 Aug. 20.00 *Usher Hall*
Brahms — Concerto for piano no.2 in B flat, op.83
Lutoslawski — Symphony no.3
Conductor — Esa-Pekka Salonen
Soloist — Krystian Zimerman (pf)

SCOTTISH NATIONAL ORCHESTRA
13 Aug. 20.00 *Usher Hall*
Glazunov — Overture solennelle, op.73
Khachaturian — Concerto for violin in D minor
Prokofiev — Symphony no.6 in E flat minor, op.111
Conductor — Neeme Järvi
Soloist — Salvatore Accardo (vn)

21 Aug. 20.00 *Usher Hall*
Parry — Blest pair of sirens
Britten — Les illuminations
V. Williams — Symphony no.1 (A sea symphony)
Conductor — Neeme Järvi
Soloists Felicity Lott (sop), Stephen Roberts (bar), EF Chorus

24 Aug. 20.00 *Usher Hall*
Josephs — The heaving bagpipe
L. Mozart — Concerto for hosepipe
Swann — Andante from Haydn's Surprise symphony
Jaja/Searle — Punkt Kontrapunkt
Josephs — Concerto d'amore
Beethoven/Strasser — Leonore overture no.4
Butterworth — Orchestral switch
Thomas — Composers' party
Reizenstein — Concerto popolare
Conductor — Toshiyuki Shimada
Soloists Michael Massey (pf), Clare McFarlane, Jagdish Mistry (vn) with Barry Tuckwell, Sir Charles Mackerras, Frank Dunlop, John Wallace and others

1 Sep. 20.00 *Usher Hall*
Delius — A mass of life (Ger)
Conductor — Sir Charles Mackerras
Soloists Heather Harper (sop), Sarah Walker (mez), Philip Langridge (ten), Jonathan Summers (bar), EF Chorus

SCOTTISH CHAMBER ORCHESTRA
13 Aug. 11.00 *Queen's Hall*
Haydn — Symphony no.6 in D (Le matin)
Henze — Aria de la folia espagñola
J.V. Cotton — Abendland
Haydn — Sinfonia concertante in B flat, op.84
Conductor — Hans Werner Henze
Soloist — Linda Hirst (mez)

20 Aug. 20.00 *Usher Hall*
Mozart — La clemenza di Tito: Overture
Britten — Symphony for cello and orchestra, op.68
Mozart — Venite populi
Mozart — Sancta Maria
Mozart — Ave verum corpus
Mozart — Veni sancte spiritus
Britten — Nocturne, op.60
Conductor — Roderick Brydon
Soloists Maldwyn Davies (ten), Raphael Wallfisch (vc), Scottish Philharmonic Singers

23 Aug. 22.45 *Ross Bandstand*
Fireworks Concert
Dvořák — Carnival - Overture
Berlioz — La damnation de Faust: Rákóczy march

Handel Music for the royal fireworks
Conductor Christopher Seaman

MOSCOW VIRTUOSI
16 Aug. 20.00 *Queen's Hall*
Vivaldi Concerti, op.6: no.5 in E minor
Vivaldi Concerti, op.3 (L'estro armonico): No.12 in E
Vivaldi Concerti, op.4 (La stravaganza): No.5 in A
Tchaikovsky Serenade for strings, op.48
Soloist Vladimir Spivakov (vn)

18 Aug. 11.00 *Queen's Hall*
Mozart Divertimento (Salzburg symphony) no.1 in D, K136
Shostakovich Concerto for piano, trumpet and strings, op.35
Respighi Il tramonto
Rossini Tarantella
Rossini Sonata for strings no.3 in C
Soloists Makvala Kasrashvili (sop), Vladimir Spivakov (vn), Vladimir Krainov (pf)

ROYAL PHILHARMONIC ORCHESTRA
17 Aug. 20.00 *Usher Hall*
Bartók Rumanian folk dances
Bartók The wooden prince - Suite
Bartók Duke Bluebeard's castle
Conductor Walter Weller
Soloists Julia Varady (sop), Dietrich Fischer-Dieskau (bar)

18 Aug. 20.00 *Usher Hall*
Tchaikovsky Symphony no.1 in G minor (Winter daydreams), op.13
Prokofiev Alexander Nevsky
Conductor Yuri Temirkanov
Soloist Irina Arkhipova (mez)
EF Chorus

BBC SYMPHONY ORCHESTRA
22 Aug. 20.00 *Usher Hall*
Bartók The miraculous mandarin
Berg Five orchestral Lieder on texts by Altenberg
Boulez Notations 1-4
Debussy Trois ballades de François Villon
Berg Three orchestral pieces, op.6
Conductor Pierre Boulez
Soloist Jessye Norman (sop)

23 Aug. 20.00 *Usher Hall*
Liszt Concerto for piano no.2 in A
Bruckner Symphony no.5 in B flat
Conductor Sir John Pritchard
Soloist Lazar Berman (pf)

AUSTRALIAN YOUTH ORCHESTRA
25 Aug. 20.00 *Usher Hall*
Smetana The bartered bride: Overture
Sculthorpe Sun music II (Ketjak)
R. Strauss Concerto for horn no.2 in E flat
Holst The planets
Conductor Sir Charles Mackerras
Soloist Barry Tuckwell (hn)
EF Chorus

BOSTON SYMPHONY ORCHESTRA
Conductor Seiji Ozawa
26 Aug. 20.00 *Usher Hall*
Dvořák Concerto for cello in B minor, op.104
Shostakovich Symphony no.10 in E minor, op.93
Soloist Yo-Yo Ma (vc)

27 Aug. 20.00 *Usher Hall*
Brahms Serenade no.1 in D, op.11
Dvořák Symphony no.9 in E minor (New World), op.95

LONDON SYMPHONY ORCHESTRA
28 Aug. 20.00 *Usher Hall*
Mozart Die Zauberflöte: Overture
Mozart Symphony no.41 in C (Jupiter), K551
Mozart Mass no.16 in C (Coronation), K317
Conductor Sir John Pritchard
Soloists Edith Mathis (sop), Carolyn Watkinson (mez), Philip Langridge (ten), John Shirley-Quirk (bar), EF Chorus

29 Aug. 20.00 *Usher Hall*
Smetana Richard III
Dvořák Symphony no.8 in G, op.88
Janáček Sinfonietta
Conductor Zdenek Macal

ENGLISH CHAMBER ORCHESTRA
29 Aug. 11.00 *Queen's Hall*
Mozart Symphony no.33 in B flat, K319
Mozart Concerto for piano no.17 in G, K453
Mozart Concerto for piano no.27 in B flat, K595
Conductor and soloist Murray Perahia (pf)

30 Aug. 20.00 *Queen's Hall*
Ravel Ma mère l'oye
Mozart Concerto for piano no.21 in C, K467
Bizet Symphony in C
Conductor Jeffrey Tate
Soloist Murray Perahia (pf)

CHAMBER CONCERTS

SMITHSONIAN CHAMBER PLAYERS
13 Aug. 15.00 *St Cecilia's Hall*
Handel Trio sonata for oboe, violin and continuo in B flat
Handel Sonata for violin and continuo in G minor
Handel Suite for harpsichord no.5 in E*
Handel Trio sonata for 2 violins and continuo in G minor (Dresden)
Marais Pièces de viole, Livre 4: Le labyrinthe
L. Couperin Les nations: L'impériale

14, 15, 17 Aug. 12.00
Royal Scottish Museum
Handel Trio sonata for oboe, violin and continuo in B flat
Handel Trio sonata for 2 violins and continuo in G minor (Dresden)
L. Couperin Les nations: L'impériale

14 Aug. 15.00 *St Cecilia's Hall*
Castello Sonata in A minor
Frescobaldi Canzona prima per basso solo
Rossi Sonata in dialogo detta la viena
Rossi Sonata sopra porto celato il mio nobil pensiero
Froberger Lamentation sur la mort sa Majesté Impériale, Ferdinand III
Buxtehude Sonata for 2 violins, viola da gamba and continuo in C
Handel Trio sonata for oboe, violin and continuo in D minor
Handel Sonata for violin and continuo in D
Handel Trio sonata for 2 violins and continuo in E

15 Aug. 15.00 *St Cecilia's Hall*
Rameau Pièces de clavecin en concerts: V. concert
F. Couperin Les goûts-réünis: X. Concert
F. Couperin Le parnasse, ou L'apothéose de Corelli

Bach Suite for cello no.1 in G
Bach Trio sonata no.2 in C (Goldberg)

BRODSKY QUARTET*
14 Aug. 11.00 *Queen's Hall*
Haydn Quartet in F minor (Razor), op.55/2*
Janáček Quartet no.1 (The Kreutzer sonata)*
Schubert Quintet in C, D956
with Alexander Baillie (vc)

16 Aug. 11.00 *Queen's Hall*
Haydn Quartet in B flat (Sunrise), op.76/4*
Britten Quartet no.3, op.94*
Mendelssohn Quartet no.2 in A minor, op.13 *

ENSEMBLE OF THE 20TH CENTURY
Director Peter Burwick
21 Aug. 11.00 *Queen's Hall*
Wagner Siegfried idyll
Webern Six pieces, op.6; arr. chamber orchestra
Dallapiccola Due lyriche anacreonte
Dallapiccola Sex carmina alcaei
Hauer Quintet, op.26
Schreker Chamber symphony
with Jill Gomez (sop)

23 Aug. 11.00 *Queen's Hall*
Eisler Septet no.2
Auric Marleborough s'en va-t-en guerre
Milhaud Actualitiés
Stravinsky Concerto in E flat (Dumbarton Oaks)
Saint-Saëns Le carnaval des animaux

SALOMON QUARTET
22 Aug. 11.00 *Queen's Hall*
Pleyel Quartet in G, op.9/10
Haydn Quartet in C, op.74/1
Mozart Quartet no.15 in D minor, K421

LONDON BRASS VIRTUOSI
24 Aug. 11.00 *Queen's Hall*
Holst A Moorside suite
V. Williams Henry V: Overture
Walton Spitfire prelude and fugue; arr. Crees
R. Strauss Festmusik der Stadt Wien
Britten Russian funeral
Grieg Funeral march
Elgar A Severn suite
Director David Honeyball

KOENIG ENSEMBLE
Director Jan Latham-Koenig
30 Aug. 11.00 *Queen's Hall*
Falla Concerto for harpsichord
Lambert Concerto for piano
Bennett Commedia 1
Poulenc Le bal masqué
Soloists David Wilson-Johnson (bar), Richard Rodney Bennett (pf)

1 Sep. 11.00 *Queen's Hall*
Debussy Danse sacrée et danse profane
Bawden Three dances (World première)
Harvey Gong-ring (EIF commission)
Nicholls Ensemble 5 (Seascape 1) (World première)
Messiaen Trois petites luturgies de la présence divine
Soloists Jeanne Loriod (ondes martenot), Paul Crossley (pf), New London Chamber Choir

BORODIN TRIO
31 Aug. 11.00 *Queen's Hall*
Beethoven Trio for piano and strings no.6 in E flat, op.70/2
Rachmaninov Trio élégiaque for piano

and strings in G minor
Shostakovich Trio for piano and strings no.2 in E minor, op.67

MUSICA ANTIQUA COLOGNE
31 Aug. 19.45 *Hopetoun House*
Vivaldi Concerto in G, R102
Vivaldi Sonata in D minor (La follia), R63
Bach Musikalisches Opfer

JOHN WILLIAMS AND FRIENDS
31 Aug. 20.00 *Usher Hall*
Handel Concerto for organ no.5, op.4/5; arr. for guitar
Vivaldi Concerto for sopranino recorder in C; arr.Harvey
B. Gascoigne Stream 2
Bach Partita for violin no.2 in D minor: Chaconne; arr. for guitar
The guitar is the song: a selection of folk songs
Gerald Garcia, Claudia Figueroa (gtr), Chris Laurence (db), Gary Kettel (perc), Richard Harvey (fl, etc), Brian Gulland (bn, etc), Mauricio Venegas (charango, quena, pan pipes), Richard Studt, Hisako Tokue (vn), Stephen Tees (va), John Heley (vc)

ROYAL THAI CLASSICAL MUSICIANS
20 Aug. 11.00 *Queen's Hall*
Introduced by Donald Mitchell

RECITALS

IRINA ARKHIPOVA (mez)
CRAIG SHEPPARD (pf)
17 Aug. 11.00 *Queen's Hall*
Mussorgsky Songs and dances of death
Songs by Glinka, Mussorgsky, Tchaikovsky, Rachmaninov

DIETRICH FISCHER-DIESKAU (bar)
HARTMUT HÖLL (pf)
19 Aug. 20.00 *Usher Hall*
Songs by Brahms

KRYSTIAN ZIMERMAN (pf)
19 Aug. 15.00 *Queen's Hall*
Bach Partita no.1 in B flat
Beethoven Sonata no.21 in C (Waldstein), op.53
Liszt Lugubre gondola
Liszt Funérailles: La notte
Liszt Nuages gris
Chopin Sonata no.2 in B flat minor (Funeral march), op.35

SALVATORE ACCARDO (vn)
MARIA TIPO (pf)
15 Aug. 11.00 *Queen's Hall*
Mozart Sonata no.32 in B flat, K454
Beethoven Sonata no.5 in F (Spring), op.24
Schubert Fantasia in C, D934

YO-YO MA (vc)
25 Aug. 11.00 *Queen's Hall*
Bach Suites nos.1, 3, 5

28 Aug. 11.00 *Queen's Hall*
Bach Suites nos.2, 4, 6

HEINZ HOLLIGER (ob)
27 Aug. 11.00 *Queen's Hall*
Telemann Der harmonische Gottendienst: 2 cantatas
Telemann Fantasias for flute; arr. for oboe
Bach Cantata no.187: Aria
Bach Cantata no.98: Aria
Bach Cantata no.202: Aria
Denisov Trio for oboe, cello and harpsichord
Holliger Trema for cello
Holliger Schwarzgewobene Trauer
with Phyllis Bryn-Julson (sop), Thomas Demenga (vc), John Constable (hpd)

EDUARDO FERNÁNDEZ (gtr)
26 Aug. 15.00 *Queen's Hall*
Naravaez Fantasias nos.3, 5, 8
Bach Prelude, fugue and allegro
Sor Sonata, op.22
Villa-Lobos 12 Études

JAZZ AND FOLK

CLEO LAINE
JOHN DANKWORTH QUINTET
16 Aug. 19.30 18 Aug. 14.30
Shakespeare and all that jazz

SWEET HONEY IN THE ROCK
17,18, 21, 22 Aug. 12.00 19 Aug. 14.30
Royal Scottish Museum
20 Aug. 22.30 *Queen's Hall*

MODERN JAZZ QUARTET
17 Aug. 20.00
17,18 Aug. 22.30 18 Aug. 20.00
19, 21 Aug. 22.30 20 Aug. 20.00
19 Aug. 20.00
21 Aug. 20.00 *Queen's Hall*
with Tommy Flanagan, Barry Harris

BEAUSOLEIL (Cajun Dance Band)
22, 24 Aug. 20.00 *Queen's Hall*
23-25 Aug. 12.00 26 Aug. 14.30
Royal Scottish Museum
with Lawrence Eller, Cas Wallin, Mike Seeger

DRAMA

SCOTTISH THEATRE COMPANY
12 Aug.-1 Sep. 19.30 (exc.14, 19, 26)
15, 18, 22, 25, 29 Aug. 1 Sep. 14.30
Assembly Hall
THE THRIE ESTAITES Lyndsay
(Adapted by Robert Kemp)
Diligence Tom Watson
King David Rintoul
Wantonness Paul Young
Placebo John Buick
Solace Tony Roper
Sensualitie Caroline Kaart
Hameliness Gerda Stevenson
Danger Fiona Kennedy
Fund-Jennet Halcro Johnston
Gude Counsel Alex McAvoy
Flatterie/Pardoner Walter Carr
Falsehood Gregor Fisher
Deceit John Grieve
Veritie Anne Kristen
Chastitie Edith Macarthur
Spiritualitie Roy Hanlon
Prioress Juliet Cadzow
Abbot Andrew Cruickshank
Parson Alexander West
Temporalitie John Shedden
Merchant Brown Derby
Soutar Ian Stewart
Soutar's wife Tricia Scott
Tailor Robert Trotter
Tailor's wife Kay Gallie
Correction's varlet Colin Gourley
Divine Correction Robert Urquhart
Poor man Phil McCall
Wilkin Widdiefow Ian Briggs
John the Common-Weal Alec Heggie
Sergeant Bill Riddoch
Scribe John Cobb
Swordbearer David Monteath
Boy Ranald Neilson
Director Tom Fleming
Designer Nadine Baylis
Lighting André Tammes
Music Cedric Thorpe Davie

THEATRE DE L'OEUVRE
14, 15, 17, 18 Aug. 19.30 Lyceum Theatre
SARAH ET LE CRI DE LA LANGOUSTE Murrell
Sarah Bernhardt Delphine Seyrig
Georges Pitou Georges Wilson
Director Georges Wilson
Scenery Koki Fregni
Costumes Fanny Verjnes

BLACK LIGHT THEATRE, Prague
20, 22, 25 Aug. 19.30 22, 25 Aug. 14.30
Lyceum Theatre
A WEEK OF DREAMS Srnec
Taxi driver/Bottom Ales Koudelka
Passenger/Puck Bohumil Dufek
Girl/Lady passenger Monika Vagnerová
Man Pavel Toman
Wife Jirina Korcacová
Woman Jana Kuracová
Titania Eva Ciharová
Director Jiri Srnec

21, 23, 24 Aug. 19.30 *Lyceum Theatre*
THE DOORS Srnec
Pierrot Pavel Toman
Harlequin Bohumil Dufek
Columbine Eva Ciharová
Director Jiri Srnec

NEGRO ENSEMBLE COMPANY, USA
27 Aug.-1 Sep. 19.30 1 Sep. 14.30
Lyceum Theatre
A SOLDIER'S PLAY Fuller
Captain Davenport Geoffrey Ewing
Sergeant Waters Douglas Turner Ward
Private Memphis Larry Riley
Director Douglas Turner Ward
Costumes Judy Dearing
Lighting Allen Hughes

15, 17, 18 Aug. 19.30 18 Aug. 14.30
King's Theatre
TWICE AROUND THE PARK Schisgal
Act 1 - A need for brussels sprouts
Leon Rose Eli Wallach
Margaret Heinz Anne Jackson
Act 2 - A need for less expertise
Edie Frazier Anne Jackson
Gus Frazier Eli Wallach
Director Arthur Storch
Designer James Tilton
(By arrangement with Peter Witt)

BERLINER ENSEMBLE
27, 28 Aug. 19.00 *King's Theatre*
GALILEO GALILEI Brecht
Galileo Galilei Ekkehard Schall
Minstrel Jaecki Schwarz
His wife Carmen-Maja Antoni
Andrea Sarti (Boy) Robert Erk
Mrs Sarti Renate Richter
Ludovico Marsili Michael Gerber
Curator Priuli Erhard Köster
Sagredo Dieter Knaup
Virginia Simone Frost
Federzoni Stefan Lisewski
Doge Peter Bause
General Georg Schweiger
Cosmo de Medici ?
Marshal Karl M. Steffens
Philosopher Victor Deiss
Mathematician Peter Tepper
Older lady of the court Doris Thalmer
Younger lady of the court Angelika Ritter
Astronomer/Official Siegfried Meyer
Fanatical monk Hans-Joachim Frank
Old cardinal Peter Kalisch

Attendant Lothar Runkel
Christopher Clavius/Rector Franz Viehmann
Little monk Hans-Peter Reinecke
Cardinal inquisitor Arno Wyzniewski
Woman Corinna Harfouch
Pope Urban VIII Günter Naumann
Cardinal Bellarmin Peter Hladik
Andrea Sarti Martin Seifert
Filippo Mucius Wolfgang Holz
Rector Gaffone Franz Viehmann
Potter Hermann Beyer
Directors Manfred Wekwerth, JoachimTenschert
Scenery Hans Ulrich Schmückle
Costumes Sylta Busse
Musical director Hans Dieter Hosalla

31 Aug. 1 Sep. 19.00 King's Theatre
SCENES FROM FAUST (URFAUST) Goethe
Prometheus/Lucifer/Erdgeist Stefan Lisewski
Satyros Heinrich Schramm
Mephistopheles Arno Wyzniewski
Faust Hermann Beyer
Wagner/Brander Peter Kalisch
Student/Valentin/Centaur Peter Bause
Frosch Wolfgang Holz
Siebel Wolfgang Arnst
Alten Peter Tepper
Margarete/Pandora Corinna Harfouch
Marthe Christine Gloger
Lieschen Angelika Ritter
Maria Petra Dobbertin
Mother Doris Thalmer
Priest Horst Wünsch
Director and designer Horst Sagert
Costumes Eduard Fischer

29 Aug. 20.00 King's Theatre
BRECHT'S SONGS AND POEMS to music by Weill, Eisler, Hosalla, Dessau, Matthus, Brecht
Carmen-Maja Antoni, Christine Gloger, Corinna Harfouch, Renate Richter, Ekkehard Schall, Hans-Peter Reinecke, Martin Seifert, Peter Tepper
Orchestra of the Berliner Ensemble
Conductor Hans Dieter Hosalla

HAROLD CLURMAN THEATRE, New York
13-15, 17-19, 23, 25 Aug. 20.30 14, 20, 22, 24 Aug. 17.00 18, 21, 23 Aug. 14.00
Church Hill Theatre
OHIO IMPROMPTU Beckett
Reader David Warrilow
Listener Rand Mitchell
CATASTROPHE Beckett
Director Donald Davis
Assistant Leigh Taylor-Young
Luke Rand Mitchell
Protagonist David Warrilow
WHAT WHERE Beckett
Bam Donald Davis
Bom David Warrilow
Bim Rand Mitchell
Bem Daniel Wirth
Director Alan Schneider
Scenery and lighting Marc D.Malamud
Costumes Carla Kramer

20 Aug. 20.30 19, 21 Aug. 17.00 22, 25 Aug. 14.00 Church Hill Theatre
A PIECE OF MONOLOGUE Beckett
David Warrilow
Directors David Warrilow, Rocky Greenberg
THAT TIME Beckett
Donald Davis
Director Alan Schneider
Scenery and lighting Rocky Greenberg

16, 21, 22, 24 Aug. 20.30 17, 18, 23, 25 Aug. 17.00 20, 24 Aug. 14.00
Church Hill Theatre
FROM ITS BEGINNING TO ITS END
A programme from the works of Beckett
Angela Pleasance, Sylvester McCoy, Leonard Fenton (rdr)
Compiled by John Calder

21-23 Aug.18.15 Church Hill Little Theatre
MALONE DIES Beckett
Excerpts read by Max Wall
Directed and compiled by John Elsom

14-24 Aug. 11.00
Church Hill Little Theatre
SAMUAL BECKETT
Talks, discussions, films, television programmes.
John Calder, Michael Billington, Ruby Cohn, Hersh Zeifman, Martin Esslin, Jack Garfein, Delphine Seyrig, John Elsom
Organized by James Knowlson

16-18 Aug. 15.00 18 Aug. 20.00
St Cecilia's Hall
COLERIDGE AND 'THE ANCIENT MARINER'
A programme from the letters and poems of Coleridge to mark the 150th anniversary of his death
Marius Goring (rdr)
Devised by John Carroll

DANCE

KOMISCHE OPER BALLET, Berlin
23-25 Aug. 19.30 25 Aug. 14.30
Playhouse
SWAN LAKE
Choreographer Tom Schilling
Music Tchaikovsky
Scenery Jochen Finke
Costumes Eleonore Kleiber
Dancers Jutta Deutschland, Angela Reinhardt, Hannelore Bey, Dieter Hülse, Thomas Kindt, Monika Lubitz, Petja Gentschewa, Jürgen Hohmann, Olaf Kaminski, Sigrid Kressmann-Brück, Mike Knospe, Werner Mente, Helga Schiele, Mario Perricone, Camilla Markwart, Jörg Simon, Britt Folk, Uta Opitz, Rose-Marie Dresel-Starke, Katrin Dix
Edinburgh Festival Theatre Orchestra
Conductor Joachim Willert

PARIS OPÉRA BALLET
29 Aug.-1 Sep. 19.30 1 Sep. 14.30
Playhouse
HARLEQUIN, MAGICIAN OF LOVE
Choreographer Ivo Cramer
Music Edouard du Pay; arr. Farncombe
Costumes Claudie Gastine
CARNAVAL
Choreographers Fokine, Nicholas Beriozoff
Music Schumann
Designer *after* Bakst
LE BOURGEOIS GENTILHOMME
Choreographer George Balanchine
Music R. Strauss
Costumes Bernard Daydé
Dancers Rudolf Nureyev, Patrick Dupond, Claude de Vulpian, Patrice Bart, Monique Loudières, Yannick Stephant, Fabienne Cerutti, Stéphane Prince, Georges Piletta, Jacques Namont, Danièle Doussard, Christine Landault, Vivianne Descoutures, Martine Vuillermoz, Véronique Arnichand, Véronique Vialar, Catherine Goffinon, Laurence Debia, Wladimir Huot, Jean-Pierre Franchetti, Pierre Darde, Félix Vivian, Thierry Mongne, Alain Bogréau, Alain Marty, Roland Juillet, Philippe Gerbert, Bertrand Berena, Guy Léonard, Gérand Lignon, Francis Malovik, Maurice Ranchet, Michel Berges, Lucien Gonzalez, Jocelyn Bosser
Edinburgh Festival Theatre Orchestra
Conductor Charles Farncombe

ROYAL THAI CLASSICAL DANCERS AND MUSICIANS
22, 24 Aug. 19.30 24 Aug. 14.30
King's Theatre

ARIFUKU KAGURA TROUPE, Japan
28, 29 Aug. 21.00
East Princes Street Gardens
29 Aug. 12.30 Ross Bandstand
Japanese traditional masked dance
Director Junichi Yoshinaga
Lighting Tateo Ozawa

EXHIBITIONS

Royal Scottish Museum
TREASURES FROM THE SMITHSONIAN INSTITUTION

Royal Scottish Academy
EDUARDO PAOLOZZI

ASSOCIATED EXHIBITIONS
(Not organized by the Festival Society)

Royal Scottish Academy
ANDREA PALLADIO

Old College, Edinburgh University
RARITIES OF CHINESE PAINTING
(From the Arthur M. Sackler collections)

City Art Centre
THE SCULPTURE OF HENRY MATISSE

THE INDISPENSABLE FAN

SCOTTISH ART

National Gallery of Scotland
DUTCH CHURCH PAINTERS

Scottish National Gallery of Modern Art
CREATION: MODERN ART AND NATURE

National Museum of Antiquities
AT HOME

Fruitmarket Gallery
JEAN MICHEL BASQUIAT: Paintings 1981-84

JOHN CAGE: Prints, drawings and books

French Institute
MAQUETTE TO MONUMENTAL: Sculpture from Rodin to our day

Printmaker's Workshop
HENRY MOORE, RECENT GRAPHICS

Fine Art Society
SIR JOHN LAVERY RA 1856-1941

Queen's Hall
A CLUTCH OF CARTOONISTS

Edinburgh College of Art
DEMARCATION '84: A programme of exhibitions, performances and a conference presented by the Richard Demarco Gallery

ANZART: Australian and New Zealand artists in Edinburgh

BOUGÉ: New French photography
Fourteen exhibitions of work by Scottish and international artists

3-14 Aug. Conference
Art and human environment

KITE FLYING

13-18 Aug.
DA AND THE KITE EXPERIENCE
Kite workshops with Da Bei Feng

1985

OPERA

OPÉRA DE LYON
12, 15, 16 Aug. 19.30 *King's Theatre*
L'ÉTOILE Chabrier
King Ouf I Georges Gautier
Sirocco Jules Bastin
Hérisson de Porc Epic Pierre-Yves le Maigat
Tapioca Antoine David
Lazuli Colette Alliot-Lugaz
Princess Laoula Ghyslaine Raphanel
Aloès Magali Damonte
Patacha Michel Fockenoy
Zalzal René Schirrer
Oasis Catherine Dubosc
Asphodele Gillian Howard
Youca Isabelle Eschenbrenner
Adza Veronique Azoulay
Sinnia Brigitte Denoues
Koukouli Valerie Marestin
Conductors John Eliot Gardiner, Claire Gibault
Directors Louis Erlo, Alain Maratrat
Designer Jacques Rapp

14, 17 Aug. 19.30 *King's Theatre*
PELLÉAS ET MÉLISANDE Debussy
Pelléas François le Roux
Mélisande Diane Montague
Golaud José van Dam
Arkel Pierre Thau
Geneviève Jocelyne Taillon
Yniold Françoise Golfier
Shepherd Franck Morazzani
Doctor René Schirrer
Conductor John Eliot Gardiner
Director and designer Pierre Strosser
Costumes Patrice Cauchetier

LES ARTS FLORISSANTS
18, 19 Aug. 19.30 *Lyceum Theatre*
ACTÉON Charpentier
Actéon Dominique Visse
Diana Agnès Mellon
Juno Marie-Claude Vallin
Arthebusia Jill Feldman
Hyale Arlette Steyer
Daphne Françoise Semellaz
ANACRÉON Rameau
Anacréon Philippe Cantor
Love Agnès Mellon
Priestess Jill Feldman
Agathocles Dominique Visse
Guest Michel Laplénie
Ris et Danceries
Conductor William Christie
Director Pierre Barrat
Scenery Claude Lemaire
Costumes Patrice Cauchetier
Lighting Philippe Arlaud
Choreographer Françoise Raffinot

CONNECTICUT GRAND OPERA
23, 24, 26, 28 Aug. 19.30 *Leith Theatre*
THE CONSUL Menotti
Magda Susan Hinshaw
John Louis Otey
Mother Beverly Evans
Police agent Ronald Hedlund
Secretary Kate Butler
Mr Kofnir Gregory Stapp
Foreign woman Bibiana Goldenthal
Anna Gomez Diane Ragains
Vera Boronel Susan Bloss
Magician Jon David Gruett
Assan Philip Cokorinos
Scottish Chamber Orchestra
Conductor Lawrence Gilgore
Director Gian Carlo Menotti
Designer Julia Trevelyan Oman

27-29 Aug. 19.30 *Playhouse*
ZARZUELA
Created and directed by Jose Tamayo
Pedro Lavirgen, Josefina Arregua, Carmen Gonzalez, Antonio Ramallo, Francisco Mudarra, Isabel Rodriguez, Emelina Lopez, Mary Carmen Ramirez, Isidoro Gavani, Jesus Castejón (sngr), Maria del Sol, Mario Lavega (dan)
Ballet Espanol Antologia
Rendalla Lirica, Madrid
Orquesta Camara Lirica, Madrid
Conductor Manuel Moreno-Buendia

ORCHESTRAL CONCERTS

ORCHESTRE NATIONAL DE FRANCE
11 Aug. 20.00 *Usher Hall*
Britten *arr.* National anthem
Lisle *arr.* Berlioz Le Marseillaise
Debussy Marche écossaise
Debussy La mer
Ravel Daphnis et Chloë
Conductor Charles Dutoit
EF Chorus

12 Aug. 20.00 *Usher Hall*
Duparc Lénore
Berlioz La mort de Cléopâtre
Schmitt La tragédie de Salomé
Conductor Thomas Fulton
Soloist Alexandrina Milcheva (mez)

13 Aug. 20.00 *Usher Hall*
Dukas La péri
Ravel Concerto for piano (Left hand)+
Ravel Concerto for piano in G
Roussel Bacchus et Ariane - Suite no.2
Conductor Thomas Fulton
Soloists Martha Argerich, Michel Béroff+ (pf)

USSR NEW SYMPHONY ORCHESTRA
Conductor Gennadi Rozhdestvensky
14 Aug. 20.00 *Usher Hall*
Saint-Saëns Symphony no.2 in A minor, op.55
Rachmaninov Concerto for piano no.4 in G minor, op.40
Glazunov Symphony no.4 in E flat, op.48
Soloist Victoria Postnikova (pf)

15 Aug. 20.00 *Usher Hall*
Prokofiev Le pas d'acier
Schnittke Concerto for violin no.4
Ravel La valse
Soloists Oleg Krysa (vn), Victoria Postnikova (pf)

SCOTTISH CHAMBER ORCHESTRA
12 Aug. 11.00 *Queen's Hall*
Bach Concerto for violin in A minor
Bach Brandenburg concerto no.6 in B flat
Bach Brandenburg concerto no.3 in G
Bach Cantata no.82
Conductor and soloist Sir Yehudi Menuhin (vn)
Soloist Nicolas Rivenq (bar)

16 Aug. 20.00 *Usher Hall*
Bach Brandenburg Concerto no.2 in F
Bach Concerto for violin in E
Bach Suite for solo cello no.3 in C+
Bach Concerto for 2 violins in D minor
Director and soloist John Tunnell (vn)
Soloists Sir Yehudi Menuhin (vn), William Conway (vc)
with Rudolf Nureyev (dan)+
Choreographer Francine Lancelot

19 Aug. 11.00 *Queen's Hall*
Bach Brandenburg concerto no.4 in G
Goehr A musical offering (J.S.B.) (EIF commission)
Handel Concerto grosso in D, op.6/5
Goehr Sinfonia, op.42
Conductor Oliver Knussen

22 Aug. 22.30 *Ross Bandstand*
Fireworks Concert
J. Strauss Unter Donner und Blitz
Beethoven Wellingtons Sieg
Handel Music for the royal fireworks
Conductor Ronald Zollman

ST MARY'S MUSIC SCHOOL ORCHESTRA
15 Aug. 15.00 *Queen's Hall*
Holst St Paul's suite
Walton Henry V: 2 pieces
G. King Little symphony
Satie Chapitres tournés en tous sens for piano
Satie Croquis et agaceries d'un gros bonhomme en bois for piano
Saint-Saëns Le carnaval des animaux
Conductors Sir Yehudi Menuhin, Nigel Murray, Geoffrey King
Soloist James Clapperton (pf)

SCOTTISH NATIONAL ORCHESTRA
17 Aug. 20.00 *Usher Hall*
Mahler Symphony no.8 in E flat
Conductor Neeme Järvi
Soloists Jill Gomez, Suzanne Murphy, Rosa Mannion (sop), Anne Collins, Alfreda Hodgson (cont), John Mitchinson (ten), Thomas Hampson (bar), Stafford Dean (bs), EF Chorus, SNO Junior Chorus

NATIONAL YOUTH BRASS BAND OF SCOTLAND
18 Aug. 15.00 *Usher Hall*
Thorpe Davie Variations on a theme of Lully
Ravel Trois chansons
Elgar A Severn suite; arr. Brand
Wilson Sinfonietta
Fauré Messe basse
P.M. Davies The peat cutters (World première)
Conductors Geoffrey Brand, Jean Kidd
SNO Junior Chorus

OPÉRA DE LYON ORCHESTRA
Conductor John Eliot Gardiner
19 Aug. 20.00 *Usher Hall*
Mozart Der Schauspieldirektor: Overture
Mozart Vado, ma dove?
Mozart Il rè pastore: L'amerò sarò costante
Mozart Così fan tutte: Per pieta
Mozart Concerto for piano no.23 in A, K488
Mozart Symphony no.38 in D (Prague), K504
Soloists Pamela Coburn (sop), Imogen Cooper (pf)

20 Aug. 20.00 *Usher Hall*
Schumann Das Paradies und die Peri
Soloists Pamela Coburn, Catherine Dubosc (sop), Brenda Boozer (mez), Patrick Power, Neil Rosenshein, Neil Jenkins (ten), Thomas Hampson (bar), EF Chorus

PITTSBURGH SYMPHONY ORCHESTRA
Conductor Lorin Maazel
21 Aug. 20.00 *Usher Hall*
Bartók Concerto for orchestra
Berlioz Symphonie fantastique

22 Aug. 20.00 *Usher Hall*
Mendelssohn A midsummer night's dream: Overture
Stravinsky Symphony in 3 movements
Franck Symphony in D

POLISH CHAMBER ORCHESTRA
Conductor Jerzy Maksymiuk
24 Aug. 11.00 *Queen's Hall*
Britten Simple symphony
Mozart Concerto for piano no.9 in E flat, K271
Lutoslawski Funeral music
Bartók Music for strings, percussion and celesta
Soloist Christian Zacharias (pf)

25 Aug. 20.00 *Usher Hall*
Mozart Eine kleine Nachtmusik
Mozart Concerto for violin no.3 in G, K216
V. Williams Fantasia on a theme by Tallis
Schubert Symphony no.5 in B flat, D485
Soloist Dmitry Sitkovetsky (vn)

LONDON PHILHARMONIC ORCHESTRA
26 Aug. 20.00 *Usher Hall*
Beethoven Symphony no.8 in F, op.93
Schubert Symphony no.9 in C (Great), D944
Conductor Christoph Eschenbach

27 Aug. 20.00 *Usher Hall*
Mozart Symphony no.36 in C (Linz), K425
Mahler Des Knaben Wunderhorn
Conductor Walter Weller
Soloists Lucia Popp (sop), Walton Groenroos (bar)*

PHILHARMONIA ORCHESTRA
Conductor Giuseppe Sinopoli
28 Aug. 20.00 *Usher Hall*
Schubert Symphony no.8 in B minor (Unfinished), D759
Mahler Symphony no.5 in C sharp minor

29 Aug. 20.00 *Usher Hall*
Mahler Symphony no.2 in C minor (Resurrection)
Soloists Lucia Popp (sop), Carolyn Watkinson (mez), EF Chorus

ORCHESTRE DE PARIS
Conductor Daniel Barenboim
30 Aug. 20.00 *Usher Hall*
Beethoven Symphony no.6 in F (Pastoral), op.68
Ravel Rapsodie espagnole
Ravel Boléro

31 Aug. 20.00 *Usher Hall*
Debussy Prélude à l'après-midi d'un faune
Boulez Rituel in memoriam Bruno Maderna
Stravinsky The rite of spring

CHAMBER CONCERTS

SCOTTISH EARLY MUSIC CONSORT
Director Warwick Edwards
15 Aug. 11.00 *Queen's Hall*
The songbook of Louis de France

22 Aug. 11.00 *Queen's Hall*
Mary's music: songs and dances from the time of Mary, Queen of Scots
Soloists Lorna Anderson (sop), Christine Cairns (mez), Paul Hindmarsh (ten), Brian Bannatyne-Scott (bs), John Kitchen (hpd) with Walter Carr as Louis de France
Staged by Frank Dunlop and Ugo Tessitore

VIA NOVA QUARTET
17 Aug. 11.00 *Queen's Hall*
Fauré Quartet in E minor, op.121
Dutilleux Quartet (Ainsi la nuit)
Ravel Quartet in F

LES ARTS FLORISSANTS
20 Aug. 15.00 *Queen's Hall*
Works by Bouzignac, Moulinié, Charpentier, Lambert
Director William Christie
Soloists Agnès Mellon, Françoise Semellaz (sop), Dominique Visse (c ten), Ian Honeyman, Michel Laplénie (ten), François Fauché, Antoine Sicot (bs), Elisabeth Matiffa (vc), Yvon Reperant (hpd)

FITZWILLIAM QUARTET
21 Aug. 11.00 *Queen's Hall*
Shostakovich Quartet no.1 in C, op.49
Tchaikovsky Quartet no.3 in E flat minor, op.30
Franck Quartet in D

NASH ENSEMBLE
27 Aug. 11.00 *Queen's Hall*
Beethoven Trio for clarinet, cello and piano, op.11
Shostakovich Trio for piano and strings no.2 in E minor, op.67
Messiaen Quatuor pour la fin du temps

CLEVELAND QUARTET
28 Aug. 11.00 *Queen's Hall*
Mozart Adagio and fugue in C minor, K546
Dvořák Quartet no.12 in F (American), op.96
Beethoven Quartet no.7 in F (Rasumovsky), op.59/1

29 Aug. 11.00 *Queen's Hall*
Schubert Quartet no.10 in E flat, D87
Dohnányi Serenade for 2 violins and viola in C, op.10
Beethoven Quartet no.16 in F, op.135

RECITALS

FELICITY LOTT (sop)
GRAHAM JOHNSON (pf)
31 Aug. 11.00 *Queen's Hall*
Schumann Frauenliebe und -leben
Debussy Fêtes galantes
Poulenc Tel jour, telle nuit
Songs by Schumann, Poulenc

SONGMAKERS' ALMANAC
13 Aug. 11.00 *Queen's Hall*
Emanuel Chabrier - 'Le bon diable en musique'
Patricia Rozario (sop), Martyn Hill (ten), Richard Jackson (bar), Graham Johnson (pf) with Neil Cunningham as Chabrier

JEAN-PHILIPPE COLLARD (pf)
14 Aug. 11.00 *Queen's Hall*
Schumann Arabesque in C, op.18
Schumann Études symphoniques, op.13
Franck Prélude, choral et fugue
Ravel Sonatine
Ravel Miroirs: Oiseaux triste *and* Alborada del gracioso

ANDRAS SCHIFF (pf)
23 Aug. 11.00 *Queen's Hall*
Bach Goldberg variations

JON KIMURA PARKER (pf)
26 Aug. 11.00 *Queen's Hall*
Bach Toccata no.6 in G minor
Mozart Sonata no.9 in D, K311
Liszt Sonata in B minor
Poulenc Novelette sur un thème de Falla
Poulenc Novelette in C
Poulenc Novelette in B flat minor
Barber Sonata in E flat, op.26

SIR YEHUDI MENUHIN (vn)
13 Aug. 22.30 *St Cuthbert's Hall*
Bach Sonata no.3 in C
Bach Partita no.3 in E
Bach Partita no.2 in D minor

14 Aug. 15.00 *Queen's Hall*
'Mr. Menuhin's delight': an exploration of Scottish fiddle playing with Mary Anne Alburger, Edna Arthur, Aly Bain, Ronald Gonella, Alastair Hardie, Bob Hobkirk, Douglas Lawrence, The Whistlebinkies

17 Aug. 11.30 *Leith Theatre*
Debussy Sonata
Beethoven Sonata no.9 in A (Kreutzer), op.47
with Paul Coker (pf)

ERNST KOVAČIČ (vn)
DAVID OWEN NORRIS (pf)
30 Aug. 11.00 *Queen's Hall*
Honegger Sonata no.2
Bach Sonata for solo violin no.2 in A minor
Elgar Sonata in E minor, op.82
Ravel Tzigane

STEVEN ISSERLIS (vc)
PETER EVANS (pf)
16 Aug. 11.00 *Queen's Hall*
Bach Suite for solo cello no.5 in C minor
Schumann Adagio and allegro, op.70
Debussy Sonata for cello and piano
Poulenc Sonata for cello and piano

CARLO CURLEY (org)
18 Aug. 19.30 *McEwan Hall*
Works by Mozart, Bach, Franck, Handel, Wagner, Widor, Dupré, Reger

CHARLES KRIGBAUM (org)
25 Aug. 14.30
St Andrew's & St George's
Bach 16 newly discovered Choral preludes
Bach Prelude and fugue in B minor

25 Aug. 19.30
St Andrew's & St George's
Bach 17 newly discovered Choral preludes
Bach Toccata and fugue in D minor (Dorian)

HÉLÈNE DELAVAULT
20, 21, 23, 24 Aug. 19.00 French Institute
19th century drawing room romances, cafe-concert songs, blues, musical dramas
with Ives Prin (pf)

JAZZ

SCOTTISH NATIONAL ORCHESTRA
McEWAN'S JAZZ FESTIVAL ALL-STARS
24 Aug. 20.00 Usher Hall
Syncopatin' symphony
When Johnny comes marching in; arr. Gould
Galloway Hot and suite: a suite in 5 sections
Conductor Russell Gloyd
with Humphrey Lyttelton, Black Eagles, Buddy Tate (ten sax), Jim Galloway (sop sax), Rosemary Galloway, Milton John Hinton (db), Warren Vaché, jun. (hn), Carl Fontana (tbn), Ray Bryant (pf), Spanky Davis (tpt), Gus Johnson, jun. (drums)

DRAMA

EDINBURGH INTERNATIONAL FESTIVAL
SCOTTISH THEATRE COMPANY
10, 12-17, 22-24 Aug. 19.30 17, 24 Aug. 14.30 Assembly Hall
THE THRIE ESTAITES Lyndsay
(Adapted by Robert Kemp)
Diligence William McCue
King David Rintoul
Wantonness David McKail
Placebo Derek Anders
Solace Jonathan Watson
Sensualitie Caroline Kaart
Hameliness Eliza Langland
Danger Corinne Harris
Fund-Jennet Halcro Johnston
Gude Counsel Alex McAvoy
Flatterie/Pardoner Walter Carr
Falsehood Angus Lennie
Deceit John Grieve
Veritie Anne Kristen
Chastitie Edith Macarthur
Spiritualitie Roy Hanlon
Prioress Juliet Cadzow
Abbot Andrew Cruickshank
Parson Alexander West
Temporalitie John Shedden
Merchant Brown Derby
Soutar Ian Stewart
Soutar's wife Sheila Latimer
Tailor Lea Ashton
Tailor's wife Pamela Kelly
Correction's varlet Billy Riddoch
Divine Correction Donald Douglas
Poor man Phil McCall
Wilkin Widdiefow David McCann
John the Common-Weal Alec Heggie
Sergeant Ian Briggs
Scribe David Gourlay
Swordbearer Kim Fenton
Boy Dolina Logan
Director Tom Fleming
Designer Nadine Baylis
Lighting André Tammes
Music Cedric Thorpe Davie

19-21, 26-31 Aug. 19.30 21, 28, 31 Aug. 14.30 Assembly Hall
THE WALLACE Goodsir Smith
William Wallace Alec Heggie
Robert Bruce John Shedden
Mirren Braidfute Vivien Heilbron
Jean Anne Kristen
Queen Margaret Edith Macarthur
Sir Thomas Braidfute John Grieve
Ailish Rae Eliza Langland
Sandy Fraser Alexander West
Sir John Mentieth Roy Hanlon
Sir John Lovell Kim Fenton
Sir John Comyn Derek Anders
Macduff/English herald Alex McAvoy
Donald Phil McCall
Sir John Graham/Sir Ralph Billy Riddoch
Andrew Murray/Earl of Angus Ian Briggs
Sir William Heselrig Donald Douglas
Sir John Stewart of Bonkill Jonathan Watson
Sir John Segrave Leon Sinden
King Edward I Leonard Maguire
Lady Isabella Corinne Harris
Earl of March/Bishop of Chichester Brown Derby
Edward, Prince of Wales James McClure
Sir Ralph de Haliburton David Gourlay
Archbishop of Canterbury Ian Stewart
Sir Peter Mallory David McKail
Thomas, Earl of Lancaster Lea Ashton
Bishop of Glasgow David Gourlay
Sir William Oliphant/Bishop of St Andrew's Lewis Allan
Bishop of Dunkeld Colin Watson
Earl of Ross David McCann
Sir John Blunt Halcro Johnston
Court jester Brian Wheeler
Singer Jean Redpath
Director Tom Fleming
Designer Nadine Baylis
Lighting André Tammes

12-15 Aug. 19.15 16,17 Aug. 20.30
Lyceum Theatre
WHEN I WAS A GIRL I USED TO SCREAM AND SHOUT... MacDonald
Morag Sheila Reid
Fiona Eleanor David
Ewan Jamie Roberts
Vari Julia Blalock
Director Simon Stokes
Designer Robin Don
Lighting Paul Denby
(In association with Jerome Minskoff)

TOHO COMPANY, Japan
22, 23, 24 Aug. 19.00 24 Aug. 14.00
Lyceum Theatre
MACBETH Shakespeare (Jap)
Macbeth Mikijiro Hira
Lady Macbeth Komaki Kurichara
Banquo Masane Tsukayama
Macduff Akira Nakao
Duncan Mizuho Suzuki
Malcolm Takayuki Sugo
Donalbain Eiichi Seike
Fleance Tsukasa Nakagoshi
Lennox Mikio Shimizu
Ross Ko Ikedo
Seyton Yukinaga Shiraishi
Doctor Yosuki Katayama
Lady Macduff Yoko Shibamura
Gentlewoman Mayuko Aoyama
Witches Tokusaburo Arashi, Goro Daimon, Shijaku Nakamura
Son to Macduff Masatoshi Murakami
Angus Ryuzaburo Otomo
Old man Tatsumi Aoyama
Murderer Naoyuki Fuchino
Cathness Ken Yamabi
Menteith Susumu Kakuma
Siward Kazuhisa Seshimo
Young Siward Tsukasa Nakagoshi
Soldier Michisuke Ida
Lord Masafumi Senoo
Director Yukio Ninagawa
Scenery Kappa Seno
Costumes Jusaburo Tsujimara
Lighting Sumio Yoshii

BAXTER THEATRE, Capetown
26, 29, 30 Aug. 19.30 27, 28 Aug. 22.30
31 Aug. 17.00 and 20.00 Lyceum Theatre
MISS JULIE Strindberg (Eng)
Miss Julie Sandra Prinsloo
John John Kani
Christine Natie Rula
Director Bobby Heaney
Designer Brian Collins
Lighting Sidney Jansen

THÉÂTRE NATIONAL DE BELGIQUE
27, 28 Aug. 19.00 Lyceum Theatre
LE MISANTHROPE Molière
Alceste Jean-Claude Frison
Philinte Michel de Warzee
Oronte Raoul de Manez
Célimène Gysele Brieuc
Eliante Nathalie van de Walle
Arsinoë Ann Marev
Acaste Jean Rovis
Clitandre Raymond Lescot
Basque André Deflandre
Dubois Paul Clairy
Un garde Jacques Burgraeve
Tanguy David
Director Jacques Huisman
Designer Thierry Bosquet
Lighting Christian Leonard

THEATRE OF COMEDY
22-24, 26-31 Aug. 19.30 24, 27, 31 Aug. 14.30 King's Theatre
TURKEY TROT or WOMEN ALL OVER Feydeau
(Adapted from *Le dindon* by John Wells)
Hattie Lachs Elin Jenkins
Glad/Maid Joanna Mackie
George "Tiggy" Wimpole Royce Mills
Agatha "Gaga" Ramsbotham Caroline Blakiston
Valerie Wimpole Eileen Atkins
Arnold Schwink Joe Melia
Helen Schwink Faith Brook
Esme Schwink John Gordon-Sinclair
Mrs Harper Elizabeth Bradley
Ronnie Savage Clive Wood
Her Honour, Judge Pamby Pat Keen
Dr Hercules Pamby Patrick Godfrey
Director Adrian Noble
Designer Bob Crowley
Lighting Robert Bryan

LA COMPAGNIE RENAUD-BARRAULT, Paris
28-31 Aug. 19.00 31 Aug. 14.00
Music Hall
ANGELO, TYRAN DE PADOUE Hugo
Angelo Jacques Dacqmine
Catarina Sylvia Berge
La Tisbé Geneviève Page
Rodolfo Gerard Ismael
Homodei Pierre Tabard
Anapesto Galeofa Jean-Paul Gonzenbach
Ordelafo Robert Lombard
Orfeo Jean-Louis Barrault
Gaboardo Dominique Virton
Reginella Lela Balenski
Dafne Marie Gwenn
Un huissier Xavier Renoult
Le doyen de Saint Antoine Pierre Hoden

Director	Jean-Louis Barrault
Designer	Ghislain Uhry
Lighting	Geneviève Soubiro

EDINBURGH INTERNATIONAL FESTIVAL
12-24 Aug. 20.00 15, 17, 22, 24 Aug. 15.00 *Church Hill Theatre*
A WEE TOUCH OF CLASS Molière
(Adapted from *Le bourgeois gentilhomme* by Coffey *and* Fulton)

Music master	Alan Vicary
Fiddler	Alan Young
Netty	Denise Coffey
Dancing master	Kenny Gardner
Archibald Jenner	Rikki Fulton
Gowrie	Kenneth Lindsay
Fleming	John Ramage
Fencing master	Peter Lincoln
Philosopher	Roger Kemp
Clementina Jenner	Janet Michael
Lord Fordell	Paul Young
Alan Foringale	Colin Gourlay
Tam Byres	Iain Stuart Robertson
Alison Jenner	Lesley Moore
Marchioness of Marchmont	Anne Kidd
Director	Joan Knight
Designer	Nigel Hook
Lighting	Simon Sewell

(In association with Perth Theatre)

POETRY AND PROSE RECITALS

13, 14 Aug. 14.45 *St Cecilia's Hall*
LOVE AMONG THE BUTTERFLIES
(Adapted by Michael Burrell from W.S. Cater's book based on the diaries of Margaret Fountaine)
Sheila Reid, John Ashton (rdr)
Directed by Michael Burrell

LATE NIGHT ENTERTAINMENT

9-11, 13-18, 20-25 Aug. 22.00
Assembly Rooms
GREATER TUNA
Joe Sears, Jaston Williams
Director Ed Howard

22-26 Aug. 23.00 *Lyceum Theatre*
28-31 Aug. 23.00 *Music Hall*
FLYING KARAMAZOV BROTHERS, USA
Juggling and cheap theatrics

DANCE

SCOTTISH BALLET
13, 17, 19, 20 Aug. 19.30 17 Aug. 14.30
Playhouse
CARMEN (World première)

Choreographer	Peter Darrell
Music	Bizet; arr. Muldowney
Designer	Terry Bartlett
Lighting	Mark Henderson

14, 15 Aug. 19.30 *Playhouse*
LA SYLPHIDE

Choreographers	Bournonville, Hans Brenaa
Music	Løvenskold
Designer	Peter Cazalet
Lighting	Charles Bristow

SYMPHONY IN D

Choreographers	Jiri Kylián, Deirdre O'Donohoe
Music	Haydn
Designer	Tom Schenk
Lighting	Joop Cabort

Dancers Rudolph Nureyev, Elaine McDonald, Robert Hampton, Christine Camillo, Davide Bombana, Linda Packer, Sally Collard-Gentle, Christopher Long, Judy Mohekey, Eleanor Moore, Noriko Ohara, Peter Royston, Paul Tyers
Conductors Guy Hamilton, David Frame

MICHAEL CLARK AND COMPANY
11-14 Aug. 22.15 *Lyceum Theatre*
OUR CACA PHONEY H
(World première)

Choreographer	Michael Clark
Music	The Fall, Jeffrey Hinton
Designers	Leigh Bowery, Bodymap
Lighting	Charles Atlas

Dancers Leslie Bryant, Michael Clark, Matthew Hawkins, Julie Hood, Ellen van Schuylenburch

RIS ET DANCERIES, France
20 Aug. 19.30 *Lyceum Theatre*
SUITTE D'UN GOÛT ÉTRANGER

Choreographers	François Raffinot, Dominique Bagouet, Andrew de Groat, Robert Kovich
Music	Marais
Scenery	Michel Brunel
Costumes	Virginie Standaert
Lighting	Françoise Michel

Dancers Ségolène Poirier, Nadège Macleay, Marie-Geneviève Masse, Jean-Christophe Bocle, Jean Charles di Zazzo, Sylvain Richard, Marc Vincent, Ien-Nio Bourrelly, Fabrice Pothier, Sophie Raffinot
Musicians Marianne Muller (va da gamba), Aline Zylberajch (hpd), Yasunori Imamura (theorbo)

GROUPE DE RECHERCHE CHORÉGRAPHIQUE DE L'OPÉRA DE PARIS
30, 31 Aug. 19.30 *Playhouse*
AUREOLE

Choreographer	Paul Taylor
Music	Handel
Costumes	Georges Tacet
Lighting	Daniel Brochier

LA COULEUR DU SECRET

Choreographer	Jean Christophe Paré
Music	Elliott Carter
Costumes	Philippe Binot
Lighting	François Gaunand

AUNIS

Choreographer	Jacques Garnier
Music	Maurice Pacher

PAS DE DEUX

Choreographer	Jacques Garnier
Music	Webern

BEETHOVEN AND BOOTH

Choreographer	David Gordon
Music	Beethoven
Scenery	Power Booth
Lighting	Michel Marie

MASSACRE ON MACDOUGAL STREET

Choreographer	Karole Armitage
Music	Rhys Chatham
Designer	Charles Atlas
Lighting	Charles Atlas, Daniel Brochier

Dancers Martine Clary, Fabienne Compet, Florence Lambert, Jean-Claude Ciappara, Jean Christophe Paré, André Lafonta, Jean-Hugues Tanto, Renaud Fauviau, Anne Pruvost, Marie Eve Edelsen, Pascale Ferrari, Loic Touze

OTHER EVENTS

21-26 Aug. 19.30 24 Aug. 11.00 and 14.30 25 Aug. 15.00 *Playhouse*
MOSCOW STATE CIRCUS
26 Aug. 10.30 *Ross Bandstand*
27 Aug. 20.00 *Leith Theatre*
KODO, Japan
Folk dancers and musicians

12-15, 19-22 Aug. 20.00 *Festival Club*
KNEE DEEP IN CLARET
The French wine trade in Scotland in poetry and song.
Rod Paterson, Jim Sutherland. Derek Hoy
Presented and arranged by Billy Kay

22-24 Aug. 20.00 24 Aug. 15.00
St Cecilia's Hall
PORTRAITS AND MINIATURES
Poetry , prose and music on themes from French and Scottish history
Gwen Watford, John Westbrook (rdr), Michael Chibbett (hpd)
Directed by John Carroll

26, 27 Aug. 15.00 *St Cecilia's Hall*
LOVE AND SONG
Edith Macarthur, John Shedden (rdr), Patricia MacMahon (sop), Lindsay Sinclair (pf)
Arranged by Paul Scott and George Bruce

SALTIRE SOCIETY
28 Aug. 15.00 *St Cecilia's Hall*
GAELIC SONG
Anne Lorne Gillies (sop), Rhona MacKay (clarsach)

30 Aug. 15.00 *St Cecilia's Hall*
THE AULD ALLIANCE
A personal view by Andrew Cruickshank

SCOTTISH POETRY LIBRARY
29 Aug. 15.00 *St Cecilia's Hall*
Michel Deguy, Sorley MacLean, Joy Hendry (rdr)
(In association with Verse Magazine)

DIRECTORS' GUILD OF GREAT BRITAIN
16 Aug. 15.00 *St Cecilia's Hall*
COPYRIGHT: Open seminar

19 Aug. 18.30 *St Cecilia's Hall*
ARE DIRECTORS REALLY NECESSARY? Public debate with leading directors, writers and performers

EXHIBITIONS

Royal Scottish Academy
COLOUR SINCE MATISSE

ASSOCIATED EXHIBITIONS
(Not organized by the Festival Society)

Royal Scottish Museum
FRENCH CONNECTIONS: Scotland and the Arts of France

National Gallery of Scotland
FRANCE AND THE NATIONAL GALLERIES

National Gallery of Scotland
TRIBUTE TO WILKIE

Scottish National Gallery of Modern Art
L'ECOLE DE PARIS 1900-1960

S.J. PEPLOE

Scottish National Portrait Gallery
A FRENCH PAINTER IN EXILE: Henry Pierre Danloux

TREASURES FROM FYVIE

City Art Centre
PRE-COLUMBIAN CERAMICS OF COSTA RICA
(From the Arthur M. Sackler Collection)

City Art Centre
AMERICAN DRAWINGS AND WATERCOLOURS
From the Carnegie Institute, Pittsburgh

A BREATH OF FRENCH AIR

National Library of Scotland
ANDREW CARNEGIE

JOHN FRANCIS CAMPBELL

Fine Art Society
CAMELS, COBWEBS AND CORMORANTS

Queen's Hall
LA PLUME DE MON CARTOONIST: Mel Calman

Demarco Gallery
7 FOKSAL GALLERY ARTISTS FROM POLAND

Talbot Rice Art Centre
ABOUT LANDSCAPE

Fruitmarket Gallery
KOMAR AND MELAMID

National Museum of Antiquities
SYMBOLS OF POWER AT THE TIME OF STONEHENGE

Edinburgh College of Art
EDINBURGH - DUBLIN 1885-1985

Royal Highland Exhibition Hall
HIGHLAND AND COUNTY '85

Dalmeny House
FRENCH FURNITURE, PORCELAIN

14, 21, 28 Aug. 18.15
National Gallery of Scotland
SCOTTISH ENSEMBLE
Concerts linking music and the visual arts

1986

OPERA

EDINBURGH INTERNATIONAL FESTIVAL
10, 12, 14 Aug. 20.00 *Usher Hall*
OBERON Weber (Eng)
Oberon Philip Langridge
Titania Gail Rolfe
Puck James Robertson
Sir Huon Paul Frey
Sherasmin Benjamin Luxon
Reiza Elizabeth Connell
Fatima Laverne Williams
Charlemagne/Haroun el Raschid/Abdallah Robert Oates
Son of Charlemagne/Babekan/Almanzor Peter Birch
Mermaid Vanessa Smith
Horn Stefan Dohr
EF Chorus
Junge Deutsche Philharmonie
Conductor Seiji Ozawa
Directors Frank Dunlop, Ugo Tessitore
Designer Carl Toms
Choreographer David Toguri
Lighting Mark Henderson

MALY THEATRE, Leningrad
18, 23 Aug. 19.15 *King's Theatre*
THE QUEEN OF SPADES Tchaikovsky
Hermann Anatoly Kapustin
Lisa Valentina Yuzvenko, Ludmilla Sirenko
Countess Irina Bogachova
Tomsky Alexander Nenadovsky
Yeletsky Nikolai Kopilov
Tchekalinsky Vladimir Naparin
Sourin Sergei Safenin
Chaplitsky Victor Lukyanov
Narumov V.I. Yushmanov
Pauline Nina Romanova
Masha S.N. Volkova
Governess Maya Kuznetsova
Master of ceremonies V.P. Korzhensky
Prilepa Y.E.V. Ustinova, T. G. Cherkasova
Milovzor Olga Korzhenskaya
Zlatagor Vladimir Pankratov
George Watson's Boys' Chorus
Conductor Valentin Kozhin
Director Stanislav Gaudasinsky

20, 24 Aug. 19.15 *King's Theatre*
EUGENE ONEGIN Tchaikovsky
Onegin Alexander Nenadovsky, Nikolai Kopilov
Tatiana Lyubov Kazarnovskaya, Ludmilla Sirenko
Olga Nina Romanova
Lensky Nikolai Ostrovsky
Madame Larina Maya Kuznetsova
Filipievna Irina Bogachova
Gremin Vladimir Ognovenko
M. Triquet Vladimir Naparin
Zaretski Leonid Gladkov
Captain Sergei Safenin, S.K. Bureyev
Conductor Valentin Kozhin
Director Stanislav Gaudasinsky

22, 25 Aug. 19.15 *King's Theatre*
MARIA STUART Slonimsky
Maria Stuart Svetlana Volkova, Valentina Yuzvenko
Elizabeth Nina Romanova
Mary Seton Maya Kuznetsova, Olga Korzhenskaya
Darnley N.N. Alexeev
Rizzio V.P. Korzhensky
Bothwell Vladimir Ognovenko
Melancholy bard Alexander Nenadovsky, Vladimir Naparin
Joyful bard Vladimir Naparin, Nikolai Kopilov
Chatelard Nikolai Vasiliev
Knox Sergei Safenin
Ruthven Leonid Gladkov
1st Baron S.K. Bureyev
2nd Baron V. Pischayev, V.P. Korzhensky
Conductor Valentin Kozhin
Director Stanislav Gaudasinsky

FOLKOPERA, Stockholm
26-29 Aug. 19.30 30 Aug. 14.30
Leith Theatre
AIDA Verdi (Swed)
Aida Irene Almén, Margareta Edström, Hillevi Martinpelto
Radames Christer Solén, Uno Stjernqvist, Robert Grundin
Amneris Ingrid Tobiasson, Anne-Marie Muehle, Catharina Olsson
Amonasro Bengt Krantz, Jan van der Schaaf
Ramfis Stephan Munkert, Staffan Rydén, Alf Häggstam
Pharaoh's spokesman Alf Häggstam, Stephan Munkert, Staffan Rydén
Priestess Anette Stridh
Messenger Rolf Knapper
Pharaoh Margareta Nilsson
Dance of the veils Rozita Auer
Conductors Glenn Mossop, Kerstin Nerbe
Director Claes Fellbom
Scenery Göran Wassberg
Costumes Eva Broms

NATIONAL YOUTH MUSIC THEATRE
20-23, 25-30 Aug. 17.00 24 Aug. 14.00
30 Aug. 10.30 *George Square Theatre*
LET'S MAKE AN OPERA Britten
Royal Academy of Music members
Director Jeremy James Taylor
Designer Alix Stone

12, 15, 17-19, 22 Aug. 14.00 11, 13-15, 20-22 Aug. 19.00 George Square Theatre
THE RAGGED CHILD Nield
Directors Jeremy James Taylor, Frank Whately
Scenery Christopher Richardson
Costumes Sheila Darlington
Lighting Peter Walters

ORCHESTRAL CONCERTS

BBC SYMPHONY ORCHESTRA
11 Aug. 20.00 *Usher Hall*
Beethoven Concerto for piano no.5 in E flat (Emperor), op.73
R. Strauss Eine Alpensinfonie
Conductor Sir John Pritchard
Soloist Jorge Bolet (pf)

MOSCOW VIRTUOSI
Conductor Vladimir Spivakov
13 Aug. 20.00 *Usher Hall*
Schubert 5 Minuets and 6 Trios
Haydn Symphony no.94 in G (Surprise)
Chorinsky Walzer Melodien; arr. Poltoratsky
Sieczynsky Wien, du Stadt meiner Träume; arr. Poltoratsky

Josef Strauss — Die Emanzipierte
Josef Strauss — Moulinet
Josef Strauss — Rudolfsheimer
Eduard Strauss — Ohne Bremse
Joh. Strauss — Leichtes Blut
Joh. Strauss — Tik Tak polka
Joh. Strauss — Unter Donner und Blitz
Joh. Strauss, *the elder* — Radetsky march
with Manchester Camerata members

15 Aug. 11.00 — *Queen's Hall*
Bach — Concerto for violin in A minor
Bach — Cantata no.53
Bach — Passion according to St Matthew: Erbarme dich
Stravinsky — Concerto in D
Shostakovich — Chamber symphony, op.110a
Shostakovich — Four preludes, op.34; arr. Poltoratsky
Soloist — Tamara Sinyavskaya (mez)

ACADEMY OF ST MARTIN-IN-THE-FIELDS
Conductor — Sir Neville Marriner
15 Aug. 20.00 — *Usher Hall*
Weber — Symphony in C
Mozart — Concerto for piano no.25 in C, K503
Beethoven — Symphony no.2 in D, op.36
Soloist — Ivan Moravec (pf)

16 Aug. 20.00 — *Usher Hall*
Mozart — Serenade no.10 in B flat (Gran partita), K361
Mozart — Zaide: Ruhe sanft
Mozart — Mass no.18 in C minor (Great), K427: Et incarnatus est
Mozart — Symphony no.25 in G minor, K183
Soloist — Margaret Marshall (sop)

SCOTTISH NATIONAL ORCHESTRA
17 Aug. 20.00 — *Usher Hall*
Gade — Echoes from Ossian - Overture
Mendelssohn — The Hebrides (Fingal's Cave) - Overture
Donizetti — Lucia di Lammermoor: Mad scene
Lesueur — Ossian ou Les bardes : Ossian's dream
Méhul — Uthal
Conductor — Neeme Järvi
Soloists — Pamela Myers (sop), Jeffrey Talbot, Mark Curtis (ten), Anthony Michaels-Moore (bar), Roderick Earle (bs), James Cairncross (narr), EF Chorus

CHAMBER ORCHESTRA OF EUROPE
Conductor — Claudio Abbado
18 Aug. 20.00 — *Usher Hall*
Prokofiev — Symphony no.1 in D (Classical), op.25
Haydn — Sinfonia concertante in B flat, op.84
Wagner — Siegfried idyll
Beethoven — Symphony no.4 in B flat, op.60
Soloists — Marieke Blakestijn (vn), Douglas Boyd (ob), Matthew Wilkie (bn), William Conway (vc)

19 Aug. 20.00 — *Usher Hall*
Schubert — Symphony no.2 in B flat, D125
Mendelssohn — Concerto for violin in E minor, op.64
Mozart — Serenade no.9 in D (Posthorn), K320
Soloist — Viktoria Mullova (vn)

OSLO PHILHARMONIC ORCHESTRA
Conductor — Mariss Jansons
20 Aug. 20.00 — *Usher Hall*
Svendsen — Carnival in Paris
Haydn — Concerto for cello no.1 in C
Tchaikovsky — Symphony no.6 in B minor (Pathétique), op.74
Soloist — Yo-Yo Ma (vc)

21 Aug. 20.00 — *Usher Hall*
Weber — Euryanthe: Overture
Beethoven — Concerto for piano no.3 in C minor, op.37
Tchaikovsky — Symphony no.2 in C minor (Little Russian), op.17
Berlioz — La damnation de Faust: Rákóczy march
Soloist — Emanuel Ax (pf)

SCOTTISH CHAMBER ORCHESTRA
21 Aug. 22.45 — *Ross Bandstand*
Fireworks Concert
Offenbach — Orphée aux enfers: Overture
P.M. Davies — An Orkney wedding
J. Strauss — Unter Donner und Blitz
Handel — Music for the royal fireworks
Conductor — Peter Maxwell Davies

26 Aug. 11.00 — *Queen's Hall*
Britten — Young Apollo
Tchaikovsky — Variations on a Rococo theme
Stravinsky — Apollon musagète
Conductor — Andrew Litton
Soloists — William Conway (vc), Peter Evans (pf)

GALA CONCERT
Celebrating 40 years of the Edinburgh Festival
24 Aug. 20.00 — *Usher Hall*
Frank Dunlop, Felicity Lott, Cleo Laine, John Dankworth, Leonard Friedman, Tom Fleming, Paul Rogers, Ian Charleson, Gary Bond, Bernard Bresslaw, National Youth Music Theatre, Royal Scottish Academy of Music and Drama, Flying Karamazov Brothers, Stanislaw Skrowaczewski, Bramwell Tovey, John Currie, EF Chorus, Hallé Orchestra
Introduced by Hannah Gordon, Denise Coffey, Sean Connery
Directed by Jeremy James Taylor

HALLÉ ORCHESTRA
25 Aug. 20.00 — *Usher Hall*
Stravinsky — Le baiser de la fée - Divertimento
Stravinsky — Concerto for piano and wind
Tchaikovsky — Symphony no.4 in F minor, op.36
Conductor — Stanislaw Skrowaczewski
Soloist — Peter Donohoe (pf)

THE TORONTO SYMPHONY
Conductor — Andrew Davis
26 Aug. 20.00 — *Usher Hall*
Berlioz — Le corsair - Overture
Tchaikovsky — Concerto for piano no.1 in B flat minor, op.23
Prokofiev — Symphony no.5 in B flat, op.100
Soloist — Ivo Pogorelich (pf)

28 Aug. 20.00 — *Usher Hall*
THE SOLDIER'S TALE — Stravinsky
Princess — Karen Kain
Soldier — Peter Ottman
Devil — Jeff Hyslop
Narrator — John Neville
Corps de ballet — Chester Fergusson, Ales Polacek
Choreographer — Brian Macdonald
OEDIPUS REX — Stravinsky
Oedipus — Robert Tear
Jocasta — Alfreda Hodgson
Creon/Messenger — Anthony Michaels-Moore
Tiresias — Stafford Dean
Shepherd — Maldwyn Davies
Narrator — John Neville
EF Chorus

CITY OF BIRMINGHAM SYMPHONY ORCHESTRA
Conductor — Simon Rattle
29 Aug. 20.00 — *Usher Hall*
Elgar — The dream of Gerontius
Soloists — Dame Janet Baker (mez), John Mitchinson (ten), John Shirley-Quirk (bar), EF Chorus

30 Aug. 20.00 — *Usher Hall*
Berio — Sinfonia
Mahler — Symphony no.2 in C minor (Resurrection)
Soloists — Felicity Lott (sop), Dame Janet Baker (mez), EF Chorus, Electric Phoenix

CHAMBER CONCERTS

MEDICI QUARTET
16 Aug. 11.00 — *Queen's Hall*
Beethoven — Quartet no.1 in F, op.18/1
Shostakovich — Two pieces for string quartet
Brahms — Quintet for clarinet and strings in B minor, op.115
with Alan Hacker (cl)

NASH ENSEMBLE
18 Aug. 11.00 — *Queen's Hall*
Mozart — Trio for piano, clarinet and viola, K498
Britten — Suite for solo cello no.3, op.87
Debussy — Rhapsody for clarinet and piano
Brahms — Trio for clarinet, cello and piano in A minor, op.114

YOUNG UCK KIM (vn), YO-YO MA (vc), EMANUEL AX (pf)
19 Aug. 11.00 — *Queen's Hall*
Beethoven — Trio for clarinet, cello and piano in B flat, op.11; transc for violin, cello and piano
Dvořák — Trio for piano and strings no.4 in E minor (Dumky), op.90
Mendelssohn — Trio for piano and strings no.2 in C minor, op.66

22 Aug. 20.00 — *Usher Hall*
Mozart — Sonata for violin and piano no.17 in C, K296
Beethoven — Sonata for cello and piano no.3 in A, op.69
Brahms — Trio for piano and strings no.1 in B, op.8

ELECTRIC PHOENIX
29 Aug. 11.00 — *Queen's Hall*
Runswick — I sing the body electric
T. Wishart — Vox II
Berio — A-Ronne
W. Brookes — Madrigals

WALLACE COLLECTION
30 Aug. 11.00 — *Queen's Hall*
Works by Mozart, Frescobaldi, Diabelli, Altenberg, Viviani, Arnold, Berio, Fantini, Keller, Ruggles

ALEXANDER GOEHR: A composer's choice
A Weekend of 20th Century Music
BRODSKY QUARTET
22 Aug. 18.00 — *Queen's Hall*
P.M. Davies — Quartet no.1
Birtwistle — Quintet for clarinet and strings
Goehr — Quartet no.3
with Nicholas Cox (cl)

23 Aug. 18.00 *Queen's Hall*
Stravinsky Three pieces
Cashian Moon of the dawn (World première)
Lutoslawski Quartet (1964)
Bartók Quartet no.3
with Carol Smith (sop)

SCOTTISH CHAMBER ORCHESTRA members
23 Aug. 11.00 *Queen's Hall*
Janáček Rikadla
Kurtág Messages of the late R.V. Troússova
Stravinsky Concertino for 12 instruments (1952 version)
Goehr Sonata about Jerusalem
Conductor Richard Bernas
Soloist Adrienne Csengery (sop)
Scottish Philharmonic Singers

ALAN FEINBERG (pf)
24 Aug. 12.00 *Queen's Hall*
Wuorinen Capriccio
Sessions Sonata no.3
Babbitt Partitions
Babbitt It takes twelve to tango
Babbitt Minute waltz
Babbitt Playing for time
Busoni Toccata

EPSILON WIND QUINTET
24 Aug. 15.00 *Queen's Hall*
Stockhausen Zeitmasse
Gerhard Quintet for wind
Carter Eight études and a fantasy

ADRIENNE CSENGERY (sop)
JOHN CONSTABLE (pf)
24 Aug. 18.00 *Queen's Hall*
Bartók Village scenes
Stravinsky Pribaoutki
Kurtág Eight pieces for piano, op.3
Bartók Five songs, op.16
Sary Magnificat
Kurtág Attila Jozsef - Fragments, op.20

LONTANO
25 Aug. 11.00 *Queen's Hall*
H. Wood Quintet
H. Eisler Fourteen ways of describing rain
B. Northcott Sextet
A. Gilbert Quartet of beasts
G. King You, always you (World première)
N. Sackman Corranach
Director Odaline de la Martinez

SCOTTISH MUSIC

ORPHEUS CALEDONIUS
11 Aug. 11.00 *Queen's Hall*
29 Aug. 19.30 *St Cecilia's Hall*
Music of the Enlightenment by McGibbon, Gow, Reid, Barsanty, Earl of Kelly, Oswald, Bremner, Schetky *and others*
with Lorna Anderson (sop), Lucy Carolan (hpd)

SCOTTISH EARLY MUSIC CONSORT
13 Aug. 11.00 *Queen's Hall*
Vocal and instrumental music with Scottish associations from 1680-1825
Director Warwick Edwards
Soloists Christine Cairns (sop), Alan Watt (bar)

McGIBBON ENSEMBLE
24, 27 Aug. 19.30 *Queen's Hall*
McGibbon Sonata no.5 in C minor
Earl of Kelly The lover's message
Oswald The maid of Selma
Earl of Kelly Trio sonata no.4 in C
McGibbon Trio sonata no.6 in D
Corelli Sonata no.9 in A
Handel Acis and Galatea: Hush ye pretty warbling choir
Anon. Sonata on 'The Lea rig' for violin
Dances on Edinburgh place names
Scots songs arr. Bremner
with Lorna Anderson (sop), Rosemary Eliot (fl)

RECITALS

NANCY ARGENTA (sop)
DAVID WILSON-JOHNSON (bar)
DAVID OWEN NORRIS (f-pf)
14 Aug. 11.00 *Queen's Hall*
Schubert Songs to settings by Scott *and* excerpts from Ossian
Schubert Ecossaises, D299, D735, D679

CATHERINE DUBOSC (sop)
RUBEN LIFSCHITZ (pf)
21 Aug. 11.00 *Queen's Hall*
Debussy Ariettes oubliées
Poulenc Fiançailles pour rire
Songs by Fauré, Debussy, Chabrier

FRANÇOIS LE ROUX (bar)
MONIQUE LAGET (pf)
22 Aug. 11.00 *Queen's Hall*
Songs by Schubert, Schumann. Duparc, Debussy, Poulenc

IRINA BOGACHOVA (mez)
IGOR LEBEDEV (pf)
27 Aug. 11.00 *Queen's Hall*
Songs and arias by Tchaikovsky, Mussorgsky, Rimsky-Korsakov, Borodin

IVO POGORELICH (pf)
27 Aug. 20.00 *Usher Hall*
Beethoven Bagatelle no.7 in A minor (Für Elise)
Bach English suite no.3 in G minor
Schumann Études symphoniques, op.13
Chopin Scherzo no.3 in C sharp minor, op.39

YOUNG UCK KIM (vn)
EMANUEL AX (pf)
20 Aug. 11.00 *Queen's Hall*
Mozart Sonata no.27 in G, K379
Webern Four pieces, op.7
Fauré Sonata no.1 in A, op.13
Beethoven Sonata no.9 in A (Kreutzer), op.47

NIGEL KENNEDY (vn)
PETER PETTINGER (pf)
28 Aug. 11.00 *Queen's Hall*
Bach Sonata for solo violin no.1 in G minor
Brahms Sonata no.2 in A, op.100
Bartók Sonata for solo violin
Stravinsky The firebird: Excerpts; arr. Dushkin
Stravinsky Petrushka: Excerpts; arr. Dushkin
Gershwin Two preludes

HEINRICH SCHIFF (vc)
ROGER VIGNOLES (pf)
12 Aug. 11.00 *Queen's Hall*
Bach Suite for solo cello no.1 in G
Shostakovich Sonata in D minor, op.40
Beethoven Sonata no.3 in A, op.69
Martinu Variations on a theme of Rossini

JAZZ

McEWAN'S JAZZ FESTIVAL ALL-STARS
23 Aug. 20.00 *Usher Hall*
The Golden Age Of Jazz
Harry 'Sweets' Edison, Buddy Tate, Milt Hinton, Al Grey, Dick Hyman, Ray Bryant, Gus Johnson, Ron Ray, Frances Cowan, Jack Falton, Brian Sheills, Ken Ellis, Janusz Kozlowski, Jerry Forde, Ricky Steele, Fapy Lafertin, Paul Sealey, Bent Persson, Bruce Adams, Bill Allred, Jim Galloway, Jack Parnell, Fionna Duncan, Warsaw Old Timers, Kustbandet of Sweden, Spanky Davis, Al Fairweather
Introduced by Dick Hyman

CLEO LAINE
JOHN DANKWORTH QUINTET
26 Aug. 19.30 *King's Theatre*

DRAMA

OXFORD PLAYHOUSE
21-30 Aug. 19.30 (exc.Sun)
Assembly Hall
HAMLET Shakespeare
Hamlet David Threlfall
Ophelia Sarah Berger
Gertrude Jean Marsh
Claudius Malcolm Rennie
Polonius/Priest Richard Kay
Horatio Michael Garner
Laertes Colin Bruce
Fortinbras/Voltimand Matthew Line
Osric/Player (King) Christopher Whittingham
Bernardo/Player (Lucianus) David Michaels
Francisco/Captain Thomas Branch
Marcellus Charles Bartholomew
Cornelius Alexander Hardy
Rosencrantz Ian Reddington
Guildenstern Peter MacQueen
Player (Queen) Clare Holman
Gravediggers John Rolfe, Charles Bartholomew
Reynaldo John Rolfe
Chorister Richard Townhill
Director Richard Williams
Designer Nadine Baylis
Lighting Raymond Cross

ROYAL SCOTTISH ACADEMY OF MUSIC AND DRAMA
12,13, 16, 17, 21, 23, 24 Aug. 18.30 14, 15, 19, 20, 22 Aug. 21.30 17, 20, 24 Aug. 14.30 *Signet Library*
THE GENTLE SHEPHERD Ramsay
Sir William Worthy Robin Begg
Patie Ramon Griffin
Roger Liam Brennan
Symon Gordon Munro
Glaud Matthew Costello
Bauldy Frank Gallagher
Peggy Hilary MacLean
Jenny Kathryn Howden
Mause Kate Cook
Madge Anne Marie Timoney
Prologue/Elspa Leone Connery
Director Toby McLauchlin
Costumes Ann Birnie, Christine Carey
Lighting Gary Brunton
Choreographer Elizabeth Henderson
Musical director John Langdon
Music Cedric Thorpe Davie

EDINBURGH INTERNATIONAL FESTIVAL
14,15, 18-20, 22 Aug. 18.30 11-13, 16, 21, 23 Aug. 21.30 14, 16, 21, 23 Aug. 14.30 *Signet Library*

DOUGLAS Home

Lady Randolph — Clare Richards
Lord Randolph — Roy Hanlon
Douglas — James Telfer
Glenalvon — Paul Young
Anna — Barbara Horne
Old Norval — John Grieve
Servant — Ian Briggs
Director — Joan Knight
Designer — Helen Wilkinson
Lighting — Simon Sewel

11-16 Aug. 19.30 14, 16 Aug. 14.30
Leith Theatre
A WEE TOUCH OF CLASS Molière
(Adapted from *Le bourgeois gentilhomme* by Coffey *and* Fulton)

Music master — Alan Vicary
Pupil — Rebecca Hawking
Netty — Maureen Carr
Dancing master — David Barclay
Archibald Jenner — Rikki Fulton
Gowrie — Kenneth Lindsay
Fleming — Forbes Masson
Fencing master — Roy Dunsire
Philosopher — Clem Ashby
Clementina Jenner — Janet Michael
Lord Fordell — Tony Roper
Alan Foringale — Ian Arthur
Tam Byres — Iain Stuart Robertson
Alison Jenner — Joyce Deans
Marchioness of Marchmont — Kate Matheson
Director — Joan Knight
Designer — Nigel Hook
Lighting — Simon Sewell
(in Association with Perth Theatre)

WORLD THEATRE SEASON

BAVARIAN STATE THEATRE
14-16 Aug. 19.15 16 Aug. 14.30
King's Theatre
JOHN GABRIEL BORKMAN Ibsen (Ger)

John Gabriel Borkman — Hans Michael Rehberg
Gunhild Borkman — Christine Buchegger
Erhart Borkman — Tobias Moretti
Ella Rentheim — Christa Berndl
Fanny Wilton — Rita Russek
Vilhelm Foldal — Heinz Bennent
Housekeeper — Heidy Förster
Frida Foldal — Anne Bennent
Director — Ingmar Bergman
Designer — Gunilla Palmstierna-Weiss

ROYAL DRAMATIC THEATRE, Stockholm
28-30 Aug. 19.30 30 Aug. 14.30
King's Theatre
MISS JULIE Strindberg

Miss Julie — Marie Göranzon
Jean — Peter Stormare
Kristin — Gerthi Kulle
Director — Ingmar Bergman
Designer — Gunilla Palmstierna-Weiss

MARKET THEATRE, Johannesburg
14-16 Aug. 19.30 16 Aug. 14.30
Lyceum Theatre
BORN IN THE RSA
Created by Barney Simon and cast

Susan — Vanessa Cooke
Zack — Timmy Kwebulana
Glen — Neil McCarthy
Sindiswa — Gcina Mhlophe
Nikki — Terry Norton
Thenjiwe — Thoko Ntshinga
Mia — Fiona Ramsay
Director — Barney Simon
Scenery — Sarah Roberts
Lighting — Mannie Manim

25-27 Aug. 20.00 27 Aug. 15.00
St Bride's Centre
28-30 Aug. 19.30 30 Aug. 14.30
Lyceum Theatre
ASINAMALI! Ngema
Solomzi Bhisholo, Thami Cele, Bongani Hlophe, Bheki Mqadi, Boy Ngema

Director — Mbongeni Ngema
Lighting — Mannie Manim

COMPAÑIA DE NURIA ESPERT, Spain
18-20 Aug. 19.30 20 Aug. 14.30
Lyceum Theatre
YERMA Lorca

Yerma — Nuria Espert
Juan — Juan Miralles
Maria — Rosa Vicente
Victor — Juan Sala
Old pagan lady — Vicky Lagos
Young girl — Karmele Aramburu
Madwoman/Female — Cristina Higueras
Sisters-in-law — Jesus Ruyman, Manuel de Benito
Dolores — Teresa Cortes
Male — Jesus Ruyman
Female voice — Ana Frau
Director — Victor Garcia
Designer — Fabia Puigserver
Lighting — Eric Teunis

COMPAÑIA DE JOSÉ LUIS GOMEZ, Spain
22-24 Aug. 19.30 23 Aug. 14.30
Lyceum Theatre
BLOOD WEDDING Lorca

Mother — Gemma Cuervo
Bridegroom — Jorge de Juan
Bride — Gloria Munoz
Neighbour/Death — Alicia Agut
Leonardo — Helio Pedregal
Leonardo's wife — Blanca Portillo
Mother-in-law — Carmen Cagigal
Father — Manuel Torremocha
Maid — Sonsoles Benedicto
Girl — Maria Jose Chacon
Boy — Antonio Morales
Girls — Lala Aguilera, Maite Chacon
Woodcutters — Ruben Tobias, Antonio Carrasco, Felipe Velez
Moon — Asuncion Sanchez
Director — José Luis Gomez
Scenery and lighting — Manfred Dittrich
Costumes — Pepe Rubio

THÉÂTRE DE LA SALAMANDRE, France
26, 27 Aug. 19.30 Lyceum Theatre
LE SAPERLEAU Bourdet

Apostasie — Françoise Benejam
El Narrador — Christian Drillaud
Morvianne — Agnes Mallèt
Le Saperleau — Guy Perrot
Directors — Alain Milianti, Gildas Bourdet
Designers — Joel Pitti, Gildas Bourdet

TOHO COMPANY, Japan
23, 25, 26, 27 Aug. 21.00
Courtyard of Old College, Edinburgh University
MEDEA Euripides (Jap)

Medea — Mikijiro Hira
Jason — Masane Tsukayama
Creon — Akihiko Shiojima
Aegeus — Ryuzaburo Otomo
Nurse — Hatsuo Yamaya, Kazuhisa Seshimo
Messenger — Takayuki Sugo
Children — Ken Osawa, Tatsuya Miura
Soldier — Fujio Higashi, Takuzo Kaneda
Director — Yukio Ninagawa
Designer — Mutsuo Takahashi
Scenery — Setsu Asakura
Lighting — Sumio Yoshii

STARY THEATRE, Cracow
9-16 Aug. 20.00 14,16 Aug. 15.00
St Bride's Centre
CRIME AND PUNISHMENT Dostoyevsky

Radyon Raskolnikov — Jerzy Radziwilowicz
Porphiry Petrovich — Jerzy Stuhr
Sonia Marmeladov — Barbara Grabowska-Oliwa
Razumihin — Krzysztof Globisz
Zamatov — Jan Monczka
Prochowich — Juliusz Grabowski
Nikolai — Andrzej Hudziak
Koch — Ryszard Lukowski
Mieszczanin — Kazimierz Borowiec
Director — Andrzej Wajda
Designer — Krystyna Zachwatowicz
Lighting — Edward Klosinski

WOOSTER GROUP, USA
12-18 Aug. 20.00 16 Aug. 15.00
Church Hill Theatre
THE ROAD TO IMMORTALITY (Part 2)
Steve Buscemi, Jim Clayburgh, Willem Dafoe, Norman Frisch, Jim Johnson, Michael Kirby, Anna Kohler, Nancy Reilly, Elion Sacker, Peyton Smith, Kate Valk, Michael Stumm, Ron Vawter, Jeff Webster

Director — Elizabeth Le Compte
Scenery — Jim Clayburgh
Costumes — Kate Valk, Peyton Smith

TAKEDA MARIONETTE THEATRE, Japan
21-23 Aug. 19.30 20, 21, 23 Aug. 14.30
Church Hill Theatre
SHISHI MAI (Dragon dance)
BAROQUE
KODOMO NO YUME (A child's dream)
LECTURE
HASHIBENKI (Duel between Benki and Ushiwaka)

Lighting — Kosaka Ikeda

FLYING KARAZAMOV BROTHERS, USA
11, 12 Aug. 19.30 12, 14-16 Aug. 23.00
King's Theatre
18-23 Aug. 19.30 Leith Theatre
JUGGLE AND HYDE: A play with words

CHINESE MAGICAL CIRCUS
26-30 Aug. 19.30 28, 30 Aug. 15.00
30 Aug. 11.00 Playhouse

TRAVERSE THEATRE
11-16 Aug. 19.30 13 Aug. 15.00
St Cecilia's Hall
HOGG: THE SHEPHERD JUSTIFIED Mohr

James Hogg — Donald Douglas

14-16, 18-23, 25-30 Aug. 19.30 16, 23, 30 Aug. 14.30 Portobello Town Hall
LAUDER
Jimmy Logan as Sir Harry Lauder
Devised and created by Jimmy Logan

Director — Clive Perry
Conductor — Patrick McCann
Lighting — Bill Cleghorn

22, 23 Aug. 23.00 28-30 Aug. 22.45
Lyceum Theatre
SCOTLAND THE WHAT - The most requested songs and sketches
Buff Hardie, Stephen Robertson, George Donald

Director — James Logan

POETRY AND PROSE RECITALS

A GALLERY OF SCOTS
Performed by Tom Fleming

18 Aug. 15.00 *St Cecilia's Hall*
BORDER AND BALLAD
with Edith Macarthur (rdr)
Devised by Tom Fleming

19 Aug. 15.00 *St Cecilia's Hall*
ROBERT FERGUSSON
with James Cairncross (rdr), Clifford Hughes (ten)
Compiled by Tom Fleming

20 Aug. 15.00 *St Cecilia's Hall*
CARLYLE AND JANE
with Edith Macarthur (rdr)
Devised by Henry Donald

21 Aug. 15.00 *St Cecilia's Hall*
WILLIAM SOUTAR
Devised by Tom Fleming *and* George Bruce

22 Aug. 15.00 *St Cecilia's Hall*
EDWIN MUIR AND WILLA
with Eileen McCallum (rdr)
Devised by Henry Donald

23 Aug. 15.00 and 19.30 *St Cecilia's Hall*
MACDIARMID A DRUNK MAN LOOKS AT THE THISTLE
Tom Fleming

24 Aug. 15.00
St Andrew and St George's
ST LUKE'S GOSPEL
(Translated into Scots by Lorimer)
Tom Fleming (rdr)

SCOTTISH POETRY LIBRARY
Northern Lights
28 Aug. 15.00 *St Cecilia's Hall*
Tom Paulin, Douglas Dunn (rdr)

29 Aug. 15.00 *St Cecilia's Hall*
Lassi Nummi, Derick Thomson (rdr)

SALTIRE SOCIETY
24, 30 Aug. 15.00 *St Cecilia's Hall*
GAELIC SONG IN THE AGE OF THE ENLIGHTENMENT
Anne Lorne Gillies (sop), Rhona MacKay (clarsach)

25, 26 Aug. 15.00 *St Cecilia's Hall*
THE TREMBLING STRING: Robert Burns and the Scottish musical tradition
Patricia MacMahon (sop), William McCue (bs), John Shedden (rdr), Lindsay Sinclair (pf), Alastair Hardie (fiddle)
Devised by George Bruce

27 Aug. 15.00 28 Aug. 11.00
St Cecilia's Hall
A HOTBED OF GENIUS
James Cairncross, Kirsty Wark (rdr)
Devised by Paul H. Scott

11-15, 18-22, 25-29 Aug. 20.00
Festival Club
THE CANTY HOLE
Mike Maran, Jack Evans, Derek Hoy, Rod Paterson

DANCE

LYON OPÉRA BALLET
12-16 Aug. 19.30 16 Aug. 14.30
Playhouse
CINDERELLA
Choreographer Maguy Marin
Music Prokofiev
Designer Montserrat Casanova
Lighting John Spradberry
Dancers Françoise Joullié, Jocelyne Mocogni, Stéphane Vessier, Gérald Joubert, Chantal Réquéna, Danièle Pater, Geneviève Reynaud, Brigitte Scheid, Inés Baroux, Sandrine Deshaie, Patricia Tolos, Lucas van Dapperen, Valerie Lacognata, Tanya Darbey
Scottish Chamber Orchestra
Conductors Bramwell Tovey, Ormsby Wilkins

BALLET OF THE GREAT THEATRE, Warsaw
18-23 Aug. 19.30 23 Aug. 14.30
Playhouse
THE SLEEPING BEAUTY
Choreographer Piotre Goussiev *after* Petipa
Music Tchaikovsky
Designer Jadwiga Jarosiewicz
Dancers Eva Glowacka, Beata Wiech, Renata Smukala, Mariusz Malecki, Anna Bialecka, Elzbieta Kwiatkowska, Lukasz Gruziel, Arkadiusz Stepien, Marek Almert, Bogdan Cholewa, Jerzy Kosjanik, Stefan Zeromski, Barbara Kryda, Barbara Sier, Barbara Klusek, Beata Nowinska, Danuta Borzecka, Kama Akucewicz, Maja Dubik, Bozena Szymanska, Edyta Wasilewska, Violetta Klimczewska, Anita Pietrewicz, Halina Wisniewska, Zbigniev Juchnowski, Bozena Szymanska, Izabela Zagorska, Julita Lubinska, Emil Wesolowski
Scottish Chamber Orchestra
Conductor Bogdan Oledzki

LONDON FESTIVAL BALLET 2
11-13 Aug. 19.30 13 Aug. 14.30
Lyceum Theatre
PETRUSHKA VARIATIONS (World première)
Choreographer and designer John Neumeier
Music Stravinsky
SONG OF A WAYFARER
Choreographer Maurice Béjart
Music Mahler; arr. Schoenberg
Lighting John van der Heyden
LAND
Choreographer Christopher Bruce
Music Nordheim
Designer Walter Nobbe
Lighting John B. Read
DROP YOUR PEARLS AND HOG IT, GIRL
Choreographer Michael Clark
Music The Fall, Saint-Saëns, Kecak Hinton
Costumes Bodymap
Lighting Charles Atlas
Dancers Peter Schaufuss, Patrick Armand, Trinidad Sevillano, Matz Skoog, Janet Mulligan, Josephine Jewkes, Karen Gee, Darryl Norton, Gretchen Newburger, Alessandro Molin, Virginie Alberti, Kevin Haigen, Pablo Savoye, Martyn Fleming, Craig Randolph, Kevin Richmond, Susan Hogard, Susan Dromisky
With Richard Jackson (bs), David Elwin, Kevin Darvas (pf)

EXHIBITIONS

Various venues
SCOTTISH ART TODAY: Artists at work 1986

Royal Museum of Scotland
A HOTBED OF GENIUS: The Scottish Enlightenment 1730-1790
Designed by John L. Paterson

Talbot-Rice Centre
PAINTING IN SCOTLAND, THE GOLDEN AGE

Royal Scottish Academy
THE ENTERPRISING SCOT

ASSOCIATED EXHIBITIONS
(Not organized by the Festival Society)

Scottish National Gallery of Modern Art
JOHN BELLANY

National Gallery of Scotland
LIGHTING UP THE LANDSCAPE: French impressionism and its origins

National Library of Scotland
SCOTLAND AND INDIA

Scottish National Portrait Gallery
THE ART AND INDUSTRY OF JAMES TASSIE

Scottish National Portrait Gallery
PRINTED LIGHT

Fine Art Society
AT HOME: Scottish interiors

City of Edinburgh Art Centre
SOFTWEAR: Commonwealth and Scottish textiles

Fruitmarket Gallery
THE MIRROR AND THE LAMP

Reid Concert Hall
THE HISTORIC CLARINET

FILM

24 Aug. 20.00 25 Aug. 15.00 *Playhouse*
GREED
Carl Davis conducts the world première of his new score
(In association with the Edinburgh Film Festival)

COMMUNITY EVENTS

The Dome
CIRCUS SENSO *and other events*

1987

OPERA

FOLKOPERA, Stockholm
11, 12, 14, 15 Aug. 19.30 13 Aug. 16.00
15 Aug. 14.30 *Leith Theatre*
DIE ZÄUBERFLÖTE Mozart (Swed)
Tamino Jan Nilsson
Arile Helleland
Pamina Katarina Pilotti
Irene Almén
Papageno Ulf Lundmark
Stefan Axelsson
Sarastro Alf Häggstam
Staffan Rydén
Queen of the Night Anette Stridh
Lena Willman
Speaker Jan van der Schaaf
1st Lady Christina Falk
Margaretha Melz
2nd Lady Anna Tomson
Marianne Myrsten
3rd Lady Catharina Olsson
Inger Stark
Papagena Marianne Andersen
Barbro Netin
Monostatos Robert Grundin
Erling Larsen
3 Boys Kasper Soila, Christopher Bjurling, Fredrik Ulfhielm
1st Colleague Thomas Annmo
Erling Larsen
Conductor Kerstin Nerbe
Director Claes Fellbom
Scenery Sören Brunes
Costumes Mathias Clason

ALTE OPER, Frankfurt
19, 21, 22 Aug. 19.30 *Leith Theatre*
THE ENGLISH CAT Henze
Lord Puff Neil Jenkins
Arnold Richard Crist
Mr Jones/Judge/Mr Fawn Alan Watt
Peter/Mr Keen/Lucian/Counsel for the Defence/Parson Julian Pike
Louise Deborah Rees
Miss Crisp Eileen Hulse
Miss Gomfit Tracey Chadwell
Lady Toodle Ameral Gunson
Mr Plunkett/Counsel for the prosecution Jonathan Best
Minette Susan Roberts
Babette Eirian James
Tom Alan Cemore
Scottish Opera Orchestra
Conductor David Shallon
Director Ian Strasfogel
Scenery Hans Hoffer
Costumes Joachim Herzog

NATIONAL OPERA OF FINLAND
26, 29 Aug. 19.30 *King's Theatre*
RIGOLETTO Verdi
Rigoletto Jorma Hynninen
Duke Pietro Ballo
Gilda Dilber
Maddalena Heljä Angervo
Sparafucile Jaakko Ryhänen
Giovanni Raija Määttänen-Falck
Count Monterone Esa Ruuttunen
Marullo Risto Hirvonen
Borsa Risto Saarman
Count Ceprano Hannu Malin
Countess Ceprano Riitta Pietarinen
Page Heli Närhi
Officer Pekka Sirola
Conductor Eri Klas
Director Jussi Tapola
Designer Seppo Nurmimaa
Lighting Petri Pylkkö

28, 30 Aug. 19.30 *King's Theatre*
JUHA Merikanto
Juha Jorma Hynninen
Tapani Valtasaari
Marja Eeva-Liisa Saarinen
Maija Lokka
Kaisa Merja Wirkkala
Juha's mother Aino Takala
Shemeikka Peter Lindroos
Shemeikka's mother Helena Salonius
Akulina Raija Määttänen-Falck
Anja Satu Vihavainen
Maura Johanna Tuomi
Nasti Riikka Rantanen
Serahviina Marjo Kuusela
Kala-Matti Matti Lehtinen
Tar-makers Heikki Saarnikko, Tuomo Häkkilä
Conductor Ulf Söderblom
Director Sakari Puurunen
Scenery Juha Lukala
Costumes Kaija Salaspuro
Lighting Tommi Kitti

THE SHANGAI KUNJU THEATRE
27, 29 Aug. 19.30 *Leith Theatre*
THE PEONY PAVILION Xianzu
(Adapted by Lu Jianzhi)
Lady Bridal Du Hua Wen Yi
Maid Fragrance Jin Caiqin
Scholar Liu Mengmei Yue Meiti
Teacher Dr Chen Ji Zhenghua
Governor Du Bao Shen Xiaoming
Flower Goddess Chu Xiang
Lord of the Underworld Zhong Waide
Taoist nun Zhu Xiaoyu
Director Hong Mo
Artistic director Yu Zhenfei
Designer Fang Chuanyun
Lighting Wang Hanru

SCOTTISH OPERA CHORUS AND ORCHESTRA
24 Aug. 20.00 *Usher Hall*
GIRL CRAZY Gershwin
Conductor John Mauceri
Soloists Harry Groener, Tudi Roche, Susan Terry

ORCHESTRAL CONCERTS

BOLSHOI THEATRE ORCHESTRA, Moscow
9 Aug. 20.00 *Usher Hall*
Rimsky-Korsakov The legend of the invisible city of Kitezh - Suite; arr. Steinberg
Mussorgsky Songs and dances of death
Tchaikovsky Symphony no.5 in E minor, op.64
Conductor Mark Ermler
Soloist Irina Arkhipova (mez)

10 Aug. 20.00 *Usher Hall*
Shostakovich Festival overture
Shostakovich Concerto for cello no.1 in E flat, op.107
Prokofiev Symphony no.5 in B flat, op.100
Conductor Mark Ermler
Soloist Alexander Rudin (vc)

12 Aug. 20.00 *Usher Hall*
Liadov From the Book of Revelation
Glazunov Concerto for piano no.1 in F minor, op.92
Rachmaninov Symphonic dances, op.45
Conductor Alexander Lazarev
Soloist Victoria Postnikova (pf)

15 Aug. 20.00 *Usher Hall*
Shostakovich Symphony no.6 in B minor, op.54
Prokofiev Concerto for violin no.2 in G minor, op.63
Scriabin Le poème de l'extase
Conductor Alexander Lazarev
Soloist Sergei Girshenko (vn)

SCOTTISH CHAMBER ORCHESTRA
11 Aug. 20.00 *Usher Hall*
P.M. Davies Sinfonietta academica
Takemitsu Nostalghia - in memory of Andrei Tarkovsky (World première)
Beethoven Symphony no.3 in E flat (Eroica), op.55
Conductor Sir Peter Maxwell Davies
Soloist Sir Yehudi Menuhin (vn)

20 Aug. 22.45 *Ross Bandstand*
Fireworks Concert
Copland Fanfare for the common man
Handel Zadok the Priest - Coronation anthem
Davis Prince Regent
Walton Henry V: Death of Falstaff *and* Agincourt song
Davis The Glenlivet fireworks music (World première)
Conductor Carl Davis
Scottish Philharmonic Singers

SCOTTISH NATIONAL ORCHESTRA
Conductor Neeme Järvi
13 Aug. 20.00 *Usher Hall*
Berlioz La damnation de Faust
Soloists Ann Murray (mez), David Rendall (ten), David Wilson-Johnson (bar), Stephen Richardson (b-bar), EF Chorus

18 Aug. 20.00 *Usher Hall*
J. McLeod The Shostakovich connection
Glazunov The seasons
Shostakovich Symphony no.5 in D minor, op.47

BBC SCOTTISH SYMPHONY ORCHESTRA
14 Aug. 20.00 *Usher Hall*
Lutoslawski Chain 3
Rachmaninov Concerto for piano no.2 in C minor, op.18
Mozart Symphony no.40 in G minor, K550
Conductor Jerzy Maksymiuk
Soloist John Ogdon (pf)

16 Aug. 15.00 *Usher Hall*
Children's Concert
Rossini Guillaume Tell: Overture
Poulenc Babar the little elephant
D. Bedford With a hundred - plus kazoos
Britten The young person's guide to the orchestra
Conductor Howard Williams
Soloist Nigel Hawthorne (narr)

PITTSBURGH SYMPHONY ORCHESTRA
(Orchestra in Residence 1987)
21 Aug. 20.00 *Usher Hall*
Beethoven Symphony no.8 in F, op.93
Beethoven Symphony no.9 in D minor (Choral), op.125
Conductor Lorin Maazel
Soloists Mechthild Gessendorf (sop), Linda Finnie (mez), Richard Leech (ten), Peter Meven (bs), EF Chorus

22 Aug. 20.00 *Usher Hall*
Gould Classical variations on colonial themes

Hindemith Mathis der Maler - Symphony
Brahms Concerto for piano no.2 in B flat, op.83
Conductor Lorin Maazel
Soloist Peter Donohoe (pf)

23 Aug. 20.00 *Usher Hall*
Schubert Rosamunde: Overture
Stravinsky The firebird - Suite
Gershwin Concerto for piano in F
Gershwin An American in Paris
Conductor Lorin Maazel
Soloist Patricia Prattis Jennings (pf)

25 Aug. 20.00 *Usher Hall*
Mozart Chi sà, chi sà qual sia
Mozart Exsultate, jubilate
Mahler Symphony no.5 in C sharp minor
Conductor Michael Tilson Thomas
Soloist Marvis Martin (sop)

26 Aug. 20.00 *Usher Hall*
Copland Billy the Kid - Suite
Gershwin For Lily Pons
Gershwin Short story
Gershwin Walking the dog
Bernstein West side story: Dances
Bernstein Chichester psalms
Conductor and soloist Michael Tilson Thomas (pf)
EF Chorus

SWEDISH RADIO SYMPHONY ORCHESTRA
Conductor Esa-Pekka Salonen
28 Aug. 20.00 *Usher Hall*
Brahms Concerto for violin in D, op.77
Schoenberg Pelleas und Melisande
Soloist Viktoria Mullova (vn)

29 Aug. 20.00 *Usher Hall*
Berwald Symphony no.4 in E flat
Lutoslawski Livre pour orchestre
Sibelius Symphony no.5 in E flat, op.82

CHAMBER CONCERTS

MELOS QUARTET OF STUTTGART
11.00 *Queen's Hall*
Beethoven String Quartets
11 Aug. Nos. 12 in E flat; 7 in F
13 Aug. Nos. 11 in F minor; 15 in A minor
3 in D
15 Aug. Nos. 1 in F; 10 in E flat
13 in B flat
17 Aug. Nos. 2 in G; 9 in C
Grosse Fuge in B flat
19 Aug. Nos. 5 in A; 14 in C sharp minor
4 in C minor
21 Aug. Nos. 6 in B flat; 16 in F
8 in E minor

BOLSHOI SEXTET
12 Aug. 11.00 *Queen's Hall*
Glinka Sextet in E flat
Glinka Divertimento brillante on themes from Bellini's 'La sonnambula'
Songs by Glinka, Tchaikovsky
Soloists Elena Shkolnikova (sop), Alexander Voroshilo (bar)

14 Aug. 11.00 *Queen's Hall*
Barkauskas Sextet
Rachmaninov Elegia
Kara-Karaev Dance
Songs by Rachmaninov, Dargomizhsky, Malashkin
Soloists Elena Shkolnikova (sop), Alexander Voroshilo (bar)

SAXOPHONE QUARTET OF NICE
20 Aug. 11.00 *Queen's Hall*
Works by Bach, Desloges, Krebs, Fjeanneau, Albinoni, Albeniz, Rivies, Scarlatti, Haydn, Beethoven, P. Woods, Mozart, Pierne, Handel

SHOSTAKOVICH QUARTET
25 Aug. 11.00 *Queen's Hall*
Shostakovich Quartet no.4 in D, op.83
Shostakovich Quartet no.7 in F sharp minor, op.108
Shostakovich Quartet no.12 in D flat, op.133

27 Aug. 11.00 *Queen's Hall*
Prokofiev Quartet no.2 in F, op.92
Stravinsky Three pieces
Ravel Quartet in F

29 Aug. 11.00 *Queen's Hall*
Borodin Quartet no.2 in D
Shostakovich Quartet no.13 in B flat minor, op.138
Schumann Quartet no.3 in A, op.41/3

EDINBURGH FESTIVAL CHORUS WALLACE COLLECTION
17 Aug. 20.00 *Usher Hall*
Works by Storace, Beethoven, Tippett, Gabrieli, Byrd, Bruckner
Conductor Arthur Oldham

SCOTTISH EARLY MUSIC CONSORT
26 Aug. 11.00 *Queen's Hall*
Medieval songs of love and war
Director Warwick Edwards
Soloists Lorna Anderson (sop), Paul Hindmarsh (ten), Alan Watt (bar)

RENAISSANCE GROUP OF ST ANDREWS
30 Aug. 22.30 31 Aug. 19.30
St Giles' Cathedral
Carver Mass for 5 voices; ed. Muriel Brown
Conductor Douglas Gifford
(Presented by the Saltire Society)

ESA-PEKKA SALONEN: A composer's choice
A Weekend of 20th Century Music
ARDITTI QUARTET
22 Aug. 11.00 *Queen's Hall*
Schnittke Quartet no.2
Carter Quartet no.4
Hakola Quartet
Gubaidulina Quartet no.3 (World première)

23 Aug. 16.00 *Queen's Hall*
Wyschnegradsky Quartet no.1
R. Reynolds Coconino... a shattered landscape
Cage Concerto for piano
Glass Quartet no.2 (Mishima)
Xenakis Tetras
Xenakis Akea for piano and strings
with Claude Helffer (pf)

ANSSI KARTTUNEN (vc)
TUIJA HAKKILA (pf)
22 Aug. 15.00 *Queen's Hall*
Wuorinen Duuiensela
Salonen YTA 2 for piano
Salonen YTA 3 for cello (World première)
Denisov Sonata
Schedrin Kadril
Carter Sonata

ELECTRONIC MUSIC
23 Aug. 12.00 *Queen's Hall*
Druckman Animus one*
Saariaho Jardin secret no.2
Denisov Chant des oiseaux
Davidovsky Synchronism no.3
with John Kenny (tbn), Tuija Hakkila (pf), Jonty Harrison

PARAGON ENSEMBLE
24 Aug. 11.00 *Queen's Hall*
Gubaidulina Jubilate
Reich Sextet
Crumb Music for a summer evening (Macrokosmos 3)

RECITALS

FELICITY LOTT (sop)
GEOFFREY PARSONS (pf)
16 Aug. 20.00 *Usher Hall*
Songs by Tchaikovsky, Wolf, Offenbach, Messager, O. Straus, Dring, Walton

IRINA BOGACHOVA, (mez)
ELENA GAUDASINSKAYA (pf)
18 Aug. 11.00 *Queen's Hall*
Mussorgsky Songs and dances of death
Arias by Saint-Saëns, Pergolesi, Cilea, Gounod, Bizet, Rossini
Songs by Shostakovich

SIR YEHUDI MENUHIN (vn)
PAUL COKER (pf)
10 Aug. 11.00 *Queen's Hall*
Brahms Sonata no.2 in A, op.100
Beethoven Sonata no.7 in C minor, op.30/2
Bartók Sonata no.1

VIKTORIA MULLOVA (vn)
ROGER VIGNOLES (pf)
27 Aug. 20.00 *Usher Hall*
Schubert Sonata in A (Duo), D574
Bach Partita for solo violin no.1 in B minor
Ravel Sonata in G
Saint-Saëns Introduction and rondo capriccioso

EVELYN GLENNIE (perc)
PHILIP SMITH (pf)
28 Aug. 11.00 *Queen's Hall*
Works by Chopin, Miki, Inns, Singer, Mayuzumi, Saint-Saëns, Abe, Helmscroot, Glennie, Musser

STOMU YAMASH'TA (perc)
26-29 Aug. 19.30 29 Aug. 22.30
St Bride's Centre

MICHAEL LAIRD, WILLIAM HOUGHTON (tpt), DENNIS TOWNHILL (org)
26 Aug. 14.30 *St Mary's Cathedral*
Trumpet sonatas by Franceschini, Purcell, Torelli, Baldassare, Vivaldi

JAZZ

McEWAN'S EDINBURGH INTERNATIONAL JAZZ FESTIVAL
19 Aug. 20.00 *Usher Hall*
A Tribute To Benny Goodman
Jay McShann, Buddy Tate, Oliver Jackson, Harry 'Sweets' Edison, Reggie Johnson, Lillian Boutté, Jim Galloway, Grover Mitchell, Al Casey, Johnny Letman, Bob Wilber Big Band with Joanne Horton, Kansas City All-Stars, Dave Shepherd Quintet

SING HEIGH HO!
26-31 Aug. 19.30 29 Aug. 14.30
Lyceum Theatre
Cleo Laine, John Dankworth Quintet, Alec Dankworth

DRAMA

WORLD THEATRE SEASON

GORKY THEATRE, Leningrad
9, 10, 15 Aug. 19.30 King's Theatre
THE HISTORY OF A HORSE Rozovsky
Kholstomer Evgeny Lebedev
Prince Serpukhovskoy Oleg Basilashvili
Vyazopurikha/Matier/Marie Valentina Kovel
Mily/Officer/Bobrinsky Mikhail Volkov
Feofan/Fritz Yuzef Mironenko
General Vladimir Medvedev
Equerry Mikhail Danilov
Vaska/Waiter Georgy Shtil
Director Georgy Tovstonogov
Designer Eduard Kochergin
Lighting E.M. Kutikov

12, 13 Aug. 19.30 King's Theatre
UNCLE VANYA Chekhov
Alexander Serebriakov Evgeny Lebedev
Elena Andreyevna Natalia Danilova
Sonya Tatiana Bedova
Maria Voinitskaya Mariya Veisbrem
Ivan Voinitsky Oleg Basilashvili
Mikhail Astrov Kirill Lavrov
Ilya Telegin Nikolai Trofimov
Marina Zinaida Sharko
Workman Evgeny Chudakov
Director Georgy Tovstonogov
Designer Eduard Kochergin

BERLINER ENSEMBLE
17-19 Aug. 19.30 King's Theatre
TROILUS AND CRESSIDA Shakespeare (Ger)
Priam Herbert Sievers
Hector Hans-Peter Reinecke
Troilus Martin Seifert
Paris Stefan Lisewski
Deiphobus Peter Tepper
Helenus Wolfgang Holz
Aeneas Franz Viehmann
Antenor Hein Trilling
Calchas Jürgen Watzke
Cressida Corinna Harfouch
Pandarus Arno Wyzniewski
Cassandra Renate Richter
Servant to Troilus Johannes Conrad
Servant to Paris Herbert Olschok
Agamemnon Dieter Knaup
Menelaus Achim Petry
Ulysses Hermann Beyer
Ajax Alejandro Quintana
Achilles Peter Bause
Nestor Michael Gerber
Patroclus Manuel Soubeyrand
Diomedes Jaecki Schwarz
Thersites Ekkehard Schall
Helen Angelika Waller
Alexander Erhard Köster
Directors Manfred Wekwerth, Joachim Tenschert
Scenery Manfred Grund
Costumes Klaus Noack

21, 22 Aug. 19.30 King's Theatre
THE CAUCASIAN CHALK CIRCLE Brecht
Expert/Old dairy farmer/Innkeeper Peter Kalisch
Alleko Bereschwili Erhard Köster
Makinä Abakidze/Farmer's wife Renate Richter
Farmer Horst Wünsch
2nd Farmer/Jussup Jaecki Schwarz
Young peasant Annemone Haase
Old peasant Surab Herman Beyer
Peasant woman Ruth Glöss
Kato Wachtang/Woman merchant Dietlind Stahl
Girl tractor driver/Ludowika Angelika Ritter
Wounded soldier Peter Hladik
Arkade Tscheidse Peter Tepper
Singers Annemone Haase, Marion Koch
Georgi Abaschwili Arno Wyzniewski
Natella Abaschwili Christine Gloger
Shalva Peter Bause
Arsen Kazbeki Dieter Knaup
Bizergan Klaus Hecke
Mikha Loladze Achim Petry
Niko Mikadze/Blackmailer Karl-Maria Steffens
Maro Corinna Harfouch
Grusche Vachnadze Franziska Troegner
Cooks Barbara Dittus, Horst Wünsch
Stable lad Harald Popig
Simon Chachav Hans-Peter Reinecke
Messenger/Doctor Heinrich Buttchereit
Lance-corporal Peter Hladik
Blockhead Johannes Conrad
Husband/Irakli Herbert Sievers
Lavrenti Vachnadze Stefan Lisewski
Aniko Vachnadze Carmen-Maja Antoni
Stable lad/Invalid Jürgen Kern
Brother Anastasius/Old refugee Jürgen Watzke
Azdak Ekkehard Schall
Schauwa Michael Gerber
Limping man Siegfried Meyer
Serving boy Harald Popig
Little mother Grusinien Ruth Glöss
Lawers Jaecki Schwarz, Franz Viehmann
Married couple Renate Richter, Erhard Köster
Director Peter Kupke
Scenery Manfred Grund
Costumes Annemarie Rost
Music Paul Dessau
Conductor Karl Heinz Nehring

20 Aug. 19.30 King's Theatre
BRECHT TO MUSIC: Songs and poems
Music by Kurt Weill and Hanns Eisler
Carmen Maja-Antoni, Peter Bause, Michael Gerber, Christine Gloger, Annemone Haase, Stefan Lisewski, Hans-Peter Reinecke, Renate Richter, Angelika Ritter, Ekkehard Schall, Peter Tepper, Franziska Troegner
Berliner Ensemble Orchestra
Conductor Rainer Böhm

GATE THEATRE, Dublin
10-15 Aug. 19.30 15 Aug. 14.30
Lyceum Theatre
JUNO AND THE PAYCOCK O'Casey
Mary Boyle Rosemary Fine
Juno Boyle Geraldine Plunkett
Johnny Boyle Joe Savino
Jerry Devine Tony Coleman
Captain Jack Boyle Donal McCann
Joxer Daly John Kavanagh
Charles Bentham Garrett Keogh
Maisie Madigan Maureen Potter
Mrs Tancred Stella McCusker
Needle Nugent Séamus Forde
An irregular mobilizer Anto Nolan
Coal-block vendor Mark O'Regan
Sewing machine man Michael Egan
Director Joe Dowling
Scenery Frank Hallinan Flood
Costumes Consolata Boyle
Lighting Rupert Murray

CAMERI THEATRE, Tel Aviv
17-19 Aug. 19.30 19 Aug. 14.30
Lyceum Theatre
MICHAEL KOLHAAS Saunders (*after* Heinrich von Kleist)
Michael Kohlhaas Joseph Carmen
Lawyer/Martin Luther Ilan Dar
Neighbour Henkel/Hinz von Tronka Ori Levi
Steward/Singer/ Kunz von Tronka Ruevan Sheffer
Elizabeth Sandra Sadeh
Junker Wenzel von Tronka Yehuda Mor
Count Wrede (narrator) Yossi Kantz
Chief of police/ Elector of Saxony Itzhak Hezkia
Herze/Meissen Rami Baruch
Director Ilan Ronen
Designer Ruth Dar

23-27 Aug. ? *Pleasance*
KIDDUSH Has'fari
Pninah Shiloni Edna Fleidel
Arieh Shiloni Yossi Graber
Yossi Shiloni Dov Navon
Director Shmuel Has'fari
Designer Yossi Ben-Ari
Lighting Avi Sabari

YUME NO YUMINSHA COMPANY, Japan
21-23 Aug. 19.30 22 Aug. 14.30
Lyceum Theatre
DESCENT OF THE BRUTES Noda (Nokemono Kitarite)
Apollo Juichi Shozo Uesugi
Princess/12 Layers/Thor Heyerdahl Hideki Noda
Boy Brian Akiko Takeshita
Rabbit in the moon Aya Enjoji
Humanitarian Institute chief Yasunori Danta
Idiot Ryosei Tayama
Kitazato Yuichi Haba
Minamizato Kazuyuki Asano
Lady Murasaki Sachiko Matsuura
Lady Sei Kaoru Mukai
Circus barker Nobuyoshi Ueda
Narrator Katsuya Kobayashi
Director Hideki Noda
Scenery Setsu Asakura
Costumes Masami Hara

THE SHANGAI KUNJU THEATRE
24 Aug. 19.30 29 Aug. 14.30
Leith Theatre
THE WOMAN WARRIOR...A martial arts performance

25, 26, 28, 30, 31 Aug.19.30 Leith Theatre
THE KUNJU MACBETH (Adapted from Shakespeare by Zheng Shifeng)
Macbeth Ji Zhenghua
Lady Macbeth Zhang Jingxian
Banquo Fang Yang
Macduff Yao Zufu
Duncan Shen Xiaoming
Malcolm Wu Dezhang
Doctor Liu Yilung
Lady Macduff Xu Yiawang
Gentlewoman Du Wanfang
Witches Wu Jijie, Liu Derong, Zhang Mingrong
Director Li Jia Yao
Kunju director Sheng Chuan Jian
Music Shen Lichun, Ku Shaolin

RAUN RAUN THEATRE, New Guinea
9, 14, 18, 21 Aug. 19.30 12, 16, 23, 25 Aug. 13.00 St Bride's Centre
SAIL THE MIDNIGHT SUN (Pidgin Eng)
10, 19 Aug. 19.30 15, 22 Aug. 15.00 12, 16, 23, 25 Aug. 17.00 St Bride's Centre
MY TIDE LET ME RIDE (Pidgin Eng)
11, 15, 20, 22 Aug. 19.30 12, 16, 23, 25 Aug. 21.00 St Bride's Centre
DANCE OF THE SNAIL (Pidgin Eng)
Seagull/Mother of swordfishes/Cockatoo Jack Puayil
Libra Betty Martin

Bwalai/Land of Hope/Flying fox/Sanguma Tony Bai
The dawn Margaret John
Young Yolina/Chief of the east/Father of Imdeduya Jacob Puas
Yolina Yalambing Namu
Chief of the west/Lord of leisure Robert Yeweh
Woman of the moons/Heron Jedda Suari
Old magic man Hitch Loape
Land of Happiness Hitch Loape, Mary Kom, Alice Molong
Land of Truth/Snail Saio Avefa
Imdeduya Tracy Pari
Mother of Imdeduya Gim Nicholas
Niugini/Robin Kakas Dimik
Secret lover/Hen Somu Koniel
Spirits of the storm Lubi Giwale, Somu Koniel, Norman Bisai
Tree/Sky Lubi Giwale
Uncles Hitch Loape, Saio Avefa
Old widow Mary Kim
Mwaga bird/Wind Nicholas Gioni
Director and choreographer Greg Murphy
Costumes Robson Ubuk, Tracy Pari, Robert Yeweh and company

TBILISI STATE PUPPET THEATRE
15, 17, 21, 23 Aug. 11.00 17, 23 Aug. 14.30 23 Aug. 19.30 Church Hill Theatre
ALFRED AND VIOLETTE Gabriadzde
18 Aug. 11.00 16, 18, 21 Aug. 14.30 Church Hill Theatre
AUTUMN OF OUR SPRINGTIME Gabriadze
19, 22 Aug. 11.00 19 Aug. 14.30 16 Aug. 19.30 Church Hill Theatre
MARSHALL DE FONTIER'S DIAMOND Gabriadze
Hamlet Jijeishvili, Vano Sharashidze (Eng commentary)

EDINBURGH INTERNATIONAL FESTIVAL
10-29 Aug. 19.30 (exc.Sun) 12, 15, 19, 22, 26, 29 Aug. 14.30 Assembly Hall
MARY STUART Schiller
(Eng. Translated by Joseph Mellish)
Mary Stuart Hannah Gordon
Queen Elizabeth Jill Bennett
Hannah Kennedy Julia McCarthy
Leicester John Fraser
Mortimer Jonathon Morris
Paulet James Cairncross
Talbot Leonard Maguire
Kent Alexander Hardy
Melvil John Grieve
Bellievre James McClure
O'Kelly Nigel Hastings
Lord Burleigh John Cairney
Sir William Davison Russell Boulter
Count Aubespine John Buick
Ladies Fenella Kerr, Rachel James
Singer Anne Foley Miller
Director Frank Dunlop
Designer Nadine Baylis
Lighting Graham Large
(In association with the Scottish Theatre Company)

ROYAL EXCHANGE THEATRE, Manchester
10-15, 17-22 Aug. 19.30 13, 15, 20, 22 Aug. 14.30 Church Hill Theatre
A WHOLLY HEALTHY GLASGOW Heggie
Donald Dick Tom Watson
Charley Hood Gerard Kelly
Murdo Caldwell Paul Higgins
Director Richard Wilson
Designer Sue Plummer
Lighting Paul Pyant

THE EDINBURGH EDITION
23, 30, 31 Aug. 19.30 30 Aug. 14.30 Assembly Hall
To celebrate the publication 200 years ago of the Edinburgh edition of *Poems chiefly in the Scottish Dialect* by Robert Burns
Fiona Galloway (sop), Jamie MacDougall (ten), William McCue (bs), Valerie Edmond, Simon Christie (rdr), Royal Scottish Country Dance Society, Festival City Fiddlers, Glencorse Pipes and Drums, Robert Black's Accordeon Trio
(A Scottish Singers Company production)

POETRY AND PROSE RECITALS

TOM FLEMING (rdr)
13 Aug. 15.00 St Cecilia's Hall
EDWIN MUIR AND WILLA
with Anne Kristen (rdr)
Devised by Henry Donald

14 Aug. 15.00 St Cecilia's Hall
THE POETRY OF EDWIN MUIR
Selected and read by Tom Fleming and introduced by George Bruce

15, 16 Aug. 15.00 St Cecilia's Hall
GUTHRIE ON GUTHRIE
(Devised by Margaret Dale from Tyrone Guthrie's *A life in the theatre*)
Tom Fleming (rdr)

SALTIRE SOCIETY
10, 11 Aug. 15.00 St Cecilia's Hall
THE RUSSIAN CONNECTION
William McCue (bs), Edith Macarthur, John Shedden, Eugenie Fraser, Paul Young (rdr), Lindsay Sinclair (pf)
Devised by George Bruce and Kevin Gibbons

17 Aug. 19.30 St Bride's Centre
A SCOTTISH POSTBAG
Edith Macarthur, John Shedden (rdr)
Devised by George Bruce and Paul Scott

24, 25 Aug. 15.00 St Cecilia's Hall
MIRROR FOR MONARCHY
Portraits of Mary, Queen of Scots and James V
Meta Forrest, Ian Gilmour (rdr), Neil Mackie (ten), Kenneth Elliott (hpd)
Devised by Isobel Dunlop

29 Aug. 11.00 and 15.00 St Bride's Centre
TRAVELLERS' TALES
Scottish folk tales in the traditional manner
Betsy Whyte, Duncan Williamson, Sheila Douglas, Andrew Douglas (rdr)

POETS FROM THE USSR
11 Aug. 11.00 St Cecilia's Hall

12 Aug. 15.00 St Cecilia's Hall
Oleg Chukhontsev, Gennadi Krasnikov with Edwin Morgan (rdr)

15 Aug. 11.00 St Cecilia's Hall
Oleg Chukhontsev, Gennadi Krasnikov with Stephen Mulrine (rdr)

13 Aug. 19.30 St Bride's Centre

14 Aug. 14.30 and 19.30 King's Theatre
Evgeny Yevtushenko (rdr)

SCOTTISH POETRY LIBRARY
24, 25 Aug. 19.30 St Cecilia's Hall
FJORD AND FIRTH
Readings by writers from Northern Europe
Marianne Larsen, Sheena Blackhall, Catriona Montgomery, Tessa Ransford, Steinunn Sigurdardottir

17, 18 Aug. 15.00 St Cecilia's Hall
IRENE HANDL
Reading from her book *The gold tip pfitzer*

19-23 Aug. 15.00 St Cecilia's Hall
SHEILA REID (rdr)
AS MISS DOROTHY PARKER ONCE SAID...
with Nigel Lillicrap (pf)
Director John Dane

26-29 Aug. 15.00 St Cecilia's Hall
DAME WENDY HILLER (rdr)
GBS REMEMBERED

DANCE

BALLET THÉÂTRE FRANÇAIS DE NANCY
18-22 Aug. 19.30 22 Aug. 14.00 and 20.15 Playhouse
Homage to Les Ballets Russes and Diaghilev
LES BICHES
Choreographer Bronislava Nijinska
Music Poulenc
Scenery Marie Laurencin
LE SPECTRE DE LA ROSE
Choreographer Mikhail Fokine
Music Weber; arr. Berlioz
Designer Léon Bakst
L'APRÈS-MIDI D'UN FAUNE
Choreographer Vaslav Nijinsky
Music Debussy
Scenery Léon Bakst
PETRUSHKA
Choreographer *after* Mikhail Fokine
Music Stravinsky
Designer Alexander Benois
Dancers Rudolf Nureyev, Alexandra Wells, Nancy Raffa, Adeline Charpentier, Laura Adami, Sophie Marquet, Philippe Anota, Henri Harent, Isabelle Bourgeais, Françoise Baffioni, Philippe Villette, Gilles Reichert, Didier Chazeau, Christine Cloux, Roberta Mazzoni, Sandrine Deshaie, Katy Maris, Geneviève Lafitte, Adriana Pous, Elisabeth Sicart, Léonardo Santos, Eric van den Abbeele, Fabio Molfesi, Nicolas Dufloux, Lionel Tardieu, J.P. Alonso, Xavier Nickler, F. Lemire, V. Lescouzeres
Scottish Philharmonic Orchestra

NATIONAL BALLET OF FINLAND
25, 27 Aug. 19.30 King's Theatre
THE NUTCRACKER
Choreographer Yuri Grigorovich
Music Tchaikovsky
Designer Anneli Qveflander
Lighting Simo Järvinen
Dancers Kirsi Aromaa, Jukka Aromaa, Jarmo Rastas, Lauri Lehto, Aku Ahjolinna, Arja Nieminen, Ulrika Hallberg, Corinna Dahlström, Tommy Kitti, Venla Konttinen, Karl Hedman, Tarja Ranta, Pia Kangasmuukko, Tero Saarinen, Maija Hänninen, Jaana Puupponen, Jyrki Järvinen, Tiina Väre, Sampo Kivelä
Conductor Kari Tikka

BLACK BALLET JAZZ, USA
12-14 Aug. 19.30 11 Aug. 20.30 15 Aug. 14.30 and 20.30 Playhouse

Choreographers Vincent Johnson, Darryl Copeland, Ronnie Marshall
Song Trina Parks
Costumes Mookie and Spudy
Lighting Stephen Bennett
Dancers Jermane Allen, Carmela Alzamie, Robbie Bradford, Claudia Bretas, Stephanie Cole, Boris Davidson, Phyllis Kent, Raymond Lewis, Velia Lockett, Carolyn McPherson, Ronnie Marshall, Joseph Threadgill, April Weeden, Gary White, Chester Whitmore

SIVERKO, USSR
Folk dancers from the far North
9-11 Aug. 19.30 10 Aug. 14.30 Playhouse
Conductor Yuri Merzenkin

XI'AN SINGING AND DANCING COMPANY
24-29 Aug. 19.30 29 Aug. 14.30 Playhouse
THE SOUL OF THE TERRACOTTA ARMY
Dance drama of the Emperor's warriors

CONFERENCE

USSR NOW

EXHIBITIONS

Scottish National Gallery of Modern Art
THE VIGOROUS IMAGINATION: New Scottish art

Royal Museum of Scotland
TBILISI TO TASHKENT: Decorative arts from Soviet Central Asia
Organized by the Museum of Oriental Art, Moscow

ASSOCIATED EXHIBITIONS
(Not organized by the Festival Society)

Royal Scottish Academy
LEADING WORKS FROM THE SAATCHI COLLECTION

National Gallery of Scotland
FRENCH MASTER DRAWINGS FROM STOCKHOLM

National Library of Scotland
IT CAM WI' A LASS: The Stuarts in literature, legend and the arts

Scottish National Portrait Gallery
THE QUEEN'S IMAGE
THE QUEEN'S WORLD
Two exhibitions commemorating the quatercentenary of the execution of Mary, Queen of Scots

WILLIAM CARRICK: 19th Century photographs of Russia

369 Gallery
MOSCOW - A PRIVATE VIEW

City Art Centre
MINIATURE MASTERPIECES: Lacquer work from Russia

City Art Centre
CHILD'S PLAY

Fruitmarket Gallery
DAVID SALLE: Paintings and drawings

Tron Kirk
P.M. - A.D.
A presentation in music, words, photographs and commentaries of survivors of the First World War

Richard Demarco Gallery
THE STORY OF THE SCOTTISH SOLDIER 1600-1914

1988

OPERA

EDINBURGH INTERNATIONAL FESTIVAL
24-27 Aug. 19.00 King's Theatre
LA GATTA CENERENTOLA Simone
Cat Cinderella Fausta Vetere
Stepmother Rino Marcelli
Hairdresser Isa Danieli
Stepsister Patrizia Giuseppe de Vittorio
Dressmaker Anna Spagnuolo
House fairy/Cuccurucù/Gay queen Giovanni Mauriello
Opening song Antonella d'Agostino
Old woman/Gypsy Ofelia de Simone
Prologue/Rosary leader/Ace of clubs Virgilio Villani
St John's dance Giuseppe de Vittorio, Lello Giulivo
Opening song of Act 2 Gianni Lamagna
Castrato voice/Soldier Walter Corda
Soldiers' song Luciano Catapano, Gianni Lamagna
Washerwomen Isa Danieli, Antonella Morea
Chambermaids Adria Mortari, Delia Viola, Anna Spagnuola, Antonella d'Agostino, Patrizia Nasini
Conductor Renato Piemontese
Director Roberto de Simone
Scenery and lighting Mauro Carosi
Costumes Odette Nicoletti

25-27 Aug. 19.30 Leith Theatre
GREEK Turnage
Mum/Waitress 2/Sphinx 1 Helen Charnock
Wife/Doreen/Waitress 1/Sphinx 2 Fiona Kimm
Eddy Quentin Hayes
Dad/Cafe manager/Chief of police Richard Suart
Almeida Ensemble
Conductor Sian Edwards
Director Jonathan Moore
Designer David Blight

FOLKOPERA, Stockholm
13, 14, 15, 17, 18, 19 Aug. 19.30 16 Aug. 16.00 18 Aug. 14.30 Leith Theatre
TURANDOT Puccini (Swed)
Turandot Anne-Lise Berntsen, Turid Nordal Haavik
Calaf Bengt Gustafsson, Erling Larsen
Liu Annika Marberg, Pia-Marie Nilsson
Timur Göran Annebring, Staffan Rydén
Ping Stefan Axelsson, Ulf Lundmark
Pong Thomas Annmo, Jan Nilsson
Pang Per-Arne Hedin, Christian Myrup
Emperor Thomas Annmo, Christian Myrup
Mandarin Jan van der Schaaf
Conductors Glenn Mossop, Kerstin Nerbe
Director Claes Fellbom
Scenery Sören Brunes
Costumes Ann-Mari Anttila
Lighting Arne Åkerström

SCHILLER THEATRE, Germany
29-31 Aug. 19.30 King's Theatre
LA PÉRICHOLE Offenbach (Ger)
La Périchole Regina Lemnitz
Piquillo Wolfgang Ransmayr
Don Andrès de Ribeira Thomas Schendel
Count Miguel de Panatellas Robert Tillian
Don Pedro de Hinoyosa Toni Slama
Old prisoner Max Buchsbaum
Notaries Harry Tchor, Eduard Wildner
Jailor Eduard Wildner
Guadalena/Frasquinella Ksenija Lukic
Berginella/Brambilla Anne-Lisa Nathan
Mastrilla/Ninetta Cornelia Geiger
Conductor Michael Rüggeberg
Director Franz Marijnen
Scenery Santiago del Corral
Costumes Mechthild Schwienhorst
Lighting Steve Kemp

HOUSTON GRAND OPERA
1, 3, 5 Sep. 19.30 Playhouse
NIXON IN CHINA Adams
Chou En-Lai Sanford Sylvan
Richard Nixon James Maddalena
Henry Kissinger Thomas Hammons
Nancy T'ang (1st Secretary) Mari Opatz
2nd Secretary Stephanie Friedman
3rd Secretary Marion Dry
Mao Tse-Tung John Duykers
Pat Nixon Carolann Page
Chiang Ch'ing Trudy Ellen Craney
Hung Chiang-Ch'ing William Wagner
Wu-Ching-Hua Heather Toma
Scottish Chamber Orchestra
Conductor John Adams
Director Peter Sellars
Scenery Adrienne Lobel
Costumes Dunya Ramicova

ENSEMBLE FOR EARLY MUSIC, USA
20, 22-25 Aug. 20.00 22, 24 Aug. 22.30 25 Aug. 15.00 Greyfriar's Kirk
DANIEL AND THE LIONS
Daniel Mark Bleeke
King Belshazzar/Habakku Frank Nemhauser
King Darius Hugo Munday
Queen/Angel Douglas Stevens
Astrologer Johnson Flucker
Lawyer Douglas Shambo
George Watson's Boys' Chorus
Conductor Frederick Renz
Director Paul Hildebrand, Jun.
Costumes Karen Matthews
Lighting Robert Graham Small

NATIONAL YOUTH MUSIC THEATRE
15-19, 21-25, 27 Aug. 19.15 16, 20, 27 Aug. 16.00 George Square Theatre
THE LITTLE RATS Allwood
Libretto J.J. Taylor, David Scott
Directors J.J. Taylor, Mark Pattenden
Designer Christopher Richardson
Costumes Sheila Darlington

ORCHESTRAL CONCERTS

SCOTTISH NATIONAL ORCHESTRA
14 Aug. 20.00 Usher Hall
R. Strauss Aus Italien
Orff Carmina burana
Conductor Neeme Järvi

Soloists Juliet Booth (sop), Neill Archer (ten), Sergei Leiferkus (bar), EF Chorus, St Mary's Cathedral Choir

ORCHESTRA GIOVANILE ITALIANA
15 Aug. 20.00 *Usher Hall*
Bussotti Il catálogo e' quésto: Part 4 - I Poemi *and* Part 3 - 'A fiesole un poema Giovanile'
Mozart Sinfonia concertante for violin and viola, K364
Brahms Symphony no.1 in C minor, op.68
Conductor Piero Bellugi
Soloists Andrea Cappelletti (vn), Olga Arzilli (va)

USSR STATE ORCHESTRA
Conductor Evgeny Svetlanov
16 Aug. 20.00 *Usher Hall*
Balakirev Symphony no.2 in D minor
Rachmaninov Symphony no.1 in D minor, op.13

18 Aug. 20.00 *Usher Hall*
Mussorgsky Khovanshchina: Overture; orch. Shostakovich
Glinka Symphony on two Russian themes
Prokofiev Symphony no.1 in D (Classical), op.25
Tchaikovsky Symphony no.3 in D (Polish), op.29

19 Aug. 20.00 *Usher Hall*
Tchaikovsky The tempest
Svetlanov Second rhapsody (For his 16th birthday)
Scriabin Symphony no.2 in C minor, op.29

NATIONAL YOUTH ORCHESTRA OF SCOTLAND
17 Aug. 20.00 *Usher Hall*
Berio La ritirata notturna di Madrid (L. Boccherini)
Rachmaninov Concerto for piano no.3 in D minor, op.30
Musgrave Concerto for orchestra
Respighi The pines of Rome
Conductor James Loughran
Soloist John Lill (pf)

SCOTTISH CHAMBER ORCHESTRA
17 Aug. 11.00 *Queen's Hall*
Vivaldi Concerto for 2 horns in F
Albinoni Adagio in G minor
Vivaldi Concerto for flute in C minor
Vivaldi Concerto for bassoon in E minor
Barber Adagio for strings, op.11
Vivaldi Concerto for 2 trumpets in C
Director Philip Ledger (hpd)

25 Aug. 22.45 *Ross Bandstand*
Fireworks Concert
Rossini Guillaume Tell: Overture
Davis The Glenlivet fireworks music
Handel Music for the royal fireworks
Conductor Bramwell Tovey
Scottish Philharmonic Singers

EDINBURGH FESTIVAL CHORUS
SCOTTISH CHAMBER ORCHESTRA Members
26 Aug. 20.00 *Usher Hall*
Schubert Three songs for men's chorus and piano
Brahms Four songs for female chorus, 2 horns and harp, op.17
Oldham In praise of the Virgin
Bruckner Mass no.2 in E minor
Soloists Lynda Towers (mez), Michael Lester Cribb (pf)

SWEDISH RADIO SYMPHONY ORCHESTRA
Conductor Esa-Pekka Salonen
A Weekend of 20th Century Music
20 Aug. 20.00 *Usher Hall*
Schoenberg Erwartung
Stravinsky The rite of spring
Soloist Karan Armstrong (sop)

21 Aug. 20.00 *Usher Hall*
Lindberg Kraft
Haydn Concerto for trumpet in E flat
Stravinsky Symphony of psalms
Soloist Håkan Hardenberger (tpt)
Toimii Ensemble, EF Chorus

22 Aug. 20.00 *Usher Hall*
Stenhammar Serenade in F, op.31
Berg Seven early songs
Ravel Shéhérazade
Debussy Images: Ibéria
Soloist Barbara Hendricks (sop)

I SOLISTI VENETI
23 Aug. 11.00 *Queen's Hall*
Albinoni Concerto in F, op.5/2
Albinoni Concerto for oboe, op.7/3
Vivaldi Concerto for mandolin in C
Vivaldi Concerti, op.3 (L'estro armonico): No.8 in A minor
Salieri Concerto for flute and oboe
Paganini Variations on 'Carnevale di Venezia'
Vivaldi Concerto for 2 mandolins in G
Conductor Claudio Scimone

ROYAL PHILHARMONIC ORCHESTRA
23 Aug. 20.00 *Usher Hall*
Brahms Variations on a theme by Haydn (St Antoni chorale), op.56a
Britten Sinfonia da requiem
Dvořák Symphony no.7 in D minor, op.70
Conductor Erich Leinsdorf

24 Aug. 20.00 *Usher Hall*
Mozart Concerto for piano no.12 in A, K414
Tchaikovsky Manfred symphony
Conductor and soloist Vladimir Ashkenazy (pf)

25 Aug. 20.00 *Usher Hall*
Sibelius Tapiola
Sibelius Symphony no.7 in C, op.105
Shostakovich Symphony no.6 in B minor, op.54
Conductor Vladimir Ashkenazy

LEIPZIG GEWANDHAUS ORCHESTRA
Conductor Kurt Masur
28 Aug. 20.00 *Usher Hall*
Beethoven Egmont: Incidental music
Beethoven Symphony no.7 in A, op.92
Soloists Friedheim Eberle (narr), Bettina Denner (mez)

29 Aug. 20.00 *Usher Hall*
Mendelssohn Symphony no.3 in A minor (Scottish), op.56
Rachmaninov Rhapsody on a theme of Paganini
R. Strauss Till Eulenspiegels lustige Streiche
Soloist Peter Rösel (pf)

SCOTTISH OPERA ORCHESTRA
31 Aug. 20.00 *Usher Hall*
R. Strauss München
Schoenberg Chamber symphony no.2, op.38
Weill Lady in the dark: Original overture
Weill Lady in the dark
Conductor John Mauceri
Soloists Patricia Hodge, Richard Griffiths, Mark Tinkler, Martin McEvoy, Forbes Masson, Scottish Opera Chorus

MAGGIO MUSICALE ORCHESTRA, Florence
Conductor James Conlon
1, 3 Sep. 20.00 *Usher Hall*
Verdi Requiem
Soloists Susan Dunn (sop), Stefania Toczyska (mez), Tonio di Paolo (ten), Gwynne Howell (bs), EF Chorus

2 Sep. 20.00 *Usher Hall*
Liszt Dante symphony
Rossini Semiramide: Overture
Rossini Guillaume Tell: Pas de six
Rossini La gazza ladra: Overture
SNO Junior Chorus

CHAMBER CONCERTS

NEW LONDON CONSORT
15 Aug. 11.00 *Queen's Hall*
Anon.(13th century) Carmina burana: 15 songs from the original manuscript
Director Philip Pickett

SHOSTAKOVICH QUARTET
11.00 *Queen's Hall*
Shostakovich String Quartets
16 Aug. Nos. 1 in C; 4 in D; 5 in B flat
18 Aug. Nos. 2 in A; 3 in F
20 Aug. Nos. 6 in G; 7 in F sharp minor 8 in C
22 Aug. Nos. 9 in E flat; 10 in A flat 11 in F minor
24 Aug. Nos.12 in D flat; 13 in B flat minor Two pieces
26 Aug. Nos.14 in F sharp 15 in E flat minor

YONIN NO KAI
(Japanese classical musicians)
1 Sep. 11.00 *Queen's Hall*
Yatsuhashi-Kengyo Midare
Nakao Kogetsucho
Ishikawa-Koto Aoyagi
Xenakis Nyuyo
Ichiyanagi Sensing the colour in the wind
Miyoshi Ryusho-kyokusui-fu

WALLACE COLLECTION
3 Sep. 11.00 *Queen's Hall*
16th century Venetian ceremonial music by Gabrieli, Banchieri, Frescobaldi

RECITALS

BARBARA HENDRICKS (sop)
ROLAND PÖNTINEN (pf)
19 Aug. 11.00 *Queen's Hall*
Songs by Haydn, Mozart, Mendelssohn, Wolf, Mahler

JORMA HYNNINEN (bar)
RALF GOTHONI (pf)
29 Aug. 11.00 *Queen's Hall*
Songs by Sibelius, Wolf, Finnish folk songs arr. Gothoni

ANNA STEIGER (sop)
ROGER VIGNOLES (pf)
2 Sep. 11.00 *Queen's Hall*
Menotti Canti della lontananza
Respighi Cinque liriche
Rossini La regata veneziana
Poulenc Poèmes de Max Jacob
Verdi Songs

VLADIMIR OVCHINIKOV (pf)
31 Aug. 11.00 *Queen's Hall*
Liszt Études d'exécution transcendante
Rachmaninov Études tableaux, op.33

PAUL COLETTI (va), HANNE-BERIT HAHNEMANN (vn), PETER EVANS (pf)
25 Aug. 11.00 *Queen's Hall*
Vivaldi Sonata for viola and piano no.6 in B flat; arr. Dallapiccola
Schumann Märchenbilder for viola and piano
Bruni Duo concertant for violin and viola, op.25
Rota Intermezzo for viola and piano
Brahms Sonata for viola and piano no.2 in E flat, op.120/2

EVELYN GLENNIE (perc)
OWEN MURRAY (accordion)
30 Aug. 11.00 *Queen's Hall*
Lundquist Duell
Fink Game for two
R. Stevenson The harlot's house (World première)
Abe Michi
Musser Étude in B
Nordheim Dinosauros
Messiaen La nativitié du Seigneur: Excerpts
Tanaka Two movements for marimba
O. Schmidt Toccata no.1
Glennie Light in darkness
Bach Prelude in B flat

JAZZ

McEWAN'S EDINBURGH INTERNATIONAL JAZZ FESTIVAL
27 Aug. 20.00 *Usher Hall*
10th Anniversary Jazz Concert
Concord All Stars, Harlem Blues and Jazz Band, Warren Vaché, Scott Hamilton, Art Hodes, Dave McKenna, Jake Hanna, Jim Galloway, George Chisholm, Buddy Tate, Dan Barret, Doc Cheatham, Carol Kidd and the Sandy Taylor Trio, Jack Lesberg, Al Fairweather, Jiving Lindy Hoppers, National Youth Jazz Orchestra, Groove Juice Special, New Orleans Parade Band
Introduced by Miles Kington

DRAMA

WORLD THEATRE SEASON

NINAGAWA COMPANY, Japan
17-21 Aug. 19.30 20 Aug. 14.30
Playhouse
THE TEMPEST Shakespeare (Jap)
Prospero Haruhiko Jo
Miranda Yuko Tanaka
Alonso Kazunaga Tsuji
Sebastian Kazuhisa Seshimo
Antonio Takeshi Wakamatsu
Ferdinand Hisashi Hatakeyama
Gonzalo Tatsumi Aoyama
Adrian Takuya Fujisaki
Francisco Yoshihiro Osaka
Caliban Yutaka Matsushige
Trinculo Kenichi Ishii
Stephano Goro Daimon
Ariel/Ceres Yoji Matsuda
Iris Hirokazu Aoyama
Juno Tokusaburo Arashi
Master Nobuyuki Tachi
Boatswain Koichi Yoshida
Director Yukio Ninagawa
Scenery Toshiaki Suzuki
Costumes Lily Komine
Lighting Tamotsu Harada

BRADLEY, FRANCIS PRODUCTIONS, Canada
15-20 Aug. 19.30 18, 20 Aug. 14.30
Lyceum Theatre
B-MOVIE: THE PLAY Wood
Art Findell Tom Wood
Stan Purdum Stephen Ouimette
Lottie Purdum Corrine Koslo
Gloria Hunt Dana Brooks
Dick Paulkickup David Elliott
Art (Understudy) Peter Anderson
Stan (Understudy) Jim Warren
Director Bob Baker
Scenery and lighting Stancil Campbell
Costumes Leslie Franklin
(In association with the Canadian Stage Company)

BAXTER THEATRE, Cape Town
22-24 Aug. 19.30 25-27 Aug. 22.30
27 Aug. 14.30 *Lyceum Theatre*
DISTRICT SIX - THE MUSICAL
Kramer *and* Peterson
Damaka Farouk Valley-Omar
Cassiem Leslie Kleinsmith
Mary Helene Joseph
Nines Paul Savage
Henry Cyril Valentine
Hester Mary Daniels
Pang Henry James
M.C. Terry Fortune
Sandy Odette Leat
Broertjie
Jody Abrahams, Loukmaan Adams
Record company executive/Swanepoel/
Vosloo John Dennison
Winston Dennis Maart
Directors
David Kramer, Taliep Peterson
Designer Brian Collins
Lighting Sidney Jansen

IL SIPARIO DI MARIO SCARPETTA, Italy
25-27 Aug. 19.00 28 Aug. 14.30
Lyceum Theatre
MISERIA E NOBILTA Scarpetta
Pupella Attilia Cirillo
Concetta Maria Izzo
Luisella Maria Basile
Don Gioacchino Ciro Capano
Don Luigino Sabino Izzo
Pasquale Michelangelo Ragni
Peppeniello Stefano Galeota
Felice Sciosciammocca Mario Scarpetta
Eugenio Favetti Pino Brancaccio
Vincenzo Francesco Sisto
Gaetano Semmolone Lello Serao
Biase Ciro Discolo
Ottavio Favetti Peppe Bosone
Gemma Stefania di Nardo
Bettina Patrizia Capuano
Director Mario Scarpetta
Scenery
Andrea Celata, Antonella de Luca
Roberto Saliola
Costumes Annamaria Morelli

LA COMPAGNIE JÉRÔME DESCHAMPS, France
31 Aug.- 4 Sep. 19.30 *Lyceum Theatre*
LES PETITS PAS Deschamps
Jean-Marc Bihour, Francis Bouc, Jean Delavalade, Yvonne Dolain, Elia Lando, Nicolas Pagniez, Christine Pignet, Philippe Roueche, Boukary Sana, Pietro Stragliati, Marie Valin, Jacques Dejean (vn), Colette Lequien (va), Louis Ingigliardi (vc), Alain Margoni (pf)
Director Jérôme Deschamps
Scenery Laurent Peduzzi
Costumes Macha Makeieff
Music
Alain Margoni, Philippe Roueche

GROUP TSE, France
29-31 Aug. 19.30 31 Aug. 14.30
Leith Theatre
LE JEU DE L'AMOUR ET DU HASARD
Marivaux
Silvia Marilu Marini
Lisette Zobeida Juau
Monsieur Orgon Larry Hager
Mario Pierre-François Pistorio
Dorante Facundo Bo
Arlequin Alain Salomon
Director Alfredo Arias
Designers
Claudie Gastine, André Colin

COMPAGNA DEI PUPI SICILIANI DI NINO CUTICCHIO, Sicily
23-27 Aug. 11.00 22, 23, 25, 26 Aug. 14.30 *Church Hill Theatre*
LA MORTE DI RUGGIERO DELL'AQUILA BIANCA

NATIVE EARTH PERFORMING ARTS, Canada
15-20 Aug. 19.30 17, 20 Aug. 14.30
St Bride's Centre
THE REZ SISTERS Highway
Pelajia Patchnose Gloria Miguel
Philomena Moosetail Muriel Miguel
Annie Cook Anne Anglin
Marie-Adele Starblanket
Shirley Cheechoo
Nanabush Rene Highway
Veronique St Pierre Margaret Cozry
Zhaboonigan Peterson Sally Singal
Emily Dictionary Gloria May Eshkibok
Bingo girl Tina Bomberry
Director Larry Lewis
Scenery and lighting Patsy Lang
Music director Tomson Highway
Music David Tomlinson

NIEUW ENSEMBLE, RAAM TEATER, Antwerp
21-24 Aug. 19.30 *St Bride's Centre*
TRAFFORD TANZI Luckham
Dean Rebel Eric Kerremans
Tanzi's dad Roger van Kerpel
Tanzi's mum Katelijn Verbeke
Referee John Willaert
Platinum Sue A'leen Cooreman
Trafford Tanzi An Nelissen
Director Walter Tillemans
Costumes Bob Verhelst

SCHILLER THEATRE, Germany
25-27 Aug. 19.30 27 Aug. 14.30
St Bride's Centre
BLOOD ON THE NECK OF THE CAT
(Marilyn Monroe against the vampires)
Fassbinder
Phoebe Zeitgeist Barbara Frey
Girl Marietta Rohrer
Model Regina Lemnitz
Lover Maria Hartmann
Dead soldier's wife Ursula Diestel
Butcher Till Hoffmann
Lover Robert Tillian
Teacher Rainer Pigulla
Soldier Achim Grubel
Policeman Toni Slama
Director Klaus Andre
Scenery Bernd Damovsky
Costumes Karin Janucek

EKKEHARD SCHALL
18-20 Aug. 22.30 *King's Theatre*
Poetry and songs by Bertolt Brecht
with Karl-Heinz Nehring (pf)

ROYAL EXCHANGE THEATRE, Manchester
15 Aug.-3 Sep. 19.30 (exc.Sun) 17, 20, 24, 27, 31 Aug. 3 Sep. 14.30
Assembly Hall
A MIDSUMMER NIGHT'S DREAM
Shakespeare

Titania	Fiona Victory
Oberon	Kenneth Cranham
Lysander	Adam Kotz
Helena	Susan Spiegel
Demetrius	Robert Clare
Hermia	Caroline Milmoe
Theseus	Stuart Richman
Hippolyta/Peaseblossom	Anna Savva
Bottom	Graham Sinclair
Starveling	Stephen Boyes
Snug/Egeus	Roy Heather
Flute	David Keys
Quince	David Allister
Snout	Phillip Walsh
Puck	Peter Lindford
Philostrate/Mustardseed	David Kiernan
Cobweb	John Bateman
Moth	Gillian Winn
Director	Gregory Hersov
Scenery	Lez Brotherston
Costumes	David Short
Lighting	Rick Fisher

BRUNTON THEATRE
15-27 Aug. 19.30 17, 20, 24, 27 Aug. 14.30 *Church Hill Theatre*
29 Aug.-3 Sep. 19.30 31 Aug. 3 Sep. 14.30 *Brunton Theatre*
HOLY ISLE Bridie

Queen Margause	Vivien Heilbron
King Lot	Michael Mackenzie
Grettir Flatface	Victor Greene
Bishop	Gordon Fulton
Father Innocence	Michael David
Torquil	Robin Begg
Ku	Anne Foley Miller
Wawa	Alexander West
Kwoo	Steve Owen
Qua	Jeffrey Daunton
She	Anne Lannan
Ba	William Steel
Trika	Lucinda Baillie
Musicians	Jack Evans, Jim Hannah
Director	Charles Nowosielski
Scenery	Nick Sargent
Costumes	Chris Orvis
Lighting	Martin Palmer

SHARED EXPERIENCE THEATRE COMPANY
29 Aug.-3 Sep. 19.30 1, 3 Sep. 14.30
St Bride's Centre
THE BACCHAE Euripides (Eng)

Dionysus	Simon Tyrrell
Teiresias/Messenger	Roger Frost
Cadmus	Wilbert Johnson
Pentheus	Peter Hamilton Dyer
Agave/Bacchae	Claire Benedict
Bacchae	Annabelle Apsion, Shona Morris, Denise Wong, Rowan Wylie
Director	Nancy Meckler
Designer	David Roger
Lighting	Rick Fisher

NATIONAL YOUTH THEATRE OF GREAT BRITAIN
24-26, 29-31 Aug. 1, 2 Sep. 20.00 26, 30 Aug. 1, 2 Sep. 23.00
St Giles' Cathedral
MURDER IN THE CATHEDRAL Eliot

Director	Edward Wilson
Designer	Brian Lee

31 Aug.-3 Sep. 22.30 3 Sep. 11.00
St Bride's Centre
PACHA MAMMA'S BLESSING (World première)
22, 23 Aug. 15.00 *St Cecilia's Hall*

BRIDIE REVISITED Mavor
James Cairncross, Ronald Mavor (rdr)

24-27 Aug. 15.00 26 Aug. 19.30
St Cecilia's Hall
CONFESSIONS OF A NIGHTINGALE
Stricklyn *and* Chandler
Ray Stricklyn as Tennessee Williams

1-3 Sep. 22.30 *Lyceum Theatre*
KIT AND THE WIDOW

DANCE

MATSUYAMA BALLET, Japan
23, 26, 27 Aug. 19.30 27 Aug. 14.30
Playhouse
GISELLE

Choreographers	Tetsutaro Shimizu, Yoshiaki Tonozaki
Music	Adam
Scenery	Naoji Kawaguchi
Costumes	Tomoko Morita
Lighting	Toshihiko Tonozaki

25, 28 Aug. 19.30 *Playhouse*
MANDALA

Choreographer	Tetsutaro Shimizu
Music	Yoshihiro Kanno
Scenery	Hideyo Tanaka
Costumes	Kimiko Yaeda
Lighting	Toshihiko Tonozaki

Dancers Yoko Morishita, Tetsutaro Shimizu, Hiroko Kurata, Kazuhiro Kaneda, Mayumi Eda, Kazuya Nakamura, Masami Sato, Akemi Sato, Akiko Yamakawa, Aki Kubo, Ayako Hashiguchi, Kumi Hiramoto, Shoichiro Sadamatsu, Tamana Sakaki, Makiko Okubo, Yoshiaki Tonosaki, Mari Shuta, Toshiyuki Miura, Hatsuo Minowa, Kenzo Kajiyama, Yumiko Fujimaki, Ayako Hamochi, Machiko Sekimoto, Yoshikazu Hiraki, Miko Suzuki, Yushiro Narita, Kenji Sato, Yushiro Nanta, Hiroyasu Sakurai
Scottish Philharmonic Orchestra
Conductor Shunsaku Tsutsumi

MICHAEL CLARK AND COMPANY
15-20 Aug. 19.30 *King's Theatre*
I AM CURIOUS, ORANGE

Choreographer	Michael Clark
Music	The Fall
Scenery	Michael Clark
Costumes	Bodymap, Leigh Bowery

Dancers Leigh Bowery, Leslie Bryant, Michael Clark, Matthew Hawkins, David Holah, Julie Hood, Amanda King, Ellen van Schuylenburch

ATERBALLETTO, Italy
2, 3 Sep. 19.30 3 Sep. 14.30
King's Theatre
PARADE

Choreographer	Léonide Massine
Music	Satie
Designer	*after* Picasso

NATURALE

Choreographer	Amedeo Amodio
Music	Berio
Costumes	Luisa Spinatelli
Lighting	Pio Troilo

LOVE SONGS

Choreographer	William Forsythe
Costumes	Eileen Brady

A SUD DI MOZART

Choreographer	Amedeo Amodio
Music	Eugenio Bennato, Carlo d'Angiò
Scenery	Lele Luzzati
Costumes	Luisa Spinatelli
Lighting	Pio Troilo

Dancers Amedeo Amodio, Christina Amodio, Raffaella Bagetto, Paola Bami, Carolina Basagni, Sveva Berti, Federico Betti, Mauro Bigonzetti, Denis Bragatto, Orazio Caiti, Giuseppe Calanni, Arturo Cannistra, Alessandra Celentano, Marie-Helene Cosentino, Corrado Giordani, Alberto Ottoboni, Paola Pagano, Roberta Pagliako, Guy Poggioli, Marc Renouard, Donatella Sturam

EXHIBITIONS

City Art Centre
REALITY AND IMAGINATION

Royal Museum of Scotland
IN THE SHADOW OF VESUVIUS

College of Art
MAKING IT!

ASSOCIATED EXHIBITIONS
(Not organized by the Festival Society)

National Gallery of Scotland
PIETRO LONGHI: The paintings of the Palazzo Leoni Montanari, Vicenza

Royal Scottish Academy
PICABIA 1879-1953

DADA & SURREALISM: A private collection

Scottish National Portrait Gallery
THE PHOTOGRAPHY OF JOHN MUIR WOOD

Royal Museum of Scotland
NEW DESIGN AND ARCHITECTURE FROM FINLAND

Richard Demarco Gallery
HUGH MacDIARMID

Talbot Rice Gallery
JOAN EARDLEY

369 Gallery
TEN YEARS OF THE 369

National Library of Scotland
SCOTLAND AND AUSTRALIA

OTHER EVENTS

15 Aug. 20.00 *St Mary's R.C. Cathedral*
SOLEMN MASS
Works by Anerio, Palestrina, Bruckner

19 Aug. 20.00 *St Giles' Cathedral*
ST.GILES' SINGERS AND ORCHESTRA

Bach	Mass in B minor
Conductor	Herrick Bunney

21 Aug. 15.00 *Leith Theatre*
SCOTTISH EARLY MUSIC CONSORT
Songs of love and war by Monteverdi, Rossi, Marini

Director	Christopher Field

2 Sep. 22.30 3 Sep. 20.30
St Mary's Cathedral
RENAISSANCE GROUP OF ST ANDREW'S

Carver	Dum sacrum mysterium
Director	Douglas Gifford

27 Aug. 11.00 *Queen's Hall*
SCOTTISH CHAMBER ORCHESTRA
Children's day

2 Sep. 19.30 *Playhouse*
RYUDOGUMI - Rock from Japan

4 Sep. 19.30 *Playhouse*
LENNY HENRY

1 Sep. 4 sessions from 11.00
St Cecilia's Hall
THE MUSIC OF MEANING
Roberto Sanesi, Edwin Morgan (rdr)
Organized by the Scottish Poetry Library

SALTIRE SOCIETY
28 Aug. 15.00 *St Cecilia's Hall*
SCOTTISH SERENADE

28 Aug. 20.00 29 Aug. 15.00 and 20.00
St Cecilia's Hall
FROM TWEED TO TIBER

30 Aug. 2 Sep. 15.00 *St Cecilia's Hall*
VOICES OF OUR KIND
Poetry of the Scottish Renaissance 1920-1980
Eileen McCallum, Meg Bateman, Paul Young (rdr)
Compiled by Alexander Scott and George Bruce.

30 Aug. 20.00 31 Aug. 15.00
St Cecilia's Hall
McGIBBON ENSEMBLE
18th century Scottish music

31 Aug. 3 Sep. 20.00 *St Cecilia's Hall*
HIGHLAND SONG OF THE '45

1989

OPERA

FESTIVAL FOLKOPERA
11, 13-19 Aug. 19.45 *Leith Theatre*
SALOME R. Strauss (Eng)
Salome — Susan Bisatt, Fiona O'Neill
Jochanaan — John Rath, Dimitri Kharitonov
Herod — Kenneth Woollam, Donald Stephenson
Herodias — Nuala Willis, Jady Pearl
Narraboth — David Aldred
Page — Helen Greenaway
5 Jews — Stephen Austin, Luigi Corvi, Barry Webb, Tom Cregan, Michael Neill
2 Nazarenes — Andrew Slater, Lyndon George
2 Soldiers — Paul Whelan, Richard Campbell
Slave — Kathleen Ferguson
Executioner — Morris Paton
Dancers — Garfield Brown, Henderson Williams
Scottish Chamber Orchestra
Conductor — Kerstin Nerbe
Director — Claes Fellbom
Scenery — Sören Brunes
Costumes — Nadine Baylis

NATIONAL OPERA OF SPAIN
(Teatro Zarzuela, Madrid)
17-19 Aug. 19.30 *Playhouse*
LA CHULAPONA Moreno Torroba
Rosario — Amalia Barrio
Chalina — Rafael Castejón
Emilia — Marisa Ruz
Organillero — Mario Martín
Don Epifanio — Luis Barbero
Venustiana — Pepa Rosado, Rosaura de Andrea
Manuela (La Chulapona) — Lola Casariego
Lolita — Rosaura de Andrea, Manolita Antolinos
Señor Antonio — José Luis Cancela
Ascensión — Juanita Ruiz
Concha — Ada Rodríguez
José María — Ricardo Muñiz
Juan de Dios — Julio Incera
Guards — José Antonio Sanguino, Ion Garayalde
Manolito — César Lucendo
Young man — José Varela
Drunkard — Jesús Alcaide
Flamenco singer — María 'La Coneja'
Ganadero — José Antonio Sanguino
Cansino — José Sánchez Cela
Peasant — Carlos Rubio
Maravilla — Pilar del Río
Guadalupe — Emilia Fuentes
Cafe owner — Andrés Fuentes
Sleeping man — Rafael del Río
Guitarist — Francisco Bohollo
Dancers — Elvira Andrés. Nuria Castejón, Paloma Moraleda, Pilar Rubio, Carlos Fernández, Isaac Fernández, Juan Manuel Lillo, Ricardo Ocaña
Conductor — Miguel Roa
Director — Gerardo Malla
Designer — Mario Bernedo
Choreographer — Goyo Montero
Lighting — Eric Teunis

OPERA NORTH
24-26 Aug. 19.30 *King's Theatre*
THE LOVE OF THREE ORANGES Prokofiev
King of Clubs — Mark Glanville
Prince — Peter Jeffes
Princess Clarissa — Patricia Payne
Leander — Andrew Shore
Truffaldino — Paul Harrhy
Pantaloon — Alan Oke
Chelio — Roger Bryson
Fata Morgana — Maria Moll
Linetta — Lesley Roberts
Nicoletta — Victoria Sharp
Ninetta — Juliet Booth
Cook — Richard Angas
Farfarello — Mark Lufton
Smeraldina — Maria Jagusz
Herald — Stephen Dowson
Conductor — David Lloyd-Jones
Director — Richard Jones
Scenery — The Brothers Quay
Costumes — Sue Blane
Lighting — Colin Smith, Peter Davison

JUTLAND OPERA
28, 29 Aug. 19.30 *Leith Theatre*
THE DIVINE CIRCUS Nørgård
Adolf Wölfli — Karl Antz
Doufi — Kim von Binzer
Saint Adolf/Doctor — Carl Chr. Rasmussen
Saint Adolf II/Alfonso XII of Spain — Troels Kold
Bianca/Lidia/Goddess Sereena/Margritt/Santa Maria — Hanne Holten
Mother/Sister Mathilda/Queen Catharina II of Spain/Holy Mother — Kirsten Buhl Møller
Conductor — Kaare Hansen
Director — Francesco Cristofoli
Designers — Charlotte Clason, Helle Rahboek, Marianne Walther
Choreographer — Dina Bjorn
Percussion — Gert Mortensen

NATIONAL YOUTH MUSIC THEATRE
TRIPLE THREAT DANCE COMPANY
14-26 Aug. 16.15 20 Aug. 14.00
George Square Theatre
EL RETABLO DE MAESE PEDRO (Master Peter's puppet show) Falla (Eng)
EL CORREGIDOR Y LA MOLINERA (The magistrate) Falla (Eng)
Conductor — Richard Dacey
Directors — Jeremy James Taylor, John Wright
Designer — Sarah Ashpole
Lighting — Richard House

SPANISH NATIONAL ORCHESTRA
Conductor Rafael Frühbeck de Burgos
13 Aug. 20.00 *Usher Hall*
ATLÁNTIDA Falla (arr. Halffter)
(Concert performance)
Isabella — Maria Oran
Pyrene — Alicia Nafé
Child — Andrew Murphy
Contralto solo — Morag Watson
Tenor solo — Kenneth Ballantine
Narrator — Enrique Baquerizo
LA VIDA BREVE Falla
(Concert performance)
Salud — Maria Oran
Paco — Josep Ruiz
Grandmother — Alicia Nafé
Uncle Salvador — Jesus Sainz Remiro
Carmela — Paloma Perez Iñigo
Manuel — Enrique Baquerizo
Flamenco singer — Gabriel Moreno
Voices in the distance — Jorge Anton
Dancer — Lucero Tena
Guitarist — Carmelo Martinez
EF Chorus

ORCHESTRAL CONCERTS

SPANISH NATIONAL ORCHESTRA
14 Aug. 20.00 *Usher Hall*
Albeniz — Española: Granada *and* Sevilla; arr. Früceck de Burgos
Albeniz — Ibéria: Corpus *and* Triana; arr. Arbós
Rodrigo — Concierto de Aranjuez for guitar
Falla — El amor brujo
Stravinsky — The firebird
Soloists Alicia Nafé (mez), Narciso Yepes (gtr)

SCOTTISH CHAMBER ORCHESTRA
14 Aug. 11.00 *Queen's Hall*
Stravinsky — Concerto in E flat (Dumbarton Oaks)
Ginastera — Variaciones concertantes, op.23
Ravel — Pavane pour une infante défunte
Beethoven — Symphony no.8 in F, op.93
Conductor — Jukka-Pekka Saraste

24 Aug. 22.45 *Ross Bandstand*
Fireworks Concert
Elgar Pomp and circumstance march no.1
Handel — Zadok the Priest - Coronation anthem
Handel — Music for the royal fireworks
Conductor — Christopher Bell

GOTHENBURG SYMPHONY ORCHESTRA
15 Aug. 20.00 *Usher Hall*
Rimsky-Korsakov — Capriccio espagnole
Sibelius — Concerto for violin in D minor, op.47
Sandström — Era
Falla — El sombrero de tres picos
Conductor — Neeme Järvi
Soloists Christine Cairns (mez), Cho-Liang Lin (vn)

OSLO PHILHARMONIC ORCHESTRA
Conductor Mariss Jansons
20 Aug. 20.00 *Usher Hall*
Kvandal Triptychon
Stravinsky Petrushka
Tchaikovsky Symphony no.4 in F minor, op.36

21 Aug. 20.00 *Usher Hall*
R. Strauss Don Juan
Grieg Concerto for piano in A minor, op.16
Brahms Symphony no.2 in D, op.73
Soloist Leif Ove Andsnes (pf)

CITY OF BIRMINGHAM SYMPHONY ORCHESTRA
Conductor Simon Rattle
22 Aug. 20.00 *Usher Hall*
Haydn Die Schöpfung (Eng)
Soloists Arleen Augér (sop), Philip Langridge (ten), Benjamin Luxon (bar), EF Chorus

23 Aug. 20.00 *Usher Hall*
Webern Six pieces, op.6
R. Strauss Concerto for oboe
Boulez Eclat
Debussy Images for orchestra
Soloist Heinz Holliger (ob)

25 Aug. 20.00 *Usher Hall*
Takemitsu Gémeaux+
Brahms Symphony no.4 in E minor, op.98
Conductor Odaline de la Martinez +
Soloists Heinz Holliger (ob), Vinko Globokar (tbn)

26 Aug. 20.00 *Usher Hall*
Adams Short ride in a fast machine
Rouse The infernal machine
Gershwin Concerto for piano in F
Gershwin Rhapsody in blue
Bernstein Prelude, fugue and riffs
A selection of jazz arrangements; arr. Whiteman
Soloists Peter Donohoe (pf), Colin Parr (cl)

NOUVEL ORCHESTRE PHILHARMONIQUE
Conductor Marek Janowski
28 Aug. 20.00 *Usher Hall*
Music of the French Revolution
De Lisle La Marseillaise; arr. Berlioz
Cherubini Requiem mass no.1 in C minor
Beethoven Symphony no.3 in E flat (Eroica), op.55
EF Chorus

29 Aug. 20.00 *Usher Hall*
Lalo Le roi d'ys: Overture
Dutilleux Concerto for violin
Messiaen L'ascension
Ravel La valse
Soloist Dmitry Sitkovetsky (vn)

CITY OF LONDON SINFONIA
1 Sep. 20.00 *Usher Hall*
Ravel Le tombeau de Couperin
Britten Serenade for tenor, horn and strings
Mozart Concerto for horn no.2 in E flat, K417
Stravinsky Pulcinella
Conductor Richard Hickox
Soloists Eiddwen Harrhy (sop), Robert Tear (ten), Stephen Varcoe (bar), Michael Thompson (hn)

BBC SCOTTISH SYMPHONY ORCHESTRA
2, 3 Sep. 20.00 *Usher Hall*
Berlioz Grande messe des morts (Requiem)
Conductor Rafael Frühbeck de Burgos
Soloist Martyn Hill (ten)
EF Chorus

CHAMBER CONCERTS

SHOSTAKOVICH QUARTET
15 Aug. 11.00 *Queen's Hall*
Haydn Quartet in D, op.33/6
Haydn Quartet in C (Bird), op.33/3
Haydn The seven last words of our Saviour from the cross; for string quartet, op.51

17 Aug. 11.00 *Queen's Hall*
Schubert Quartet no.13 in A minor, D804
Schubert Quartet no.12 in C minor (Quartetsatz), D703
Schubert Quartet no.14 in D minor (Death and the maiden), D810

19 Aug. 11.00 *Queen's Hall*
Schumann Quartet no.1 in A minor, op.41/1
Schumann Quartet no.2 in F, op.41/2
Schumann Quartet no.3 in A, op.41/3

21 Aug. 11.00 *Queen's Hall*
Glinka Quartet no.2 in F
Balashov Quartet no.2
Tchaikovsky Quartet no.3 in E flat minor, op.30

23 Aug. 11.00 *Queen's Hall*
Rimsky-Korsakov *and others* Quartet (B-la-f)
Lobanov Quartet no.4, op.49
Borodin Quartet no.1 in A

25 Aug. 11.00 *Queen's Hall*
Collective work Variations on a Russian theme (dedicated to Mitrofan Belyaev)
Gretchaninov Quartet no.1 in G, op.2
Ermolayev Quartet no.2 (The praise), op.22

NEW LONDON CONSORT
Director Philip Pickett
16 Aug. 11.00 *Queen's Hall*
Music at the Court of Ferdinand and Isabella from the great songbooks of Renaissance Spain

18 Aug. 11.00 *Queen's Hall*
Music from the pilgrim road to Santiago de Compostella

ENSEMBLE STRADIVARIA
26 Aug. 11.00 *Queen's Hall*
French Symphonies of the 18th Century
Gossec Symphonie à 4 in A
Saint Georges Symphonie concertante in G, op.2/6
Breval Symphonie concertante in D, op.4/1
Ozi Symphonie concertante in F, op.10
Cambini Symphonie concertante in D (La patriote)

TOKYO QUARTET
30 Aug. 11.00 *Queen's Hall*
Beethoven Quartet no.2 in G, op.18/2
Borodin Quartet no.2 in D
Bartók Quartet no.1

31 Aug. 11.00 *Queen's Hall*
Haydn Quartet in G minor (Rider), op.74/3
Ravel Quartet in F
Smetana Quartet no.1 in E minor (From my life)

L'ITINÉRAIRE
30 Aug. 20.00 Royal Museum of Scotland
Works by Murail, Grisey, Levinas, Scelsi

LA MUSE EN CIRCUIT
31 Aug. 20.00 Royal Museum of Scotland
The Spanish lesson including music by Ferrari, Musseau, Foures, Jisse
Director Luc Ferrari

WALLACE COLLECTION
1 Sep. 11.00 *Queen's Hall*
Music from the Spanish Renaissance

ENSEMBLE INTERCONTEMPORAIN Members
2 Sep. 11.00 *Queen's Hall*
Messiaen Catalogue d'oiseaux: L'alouette lulu *and* La bouscarle
Messiaen Thème et variations
Messiaen Quatuor pour la fin du temps

RECITALS

MONTSERRAT CABALLE (sop)
MIGUEL ZANETTI (pf)
16 Aug. 20.00 *Usher Hall*
Songs by Vivaldi, Bellini, Mercadante, Rossini, Granados, Mompou, Obradors, Turina

PETER DONOHOE (pf)
28 Aug. 11.00 *Queen's Hall*
Beethoven Sonata no.17 in D minor (Tempest), op.31/2
Berg Sonata, op.1
Bartók Sonata
Rachmaninov Preludes nos.12-24, op.32

HEINZ HOLLIGER (ob)
JOHN CONSTABLE (pf)
22 Aug. 11.00 *Queen's Hall*
Koechlin Au loin: chants, op.20; arr. for oboe and piano
Koechlin Le repos au Tityre; monoday for oboe d'amore
Koechlin Sonata for oboe and piano, op.58
Dorati Five pieces for oboe
Pasculli Gran concerto su temi dall'opera 'La Favorita' (Donizetti); arr. for oboe and piano

GERT MORTENSEN (perc)
29 Aug. 11.00 *Leith Theatre*
Másson Prim for snare drum
Ruders Cha-cha-cha
Holten Valsevaerk
Xenakis Psappha
Nørgård I ching

RAVI SHANKAR (sitâr)
31 Aug. 20.00 *Usher Hall*
with Durga Lal (pakhawaj), Shubho Shankar (sitâr), Kumar Bose (tabla)
(In Foyer - Kathak Dance by Renu Bassi)

JAZZ

McEWAN'S EDINBURGH INTERNATIONAL JAZZ FESTIVAL
24 Aug. 20.00 *Usher Hall*
A Duke Ellington Celebration
Stan Tracey Big Band, The World's Greatest Jazz Band, Yank Lawson (tpt), Bob Haggart (db), Kenny Davern, Peanuts Hucko (cl), Rufus Harley (bp. ten sax), Humphrey Lyttelton and his Band, Lillian Boutté (vocals), Guy Lafitte, Scott Hamilton (ten sax), Jake Hanna (drums), Brian Lemon (pf), Ray Williams (tbn),

Warren Vaché, jun. (cornet), The Hot Antic Jazz Band.
Introduced by Humphrey Lyttelton

27 Aug. 20.00 *Usher Hall*
STEPHANE GRAPPELLI (vn)
with Martin Taylor (electric gtr), Jack Sewing (db), Marc Fosset (acoustic gtr)

DRAMA

WORLD THEATRE SEASON

GATE THEATRE, Dublin
14, 17-19 Aug. 19.30 15 Aug. 21.30
16 Aug. 18.30 17, 19 Aug. 14.30
Lyceum Theatre
SALOMĖ Wilde (Eng)
Salomé — Olwen Fouere
Jokanaan — Joe Savino
Herod — Alan Stanford
Herodias — Barbara Brennan
Page — Michael James Ford
Young Syrian — David Heap
Tigellinus — Jonathan Ryan
Naaman — The Diceman
Piano player — Roger Doyle
Other parts played by Catherine Crowe. Fiona Douglas-Stewart, Bairbre Ní Chaoimh
Director — Steven Berkoff
Scenery — Robert Ballagh
Costumes — Nigel Boyd
Lighting — Trevor Dawson

ELS COMEDIANTS, Spain
15 Aug. 18.30 16 Aug. 21.30
Lyceum Theatre
LA NIT

13, 17 Aug. 21.30
George Heriot's School Grounds
DIMONIS
Xavier Amatller, Jaume Bernadet, Jordi Bulbena, Montserrat Catala, Montserrat Colome, Joan Font, Angeles Julian, Rita Kuan, Matilde Muñiz, Andres Sanchez (act), Ramon Calduch, Carlos Elmeua, Joan Montañez, Jordi Riera, Rafael Zaragueta (mus)

COMPAÑIA NACIONAL TEATRO CLASICO, Spain
22, 23 Aug. 19.30 *Lyceum Theatre*
LA CELESTINA Rojas
Calisto — Juan Gea
Melibea — Adriana Ozores
Sempronio — Jesus Puente
Celestina — Amparo Rivelles
Elicia — Resu Morales
Crito — Angel Garcia Suarez
Pármeno — Cesar Dieguez
Lucrecia — Blanca Apilanez
Alisa — Charo Soriano
Areúsa — Pilar Barrera
Tristán — Antonio Carrasco
Sosia — Felix Casales
Pleberio — Vicente Gisbert
Centurio — Enrique Navarro
Ruffians — Joaquin Climent, Carlos Alberto Abad, Carlos Moreno
Director — Adolfo Marsillach
Designer — Carlos Cytrynowski

25, 26 Aug. 19.30 *Lyceum Theatre*
EL ALCALDE DE ZALAMEA Calderón de la Barca
Rebolledo — Enrique Navarro
Soldiers — Carlos Alberto Abad, Carlos Moreno
La Chispa — Resu Morales
Don Alvaro de Ataide — Juan Gea
Sergeant — Felix Casales
Don Mendo — Miguel Palenzuela
Nuño — Cesar Dieguez
Isabel — Adriana Ozores
Inés — Blanca Apilanez
Pedro Crespo — Jesus Puente
Juan — Antonio Carrasco
Don Lope — Angel Picazo
Clerk — Angel Garcia Suarez
King Philip II — Vicente Gisbert
Director — José Luis Alonso
Designer — Pedro Moreno
Lighting — Juan Gomez Cornejo

MUSIC-THEATRE GROUP, New York
29, 31 Aug. 20.00 30 Aug. 1, 2 Sep. 19.00 and 21.30 *Lyceum Theatre*
THE GARDEN OF EARTHLY DELIGHTS Clarke
Rob Besserer, Felix Blaska, Margie Gillis, Marie Fourcaut, Raymond Kurshal, Matthias Naegele, Bill Ruyle, Peggy Scales, Steven Silverstein, Paola Sytron
Director and choreographer — Martha Clarke
Costumes — Jane Greenwood
Lighting — Paul Gallo
Music — Richard Peaslee

LA COMPAGNIE JÉRÔME DESCHAMPS, France
19-21 Aug. 19.30 21 Aug. 14.30
King's Theatre
C'EST DIMANCHE Deschamps
Jean-Marc Bihour, Jérôme Deschamps, Christine Pignet
Director — Jérôme Deschamps
Music — Philippe Roueche
Lighting — Dominique Bruguieré

STARY THEATRE, Cracow
28-30 Aug. 19.30 *King's Theatre*
THE DYBUK Ansky (Pol)
Rabbi Sender — Jerzy Radziwilowicz, Jerzy Gralek
Lea — Aldona Grochal
Frade — Izabela Olszewska
Gittel — Dorota Pomykala
Menashe — Jan Korwin-Kochanowski
Nakhman — Stanislaw Gronkowski
Meshulach — Jerzy Trela
Rabbi Azriel — Jan Peszek
Michael — Ryszard Lukowski
Meyer — Jan Monczka
Chanan — Krzysztof Globisz
Henoch — Marek Kalita
Rabbi Szymszon — Tadeusz Huk
Messenger — Stefan Szramel
Hunchback — Tadeusz Malak
Man on crutches — Pawel Kruszelnicki
Jewess — Ewa Kolasinska
Paralytic — Grazyna Laszczyk
Blind woman — Marta Jurasz
Director — Andrzej Wajda
Designer — Krystyna Zachwatowicz

1, 2 Sep. 19.30 2 Sep. 14.30
King's Theatre
LIFE IS A DREAM Calderón de la Barca (Pol)
Basilio (Polish King) — Jerzy Binczycki
Segismundo (Prince) — Krzysztof Globisz
Astolfo — Jerzy Radziwilowicz
Clotaldo — Aleksander Fabisiak
Clarin — Jerzy Trela, Jerzy Gralek
Estrella — Danuta Maksymowicz, Urszula Kiebzak-Debogorska
Rosaura — Dorota Pomykala
Director — Jerzy Jarocki
Designer — Jerzy Juk-Kowarski

TAGANKA THEATRE, USSR
22, 23, 25, 26 Aug. 19.30 *Leith Theatre*
BORIS GODUNOV Pushkin
Boris — Nikolai Gubenko
Varlaam — Felix Antipov
Shuisky — Yuri Belyaev
Pimen — Ivan Borgnik
Marina — Alla Demidova
Missail — Rasmi Dzabrailov
Xenia — Natalia Petrovna Saiko
Dimitri — Valery Zolotukhin
Director — Yuri Lyubimov
Designer — David Borovski

HELIOTROPE PRODUCTIONS
31 Aug.-3 Sep. 19.30 2 Sep. 14.30
Leith Theatre
TORCHLIGHT AND LASER BEAMS Nolan *and* Scott
Joseph Meehan — Conor Mullen
Joseph Too — Frank McCusker
Matthew Meehan — Clive Geraghty
Nora Meehan — Geraldine Plunkett
Mosaim Poaberry/Necromancer/Father Flynn — Frank Kelly
Yvonne Meehan — Ann Slattery
Grandmother/Lamp woman — Eve Watkinson
Paul Browne — Risteard Cooper
Deirdre Devine — Maggie Naughter
Stephen Monahan — Peter Vollebregt
Doctor/Mono — Hugh Martigan
Music played by — Roger Doyle
Director — Michael Scott
Designer — Bronwen Casson
Lighting — Leslie Scott
(Dublin Theatre Festival/Gaiety Theatre Prod.)

YOKOHAMA BOAT THEATRE, Japan
21-26 Aug. 19.30 24, 26 Aug. 14.30
St Bride's Centre
OGURI HANGAN, TERUTE HIME Endo
Oguri Hangan — Akihiko Yamashita
Terute Hime/Snake — Michiko Tonomiya
Oguri's corpse — Hiroshi Matsunobu
Lord Kaneiye/Shaman — Kazuko Furuya
Kord Kaneiye's wife/Goddess — Mija Choi
Other parts played by Ei Noguchi, Yuji Toki, Chomasa Tamayose, Akiko Shima, Sunchoru Kan, Hiroko Nagai, Tomoe Irino
Musicians — Makoto Yabuki, Yuko Yoshikawa, Takashi Wada
Director — Takuo Endo
Scenery — Yukio Horio
Costumes — Kikuko Ogata

ACTORS' GANG, USA
29 Aug. 19.30 30 Aug.-2 Sep. 22.30
31 Aug. 14.30 3 Sep. 16.00 and 20.00
St Bride's Centre
CARNAGE Simon *and* Robbins
Rev. Doctor Cotton Slocum — Lee Arenberg
Deacon Tack — Ned Bellamy
Ralph — Brent Hinkley
Dot — Shannon Holt
Other parts played by Jack Black, Cynthia Ettinger, Jeff Foster, Kyle Gass, Lisa Moncure, Dean Robinson, Cari Dean Whittemore
Music composed and performed by David Robbins, Darryl Tewes, Kyle Gass

ROYAL NATIONAL THEATRE STUDIO
14-19 Aug. 19.30 16, 19 Aug. 14.30
St Bride's Centre
SCHISM IN ENGLAND Calderón de la Barca (Eng. Translated by John Clifford)
King Henry VIII — Geoffrey Bateman
Anne Boleyn — Miranda Foster
Cardinal Wolsey — Michael N. Harbour
Thomas Boleyn — Peter Sproule

Charles — Jeremy Flynn
Dionis — Ian Fitzgibbon
Pasquin — Karl Johnson
Queen Catherine — Linda Bassett
Princess Mary — Hilary Dawson
Margaret Pole — Jacquetta May
Jane Seymour — Kate Gielgud
Captain — Metin Marlowe
Soldiers
David Solomon, Christopher Priest
Director — John Burgess
Designer — Alison Chitty
Lighting — Ben Ormerod

28, 30, 31 Aug. 1, 2 Sep. 19.30
29 Aug. 22.30 30 Aug. 2 Sep. 14.30
St Bride's Centre
WHEN WE WERE WOMEN MacDonald
Maggie — Mary MacLeod
Isla — Joanna Roth
Alec — Henry Stamper
Mackenzie — Ewan Stewart
Woman/Cath — Jan Shand
Director — John Burgess
Designer — Alison Chitty
Lighting — Ben Ormerod

TRON THEATRE, Glasgow
14-19, 21-23 Aug. 19.30 18, 19, 22 Aug. 14.30 Church Hill Theatre
CLYDE NOUVEAU Heggie
Gordon Carlyle — Sean Scanlan
Stuart Bone — Kevin McMonagle
Danny Noble — Douglas Henshall
Hugh Auld — Jake D'Arcy
Grace Dear — Gaylie Runciman
Catriona Steel — Muriel Romanes
Jim Steel — Charles Kearney
Director — Michael Boyd
Designer — Graham Johnston

POETRY AND PROSE RECITALS

15-19 Aug. 15.00
Royal Museum of Scotland
DAME WENDY HILLER (rdr)
GBS remembered

22-26 Aug. 15.00 23, 25 Aug. 19.30
Royal Museum of Scotland
MIRIAM MARGOLYES (rdr)
Wooman, lovely wooman, what a sex you are - a look at the women in Dickens with David Timson (act), Helen Crawford (pf)
Director — Sonia Fraser

29, 30 Aug. 15.00 29 Aug. 19.30
Royal Museum of Scotland
JOHN FRASER (rdr)
J.M. Barrie - The man who wrote Peter Pan
Director — Frank Barrie

31 Aug.-2 Sep. 15.00 1 Sep. 19.30
Royal Museum of Scotland
IRENE WORTH (rdr)
Letters of love and affection
(From letters in the Pierpont Morgan Library, New York)

LATE NIGHT ENTERTAINMENT

22, 23 Aug. 23.00 St Bride's Centre
EPO

DANCE

BREMER THEATER, Bremen
15-17 Aug. 19.30 17 Aug. 14.30
King's Theatre
MACBETH
Choreographer — Johann Kresnik
Music — Kurt Schwertsik
Scenery — Gottfried Helnwein
Costumes — Anne Steiner
Dancers Joachin Siska, Susana Ibanez, Maverick Quek, Amy Coleman, Susan Barnett, Harald Beutelstahl, Roberto A. Giovanetti, Regine Fritschi, Kate Antrobus

SPANISH NATIONAL BALLET
12-14 Aug. 19.30 14 Aug. 14.30
Playhouse
DANZA Y TRONIO
Choreographer — Mariemma
Music — Soler, Boccherini, Abril
Costumes — Peris Hermanos
ALBORADA DEL GRACIOSO
Choreographer — Jose Granero
Music — Ravel
Lighting
Carlos Guerrero, Rafael Yunta
BOLERO
Choreographer, costumes and lighting
Jose Granero
Music — Ravel
SOLEA
Choreographer and Lighting
Jose Antonio
Music — Manolo Sanlucar
Designer — Pedro Moreno
Dancers Merche Esmeralda, José Antonio, Conchita Cerezo, Maribel Gallardo, Aida Gomez, Ana Gonzalez, Cristina Hernando, Juan Mata, Paco Morell, Adelaida Calvin, Adoracion Carpio, Guadalupe Gomez, Montserrat Marin, Joaquin Cortes, Antonio Marquez
Scottish Philharmonic Orchestra
Conductor — Benito Lauret

BALLET CRISTINA HOYOS, Spain
17-19 Aug. 20.00 19 Aug. 14.30
Usher Hall
SINTESIS SOBRE CARMEN
SUEÑOS FLAMENCOS
Choreographers
Cristina Hoyos, Manolo Marin
Costumes — Justo Salao-Cornejo
Lighting — Paco Doniz
Dancers Cristina Hoyos, Juan Ortega, Macarena Béjar, Manuela Reyes, Rosario Cala, Juan A. Jimenez, Fernando Romero, Juan Paredes
with Juan Jose Amador, El Extremeño (sngr), Paco Arriaga, Carlos Heredia, Diego Franco (gtr)

HOUSTON BALLET
22, 24, 25 Aug. 19.30 Playhouse
GAUTAMA BUDDHA
Choreographer — Christopher Bruce
Music — Naresh Sohal
Costumes — Walter Nobbe
Lighting — John B. Read
ESMERALDA: Pas de deux
Choreographer — Ben Stevenson
Music — Pugni; arr. Drigo
Costumes — Ray Delle Robbins

PIR SQUARED
Choreographer — Lois Bewley
Music — Varèse
Lighting — William Banks

GHOST DANCES
Choreographer — Christopher Bruce
Music
South American folk songs; arr. Carr
Scenery — Christopher Bruce
Costumes — Belinda Scarlett
Lighting — Nick Chelton

23, 26 Aug. 19.30 26 Aug. 14.30
Playhouse
SWAN LAKE
Choreographer — Ben Stevenson *after* Petipa *and* Ivanov
Music — Tchaikovsky
Designer — David Walker
Dancers Rachel Jonell Beard, Li Cunxin, John Grensback, Paul Le Gros, Kenneth McCombie, Mary McKendry, Koen Onzia, Janie Parker, Dorio Perez, Carmen Mathe, Kerri McClatchy Hogue, Mark Arvin, Sean Kelly, Timothy O'Keefe, Sandra Organ, Kristine Richmond
BBC Scottish Symphony Orchestra
Conductor — Glenn Langdon

RED NOTES DANCE COMPANY, France
25, 26 Aug. 19.30 Church Hill Theatre
L'AN UN (opera-ballet) Youngerman
Veronique Berri (sop), Caroline Faro (narr), Ensemble Vocal de la Maitrise Gabriel Fauré
Conductor — Marc Florian
Director — Duncan Youngerman
Designer — Jean-Luc Simonini
Costumes — Laurence Perquy
Choreographer — Andrew Degroat

EXHIBITIONS

National Gallery of Scotland
EL GRECO: Mystery and illumination

Old College, Edinburgh University
TARTAN EXHIBITION

ASSOCIATED EXHIBITIONS
(Not organized by the Festival Society)

Royal Museum of Scotland
OUR PHOTOGRAPHIC LEGACY

Scottish National Gallery of Modern Art
SCOTTISH ART SINCE 1900

Royal Scottish Academy
WILLIAM McTAGGART (1835-1910)

Royal Museum of Scotland
THE WEALTH OF A NATION

Scottish National Portrait Gallery
WILLIAM ADAM (1689-1748)

PATRONS AND PAINTERS: Art in Scotland 1650-1760

City of Edinburgh Art Centre
WHEN WE WERE YOUNG

EDVARD MÜNCH

Richard Demarco Gallery
CONTEMPORARY ART FROM THE NETHERLANDS

369 Gallery
NORTHERN HORIZONS: Norwegian contemporary art

Fine Art Society
THE McTAGGARTS AND OTHER ARTIST FAMILIES

Edinburgh College of Art
ROBIN PHILIPSON RETROSPECTIVE

Calton Gallery
EDINBURGH AND ITS STORY: J. Ayton Symington

National Library of Scotland
300 YEARS 300 BOOKS

OTHER EVENTS

15 Aug. 19.30 St Mary's R.C. Cathedral
SOLEMN MASS
Works by Victoria, Johnson, Oldham

1 Sep. 22.30 2 Sep. 20.30
St Mary's Cathedral
RENAISSANCE GROUP OF ST ANDREW'S
A celebration of great Renaissance masses from Scotland and Spain
Director Douglas Gifford

SALTIRE SOCIETY
14, 16 Aug. 15.00 19 Aug. 20.00
St Andrew's & St George's
SCOTLAND AND THE FRENCH REVOLUTION
Gerda Stevenson, James Cairncross, Paul Young (rdr)
Arranged by Kevin Gibbons

15, 18 Aug. 15.00
St Andrew's & St George's
LAND OF MacLEOD
Kathleen MacDonald (sngr), Rhona MacKay (hp, clarsach), Robert Wallace (bp)

17, 19 Aug. 15.00
St Andrew's & St George's
SEA TALK, SEA SONG
Mary Sandeman, William McCue (sngr), Rose McBain, John Shedden (rdr)
Arranged by George Bruce

1990

OPERA

BOLSHOI OPERA, Moscow
14-16 Aug. 19.00 Playhouse
BETROTHAL IN A MONASTERY
Prokofiev
Don Jerome Alexei Maslennikov
Vladimir Kudriashov
Ferdinand Igor Morozov
Vladimir Redkin
Louisa Galina Chernoba
Natalya Pustovaya
Duenna to Louisa Galina Borisova
Nina Galonova
Antonio Arkady Mishenkin
Alexander Fedin
Clara Marina Shutova
Olga Terushnova
Mendoza Mikhail Krutikov
Nikolai Nizienko
Don Carlos Vladimir Malchenko
Movsar Mintsayev
Father Augustine Anton Dzhaparedze
Yuri Netchaev
Father Elixir Alexander Arkhipov
Andrei Salnikov
Father Chartreuse Mikhail Maslov
Vladimir Malchenko
Father Benedictine Viacheslav Pochansky
Maxim Mikhailov
1st Monk/Pablo Andrei Salnikov
Yuri Markolov
2nd Monk/Pedro Vladislav Pazhinsky
Lauretta Nina Larionova
Rosina Larissa Yurchenko
Lopez Konstantin Baskov
Nikolai Maiboroda
Miguel Maxim Mikhailov
Peter Gluboky
Conductor Alexander Lazarev
Director Boris Pokrovsky
Designer Valery Leventhal

SLOVAK NATIONAL OPERA AND BALLET
20, 24, 25 Aug. 19.00 Playhouse
FAUST Gounod
Faust Jozef Kundlák
Miroslav Dvorský
Marguerite Eva Jenisová
Ľudmilla Hudecová
Lívia Ághová
Mephistopheles Peter Mikuláš
Ján Galla
Valentin Richard Haan
Ján Ďurčo
Siebel Ida Kirilová
Jitka Saparová
Marthe Marta Nitranová
Denisa Šlepkovská
Brander Vladimír Kubovčík
Dancers
Mephistopheles Mario Radačovský
Juraj Šiška
Sex Irina Čierniková
Dália Gáliková
Power Jozef Šoltés
Dušan Nebyla
Marguerite Eva Horáková
Conductor Oliver Dohnányi
Director Jozef Bednárik
Designer Ladislav Vichodil
Choreographer Libor Vaculik

22, 23 Aug. 19.00 Playhouse
PRINCE IGOR Borodin
Igor František Caban
Róbert Szucs
Yaroslavna Ľubica Rybárska
Magdaléna Blahušiaková
Vladimir Sergei Larin
Galitzky Ján Galla
Josef Špaček
Kontchak Sergey Kopchák
Ondrej Malachovský
Kontchakovna Ida Kirilová
Skoula Pavol Mauréry
Rastislav Uhlár
Eroshka Pavol Gábor
Ivan Ožvát
Ovlour Miroslav Dvorský
Yaroslavna's nurse Alžbeta Michálková
Polovtsian girl Jitka Saparová
Solo dancers Irina Čierniková, Eva Šenkýriková, Ingrid Murceková, Dušan Nebyla, Michal Mikeš, J.I. Vasilenko
Conductor Oliver Dohnányi
Director Július Gyermek
Designer Vladimír Suchánek
Choreographer Karol Tóth *after* Fokine

27 Aug. 19.30 King's Theatre
THE WHIRLPOOL Suchoň
Katrena Ľubica Rybárska
Ondrej Josef Abel
Štelina Ondrej Malachovský
Zimon Rastislav Uhlár
Zimonka Alžbeta Michálková
Zalcicka Jaroslava Sedlářová
Školnica Ľuba Baricová
Marka Anna Czaková
Zuzka Jitka Saparová
Shepherd Jana Valášková
Krupa Pavol Gábor
Hrín František Caban
Olen Jozef Špaček
Master (wedding ceremony)
Stanislav Beňačka
Mistress (wedding ceremony)
Mária Borbeľová
Woman/Cook Anna Kľuková
Bridesman Ján Konstanty
Gendarme Juraj Volgyi
Conductor Jonas Alexa
Director Branislav Kriška
Designer Ladislav Vichodil
Choreographer Jozef Dolinský

29, 30 Aug. 19.30 King's Theatre
JULIETTA Martinů
Julietta Eva Jenisová
Elena Holičková
Michel Juraj Ďurdiak
Miroslav Švejda
Commissioner of police Milan Kopačka
Old Arab Jozef Špaček
Man with a helmet Ján Ďurčo
Man at the window Juraj Hrubant
Shopkeeper with birds Marta Nitranová
Shopkeeper with fishes Anna Czaková
Gentlemen Ľudmila Hudecová, Anna Kľuková, Jitka Saparová
Grandfather Rastislav Uhlár
Old man Vladimír Kubovčík
Seller of memories Juraj Oniščenko
Old sailor Stanislav Beňačka
Young sailor Jitka Saparová
Little Arab Silvia Virágová
Engineer Ján Konstanty
Conductor Viktor Málek
Director Miroslav Fischer
Designer Milan Ferenčík

JUTLAND OPERA
18 Aug. 18.00 Usher Hall
TRISTAN UND ISOLDE Wagner
(Concert performance.)
Tristan Matti Kastu
Isolde Lisbeth Balslev
Brangäne Karin Mang-Habash
Kurwenal Lars Waage

King Mark — Aage Haugland
Melot/Young sailor — Ole Hedegaard
Shepherd — Kai Hansen
Steersman — Carl Christian Rasmussen
Conductor — Francesco Cristofoli

PRAGUE SYMPHONY ORCHESTRA
13 Aug. 20.00 *Usher Hall*
THE GREEK PASSION Martinů (Eng)
(Concert performance)
Maniolos — Alan Woodrow
Katerina — Phyllis Cannan
Grigoris — Stephen Richardson
Kostandis/Ladas — John Hancorn
Fotis — Geoffrey Moses
Yannakos — Arthur Davies
Lenio — Christine Bunning
Nikolios — Beverley Mills
Panais — Jeffrey Lawton
Michelis — John Harris
Old man/Patriarcheas — David Gwynne
Andonis — Neville Ackerman
Despinio — Morag Watson
Conductor — Jiří Belohlávek

ORCHESTRAL CONCERTS

PRAGUE SYMPHONY ORCHESTRA
14 Aug. 20.00 *Usher Hall*
Janáček — Sinfonietta
Martinů — Concerto for piano no.2
Debussy — La mer
Conductor — Jiří Belohlávek
Soloist — Rudolf Firkušný (pf)

16 Aug. 20.00 *Usher Hall*
Suk — Fantastic scherzo
Martinů — Rhapsody concerto for viola
Rimsky-Korsakov — Schéhérazade
Conductor — Petr Altrichter
Soloist — Josef Suk (va)

SAITO KINEN ORCHESTRA, Japan
12 Aug. 20.00 *Usher Hall*
Dvořák — Concerto for cello in B minor, op.104
Brahms — Symphony no.1 in C minor, op.68
Conductor — Seiji Ozawa
Soloist — Mstislav Rostropovich (vc)

BBC SCOTTISH SYMPHONY ORCHESTRA
15 Aug. 20.00 *Usher Hall*
Sibelius — Symphony no.4 in A minor, op.63
Tan Dun — Orchestral theatre (World première)
Debussy — Marche écossaise
Dukas — L'apprenti sorcier
Conductor — Jerzy Maksymiuk
Magician — Topper Martyn

BOLSHOI THEATRE ORCHESTRA, Moscow
Conductor — Alexander Lazarev
17 Aug. 20.00 *Usher Hall*
Rachmaninov — Concerto for piano no.3 in D minor, op.30
Prokofiev — Ivan the terrible
Soloists Elena Zaremba (mez), Mikhail Krutikov (bass), Grigory Sokolov (pf), Boris Morgunov (narr), Bolshoi Theatre Chorus

21 Aug. 20.00 *Usher Hall*
Tchaikovsky — Suite no.3 in G, op.55
Prokofiev — Alexander Nevsky
Soloist — Elena Zaremba (mez)
EF Chorus

SCOTTISH NATIONAL ORCHESTRA
19 Aug. 15.00 *Usher Hall*
Enescu — Rumanian rhapsody no.1 in A, op.11/1
Bartók — Concerto for orchestra
Khachaturian — Symphony no.2 in E minor (The bell)
Conductor — Neeme Järvi

CITY OF LONDON SINFONIA
20 Aug. 20.00 *Usher Hall*
Elgar — Introduction and allegro, op.47
R. Strauss — Concerto for horn no.2 in E flat
Grainger — Songs
Conductor — Richard Hickox
Soloists Lynton Atkinson (ten), Richard Jackson (bar), Barry Tuckwell (hn), EF Chorus

ENGLISH CHAMBER ORCHESTRA
24 Aug. 20.00 *Usher Hall*
Bach — Concerto for violin and oboe in D minor
Bach — Concerto for violin in E
Bach — Concerto for 2 violins in D minor
Mozart — Symphony no.39 in E flat, K543
Director and soloist — Pinchas Zukerman (vn)
Soloists José-Luis García (vn), Neil Black (ob)

ROTTERDAM PHILHARMONIC ORCHESTRA
Conductor — James Conlon
25 Aug. 20.00 *Usher Hall*
Martinů — Concerto for double string orchestra, piano and timpani
R. Strauss — Ein Heldenleben
Soloists Peter Donohoe (pf), Randy Max (timp)

26 Aug. 20.00 *Usher Hall*
Dvořák — Requiem mass
Soloists Carolyn James (sop), Alexandrina Milcheva (mez), Vinson Cole (ten), Gwynne Howell (bass), EF Chorus

SAN FRANCISCO SYMPHONY ORCHESTRA
Conductor — Herbert Blomstedt
28 Aug. 20.00 *Usher Hall*
Mozart — Symphony no.32 in G, K318
Haydn — Concerto for cello no.1 in C
Nielsen — Symphony no.4 (Inextinguishable), op.29
Soloist — Yo-Yo Ma (vc)

29 Aug. 20.00 *Usher Hall*
Mozart — Concerto for piano no.23 in A, K488
Bruckner — Symphony no.5 in B flat
Soloist — Emanuel Ax (pf)

SCOTTISH CHAMBER ORCHESTRA
30 Aug. 22.45 *Ross Bandstand*
Fireworks Concert
McIlwham — Alba
Tchaikovsky — 1812 overture
Handel — Music for the royal fireworks
Offenbach — Orphée aux enfers: Overture
Conductor — Ivor Bolton
Soloist — George McIlwham (bp)

BERLIN SYMPHONY ORCHESTRA
Conductor — Claus Peter Flor
31 Aug. 20.00 *Usher Hall*
Mozart — Symphony no.34 in C, K338
Martinů — Concerto for piano no.3
R. Strauss — Tod und Verklärung
Soloist — Rudolf Firkušný (pf)

1, 2 Sep. 20.00 *Usher Hall*
Brahms — Ein deutsches Requiem
Soloists Arleen Augér (sop), Thomas Allen (bar), EF Chorus

ACADEMY OF ANCIENT MUSIC
1 Sep. 11.00 *Queen's Hall*
Telemann — Burlesque de Quichotte, Hoffman
Bach — Suite no.1 in C
Handel — Concerto grosso in B flat, Op.3/2
Handel — Silete venti
Director — Christopher Hogwood
Soloist — Lynne Dawson (sop)

CHAMBER CONCERTS

NASH ENSEMBLE
13 Aug. 11.00 *Queen's Hall*
Hummel — Septet in C (Military), op.114
Martinů — La rêvue de cuisine
Brahms — Serenade no.1 in D, op.11

14 Aug. 11.00 *Queen's Hall*
R. Strauss — Till Eulenspiegels lustige Streiche (chamber version)
Mozart — Quintet for horn and strings in E flat, K407
Schubert — Octet in F, D803

SUK QUARTET OF PRAGUE
15 Aug. 11.00 *Queen's Hall*
Schumann — Quartet no.1 in A minor, op.41/1
Martinů — Quartet no.4
Mozart — Quintet no.3 in G minor, K516
with Josef Suk (va)

17 Aug. 11.00 *Queen's Hall*
Beethoven — Quartet no.5 in A, op.18/5
Martinů — Quartet no.6
Suk — Quartet no.2, op.31

SCOTTISH CHAMBER ORCHESTRA members
18 Aug. 11.00 *Queen's Hall*
D. Horne — towards dharma
J. Weir — A Serbian cabaret
P.M. Davies — Miss Donnithorne's maggot
Conductor — Mark Wigglesworth
Soloists Jane Manning (sop), David Horne (pf)

18 Aug. 14.30 *Queen's Hall*
P. Nelson — Tournoiements de spectres
G. King — Message from nowhere
J.M. Geddes — Leo, dreaming
W. Sweeney — Sharakan
MacMillan — Búsqueda
Conductor — James MacMillan
Soloists John Kenny (tbn), Diana Rigg (narr)

PANOCHA QUARTET
21 Aug. 11.00 *Queen's Hall*
Haydn — Quartet in C, op.76/3
Martinů — Quartet no.5
Dvořák — Quintet for piano and strings in A, op.81
with Rudolf Firkušný (pf)

23 Aug. 11.00 *Queen's Hall*
Haydn — Quartet in D, op.76/5
Martinů — Quartet no.7 (Concerto da camera)
Janáček — Quartet no.2 (Intimate letters)

CZECH NONET, PANOCHA QUARTET
25 Aug. 11.00 *Queen's Hall*
Martinů — Nonet fragment
Martinů — Promenádý
Martinů — Two pieces for harpsichord
Martinů — Sonata for harpsichord

Martinů — Two impromptus
Martinů — Concerto for harpsichord
Soloists Zuzana Ruzicková (hpd), Steven Osborne (pf), Rudolf Firkušný (pf)

CZECH NONET
27 Aug. 20.00 — *Greyfriar's Kirk*
Martinů — Nonet
Jaroch — Nonet no.2
Beethoven — Septet, op.20

ST GILES' SINGERS
17 Aug. 20.00 — *St Giles' Cathedral*
Bach — Mass in B minor
Conductor — Herrick Bunney

RENAISSANCE GROUP OF ST ANDREW'S
31 Aug. 22.30 1 Sep. 20.30
St Mary's Cathedral
Carver — Mass for 6 voices
Carver — Mass for 19 voices
Carver — O bone Jesu

RECITALS

MONTSERRAT CABALLE (sop)
MIGUEL ZANETTI (pf)
19 Aug. 20.00 — *Usher Hall*
Songs by Stradella, Gasparini, Giordani, Galuppi, Puccitta, Donizetti, Rossini, Pacini, Debussy, Montsalvatge, Serrano, Chapi

TERESA BERGANZA (mez)
JUAN ANTONIO ALVAREZ PAREJO (pf)
23 Aug. 20.00 — *Usher Hall*
Rossini — Giovanna d'Arco
Songs by Leoz, Granados, Rodrigo, Rossini

THOMAS ALLEN (bar)
ROGER VIGNOLES (pf)
28 Aug. 11.00 — *Queen's Hall*
V. Williams — Songs of travel
Songs by Wolf, Schumann, folk songs

ARLEEN AUGÉR (sop)
IRWIN GAGE (pf)
31 Aug. 11.00 — *Queen's Hall*
Songs by Ravel, R. Strauss, Mahler, Wolf

PETER DONOHOE (pf)
16 Aug. 11.00 — *Queen's Hall*
Prokofiev — Sonatas nos.1-3
Shostakovich — Sonata no.2 in B minor, op.61
Shostakovich Preludes and fugues, op.87: No.24 in D

20 Aug. 11.00 — *Queen's Hall*
Haydn — Sonata no.60 in C
Prokofiev — Sonatas nos. 5, 9, 4

24 Aug. 11.00 — *Queen's Hall*
Mozart — Sonata no.11 in A, K331
Prokofiev — Sonatas nos. 6-8

ZUZANA RŮŽIČKOVÁ (hpd)
22 Aug. 19.30 — *St Cecilia's Hall*
26 Aug. 15.00 — *St Cecilia's Hall*
Two recitals featuring the Russell Collection of early keyboard instruments

27 Aug. 11.00 — *Queen's Hall*
Bach — Goldberg variations

RUDOLF FIRKUŠNÝ (pf)
29 Aug. 11.00 — *Queen's Hall*
Janáček — Sonata 1 X 1905
Janáček — On a overgrown path: Book 1
Martinů — Fantasia and Toccata
Dvořák — Theme and variations in A flat, op.36
Smetana — Czech dances: Furiant
Smetana — Souvenirs de Bohème en forme de polka
Smetana — Macbeth and the witches

STEVEN ISSERLIS (vc)
PETER EVANS (pf)
22 Aug. 11.00 — *Queen's Hall*
Bach — Suite for solo cello no.3 in C
Schubert — Sonata in A minor (Arpeggione), D821
Janáček — Fairy tale (Pohádka)
Martinů — Sonata no.2

YO-YO MA (vc), EMANUEL AX (pf)
30 Aug. 19.00 — *Usher Hall*
Beethoven — Variations on 'Ein Mädchen oder Weibchen' (Mozart)
Beethoven — Sonatas nos. 1-5
Beethoven — Variations on 'Bei Männern' (Mozart)
Beethoven — Variations on 'See the conquering hero comes' (Handel)

EVELYN GLENNIE (perc)
30 Aug. 11.00 — *Queen's Hall*
Works by Cauberghs, Green, Kurka, McLeod, Abe, Rosauro, Sueyoshi
with Philip Smith (pf)

YOUNG MUSICIANS LATE NIGHT CONCERTS
Informal evenings by former pupils of St Mary's Music School
22.45 — *St Andrew's & St George's*
13 Aug. Claire Docherty (vn), Alexandra Andrievsky (pf)
14 Aug. Edmund Coxon (vn), Julia Lynch (pf)
15 Aug. Paul Galbraith (gtr)
16 Aug. David Horne, Steven Osborne (2 pianos)
17 Aug. Bridget Evans (vc)

MASTER CLASSES

17 Aug. 14.30
St Andrew's & St George's
PETER DONOHOE (pf)

28 Aug. 15.00 — *Reid Concert Hall*
EVELYN GLENNIE (perc)

JAZZ

McEWAN'S EDINBURGH INTERNATIONAL JAZZ FESTIVAL
22 Aug. 20.00 — *Usher Hall*
Gala Concert 'East Meets West'
Original Prague Syncopated Orchestra, Nat Pierce All-Stars, Harry 'Sweets' Edison (tpt), Joe Temperley (sax), Danny Moss (sax), Eddie Condon Celebration Band, Budapest Ragtime Orchestra
Introduced by Peter Clayton

CLEO LAINE, JOHN DANKWORTH
27 Aug. 20.00 — *Usher Hall*
John Dankworth Quintet, Guy Barker (tpt, flugel hn), Mark Nightingale (tbn)

DRAMA

EDINBURGH INTERNATIONAL FESTIVAL
10 Aug.-1 Sep. 19.30 (exc.Sun) 18, 22, 25, 29 Aug. 1 Sep. 14.30 — *Assembly Hall*
TREASURE ISLAND Stevenson (Adapted by Frank Dunlop) (World première)
Jim Hawkins — Peter Duncan
Captain Billy Bones — Jimmy Logan
Mrs Hawkins — Bridget McCann
Jim Hawkins (Boy) — Graham McInnes, Iain Hathorn
Black dog — Keith Hutcheon
Dr Livesay — Richard Warwick
Blind Pew/Benn Gunn — Walter Carr
Ben — Norman Chalmers
George Merry — Richard Lintern
Johnny/Dick — Paul Morrow
Harry — Gordon MacArthur
Dirk — Graham MacGregor
Squire Trelawney — Harold Innocent
Redruth/Red night cap — Paul Benzing
Joyce — Gerard Gray O'Brien
Hunter — Paul Gilmore
Long John Silver — Hywel Bennett
Tom Morgan — Neil Patterson
Captain Alexander Smollett — Frank Barrie
Arrow — Greig Alexander
Job Anderson — Jonathan Howell
Israel Hands — Desmond McNamara
Tom Friendly — Ashley Ashworth
Abraham Day — David Harewood
John — Greig Alexander
Pirate — Sedhar Chozam
Director — Frank Dunlop
Designer — Nadine Baylis
Lighting — Leonard Tucker

RENAISSANCE THEATRE COMPANY
6, 9, 11, 13, 16, 18 Aug. 19.30 8, 15 Aug. 14.30 — *King's Theatre*
A MIDSUMMER NIGHT'S DREAM Shakespeare
Titania/Hippolyta — Siobhán Redmond
Theseus/Oberon — Simon Roberts
Lysander — James Larkin
Helena — Emma Thompson
Demetrius — Max Gold
Hermia — Francine Morgan
Bottom — Richard Briers
Starveling — Edward Jewesbury
Snug — Karl James
Flute — Gerard Horan
Quince — Kenneth Branagh
Snout — Bryan Kennedy
Puck — Ethna Roddy
Philostrate/Egeus/Mustardseed — Jimmy Yuill
Peaseblossom — Ann Davies
Cobweb — Sue Long
Moth — Christopher Armstrong
Director — Kenneth Branagh
Designer — Jenny Tiramani
Lighting — Jon Linstrum

7, 8, 10, 14, 15, 17 Aug. 19.30 11, 18 Aug. 14.30 — *King's Theatre*
KING LEAR Shakespeare
King Lear — Richard Briers
Goneril — Siobhán Redmond
Regan — Francine Morgan
Cordelia — Ethna Roddy
Edgar — Kenneth Branagh
Edmund — Simon Roberts
Duke of Burgundy — Bryan Kennedy
Duke of Albany — Karl James
Duke of Cornwall — Gerard Horan
Earl of Kent — Jimmy Yuill
Earl of Gloucester — Edward Jewesbury
Fool — Emma Thompson
King of France/Curan — Max Gold
Oswald — James Larkin
Messenger — Christopher Armstrong
Director — Kenneth Branagh
Designer — Jenny Tiramani
Lighting — Jon Linstrum

COMMUNICADO THEATRE COMPANY
11, 12, 14-19 Aug. 19.30 18, 19 Aug. 14.30 St Bride's Centre
DANTON'S DEATH Büchner (Eng)
Lacroix James Bryce
Georges Danton Robert Carr
Lucile Maureen Carr
Simon Matthew Costello
Legendre Vincent Friell
Camille Desmoulins Kenneth Glenaan
Marion Kathryn Howden
Singer Frances Lynch
Simon's wife Irene MacDougall
St Just Andrew Price
Julie Patricia Ross
Cellist Ron Shaw
Robespierre Laurie Ventry
Director Gerry Mulgrew
Designer Paul Ambrose
Lighting John Robb

WORLD THEATRE SEASON

KOREAN NATIONAL THEATRE AND DANCE COMPANY
31 Aug. 1 Sep. 19.30 1 Sep. 14.30
King's Theatre
STORY OF CH'UNHYANG
Ch'unhyang Suk-Son Ahn
Yi Mong-Ryong Hee-Jin Eun
Wolmae Chong-Suk Oh
Byun Hak-Do Kang Jong-Chol
Bangja Kee-Sok Wang
Hyangdan Mi-Jong Jong
MADAME TOMI (A dance drama)
Madame Tomi Yang Sung-Ok
Tome Son Byung-Woo
Sadangnyo Seung-Mi Yang
Chief Shaman Yi Ji-Young
King Jung-Mok Park
Queen Choi Jung-Im
Choreographer and Director Bom Song

CHIJINKAI THEATRE COMPANY, Japan
12-14 Aug. 19.30 14 Aug. 14.30
Lyceum Theatre
THE GREAT DOCTOR YABUHARA (Yabuhara Kengyo) Inoue
Blind narrator Kikuo Kaneuchi
Suginoichi Yasuyoshi Hara
Shichibei/ Hanawa Hokiichi/Father/Lover Takashi Fujiki
Oshiho Kyoko Mitsubayashi
Kumanoichi/Sakuma-Kengyo Nobuyoshi Matsukuma
Kotonoichi/Zenbei Shinpei Suzuki
Oichi Akiko Iwase
Kekke/Matsudaira Sadanobu Kyoji Naka
Widow Kyoko Yamaguchi
Daughter of widow Mie Koga
Guitarist Naoya Mizumura
Director Koichi Kimura
Scenery Setsu Asakura

KATHAKALI THEATRE, India
15-18 Aug. 19.15 Lyceum Theatre
KING LEAR Shakespeare
(Adapted by David McRuvie)
King Lear Keezhapadam Kumaran Nair
Kalamandalam Padmanabhan Nair
Goneril Nelliyode Vasudevan Namboodiri
Regan Kalamandalam Unnikrishnan Nair
Cordelia Sadanam Annette Leday
Fool Kalamandalam Manoj Kumar
King of France Sadanam Krishnankutty
Tom Sadanam Bhasi
Soldier Hari Nelliyode
Vocalists Kalamandalam Haridas, Udyogamandal Damodaran
Percussion Mattanur Sankara, Kottaikal Ravindran
Directors Annette Leday, David McRuvie
Lighting Gerard Espinosa

NINAGAWA COMPANY, Japan
20-22 Aug. 19.30 22 Aug. 14.30
Lyceum Theatre
SOTOBA KOMACHI Mishima
Old woman Haruhiko Joh
Poet Norihiro Inoue
Men Haruyoshi Nishikubo, Keita Oishi, Kazuhiro Kikuchi,Yukio Tsukamoto, Masato Mochizuki
Women Eiichi Seike, Ken Shibuya, Tadashi Okada, Tomoyuki Yamada, Jun Nishihara
Policeman Susumu Kakuma
SEKIDERA KOMACHI
(A Japanese traditional dance)
Dancer Yukio Yoshimura
with Seisho Tosha (Jap flute)
Director Yukio Ninagawa
Scenery Kaoru Kanamori
Lighting Tamotsu Harada

MUSIC-THEATRE GROUP, New York
26, 29 Aug. 19.00 and 21.30 25, 27, 28 Aug. 19.30 28 Aug. 14.30
Lyceum Theatre
JUAN DARIÉN Taymor *and* Goldenthal
Vocal soloist/Circus barker David Toney
Mother/Old woman Ariel Ashwell
Hunter/Senor Teledo Kristofer Batho
Mr Bones/Schoolteacher Lenard Petit
Juan (Puppet) Kristofer Batho, Andrea Kane, Stephen Kaplin
Juan (Boy) Nik Nackley
Schoolchildren David Toney, Nancy Mayans, Irene Wiley
Moth Olga Meredíz
Drunken couple Kristofer Batho, Andrea Kane
Green dwarf Andrea Kane
Director Julie Taymor
Designer G.W. Mercier
Conductor Richard Cordova

YUME NO YUMINSHA COMPANY, Japan
31 Aug.-2 Sep. 19.30 1 Sep. 14.30
Lyceum Theatre
HALF GODS (Hanshin) Noda
Mathematician/Doctor Hideki Noda
Maria Akiko Takeshita
Shura Aya Enjoji
Tutor Yuichi Haba
Father Ryosei Tayama
Mother Shinobu Kawamata
Sphinx Kenta Satoi
Migiko/Gabriel Yorie Yamashita
Hidariko/Mermaid Kaoru Mukai
Unicorn Kazuyuki Asano
Harpy Nobuyoshi Ueda
Geryon Tosho Monma
Director Hideki Noda
Scenery Masahiro Iwai
Costumes Masami Hara
Lighting Takashi Kitakizaki

STOMU YAMASH'TA
23-25 Aug. 19.30 24 Aug. 22.30
St Bride's Centre
SOLAR DREAM
with Naome Matsumoto (dancer)

DOWNSTAGE THEATRE COMPANY, New Zealand
27 Aug.-1 Sep. 19.30 30 Aug. 1 Sep. 14.30 St Bride's Centre
HEDDA GABLER Ibsen (Eng)
Hedda Catherine Wilkin
George Tesman Peter McCauley
Judge Brack Ray Henwood
Thea Elvsted Joanne Simpson
Eilert Lövberg Jim Moriarty
Julia Tesman Glenis Levestam
Bertha Kate Harcourt
Director Colin McColl
Scenery and lighting Tony Rabbit
Costumes Jane Woodall

BELVOIR STREET THEATRE, Australia
13-25 Aug.19.30 (exc.Sun) 16, 18, 23, 25 Aug. 14.30 Church Hill Theatre
GREEK TRAGEDY Leigh
Kalliope Evdokia Katahanas
Alex Adam Hatzimanolis
Perri Nicholas Papademetriou
Vicki Christina Totos
Larry George Spartels
Toni Zoe Carides
Director Mike Leigh
Designer Stephen Curtis
Costumes Edie Kurzer
Lighting Paul O'Leary
(In association with the Theatre Royal, Stratford East)

HOTEL PRO FORMA, Denmark
15-18 Aug. 21.30
Royal Museum of Scotland
WHY DOES NIGHT COME, MOTHER?
(Concept by Tomas Lahoda and K.T. Dehlholm)
Soprano Eva Hess Thaysen
Dancer Marie Huda Fogtdal
Stuntman Knud Schirmer
Acrobat Louise Schytte
Emigrant Daniel Okine
Reader Finn Andersen
Director Kirsten Tomas Dehlholm
Costumes Anne-Grethe Brunn
Music Karl Aage Rasmussen

ARCHAOS and THE CHIHUAHUAS, France
11 Aug.-2 Sep. 20.30 (exc.Mon) 12, 18, 19, 25, 26 Aug. 1, 2 Sep.15.00 Leith Links
BOUINAX

FLYING KARAMAZOV BROTHERS, USA
16-18, 27, 28 Aug. 22.30 17, 18, 26, 29 Aug. 14.30 Lyceum Theatre
20, 21 Aug. 19.30 21 Aug. 14.30
St Bride's Centre
CLUB

NATIONAL YOUTH MUSIC THEATRE
10, 12-17, 20, 22, 24, 25 Aug. 19.00 14, 17-22, 25 Aug. 16.00
George Square Theatre
OCTOBER'S CHILDREN (A musical play)
Written and directed by Jeremy James Taylor *and* Frank Whateley
Music by David Nield

WORDS BEYOND WORDS
13 Aug. 19.30 14-17 Aug. 14.30
St Bride's Centre
THE BRUCE Silver (A rehearsed reading)
Alexander Morton, Bill Riddoch, Muriel Romanes, Tony Cownie, Lewis Howden, Tom Smith, Alan Vicary, Iain Macrae
Director Tom McGrath
(In association with the Saltire Society)

22-25 Aug. 15.00 24, 25 Aug. 19.30
HONOR BLACKMAN
Royal Museum of Scotland
YVETTE - the life and times of Yvette Guilbert
Director Richard Digby Day
Musical director William Blezard

27, 28 Aug. 19.30 28 Aug. 15.00
Royal Museum of Scotland
SALLY ANN HOWES
FROM THIS MOMENT ON
Arranged and accompanied by Martin Smith
Director Nica Burns

29 Aug.-1 Sep. 15.00 31 Aug. 1 Sep. 19.30 Royal Museum of Scotland
RON BERGLAS
THE DOUBLE BASS Süskind
(Eng. Translated by Michael Hofmann)
Director Edward Hardwicke

POETRY AND PROSE RECITALS

SALTIRE SOCIETY
13, 14 Aug. 15.00 St Cecilia's Hall
ROBERT LOUIS STEVENSON IN THE SOUTH SEAS
Robert Louis Stevenson John Shedden
Compiled by Jenni Calder

15, 16 Aug. 15.00 St Cecilia's Hall
GAELIC SONG RECITAL
Anne Lorne Gillies (sop), Rhona Mackay (clarsach)

17, 18 Aug. 15.00 St Cecilia's Hall
ROBERT BURNS AND NEIL GOW MEET
Patricia MacMahon (sop), Alastair Hardie (fiddle), Patrica Hair (vc)

SCOTTISH POETRY LIBRARY: International poetry readings
21 Aug. 15.00 St Cecilia's Hall
PABLO NERUDA: A celebration
Devised and presented by Alastair Reid

23 Aug. 15.00 St Cecilia's Hall
FLYING CARPET: Poetry from Romania 1990
Grete Tartler, Daniela Crasnaru, Fleur Adcock, Nancy Nicholson (rdr)

15-18 Aug. 15.00 17,18 Aug. 19.30
Royal Museum of Scotland
NICHOLAS PARSONS (rdr)
HOW PLEASANT TO MEET MR LEAR

THE THEATRE OF LITERATURE
20, 21 Aug. 15.00 21 Aug. 19.30
Royal Museum of Scotland
THE GREAT McGONAGALL AND WORSE VERSE
Angela Pleasance, Sean Barrett (rdr)
Devised and directed by John Calder

24, 25 Aug. 15.00 25 Aug. 19.30
St Cecilia's Hall
TO ITS BEGINNING TO ITS END
The journey of life as seen by Samuel Beckett
Angela Pleasance, Sean Barrett, Leonard Fenton (rdr)
Devised and narrated by John Calder

LATE NIGHT ENTERTAINMENT

20-25 Aug. 22.30 King's Theatre
SCOTLAND THE WHAT?
MANY HAPPY RETURNS: 21st birthday show
Buff Hardie, George Donald, Stephen Robertson
Director James Logan

DANCE

CLEVELAND SAN JOSE BALLET
28-30 Aug. 19.30 29 Aug. 14.30
Playhouse
QUICKSILVER
Choreographer Dennis Nahat
Music Mendelssohn
Designer Nicholas J. Cavallaro
THE OVERCOAT
Choreographer Flemming Flindt
Music Shostakovich
Designer Beni Montresor
Lighting Christina Giannelli

31 Aug. 1 Sep. 19.30 1, 2 Sep. 14.30
Playhouse
COPPÉLIA
Choreographer Dennis Nahat
Music Delibes
Designer David Guthrie
Lighting Nicholas J. Cavallaro
Dancers Rudolf Nureyev, Cynthia Gregory, Karen Gabay, Nadia Bourman, Melissa Mitchell, Cynthia Graham, Raymond Rodriguez, Olivier Munoz, Peter di Bonaventura, Linda Jackson, Robert Gardner, Kristina Windom, Mark Otloski, Lisa Alfieri, Elizabeth Mackin, Laurie Miller, Kay Eichman, Suzanne Lownsbury, Paula Nunez, Pamela Reyman, Karyn Connell, William Baierbach, Rafael Delgado, Alexandrous Ballard, David Allan Cook, Kevin Thomas, Jeffrey Hughes, Laura Moore, Steven Voznick, Curtis Dick, Jon Carlo Franchi, Charles Calhoun, Austin St John, Michael Hauser, Courtney Laves, Ginger Thatcher, Julie Nakagawa, Glen Tarachow
Scottish Philharmonic Orchestra
Conductor Dwight Oltman

KOREAN CLASSICAL MUSIC AND DANCE COMPANY
13, 14 Aug. 19.30 14 Aug. 15.00
Royal Museum of Scotland
Traditional music and dances

CUMBRE FLAMENCA, Spain
17, 18 Aug. 19.30 Playhouse
EL BAILE
Choreographer Cristobal Reyes
Lighting Felipe Rodriguez
Dancers Juana Amaya, Antonio Canales, La Chana, Angela Granados, Cristobal Reyes
with Rafael Fajardo, La Tobala, Alfonso 'El Veneno', Pedro Montoya (sngr), Diego Losada, Tito Losada, Pedro Sierra, Nino del Tupe (gtr)

LA COMPAGNIE PHILIPPE GENTY, France
19-22 Aug. 19.30 King's Theatre
DRIFTINGS
Choreographer Mary Underwood
Music Rene Aubry
Costumes Annick Baudelin
Lighting Eric Würtz
Dancers Kathy Deville, Pascale Blaison, Eric de Sarria, Christian Carignon, Gabriel Guimard

AMERICAN INDIAN DANCE THEATRE, USA
23-25 Aug. 19.30 25 Aug. 14.30
King's Theatre
Traditional dances of the American Indians
Joe Bellanger, Rudy Bob, Lavina Colwash, Fabian Fontenelle, Kevin Haywahe, Chester Mahooty, John Meninick, Edmond Tate Nevaquaya, Marty Pinnecoose, Norman Roach, Ramona Roach, Eric Sampson, Cassie Soldierwolf, Eddie Swimmer, Danell Tailfeathers, Morgan Tosee, Andy Vasquez, Dwight Whitebuffalo, Lloyd Yellowbird
Director Hanay Geiogamah
Lighting Alan Adelman

ASSOCIATED EXHIBITIONS
(Not organized by the Festival Society)

Including
City Art Centre
SWEAT OF THE SUN: The gold of Peru

Lady Stair's House
ROBERT LOUIS STEVENSON

National Gallery of Scotland
CÉZANNE AND POUSSIN

Royal Scottish Academy
SCOTLAND'S PICTURES

National Portrait Gallery
DYNASTY: The royal house of Stewart

National Library of Scotland
THE HEBRIDES SURVEYED

Royal Incorporation of Architects
ARCHITECTURE OF THE SCOTTISH RENAISSANCE

Fruitmarket Gallery
MAX ERNST

1991

OPERA

BOLSHOI OPERA, Moscow
21, 22 Aug. 19.00 *Playhouse*
EUGENE ONEGIN Tchaikovsky
Onegin Vladimir Redkin
Pavel Chernykh
Tatiana Nina Rautio
Maria Gavrilova
Olga Elena Zaremba
Lensky Arkady Mishenkin
Oleg Kulko
Mme Larina Ludmilla Sergienko
Nina Fomina
Filipievna Ludmilla Nam
Tatiana Pegura
Gremin Gleb Nikolsky
M. Triquet Oleg Biktimirov
Andrei Salnikov
Zaretski Nikolai Nizienko
Anatoly Babykin
Captain Vladimir Bukin
Maxim Mikhailov
Conductor Alexander Lazarev
Director Boris Pokrovsky
Designer Valery Leventhal
Lighting Pavel Volbenkov

24, 25 Aug. 19.00 *Playhouse*
CHRISTMAS EVE Rimsky-Korsakov
Oksana Ekaterina Kudriavchenko
Nina Rautio
Vakula Paolo Kudriavchenko
Lev Kuznetsov
Chub Arthur Eizen
Boris Morozov
Solokha Galina Borisova
Marina Shutova
Devil Oleg Biktimirov
Panas Peter Gluboky
Maxim Mikhailov
Golova Mikhail Maslov
Diak Vladimir Kudriashov
Nikolai Maiboroda
Woman with a violet nose Ludmilla Nam
Raisa Kotova
Woman with a normal nose
Nina Larionova
Zoya Smolianinova
Patsiuk Anatoly Babykin
Nikolai Nizienko
Tsarina Tatiana Erastova
Galina Borisova
Conductor Alexander Lazarev
Director Alexander Titel
Designer Valery Leventhal

SCOTTISH OPERA
29, 31 Aug. 19.00 *King's Theatre*
LA CLEMENZA DI TITO Mozart
Tito Glenn Winslade
Vitellia Juliana Gondek
Sesto Anne Mason
Servilia Claire Daniels
Annio Cheryl Barker
Publio Robert Poulton
Conductor Nicholas McGegan
Director Stephen Wadsworth
Scenery Thomas Lynch
Costumes Dunya Ramicova
Lighting Peter Kaczorowski

KIROV OPERA, Leningrad
10, 12 Aug. 19.00 *Playhouse*
KHOVANSHCHINA Mussorgsky
(Orchestrated by Shostakovich)
Prince Ivan Khovansky Bulat Minzhilkiev
Prince Vassily Galitsin Alexei Steblianko
Prince Andrei Khovansky Yuri Marusin
Vladimir Galusin
Shaklovity Viacheslav Trofimov
Valery Alexeev
Dosifei Nikolai Okhotnikov
Alexander Morozov
Marfa Olga Borodina
Evgenia Gorokhovskaya
Scribe Konstantin Pluzhnikov
Emma Elena Prokina
Tatiana Kravtsova
Susanna Evgenia Chelovalnik
Varsonofiev Andrei Hramcov
Mikhail Chernozukov
Kouzka Nikolai Gassiev
1st Streltsy Evgeny Fedotov
2nd Streltsy Grigory Karasev
Andrei Hramcov
Streshniev Vasily Gerelo
Viacheslav Trofimov
Pastor Valery Lebed
Vasily Gerelo
Klevret Igor Yan
Dancer Elena Bagenova
Conductor Valery Gergiev
Director Leonid Baratov
Designer Feodor Federovsky
Choreographer Feodor Lopulov

14 Aug. 19.00 *St Bride's Centre*
THE MARRIAGE Mussorgsky
Podkolyosin Valery Alexeev
Kochkaryov Vladimir Galusin
Fyokla Ivanovna Larissa Diadkova
Stepan Grigory Karasev
Conductor Alexander Polianichko
Director Yuri Aleksandrov
Designer Galina Solovyova

16 Aug. 19.00 *Usher Hall*
BORIS GODUNOV Mussorgsky
(Concert performance)
Boris Sergei Aleksashkin
Grigory Yuri Marusin
Marina Olga Borodina
Pimen Alexander Morozov
Varlaam Vladimir Ognovenko
Missail Nikolai Gassiev
Shuisky Alexander Dedik
Rangoni Valery Alexeev
Feodor Larissa Diadkova
Xenia Olga Kondina
Nurse Evgenia Perlasova
Hostess Ludmilla Filatova
Simpleton Vladimir Solodovnikov
Shchelkalov Mikhail Kit
Nikitich Evgeny Fedotov
Mityukha Mikhail Chernozukov
Guard Evgeny Fedotov
Boyar Nikolai Gassiev
Jesuits
Georgy Zastavny, Viacheslav Trofimov
Krushchov Yuri Zhikalov
Peasants Evgenia Perlasova, Tatiana Filimonova
Jolly young man Andrei Hramcov
Deaf old man Grigory Karasev
Conductor Valery Gergiev

13 Aug. 20.00 *Usher Hall*
SOROCHINSKY FAIR Mussorgsky
(Concert performance)
Tcherevik Mikhail Kit
Parassia Larissa Shevchenko
Khivria Olga Korzhenskaya
Kum Sergei Aleksashkin
Gritzko Yuri Marusin
Afanasi Ivanitch Konstantin Pluzhnikov
Gypsy/Black God Viacheslav Trofimov
Mussorgsky Pictures at an exhibition; orch. Gorchakov
Conductor Valery Gergiev

15 Aug. 20.00 *Usher Hall*
SALAMMBÔ Mussorgsky
(Concert performance)
Salammbô Olga Borodina
Mathô Bulat Minzhilkiev
Balearic islander Vasily Gerelo
Spendius Valery Lebed
High Priest of Moloch
Vladimir Solodovnikov
Priests Nikolai Gassiev, Sergei Aleksashkin, Evgeny Fedotov
Mussorgsky A night on the Bare Mountain
Conductor Valery Gergiev

ORCHESTRAL CONCERTS

SCOTTISH CHAMBER ORCHESTRA
11 Aug. 20.00 *Usher Hall*
Mozart Concerto for piano no.24 in C minor, K491
Mozart Mass no.18 in C minor (Great), K427
Conductor Sir Yehudi Menuhin
Soloists Eileen Hulse, Adrianne Pieczonka (sop), Andrew Tusa (ten), Johannes Mannov (bs), Jeremy Menuhin (pf), EF Chorus

29 Aug. 22.45 *Ross Bandstand*
Fireworks Concert
Suppe Light cavalry: Overture
Sibelius Finlandia
Berlioz Symphonie fantastique
Tchaikovsky Marche slave
Tchaikovsky 1812 overture
Conductor Christopher Bell

ROYAL SCOTTISH ORCHESTRA
14 Aug. 20.00 *Usher Hall*
Britten War requiem
Conductor Sir Alexander Gibson
Soloists Galina Simkina (sop), David Rendall (ten), Willard White (bs), EF Chorus, RSO Junior Chorus

LENINGRAD PHILHARMONIC ORCHESTRA
Conductor Yuri Temirkanov
17 Aug. 20.00 *Usher Hall*
Tchaikovsky The nutcracker: Pas de deux
Tchaikovsky Concerto for violin in D, op.35
Tchaikovsky Symphony no.5 in E minor, op.64
Soloist Zino Vinnikov (vn)

18 Aug. 20.00 *Usher Hall*
Prokofiev Symphony no.1 in D (Classical), op.25
Prokofiev Concerto for piano no.3 in C, op.26
Prokofiev Romeo and Juliet - Suite
Soloist Alexander Slabodianik (pf)

20 Aug. 20.00 *Usher Hall*
Beethoven Concerto for piano no.1 in C, op.15
Mozart Requiem, K626
Soloists Tatiana Novikova (sop), Evgenia Gorokhovskaya (mez), Alexei Martinov (ten), Sergei Leiferkus (bar), Dmitri Alexeev (pf), EF Chorus

ENGLISH CHAMBER ORCHESTRA
19 Aug. 20.00 *Usher Hall*
Mozart Cassation in G, K63
Mozart Concerto for piano no.20 in D minor, K466
Haydn Symphony no.69 in C (Loudon)
Dvořák Serenade for wind in D minor, op.44
Conductor Leopold Hager
Soloist Elisabeth Leonskaja (pf)

PHILHARMONIA ORCHESTRA
Conductor Esa-Pekka Salonen
22 Aug. 20.00 *Usher Hall*
Debussy Images: Gigues
Shostakovich Concerto for cello no.2 in G, op.126
Stravinsky The firebird (1910 version)
Soloist Heinrich Schiff (vc)

23 Aug. 20.00 *Usher Hall*
Debussy Images: Ibéria
Bartók Concerto for viola
Stravinsky The rite of spring
Soloist Yuri Bashmet (va)

24 Aug. 20.00 *Usher Hall*
Debussy Images: Rondes de printemps
Bartók Concerto for piano no.3
Stravinsky Petrushka
Soloist Barry Douglas (pf)

ROYAL LIVERPOOL PHILHARMONIC ORCHESTRA
26 Aug. 20.00 *Usher Hall*
Suk Praga
Shostakovich Concerto for violin no.1 in A minor, op.99
Dvořák Symphony no.8 in G, op.88
Conductor Libor Pešek
Soloist Igor Oistrakh (vn)

CZECH PHILHARMONIC ORCHESTRA
28 Aug. 20.00 *Usher Hall*
Matoušek Fanfare for 17 November
Dvořák Symphony no.7 in D minor, op.70
Janáček Glagolitic mass
Conductor Sir Charles Mackerras
Soloists Zora Jehličková (sop), Eva Randová (mez), Leo Marian Vodička (ten), Peter Mikuláš (bs), Jaroslav Tvrzský (org), EF Chorus

30 Aug. 20.00 *Usher Hall*
Janáček Taras Bulba
Beethoven Concerto for violin, cello and piano in C, op.56
Dvořák Symphony no.5 in F, op.78
Conductor Jiří Belohlávek
Soloists Israel Piano Trio

31 Aug. 20.00 *Usher Hall*
In Honour of Prague
Mozart Don Giovanni: Overture
Mozart Symphony no.38 in D (Prague), K504
Eben Prague nocturnes
Dvořák Slavonic dances, op.46
Conductor Jiří Belohlávek

ACADEMY OF ANCIENT MUSIC
29 Aug. 20.00 *Usher Hall*
Vivaldi Concerto for flute in G minor (La notte), R439
Vivaldi Cessate, omai cessate
Vivaldi Concerto for oboe in A minor, R463*
Vivaldi Concerto for bassoon in B flat (La notte), R501
Vivadli Clarae stellae
Vivaldi Concerto for flute, oboe and bassoon in F (La tempesta di mare), R570
Director Christopher Hogwood
Soloists James Bowman (c ten), Rachel Brown (fl), Frank de Bruine (ob), Jeremy Ward (bn)

CHAMBER CONCERTS

KIROV CHAMBER ENSEMBLE
12 Aug. 11.00 *Queen's Hall*
Balakirev Octet
Glinka Serenade on themes from Donizetti's 'Anna Bolena'
Rogalyov If Schubert read Pravda
Popov Septet

CZECH NONET
14 Aug. 11.00 *Queen's Hall*
Lutoslawski Dance preludes
Teml Capricious summer (World première)
Mozart Quartet for oboe and strings in F, K370
Reicha Octet in E flat, op.96

16 Aug. 11.00 *Queen's Hall*
Prokofiev Quintet for oboe, clarinet and strings in G minor, op.39
Kalabis Nonet no.2
Spohr Nonet in F, op.31

LES PERCUSSIONS DE STRASBOURG
15 Aug. 11.00 *Queen's Hall*
Varèse Ionisation
Cage First construction (in metal)
Xenakis Pléiades

HEBRIDES ENSEMBLE
17 Aug. 11.00 *Queen's Hall*
Prokofiev Overture on Jewish themes
Knussen Cantata for oboe and string trio, op.15
Poulenc Trio for oboe, bassoon and piano
J.B. Baker Duo for oboe and cello
Janáček Concertino for piano and chamber ensemble

PANOCHA QUARTET
20 Aug. 11.00 *Queen's Hall*
Haydn Quartet in D, op.33/6
Sommer Quartet no.2 in D minor
Dvořák Sextet in A, op.48
with Milan Škampa (va), Marek Jerie (vc)

23 Aug. 11.00 *Queen's Hall*
Dvořák Terzetto in C, op.74
Dvořák Quartet no.14 in A flat, op.105
Dvořák Quintet in E flat (American), op.97
With Milan Škampa (va)

26 Aug. 11.00 *Queen's Hall*
Dvořák Quartet no.10 in E flat, op.51
Mozart Quartet no.14 in G, K387
Schubert Quartet no.10 in E flat, D87

TAN DUN
24, 26 Aug. 15.00 *Edinburgh Academy*
Soundshape for ceramics, voice and movement
Demonstrations of ceramic instruments
Silent earth for ceramics (World première)

LIVE MUSIC NOW!
15.00 *St Andrew's & St George's*
28 Aug. Nielsen Wind Consort
29 Aug. Mary Ann Kennedy, Charlotte Petersen (Clarsach duo)
30 Aug. Athenaeum Brass Quintet

ROYAL SCOTTISH ACADEMY OF MUSIC AND DRAMA
15-17 Aug. 22.00 *Signet Library*
Salieri: Friends, enemies and pupils

27-29 Aug. 22.00
Royal College of Physicians
Rossini at home
Bernard Bresslaw as Rossini, Sarah Pring (sop), Christine Botes (mez), Colin McKerracher (ten), Alan Watt (bar), Scott Mitchell (pf)

KIROV OPERA SOLOISTS AND CHORUS
14 Aug. 22.30 *St Giles' Cathedral*
Russian church music
Soloists Olga Kondina (sop), Larissa Diadkova (mez), Vladimir Solodovnikov (ten), Sergei Aleksashkin (bs)

ST GILES' SINGERS AND ORCHESTRA
16 Aug. 20.00 *St Giles' Cathedral*
Bach Mass in B minor
Conductor Herrick Bunney

SONGS FOR THE FALLING ANGEL: A requiem for Lockerbie
18 Aug. 18.00 *Greyfriar's Kirk*
Music Karen Wimhurst
Libretto and poems Douglas Lipton
Visual artist Keith McIntyre
Conductor Ian McCrorie
Soloists Frances Lynch, Sarah Watson (sop), Steve Kettley (sax), Mary Ann Kennedy (hp), Derek Brockett (narr), Vocem

RENAISSANCE GROUP OF ST ANDREW'S
30, 31 Aug. 20.30 *St Mary's Cathedral*
Carver Mass for 10 voices for St Michael's Day
Conductor David Gascoigne

RECITALS

MARGARET PRICE (sop)
PHILLIP MOLL (pf)
12 Aug. 20.00 *Usher Hall*
Schumann Liederkreis, op.39
Songs by Schubert

FELICITY LOTT (sop)
ROGER VIGNOLES (pf)
25 Aug. 15.00 *Usher Hall*
Songs by R. Strauss, Poulenc, Hahn, Offenbach, O. Straus

THOMAS ALLEN (bar)
ROGER VIGNOLES (pf)
31 Aug. 11.00 *Queen's Hall*
Songs by Haydn, Wolf, Barber, Ives, Copland

JESSYE NORMAN (sop)
PHILLIP MOLL (pf)
1 Sep. 20.00 *Usher Hall*
Wagner Wesendonck Lieder
Schoenberg Cabaret songs
Songs by R. Strauss, Tchaikovsky

PETER DONOHOE (pf)
19 Aug. 11.00 *Queen's Hall*
Gershwin Gershwin songbook
Stravinsky Petrushka: 3 movements; arr. for piano
Debussy Estampes
Debussy Masques
Debussy D'un cahier d'esquisses
Debussy L'isle joyeuse

PETER DONOHOE
MARTIN ROSCOE (pf)
21 Aug. 11.00 *Queen's Hall*
Stravinsky Concerto for 2 solo pianos
Debussy En blanc et noir
Debussy Nocturnes; arr. Ravel
Rachmaninov Symphonic dances, op.45

TATYANA NIKOLAEVA (pf)
28 Aug. 11.00 *Queen's Hall*
Shostakovich Preludes and fugues, op.87: Nos. 1-12

30 Aug. 11.00 *Queen's Hall*
Shostakovich Preludes and fugues, op.87: Nos. 13-24

JOSEF SUK (vn)
RUDOLF FIRKUŠNÝ (pf)
22 Aug. 11.00 *Queen's Hall*
Smetana From the homeland
Dvořák Sonatina in G, op.100
Janáček Sonata
Mozart Sonata no.21 in E minor, K304
Beethoven Sonata no.10 in G, op.96

IGOR OISTRAKH (vn)
NATALIA ZERTSALOVA (pf)
27 Aug. 11.00 *Queen's Hall*
Brahms Sonata no.2 in A, op.100
Beethoven Sonata no.7 in C minor, op.30/2
Hindemith Sonata in E
Chausson Poème
Waxman Carmen fantasia

STEVEN ISSERLIS (vc)
PETER EVANS (pf)
24 Aug. 11.00 *Queen's Hall*
Schumann 5 Stücke im Volkston, op.102
Britten Suite for solo cello no.3, op.87
Tavener Thrénos for solo cello (World première)
Prokofiev Sonata in C, op.119

PETR EBEN (org)
25 Aug. 19.00 *Greyfriar's Kirk*
Themes and improvisations on texts from *The labyrinth of the world* and *The paradise of the heart* by J.A. Komenský
with Tom Fleming (rdr)

SHEILA ARMSTRONG (sop)
BARRY TUCKWELL (hn)
ROGER VIGNOLES (pf)
13 Aug. 11.00 *Queen's Hall*
Beethoven Sonata for horn and piano in F, op.17
R. Strauss Alphorn
R. Strauss Songs
R. Strauss Andante for horn and piano, op.posth.
Schubert Auf dem Strom, D943
Rossini La regata veneziana
Dukas Villanelle for horn and piano
Donizetti L'amor funesto

MASTER CLASSES

14.30 *St Andrew's & St George's*
21 Aug. Panocha Quartet
22 Aug. Peter Donohoe
27 Aug. Roger Vignoles

JAZZ AND FOLK

21 Aug. 20.00 *Usher Hall*
EDINBURGH INTERNATIONAL JAZZ FESTIVAL
The Roots of Jazz and Blues
Barney Kessel Trio, Yank Lawson All Stars, Leon Redbone, Rebirth Brass Band, Oliver Jones Trio.
Introduced by Humphrey Lyttelton

25 Aug. 19.30 26, 27, 29-31 Aug. 22.00
St Bride's Centre
29 Aug. 11.00 *Queen's Hall*
BRATSCH
Gypsy music from Central Europe

16, 17 Aug. 19.30 17 Aug. 15.00
Edinburgh Academy
SAMULNORI, Korea

DRAMA

EDINBURGH INTERNATIONAL FESTIVAL/SCOTTISH THEATRE COMPANY
12-31 Aug. 19.30 (exc.Sun) 14, 17, 21, 24, 28, 31 Aug. 14.30 *Assembly Hall*
THE THRIE ESTAITES Lyndsay
(Adapted by Robert Kemp)
Diligence David Kincaid
King Stuart McQuarrie
Wantonness Sandy Welch
Placebo Jake D'Arcy
Solace Iain Andrew
Sensualitie Caroline Kaart
Hameliness Eliza Langland
Danger Emma Dingwall
Fund-Jennet Halcro Johnston
Gude Counsel Robert James
Flatterie/Pardoner Andrew Dallmeyer
Falsehood Angus Lennie
Deceit Jackie Farrell
Veritie Ann-Louise Ross
Chastitie Edith Macarthur
Spiritualitie Roy Hanlon
Prioress Juliet Cadzow
Abbot Joseph Brady
Parson Gregor Duncan
Temporalitie Finlay Welsh
Merchant Brown Derby
Soutar Ian Stewart
Tailor Norman Fraser
Tailor's wife Sandra McNeeley
Correction's varlet Ian Briggs
Divine Correction David Rintoul
Poor man Phil McCall
Wilkin Widdiefow Tom McGovern
John the Common-Weal Alexander Morton
Sergeant Bill Riddoch
Prelate Patrick Stephen-Samuels
Boy Robert Norman/Stefan Nowosielski
Director Tom Fleming
Designer Nadine Baylis
Lighting Jenny Cane
Music Cedric Thorpe Davie
Scottish Pro Musica Players

NINAGAWA COMPANY
8-10, 12-17 Aug. 19.30 10, 13, 17 Aug. 14.30 *King's Theatre*
TANGO AT THE END OF WINTER
Shimizu
Kiyomura Sei Alan Rickman
Gin Suzanne Bertish
Shigeo Robert Glenister
Miyakoshi Nobuko Anne Marie Cavanagh
Kiyomura Hana Diana Fairfax
Nawa Mizuo Beatie Edney
Nawa Ren Barry Stanton
Tamami Mandy Cheshire
Touta Rupert Mason
Uncle Kamihida Peter Bayliss
Uncle Kitahida Peter Whitbread
Cousin Nishihida Timothy Bateson
Director Yukio Ninagawa
Scenery Setsu Asakura
Costumes Lily Komine
Lighting Sumio Yoshii

LENKOM THEATRE, Moscow
11-14 Aug. 19.30 *Empire Theatre*
TOO CLEVER BY HALF (Mudrets)
Ostrovsky
Yegor Gloumov Victor Rakov
Mme Gloumova Tatiana Kravchenko
Kroutitzky Leonid Bronevoy
Mamaev Vlevolod Larionov
Yuri Kolchef
Kleopatra Mamaeva Ena Chucova
Gorodoulin Alexander Zaryev
Mme Maniefa Elena Fadeva
Mme Tourousina Margarita Strunova
Mashenka Ludmila Arteneva
Kourchaev Sergei Chonshvily
Golutvin Denis Karasev
Companions Tatiana Zakava, Nina Paladina, Inadia Schenikova
Styopka Stanislav Guitarev
Grigory Yuri Fokin
Director Mark Zakharov
Scenery Olega Sheintsis
Costumes Valentine Komolova
Lighting Mikhail Babenko

NATIONAL THEATRE OF CRAIOVA, Romania
16, 18-20 Aug. 19.30 *Empire Theatre*
UBU REX WITH SCENES FROM MACBETH Jarry *and* Shakespeare
Pa Ubu Ilie Gheorghe
Ma Ubu Valler Dellakeza
Captain MacNure/The bear Angel Rababoc
King Wenceslas Remus Margineanu
Queen Rosamund Tamara Popescu
Boggerlas Mirela Cioaba
Tsar Alexis Ion Colan
Michael Feodorovitch Vladimir Juravle
Count of Vitebsk Tudorel Petrescu
Duke of Courland Lucian Albanezu
Tails Theodor Marinescu
Heads Constantin Cicort
Gyron Marian Negrescu
Polish nobleman Anghel Popescu
Ladislas Minela Zamfir
Boleslas Roxana Pera
Macbeth Tudor Gheorghe
Lady Macbeth Leni Pintea-Homeag
Duncan Remus Margineanu
Gentleman compère Valeriu Dogaru
Lady compère Smaragda Olteanu
Musician and other characters Anca Baloiu
Director and designer Silviu Purcarete
Lighting Vadim Levinski
Music Nicu Alifantis

MUMMENSCHANZ COMPANY
17 Aug. 15.00 and 20.00 19-21 Aug. 14.30 21 Aug. 19.30 *Empire Theatre*
THE BEST OF MUMMENSCHANZ
Created by Andres Bossard, Floriana Frassetto, Bernie Schürch
Performed by Barbara Karger, Tina Kronis, Thomas Prattki

CRICOT 2, Poland
23-27 Aug. 19.30 27 Aug. 14.30
Empire Theatre
TODAY IS MY BIRTHDAY Kantor
Proprietor Tadeusz Kantor
His self portrait/Meyerhold Andrzej Welminski
Shadow Loriano della Rocca
Cleaning woman Ludmila Ryba
Father Waclaw Janicki
Individual Leslaw Janicki
Mother Maria Krasicka
Uncle Stasio Roman Siwulak
Priest Smietana Zbigniew Bednarcyk
Maria Jarema Ewa Janicka
Jonasz Stern Zbigniew Gostomski
Dr Klein-Jehova Mira Rychlicka
Water carrier Jan Ksiazek
Infanta Teresa Welminska
Newspaper boy Lech Stangret
Beadle Stanislaw Michno

NATIONAL THEATRE OF MARTIN, Czechoslovakia
19, 22, 23 Aug. 19.30 22 Aug. 14.30
St Bride's Centre
BAAL Brecht (Slovak)
Baal Matej Landl

Ekart Milan Bahul
Johannes Jindrich Obsil
Sefia Olga Sulikova
Johanna Katarina Zatovicova
Landlady Gita Mazalova
Lujza Emilia Cizova
1st Sister Michaela Csillaghyova
2nd Sister Lubomira Hlavacova-Krkosova
Other parts played by Michal Gazdik, Frantisek Vyrostko, Martin Hornak, Petronela Valentova
Dancers Eva Gasparova, Jana Domkova, Sona Sicakova, Jana Rusinakova, Anna Dankova, Jana Zambojova
Director Roman Polak
Scenery Jozef Ciller
Costumes Maria Cillerova

20, 21, 24 Aug. 19.30 24 Aug. 14.30
St Bride's Centre
LA DISPUTE Marivaux (Slovak)
Mesrou Jan Kozuch
Carisa Petronela Valentova
Eglé Lubomira Hlavacova-Krkoskova
Azor Milan Bahul
Adina Daniela Kuffelova
Mesrin Frantisek Vyrostko
Director Roman Polak
Scenery Jozef Ciller
Costumes Maria Cillerova

OPEN THEATRE OF BELGRADE
26-31 Aug. 19.15 28, 31 Aug. 14.30
St Bride's Centre
L'ORCHESTRE Anouilh (S.Croat)
Patricia Ruzjca Sokic
Pamela Ivana Zigon
Madame Ortange Olivera Markovic
Susanne Delicia Elisaveta Sablic
Hermiline Milica Isakovic
Leona Zoran Cvijanovic
Leon Tihomir Stanic
M. Lebonge Zivojin-Zika Milenkovic
Director Petar Zec
Scenery Geroslav Zarjc
Costumes Bozana Jovanovic
Choreographer Sonja Lapatanov

BRUNTON THEATRE
9-13, 15-17 Aug. 19.30 10, 15, 17 Aug. 14.30 St Bride's Centre
21-24, 26-31 Aug. 19.30 22, 24, 29, 31 Aug. 14.30 Brunton Theatre
THE BRUCE Silver
Robert Bruce Paul Samson
Robert I Alec Heggie
Queen Elizabeth Melanie O'Reilly
Isabel, Countess of Buchan/Jean Muriel Romanes
David, Bishop of Moray/Brother David/Neil Ross Mackay
Robert Wishart, Bishop of Glasgow Alec Monteath
William Lamberton Gordon Fulton
Sir Henry de Bohun/Edward I Dominic Grant
Sir David Brechin/Sir Edward Bruce David Monteath
Kirkpatrick/Sir James Douglas Gregor Powrie
Neil Bruce/Alexander Bruce/Earl of Buchan/ Prince of Wales Liam Brennan
Red John Comyn/Sir Thomas Randolph/ John Lewis Howden
Boy Stuart Wilkinson
Girl Dawn Hazel
Director Charles Nowosielski
Designer Nick Sargent
Lighting Martin Palmer

NATIONAL YOUTH MUSIC THEATRE
12-17, 19-20 Aug. 19.30 14, 16, 17, 20 Aug. 14.30 Church Hill Theatre
ONCE UPON A WAR Coffey
Music Richard Taylor
Directors Jeremy James Taylor, Russell Labey
Scenery Simon Elliott, Bernadette Roberts
Costumes Sheila Darlington
Lighting Richard House

THEATRE ROYAL, Stratford East
22-24, 26-31 Aug. 19.30 24, 29, 31 Aug. 14.30 Church Hill Theatre
SHOOTING DUCKS Vampilov
(Eng. Translated by Peter Tegel)
Zilov Karl Howman
Boy Russell Jones
Sayapin Steve Edwin
Kusakov Stephen Bent
Valeria Michelle Fine
Vera Kathryn Howden
Kushak Robert Putt
Galina Candida Gubbins
Irina Sheri Graubert
Dima Louis Mellis
Director Philip Hedley
Designer Jenny Tiramani
Lighting Stephen Watson

12-15 Aug. 15.00 13, 14 Aug. 19.30
Royal College of Physicians
THE MINSTREL AND THE SHIRRA Massie
Sir Walter Scott Robert Paterson
with Elspeth Smellie (clarsach)
Director Judy Steel

14, 15, 17 Aug. 11.00
Royal College of Physicians
THE WINEMAKERS' STORY
Michael Buller and the Winemakers of Bordeaux

16-18 Aug. 15.00 17, 18 Aug. 19.30
Royal College of Physicians
THE TOWERS OF TREBIZOND
Whitemore (From the novel by Rose Macaulay)
Rohan McCullough
Director Wyn Jones

19, 21, 22 Aug. 19.30 20-22 Aug. 15.00
Royal College of Physicians
GLITTER CITY Jonič
Bettina Jonič
with David Craven (pf)

23-25, 27 Aug. 19.30 24-27 Aug. 15.00
Royal College of Physicians
FENELLA FIELDING in INSIDE STORIES
with Colin Starkey
Director Peter Benedict

28, 30 Aug. 19.30 29-31 Aug. 15.00
Royal College of Physicians
NIJINSKY: DEATH OF A FAUN Pownall
Nijinsky Nicholas Johnson
Director Jane McCulloch
Designer Jennie Norman

ARCHAOS, France
10 Aug.-1 Sep. (exc.Mon) 20.30 (Sat and Sun 15.00) Leith Links
BX-91: Beau comme la guerre

PROSE AND POETRY RECITALS

SCOTTISH POETRY LIBRARY
16 Aug. 15.00 St Cecilia's Hall
THE OTHER HALF: poets from Germany
Heinz Czechowski, Werner Durrson, Michael Hamburger (rdr)

30 Aug. 15.00 St Cecilia's Hall
A COMPASS OF SCOTTISH VOICES
Norman MacCaig, Sorley MacLean, George Bruce, Tom Leonard (rdr)

SALTIRE SOCIETY
19, 26 Aug. 15.00 St Cecilia's Hall
'AULD REEKIE': Edinburgh in words and music
Edith Macarthur, James Cairncross (rdr), Alastair Hardie (fiddle)
Devised by Paul Scott

20, 27 Aug. 15.00 St Cecilia's Hall
HARP OF THE NORTH: The clarsach celebrated in music and verse
Rhona Mackay, Isobel Mieras (clarsach), John Shedden (rdr)
Compiled by Peter Freshwater

21, 28 Aug. 15.00 St Cecilia's Hall
THE WINTER QUEEN: The story of Elizabeth of Bohemia, Princess of Scotland
Meta Forrest, Ian Gilmour (rdr), Ian Paton (ten), Kenneth Elliott (hpd)
Compiled by Isobel Dunlop

22, 29 Aug. 15.00 St Cecilia's Hall
NEIL GUNN: A celebration in words and music
Rose McBain, John Shedden (rdr)
Compiled by Margery McNeill

DANCE

NATIONAL BALLET OF CUBA
20, 22, 24 Aug. 19.30 24 Aug. 14.30
King's Theatre
DON QUIXOTE
Choreographers Petipa, Alexander Gorski
Music Minkus

21, 23 Aug. 19.30 25 Aug. 15.00
King's Theatre
LES SYLPHIDES
Choreographer Mikhail Fokine
Music Chopin
LA CASA DI BERNARDA ALBA
Choreographer Ivan Tenorio
Music S. F. Barosso
DIDO ABANDONADO
Choreographer Alicia Alonso
Music Gasparo Angiolini
Designer (all ballets) Salvador Fernández
Dancers Alicia Alonso, Ofelia Gonzalez, María Elena Llorente, Rosario Súarez, Marta García, Lázaro Carreño, Jorge Vega, Lienz Chang, Ernesto Quenedith, Orlando Salgado, Lorena Feijoo, Svetlana Ballester, Galina Alvarez, Loipa Araújo, Mercedes Vergara, Maydee Peña, Haydee Delgado, Moraima Martínez, Gladys Acosta, Anael Martín, Rafael Padilla, José Medina, Emilio Manzano, Gabriel Sánchez, Georgina Ramos, Jesús Corrales, Rosa Ochoa, Tamara Villareala, Aymara Cabrera, Alena Carmentates, Ivette Gonzalez, Julia Maya, Felix Rodríguez, Alberto Terrero, Vladimir Alvarez, Ana Leyte
BBC Scottish Symphony Orchestra
Conductor Jose Ramon Urbay

BALLET OF THE DEUTSCHE OPER, Berlin
30, 31 Aug. 19.30 31 Aug. 14.30
1 Sep. 15.00 Playhouse

GISELLE
Choreographer Peter Schaufuss *after* Jean Coralli *and* Jules Perrot
Music Adam
Designer Desmond Healey

28, 29 Aug. 18.45 *Playhouse*
RING ROUND THE RING
Choreographer Maurice Béjart
Music Wagner
Designer Peter Sykora
Lighting Jean-Claude Asquie
Dancers Peter Schaufuss, Lisa Cullum, Leanne Benjamin, Christine Camillo, Bart de Block, Alessandro Molin, Martin James, Susan Hogard, Arantxa Arguelles, Yulia Makhalina, Igor Zelensky, Silke Sense, Marek Rozycki, Vladimir Damianov, Johnny Eliasen, Charlotte Butler, Patrick de Bana, Yannick Boquin, Janet Wong, Arkardiusz Duch, Stefan Zeromski, Marguerite Donlon, Theresa Jarvis, Piotr Lutrosinski, Kathy Kepler, Katarzyna Gdaniec, Stefano Giannetti, Joakim Svalberg, Kathlyn Pope, Xavier Ferla, Tomas Karlborg, Felicitas Binder, Sara Rendall, Julia Lawrenz
with Michael Denard (narr), Elizabeth Cooper (pf)
Northern Sinfonia
Conductor Peter Ernst Lassen

LA LA LA HUMAN STEPS
14-17 Aug. 19.30 *Playhouse*
INFANTE C'EST DESTROY
Choreographer Edouard Lock
Dancers Edouard Lock, Louise Lecavalier, Donald Weikert, Marito Olsson-Forsberg, Pim Boonprakob, Sarah Williams, Bernardus Bartels

TEATR EKSPRESJI, Poland
26, 27 Aug. 19.30 *King's Theatre*
ZUN
Choreographer Wojciech Misiuro
Designer Barbara Hanicka
Lighting Marek Mroczkowski
Cast Krzysztof Balinski, Andrzej Chorab, Krzysztof Dziemaszkiewicz, Bozena Eltermann, Wojciech Misiuro, Wojciech Osowski, Zenon Zwirski, Jaroslawa Pozorska, Aleksandra Trytko

LA COMPAGNIE PHILIPPE GENTY, France
28 Aug.-1 Sep. 19.30 31 Aug. 14.30
Empire Theatre
DÉSIRS PARADE
Choreographer Mary Underwood
Music René Aubrey
Dancers Alain Clement, Agnès Neel, Patrick Henniquau, Emmanuel Plassard

ASSOCIATED EXHIBITIONS
(Not organized by the Festival Society)

Including

National Museum of Scotland
BEHIND GOLDEN SCENES

Fine Art Society
BRITISH ARTISTS IN MEIJI JAPAN 1880-1900

Talbot Rice Gallery
ZEN BUDDHISM AND THE RYU GROUP

Edinburgh College of Art
RESTLESS SHADOWS

1992

OPERA

EDINBURGH INTERNATIONAL FESTIVAL
23, 24 Aug. 20.00 *King's Theatre*
IL MAESTRO DI CAPPELLA Cimarosa
Maestro Claudio Desderi
LA VOIX HUMAINE Poulenc
Elle Elisabeth Söderström
Scottish Chamber Orchestra
Conductor Richard Armstrong

OPERA NORTH
26, 28, 29 Aug. 19.00 *King's Theatre*
YOLANTA Tchaikovsky (Eng)
Yolanta Joan Rodgers
Vaudémont Kim Begley
René Norman Bailey
Robert Robert Hayward
Ibn-Hakia Clive Bayley
Alméric Philip Mills
Bertrand David Gwynne
Marthe Tamsin Dives
Brigitte Anne-Marie Ives
Laure Lesley Roberts

ADVENTURES IN MOTION PICTURES
THE NUTCRACKER Tchaikovsky
Choreographer Matthew Bourne
Dancers Etta Murfitt, Scott Ambler, Ally Fitzpatrick, Barry Atkinson, Andrew George, Rosie Allen, Maxine Fone, Misha Downey, Teresa Barker, Simon Murphy, Friedrich Gehrig, Anton Skrzypiciel
English Northern Philharmonia
RSO Children's Chorus
Conductor David Lloyd-Jones
Director Martin Duncan
Designer Anthony Ward
Lighting Ian Sommerville

BBC SCOTTISH SYMPHONY ORCHESTRA
16 Aug. 20.00 *Usher Hall*
MOSES UND ARON Schoenberg (Eng)
(Concert performance)
Moses Willard White
Aron William Cochran
Young girl/1st Naked virgin Rebecca Evans
Young man/Naked youth Paul Charles Clarke
Ephraimite/Man Jonathan Best
Priest Alastair Miles
Conductor Richard Armstrong
Cappella Nova, EF Chorus, RSO Children's Chorus

SCOTTISH OPERA
20 Aug. 19.00 *Usher Hall*
THE OPRICHNIK Tchaikovsky
(Concert performance)
Prince Zhemchuzhny Piotr Nowacki
Natalia Galina Gorchakova
Andrei Morozov Paolo Kudriavchenko
Morozova Ludmilla Nam
Zakharevna Fiona Kimm
Prince Vyazminsky Vladimir Glushchak
Fedor Basmanov Anne Collins
Molchan Mitkov David Morrison
Conductor Mark Ermler

ORCHESTRAL CONCERTS

DANISH NATIONAL RADIO SYMPHONY ORCHESTRA
17 Aug. 20.30 *Usher Hall*
Tchaikovsky Festival overture on the Danish national anthem
Tchaikovsky Concerto for violin in D, op.35
Tchaikovsky Symphony no.1 in G minor (Winter daydreams), op.13; arr. Rozhdestvensky
Conductor Dmitri Kitaenko
Soloist Joshua Bell (vn)

SCOTTISH CHAMBER ORCHESTRA
18 Aug. 20.00 *Usher Hall*
Stravinsky Apollon musagète
Tchaikovsky Variations on a Rococo theme
Tchaikovsky The sleeping beauty: Pas de deux; arr. Stravinsky
Tchaikovsky Souvenir de Florence
Conductor Yuri Simonov
Soloist Raphael Wallfisch (vc)

26 Aug. 19.30 *Usher Hall*
Tchaikovsky Suite no.4 in G (Mozartiana), op.61
Berlioz Les nuits d'été
Schoenberg Verklärte Nacht
Conductor Donald Runnicles
Soloist Isabelle Vernet (sop)

27 Aug. 23.00 *Ross Bandstand*
Fireworks Concert
Orff Carmina Burana: 3 choruses
Tchaikovsky Festival coronation march
Tchaikovsky Eugene Onegin: Waltz and Polonaise
Sibelius Finlandia
Tchaikovsky Marche slave
Bizet Carmen: March
Conductor David Angus
Scottish Chamber Orchestra Chorus

ST PETERSBURG PHILHARMONIC ORCHESTRA
21 Aug. 20.00 *Usher Hall*
Weber Oberon: Overture
Tchaikovsky Serenade for strings, op.48
Shostakovich Symphony no.5 in D minor, op.47
Conductor Mariss Jansons

22 Aug. 20.00 *Usher Hall*
Rachmaninov Concerto for piano no.2 in C minor, op.18
Tchaikovsky Symphony no.4 in F minor, op.36
Conductor Mariss Jansons
Soloist Mikhail Rudy (pf)

23 Aug. 20.00 *Usher Hall*
Tchaikovsky Marche slave
Tchaikovsky Swan lake - Suite
Tchaikovsky Manfred symphony
Conductor Yuri Temirkanov

LONDON PHILHARMONIC
24 Aug. 20.00 *Usher Hall*
Bruckner Symphony no.8 in C minor; ed. Nowak
Conductor Franz Welser-Möst

25 Aug. 20.00 *Usher Hall*
Beethoven Egmont: Overture
R. Strauss Vier letzte Lieder
Beethoven Symphony no.7 in A, op.92
Conductor Klaus Tennstedt
Soloist Felicity Lott (sop)

ENGLISH NORTHERN PHILHARMONIA
27 Aug. 20.00 *Usher Hall*
Tchaikovsky Symphony no.2 in C minor (Little Russian), op.17 (original version 1872)
Tchaikovsky Songs: Legend; Was I not a little blade of grass; Does the day reign?

Tchaikovsky Concert fantasia for piano and orchestra, op.56
Tchaikovsky Concerto for piano no.3 in E flat, op.75
Conductor Paul Daniel
Soloists Elena Prokina (sop), Peter Donohoe (pf)

ROYAL SCOTTISH NATIONAL ORCHESTRA
28 Aug. 20.00 *Usher Hall*
Tchaikovsky Hamlet - Fantasy overture
Prokofiev Hamlet: Incidental music
Shostakovich Hamlet: Concert scenario (World première)
Conductor Gennadi Rozhdestvensky
Soloists Elena Prokina (sop), Neal Davies (b-bar)

30 Aug. 20.00 *Usher Hall*
Tchaikovsky The storm - Overture
Tchaikovsky Concerto for piano no.1 in B flat minor, op.23
Tchaikovsky Symphony no.6 in B minor (Pathétique), op.74
Conductor Neeme Järvi
Soloist Peter Donohoe (pf)

3 Sep. 19.30 *Usher Hall*
Tchaikovsky Concerto for piano no.2 in G, op.44
Tchaikovsky Symphony no.3 in D (Polish), op.29
Tchaikovsky Cantata Moscow
Conductor Yuri Simonov
Soloists Peter Donohoe (pf), Olga Borodina (mez), Dimitri Kharitonov (bar), EF Chorus

ROYAL CONCERTGEBOUW ORCHESTRA, Amsterdam
Conductor Riccardo Chailly
31 Aug. 20.00 *Usher Hall*
Haydn Symphony no.45 in F sharp minor (Farewell)
Berio Requies
Beethoven Symphony no.4 in B flat, op.60

1 Sep. 19.30 *Usher Hall*
Webern Passacaglia, op.1
Beethoven Concerto for piano no.4 in G, op.58
Tchaikovsky Symphony no.5 in E minor, op.64
Soloist Maria João Pires (pf)

SCOTTISH MUSIC THROUGH THE CENTURIES

CAPPELLA NOVA
19 Aug. 20.30 *Greyfriar's Kirk*
From Columba to Carver (8th-16th centuries)
Celtic chants. Excerpts from St Andrew's Music Book. Readings from Celtic texts
Carver Gaude Flore
Carver O bone Jesu
Conductor Alan Tavener
Soloists Judith Peacock (clarsach), Tom Fleming (rdr)

CONCERTO CALEDONIA
23 Aug. 15.00 *Queen's Hall*
From Rome to home (17th and 18th centuries)
Clerk Eheu Eheu!
Clerk Sonata for solo violin
Abell Aloud proclaim: Coronation ode for Queen Anne
Clerk Odo di mesto intorno
Abell Songs
Lute and harpsichord solos from the Balcarres and other manuscripts
Soloists Lynne Dawson (sop), Renald Laban (male sop), Jakob Lindberg (lute)

SCOTTISH CHAMBER ORCHESTRA
29 Aug. 20.00 *Usher Hall*
Thistles, kisses and crescendos: (Mid 18th century)
Oswald March and Minuet and Cardiganshire march
McGibbon Sonata no.3 in G
Oswald Colin's kisses
Oswald The seasons: Excerpts
Oswald The dustcart cantata
Earl of Kelly Symphony in B flat
Anon. The celebrated trumpet tune
Oswald Cambridge and Buckinghamshire marches
Oswald Sonata on Scots tunes
Oswald The dancing master
Oswald The wheelbarrow cantata
Earl of Kelly Minuets
Earl of Kelly Death is now my only treasure
Earl of Kelly Symphony in C
Director James Clark
Soloists Patricia MacMahon (sop), John Mark Ainsley (ten), Ursula Smith (vc), David McGuinness (hpd)

HEBRIDES ENSEMBLE members
2 Sep. 19.30 *Queen's Hall*
Scotus Germanicus (Early to mid 19th century)
Thomson Trio for piano and strings in G minor
Thomson Bagatelle
Thomson Mazurka
Thomson Songs
Hogg Lie still my love; arr. Dewar
MacCunn Songs
A.C. MacKenzie Quartet for piano and strings
Soloists Marie McLaughlin (sop), Malcolm Martineau (pf)

SCOTTISH CHAMBER ORCHESTRA
5 Sep. 20.00 *Usher Hall*
The Scottish virtuoso (19th and 20th centuries)
Wallace The passing of Beatrice
MacMillan Veni, veni Emmanuel+
Musgrave Concerto for horn
A.C. MacKenzie Scottish concerto
Whyte Donald of the Burthens: Finale
Conductors Sir Alexander Gibson, Jukka-Pekka Saraste+
Soloists Evelyn Glennie (perc), Barry Tuckwell (hn), Steven Osborne (pf), George McIlwham (bp)

CHAMBER MUSIC

BORODIN QUARTET
17 Aug. 11.00 *Queen's Hall*
Tchaikovsky Quartet movement in B flat
Tchaikovsky Quartet no.1 in D, op.11
Brahms Quartet no.1 in C minor, op.51/1

18 Aug. 11.00 *Queen's Hall*
Tchaikovsky Quartet no.2 in F, op.22
Brahms Quartet no.2 in A minor, op.51/2

19 Aug. 11.00 *Queen's Hall*
Tchaikovsky Quartet no.3 in E flat minor, op.30
Brahms Quartet no.3 in B flat, op.67

BARTÓK QUARTET
27 Aug. 11.00 *Queen's Hall*
Bartók Quartets nos.1, 4, 6

28 Aug. 11.00 *Queen's Hall*
Bartók Quartets nos. 2, 3, 5

RAPHAEL ENSEMBLE
29 Aug. 11.00 *Queen's Hall*
Brahms Sextet no.1 in B flat, op.18
Tchaikovsky Souvenir de Florence: string sextet, op.70

PETER FRANKL (pf), GYÖRGY PAUK (vn), RALPH KIRSHBAUM (vc)
5 Sep. 11.00 *Queen's Hall*
Janáček Fairy tale (Pohádka) for cello and piano
Janáček Sonata for violin and piano
Tchaikovsky Trio for piano and strings in A minor, op.50

EDINBURGH FESTIVAL CHORUS
24, 25 Aug. 22.30 *St Giles' Cathedral*
Tchaikovsky Liturgy of St John Chrysostom
Conductor Arthur Oldham

DIANA MONTAGUE (mez)
ANTHONY ROLFE JOHNSON (ten)
SIR CHARLES MACKERRAS (cond)
3 Sep. 22.30 *Usher Hall*
Mahler Das Lied von der Erde; arr. Schoenberg
with Edinburgh Festival Ensemble

ANN MURRAY (mez)
PHILIP LANGRIDGE (ten)
PETER DONOHOE (pf)
17 Aug. 22.30 *Usher Hall*
Mahler Das Lied von der Erde

RECITALS

DMITRI HVOROSTOVSKY (bar)
JULIAN REYNOLDS (pf)
19 Aug. 20.00 *Usher Hall*
Songs by Tchaikovsky, Borodin, Rimsky-Korsakov, Rachmaninov

BARBARA BONNEY (sop)
GEOFFREY PARSONS (pf)
22 Aug. 11.00 *Queen's Hall*
Songs by Mendelssohn, Grieg, R. Strauss, Berg, Barber

ISABELLE VERNET (sop)
MARIE-JEANNE SERERO (pf)
25 Aug. 11.00 *Queen's Hall*
French songs by Fauré, Poulenc, Hahn, Duparc, Satie, Rosenthal

ANDREAS SCHMIDT (bar)
GEOFFREY PARSONS (pf)
26 Aug. 11.00 *Queen's Hall*
Schubert Die schöne Müllerin

ELENA PROKINA (sop)*
IAIN BURNSIDE (pf)
31 Aug. 11.00 *Queen's Hall*
Arias and songs by Tchaikovsky, Rachmaninov

OLGA BORODINA (mez)
LARISSA GERGIEVA (pf)
1 Sep. 11.00 *Queen's Hall*
Songs by Tchaikovsky

JANICE WATSON (sop)
IAIN BURNSIDE (pf)
3 Sep. 11.00 *Queen's Hall*
Songs by Liszt, Tchaikovsky, Rachmaninov

STEVEN OSBORNE (pf)
20 Aug. 11.00 *Queen's Hall*
Haydn Sonata no.48 in C
Messiaen Vingt regards sur l'enfant Jesus: Nos. 1, 8, 10, 14, 15
Schubert Sonata no.18 in G, D894

PETER DONOHOE (pf)
21 Aug. 11.00 *Queen's Hall*
Tchaikovsky Scherzo à la russe, op.1/1
Tchaikovsky Two pieces, op.2
Tchaikovsky Sonata no.1 in F minor
Tchaikovsky Eighteen pieces, op.72: Un poco di Chopin
Chopin Scherzo no.4 in E, op.54
Chopin Berceuse in D flat, op.57
Chopin Études nos.1-12, op.10

24 Aug. 11.00 *Queen's Hall*
Schumann Études symphoniques, op.13
Piano works by Tchaikovsky and Schumann

2 Sep. 11.00 *Queen's Hall*
Tchaikovsky Two pieces, op.10
Tchaikovsky Sonata no.2 in G (Grande sonata), op.37
Tchaikovsky Eighteen pieces, op.72: Valse à cinq temps
Rachmaninov Études tableaux: Excerpts
Stravinsky Petrushka: 3 movements; arr. for piano

BENJAMIN FRITH (pf)
26 Aug. 22.30 *Usher Hall*
Beethoven Variations on a waltz by Diabelli

RICHARD GOODE (pf)
1 Sep. 22.30 *Usher Hall*
Beethoven Sonata no.29 in B flat (Hammerklavier), op.106

4 Sep. 11.00 *Queen's Hall*
Mozart Sonata no.15 in F, K533
Schubert Sonata no.19 in C minor, D958
Debussy Preludes for piano: Excerpts
Schubert Sonata no.21 in B flat, D960

LATE NIGHT ENTERTAINMENT

MUSIC BOX
19 Aug. 22.30 *Lyceum Theatre*
A not so serious look at music: Linda Ormiston, Donald Maxwell and Wyn Davies preview the 1992 Festival

DENNIS O'NEILL (ten)
INGRID SURGENOR (pf)
21 Aug. 22.30 *Lyceum Theatre*
Neapolitan songs and ballads

ELISABETH SÖDERSTRÖM (sop)
28 Aug. 22.30 *Lyceum Theatre*
In cabaret with Lars Roos (pf)

DRAMA

ROYAL NATIONAL THEATRE
18 Aug.-5 Sep. 19.30 (exc. Sun) 25 Aug. 14.30 22, 29 Aug. 5 Sep. 16.30 and 20.30 *Assembly Hall*
FUENTE OVEJUNA Lope de Vega
(Eng. In a version by Adrian Mitchell)
Fernando Gomez du Guzman James Laurenson
Captain Flores Mark Strong
Sergeant Ortuno David Hounslow
Grand Master of Calatrava Karl Collins
Queen Isabella Mona Hammond
King Ferdinand Jon Rumney
Don Manrique Stephen Hattersley
Cimbranos Nigel Leach
Soldiers James Kerr, Aaron Shirley, Dominic Taylor
Laurencia Rachel Joyce
Pascuala Pamela Nomvete
Frondoso Wilbert Johnson
Barrildo Jo Stone-Fewings
Mengo Clive Rowe
Juan Rojo Michael Gardiner
Esteban Ben Thomas
Alonso Stefan Kalipha
Jacinta Helen McCrory
Boy Thomas Murrill
Anthony Walters
Ines Clara Onyemere
Olalla Teresa McElroy
Peasant Ignatius Anthony
Leonelo Ben Miles
Farmer Nicholas Caunter
Aldermen Dominic Taylor, Dominic Rickhards
Director Declan Donnellan
Designer Nick Ormerod
Lighting Mick Hughes

26, 27 Aug. 14.30 *Lyceum Theatre*
THE SECRET LIFE Barker
(A rehearsed reading)
Stephen Serecold James Laurenson
Evan Strowde Alan Howard
Eleanor Strowde Rosemary Martin
Joan Westbury Brenda Blethyn
Countess of Peckham Mary Mitchell
Oliver Gauntlett Jo Stone-Fewings
Mr Kittredge Manning Redwood
Susan Kittredge Rachel Joyce
Dorothy Gauntlett/Parlour maid Helen McCrory
Sir Leslie Heriot/Lord Clumbermere/Sir Geoffrey Salomons Michael Gardiner

3, 4 Sep. 14.30 *Lyceum Theatre*
THE MARRYING OF ANN LEETE Barker
(A rehearsed reading)
Ann Leete Helen McCrory
Lord John Carp James Laurenson
George Leete Nigel Leach
Daniel Tatton/Mr Crowe Michael Gardiner
Lady Sarah Cottesham Rachel Joyce
Carnaby Leete Patrick O'Connell
John Abud Rupert Graves
Rev. Dr Remnant Steven Beard
Mr Smallpiece Stephen Hattersley
Sir George Leete John Rumney
Mrs Opie/Lady Leete/Mrs Prestige Di Langford
Mr Tetgeen/Mr Prestige Allan Mitchell
Lord Arthur Carp Ben Thomas
Dolly Clara Onyemere
Rev. Mr Tozer/Dimmuck Aaron Shirley

EDINBURGH INTERNATIONAL FESTIVAL
ROYAL LYCEUM THEATRE COMPANY
17-22 Aug. 19.00 18, 22 Aug. 14.00
Lyceum Theatre
THE VOYSEY INHERITANCE Barker
Mr Voysey Tenniel Evans
Peacey Ron Pember
Edward Voysey Peter Lindford
Major Booth Voysey Peter Blythe
Mr George Booth Frank Middlemass
Denis Tregoning Matthew Byam Shaw
Rev. Evan Colpus Peter Halliday
Ethel Voysey Sandra Butterworth
Alice Maitland Katharine Rogers
Honor Voysey Tricia Kelly
Beatrice Voysey Harriet Bagnall
Phoebe Liz Moscrop
Mary Phoebe Burridge
Mrs Voysey Gillian Martell
Trenchard Voysey Christopher Good
Hugh Voysey Michael Grandage
Emily Voysey Anne White
Director William Gaskill
Scenery Hayden Griffin
Costumes Annie Smart
Lighting Andy Phillips

19 Aug. 17.00 *Lyceum Theatre*
ROCOCO Barker
(A rehearsed reading)
Miss Underwood Gillian Martell
Mrs Underwood Liz Moscrop
Mrs Reginald Anne White
Reginald Peter Blythe
Vicar Peter Halliday
Mr Uglow Frank Middlemass
Scene narrator Christopher Good
Director William Gaskill

20 Aug. 17.00 *Lyceum Theatre*
FAREWELL TO THE THEATRE Barker
(A rehearsed reading)
Dorothy Susan Engel
Edward Tenniel Evans
Scene narrator Christopher Good
Director William Gaskill

LYRIC THEATRE, Hammersmith
25-29 Aug. 19.00 28, 29 Aug. 14.00
Lyceum Theatre
THE MADRAS HOUSE Barker
Philip Madras Roger Allam
Major Hippisly Thomas Thomas Wheatley
Julia Huxtable/Miss Belhaven Charlotte Harvey
Laura Huxtable/Mrs Brigstock Kate Lock
Emma Huxtable Alexandra Mathie
Jane Huxtable/Miss Yates Suzanna Hamilton
Henry Huxtable Sam Kelly
Katherine/Miss Chancellor Frances Cuka
Amelia Madras Helen Ryan
Minnie Huxtable/Jessica Madras Eve Matheson
Clara Huxtable/Maid Trilby James
Mr Brigstock/Mr Windlesham Jim Hooper
Eustace Perrin State Bill Bailey
Constantine Madras John Hallam
Director Peter James
Designer Pamela Howard
Lighting Mick Hughes

ORANGE TREE THEATRE, Richmond
25-29 Aug. 19.30 26, 29 Aug. 14.30
St Bride's Centre
HIS MAJESTY Barker (World première)
King Henry XIII of Carpathia Sam Dastor
Queen Rosamund Caroline John
Colonel Guastalla Brian Hickey
Mr Henry Dwight Osgood/Mayor of Zimony/Jakab David Timson
Count Zapolya Barrie Cookson
Countess Czernyak Auriol Smith
Dominica Czernyak Janine Wood
Ella Caroline Gruber
Colonel Hadik Peter Wyatt
Dr Madrassy Morris Perry
Count Stephen Czernyak Geoffrey Church
Gen. Horvath/Sgt Maj. Bakay Richard Owens
Mr Bruckner Frank Moorey
Captain Roger Dad Timothy Watson
Lieutenant Vida/Sir Charles Vincent Brimble
Director Sam Walters
Designer Tom Piper
Lighting Dickon O'Mara, Paul Smailes

GREENWICH THEATRE COMPANY
17-22 Aug. 19.30 19, 22 Aug. 14.30
Church Hill Theatre
SCHIPPEL Taylor

Hiketier — David Bamber
Thekla — Kate Buffery
The Prince — Michael Simkins
Krey — Richard Freeman
Wolke — Brian Protheroe
Schippel — James Saxon
Jenny — Sadie Shimmin
Director — Jeremy Sams
Designer — Lez Brotherston
Lighting — Leonard Tucker

KING'S HEAD THEATRE CLUB, Islington
24-29 Aug. 19.30 26, 29 Aug. 14.30
Church Hill Theatre
THE BLACK AND WHITE MINSTRELS
Taylor
Cyril — Jason Isaacs
Gil — Katy Murphy
Harry — James McKenna
Pat — Andrea Gibb
Atara — Yvonne Gidden
Max — David Solomon
Director — Linda Marlowe
Scenery — Nick Burnell
Costumes — Jacqui Hubbard
Lighting — Nick Brownlie

NORTHERN STAGE COMPANY, Newcastle
31 Aug.-5 Sep. 19.30 2, 5 Sep. 14.30
Church Hill Theatre
AND A NIGHTINGALE SANG Taylor
Helen Scott — Denise Welch
Joyce Scott — Angela Lonsdale
George — David Whitaker
Peggy — Val McLane
Andie — Stephen Hancock
Eric — Robson Green
Norman — Ian Sharrock
Musicians — Tony McNally, Mike Watson
Director — Alan Lyddiard
Designer — Neil Murray
Lighting — Gerry Jenkinson

FIFTH ESTATE
17-22 Aug. 19.30 21, 22 Aug. 14.30
Corn Exchange
THE BALLACHULISH BEAT Taylor
Ron Green — Robert Carr
Jimmie Hill — Justin Greer-Spencer
Connie — Julia Dow
Walter — Suzanne Bonnar
Andy Stalin — Andrew Barr
The Keelies
Martin — George Drennan
Derek — Gary Grochla
Alan — Gordon Dougall
Musicians — Rab Handleigh, Nick Jones, Margaret Marshall
Director — Allan Sharpe
Scenery — Paul Ambrose Wright
Costumes — Michael Sisson
Lighting — John Cassidy
Musical director — David McNiven

EDINBURGH INTERNATIONAL FESTIVAL/ BYRE THEATRE
24-26 Aug. 14.30 25-27 Aug. 11.00
Corn Exchange
OPERATION ELVIS Taylor
Malcolm — Andy Milarvie
Mum/Lynn/Hospital sister — Cathy Davidones
Alex/Headteacher/Jackie — Brian Cowan
Michelle — Annalu Waller
Director — Maggie Kinloch
Designer — Minty Donald

EDINBURGH INTERNATIONAL FESTIVAL
18-22 Aug. 19.30 20, 22 Aug. 14.30
St Brides's Centre
WALTER Taylor
(Adapted by Michael Wilcox)
Eric — Vincent Friell
Rikkie/Doctor — Phil McCall
Ian — Tom McGovern
Doris — Sandra Voe
Walter — Tom Watson
Joyce — Tracey Wilkinson
Director — Hamish Glen
Designer — Kenny Miller
Lighting — Gerry Jenkinson
Musical director — David Trouton

TRON THEATRE, Glasgow
31 Aug.-5 Sep. 19.30 3, 5 Sep. 14.30
St Bride's Centre
GOOD Taylor
Bouller/Eichmann — Derek Anders
Halder — Conrad Asquith
Anne — Fiona Bell
Helen — Jennifer Black
Freddie the Major — Jimmy Chisholm
Nurse/Elisabeth — Alexis Leighton
Maurice — Ronnie Letham
Mother — Edith Macarthur
Hitler/Bok — Billy McColl
Clerk/Doctor/Despatch rider — Tom Smith
Director — Michael Boyd
Designer — Graham Johnston
Lighting — Nick McCall
Musical director — Gordon Dougall

EIN TRAUM, WAS SONST Syberberg and Clever
21-22 Aug. 19.30 *King's Theatre*
Edith Clever, Hans Jürgen Syberberg

NATIONAL THEATRE OF RUMANIA
30, 31 Aug. 1, 3-5 Sep. 18.30
Corn Exchange
AN ANCIENT TRILOGY:
MEDEA Inspired by Euripides
Medea — Maia Morgenstern, Olga Delia Mateescu
Jason — Ovidiu Juliu Moldovan, Mircea Rusu
Aegeus/Messenger — Vasile Filipescu, Eugen Cristea, Alexandru Hasnas
Nurse — Simona Bondoc, Maria Filimon
Tutor — Grigore Magaceveschi
Children — Natalia Dumitru, Robert Dumitru
Creusa — Tatiana Constantin, Juliana Moise
THE TROJAN WOMEN Inspired by Euripides
Hecuba — Ileana Siana Ionescu, Iona Bulca
Cassandra — Raluca Penu, Tatiana Constantin
Helen — Carmen Ionescu, Juliana Moise
Andromache — Silvia Nastase, Ecaterina Nazare, Liliana Hoduregea
Achilles — Dan Puric, Vasile Filipescu, Claudiu Istodor
Pallas Athene — Simona Maicanescu, Maria Filimon
Polyxena — Tatiana Constantin, Juliana Moise
Helen's guardian — Claudiu Istodor
Astyanax — Robert Dumitru
Dance of the drowned girl — Juliana Moise
ELECTRA Inspired by Sophocles
Electra — Carmen Galin, Ana Ciontea
Orestes — Claudiu Bleont, Mircea Anca
Chrysothemis — Simona Maicanescu, Cerasela Stan
Clytemnestra — Florina Cercel, Ilinca Tomorovean
Aegisthus — Costel Constantin, Andrei Finji
Pylades — Vasile Filipescu, Dan Puric
Tutor — Constantin Dinulescu, Alexandru Hasnas
Agamemnon — Claudiu Istodor
Wanderer — Dan Puric, Vasile Filipescu
Antigone — Natalia Dumitru
Director — Andrei Serban
Scenery — Dan Jitianu
Costumes — Doina Levinta
Lighting — Robert Valiescu, Alexandru Dobrogeanu
Music — Liz Swados

ELS JOGLARS, Spain
1-5 Sep. 20.00 *Lyceum Theatre*
YO TENGO UN TIO EN AMÉRICA
Jesus Agelet, Eduard Fernandez, Josep M. Fontseré, Ramón Fontseré, Pilár Saenz, Joan Serrats, Xevi Vilar (act), Jordi Pauli (ten sax), Paulina Gálvez, Helena Llauradó, Alberto Sierra, Susana Trujillo, Esperanza de la Vega, Ferando Villalobos (dancers)
Director and choreographer — Albert Boadella

A DRUNK MAN LOOKS AT THE THISTLE MacDiarmid
2 Sep. 22.30 *Lyceum Theatre*
Tom Fleming

DANCE

BALLET CRISTINA HOYOS, Spain
17-20 Aug. 19.30 *Playhouse*
YERMA
Choreographers — Cristina Hoyos, Manolo Marin
Music — Paco Arriaga
Scenery — Gerardo Vera
Costumes — Franca Squarciapino
Lighting — Freddy Gerlache
LO FLAMENCO
Choreographers — Cristina Hoyos, Manolo Marin
Music — Paco Arriaga
Lighting — Paco Dóniz
Dancers — Cristina Hoyos, Juan A. Jiménez, Juan Paredes, Manuela Reyes, Hiniesta Cortés, Rosario Cala, Macarena Béjar, Juan Ortega, Esperanza Galán, Charo Cruz, Javier Venegas
with Paco Arriaga, Eugenio Iglesias, Diego de Bormujos (gtr), 'El Extremeño', Manolo Sevilla, Segundo Falcón (sngr)

MARK MORRIS DANCE GROUP, USA
18-20 Aug. 20.00 20 Aug. 14.30
King's Theatre
DIDO AND AENEAS
Choreographer — Mark Morris
Music — Purcell
Scenery — Robert Bordo
Costumes — Christine van Loon
with Rebecca Evans, Rosemary Joshua (sop), Della Jones (mez), James Maddalena (bar)

22-24 Aug. 19.30 23 Aug. 14.30
Playhouse
A LAKE
Music — Haydn
Costumes — Martin Pakledinaz

THREE PRELUDES
Music Gershwin
Costumes Isaac Mizrahi
BEDTIME
Music Schubert
Costumes Susan Ruddie
BEAUTIFUL DAY
Music Bach
Costumes Susan Ruddie
POLKA
Music Lou Harrison
Costumes Susan Ruddie
GLORIA
Music Vivaldi
Choreographer (all ballets) Mark Morris
with Lorraine Hunt, Rebecca Evans (sop), Jonathan Rees (vn), David McClenaghan (hn), Linda Dowdell (pf)
Lighting (all ballets) James F. Ingalls
Dancers Alyce Bochette, Joe Bowie, Ruth Davidson, Tina Fehlandt, Penny Hutchinson, Dan Joyce, Olivia Maridjan-Koop, Clarice Marshall, Mark Morris, Rachel Murray, June Omura, Kraig Patterson, Mireille Radwan-Dana, Guillermo Resto, Keith Sabado, William Wagner, Jean-Guillaume Weis, Megan Williams
Schola Cantorum of Edinburgh, Scottish Ensemble
Conductor Gareth Jones

TANZTHEATER WUPPERTAL
3-5 Sep. 20.00 *King's Theatre*
CAFE MÜLLER
Choreographer Pina Bausch
Music Purcell
Designer Rolf Borzik
Dancers Malou Airaudo, Pina Bausch, Finola Cronin, Dominique Mercy, Jan Minarik, Jean-Laurent Sasportes

SYMPOSIA

2.30 *St Andrew's & St George's*
21 Aug. TCHAIKOVSKY
Anthony Holden, Leslie Howard, David Brown
25 Aug. HARLEY GRANVILLE BARKER
Prof. Jan McDonald, Margery Morgan, Peter Whitebrook
27 Aug. SCOTTISH MUSIC
John Purser
1 Sep. C.P. TAYLOR
Stewart Conn, Tom McGrath, Michael Wilcox

LECTURES

13.10 *Queen's Hall*
17 Aug. Spain as a world culture Richard MacKenney
18 Aug. Scotland's music John Purser
19 Aug. Schoenberg Neil Mackay
20 Aug. C.P. Taylor Cordelia Oliver
21 Aug. Lieder: the art of song John Miller
24 Aug. Tchaikovsky Anthony Holden
25 Aug. Dutch art and Scotland Julia Lloyd Williams
26 Aug. Harley Granville Barker Prof. Jan McDonald
27 Aug. Yolanta *and* The nutcracker Nicholas Payne
28 Aug. Dance: Images and ideas Bob Lockyer
31 Aug. Greek tragedy Olga Taxidou
1 Sep. Hammerklavier *and* Diabelli variations Bill Alexander
2 Sep. Mahler and Das lied von der Erde Prof. David Kimbell
3 Sep. Allan Ramsay Alastair Smart
4 Sep. Festival '92 - a retrospective Owen Dudley Edwards
(In association with Edinburgh University)

ASSOCIATED EXHIBITIONS
(Not organized by the Festival Society)

National Gallery of Scotland
DUTCH ART AND SCOTLAND

McEwan Hall
SCOTTISH MUSIC

Scottish National Gallery of Modern Art
JAMES PRYDE

Royal Scottish Academy
MIRO SCULPTURES

Scottish National Portrait Gallery
ALLAN RAMSAY

1993

OPERA

SCOTTISH OPERA
16, 18 Aug. 19.30 *King's Theatre*
I DUE FOSCARI Verdi
Francesco Foscari Frederick Burchinal *sung by* Phillip Joll*
Jacopo Foscari Deng
Lucrezia Contarini Ekaterina Kudriavchenko
Jacopo Loredano Nicolas Cavallier
Barbarigo Richard Coxon
Pisana Jill-Maria Marsden
Attendant Robert Crowe
Servant David Morrison
Conductor Richard Armstrong
Director Howard Davies
Designer Ashley Martin-Davis
Lighting Alan Burrett

EDINBURGH INTERNATIONAL FESTIVAL/ TRAVERSE THEATRE
14, 17, 18, 20, 21 Aug. 19.00
Traverse Theatre
TOURIST VARIATIONS MacMillan
(World première)
Gerry Alasdair Elliott
Gina Eirian Davies
Director Francisco Negrin
ANNA Armstrong (World première)
Anna Pamela Helen Stephen
North/West Alasdair Elliott
South/East Eirian Davies
Director Ian Brown
Lighting Davy Cunningham
Edinburgh Festival Ensemble
Conductor Martin André

EDINBURGH INTERNATIONAL FESTIVAL
25, 26 Aug. 19.30 *King's Theatre*
BÚSQUEDA MacMillan
(Concert performance)
Ruth Anderson, Charlotte Spink, Katie Tearle (sngr), Amanda Crossley, Juliette Gilmour, Katy Hale, Miureann Kelly, Derek Johnston, Colin Lowden, David Arneil, Mark Petrie (act), Juliet Stevenson (narr)
VISITATIO SEPULCHRI MacMillan
1st Woman Olivia Blackburn
2nd Woman Christine Bunning
3rd Woman Tamsin Dives
1st Angel Rupert Oliver Forbes
2nd Angel Alan Oke
3rd Angel Stephen Richardson
Cantor Roger Bryson
Dancers Fin Walker, Andrew Fifield, Tom Roden
Scottish Chamber Orchestra
Conductor Ivor Bolton
Director Francisco Negrin
Designer Aldona Cunningham
Lighting Heather Carson
Choreographer Gregory Nash

CANADIAN OPERA COMPANY
28, 29 Aug. 19.30 *Playhouse*
DUKE BLUEBEARD'S CASTLE Bartók
Judith Jane Gilbert
Duke Victor Braun
ERWARTUNG Schoenberg
Woman Rebecca Blankenship
Conductor Richard Bradshaw
Director Robert Lepage
Designer Michael Levine
Lighting Robert Thomson

WELSH NATIONAL OPERA
2, 4 Sep. 19.30 *Playhouse*
FALSTAFF Verdi
Falstaff Donald Maxwell
Alice Suzanne Murphy
Meg Wendy Verco
Mistress Quickly Claire Powell
Nanetta Nuccia Focile
Ford Bryn Terfel
Fenton Paul Charles Clarke
Dr Caius Peter Bronder
Bardolph John Harris
Pistol Geoffrey Moses
Innkeeper Paul Gyton
Robin Christopher Hall/Luke Trolley
Conductor Richard Armstrong
Director Peter Stein
Scenery Lucio Fanti
Costumes Moidele Bickel
Lighting Robert Bryan

SCOTTISH CHAMBER ORCHESTRA
16 Aug. 19.00 *Usher Hall*
COSÌ FAN TUTTE Mozart
(Concert performance)
Fiordiligi Felicity Lott
Dorabella Marie McLaughlin
Ferrando Jerry Hadley
Guglielmo Alessandro Corbelli
Despina Nuccia Focile
Don Alfonso Gilles Cachemaille
EF Chorus
Conductor Sir Charles Mackerras

BBC SCOTTISH SYMPHONY ORCHESTRA
24 Aug. 19.00 *Usher Hall*
DIE FREUNDE VON SALAMANKA Schubert (Concert performance)
Countess Olivia Anne Dawson
Laura Rebecca Evans
Eusebia Alwyn Mellor
Alonso Rufus Müller
Diego Christopher Ventris
Count Tormes Richard Coxon
Fidelio/1st Robber Neal Davies
Alcade/2nd Robber Peter Sidhom
Manuel Jonathan Best
Narrator Juliet Stevenson
ŠÁRKA Janáček (Concert performance)
Šárka Helena Kaupová
Ctirad William Kendall
Lumír Christopher Ventris
Přemysl Neal Davies
Scottish Opera Chorus
Conductor David Robertson

ROYAL SCOTTISH NATIONAL ORCHESTRA
26 Aug. 20.00 *Usher Hall*
OBERTO Verdi (Concert performance)
Cuniza Jane Henschel
Riccardo Dennis O'Neill
Oberto Alastair Miles
Leonora Maria Guleghina
Imelda Fiona Kimm
EF Chorus
Conductor David Robertson

ORCHESTRAL CONCERTS

ROYAL SCOTTISH NATIONAL ORCHESTRA
15 Aug. 20.00 *Usher Hall*
Janáček The cunning little vixen - Suite
Janáček Amarus
Schubert Mass no.5 in A flat, D678
Conductor Walter Weller
Soloists Yvonne Kenny (sop), Fiona Janes (mez), Stefan Margita, John Mark Ainsley (ten), Andreas Schmidt (bar), EF Chorus

29 Aug. 20.00 *Usher Hall*
Verdi Requiem
Conductor Carlo Rizzi
Soloists Jane Eaglen (sop), Olga Borodina (mez), Dennis O'Neill (ten), Alastair Miles (bs), EF Chorus

SCOTTISH CHAMBER ORCHESTRA
17 Aug. 19.30 *Usher Hall*
Janáček Rikadla
Janáček Capriccio for piano (left hand) and chamber ensemble
Schubert Rosamunde: Incidental music
Conductor Sir Charles Mackerras
Soloists Ann Taylor-Morley (mez), Peter Donohoe (pf), SCO Chorus

2 Sep. 22.30 *Ross Bandstand*
Fireworks Concert
Glinka Ruslan and Ludmilla: Overture
Falla El amor brujo: Ritual fire dance
Sibelius Karelia suite: Excerpts
Khachaturian Gayaneh: Sabre dance
Stravinsky The firebird: Finale
Davis Stars and stripes
Conductor Carl Davis

LONDON PHILHARMONIC
18 Aug. 20.00 *Usher Hall*
Beethoven Leonore: Overture no.3
Beethoven Concerto for violin in D, op.61
Brahms Symphony no.4 in E minor, op.98
Conductor Franz Welser-Möst
Soloist Frank Peter Zimmermann (vn)

19 Aug. 20.00 *Usher Hall*
Mahler Symphony no.5 in C sharp minor
Conductor Franz Welser-Möst

ORQUESTA DE CAMBRA TEATRE LLIURE
Conductor Josep Pons
20 Aug. 20.00 *Usher Hall*
Falla El corregidor y la molinera
Falla Concerto for harpsichord
Falla El amor brujo (original version)
Soloists Ginesa Ortega (flamenco sngr), Lluis Vidal (pf)

23 Aug. 11.00 *Queen's Hall*
Gerhard Alegrías
Gerhard Cancionero de Pedrell
Gerhard Seven haiku
Gerhard Pandora
Soloist Josep Benet (ten)

OSLO PHILHARMONIC ORCHESTRA
22 Aug. 20.00 *Usher Hall*
Stravinsky The firebird - Suite (1919)
Bartók Concerto for viola
Dvořák Symphony no.8 in G, op.88
Conductor Mariss Jansons
Soloist Yuri Bashmet (va)

PHILHARMONIA ORCHESTRA
23 Aug. 20.00 *Usher Hall*
Janáček Sinfonietta
Schubert Symphony no.9 in C (Great), D944
Conductor Marek Janowski

25 Aug. 20.00 *Usher Hall*
Elgar Concerto for cello in E minor, op.85
R. Strauss Don Quixote
Conductor Mark Elder
Soloist Steven Isserlis (vc)

27 Aug. 20.00 *Usher Hall*
MacMillan Sinfonietta
Haydn Symphony no.94 in G (Surprise)
Dvořák Symphony no.9 in E minor (New World), op.95
Conductor Leonard Slatkin

28 Aug. 20.00 *Usher Hall*
MacMillan The confession of Isobel Gowdie
MacMillan Epiclesis: a concerto for trumpet (World première)
Stravinsky The rite of spring
Conductor Leonard Slatkin
Soloist John Wallace (tpt)

SWF SYMPHONY ORCHESTRA, Baden-Baden
Conductor Michael Gielen
30 Aug. 19.30 *Usher Hall*
Rachmaninov The isle of the dead
Schnittke Concerto grosso no.2 for violin and cello
Suk A summer fairy tale
Soloists Christian Tetzlaff (vn), Heinrich Schiff (vc)

31 Aug. 20.00 *Usher Hall*
Schoenberg Concerto for piano, op.42
Mahler Symphony no.7 in E minor
Soloist Alfred Brendel (pf)

LEIPZIG GEWANDHAUS ORCHESTRA
Conductor Kurt Masur
1 Sep. 19.30 *Usher Hall*
Brahms Concerto for piano no.2 in B flat, op.83
Mussorgsky Pictures at an exhibition; orch. Gorchakov
Soloist Peter Donohoe (pf)

2 Sep. 20.00 *Usher Hall*
Beethoven Symphony no.1 in C, op.21
Bruckner Symphony no.4 in E flat (Romantic)

SCOTTISH OPERA ORCHESTRA
3 Sep. 20.00 *Usher Hall*
Dvořák Othello - Overture
Janáček The fiddler's child
Janáček The ballad of Blaník
Schubert Mass no.6 in E flat, D950
Conductor Richard Armstrong
Soloists Dawn Upshaw (sop), Patricia Bardon (mez), John Mark Ainsley, Philip Salmon (ten), Alastair Miles (bs), EF Chorus

ROYAL LIVERPOOL PHILHARMONIC ORCHESTRA
4 Sep. 20.00 *Usher Hall*
Janáček Schluck und Jau
Schubert Symphony no.8 in B minor (Unfinished), D759
Janáček Concerto for violin (The pilgrimage of the soul)
Janáček Taras Bulba
Conductor Libor Pešek
Soloist Christian Tetzlaff (vn)

CHAMBER CONCERTS

CHAMBER GROUP OF SCOTLAND
17 Aug. 11.00 *Queen's Hall*
MacMillan Study on two planes
MacMillan The road to Ardtalla
MacMillan Three dawn rituals
MacMillan Sonata for piano
MacMillan ...As others see us...
Conductor James MacMillan
Soloist Graeme McNaught (pf)

GOULD TRIO
19 Aug. 11.00 *Queen's Hall*
Janáček Sonata for violin and piano
Schubert Notturno in E flat, D897
Schubert Trio for piano and strings no.1 in B flat, D898

25 Aug. 11.00 *Queen's Hall*
Schubert Trio for piano and strings in B flat (one movement), D28
Janáček Fairy tale (Pohádka)
Schubert Trio for piano and strings no.2 in E flat, D929

CARMINA QUARTET
27 Aug. 11.00 *Queen's Hall*
Schubert Quartet no.12 in C minor (Quartetsatz), D703
Janáček Quartet no.1 (The Kreutzer sonata)
Schubert Quartet no.15 in G, D887

LONDON WINDS, SCOTTISH CHAMBER ORCHESTRA QUARTET
28 Aug. 11.00 *Queen's Hall*
MacMillan Untold
MacMillan Tuireadh
Mozart Serenade no.10 in B flat (Gran partita), K361
Director Michael Collins (cl)

GAUDIER ENSEMBLE
30 Aug. 11.00 *Queen's Hall*
Janáček Mládi
Janáček Concertino for piano and chamber ensemble
Schubert Octet, D803
with Susan Tomes (pf)

LINDSAY QUARTET
30 Aug. 22.30 *Usher Hall*
Schubert Quintet in C, D956
with Alexander Baillie (vc)

1 Sep. 11.00 *Queen's Hall*
Janáček Quartet no.2 (Intimate letters)
Schubert Quartet no.14 in D minor (Death and the maiden), D810

RSNO CHORUS
EDINBURGH FESTIVAL ENSEMBLE
27 Aug. 22.30 *St Giles' Cathedral*
MacMillan They saw the stone had been rolled away (World première)
MacMillan Divo Aloysio sacrum (World première)
MacMillan Beatus vir
MacMillan Cantos sagrados
MacMillan Catherine's lullabies
Conductor Christopher Bell

Soloists Irene Drummond (sop), John Kitchen (org)

ANN MURRAY (mez)
PHILIP LANGRIDGE (ten)
PETER DONOHOE (pf)
1 Sep. 22.30 *Usher Hall*
Schubert Viola
Janáček The diary of one who disappeared
with Cappella Nova members

RECITALS

ANNE EVANS (sop)
LIONEL FRIEND (pf)
16 Aug. 11.00 *Queen's Hall*
Berg Seven early songs
Schumann Frauenliebe und -leben
Wagner Wesendonck Lieder

FELICITY LOTT (sop)
GEOFFREY PARSONS (pf)
18 Aug. 22.30 *Lyceum Theatre*
Songs by Hahn, Messager, Lecocq

ROBERT HOLL (bar)
ANDRÁS SCHIFF (pf)
20 Aug. 11.00 *Queen's Hall*
Janáček On an overgrown path: Book 1
Janáček In the mist
Songs by Schubert

ROBERT HOLL (bar)
OLEG MAISENBERG (pf)
22 Aug. 14.30 *Queen's Hall*
Schubert Winterreise

THOMAS HAMPSON (bar)
GEOFFREY PARSONS (pf)
20 (Mat), 21 Aug. 20.00 *Usher Hall*
Beethoven An die ferne Geliebte
Schumann Dichterliebe
Songs by Franz, Loewe, Schumann, Grieg

SYLVIA McNAIR (sop)
ROGER VIGNOLES (pf)
21 Aug. 11.00 *Queen's Hall*
Songs by Purcell, Schubert, Wolf, Debussy, Bernstein

DAWN UPSHAW (sop)
MARGO GARRETT (pf)
31 Aug. 11.00 *Queen's Hall*
Songs by Copland, Schumann, Wolf, Schubert, Debussy

THOMAS QUASTHOFF (bar)
PETER LANGEHEIN (pf)
3 Sep. 11.00 *Queen's Hall*
Brahms Vier ernste Gesänge
Songs by Schubert

ANNE SOFIE VON OTTER (mez)
MELVYN TAN (f-pf)
4 Sep. 11.00 *Queen's Hall*
Haydn Arianna a Naxos
Schubert Sonata no.13 in A, D664
Songs by Mozart, Haydn, Schubert

RICHARD GOODE (pf)
17 Aug. 22.30 *Usher Hall*
Beethoven Bagatelles nos.19-24, op.126
Schubert Sonata no.17 in D, D850

ANDRÁS SCHIFF (pf)
18 Aug. 11.00 *Queen's Hall*
Schubert Sonata no.7 in E flat, D568
Janáček Sonata 1 X 1905
Schubert Sonata no.19 in C minor, D958

STEVEN OSBORNE (pf)
24 Aug. 11.00 *Queen's Hall*
Schubert Impromptus, D935
Beethoven Sonata no.31 in A flat, op.110
Chopin Preludes nos.1-24, op.28

LEONIDAS KAVAKOS (vn)
PÉTER NAGY (pf)
2 Sep. 11.00 *Queen's Hall*
Mozart Sonata no.35 in A, K526
Beethoven Sonata no.10 in G, op.96
Ravel Sonata no.1
Bartók Rhapsody no.1
Sarasate Zigeunerweisen

YURI BASHMET (va)
MIKHAIL MUNTIAN (pf)
26 Aug. 11.00 *Queen's Hall*
Marais Suite in D minor; arr. Dalton
Schumann Märchenbilder
Schubert Sonata in A minor (Arpeggione), D821

JOHN WALLACE (tpt)
SIMON WRIGHT (org)
24 Aug. 22.30 *St Giles' Cathedral*
Music for trumpet and organ by Tartini, Cabanilles, Olague, Bruna, Eben, Purcell, Handel, Clarke

LATE NIGHT ENTERTAINMENT

THE RETURN OF THE MUSIC BOX
16 Aug. 22.30 *Lyceum Theatre*
Linda Ormiston, Donald Maxwell and Wyn Davies present an irrelevant (sorry) irreverent look at the 1993 Festival

LLUÍS LLACH
3 Sep. 22.30 *Lyceum Theatre*

DRAMA

TAG THEATRE COMPANY, Glasgow
A SCOTS QUAIR Gibbon
(Adapted by Alastair Cording)
17, 20, 24, 27 Aug. 19.30 25 Aug.1 Sep. 14.00 21, 28 Aug. 4 Sep. 13.00
Assembly Hall
SUNSET SONG
Chris Guthrie Pauline Knowles
Tink/Ewan Tavendale Stuart Bowman
Rev. Colquohoun/Mr. Semple Stewart Porter
Marget Strachan Jacqueline Anderson
Kirsty Strachan Nicola Burnett Smith
Jean Guthrie/Aunt Janet Anne Kidd
Uncle Tam Kris Koren
Will Guthrie/Rev. Gibbon Dougal Lee
John Guthrie Michael Mackenzie
Long Rob Iain Stuart Robertson
Chae Strachan Malcolm Shields
18, 25, 30 Aug. 1 Sep. 19.30 21, 28 Aug. 4 Sep. 16.30 *Assembly Hall*
CLOUD HOWE (World première)
Chris Colquohoun Pauline Knowles
Ewan Tavendale Stuart Bowman
Rev. Colquohoun Stewart Porter
Young Ewan/Charlie Cronin Jacqueline Anderson
'The Blaster'/Jeannie Grant Nicola Burnett Smith
Else/Mrs Geddes/Mrs Kindness Anne Kidd
Catcraig Kris Koren
Provost Hogg/Mr Geddes/Mowat Dougal Lee
Jim the Sourock/Brown Lionel McClelland
Ake Ogilvie/Mr Kindness Michael Mackenzie
Meiklebogs/Sgt Feet Iain Stuart Robertson
Jock Cronin/Doctor Malcolm Shields
19, 26, 31 Aug. 3 Sep. 19.30 21, 28 Aug. 4 Sep. 20.00 *Assembly Hall*
GREY GRANITE (World première)
Chris Colquohoun Pauline Knowles
Ewan Tavendale Stuart Bowman
Meg Watson/Geordie Jacqueline Anderson
Ellen Johns Nicola Burnett Smith
Ma Cleghorn Anne Kidd
Cushnie Kris Koren
Piddle/Norman/Will Guthrie Dougal Lee
Watson/Archie Lionel McClelland
Foreman/Ake/John Guthrie Michael Mackenzie
Trease Stewart Porter
Sgt Feet/Provost Speight/Long Rob Iain Stuart Robertson
Miss Murgatroyd/Alick Watson Malcolm Shields
Musicians Kris Koren, Lionel McClelland
Directors Tony Graham, Andy Howitt
Designer Sally Jacobs
Lighting Jeanine Davies
Music Dougie MacLean

SALZBURG FESTIVAL
1, 2 Sep. 14.30
Royal Highland Exhibition Hall
JULIUS CAESAR Shakespeare (Ger)
Julius Caesar Martin Benrath
Brutus Thomas Holtzmann
Portia Elisabeth Orth
Mark Antony Gert Voss
Cassius Hans Michael Rehberg
Casca Branko Samarovski
Calpurnia Rosel Zech
Cinna the conspirator Werner Friedl
Cimber Manfred Andrae
Cicero Hans Henning Heers
Octavius Caesar Daniel Friedrich
Artemidorus/Lucilius Wolfgang Schwarz
Cinna the poet Karl Lieffen
Decius Brutus Kurt Meisel
Marullus Hans Josef Eich
Flavius Wolfgang Dehler
Pindarus Lusako Karonga
Soothsayer Walter Schmidinger
Lepidus Oliver Stern
Titinius Sven-Erik Bechtolf
Clitus Frank Asamus
Dardanius Marcus Kaloff
Publius Heinrich Strobele
Lena Gerhard Paul
Trebonius Jörg Holm
Ligarius Peter Neubauer
Messala Michael Mendl
Young Cato Sylvan Pierre Leirich
Volumnius Hermann Schmid
Lucius Carsten Voigt
Other parts played by Dietrich Adam, Franz Xaver Zach, Timo Dierkes, Tim Kramer, Joachim Paul Schulze
Director Peter Stein
Scenery Dionissis Fotopoulos
Costumes Moidele Bickel
Music Peter Fischer

SALZBURG FESTIVAL/MC 93 BOBIGNY
16-21 Aug. 19.30 19, 21 Aug. 14.30
Lyceum Theatre
THE PERSIANS Aeschylus (Eng.
A modern version by Robert Auletta)
Xerxes John Ortiz
Atossa Cordelia Gonzalez
Ghost of Darius Howie Seago
Chorus Ben Hailey jun., Joseph Haj, Martinus Miroto
Director Peter Sellars
Costumes Dunya Ramicova
Lighting James F. Ingalls

HEBBEL-THEATER, Berlin
25-28 Aug. 19.30 *Lyceum Theatre*
DR FAUSTUS LIGHTS THE LIGHTS
Stein
Dr Faustus Thilo Mandel, Christian Ebert, Thomas Lehmann
Mephisto in red Heiko Senst
Mephisto in black Florian Fitz
Marguerite Ida and Helena Annabel Katrin Heller, Wiebke Kayser, Gabriele Völsch
Little boy Christian Schmidt
Dog Karla Trippel
Boy Christian Ebert
Girl Wiebke Kayser
Country woman Martin Vogel
Mr Viper Moritz Sostmann
Man from over the seas Thomas Lehmann
Director Robert Wilson
Costumes Hans Thiemann
Lighting Heinrich Brunke, Andreas Fuchs

CITIZENS' THEATRE, Glasgow
31 Aug.- 4 Sep. 19.30 1, 4 Sep. 14.30
Lyceum Theatre
THE SOLDIERS Lenz (Eng. Translated by Robert David MacDonald)
Marie Helen Baxendale
Charlotte Nada Sharp
Madame Wesener Angela Chadfield
Wesener Gerard Murphy
Stolzius Henry Ian Cusick
Madame Stolzius Sybil Allen
Count von Spannheim Derwent Watson
Desportes Mark Bazeley
Captain Pirzel Adrian Howells
Eisenhardt Gerrard McArthur
Major Hardy Mark Lewis
Count de la Roche Allan Henderson
Lieutenant O'Murphy Benedick Bates
Lieutenant Rammler Sean Harris
Countess de la Roche Jane Bertish
Groom Owen Gorman
Mme Bischof Irene Sunters
Mlle Bischof Andrea Hart
Mlle Zipfersaat Gemma Douglas
Grandmother Ida Schuster
Director and designer Philip Prowse
Lighting Gerry Jenkinson

GATE THEATRE, London
2 Sep. 14.30 *Lyceum Theatre*
THE NEW MENOZA Lenz
(Eng. Translated by Meredith Oakes)
(A rehearsed reading)

3 Sep. 14.30 *Lyceum Theatre*
THE TUTOR Lenz
(Eng. Translated by Anthony Meech)
(A rehearsed reading)
Tristram Jellinek, Tom Chadbon, Mark Aiken, Pearce Quigley, Robert Bowman, Stephen Boxer, Linda Bassett, Sara Mair Thomas, Marjorie Yates, Deborah Findlay
Director David Fielding

DEUTSCHES THEATER, Berlin
2-4 Sep. 19.30 *King's Theatre*
DER ZERBROCHNE KRUG Von Kleist
Walter Klaus Piontek
Adam Jörg Gudzuhn
Licht Thomas Neumann
Frau Marthe Rull Gudrun Ritter
Eve Ulrike Krumbiegel
Veit Tümpel Horst Weinheimer
Ruprecht Bernd Stempel
Frau Brigitte Käthe Reichel
Servant Wolf-Dietrich Köllner
Court bailiff Walter Lendrich
Maids Heidrun Perdelwitz, Annelene Hischer
Director Thomas Langhoff
Scenery Pieter Hein
Costumes Christine Stromberg
Lighting Hilmar Koppe

SCOTTISH VARIETY
20-23 Aug. 18.00 and 20.45
King's Theatre
THE FABULOUS FIFTIES
William Armour, George Armstrong, Johnny Beattie, Walter Carr, Anne Fields, Adrian Fleming, Flipside, Karen Hunter, Mary Lee, Maggi Lindsay, Jimmy Logan, Susan Maughan, Jack Milroy, The Sounds of The Platters, The Tiller Girls, Wax 'n' Wain
Devised by Jimmy Logan
Director Douglas Squires
Designer Reg Allen
Costumes Betty Dunlop
Conductor Patrick McCann

DANCE

MARK MORRIS DANCE GROUP, USA
17-19 Aug. 19.30
Meadowbank Sports Centre
NEW LOVE SONG WALTZES
LOVE SONG WALTZES
Music Brahms
Lighting James F. Ingalls
with Amanda Roocroft (sop), Felicity Palmer (mez), John Mark Ainsley (ten), Thomas Allen (bar), Linda Dowdell, Malcolm Martineau (pf)
A SPELL (World première)
Music John Wilson
Costumes Susan Ruddie
Lighting Michael Chybowski
with Tom Finucane (lute), Christopher Robson (c ten)
MOSAIC AND UNITED
Music Henry Cowell
Costumes Isaac Mizrahi
Lighting Michael Chybowski
with Emperor Quartet

21-23 Aug. 19.30
Meadowbank Sports Centre
JESU, MEINE FREUDE
Music Bach
Lighting Michael Chybowski
with Kevin McCrae (vc), John Steer (db), Stuart Hope (org), Schola Cantorum of Edinburgh
Conductor Eric Ibler
HOME
Costumes Susan Ruddie
Lighting Michael Chybowski
Music composed and performed by Michelle Shocked, Rob Wasserman (fiddle)
GRAND DUO
Music Lou Harrison
Costumes Susan Ruddie
Lighting Michael Chybowski
with James Clark (vn), Linda Dowdell (pf)
Choreographer Mark Morris
Dancers Alyce Bochette, Joe Bowie, Ruth Davidson, Tina Fehlandt, Dan Joyce, Olivia Maridjan-Koop, Clarice Marshall, Rachel Murray, June Omura, Kraig Patterson, Mireille Radwan-Dana, Guillermo Resto, Keith Sabado, William Wagner, Megan Williams

BILL T. JONES/ARNIE ZANE DANCE COMPANY, USA
28, 29 Aug. 19.30 29 Aug. 14.30
King's Theatre
FÊTE
Choreographer Bill T.Jones
Music RichardGoodheart, Paul Lansky
Scenery Gregory Bain
Costumes Liz Prince
SPEEDING AND TANTRUM
Choreographer Sean Curran
Music Michael Nyman
SOON
Choreographer Bill T. Jones
Music Weill, S.Williams, F. Longshaw
Costumes Joseph Jones, Valerie Williams
LAST NIGHT ON EARTH
Choreographer Bill T. Jones
Music Weill, Blitzstein *and others*
Scenery Ross Bleckner
Costumes Rifat Ozbek
D-MAN IN THE WATERS
Choreographer Bill T. Jones
Music Mendelssohn
Costumes The Company
Lighting (all ballets) Robert Wierzel
Dancers Bill T. Jones, Arthur Aviles, Torrin Cummings, Sean Curran, Eric Geiger, Lawrence Goldhuber, Heidi Latsky, Jeffery McLamb, Odile Reine-Adelaide, Maya Saffrin, Andrea Woods
Scottish Chamber Orchestra Octet

TRADITIONAI SCOTTISH STORYTELLING

16 Aug.- 4 Sep. 22.30 (exc.Sun)
Glasite Meeting House
George MacPherson, David Campbell, Duncan Williamson, Willie MacPhee, Fiona Macleod, Sheila Douglas, Padraig MacNeill, Alison Millen, Sheila Stewart, Stanley Robertson

LECTURES

13.10 *Queen's Hall*
16 Aug. The Persians Olga Taxidou
17 Aug. Janáček Dr John Tyrell
18 Aug. Schubert Lieder Dr John Miller
19 Aug. Scottish variety Vivien Devlin
20 Aug. Roberto Gerhard Neil MacKay
23 Aug. Photography's first century Julie Lawson
24 Aug. Verdi Prof. David Kimbell
25 Aug. James MacMillan Michael Tumelty
26 Aug. A Scots quair Prof. Ian Campbell
27 Aug. American modern dance Bill T. Jones
30 Aug. Julius Caesar James Spalding
31 Aug. J.M.R. Lenz Dr Fiona Elliott
1 Sep. Schubert chamber music Prof. David Kimbell
2 Sep. Storytelling David Campbell
3 Sep. Festival '93 - A retrospective Owen Dudley Edwards
(In association with Edinburgh University)

THE FESTIVAL IN FOCUS

Chaired by Sheena McDonald
14.30 Senate Room, Edinburgh University
15 Aug. Peter Sellars, Mark Morris, Dr John Tyrell on Janáček, Prof. Robert Pascall on Schubert
22 Aug. James MacMillan, Jimmy Logan, Sir Edward Downes on Verdi,
29 Aug. Peter Stein, Robert Lepage, Robert David MacDonald on Lenz,

EXHIBITIONS

City Art Centre
THE WAKING DREAM: Photography's first century
Lyceum Theatre
SCOTTISH VARIETY EXHIBITION

1994

OPERA

SCOTTISH OPERA
15, 17 Aug. 19.15 *Festival Theatre*
FIDELIO Beethoven
Leonore Elizabeth Whitehouse
Florestan Michael Pabst
Rocco Stafford Dean
Don Pizarro Matthew Best
Marzelline Ai-Lan Zhu
Jacquino Richard Coxon
Don Fernando Carsten Stabell
Prisoners
Campbell Russell, Graeme Danby
Conductor Richard Armstrong
Director Tim Albery
Designer Stewart Laing
Lighting Peter Mumford

AUSTRALIAN OPERA
25-27 Aug. 19.15 *Festival Theatre*
A MIDSUMMER NIGHT'S DREAM
Britten
Tytania Kathryn McCusker
Oberon Michael Chance
Lysander Ian Bostridge
Helena Elisa Wilson
Demetrius Paul Whelan
Hermia Kirsti Harms
Theseus Bruce Martin
Hippolyta Ingrid Silveus
Bottom Gary Rowley
Starveling Neil Kirkby
Snug Richard Alexander
Flute Michael Martin
Quince Geoffrey Crook
Snout Graeme MacFarlane
Puck Tyler Coppin
Peaseblossom Stephen Mansour
Cobweb Timothy Cross
Moth Benjamin Namdarian
Mustardseed Michael Sykes
Indian prince Joel Scammell
Scottish Chamber Orchestra
Conductor Roderick Brydon
Director Baz Luhrmann
Designers
Catherine Martin, Bill Marron
Lighting Nigel Levings

OPERA NORTH
31 Aug. 2 Sep. 19.15 *King's Theatre*
L'ÉTOILE Chabrier (Eng)
King Ouf I Paul Nilon
Sirocco Clive Bayley
Hérisson de Porc Epic Alan Oke
Tapioca Mark Curtis
Lazuli Maria Jagusz*
Princess Laoula Mary Hegarty
Aloès Kate Flowers
Chief of police Paul Wade
Conductor Valentin Reymond
Director Phyllida Lloyd
Designer Anthony Ward
Lighting Rick Fisher

1, 3 Sep. 19.15 *King's Theatre*
LE ROI MALGRÉ LUI Chabrier (Eng)
Minka Rosa Mannion
Alexina Juliet Booth
Basile Keith Mills
Henri de Valois Russell Smythe
Duc de Fritelli Geoffrey Dolton
Count Laski Nicholas Folwell
Nangis Justin Lavender
Liancourt Brian Cookson
D'Elbeuf Peter Bodenham
Caylus Bruce Budd
Villequier Galloway Bell
Max James Thornton
Prince Albert Maurice Bowen
Conductor Paul Daniel
Director Jeremy Sams
Designer Lez Brotherston
Lighting Paul Pyant

SCOTTISH CHAMBER ORCHESTRA
15 Aug. 19.00 *Usher Hall*
LE NOZZE DI FIGARO Mozart
(Concert performance)
Figaro Alastair Miles
Susanna Nuccia Focile
Count Alessandro Corbelli
Countess Carol Vaness
Cherubino Susanne Mentzer
Dr Bartolo/Antonio Alfonso Antoniozzi
Marcellina Suzanne Murphy
Don Basilio/Don Curzio Ryland Davies
Barbarina Rebecca Evans
Scottish Chamber Opera Chorus
Conductor Sir Charles Mackerras

17 Aug. 14.30 *Usher Hall*
LEONORE Beethoven
(Concert performance)
Leonore Janice Watson
Florestan William Kendall
Rocco Franz Hawlata
Don Pizarro Donald Maxwell
Marzelline Rebecca Evans
Jacquino Paul Charles Clarke
Don Fernando Neal Davies
Prisoners Ivor Klayman, William Durran
EF Chorus
Conductor Sir Charles Mackerras

BBC SCOTTISH SYMPHONY ORCHESTRA
18 Aug. 20.00 *Usher Hall*
BRISËÏS Chabrier (Concert performance)
Briséïs Joan Rodgers
Hylas Mark Padmore*
Catechist Simon Keenlyside
Stratocles Michael George
Thanasto Kathryn Harries
Servants Gillian Taylor, Ann Hetherington
Sailors Graeme Danby, John Prince
Scottish Opera Chorus
Chabrier España
Chabrier Ode à la musique
Chabrier La sulamite
Conductor Jean Yves Ossonce

ORCHESTRAL CONCERTS

ROYAL SCOTTISH NATIONAL ORCHESTRA
14 Aug. 20.00 *Usher Hall*
Mahler Symphony no.8 in E flat
Conductor Donald Runnicles
Soloists Janice Watson, Jane Eaglen, Susan Chilcott (sop), Catherine Keen, Patricia Bardon (mez), Peter Svensson (ten), Gregory Yurisich (bar), Gwynne Howell (bs), EF Chorus, RSNO Junior Chorus

3 Sep. 20.00 *Usher Hall*
Elgar The dream of Gerontius
Conductor Sir Charles Mackerras
Soloists Ann Murray (mez), Philip Langridge (ten), Alastair Miles (bs), EF Chorus

SCOTTISH CHAMBER ORCHESTRA
17 Aug. 10.00 *Usher Hall*
Introduction by Prof. H.C. Robbins Landon
Beethoven Leonore: Overture no.1
Beethoven Cantata on the death of Emperor Joseph II
Beethoven Leonore: Overture no.3
Conductor Martin André
Soloists Alwyn Mellor (sop), Phillip Joll (b-bar), Scottish Chamber Orchestra Chorus

1 Sep. 22.30 *Ross Bandstand*
Fireworks Concert
Shostakovich Festival overture
Handel Water music: Excerpts
Beethoven Symphony no.7 in A, op.92: Finale
Chabrier España
Conductor Martin André

EUROPEAN COMMUNITY YOUTH ORCHESTRA
19 Aug. 20.00 *Usher Hall*
Brahms Symphony no.2 in D, op.73
Brahms Symphony no.4 in E minor, op.98
Conductor Carlo Maria Giulini

STAVANGER SYMPHONY ORCHESTRA
20 Aug. 20.00 *Usher Hall*
Conductor Frans Brüggen
Haydn Symphony no.93 in D
Mozart Concerto for violin no.2 in D, K211
Beethoven Symphony no.2 in D, op.36
Soloist Thomas Zehetmair (vn)

21 Aug. 20.00 *Usher Hall*
Schubert Adagio and Rondo for violin and orchestra in A, D438
Schubert Symphony no.8 in B minor (Unfinished), D759
Beethoven Romance for violin and orchestra no.2 in F, op.50
Beethoven Symphony no.8 in F, op.93
Soloist Thomas Zehetmair (vn)

NDR SYMPHONY ORCHESTRA, Hamburg
23 Aug. 20.00 *Usher Hall*
Beethoven Symphony no.6 in F (Pastoral), op.68
Beethoven Symphony no.5 in C minor, op.67
Conductor Günter Wand

ORCHESTRA OF THE AGE OF ENLIGHTENMENT
Conductor Sir Charles Mackerras
25 Aug. 20.00 *Usher Hall*
Beethoven Symphony no.4 in B flat, op.60
Beethoven Symphony no.7 in A, op.92

26 Aug. 20.00 *Usher Hall*
Beethoven Symphony no.9 in D minor (Choral), op.125
Soloists Amanda Roocroft (sop), Fiona Janes (mez), John Mark Ainsley (ten), Neal Davies (b-bar), New Company

LONDON PHILHARMONIC
27 Aug. 20.00 *Usher Hall*
Beethoven Concerto for piano no.2 in B flat, op.19
Beethoven Concerto for piano no.3 in C minor, op.37
Beethoven Concerto for piano no.4 in G, op.58
Conductor Bernard Haitink
Soloist András Schiff (pf)

29 Aug. 20.00 *Usher Hall*
Beethoven Egmont: Overture
Beethoven Concerto for piano no.1 in C, op.15
Beethoven Concerto for piano no.5 in E flat (Emperor), op.73
Conductor Bernard Haitink
Soloist András Schiff (pf)

30 Aug. 19.30 *Usher Hall*
Schumann Scenes from Goethe's Faust
Conductor John Nelson*
Soloists Susan Gritton*, Anne Dawson, Alwyn Mellor, Ann Taylor-Morley (sop), Catherine Denley (mez), Rufus Müller (ten), Boje Skovhus (bar), Neal Davies (b-bar), Alastair Miles (bs), EF Chorus, RSNO Junior Chorus

CLEVELAND ORCHESTRA
Conductor Christoph von Dohnányi
31 Aug. 19.30 *Usher Hall*
Beethoven Symphony no.1 in C, op.21
Beethoven Symphony no.3 in E flat (Eroica), op.55

1 Sep. 20.00 *Usher Hall*
Ives Central Park in the dark
Hindemith Symphonic metamorphosis on themes of Weber
Dvořák Symphony no.9 in E minor (New World), op.95

2 Sep. 20.00 *Usher Hall*
Bach Musikalisches Opfer: Ricercar à 6; arr. Webern
Stravinsky Concerto for violin in D
Mahler Symphony no.1 in D
Soloist Christian Tetzlaff (vn)

CHAMBER MUSIC

BORODIN STRING QUARTET
15 Aug. 11.00 *Queen's Hall*
Beethoven Quartet no.4 in C minor, op.18/4
Beethoven Quartet no.13 in B flat, op.130

16 Aug. 22.30 *Usher Hall*
Beethoven Quartet no.15 in A minor, op.132

18 Aug. 11.00 *Queen's Hall*
Beethoven Quartet no.1 in F, op.18/1
Beethoven Quartet no.7 in F (Rasumovsky), op.59/1

20 Aug. 11.00 *Queen's Hall*
Beethoven Quartet no.8 in E minor (Rasumovsky), op.59/2
Beethoven Quartet no.9 in C (Rasumovsky), op.59/3

22 Aug. 11.00 *Queen's Hall*
Beethoven Quartet no.5 in A, op.18/5
Beethoven Quartet no.11 in F minor (Serioso), op.95
Beethoven Grosse Fuge in B flat, op.133

OLLI MUSTONEN (pf)
JOSHUA BELL (vn)
STEVEN ISSERLIS (vc)
25 Aug. 11.00 *Queen's Hall*
Rachmaninov Trio elégiaque for piano and strings in G minor
Ravel Trio for piano and strings in A minor
Shostakovich Trio for piano and strings no.2 in E minor, op.67

CASTALIAN BAND
27, 28 Aug. 18.00 *St Cecilia's Hall*
A re-creation of an Edinburgh Musical Society concert given on 28 January 1780
Maldere Overture in C, op.4/2
Handel Rinaldo: Lascia ch'io pianga
Davaux Sinfonia concertante in D, op.5/2
Handel Alexander Severus: Overture
Veracini Sonata, op.2/9
Handel Messiah: Rejoice greatly
Corelli Concerto grosso in C minor, op.6/3
Trad. Corn riggs
Earl of Kelly Overture in C, op.1/2

TRANSYLVAN QUARTET
30 Aug. 11.00 *Queen's Hall*
Haydn Quartet in D minor (Fifths), op.76/2
Ravel Quartet in F
Bartók Quartet no.4

ENSEMBLE INTERCONTEMPORAIN
2 Sep. 11.00 *Queen's Hall*
Boulez Le marteau sans maître
Conductor David Robertson
Soloists Randi Stene (mez), André Trouttet (cl)

3 Sep. 17.00 *Playhouse*
Boulez Dialogue de l'ombre double
Boulez Improvisations sur Mallarmé 1 and II
Boulez ...explosante fixe...
Conductor Pierre Boulez
Soloist Christine Whittlesey (sop), Alain Damiens (cl)

NEW COMPANY
27 Aug. 22.30 *Greyfriar's Kirk*
Sacred Music from the Court of Philip II
A. Lôbo Versa est in luctum
Margalhães Commissa mea pavesco
D. Lôbo Audivi vocem de caelo
Vivanco Versa est in luctum
Victoria Requiem mass
Director Harry Bicket

BARBARA BONNEY (sop), ANNE SOFIE VON OTTER (mez), KURT STREIT (ten), OLAF BÄR (bar), BENGT FORSBERG, HELMUT DEUTSCH (pf)
31 Aug. 22.30 *Usher Hall*
Brahms Liebeslieder Walzer
Brahms Neue Liebeslieder Walzer
Schumann Spanische Liebeslieder

RECITALS

OLGA BORODINA (mez)
LARISSA GERGIEVA (pf)
16 Aug. 11.00 *Queen's Hall*
Shostakovich Spanish songs, op.100
Falla Siete canciones populares españolas
Rachmaninov Songs

GALINA GORCHAKOVA (sop)
LARISSA GERGIEVA (pf)
19 Aug. 11.00 *Queen's Hall*
Songs by Glinka, Dargomizhsky, Balakirev, Rimsky-Korsakov, Tchaikovsky, Rachmaninov

NUCCIA FOCILE (sop)
INGRID SURGENOR (pf)
27 Aug. 11.00 *Queen's Hall*
Schumann Frauenliebe und -leben
Songs by Bellini, Verdi, Ravel, Brahms, Wolf

BOJE SKOVHUS (bar)
HELMUT DEUTSCH (pf)
1 Sep. 11.00 *Queen's Hall*
Goethe settings by Beethoven, Wolf, Schubert

FELICITY LOTT (sop)
GRAHAM JOHNSON (pf)
3 Sep. 11.00 *Queen's Hall*
Songs by Schubert, Wolf, Gounod, Chabrier

ALFRED BRENDEL (pf)
22 Aug. 20.00 *Usher Hall*
Beethoven Sonata no.25 in G, op.79
Beethoven Sonata no.24 in F sharp, op.78
Beethoven Sonata no.15 in D (Pastoral), op.28
Beethoven Sonata no.27 in E minor, op.90
Beethoven Sonata no.4 in E flat, op.7

RICHARD GOODE (pf)
23 Aug. 11.00 *Queen's Hall*
Beethoven Sonata no.7 in D, op.10/3
Beethoven Sonata no.18 in E flat, op.31/3
Beethoven Sonata no.14 in C sharp minor (Moonlight), op.27/2
Beethoven Sonata no.28 in A, op.101

26 Aug. 11.00 *Queen's Hall*
Beethoven Sonata no.9 in E, op.14/1
Beethoven Sonata no.17 in D minor (Tempest), op.31/2
Beethoven Sonata no.26 in E flat (Farewell), op.81a
Beethoven Sonata no.30 in E, op.109

29 Aug. 11.00 *Queen's Hall*
Beethoven Sonata no.13 in E flat, op.27/1
Beethoven Sonata no.23 in F minor (Appassionata), op.57
Beethoven Sonata no.6 in F, op.10/2
Beethoven Sonata no.31 in A flat, op.110

PIOTR ANDERSZEWSKI (pf)
24 Aug. 22.30 *Usher Hall*
Beethoven Sonata no.8 in C minor (Pathétique), op.13
Beethoven Sonata no.21 in C (Waldstein), op.53

JOANNA MacGREGOR (pf)
31 Aug. 11.00 *Queen's Hall*
Bach French suite no.5 in G
Berio Sequenza IV
Bartók Sonata
Bach French suite no.3 in B minor
Boulez Sonata no.1
Debussy Études nos.1-6

MAXIM VENGEROV (vn)
ITAMAR GOLAN (pf)
24 Aug. 11.00 *Queen's Hall*
Mozart Sonata no.22 in A, K305
Beethoven Sonata no.5 in F (Spring), op.24
Works by Kreisler, Hubay, Tchaikovsky, Prokofiev, Paganini, Wieniawski

MISCHA MAISKY (vc)
MARTHA ARGERICH (pf)
28 Aug. 20.00 *Usher Hall*
Beethoven Sonata no.5 in D, op.102/2
Stravinsky Pulcinella: Suite Italienne
Schumann Fantasiestücke, op.73; arr. for cello and piano
Shostakovich Sonata in D minor, op.40

THOMAS TROTTER (org)
19 Aug. 22.30 *St Giles' Cathedral*
Messiaen La nativité du Seigneur

26 Aug. 22.30 *St Giles' Cathedral*
Messiaen Apparition de l'église éternelle
Messiaen Les corps glorieux

2 Sep. 22.30 *St Giles' Cathedral*
Messiaen L'ascension
Messiaen Messe de la Pentecôte
Messiaen Le livre du Saint Sacrement: 2 Movements

LATE NIGHT ENTERTAINMENT

15 Aug. 22.45 *Lyceum Theatre*
MUSIC BOX
The hour we knew nothing
Linda Ormiston, Donald Maxwell and John Scrimger preview the 1994 Festival

18 Aug. 22.30 *Lyceum Theatre*
A CHABRIER CABARET
Chabrier Denis Quilley
with Linda Kitchen (sop), Philip Salmon (ten), Malcolm Martineau (pf)
Devised by Gerald Larner

21, 22 Aug. 22.30 *Festival Theatre*
UTE LEMPER
with Bruno Fontaine (pf)

30 Aug. 22.30 *Lyceum Theatre*
MICHEL HERMON SINGS PIAF
with Gérard Barreaux (accordion)

DRAMA

EDINBURGH INTERNATIONAL FESTIVAL
13, 15-21 Aug. 19.30 20 Aug. 14.30
Meadowbank Sports Centre
THE SEVEN STREAMS OF THE RIVER OTA (World première)
Conceived and performed by Éric Bernier, Normand Bissonnette, Rebecca Blankenship, Martina Bovet, Marie Brassard, Anne-Marie Cadieux, Robert Caux, Normand Daneau, Marie Gignac, Ghislaine Vincent
Director Robert Lepage
Scenery Carl Fillion
Costumes Yvan Gaudin, Marie-Chantal Vaillancourt
Lighting Sonoyo Nishikawa
(Co-production with Wiener Festwochen, La Maison des Arts de Créteil, Manchester City of Drama)

15-20 Aug. 19.30 18, 20 Aug. 14.30
Lyceum Theatre
TORQUATO TASSO Goethe (Eng. Translated by Robert David MacDonald)
Torquato Tasso Henry Ian Cusick
Alfonso II Andrew Wilde
Leonora d'Este Kathy-Kiera Clarke
Leonora Sanvitale Irina Brook
Antonio Montecatino Mark Lewis
Footmen Brendan Hooper, Stephen Wale
Director Robert David MacDonald
Scenery Julian McGowan
Costumes Hilary Baxter
Lighting Gerry Jenkinson

25, 27, 28 Aug. 15.00 Murrayfield Ice Rink
ORESTEIA Aeschylus
(Rus. Translated by Boris Shekassiouk)
Orestes Evgeny Mironov
Apollo Igor Kostolevsky
Aegisthus Sergei Sazontiev
Agamemnon Anatoly Vassiliev
Pylades Vladislav Sytch
Guard Vitaly Stremovsky
Messenger Viacheslav Rasbegaiev
Servant Alexander Kutepov
Clytemnestra Ekaterina Vassilieva
Electra Tatiana Doguileva
Athena Elena Maiorova
Cassandra Natalia Kochetova
Pythia Ludmilla Tchursina
Nurse Olga Dzisko
Director Peter Stein
Designer Moidele Bickel
(Co-production with Kunstfest Weimar, Rotterdamse Schouwburg, Maison des Arts et de la Culture Créteil, La Manège, Maubeuge)

BERLINER ENSEMBLE
16-18 Aug. 19.00 *King's Theatre*
ANTONY AND CLEOPATRA
Shakespeare
(Ger. Translated by Elisabeth Plessen)
Cleopatra Eva Mattes
Antony Gert Voss
Enobarbus Hermann Beyer
Octavius Caesar Veit Schubert
Soothsayer/Schoolmaster/Clown/Menas Urs Hefti
Lepidus Jaecki Schwarz
Pompey/Taurus/Diomedes Georg Bonn
Dolabella/Alexas Götz Schulte
Scarus/Messenger Hans Fleischmann
Demetrius/Gallus Thomas Sicker
Agrippa Dieter Knaup
Proculeius/Thidias Rüdiger Kuhlbrodt
Ventidius/Menecrates Axel Werner
Canidius/Seleucas Stefan Lisewski
Maecenas Martin Seifert
Mardian Nino Sandow
Eros Uwe Bohm
Iras/Octavia Gaby Herz
Charmian Deborah Kaufmann
Varrius/Egyptian soldier Patrick Lanagan
Old soldier Hans-Peter Reinecke
Director Peter Zadek
Scenery Wilfried Minks
Costumes Norma Moriceau
Lighting André Diot

ABBEY THEATRE, Dublin
24-28 Aug. 19.30 27, 28 Aug. 14.30
King's Theatre
THE WELL OF THE SAINTS Synge
Mary Doul Pat Leavy
Martin Doul Derry Power
Timmy Patrick Laffan
Molly Byrne Derbhle Crotty
Bride Bríd Ní Neachtain
The Saint Stuart Graham
Holy women Kathleen Barrington, Máire Ní Ghráinne, Máire O'Neill
Mat Simon Macdara Ó Fátharta
Patch Ruadh Ronan Leahy
Seán Dubh John Bergin
Director Patrick Mason
Designer Monica Frawley
Lighting Trevor Dawson

CENTRE DRAMATIQUE NATIONAL ORLEANS-LOIRET-CENTRE
23-25 Aug. 19.00 *Lyceum Theatre*
THE WINTER'S TALE Shakespeare
(Fr. Translated by Jean-Michel Déprats)
Leontes Pierre-Alain Chapuis
Hermione/Mopsa/Time Irina Dalle
Paulina/Dorcas Sophie Daull
Antigonus/Old shepherd/Lord Yedwart Ingey
Perdita/Mamillius/Emilia Chantal Lavallée
Florizel/Gentleman/Archidamus/Bear Christophe Guichet
Autolycus/Gaoler/Mariner Léon Napias
Camillo/Dion Olivier Cruveiller
Polixenes/Cleomenes Vincent Massoc
Clown/Lord Jean-Marc Eder
Director Stéphane Braunschweig
Scenery Giorgio Barberio Corsetti
Costumes Frédéric Rebuffat
Lighting Marion Hewlett

ROYAL LYCEUM THEATRE COMPANY
30 Aug.-3 Sep. 19.00 1, 3 Sep. 14.30
Lyceum Theatre
ARMSTRONG'S LAST GOODNIGHT
Arden
Sir David Lindsay David Robb
James Johnstone Graham McTavish
John Armstrong Stuart Hepburn
Meg Eliot Sharon Small
Alexander McGlass Tom McGovern
Janet Carol Brannan
Lindsay's mistress Alison Peebles
Maid Veronica Leer
James V of Scotland Joel Strachan
Piper Ian Kinnear
Other parts played by Andrew Barr, Alan Caig, Malcolm Shields, Cameron Stewart, Michael Mackenzie, Sandy Neilson
Director William Gaskill
Designer Henk Schut
Lighting Andy Phillips

SCHAUBÜHNE AM LEHNINER PLATZ, Berlin
31 Aug.-3 Sep. 20.00 *Festival Theatre*
THE HOUR WE KNEW NOTHING OF EACH OTHER Handke
Armelle Bérengier, Françoise Brion, Andrea Clausen, Lorella Cravotta, Karoline Eichhorn, Tina Engel, Dominique Frot, Diana Greenwood, Anne Koren, Myriam Lebreton, Dörte Lyssewski, Swetlana Schönfeld, Odile Seitz, Katharina Tüschen, Pierre Aussedat, Matthias Bundschuh, Geoffrey Carey, Hans Diehl, Pascal Elso, Uwe Kockisch, Roch Leibovici, Hans-Werner Meyer, Jean Nanga, Jérome Nicolin, Cornelius Obonya, Rainer Philippi, Kurt Radeke, Werner Rehm, Alexander Schröder, Peter Simonischek, Juan Manuel Vicente, Jacques Vincey, Sven Walser
Director Luc Bondy
Scenery Gilles Aillaud
Costumes Susanne Raschig
Lighting Konrad Lindenburg

DANCE

MIAMI CITY BALLET
15-17 Aug. 19.30 *Playhouse*
JEWELS
Choreographer George Balanchine
Music Fauré, Stravinsky, Tchaikovsky
Scenery Carlos Arditti, Robert Darling
Costumes Barbara Karinska
Lighting James Leitner

19, 20 Aug. 19.30 20 Aug. 14.30
Playhouse
SERENADE
Choreographer George Balanchine
Music Tchaikovsky
Costumes Barbara Karinska
Lighting James Leitner
TCHAIKOVSKY PAS DE DEUX
Choreographer George Balanchine
Music Tchaikovsky
Costumes Haydée Morales
Lighting Randall Henderson
THE FOUR TEMPERAMENTS
Choreographer George Balanchine
Lighting James Leitner
WESTERN SYMPHONY
Choreographer George Balanchine
Music Hershy Kay
Scenery John Boyt
Costumes Barbara Karinska
Lighting James Leitner
Dancers Marin Boieru, Alexander Brady, Benjamin Istvan Cseko, Paige Fulleton, Franklin Gamero, Douglas Gawriljuk, Melissa Gerson, Marjorie Hardwick, Sally Ann Isaacks, Myrna Kamara, Tiffany Kmet, Shari Little, Iliana Lopez, Mabel Modrono, Maribel Modrono, Arnold Quintane, Christopher Román,

Gregory Schramél, Deanna Seay, Eric Sparks, Lin Zhen
with Karl Moraski (pf)
Royal Scottish National Orchestra
Conductor Akira Endo

MARK MORRIS DANCE GROUP, USA
20-22 Aug. 19.30 22 Aug. 14.30
Festival Theatre
L'ALLEGRO, IL PENSEROSO ED IL MODERATO
Choreographer Mark Morris
Music Handel
Scenery Adrianne Lobel
Costumes Christine van Loon
Lighting James F. Ingalls
Dancers Katharina Bader, Alyce Bochette, Joe Bowie, Charlton Boyd, Derrick Brown, Juliet Burrows, Ruth Davidson, Tina Fehlandt, Shawn Gannon, Ruben Graciani, John Heginbotham, Dan Joyce, Victoria Lundell, Marianne Moore, Donald Mouton, Rachel Murray, Mark Nimkoff, Deniz Oktay, June Omura, Kraig Patterson, Mireille Radwan-Dana, Guillermo Resto, Vernon Scott, William Wagner, Megan Williams, Julie Worden, Daniel Gwirtzman, Jordana Toback
with Anne Dawson, Rosemary Joshua (sop), Fiona Janes (mez), Rufus Müller (ten), Neal Davies (b-bar)
Schola Cantorum of Edinburgh
Scottish Chamber Orchestra
Conductor Gareth Jones

FONDATION JEAN-PIERRE PERREAULT, Canada
20-22 Aug. 20.00 King's Theatre
LA VITA
Choreographer and Designer Jean-Pierre Perreault
Music Bertrand Chénier
Lighting Jean Gervais
Dancers Christine Charles, Anne Bruce Falconer, Lina Malenfant, Sylviane Martineau, Luc Quellette, Sylvain Poirier, David Rose, Ken Roy, Yves Saint-Pierre, Mark Shaub, Daniel Soulieres, Tassy Teekman

LUCINDA CHILDS DANCE COMPANY, USA
23 Aug. 19.30 Playhouse
CONCERTO
Music Gorecki
Costumes Anne Masset
Lighting Eric Cornwell
DANCE
Music Glass
Film/Scenery Sol Lewitt
Costumes and Lighting A. Christina Giannini

24 Aug. 19.30 Playhouse
IMPROMPTU
Music Andrzej Kurylewicz
Costumes Ronaldus Shamask
Lighting Eric Cornwell
DANCE

25 Aug. 19.30 Playhouse
RHYTHM PLUS
Music Ligeti, Luc Ferrari
Costumes Christophe de Menil
Lighting Beverly Emmons
ONE AND ONE
Music Xenakis
Costumes Anne Masset
Scenery and Lighting Nan Hoover, Eric Cornwell
CONCERTO
Choreographer (all ballets) Lucinda Childs

Dancers Susan Blankensop, Ty Boomershine, Lucinda Childs, Bruce Jones, Claire Kaplan, Janet L. Kaufman, Gabriel Masson, Michele Pogliani, Garry Reigenborn, Amy Schwartz, Margaret Wallin
with Elisabeth Chojnacka (hpd)

MERCE CUNNINGHAM DANCE COMPANY, USA
27-28 Aug. 19.30 28 Aug. 14.30
Playhouse
CARGO X
Choreographer Merce Cunningham
Music Takehisa Kosugi
Design and Lighting Dove Bradshaw
ENTER
Choreographer Merce Cunningham
Music David Tudor, John Cage
Designer Elliot Caplan
Lighting Marsha Skinner
Dancers Kimberly Bartosik, Lisa Boudreau, Thomas Caley, Michael Cole, Merce Cunningham, Jean Freebury, Frederic Gafner, Chris Komar, China Laudisio, Matthew Mohr, Banu Ogan, Jared Phillips, Glen Rumsey, Jeannie Steele, Robert Swinston, Cheryl Therrien, Jenifer Weaver

FESTIVAL IN FOCUS

(Chaired by Sheena McDonald)
Empire Rooms, Festival Theatre
14 Aug. 17.00 Edward Villella, Tim Albery, Robert David MacDonald, Richard Armstrong
21 Aug. 15.00 Mark Morris, Jean-Pierre Perreault
21 Aug. 17.00 Peter Stein, Robert Lepage, Stéphane Braunschweig, Baz Luhrmann
28 Aug. 17.00 Gerald Larner, Jeremy Sams, Dr Bernd Sucher, John Nelson

LECTURES

1.10 Queen's Hall
15 Aug. Shakespeare James Spalding
16 Aug. Balanchine Edward Villella
18 Aug. Chabrier Gerald Larner
19 Aug. Beethoven quartets Leon Coates
22 Aug. Beethoven piano sonatas Dr Colin Kingsley
23 Aug. J.M. Synge Antoinette Butler
24 Aug. Oresteia Dr Olga Taxidou
25 Aug. American dance Lucinda Childs
26 Aug. St Cecilia's 1780 Richard Gwilt
29 Aug. Beethoven symphonies Dr John Miller
30 Aug. Goethe Prof. James Trainer
31 Aug. Messiaen Dr Neil Mackay
1 Sep. Boulez David Robertson
2 Sep. Festival '94 - A retrospective Owen Dudley Edwards

1995

OPERA

SCOTTISH OPERA
14, 16 Aug. 19.15 Festival Theatre
THE JACOBIN Dvořák (Eng)
Bohus of Harasov Peter Sidhom
Julie Rita Cullis
Filip Donald Maxwell
Benda Alasdair Elliott
Terinka Claire Rutter
Jirí Richard Coxon
Adolf of Harasov Robert Hayward
Count Vilém of Harasov Stafford Dean
Lotinka Ann Hetherington
Conductor Richard Armstrong
Director Christine Mielitz
Scenery Reinhart Zimmermann
Costumes Eleonore Kleiber
Lighting Chris Ellis

AVANTI!
14-19 Aug. 19.30 Lyceum Theatre
I WAS LOOKING AT THE CEILING AND THEN I SAW THE SKY Adams
Consuelo Sophia Salguero
Dewain Jerry Dixon
Rick Welly Yang
Leila Kennya J. Ramsey
David Darius de Haas
Tiffany Kaitlin Hopkins
Mike Michael Christopher Ness
Conductor Grant Gershon
Director Peter Sellars
Costumes Dunya Ramicova
Lighting James F. Ingalls
Sound François Bergeron
(Co-production by Cal Performances, Helsinki Festival, Lincoln Center, MC 93 Bobigny, Thalia Theater, Hamburg)

KIROV OPERA, St.Petersburg
18, 19 Aug. 18.30 Festival Theatre
THE LEGEND OF THE INVISIBLE CITY OF KITEZH Rimsky-Korsakov
Fevronia Galina Gorchakova
Marina Shaguch
Prince Vsevolod Yurievich Sergei Naida*
Prince Yuri Vsevolodovich Nikolai Okhotnikov
Grishka Kuterma Konstantin Pluzhnikov
Nikolai Gassiev
Feodor Poyarok Nikolai Putilin
Man with a bear Nikolai Gassiev
Alexander Shubin
Gusliar Viacheslav Lukhanin
Beggar singer Alexander Gergalov
Best people Grigory Karasev, Victor Vikhrov
Young boy Olga Korzhenskaya
Burundai Alexander Morozov
Biediai Bulat Minzhilkiev
Alkanost Larissa Diadkova
Sirin Marina Shaguch
Tatiana Kravtsova
Conductor Valery Gergiev
Director Andris Liepa
Scenery Anatole Nezhny
Costumes Irina Cherednikova
Lighting Vladimir Lukasevich

21, 22 Aug. 18.30 Festival Theatre
SADKO Rimsky-Korsakov
Sadko Vladimir Galusin
Lyubava Buslayevna Evgenia Tselovalnik
Olga Korzhenskaya
Okian-More Alexander Morozov
Volkhova Valentina Tsidipova*
Nezhata Olga Markova-Mikhailenko

Duda — Grigory Karasev
Sopel — Nikolai Gassiev
Foma Nazarich — Victor Vikhrov
Viacheslav Lukhanin
Viking merchant — Bulat Minzhilkiev
Venetian merchant — Alexander Gergalov
Indian guest — Sergei Cunaien*
Apparition — Nikolai Putilin
Skomoroshiny — Svetlana Volkova, Tatiana Filimonova, Tatiana Kravtsova
Conductor — Valery Gergiev
Director — Alexei Stepaniuk
Designer — Viacheslav Okuniev *after* Korovin
Choreographer — Oleg Ignatiev

17 Aug. 19.00 — *Usher Hall*
RUSLAN AND LUDMILLA Glinka
(Concert performance)
Ruslan — Alexander Morozov
Ludmilla — Marina Shaguch
Ratmir — Larissa Diadkova
Gorislava — Galina Gorchakova
Svetozar — Nikolai Okhotnikov
Farlaf — Georgy Seleznev
Finn — Grayer Khanedanian
Naina — Evgenia Tselovalnik
Bayan — Konstantin Pluzhnikov
Conductor — Valery Gergiev

SCOTTISH CHAMBER ORCHESTRA
14 Aug. 19.00 — *Usher Hall*
DON GIOVANNI Mozart
(Concert performance)
Don Giovanni — Boje Skovhus
Donna Anna — Christine Brewer
Donna Elvira — Felicity Lott
Don Ottavio — Jerry Hadley
Leporello — Alessandro Corbelli
Zerlina — Nuccia Focile
Masetto/The Commendatore — Umberto Chiummo
Scottish Chamber Orchestra Chorus
Conductor — Sir Charles Mackerras

ORCHESTRAL CONCERTS

ROYAL SCOTTISH NATIONAL ORCHESTRA
24 Aug. 19.30 — *Usher Hall*
Wagner — Siegfried: Act 3 Scene 3
Wagner — Götterdämmerung: Act 3
Conductor — Donald Runnicles
Soloists — Jane Eaglen, Janice Watson, Susan Chilcott (sop), Jane Irwin* (mez), Heinz Kruse (ten), Phillip Joll (bar), John Tranter (bs)*, EF Chorus

19 Aug. 19.30 — *Usher Hall*
Dvořák — Requiem mass
Conductor — Sir Charles Mackerras
Soloists — Jane Eaglen (sop), Randi Stene (mez), Thomas Moser (ten), Alastair Miles (bs), EF Chorus

26 Aug. 19.30 — *Usher Hall*
Mahler — Des Knaben Wunderhorn
Bruckner — Symphony no.4 in E flat (Romantic)
Conductor — Donald Runnicles
Soloists — Anne Sofie von Otter (mez), Boje Skovhus (bar)

GUSTAV MAHLER JUGENDORCHESTER
13 Aug. 20.00 — *Usher Hall*
Bruckner — Symphony no.9 in D minor
Bruckner — Te deum in C
Conductor — Claudio Abbado
Soloists — Jane Eaglen (sop), Liliana Nichiteanu (mez), Endrik Wottrich (ten), Robert Lloyd (bs), EF Chorus

PHILHARMONIA ORCHESTRA
15 Aug. 20.00 — *Usher Hall*
Dvořák — Stabat Mater
Conductor — John Eliot Gardiner
Soloists — Judith Howarth (sop)*, Anne Sofie von Otter (mez), Anthony Rolfe Johnson (ten), Alastair Miles (bs), EF Chorus

ROYAL LIVERPOOL PHILHARMONIC ORCHESTRA
18 Aug. 19.30 — *Usher Hall*
Dvořák — In nature's realm - Overture
Dvořák — Carnival - Overture
Dvořák — Othello - Overture
Dvořák — Biblical songs
Dvořák — Symphony no.6 in D
Conductor — Libor Pešek
Soloist — Peter Mikuláš (bar)

ENSEMBLE CONTRECHAMPS
19 Aug. 17.00 — *St Bernard's Church*
Nunes — Versus I
Nunes — Nachtmusik I
Conductor — Zsolt Nagy

BBC SCOTTISH SYMPHONY ORCHESTRA
19 Aug. 22.30 — *McEwan Hall*
Nunes — Quodlibet
Conductors — Kasper de Roo, Emilio Pomárico

ST PETERSBURG PHILHARMONIC ORCHESTRA
20 Aug. 20.00 — *Usher Hall*
Dvořák — Symphony no.8 in G, op.88
Prokofiev — Romeo and Juliet: Excerpts
Conductor — Mariss Jansons

22 Aug. 20.00 — *Usher Hall*
Dvořák — Symphony no.7 in D minor, op.70
Elgar — Variations on an original theme (Enigma)
Conductor — Yuri Temirkanov

SCOTTISH CHAMBER ORCHESTRA
21 Aug. 20.00 — *Usher Hall*
Dvořák — Concerto for piano in G minor, op.33
Dvořák — Concerto for violin in A minor, op.53
Dvořák — The noonday witch
Dvořák — Concerto for cello in B minor, op.104
Conductor — Sir Charles Mackerras
Soloists — András Schiff (pf), Yuuko Shiokawa (vn), Boris Pergamenschikow (vc)

1 Sep. 22.30 — *Ross Bandstand*
Fireworks Concert
Handel — Zadok the Priest - Coronation anthem
Bach — Brandenburg concerto no.2: Allegro assai
Dvořák — Slavonic dance no.8 in G minor, op.46/8
Dvořák — Slavonic dance no.15 in C, op.72/7
Mussorgsky — Pictures at an exhibition: The great Gate of Kiev
Beethoven — Symphony no.5 in C minor: Finale
Conductor — Max Pommer
Scottish Chamber Orchestra Chorus

SWF SYMPHONY ORCHESTRA, Baden-Baden
29 Aug. 20.00 — *Usher Hall*
Zimmermann — Requiem for a young poet
Conductor — Michael Gielen
Soloists — Vlatka Orsanic (sop), James Johnson (bar), Bernhard Schir, Michael Rotschopf (spk), EF Chorus, Cologne Radio Chorus, South German Radio Chorus, Slovakian Philharmonic Chorus, Bratislava
(Co-production between EIF, Salzburg Festival, Festival d'Automne Paris, Berlin Festwochen *and* SWF Symphony Orchestra, Baden-Baden)

CAMERATA ACADEMICA, Salzburg
Conductor — Sándor Végh
30 Aug. 20.00 — *Usher Hall*
Schubert — Symphony no.2 in B flat, D125
Haydn — Symphony no.103 in E flat (Drumroll)
Schubert — Symphony no.3 in D, D200

1 Sep. 20.00 — *Usher Hall*
Schubert — Symphony no.1 in D, D82
Mozart — Concerto for piano no.27 in B flat, K595
Schubert — Symphony no.6 in C, D589
Soloist — Alfred Brendel (pf)

NDR SYMPHONY ORCHESTRA, Hamburg
Conductor — Günter Wand
31 Aug. 20.00 — *Usher Hall*
Schubert — Symphony no.8 in B minor (Unfinished), D759
Schubert — Symphony no.9 in C (Great), D944

2 Sep. 20.00 — *Usher Hall*
Bruckner — Symphony no.8 in C minor

CHAMBER CONCERTS

PANOCHA QUARTET
18 Aug. 11.00 — *Queen's Hall*
Dvořák — Quartet no.9 in D minor, op.34
Dvořák — Quartet no.10 in E flat, op.51
Dvořák — Quartet no.12 in F (American), op.96

21 Aug. 11.00 — *Queen's Hall*
Dvořák — Quartet no.14 in A flat, op.105
Dvořák — Quartet no.13 in G, op.106

ANDRÁS SCHIFF (pf), YUUKO SHIOKAWA, ANNA KANDINSKAIA (vn), BORIS FAUST (va)
BORIS PERGAMENSCHIKOW (vc)
19 Aug. 11.00 — *Queen's Hall*
Dvořák — Terzetto in C for 2 violins and viola, op.74
Dvořák — Trio for piano and strings no.3 in F minor, op.65
Dvořák — Quintet for piano and strings in A, op.81

RAPHAEL ENSEMBLE
24 Aug. 11.00 — *Queen's Hall*
Dvořák — Sextet in A, op.48
Bruckner — Quintet in F

MARKUS STOCKHAUSEN (tpt), PETER RIEGELBAUER (db), MAJELLA STOCKHAUSEN (pf, celeste), MARCUS CREED (pf, celeste, hpd)
27 Aug. 17.00 — *St Bernard's Church*
Kurtág — Rückblick: Hommage à Stockhausen

ENSEMBLE INTERCONTEMPORAIN
28 Aug. 19.30 — *Queen's Hall*
Berg — Four pieces for clarinet and piano, op.5
Webern — Concerto, op.24
Webern — Five pieces, op.10

Mahler Lieder eines fahrenden Gesellen; arr. Schoenberg
Schoenberg Gurrelieder: Song of the Wood Dove
Schoenberg Chamber symphony no.1, op.9
Conductor Pierre Boulez
Soloists Nadine Denize (mez), André Trouttet (cl), Dimitri Vassilakis (pf)

CHAMBER ORCHESTRA OF EUROPE WIND SOLOISTS
30 Aug. 11.00 *Queen's Hall*
Kramář Octet-partita in F, op.57
Mozart Serenade no.12 in C minor, K388
Dvořák Serenade in D minor, op.44

EMPEROR QUARTET
31 Aug. 11.00 *Queen's Hall*
Haydn Quartet in B minor, op.33/1
Britten Quartet no.3, op.94
Haydn Quartet in G, op.77/1

SCOTTISH PREMIÈRE SERIES
(Introduced by Geoffrey Baskerville)

CHAMBER GROUP OF SCOTLAND
13 Aug. 14.30 BBC Broadcasting House
W. Sweeney Life studies 1-IV
S. Beamish Iasg
J. McLeod Songs of Dionysius
J. Lunn A tonic for the dominant+

HEBRIDES ENSEMBLE
20 Aug. 14.30 BBC Broadcasting House
K. Leighton Fantasy on an American hymn tune
J. Weir Distance and enchantment
J. Clapperton Elrich fantasyis+

YGGDRASIL QUARTET OF ABERDEEN
27 Aug. 14.30 BBC Broadcasting House
J. Weir Quartet
R. Crawford Quartet no.2
M. Robb Blood foliage+
+BBC Commission - world première
(In association with BBC Radio Scotland)

RECITALS

RANDI STENE (mez)
HÄVARD GIMSE (pf)
15 Aug. 11.00 *Queen's Hall*
Songs by Schubert, Brahms, Zemlinsky, Dvořák, Grieg

WOLFGANG HOLZMAIR (bar)
GÉRARD WYSS (pf)
17 Aug. 11.00 *Queen's Hall*
Fauré La bonne chanson
Songs by Schubert, Duparc

NEAL DAVIES (b-bar)
IAIN BURNSIDE (pf)
22 Aug. 11.00 *Queen's Hall*
Schumann Liederkreis, op.39
Songs by Rachmaninov, Dargomizhsky, Wolf, Poulenc, Ibert

PETER SCHREIER (ten)
ANDRÁS SCHIFF (pf)
23 Aug. 19.30 *Usher Hall*
Schubert Die schöne Müllerin

25 Aug. 19.30 *Usher Hall*
Schubert Winterreise

27 Aug. 19.30 *Usher Hall*
Schubert Schwanengesang
Schubert settings of Goethe

THOMAS QUASTHOFF (bar)
PETER LANGEHEIN (pf)
25 Aug. 11.00 *Queen's Hall*
Schumann Dichterliebe
Songs by Brahms, Wolf

GALINA GORCHAKOVA (sop)
LARISSA GERGIEVA (pf)
28 Aug. 11.00 *Queen's Hall*
Songs by Glazunov, Grechaninov, Taneyev, Rubinstein, Arensky, Cui

ITXARO MENTXAKA (mez)
JORDI GALOFRÉ (ten)
BARTOMEU JAUME (pf)
29 Aug. 11.00 *Queen's Hall*
Songs by Falla, Halffter, Toldrá, Montsalvatge. Zarzuela arias by Chapi, Sorozabal, Serrano, Fernández-Caballero, Chueca, Valverde

SOLVEIG KRINGELBORN (sop)
EINAR STEEN-NØKLEBERG (pf)
2 Sep. 11.00 *Queen's Hall*
Grieg Haugtussa
Songs and arias by Mozart, Rangström, Nielsen, Sibelius, Grieg

ALICIA DE LARROCHA (pf)
16 Aug. 11.00 *Queen's Hall*
Soler Sonata no.15 in D minor
Soler Sonata no.12 in C sharp minor
Granados Spanish dances nos. 1, 2, 5-8
Schumann Carnaval

ANDRÁS SCHIFF (pf)
23 Aug. 22.30 *Usher Hall*
Schubert Sonata no.18 in G, D894

25 Aug. 22.30 *Usher Hall*
Schubert Sonata no.20 in A, D959

27 Aug. 22.30 *Usher Hall*
Schubert Sonata no.21 in B flat, D960

MARIA JOÃO PIRES (pf)
23 Aug. 11.00 *Queen's Hall*
Schumann Romances, op.28
Mozart Sonata no.13 in B flat, K333
Chopin Nocturnes nos.1-10

THOMAS ZEHETMAIR (vn)
20 Aug. 22.30 *Greyfriars Kirk*
Bach Sonata no.1 in G minor
Bach Partita no.1 in B minor

22 Aug. 22.30 *Greyfriars Kirk*
Bach Sonata no.2 in A minor
Bach Partita no.2 in D minor

24 Aug. 22.30 *Greyfriars Kirk*
Bach Partita no.3 in E
Bach Sonata no.3 in C

DMITRY SITKOVETSKY (vn)
PAVEL GILILOV (pf)
1 Sep. 11.00 *Queen's Hall*
Prokofiev Cinq melodies, op.35b
Shostakovich Sonata, op.134
Schnittke Sonata no.1
Stravinsky Duo concertant

YO-YO MA (vc)
14 Aug. 14.00 *Greyfriars Kirk*
Bach Suites nos.1-6

THE MUSIC BOX
14 Aug. 22.45 *Lyceum Theatre*
A guide to the 1995 Festival with Linda Ormiston, Donald Maxwell, John Scrimger, Wyn Davies

FOLK MUSIC

13 Aug.-2 Sep. 23.00 (exc. 25 Aug. 19.00 26 Aug. 17.00) *Festival Theatre*
FOLK SONGS OF NORTH-EAST SCOTLAND
21 programmes of songs from the Greig-Dunbar Collection
Margaret Bennett, Aileen Carr, Sheila Douglas, Jock Duncan, Dick Gaughan, Peter Hall, Hamish Henderson, Heather Heywood, Andy Hunter, Norman Kennedy, Cy Lawrie, Emily Lyle, Brian Miller, Jo Miller, Ailie Munro, Gordeanna McCulloch, Tom McKean, Alison McMorland, Adam McNaughtan, Willie McPhee, Anne Neilson, Ian Olson, Palaver, Eileen Penman, Elaine Petrie, Ted Poletyllo, Tam Reid, Irene Riggs, Davie Robertson, Stanley Robertson, Isla St Clair, Elizabeth Stewart, Sheila Stewart, Stramash, Jane Turriff, Arthur Watson, Sheena Wellington

25 Aug. 22.30 27 Aug. 20.00
Festival Theatre
MARIA DEL MAR BONET
with Javier Mas (gtr)

26 Aug. 19.30 and 22.30 *Festival Theatre*
FADOS
Carlos Zel, Argentina Santos (sngr), José Luis Nobre Costa, Pedro Caldeira Cabral, Francisco Gonçalves, Joel Pina (gtr)

DRAMA

TAG THEATRE COMPANY, Glasgow
14-19, 22-27 Aug. 19.30 19, 24, 26 Aug. 14.30 *Assembly Hall*
LANARK Gray (Adapted by Alastair Cording) (World première)
Painter/McPhedron Stuart MacIntyre
Lanark Laurance Rudic
Catalyst Carole Irvine
Rima/Marjorie Carol Brannan
Duncan Thaw Tom Smith
Thaw's father/Ozenfant Ross Mackay
Gloopy/Drummond/Dr Munro/Ritchie/ Smollett/Nastler Tony Cownie
Gay/Thaw's mother/Mrs Fleck/Peggy Byres/Grant/Libby Linda Duncan McLaughlin
Sludden/Watt/Cowlairs minister/ Monsignor Noakes Kern Falconer
Director Tony Graham
Designer Angela Davies
Lighting Jeanine Davies
Music Alasdair Nicolson

ABBEY THEATRE, Dublin
18-23 Aug. 19.30 19, 21, 23 Aug. 14.30
King's Theatre
OBSERVE THE SONS OF ULSTER MARCHING TOWARDS THE SOMME
McGuinness
Kenneth Pyper (the elder) Clive Geraghty
Kenneth Pyper (the younger) Peter Gowen
David Craig Conor McDermottroe
John Millen Gerard Byrne
William Moore Patrick O'Kane
Christopher Roulston Sean Campion
Martin Crawford David Parnell
George Anderson Frank McCusker
Nat McIlwaine Lalor Roddy
Director Patrick Mason
Scenery Joe Vanek
Costumes Joan O'Clery
Lighting Nick Chelton

LA COMPAGNIE JÉRÔME DESCHAMPS, France
26-28 Aug. 19.30 27 Aug. 14.30
King's Theatre
C'EST MAGNIFIQUE Deschamps *and* Makeieff
Jean-Marc Bihour, Robert Horn, Atmen Kelif, Bruno Lochet, Yolande Moreau, François Morel, Philippe Rouèche
Directors Jérôme Deschamps, Macha Makeieff
Artistic collaboration Bernard Giraud
Costumes Macha Makeieff
Music Philippe Rouèche

SCHAUBÜHNE AM LEHNINER PLATZ, Berlin
1 Sep. 17.00 2 Sep. 16.30 King's Theatre
THE ILLUSIONIST Guitry
(Ger. Translated by Luc Bondy)
Paul Dufresne (Teddy Brooks) Gert Voss
Albert Cahen Peter Simonischek
Jacqueline Beauchamps Dörte Lyssewski
Gabrielle (Miss Hopkins) Claudia Michelsen
Gérome Werner Rehm
Gosset Oliver Stern
Honorine (Maid) Libgart Schwarz
Old variety artist Kurt Radeke

1 Sep. 21.30 2 Sep. 21.00 King's Theatre
LET'S DREAM Guitry
(Ger. Translated by Luc Bondy)
The Husband Peter Simonischek
The Wife Libgart Schwarz
The Servant Kurt Radeke
Himself Otto Sander
Director Luc Bondy
Scenery Gilles Aillaud
Costumes Moidele Bickel
Lighting Konrad Lindenberg, Alexander Koppelmann

CITIZENS' THEATRE, Glasgow
22-26 Aug. 19.30 26 Aug. 14.00
Lyceum Theatre
DON CARLOS Schiller (Eng. Translated by Robert David MacDonald)
Philip II Giles Havergal
Elizabeth of Valois Sophie Ward
Don Carlos Benedick Bates
Marquis of Posa Andrew Woodall
Princess of Eboli Julie Saunders
Duke of Alba Matthew Zajac
Domingo Murray Melvin
Count Lerma Stephen MacDonald
Duchess of Olivarez Jill Spurrier
Marchioness of Mondecar Victoria Davar
Hénarez Bambos Karayanis
Grand Inquisitor Tristram Jellinek
Director and designer Philip Prowse
Lighting Gerry Jenkinson

BERLINER ENSEMBLE
29, 30 Aug. 19.30 Lyceum Theatre
THE MERCHANT OF VENICE
Shakespeare
(Ger. Translated by Elisabeth Plessen)
Duke of Venice Martin Seifert
Antonio/Prince of Morocco Ignaz Kirchner
Bassanio Paulus Manker
Salarino Veit Schubert
Salanio/Old Gobbo Urs Hefti
Gratiano Stefan Lisewski
Lorenzo Götz Schulte
Shylock/Prince of Arragon Gert Voss
Tubal Jaecki Schwarz
Portia Eva Mattes
Nerissa Wiebke Frost
Jessica Deborah Kaufmann
Launcelot Gobbo Uwe Bohm
Stephano Georg Bonn
Balthazar Patrick Lanagan
Policeman Michael Rohner
Officer of the court Maik Kittel
Director Peter Zadek
Scenery Wilfried Minks
Costumes Johannes Grützke
Lighting André Diot
Music Luciano Berio

THÉÂTRE DE L'EUROPE
30 Aug.-2 Sep. 21.00 Drill Hall
DANS LA SOLITUDE DES CHAMPS DE COTON Koltès
The Dealer Patrice Chéreau
The Client Pascal Greggory
Director Patrice Chéreau
Scenery Richard Peduzzi
Costumes Moidele Bickel
Lighting Jean-Luc Chanonat
(Co-production with Azor Films Sarl, Festival de Otoño de la Communidad de Madrid, La Biennale di Venezia, Festival d'Automne Paris)

DANCE

MIAMI CITY BALLET
14-16 Aug. 19.30 16 Aug. 14.30
Playhouse
THE NUTCRACKER
Choreographer George Balanchine
Music Tchaikovsky
Scenery José Varona
Costumes José Varona, Haydée Morales
Lighting Thomas Skelton
Dancers Marin Boieru, Alexander Brady, Edward Cox, Benjamin Istvan Cseko, Amy Foster, Laurel Foster, Paige Fulleton, Franklin Gamero, Douglas Gawriljuk, Melissa Gerson, Marifé Gimenez, Sally Ann Isaacks, Todd Jost, Myrna Kamara, Joan Latham, Shari Little, Iliana Lopez, Mabel Modrono, Maribel Modrono, Amy Seawright Moreno, Kareen Pauld, Jonathan Pessolano, Jennifer Polyocan, Arnold Quintane, Jacob Rice, Deanna Seay, Thomas M. Shoemaker, Kendall Sparks, Bruce K. Thornton
Schola Cantorum of Edinburgh
Royal Scottish National Orchestra
Conductor Akira Endo

MARK MORRIS DANCE GROUP, USA
14-16 Aug. 20.00 King's Theatre
SOMEBODY'S COMING TO SEE ME TONIGHT
Music Foster
Costumes Susan Ruddie
Lighting Michael Chybowski
THE OFFICE
Music Dvořák
Costumes June Omura
Lighting Michael Chybowski
LUCKY CHARMS
Music Ibert
Lighting Michael Chybowski
ONE CHARMING NIGHT
Music Purcell
Lighting Phil Sandstrom
POLKA
Costumes Susan Ruddie
Music Lou Harrison
Lighting Michael Chybowski
Choreographer (all ballets) Mark Morris
with Drew Minter (c ten), Jayne West (sop), Stephen Salters (bar), Emperor Quartet, Schola Cantorum of Edinburgh, Edinburgh Festival Ensemble
Conductor Gareth Jones

29 Aug.-2 Sep. 19.30 2 Sep. 14.30
Festival Theatre
THE HARD NUT
Choreographer Mark Morris
Music Tchaikovsky
Scenery Adrianne Lobel
Costumes Martin Pakledinaz
Lighting James F. Ingalls
Schola Cantorum of Edinburgh
Royal Scottish National Orchestra
Conductor Donald York
Dancers Katharina Bader, Rob Besserer, Joe Bowie, Charlton Boyd, Derrick Brown, Juliet Burrows, Derek Clifford, Ruth Davidson, Tina Fehlandt, Shawn Gannon, Ruben Graciani, Daniel Gwirtzman, Peter Wing Healey, John Heginbotham, Dan Joyce, Victoria Lundell, Clarice Marshall, Marianne Moore, Rachel Murray, Deniz Oktay, June Omura, Kraig Patterson, Mireille Radwan-Dana, Guillermo Resto, Susan Shields, Utafumi Takemura, Jordana Toback, William Wagner, Teri Weksler, Megan Williams, Julie Worden

BILL T. JONES/ARNIE ZANE DANCE COMPANY, USA
25-27 Aug. 19.30 Playhouse
STILL/HERE
Choreographer Bill T. Jones
Music Kenneth Frazelle, Vernon Reid
Visual concept Gretchen Bender
Costumes Liz Prince
Lighting Robert Wierzel
Dancers Arthur Aviles, Gabri Christa, Josie Coyoc, Mark Davis, Lawrence Goldhuber, Rosalynde LeBlanc, Odile Reine-Adelaide, Daniel Russell, Maya Saffrin, Gordon F. White

TANZTHEATER WUPPERTAL
31 Aug.-2 Sep. 19.30 Playhouse
NELKEN
Choreographer Pina Bausch
Music Gershwin *and others*
Scenery Peter Pabst
Costumes Marion Cito
Dancers Elena Adaeva, Regina Advento, Ruth Amarante, Jakob Andersen, Andrei Berezine, Antonio Carallo, Lutz Förster, Mechthild Grossmann, Barbara Hampel, Kyomi Ichida, Urs Michael Kaufmann, Daphnis Kokkinos, Marigia Maggipinto, Bernd Marszan, Dominique Mercy, Jan Minarik, Cristiana Morganti, Nazareth Panadero, Jean Laurent Sasportes, Julie Shanahan, Julie Anne Stanzak, Aida Vainiere, Michael Whaites
Stuntmen Michael Mohr, Salvatore Pascale, Reinhard Steinmeier, Jürgen Sücker

MASTER CLASS

31 Aug. 14.30 Festival Theatre
VIOLETTE VERDY
with dancers from Scottish Ballet

FESTIVAL IN FOCUS

(Chaired by Sheena McDonald)
17.00 Festival Theatre
13 Aug. Richard Armstrong, Tony Graham, Peter Sellars, Boje Skovhus
20 Aug. Peter A. Hall, Robert David MacDonald, Patrick Mason
27 Aug. Pierre Boulez, Patrice Chéreau

IN CONVERSATION WITH

13 Aug. 14.00 Festival Theatre
Mark Morris *and* Edward Villella talk to Ruth Mackenzie
14 Aug. 17.00 Lyceum Theatre
Peter Sellars talks to Ruth Mackenzie

16 Aug. 17.00 *Lyceum Theatre*
Sir Charles Mackerras talks to Conrad Wilson
21 Aug. 17.00 *Lyceum Theatre*
Patrick Mason talks to Ruth Mackenzie
25 Aug. 17.00 *Lyceum Theatre*
Bill T. Jones talks to Ruth Mackenzie
30 Aug. 17.00 *Lyceum Theatre*
Luc Bondy talks to Ruth Mackenzie

WORKSHOPS AND STUDY DAYS

17 Aug. 16.00 *Assembly Hall*
LANARK: From page to stage
Alastair Cording, Alasdair Nicolson, Angela Davies, Jeanine Davies, Tony Graham

28 Aug. 10.00 *Lyceum Theatre*
KOLTÈS STUDY DAY

LECTURES

14 Aug. Contemporary Scottish music — Michael Tumelty
15 Aug. Lanark — Alastair Cording
16 Aug. Dvořák's symphonies — Dr John Miller
17 Aug. Schubert song cycles — Prof. Peter Branscombe
18 Aug. Rimsky-Korsakov — Derek Watson
21 Aug. Bach solo suites — Dr John Kitchen
22 Aug. Irish theatre — Owen Dudley Edwards
23 Aug. Schiller's Don Carlos — Dr Fiona Elliott
24 Aug. Dvořák chamber music — Dr Stuart Campbell
25 Aug. Fados — Pedro Caldeira Cabral
28 Aug. Greig-Dunbar collection — Emily Lyle
29 Aug. Zimmermann — Andreas Breitscheid
30 Aug. The merchant of Venice — James Spaulding
31 Aug. Guitry
1 Sep. Bruckner — Prof. David Kimbell
(In association with Edinburgh University)

1996

Correct at the time of printing (March 1996) but subject to change

OPERA

EDINBURGH INTERNATIONAL FESTIVAL
16, 17, 19, 20 Aug. 19.15 Festival Theatre
ORFEO ED EURIDICE Gluck
(Vienna version 1762)
Orfeo — Michael Chance
Euridice — Dana Hanchard
Amor — Christine Brandes
Mark Morris Dance Group
Handel & Haydn Society Chorus and Orchestra, Boston
Conductor — Christopher Hogwood
Director and choreographer — Mark Morris
Designer — Adrianne Lobel
Costumes — Martin Pakledinaz
Lighting — Michael Chybowski

29-31 Aug. 19.15 Festival Theatre
IPHIGÉNIE EN TAURIDE Gluck
(Vienna version 1781 - Ger)
Iphigenie — Christine Brewer
Oreste — William Kendall
Pylade — Peter Bronder
Thoas — David Barrell
Dancers
Iphigenie — Malou Airaudo
Oreste — Dominique Mercy
Pylade — Bernd Marzan
Thoas — Lutz Förster, Andrei Berezine
Tanztheater Wuppertal
Scottish Opera Chorus
Scottish Chamber Orchestra
Conductor — Jan Michael Horstmann
Director and choreographer — Pina Bausch
Designer — Pina Bausch, Jürger Dreier *in collaboration with* Rolf Borzik
(In association with Cultural Industry)

SCOTTISH OPERA
23, 25 Aug. 19.15 *Festival Theatre*
INES DE CASTRO MacMillan
(World première)
Ines de Castro — Helen Field
Blanca — Elizabeth Byrne
Pedro — Jeffrey Lawton
The King — Stafford Dean
Conductor — Richard Armstrong
Director — Jonathan Moore
Designer — Chris Dyer
Lighting — Paule Constable

HOUSTON GRAND OPERA
29-31 Aug. 19.30 31 Aug. 14.30
Festival Theatre
FOUR SAINTS IN THREE ACTS Thomson
St Teresa I — Ashley Putnam
St Teresa II — Suzanna Guzman
St Ignatius — Sanford Sylvan
Commère — Marietta Simpson
Compère — Wilbur Pauley
St Chavez — Gran Wilson
Royal Scottish National Orchestra
Conductor — Richard Bado
Director and designer — Robert Wilson
Costumes — Francesco Clemente
Lighting — Jennifer Tipton
(Co-production between EIF, Houston Grand Opera and Lincoln Centre, NY)

SCOTTISH CHAMBER ORCHESTRA
12 Aug. 19.30 *Usher Hall*
FIDELIO Beethoven
(Concert performance)
Leonore — Gabriela Beňačková
Florestan — Anthony Rolfe Johnson
Rocco — Siegfried Vogel
Don Pizarro — Franz-Josef Kapellmann
Marzelline — Ildiko Raimondi
Jacquino — John Mark Ainsley
Don Fernando — David Wilson-Johnson
EIF Chorus
Conductor — Sir Charles Mackerras

ORCHESTRAL CONCERTS

ROYAL SCOTTISH NATIONAL ORCHESTRA
11 Aug. 20.00 *Usher Hall*
Schoenberg — A survivor from Warsaw
Beethoven — Symphony no.9 in D minor (Choral), op.125
Conductor — Donald Runnicles
Soloists Hillevi Martinpelto (sop), Jane Irwin (mez), Heinz Kruse (ten), Bryn Terfel (b-bar), Olaf Bär (narr), EIF Chorus

19 Aug. 20.00 *Usher Hall*
Britten — War requiem
Conductor — Donald Runnicles
Soloists Elena Prokina (sop), Anthony Rolfe Johnson (ten), Thomas Quasthoff (bar), EIF Chorus, RSNO Junior Chorus

RUSSIAN NATIONAL ORCHESTRA
Conductor Mikhail Pletnev
13 Aug. 20.00 *Usher Hall*
Haydn — Symphony no.93 in D
Shostakovich — Concerto for cello no.1 in E flat, op.107
Tchaikovsky — Symphony no.1 in G minor (Winter daydreams), op.13
Soloist — Natalia Gutman (vc)

14 Aug. 20.00 *Usher Hall*
Haydn — Symphony no.104 in D (London)
Shostakovich Symphony no.10 in E minor, op.93

BBC SCOTTISH SYMPHONY ORCHESTRA
15 Aug. 22.30 *Usher Hall*
Nunes — Ruf
Conductor — Emilio Pomárico

NEW YORK PHILHARMONIC ORCHESTRA
Conductor Kurt Masur
17 Aug. 20.00 *Usher Hall*
R. Strauss — Till Eulenspiegels lustige Streiche
Rorem — Concerto for cor anglais
Beethoven — Symphony no.7 in A, op.92
Soloist — Thomas Stacy (cor ang)

18 Aug. 20.00 *Usher Hall*
Prokofiev — Romeo and Juliet - Suite
Tchaikovsky — Symphony no.5 in E minor, op.64

OSLO PHILHARMONIC ORCHESTRA
20 Aug. 20.00 *Usher Hall*
Rossini — L'Italiana in Algeri: Overture
Grieg — Songs
Beethoven — Symphony no.5 in C minor, op.67
Conductor — Maris Janssons
Soloist — Barbara Bonney (sop)

GUSTAV MAHLER JUGENDORCHESTER
21 Aug. 19.30 *Usher Hall*
Schoenberg Gurrelieder
Conductor Claudio Abbado
Soloists Jane Eaglen (sop), Marjana Lipovsek (mez), Thomas Moser, Philip Langridge (ten), Franz Grundheber (bar), Hans Hotter (narr), ElF Chorus, Arnold Schoenberg Choir

HANOVER BAND
Conductor Sir Charles Mackerras
Haydn - Paris Symphonies
21 Aug. 22.30 *Usher Hall*
Haydn Symphony no.85 in B flat (La reine)
Haydn Pieta di me
Haydn Symphony no.87 in A
Soloists Nuccia Focile (sop), Katarina Karnéus (mez), Toby Spence (ten)

22 Aug. 22.30 *Usher Hall*
Haydn Symphony no.83 in G minor (The hen)
Haydn Se ti perdo
Haydn Symphony no.84 in E flat
Soloist Nuccia Focile (sop)

23 Aug. 22.30 *Usher Hall*
Haydn Symphony no.82 in C (The bear)
Haydn Berenice che fai
Haydn Symphony no.86 in D
Soloist Katarina Karnéus (mez)

25 Aug. 20.00 *Usher Hall*
Haydn Die Schöpfung
Soloists Felicity Lott (sop), John Mark Ainsley (ten), Neal Davies (b-bar), ElF Chorus

PHILHARMONIA ORCHESTRA
Conductor Kurt Sanderling
22 Aug. 19.30 *Usher Hall*
Brahms Concerto for piano no.1 in D minor, op.15
Brahms Concerto for piano no.2 in B flat, op.83
Soloist András Schiff (pf)

23 Aug. 19.30 *Usher Hall*
Haydn Symphony no.39 in G minor
Bruckner Symphony no.4 in E flat (Romantic)

ORCHESTRA OF THE EIGHTEENTH CENTURY
Conductor Frans Brüggen
27 Aug. 20.00 *Usher Hall*
Haydn Symphony no.103 in E flat (Drumroll)
Haydn Symphony no.101 in D (Clock)
Haydn Symphony no.100 in G (Military)

28 Aug. 20.00 *Usher Hall*
Haydn Symphony no.94 in G (Surprise)
Beethoven Concerto for violin in D, op.61
Soloist Thomas Zehetmair (vn)

30 Aug. 22.30 *Usher Hall*
Rameau Les fêtes d'Hébé

31 Aug. 14.30 *Usher Hall*
Children's Concert
Works by Bach, Gluck, Haydn, Mozart, Beethoven, Schubert, Mendelssohn

SCOTTISH CHAMBER ORCHESTRA
29 Aug. 22.30 *Ross Bandstand*
Handel Zadok the Priest - Coronation anthem
Brahms Academic festival overture
Handel Music for the royal fireworks
Conductor Gareth Jones
Scottish Chamber Orchestra Chorus

CLEVELAND ORCHESTRA
Conductor Christoph von Dohnányi
29 Aug. 20.00 *Usher Hall*
Beethoven Quartet no.11 in F minor (Serioso), op.95; orch. Mahler
Mahler Symphony no.5 in C sharp minor

30 Aug. 19.30 *Usher Hall*
Ives The unanswered question
Beethoven Concerto for piano no.1 in C, op.15
Brahms Symphony no.1 in C minor, op.68
Soloist Alfred Brendel (pf)

ORCHESTRA OF THE AGE OF ENLIGHTENMENT
31 Aug. 20.00 *Usher Hall*
Mendelssohn Elijah
Conductor Sir Charles Mackerras
Soloists Renée Fleming, Catrin Wyn-Davies (sop), Hilary Summers, Patricia Bardon (mez), John Mark Ainsley, John Bowen (ten), Bryn Terfel, Neal Davies (b-bar), Geoffrey Moses (bs), ElF Chorus

CHAMBER MUSIC

HAYDN STRING QUARTETS

VELLINGER QUARTET
12 Aug. 18.00 *St Cuthbert's Church*
Quartet in G, op.54/1
Quartet in B flat, op.71/1

13 Aug. 18.00 *St Cuthbert's Church*
Quartet in E, op.54/3
Quartet in D, op.71/2

14 Aug. 18.00 *St Cuthbert's Church*
Quartet in C, op.54/2
Quartet in E flat, op.71/3

EMPEROR QUARTET
15 Aug. 18.00 *St Cuthbert's Church*
Quartet in F sharp minor, op.50/4
Quartet in D (Frog), op.50/6

16 Aug. 18.00 *St Cuthbert's Church*
Quartet in B flat, op.50/1
Quartet in F (Dream), op.50/5
Quartet in E flat, op.50/3

23 Aug. 18.00 *St Cuthbert's Church*
Quartet in D minor, op.42
Quartet in C, op.50/2
Quartet in E flat, op.64/6

24 Aug. 18.00 *St Cuthbert's Church*
Quartet in E flat, op.76/6
Quartet in F, op.74/2

QUATUOR MOSAÏQUES
17 Aug. 18.00 *St Cuthbert's Church*
Quartet in G minor, op.20/3
Quartet in E flat (Joke), op.33/2
Quartet in G, op.77/1

19 Aug. 18.00 *St Cuthbert's Church*
Quartet in B flat, op.33/4
Quartet in D, op.20/4
Quartet in C (Bird), op.33/3

20 Aug. 18.00 *St Cuthbert's Church*
Quartet in D, op.33/6
Quartet in D minor, op.103
Quartet in C, op.20/2

21 Aug. 18.00 *St Cuthbert's Church*
Quartet in E flat, op.20/1
Quartet in B minor, op.33/1
Quartet in A, op.20/6

22 Aug. 18.00 *St Cuthbert's Church*
Quartet in G, op.33/5
Quartet in F minor, op.20/5
Quartet in F, op.77/2

ORLANDO QUARTET
26 Aug. 18.00 *St Cuthbert's Church*
Quartet in B flat, op.64/3
Quartet in G, op.64/4
Quartet in D (The lark), op.64/5

27 Aug. 18.00 *St Cuthbert's Church*
Quartet in D minor (Fifths), op.76/2
Quartet in B flat (Sunrise), op.76/4
Quartet in D, op.76/5

LINDSAY QUARTET
28 Aug. 18.00 *St Cuthbert's Church*
Quartet in F minor (Razor), op.55/2
Quartet in B flat, op.55/3

29 Aug. 18.00 *St Cuthbert's Church*
Quartet in A, op.55/1
Quartet in C, op.64/1
Quartet in B minor, op.64/2

30 Aug. 18.00 *St Cuthbert's Church*
Quartet in C, op.74/1
Quartet in G minor (Rider), op.74/3

31 Aug. 18.00 *St Cuthbert's Church*
Quartet in G, op.76/1
Quartet in C (Emperor), op.76/3

28 Aug. 22.30 *St Giles' Cathedral*
The seven last words of our Saviour from the cross; for string quartet, op.51 with Tom Fleming (rdr)

THOMAS ZEHETMAIR (vn), HEINRICH SCHIFF (vc), TILL FELLNER (pf)
17 Aug. 11.00 *Queen's Hall*
Beethoven Variations on 'Die Zauberflöte' (Mozart) for cello and piano?
Webern Three little pieces for cello and piano, op.11
Webern Four pieces for violin and piano, op.7
Schubert Rondo brillant for violin and piano in B minor, D895
Schubert Trio for piano and strings no.1 in B flat, D898

BENJAMIN FRITH EMPEROR QUARTET
22 Aug. 11.00 *Queen's Hall*
Mozart Concerto for piano no.11 in F, K413; arr. for piano and strings
Mozart Concerto for piano no.12 in A, K414; arr. for piano and strings
Mozart Concerto for piano no.13 in C, K415; arr. for piano and strings

ANDRÁS SCHIFF (pf), YUUKO SHIOKAWA, ERICH HÖBARTH (vn), NOBUKO IMAI (va), MIKLÓS PERENYI, BORIS PERGAMENSCHIKOW (vc), ELMAR SCHMID (cl), RADOVAN VLATKOVIC (hn)
Brahms Chamber Music
24 Aug. 11.00 *Queen's Hall*
Trio for clarinet, cello and piano in A minor, op.114
Sonata for violin and piano no.1 in G, op.78
Quartet for piano and strings no.1 in G minor, op.25

26 Aug. 11.00 *Queen's Hall*
Sonata for cello and piano no.1 in E minor, op.38
Sonata for clarinet and piano no.1 in F minor, op.120/1
Trio for piano and strings no.1 in B, op.8

27 Aug. 11.00 *Queen's Hall*
Sonata for viola and piano no.2 in E flat, op.120/2
Trio for piano and strings no.3 in C minor, op.101
Quartet for piano and strings no.2 in A, op.26

29 Aug. 11.00 *Queen's Hall*
Sonata for violin and piano no.3 in D minor, op.108
Sonata for cello and piano no.2 in F, op.99
Trio for horn, violin and piano in E flat, op.40

31 Aug. 11.00 *Queen's Hall*
Sonata for violin and piano no.2 in A, op.100
Trio for piano and strings no.2 in C, op.87
Quartet for piano and strings no.3 in C minor, op.60

CONCERTO ITALIANO
13 Aug. 11.00 *Queen's Hall*
Monteverdi Madrigals
Director Rinaldo Alessandrini

BURNS SONG
18 Aug. 19.30 *Festival Theatre*
Unaccompanied folk songs, songs and arrangements for chamber ensemble
Mhairi Lawson (sop), Neal Davies (bar), David McGuinness (pf, f-pf), Lucy Russell (baroque vn)

ORLANDO QUARTET
EDINBURGH FESTIVAL SINGERS
24 Aug. 20.00 *Usher Hall*
Kurtág Játékok
Kurtág Twelve microludes
Kurtág Songs of despair and sorrow (World première of complete version)
Kurtág Officium breve in memoriam Andreae Szervánszky
Kurtág Songs of despair and sorrow with Marta Kurtág, György Kurtág (pf)

RECITALS

BOJE SKOVHUS (bar)
HELMUT DEUTSCH (pf)
12 Aug. 11.00 *Queen's Hall*
Schumann Liederkreis, op.24
Songs by Schubert, R. Strauss

BRYN TERFEL (b-bar)
MALCOLM MARTINEAU (pf)
15 Aug. 19.30 *Usher Hall*
Schubert Songs
Ibert 4 Chansons de Don Quichotte
V. Williams Songs of travel

TOM KRAUSE (bar)
EERO HEINONEN (pf)
16 Aug. 11.00 *Queen's Hall*
Mussorgsky Songs and dances of death
Songs by Schubert, R. Strauss, Sibelius

MICHELLE DeYOUNG (mez)
KEVIN MURPHY (pf)
19 Aug. 11.00 *Queen's Hall*
Songs by Haydn, Debussy, Schoenberg, R. Strauss, Grieg

RENÉE FLEMING (sop)
HELEN YORKE (pf)
21 Aug. 11.00 *Queen's Hall*
Songs by Schubert, Schumann, Fauré, Turina and American composers

IAN BOSTRIDGE (ten)
GRAHAM JOHNSON (pf)
23 Aug. 11.00 *Queen's Hall*
Schubert Winterreise

ANN MURRAY (mez)
GRAHAM JOHNSON (pf)
30 Aug. 11.00 *Queen's Hall*
Songs by Brahms, Haydn, Fauré, Hahn, Irish folksongs

PAUL CROSSLEY (pf)
14 Aug. 11.00 *Queen's Hall*
Piano works by Ravel

20 Aug. 11.00 *Queen's Hall*
Piano works by Ravel

ALICIA DE LARROCHA (pf)
15 Aug. 11.00 *Queen's Hall*
Piano works by Mompou, Falla

EVGENY KISSIN (pf)
16 Aug. 20.00 *Usher Hall*
Bach Partita for violin no.2 in D minor: Chaconne; arr. for piano by Busoni
Beethoven Sonata no.14 in C sharp minor (Moonlight), op.27/2
Schumann Fantasia in C, op.17
Schumann Toccata in C, op.7

RICHARD GOODE (pf)
26 Aug. 20.00 *Usher Hall*
Bach Partita no.4 in D
Chopin 5 Mazurkas
Chopin Polonaise for piano no.7 in A flat (Polonaise fantasia), op.61
Brahms Intermezzos and capriccios
Beethoven Sonata no.32 in C minor, op.111

CHRISTIAN ZACHARIAS (pf)
28 Aug. 11.00 *Queen's Hall*
Debussy Preludes: Book.1
Bach 15 Preludes without fugues

SCOTTISH FIDDLE MUSIC
13 Aug. 22.30 *Greyfriars Kirk*
Scotland takes up the fiddle (c1670-1770)
Bonnie Rideout, Lucy Cowan

17 Aug. 22.30 *Greyfriars Kirk*
The age of patronage (c1770-1831)
Alasdair Fraser, Maureen Turnbull

19 Aug. 22.30 *Greyfriars Kirk*
The Highland inheritance
Bonnie Rideout, Alasdair Fraser

24 Aug. 22.30 *Greyfriars Kirk*
The North East tradition
Douglas Lawrence, Alastair Hardie, Paul Anderson

27 Aug. 22.30 *Greyfriars Kirk*
The Northern fiddler
Aly Bain, Jerry Holland

MUSIC BOX
12 Aug. 22.30 *Lyceum Theatre*
Linda Ormiston and Donald Maxwell present a hilarious preview of the Festival programme in words and music

DRAMA

TEATRO STABILE, Parma
24-25 Aug. 19.30 *Lyceum Theatre*
PIERROT
Schoenberg Pierrot lunaire
Seven canzonas
Soloist Maddalena Crippa
Orchestra Sinfonica dell'Emilia Romagna 'Arturo Toscanini'
Conductor Denise Fedeli
Director Walter Le Moli
Designer Bruno Buonincontri
Costumes Moidele Bickel
Lighting Claudio Coloretti
(In collaboration with Teatro Regio, Parma)

TEATRO DI ROMA
TEATRO STABILE, Parma
29-31 Aug. 19.00 *King's Theatre*
UNCLE VANYA Chekhov (It. Translated by Milli Martinelli and Peter Stein)
Alexander Serebriakov Renzo Giovampietro
Elena Andreyevna Maddalena Crippa
Sonya Elisabetta Pozzi
Maria Voinitskaya Tania Rocchetta
Ivan Voinitsky Roberto Herlitzka
Mikhail Astrov Remo Girone
Ilya Telegin Michele de Marchi
Marina Bianca Sollazzo
Workman Giovanni Fochi
Director Peter Stein
Designer Ferdinand Wögerbauer
Costumes Moidele Bickel
Lighting Claudio Coloretti

EX MACHINA, Montreal
12-16 Aug. 19.30 *King's Theatre*
ELSINORE: Variations on Shakespeare's *Hamlet*
Created, directed and performed by Robert Lepage
Designer Carl Fillion
Costumes Yvan Gaudin
Lighting Alain Lortie, Nancy Mongrain
Multimedia systems Jacques Collin
(in association with Cultural Industry)

EDINBURGH INTERNATIONAL FESTIVAL
13-17, 19-21 Aug. 19.30 *Lyceum Theatre*
ORLANDO (Adapted from Virginia Woolf's novel by Pinckney and Wilson)
Orlando Miranda Richardson
Director and designer Robert Wilson *in collaboration with* Ann-Christian Rommen
Costumes Susanne Raschig
Lighting Heinrich Brunke, Robert Wilson
Music Hans Peter Kuhn

NOTTINGHAM PLAYHOUSE
27-31 Aug. 19.30 31 Aug. 14.30
Lyceum Theatre
TIME AND THE ROOM Strauss
(Eng. Translated by Jeremy Sams)
Directed and designed by Martin Duncan and David Fielding

WILDCAT
16-18, 20-24, 26-28 Aug. 19.30 24 Aug. 14.30 Edinburgh International Conference Centre
A SATIRE OF THE FOUR ESTAITES
McGrath
Director John McGrath

L'ESPLÈNDIDA VERGONYA DEL FET MAL FET Santos
23-25 Aug. 20.00 *King's Theatre*

THE SEVEN SACRAMENTS OF NICOLAS POUSSIN
12-18 Aug. 22.30
Meadows Lecture Theatre
A solo performance by Neil Bartlett
Designer Robin Whitmore

DANCE

MARK MORRIS DANCE GROUP, USA
12-14 Aug. 19.30 14 Aug. 14.00
Festival Theatre
BEHEMOTH
TEN SUGGESTIONS
Music Tcherepnin
WORLD POWER
Music Lou Harrison
NEW WORK (World première)
Music Monteverdi
Choreographer (all ballets) Mark Morris
with Concerto Italiano

NETHERLANDS DANCE THEATRE
13, 14 Aug. 19.30 *Playhouse*
BELLA FIGURA
Music Lukas Foss and Italian Baroque
NEW WORK
SYMPHONY OF PSALMS
Music Stravinsky

15, 16 Aug. 19.30 *Playhouse*
WHEREABOUTS UNKNOWN
Music
Pårt, Reich, Webern, Ives, de Roo
SARABANDE
Music Bach; arr. Dick Heuff
FALLING ANGELS
Music Steve Reich
SIX DANCES
Music Mozart
Choreographer (all ballets) Jiří Kylián

MARTHA GRAHAM DANCE COMPANY, USA
18, 20 Aug. 19.30 *Playhouse*
SERENATA MORISCA
Music Mario Tarenghi; arr. McPhee
LAMENTATION
Music Kodály
EL PENITENTE
Music Louis Horst
DIVERSION OF ANGELS
Music Norman Dello-Joio
ERRAND INTO THE MAZE
Music Menotti
CHRONICLE
Music Wallingford Riegger

19, 21 Aug. 19.30 *Playhouse*
DEEP SONG
Music Henry Cowell
HERETIC
Music Anon.
SATYRIC FESTIVAL SONG
Music Fernando Palacios
CELEBRATION
Music Louis Horst
CAVE OF THE HEART
Music Barber
APPALACHIAN SPRING
Music Copland
Choreographer (all ballets)
Martha Graham

TOMOE SHIZUNE AND HAKUTOBO
18-20 Aug. 19.30 *King's Theatre*
RENYO - Far from the Lotus
Choreographer, designer and composer Tomoe Shizune
Lighting Takuro Osaka, Tai Morishita
Sound Sanae Kagaya

FILM

DER ROSENKAVALIER
(A silent film with live music)
24 Aug. 14.00 and 20.00 *Festival Theatre*
Music R. Strauss
Conductor Manfred Reichert
(in association with the Edinburgh Film Festival

FESTIVAL INSIGHTS

A series of talks, discussions and 'In conversation' events

17.00 *Festival Theatre*
12 Aug. 20th century choreographers - Jiří Kylián and Netherlands Dance Company members in conversation
13 Aug. Nicolas Poussin
Timothy Clifford and Neil Bartlett
14 Aug. Robert Lepage in conversation with David Stenhouse
15 Aug. The music of Emmanuel Nunes
Brian Morton
16 Aug. 20th century choreographers - The work of Martha Graham
Diane Gray and Ron Protas
17 Aug. 20th century choreographers - Mark Morris in conversation with Lynne Walker
18 Aug. Christopher Hogwood in conversation with Conrad Wilson
19 Aug. Butoh. Lindsay John
20 Aug. Jane Eaglen in conversation with Dr Guy Goodwin
21 Aug. John McGrath and David McLennan in conversation with David Stenhouse
22 Aug. Ravel piano music: a discussion
Paul Crossley and Gerald Larner
23 Aug. Scottish fiddle music: a lecture demonstration. Alastair Hardie and colleagues
24 Aug. Ines de Castro: a symposium
James MacMillan and Richard Armstrong
25 Aug. Carlos Santos in conversation with Ruth Mackenzie
26 Aug. 20th century choreographers - The work of Pina Bausch.
Annie Griffin
27 Aug. Four saints in three acts
Mark Pappenheim
28 Aug. Botho Strauss: a symposium
Led by Martin Duncan
29 Aug. Robert Wilson in conversation with Ruth Mackenzie
30 Aug. Peter Stein in conversation with Michael Billington

LECTURES

11 Aug. 14.30 *McEwan Hall*
The University Festival lecture
Prof. George Steiner

1.10 *Queen's Hall*
12 Aug. Monteverdi madrigals
Svend Brown
13 Aug. Hamlet James Spalding
14 Aug. Gluck Prof. Peter Branscombe
15 Aug. Orlando Dr Halla Beloff
16 Aug. Britten's War requiem
Dr John Evans
19 Aug. Martha Graham Sara Porter
20 Aug. Schoenberg's Pierrot lunaire
Neil McKay
21 Aug. Ane Satyre of the thrie estaites
Owen Dudley Edwards
22 Aug. Ines de Castro David Munrow
23 Aug. Brahms John Miller
26 Aug. Four saints in three acts
Derek Watson
27 Aug. Uncle Vanya
Emilia Vosnesenskaya
28 Aug. Botho Strauss Dr Alison Phipps
29 Aug. Haydn Quartets Peter Cropper
30 Aug. Mendelssohn's Elijah
Prof. David Kimbell
(In association with Edinburgh University)

SUMMER COURSES

(Edinburgh University)
10-16 Aug. Festival drama
24-30 Aug. Festival music

Operas, Plays and Ballets 1947-1996

OPERAS

Adams, John
I was looking at the ceiling and then I saw the sky 1995
Nixon in China 1988
Allwood, Peter
The little rats 1988
Anonymous
Daniel and the lions 1988
Armstrong, Craig
Anna 1993
Bartók, Béla
Duke Bluebeard's castle 1963, 67 (con perf), 73, 84 (con perf), 93
Beethoven, Ludwig van
Fidelio 1952, 94, 96 (conc perf)
Leonore 1994 (conc perf)
Bellini, Vincenzo
I Capuleti ed i Montecchi 1967
I puritani 1960
La sonnambula 1957
La straniera 1972
Berg, Alban
Lulu 1966, 75
Wozzeck 1959, 66, 80
Berlioz, Hector
Les Troyens 1972 (Eng)
Bernstein, Leonard
Candide 1981
Birtwistle, Harrison
Punch and Judy 1968
Bizet, Georges
Carmen 1977, 78
Blomdahl, Karl Birger
Aniara 1959
Borodin, Alexander
Prince Igor 1962 (S.Croat), 90
Britten, Benjamin, *Lord*
Albert Herring 1965
The burning fiery furnace 1968
Curlew River 1968
Death in Venice 1973, 83
Let's make an opera 1986
A midsummer night's dream 1961, 94
Noye's fludde 1982
Peter Grimes 1968
The prodigal son 1968
The rape of Lucretia 1963
The turn of the screw 1962, 79
Busoni, Ferruccio
Arlecchino 1960
Cavalieri, Emilio de
Il rappresentazione di anima e di corpo 1972
Cavalli, Pier Francesco
Orion 1984 (Eng)
Chabrier, Emmanuel
Briséïs 1994 (conc perf)
L'Étoile 1985, 94 (Eng)
Le roi malgré-lui 1994 (Eng)
Charpentier, Marc-Antoine
Actéon 1985
Cikker, Ján
Resurrection 1964
Cilea, Francesco
Adriana Lecouvreur 1963
Cimarosa, Domenico
Il maestro di cappella 1992
Il matrimonio segreto 1957, 80
Cornelius, Peter
Der Barbier von Bagdad 1956
Dallapiccola, Luigi
Il prigioniero 1969
Davies, *Sir* Peter Maxwell
The lighthouse (World première) 1980
Debussy, Claude
Pelléas et Mélisande 1978, 85
Delius, Frederick
Fennimore and Gerda 1983
Donizetti, Gaetano
Don Pasquale 1963
L'elisir d'amore 1957
Lucia di Lammermoor 1961
Maria Stuarda 1969
Dvořák, Antonín
The Jacobin 1995 (Eng)
Rusalka 1964
Falla, Manuel de
Atlántida 1962 (conc perf), 89 (conc perf)
El retablo de Maese Pedro 1989 (Eng)
La vida breve 1958, 89 (conc perf)
Gay, John
The beggar's opera 1963, 68, 81
Gershwin, George
Girl crazy 1987 (conc perf)
Glinka, Mikhail
Ruslan and Ludmilla 1995 (conc perf)
Gluck, Christoph Willibald von
Alceste 1974
Iphigénie en Tauride 1961, 79 (Eng)
Iphigénie en Tauride (Vienna version 1781 - Ger) 1996
Orfeo ed Euridice (Vienna version 1762) 1996
Goehr, Alexander
Triptych 1971
Triptych: Naboth's vineyard 1969
Gounod, Charles
Faust 1990
Hamilton, Iain
Pharsalia (World première) 1969
Handel, George Frederick
Ariodante 1982
Il pastor fido 1974
Tamerlano 1982 (Eng)
Haydn, Franz Joseph
Orfeo ed Euridice 1967
Le pescatrici 1965
Henze, Hans Werner
Elegy for young lovers 1970
The English cat 1987
Hindemith, Paul
Mathis der Maler 1952
Janáček, Leoš
The cunning little vixen 1970, 80 (Eng)
The excursions of Mr Broucek 1970
From the house of the dead 1964
Jenůfa 1974 (Swed)
Káta Kabanová 1964, 78 (Ger)
The Makropoulos affair 1970
Šárka 1993 (conc perf)
Lortzing, Albert
Der Wildschütz 1958
MacMillan, James
Búsqueda 1993
Ines de Castro (World première) 1996
Tourist variations 1993
Visitatio sepulchri 1993
Malipiero, Gian Francesco
Sette canzoni 1969
Martinů, Bohuslav
The Greek passion 1990 (conc perf)
Julietta 1990
Massenet, Jules
Don Quichotte 1962 (S.Croat)
Menotti, Gian Carlo
The consul 1985
The medium 1984
The telephone 1984
Merikanto, Aarre
Juha 1987
Mitchell, Joseph
The Highland fair (a ballad opera) 1952, 53
Monteverdi, Claudio
Il combattimento di Tancredi e Clorinda 1969
L'incoronazione di Poppea 1978
L'Orfeo 1978
Il ritorno d'Ulisse in patria 1978
Moreno Torroba, Fernando
La Chulapona 1989
Mozart, Wolfgang Amadeus
La clemenza di Tito 1981, 91
Così fan tutte 1948, 49, 54, 65 (Ger), 80, 93 (conc perf)
Don Giovanni 1948, 51, 65, 73, 74, 95 (conc perf)
Die Entführung aus dem Serail 1958, 71, 82
Idomeneo 1953
Le nozze di Figaro 1947, 50, 75, 76, 94 (conc perf)
Die Zauberflöte 1952, 56, 66, 83, 87 (Swed)
Musgrave, Thea
Mary, Queen of Scots (World première) 1977
The voice of Ariadne 1981
Mussorgsky, Modest
Boris Godunov 1991 (conc perf)
Khovanshchina 1962 (S.Croat), 91
The marriage 1982, 91
Salammbó 1991 (conc perf)
Sorochinsky Fair 1991 (conc perf)
Nield, David
The ragged child 1986
The tower of Babel 1984
Nono, Luigi
Al gran sole carico d'amore 1978 (conc perf)
Nørgård, Per
The divine circus 1989
Offenbach, Jacques
La Périchole 1988 (Ger)
Orr, Robin
Hermiston (World première) 1975
Paulus, Stephen
The postman always rings twice 1983
Poulenc, Francis
La voix humaine 1960, 92
Prokofiev, Serge
Betrothal in a monastery 1990
The fiery angel 1970
The gambler 1962 (S.Croat)
The love of three oranges 1962 (S.Croat), 1989 (Eng)
Puccini, Giacomo
Gianni Schicchi 1969
Manon Lescaut 1982
Turandot 1988 (Swed)
Rameau, Jean-Philippe
Anacréon 1985
Reimann, Aribert
Melusine 1971
Rimsky-Korsakov, Nikolay
Christmas eve 1991
The golden cockerel 1979 (Eng)
The legend of the invisible city of Kitezh 1995
Sadko 1995
Rossini, Gioacchino
Il barbiere di Siviglia 1955, 61, 81
La Cenerentola 1953, 71
Le Comte Ory 1954
Elisabetta, Regina d'Inghilterra 1972
L'Italiana in Algeri 1976
La pietra del paragone 1982
Il Signor Bruschino 1969
Il Turco in Italia 1957
Schoenberg, Arnold
Erwartung 1993
Moses und Aron 1976, 92 (conc perf)

PLAYS

Wilder, Thornton
A life in the sun (World première) 1955
The matchmaker (World première) 1954
Williams, Jaston
Greater Tuna 1985
Wilson, John
Hamp 1964
Wood, Tom
B-Movie: the play 1988
Wright, David
Would you look at them smashing all those lovely windows 1969
Wymark, Olwen
Triple image 1967
Wyspianski, Stanislaw
Acropolis 1968

BALLETS

3 epitaphs (Taylor) 1966
13 dances (Petit) 1949
A sud di Mozart (Amodio) 1988
Acrobats of God (Graham) 1963
Adagio (Ohn) 1959
Afternoon of a faun (Robbins) 1959
Agon (Balanchine) 1967
Alborada del gracioso (Granero) 1989
Allegro, il penseroso ed il moderato, L' (Morris) 1994
Amor brujo, El (Wright) World première 1975
Amour et son amour, L' (Babilée) 1949
Amours de Jupiter, Les (Petit) 1949
An un, L' (Degroat) 1989
And after (Sagan) 1974
Appalachian spring (Graham) 1996
Apollo (Balanchine) 1967, 75, 79
Aprés midi d'un faune, L' (Nijinsky) 1987
Aunis (Garnier) 1985
Aureole (Taylor) 1966, 85
Bagatai 1964
Baile, El (Reyes) 1990
Baiser de la fée, La (MacMillan) 1960
Bal des blanchisseuses, Le (Petit) 1949
Balance à trois (Babilée) 1959
Ballabile (Petit) 1960
Ballad of a medieval love, The: Scenes (Mlakar) 1951
Ballad of Carmen and Don José, The 1960
Ballet imperial (Balanchine) 1951
Balletino (Sanders) 1959
Beau Danube, Le (Massine) 1950, 60
Beautiful day (Morris) 1992
Bedtime (Morris) 1992
Beethoven and Booth (Gordon) 1985
Behemoth (Morris) 1996
Bella figura (Kylián) 1996
Belle dame sans merci, La (Howard) World première) 1958
Biches, Les (Nijinska) 1987
Billy the Kid (Loring) 1953
Birthday offering (Ashton) 1956
Black district (Beatty) 1968
Blood wedding (Gades) 1979, 82
Blood wedding (Rodrigues) 1953
Bolero (Granero) 1989
Boucle, La (Babilée) 1959
Bourgeois gentilhomme, Le (Balanchine) 1984
Bourrée fantasque (Balanchine) 1952
Boutique fantasque, La (Massine) 1948, 54
Brandenburg (Czarny) 1970
Bride's kerchief, The: Pas de deux (Harangozó) 1963
Bugaku (Balanchine) 1967
Cafe Müller (Bausch) 1992
Cage, The (Robbins) 1952
Canto vital (Plissetsky) 1979
Capricious Lucinda (Larsen) 1955
Caracole (Balanchine) 1952
Cargo X (Cunningham) 1994
Carmen (Darrell) World première 1985
Carmen (Petit) 1971
Carnaval (Fokine, Beriozoff) 1984
Carte blanche (Gore) World première 1953
Casa di Bernarda Alba, La (Tenorio) 1991
Catalyst, The (Cranko) 1963
Cave of the heart (Graham) 1996
Celebration (Graham) 1996
Changement de pieds (Carter) World première 1958
Checkmate (de Valois) 1948, 51
Chéri (Darrell) World première 1980
Chicago brass (Alston) 1983
Choreartium (Massine) 1960
Chronicle (Graham) 1996
Cinderella (Marin) 1986
Circle of love (Cullberg) World première 1958
Circle of roses (Sylvestersson) 1959
Circo de Espana (Maracci) 1953
Clock symphony (Massine) 1948
Clytemnestra (Graham) 1963
Colour moves (North) World première 1983
Commedia umana, La (Massine) 1960
Con amore (Christensen) 1981
Concert, The (Robbins) 1959
Concertino (Bruce) 1983
Concerto (Childs) 1994
Concerto (MacMillan) 1975, 79
Concerto barocco (Balanchine) 1952, 57, 67
Concerto for dancers (Toye) World première 1958
Concierto de aranjuez (López) 1953
Congo tango palace (Beatty) 1968
Conservatoire, Le (Bournonville) 1971
Constantia (Dollar) 1953
Coppélia (Nahat) 1990
Coppélia (Petipa, Cecchetti) 1948, 52, 56
Coppélia: Act 2 (St.Léon) 1949
Couleur du secret, La (Paré) 1985
Country dances (Tharp) 1976
Couples (Van Dantzig) 1974
Création, La (Lichine) 1949, 59
Credo (Fealy) 1968
Cross-fade (Nikolais) 1975
Cupid out of his humour (Skeaping) 1957
D-man in the waters (Jones) 1993
Dance (Childs) 1994
Dance of the spider (Koskinen) 1959
Dances of love and death (Cohan) World première 1981
Danses concertantes (MacMillan) 1960
Danza y tronio (Mariemma) 1989
Daphnis and Chloë (Cranko) 1963
Deep song (Graham) 1996
Del amor y de la muerte (Ricarda) 1952
Désirs parade (Underwood) 1991
Dido abandonado (Alonso) 1991
Dido and Aeneas (Morris) 1992
Diversion of angels (Graham) 1963, 96
Divertimento (Babilée) 1959
Divertimento no.15 (Balanchine) 1981
Don Quichotte (Gé) 1959
Don Quixote (de Valois) 1951
Don Quixote (Petipa, Gorski) 1991
Don Quixote: Pas de deux (*after* Petipa) 1977
Donizetti variations (Balanchine) 1967
Doundoumba (Dance of retired warriors) 1964
Dream, The (Ashton) 1975
Dreams (Parlič) World première 1958
Driftings (Underwood) 1990
Drop your pearls and hog it, girl (Clark) 1986
Duet (Taylor) 1966
Ebony concerto (Taras) 1967
Eight jelly rolls (Tharp) 1976
Elite syncopations (MacMillan) 1979
Embattled garden (Graham) 1963
Emprise, L' (Sanders) 1959
Enter (Cunningham) 1994
Epreuve d'amour, L' (Gé *after* Fokine) 1959
Errand into the maze (Graham) 1996
Esmeralda: Pas de deux (Stevenson) 1989
Estro armonico, L' (Cranko) 1963
Facheuses rencontres, Les (Skibine) World première 1958
Fall River legend (de Mille) 1950
Falling angels (Kylián) 1996
Fancy free (Robbins) 1950
Fantasia Goyesca (López) 1953
Femme muette, La (Cobos) 1957
Fête (Jones) 1993
Fête étrange, La (Howard) 1953

Exhibitions

7 Foksal Gallery artists from Poland 1985
17th century Italian drawings 1972
18th century musical instruments 1974
1826 - 1976 1976
300 years 300 books 1989
Aachen international 70/74 1974
About landscape 1985
Alan Davie: Paintings 1952-1972 1972
Allan Ramsay 1992
America America 1977
American abstract expressionists 1981
American drawings and watercolours 1985
Andrea Palladio 1984
Andrew Carnegie 1985
Angels, nobles and unicorns 1982
Anzartbougé: New French photography 1984
Armand Hammer collection 1978
Art and industry of James Tassie, The 1986
Art nouveau In Finland 1979
Art of the Andes 1983
Art of the doll-maker, The 1983
At home 1984
At home: Scottish interiors 1986
Behind golden scenes 1991
Belgian contribution to Surrealism, The 1971
Blue Rider Group 1960
Boudin to Picasso 1968
Braque 1956
Breath of French air, A 1985
British artists in Meiji Japan 1880-1900 1991
British watercolours and drawings 1982
Bulgarian icons 1978
Byzantine art 1958
Camels, cobwebs and cormorants 1985
Canada 101 1968
Centre stage 1983
Ceri Richards 1975
Cézanne 1954
Cézanne and Poussin 1990
Charles Rennie Mackintosh 1968
Child's play 1987
Circles of the world: Traditional art of the Plains Indians 1982
Clutch of cartoonists, A 1984
Codex Hammer 1982
Coia caricatures 1971
Colour since Matisse 1985
Contemporary art from the Netherlands 1989
Contemporary German art from Düsseldorf 1970
Contemporary Polish art 1969
Contemporary Rumanian art 1971
Corot Exhibition 1965
Creation: Modern art and nature 1984
Dada & Surrealism 1988
David Salle: Paintings and drawings 1987
Degas 1952
Degas 1879 1979
Delacroix Exhibition 1964
Demarcation '84 1984
Derain 1967
Dovecot tapestry 1980
Dutch art and Scotland 1992
Dutch church painters 1984
Dynasty: The royal house of Stewart 1990
Early Celtic art 1970
L'ecole de Paris 1900-1960 1985
Edinburgh - Dublin 1885-1985 1985
Edinburgh and its story: J. Ayton Symington 1989
Edinburgh open 100 1967
Eduardo Paolozzi 1984
Edvard Münch 1989
Eight from Berlin 1975
El Greco: Mystery and illumination 1989
Eleven Dutch artists 1974
Enterprising Scot, The 1986
Epstein memorial exhibition 1961
France and the National Galleries 1985
French connections: Scotland and the arts of France 1985
French furniture, Porcelain 1985
French master drawings from Stockholm 1987
French painter in exile, A: Henry Pierre Danloux 1985
Fritz Wotruba 1968
Gauguin 1955
Georges Rouault 1966
Giam Bologna 1978
Hebridean light 1982
Hebrides surveyed, The 1990
Henry Moore, recent graphics 1984
Henryk Stazewski Recent paintings 1979
Hepworth 1976
Heritage 1975
Highland and County '85 1985
Historic clarinet, The 1986
Hoffnung 1968
Homage to Diaghilev 1954
Honoré Daumier, 1808-1879 1981
Hotbed of genius, A 1986
Hugh MacDiarmid 1988
Hundertwasser 1983
Imperial images in Persian miniature painting 1977
In the shadow of Vesuvius 1988
Indispensable fan, The 1984
It cam wi' a lass 1987
Italian sixteenth century drawings from British private collections 1969
Jack Bush 1980
Jack Coia 1969
James VI and I 1975
James Pryde 1992
Jean Michel Basquiat: Paintings 1981- 84 1984
Joan Eardley 1988
John Bellany 1986
John Cage 1984
John Francis Campbell 1985
John Michael Wright: The King's painter 1982
Joseph Beuys 1980
Kandinsky 1975
Kandinsky: The Munich years 1900-14 1979
Kind of gentle painting, A 1975
Komar and Melamid 1985
Leading works from the Saatchi collection 1987
Legacy, The 1980
Lighting up the landscape: French Impressionism and its origins 1986
Lion rugs of Fars 1980
Lookalike: Themes and variations in art 1982
Macchiaioli, I: Italian Impressionists 1982
McTaggarts and other artist families, The 1989
Making it! 1988
Man and music 1983
Man Ray 1982
Maquette to monumental 1984
Masterpieces of Czech art 1959
Masterpieces of French painting from the Bührle collection 1961
Max Ernst 1990
Medieval frescoes from Yugoslavia 1953
Miniature masterpieces: Lacquer work from Russia 1987
Miro sculptures 1992
Miró's people 1982
Mirror and the lamp, The 1986
Mirrors and windows 1981
Modern spirit: American painting, The 1908-35 1977
Modigliani 1963
Moltzau collection: Cézanne to Picasso 1958
Monet 1957
Moscow - A private view 1987
Mouton Rothschild: Paintings for the labels 1945-1981 1983
Music and dance in Indian art 1963
New design and architecture from Finland 1988
New new Mexico 1980
Northern horizons: Norwegian contemporary art 1989
Objects Usa 1973
Our photographic legacy 1989
Painting in Scotland, The golden age 1986
Parade: Dance costumes of three centuries 1979
Parliament House exhibition, The 1971
Patrons and painters: Art in Scotland 1650-1760 1989
Paul-Emile Borduas 1905-1960 1983
Photography of John Muir Wood, The 1988
Picabia 1879-1953 1988
Pietro Longhi 1988
Piranesi drawings and etchings 1982
Plume de mon cartoonist, La: Mel Calman 1985
P.M. - A.D. 1987
Polish contemporary art 1972
Pomp 1969
Pre-Columbian ceramics of Costa Rica 1985
Prescote in Edinburgh 1980
Printed light 1986
Proud bassoon, The 1983
Queen's image, The 1987
Queen's world, The 1987
Rarities of Chinese painting 1984
Reality and imagination 1988
Rembrandt van Rhyn 1950
Renoir 1953
Restless shadows 1991
Robert Louis Stevenson 1990
Robert Scott Lauder's master class 1983
Robin Philipson retrospective 1989
Rumanian art treasures 1965
Russian non-objective art 1978
S.J. Peploe 1985
Sandro Chia 1983
Scotch myths 1981
Scotland and Australia 1988
Scotland and India 1986
Scotland's pictures 1990
Scottish art 1984
Scottish art since 1900 1989
Scottish art today: Artists at work 1986
Scottish arts now 1982
Scottish crafts now 1983
Scottish Expressionism 1983
Scottish music 1992
Scottish Variety exhibition 1993
Sculpture of Henry Matisse, The 1984
Seeing is not believing 1981
Shakespeare exhibition, The 1964
Sir John Lavery RA 1856-1941 1984

World Premières

MUSIC

Armstrong, Craig
  Anna 1993
Arnell, Richard
  Landscapes and figures 1956
Bainbridge, Simon
  Landscapes and magic words 1981
Banks, Don
  Trio for horn, violin and piano 1962
Bawden, Rupert
  Three dances 1984
Bennett, Richard Rodney
  Sonata for horn 1979
  Sonnets to Orpheus 1979
Berio, Luciano
  Bewegung (Definitive version) 1971
  'Cries' of London 1976
Berkeley, *Sir* Lennox
  Sonata for flute and piano 1978
Berkeley, Michael
  Sonata for guitar 1982
Birtwistle, Harrison
  Chanson de geste for basset horn and pre-recorded tape 1973
Blacher, Boris
  Inventions for orchestra 1954
Bliss, *Sir* Arthur
  Edinburgh overture 1950
  Quartet no.2 1950
Bloch, Ernest
  Concerto symphonique 1949
Burkhard, Willy
  Concertino for 2 flutes, harpsichord and string orchestra 1954
Cashian, Philip
  Moon of the dawn 1986
Chisholm, Erik
  Concerto for violin 1952
Clapperton, James
  Elrich fantasyis 1995
Crosse, Gordon
  Dream songs 1979
Daiken, Melanie
  Mayakovsky and the sun 1971
Dalby, Martin
  The keeper of the pass 1971
  O bella e vaga aurora 1982
Davies, *Sir* Peter Maxwell
  The lighthouse 1980
  The peat cutters 1985
Davis, Carl
  Countdown 1974
  The Glenlivet fireworks music 1987
  Greed: incidental music to the film 1986
Druckman, Jacob
  Other voices 1976
Eastwood, Thomas
  Capriccio 1961
  Solitudes 1964
Forbes, Sebastian
  Symphony in two movements 1972
Frankel, Benjamin
  Five bagatelles for 11 instruments 1959
  A Shakespeare overture 1956
Fricker, Peter
  Concerto for viola, op.18 1953
Gal, Hans
  Quartet no.3 1970
Gershwin, George
  Lullaby for harmonica and string quartet 1963
Goehr, Alexander
  Introduction and fugue for 3 clarinets 1978
  A musical offering (J.S.B.) 1985
  Paraphrase on 'Il combattimento di Tancredi e Clorinda' (Monteverdi) for clarinet 1969
Gubaidulina, Sofia
  Quartet no.3 1987
Hamilton, Iain
  Concerto for violin no.2 (Amphion) 1972
  Pharsalia 1969
  Sinfonia for 2 orchestras 1959
  The spirit of delight 1979
Harper, Edward
  Intrada after Monteverdi 1982
  Ricercare in memoriam Luigi Dallapiccola 1975
Harvey, Jonathan
  Gong-ring 1984
Henze, Hans Werner
  Ariosi 1964
Jirák, Karel
  Symphony no.5 1951
King, Geoffrey
  You, always you 1986
Kurtág, György
  Songs of despair and sorrow (Complete version) 1996
Leighton, Kenneth
  Octet (Homage to Percy Grainger), op.87 1982
Lunn, John
  A tonic for the dominant 1995
McEwen, J.B.
  Trio for strings no.5 (Attica) 1948
McGuire, Edward
  Euphoria - a sense of well-being 1980
MacMillan, James
  Epiclesis: a concerto for trumpet 1993
  Ines de Castro 1996
  They saw the stone had been rolled away 1993
  Tourist variations 1993
Mainardi, Enrico
  Sonata for solo cello 1960
Maw, Nicholas
  The ruin 1980
Menotti, Gian Carlo
  Moans, groans, cries, sighs, or a composer at work 1981
Muldowney, Dominic
  Quartet no.2 1982
Musgrave, Thea
  Mary Queen of Scots 1977
Nicholls, David
  Ensemble 5 (Seascape 1) 1984
Nono, Luigi
  Intolleranza - Suite 1969
  Sul Ponte di Hiroshima 1962
Oldham, Arthur
  Psalms in times of war 1977
Oliver, Stephen
  Namings 1981
Orr, Robin
  Hermiston 1975
  Sonatine in 1 movement for cello and piano 1948
Penderecki, Krzysztof
  Concerto for cello no.1 1972
Poulenc, Francis
  Le travail du peintre 1957
Rainier, Priaulx
  Concerto for violin - Due canti e finale 1977
Rawsthorne, Alan
  Practical cats 1954
Robb, Magnus
  Blood foliage 1995
Rueff, Jeanine
  Quartet 1950
Salonen, Esa-Pekka
  YTA 3 for cello 1987
Searle, Humphrey
  Symphony no.3, op.36 1960
Shostakovich, Dmitri
  Hamlet: Concert scenario 1992
  Lady Macbeth of Mtsensk - Suite 1962
Stevenson, Ronald
  The harlot's house 1988
Takemitsu, Toru
  Nostalghia - in memory of Andrei Tarkovsky 1987
Tan Dun
  Orchestral theatre 1990
  Silent earth for ceramics 1991
Tavener, John
  Akhmatova requiem 1981
  Thrénos for solo cello 1991
Teml
  Capricious summer 1991
Tippett, *Sir* Michael
  Concerto for orchestra 1963
  Fantasia concertante on a theme of Corelli 1953
Walton, *Sir* William
  Symphony no.2 1960
Whyte, Ian
  Biblical songs 1950
Wilkins, Margaret
  Circus 1975
Williams, Grace
  Penillion 1955
Williamson, Michael
  Birthday ode to Queen Elizabeth, the Queen Mother 1980
  Symphonic variations 1965
Wilson, Thomas
  Concerto for orchestra 1967
  Ritornelli per archi 1972
  Te deum 1971
Wordsworth, William
  Quintet for clarinet and strings 1955
  Symphony no.2 in D, op.34 1951
  Symphony no.4 in E flat, op.54 1954

PLAYS

Anonymous and Collective works
Pacha Mammas's blessing 1988
The passion: Part 1 1980
The seven streams of the River Ota 1995
Barker, Harley Granville
His majesty 1992
Bridie, James
The Queen's comedy 1950
Brown, Ian
The knife 1973
Connolly, Billy
The red runner 1979
Dennis, Nigel
August for the people 1961
Dostoyevsky, Fyodor
The brothers Karamazov 1981 (Eng)
Dufton, Bill *and* Thorne, Ian
Boswell's life of Johnson 1970
Eliot, T. S.
The cocktail party 1949
The confidential clerk 1953
The elder statesman 1958
Foster, Paul
Tom Paine 1967+
Gibbon, Lewis Grassic
A Scots quair: Parts 2 and 3 1993
Goodsir Smith, Sydney
The Wallace 1960, 85
Gray, Alasdair
Lanark (Adapted by Cording) 1995
Griffin, Jonathan
The hidden king 1957
Hailstone, John
A present for the past 1966+
Hassall, Christopher
The player king 1952
Hogg, James (Adapted by Jack Ronder)
Confessions of a justified sinner 1971
Jonic, Bettina
Glitter city 1991
Lorca 1966
Josipovici, Gabriel
Flow 1973
Kops, Bernard
The dream of Peter Mann 1960
Laing, R.D.
Knots 1973
Lawler, Ray
The unshaven cheek 1963
Linklater, Eric
The atom doctor 1950
Breakspear in Gascony 1959
McCarthy, Sean
The fantastical feats of Finn MacCool 1974
McGrath, John
Animal 1979
Random happenings in the Hebrides 1970
McLarnon, Gerard
The bonefire 1958
Morgan, Charles
The river line 1952
Sieveking, Lance *and* Cottrell, Richard
A room with a view 1967
Stevenson, R.L.
Treasure island (Adapted by Frank Dunlop) 1990
Stoppard, Tom
On the razzle 1981
Thomas, Dylan
Under Milk Wood (1st stage prod.) 1956
Wilder, Thornton
A life in the sun 1955
The matchmaker 1954+

BALLETS

Amor brujo, El (Wright) 1975
Belle dame sans merci, La (Howard) 1958
Carmen (Darrell) 1985
Carte blanche (Gore) 1953
Changement de pieds (Carter) 1958
Chéri (Darrell) 1980
Circle of love (Cullberg) 1958
Colour moves (North) 1983
Concerto for dancers (Toye) 1958
Dances of love and death (Cohan) 1981
Dreams (Parlic) 1958
Facheuses recontres, Les (Skibine) 1958
Great peacock, The (Wright) 1958
Knoxville: Summer 1915 (Ailey) 1968
Midsummer's vigil (Holmgren) 1958
Night and silence, The (Gore) 1958
Octet (Taras) 1958
Our caca phoney h (Clark) 1985
Petrushka variations (Neumeier) 1986
Playground (MacMillan) 1979
Punch and the street party (Bintley) 1979
Reflection (Cranko) 1952
Secrets (Cranko) 1958
Seventh sacrament, The (Mendel) 1958
Soldier's tale, The (Helpmann) 1954
Song of unending sorrow (Ricarda) 1957
Spell, A (Morris) 1993
Stop stars (Wagoner) 1981
New work? (Kylián) 1996
New work? (Morris) 1996

+Query World première

Artists 1947-1996

At the time of printing detailed cast lists for the 1996 Festival were not available and therefore the list of artists for that year is incomplete. There is also a possibility that some of the artists included may have been changed at a late stage.

59 THEATRE COMPANY 1963
69 THEATRE COMPANY 1968
7.84 1983
AARON, Janet (dan) 1966
ABAD, Carlos Alberto (act) 1989
ABBADO, Claudio (cond) 1966, 67, 68, 69, 71, 75-83, 86, 95, 96
ABBADO, Roberto (cond) 1982
ABBEELE, Eric van den (dan) 1987
ABBEY THEATRE, Dublin 1968, 74, 94, 95
ABBOTT, Tommy (dan) 1959
ABRAHAMS, Jody (act) 1988
ABRAMISHVILI, S. (act) 1979
ABRIL, Anton Garcia (comp) 1983
ABSE, Dannie (rdr) 1979
ABU-WARDA, Yusof (act) 1983
ACADEMY OF ANCIENT MUSIC 1979, 90, 91
ACADEMY OF ST MARTIN-IN-THE-FIELDS 1970, 83, 86
ACCADEMIA MONTEVERDIANA 1962
ACCARDO, Salvatore (vn) 1979, 80, 81, 82, 84
ACCLAIM PRODUCTIONS LTD 1983
ACEVEDO, Miriam (act) 1975
ACKER, Sharon (act) 1956
ACKERMAN, Neville (ten) 1990
ACKLAND, Joss (act) 1958, 59
ACKROYD, Ronnie (act) 1975
ACOSTA, Gladys (dan) 1991
ACTORS' COMPANY 1972-74
ACTORS GANG, USA 1989
ADAEVA, Elena (dan) 1995
ADAM, Dietrich (act) 1993
ADAM, Theo (b-bar) 1968
ADAMI, Laura (dan) 1987
ADAMOV, Arthur 1963
ADAMS, Bruce (mus) 1986
ADAMS, Carolyn (dan) 1966
ADAMS, Christopher (sngr) 1979
ADAMS, Desmond (act) 1978
ADAMS, Diana (dan) 1952
ADAMS, John (cond) 1988
ADAMS, Loukmaan (act) 1988
ADAMS, Stephen James (sngr) 1973
ADANI, Mariella (sop) 1960, 65
ADCOCK, Fleur (rdr) 1990
ADDISON, John (comp) 1961
ADELMAN, Alan (light) 1990
ADLER, Larry (harmonica) 1963, 65
ADRIAN, Max (act) 1962, 63, 66
ADSHEAD, Kay (act) 1977
ADVENTO, Regina (dan) 1995
ADVENTURES IN MOTION PICTURES 1992
ADWALL, Allan (act) 1967
AEOLIAN QUARTET 1969, 72
AGELET, Jesus (act) 1992
ÁGHOVÁ, Livia (sop) 1990
AGNEW, Iain (act) 1970
AGOSTINO, Antonella d' (sngr) 1988
AGUILERA, Lala (act) 1986
AGUIRRE, Jesús (sngr) 1958
AGUT, Alicia (act) 1986
AHJOLINNA, Aku (dan) 1987
AHLBURG, John (act) 1976
AHLERSMEYER, Mathieu (bar) 1952
AHLIN, Cvekta (mez) 1968
AHN, Suk-Son (act) 1990
AIKEN, Mark (act) 1993
AILEY, Alvin (chor) 1968
AILLAUD, Gilles (des) 1994, 95
AIMÉE, J. Ch. (des) 1979
AINLEY, Pekoe (act) 1964
AINSLEY, John Mark (ten) 1992, 93, 94, 96
AIRAUDO, Malou (dan) 1978, 92, 93
AITKEN, Christine (dan) 1979
AITKEN, Malcolm (ten) 1981, 83
AJIBADE, Yemi (act) 1961
AKERS, William (light) 1980
ÅKERSTRÖM, Arne (light) 1987, 88
AKROAMA, Teatro Laboratorio Sardinia, 1982
AKUCEWICZ, Kama (dan) 1986
AL FAIRWEATHER-SANDY BROWN ALL STARS 1962
ALAN, Hervey (bs) 1949, 53, 55
ALARIE, Pierrette (sop) 1951
ALBALAT, Manuel (bs) 1958
ALBAN BERG QUARTET 1976, 80
ALBAN TRIO 1953
ALBANACHS 1967
ALBANEZU, Lucian (act) 1991
ALBANI, Maria Teresa (act) 1975
ALBEE, Edward (spk) 1963
ALBERTI, Virginie (dan) 1986
ALBERY, Tim (dir) 1994
ALBION BAND 1980
ALBRECHT, Gerd (cond) 1975, 83
ALBRECHT, Richard (act) 1979
ALBURGER, Mary Anne (vn) 1985
ALCAIDE, Jesús (sngr) 1989
ALDEN, David (dir) 1980
ALDER, Robert (boy sop) 1968
ALDERSON, Robert (bs) 1981
ALDOUS, Robert (act) 1957
ALDRED, David (ten) 1981, 89
ALDREDGE, Theoni V. (des) 1977
ALEKSANDROV, Yuri (dir) 1991
ALEKSASHKIN, Sergei (bs) 1991
ALESSANDRINI, Rinaldo (mus dir) 1996
ALEXA, Jonas (cond) 1990
ALEXANDER, Bill (dir) 1980
ALEXANDER, Bill (lect) 1992
ALEXANDER, Bruce (act) 1981
ALEXANDER, Carlos (bar) 1966
ALEXANDER, George (va) 1951
ALEXANDER, Greig (act) 1990
ALEXANDER, Joan (sop) 1948, 49, 51, 52, 53, 56, 59
ALEXANDER, Richard (bs) 1994
ALEXANDER, Roberta (sop) 1983
ALEXANDRE, Anne (act) 1970
ALEXEEV, Dmitri (pf) 1980, 91
ALEXEEV, N.N. (sngr) 1986
ALEXEEV, Valery (bs) 1991
ALFIERI, Lisa (dan) 1990
ALGAROFF, Youly (dan) 1949
ALGERANOVA, Claudie (dan) 1958
ALIBERTI, Lucia (sop) 1982
ALIFANTIS, Nicu (comp) 1991
ALLAM, Roger (act) 1992
ALLAN, Alexander (act) 1959, 60, 61, 65
ALLAN, Lewis (act) 1985
ALLDIS, John (cond) 1968, 78
ALLEGRI QUARTET 1961, 62, 64, 75
ALLEN, Jermane (dan) 1987
ALLEN, John (act) 1951
ALLEN, Paschal (bs) 1968
ALLEN, Patrick (act) 1962
ALLEN, Reg (des) 1993
ALLEN, Richard (bar) 1972
ALLEN, Ronald (act) 1955
ALLEN, Rosie (dan) 1992
ALLEN, Sheila (rdr) 1980
ALLEN, Sybil (act) 1993
ALLEN, Thomas (bar) 1973, 76, 77, 78, 80, 81, 90, 91, 93
ALLEN, William (pf) 1947
ALLEYN, Barbara (act) 1956
ALLIO, René (des) 1960
ALLIOT-LUGAZ, Colette (mez) 1985
ALLISTER, David (act) 1988
ALLOCCA, Lucia (act) 1976
ALLRED, Bill (mus) 1986
ALMEIDA ENSEMBLE 1988
ALMÉN, Irene (sop) 1986, 87
ALMERT, Marek (dan) 1986
ALNAR, Ayhan (sop) 1947
ALONSO, Alicia (dan, chor) 1950, 53, 79, 91
ALONSO, J.P. (dan) 1987
ALONSO, José Luis (dir) 1989
ALSTON, Richard (chor, des) 1983
ALTE OPER, Frankfurt 1987
ALTRICHTER, Petr (cond) 1990
ALUM, Manuel (chor, des) 1974
ALVA, Luigi (ten) 1957, 61, 71, 73, 74, 81, 82
ALVAREZ, Arnaldo (dan) 1978
ÁLVAREZ, Cristina (dan) 1979
ALVAREZ, Galina (dan) 1991
ALVAREZ, Vladimir (dan) 1991
ALVAREZ PAREJO, Juan Antonio (pf) 1990
ALVIN AILEY AMERICAN DANCE THEATER 1968
ALZAMIE, Carmela (dan) 1987
AMADE, Raymond (ten) 1954
AMADEUS QUARTET 1951, 52, 54, 56, 59, 61, 63, 66, 68, 70, 73, 75, 77, 78, 80
AMADEUS TRIO 1960
AMADOR, Juan José (sngr) 1989
AMAGATSU, Ushio (chor, dir, dan) 1982
AMALA (dan) 1956
AMARA, Lucine (sop) 1954
AMARANTE, Ruth (dan) 1995
AMATLLER, Xavier (act) 1989
AMAYA, Juana (dan) 1990
AMBASH, Elinor (dan) 1974
AMBLER, Scott (dan) 1992
AMBROSE, Paul (des) 1990
AMBROSINI, Jean-Claude (pf) 1972
AMELING, Elly (sop) 1968, 79
AMER, Nicholas (act) 1954, 67
AMERICAN BALLET THEATRE 1950, 53
AMERICAN BRASS QUINTET 1976
AMERICAN INDIAN DANCE THEATRE 1990
AMERICAN REPERTORY THEATRE 1982
AMFITHEATROFF, Massimo (vc) 1950
AMICI QUARTET 1959
AMIEL, Jon (dir) 1978
AMIS, Kingsley (spk) 1980
AMIT, Sheila (sop) 1965
AMNER, Richard (pf) 1982
AMODIO, Amedeo (chor, dan) 1988
AMODIO, Christina (dan) 1988
AMPHI-THEATRE 1981
AMY, Gilbert (cond) 1973
ANCA, Mircea (act) 1992
ANCHÓRIZ, Leo (des) 1958
ANDA, Géza (pf) 1955, 70
ANDERS, Derek (act) 1969, 85, 92
ANDERS, Peter (ten) 1950, 52
ANDERSEN, Finn (act) 1990
ANDERSEN, Jakob (dan) 1995
ANDERSEN, Marianne (sop) 1987

ANDERSON, Alexander (org) 1964
ANDERSON, Ande (dir) 1966
ANDERSON, Clinton (act) 1968
ANDERSON, David (pf) 1948, 49, 50
ANDERSON, Georgine (act) 1960
ANDERSON, Graeme (dan) 1963
ANDERSON, Hedli (sop) 1956
ANDERSON, Jacqueline (act) 1993
ANDERSON, Jean (act) 1967
ANDERSON, John (ob) 1981
ANDERSON, Judith (act) 1960, 63
ANDERSON, Lindsay (dir) 1983
ANDERSON, Lorna (sop) 1985, 87
ANDERSON, Miles (act) 1979
ANDERSON, Paul (fiddle) 1996
ANDERSON, Peter (act) 1988
ANDERSON, Robert (act) 1951
ANDERSON, Rona (act) 1950, 60
ANDERSON, Ruth (sngr) 1993
ANDERSSON, Bengt (dan) 1957
ANDERSSON, Gerd (dan) 1957
ANDERSSON, Laila (sop) 1974
ANDERSZEWSKI, Piotr (pf) 1994
ANDOR, Eva (sop) 1973
ANDRADE, Adolfo (chor, dan) 1959, 60
ANDRAE, Manfred (act) 1993
ANDRAŠEVIĆ, Stjepan (ten) 1962
ANDRÉ, Francis (des) 1962
ANDRÉ, Klaus (dir) 1988
ANDRÉ, Martin (cond) 1993, 94
ANDRÉ, Maurice (tpt) 1975
ANDREA, Rosaura de (sngr) 1989
ANDREAE, Hans (hpd) 1954
ANDRÉS, Elvira (dan) 1989
ANDREW, Iain (act) 1991
ANDREW, Milla (sop) 1979
ANDREWS, Harry (act) 1947
ANDRIANOVA, Maria (act) 1978
ANDRIEVSKY, Alexandra (pf) 1990
ANDSNES, Leif Ove (pf) 1989
ANGAS, Richard (bs) 1989
ANGELES, Victoria de los (sop) 1950, 51, 57, 58, 60, 71
ANGELL, Donna (act) 1980
ANGERVO, Heljä (mez) 1987
ANGLADA, Rafael (act) 1983
ANGLIN, Anne (act) 1988
ANGUS, David (cond) 1992
ANGUS, Jennifer (act) 1965
AÑIBARRO, José Roberto (act) 1983
ANISSIMOVA, Nina (chor) 1963
ANKERS, Kathleen (des) 1947
ANNALS, Michael (des) 1961, 63, 64, 74, 81
ANNEAR, Gwenyth (sop) 1965, 66
ANNEBRING, Göran (sngr) 1988
ANNICELLI, Corrado (act) 1976
ANNING, Linda (dan) 1977
ANNMO, Thomas (sngr) 1987, 88
ANOTA, Philippe (dan) 1987
ANRIEU, Paul (narr) 1962
ANSERMET, Ernest (cond) 1949, 54, 58
ANTHONY, Ignatius (act) 1992
ANTHONY, Trevor (bs) 1950, 61
ANTIPOV, Felix (act) 1989
ANTOLINOS, Manolita (sngr) 1989
ANTON, Jorge (ten) 1989
ANTONI, Carmen-Maja (act) 1984, 87
ANTONIO (dan, chor) 1950, 58
ANTONIO, José (chor, des, dan) 1989
ANTONIO, Juan (dan) 1982
ANTONIO AND HIS SPANISH BALLET COMPANY 1958
ANTONIO GADES BALLET, Spain 1982
ANTONIOZZI, Alfonso (b-bar) 1994
ANTONUTTI, Omero (act) 1965
ANTROBUS, Kate (dan) 1989
ANTROBUS, Yvonne (act) 1969
ANTTILA, Ann-Mari (des) 1988
AOYAMA, Hirokazu (act) 1988
AOYAMA, Mayuko (act) 1985
AOYAMA, Tatsumi (act) 1985, 88
APILANEZ, Blanca (act) 1989
APOLLO SOCIETY 1948, 58, 59
APPEL, Wolf (ten) 1972
APPLEBAUM, Louis (comp) 1956
APPLEGREN, Curt (bs) 1980
APPS, Edwin (act) 1952
APSION, Annabelle (act) 1988
ARAGALL, Giacomo (ten) 1965, 67
ARAIZA, Francisco (ten) 1978, 84
ARAMBURU, Karmele (act) 1986
ARASHI, Tokusaburo (act) 1985, 88
ARAÚJO, Loipa (dan) 1979, 91
ARAUZO, Stella (dan) 1982
ARCHAOS 1990, 91
ARCHER, Neill (ten) 1988
ARCHER, Robin (des) 1967, 70-73, 75-78
ARDEN, John (spk) 1963
ARDITTI, Carlos (des) 1994
ARDITTI QUARTET 1987
ARDIZZONE, Enrico (act) 1965
ARENBERG, Lee (act) 1989
ARENI, Nunzio (sngr) 1975
ARGENT, Edward (act) 1962
ARGENTA, Nancy (sop) 1986
ARGERICH, Martha (pf) 1966, 67, 69, 73, 85, 94
ARGUELLES, Arantxa (dan) 1991
ARIAS, Alfredo Rodriguez (dir) 1979, 88
ARIE, Raffaele (bs) 1969, 72, 74
ARIFUKU KAGURA TROUPE 1984
ARIOSTINI, Armando (bar) 1982
ARKHIPOV, Alexander (bar) 1990
ARKHIPOVA, Irina (mez) 1984, 87
ARLAUD, Philippe (light) 1985
ARMAND, Patrick (dan) 1986
ARMITAGE, Karole (chor, dan) 1979, 85
ARMOUR, William (act) 1973, 75, 93
ARMSTRONG, Alun (act) 1975
ARMSTRONG, Christopher (act) 1990
ARMSTRONG, Frankie (folk sngr) 1965
ARMSTRONG, Gareth (act) 1970
ARMSTRONG, George (ent) 1993
ARMSTRONG, Karan (sop) 1988
ARMSTRONG, Malcolm (act) 1974
ARMSTRONG, Richard (cond, spk) 1980, 92-96
ARMSTRONG, Sheila (sop) 1973, 75, 76, 78, 80, 91
ARMSTRONG, William (light) 1983
ARNAC, Béatrice (ent) 1969
ARNAUD, Philippe (light) 1984
ARNEIL, David (act) 1993
ARNELL, Richard (cond, comp) 1953
ARNICHAND, Véronique (dan) 1984
ARNOLD, Robert (act) 1959
ARNOLD SCHOENBERG CHOIR 1996
ARNST, Wolfgang (act) 1984
AROLDINGEN, Karin von (dan) 1967
AROMAA, Jukka (dan) 1987
AROMAA, Kirsi (dan) 1987
ARONOWITZ, Cecil (va) 1954, 56, 62, 63, 72, 73
ARPINI, Luigi (act) 1980
ARRAU, Claudio (pf) 1950, 54, 58, 60, 65, 67, 69, 80
ARREGUA, Josefina (sngr) 1985
ARRIAGA, Paco (gtr) 1989, 92
ARRINDELL, Clive (act) 1978
ARROYO, Martina (sop) 1974
ARS MUSICAE ENSEMBLE 1960
ARTENEVA, Ludmila (act) 1991
ARTHUR, Edna (vn) 1951, 75, 85, 86
ARTHUR, Edward (act) 1967
ARTHUR, Ian (act) 1986
ARTS FLORISSANTS, Les 1985
ARTUR, Claude (pf) 1966
ARVIDSSON, Lillemor (dan) 1974
ARVIN, Mark (dan) 1989
ARZILLI, Olga (va) 1988
ASAKAWA, Takako (dan) 1963
ASAKURA, Setsu (des) 1986, 87, 90, 91
ASAMUS, Frank (act) 1993
ASANO, Kazuyuki (act) 1987, 90
ASANTE, Christopher (act) 1975
ASHBOURNE, Caroline (act) 1981
ASHBRIDGE, Bryan (dan) 1954, 56
ASHBY, Clem (act) 1986
ASHCROFT, *Dame* Peggy (act, rdr) 1948, 58, 72, 80
ASHE, Rosemary (sop) 1981
ASHER, Jane (act) 1966
ASHERSON, Renée (act) 1947, 66
ASHKENAZY, Vladimir (cond, pf) 1971, 81, 88
ASHMOLE, David (dan) 1979
ASHMOLE, Silvia (sngr) 1960
ASHPOLE, Sarah (des) 1989
ASHTON, *Sir* Frederick (chor) 1948, 51, 52, 54, 55, 56, 60, 73, 75, 79
ASHTON, John (rdr) 1985
ASHTON, Lea (act) 1950, 63, 85
ASHWELL, Ariel (act) 1990
ASHWOOD, Denise (sop) 1980
ASHWORTH, Ashley (act) 1990
ASHWORTH, Dee (light) 1977
ASKER, Björn (bs) 1974
ASLANIDIS, Dorotea (act) 1970
ASMUS, Frank (act) 1993
ASPROUDIS, Elias (act) 1981
ASQUITH, Conrad (act) 1992
ASRIEL, Andre (comp) 1970
AST, Margarete (mez) 1956
ATERBALLETTO 1988
ATHENAEUM BRASS QUINTET 1991
ATHERTON, David (cond) 1968, 69, 72, 74
ATIENZA, Edward (act) 1967
ATKINS, Eileen (act) 1963, 85
ATKINS, James (bar) 1954, 55
ATKINS, Robert (act) 1961
ATKINS, Tom (act) 1971
ATKINSON, Barry (dan) 1992
ATKINSON, Lynton (ten) 1990
ATKINSON, Michael (act) 1966
ATKINSON, Rosalind (act) 1947, 57, 58, 61
ATLAS, Charles (des, light) 1985, 86
ATLAS, Consuela (dan) 1968
ATTFIELD, Helen (mez) 1973
AUBRÉE, Blanche (dan) 1962
AUBREY, Diane (act) 1961
AUBREY, James (act) 1972
AUBREY, Larry (act) 1969
AUDEN, W.H. (rdr) 1965
AUDEOUD, Susana (dan) 1960
AUDLEY, Maxine (act) 1961, 62
AUDSLEY, Alastair (act) 1962
AUENMÜLLER, Gabriele (sop) 1982
AUER, Rozita (dan) 1986
AUGÉR, Arleen (sop) 1989, 90
AUSENSI, Manuel (bs) 1958
AUSSEDAT, Pierre (act) 1994
AUSTIN, Clare (act) 1957
AUSTIN, Stephen (ten) 1989
AUSTRALIAN DANCE THEATRE 1980
AUSTRALIAN OPERA 1994
AUSTRALIAN YOUTH ORCHESTRA 1984
AVANTI 1995
AVEFA, Saio (act) 1987
AVILES, Arthur (dan) 1993, 95
AVOGARDO, Mauro (act) 1975
AX, Emanuel (pf) 1975, 80, 83, 86, 90
AXELSSON, Stefan (bar) 1987, 88
AYARS, Ann (sop) 1948
AYER, *Sir* Alfred (lect) 1983
AYR JUNIOR GAELIC CHOIR 1962, 63
AZARMI, Nassrin (sop) 1976
AZNAVOUR, Charles (sngr) 1967
AZOULAY, Veronique (sngr) 1985
AZUMA, Haruyo (dan) 1955
AZUMA, Tokuho (dan) 1955
AZUMA, Tomiko (dan) 1955
AZUMA, Yukiko (dan) 1955
AZUMA KABUKI DANCERS AND MUSICIANS 1955

BRZOZOWSKI, Stanislaw (act) 1966
BUBULAC, Ovidiu (des) 1971
BUCCARELLA, Lucio (db) 1969
BUCHAN, Cynthia (mez) 1979
BUCHAN, Sandra (act) 1970
BUCHAN,Tom (act) 1971
BUCHANAN, Graham (act) 1951
BUCHANAN, Isobel (sop) 1981, 83
BUCHANAN, Meg (act) 1954
BUCHANAN, Robert (act) 1952
BUCHANAN, Una (sop) 1977, 80, 81, 83
BUCHEGGER, Christine (act) 1986
BUCHSBAUM, Max (act) 1988
BUCHTA, Hubert (ten) 1958, 66
BUCK, David (act) 1962
BUCKLE, Richard (dir, lect) 1954, 61, 64, 79
BUCKMAN, Pamela (dan) 1980
BUDAPEST QUARTET 1950
BUDAPEST RAGTIME ORCHESTRA 1990
BUDD, Bruce (bs) 1975, 94
BUFFERY, Kate (act) 1992
BUGARINOVIĆ, Melanija (mez) 1962
BUICK, John (act) 1984, 87
BUJONES, Fernando (dan) 1977
BUKIN, Vladimir (bar) 1991
BULANDRA THEATRE, Bucharest 1971
BULBENA, Jordi (act) 1989
BULCA, Iona (act) 1992
BULL, Peter (act) 1957, 61
BULLER, Michael (rdr) 1991
BUNDSCHUH, Matthias (act) 1994
BUNDY, William (light) 1965
BUNNAGE, Avis (act) 1964
BUNNEY, Herrick (org, hpd, cond) 1949, 51, 54, 56, 58, 59, 61, 62, 64, 66, 67, 71, 88, 90, 91
BUNNING, Christine (sop) 1990, 93
BUNRAKU, National Puppet Theatre, Japan 1976
BUNTING, Heidi (dan) 1981
BUONINCONTRI, Bruno (des) 1996
BURBAGE, Robert (act) 1979
BURBRIDGE, Edward (des) 1968
BURBUTASHVILI, L. (act) 1979
BURCHFIELD, Robert 1980
BURCHINAL, Frederick (bar) 1983, 93
BUREYEV, S.K. (sngr) 1986
BURGE, Lucy (dan) 1983
BURGE, Stuart (dir) 1962, 64, 76
BURGESS, Anthony (spk) 1980
BURGESS, Christian (act) 1979
BURGESS, Christopher (act) 1959
BURGESS, John (act, dir) 1980, 89
BURGESS, John (bp) 1954, 56
BURGRAEVE, Jacques (act) 1985
BURKE, Alfred (act) 1970
BURKE, David (act) 1969, 70, 76, 80
BURKE, Georgia (act) 1965
BURKE, Kenneth (dan) 1977
BURKE, Patricia (act) 1947, 50
BURKE, Patrick (act) 1976
BURKE, Traugott (act) 1977
BURKHARD, Ursula (fl) 1954
BURNE, Gary (dan) 1956, 60
BURNELL, Nick (des) 1992
BURNHAM, Edward (dir) 1956
BURNS, Louise (dan) 1979
BURNS, Nica (dir) 1990
BURNSIDE, Iain (pf) 1992, 95
BURRA, Edward (des) 1948, 51
BURRELL, John (dir) 1947
BURRELL, Michael (dir) 1985
BURRELL, Sheila (act) 1974
BURRETT, Alan (light) 1993
BURRIDGE, Geoffrey (act) 1975
BURRIDGE, Phoebe (act) 1992
BURROUGHS, William 1962
BURROWS, Juliet (dan) 1994, 95
BURROWS, Stuart (ten) 1978
BURTON, Humphrey (spk) 1981
BURTON, Miriam (act) 1967
BURTON, Richard (act) 1953
BURWICK, Peter, (cond) 1984
BURY, John (des) 1964, 84
BUSCEMI, Steve (act) 1986
BUSCH, Adolf (vn) 1949
BUSCH, Fritz (cond) 1950, 51
BUSCH QUARTET 1949
BUSSE, Sylta (des) 1972, 84
BUSSON, René (act) 1947
BUSTABAD, Raúl (dan) 1979
BUTCHER, Veronica (dan) 1977, 80
BUTHION, Hubert (act) 1947
BUTLER, Antoinette (lect) 1994
BUTLER, Charlotte (dan) 1991
BUTLER, Kate (mez) 1985
BUTLER, Richard (act) 1976
BUTLIN, Roger (des) 1979
BUTLIN, Ron (spk) 1980
BUTOR, Michel (spk) 1962
BUTTCHEREIT, Heinrich (act) 1987
BUTTERWORTH, Sandra (act) 1992
BUTTON, Jeanne (des) 1967
BYATT, Andrew (act) 1973
BYRE THEATRE 1992
BYRNE, Elizabeth (sop) 1996
BYRNE, Gerard (act) 1995
BYRNE, John (des) 1974
BYRNE, John (spk) 1980
BYRNE, Patsy (act) 1962
BYRON, John (act) 1967, 70
BYUNG-WOO, Son (dan) 1990

CABALLE, Montserrat (sop) 1989, 90
CABALLERO, José (des) 1958
CABAN, František (bar) 1990
CABARET RIVE GAUCHE 1969
CABAYO, Ena (act) 1975
CABORT, Joop (light) 1985
CABOT, Christopher (act) 1967, 68
CABRAL, Pedro Caldeira (gtr, lect) 1995
CABRERA, Aymara (dan) 1991
CACHEMAILLE, Gilles (bar) 1993
CACOYANNIS, Michael (dir) 1974
CADELL, Jean (act) 1949
CADENAS, Covadonga (act) 1983
CADIEUX, Anne-Marie (act) 1994
ČADIKOVIČOVÁ, Milada (sngr) 1964
CADONI, Fernanda (mez) 1953, 54, 55
CADZOW, Joan (dan) 1976
CADZOW, Juliet (act) 1984, 85, 91
CAGIGAL, Carmen (act) 1986
CAHILL, Teresa (sop) 1969
CAIG, Alan (act) 1994
CAIN, William (act) 1968
CAIRNCROSS, James (act, rdr) 1949-53, 61, 67, 73-75, 79, 86-89, 91
CAIRNEY, John (act) 1953, 59, 62, 70, 73, 87
CAIRNS, Christine (mez) 1980, 85-86, 89
CAITI, Orazio (dan) 1988
ČAKAREVIĆ, Djurdjevka (cont) 1962
CALA, Rosario (dan) 1989, 92
CALABRESE, Franco (bs) 1957
CALABRO, Suzanne (sop) 1978
CALANNI, Giuseppe (dan) 1988
CALDER, David (act) 1968, 69
CALDER, John (dir, narr) 1962, 84, 90
CALDER-MARSHALL, Anna (act) 1968, 69, 70, 76
CALDICOTT, Margery (act) 1957
CALDUCH, Ramon (mus) 1989
CALEY, Thomas (dan) 1994
CALHOUN, Charles (dan) 1990
CALLAS, Maria (sop) 1957
CALLENDER, Antonio (drums) 1967
CALLOW, Simon (act) 1973
CALVET QUARTET 1947
CALVIN, Adelaida (dan) 1989
CALVO, Pilar (dan) 1953
CAMACHO, Leu (act) 1965
CAMARINHA, Domingos Augusto (gtr) 1962
CAMBLE, Alwyne (des) 1958
CAMBRIDGE UNIVERSITY MADRIGAL SINGERS 1953
CAMDEN, Archie (bn) 1948, 63
CAMERATA ACADEMICA, Salzburg 1995
CAMERATA LYSY, Gstaad 1981
CAMERI THEATRE, Tel Aviv 1987
CAMERON, Angus (fiddle) 1969
CAMERON, Calum (sngr) 1962
CAMERON, Doreen (act) 1975, 79
CAMERON, John (bar) 1953, 59, 68
CAMERON, Matthew (des) 1968
CAMILLO, Christine (dan) 1985, 91
CAMPAN, Zanie (act) 1953
CAMPBELL, David (story-teller, lect) 1993
CAMPBELL, Donald (spk) 1980
CAMPBELL, Douglas (act) 1948-50, 56
CAMPBELL, Evelyn (sngr) 1947, 48, 61, 62, 63, 65, 66, 69
CAMPBELL, *Prof.* Ian (lect) 1993
CAMPBELL, James (sngr) 1947, 56
CAMPBELL, Jean (pf) 1961
CAMPBELL, Judy (act) 1968
CAMPBELL, Kenna (sngr) 1961, 62, 66
CAMPBELL, Richard (sngr) 1989
CAMPBELL, Stancil (des) 1988
CAMPBELL, *Dr* Stuart (lect) 1995
CAMPBELL-MOORE, Roy (dan) 1977, 80
CAMPBELTOWN GAELIC CHOIR 1948, 54
CAMPI, Enrico (bs) 1963, 72
CAMPION, Sean (act) 1995
CAMPISI, Gaetano (act) 1970
CAMPOLI, Alfredo (vn) 1956
CANADIAN BRASS 1980
CANADIAN OPERA COMPANY 1993
CANADIAN STAGE COMPANY 1988
CANALES, Antonio (dan) 1990
CANCELA, José Luis (sngr) 1989
CANE, Jenny (light) 1991
ČANGALOVIĆ, Miroslav (bs) 1962
CANINO, Bruno (pf) 1969, 73, 75, 79
CANIPAROLI, Val (dan) 1981
CANNAN, Phyllis (sop) 1971, 90
CANNING, Robert (dan) 1980
CANNISTRA, Arturo (dan) 1988
CANO, Antonio (dan) 1962
CANTELLI, Guido (cond) 1950, 54, 55
CANTELO, April (sop) 1949, 50, 52, 64, 65, 68, 69
CANTILENA 1975
CANTOR, Philippe (bar) 1985
CANTORES DE MADRID 1958
CAPANO, Ciro (act) 1988
CAPECCHI, Renato (bar) 1963, 65, 69, 71
CAPITANO, Francesco (act) 1975
CAPLAN, Elliot (des) 1994
CAPLAT, Moran (spk) 1953
CAPPELLA NOVA 1992, 93
CAPPELLA SINGERS 1976
CAPPELLETTI, Andrea (vn) 1988
CAPPUCCILLI, Piero (bar) 1963
CAPPUCCIO, Emilio (act) 1965
CAPRICORN 1981
CAPUANO, Patrizia (act) 1988
CAPULETTI (des) 1957
CARAGIU, Toma (act) 1971
CARALLO, Antonio (dan) 1995
CARAMITRU, Ion (act) 1971
CARBY, Fanny (act) 1964
CARCANO, Emilio (des) 1979
CARCANO, Gianfilippo (act) 1975
CARD, June (sop) 1978
CARDIN, Pierre (des) 1961
CARDUS, Anita (dan) 1963
CAREWE, John (cond) 1960, 61
CAREY, Brian (dir, act) 1956-59, 60, 65
CAREY, Christine (des) 1986
CAREY, Denis (dir) 1957
CAREY, Geoffrey (act) 1994
CAREY, Judith (act) 1965
CARIDES, Zoe (act) 1990

CARIGNON, Christian (dan) 1990
CARIN, Victor (act, dir) 1962, 63, 64, 65
CARLEHED, Ingemar (act) 1974
CARLILE, Bob (act) 1974
CARLIN, Joanna (act) 1975
CARLIN, John (act) 1959
CARLIN, Mario (ten) 1960
CARLSON, Lenus (bar) 1975, 78
CARLSSON, Sonja (des) 1958
CARLTON, Timothy (act) 1975
CARLYLE, Joan (sop) 1961
CARMEN, Joseph (act) 1985
CARMENTATES, Alena (dan) 1991
CARMICHAEL, Alexander (sngr) 1948, 49, 51
CARMICHAEL, Ian A. (sngr) 1964
CARMICHAEL, Peter (fiddler) 1965
CARMINA QUARTET 1993
CARMON, Joseph (act) 1987
CAROLAN, John (ten) 1953, 54, 55
CAROLAN, Lucy (hpd) 1986
CARON, Leslie (dan) 1949
CARON, Sandra (act) 1969
CAROSI, Mauro (des) 1988
CARPI, Fiorenzo (comp) 1956
CARPIO, Adoracion (dan) 1989
CARR, Aileen (folk sngr) 1995
CARR, Maureen (act) 1986, 90
CARR, Nicholas (cond) 1983
CARR, Robert (act) 1990, 92
CARR, Walter (act) 1957-63, 73, 84, 85, 90, 93
CARRANCO, Clara (dan) 1979
CARRANZA, Fernando (gtr) 1977
CARRARO, Tino (act) 1956
CARRASCO, Antonio (act) 1986, 89
CARREÑO, Lázaro (dan) 1979, 91
CARRERAS, José (ten) 1982
CARRERE, Anne (act) 1957
CARRIÉ, Marie-Claire (dan) 1962
CARROL, Jean (act, sngr) 1948, 49, 51
CARROLL, Christina (sop) 1948
CARRON, Elisabeth (sop) 1984
CARRUCCIU, Anna Lughia (des) 1982
CARSON, David (act) 1968
CARSON, Heather (light) 1993
CARTER, Alan (chor, des) 1958
CARTER, Jack (chor) 1977
CARTER, Laurence (act) 1967
CARTER, Mary (vn) 1947, 49
CARTER TRIO 1947, 48, 53
CARTERI, Rosanna (sop) 1957
CARTIER, Jean-Albert 1982
CARTIER, Yvonne (dan) 1958
CARTURAN, Gabriella (mez) 1957
CARTWRIGHT, Bill (act) 1960
CARTWRIGHT, Percy (act) 1949, 57
CARTY, Frances (dan) 1983
CARUBBI, Luigi (act) 1965
CASA, Lisa della (sop) 1952
CASADESUS, Robert (pf) 1947, 50-51, 56
CASADO, Germinal (des, dan) 1962
CASALES, Felix (act) 1989
CASANOVA, Montserrat (des) 1986
CASARIEGO, Lola (mez) 1989
CASE, Geoffrey (act) 1968
CASE, John Carol (bar) 1972
CASEY, Al 1987
CASH, Jessica (sop) 1968
CASONI, Bianca-Maria (mez) 1961
CASPAR, Horst (act) 1949
CASSADÓ, Gaspar (vc) 1958
CASSIDY, John (light) 1992
CASSILLY, Richard (ten) 1968
CASSON, Bronwen (des) 1989
CASSON, John (dir) 1950
CASSON, Lewis (act) 1950, 51, 52
CASTALIAN BAND 1994
CASTEJÓN, Jesus (sngr) 1985
CASTEJÓN, Nuria (dan) 1989
CASTEJÓN, Rafael (sngr) 1989
CASTELLANO, Franco (act) 1982
CASTLE, John (act) 1970
CASTRO MOTA, Guilermino Antonio de (gtr) 1962
CATALA, Montserrat (act) 1989
CATAPANO, Luciano (sngr) 1988
CATER, John (act) 1968
CATHERINE MURRAY'S WAULKING TEAM 1980
CATTAND, Gabriel (act) 1948, 57
CAUCHETIER, Patrice (des) 1985
CAUNTER, Nicholas (act) 1992
CAUSLEY, Charles (rdr) 1965, 71
CAUX, Robert (act, comp) 1994, 96
CAVALLARO, Nicholas J. (des) 1990
CAVALLIER, Nicolas (sngr) 1993
CAVANAGH, Anne Marie (act) 1991
CAVAZOS, Bree (act) 1968
CAVE, Desmond (act) 1974
CAVELL, Dallas (act) 1960
CAVELLERO, Jacky (db) 1971
CAZALET, Peter (chor, dan, des) 1958, 61, 77, 80
CECCATO, Aldo (cond) 1969
CECCHETTI, Enrico (chor) 1948
CECCHI, Nana (des) 1982
CELA, José Sánchez (sngr) 1989
CELADA, Raoul (dan) 1950
CELATA, Andrea (des) 1988
CELE, Thami (act) 1986
CELENTANO, Alessandra (dan) 1988
CELLIER, Peter (act) 1958, 63
CELLINI, Renato (cond) 1947
CEMORE, Alan (bar) 1987
CENSI, Francesco (act) 1970
CENTRAL PUPPET THEATRE, Sofia 1969
CENTRE DRAMATIQUE NATIONAL ORLEANS-LOIRET-CENTRE 1994
CERCEL, Florina (act) 1992
CEREZO, Conchita (dan) 1989
CERNOVITCH, Nikola (light) 1967, 68
CERUTTI, Fabienne (dan) 1984
CERVENA, Sona (mez) 1966, 67, 70, 78
CERVENKA, Jan (pf) 1958
CHACON, Maite (act) 1986
CHACON, Maria Jose (act) 1986
CHADBON, Tom (act) 1993
CHADFIELD, Angela (act) 1972, 93
CHADWELL, Tracey (sop) 1987
CHAGRIN, Claude (des) 1964
CHAGRIN, Julian (ent) 1964
CHAGRIN, Nicholas (act) 1961, 66
CHAILLY, Riccardo (cond) 1979, 81, 92
CHAKRAVARTY, Kamala (tambura) 1971
CHALLENOR, Carla (act) 1969
CHALLIS, John (act) 1981
CHALMERS, Norman (act) 1990
CHAMARAT, Georges (act) 1954
CHAMBER GROUP OF SCOTLAND 1993, 95
CHAMBER ORCHESTRA OF EUROPE 1983, 86
CHAMBER ORCHESTRA OF EUROPE Wind Soloists 1995
CHAMBORD, Simone (act) 1951
CHANA, La (dan) 1990
CHANCE, Michael (c ten) 1994, 96
CHANDOS, John (act) 1963
CHANEY, Stewart (des) 1953
CHANG, Lienz (dan) 1991
CHANNON, Paul (spk) 1982
CHANNON, Waldo (vc) 1949
CHANONAT, Jean-Luc (light) 1995
CHAOIMH, Bairbre Ní (act) 1989
CHAPMAN, Derek (act) 1989
CHAPMAN, Paul (act) 1966
CHAPPELL, William (des) 1948, 51, 52, 79
CHAPUIS, Pierre-Alain (act) 1994
CHARBA, Mari-Claire (act) 1967
CHARD, Geoffrey (bar) 1968
CHARLES, Christine (dan) 1994
CHARLES, Joseph (act) 1970
CHARLESON, Ian (act) 1972, 73, 86
CHARNOCK, Helen (sop) 1988
CHARON, Jacques (act) 1954
CHARPENTIER, Adeline (dan) 1987
CHARRAT, Janine (chor) 1949, 59, 62
CHARUP, Remy (des) 1981
CHASE, Lucia (dan) 1950
CHASE, Ronald (des) 1983
CHATER, Geoffrey (act) 1954
CHATFIELD, Philip (dan) 1951, 54, 56
CHAUDHARI, Reva (dan) 1960
CHAUMEAU, André (act) 1970
CHAUMETTE, Monique (act) 1953
CHAUSSAT, Geneviève (dan) 1976
CHAUVERON, Andrée de (act) 1954
CHAVCHAVADZE, M.E. (act) 1979
CHAVDA, Hasmukh (dan) 1960
CHAZALETTES, Giulio (act) 1956
CHAZEAU, Didier (dan) 1987
CHEATHAM, Doc (mus) 1988
CHEECHOO, Shirley (act) 1988
CHELOVALNIK, Evgenia (sop) 1991
CHELTON, Nick (light) 1976, 79, 80, 89, 95
CHÉREAU, Patrice (dir, act) 1995
CHEREDNIKOVA, Irina (des) 1995
CHERKASOVA, T.G. (sngr) 1986
CHERKASSKY, Shura (pf) 1972, 83
CHERNOBA, Galina (sop) 1990
CHERNOZUKOV, Mikhail (sngr) 1991
CHERNYKH, Pavel (bar) 1991
CHERRELL, Gwen (act) 1954
CHESEAUD, Monique (des) 1957
CHESHIRE, Mandy (act) 1991
CHESTER, Richard (fl) 1978
CHETWYN, Robert (dir) 1966
CHEVALIER, Françoise (des) 1981
CHIARAPPA, Carlo (vn) 1982
CHIARI, Mario (des) 1982
CHIBBETT, Michael (hpd) 1981, 85
CHICAGO SYMPHONY ORCHESTRA 1971, 78
CHICHESTER FESTIVAL THEATRE 1963
CHICO-BONET, Francesch (sngr) 1978
CHIESA, Norberto (des) 1981
CHIHUAHUAS 1990
CHIJINKAI THEATRE COMPANY, Japan 1990
CHILCOTT, Susan (sop) 1994, 95
CHILDREN'S MUSIC THEATRE *See* National Youth Music Theatre
CHILDS, Lucinda (chor, dan, lect) 1994
CHILINGIRIAN QUARTET 1977
CHILTON, Mary (act) 1981
CHINCHALADZE, N. (act) 1979
CHINESE MAGICAL CIRCUS 1986
CHING, James (pf) 1954
CHINNERY, Dennis (act) 1958
CHISHOLM, George (mus) 1988
CHISHOLM, Jimmy (act) 1983, 92
CHISWICK, Jeffrey (act) 1980
CHITTY, Alison (des) 1989
CHIUMMO, Umberto (bs) 1995
CHKHAIDZE, R. (act) 1979
CHKHEIDZE, L. (act) 1979
CHKHIKVADZE, D. (act) 1979
CHKHIKVADZE, R. (act) 1979
CHMIELEWSKI, Tadeusz (pf) 1976
CHOËL, Bruno (act) 1981
CHOEURS DE LA RADIODIFFUSION FRANÇAISE 1964
CHOI, Mija (act) 1989
CHOILEAIN, Aedin Ní (?) 1967
CHOJNACKA, Elisabeth (hpd) 1994
CHOLEWA, Bogdan (dan) 1986
CHONSHVILY, Sergei (act) 1991
CHORAB, Andrzej (dan) 1991
CHOZAM, Sedhar (act) 1990
CHRISTA, Gabri (dan) 1995
CHRISTE, Nils (dan) 1970
CHRISTENSEN, Lew (chor) 1981
CHRISTIANS, Heide (sop) 1983

CHRISTIE, Bob (mus) 1980
CHRISTIE, George (spk) 1982
CHRISTIE, Gordon (ten) 1980, 82
CHRISTIE, Madeleine (act) 1950-52, 53, 55
CHRISTIE, Nan (sop) 1977, 78
CHRISTIE, Robert (act) 1956
CHRISTIE, Simon (rdr) 1987
CHRISTIE, William (cond) 1985
CHRISTOFF, Boris (bs) 1961
CHRISTOPH, Rudolph (act) 1970
CHRISTOU, Francis (cl, bas hn) 1971, 78
CHU XIANG (act) 1987
CHUCOVA, Ena (act) 1991
CHUDAKOV, Evgeny (act) 1987
CHUKHONTSEV, Oleg (rdr) 1987
CHUNG, Kyung-Wha (vn) 1975, 81, 82
CHURCH, Esmé (act) 1954
CHURCH, Geoffrey (act) 1992
CHURCH, Tony (rdr) 1979
CHURCHILL, Diana (act) 1966
CHYBOWSKI, Michael (light) 1993, 95, 96
CIAPPARA, Jean-Claude (dan) 1985
CICERI, Leo (act) 1957
ČICORT, Constantin (act) 1991
ČIERNIKOVÁ, Irina (dan) 1990
CIEŚLAK, Ryszard (act) 1968
CIFUENTES, Horacio (dan) 1981
CIHAROVA, Eva (act) 1984
CILLER, Jozef (des) 1991
CILLEROVA, Maria (des) 1991
CIOABA, Mirela (act) 1991
CIONI, Renato (ten) 1963, 69
CIONTEA, Ana (act) 1992
CIORANU, Aurel (act) 1971
CIRILLO, Attilia (act) 1988
CISNEROS, Evelyn (dan) 1981
CITIZENS' THEATRE, Glasgow 1950-53, 59, 60, 68, 72, 79, 83, 93, 95
CITO, Marion (des) 1995
CITY OF BIRMINGHAM SYMPHONY ORCHESTRA 1960, 83, 84, 89
CITY OF LONDON SINFONIA 1989, 90
CIULEI, Liviu (des) 1971
CIVIL, Alan (hn) 1961
CIZOVA, Emilia (act) 1991
CLABASSI, Plinio (bs) 1969
CLAIRE, Jennifer (act) 1965
CLAIRE, Stella (dan) 1952
CLAIRY, Paul (act) 1985
CLAM, Leopold (bs) 1975
CLANCY, Deirdre (des) 1973, 75, 79
CLAPPERTON, James (pf) 1985
CLARE, Maurice (vn) 1948, 51
CLARE, Robert (act) 1988
CLARK, Bruce 1952
CLARK, Ernest (act) 1949, 52
CLARK, Foster (cond) 1957
CLARK, Graham (ten) 1976, 83
CLARK, James (con, vn) 1992, 93
CLARK, Jameson (sngr) 1956
CLARK, Michael (chor,dan,des) 1985, 86, 88
CLARK, Ruth (act) 1953
CLARK, Wynne (act) 1970
CLARKE, Elisabeth (dan) 1978
CLARKE, Harold (fl) 1949
CLARKE, Kathy-Kiera (act) 1994
CLARKE, Martha (dir) 1989
CLARKE, Oz (act) 1978
CLARKE, Paul Charles (ten) 1992, 93, 94
CLARKE, Raymond (act) 1963
CLARKSON, Joan (mez) 1971
CLARY, Martine (dan) 1985
CLAS, Johanna (act) 1970
CLASIS, Charlotte (act) 1955
CLASON, Charlotte (des) 1989
CLASON, Mathias (des) 1987
CLAUDE, Ferna (act) 1960
CLAUSEN, Andrea (act) 1994
CLAVÉ, Antoni (des) 1960, 71
CLAVEY, George J. (sngr) 1962, 63-65
CLAVIER, Josette (dan) 1959
CLAY, Nicholas (act) 1969
CLAY, Peter (act) 1970
CLAYBURGH, Jim (act, des) 1986
CLAYDEN, Pauline (dan) 1947, 48, 51, 54
CLAYTON, Peter (spk) 1990
CLEGG, Peter (dan) 1954, 56
CLEGHORN, Bill (light) 1986
CLEMENT, Alain (dan) 1991
CLÉMENT, Willy (bar) 1951
CLEMENTE, Francesco (des) 1996
CLERMONT, René (act) 1951
CLERVANNE, Madeleine (act) 1955
CLEVA, Fausto (cond) 1959
CLEVELAND ORCHESTRA 1967, 94, 96
CLEVELAND QUARTET 1977, 82, 85
CLEVELAND SAN JOSE BALLET 1990
CLEVER, Edith (act) 1992
CLEVERDON, Douglas (dir) 1956
CLIFFORD, Derek (dan) 1995
CLIFFORD, Timothy (lect) 1996
CLIMENT, Joaquin (act) 1989
CLOEZ, Gustave (cond) 1950, 57
CLOISTER SINGERS OF ST ANDREWS 1949
CLOSE THEATRE CLUB 1967
CLOUGH, Peter (act) 1971
CLOUX, Christine (dan) 1987
CLUNES, Alec (act) 1950
CLURMAN, Harold (spk) 1963
CLUYTENS, André (cond) 1949
COATES, Edith (cont) 1963
COATES, Leon (lect) 1994
COBB, John (act) 1984
COBOS, Antonia (chor) 1957
COBURN, Brian (act) 1966
COBURN, Mary-Anne (act) 1983
COBURN, Pamela (sop) 1985
COCHRAN, William (ten) 1978, 92
COCTEAU, Jean (dir, des) 1949, 60
CODA, Frank (act) 1964
CODLING, Teresa (act) 1981
COE, Tony (cl) 1971
COFFEY, Denise (act) 1967, 71-72, 85-86
COHAN, Robert (chor, dan) 1963, 81
COHEN, Shura (des) 1983
COHN, Ruby (spk) 1984
COIA, Gino (act) 1958, 60
COKER, Paul (pf) 1981, 85, 87
COKORINOS, Philip (sngr) 1985
COLAN, Ion (act) 1991
COLE, George (act) 1965
COLE, Michael (dan) 1994
COLE, Stephanie (dan) 1987
COLE, Vinson (ten) 1990
COLEMAN, Amy (dan) 1989
COLEMAN, Basil (dir) 1962
COLEMAN, Noel (act) 1964
COLEMAN, Tony (act) 1987
COLEMAN, Violet (act) 1948
COLERIDGE, Sylvia (act) 1960, 61
COLETTI, Paul (va) 1981, 88
COLIN, André (des) 1988
COLLARD, Jean-Philippe (pf) 1979, 85
COLLARD-GENTLE, Sally (dan) 1977, 80, 85
COLLEDGE, Alistair (act) 1960
COLLEGIUM MUSICUM, Zürich 1954
COLLIER, Marie (sop) 1962
COLLIER, Sarah (act) 1979
COLLIN, Jacques (des) 1996
COLLINS, Alan (act) 1964
COLLINS, Anne (cont) 1978, 85, 92
COLLINS, Brian (des) 1968, 85, 88
COLLINS, Elaine (act) 1979
COLLINS, Jonathan (act) 1961
COLLINS, Karl (act) 1992
COLLINS, Kevin (act) 1970
COLLINS, Lewis (act) 1972
COLLINS, Michael (dir, cl) 1993
COLLINS, Paul (vn) 1953
COLLINSON, Francis (arr) 1956
COLLIS, David (des) 1971
COLMANT, Alexandra (sngr) 1981
COLOGNE OPERA 1980, 81
COLOGNE OPERA STUDIO 1981
COLOGNE RADIO CHORUS 1995
COLOMBAIONI, Carlo *and* Alberto 1976, 83
COLOMBO, Scipio (bar) 1969
COLOME, Montserrat (act) 1989
COLONNA, Robert (act) 1968
COLONNELLO, Attilio (des) 1963
COLORETTI, Claudio (light) 1996
COLTELLACCI, Giulio (des) 1972
COLWASH, Lavina (dan) 1990
COMBINE, The 1970
COMBOY, Ian (bs) 1977
COMEDIANTS, Els 1989
COMÉDIE FRANÇAISE 1954
COMMICHAU, Jürgen (bar) 1982
COMMUNICADO THEATRE COMPANY 1990
COMPAGNIA DEI PUPI SICILIANI DI NINO CUTICCHIO 1988
COMPAGNIA MARIONETTISTICI CARLO COLLA 1982
COMPAGNIE DE MIME MARCEL MARCEAU 1953
COMPAGNIE DE THÉÂTRE DU CENTRE NATIONAL DES ARTS, Ottawa 1980
COMPAGNIE EDWIGE FEUILLÈRE 1955
COMPAGNIE JÉRÔME DESCHAMPS 1988, 89, 95
COMPAGNIE JOUVET DE THÉATRE DE L'ATHÉNÉE 1947
COMPAGNIE PHILIPPE GENTY 1990, 91
COMPAGNIE RENAUD-BARRAULT 1948, 57, 85
COMPAGNIE ROGER PLANCHON 1960
COMPAÑIA DE JOSÉ LUIS GOMEZ, Spain 1986
COMPAÑIA DE NURIA ESPERT 1983, 86
COMPAÑIA NACIONAL TEATRO CLASICO, Madrid 1989
COMPET, Fabienne (dan) 1985
COMPTE, Elizabeth Le (act) 1974, 86
COMPTON, Fay (act) 1953
COMSUDI, Elaine (dan) 1967
CONCERTGEBOUW ORCHESTRA *See* Royal Concertgebouw Orchestra
CONCERTGEBOUW WIND QUINTET 1961
CONCERTO CALEDONIA 1992
CONCERTO ITALIANO 1996
CONCORD ALL STARS 1988
'La CONEJA', María (sngr) 1989
CONKLIN, John (des) 1983
CONLON, James (cond) 1982, 88, 90
CONN, Stewart (spk) 1992
CONNECTICUT GRAND OPERA 1985
CONNELL, Elizabeth (sop) 1986
CONNELL, Karyn (dan) 1990
CONNERY, Leone (act) 1986
CONNERY, Sean (act) 1986
CONNOR, Edric (act) 1961
CONNOR, Kenneth (act) 1947
CONNOR, Patrick (act) 1979
CONOLEY, Anne (sop) 1973
CONOLEY, Terence (act) 1952, 53
CONRAD, Johannes (act) 1987
CONSONNI, Raoul (act) 1956
CONSORT OF MUSICKE 1975, 81
CONSTABLE, John (pf, hpd) 1984, 86, 89
CONSTABLE, Paule (light) 1996
CONSTANTIN, Anatol (act) 1983
CONSTANTIN, Costel (act) 1992
CONSTANTIN, Rudolf (bar) 1970
CONSTANTIN, Tatiana (act) 1992
CONSTANTINE, Hélène (dan) 1949
CONTI, Tom (act) 1962
CONTRADE DI CORI 1979

CONVIVIUM MUSICUM 1957
CONWAY, Jeremy (act) 1964
CONWAY, William (vc) 1986
COOK, David Allan (dan) 1990
COOK, Deborah (sop) 1978
COOK, Kate (act) 1986
COOK, Peter (ent) 1960
COOKE, Alistair (rdr) 1980, 83
COOKE, Vanessa (act) 1975, 86
COOKSON, Barrie (act) 1992
COOKSON, Brian (ten) 1994
COOKSON, Michael (va) 1982
COOPER, Douglas (exh dir) 1955, 57, 61
COOPER, Elizabeth (pf) 1991
COOPER, George (act) 1964
COOPER, Imogen (pf) 1985
COOPER, Joseph (pf) 1957
COOPER, Risteard (act) 1989
COOPER, Rowena (act) 1959, 64
COOPERATIVA TEATROMUSICA, Rome 1982
COOPERATIVA TUSCOLANO 1975
COOREMAN, A'leen (act) 1988
COPELAND, Darryl (chor) 1987
COPELAND, James (act) 1951
COPLEY, Peter (act) 1947, 50
COPPEN, Hazel (act) 1967
COPPIN, Tyler (sngr) 1994
COQ, Pierre Le (act) 1955
CORALLI, Jean (chor) 1950, 57, 59, 79, 91
CORBELLI, Alessandro (bar) 1982, 93-95
CORBETT, Geoffrey (cond) 1947
CORBETT, Harry H. (act) 1957
CORBETT, Tony (light) 1968
CORDA, Walter (sngr) 1988
CORDING, Alastair (lect) 1995
CORDING, John (act) 1969, 73, 78
CORDOBA, Faiquillo de (dan) 1977
CORDOVA, Richard (cond) 1990
CORDUNER, Allan (act) 1976
CORENA, Fernando (bs) 1955, 57, 61, 63
CORMACK, George (act) 1962, 65, 66
CORNEJO, Juan Gomez (light) 1989
CORNELL, Gwynn (cont) 1972
CORNFIELD, Ellen (dan) 1979
CORNWELL, Eric (light) 1994
CORRADI, Gian Paolo (ten) 1972
CORRAL, Santiago del (des) 1988
CORRALES, Jesús (dan) 1991
CORRIES, The 1971
CORRY, Graham (act) 1963
CORSARO, Frank (dir) 1983
CORSETTI, Giorgio Barberio (des) 1994
CORTÉS, Hiniesta (dan) 1992
CORTES, Joaquin (dan) 1989
CORTES, Teresa (act) 1986
CORTIZO, Fernando (dan) 1978
CORTOT, Alfred (pf) 1948
CORVI, Luigi (sngr) 1989
COSENTINO, Marie-Helene (dan) 1988
COSSINS, James (act) 1964, 68
COSSOTTO, Fiorenza (mez) 1957, 60, 74
COSTA, José Luis Nobre (gtr) 1995
COSTA, Michael da (act) 1970
COSTELLO, Kevin (act) 1974
COSTELLO, Matthew (act) 1986, 90
COSTELLO, Tom (act) 1971
COSTER, Janet (mez) 1961
COSULICH, Guido 1972
COTEAU, Denis de (cond) 1981
COTESCU, Octavian (act) 1971
COTRUBAS, Ileana (sop) 1975, 78, 82, 83
COTTER, Sean (act) 1962
COTTRELL, Richard (dir) 1967, 69, 72, 79
COULETTE, Yvonne (act) 1952, 57
COULOURIS, George (act) 1949
COULSON, Sidney (act) 1967
COURAUD, Marcel (cond) 1960
COURTENAY, Margaret (act) 1954
COURTENAY, Tom (act) 1960, 68
COURTNEY, Barbara (act) 1971, 72
COURTNEY, Nigel (dan) 1981
COUSINS, Michael (ten) 1976
COUSSONNEAU (act) 1953
COUSTE, Raymond (gtr) 1979
COUTU, Jean (act) 1956
COVENT GARDEN OPERA *See* Royal Opera, Covent Garden
COWAN, Brian (act) 1992
COWAN, Francis 1986
COWAN, Ian (act) 1959
COWAN, Lucy (fiddle) 1996
COWIE, Douglas (sngr) 1980
COWNIE, Tony (act) 1990, 95
COX, Arthur (act) 1967, 70
COX, Brian (act) 1966, 68, 69
COX, Edward (dan) 1995
COX, John (dir) 1969, 71, 82
COX, Michael Graham (act) 1971
COX, Nicholas (cl) 1986
COX, Philip (bs) 1981
COXON, Edmund (vn) 1990
COXON, Richard (ten) 1993, 94, 95
COYOC, Josie (dan) 1995
COZRY, Margaret (act) 1988
CRACCO, Alberto (act) 1975
CRACOW PHILHARMONIC CHORUS 1972
CRACOW PHILHARMONIC ORCHESTRA 1972
CRAGUN, Richard (dan) 1963
CRAIG, Charles (ten) 1964, 71
CRAIG, Douglas (bar) 1950
CRAIG, Hugh (dan) 1983
CRAIG, Peter (act) 1967
CRAMER, Francine (dan) 1962
CRAMER, Heinz (bs) 1958, 66
CRAMER, Ivo (chor) 1957, 84
CRANEY, Trudy Ellen (sop) 1988
CRANHAM, Kenneth (act) 1988
CRANITCH, Lorcan (act) 1983
CRANKO, John (chor) 1952, 53, 56, 58, 60, 63, 71, 76
CRASNARU, Daniela (rdr) 1990
CRAVEN, David (pf) 1991
CRAVOTTA, Lorella (act) 1994
CRAWFORD, Andrew (act) 1969, 71
CRAWFORD, Helen (pf) 1989
CRAXTON, Janet (ob) 1964
CREED, Marcus (pf, celeste, hpd) 1995
CREGAN, Tom (sngr) 1989
CREIGHTON, Anthony (act) 1957
CRESPIN, Régine (sop) 1973
CRESSWELL, Pat (act) 1964
CRETULESCU, Tamara (act) 1981
CREWE, Nigel (act) 1969
CRICHTON, Bill (act) 1954
CRICHTON-SMITH, Iain (rdr) 1979, 80
CRICOT 2 1980, 91
CRIDDLE, Tom (act) 1960
CRIPPA, Maddalena (act, sngr) 1996
CRISA, Gail (dan) 1967
CRIST, Richard (ten) 1987
CRISTEA, Eugen (act) 1992
CRISTOFOLI, Francesco (dir, cond) 1989, 90
CRISWELL, Michael (act) 1976
CRIVELLI, Filippo (dir) 1969
CROAN, Margo (act) 1961
CROCKER, Gary Austin (dan) 1978
CROCKER, John (act) 1963
CROFT, John (act) 1964
CROFUT, Bill (banjo) 1979
CROMBIE, Josephine (act) 1951
CROMBIE, Ogilvie (act) 1964
CROMWELL, John (act) 1971
CRONIN, Finola (dan) 1992
CROOK, Geoffrey (sngr) 1994
CROOKE, Frederick (des) 1958
CROOM, Jim (ten) 1982
CROPLEY, Eileen (dan) 1966
CROPPER, Peter (lect) 1996
CROSS, Ben (act) 1975
CROSS, Gerald (act) 1955
CROSS, Hugh (act) 1957, 60
CROSS, Raymond (light) 1986
CROSS, Timothy (sngr) 1994
CROSSLEY, Amanda (act) 1993
CROSSLEY, Paul (pf, org, spk) 1971, 84, 96
CROTTY, Derbhle (act) 1994
CROUCHER, Roger (act) 1962
CROW, Angela (act) 1956
CROWDEN, Graham (act) 1963, 76
CROWE, Catherine (act) 1989
CROWE, Robert (ten) 1981, 93
CROWLEY, Bob (des) 1979, 85
CROWLEY, Dermot (act) 1974, 75
CROWLEY, Jeananne (act) 1974
CROWSON, Lamar (pf) 1961
CRUDDAS, Audrey (des) 1947, 54, 55, 60, 61
CRUFT, Eugene (db) 1963
CRUICKSHANK, Andrew (act, narr) 1979, 84, 85
CRUICKSHANK, Marty (act) 1967
CRUVEILLER, Olivier (act) 1994
CRUZ, Charo (dan) 1992
CSARNÓY, Katalin (dan) 1973
CSEKO, Benjamin Istvan (dan) 1994, 95
CSENGERY, Adrienne (sop) 1986
CSILLAGHYOVA, Michaela (act) 1991
CUBA, National Ballet *See* National Ballet Of Cuba
CUBERLI, Lella (sop) 1982
CUENOD, Hugues (ten) 1960
CUERVO, Gemma (act) 1986
CUESTA, Oliva (act) 1983
CUKA, Frances (act) 1968, 92
CULLBERG, Birgit (chor) 1957, 58
CULLBORG, Leo (act) 1974
CULLEN, Ailie (pf) 1947, 48, 49, 52
CULLIFORD, James (act) 1958, 67
CULLIS, Rita (sop) 1995
CULLUM, Lisa (dan) 1991
CULSHAW, Bernard (des) 1969, 71, 79
CUMANI-QUASIMODO, Maria (act) 1975
CUMBRE FLAMENCA 1990
CUMMINGS, Douglas (vc) 1972
CUMMINGS, Torrin (dan) 1993
CUNAIEN, Sergei (ten) 1995
CUNLIFFE, Jerry (act) 1967, 76
CUNNINGHAM, Aldona (des) 1993
CUNNINGHAM, Dan (act) 1952
CUNNINGHAM, Davy (light) 1993
CUNNINGHAM, Margo (act) 1957
CUNNINGHAM, Merce (chor, dan) 1979, 83, 94
CUNNINGHAM, Neil (rdr) 1985
CUNXIN, Li (dan) 1989
CURLEY, Carlo (org) 1985
CURLEY, Wilma (dan) 1959
CURNOCK, Richard (act) 1956, 64
CURNOW, Neil (act) 1959
CURR, A. Maxwell (act) 1952
CURR, Rosemary (act) 1964, 65
CURRAH, Brian (des) 1970
CURRAM, Roland (act) 1970
CURRAN, Paul (act) 1951
CURRAN, Sean (chor, dan) 1993
CURREY, Linden (dan) 1977, 80
CURRIE, John (cond) 1981, 86
CURRY, Julian (act) 1964
CURRY, Shaun (act) 1962
CURTIN, Phyllis (sop) 1968
CURTIS, Mark (ten) 1986, 94
CURTIS, Philip (sngr) 1979
CURTIS, Stephen (des) 1990
CURZON, *Sir* Clifford (pf) 1950, 52, 55, 56, 61, 63, 67, 70, 74, 76, 77, 78, 79
CUSICK, Henry Ian (act) 1993, 94
CUTHBERT, Andrew (act) 1981
CUTHBERTSON, Iain (act) 1957, 59, 60, 62, 66
CVEJIĆ, Biserka (mez) 1962

DENNIS BRAIN WIND ENSEMBLE 1957
DENNISON, John (act) 1988
DENOUES, Brigitte (sngr) 1985
DENT, Josephine (act) 1948
DERAIN, André (des) 1948, 54
DERBY, Brown (act) 1960, 62, 64, 65, 69, 70, 71, 73, 84, 85, 91
DERMOTA, Anton (ten) 1957
DERMOTA, Hilde (pf) 1957
DERMOTT, Mac (cond) 1952
DERNESCH, Helga (sop) 1970, 71, 72
DEROUBAIX, Jeanne (vocalist) 1965
DERRAH, Thomas (act) 1982
DERRINGTON, Michael (act) 1979
DESAI, Yogen (chor, dan) 1956
DESAILLY, Jean (act) 1948
DESCHAMPS, Jean (act) 1953
DESCHAMPS, Jérôme (dir, act) 1988, 89, 95
DESCOMBEY, Michael (chor) 1974
DESCOUTURES, Vivianne (dan) 1984
DESDERI, Claudio (bar) 1969, 82, 92
DESHAIE, Sandrine (dan) 1986, 87
DESMARE, Roger (act) 1953
DÉSORMIÈRE, Roger (cond) 1950
DEUS, Joaquín (bs) 1958
DEUTSCH, Helmut (pf) 1994, 96
DEUTSCHE OPER, Berlin 1971, 75
DEUTSCHE OPERA AM RHEIN, Düsseldorf-Duisburg 1972, 76
DEUTSCHES THEATER, Berlin 1970, 93
DEUTSCHLAND, Jutta (dan) 1984
DEVI, Kumudini (dan) 1956
DEVI, Ritha (chor, dan) 1980
DEVI, Shevanti (dan) 1956
DEVI, Suryamukhi (dan) 1960
DEVILLE, Kathy (dan) 1990
DEVINE, George (dir) 1950, 57, 59, 61, 63
DEVLIN, J.G. (act) 1958, 59, 80
DEVLIN, Vivien (lect) 1993
DEVLIN, William (act) 1950, 52
DEWEY, Kenneth (dir) 1963
DEXTER, John (dir) 1963
DeYOUNG, Michelle (mez) 1996
DHANALAKSHMI, S. (tambura) 1963
DHÉRAN, Bernard (dir, act) 1948, 61
DHOMHNAILL, Máire Ní (act) 1968
DIADKOVA, Larissa (mez) 1991, 95
DIAMOND, Marian (act) 1962, 72, 73
DIANA, Angela (des, act) 1972
DIAZ, Justino (bs) 1981, 82
DIBERTI, Luigi (act) 1970
DICEMAN, The (act) 1989
DICHTER, Misha (pf) 1969
DICK, Curtis (dan) 1990
DICKERSON, Bernard (ten) 1963, 68
DICKIE, Murray (ten) 1950, 53, 54, 61
DICKS, Walter (bs) 1971, 75
DICKSON, Bettina (act) 1963
DICKSON, Hester (pf) 1950, 60, 64
DICKSON, Joan (vc) 1950, 53, 60, 61, 62, 64, 65
DICKSON, Nancy (dan) 1981
DICKSON, Stephen (bar) 1983
DICKSON MacLEOD DANCERS AND PIPERS 1967
DIDIER, Armand (act) 1981
DIDUSCH, Reingard (sop) 1976
DIEBEL, John (des) 1958
DIEGUEZ, Cesar (act) 1989
DIEHL, Hans (act) 1994
DIEMER, Guido (sngr) 1952
DIERKES, Timo (act) 1993
DIESTEL, Ursula (act) 1988
DIETRICH, Marlene (ent) 1964, 65
DIGNAM, Mark (act) 1947, 50, 66
DIJK, Cornelis van (ten) 1975
DILBER (sop) 1987
DiLENA, Mari (dan) 1978
DIMIK, Kakas (act) 1987
DIMITRIJEVIĆ, Dragi (sngr) 1962
DINGWALL, Emma (act) 1991
DINSDALE, Reece (act) 1981
DINULESCU, Constantin (act) 1992
DIONISOTTI, Paola (act) 1972, 73, 74
DIOR, Christian (des) 1949
DIOT, André (light) 1994, 95
DISCOLO, Ciro (act) 1988
DISMOND, Larry (gtr) 1967
DISPERATI, Giuliano (act) 1965
DISS, Eileen (des) 1980
DITTA, Douglas (act) 1961
DITTRICH, Manfred (des) 1986
DITTUS, Barbara (act) 1987
DIVES, Tamsin (mez) 1992, 93
DIX, Katrin (dan) 1984
DIXON, Jerry (sngr) 1995
DIXON, Shirley (act) 1969
DJOKIĆ, Aleksandar (bs) 1962
DJORDJEVIĆ, Mira (sngr) 1962
DJORDJEVIĆ, Višnja (dan) 1962
DJURDJEVIĆ, Djordje (bs) 1962
DMITREYEVA, Antonina (act) 1978
DOBBERTIN, Petra (act) 1984
DOBBS, Mattiwilda (sop) 1954, 65, 71
DOBIE, Alan (act) 1952, 54, 62, 78
DOBOUJINSKY, Mstislav (des) 1952
DOBOUJINSKY, Rostislav (des) 1952, 79
DOBRÁ, Jaroslava (sop) 1964, 70
DOBRIEVICH, Louba (dan) 1962
DOBRIEVICH, Pierre (dan) 1962
DOBROGEANU, Alexandru (light) 1992
DOBSON, John (ten) 1961
DOBTCHEFF, Vernon (act) 1961
DOCHERTY, Claire (vn) 1990
DOCHEVA, Liliana (dir) 1969
DODIMEAD, David (act) 1964, 69
DOGARU, Valeriu (act) 1991
DOGGETT, Alan (comp) 1972
DOGHAN, Philip (ten) 1982
DOGUILEVA, Tatiana (act) 1994
DOHNÁNYI, Christoph von (cond) 1970, 83, 94, 96
DOHNÁNYI, Ernst von (pf) 1956
DOHNÁNYI, Oliver (cond) 1990
DOHR, Stefan (hn) 1986
DOIG, Alison (mez) 1981
DOKTOR, Paul (va) 1963
DOLAIN, Yvonne (act) 1988
DOLAN, Catherine (act) 1956
DOLIDZE, T. (act) 1979
DOLIN, *Sir* Anton (lect) 1979
DOLINSKÝ, Jozef (chor) 1990
DOLLAR, William (chor) 1953
DOLTON, Geoffrey (bar) 1994
DOMANÍNSKÁ, Libuše (sop) 1964
DOMINGO, Placido (ten) 1970, 77
DOMINGUEZ, Angeles Gulin (sop) 1969
DOMINGUEZ, Oralia (mez) 1955, 60
DOMINIQUE (dan) 1958
DOMKOVA, Jana (dan) 1991
DOMMISCH, Peter (act) 1970
DOMPIETRINI, Colette (act) 1960
DON, Robin (des) 1977, 85
DONAGHY, Philip (act) 1980
DONALD, George (ent) 1986, 90
DONALD, Mary Helen (act) 1956
DONALD, Minty (des) 1992
DONALD, Sheila (act) 1956
DONALDSON, Gail (dan) 1961
DONATH, Helen (sop) 1967, 73, 75, 80, 82, 83
DONCASTER, Stephen (des) 1961, 73
DONCASTER, Wendy (des) 1959, 73
DÓNIZ, Paco (light) 1992
DONLON, Marguerite (dan) 1991
DONNELLAN, Declan (dir) 1992
DONNELLY, Malcolm (bar) 1980
DONNELLY, Patrick (dan) 1952, 53, 75, 76
DONOHOE, Peter (pf) 1982, 86, 87, 89-93
DONOVAN, John (act) 1968
DOOLEY, William (bar) 1975
DORATI, Antol (cond) 1970, 77
DORÉ, Edna (act) 1980
DORLIAK, Dmitry (act) 1978
DORNÉS, Roger (des) 1961
DOROW, Dorothy (sop) 1961, 62
DORWARD, David (comp) 1969
DORWARD, Helen (act) 1969
DOTRICE, Roy (act) 1962
DOTTI, Maurizio (des) 1982
DOUGALL, Gordon (sngr) 1992
DOUGLAS, Andrew (rdr) 1987
DOUGLAS, Barry (pf) 1991
DOUGLAS, Bill (pf ?) 1980
DOUGLAS, Donald (act) 1959, 68, 85, 86
DOUGLAS, Gemma (act) 1993
DOUGLAS, Iain R. (sngr) 1961
DOUGLAS, Nigel (ten) 1968, 75, 80
DOUGLAS, Paul (dan) 1981
DOUGLAS, Scott (dan) 1953
DOUGLAS, Sheila (rdr, story teller, folk sngr) 1987, 93, 95
DOUGLAS-STEWART, Fiona (act) 1989
DOUSE, Anthony (act) 1975
DOUSSARD, Danièle (dan) 1984
DOW, Julia (act) 1992
DOWD, Ronald (ten) 1963, 70
DOWDELL, Linda (pf) 1992, 93
DOWLING, Joe (dir) 1987
DOWLING, Vincent (act) 1968
DOWNER, James (act) 1980
DOWNES, *Sir* Edward (cond, pf) 1961, 70
DOWNEY, Misha (dan) 1992
DOWNIE, Andrew (sngr, act) 1949, 51, 52, 59
DOWNS, Jane (act) 1957, 58, 61
DOWNSTAGE THEATRE COMPANY 1990
DOWSON, Stephen (bs) 1989
DOYLE, Desmond (dan) 1954, 56
DOYLE, Pat (act) 1981
DOYLE, Roger (pf) 1989
DÓZSA, Imre (dan) 1973
DRACH, Michel (des) 1959
DRAGADZE, Ivan (dan) 1960
DRAGE, Mary (dan) 1954, 56
DRAKE, Bryan (bar) 1963, 65, 68
DRANCOURT, Arsène (act) 1954
DRAPER, Paul (bn) 1949
DREIER, Jürger (des) 1996
DREIS, Renate (sngr) 1972
DRENNAN, George (sngr) 1992
DRESDEL, Sonia (act) 1950
DRESDEN STAATSKAPELLE 1978, 82
DRESDEN STATE OPERA 1982
DRESEL-STARKE, Rose-Marie (dan) 1984
DRESEN, Adolf (dir) 1983
DRESSLER, Günter (bs) 1982
DREW, David (chor) 1969
DRILLAUD, Christian (act) 1986
DRISCOLL, Loren (ten) 1967, 71, 75
DROLC QUARTET 1961
DROMISKY, Susan (dan) 1986
DROR, Ora (dan) 1974
DRUMMOND, Alasdair (dan) 1952
DRUMMOND, Irene (sop) 1993
DRUMMOND, *Sir* John (lect, spk) 1979, 80, 81, 82
DRURY, Ken (act) 1980
DRY, Marion (sngr) 1988
DU PRÉ, Jacqueline *See* Pré, Jacqueline du
DU WANFANG (act) 1987
DUBIK, Maja (dan) 1986
DUBOIS, Françoise (dan) 1962
DUBOSC, Catherine (sop) 1985, 86
DUBREUIL, Alain (dan) 1975, 79
DUCAR, François (act) 1955
DUCE, Sharon (act) 1973, 74
DUCH, Arkardiusz (dan) 1991
DUDA, Zdeněk (sngr) 1964
DUDICOURT, Marc (act) 1960
DUDLEY, William (des) 1975, 77, 80
DUESING, Dale (bar) 1982

DUFALLO, Richard (cond) 1980
DUFEK, Bohumil (act) 1984
DUFF-GRIFFIN, William (act) 1976
DUFLOUX, Nicolas (dan) 1987
DÜGGELIN, Werner (dir) 1965
DUGUID, Peter (act, dir) 1950, 55, 59, 61
DUHAMEL, Jacques (light) 1979
DULOVIĆ, Ljiljana (dan) 1962
DUMAKUDE, Thuli (act) 1983
DUMITRU, Constantin (bs) 1976
DUMITRU, Natalia (act) 1992
DUMITRU, Robert (act) 1992
DUNBAR, John (act) 1957, 64
DUNCAN, Agnes (cond) 1952
DUNCAN, Archie (act) 1948
DUNCAN, Fionna (mus) 1986
DUNCAN, Frank (act) 1947
DUNCAN, Gregor (act) 1991
DUNCAN, Jock (folk sngr) 1995
DUNCAN, Lindsay (act) 1979
DUNCAN, Martin (dir, des, spk) 1992, 96
DUNCAN, Peter (act) 1990
DUNCAN, Ronald (spk) 1963
DUNCAN, Sandra (act) 1966
DUNCAN, Todd (bar) 1947
DUNCANSON, John (act) 1961
DUNDEE REPERTORY THEATRE 1959
DUNHAM, Rosemarie (act) 1960, 61
DUNKEEL, Eugene (des) 1957
DUNKLEY, Chris (spk) 1981
DUNLEAVY, Rosemary (dan) 1967
DUNLOP, Betty (des) 1993
DUNLOP, Frank (dir) 1960, 65, 66, 67, 69, 71, 72, 82, 84, 85, 86, 87, 90
DUNLOP, Joseph (act) 1962, 64
DUNN, Douglas (rdr) 1986
DUNN, Geoffrey (act) 1955
DUNN, Iain (bar) 1971, 72
DUNN, Patricia (dan) 1959
DUNN, Susan (sop) 1988
DUNNE, Eithne (act) 1964
DUNNETT, Iain (act) 1960, 62
DÜNNWALD, Josef (cond) 1963
DUNSIRE, Roy (act) 1986
DUNSTER, Wilson (act) 1975
DUPOND, Patrick (dan) 1984
DUPONT, Jacques (des) 1979
DUPOUY, Jean (ten) 1976
DUPRÉ, Desmond (lute,cittern) 1957
DUPRÉ, Marcel (org) 1950
DURANT, Andrea (dan) 1977
DURAS, Marguerite (spk) 1963
ĎURČO, Ján (bar) 1990
DURDEN, Richard (act) 1968
ĎURDIAK, Juraj (ten) 1990
DÜREN, Fred (act) 1970
DURKIN, Peter (act) 1976
DUROV, Lev (act) 1978
DURRAN, William (sngr) 1994
DURRANT, Hugh (des) 1977, 81
DURRELL, Lawrence (spk) 1962
DÜRRLER, Brigitte (sop) 1976
DURRSON, Werner (rdr) 1991
DUSKE, Erna Maria (sop) 1956
DÜSSELDORF SYMPHONY ORCHESTRA 1976
DÜSSELDORF THEATRE COMPANY 1950
DUTOIT, Charles (cond) 1981, 85
DUVAL, Denise (sop) 1960
DUYKERS, John (ten) 1988
DVIR, Dahlia (dan) 1974
DVIR, David (dan) 1974
DVORSKÝ, Miroslav (ten) 1990
DYCK, Wendy van (dan) 1981
DYER, Chris (des) 1996
DYKES, Ivor (light) 1969
DZABRAILOV, Rasmi (act) 1989
DZHAPAREDZE, Anton (bar) 1990
DZIEMASZKIEWICZ, Krzysztof (dan) 1991
DZIGRASHVILI, L. (act) 1979
DZISKO, Olga (act) 1994

EAGAN, Michael (des) 1980
EAGLE PIPERS' SOCIETY 1965
EAGLEN, Jane (sop) 1993, 94, 95, 96
EAGLES, Leon (ent) 1964
EALES, Daphne (des) 1967
EARLE, Roderick (bs) 1986
EARLE, Stephen (act) 1975
EARLY MUSIC CONSORT 1971
EASDALE, Brian (comp) 1954
EASSON, Margaret (act) 1952
EASTON, Richard (act) 1956, 78
EASTON, Robert Nicholl (bar) 1949, 52
EASTWOOD, Thomas (comp) 1957
EBDON, John (act) 1950
EBEN, Petr (org) 1991
EBERLE, Friedheim (narr) 1988
EBERS, Clara (sop) 1950, 52
EBERT, Carl (dir) 1947-51, 53-55
EBERT, Christian (act) 1993
EBERT, Joyce (act) 1971
EBERT, Peter (dir) 1954-55, 60, 67, 71-72
EBERZ, Alfons (ten) 1981
ECHÁNIZ, Abraham Thevenet (pf) 1953
ECK, Imre (dan) 1983
ECKARD, Max (act) 1949
EDA, Mayumi (dan) 1988
EDA-PIERRE, Christiane (sop) 1973
EDDIE CONDON CELEBRATION BAND 1990
EDDISON, Robert (act) 1950, 51, 57, 61, 69, 72, 73, 74, 77
EDDY, Jenifer (sop) 1961
EDELMANN, Otto (bs) 1952
EDELSEN, Marie Eve (dan) 1985
EDER, Jean-Marc (act) 1994
EDGELL, Yvonne (act) 1981
EDINBURGH CITY POLICE PIPE BAND 1964, 66
EDINBURGH FESTIVAL CHORUS 1965-1996
EDINBURGH FESTIVAL ENSEMBLE 1992, 93, 95
EDINBURGH FESTIVAL OPERA 1967, 71, 73-78, 93
EDINBURGH FESTIVAL PRODUCTIONS 1978
EDINBURGH FESTIVAL SINGERS 1996
EDINBURGH GAELIC CHOIR 1961-2, 64
EDINBURGH HIGHLAND REEL AND STRATHSPEY SOCIETY 1961
EDINBURGH INTERNATIONAL BALLET 1958
EDINBURGH INTERNATIONAL JAZZ FESTIVAL 1991
EDINBURGH PLAYERS 1963, 64
EDINBURGH QUARTET 1963, 70, 80
See also New Edinburgh Quartet
EDINBURGH ROYAL CHORAL UNION 1950-63
EDINBURGH UNIVERSITY SINGERS 1950, 51, 56, 58, 59, 61, 64, 66
EDISON, Harry 'Sweets' (tpt) 1986, 87, 90
EDLER, Graeme (act) 1977
EDMOND, Valerie (rdr) 1987
EDMONDS, Gwendoline (dan) 1980
EDMONDS, Thomas (ten) 1973
EDMUNDSON, Keith (light) 1977, 78
EDNEY, Beatie (act) 1991
EDSTRÖM, Margareta (sop) 1986
EDWARDS, Anne (act) 1952, 53
EDWARDS, Geoffrey (sngr) 1981
EDWARDS, Hilton (spk) 1963
EDWARDS, Joan (cont) 1963
EDWARDS, Kenneth (act) 1947, 51, 52
EDWARDS, Leslie (dan) 1947, 48, 51, 54, 56, 60
EDWARDS, Meredith (act) 1954
EDWARDS, Owen Dudley (lect, spk) 1981, 92, 93, 94, 95, 96
EDWARDS, Paddy (act) 1960
EDWARDS, Sian (cond) 1988
EDWARDS, Warwick (cond) 1985, 86-87

EDWIN, Steve (act) 1991
EFROS, Anatoli (dir) 1978
EGAN, Michael (act) 1987
EGERTON, Francis (ten) 1967, 79, 80, 82
EGINTON, Meg (dan) 1979
EGLEVSKY, André (dan) 1950
EGOROV, Youri (pf) 1981
EGÜES, Rembert (cond) 1979
EHRLING, Sixten (cond) 1957, 59
EICH, Hans Josef (act) 1993
EICHEL, Kaspar (act) 1970
EICHELBERGER, James (act) 1968
EICHHORN, Karoline (act) 1994
EICHMAN, Kay (dan) 1990
EISINGER, Irene (sop) 1949
EISLER, Georg (lect) 1983
EISLER, Hans (comp) 1984
EIZEN, Arthur (bs) 1991
EKLUND, Nils (act) 1967
EKSTRÖM, Henny (mez) 1972
ELDER, Mark (cond) 1976, 93
ELDER, Michael (act) 1954, 56-57, 59-60
ELDRIDGE, Howard (light) 1973, 74
ELECTRIC PHOENIX 1986
ELÈS, Sandor (act) 1980
ELGAR, Avril (act) 1963
ELIASEN, Johnny (dan) 1991
ELIASSON, Sven Olof (ten) 1970, 76
ELIOT, Rosemary (fl) 1986
ELKINS, Margreta (mez) 1961, 71
ELLER, Lawrence (mus) 1984
ELLIOT, Faith (sop) 1984
ELLIOTT, Alasdair (ten) 1993, 95
ELLIOTT, David (act) 1988
ELLIOTT, Denholm (act) 1953
ELLIOTT, *Dr* Fiona (lect) 1993, 95
ELLIOTT, Kenneth (hpd) 1972, 87, 91
ELLIOTT, Michael (dir) 1963, 68, 76
ELLIOTT, Simon (des) 1991
ELLIS, Chris (light) 1995
ELLIS, Ken (mus) 1986
ELLIS, James (act) 1958
ELLIS, Mary (act) 1949
ELLIS, Osian (hp) 1958, 76
ELLIS, Peter (act) 1961
ELLIS, Richard (dan) 1947, 48, 51
ELLIS, Robin (act) 1969, 72, 73, 74
ELLMANN, Richard (spk) 1980
ELMEUA, Carlos (mus) 1989
ELPHICK, Michael (act) 1967
ELSO, Pascal (act) 1994
ELSOM, John (dir) 1984
ELTERMANN, Bozena (dan) 1991
ELVERY, John (des) 1969
ELVIN, Violetta (dan) 1947, 48, 51, 54
ELWIN, David (pf) 1986
ELY, Joey (act) 1970
EMERY, Jack (dir) 1983
EMERY, Susan (dan) 1979
EMMERLICH, Gunter (bs) 1982
EMMONS, Beverly (light) 1994
EMPEROR QUARTET 1993, 95, 96
ENARDU, Marcello (act) 1982
ENCK, Wolfgang (dan) 1976
ENDERLÉ, Tutti (dan) 1949
ENDICOTT, Jo-Anne (dan) 1978
ENDO, Akira (cond) 1994, 95
ENDO, Takuo (dir) 1989
ENGEL, Susan (act) 1962, 80, 92
ENGEL, Tina (act) 1994
ENGELSKAMP, Josephine (sop) 1972
ENGEN, Keith (bs) 1965
ENGLISH, Gerald (ten) 1962, 65, 67, 71
ENGLISH, John (act) 1966
ENGLISH QUARTET 1962
ENGLISH BAROQUE SOLOISTS 1982
ENGLISH CHAMBER ORCHESTRA 1961, 63-65, 68, 72-76, 78, 84, 90, 91
ENGLISH CHAMBER ORCHESTRA WIND ENSEMBLE 1973
ENGLISH CONSORT OF VIOLS 1971
ENGLISH NORTHERN PHILHARMONIA 1992

GEORGE, Andrew (dan) 1992
GEORGE, Lyndon (mime) 1989
GEORGE, Michael (bs) 1984, 94
GEORGE, Radu (act) 1981
GEORGE WATSON'S BOYS' CHORUS 1977, 78, 86, 88
GEORGESCU, Alexander (act) 1981
GEORGIADIS, John (vn) 1977
GEORGIADIS, Nicholas (des) 1956, 60, 63, 75, 77
GERAGHTY, Clive (act) 1974, 89, 95
GÉRARD, Rolf (des) 1948, 49, 50, 54
GERBER, Michael (act) 1984, 87
GERBER, René (perc) 1960
GERBERT, Philippe (dan) 1984
GERELO, Vasily (b-bar) 1991
GERETY, Peter (act) 1968
GERGALOV, Alexander (bar) 1995
GERGIEV, Valery (cond) 1991, 95
GERGIEVA, Larissa (pf) 1992, 94, 95
GERLACHE, Freddy (light) 1992
GÉRÔME, Raymond (act) 1961
GERRARD, Patricia (act) 1973
GERSHON, Grant (cond) 1995
GERSON, Jack (spk) 1963
GERSON, Melissa (dan) 1994, 95
GERTH, Hansjürgen (act) 1977
GERUSSI, Bruno (act) 1956
GERVAIS, Jean (light) 1994
GESSENDORF, Mechthild (sop) 1987
GESTER, Kurt (bar) 1954, 76
GESZTY, Sylvia (sop) 1966, 68
GHAZARIAN, Sona (sop) 1976
GHELLI, Ferdinando (des) 1969
GHEORGHE, Ilie (act) 1991
GHEORGHE, Tudor (act) 1991
GHIUSELEV, Nicola (bs) 1979
GIACOBBE, Gabriella (act) 1956
GIANNELLI, Christina (light) 1990
GIANNETTI, Stefano (dan) 1991
GIANNINI, A. Christina (des, light) 1994
GIANNOTTI, Claudia (act) 1975
GIBAULT, Claire (cond) 1985
GIBB, Andrea (act) 1992
GIBBS, Ernest Clark (act) 1949
GIBSON, *Sir* Alexander (cond) 1959-83, 91, 92
GIBSON, Catherine (act) 1958
GIBSON, Chloe (dir) 1963
GIBSON, James (dir, act, rdr) 1948-53, 56-62, 64, 65, 68
GIBSON, John (dir) 1964
GIBSON, Neil (act) 1978
GIDDEN, Yvonne (act) 1992
GIELEN, Michael (cond) 1978, 93, 95
GIELGUD, *Sir* John (dir, act)) 1948, 51, 57, 61
GIELGUD, Kate (act) 1989
GIERSTER, Hans (cond) 1965
GIESECKE, Siegmund (act) 1949
GIESEN, Hubert (pf) 1966
GIFFEN, Jeni (act) 1973, 74
GIFFIN, John (dan) 1978
GIFFORD, Douglas (cond) 1987, 88, 89
GIGNAC, Marie (act) 1994
GILBERT, Geoffrey (fl, cond) 1949, 54
GILBERT, James (act) 1950, 51
GILBERT, Jane (mez) 1993
GILBERT, Kenneth (act) 1977
GILBERT, Max (va) 1948
GILBERT, Natalie (sngr) 1981
GILBERT, Simon (sngr) 1967
GILBERTSON, Clive (act) 1977
GILCRIST, Anna (act) 1967
GILELS, Emil (pf) 1966, 80
GILES, David (dir) 1972, 73, 78
GILFEATHER, Doris (?) 1963
GILGORE, Lawrence (cond) 1985
GILILOV, Pavel (pf) 1995
GILL, John (act) 1956
GILL, Peter (dir) 1975
GILL, Richard (bs) 1976
GILLARD, Christopher (dan) 1980
GILLESPIE, Robert (act) 1954, 71
GILLIES, Alasdair B. (sngr) 1961, 62, 66
GILLIES, Anne (sngr) 1963, 64, 65
GILLIES, Anne Lorne (sop) 1985, 86, 90
GILLIES, Aunice M. (sngr) 1961
GILLIES, Carol (act) 1968, 70
GILLIES, Valerie (spk) 1980
GILLIS, Margie (?) 1989
GILMORE, Murray (act) 1962
GILMORE, Paul (act) 1990
GILMORE, Peter (act) 1967, 68
GILMOUR, Gordon (act) 1957
GILMOUR, Ian (rdr) 1959, 61, 87, 91
GILMOUR, Juliette (act) 1993
GILPIN, Jean (act) 1974
GIMENEZ, Marifé (dan) 1995
GIMENEZ, Mercedes (act) 1983
GIMSE, Hävard (pf) 1995
GINIVAN, Garry (act) 1976
GIONI, Nicholas (act) 1987
GIORDANI, Corrado (dan) 1988
GIORGETTI, Giorgio (bar) 1969
GIOVAMPIETRO, Renzo (act) 1996
GIOVANETTI, Roberto A. (dan) 1989
GIRARD, André (cond) 1949
GIRAUD, Bernard (dir) 1995
GIRAUDEAU, Philippe (dan) 1981
GIRONE, Remo (act) 1996
GIROUX, Germaine (act) 1956
GIRSHENKO, Sergei (vn) 1987
GISBERT, Vicente (act) 1989
GISCHIA, Léon (des) 1953
GIULINI, Carlo Maria (cond) 1955, 60, 61, 62, 65, 67-78, 94
GIULIVO, Lello (sngr) 1988
GIURANNA, Bruno (va) 1961, 82
GIUSTI, Graziano (act) 1970
GIWALE, Lubi (act) 1987
GLADKOV, Leonid (sngr) 1986
GLADSTEIN, Robert (chor) 1981
GLANISTER, Suzanne (des) 1964
GLANVILLE, Mark (sngr) 1989
GLASGOW ANGUS DANCE BAND 1963
GLASGOW GAELIC MUSICAL ASSOCIATION 1961, 62, 64, 66
GLASGOW ISLAY GAELIC CHOIR 1964
GLASGOW ORPHEUS CHOIR 1947, 48, 49, 50
GLASS, Kalman (act) 1960
GLAZUNOV, Kyrill (act) 1978
GLEN, Hamish (dir) 1992
GLENAAN, Kenneth (act) 1990
GLENCORSE PIPES AND DRUMS 1987
GLENISTER, Robert (act) 1991
GLENNIE, Evelyn (perc) 1987, 88, 90, 92
GLIGORIJEVIĆ, Ilija (bs) 1962
GLIGORIJEVIĆ, Jovan (bar) 1962
GLIŠIĆ, Mira (des) 1962
GLOAG, David (act) 1955
GLOAG, Helena (act) 1951, 59
GLOBISZ, Krzysztof (act) 1986, 89
GLOBOKAR, Vinko (tbn) 1989
GLOGER, Christine (act) 1984, 87
GLÖSS, Ruth (act) 1987
GLOSSOP, Peter (bar) 1961, 63
GLOVER, Brian (act) 1977, 80
GLOVER, Julian (act) 1961, 64, 70, 82
GLOWACKA, Eva (dan) 1986
GLOYD, Russell (cond) 1985
GLUBOKY, Peter (bs) 1990, 91
GLUSHCHAK, Vladimir (bar) 1992
GLYNDEBOURNE OPERA 1947-51, 1953-55, 60
GOBBI, Tito (dir, bar) 1969
GODDARD, Renee (act) 1977
GODDARD, Willoughby (act) 1961, 73
GODFREY, Derek (act) 1962
GODFREY, Michael (act) 1969
GODFREY, Patrick (act) 1960, 78, 85
GODFREY, Victor (b-bar) 1961
GODINHO, Rafael (act) 1972
GODKIN, Paul (dan) 1950
GODLEY, Adam (act) 1980
GODLEY, Campbell (act) 1962
GODREAU, Miguel (dan) 1968
GODSON, Daphne (vn) 1981
GODWIN, Howard (pf) 1960
GOEHR, Alexander (cond, lect) 1969, 71, 78, 83
GOFFINON, Catherine (dan) 1984
GOGITIDZE, V. (act) 1979
GOLAN, Itamar (pf) 1994
GOLD, Max (act) 1990
GOLDBERG, Bernard (fl) 1964
GOLDBERG, Reiner (ten) 1982
GOLDBERG, Szymon (cond, vn) 1955, 57, 61, 65, 67, 69, 74
GOLDBLATT, Harold (act) 1958
GOLDEN, Geoffrey (act) 1968, 74
GOLDEN AGE SINGERS 1954
GOLDENBERG, Eliahu (dir, act) 1966
GOLDENTHAL, Bibiana (sop) 1985
GOLDHUBER, Lawrence (dan) 1993, 95
GOLDIE, Michael (act) 1961
GOLDING, William (spk) 1962
GOLDSCHMIDT, Berthold (cond) 1947
GOLDSTONE, Anthony (pf) 1973, 76
GOLFIER, Françoise (sop) 1985
GÖLLNITZ, Fritz (ten) 1952
GOLOVINA, Solange (dan) 1957
GOLOVINE, Serge (dan) 1950, 52, 57
GOMEZ, Aida (dan) 1989
GOMEZ, Guadalupe (dan) 1989
GOMEZ, Jill (sop) 1970, 79, 81, 84, 85
GOMEZ, José Luis (dir) 1986
GÓMEZ, Rosario (mez) 1958
GONÇALVES, Francisco (gtr) 1995
GONCHAROVA, Nathalia (des) 1954
GONDEK, Juliana (sop) 1991
GONELLA, Ronald (fiddle) 1963, 64, 85
GONTA, Grigore (dir) 1981
GONZALEZ, Ana (dan) 1989
GONZALEZ, Carmen (mez) 1985
GONZALEZ, Cordelia (act) 1993
GONZALEZ, Ivette (dan) 1991
GONZALEZ, Lucien (dan) 1984
GONZÁLEZ, Ofelia (dan) 1979, 91
GONZENBACH, Jean-Paul (act) 1985
GOOD, Alan (dan) 1979
GOOD, Christopher (act) 1992
GOOD, Maurice (act) 1961
GOODALL, Jonathan (hn) 1980
GOODCHILD, Tim (des) 1969
GOODE, Coleridge (?) 1963
GOODE, Richard (pf) 1974, 92-94, 96
GOODIER, Robert (act) 1956
GOODLIFFE, Michael (act) 1951, 52, 61
GOODMAN, Keith (act) 1963
GOODWIN, *Dr* Guy (interviewer) 1996
GOODWIN, *Lord* (spk) 1982
GOODWIN, Noël (lect) 1979
GOODY, Kim (act) 1975
GOORNEY, Howard (act) 1964
GOORNEY, Richard (act) 1964
GOOSSENS, Eugene (cond) 1949
GOOSSENS, Leon (ob) 1947, 48, 49, 51, 53, 54, 56
GOPAL, Ram (chor, dan) 1956
GÖRANZON, Marie (act) 1986
GORCHAKOVA, Galina (sop) 1992, 94, 95
GORDON, Alan (act) 1950
GORDON, Brian (c ten) 1982
GORDON, Cliff (act) 1956
GORDON, David (dan, chor) 1970, 85
GORDON, Hannah (act) 1986, 87
GORDON, Ruth (act) 1954
GORDON, Stafford (act) 1975
GORE, Walter (chor) 1953, 58
GÓRECKI, Leon (act) 1966
GORING, Marius (rdr) 1984
GORKY THEATRE 1987
GORMAN, Owen (act) 1993
GÖRNER, Christine (sop) 1952
GOROKHOVSKAYA, Evgenia (mez) 1991

GORR, Rita (mez) 1961
GORSKI, Alexander (chor) 1991
GOSSCHALK, Kathy (dan) 1970
GOSTELOW, Gordon (act) 1962
GOTHENBURG CITY THEATRE 1974
GOTHENBURG SYMPHONY ORCHESTRA 1989
GOTHONI, Ralf (pf) 1983, 88
GOTTSCHALK, Nancy (sop) 1971
GOTTWALD, Clytus (cond) 1973
GÖTZ, Werner (ten) 1976, 78, 83
GOUGALOFF, Peter (ten) 1975
GOULD TRIO 1993
GOUPIL, Pierre-René (light) 1980
GOURLAY, Colin (act) 1984, 85
GOURLAY, David (act) 1985
GOURLEY, Meryl (act) 1961
GOUSSIEV, Piotre (chor) 1986
GOUSTIS, Vassilis (act) 1981
GOUTAS, Pierre (act) 1951
GOVAN GAELIC CHOIR 1963, 64, 69
GOVILOFF, Georges (dan) 1957
GOVRIN, Gloria (dan) 1967
GOWEN, Peter (act) 1995
GOWING, Lawrence (dir) 1954
GRABER, Yossi (act) 1987
GRABOWSKA-OLIWA, Barbara (act) 1986
GRABOWSKI, Juliusz (act) 1986
GRACE, Nickolas (act) 1981
GRACE, *Princess of Monaco* (rdr) 1976
GRACHYOV, Anatoly (act) 1978
GRACIANI, Ruben (dan) 1994, 95
GRADUS, Lawrence (dan) 1959
GRAETZ, Emmy (act) 1949
GRAF, Peter Lukas (fl) 1971
GRAHAM, Alasdair (pf) 1971
GRAHAM, Colin (dir, des) 1963, 65, 68, 73, 77, 78, 83
GRAHAM, Cynthia (dan) 1990
GRAHAM, Denys (act) 1956
GRAHAM, James (sngr) 1973
GRAHAM, Jane (des) 1961
GRAHAM, John (bs) 1967, 68, 70, 72
GRAHAM, Laura (act) 1961
GRAHAM, Martha (chor, dan) 1963, 96
GRAHAM, Stuart (act) 1994
GRAHAM, Tony (dir) 1993, 95
GRAHAM, Virginia (act) 1956
GRAINGER, Roger (act) 1961
GHRÁINNE, Máire Ní (act) 1968, 94
GRALEK, Jerzy (act) 1989
GRANADOS, Angela (dan) 1990
GRANATA, Paulo (act) 1975
GRAND BALLET DU MARQUIS DE CUEVAS 1950, 52, 57
GRANDAGE, Michael (act) 1992
GRANDI, Margherita (sop) 1947, 49
GRANERO, José (chor, des) 1989
GRANT, Alexander (dan) 1947, 48, 51, 54, 56, 60, 69
GRANT, Deborah (act) 1980
GRANT, Dominic (act) 1991
GRANT, James (act) 1960, 63, 73, 75
GRANT, Kirsteen (sngr) 1965, 66
GRANT, Sheila (act) 1968, 69
GRANVAL, Jean-Pierre (act) 1948
GRAPPELLI, Stephane (vn) 1989
GRASES, Esperanza (act) 1983
GRASSINI, Maria Grazia (act) 1970
GRAUBERT, Sheri (act) 1991
GRAVES, Rupert (act) 1992
GRAY, Andrew (act) 1948
GRAY, Charles (act) 1955
GRAY, Diane (lect) 1996
GRAY, John (act) 1966
GRAY, John (dir) 1980
GRAY, Linda Esther (sop) 1983
GRAY, Marillyn (act) 1954, 56
GRAY, Natalie (act) 1976
GRAY, Nicholas Stuart (act) 1966
GRAY, Spalding (act) 1974
GRAY, Willoughby (act) 1980
GRAZIOSI, Franco (act) 1956
GREATOREX, Christopher (act) 1964
GRECO, Juliette (sngr) 1961
GREEN, Dorothy (act) 1950
GREEN, Lars (act) 1974
GREEN, Philip (cl) 1966
GREEN, Robson (act) 1992
GREENAWAY, Helen (sngr) 1989
GREENBERG, Rocky (dir, des) 1984
GREENBERG, Sylvia (sop) 1978
GREENE, Daryl (sop) 1976, 79
GREENE, Eric (ten) 1947, 48
GREENE, Gayle (sngr) 1983
GREENE, Reginald (act) 1963
GREENE, Victor (act) 1988
GREENOCK GAELIC CHOIR 1961, 62, 64
GREENOCK GAELIC CHORAL SOCIETY 1961, 62
GREENOCK HIGH SCHOOL GAELIC CHOIR 1966
GREENSLADE, Hubert (pf) 1948
GREENWICH THEATRE COMPANY 1992
GREENWOOD, Diana (act) 1994
GREENWOOD, Jane (des) 1989
GREENWOOD, Joan (spk) 1963
GREENWOOD, John (act) 1955
GREENWOOD, Rosamund (act) 1954
GREER-SPENCER, Justin (act) 1992
GREEVY, Bernadette (mez) 1972, 76
GREFVEBERG, Birgit (dan) 1957
GREGG, Hubert (rdr) 1979
GREGG SMITH SINGERS 1961
GREGGORY, Pascal (act) 1995
GREGOR, Bohumil (cond) 1964, 70
GREGORY, André (dir) 1971
GREGORY, Cynthia (dan) 1990
GREGORY, Paul (act) 1981
GREIF, Stephen (act) 1969
GREIG, Joseph (act) 1960, 70
GREIG, Patricia (sop) 1978
GREINDL, Josef (bs) 1968, 71, 75
GRENSBACK, John (dan) 1989
GREY, Beryl (dan) 1947, 48, 56
GREY, Al (mus) 1986
GRIERSON, Mary (pf) 1952
GRIEVE, John (act) 1959, 60, 63, 73, 75, 84, 85, 86, 87
GRIFFIN, Anita (dan) 1981
GRIFFIN, Annie (lect) 1996
GRIFFIN, Hayden (des) 1975, 92
GRIFFIN, Josephine (act) 1952
GRIFFIN, Ramon (act) 1986
GRIFFIN, Rodney (act) 1967
GRIFFITHS, Dennis (dan) 1958, 61
GRIFFITHS, Elizabeth (sngr) 1973
GRIFFITHS, Gwyn (bar) 1954, 55, 60
GRIFFITHS, Hilary (cond) 1981
GRIFFITHS, James (act) 1974
GRIFFITHS, Michael (act) 1971
GRIFFITHS, Richard (act) 1988
GRIGOR, Murray *and* Barbara 1981
GRIGORIEV, Serge (chor) 1954
GRIGOROVICH, Yuri (chor) 1987
GRILLER QUARTET 1949, 50, 51, 55
GRILLI, Umberto (ten) 1965, 72
GRIMES, Frank (act) 1983
GRIMES, Jerry (act) 1967
GRINLING, Amanda (act) 1959
GRITTON, Susan (sop) 1994
GROAT, Andrew de (chor) 1985
GROBE, Donald (ten) 1965, 71, 75
GROBSTAS, Eva (dan) 1976
GROCHAL, Aldona (act) 1989
GROCHLA, Gary (sngr) 1992
GROENER, Harry (sngr) 1987
GROENROOS, Walton (bar) 1985
GROIS, Liuben (dir) 1969
GRONKOWSKI, Stanislaw (act) 1989
GRONWALD, Wilfried (des) 1963
GROOVE JUICE SPECIAL 1988
GROPMAN, David (des) 1980
GRÖSCHEL, Werner (bs) 1978
GROSS, Arthur (act) 1959
GROSSMANN, Ferdinand (cond) 1951
GROSSMANN, Mechthild (dan) 1995
GROTOWSKI, Jerzy (dir) 1968
GROUPE DE RECHERCHE CHORÉGRAPHIQUE DE L'OPÉRA DE PARIS 1985
GROUPE TSE, Paris 1979, 88
GROUT, James (act) 1950
GROVES, Alison (act) 1971, 72
GROVES, Bill (dan) 1975
GROVES, *Sir* Charles (cond) 1977
GRUBE-DEISTER, Elsa (act) 1970
GRUBEL, Achim (act) 1988
GRUBER, Caroline (act) 1992
GRUBER, Ferry (ten) 1965
GRÜBLER, Ekkehard (des) 1978
GRUETT, Jon David (sngr) 1985
GRUMBACH, Raimund (bs) 1965
GRÜMMER, Elisabeth (sop) 1952, 56
GRUND, Manfred (des) 1987
GRÜNDGENS, Gustaf (dir, act) 1949
GRUNDHEBER, Franz (bar) 1968, 96
GRUNDIN, Robert (ten) 1986, 87
GRUPPO SPERIMENTAZIONE TEATRALE 1972
GRUSIN, Richard (act) 1982
GRÜTZKE, Johannes (des) 1995
GRUZIEL, Lukasz (dan) 1986
GSOVSKY, Victor (chor) 1949
GUADASINSKAYA, Elena (pf) 1987
GUARD, Philip (act) 1951, 54, 55
GUBBINS, Candida (act) 1991
GUBENKO, Nikolai (act) 1989
GÜDEN, Hilde (sop) 1948
GUDRUN, Ann (act) 1959
GUDZUHN, Jörg (act) 1993
GUELI, Maurizio (act) 1982
GUÉROULT, Jean-Jacques (va) 1979
GUERRERO, Carlos (light) 1989
GUFFANTI, Hugo (dan) 1979
GUGLIELMI, Margherita (sop) 1971, 72
GUI, Vittorio (cond) 1948, 49, 52, 53, 54, 60
GUICHET, Christophe (act) 1994
GUILD, Charles (cond) 1949
GUILLOU, Jean (org) 1976
GUIMARD, Gabriel (dan) 1990
GUINEE, Christopher (act) 1960
GUINNESS, *Sir* Alec (act) 1947, 49, 63
GUITAREV, Stanislav (act) 1991
GUITTIER, Marief (act) 1981
GULEDANI, F. (act) 1979
GULEGHINA, Maria (sop) 1993
GULLAND, Brian (bn, etc) 1984
GUNN, Elise (act) 1953
GUNSON, Ameral (sngr) 1987
GÜNTER, Horst (bar) 1952, 56
GUNTER, John (des) 1970
GURA, Hedy (mez) 1952
GURAWSKI, Jerzy (des) 1968
GÜRZENICH ORCHESTRA, Cologne 1980, 81
GUSTAFSON, Björn (act) 1967
GUSTAFSSON, Bengt (ten) 1988
GUSTAV MAHLER JUGENDORCHESTER 1995, 96
GUSTAVSSON, Elis (dan) 1957
GUTELIUS, Phyllis (dan) 1963
GUTHRIE, David (des) 1990
GUTHRIE, Frederick (bs) 1962
GUTHRIE, Tyrone (dir) 1948-56, 58-59
GUTIÉRREZ, Enrique (dan) 1958
GUTMAN, Natalia (vc) 1980, 96
GUY, Jane (mez) 1980, 81, 83
GUYS, Constantin (des) 1950, 60
GUZMAN, Suzanna (mez) 1996
GUZZINATI, Margherita (act) 1965
GWENN, Marie (act) 1985
GWILLIM, Jack (act) 1955
GWILT, Richard (cond, lect) 1994
GWILYM, Mike (act) 1972

HAVRÁNEK, Otakar (sngr) 1964, 70
HAWKING, Rebecca (act) 1986
HAWKINS, Leader (act) 1959, 61, 64
HAWKINS, Matthew (dan) 1985, 88
HAWKSLEY, Brian (act) 1961
HAWLATA, Franz (bs) 1994
HAWTHORNE, Denys (act) 1958, 81
HAWTHORNE, Nigel (narr) 1987
HAY, Patricia (sop) 1968, 71, 72, 81
HAYDÉE, Marcia (dan) 1963
HAYDEN, Melissa (dan) 1952, 53
HAYES, Annie (act) 1977
HAYES, Deborah (act) 1972
HAYES, Malcolm (act) 1966
HAYES, Quentin (bar) 1988
HAYGARTH, Tony (act) 1974, 80
HAYMAN, David (act) 1979
HAYMAN, Lillian (act) 1965
HAYMAN, Ronald (dir) 1966
HAYS, Bill (dir) 1969, 70, 76
HAYS, David (des) 1958, 67
HAYTHORNE, Harry (dan) 1960
HAYWAHE, Kevin (dan) 1990
HAYWARD, Charles (act) 1976
HAYWARD, Robert (bar) 1992, 95
HAYWOOD, Alan (act) 1981
HAYWOOD, Simon (act) 1980
HAZEL, Dawn (act) 1991
HAZELDINE, James (act) 1975
HAZELL, Hy (act) 1968
HAZINSKI, Michael (dan) 1981
HÁZY, Erzsébet (sop) 1973
HEAL, Joan (act) 1971, 72
HEALEY, Desmond (des) 1991
HEALEY, Peter Wing (dan) 1995
HEANEY, Bobby (dir) 1985
HEANEY, Seamus (spk) 1980
HEAP, David (act) 1989
HEAP, Douglas (des) 1975, 80
HEARD, Daphne (act) 1952
HEARD, Douglas (act) 1972
HEARNE, Reginald (act) 1947
HEATH, *Sir* Edward (cond) 1980
HEATH, Kenneth (vc) 1961
HEATH, Suzanne (act) 1968
HEATHCOTE, Thomas (act) 1955
HEATHCOTT, Roger (act) 1963
HEATHER, Roy (act) 1988
HEATON, Anne (dan) 1951, 54
HEBBEL-THEATER, Berlin 1993
HEBEL, Jacqueline (act) 1947
HEBRIDES ENSEMBLE 1991, 92, 95
HECKE, Klaus (act) 1987
HECKER, Werner (sngr) 1956
HECKROTH, Hein (des) 1948
HEDEBY, Kerstin (des) 1974
HEDEGAARD, Ole (ten) 1990
HEDIN, Per-Arne (sngr) 1988
HEDLEY, Philip (dir) 1976, 91
HEDLUND, Ronald (bs) 1985
HEDMAN, Karl (dan) 1987
HEELEY, Desmond (des) 1958, 59, 60, 62
HEERS, Hans Henning (act) 1993
HEFTI, Urs (act) 1994, 95
HEGARTY, Mary (sop) 1994
HEGGIE, Alec (act) 1973, 75, 84, 85, 91
HEGINBOTHAM, John (dan) 1994, 95
HEGT, Saskia Noordhoek (act) 1971
HEIDLER, Maria (act) 1976
HEILBRON, Vivien (act) 1973, 75, 85, 88
HEIN, Pieter (des) 1993
HEINONEN, Eero (pf) 1996
HEJBALOVA, Valerija (sop) 1962
HELEY, John (vc) 1984
HELFFER, Claude (pf) 1987
HELIOTROPE PRODUCTIONS 1989
HELLELAND, Arile (ten) 1987
HELLER, Katrin (act) 1993
HELLER, Martin (act) 1960, 66, 70
HELLEWELL, Louise (dan) 1977, 80
HELLMANN, Claudia (mez) 1966
HELLMANN, Lillian 1963
HELMA, Robert (ten) 1952
HELMOND, Katherine (act) 1968
HELNWEIN, Gottfried (des) 1989
HELPMANN, Max (act) 1956
HELPMANN, *Sir* Robert (chor, dan, act) 1948, 54, 57
HELROYD, Michael (spk) 1981
HEMSLEY, Thomas (bar) 1955, 62, 64, 68, 79
HENDERSON, Allan (act) 1993
HENDERSON, Betty (act) 1950
HENDERSON, Elizabeth (chor) 1986
HENDERSON, Hamish (des) 1965-67
HENDERSON, Hamish (spk) 1995
HENDERSON, Janet (sngr) 1981
HENDERSON, Mark (light) 1985, 86
HENDERSON, Michael (act) 1966
HENDERSON, Randall (light) 1994
HENDERSON, Roy (bar) 1947, 48
HENDERSON, Wight (pf) 1958, 59
HENDRICKS, Barbara (sop) 1983, 88
HENDRIKS, Marijke (mez) 1981
HENDRY, Joy (rdr) 1985
HENFREY, Janet (act) 1978
HENGEVELD, Gerard (pf) 1957
HENNEY, Del (act) 1968
HENNIQUAU, Patrick (dan) 1991
HENRI PATTERSON ENSEMBLE 1961
HENRIOT, Nicole (pf) 1954
HENRY, Edward (dan) 1981
HENRY, Lenny (ent) 1988
HENRY, May (act) 1970
HENRY, Stuart (act) 1957, 62
HENRY SHEREK 1949-53, 56-58
HENSCHEL, Jane (mez) 1993
HENSHALL, Douglas (act) 1989
HENSON, Nicky (act) 1967, 69
HENTY, Thomas (act) 1981
HENWOOD, Ray (act) 1990
HENZE, Hans Werner (cond) 1963, 70, 81, 82, 84
HEPBURN, Stuart (act) 1994
HEPPENSTALL, Rayner 1962
HEPPLE, Jeanne (act) 1959
HEPTON, Bernard (dir) 1959
HERBAULT, Michel (act) 1951
HERBERT, Jocelyn (des) 1961, 63
HERBERT, William (ten) 1949, 52, 53, 54
HERBIET, Jean (dir) 1980
HERCZOG, István (dan) 1976
HEREDIA, Carlos (gtr) 1989
HERIBAN, Josef (bs) 1970
HERINCX, Raimund (bar) 1970, 82
HERINGTON, Julian (dir) 1959
HERITAGE, Leslie (act) 1969
HERLIE, Eileen (act) 1948, 54
HERLITZKA, Roberto (act) 1996
HERMANN, Roland (bar) 1978
HERMANOS, Peris (des) 1989
HERMON, Michel (sngr) 1994
HERNANDEZ, Paco (dan) 1960
HERNANDO, Cristina (dan) 1989
HERRING, Elisabeth (act) 1970
HERRMANN, Theo (bs) 1952
HERSOV, Gregory (dir) 1988
HERZ, Gaby (act) 1994
HERZ, Joachim (dir) 1982
HERZOG, Joachim (des) 1987
HESS, *Dame* Myra 1951, 55, 56, 60
HESTER, Carolyn (mus) 1962
HETHERINGTON, Ann (mez) 1994, 95
HEWGILL, Roland (act) 1956
HEWLETT, Marion (light) 1994
HEYDEN, John van der (light) 1986
HEYWOOD, Heather (sngr) 1995
HEYWOOD, Pat (act) 1959
HEZKIA, Itzhak (act) 1987
HICK, Timothy (act) 1981
HICKEY, Brian (act) 1992
HICKOX, Richard (cond) 1989, 90
HICKS, Grant (des) 1979
HICKS, Zoë (act) 1967, 69, 70, 77
HICKSON, Joan (act) 1981
HICKSON, Robert (act) 1977
HIGASHI, Fujio (act) 1986
HIGGINS, Benjamin Pearce (arr) 1968
HIGGINS, Paul (act) 1987
HIGHTOWER, Rosella (dan, chor) 1950, 52, 57
HIGHWAY, Rene (act) 1988
HIGHWAY, Tomson (cond) 1988
HIGHWOOD, June (dan) 1979
HIGNETT, Mary (act) 1954
HIGUERAS, Cristina (act) 1983, 86
HILDEBRAND, Paul, jun. (dir) 1988
HILL, Arthur (act) 1954
HILL, Dave (act) 1980
HILL, Derek (exh dir) 1952
HILL, Jenny (sop) 1968
HILL, Margaret (dan) 1953
HILL, Martyn (ten) 1971, 85, 89
HILL, Rose (act) 1978
HILL, Stephen (act) 1983
HILL-BOYLE, Margaret (pf) 1948
HILLEBRAND, Nikolaus (bar) 1983
HILLEBRECHT, Hildegard (sop) 1966
HILLER, *Dame* Wendy (act) 1955, 66, 68, 69, 76, 87, 89
HILLMAN, David (ten) 1970, 76, 77
HILSDORF, Hans (pf) 1969
HILTON, Andrew (act) 1979
HILTON, Janet (cl) 1979
HINDEMITH, Paul (cond) 1955
HINDMARSH, Paul (ten) 1985, 87
HINDS, Ciaran (act) 1983
HINES, Jerome (bs) 1953
HINES, Ronald (act) 1953
HINKLEY, Brent (act) 1989
HINKSON, Mary (dan) 1963
HINSHAW, Susan (sop) 1985
HINTON, Milt (db) 1985, 86
HINTON, Paula (dan) 1958
HIOLSKI, Andrzej (bar) 1972
HIRA, Mikijiro (act) 1985, 86
HIRAKI, Yoshikazu (dan) 1988
HIRAMOTO, Kumi (dan) 1988
HIRSCH, Robert (act) 1954
HÍRSCHOVÁ, Jindřiška (des) 1970
HIRST, Linda (mez) 1984
HIRSTI, Marianne (sop) 1983
HIRT, Eleonore (act) 1948
HIRTE, Klaus (ten) 1966
HIRVONEN, Risto (sngr) 1987
HISCHER, Annelene (act) 1993
HJULSTRÖM, Lennart (dir) 1974
HLADIK, Peter (act) 1984, 87
HLAVACOVA-KRKOSOVA, Lubomira (act) 1991
HLAVSA, Jan (ten) 1970
HLOBILOVÁ, Eva (sngr) 1970
HLOPHE, Bongani (act) 1986
HO, Michael (dan) 1983
HÖBARTH, Erich (vn) 1996
HOBBS, Carleton (act) 1961
HOBI, Frank (dan) 1952
HOBKIRK, Bob (fiddle) 1985
HODEN, Pierre (act) 1985
HODGE, Patricia (act) 1976, 88
HODES, Art (mus) 1988
HODES, Linda (dan) 1963
HODGSON, Alfreda (cont) 1975, 80, 81, 85, 86
HODGSON, Charles (act) 1964
HODUREGEA, Liliana (act) 1992
HOENE, Barbara (sop) 1982
HOFFER, Hans (des) 1987
HÖFFGEN, Marga (cont) 1962
HOFFMAN, Adolf-Peter (act) 1970
HOFFMAN, Grace (mez) 1958, 66
HOFFMAN, Guy (act) 1956
HOFFMANN, Till (act) 1988
HOFSTÄTTER, Elfriede (pf) 1951
HOGAN, Bosco (act) 1974
HOGARD, Susan (dan) 1986, 91
HOGARTH, William (des) 1953
HÖGLUND, Paul (bar) 1974

HOGUE, Kerry McClatchy (dan) 1989
HOGWOOD, Christopher (cond) 1979, 90, 91, 96
HOHMANN, Jürgen (dan) 1984
HÖISETH, Kolbjörn (ten) 1974
HOLAH, David (dan) 1988
HOLBROOK, Hal (act) 1960
HOLDAWAY, Caroline (act) 1979
HOLDEN, Anthony (lect) 1992
HOLDEN, June (mez) 1962
HOLDEN, Stanley (dan) 1952, 53, 60
HOLDER, Geoffrey (chor, comp, des) 1968
HOLIČKOVÁ, Elena (sop) 1990
HÖLL, Hartmut (pf) 1984
HOLL, Robert (bar) 1993
HOLLAND, Anthony (act) 1949, 52
HOLLAND, James (perc) 1981
HOLLAND, Jeffrey (act) 1978
HOLLAND, Jerry (fiddle) 1996
HOLLEMAN, Gordon (bs) 1983
HOLLEY, William (ten) 1972
HOLLIGER, Heinz (ob) 1963, 65, 70, 73, 76, 84, 89
HOLLIGER, Ursula (hpd) 1973
HOLLIGER ENSEMBLE 1973
HOLLINGSWORTH, John (cond) 1951, 56
HOLLOWAY, Laurie (pf) 1966, 67
HOLLOWAY, Stanley (act) 1954
HOLLREISER, Heinrich (cond) 1966, 71
HOLLWEG, Ilse (sop) 1950
HOLLWEG, Werner (ten) 1971, 78, 81
HOLLYWOOD QUARTET 1957
HOLM, Ian (act) 1962
HOLM, Jörg (act) 1993
HOLM, Richard (ten) 1966
HOLMAN, Clare (act) 1986
HOLMES, Denis (act) 1955, 74, 81
HOLMES, Eda (dan) 1981
HOLMES, Michael (chor) 1950
HOLMGREN, Björn (dan, chor) 1957, 58
HOLMGREN, Jan (light) 1974
HOLMIN, Lorrie (act) 1967
HOLT, Hazel (sop) 1971
HOLT, Patrick (act) 1975
HOLT, Shannon (act) 1989
HOLTZMANN, Thomas (act) 1993
HOLZ, Wolfgang (act) 1984, 87
HÖLZKE, Karl Friedrich (ten) 1982
HOLZMAIR, Wolfgang (bar) 1995
HOMES, Peter (act) 1980
HOMEWOOD, Bill (dir, act) 1983
HONEGGER, Henri (vc) 1949
HONEY, Albert (fl) 1950
HONEYBALL, David (cond) 1984
HONEYMAN, Ian (ten) 1985
HONMA, Fusataka (act) 1972
HONG MO (dir) 1987
HØNNINGEN, Mette (dan) 1971
HOOD, Julie (dan) 1985, 88
HOOK, Nigel (des) 1985, 86
HOOPER, Brendan (act) 1994
HOOPER, Jim (act) 1977, 92
HOOPER, Robin (act) 1983
HOOPER-ROE, Janice (mez) 1973
HOOPMANN, Frank (sngr) 1952
HOOVER, Nan (des) 1994
HOPE, Gary (act) 1960
HOPE, Stuart (org) 1993
HOPE-WALLACE, Philip (lect) 1952
HÖPER, Wolfgang (act) 1977
HOPKINS, Bernard (act) 1963, 67
HOPKINS, Kaitlin (sngr) 1995
HOPPE, Heinz (ten) 1956
HOPPS, Stuart (act, chor) 1979, 89
HORÁČEK, Jaroslav ((bs) 1964, 70
HORÁKOVÁ, Eva (dan) 1990
HORAN, Gerard (act) 1990
HORDERN, *Sir* Michael (act) 1953, 62
HORENSTEIN, Jascha (cond) 1961
HORIO, Yukio (des) 1989
HÖRLIN, Tor (des) 1957, 59
HORN, Robert (act) 1995
HORNAK, Martin (act) 1991
HORNE, Barbara (act) 1986
HORNE, David (pf) 1990
HORNE, Marilyn (mez) 1964, 75
HORNE, William (ten) 1949
HORNIMAN, Christina (act) 1949
HORNUNG, Elisabeth (mez) 1982
HOROVITCH, David (act) 1968
HOROVITZ, Joseph (cond) 1958, 68
HORSEY, Helen (act) 1948
HORSFALL, Bernard (act) 1953, 57
HORSFALL, Brian (act) 1953
HORSTMANN, Jan Michael (cond) 1996
HORTEK, Pavel (dir) 1984
HÖRTNAGEL, Georg (db) 1977
HORTON, Joanne (mus) 1987
HORVATH, Janos (des) 1959
HOSALLA, Hans Dieter (cond) 1984
HOSHO, Fusao (act) 1972
HOSHO, Fusateru (act) 1972
HOSHO, Kan (act) 1972
HOSHO, Yaichi (act) 1972
HOSHO NOH THEATRE 1972
HOSSACK, Grant (cond) 1981
HOT ANTIC JAZZ BAND 1989
HOTCHKIS, John (comp) 1958
HOTEL PRO FORMA 1990
HOTTER, Hans (b-bar, narr) 1954, 65, 83, 96
HOUGHTON, William (tpt) 1987
HOUNSLOW, David (act) 1992
HOUSE, Eric (act) 1956
HOUSE, Richard (light) 1989, 91
HOUSTON, Donald (act) 1949, 56, 59
HOUSTON, Jean (sngr) 1948
HOUSTON, Roxane (sop) 1951
HOUSTON BALLET 1989
HOUSTON GRAND OPERA 1988, 96
HOVING, Lucas (chor) 1968
HOWARD, Alan (act) 1992
HOWARD, Andrée (chor, des) 1953, 58
HOWARD, Ann (mez) 1984
HOWARD, Ed (dir) 1985
HOWARD, Gillian (sngr) 1985
HOWARD, Leslie (spk) 1992
HOWARD, Michael (cond) 1956
HOWARD, Pamela (des) 1977, 83, 92
HOWARD, Richard (act) 1969
HOWARD, Trevor (act) 1947
HOWARTH, Elgar (cond) 1971, 74
HOWARTH, Judith (sop) 1995
HOWARTH, Kristine (act) 1977
HOWARTH, Michael (act) 1977
HOWDEN, Kathryn (act) 1986, 90, 91
HOWDEN, Lewis (act) 1990, 91
HOWE, George (act) 1951
HOWELL, Gillian (act) 1951
HOWELL, Gwynne (bs) 1976, 80, 81, 83, 88, 90, 94
HOWELL, Jonathan (act) 1990
HOWELLS, Adrian (act) 1993
HOWELLS, Anne (mez) 1972, 78, 84
HOWELLS, Martin (act) 1980
HOWELLS, R.C. (org) 1948
HOWES, Sally Ann (act) 1990
HOWITT, Andy (dir) 1993
HOWLETT, Neil (bar) 1964
HOWLETT, Noel (act) 1952
HOWMAN, Karl (act) 1991
HOWSON, Heather (sop) 1971
HOY, Derek (?) 1985, 86
HOYLAND, William (act) 1979
HOYOS, Cristina (chor, dan) 1977, 82, 89, 92
HRAMCOV, Andrei (bs) 1991
HRISTIĆ, Jovan (spk) 1963
HRISTIĆ, Stevan (cond) 1951
HRUBANT, Juraj (bs) 1990
HRUŠKA, Emanuel (sngr) 1964
HUA WEN YI, (act) 1987
HUBBARD, Celia (des) 1952
HUBBARD, Jacqui (des) 1992
HUCKO, Peanuts ((cl)) 1989
HUDD, Walter (act) 1961
HUDDERSFIELD CHORAL SOCIETY 1948
HUDEC, Christian (dan) 1962
HUDECOVÁ, Ľudmilla (sop) 1990
HUDZIAK, Andrzej (act) 1986
HUGHES, Allen (light) 1984
HUGHES, Christian (act) 1966
HUGHES, Clifford (ten) 1973, 74, 75, 78, 86
HUGHES, David (ten) 1968
HUGHES, Grace *and* Eric 1967
HUGHES, Hazel (act) 1966, 67
HUGHES, Jeffrey (dan) 1990
HUGHES, Malcolm (act) 1978
HUGHES, Mick (light) 1974, 76, 77, 78, 80, 92
HUGHES, Robert (spk) 1981
HUGHES, Ted (rdr) 1965
HUGO, Jean (des) 1949
HUGUENIN, Robert (act) 1973
HUISMAN, Jacques (dir) 1985
HUK, Tadeusz (act) 1989
HULBERT, Anthony (dan) 1962
HULKE, Sally (des) 1960, 62, 69
HÜLSE, Dieter (dan) 1984
HULSE, Eileen (sop) 1987, 91
HULTON, Celia (dan) 1981
HUMBIE, Betty (Lady Beecham) (pf) 1950
HUMPHREY LYTTELTON and his Band 1989
HUMPHREYS, Sheila (sngr) 1973
HUMPHRY, John (act) 1958
HUNGARIAN QUARTET 1948, 55, 65
HUNGARIAN STATE BALLET 1963, 73, 83
HUNGARIAN STATE OPERA 1963, 73
HUNT, Derek (act) 1959
HUNT, Hugh (dir) 1952
HUNT, Karen (sop) 1983
HUNT, Lorraine (sop) 1992
HUNT, Wish Mary (dan) 1958
HUNTER, Alan (act) 1973
HUNTER, Alastair (act) 1969
HUNTER, Andy (folk singer) 1995
HUNTER, Isla (pf) 1949
HUNTER, James (act) 1973
HUNTER, Karen (ent) 1993
HUNTER, Nan D. (sngr) 1961, 63
HUNTER, Rita (sop) 1974
HUNTER, Russell, (act) 1964, 68, 71, 73, 76
HUOT, Wladimir (dan) 1984
HURREN, Bonnie (act) 1964
HURRY, Leslie (des) 1948, 51, 55 - 58, 62
HURST, Christopher (act) 1979
HURT, John (act) 1964
HURWITZ, Emanuel (vn) 1954, 63
HURWITZ CHAMBER ENSEMBLE 1963
HÜSCH, Gerhard (bar) 1956
HUSSEY, John (act) 1962
HUTCHEON, Keith (act) 1990
HUTCHINSON, Penny (dan) 1992
HUTCHISON, Caroline (act) 1975
HUTT, William (act) 1956
HUTTENLOCHER, Philippe (bar) 1978
HUXLEY, Aldous (spk) 1962
HVOROSTOVSKY, Dmitri (bar) 1992
HYDE, Jonathan (act) 1973, 79
HYDE, Kenneth (act) 1952
HYDE, Margaret Field (sop) 1947, 54
HYE-KNUDSEN, Johan (cond) 1955
HYLAND, Frances (act) 1951
HYMAN, Dick (mus) 1986
HYND, Ronald (dan) 1954, 56, 60
HYNNINEN, Jorma (bar) 1987, 88
HYSLOP, Jeff (dan) 1986

IBANEZ, Susana (dan) 1989
IBLER, Eric (cond) 1993

ICHIDA, Kyomi (dan) 1995
ICTUS, Raducu (act) 1981
IDA, Michisuke (act) 1985
IGLESIAS, Eugenio (gtr) 1992
IGNATIEV, Oleg (chor) 1995
IHLE, Andrea (sop) 1982
IKEDA, Kosaka (light) 1986
IKEDO, Ko (act) 1985
ILOSVAY, Maria von (cont) 1952, 56
IMAI, Nobuko (va) 1996
IMAI, Yasuo (act) 1972
IMAMURA, Yasunori (theorbo) 1985
IMBUSCH, Paul (act) 1981
IMLACH, Hamish (act) 1974
IMRIE, Celia (act) 1979
INCERA, Julio (sngr) 1989
INGA-LISE (trapeze artist) 1979
INGALLS, James F. (light) 1982, 92-95
INGEY, Yedwart (act) 1994
INGHAM, Barrie (act) 1958, 70
INGIGLIARDI, Louis (vc) 1988
INGMAN, Trevor (act) 1977
INGRAM, Malcolm (act) 1975
INIGO, Paloma Perez (sop) 1989
INNES, George (act) 1960
INNIS GAELS 1967
INNOCENT, Harold (act) 1958, 68, 73, 81, 90
INOUE, Norihiro (act) 1990
INTERNATIONAL YOUTH CHORUS 1978
INTERNATIONAL YOUTH ORCHESTRA 1978
IONESCU, Carmen (act) 1992
IONESCU, Ileana Siana (act) 1992
IRELAND, Ian (act, dir) 1970, 73, 74, 75
IRELAND, Kenny (act) 1980
IRINO, Tomoe (act) 1989
IRMER, Patrick Harding (dan) 1981
IRONSIDE, Christopher (des) 1954
IRONSIDE, Robin (des) 1954
IRUZUBIETA, Raquel (act) 1979
IRVINE, Carole (act) 1995
IRVINE, Thom (bs) 1981, 83
IRVING, Ian (light) 1980
IRVING, Michael (act) 1966
IRVING, Robert (cond) 1951, 56, 63, 67
IRWIN, James (act) 1976
IRWIN, Jane (mez) 1995, 96
IRWIN, Robert (bar) 1947
ISAACKS, Sally Ann (dan) 1994, 95
ISAACS, Jason (act) 1992
ISAACS, Jeremy (spk) 1981
ISADOR, Michael (pf) 1977
ISAKOVIC, Milica (act) 1991
ISBISTER, Claire (act) 1959
ISELER, Elmer (cond) 1980
ISEPP, Martin (pf) 1976, 79
ISHII, Kenichi (act) 1988
ISMAEL, Gerard (act) 1985
ISOTTA, Riccardo (des) 1982
ISRAEL, Alain (dan) 1980
ISRAEL, George (sngr) 1949
ISRAEL PHILHARMONIC ORCHESTRA 1971, 75
ISRAEL PIANO TRIO 1991
ISSERLIS, Steven (vc) 1985, 90-91, 93-94
ISTODOR, Claudiu (act) 1992
ISTOMIN, Eugene (pf) 1963, 68
ITALIAN YOUTH ORCHESTRA *See* Orchestra Giovanile Italiana
ITINÉRAIRE, L' 1989
IVANOV, Lev (chor) 1949, 50, 51, 56, 59, 63, 79
IVERIA, Miki (rdr) 1981
IVES, Anne-Marie (sop) 1992
IVESON, Colin (bs) 1979
IWAI, Masahiro (des) 1990
IWASE, Akiko (act) 1990
IYER, Palghat Mani (mridangam) 1965
IZUMI, Yasuyuki (act) 1972
IZZO, Maria (act) 1988
IZZO, Sabino (act) 1988

JABLONSKI, Roman (vc) 1979
JACCOTTET, Christiane (hpd) 1970
JACKSON, Alan (rdr) 1971
JACKSON, Anne (act) 1984
JACKSON, Arthur (bs) 1974, 75, 76
JACKSON, Brian (act) 1958
JACKSON, Ellen (sop) 1981, 83
JACKSON, Gordon (act) 1967
JACKSON, Linda (dan) 1990
JACKSON, Michael (act) 1976
JACKSON, Nancie (act) 1959
JACKSON, Oliver (mus) 1987
JACKSON, Richard (bar) 1979, 83, 85, 86, 90
JACKSON, Rowena (dan) 1951, 54, 56
JACKSON, Walter (act) 1968
JACOB, Gordon (comp) 1958
JACOBEAN ENSEMBLE 1957
JACOBI, *Sir* Derek (act) 1973, 77, 78
JACOBS, Olu (act) 1980
JACOBS, Sally (des) 1961, 93
JACOBSEN, Palle (dan) 1971
JACOBSSON, John-Erik (ten) 1974
JACQUEMONT, Maurice (act) 1951
JACQUES, Reginald (cond) 1947, 49, 54
JACQUES LOUSSIER TRIO 1967
JACQUES ORCHESTRA 1947, 49, 54
JACQUET, Guy (act) 1961
JAGO, June (act) 1963, 67
JAGUSZ, Maria (mez) 1989, 94
JAHOLKOWSKI, Antoni (act) 1968
JAKAMEIT, Rosemarie (des) 1952
JAKIEL, Richard (act) 1976
JAKOWICZ, Krzysztof (vn) 1981
JALAS, Jussi (pf, cond) 1949, 59
JAMES, Carolyn (sop) 1990
JAMES, Eirian (mez) 1979, 87
JAMES, Emrys (act) 1961, 74
JAMES, Finlay (des) 1956, 80
JAMES, George (bs) 1950, 53
JAMES, Gerald (act) 1958, 60
JAMES, Graham (act) 1967
JAMES, Henry (act) 1988
JAMES, Karl (act) 1990
JAMES, Martin (dan) 1991
JAMES, Peter (dir) 1971, 74, 92
JAMES, Rachel (act) 1987
JAMES, Robert (act) 1960, 65, 71, 91
JAMES, Trilby (act) 1992
JAMESON, Pauline (act) 1957, 80
JAMISON, Judith (dan) 1968
JANÁČEK QUARTET 1964
JANČIĆ, Nikola (ten) 1962
JANES, Fiona (mez) 1993, 94
JANES, Hugh (act) 1961, 62
JANEVA, Magdalena (dan) 1962
JANICKA, Ewa (act) 1980
JANICKI, Leslaw (act) 1980
JANICKI, Waclaw (act) 1980
JANIGRO, Antonio (cond, vc) 1958
JANKOVIĆ, Stanoje (bar) 1962
JANOTTA, Monique (dan) 1976
JANOWITZ, Gundula (sop) 1966, 75
JANOWSKI, Marek (cond) 1989, 93
JANSEN, Sidney (light) 1985
JANSONS, Mariss (cond) 1986, 89, 92, 93, 95, 96
JANSSEN, Armin (pf) 1960
JANUCEK, Karin (des) 1988
JANVIER, Josiane (dan) 1962
JAROCKI, Jerzy (act) 1989
JAROSIEWICZ, Jadwiga (des) 1986
JARRE, Maurice (comp) 1953
JARRED, Mary (cont) 1953
JÄRVI, Neeme (cond) 1983-90, 92
JÄRVINEN, Jyrki (dan) 1987
JÄRVINEN, Simo (light) 1987
JARVIS, Andrew (act) 1980
JARVIS, Bill (act) 1967
JARVIS, Theresa (dan) 1991
JASPER, Bella (sop) 1971
JAUME, Bartomeu (pf) 1995
JAUNET, André (fl) 1954

JAYARAMAN, Lalgudi (vn) 1965
JAYSTON, Michael (act) 1964
JEAN CARNIE SCHOOL OF DANCING 1966
JEAN REYNOLDS SCHOOL OF DANCING 1963
JEANES, Rosemary (act) 1976
JEANS, Isabel (act) 1953
JEANS, Ursula (act) 1949, 50, 59
JEDLIČKA, Dalibor (bs) 1964, 70
JEDLIČKA, Rudolf (bar) 1970
JEFFERIES, Stephen (dan) 1975
JEFFERSON-HAYES, John (act) 1983
JEFFES, Peter (ten) 1984, 89
JEFFORD, Barbara (act) 1958, 77, 80
JEHLIČKOVÁ, Zora (sop) 1991
JEHRLANDER, Kåge (ten) 1974
JELINEK, Anica (sngr) 1962
JELÍNKOVÁ, Štěpánka (sngr) 1970
JELLINEK, Tristram (act) 1993, 95
JENISOVÁ, Eva (sop) 1990
JENKINS, Elin (act) 1985
JENKINS, Margo (act) 1956
JENKINS, Martin (dir) 1977
JENKINS, Neil (ten) 1980, 85, 87
JENKINS, Robin (spk) 1962
JENKINSON, Gerry (light) 1972, 79, 82, 83, 92, 93, 94, 95
JENN, Myfanwy (act) 1964
JENNER, Alexander (pf) 1958
JENNINGS, Gloria (mez) 1969
JENNINGS, Patricia Prattis (pf) 1987
JENNINGS, Robert (act) 1962
JENNINGS, Sandra (act) 1948
JENSEN, Svend Erik (dan) 1955
JENSEN, Thomas (cond) 1954
JEREZ, Gomez de (sngr) 1982
JERIE, Marek (vc) 1991
JERNEC, Karel (dir) 1964
JEROME, Roger (sngr) 1963
JERUSALEM, Siegfried (ten) 1982, 83
JESSETT, Michael (gtr) 1965
JEWESBURY, Edward (act) 1966, 67, 71, 90
JEWKES, Josephine (dan) 1986
JEZIL, Milos (ten) 1982
JHONES, Fernando (dan) 1979
JI ZHENGHUA (act) 1987
JI-YOUNG, Yi (dan) 1990
JIJEISHVILI, Hamlet (narr) 1987
JIMÉNEZ, Juan A. (dan) 1989, 92
JIN CAIQIN (act) 1987
JINDRÁK, Jindřich (bar) 1964, 70
JITIANU, Dan (des) 1992
JIVING LINDY HOPPERS 1988
JO, Haruhiko (act) 1988
JOANNOU, Ulrike (sop) 1982
JOBE, Tom (dan) 1981
JOCHUM, Eugen (cond) 1957, 70
JOE HARRIOTT BAND 1963
JOGLARS, Els 1992
JOH, Haruhiko (act) 1990
JOHN, Billy (act) 1963
JOHN, Caroline (act) 1961, 92
JOHN, Lindsay (lect) 1996
JOHN, Margaret (act) 1987
JOHN, Robin (act) 1965
JOHN ALLDIS CHOIR 1967, 68, 76, 78
JOHN DANKWORTH QUINTET 1965, 84, 86, 87, 90
JOHNSON, Bernard (des) 1967
JOHNSON, Graham (pf) 1983, 85, 94, 96
JOHNSON, Gus, (drums) 1985, 86
JOHNSON, James (bar) 1995
JOHNSON, Jim (act) 1986
JOHNSON, Karl (act) 1989
JOHNSON, Louis (chor) 1967
JOHNSON, Nicholas (dan) 1975, 91
JOHNSON, Onni (act) 1976
JOHNSON, Patricia (mez) 1975, 82
JOHNSON, Peter (act) 1954
JOHNSON, Reggie (mus) 1987
JOHNSON, Richard (act) 1962

KELMAN, James (spk) 1959
KELSALL, Moultrie (act) 1948, 49, 51
KELSEY, David (act) 1967
KEMBALL, Colin (act) 1964
KEMP, Jeremy (act) 1958
KEMP, Robert (lect, act) 1951
KEMP, Roger (act) 1976, 85
KEMP, Steve (light) 1988
KEMPE, Rudolf (cond) 1956, 59, 61, 72
KEMPFF, Wilhelm (pf) 1959
KENDAL, Felicity (act) 1972, 81
KENDALL, William (act) 1961
KENDALL, William (ten) 1982, 93, 94, 96
KENNEDY, Bryan (act) 1990
KENNEDY, Fiona (act) 1984
KENNEDY, James (act) 1968, 71, 73
KENNEDY, Jim (act) 1979
KENNEDY, John (vc) 1956
KENNEDY, Laurie (act) 1971
KENNEDY, *Sir* Ludovic (rdr) 1974, 75
KENNEDY, Mary Ann (clarsach, hp) 1991
KENNEDY, Maxwell (sngr) 1948
KENNEDY, Nigel (vn) 1986
KENNEDY, Norman (folk sngr) 1995
KENNEDY, Roderick (bs) 1980
KENNEDY, Sherilyn (dan) 1979
KENNY, John (tbn) 1987, 90
KENNY, Sean (des) 1959, 62
KENNY, Yvonne (sop) 1977, 78, 82, 93
KENT, Jonathan (act) 1972, 77, 79
KENT, Linda (dan) 1968
KENT, Phyllis (dan) 1987
KENT OPERA 1979
KENTISH, David (act) 1947
KENTISH, John (ten) 1960
KENTNER, Louis (pf) 1948, 56, 58, 77
KENTON, Peter (act) 1968
KEOGH, Garrett (act) 1987
KEOGH, Tom (des) 1949, 59
KEPLER, Kathy (dan) 1991
KÉRENDI, Jaleh (dan) 1962
KERMACK, Paul (act) 1960
KERN, Jürgen (act) 1987
KERN, Patricia (mez) 1975, 79
KERPEL, Roger van (act) 1988
KERR, Alistair (act) 1964
KERR, Catherine (dan) 1979
KERR, Fenella (act) 1987
KERR, Fraser (act) 1969
KERR, Geoffrey (act) 1958
KERR, James (act) 1992
KERR, Nan (act) 1962
KERREMANS, Eric (act) 1988
KERTÉSZ, István (cond) 1963, 67, 68
KERTÉSZ-GABRY, Edith (sop) 1981
KERYSE, Gerard (light) 1984
KESSELHEIM, Silvia (dan) 1978
KESTEREN, John van (ten) 1980
KETTEL, Gary (perc) 1984
KETTLEY, Steve (sax) 1991
KEVEHÁZI, Gábor (dan) 1983
KEY, Peter (des) 1967
KEYS, David (act) 1988
KEYS, Robert (pf) 1961, 64
KEYTE, Christopher (bs) 1967
KFIR, Michael (act) 1983
KHAN, Ali Akbar (sarode) 1963
KHAN, Bismillah (shahnai) 1965
KHAN, Imrat (surbahar) 1965
KHAN, Vilayat (sitâr) 1965
KHANEDANIAN, Grayer (ten) 1995
KHARABADZE, G. (act) 1979
KHARITONOV, Dimitri (bar) 1989, 92
KHIDASHELI, A. (act) 1979
KHOURI, Rhida El (act) 1976
KIDD, Anne (act) 1985, 93
KIDD, Carol (act) 1988
KIDD, Jean (cond) 1985
KIDD, John (act) 1955
KIEBZAK-DEBOGORSKA, Urszula (act) 1989
KIENZL, Monika (sngr) 1965
KIERNAN, David (act) 1988
KIHLGREN, Vera (dan) 1957
KIKUCHI, Kazuhiro (act) 1990
KILBURN, Weldon (pf) 1957
KILEY, Richard (rdr) 1976
KILGER, Heinrich (des) 1970
KILGOUR, Murray (dan) 1979
KILMER, Paul (sngr) 1983
KILOVITZ, Katherine (act) 1983
KIM, Mary (act) 1987
KIM, Willa (des) 1981
KIM, Young Uck (vn) 1983, 86
KIMBELL, *Prof.* David (lect) 1992, 93, 95, 96
KIMM, Fiona (mez) 1988, 92, 93
KIMURA, Koichi (dir) 1990
KIMURA, Toshimitsu (bar) 1972, 76
KINCAID, David (act) 1965, 66, 83, 91
KINDT, Thomas (dan) 1984
KINEYA, Katsusaburo (cond) 1955
KING, Amanda (dan) 1988
KING, Geoffrey (cond) 1985
KING, Joan (act) 1954
KING, Malcolm (bs) 1967
KING, Thea (cl) 1963
KING-WOOD, David (act) 1950
KINGHORN CHOIR 1963
KING'S HEAD THEATRE CLUB 1992
KING'S SINGERS 1972, 73, 74, 76, 81
KINGSLEY, *Dr* Colin (lect) 1994
KINGSLEY, Margaret (sop) 1974
KINGSTON, Mark (act) 1959
KINGTON, Miles 1988
KINLOCH, Maggie (dir) 1992
KINMAN, Chris (des) 1974
KINMONT, Meredith (act) 1961
KINNAIRD, Alison (mus) 1980
KINNAIRD, Cora (act) 1983
KINNEAR, Ian (bp) 1994
KINNIE, Tony (act) 1965
KINSELLA, Thomas (rdr) 1965
KIRBY, Johanna (act) 1979, 83
KIRBY, Michael (act) 1986
KIRBY, Nicholas (sngr) 1973
KIRCHNER, Ignaz (act) 1977, 95
KIRICHENKO, Irena (act) 1978
KIRILOVÁ, Ida (sop) 1990
KIRKBY, Emma (sop) 1981
KIRKBY, Neil (sngr) 1994
KIRKCALDY CHORAL UNION members 1952
KIRKPATRICK, Charlotte (dan) 1981
KIRKPATRICK, Ralph (hpd) 1955
KIRKWOOD, John (act) 1964
KIRKWOOD, Pat (act) 1976
KIROV OPERA 1991, 95
KIROV ORCHESTRA SOLOISTS 1991
KIRSCHSTEIN, Leonore (sop) 1971
KIRSHBAUM, Ralph (vc) 1973, 78, 92
KISSIN, Evgeny (pf) 1996
KISSOON, Jeffery (act) 1972
KIT, Mikhail (bs) 1991
KIT AND THE WIDOW 1988
KITAENKO, Dmitri (cond) 1992
KITAKIZAKI, Takashi (light) 1990
KITCHEN, *Dr* John (lect) 1995
KITCHEN, John (hpd,org) 1985, 93
KITCHEN, Linda (sop) 1994
KITCHEN, Michael (act) 1981
KITCHIN, Margaret (pf) 1962, 65, 71, 72
KITOVITZ, Katherine (act) 1983
KITTEL, Maik (act) 1995
KITTI, Tommi (dan, light) 1987
KIVELÄ, Sampo (dan) 1987
KJELLGREN, Ingeborg (mez) 1959
KJELLSON, Ingvar (act) 1967
KLAFF, Jack (act) 1979
KLAS, Eri (cond) 1987
KLAVSEN, Verner (dan) 1957
KLAYMAN, Ivor (bs) 1994
KLECHOT, Rajmund (act) 1966
KLEE, Bernhard (cond) 1968
KLEIBER, Carlos (cond) 1966
KLEIBER, Eleonore (des) 1984, 95
KLEIMERT, Dorrit (sop) 1974
KLEIN, Allen Charles (des) 1982
KLEINDIENST, Stella (sop) 1981
KLEINSMITH, Leslie (act) 1988
KLEMPERER, Otto (cond) 1957, 58, 61, 68
KLIEN, Walter (pf) 1971
KLIMCZEWSKA, Violetta (dan) 1986
KLOBUCAR, Berislav (cond) 1974
KLOSINSKI, Edward (light) 1986
KLOTZ, Florence (des) 1959
KĽUKOVÁ, Anna (sngr) 1990
KLUSEK, Barbara (dan) 1986
KMENTT, Waldemar (ten) 1966
KMET, Tiffany (dan) 1994
KNAPP, Josef (ten) 1965
KNAPP, Peter (bar) 1978
KNAPP, Terence (act) 1963
KNAPPER, Rolf (sngr) 1986
KNAUP, Dieter (act) 1984, 87, 94
KNEALE, Patricia (act) 1960
KNEEBONE, Tom (act) 1955
KNEELAND, Richard (act) 1968
KNIGHT, Alan (act) 1964
KNIGHT, David (act) 1966
KNIGHT, Esmond (act) 1950, 66
KNIGHT, Gillian (mez) 1978
KNIGHT, Joan (dir) 1966, 85, 86
KNIGHT, Michael (des) 1971
KNIGHTLY, Will (act) 1971
KNILL, Hans (dan) 1970
KNIPLOVÁ, Naděžda (sop) 1964, 70
KNOBEL, Marita (mez) 1981
KNODE, Charles (des) 1973
KNOLL, Rudolf (bar) 1966
KNOSPE, Mike (dan) 1984
KNOWLES, Pauline (act) 1993
KNOWLSON, James 1984
KNOX, Alexander (act) 1968
KNUSSEN, Oliver (cond) 1985
KOBAKHIDZE, B. (act) 1979
KOBAYASHI, Katsuya (narr) 1987
KOBAYASHI, Yoshiro (act) 1972
KOCH, Inge (dan) 1976
KOCH, Karl-Heinz (ten) 1982
KOCH, Marion (act) 1987
KOCHERGIN, Eduard (des) 1987
KOCHETOVA, Natalia (act) 1994
KOČÍ, Přemysl (bar) 1964
KOČÍ, Viktor (ten) 1964, 70
KOCKISCH, Uwe (act) 1994
KOCSIS, Zoltán (pf) 1978, 81, 83
KODETOVÁ, Sylvia (sop) 1964
KODO 1985
KOECKERT QUARTET 1960
KOEGEL, Ilse (mez) 1952
KOENIG, Monica (des) 1958
KOENIG ENSEMBLE 1984
KOESUN, Ruth Ann (dan) 1953
KOGA, Mie (act) 1990
KOGAN, Leonid (vn) 1967
KÖHL, Uschi (des) 1981
KOHLER, Anna (act) 1986
KOHLER, Estelle (act) 1983
KOHN, Karl Christian (bs) 1965
KOKKINOS, Daphnis (dan) 1995
KOLÁŘ, Zbyněk (des) 1964
KOLASINSKA, Ewa (act) 1989
KOLCHEF, Yuri (act) 1991
KOLLNER, Alfredo (dan) 1960
KÖLLNER, Wolf-Dietrich (act) 1993
KOLLO, René (ten) 1972
KOLTAI, Ralph (des) 1967, 70, 76
KOM, Mary (act) 1987
KOMAR, Chris (dan) 1979, 94
KOMINE, Lily (des) 1988, 91
KOMISCHE OPER BALLET, Berlin 1984
KOMLÓSSY, Erzsébet (cont) 1973
KOMOLOVA, Valentine (des) 1991
KONDINA, Olga (sop) 1991
KONDRASHIN, Kyril (cond) 1977
KONEČNÁ, Jarmila (des) 1964, 70
KONIEL, Somu (act) 1987

McLELLAN, Robert (spk) 1963
MacLENNAN, Dolina (rdr) 1974, 79, 80-81
MacLENNAN, Elizabeth (act) 1970
MacLENNAN, Neiliann (sngr) 1961
MacLEOD, Angus C. (sngr) 1963, 66
MacLEOD, Anna (act) 1976
MacLEOD, Donald (sngr) 1962
MacLEOD, Pipe-Major Donald (bp) 1964
MacLEOD, Donnie (sngr) 1980
MacLEOD, Fiona (story-teller) 1993
MacLEOD, Johan (sngr) 1962
MacLEOD, Kitty (sngr) 1947
MacLEOD, Mary (act) 1989
McLEOD, Norman (act) 1959
MacLEOD, Rhona (sngr) 1961, 63, 65
MacLEOD, Seonaid (dan) 1980
McLERIE, Allyn (dan) 1950
MacLIAMMÓIR, Michéal (act) 1957
McLURE, James (act) 1985
MacMAHON, Patricia (sop) 1969, 85, 86, 90, 92
McMANUS, Mark (act) 1974
MacMILLAN, David (act) 1959, 66
McMILLAN, Dougald (spk) 1980
MacMILLAN, Helen (sngr) 1948, 62
MacMILLAN, *Sir* Kenneth (dan, chor) 1951, 53, 56, 60-63, 75, 79
MacMILLAN, James (cond, spk) 1990, 93, 96
McMILLAN, Roddy (act) 1950, 51, 53, 54, 56, 57, 59, 73, 75
McMONAGLE, Kevin (act) 1989
McMONAGLE, Walter (act) 1971
McMORLAND, Alison (folk sngr) 1995
McMURRAY, John (des) 1979
McNAIR, Sylvia (sop) 1993
McNALLY, Tony (mus) 1992
McNAMARA, Desmond (act) 1990
McNAUGHT, Graeme (pf) 1993
McNAUGHTAN, Adam (folk sngr) 1995
McNAUGHTON, David (dan) 1981
MacNAUGHTON, Ian (act) 1950, 51, 53
MacNEACAIL, Aonghas (rdr) 1980
MacNEE, Patrick (act) 1954
McNEELEY, Sandra (act) 1991
McNEIL, Claudia (act) 1965
MacNEIL, Dorothy (sop) 1951
MacNEIL, Flora (sngr) 1962, 80
MacNEILL, Padraig (story-teller) 1993
McNICOL, Henry (spk) 1963
MacNIVEN, Catherine A. (sngr) 1961, 62
McNIVEN, David (mus dir) 1992
McNULTY, Pat 1967
MacOWAN, Michael (dir) 1952
MacPHEE, James (sngr) 1951
McPHEE, Willie (folk sngr, storyteller) 1993, 95
McPHERSON, Carolyn (dan) 1987
MacPHERSON, George (story-teller) 1993
McPHERSON, William (vn) 1961
McQUARRIE, Stuart (act) 1991
MacQUEEN, Peter (act) 1986
MacRAE, Donald (sngr) 1963
MacRAE, Duncan (act) 1948, 49, 50, 51, 57, 59, 61, 63, 65, 66
MacRAE, Iain (act) 1990
MacRAE, John A. (sngr) 1961, 63
MacRAE, Kenneth (sngr) 1963
MACREADY, Susan (act) 1970
MacRITCHIE, Allan (sngr) 1947
McRUVIE, David (dir) 1990
MacSWEEN, Gayrie (dan) 1958
McTAGGART, Archie (sngr) 1966
McTAVISH, Graham (act) 1994
MacVICAR, Donald (sngr) 1961
MADAU-DIAZ, Antonello (dir) 1967
MADDALENA, James (bar) 1988, 92
MADDOX, Diana (act) 1956
MADEJSKY, Evaryste (dan) 1950
MADEY, Boguslav (cond) 1976
MADRID, Tomas de (dan) 1977, 78
MADSEN, Egon (dan) 1963

MAEDA, Haruhiro (act) 1972
MAEDA, Jun (des) 1976
MAEDA, Seison (des) 1955
MAEDER, Armin (sngr) 1970
MAESTRI, Giancarlo (act) 1965
MAGACEVESCHI, Grigore (act) 1992
MAGALLANES, Nicholas (dan) 1952
MAGALOFF, Nikita (pf) 1969
MAGDALEN COLLEGE, CHOIR, Oxford members 1984
MAGEE, Patrick (act) 1959
MAGGIO MUSICALE ORCHESTRA, 1988
MAGGIPINTO, Marigia (dan) 1995
MAGNUSSON, Magnus (spk) 1981
MAGUIRE, Hugh (vn) 1961
MAGUIRE, Jack (act) 1948
MAGUIRE, James (act) 1963
MAGUIRE, Leo (act) 1963
MAGUIRE, Leonard (act) 1951, 58, 59, 60, 62, 63, 65, 69, 85, 87
MAGYAR, Thomas (vn) 1965
MAHILLON, Didi (des) 1962
MAHLAU, Alfred (des) 1954
MAHLER, Donald (dan) 1962
MAHOOTY, Chester (dan) 1990
MAIBORODA, Nikolai (ten) 1990, 91
MAICANESCU, Simona (act) 1992
MAICH, Giorgio (act) 1970
MAIER, Tracy-Kai (dan) 1981
MAIGAT, Pierre-Yves le (b-bar) 1985
MAILER, Norman (spk) 1962
MAIN, John (act) 1948
MAINARDI, Enrico (vc) 1948, 55, 60
MAIORANO, Robert (dan) 1967
MAIOROVA, Elena (act) 1994
MAIRENE, Manuel (dan) 1960
MAISENBERG, Oleg (pf) 1993
MAISKY, Mischa (vc) 1994
MAJIMA, Miya (sngr) 1976
MAJOR, Aime (act) 1956
MAKAROVA, Natalia (dan) 1977
MAKEHAM, Eliot (act) 1954
MAKEIEFF, Macha (des) 1988, 95
MAKHALINA, Yulia (dan) 1991
MAKHARADZE, A. (act) 1979
MAKSIMOVIĆ, Velizar (bar) 1962
MAKSYMIUK, Jerzy (cond) 1979, 81, 85, 87, 90
MAKSYMOWICZ, Danuta (act) 1989
MALACHOVSKÝ, Ondrej (bs) 1990
MALAHIDE, Patrick (act) 1973, 74
MALAIMARE, Mihai (act) 1981
MALAK, Tadeusz (act) 1989
MALAMUD, Marc D. (des) 1984
MALAS, Spiro (bs) 1967
MALATESTA, Giuseppe Crisolini (des) 1982
MALBIN, Elaine (sop) 1954
MALCHENKO, Vladimir (bar) 1990
MALCLÈS, Jean-Denis (des) 1949, 57, 60, 61
MALCO, Paolo (act) 1970
MALCOLM, Douglas (act) 1968
MALCOLM, George (hpd) 1960-61, 63, 67
MALCUZYNSKI, Witold (pf) 1960
MALDONADO, Rafael (sngr) 1958
MALECKI, Mariusz (dan) 1986
MÁLEK, Viktor (cond) 1990
MALENFANT, Lina (dan) 1994
MALEY, Ann (act) 1973
MALEY, Leonard (act) 1950
MALIN, Hannu (bs) 1987
MALLA, Gerardo (dir) 1989
MALLESON, Miles (act) 1950, 59
MALLET, Agnès (act) 1981, 86
MALLETT, Alfred (sngr) 1961
MALLIER, Julien (act) 1960
MALONE, Carol (sop) 1971
MALOVIK, Francis (dan) 1984
MALY THEATRE 1986
MAMA COMPANY, La, 1967, 76
MANCHESTER CAMERATA members 1986

MANDAK, Rudolf (sngr) 1968
MANDAUS, Luděk (dir) 1970
MANDEL, Thilo (act) 1993
MANDIKIAN, Arda (cont) 1952
MANEN, Hans van (chor,des) 1970, 75
MANESSIER, Alfred (des) 1960
MANETTI, Giuliano (act) 1975
MANEZ, Raoul de (act) 1985
MANFORD, John (act) 1969
MANG-HABASHI, Karin (mez) 1990
MANGIN, Noel (bs) 1968
MANHATTAN PROJECT 1971
MANIM, Mannie (light) 1986
MANKER, Paulus (act) 1995
MANKOWITZ, Wolf (spk) 1963
MANN, Karen (act) 1979
MANNING, Jane (sop) 1971, 74, 79, 90
MANNING, Judy (act) 1956
MANNINI, Elena (des) 1970
MANNION, Rosa (sop) 1985, 94
MANNONI, Paola (act) 1965
MANNOV, Johannes (bs) 1991
MANSOUR, Stephen (sngr) 1994
MANTOVANI, Dino (bs) 1957
MANUEL, Robert (act) 1954
MANZANARES, Emilia Garcia (sngr) 1958
MANZANO, Emilio (dan) 1991
MAOR, Yehuda (dan) 1974
MAR, Norman del (cond) 1961, 62-65
MARACCI, Carmelita (chor) 1953
MARAGLIANO, Luisa (sop) 1972
MARAKOFF, Serge (dan) 1962
MARAN, Mike (?) 1986
MARANO, Ezio (act) 1956
MARATRAT, Alain (dir) 1985
MARAVILLA, Luis (gtr) 1953
MARBAUX, Jacqueline (act) 1955
MARBERG, Annika (sop) 1988
MARCEAU, Marcel (act, dir) 1948, 53, 67
MARCELLI, Rino (sngr) 1988
MARCH, Elspeth (act) 1948
MARCHAIX, Jacques (ent) 1969
MARCHAND, Lucienne le (act) 1953
MARCHI, Mario Vellani (des) 1957
MARCHI, Michele de (act) 1996
MARESCA, Rosalia (sop) 1963
MARESTIN, Valerie (sngr) 1985
MARET, Jean-Claude (des) 1983
MAREV, Ann (act) 1985
MARGARITA (dan) 1977
MARGINE, Marzio (act) 1970
MARGINEANU, Remus (act) 1991
MARGITA, Stefan (ten) 1993
MARGOLYES, Miriam (act) 1989
MARGONI, Alain (pf) 1988
MARHEINEKE, Regina (sop) 1968
MARIDJAN-KOOP, Olivia (dan) 1992, 93
MARIE, Michel (light) 1985
MARIEMMA (chor, dan) 1977, 78, 89
MARIJNEN, Franz (dir) 1988
MARIN, Maguy (chor) 1986
MARIN, Manolo (chor) 1989
MARIN, Montserrat (dan) 1989
MARINESCU, Theodor (act) 1991
MARINI, Anita (act) 1982
MARINI, Marilù (act) 1979, 88
MARIONETTEATERN, Stockholm 1967
MARIS, Katy (dan) 1987
MARJORIBANKS, Brian (act) 1964
MÁRK, Tivadar (des) 1963, 73
MARK MORRIS DANCE GROUP 1992-96
MARKET THEATRE, Johannesburg 1986
MARKEVICH, Igor (cond) 1962
MARKHAM, Gervase (fl) 1951
MARKOLOV, Yuri (sngr) 1990
MARKOVA-MIKHAILENKO, Olga (sngr) 1995
MARKOVIĆ, Branko (dan) 1951, 62
MARKOVIĆ, Olivera (act) 1991
MARKOVIĆ, Vjera (dan) 1960
MARKS, Alfred (act) 1963, 80
MARKS, Frederick (act) 1976

NIGHTINGALE, Michael (act) 1951
NIJINSKA, Bronislava (chor) 1953, 57, 87
NIJINSKY, Vaslav (chor) 1987
NIKOLAEVA, Tatyana (pf) 1991
NIKOLAIS, Alwin (chor, des) 1975
NIKOLAIS DANCE THEATER 1975
NIKOLSKY, Gleb (bs) 1991
NILON, Paul (ten) 1994
NILSSON, Birgit (sop) 1959, 74
NILSSON, Jan (ten) 1987, 88
NILSSON, Margareta (sngr) 1986
NILSSON, Pia-Marie (sop) 1988
NIMKOFF, Mark (dan) 1994
NIMMO, Derek (act) 1957
NINAGAWA, Yukio (dir) 1985, 86, 88, 90, 91
NINAGAWA THEATRE COMPANY 1988, 90-91
See also Toho Theatre Company
NINIDZE, M. (act) 1979
NINIDZE, V. (act) 1979
NISHIHARA, Jun (act) 1990
NISHIKAWA, Sonoyo (light) 1994
NISHIKUBO, Haruyoshi (act) 1990
NISSEN, Hans Hermann (bar) 1965
NITRANOVÁ, Marta (mez) 1990
NIZIENKO, Nikolai (bs) 1990, 91
NOACK, Klaus (act) 1987
NOAR, Doria (act) 1960
NOBBE, Walter (des) 1983, 86, 89
NOBBS, John (dan) 1980
NOBEL, Felix de (cond) 1951, 65
NOBILI, Lila de (des) 1959
NOBLE, Adrian (dir) 1979, 85
NOBLE, Larry (act) 1969
NÖCKER, Hans Günter (b-bar) 1958, 75
NODA, Hideki (dir, act) 1987, 90
NOEL, Bernard (act) 1948
NOËL, Jacques (des) 1953, 64, 71
NOEL, Wendy (act) 1950
NOGARA, Anna (act) 1970
NOGARET, Nicole (dan) 1960
NOGUCHI, Ei (act) 1989
NOGUCHI, Isamu (des) 1963
NOGUCHI, Yoshihisa (act) 1972
NOIRET, Philippe (act) 1953
NOLAN, Anto (act) 1987
NOLTE, Pietro (act) 1947
NOMVETE, Pamela (act) 1992
NONI, Alda (sop) 1949, 53, 54
NOONE, Jennifer (des) 1967
NOOTEBLOOM, Cees (spk) 1963
NORDIN, Birgit (sop) 1959
NORDMO-LÖVBERG, Aase (sop) 1959
NORMAN, Jay (dan) 1959
NORMAN, Jennie (des) 1991
NORMAN, Jessye (sop) 1972, 74, 77-82, 84, 91
NORMAN, Robert (act) 1991
NORMINGTON, John (act) 1975
NORRINGTON, Roger (cond) 1979, 80, 82
NORRIS, David Owen (pf) 1985, 86
NORRIS, Peter (des) 1956, 57
NORTH, Robert (chor, dan) 1975, 83
NORTH, Wendy (des) 1959
NORTHERN SINFONIA 1991
NORTHERN STAGE COMPANY, 1992
NORTON, Alex (act) 1974
NORTON, Darryl (dan) 1986
NORTON, Deborah (act) 1981
NORTON, Martin (act) 1962
NORTON, Terry (act) 1986
NORWICH, John Julius 1981
NOTTINGHAM PLAYHOUSE 1969, 75, 77, 96
NOUVEL ORCHESTRE PHILHARMONIQUE 1989
NOVIKOVA, Tatiana (sop) 1991
NOVOTNÁ, Božena (sngr) 1964
NOWACKI, Piotr (bar) 1992
NOWAKOWSKI, Marian (bs) 1952
NOWINSKA, Beata (dan) 1986
NOWOSIELSKI, Charles (dir) 1988, 91
NOWOSIELSKI, Stefan (act) 1991
NTSHINGA, Thoko (act) 1986
NUCCI, Leo (bar) 1981
NUGUE, Charles (act) 1951
NUMMI, Lassi (rdr) 1986
NUNEZ, Paula (dan) 1990
NUNN, Trevor (dir) 1978
NUOVA COMPAGNIA DI CANTO POPOLARE 1975
NUREYEV, Rudolf (dan, chor) 1975, 84, 85, 87, 90
NURMIMAA, Seppo (des) 1959, 81, 87
NUTTGENS, Patrick (spk) 1981
NUYTS, Jan (dan) 1970
NYE, Palma (dan) 1947, 48
NÝVLT, Vladimir (des) 1964, 70

O AONGHUSA, Micheal (act) 1974
O'BRIAIN, Michéal (act) 1968, 74
O'BRIEN, Gerard Gray (act) 1990
O'BRIEN, Mary (sop) 1967
O'BRIEN, Niall (act) 1974
O'CALLAGHAN, Maurice (act) 1958
O'CALLAGHAN, Patrick (act) 1968
O'CLERY, Joan (des) 1995
O'CONNELL, Patrick (act) 1992
O'CONNOR, Kevin (act) 1967
O'DELL, Etain (act) 1958, 59
O'DONOHOE, Deirdre (chor) 1985
O'HALLORAN, Michael (act) 1956
O'HARA, Joan (act) 1959
O'HARA, Mary (sngr) 1956
O'HARA, Riggs (act) 1961, 72
O'HARA, Steve (act) 1981
O'HORGAN, Tom (dir) 1967
O'KANE, Patrick (act) 1995
O'KEEFE, Timothy (dan) 1989
O'KELLY, Aideen (act) 1968
O'LEARY, Paul (light) 1990
O'MAHONEY, Robert (act) 1979
O'MARA, Dickon (light) 1992
O'NEAL, Alison (dan) 1980
O'NEILL, Dennis (ten) 1980, 92, 93
O'NEILL, Fiona (sop) 1989
O'NEILL, Máire (act) 1994
O'NEILL, Patricia (sop) 1975, 76
O'NEILL, Sheila (ent) 1964
O'REGAN, Mark (act) 1987
O'REILLY, Melanie (act) 1991
O'REILLY, Sheilah (dan) 1952, 53
O'SHAUGHNESSY, Peter (act) 1963
O'SULLIVAN, Philip (act) 1974
OAKLAND, Jane (sop) 1981, 83
OATES, Robert (act) 1979, 86
OBAN GAELIC CHOIR 1963
OBERDORFER, Bert (act) 1977
OBERLIN, Jean-Jacques (spk) 1954
OBERLIN, Russell (c ten) 1961
OBONYA, Cornelius (act) 1994
OBORIN, Lev (pf) 1962
OBRADOVIĆ, Katarina (dan) 1951, 62
OBRAZTSOV, Sergei (dir) 1966
OBRAZTSOVA, Olga (pf) 1966
OBSIL, Jindrich (act) 1991
OCAÑA, Ricardo (dan) 1989
OCHOA, Rosa (dan) 1991
OCKRENT, Mike (dir) 1980
OGAN, Banu (dan) 1994
OGASANU, Virgil (act) 1971
OGATA, Atsushi (dan) 1982
OGATA, Kikuko (des) 1989
OGDON, John (pf) 1961-63, 65, 74, 87
OGILVIE, George (ent) 1964
OGNOVENKO, Vladimir (bs) 1986, 91
OH, Chong-Suk (act) 1990
OHARA, Noriko (dan) 1977, 80, 85
OHLSON, Arne (ten) 1959
OHN, Gérard (chor, dan) 1959
OISHI, Keita (act) 1990
OISTRAKH, David (vn) 1962, 68
OISTRAKH, Igor (vn) 1991
OKADA, Tadashi (act) 1990
OKE, Alan (bar) 1981, 82, 83, 89, 93, 94
OKHOTNIKOV, Nikolai (bs) 1991, 95
OKINE, Daniel 1990
OKTAY, Deniz (dan) 1994, 95
OKUBO, Makiko (dan) 1988
OKUNIEV, Viacheslav (des) 1995
OLAFSEN, Inge (dan) 1971
OLD VIC 1947, 50, 52-55, 58-61
OLDHAM, Arthur (cond) 1987, 92
OLDMAN, Gary (act) 1983
OLIVER, Alexander (ten) 1969, 78, 80
OLIVER, Anthony (act) 1965
OLIVER, Cordelia (lect) 1992
OLIVER, John (rdr) 1947
OLIVER, Roland (act) 1973
OLIVER, Stephen (act) 1977
OLIVER JONES TRIO 1991
OLIVERO, Magda (sop) 1963, 69
OLIVIER, Laurence, *Lord* (spk) 1963
OLIVIER, Nicolas (act) 1969
OLLENDORF, Fritz (bs) 1954
OLSCHOK, Herbert (act) 1987
OLSON, Ian (folk sngr) 1995
OLSSON, Catharina (mez) 1986, 87
OLSSON, Diana (act) 1966
OLSSON-FORSBERG, Marito (dan) 1991
OLSZEWSKA, Izabela (act) 1989
OLTEANU, Smaragda (act) 1991
OLTMAN, Dwight (cond) 1990
OMAN, Julia Trevelyan (des) 1967, 85
OMURA, June (dan, des) 1992-95
ONAFRI, Stefano (act) 1982
ONCINA, Juan (ten) 1953, 54, 55, 60, 63
ONIŠČENKO, Juraj (bar) 1990
ONKINEN, Uno (dan) 1959
ONOE, Umesuke (dan) 1955
ONYEMERE, Clara (act) 1992
ONZIA, Koen (dan) 1989
OPATZ, Mari (sngr) 1988
OPEN THEATRE, Belgrade 1991
OPÉRA DE LYON 1985
OPÉRA DE LYON BALLET 1986
OPÉRA DE LYON ORCHESTRA 1985
OPERA NORTH 1989, 92, 94
OPERA THEATER OF ST LOUIS 1983
OPITZ, Uta (dan) 1984
OPP, Kurt-Egon (sngr) 1958, 66
OPPENHEIM, Hans (cond) 1949, 50, 52, 53, 55, 59
OPRINA, Gheorghe (act) 1971
ORAM, Daphne (electronic music) 1961
ORAN, Maria (sop) 1989
ORANGE TREE THEATRE 1992
ORBACH, Judith (act) 1974
ORCHESTRA AMBROSIANA 1982
ORCHESTRA CAMERA LIRICA OF MADRID 1985
ORCHESTRA GIOVANILE ITALIANA 1988
ORCHESTRA OF THE AGE OF ENLIGHTENMENT 1994
ORCHESTRA OF THE EIGHTEENTH CENTURY 1983, 96
ORCHESTRE DE LA SUISSE ROMANDE 1949
ORCHESTRE DE PARIS 1973, 76, 85
ORCHESTRE DES CONCERTS COLONNE 1947
ORCHESTRE NATIONAL DE FRANCE 1975, 85
ORCHESTRE NATIONAL DE LA RADIODIFFUSION FRANÇAISE 1950, 54, 64
ORCHESTRE NATIONAL DE LA RADIODIFFUSION FRANÇAISE WIND QUINTET 1950
ORD, Boris (cond) 1953
ORDMAN, Jeanette (dan) 1974
ORFEON DONOSTIARRA 1962
ORGAL, Yehiel (light) 1983
ORGAN, Sandra (dan) 1989
ORIGINAL PRAGUE SYNCOPATED ORCHESTRA 1990

PEDANI, Paolo (bar) 1969
PEDEN, Elizabeth (dan) 1977
PEDERSEN, Ove Christian (des) 1955, 71
PEDRAZZI, Elisabetta (act) 1975
PEDRAZZINI, Horacio (act) 1979
PEDREGAL, Helio (act) 1986
PEDUZZI, Laurent (des) 1988
PEDUZZI, Richard (des) 1995
PEEBLES, Alison (act) 1994
PEEL, Eileen (act) 1958
PEGURA, Tatiana (mez) 1991
PEJSKOVA, Helena (dan) 1976
PELLE, Nadia (mez) 1984
PELLEGRINI, Carlo (dan) 1975
PEMBER, Roy (act) 1992
PEMBERTON, Charles (act) 1964
PEN DU BOIS, Raoul (des) 1952
PEÑA, Maydee (dan) 1991
PEÑA, Paco (gtr) 1977
PENCIULESCU, Radu (dir) 1973
PENDERECKI, Krzysztof (comp) 1967
PENMAN, Eileen (folk sngr) 1995
PENRY-JONES, Peter (act) 1959
PENTELOW, Arthur (act) 1959
PENU, Raluca (act) 1992
PEPER, Uwe (ten) 1982
PEPINO, Marius (act) 1971
PERA, Roxana (act) 1991
PERAHIA, Murray (pf, cond) 1973, 81, 84
PERCEVAL, Robert (act) 1947
PERCUSSIONS DE STRASBOURG, Les 1973, 91
PERDELWITZ, Heidrun (act) 1993
PERENYI, Miklós (vc) 1996
PEREZ, Dorio (dan) 1989
PERFORMANCE GROUP 1974
PERGAMENSCHIKOW, Boris (vc) 1995, 96
PERIĆ, Boyana (dan) 1951
PERIĆ, Dragomir (sngr) 1962
PERLASOVA, Evgenia (sop) 1991
PERLMAN, Itzhac (vn) 1969, 75
PERNERSTORFER, Alois (bar) 1951
PERQUY, Laurence (des) 1989
PERRAS, John (cond) 1966
PERREAULT, Jean-Pierre (chor, des) 1994
PERRET, Edith (act) 1953
PERRETT, Richard (sngr) 1983
PERRICONE, Mario (dan) 1984
PERRIERS, Danièle (sop) 1974, 75
PERRONE, Luigi (act) 1972
PERROT, Guy (act) 1981, 86
PERROT, Jules (chor) 1950, 59, 79, 91
PERRY, Clive (dir) 1981, 86
PERRY, Igal (dan) 1974
PERRY, Morris (act) 1957, 92
PERSSON, Bent (mus) 1986
PERSSON, Tore (sngr) 1959
PERTH THEATRE 1959, 85, 86
PEŠEK, Libor (cond) 1991, 93, 95
PESELEV, Arcady (act) 1978
PEŞINA, Victor (dan) 1981
PEŠKOVÁ, Jana (act) 1969
PESSOLANO, Jonathan (dan) 1995
PESZEK, Jan (act) 1989
PETAROZZI, Jacques Antoine (dan) 1978
PETER, Fritz (ten) 1978
PETER, Zoltan (dan) 1981
PETERS, Johanna (cont) 1965, 67, 68, 71
PETERS, Karlheinz (bar) 1966
PETERS, Lorraine (act) 1977
PETERS, Michael (dan) 1968
PETERS, Reinhard (cond) 1971, 75
PETERSEN, Charlotte (clarsasch) 1991
PETERSEN, Madonna (dan) 1980
PETERSON, Bengt (dir) 1959, 74
PETERSON, Eric (act, dir) 1980
PETERSON, Ileana (mez) 1974
PETERSON, Kirk (dan) 1981
PETERSON, Oscar 1980, 81
PETERSON, Taliep (dir) 1988
PETHERBRIDGE, Edward (act, dir) 1972, 73, 74, 78
PETHÓ, László (dan) 1973
PETIPA, Marius (chor) 1947-51, 53, 56, 57, 59, 75, 77, 86, 91
PETIT, Lenard (act) 1990
PETIT, Roland (chor) 1949, 59, 60, 71
PETRASSI, Goffredo (cond) 1974
PETRESCU, Irina (act) 1971
PETRESCU, Tudorel (act) 1991
PETRI, Mario (bs) 1951
PETRIE, Elaine (folk sngr) 1995
PETRIE, Mark (act) 1993
PETROV, Nicolas (dan) 1960
PETROV, Nikolai (pf) 1966
PETRY, Achim (act) 1987
PETTERSSON, Ann-Margret (dir) 1974
PETTIGREW, Robert (mus dir) 1983
PETTINGER, Peter (pf) 1986
PEYER, Gervase de (cl) 1959, 63, 68, 71, 75
PEYMANN, Claus (dir) 1977
PFEIFLE, Alfred (ten) 1958
PFENDT, Jean (bs) 1952, 56
PHIPPS, *Dr* Alison (lect) 1996
PHILADELPHIA ORCHESTRA 1982
PHILHARMONIA CHORUS 1960, 67, 69
PHILHARMONIA ORCHESTRA 1949, 53-54, 57-58, 60-63, 65, 66, 68-70, 73, 76-85, 91, 93, 95, 96
PHILIP, John (dir) 1960
PHILIP JONES BRASS ENSEMBLE 1979
PHILIPPART, Nathalie (dan) 1949
PHILIPPE, Pierre (pf) 1960
PHILIPPI, Rainer (act) 1994
PHILLIPS, Andy (light) 1970, 75, 80, 92, 94
PHILLIPS, Dorothea (act) 1956, 58
PHILLIPS, Harvey (vc) 1947, 51
PHILLIPS, Jared (dan) 1994
PHILLIPS, John (act) 1952, 58
PHILLIPS, Leslie (act) 1983
PHILLIPS, Melanie (sngr) 1973
PHILLIPS, Norman (sngr) 1981
PHILLIPS, Robin (act) 1961
PHILOMUSICA OF LONDON 1963
PIAT, Jean (act) 1954
PIATIGORSKY, Gregor (vc) 1948
PICASSO, Pablo (des) 1948, 54
PICAZO, Angel (act) 1989
PICCHI, Mirto (ten) 1949, 69
PICCOLA SCALA, La, Milan 1957, 82
PICCOLO TEATRO, Milan 1956
PICCOLOMINI, Elisabetta (act) 1982
PICKETT, Philip (mus dir) 1988, 89
PIECZONKA, Adrianne (sop) 1991
PIECZURO, Janusz (act) 1966
PIEMONTESE, Renato (cond) 1988
PIERIS, Niloufer (dan) 1976
PIERRE, Francis (hp) 1982
PIERRE, John La (sngr) 1983
PIETARINEN, Riitta (sngr) 1987
PIETREWICZ, Anita (dan) 1986
PIETROPINTO, Angela (act) 1971
PIGGOTT, *Prof.* Stuart (exh dir) 1970
PIGGOTT-SMITH, Tim (act) 1970
PIGNET, Christine (act) 1988, 89
PIGULLA, Rainer (act) 1988
PIKE, Julian (sngr) 1987
PILARCZYK, Helga (sop) 1956, 60, 68, 70
PILARRE, Susan (dan) 1967
PILBROW, Richard (light) 1960, 68
PILETTA, Georges (dan) 1984
PILIPENKO, Lidia (dan) 1962
PILLINGER, Edward (cl, bas hn) 1978
PILOTTI, Katarina (sop) 1987
PILZ, Gottfried (des) 1971
PINA, Joel (gtr) 1995
PINE, Larry (act) 1971
PINET, Lise (dan) 1962
PINI, Amalia (mez) 1949
PINI, Anthony (vc) 1950
PINI, Carl (cond) 1975
PINNECOOSE, Marty (dan) 1990
PINNOCK, Trevor (cond) 1982
PINTEA-HOMEAG, Leni (act) 1991
PINTER, Harold (spk) 1963
PINTILIE, Lucian (dir) 1971
PINTO, Nicola di (act) 1976
PIONTEK, Klaus (act) 1970, 93
PIPER, John (des) 1948, 51, 53, 58, 60, 61, 62, 65, 73
PIPER, Tom (des) 1992
PIRAIKON THEATRE 1966
PIRAS, Rosalba (act) 1982
PIRES, Maria Joao (pf) 1992, 95
PISCHAYEV, V. (sngr) 1986
PISTORIO, Pierre-François (act) 1988
PITHY, Wensley (act) 1950
PITKIN, William (des) 1981
PITT, Prior (act) 1961
PITT-WATSON, Ian (cond) 1950, 51
PITTI, Joel (des) 1986
PITTIS, Florian (act) 1971
PITTMAN, Richard (cond) 1983
PITTSBURGH SYMPHONY ORCHESTRA 1964, 85, 87
PIZZI, Pier Luigi (des) 1969, 82
PLA, Mirta (dan) 1979
PLAISTED, Ronald (dan) 1960
PLANCHON, Paul (act) 1960
PLANCHON, Roger (dir, act) 1960
PLANE, Liane (dan) 1953
PLANXTY 1974
PLASSARD, Emmanuel (dan) 1991
PLATE, Wilfried (sngr) 1968
PLATONOFF, Martha (des) 1959
PLATT, Norman (dir) 1979
PLATTS, Kevin (boy sop) 1962
PLEASANCE, Angela (act) 1984, 90
PLEETH, William (vc) 1954, 75, 78
PLETNEV, Mikhail (cond) 1996
PLISSETSKY (chor) 1979
PLOWRIGHT, Joan (act) 1963, 83
PLOWRIGHT, Rosalind (sop) 1983
PLÜMACHER, Hetty (cont) 1958, 66
PLUMMER, Christopher (act) 1956
PLUMMER, Sue (des) 1987
PLUNKETT, Geraldine (act) 1987, 89
PLUZHNIKOV, Konstantin (ten) 1991, 95
POCHANSKY, Viacheslav (sngr) 1990
PODDA, Elisabetta (act) 1982
POELS, Arnold (dan) 1962
POELVOORDE, Rita (dan) 1970
POGGIALI, Giovanni (act) 1976
POGGIOLI, Guy (dan) 1988
POGLIANI, Michele (dan) 1994
POGORELICH, Ivo (pf) 1986
POGSON, Geoffrey (ten) 1977, 78
POINDEXTER, H.R. (des) 1977
POIRIER, Ségolène (dan) 1985
POIRIER, Sylvain (dan) 1994
POKORNI, Temira (dan) 1962
POKORNÝ, Jirí (pf) 1964
POKORNÝ, Marcel (des) 1964, 70
POKORNÝ, Vaclav (sngr) 1964
POKROVSKY, Boris (dir) 1990, 91
POLACEK, Ales (dan) 1986
POLAJENKO, Nicholas (dan) 1949, 57
POLAK, Roman (dir) 1991
POLERI, David (ten) 1951, 55
POLETYLLO, Ted (folk sngr) 1995
POLGÁR, László (bs) 1973
POLIANICHKO, Alexander (cond) 1991
POLISH CHAMBER ORCHESTRA 1979, 81, 84, 85
POLISH MIME THEATRE 1966
POLISH RADIO SYMPHONY ORCHESTRA 1962
POLLAK, Anna (cont) 1963
POLLINI, Maurizio (pf) 1976, 77, 79-82
POLLITT, Clyde (act) 1978
POLYOCAN, Jennifer (dan) 1995

RANDIN, Gunnar (dan) 1957
RANDOLPH, Craig (dan) 1986
RANDOVÁ, Eva (mez) 1976, 83, 91
RANGANATHAN, T. (mridangam) 1963
RANISON, Paul (narr) 1989
RANKIN, Eugene (pf) 1959
RANKIN, Nell (mez) 1961
RANKL, Karl (cond) 1953, 54, 55, 56
RANSFORD, Tessa (rdr) 1987
RANSMAYR, Wolfgang (act) 1988
RANTA, Tarja (dan) 1987
RANTANEN, Riikka (sngr) 1987
RAO, Rekha (dan) 1960
RAO, Vatsala (dan) 1960
RAPHAEL ENSEMBLE 1992, 95
RAPHANEL, Ghyslaine (sop) 1985
RAPISARDI, Greta (sop) 1957
RAPOPORT, David (dan) 1974
RAPP, Jacques (des) 1985
RAPP, Richard (dan) 1967
RASBEGAIEV, Viacheslav (act) 1994
RASCHIG, Susanne (des) 1994, 96
RASHID, Justin (act) 1976
RASMUSSEN, Carl Christian (bar) 1990
RASMUSSEN, Karl Aage (comp) 1990
RASSINE, Alexis (dan) 1947, 48, 51, 54, 56
RASTAS, Jarmo (dan) 1987
RATCLIFFE, Mandy (act) 1974
RATCLIFFE, Stanley (act) 1960
RATH, John (bar) 1989
RATTI, Eugenia (sop) 1955, 57, 71
RATTLE, *Sir* Simon (cond) 1979, 81-83, 86, 89
RAUN RAUN THEATRE, New Guinea 1987
RAUPACH, Elizabeth (des) 1980
RAUSCHENBERG, Robert (des) 1966
RAUTAWAARA, Aulikki (sop) 1949
RAUTIO, Nina (sop) 1991
RAVINDRAN, Kottaikal (perc) 1990
RAWE, Tom (dan) 1976
RAWLINGS, John (des) 1966
RAWLINGS, Margaret (act) 1961
RAWLINSON, Brian (act) 1954
RAWSON, Nicholas (act) 1970
RAWSON, Philip (exh dir) 1963
RAY, Robin (ent) 1961
RAY, Ron (mus) 1986
RAYBOULD, Clarence (cond) 1955
RAYMOND, Cyril (act) 1961
RAYNER, Kenneth (light) 1980
RE, Carla del (sop) 1983
REA, Gaetano (sngr) 1977
REA, Tano (act) 1981
READ, John B. (light) 1967, 68, 69, 70, 74, 75, 80, 81, 83, 86, 89
REAL, Elvira (dan) 1953
REAY, Ronald (dan) 1958
REBIRTH BRASS BAND 1991
REBMANN, Liselotte (sop) 1966
REBUFFAT, Frédéric (des) 1994
RECKFORD, Barry (spk) 1963
RECKORD, Lloyd (act) 1952
RED NOTES DANCE COMPANY 1989
REDBONE, Leon (mus) 1991
REDDICK, Grant (act) 1956
REDDINI, Angela (des) 1972
REDGRAVE, Lynn (act) 1969
REDINGTON, Michael (act) 1954
REDKIN, Vladimir (bar) 1990, 91
REDMOND, Moira (act) 1966, 72
REDMOND, Siobhán (act) 1990
REDPATH, Jean (folk sngr) 1978, 85
REDWOOD, Manning (act) 1992
REECE, Arley (ten) 1978, 80
REED, Gavin (act) 1966, 67, 71, 72
REEDER, Kim (dan) 1979
REES, Allyson (act) 1981
REES, David (act) 1956
REES, Deborah (sop) 1987
REES, Jonathan (vn) 1992
REES, Roger (act) 1978
REEVES, George (pf) 1950, 55
REEVES, Michael (cond) 1974
REEVES, Peter (act) 1972
REFN, Helge (des) 1955
REHBERG, Hans Michael (act) 1986, 93
REHFUSS, Heinz (bar) 1957
REHM, Werner (act) 1994, 95
REICH, Günter (bar) 1967, 76
REICHEL, Käthe (act) 1993
REICHENBERG, Harry (boy sop) 1956
REICHERT, Gilles (dan) 1987
REICHERT, Manfred (cond) 1996
REID, Alastair (rdr) 1990
REID, Alex (des) 1977, 81
REID, Alexander (spk) 1962, 63
REID, Christine (act) 1967
REID, Francis (light) 1966, 79
REID, Gordon (act) 1968
REID, Jamie MacDonald (act) 1973
REID, Pipe-Major Robert (bp) 1954
REID, Sheila (act) 1972, 73, 74, 85, 87
REID, Tam (folk sngr) 1995
REIDY, Gabrielle (act) 1974
REIGENBORN, Garry (dan) 1994
REILLY, Bill (dan) 1959
REILLY, Charles Nelson (dir) 1977
REILLY, Nancy (act) 1986
REIMANN, Aribert (pf) 1972, 74, 75
REINE-ADELAIDE, Odile (dan) 1993, 95
REINECKE, Hans-Peter (act) 1984, 87, 94
REINHARDT, Angela (dan) 1984
REINHARDT, Georg (dir, des) 1972, 76
REINHART, Molly (dan) 1966
REINKING, Wilhelm (des) 1971
REISNER, Chris (dan) 1975
REISS, Amanda (act) 1963
REITHERMANN, Myles (act) 1969
RELPH, George (act) 1947
RELTON, William (act) 1981
REMIRO, Jesus Sainz (sngr) 1989
REMLEY, Robert (dan) 1979
RENAISSANCE GROUP OF ST ANDREWS 1987-91
RENAISSANCE SINGERS 1956
RENAISSANCE THEATRE COMPANY 1990
RENAUD, Madeleine (act) 1948, 57, 70
RENCHER, Derek (dan) 1960
RENDALL, David (ten) 1980, 87, 91
RENDALL, Sara (dan) 1991
RENDALLA LIRICA OF MADRID 1985
RENGUET, Jeanine (dan) 1962
RENNERT, Günther (dir, lect) 1952, 54, 56, 58, 66
RENNIE, Malcolm (act) 1968, 86
RENOIR, Pierre (act) 1947
RENOUARD, Marc (dan) 1988
RENOULT, Xavier (act) 1985
RENZ, Dayne (sngr) 1983
RENZ, Frederick (cond) 1988
REPERANT, Yvon (hpd) 1985
RÉQUÉNA, Chantal (dan) 1986
RESICK, Georgine (sop) 1980, 81
RESNIK, Regina (mez) 1968
RESTO, Guillermo (dan) 1992, 93, 94, 95
REVILL, Elizabeth (act) 1976
REVOIL, Fanély (sop) 1951
REX, Sheila (cont) 1965
REYES, Andre (dan) 1981
REYES, Cristobal (chor, dan) 1990
REYES, Manuela (dan) 1989, 92
REYMAN, Pamela (dan) 1990
REYMOND, Valentin (cond) 1994
REYNAUD, Geneviève (dan) 1986
REYNOLD, Dorothy (act) 1951
REYNOLDS, Anna (mez) 1964, 71, 76
REYNOLDS, Julian (pf) 1992
REZNIKOFF, Michel (dan) 1950, 52
RHODES, Dorothy (sngr) 1983
RHODIE, George (light) 1967
RHODIN, Michel (act) 1959
RHODIN, Teddy (dan) 1957
RHUBARB THE CLOWN (mime, juggler) 1978
RICARDA, Ana (dan, chor) 1950, 52, 57
RICCI, Mario (dir) 1972
RICCI, Ruggiero (vn) 1970
RICCIARDI, Franco (ten) 1957
RICE, Jacob (dan) 1995
RICE, Peter (des) 1955, 57, 60, 63, 68
RICE, Tim (act) 1975
RICH, Roy (dir) 1956
RICHARD, Emily (act) 1978
RICHARD, Jean (act) 1947
RICHARD, Lawrence (bs) 1970
RICHARD, Sylvain (dan) 1985
RICHARDS, Angela (act) 1968
RICHARDS, Aubrey (act) 1947, 56, 57
RICHARDS, Clare (act) 1964, 65, 71, 73, 86
RICHARDS, Grant (ten) 1981, 83
RICHARDS, Irene (vn) 1949
RICHARDS, Lloyd (dir) 1965
RICHARDS, Ted (act) 1965
RICHARDSON, Alan (pf) 1949
RICHARDSON, Christopher (des) 1984, 86, 88
RICHARDSON, Elizabeth (act) 1979
RICHARDSON, Ian (act) 1959
RICHARDSON, Lynda (sop) 1981
RICHARDSON, Miranda (act) 1996
RICHARDSON, *Sir* Ralph (act) 1947
RICHARDSON, Robin (spk) 1964
RICHARDSON, Stephen (b-bar) 1983, 87, 90, 93
RICHARDSON, Tony (dir) 1961
RICHEY, Angela (vn) 1953
RICHMAN, Stuart (act) 1988
RICHMOND, Kevin (dan) 1986
RICHMOND, Kristine (dan) 1989
RICHTER, Gerd (des) 1958
RICHTER, Renate (act) 1984, 87
RICHTER, Sviatoslav (pf) 1964
RICHTER, Wilhelm (bar) 1976
RICHTER-HAASER, Hans (pf) 1958, 59
RICKETTS, Ian (act) 1962
RICKHARDS, Dominic (act) 1992
RICKMAN, Alan (act) 1976, 81, 91
RIDDER, Anton de (ten) 1972
RIDDINGTON, Ian (act) 1986
RIDDLE, Frederick (va) 1956
RIDDOCH, Bill (act) 1984, 85, 90, 91
RIDEOUT, Bonnie (fiddle) 1996
RIDONI, Relda (act) 1956
RIEDMAN, Andreas (boy sop) 1978
RIEGEL, Kenneth (ten) 1983
RIEGELBAUER, Peter (db) 1995
RIEGER, Paul (act) 1947
RIERA, Jordi (mus) 1989
RIGG, *Dame* Diana (narr, rdr) 1978, 90
RIGGS, Irene (folk sngr) 1995
RIGILLO, Mariano (act) 1976
RIGIRI, Guerrando (bar) 1969
RIGNOLD, Hugo (cond) 1947, 54
RIGOPOULOU, Zoe (act) 1981
RILEY, Bridget (des) 1983
RILEY, Judy (act) 1977
RILEY, Larry (act) 1984
RIMBOLD, Michèle (dan) 1962
RINALDI, Alberto (bar) 1973, 74
RING, Joy (act) 1964, 66
RINGBOM, Jon (des) 1983
RINGLAND, Dave (act) 1970
RINKAMA, Nisse (cond) 1959
RINKER, Kenneth (dan) 1976
RINTOUL, David (act) 1973, 80, 81, 83-85, 91
RINTZLER, Marius (bs) 1972, 75, 76, 78, 81, 82
RIO, Pilar del (sngr) 1989
RÍO, Rafael del (sngr) 1989
RIPPON, Michael (bs) 1969, 71, 78, 80, 81
RIQUIER, Georges (act) 1947, 53
RIS ET DANCERIES 1985

RISSONE, Checco (act) 1956
RISTIĆ, Dušan (des) 1958, 62
RISTIĆ, Marica (dan) 1962
RITCHIE, Elizabeth (sop) 1975, 76
RITCHIE, June (act) 1965
RITTER, Angelika (act) 1984, 87
RITTER, Gudrun (act) 1993
RIVELLES, Amparo (act) 1989
RIVENQ, Nicolas (bar) 1985
RIVERS, Malcolm (bar) 1968
RIVLIN, Leora (act) 1983
RIZZI, Carlo (cond) 1993
ROA, Miguel (cond) 1989
ROACH, Norman (dan) 1990
ROACH, Ramona (dan) 1990
ROANNE, Gabrielle (act) 1951
ROAR, Leif (bar) 1976
ROBB, David (act) 1994
ROBB, John (light) 1990
ROBBE-GRILLET, Alain (spk) 1963
ROBBINS, David (mus) 1989
ROBBINS, Jerome (chor) 1950, 52, 59
ROBBINS, Ray Delle (des) 1989
ROBERT BLACK'S ACCORDEON TRIO 1987
ROBERT MASTERS PIANO QUARTET 1947, 48, 52, 57
ROBERTI, Margherita (sop) 1963
ROBERTON, *Sir* Hugh (cond) 1947-50
ROBERTS, Bernadette (des) 1991
ROBERTS, Graham (act) 1959
ROBERTS, Howard A. (cond, comp) 1965, 67
ROBERTS, Jamie (act) 1985
ROBERTS, Janet Etta (des) 1977
ROBERTS, Lesley (sngr) 1989, 92
ROBERTS, Marilyn (act) 1967
ROBERTS, Rachel (act) 1954, 61
ROBERTS, Sarah (des) 1986
ROBERTS, Simon (act) 1990
ROBERTS, Stephen (bar) 1984
ROBERTS, Susan (sop) 1987
ROBERTSON, Andrew (act) 1967, 71, 72
ROBERTSON, Annette (ent) 1961
ROBERTSON, David (cond, lect) 1993-94
ROBERTSON, Davie (folk sngr) 1995
ROBERTSON, Duncan (ten) 1964, 68
ROBERTSON, Iain Stuart (act) 1985, 86, 93
ROBERTSON, Ian (pf) 1978
ROBERTSON, James (boy sop) 1986
ROBERTSON, Jeannie (folk sngr) 1956
ROBERTSON, John (ten) 1968, 72, 75, 76, 77, 79, 80, 83
ROBERTSON, Joshua (act) 1977
ROBERTSON, Margaret (act) 1960
ROBERTSON, Moira (act) 1949, 50
ROBERTSON, Patrick (des) 1969
ROBERTSON, Rae (pf) 1951
ROBERTSON, Sasha (act) 1977
ROBERTSON, Stanley (sngr, story teller) 1993, 95
ROBERTSON, Stephen (ent) 1986, 90
ROBERTSON, Toby (dir) 1967, 68-71, 73, 75, 77, 78
ROBIER, Jean (des) 1950, 52, 57
ROBIN, Michel (act) 1960
ROBINSON, Alma (dan) 1968
ROBINSON, Dean (act) 1989
ROBINSON, Forbes (bs) 1961, 63, 65, 66
ROBINSON, Robert (act) 1961
ROBINSON, Sharon (vc) 1980
ROBINSON, Stanford (pf) 1951
ROBINSON, Tony (act) 1968, 70
ROBSON, Christopher (c ten) 1993
ROBSON, Elizabeth (sop) 1963, 64, 67
ROBSON, *Dame* Flora (act) 1951, 66, 70
ROCCA, Loriano della (act) 1980
ROCCHETTA, Tania (act) 1996
ROCHAIX, François (dir) 1983
ROCHE, Tudi (sngr) 1987
ROCKSTROH, Heinz (cond) 1949
RODDY, Ethna (act) 1990
RODDY, Lalor (act) 1995
RODEN, Anthony (ten) 1979
RODEN, Tom (dan) 1993
RODGER-BOWEN, Anne (sngr) 1984
RODGERS, Anton (ent) 1961
RODGERS, Joan (sop) 1992, 94
RODGERS, Joy (act) 1951
RÖDIN, Margot (mez) 1974
RODNEY, Prudence (dan) 1958
RODOLPHE, Teddy (dan) 1949
RODRIGUE, Camille (act) 1947
RODRIGUES, Alfred (dan, chor) 1951, 53, 56, 61, 68
RODRIGUES, Amalia (sngr) 1962
RODRIGUEZ, Ada (sngr) 1989
RODRIGUEZ, Felipe (light) 1990
RODRIGUEZ, Felix (dan) 1991
RODRIGUEZ, Isabel (sngr) 1985
RODRIQUEZ, Manuel (gtr) 1982
RODRIGUEZ, Raymond (dan) 1990
RODWAY, Norman (act) 1959
ROE, Wendy (dan) 1977, 80
ROFRANO, Albert (act) 1967
ROGAN, John (act) 1970
ROGÉ, Pascal (pf) 1982
ROGER, David (des) 1988
ROGERS, John (act) 1963
ROGERS, Katharine (act) 1992
ROGERS, Paul (act) 1950, 53-55, 58, 86
ROGERS, Sandra (act) 1992
ROHNER, Michael (act) 1995
ROHR, Otto von (bs) 1958, 66
ROHR, Tony (act) 1974
ROHRER, Marietta (act) 1988
ROLFE, Gail (sngr) 1986
ROLFE, John (act) 1986
ROLFE JOHNSON, Anthony (ten) 1973, 75, 76, 79, 82, 83, 92, 95, 96
ROLL, Michael (pf) 1964, 71
ROLLÁN, Carmen (dan) 1958
ROLLINGS, Gordon (act) 1961
ROMÁN, Christopher (dan) 1994
ROMANELLI, Rita (dan) 1963
ROMANES, Muriel (act) 1974, 89, 90, 91
ROMANO, Franco (dan) 1962
ROMANO, Mario (des) 1972
ROMANO, Sergio (spk) 1982
ROMANOVA, Nina (mez) 1986
ROMERO, Fernando (dan) 1989
ROMERO, Freddy (dan) 1968
ROMMEN, Ann-Christian (dir, des) 1996
RÓNA, Viktor (dan) 1963, 73
RONANE, John (act) 1962
RONCONI, Luca (dir) 1970, 75
RONDA, Paco de (dan) 1953
RONDER, Tanya (act) 1980
RONDIRIS, D. (dir) 1966
RONEN, Ilan (dir) 1987
RÖNNLUND, Lennart (pf) 1982
ROO, Kasper de (cond) 1995
ROOCROFT, Amanda (sop) 1993, 94
ROOLEY, Anthony (lute, cond) 1971, 81
ROOPE, Clover (dan) 1961
ROOS, Lars (pf) 1992
ROOSE-EVANS, James (dir) 1967
ROOST, Garry (act) 1983
ROPER, Tony (act) 1973, 79, 84, 86
ROPER-KNIGHT, Courtney (act) 1981
ROS, Mireia (act) 1983
ROSADO, Pepa (sngr) 1989
ROSARIO (dan) 1950
ROSCOE, Martin (pf) 1991
ROSE, Alexander (sngr) 1976
ROSE, Clifford (act) 1970
ROSE, David (dan) 1994
ROSE, Geoffrey (act) 1959
ROSE, George (act) 1947, 51
ROSE, Jürgen (des) 1975, 79
ROSE, Leonard (vc) 1951, 63, 68
RÖSEL, Peter (pf) 1988
ROSEN, Charles (pf) 1983
ROSEN, Elsa Marianne von (dan)1957-58
ROSENBERG, Sylvia (vn) 1982
ROSENSHEIN, Neil (ten) 1985
ROSENTHAL, Jean (light) 1959, 63
ROSENTHAL, Martin (sngr) 1975
ROSMER, Milton (act) 1952
ROSS, Alan (act) 1971
ROSS, Ann-Louise (act) 1991
ROSS, Bertram (dan) 1963
ROSS, Elise (sop) 1980
ROSS, Kenneth (sngr) 1965
ROSS, Patricia (act) 1990
ROSSACK, Roswitha (dan) 1976
ROSSI, Massimo de (act) 1975
ROSSI, Sandro (act) 1965
ROSSINGTON, Norman (act) 1954, 63
ROSSINI, Anna (act) 1970, 76
ROSSITER, Leonard (act) 1964, 68
ROSSON, Keith (dan) 1960
ROST, Annemarie (des) 1987
ROSTAL, Max (vn) 1950, 52, 53
ROSTROPOVICH, Mstislav (vc, pf, cond) 1960, 62, 64, 68, 75, 76, 90
ROTA, Anna Maria (mez) 1960, 63
ROTARDIER, Kelvin (dan) 1968
ROTH, George (vc) 1950
ROTH, Joanna (act) 1989
ROTHENBERGER, Anneliese (sop) 1952, 56
RÖTHLISBERGER, Max (des) 1960
ROTHMÜLLER, Marko (bar) 1949, 50, 51, 55
ROTHWELL, Michael (act) 1963
ROTSCHOPF, Martin (narr) 1995
ROTTERDAM PHILHARMONIC ORCHESTRA 1990
ROTTSIEPER, Wolfgang 1952
ROUAULT, Georges (des) 1975, 79
ROUBA, Pawel (act) 1966
ROUECHE, Philippe (act, mus) 1988, 89, 95
ROUGERIE, Jean (dir, act) 1970
ROUGHEAD, Hamish (act) 1969
ROULEAU, Joseph (bs) 1961, 64, 69, 72, 78
ROUMER, Emile (?) 1963
ROUSKOVÁ, Anna (sngr) 1964
ROUSTAN, Joëlle (des) 1962
ROUX, François le (bar) 1985, 86
ROUX, Jean Louis (act) 1956
ROVERE, Anna Maria (sop) 1955
ROVIS, Jean (act) 1985
ROWALLAN SINGERS 1964
ROWAN, Peggy (act) 1960
ROWANN, Judith (dan) 1979
ROWE, Beatrice (act) 1952
ROWE, Clive (act) 1992
ROWE, John (act) 1977, 78
ROWE, Stephen (act) 1982
ROWE, Thomas (light) 1981
ROWELL, Kenneth (des) 1953, 60, 69
ROWLANDS, Carol (sngr) 1983
ROWLANDS, Patsy (ent) 1964
ROWLEY, Gary (sngr) 1994
ROY, Georges le (act) 1948
ROY, Jean-Philippe (light) 1983
ROY, Ken (dan) 1994
ROY, Pierre (des) 1949
ROYAL ACADEMY OF MUSIC members 1986
ROYAL BALLET 1947, 48, 51, 54, 56, 60, 75
ROYAL CONCERTGEBOUW ORCHESTRA 1948, 52, 57, 63, 70, 77, 83, 92
ROYAL DANISH BALLET 1955, 71
ROYAL DANISH CHAPEL CHOIR 1958
ROYAL DANISH ORCHESTRA 1958
ROYAL DRAMATIC THEATRE, Stockholm 1986
ROYAL EXCHANGE THEATRE, Manchester 1976, 87, 88
ROYAL LIVERPOOL PHILHARMONIC ORCHESTRA 1947, 48, 60, 91, 93, 95

SCOTTISH SINGERS 1948, 49, 51
SCOTTISH THEATRE+ 1948, 49
SCOTTISH THEATRE BALLET
See SCOTTISH BALLET
SCOTTISH THEATRE COMPANY 1984, 85, 91
SCOTTO, Renata (sop) 1957, 69, 72
SCRIMGER, John (pf) 1992, 94, 95
SCUDELLARO, Enzo (act) 1976
SCULLY, Terry (act) 1965, 67
SCURFIELD, Matthew (act) 1975
SEAGO, Howie (act) 1993
SEAL, Elizabeth 1965
SEALE, Douglas (dir) 1956
SEALEY, Paul (mus) 1986
SEAMAN, Christopher (cond) 1972, 73, 74, 84
SEARLE, Humphrey (comp) 1962
SEARLE, Peter (light) 1977, 80
SEARS, Joe (act) 1985
SEAY, Deanna (dan) 1994, 95
SEBESTÉNY, Katalin (dan) 1973
SECCHI, Adrian (comp) 1970
SECOMB, Don (dan) 1980
SEDGWICK, Toby (mime) 1980
SEDLÁŘOVÁ, Jaroslava (sngr) 1990
SEEAR, Andrew (act) 1977
SEEFRIED, Irmgard (sop) 1951-54, 56, 59, 64, 66
SEEGER, Mike (mus) 1984
SEEMANN, Carl (pf) 1956, 59
SEFEROVIĆ, Dragan (dan) 1962
SEGAL, Gilles (act) 1953
SEGAL, Guri (act) 1983
SEGAL, Uri (cond) 1972
SEGOVIA (gtr) 1948, 55
SEGOVIA, Rosita (dan) 1958
SEHLMARK, Margit (mez) 1959
SEIFERT, Martin (act) 1984, 87, 94, 95
SEIGNER, Louis (act) 1954
SEIGNIOUS, Geraldine (act) 1967
SEIKE, Eiichi (act) 1985, 90
SEITZ, Odile (act) 1994
SEKIMOTO, Machiko (dan) 1988
SELEZNEV, Georgy (bs) 1995
SELF, Jim (dan) 1970
SELLARS, Peter (dir) 1988, 93, 95
SELLING, Caj (dan) 1957
SELLNER, Gustav Rudolf (dir) 1971, 75
SEMELLAZ, Françoise (sngr) 1985
SENKÝRIKOVÁ, Eva (dan) 1990
SENO, Kappa (des) 1985
SENOO, Masafumi (act) 1985
SENSE, Silke (dan) 1991
SENST, Heiko (act) 1993
SENTPAUL, Frithjof (bs) 1966
SEQUI, Sandro (dir) 1969, 82
SERAO, Lello (act) 1988
SERBAN, Andrei (dir) 1976, 82, 92
SEREBRIAKOV (des) 1949
SEREGI, László (chor) 1973
SERERO, Marie-Jeanne (pf) 1992
SERGENT, Yves (act) 1955
SERGEYEV, Nicholas (chor) 1947, 48, 52, 75
SERGIENKO, Ludmilla (sop) 1991
SERKIN, Peter (pf) 1964
SERKIN, Rudolf (pf) 1949, 64
SERNER, Hakan (act) 1967
SERRATS, Joan (act) 1992
SESHIMO, Kazuhisa (act) 1985, 86, 88
SESTETTO ITALIANO LUCA MARENZIO 1959, 69
SEVILLA, Manolo (sngr) 1982, 92
SEVILLANO, Trinidad (dan) 1986
SEWELL, George (act) 1964
SEWELL, Simon (light) 1985, 86
SEWING, Jack (db) 1989
SEYLER, Athene (act) 1952, 65
SEYMOUR, Lynn (dan) 1975
SEYRIG, Delphine (act) 1984
SGOURDA, Antigone (sop) 1973, 74
SHA, Tamae (chor) 1990
SHACKLOCK, Constance (cont) 1954
SHADOWS 1990
SHAFFER, Elaine (fl) 1967
SHAFFER, Peter 1963, 80
SHAGUCH, Marina (sop) 1995
SHAHN, Ben (des) 1959
SHAKHOVSKAYA, Natalia (vc) 1966
SHALHOUB, Tony (act) 1982
SHALLON, David (cond) 1987
SHAMASK, Ronaldus (des) 1994
SHAMBO, Douglas (sngr) 1988
SHANAHAN, Julie (dan) 1995
SHAND, Jan (act) 1989
SHAND, Jimmy (accordion) 1951, 63
SHANGHAI KUNJU THEATRE 1987
SHANKAR, Ravi (sitâr), 63, 71, 80, 89
SHANKAR, Shubho (sitâr) 1989
SHANLEY, Kenneth (act) 1968
SHANLEY, Patrick (act) 1970
SHARAFF, Irene (des) 1959
SHARASHIDZE, Vano (narr) 1987
SHARED EXPERIENCE THEATRE COMPANY 1988
SHARKO, Zinaida (act) 1987
SHARMA, Gyan (dan) 1960
SHARMAN, Bruce (act) 1953
SHARMAN, Marigold (act) 1959, 64
SHARP, Nada (act) 1993
SHARP, Victoria (sngr) 1989
SHARPE, Allan (dir) 1992
SHARROCK, Ian (act) 1992
SHATNER, William (act) 1956
SHAUB, Mark (dan) 1994
SHAUGHNESSY, David (act) 1977
SHAVEN, Daphne (act) 1956
SHAW, Brian (dan) 1951, 54, 56, 60
SHAW, Elspeth (dan) 1980
SHAW, John (bar) 1961, 68
SHAW, Kenneth (act) 1970
SHAW, Lauriston (act) 1960
SHAW, Lois (act) 1960
SHAW, Matthew Byam (act) 1992
SHAW, Nigel Hamilton (sngr) 1980, 81
SHAW, Ron (act) 1990
SHAW, Sebastian (rdr, act) 1956, 57
SHAW-PARKER, David (act) 1980
SHEARER, Moira (dan, act, rdr, lect) 1948, 51, 54, 57, 74, 75, 79
SHEBBEARE, Norma (act) 1947
SHEDDEN, John (act) 1970, 73, 84, 85-87, 89-91
SHEFFER, Ruevan (act) 1987
SHEFFIELD PHILHARMONIC CHORUS 1954
SHEILLS, Brian 1986
SHEINTSIS, Olega (des) 1991
SHELLEY, Howard (pf) 1978
SHELTON, Timothy (act) 1974
SHELVING, Paul (des) 1959
SHEN LICHUN (comp) 1987
SHEN XIAOMING (act) 1987
SHENG CHUAN JIAN (dir) 1987
SHEPHERD, Adrian (vc) 1975, 78
SHEPHERD, Jack (act) 1971, 72, 80
SHEPPARD, Craig (pf) 1984
SHEPPERDSON, Leon (act) 1961
SHER, Antony (act) 1977
SHERIDAN, Dennis (act) 1968
SHERMAN, Bob (act) 1976
SHEVCHENKO, Larissa (sop) 1991
SHIBAMURA, Yoko (act) 1985
SHIBUYA, Ken (act) 1990
SHIELDS, Malcolm (act) 1993, 94
SHIELDS, Susan (dan) 1995
SHILLING, Eric (bar) 1968
SHIMA, Akiko (act) 1989
SHIMADA, Toshiyuki (cond) 1984
SHIMELL, William (bar) 1979
SHIMIZU, Mikio (act) 1985
SHIMIZU, Tetsutaro (chor, dan) 1988
SHIMKO, Dalia (act) 1983
SHIMMIN, Sadie (act) 1992
SHIOJIMA, Akihiko (act) 1986
SHIOKAWA, Yuuko (vn) 1995, 96
SHIRAISHI, Yukinaga (act) 1985
SHIRLEY, Aaron (act) 1992
SHIRLEY, George (ten) 1979
SHIRLEY-QUIRK, John (bar) 1961, 63, 68, 70, 71, 73, 75, 77-79, 81, 84, 86
SHIVAS, Andrew (perc) 1966
SHIZUNE, Tomoe (chor) 1996
SHIZURU, Eiho (interp) 1972
SHKOLNIKOVA, Elena (sop) 1987
SHOCKED, Michelle (vocals) 1993
SHOEMAKER, Thomas M. (dan) 1995
SHOLEM, Ann (dan) 1977, 80
SHORE, Andrew (bar) 1979, 89
SHORT, David (des) 1988
SHORTT, Bernadette (act) 1983
SHOSTAKOVICH, Maxim (cond) 1982
SHOSTAKOVICH QUARTET 1987, 88-89
SHRAPNEL, John (act) 1969, 71, 77
SHTIL, Georgy (act) 1987
SHUBIN, Alexander (sngr) 1995
SHUTA, Mari (dan) 1988
SHUTOVA, Marina (mez) 1990
SHVELIDZE, M. (des) 1979
SIBANDA, Seth (act) 1983
SIBERRY, Michael (act) 1983
SIBLEY, *Dame* Antoinette (dan) 1960
SICAKOVA, Sona (dan) 1991
SICART, Elisabeth (dan) 1987
SICHEL, Diann (dan) 1981
SICKER, Thomas (act) 1994
SICOT, Antoine (bs) 1985
SIDEY, David (des) 1958
SIDHOM, Peter (bar) 1993, 95
SIEGFRIED, Irene (dan) 1958
SIEPI, Cesare (bs) 1950
SIER, Barbara (dan) 1986
SIERCKE, Alfred (des) 1952, 56, 58
SIERING, James (act) 1976
SIERRA, Alberto (dan) 1992
SIERRA, Pedro (gtr) 1990
SIEVELING, Earle (dan) 1967
SIEVERS, Herbert (act) 1987
SIFAKI, K. (act) 1966
SIFAKI, Rika (act) 1966, 81
SIFNIOS, Duška (dan) 1960, 62
SIGURDARDOTTIR, Steinunn (rdr) 1987
SIKMASHVILI, L. (act) 1979
SILJA, Anja (sop) 1966, 70, 74
SILKIN, Jon (rdr) 1965
SILLEM, Maurits (pf, cond) 1958
SILLITOE, Kenneth (vn) 1972
SILLS, Bettijane (dan) 1967
SILVER, Millicent (hpd) 1950
SILVERI, Paolo (bar) 1948, 49
SILVERSTEIN, Steven (?) 1989
SILVESTRI, Constantin (cond) 1963
SILVEUS, Ingrid (sngr) 1994
SIM, Alastair (act) 1965
ŠIMÁČEK, Oldřich (des) 1970
SIMANDI, David 1980
SIMIONATO, Giulietta (mez) 1947
SIMKINA, Galina (sop) 1991
SIMKINS, Michael (act) 1992
SIMON, Barney (dir) 1986
SIMON, Jörg (dan) 1984
SIMONE, Kirsten (dan) 1958, 71
SIMONE, Ofelia de (sngr) 1988
SIMONE, Roberto de (dir, comp) 1975, 76, 88
SIMONEAU, Léopold (ten) 1951, 52
SIMONINI, Jean-Luc (des) 1989
SIMONISCHEK, Peter (act) 1994, 95
SIMONOV, Yuri (cond) 1992
SIMONS, William (act) 1968, 69
SIMPSON, Derek (vc) 1963
SIMPSON, Glenda (mez) 1982
SIMPSON, Joanne (act) 1990
SIMPSON, Marietta (mez) 1996
SIMPSON, William (act) 1957, 58, 59
SINCLAIR, Ann (des) 1980
SINCLAIR, Graham (act) 1988

STAN TRACEY BIG BAND 1989
STANDAERT, Virginie (des) 1985
STANFORD, Alan (act) 1989
STANGRET, Lech (act) 1980
STANIC, Tihomir (act) 1991
STANNARD, Heather (act) 1950, 52
STANOEVICI, Bogdan (act) 1981
STANTON, Barry (act) 1991
STANYON, Bryan (act) 1969, 70
STANZAK, Julie Anne (dan) 1995
STAPP, Gregory (bs) 1985
STARC, Drago (ten) 1962
STARK, Graham (act) 1950
STARK, Inger (cont) 1987
STARKER, Janos (vc) 1957
STARKEY, Colin (act) 1991
STARKOVÁ, Věra (sngr) 1970
STARR, Dolores (dan) 1952
STARY THEATRE, Cracow 1986, 89
STASIO, Anna di (mez) 1963, 69
STAVANGER SYMPHONY ORCHESTRA 1994
STAW, Ryszard (act) 1966
STEBBING, Margot (va) 1949
STEBER, Eleanor (sop) 1947, 53
STEBLIANKO, Alexei (ten) 1991
STECKMAN, Larry (light) 1976
STEEL, David (spk) 1982
STEEL, Judy (dir) 1991
STEEL, William (act) 1988
STEELE, Anna (act) 1957
STEELE, James (act) 1957
STEELE, Jeannie (dan) 1994
STEELE, Ricky (mus) 1986
STEELE-PERKINS, Crispian (tpt) 1982
STEEN-NØKLEBERG, Einar (pf) 1995
STEER, John (db) 1993
STEFANO, Giuseppe di (ten) 1957
STEFANONI, Marco (sngr) 1955, 60
STEFANOPOULOS, D. (act) 1966
STEFANOVIĆ, Liubitza (dan) 1951
STEFANOVIĆ, Nikola (sngr) 1962
STEFFEK, Hanny (sop) 1965
STEFFENS, Karl Maria (act) 1984, 87
STEGERS, Bernice (act) 1977
STEIGER, Anna (sop) 1988
STEIN, Leonard (lect) 1983
STEIN, Peter (dir) 1993, 94, 96
STEINBERG, Saul (des) 1959
STEINBERG, William (cond) 1964
STEINER, Anne (des) 1989
STEINER, Elisabeth (sop) 1983
STEINER, George (spk) 1980, 96
STEINMEIER, Reinhard (stuntman) 1995
STEMPEL, Bernd (act) 1993
STENDER, Paul (act) 1970
STENE, Randi (mez) 1994, 95
STENHOUSE, David (interviewer) 1996
STEPANIUK, Alexei (dir) 1995
STEPHANT, Yannick (dan) 1984
STEPHEN, Pamela Helen (mez) 1993
STEPHEN-SAMUELS, Patrick (act) 1991
STEPHENS, Robert (act) 1963
STEPHENSON, Donald (ten) 1984, 89
STEPIEN, Arkadiusz (dan) 1986
STEPNER, Daniel (vn) 1983
STERBINSZKY, László (dan) 1973
STERN, Isaac (vn) 1953, 54, 56, 60, 63, 68, 73, 78
STERN, Oliver (act) 1993, 95
STERN, Tim (act) 1980
STERNBERGER, Barbara (sop) 1982
STEUART, David (act) 1951, 59
STEUART, Douglas (dan) 1954, 56, 60
STEVENS, Denis (cond) 1962
STEVENS, Douglas (c ten) 1988
STEVENS, Ronnie (act) 1971, 72, 73
STEVENSON, Ben (chor) 1989
STEVENSON, Gerda (act) 1984, 89
STEVENSON, Harry (sngr) 1966
STEVENSON, Hugh (des) 1953
STEVENSON, Juliet (act, narr) 1980, 83
STEVENSON, Ronald (pf) 1978
STEWART, Cameron (act) 1994
STEWART, Elizabeth (folk sngr) 1995
STEWART, Ewan (act) 1989
STEWART, Hugh (act) 1951
STEWART, Ian (act) 1948, 49, 73, 84, 85, 91
STEWART, Job (act) 1953, 54, 55, 67
STEWART, Sheila (folk sngr, storyteller) 1993, 95
STEWART, Stanley (act) 1964
STEWART, Tara (dan) 1980
STEWART-KELLOGG, Cal (cond) 1984
STEYER, Arlette (sngr) 1985
STIERLE, Bernhard (act) 1966
STIRLING GAELIC CHOIR 1965
STIRN, Daniel (cond) 1959
STIVELL, Alan (folk ensemble) 1974
STJERNQVIST, Uno (ten) 1959, 86
STOCK, Nigel (rdr) 1978, 79, 83
STOCKHAUSEN, Majella (pf, celeste) 1995
STOCKHAUSEN, Markus (tpt) 1995
STOCKHOLM OPERA
See Royal Opera, Stockholm
STOCKHOLM PHILHARMONIC CHOIR 1970
STOCKHOLM PHILHARMONIC ORCHESTRA 1970
STODDART, George (bp) 1963, 64-65, 80
STODDART, John (des) 1974, 79
STOJANOVIC, Milka (sop) 1962
STOKES, Simon (dir) 1985
STOKOWSKI, Leopold (cond) 1961
STOKVIS, Joop (des) 1968, 70
STOLTZMAN, Richard (cl) 1980
STOLZE, Gerhard (ten) 1966
STOLZE, Kurt-Heinz (hpd, cond) 1963
STONE, Alix (des) 1947, 58, 63, 68, 82, 84, 86
STONE, Paddy (dan) 1958
STONE-FEWINGS, Jo (act) 1992
STONIER, Claire (dan) 1980
STOPCZYNSKI, Alice (act) 1977
STORCH, Arthur (dir) 1984
STORER, Andrew (des) 1983
STORER, Dianne (dan) 1977
STORMARE, Peter (act) 1986
STORRY, Malcolm (act) 1977
STORTI, Giovan Battista (act) 1980
STRACHAN, Joel (act) 1994
STRAGLIATI, Pietro (act) 1988
STRAKA, Peter (ten) 1978
STRAKER, Peter (act) 1975
STRAMASH 1995
STRASFOGEL, Ian (dir) 1987
STRATFORD ONTARIO FESTIVAL COMPANY 1956
STRATHEARN, Paul (ten) 1981, 82
STRAUDO, Yolande (dan) 1976
STRAUSS, Paul (cond) 1953
STREETON, Jane (sop) 1983
STREHLER, Giorgio (dir) 1956, 57
STREIT, Kurt (ten) 1994
STREMOVSKY, Vitaly (act) 1994
STRICKER, Frieder ((ten) 1983
STRICKLAND, Elaine (act) 1973
STRICKLYN, Ray (act) 1988
STRIDE, John (rdr) 1978
STRIDH, Anette (sop) 1986, 87
STRIKE, Lois (dan) 1975, 79
STŘÍŠKA, Jaroslav (ten) 1964
STROBELE, Heinrich (act) 1993
STROMBERG, Christine (des) 1993
STRONG, David (act) 1965, 66
STRONG, Mark (act) 1992
ŠTROS, Ladislav (dir) 1964
STROSS QUARTET 1959
STROSSER, Pierre (dir, des) 1985
STRUNOVA, Margarita (act) 1991
STUART, Eleanor (act) 1956
STUART, James (act) 1948, 49, 51
STUART, Josephine (act) 1966
STUBBING, N.H. (des) 1957
STUBBS, Annena (des) 1965, 68
STUBBS, Una (act) 1967
STUDHOLME, Marion (sop) 1952, 53, 63
STUDT, Richard (vn) 1984
STUHR, Jerzy (act) 1986
STULEN, Jan (cond) 1970
STUMM, Michael (act) 1986
STUMPF, Thomas (pf) 1973
STURAM, Donatella (dan) 1988
STURUA, R. (dir) 1979
STUTTGART BALLET 1963
STUTTGART CHAMBER ORCHESTRA 1952
STUTTGART PIANO TRIO 1979
STUTTGART STATE OPERA
See Württemberg State Opera
SUAREZ, Angel Garcia (act) 1989
SUÁREZ, Rosario (dan) 1979, 91
SUARI, Jedda (act) 1987
SUART, Richard (bar) 1988
SUBBULAKSHMI (sop) 1963
ŠUBRTOVÁ, Milada (sop) 1964
SUCHÁNEK, Vladimir (des) 1990
SUCHER, *Dr* Bernd (spk) 1994
SUCHET, David (act) 1976
SÜCKER, Jürgen (stuntman) 1995
SUGGIA, Guilhermina (vc) 1949
SUGO, Takayuki (act) 1985, 86
SUK, Josef (va, vn) 1970, 90, 91
SUK QUARTET 1990
SUKIS, Lilian (sop) 1979
SULICH, Wassili (dan) 1960
SULIKOVA, Olga (act) 1991
SULLEY, Edmund (act) 1959, 60, 69
SULLIVAN, Charles (tpt) 1967
SULLIVAN, Daniel (bar) 1983
SULLIVAN, Hugh (act) 1960
SULLIVAN, John Carver (des) 1983
SUMMERS, Hilary (mez) 1996
SUMMERS, Joan (act) 1959
SUMMERS, Jonathan (bar) 1979, 84
SUMMERS, Michael (cond) 1982
SUMNER, Bernard (hpd) 1966
SUMNER, Carol (dan) 1967
SUMNER, David (act) 1966
SUND, Robert (dan) 1981
SUNDE, Erling (dan) 1961
SUNDMAN, Margareta (sngr) 1974
SUNG-OK, Yang (dan) 1990
SUNTERS, Irene (act) 1963, 93
SUOMINEN, Paul (des) 1959
SURGENOR, Ingrid (pf) 1992, 94
SUSANA (dan) *See* Audeoud, Susana
SUSANA Y JOSÉ 1960
SUSSKIND, Walter (cond) 1947, 51, 52, 56, 59, 66
SUSSMAN, Stanley (cond) 1996
SUTHERLAND, Don (act) 1961
SUTHERLAND, Iain (cond) 1969, 71
SUTHERLAND, James (act) 1948, 49, 51
SUTHERLAND, Jim (?) 1985
SUTHERLAND, Joan (sop) 1960, 61, 67
SUTHERLAND, Robert (pf) 1967
SUTTON, Alison Mary (sngr) 1979
SUZMAN, Janet (act) 1970, 77, 83
SUZUKI, Miko (dan) 1988
SUZUKI, Mizuho (act) 1985
SUZUKI, Shinpei (act) 1990
SUZUKI, Toshiaki (des) 1988
SVALBERG, Joakim (dan) 1991
SVANHOLM, Set (ten) 1959
ŠVEHLÁ, Zdeněk (ten) 1964
ŠVEJDA, Miroslav (ten) 1990
SVENSSON, Peter (ten) 1994
SVETLANOV, Evgeny (cond) 1968, 78, 88
SVOBODA, Josef (des) 1964, 70
SVOLINSKÝ, Karel (des) 1970
ŠVORC, Antonín (bar) 1964
SWADOS, Elizabeth (comp) 1976, 92
SWAINE, Roger (act) 1968
SWAMI, Narayan (dan) 1960
SWANN, Donald (ent) 1959
SWANSON, Philip (lect) 1992

VOYTEK (des) 1968
VOZNICK, Steven (dan) 1990
VRIES, Peter Jon de (act) 1976
VRONSKY *and* BABIN (pf) 1959
VROOM, Jean-Paul (des) 1970, 75
VRSAIKOV, Ljubica (mez) 1962
VUILLERMOZ, Martine (dan) 1984
VÜLLINGS, Karl (sngr) 1972
VULPIAN, Claude de (dan) 1984
VUOTO, Aurora (dan) 1963
VYROSTKO, Frantisek (act) 1991
VYROUBOVA, Nina (dan) 1949, 57
VYVYAN, Jennifer (sop) 1953, 58, 59, 62

WAAGE, Lars (bar) 1990
WAAS, Annelie (sop) 1965
WACHMANN, Franzinska (sop) 1966
WACKER, Monika (dan) 1978
WADA, Hiroshi (act) 1972
WADA, Takashi (mus) 1989
WADE, Charles (act) 1959
WADE, Paul (ten) 1994
WADSWORTH , Stephen (dir) 1991
WAGNER, Kurt (sngr) 1972
WAGNER, Robin (des) 1967
WAGNER, Wieland (dir, des) 1958, 66, 68, 75
WAGNER, William (dan) 1992, 93-95
WAGNER, William (sngr) 1988
WAGONER, Dan (chor, dan) 1966, 81
WAHLROTH, Ragne (sngr) 1974
WAHLUND, Sten (bs) 1974
WAIMAN, Mikhail (vn) 1966
WAIN, John 1965
WAISTNAGE, Harry (des) 1967
WAJDA, Andrzej (dir, act) 1986, 89
WAKAMATSU, Takeshi (act) 1988
WAKASUGI, Hiroshi (cond) 1982
WAKE, Joanna (act) 1966, 71, 72
WAKHEVITCH, Georges (des) 1949, 52, 56, 59
WAL, Jan van der (des) 1970
WALBERG, Betty (pf) 1959
WALBROOK, Anton (act) 1957
WALCOTT, Derek (?) 1963
WALE, Stephen (act) 1994
WALFORD, Ann (act) 1954
WALKER, Amanda (act) 1960
WALKER, David (des) 1965, 74, 89
WALKER, Diane (dan) 1983
WALKER, Fin (dan) 1993
WALKER, Fiona (act) 1967, 71
WALKER, Harry (act) 1963, 66
WALKER, Larry (act) 1977
WALKER, Lynne (interviewer) 1996
WALKER, Penelope (mez) 1981
WALKER, Sarah (mez) 1968, 76, 77, 80, 81, 82, 84
WALKER, Timothy (gtr) 1976, 81
WALKLETT, Mary (act) 1951
WALL, Max (act) 1977, 84
WALLACE, Ian (bs) 1948, 49, 50, 52-55, 60, 76
WALLACE, John (tpt) 1984, 93
WALLACE, Robert (bp) 1989
WALLACE, Ronald (light) 1971
WALLACE COLLECTION 1986-89
WALLACH, Eli (act) 1984
WALLE, Nathalie van de (act) 1985
WALLENSTEIN, Alfred (cond) 1953
WALLENSTEIN, Ilse (sop) 1952
WALLER, Angelika (act) 1987
WALLER, Annalu (act) 1992
WALLER, Gordon (act) 1969, 72
WALLFISCH, Ernst (va) 1960, 63, 75
WALLFISCH, Lory (pf) 1960
WALLFISCH, Raphael (vc) 1984, 92
WALLIN, Anne-Marie (dan) 1957
WALLIN, Cas (mus) 1984
WALLIN, Margaret (dan) 1994
WALLIS, Alec (act) 1978
WALLIS, Bill (ent) 1964
WALLIS, Delia (mez) 1973
WALLWORTH, Brian (act) 1971
WALSER, Martin (spk) 1963
WALSER, Sven (act) 1994
WALSH, Phillip (act) 1988
WALTER, Bruno (cond, pf) 1947, 49, 51, 53
WALTER, Erich (des, chor) 1972, 76
WALTER, Naum (pf) 1967
WALTER, Richard (act) 1950
WALTERS, Anthony (act) 1992
WALTERS, John (act) 1959
WALTERS, Peter (light) 1986
WALTERS, Sam (dir) 1992
WALTERS, Stevie (act) 1963
WALTERS, Sylvia (act) 1967
WALTHER, Marianne (des) 1989
WALTHER, Ute (mez) 1982
WALTON, John (db) 1949
WALTON, Tony (des) 1963
WALTON, *Sir* William (cond) 1959
WAND, Günter (cond) 1994, 95
WANDA (act) 1947
WANG HANRU (light) 1987
WANG, Kee-Sok (act) 1990
WARD, Anthony (des) 1992, 94
WARD, David (bs) 1960, 63, 68, 71, 76
WARD, Douglas Turner (dir, act) 1984
WARD, Eliza (act) 1966
WARD, James (act) 1959
WARD, Jeremy (bn) 1991
WARD, Joseph (ten) 1961
WARD, Paddy (act) 1978
WARD, Richard (act) 1965
WARD, Sophie (act) 1995
WARE, Derek (act) 1976
WARK, Kirsty (rdr) 1986
WARNER, Genevieve (sop) 1951
WARNER, John (act) 1951, 52, 57, 79, 81
WARRACK, John (lect) 1982
WARRE, Michael (des) 1947, 60
WARREN, Barry (act) 1967, 73
WARREN, Jim (act) 1988
WARREN, Polly (act) 1977
WARRILOW, David (act) 1984
WARRINGTON, Don (act) 1980
WARSAW OLD TIMERS 1986
WARWAS, Ewa (act) 1966
WARWICK, Richard (act) 1969, 90
WARZEE, Michel de (act) 1985
WASHINGTON, Paolo (bs) 1963
WASHINGTON, Shelley (dan) 1976
WASHINGTON OPERA 1984
WASILEWSKA, Edyta (dan) 1986
WASSBERG, Göran (des) 1986
WASSERMAN, Rob (fiddle) 1993
WASSERTHAL, Elfriede (sop) 1952
WATERBOLK, Yteke (dan) 1970
WATERHOUSE, Ellis (exh dir) 1950, 51
WATERHOUSE, William (bn) 1961
WATERS, Jan (act) 1968, 73, 77
WATERS, Sylvia (act) 1967
WATERSON, Juanita (des) 1964
WATFORD, Gwen (rdr) 1985
WATKINSON, Carolyn (mez) 1982-85
WATKINSON, Eve (act) 1989
WATKINSON, Seanna (act) 1977
WATSON, Arthur (sngr) 1995
WATSON, Betty (sngr) 1947, 48, 49
WATSON, Claire (sop) 1965
WATSON, Colin (act) 1985
WATSON, Derek (lect) 1995, 96
WATSON, Derwent (act) 1983, 93
WATSON, Derwent (act) 1993
WATSON, Greta (act) 1981
WATSON, Janice (sop) 1992, 94, 95
WATSON, Jean (cont) 1949, 50
WATSON, Jonathan (act) 1985
WATSON, June (act) 1971
WATSON, Lillian (sop) 1984
WATSON, Mike (mus) 1992
WATSON, Morag (mez) 1989, 90
WATSON, Roslyn (dan) 1980
WATSON, Sarah (sop) 1991
WATSON, Stephen (light) 1991
WATSON, Timothy (act) 1992
WATSON, Tom (act) 1964, 70, 83, 84, 87, 92
WATT, Alan (bar) 1986, 87, 91
WATT, Andrew (boy sop) 1980
WATTS, Andre (pf) 1971
WATTS, Helen (cont) 1963, 65, 68, 74, 76-79
WATZKE, Jürgen (act) 1987
WAX 'n' WAIN 1993
WAY, Eileen (act) 1960
WAY, Jennifer (dan) 1976
WEAVER, Jenifer (dan) 1994
WEBB, Alan (act) 1951, 53
WEBB, Barry (sngr) 1989
WEBER, Diana (dan) 1981
WEBER, Richard (act) 1969
WEBSTER, Jeff (act) 1986
WEEDEN, April (dan) 1987
WEGENAST, Róbert (des) 1983
WEGNER, Horst (bar) 1952
WEGNER, Walburga (sop) 1951
WEHRLE, Lothar (sngr) 1971
WEIDMANN, Ilse (dan) 1963
WEIKENMEIER, Albert (ten) 1972
WEIKERT, Donald (dan) 1991
WEIL, Terence (vc) 1962, 72
WEINHEIMER, Horst (act) 1993
WEIR, *Dame* Gillian (org) 1980
WEIS, Jean-Guillaume (dan) 1992
WEISGERBER, Antje (act) 1949
WEISSELBERG, Kiffer (act) 1968
WEISSENBERG, Alexis (pf) 1974
WEKSLER, Teri (dan) 1995
WEKWERTH, Manfred (dir) 1984, 87
WELCH, Denise (act) 1992
WELCH, Sandy (act) 1991
WELCOME, Josephine (act) 1975, 79
WELCZ, Nicky (act) 1971
WELITSCH, Alexander (bs) 1958
WELITSCH, Ljuba (sop) 1948, 49
WELKER, Hartmut (bar) 1983
WELLER, Dieter (bs) 1970, 76, 83
WELLER, Walter (cond) 1984, 85, 93
WELLES, Robert (act) 1952
WELLINGTON, Sheena (folk sngr) 1995
WELLMAN, James (act) 1950
WELLMAN, Sylvia (dan) 1961
WELLS, Alexandra (dan) 1987
WELLS, Elaine (act) 1959
WELLS, John (spk) 1980
WELMINSKI, Andrzej (act) 1980
WELSER-MÖST, Franz (cond) 1992, 93
WELSH, Finlay (act) 1991
WELSH, Moray (vc) 1975, 79
WELSH, Norman (act) 1950
WELSH NATIONAL OPERA 1982, 93
WELTY, James (des) 1981
WENDEL, Heinrich (des) 1972, 76
WENDELS, Marlise (sngr) 1970
WENHAM, Brian (spk) 1981
WENK, Ulrich (dir) 1968
WENKEL, Ortrun (cont) 1978
WENSAK, Annie (act) 1981
WENT, Anne (dan) 1981
WENTWORTH, Robin (act) 1981
WENZINGER, August (cond) 1962
WERBA, Erik (pf) 1956, 59, 64
WERING, Janny van (hpd) 1967
WERNER, Axel (act) 1994
WERNER, Margot (dan) 1958
WESKER, Arnold (spk) 1963
WESOLOWSKI, Emil (dan) 1986
WEST, Alexander (act) 1984, 85, 88
WEST, Anne (act) 1972
WEST, Charles (act) 1958, 59, 60, 61
WEST, Christopher (dir) 1957
WEST, Jayne (sop) 1995
WEST, Jon Frederic (ten) 1983
WEST, Rebecca (spk) 1962

WRIGHT, Geoffrey (comp) 1959
WRIGHT, John (dir) 1989
WRIGHT, Paul Ambrose (des) 1992
WRIGHT, Peter (dan, chor) 1958, 63, 75
WRIGHT, Richard (?) 1963
WRIGHT, Rose Marie (dan) 1976
WRIGHT, Sheila (act) 1954
WRIGHT, Simon (org) 1993
WRIGHT, Teresa (act) 1971
WRINGER, Leo (act) 1979
WRONSKI, Tadeusz (vn) 1962
WU, William (sngr) 1975
WU DEZHANG (act) 1987
WU JIJIE (act) 1987
WUNDERLICH, Fritz (ten) 1958, 65, 66
WÜNSCH, Horst (act) 1984, 87
WÜRTTEMBERG STATE OPERA 1958, 66
WÜRTTEMBERG STATE THEATRE 1977
WÜRTZ, Eric (dan) 1990
WYATT, Peter (act) 1992
WYLIE, Frank (act) 1958, 60, 62
WYLIE, Rowan (act) 1988
WYMARK, Jane (act) 1978
WYMARK, Patrick (act) 1967
WYN-DAVIES, Catrin (sop) 1996
WYNN, David (act) 1971, 72
WYNNE, Gilbert (act) 1961
WYNNE, Ken (act) 1962
WYNTER, Mark (act) 1981
WYNYARD, Diana (act) 1951
WYSS, Gérard (pf) 1995
WYSS, Sophie (sop) 1952
WYTTENBACH, Jörg (pf, hpd) 1973
WYZNIEWSKI, Arno (act) 1984, 87

XENAKIS, A. (act) 1966
XI'AN SINGING AND DANCING COMPANY 1987
XIMÉNEZ, Roberto (dan) 1953
XU YIAWANG (act) 1987

YABUKI, Makoto (mus) 1989
YAEDA, Kimiko (des) 1988
YAKAR, Rachel (sop) 1972, 76, 78
YAKOVLEVA, Olga (act) 1978
YALTON, Jaron (dan) 1956
YAMABI, Ken (act) 1985
YAMADA, Tomoyuki (act) 1990
YAMAGUCHI, Kyoko (act) 1990
YAMAKAWA, Akiko (dan) 1988
YAMASH'TA, Stomu (perc) 1970, 87, 90
YAMASHITA, Akihiko (act) 1989
YAMASHITA, Yorie (act) 1990
YAMAYA, Hatsuo (act) 1986
YAN, Igor (ten) 1991
YANG, Seung-Mi (dan) 1990
YANG, Welly (sngr) 1995
YANK LAWSON ALL-STARS 1991
YANO, Keiko (sop) 1976
YAO ZUFU (act) 1987
YASUFUKU, Haruo (mus) 1972
YATES, Marjorie (act) 1977, 93
YEARGAN, Michael H. (des) 1982
YEEND, Frances (sop) 1951
YELLAND, Dave (act) 1972
YELLOWBIRD, Lloyd (dan) 1990
YEPES, Narciso (gtr) 1989
YEVTUSHENKO, Evgeny (rdr) 1987
YEWEH, Robert (act) 1987
YFANTIS, Tassos (act) 1981
YGGDRASIL QUARTET 1995
YOKOHAMA BOAT THEATRE 1989
YONIN NO KAI 1988
YORK, Donald (cond) 1995
YORK, Philip (act) 1977
YORKE, Helen (pf) 1996
YORKE, Vincent (des) 1969
YOSHIDA, Kae (des) 1981
YOSHIDA, Koichi (act) 1988
YOSHII, Sumio (light) 1985, 86, 91
YOSHIKAWA, Yuko (mus) 1989
YOSHIMURA, Yukio (dan) 1990
YOSHINAGA, Junichi (dir) 1984
YOUNG, Alan (act) 1985
YOUNG, Alexander (ten) 1950, 62, 63, 64, 67
YOUNG, Benny (act) 1973, 75, 79
YOUNG, Douglas (spk) 1962
YOUNG, Jeremy (act) 1965
YOUNG, John (act) 1950, 56, 57, 58, 60, 62, 73, 75
YOUNG, Johnny (act) 1967
YOUNG, Lola (act) 1977
YOUNG, Malcolm (act) 1966
YOUNG, Paul (act) 1958, 73, 75, 83-87, 88, 89
YOUNG, William (act) 1948, 49
YOUNG LYCEUM COMPANY 1973, 74
YOUNG VIC 1971, 72
YOUNGER, Shane (act) 1966
YOUNGERMAN, Duncan (dir) 1989
YOUSKEVITCH, Igor (dan) 1950, 53
YU ZHENFEI (act) 1987
YUE MEITI (mez) 1987
YUGOSLAV BALLET
See Belgrade Opera Ballet
YUILL, Jimmy (act) 1990
YUME NO YUMINSHA COMPANY 1987, 90
YUNTA, Rafael (light) 1989
YURCHENKO, Larissa (sngr) 1990
YURIKO (dan) 1963
YURISICH, Gregory (bar) 1994
YUSHMANOV, V.I. (sngr) 1986
YUZVENKO, Valentina (sop) 1986

ZABALETA, Nicanor (hp) 1959
ZACCARIA, Nicola (bs) 1957
ZACH, Franz Xaver (act) 1993
ZACHARIAS, Christian (pf) 1985, 96
ZACHWATOWICZ, Krystyna (act) 1986, 89
ZADEK, Hilde (sop) 1950, 51
ZADEK, Peter (dir) 1994, 95
ZAGORSKA, Izabela (dan) 1986
ZAGREB SOLOISTS' ENSEMBLE 1958
ZAJAC, Matthew (act) 1995
ZAKAVA, Tatiana (act) 1991
ZAKHAROV, Mark (dir) 1991
ZAKIN, Alexander (pf) 1954, 56
ZAKOWSKY, Rainer (ten) 1982
ZALLINGER, Meinhard von (cond) 1965
ZAMBOJOVA, Jana (dan) 1991
ZAMENGO, Renata (act) 1970
ZAMFIR, Minela (act) 1991
ZAMIR, Miriam (dan) 1974
ZAMORANO, José (dan) 1979
ZAMPARINI, Gabriella (act) 1975
ZANASI, Mario (bar) 1969
ZANAZZO, Alfredo (bs) 1982
ZANETTI, Miguel (pf) 1971, 89, 90
ZANG, Edward (act) 1967
ZANI, Giacomo (cond) 1972
ZANIBELLI, Biancarosa (mez) 1969
ZANNINI, Laura (mez) 1971
ZAPF, Rosl (sngr) 1970
ZARAGUETA, Rafael (mus) 1989
ZAREMBA, Elena (mez) 1990, 91
ZARESKA, Eugenia (mez) 1948
ZARJC, Geroslav (des) 1991
ZARYEV, Alexander (act) 1991
ZASTAVNY, Georgy (sngr) 1991
ZATOVICOVA, Katarina (act) 1991
ZAUTACHVILI, O. (act) 1979
ZAZZO, Jean Charles di (dan) 1985
ZEC, Petar (dir) 1991
ZECCHI, Carlo (cond) 1948
ZECH, Rosel (act) 1993
ZECHA, Chesterina Sim (dan) 1963
ZEFFIRELLI, Franco (dir, des) 1957, 61
ZEGARELLI, Carmela (dan) 1981
ZEHETMAIR, Thomas (vn) 1994, 95, 96
ZEIFMAN, Hersh 1984
ZEL, Carlos (sngr) 1995
ZELENSKY, Igor (dan) 1991
ZEROMSKI, Stefan (dan) 1986, 91
ZERTSALOVA, Natalia (pf) 1991
ZHANG JINGXIAN (act) 1987
ZHANG MINGRONG (act) 1987
ZHEN, Lin (dan) 1994
ZHIKALOV, Yuri (sngr) 1991
ZHONG WAIDE (act) 1987
ZHU, Ai-Lan (sop) 1994
ZHU XIAOYU (act) 1987
ZIAHI, Győző (dan) 1973
ŽIDEK, Ivo (ten) 1964, 70
ZIGON, Ivana (act) 1991
ZIKMUNDOVÁ, Eva (mez) 1964, 70
ZILIO, Elena (sop) 1972
ZIMERMAN, Krystian (pf) 1978, 79, 84
ZIMMERMAN, Jamie (dan) 1981
ZIMMERMANN, Erich (ten) 1952, 56
ZIMMERMANN, Frank Peter (vn) 1993
ZIMMERMANN, Jörn (des) 1965
ZIMMERMANN, Reinhart (des) 1974, 95
ZINA, Joe (dan) 1975
ZIPPEL, Dorothee (des) 1971
ZOBEIDA *See* JUAU, Zobeida
ZÖLLER, Karlheinz (fl) 1970
ZOLLMAN, Ronald (cond) 1985
ZOLOTUKHIN, Valery (act) 1989
ZORITCH, George (dan) 1952
ZSCHAU, Marilyn (sop) 1983
ZUKERMAN, Eugenia (fl) 1980
ZUKERMAN, Pinchas (vn, va, cond) 1971, 72, 78, 83, 90
ZUKOFSKY, Paul (vn) 1972
ZUKOWSKI, Zbigniew (act) 1966
ŽUNAC, Stevan (dan) 1962
ZÜRICH OPERA 1978
ZWIRSKI, Zenon (dan) 1991
ZYLBERAJCH, Aline (hpd) 1985
+ Formed for the occasion

Financial Statistics

1947	Donations	
	Edinburgh Corporation	22 000
	Arts Council	20 000
	Donors	19 791
		61 791
	Deficit 20 776	
1948	Donations	
	Edinburgh Corporation	15 000
	Arts Council	5 000
	Donors	6 122
		26 122
	Deficit 10 465	
1949	Donations	
	Edinburgh Corporation	15 000
	Arts Council	3 000
	Donors	4 054
		22 054
	Deficit 24 206	
1950	Donations	
	Edinburgh Corporation	15 000
	Arts Council	3 000
	Donors	8 496
		26 496
	Deficit 19 993	
1951	Donations	
	Edinburgh Corporation	15 000
	Arts Council	3 000
	Donors	10 446
		28 446
	Deficit 38 833	
1952	Donations	
	Edinburgh Corporation	15 000
	Scottish Arts Council	5 000
	Donons	23 694
		43 694
	Deficit 17 645	
1953	Donations	
	Edinburgh Corporation	15 000
	Scottish Arts Council	7 500
	Donors	23 379
		46 879
	Deficit 18 992	
1954	Donations	
	Edinburgh Corporation	15 000
	Scottish Arts Council	7 500
	Donors	21 185
		43 685
	Deficit 30 779	
1955	Donations	
	Edinburgh Corporation	15 000
	Scottish Arts Council	7 500
	Donors	18 243
		40 743
	Deficit 27 112	
1956	Donations	
	Edinburgh Corporation	15 000
	Scottish Arts Council	7 500
	Donors	18 836
		41 336
	Deficit 15 895	
1957	Donations	
	Edinburgh Corporation	15 000
	Scottish Arts Council	7 500
	Donors	19 766
		42 266
	Deficit 22 606	
1958	Donations	
	Edinburgh Corporation	25 000
	Scottish Arts Council	10 000
	Donors	32 245
		67 245
	Deficit 7 436	
1959	Donations	
	Edinburgh Corporation	25 000
	Scottish Arts Council	12 000
	Donors	30 922
		67 922
	Deficit 7 141	
1960	Donations	
	Edinburgh Corporation	25 000
	Scottish Arts Council	15 000
	Donors	30 941
		70 941
	Deficit 24 204	
1961	Donations	
	Edinburgh Corporation	50 000
	plus Special contrib.	20 000
	Scottish Arts Council	15 000
	plus Special contrib.	5 000
	Donors	37 192
		127 192
	Deficit 2 604	
1962	Donations	
	Edinburgh Corporation	50 000
	Scottish Arts Council	20 000
	Donors	34 312
		104 312
	Deficit 17 995	

1963	Donations	
	Edinburgh Corporation	50 000
	Scottish Arts Council	20 000
	Donors	37 484
		107 484
	Deficit 23 204	

1964	Donations	
	Edinburgh Corporation	50 000
	Scottish Arts Council	20 000
	Donors	37 403
		107 403
	Surplus 35 637	

1965	Donations	
	Edinburgh Corporation	50 000
	plus Special contrib.	25 000
	Scottish Arts Council	30 000
	Donors	38 336
		143 336
	Deficit 13 383	

1966	Donations	
	Edinburgh Corporation	75 000
	plus Special contrib.	25 000
	Scottish Arts Council	35 000
	Donors	36 610
		171 610
	Surplus 25 881	

1967	Donations	
	Edinburgh Corporation	75 000
	Scottish Arts Council	50 000
	Donors	31 452
		156 452
	Deficit 34 479	

1968	Donations	
	Edinburgh Corporation	75 000
	Scottish Arts Council	50 000
	Capital fund	3 189
	Donors	29 922
		158 111
	Deficit 9 500	

1969	Donations	
	Edinburgh Corporation	80 000
	Scottish Arts Council	60 000
	Capital fund	5 467
	Donors	27 656
		173 123
	Deficit 24 221	

1970	Donations	
	Edinburgh Corporation	100 000
	Scottish Arts Council	70 000
	Capital fund	9 412
	Donors	28 841
		208 253
	Deficit 5 034	

1971	Donations	
	Edinburgh Corporation	110 000
	Scottish Arts Council	80 000
	Capital fund	4 400
	Donors	27 151
		221 551
	Surplus 21 940	
£10,000 transferred to Capital Fund		11 940

1972	Donations	
	Edinburgh Corporation	120 000
	Scottish Arts Council	88 000
	Capital fund	4 743
	Donors	32 035
		244 778
	Surplus 24 149	

1973	Donations	
	Edinburgh Corporation	120 000
	Scottish Arts Council	100 000
	Capital fund	5 117
	Donors	42 072
		267 189
	Surplus 6 675	

1974	Donations	
	Edinburgh Corporation	145 000
	Scottish Arts Council	125 000
	plus Special contrib.	10 000
	Capital fund	5 561
	Donors	42 847
		328 408
	Deficit 15 091	

1975	Donations	
	Edinburgh Dist. Council	90 000
	Lothian Regional Council	90 000
	Scottish Arts Council	150 000
	plus Special contrib.	5 000
	Capital fund	6 506
	Donors	43 643
		385 149
	Surplus 721	

1976	Donations	
	Edinburgh Dist. Council	106 500
	Lothian Regional Council	90 000
	Scottish Arts Council	225 000
	Capital fund	6 000
	Donors	64 349
		491 849
	Deficit 6 365	

1977	Donations	
	Edinburgh Dist. Council	222 620
	Scottish Arts Council	230 000
	Capital fund	6 356
	Sponsors and donors	80 127
		539 103
	Deficit 22 680	

1978	Donations	
	Edinburgh Dist. Council	300 000
	Special contrib.	22 680
	Scottish Arts Council	270 000
	Capital fund	7 777
	Sponsors and donors	87 437
		687 894
	Deficit 25 033	
1979	Donations	
	Edinburgh Distr. Council	330 000
	Scottish Arts Council	300 000
	Capital fund	8 105
	Sponsors and donors	89 738
		727 843
	Deficit 2 554	
1980	Donations	
	Edinburgh Distr. Council	363 000
	Scottish Arts Council	330 000
	Sponsors and donors	81 177
		774 177
	Surplus 15 247	
1981	Donations	
	Edinburgh Distr. Council	400 000
	Scottish Arts Council	378 000
	Capital fund	22 910
	Sponsors and donors	201 145
		1 002 055
	Deficit 46 277	
1982	Donations	
	Edinburgh Dist. Council	471 000
	Scottish Arts Council	390 000
	Sponsors and donors	197 783
		1 058 783
	Surplus 24 862	
1983	Donations	
	Edinburgh Dist. Council	564 550
	Plus Special contrib.	70 000
	Scottish Arts Council	426 990
	Plus Special contrib.	10 000
	Capital fund	26 498
	Sponsors and donors	245 516
		1 343 554
	Deficit 68 991	
1984	Donations	
	Edinburgh Distr. Council	560 000
	Scottish Arts Council	437 800
	Military Tattoo	10 000
	Donors	70 205
	Sponsors	210 955
		1 288 960
	Surplus 75 144	
1985	Donations	
	Edinburgh Distr. Council	600 500
	Scottish Arts Council	446 550
	Sponsors and donors	316 027
		1 363 077
	Surplus 114 685	
1986	Donations	
	Edinburgh Dist. Concil	633 000
	Scottish Arts Council	464 410
	Capital fund	50 000
	Sponsors and donors	276 085
		1 423 495
	Deficit 159 826	
1987	Donations	
	Edinburgh Dist. Council	553 000
	Scottish Arts Council	473 700
	Sponsors and donors	512 873
		1 539 573
	Deficit 88 669	
1988	Donations	
	Edinburgh Dist. Council	553 000
	Scottish Arts Council	493 000
	Other grants	5 000
	Sponsors and donors	597 569
		1 648 569
	Deficit 97 399	
1989	Donations	
	Edinburgh Dist. Council	600 000
	Scottish Arts Council	503 000
	Other grants	4,500
	Sponsors and donors	783 687
		1 891 187
	Deficit 112 313	
1990	Donations	
	Edinburgh Dist. Council	650 000
	Lothian Regional Council	100 000
	Scottish Arts Council	553 300
	Other grants	21 862
	Sponsors and donors	603 745
		1 928 907
	Surplus 91 865	
1991	Donations	
	Edinburgh Dist. Council	695 500
	Lothian Regional Council	106 000
	Scottish Arts Council	592 584
	Other grants	105 950
	Sponsors and donors	796 681
		2 296 715
	Deficit 245 628	

1992	Donations	
	Edinburgh Dist. Council	723 320
	Lothian Regional Council	157 500
	Scottish Arts Council	651 840
	Enhancement award	112 500
	Sponsors and donors	798 219
		2 443 379
	Surplus 189 831	
1993	Donations	
	Edinburgh Dist. Council	850 000
	Lothian Regional Council	250 000
	Scottish Arts Council	684 500
	Enhancement award	112 500
	Sponsors and donors	870 944
		2 767 944
	Surplus 12 742	
1994	Donations	
	Edinburgh Dist. Council	950 000
	Lothian Regional Council	350 000
	Scottish Arts Council	735 000
	Sponsors and donors	1078 555
		3 113 555
	Surplus 1 482	
1995	Donations	
	Edinburgh Dist. Council	950 000
	Lothian Regional Council	350 000
	Scottish Arts Council	747,000
	Sponsors and donors	1 041 678
		3 088 678
	Deficit 34 440	

Sponsors and Donors 1980-1996

20/20 Systems Ltd, 1991
Abbey National Building Society, 1983
Lady June Aberdeen, 1984
Aer Lingus, 1995
Air Afrique, 1983
Air France, 1987, 91
Air India, 1983
Air UK, 1991, 95-96
Aitken & Niven Ltd, 1980-82, 84-96
Walter Alexander & Co. (Coachbuilders) Ltd, 1980-83
Matthew Algie Ltd, 1991-96
Miss Grace Alison, 1989, 93
James Allan & Son Ltd, 1980-85
Amerada Hess Ltd, 1986-91
American Express, 1982
Anglo World Travel Ltd, 1980
Appleyard of Edinburgh, 1987
AT & T, 1992-93

BAA, 1981-82
The Bacher Trust, 1996
Baillie Gifford & Co. 1988-96
Balmoral Hotel, 1992-96
Banco Santander, 1989
Band Three Radio Ltd, 1991
Bank of Scotland, 1981-96
Banque Nationale de Paris, 1980-82
Barclays Bank PLC, 1980-93
Mrs Barr, 1992
John Bartholomew & Son Ltd, 1980-86, 89
BAT Industries, 1994
BBC Scotland, 1989
Beck's, 1994
Bell Lawrie White & Co. Ltd, 1989-95
Bennett & Robertson, 1995
A & J Beveridge, 1984
Bikubenfonden, 1989
The Binks Trust, 1983-84, 87-96
Blyth & Blyth Associates, 1994-95
Bollinger Champagne, 1986-90
Boots the Chemists Ltd, 1980-87
James Bowen & Sons Ltd, 1980, 82, 84
BP in Scotland, 1980-83, 87-96
Brechin Brothers Ltd, 1980-82
British Airways PLC, 1984, 88, 92, 94-95
British Alcan Aluminium PLC, 1987
British Caledonian, 1980-83
British Gas (Scotland) PLC, 1980-93
British Midland Airways Ltd, 1986-87, 90-93
British Transport Hotels Ltd, 1980-81
Britoil & Partners, 1985
Bruntons, 1984-87
BSIS, 1994
BT, 1986, 88-96
BT East of Scotland, 1990
BT West End Mobile Communications Dept, 1989
W & J Burness WS, 1995
R R J Burns, 1989-90, 92

Cairncross Ltd, Jewellers, 1992
Caledonian Bank PLC, 1992-95
Caledonian Hotel, 1987-96
Caledonian Paper PLC, 1993-96
Caltrust, 1984-86
Canon (UK), Edinburgh, 1984
Canon Scotland Business Machines Ltd, 1991-92
Capital Copiers Ltd, 1992-96
Carlsberg & Scottish Importers Ltd, 1980
Carlton Highland Hotel, 1995
CDL Car Parks, 1991
Christian Salvesen PLC, 1980-83, 85-96
Citibank, 1980, 94-95
Cluff Oil Ltd, 1981-82
Clydesdale Bank PLC, 1981-88, 95-96

Compaq, 1996
Conoco (UK) Ltd, 1984
Coopers & Lybrand, 1994-96
The Craignish Trust, 1980-81
Cramond Inn Ltd, 1980
D S Crawford Ltd, 1980, 91
Crédit Lyonnais, 1980-81
Creditanstalt Bankverein, 1983
Cruden Foundation Ltd, 1980-96
Cummins Engine Company Ltd, 1994

Danske Bank, 1995
Datapost Scotland, 1988-89
Davison at Newington, 1980-82, 85
Dawson International PLC, 1987-92, 94-95
Mr Maxwell D Deans, 1986
Miss W M Deans, 1985
Digital Equipment Co. (DEC), 1987
Distillers Company, 1981-85
Doric Tavern, 1980-82
Evelyn Drysdale Charitable Trust, 1983-84, 87, 90-96
Dunard Fund, 1989, 92-96
Dunard Fund USA, 1989-91
Alexander Dunbar, 1984
Prof. J D Dunbar-Nasmith, 1995
Dundas and Wilson, Solicitors, 1996
Dunfermline Building Society, 1995-96
Mrs A Marion Dunnett, 1995

Edinburgh Airports Ltd, 1991-92
Edinburgh Chamber of Commerce, 1993-96
Edinburgh Crystal, 1987
Edinburgh Development & Investment, 1994
Edinburgh Indian Association, 1983
Edinburgh International Festival Endowment Fund, 1991-96
Edinburgh Licensed Trade Association, 1984
Edinburgh Military Tattoo, 1989-96#
Edinburgh Photographic Society, 1980-82, 84-88
Elf Aquitaine UK, 1980-86
Mrs M M Elmslie, 1989-94
Lady Erskine-Hill, 1985
Esso Petroleum Co. Ltd, 1980, 82
Ethicon Ltd, 1990-96
Europcar Car Rental, 1987-89
European Arts Festival, 1992
Ever Ready Ltd, 1989, 91-92, 95-96

Esmée Fairbairn Charitable Trust, 1994
The Famous Grouse Finest Scotch Whisky, 1992-94
Featherhall Press Ltd, 1980-82, 84
J E Fells (Antonio Barbadillo), 1989
Ferranti, 1986-90
Festival Club, 1984-89
Financial Times, 1996
Finlay & Company Ltd, 1980-82
Flowers by Maxwell, 1990
Mrs Forsyth, 1989
R W Forsyth, 1980
Foundation for Sport and the Arts, 1993-95
Friends of the Edinburgh International Festival, 1983-96

Garuda Indonesian Airways, 1983
GEC Scotland Ltd, 1991-93
General Accident PLC, 1980-84, 96
George Hotel, 1991
Glaxo Welcome PLC, 1989-91, 93-96
Gleneagles Hotels PLC, 1982

Glenlivet Whisky Company, 1981-94
Glenrothes Development Corporation, 1992
Matthew Gloag & Son Ltd, 1996
Goethe-Institut, 1989
A Goldberg and Sons Ltd, 1980, 81
Fiona Grant, 1993, 95, 96
James Gray & Son Ltd, 1984, 86
Greig Middleton & Company Ltd, 1995, 96
Guinness PLC, 1986-88
Calouste Gulbenkian Foundation, 1996

Mr & Mrs Wallace Halladay, 1984
Hamada Edinburgh Festival Foundation, 1991, 92, 94, 96
Hamilton & Inches, 1987-88
Armand Hammer Foundation, 1982
Hammerson Group, 1990
Heatkeeper Homes, 1989
Mr & Mrs H J Heinz II, 1984
Hertz (UK) Ltd, 1991-95
HFC Trust Ltd, 1982
Highlands and Islands Development Board, 1980
Hitachi Ltd, 1986
Hongkong and Shanghai Banking Corporation, 1981, 82
Hope Scott Trust, 1981, 87
House of Fraser (Stores) Ltd, 1983-91
House of Hair, 1980, 81
Howard Hotel, 1991
Howard Smith Papers (Scotland) Ltd, 1995

IBM, 1980-96
ICI, 1980-96
ICL (UK) Ltd, 1991
IMI Computing Ltd, 1990
Indian Council for Cultural Relations, 1983
Indian Government Tourist Board, 1983
Insider Publications, 1993, 94
L'Institut Français d'Ecosse, 1989
InterCity, 1983-85, 91-94

Jaguar Cars, 1988, 90, 93, 94
Brian M Jamieson, 1990
The Japan Foundation, 1982
Eda, Lady Jardine Charitable Trust, 1980-84, 86-87, 89-96
Jeffreys Ltd, 1980-82, 85
Jenners Ltd, 1980-96
Jerzees American Active Wear, 1995
John Menzies PLC, 1980-96
Stanley Thomas Johnson Foundation, 1994
The late Ian T Johnstone, 1993
Justerini & Brooks Ltd, 1980-82, 84, 89, 91-92
JVC, 1988

King James Thistle Hotel, 1991
KPMG Peat Marwick, 1989-96

Laskys, 1980
Law & Dunbar-Nasmith Partnership, 1989
Leamington Hotel, 1980
Lever Brothers Ltd, 1991-92, 94-96
Life Association of Scotland, 1980-84, 86-90
Lillywhites Ltd, 1980-81
J C Lindsay & Co. Ltd, 1980-82, 85
Littlewoods Ltd, 1980-85, 87
London Law Trust, 1984-85
Lothian & Edinburgh Enterprise Ltd, 1992-93
Lothian Regional Council, 1989-90
Lufthansa Airways, 1984

MacDonald Orr Ltd, 1996
McEwan's 80/-, 1990
Macfarlan Smith Ltd, 1984-96
The N S MacFarlane Charitable Trust, 1994, 96
McGrigor Donald, 1989-96
A H McIntosh & Co. Ltd, Kirkcaldy, 1981
Mackenzie & Storrie Ltd, 1980-82, 84-92
Mackenzie's Sports Shop Ltd, 1980-82, 84
McKirdy's Seafood Bar, 1990
Maclay Murray & Spens, 1988-90, 93-96
Mrs C P Macnaughton, 1984
MacRoberts Solicitors, 1995-96
Mactaggart & Mickel, 1980, 82-96
Manca Associates, 1991
Joseph Mann, 1980
Marks & Spencer PLC, 1980-81, 88-89, 93-96
D B Marshall (Newbridge), 1984-87
Marshall's Food Group Ltd, 1994
Martin's Restaurant, 1989-92, 94, 96
Nancie Massey Charitable Trust, 1990-96
C Menzies, 1983-86
Mid Wales Development, 1984
Midland Bank PLC, 1980-82, 95
James Miller & Partners Ltd, 1980-82, 84-86
Sir James Miller Edinburgh Trust, 1983
Miller Group Ltd, 1988-96
Ministero del Turismo e dello Spettacolo Italiano, 1982
Mitsubishi Electric UK Ltd, 1996
Mobil North Sea Ltd, 1982, 86
Moët & Chandon, 1995
Peter Moores Foundation, 1993
Morgan Grenfell Development Capital Ltd, 1996
Morrison Construction Group PLC, 1994-96
William Muir (Bond 9) Ltd, 1980-82, 84-87

National Endowment for the Arts, 1982
National Endowment for the Humanities, 1982
National Westminster Bank Ltd, 1980-82, 84
Nationwide Building Society, 1980-81
NEC Semiconductors (UK) Ltd, 1995-96
Wm. Nicol & Sons (Ironmongers) Ltd, 1980
Nimmo's Colour Printers, 1995
North British Hotel, 1987-88
North British Steel Group Ltd, 1980-83
North West Orient Airlines, 1984-85

Observer, 1982
Orr Macqueen WS, 1995
Oxygen, 1996

P A Consulting Group, 1986
Pastime Publications Ltd, 1984
PepsiCo Inc. 1984
Pillans & Wilson, 1980-84, 94-96
Polton House Press, 1995
Press Data Bureau, 1995-96
Press Papers Ltd, 1986
Prestonfield House Hotel, 1991-92, 95-96

Mrs S Pringle, 1980
Rae Mackintosh (Music) Ltd, 1982-84
Rank Xerox, 1984
Rankins' Fruit Markets Ltd, 1980
J & B Rare, 1985
Registered Estate Agents Ltd, 1988
Donald & Brenda Rennie, 1995-96
Reuters Ltd, 1994
Irvine Robertson Wines Ltd, 1989
Romanes & Paterson Ltd, 1980
Ross's of Edinburgh, 1980-82, 84-87, 89-96
Rowntree Mackintosh PLC, 1980-90
Royal Bank of Canada, 1986
Royal Bank of Scotland PLC, 1981-96
Royal Insurance (UK) Ltd, 1980-84, 86, 89
Royal Mail, 1989, 93-96
Royal Mail Parcels, 1989
Royal Terrace Hotel, 1991-92
The Hon. Sir Steven Runciman, 1995-96
Ryden, 1994

Arthur M Sackler Foundation, 1982, 84
Saison Foundation, 1989
Mrs Marion H Salvesen's Charitable Trust, 1987-96
Sanderson Travel Service Ltd, 1980
Santa Fe UK Ltd, 1984
Scandic Crown Hotel, 1991
Schroder Charity Trust, 1994
Scobie & McIntosh Ltd, 1984
Scotia Office Machines Ltd, 1993
Scotiabank, 1980
Scotsman, 1988
Scott-Moncrieff, CA, 1993, 96
Scottish Airports Ltd, 1980-91
Scottish Amicable, 1982
Scottish & Newcastle PLC, 1981-96
Scottish Brewers Ltd, 1986-89
Scottish Equitable Life Assurance Society, 1987-91
Scottish Express International, 1989
Scottish Financial Enterprise, 1987-91
Scottish Investment Trust, 1994
Scottish Life, 1980-83, 89-90, 92-96
Scottish Post Office, 1984-88
Scottish Power PLC, 1990-96
Scottish Pride Ltd, 1995
Scottish Provident, 1980-81, 84-85, 89-90, 94
Scottish Television, 1985-89, 93-95
Scottish Tourist Board, 1989
Scottish Transport Group, 1981-91
Scottish Widows, 1987, 95-96
Scottish Woollen Publicity Council, 1989
Sears Foundation, 1994
Secret Garden Behind the Witchery, 1993
Securicor Communications, 1989-90
Sedan Chauffeur Drive, 1980-82
SEEL Ltd, 1984-85
Sheerspeed UK Ltd, 1989
Shell UK Ltd, 1986-87, 92-96
Sheraton Caltrust PLC, 1989
Sheraton Grand Hotel, 1987-96
Sidlaw Group PLC, 1994
Dr Janet Mary Smith, 1993
Smithkline Beckman Corporation, 1982
SMT Sales and Service, 1980-88
Sony (UK) Ltd, 1982
South of Scotland Electricity Board, 1981-89

Sovscot Tours Ltd, 1981-82, 84, 86-87
Spanish Consul General, 1992
Speedbird Holidays, 1988
Spider Systems Ltd, 1989, 95
Standard Life, 1984-96
Steensen, Varming, Mulcahy & Partners, 1980-82
The Stevenson Trust, 1995-96
Strathern & Blair, 1985
Strathmore Mineral Water Company, 1989-92, 94-96
Sun Alliance, 1982, 85, 87, 88, 92-96
Swiss Bank Corporation, 1981
Miss C A M Sym's Charitable Trust, 1986-87, 89-90, 92-96

Tandon PLC, 1991
The Tartan Gift Shops, 1980-84
Tate & Lyle PLC, 1986-92
Taylors Corporate Scotland, 1993
Tennent Caledonian, 1980-83, 85-89
Thistle Hotels Ltd, 1987
Grant Thornton, 1992-93
Total Oil Marine, 1980-92
Town & Country Car Rental, 1986-87
G Percy Trentham, 1983
Trunk Trailer Company, 1983
Trusthouse Forte Ltd, 1980-82
TSB Bank Scotland, 1989-91, 93-96
TSB Group PLC, 1987-88

United Biscuits (Holdings) PLC, 1986-89
University of Edinburgh, 1989-96

T K Valve Ltd, 1990-92
Valvona & Crolla Ltd, 1988-89
Mrs Nora Veitch, 1989-90
Virgil Thomson Foundation, Ltd, 1996
Visiting Arts, 1987, 89-96

W & P Charitable Trust, 1996
Wagstaff & Roy Creative Consultants, 1995
Hiram Walker & Sons (Scotland) PLC, 1980-86, 90-91
S G Warburg Group PLC, 1994
Waterstones Booksellers, 1988-89
Watson & Philip Charities Trust, 1995
Weatherall Green & Smith, 1993, 95
Whiley Foils Ltd, 1995-96
Whitbread PLC, 1994
Who's Who in Business in Scotland Ltd, 1992
Whytock & Reid, 1989-90
The Wilfred Owen Association, 1996
Wimpey Homes Holdings Ltd, 1980-87
The W M Company PLC, 1987-95
F W Woolworth & Co. Ltd, 1980-83

YBT Support Society, 1989
Sir Roger W Young, 1984-86
John Younger, 1984

This list has been compiled from information given in the Festival programmes. Any donations received after the programmes were printed have not been included.

Only these dates were listed in the programmes, but donations were received for earlier years.

Index